MW00759774

THE COMPLETE MUSICIAN

THE COMPLETE MUSICIAN

AN INTEGRATED APPROACH TO TONAL THEORY, ANALYSIS, AND LISTENING

Second Edition

Steven G. Laitz

Eastman School of Music

New York Oxford
OXFORD UNIVERSITY PRESS
2008

Oxford University Press, Inc., publishes works that further Oxford University's objective of excellence in research, scholarship, and education.

Oxford New York

Auckland Cape Town Dar es Salaam Hong Kong Karachi
Kuala Lumpur Madrid Melbourne Mexico City Nairobi
New Delhi Shanghai Taipei Toronto

With offices in
Argentina Austria Brazil Chile Czech Republic France Greece
Guatemala Hungary Italy Japan Poland Portugal Singapore
South Korea Switzerland Thailand Turkey Ukraine Vietnam

Published by Oxford University Press, Inc.
198 Madison Avenue, New York, New York 10016
http://www.oup.com
Oxford is a registered trademark of Oxford University Press

Library of Congress Cataloging-in-Publication Data
Laitz, Steven G. (Steven Geoffrey)
The complete musician : an integrated approach to tonal theory, analysis, and listening / Steven G. Laitz.
p. cm.
Includes indexes.

ISBN 978-0-19-530108-3 (cloth : alk. paper) 1. Music theory -- Textbooks. 2. Tonality. 3. Musical analysis. I. Title.

MT6.L136C66 2007

781.2–dc22

2006050725

Printing number: 9 8 7 6 5

Printed in the United States of America
on acid-free paper

To my family
Anne-Marie, Maddie, and Winn Dixie

CONTENTS

PART 3 A NEW HARMONIC FUNCTION AND ADDITIONAL MELODIC AND HARMONIC EMBELLISHMENTS

PART 5 CREATING LARGER FORMS

PART 6 CHROMATICISM

PART 9 INTRODUCTION TO NINETEENTH-CENTURY HARMONY: THE SHIFT FROM ASYMMETRY TO SYMMETRY

PREFACE

Music students often suffer through their tonal theory and ear-training courses, viewing them as not particularly relevant—perhaps even painful—sidelines of their musical studies. This is a shame, since an unsatisfying experience early on usually has an adverse effect on students' attitudes in subsequent academic courses. Some do in fact express a legitimate concern that much of the standard undergraduate theory and ear-training curriculum has little bearing on their music making. For example, students often view part writing and figured bass as arcane and antiquated activities, and ear-training and dictation—activities that should be intimately linked to music making—as scarcely more meaningful. Intervals out of context and chords strung together in disembodied harmonic progressions strip music of its very life. Arguably the most important component of any theory curriculum, analysis, is sometimes reduced to nothing more than roman numerals and form labeling. Reading and comprehending theory texts can be especially daunting, given that these are often encyclopedic in nature, encompassing details that represent exceptions rather than the norms of tonal music. *The Complete Musician* addresses each of these concerns in various ways.

Underlying Approach

The Complete Musician is founded on three simple premises. First, I believe students can learn to hear, comprehend, and model the structure and syntax of the music they love. Second, I take the tack that the same simple processes underlie all tonal music, and are fleshed out in wondrously diverse ways. Third, I believe that students will rise to the challenge when all of their senses are stimulated and they are immersed in instrumental and vocal music from the tonal repertoire.

A hierarchical approach that illuminates how the harmony of a given passage emerges from the combination of melodic lines is central to *The Complete Musician*. The book's view of tonal music as a fusion of melody, counterpoint, and harmony will appeal to single-line players and singers, as well as to keyboard players. The text develops a multistage writing and aural process through which students discern the harmonic flow of a passage by considering its outer-voice counterpoint and metrical setting. With a foundation of the tonal norms, students should be able to connect their basic musical instincts with what they hear and see. For example, students will learn to notate the missing cello line of a string quartet when the given score contains only the upper instruments, but the recorded performance includes all four. By integrating an understanding of tonal procedures, analytical strategies, and the ability to read music with singing, playing, and listening, students should emerge from the course as independent and well-rounded musicians.

The book's user-friendly, multitiered analytical approach stresses the distinction between description (i.e., using roman numerals and figured bass to label a given sonority according to its scale-degree relation to the tonic) and interpretive analysis (i.e., exploring the metric-rhythmic placement, spacing, voicing, duration, and possible motivic context of a sonority to determine its function). Interpretive analysis, then, draws heavily on students' musical instincts and experiences. Students should be given significant responsibility in class, to allow them to discover that successfully negotiating an exercise depends more on a series of well-supported musical decisions than on yes and no answers. The role of the students as active participants, whose opinions matter, is central to the spirit of this text.

Audience

The Complete Musician should appeal to music majors with varied levels of experience. For those with little theory background, an extensive 150-page fundamentals unit emphasizes function and context and provides a strong foundation for what follows. For students with more expertise and the desire to learn what happens beyond the common-practice harmonic spectrum, the final four chapters of the text introduce them to nineteenth- and early twentieth-century tonal practices. The text implicitly assumes that there are as many levels of student experience and background as there are students using the text. To that end, every topic is presented in a graduated fashion and may be tailored to meet specific student needs.

Examples

The driving force behind the book is the music literature, since, obviously, this is what theory illuminates. The repertoire included ranges from Wipo's eleventh-century setting of "Victimae pachali laudes" to Chicago's "Saturday in the Park," from solo vocal and instrumental music to the orchestral repertoire, from Haydn's London symphonies to Scriabin's later piano preludes. The inclusion of music from an entire millennium (focusing on the common-practice repertoire), dramatically underscores the fact that finite and specific contrapuntal and harmonic procedures form a common thread that runs through the stylistic differences of this music. Further, though examples in a purely homophonic texture tidily illustrate common-practice harmonic idioms, they do not develop students' ability to negotiate the panoply of textures and styles fundamental to the repertoire they listen to and perform. Over 500 recorded examples and exercises in DVD format are included with each copy of the textbook, and more than 2,000 additional examples are presented in DVDs that accompany the two workbooks. All of the music is performed by soloists and ensembles from the Eastman School of Music and the Rochester Philharmonic Orchestra.

Integration

The Complete Musician integrates the tasks that comprise a tonal theory curriculum, explicitly connecting written theory (part writing, composition, and analysis), musicianship skills (singing, playing, improvisation, and dictation), and music making outside of theory class. Given the emphasis on tonal harmony and the array of musical examples drawn from the literature (both excerpts and complete pieces) as well as the detailed treatment of both small and large forms and keyboard application, the only supplements needed are sight-singing and rhythmic reading materials. These would most likely be used in separate aural skills classes that address sight and prepared singing, conducting, and rhythmic and melodic dictation.

The workbooks further support this integration (see Ancillaries).

Introduction and Pacing of Important Topics

The Complete Musician begins with a thorough introduction to fundamentals that includes a discussion of melody writing and analysis, hierarchy, and species counterpoint. In addition to diatonic and chromatic procedures, other dimensions of the tonal tradition receive full treatment, including small formal structures (e.g., motive, phrase, period, and sentence) as well as larger forms (binary, ternary, rondo, and sonata), and stylistic distinctions between eighteenth- and nineteenth-century tonal practice.

The Complete Musician is neither an overview of the high points of music theory nor a survey of every topic associated with tonal music. Rather, it strives to develop a deep understanding of concepts by devoting one or more chapters to such crucial topics related to the tonal tradition as sequences, compound melody, and invertible counterpoint. The materials are presented at a pace that maximizes learning. Concepts are introduced in their most common musical contexts and then immediately reinforced with a broad array of exercises that include singing, writing, analyzing, listening, and playing. Exercises progress from more passive written, aural, and tactile activities (such as identifying, correcting, and comparing) to those requiring active understanding (such as unfigured basses, melody harmonization, and model composition), carefully arranged so that the skills the students develop lead from identification to composition.

Topics such as voice-leading norms and harmonic usage are presented in order of importance so that students never feel overwhelmed by endless rules, nor misled into thinking that all harmonies occur with equal frequency and are of equal importance. The emphasis on varied styles and genres illuminates the ways in which a small number of consistent contrapuntal and harmonic procedures are immutable throughout the tonal tradition. To counter any misconception that tonal pieces are cut from the same musical cloth with a limited range of compositional possibilities, emphasis is placed on motivic relationships that make a given work unique. Students learn that only through active study of the score can one discover such musical processes.

New to the Second Edition

This new edition contains many changes, both subtle and obvious. Each textbook chapter has undergone either significant revision or has been rewritten to improve general ordering between large topics (e.g., the pre-dominant function is introduced earlier) and organization within chapters (particularly in Parts 1–4).

- There are several new topics and expansions: a new chapter (16) devoted exclusively to the motive; new sections on analytical decision making through Gestalt techniques (in Chapters 2 and 7); lead sheet notation (Chapter 6); harmonizing florid melodies (beginning in Chapter 9); and an expanded section on musical texture and harmonic analysis (Chapter 6).
- Numerous analyses throughout the book, including thirteen "Model Analysis" sections, provide extended analyses of canonical pieces.
- Music examples include more from the wind and brass literature.
- Careful attention has been paid to the simplifying of explanations and definitions, with added summary charts and step-by-step procedures.
- The easier-to-read layout and format and nearly 200 new examples will make working through the text more enjoyable.
- There are also new types of exercises (also in the workbooks): for example, exercises for single-line instrumentalists, such as exploring the complementary processes of elaborating homophony and reducing florid textures, all of which are taken from the literature; listening exercises that vividly demonstrate how four-voice harmony is derived from outer-voice counterpoint (bass and soprano); and many new, more-graduated exercises. They include many written, aural, and playing exercises crafted for students with a wide range of abilities.
- The workbooks and Instructor's Manual have been significantly revamped (see Ancillaries).
- The recording format has undergone significant changes as well. The ten CDs that accompanied the first edition of *The Complete Musician* (eight of which needed to be purchased separately) have been expanded, with five additional hours of examples, so that approximately 90% of the music included in text and workbooks has been recorded. Further, all music is now presented on five easy-to-navigate, high-density music DVDs. Finally, all of this music is now packaged along with the text (two DVDs included—DVD 1 contains recordings of the text examples and DVD 2 contains recordings of text exercises) and workbooks (two DVDs in Workbook 1 and one DVD in Workbook 2). All examples and exercises are included on the DVDs in MP3 format (i.e., downloadable to other devices: MP3 players, iPods, etc.). There are many more excerpts and complete works included in the second edition's musical examples and exercises than there were in the first edition, and the sound quality has been significantly improved.

Ancillaries

The two workbooks that supplement the exercises in the text have been completely reorganized. Crafted for students of all abilities, the exercises have been provided in a format in which each chapter presents from four to eight complete and integrated assignments that fit on either one or two pages (front and back). Each assignment contains four or more diverse tasks, including single-line singing (single-line players may use their own instrument), two- and four-voice writing (figured bass, melody harmonization, freer illustrations, etc.), analysis, dictation, and keyboard. Supplementary exercises appear in the final portion of each workbook chapter. There are also new types of exercises (also in the textbook): for example, exercises for single-line instrumentalists, such as exploring the complementary processes of elaborating homophony and reducing florid textures, all of which are taken from the literature; listening exercises that vividly demonstrate how four-voice harmony is derived from outer-voice counterpoint (bass and soprano); and many new, more graduated exercises. There are many written, aural, and playing exercises crafted for students with a wide range of abilities.

A 450-page Instructor's Manual provides solutions to all of the ear-training exercises, sample solutions for more than 200 various writing exercises (e.g., figured bass and melody harmonization) and analyses, and supplementary examples, exercises, and teaching guidelines that detail effective strategies for each chapter.

Terminology and Scope

For those activities that fall in the crosshairs of an instructor's penchant for one underlying system or another, *The Complete Musician* aims to take a neutral, and hopefully ecumenical, path. For example, no particular system is espoused for singing harmonic patterns. Students should employ whatever system is used in class: scale-degree numbers, movable- or fixed-do *solfège*, and so on. Whenever possible, established terminology is used. However, when current terminology is felt to be insufficient or vague, the reader will encounter departures from and additions to what is usually taught. For example, considerable time is spent on harmonic sequences, given the ubiquitous presence and crucial role they play in tonal music. To help students master hearing and writing sequences, I have devised a nomenclature system that captures both their general rise and fall, and the chord-to-chord root intervals that create these motions.

Another reason to depart occasionally from established terminology results from the desire to reveal tonal music's hierarchical processes and to model how we hear various harmonic motions. To that end, the analytical method employed in *The Complete Musician* involves considering a chord's relative importance within a given musical context. For example, a dominant harmony that leads conclusively to tonic as part of a strong authentic cadence is a different type of dominant from one that occurs within a phrase and merely helps connect tonic and submediant, or one that occurs at the half-cadence but does not actually move to the following tonic. It might be more profitable, then, to view such a dominant as referring back to the initial tonic and therefore not moving the progression ahead. By distinguishing between such functions, students should learn that analysis is a creative enterprise that embraces their instincts and has implications for their own music making.

A few topics usually found in harmony texts are not covered here, but the reader will encounter others that seldom appear in texts. For example, there is no discussion of ninth and eleventh chords, since such sonorities are usually more apparent than real in common-practice music. On the other hand, topics such as two-voice counterpoint, invertible counterpoint, compound melody, and late-nineteenth-century intervallic motivic cells receive detailed treatment, since they are crucial compositional procedures in eighteenth- and nineteenth-century music. Knowledge of their use will not only impact students' ability to hear harmony in time, but also will have a profound impact on their playing and singing.

Acknowledgments

For each stage of preparation of this new edition, Christopher Bartlette has been an enormous help and pedagogical influence. His keen and perceptive mind and deep musicality both inspired and guided me. I also thank my colleagues William Marvin (at the Eastman School) and Deborah Stein (at the New England Conservatory) for their many helpful suggestions. Finally, I thank the following reviewers, who made more than one pass through the new manuscript provided sage theoretical and pedagogical advice:

Mary I. Arlin, Ithaca College
Tom Baker, University of Washington
Amy Bauer, University of California, Irvine
Gene Biringer, Lawrence University
Karl Braunschweig, Wayne State University
Matthew Bribitzer-Stull, The University of Minnesota
Lora Dobos, The Ohio State University
Robert Knupp, Mississippi College
Thomas MacFarlane, New York University
Paul Murphy, State University of New York, Fredonia
Jocelyn Neal, The University of North Carolina at Chapel Hill
Robert Peck, Louisiana State University
J. Brian Post, Humboldt State University
Steven Strunk, Catholic University
Kevin Swinden, Wilfred Laurier University
Eliyahu Tamar, Duquesne University
Gerard Yun, Georgetown University

Once again, I thank my students and colleagues who were instrumental in the first edition. They include: Norman Carey, Evan Jones, Su Yin Mak, William Marvin, Neil Minturn, Gordon Sly, and Deborah Stein. Special thanks are due Brent Auerbach and Lisa Campi, who made countless crucial suggestions.

I thank the staff at Oxford University Press for their continued faith in this project. Jan Beatty, executive editor, worked tirelessly on all stages of both the first and the second editions. Her instincts and savvy and especially her ability to keep me nearly sane will not be forgotten. Karen Shapiro, managing editor, oversaw the production of both editions; anything short of sainthood would not aptly acknowledge her patience and guidance throughout the production stages of this bulky project.

I also express my gratitude to the Eastman School of Music, especially the past directors, Robert Freeman and James Undercofler, who supported this project in countless ways. Jamal Rossi, Eastman's interim director, has been a source of inspiration. A special debt of gratitude is due the students and faculty of Eastman, who played and sang the countless musical examples so artfully. Jun Qian both produced the nearly 18 hours of recorded music for the second edition and performed as a member of the wind quartet; his recording of such works as Mozart's Clarinet Quintet will surely inspire students and teachers alike. Nancia D'Alimonte, producer of the recordings for the first edition, will be pleased to learn that many of those recordings found their way into the second edition. Mike Farrington, the recording engineer and supervisory editor for both editions, continues to amaze me. His absolute cool through all stages of the recording process kept us all on track. Thanks also go to Helen Smith, director of Eastman's Recording Services, for her help and support.

I also thank the wonderful musicians heard on the DVDs included with this project:

Arciola, Marissa	Bass
Beaudry, Chris	Bass Trombone
Berkebile, Jennifer	Mezzo Soprano
Bezuidenhout, Kris	Piano, harpsichord, forte piano
Binkley, Jennifer	Horn
Block, Christina	Clarinet
Boover, Alta	Alto
Brooks, Liz	Mezzo Soprano
Burhans, Caleb	Viola, Violin
Cheetham, Andy	Trumpet
Chen, Po Yao (Richard)	Bassoon
Choi, Hyunji	Cello
Dawson, Andrea	Violin
Franco, Allison	Oboe
Fulton, John	Baritone
Gliere, Jennifer	Soprano
Grandey, Ali	Soprano
Hennings, Dieter	Guitar
Hermanson, Brian	Clarinet
Hileman, Lynn	Bassoon
Jin, Min	Tenor
Jorgensen, Michael	Violin
Karney, Laura	Oboe
Kellogg, Mark	Bass Trombone
Kelly, Mike	Tenor
Kelly, Susie	Cello
Kim, Sophia	Flute
Kohfeld, Cheryl	Viola
Laitz, Steve	Piano
Lange, Amy	Bassoon
Leung, Chun Chim (David)	Violin
Manolov, Emanouil	Violin
Marks, Matt	Horn
Martin, Rob	Violin
Nulty, Dennis	Tuba

Orlando, Courtney	Violin
OuYang, Angel	Violin
Penneys, Rebecca	Piano
Pritchard, Jillian	Timpani
Qian, Jun	Clarinet
Prosser, Doug	Trumpet
Radnofsky, Lauren	Cello
Richards, John	Viola
Salatino, Mark	Trombone
Salsbury, Josh	Trombone
Schneider, Nicolas	Cello
Shaw, Brian	Trumpet
Sheldrick, Braunwin	Viola
Shewan, Paul	Trumpet
Sugitani, Mune	Baritone
Traficante, Sara	Flute
Wensel, Ben	Cello
Widmer, John	Trombone
Wilcox, Kathy	Oboe
Winchell, Katie	Flute
Wish, David	Violin
Wood, Lindsey	Horn
Zabenova, Ainur	Violin
Nancia D'Alimonte	Conductor and Producer, First Edition
Jun Qian	Producer and clarinet, Second Edition

Once again, I thank Carl Schachter and acknowledge with gratitude the late Edward Aldwell for providing a spectacular model of scholarship, musicality, and pedagogy that plays no small role in the philosophic undergirding of this book.

I owe a special debt of gratitude to Joyce Shannon, who, since my first day in her freshman theory class at Chaffey College, has inspired me in all ways musical. Finally, to my best friend and soul mate, my wife, Anne-Marie, who after thirty years together can still make me laugh.

PART 1

THE FOUNDATION OF TONAL MUSIC

The diverse and magnificent body of tonal music that has come down to us over the centuries (and that continues to grow to this day) is one of the greatest and most enduring of all human achievements. You have recognized this fact and have decided to immerse yourself in learning about this form of human expression. Perhaps you have chosen to study music seriously because of its power to move you as no other earthly stimulus can. Or perhaps you have discovered that experiencing music allows unknown dimensions of your self to emerge, and you begin to realize the depth, complexity, and potential you possess as a human being.

That you are drawn to music to the degree that you are willing to invest the necessary effort and time to understand the syntax and structure of tonal music is testimony to music's power, and you are to be congratulated in taking this step. Clearly, you realize that just as the budding painter or sculptor must immerse herself in the study of anatomy and physiology in order to understand how to project this structure on canvas or in marble, so, too, must the musician understand the music's structure and process in order to play artistically.

There is only one—very important—requirement for you to complete this text successfully. You must have faith that the reward is worth the effort. Specifically, by working through this book, you will not only possess a strong foundation of the principles of writing, analyzing, hearing, singing, and playing tonal harmony and understanding the most important musical forms, but you also will be able to apply these principles to your performance and to any tonal pieces you will encounter throughout your life. There will, of course, be many occasions when you will be tempted to eject this book from the window of a quickly moving car, or to selflessly donate it to any scout group needing to add life to a smoldering campfire, but you will probably stop short of acting on these natural impulses. You will realize that your faith in this project is similar to the faith you demonstrate every day in the practice room: that long and lonely hours filled with trial and error and sustained concentration will eventually pay off. Indeed, even the most pedantic tasks, like practicing scales—which has occupied more of your practice time over the years than probably any other practice activity—are still part of your daily regimen. And why? Because you have faith that scales are important. A bit of this faith needs to be applied to the study of music theory. This book attempts to provide a clear path that will make the task as musical as possible. We know the truth and wisdom of proverbs such as "the journey of a thousand miles begins with the first step." Let's begin.

Part 1 presents the building blocks of music theory, including the terminology and concepts required for everyday musical discourse.

CHAPTER 1

The Pitch Realm: Tonality, Notation, and Scales

Western music written during the Baroque, Classical, and Romantic periods (c. 1650–c. 1900) is called **tonal music**, or music of the **common-practice period**. Compositions written during these three centuries have a point of gravitation, an explicit or implicit center around which all its pitches orbit. This phenomenon is called **tonality,** and the **gravitational center**—a single pitch (labeled using letters of the alphabet from A through G, plus various possible modifiers, including "flat", "sharp," "major," and "minor")—is called the **tonic**. Music with some sort of gravitational center has existed since antiquity and continues to flourish to the present day in film scores, popular and commercial music, folk music, and jazz. Furthermore, music with a tonal center or other such point of reference can be found throughout the world. In our studies here, however, we focus on the repertory that emerged in Europe during the common-practice period.

Charting Musical Sound: Staff and Clef

Tonal music is often written down in order to preserve it and to ensure that its **pitches** (the musical sound generated by a vibrating body) and their placement in time, or **rhythm**, receive relatively consistent performance. Such musical **scores** begin with several defining elements, including the staff and clef, which make it possible to fix pitches and define the relationships between them. A **staff** (plural: **staves**) contains horizontal lines and spaces, each of which, in conjunction with a **clef,** represents a specific pitch, thus permitting the performer to see exactly how much higher or lower a given pitch is in relation to some other pitch. The earliest clefs indicated the location of what has become middle C. Example 1.1 shows what the C clef looks like in modern notation.

EXAMPLE 1.1 C Clefs

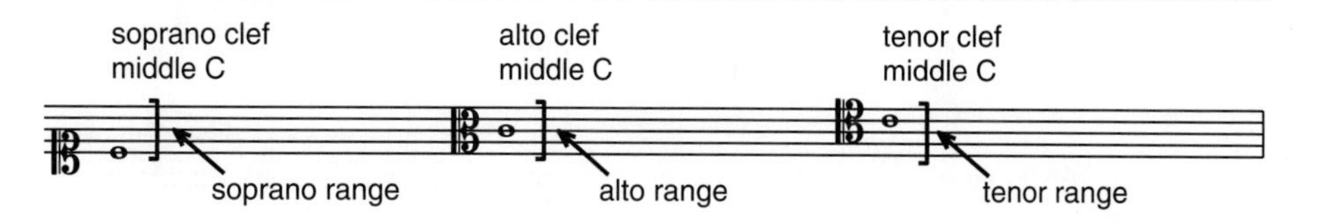

C clefs may occur on any of the five lines of the staff. Notice that the names of the sample C clefs in Example 1.1 correspond to the names of the voice ranges. This indicates why C clefs are useful: The range of the vocal melodies written in these clefs rarely exceeds the limits of the staves. Today, only two C clefs are commonly found: the alto (in which viola music is written) and the tenor (in which some trombone, bassoon, and cello music is written).

Two other clefs came into prominence centuries after the C clefs were well established, and they represent a good compromise for notating all vocal music since they can accommodate the bass and soprano voices at their extremes, with alto and tenor within. The **treble** (or G clef) indicates the location of G above middle C, and the **bass** (or F clef) the location of F below middle C. The G clef encircles the G staff line, and the two dots of the F clef demark the F line. These two clefs have become the most widely used in the twentieth and twenty-first centuries, and it is therefore imperative that you are able to read them both fluently. Bass and treble clefs often appear one above the other, in the **grand staff** (Example 1.2).

EXAMPLE 1.2 Grand Staff

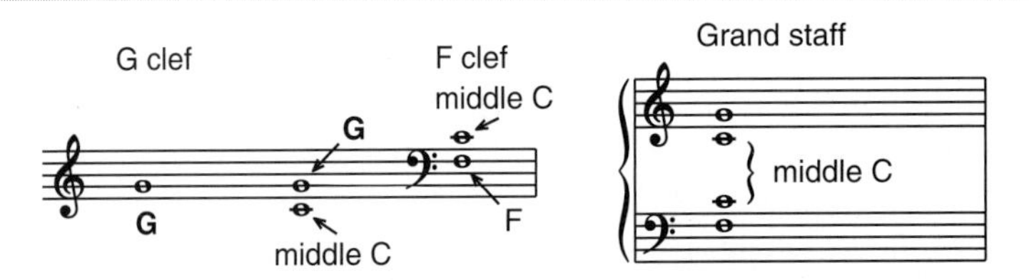

Ledger lines extend a staff in order to accommodate pitches that exceed its range. Since so many instruments and voices are now commonly written in either the bass or treble clef, ledger lines are commonplace. When composers write extended passages of music that would require a performer to navigate numerous pitches above or below the treble or bass staves, they often notate them comfortably within the staff and simply add the **octave sign** ("ottava," ***8va*** or ***8vb***), which specifies that the pitches that follow are to be performed one octave higher or one octave lower than written ("8va" above a pitch indicates performing the pitch one octave higher; "8vb" [or "8va" *below*] or "8va bassa" indicates performance one octave lower). Example 1.3A contains ottavas in both the bass and treble clefs because Liszt takes advantage of the piano's huge range, yet the use of the ottavas makes it much easier to read than the alternate version, notated without the octave signs (Example 1.3B). In vocal music, octave indications are shown most often in the treble clef and are intended for the tenors; the "8" appended to the bottom of the treble clef indicates performance of pitches one octave lower.

EXAMPLE 1.3 Liszt, "Sursum corda" from *Annees de Pelerinage*, Year 3

DVD 1
CH 1
TRACK 1

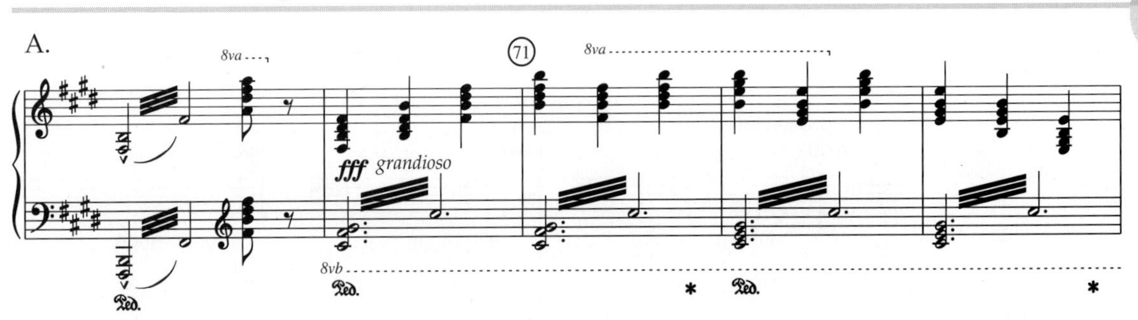

Continued

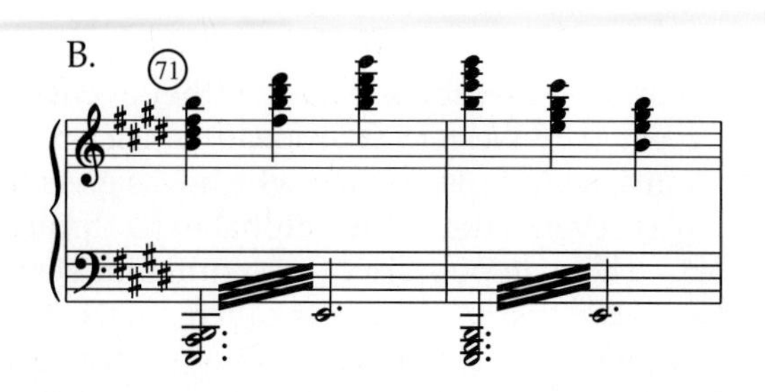

Pitch and Pitch Class

EXAMPLE 1.4 Pitch v. Pitch Class

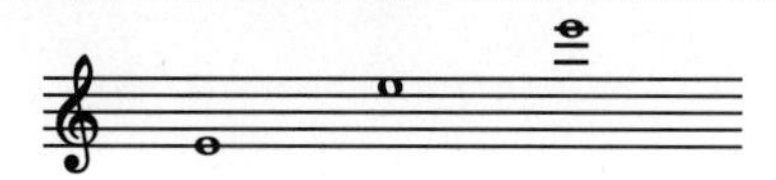

In Example 1.4, the note E appears in various locations relative to the staff: high, middle, and low. By referring to specific Es that are higher or lower than one another, we are referring to each E as a distinct **pitch**. A pitch is generated by a vibrating body, whether it be a violin string or a clarinet reed. The speed of the regularly recurring vibrations—called the *frequency*— determines the pitch: The faster the vibrations, the higher the pitch; and the slower the vibrations, the lower the pitch (and the shape, or *waveform*, of the vibrating body creates the *timbre*, or tone quality, that gives the characteristic sound of individual instruments). Pitch refers to the relative highness or lowness of sound, and it allows us to specify both the name and placement of E in relation to other Es. This placement, called **register**, refers to the specific area in which musical activity takes place. If you are seated at the middle of the piano keyboard, your body is usually aligned with middle C. As you play the Cs above and below middle C, you change register.

The term **pitch class** refers to all pitches with the same letter name. Pitches with the same name are separated by the distance of an **octave** (from *ottava*, or "eight"). When played together, pitches at a distance of one or more octaves sound very similar, which is why they have the same letter name. The reason that octave-related pitches sound nearly identical has to do with the relationship of the frequencies: For every pitch, the frequency of the pitch one octave higher is doubled, and the frequency of the pitch one octave lower is halved. In Example 1.4, all of the Es are represented by the pitch class E, no matter how high or low in the score. Still, the registral distinctions between the various representatives of pitch class E can mark important moments in the musical flow.

The Division of Musical Space: Intervals

The distance between any two pitches is called an **interval**. Musicians have been exploring different-size intervals for more than two millennia. They universally considered the octave to be a crucial interval, for it marks an important sonic boundary: Pitches separated by one or more octaves are considered to be so closely related that they share the same name. With the octave in place, musicians parsed this distance in various ways, most of which were attempts to distribute pitches rather evenly over its span. Eventually, the music created by Western (European) musicians used pitches that divided the octave into seven **steps**, each of which was given its own name, corresponding to the first seven letters of the alphabet (A through G).

These steps were of two different sizes, one exactly twice as large as the other. The smaller step is called a **half step** (half steps on the keyboard occur between any two adjacent keys, such as E and F or B and C). The larger step is called a **whole step**, defined as two half steps (whole steps on the keyboard occur between any two keys separated by one intervening key, such as between C and D or A and B). See Example 1.5, which marks various half (H) and whole (W) steps on the keyboard.

EXAMPLE 1.5 Half and Whole Steps, Musical Registers, Octave Designations, and the Keyboard

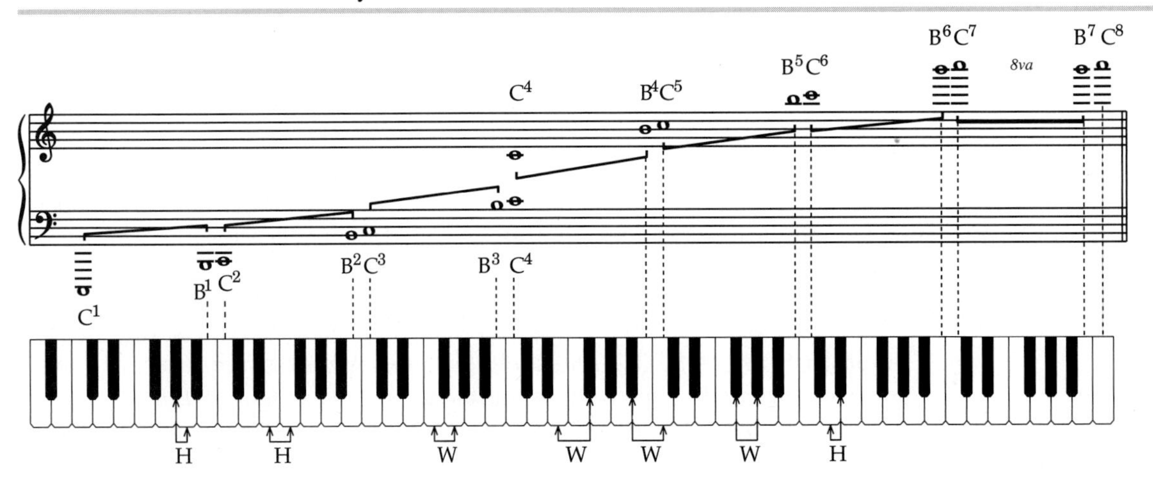

Example 1.5 also shows a common way of describing pitches: Each octave, moving upward from C to B, is assigned a number. We use the piano keyboard to illustrate these names and numbers because of its large range (88 pitches) and clarity of pitch representation (each key represents a single pitch). The lowest C on the piano is designated C^1, and each higher octave is incremented by 1: middle C is C^4. C is the lowest pitch in each octave; pitches above C in that octave will have the same octave designation, as shown in Example 1.5.

Accidentals

There are seven different pitch names within an octave (A–G), but a glance at the keyboard reveals twelve different keys: seven white and five black. In order to name each of the 12 keys, we refine the names of the seven basic (or *natural*) keys by adding various modifiers, which we refer to as **chromatic alterations** or **accidentals**. Two common accidentals are the flat (♭), which lowers a pitch one half step, and the sharp (♯), which raises it one half step. The **natural** (♮) is another common accidental, the purpose of which is to cancel a previous accidental. For example, an F♮ following an F♯ removes the sharp, resulting in a pitch that is one half step lower.

Two more accidentals complete the alteration family. A **double sharp** (𝄪) will raise a pitch by two half steps (or an already-sharped pitch by one half step). By the same token, a **double flat** (♭♭) will lower a pitch by two half steps (or an already-flatted pitch by one half step). When you encounter a chromatic alteration, it will be applied only in the octave register in which it occurs and will remain in effect until the end of the measure. If a composer wishes to continue the alteration, he or she must repeat it in subsequent measures. Example 1.6 summarizes all the accidentals and demonstrates how various notated examples would correlate with the keyboard. Note that each of five possible accidentals has been applied to F.

EXAMPLE 1.6 Accidentals

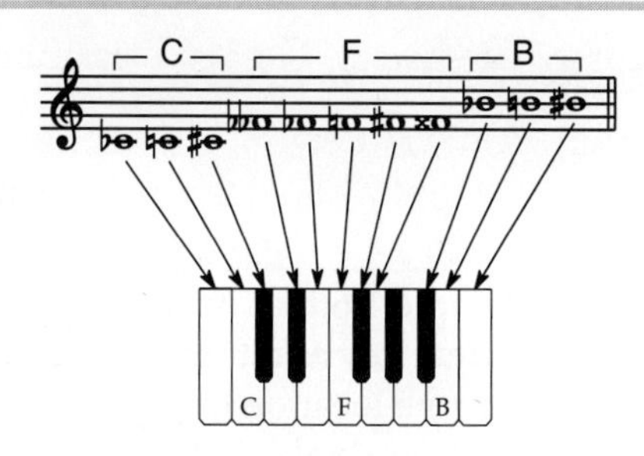

♯ sharp	raises a pitch a half step
♭ flat	lowers a pitch a half step
♮ natural	cancels a previous accidental or indicates an unaltered pitch
𝄪 double sharp	raises an unaltered pitch two half steps or a sharped pitch one half step
♭♭ double flat	lowers an unaltered pitch two half steps or a flatted pitch one half step.

Scales

Thus, the octave has been divided into 12 pitches, each equidistant from the next by the interval of a half step. We refer to the entire collection of 12 possible pitch classes as the **chromatic system**; arranged in order, these pitch classes form the **chromatic scale**, as shown in Example 1.7. This ordering looks like a staircase or ladder, and it is from this representation that the Latin term for scale, *scala*, was derived. However, the large, 12-pitch-class chromatic system is really more a collection of *possible* pitches; composers tended to use a seven-pitch-class scale that mixes half and whole steps. Consider the pitch classes E-F♯-G♯-A-B-C♯-D♯ (notated as unfilled pitches in Example 1.7). Notice that there are five whole steps (W) and two half steps (H) (occurring between G♯/A and D♯/E).

EXAMPLE 1.7 The Chromatic and Diatonic Scales

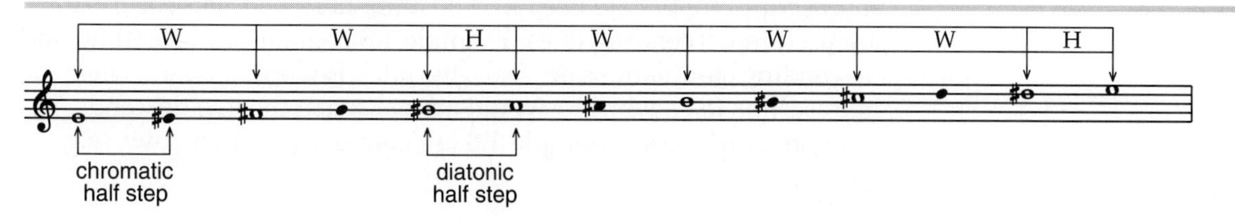

This scale, based on the ordered succession of the seven different letter names, is the foundation of Western music. A composition based on such a scale is said to be in a **key**. Thus, a composition is in the key of E if it is based on a scale generated from the pitch class E. Since each letter of the musical alphabet is represented once and only once, we refer to this type of scale as **diatonic** (or "through the tones"). A diatonic scale may begin on any of the 12 different pitch-classes and may ascend or descend. Thus, pitches that are members of the seven-pitch-class scale are **diatonic** (shown as unfilled pitches), and pitches that lie outside the scale are **chromatic** (from Latin, *chroma*, or "color").

There are two different names for half steps: **Diatonic half steps** include two different letter names (e.g., G♯ and A, as in the E scale in Example 1.7) and **chromatic half steps**, which share the same letter name (e.g., A♭ and A). See Example 1.7.

Enharmonicism

You may have observed in Example 1.6 that on the keyboard, pitches such as C♭ and B, and B♯ and C are the same key and therefore sound the same. Pitches and pitch classes that have the same location on the keyboard but have different names are **enharmonically equivalent**. Since enharmonically related pitches sound the same as one another, we consider them to be the same pitch class.

EXAMPLE 1.8 Enharmonically Equivalent Pitches

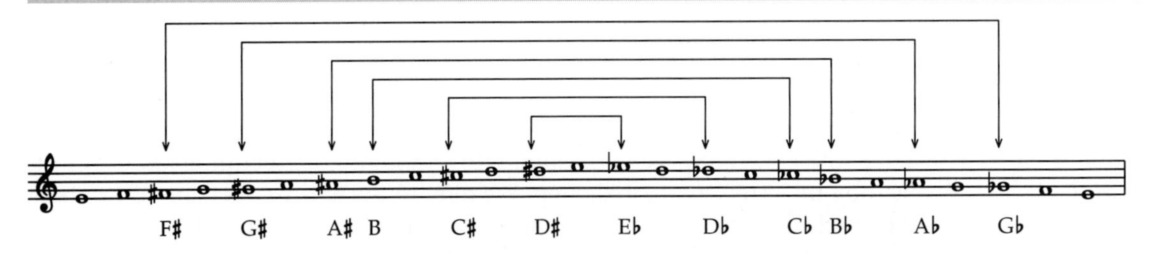

Given that C♭ and B are enharmonically equivalent (and the same pitch class), you may have wondered why one was chosen over the other in Example 1.7. The specific name we give to a pitch is determined by how it functions within a musical context. There are two general principles for determining whether to use one enharmonically equivalent pitch rather than another.

1. Use the note name that represents membership within the prevailing key; thus, we would use B rather than C♭ in Example 1.7)
2. In a chromatic environment, employ the notation convention in which sharps (or naturals) are used in ascending lines and flats (or naturals) are used in descending lines. Example 1.8 contains an ascending and descending chromatic scale. Thus, the pitch F♯ would be used when the line ascends to G, while G♭ would appear when the line descends. Enharmonic pitches in Example 1.8 are connected with arrows (e.g., F♯ and G♭).

Enharmonicism is more abstract than real. For fixed-pitch instruments, such as the piano, enharmonically related pitches are identical; but for moveable-pitch instruments, players will slightly alter, or *temper*, the pitches according to the context (e.g., string players would most likely play a G♯ somewhat higher than an A♭ in order to intensify the expected ascending motion to A).

Common-practice composers draw most of their pitch material from the diatonic scale, but they also incorporate elements from the chromatic system. When most of the pitch material comes from the seven pitch classes of a scale, we refer to the music as diatonic. As more nondiatonic pitches are used in a composition, it becomes increasingly chromatic. Later, we will learn how composers incorporate chromatic elements into their music.

Scale Degree Numbers and Names

As shown in Example 1.9, each of the seven members—or **scale degrees**—of the scale can be numbered in ascending order, beginning with the tonic. Such **scale degree numbers** are distinguished by the caret, or cap, that is placed above each number in order to avoid confusion with other numbers that have different meanings. Scale degrees may also be identified by names that reflect their relationship to the tonic pitch class. In order of importance, the next scale members are the **dominant** and the **mediant**. If we call the tonic the first step, the dominant lies five steps above the tonic and the mediant lies three steps above the tonic. The mediant's name is logically derived from the fact that it lies midway between the tonic and the dominant. The **supertonic,** as the name implies, lies immediately above the tonic. The **subdominant**, the fourth scale degree, derives its name from the fact that it can also be viewed as lying five steps below the tonic, just as the dominant lies five above. Similarly, the **submediant,** the sixth scale degree, lies three steps below the tonic, just as the mediant lies three above. Finally, the **leading tone**, scale degree 7, lies one step below the tonic, to which it usually leads.

EXAMPLE 1.9 The E Scale with Scale Degree Numbers and Names

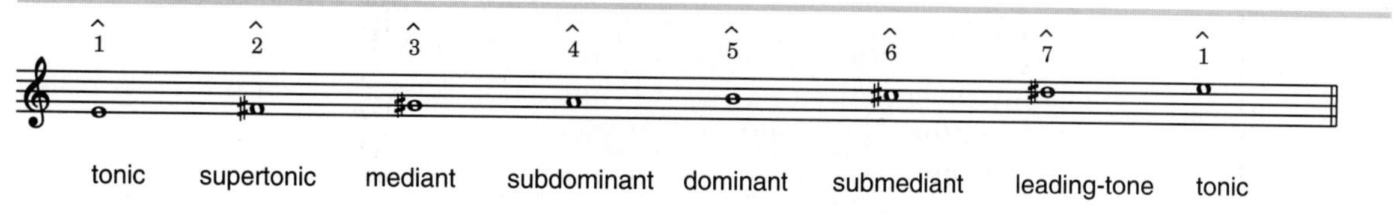

Specific Scale Types: Major and Minor

An easy way to memorize scale patterns is to arrange the pitch classes in ascending order, as we did in the previous examples. It is crucial that this ordering use *every pitch letter name once and only once.* A major scale consists of a collection of seven different pitch classes with the intervallic order w–w–h–w–w–w–h. **Major** and its companion, **minor** (which has a slightly different intervallic ordering), refer to the **mode** of the piece. The major mode is sometimes considered brighter than the minor mode and more stable. Example 1.10A illustrates a passage in D major from Schubert's "Gute Nacht," followed by the passage cast in the minor mode (Example 1.10B).

EXAMPLE 1.10 **Schubert, "Gute Nacht" from *Winterreise***

Although the term *mode* has been used since antiquity to refer to many different scalar constructions, nowadays we also use *mode* to refer to the two types of scales that occur regularly in tonal music: major and minor. Memorize the intervallic pattern that creates a major scale, especially the location of the half steps (between $\hat{3}$ and $\hat{4}$ and between $\hat{7}$ and $\hat{1}$). The name of a key provides two kinds of information: It identifies both the tonic pitch and the mode (major or minor).

Building Scales in the Major Mode

We can generate a major scale on each of the remaining 11 pitch classes by using the same pattern of half and whole steps found in the E-major scale. Moving any pitch pattern so that it begins on a different set of pitches is called **transposition**. Let's build a major scale on A.

First, since a scale consists of stepwise motion, we will use every letter name in turn, and we will end our scale by repeating the tonic pitch one octave higher in order to create closure: A–B–C–D–E–F–G–A.

Next, we refine our scale and create the sound of the major mode by using the pattern of half and whole steps that we learned in the context of E major (w–w–h–w–w–w–h). A to B, the first interval, is a whole step, so we move on to the next, which must also be a whole step. However, B to C is only a half step, so we must increase its size. We can do this by adding a sharp to C, raising the pitch a half step (C♯). B to C♯ is a whole step, so we move on to the next interval, which should be a half step, and, indeed, C♯ moves a half step to D. Continuing this process, we determine that the pitches of the major scale on A are A–B–C♯–D–E–F♯–G♯–A (Example 1.11). Since the scale of A major contains three sharped pitches, we say that "the scale of A major contains three sharps."

EXAMPLE 1.11 The A-Major Scale

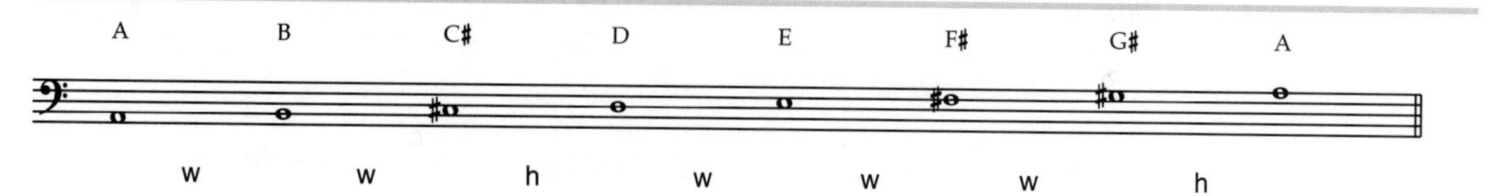

Let's try building one more major scale, this time on F, beginning with the ordering F–G–A–B–C–D–E–F. Applying our formula of whole and half steps to the first two intervals, we find that F to G and G to A are both whole steps, as they should be. Moving ahead, the distance from A to B is another whole step, rather than the requisite half step. Therefore, we must lower B one half step by adding a flat, changing B to B♭. Next, we need another whole step, which B♭ to C provides. By continuing this process, we see that the major scale on F requires just one flat: F–G–A–B♭–C–D–E–F (Example 1.12).

EXAMPLE 1.12 The F-Major Scale

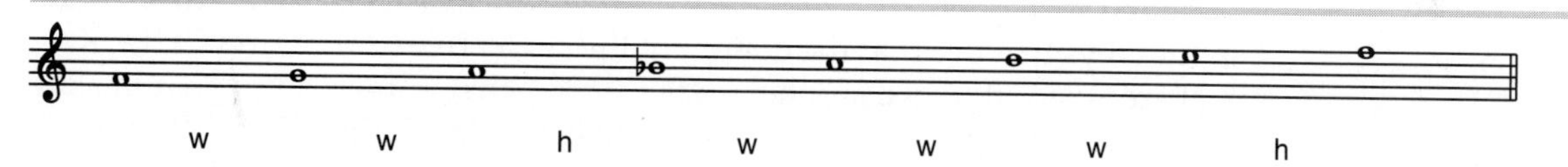

Key Signatures and the Circle of Fifths

The **key signature** is a symbol that appears at the beginning of each musical staff, to the right of the clef. It presents a pattern of either sharps or flats that is a helpful musical shorthand for conveying pitch classes of a key. Indeed, the key signature often implies the key of the composition (keys are made explicit by how the pitches are actually used). Imagine the notational nightmare one would encounter when writing a piece in C♯ major without a key signature: Every pitch in the piece would need to be preceded by a sharp sign. Example 1.13 shows the four-sharp key signature for E major. Note that there is only one F♯, one C♯, one G♯, and one D♯ shown in the key signature; when you indicate a sharp or flat in a key signature, the accidental applies to the entire pitch class (if you write a sharp for one F♯, then all Fs become F♯s).

EXAMPLE 1.13 The Key Signature for E Major

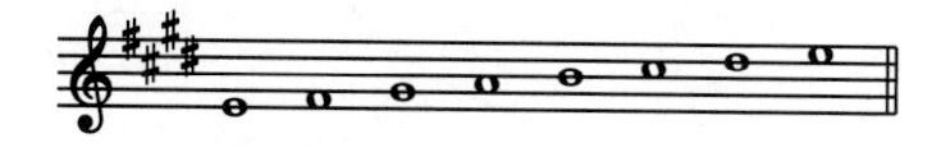

G major has one altered pitch (F♯), so its key signature has one sharp; D major has two altered pitches (F♯, C♯), so its key signature has two sharps. The complete list of major keys with sharps is: G (1 sharp), D (2), A (3), E (4), B (5), F♯ (6), C♯ (7). Note that the tonic note for each key on the list is five steps (or a "fifth") higher than in the previous key. The sharps in a key signature—when read from left to right—are also a fifth apart: F♯, C♯, G♯, D♯, A♯, E♯, B♯.

A way of memorizing the relationship between the key signature and the tonic is to note that the pitch one half step above the final sharp in the key signature is the tonic. For example, if the last sharp is F♯, the tonic is G; if the last sharp is B♯, the tonic is C♯.

The flat keys follow the same pattern of fifths, but in the opposite direction from C: F, B♭, E♭, A♭, D♭, G♭, C♭. Flats are added in a specific order of descending fifths: B♭, E♭, A♭, D♭, G♭, C♭, F♭. For flat keys, the tonic can be determined by reading the penultimate flat in the key signature. If the key signature contains B♭ and E♭, the second-to-last flat, B♭, is the tonic. Likewise, if the key signature contains B♭, E♭, A♭, and D♭, than the tonic is A♭. Note that when we ascend by fifths, we end with C♯ major; when we descend by fifths, we end with C♭ major.

The opposing process of flat and sharp key relations may be represented graphically as in Example 1.14, using a circle that illustrates both the key signatures and their relationships to one another. This diagram is called the **circle of fifths**, since each key on the circle lies a fifth above the preceding key (if you move clockwise around the circle) or a fifth below the preceding (if you move counterclockwise around the circle). Notice that there are 15 keys listed, although there are only 12 chromatic pitches. This is because of three enharmonic keys that occur at the bottom of the circle: B/C♭, F♯/G♭, and C♯/D♭. Keys that are adjacent to one another on the circle—that is, their key signatures differ by one sharp or flat—are called **closely related keys** (e.g., A♭ major is closely related to both D♭ major and E♭ major).

EXAMPLE 1.14 The Circle of Fifths

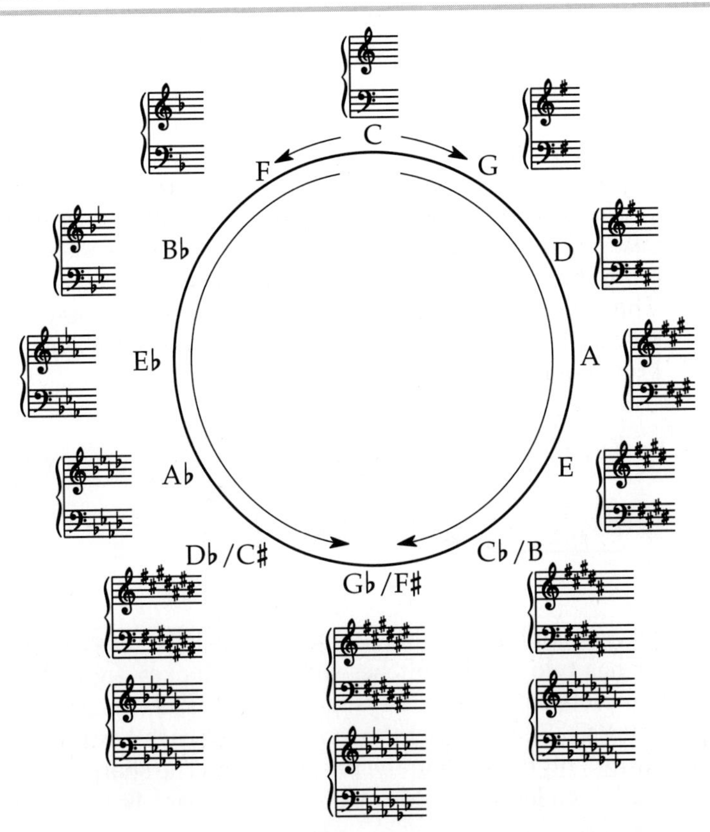

Building Scales in the Minor Mode

The **minor mode** is the other mode used in tonal music, and, like its major counterpart, it comprises a particular sequence of half steps and whole steps. The minor mode is distinguished primarily by its mediant ($\hat{3}$), which lies one half step lower than the third scale degree of the major mode. For example, in the key of D major, the third scale degree is F♯, while in the key of D minor, the third scale degree is F natural. Another important difference between the major and the minor modes is that $\hat{6}$ and $\hat{7}$ in the minor mode are variable; depending on the melodic line's direction, their scale degrees may be raised or lowered, which is why the minor mode is often considered to be more flexible than the major mode. The minor mode is characterized by a darker sound, in contrast to the bright sound of the major scale. Listen again to Example 1.10.

Example 1.15 presents D-major and D-minor scales. Notice that the minor scale has a different pattern of half and whole steps than the major. Pitch differences are shown as filled-in notes. We refer to this form of the minor scale—with a half step between $\hat{2}$ and $\hat{3}$ and between $\hat{5}$ and $\hat{6}$—as the **natural minor scale**. Notice that both $\hat{6}$ and $\hat{7}$ are a half step lower than in major.

EXAMPLE 1.15 Major and Natural Minor Scales

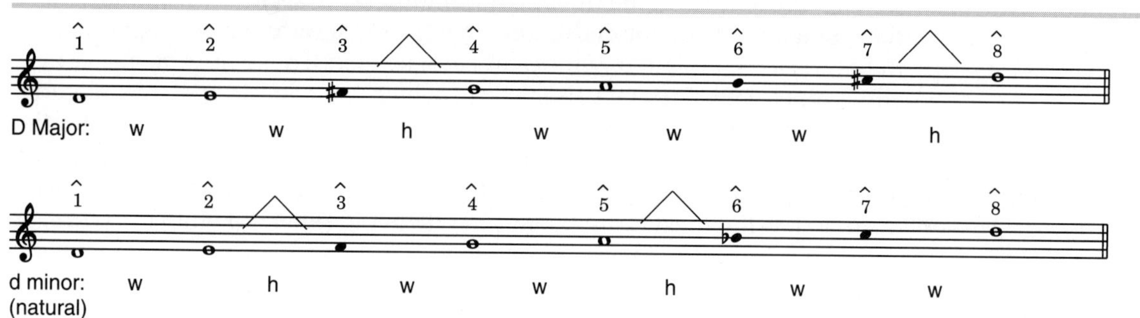

Composers often intensify melodic motion in the minor mode, resulting in the slight rearrangement of half steps and whole steps in the final three pitches. These variations take two forms and result in what are traditionally called the **harmonic minor scale** and the **melodic minor scale**. Example 1.16 presents the three forms of the minor scale: natural, harmonic, and melodic. The differences are based on the natural tendency for melodic lines to move toward a goal. That is, raising pitches enhances the pull of an ascending line, and lowering pitches enhances the direction of a descending line.

EXAMPLE 1.16 Natural, Harmonic, and Melodic Minor Scales

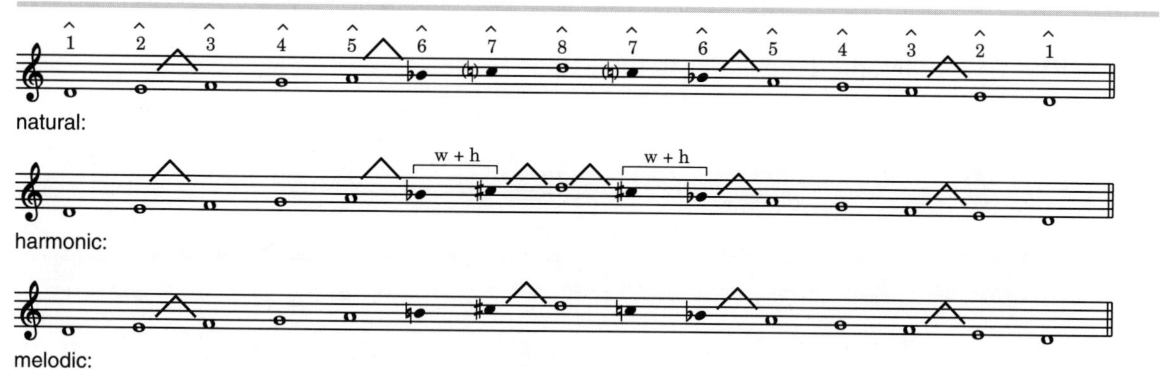

One can view these two variations of the minor scale as a means of creating both this goal-directed motion and a smooth melodic line, because forward motion in tonal music is generally enhanced by half-step motion. For example, the natural minor scale, with its smooth stepwise motion from $\hat{5}$ to $\hat{8}$ does not possess much goal-oriented motion in its ascent because it does not contain a leading tone. The **harmonic minor scale** remedies this situation by raising $\hat{7}$ to create a leading tone. Notice in Example 1.10 that Schubert adds the leading tone (C♯) in the piano accompaniment (m. 10) in order to create a sense of musical closure that complements the end of the first line of text. However, as shown in Example 1.16, the addition of the leading tone sacrifices the smooth melodic motion between $\hat{6}$ and $\hat{7}$ by producing a gap of one and a half steps. The **melodic minor scale** contains both smooth stepwise motion and the leading tone, since $\hat{6}$ as well as $\hat{7}$ are raised, which leads nicely upward to $\hat{1}$, the primary tonal pillar and point of stability. The descending version of the melodic minor scale is different from its ascending version: In order to enhance the descent toward the secondary tonal pillar, ($\hat{5}$), $\hat{6}$ and $\hat{7}$ are lowered. We call the lowered $\hat{7}$ the **subtonic** rather than the leading tone; the subtonic does not rise to the tonic as the leading tone does; rather, it is the crucial first step in a falling line that leads toward the dominant.

The three forms of the minor scale should be viewed more as slight variations of a single "minor collection" than as three different scales, because of their constant circulation within a musical context. Thus, the minor scale is really a nine-pitch-class repository from which the composer draws material. Indeed, as shown in Example 1.17A, Mozart's descending chromatic line touches on both forms of $\hat{7}$ and $\hat{6}$ on its way to an arrival on $\hat{5}$; the musical "point" is less what form of minor is used than what musical procedure creates the most dramatic tension (to avoid potential ambiguity, up and down arrows will represent raised and lowered scale degrees, respectively). Example 1.17B arranges the entire minor collection in ascending order. Example 1.17C illustrates how the minor collection is really a byproduct of the melodic requirements of individual lines. For example, the opening descending bass line is intensified by the lowered forms of $\hat{6}$ and $\hat{7}$, while the following ascent is supported by using their raised forms. Notice that the unwieldy interval of three half steps that occurs between lowered $\hat{6}$ and raised $\hat{7}$ of the harmonic form of minor is actually moot, since this interval rarely occurs within a single melodic line. In the Bach chorale, $\uparrow\hat{7}$ (E♯) arises either from a stepwise ascent through $\uparrow\hat{6}$ (D♯) or from the half-step descent from $\hat{1}$ to $\hat{7}$ and return to $\hat{1}$ (F♯–E♯–F♯); E♯ is not in any way connected to $\downarrow\hat{6}$ (D natural). Similarly, $\downarrow\hat{6}$ arises from an upward movement from $\hat{5}$, to which it returns. Thus, $\downarrow\hat{6}$ gravitates toward $\hat{5}$ and $\uparrow\hat{7}$ gravitates toward $\hat{1}$.

EXAMPLE 1.17 Melodic Tendencies in the Minor Mode

DVD 1 CH 1 TRACK 3

A. Mozart, Piano Sonata in D major, K. 284, Polonaise en Rondeau

B. Scale

C. Bach, "Verleih' uns Frieden gnädiglich"

Key Signatures in Minor

Minor keys are represented by key signatures derived from the natural minor scale. The order of minor key signatures proceeds in exactly the same pattern as the major key signatures. See Example 1.18, which summarizes the number and names of the sharps or flats for all major and minor keys; C, with no flats or sharps, is in the middle, with added sharps and flats fanning out above and below C. That is, one sharp is added to the key signature for each scale that lies a fifth higher than the previous scale (i.e., from $\hat{1}$ up to $\hat{5}$). One flat is added to the key signature that lies a fifth lower than the previous scale (i.e., from $\hat{1}$ down to $\hat{4}$).

EXAMPLE 1.18 **Sharps and Flats in Major and Minor Keys**

MAJOR KEY	MINOR KEY	NUMBER OF ACCIDENTALS	ACCIDENTALS IN KEY
C♯	a♯	7 sharps	F♯ C♯ G♯ D♯ A♯ E♯ B♯
F♯	d♯	6 sharps	F♯ C♯ G♯ D♯ A♯ E♯
B	g♯	5 sharps	F♯ C♯ G♯ D♯ A♯
E	c♯	4 sharps	F♯ C♯ G♯ D♯
A	f♯	3 sharps	F♯ C♯ G♯
D	b	2 sharps	F♯ C♯
G	e	1 sharp	F♯
→ C	a	0	
F	d	1 flat	B♭
B♭	g	2 flats	B♭ E♭
E♭	c	3 flats	B♭ E♭ A♭
A♭	f	4 flats	B♭ E♭ A♭ D♭
D♭	b♭	5 flats	B♭ E♭ A♭ D♭ G♭
G♭	e♭	6 flats	B♭ E♭ A♭ D♭ G♭ C♭
C♭	a♭	7 flats	B♭ E♭ A♭ D♭ G♭ C♭ F♭

Relative Major and Minor Keys

We refer to major and minor keys with the same key signatures as **relative**. The relative major key of a minor key lies three half steps (i.e., skipping one letter name) above the tonic of the minor key; of course, we also can think of relative minor keys as lying three half steps below the tonic of the major key. Example 1.19A, from one of Beethoven's piano sonatas, illustrates the relative major relationship between D minor and F major. Usually, however, such literal restatements of material in a different harmonic area are not as common as the use of contrasting material, as illustrated in another example from Beethoven's piano sonatas (Example 1.19B). Here, the relative relationship works the other way: from a major key (D major) to a minor key (B minor). Beethoven's dramatic statement of the D-major opening theme in octaves is followed by a tumultuous theme in B minor.

EXAMPLE 1.19 Relative Key Relations

DVD 1
CH 1
TRACK 4

A. Beethoven, Piano Sonata in D major, op. 28, *Andante*

B. Beethoven, Piano Sonata in D major, op. 10, no. 3

Such dramatic harmonic shifts, however, are uncommon. The diagram in Example 1.20 illustrates the pairing of relative major and minor keys around the circle of fifths. Major keys are represented by uppercase letters and minor keys by lowercase letters on the circle of fifths.

EXAMPLE 1.20 Relative Major and Minor Key Signatures

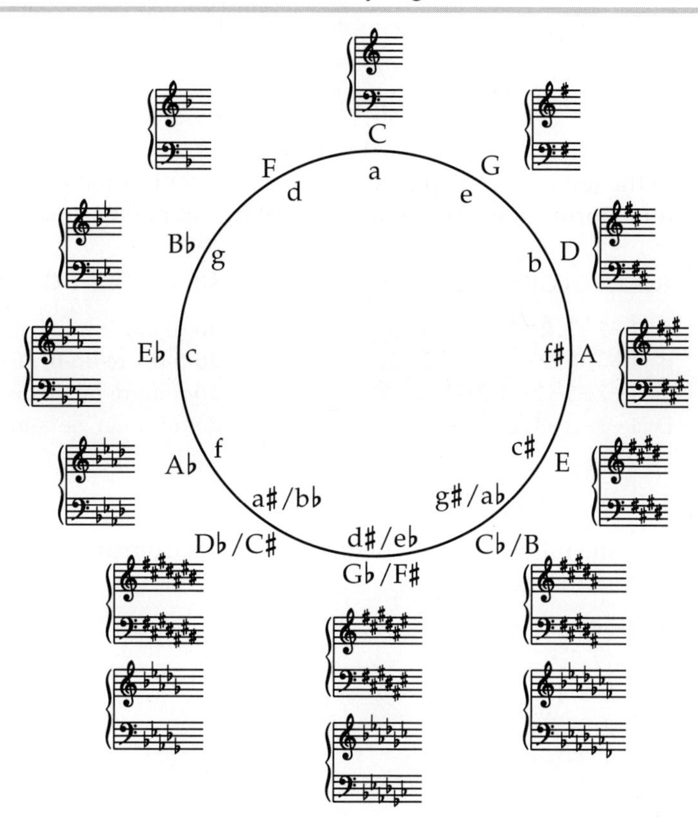

Parallel major and **parallel minor** scales and keys are those that share the same tonic but do not share the same key signatures. For example, the parallel minor of D major is D minor, and the parallel major of B♭ minor is B♭ major. The key signatures of parallel keys differ by three accidentals (e.g., the D major and d minor of Schubert's "Gute Nacht" in Example 1.10 contain two sharps and one flat respectively [i.e., two sharps plus one flat equals three accidentals]). Example 1.21 illustrates back-to-back statements of material in the parallel keys of G major and G minor.

EXAMPLE 1.21 Mozart, Piano Sonata in C major, K. 545, *Allegro*

DVD 1
CH 1
TRACK 5

EXERCISE INTERLUDE

PERFORMING

1.1 Scales: Pattern Continuation

Study the following scale degree patterns, and continue them until you return to the tonic. Sing or play on your instrument in both the major mode and the three forms of the minor mode. Feel free to make up some of your own.

SCALE DEGREE NUMBERS:	MOVEABLE DO SOLFÈGE:
A. $\hat{1}-\hat{2}-\hat{3}, \hat{2}-\hat{3}-\hat{4}, \hat{3}-\hat{4}-\hat{5}, \ldots$	do-re-mi, re-mi-fa, mi-fa-sol, . . .
B. $\hat{1}-\hat{7}-\hat{1}, \hat{2}-\hat{1}-\hat{2}, \hat{3}-\hat{2}-\hat{3}, \ldots$	do-ti-do, re-do-ti, mi-re-mi, . . .
C. $\hat{1}-\hat{7}-\hat{1}-\hat{2}-\hat{3}, \hat{2}-\hat{1}-\hat{2}-\hat{3}-\hat{4}, \ldots$	do-ti-do-re-mi, re-do-re-mi-fa, . . .
D. $\hat{1}-\hat{3}-\hat{2}-\hat{1}, \hat{2}-\hat{4}-\hat{3}-\hat{2}, \hat{3}-\hat{5}, \ldots$	do-mi-re-do, re-fa-mi-re, mi-sol, . . .

1.2 Scale Degree Patterns

Sing the following scale degree fragments from any given pitch in both major and minor modes.

A. $\hat{1}$–$\hat{2}$–$\hat{3}$
B. $\hat{1}$–↑$\hat{7}$–$\hat{1}$
C. $\hat{1}$–$\hat{3}$–$\hat{5}$–$\hat{1}$
D. $\hat{1}$–$\hat{2}$–$\hat{3}$–↑$\hat{7}$–$\hat{1}$
E. $\hat{5}$–$\hat{4}$–$\hat{3}$–$\hat{1}$–♭$\hat{6}$–$\hat{5}$
F. $\hat{3}$–$\hat{2}$–$\hat{1}$–$\hat{5}$
G. $\hat{3}$–$\hat{1}$–$\hat{4}$–$\hat{5}$–$\hat{1}$

1.3 Transposition

Perform each given melodic fragment, and then label the scale degree numbers. Then, on your instrument, perform the fragment, transposing it to the key implied by the given pitch. *Note:* the given pitch will be the first pitch of the fragment but, like the fragment may not necessarily be the tonic.

For example, given the fragment D–G–A–B–F♯–G and the first pitch of the transposed version (B♭), you would:

1. Perform and study the melody to determine the key. The sample solution is in G major.
2. Label the scale degrees of the melody ($\hat{5}$–$\hat{1}$–$\hat{2}$–$\hat{3}$–$\hat{7}$–$\hat{1}$).
3. Transfer the scale degree number of the first pitch of the original melody to the given new pitch, since this will be the first pitch of the transposed version. Given that the first pitch of the original melody is D, which functions as $\hat{5}$ in G, then the given B♭ will also function as $\hat{5}$, but now in the key of E♭ major.
4. Play the transposed version: B♭–E♭–F–G–D–E♭

Sample solution:

When transposing by a fifth, use the circle of fifths to guide you.
A1.
A2.
B1.
B2.
C.
C1.
C2.
D. Mozart, Piano Sonata in C major, K. 545, *Allegro*
D1.
D2.
Allegro
tr
E. Mozart, Sinfonia Concertante in E♭ major, K. 364, *Andante*
E1.
E2.
p
F. Schumann, "Das verlassne Mägdelein", op. 64, no.2
F1.
F2.
p
Früh wann die Häh-ne kräh'n, eh' die Stern-lein schwin-den,
G. Bach, French Suite in B minor, BWV 814, Sarabande
G1.
G2.
H. Beethoven, Symphony no. 3 in E♭ major, op. 55, *Marcia Funebre*
H1.
H2.
Marcia funebre
Adagio assai

LISTENING

1.4 Half v. Whole Steps (I)

Sing the two pitches that you hear in a comfortable register. Determine whether the pitches lie the intervallic distance of a half step or a whole step from one another. You may wish to listen in terms of function: a half-step relationship will sound like leading tone to tonic ($\hat{7}$–$\hat{8}$), or vice versa. A whole-step relationship will sound like the beginning ascent of a scale ($\hat{1}$–$\hat{2}$) or the ending descent ($\hat{2}$–$\hat{1}$). Identify using "H" or "W."

A. _____ B. _____ C. _____ D. _____ E. _____ F. _____ G. _____ H. _____ I. _____ J. _____

DVD 2
CH 1
TRACK 2

1.5 Half v. Whole Steps (II)

This exercise is identical to exercise 1.4, but this time you will notate the second pitch of the pair of pitches.

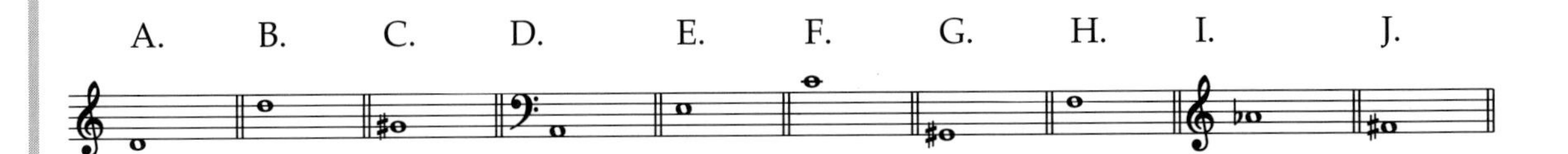

DVD 2
CH 1
TRACK 3

1.6 Aural and Visual Comparison

You will hear melodic fragments. Circle the score that corresponds with what was played.

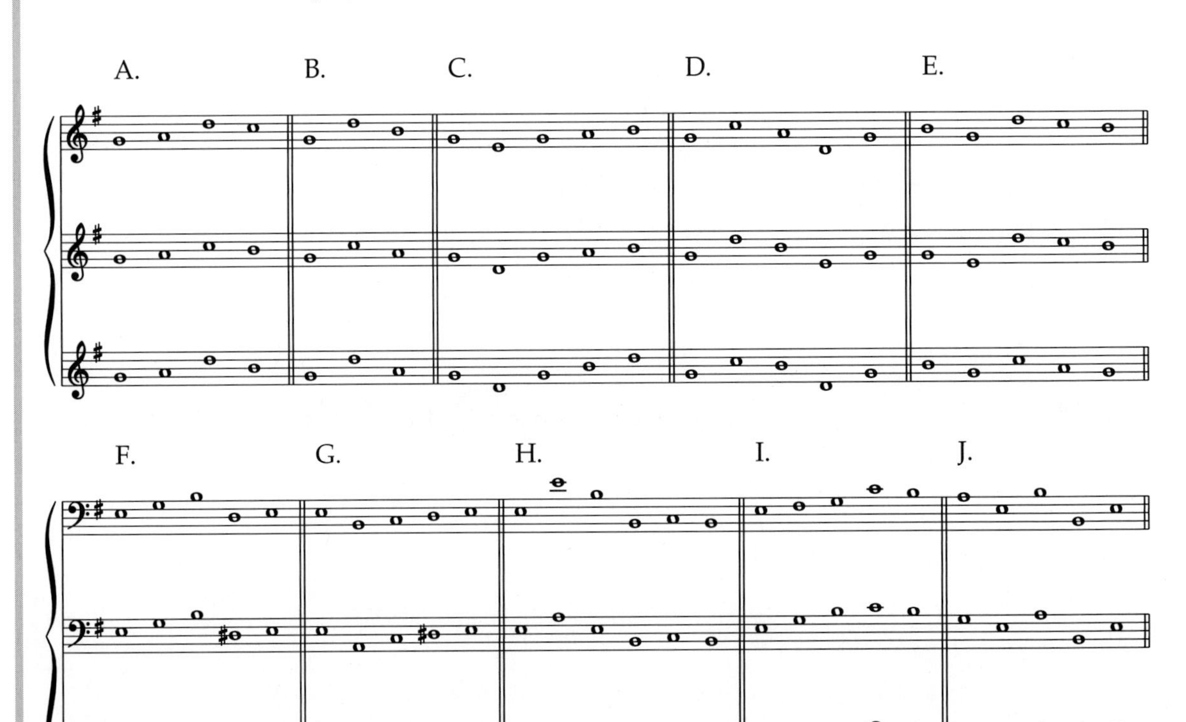

DVD 2
CH 1
TRACK 4

1.7. Mode Identification

Identify the mode (major or minor) for each of the musical excerpts drawn from well-known theme-and-variation movements. What is unusual about F?

A. _____ B. _____ C. _____ D. _____ E. _____ F. _____

DVD 2
CH 1
TRACK 5

1.8 Ear Training: Melodic Dictation

You will hear five-pitch major-mode melodies. Listen to the entire melody and be able to sing (1) the tonic pitch and (2) the entire fragment. Then, on a separate sheet of manuscript paper, notate the pitches using scale degree numbers. $\hat{1}$ is played before you hear each example.

WRITING

1.9 Writing Scales (I)

Notate the following scales on manuscript paper. Use accidentals instead of key signatures, and mark each half and whole step. Begin by writing the first scale (B♭ major) in bass clef and the next in treble clef. Continue alternating clefs for each scale.

A. Major:

1. D (sample solution):

2. B♭ 3. E♭ 4. G 5. B 6. E 7. D♭

B. Melodic minor:

1. F 2. A 3. B

C. Harmonic minor:

1. G 2. B♭ 3. C♯

D. Natural minor:

1. D 2. E♭ 3. E

1.10 Writing Scales (II)

Write the following scales on manuscript paper, using accidentals instead of key signatures.

A. The major scale in which:

1. G♯ is $\hat{3}$ (sample solution):

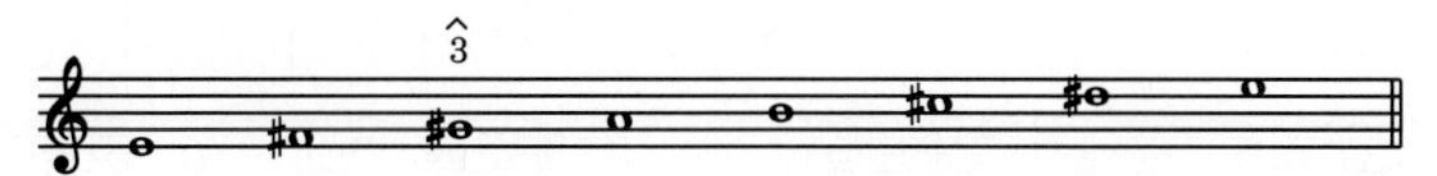

2. C is $\hat{4}$ 3. G♯ is $\hat{6}$ 4. C♯ is $\hat{6}$ 5. B♭ is $\hat{2}$ 6. B♭ is $\hat{4}$ 7. B♭ is $\hat{7}$

B. The major scale in which:

1. A is supertonic 2. D is mediant 3. F is submediant 4. B is dominant
5. E is supertonic 6. E is subdominant 7. E is leading tone

C. The harmonic minor scale in which:

1. A is $\hat{3}$ 2. C♯ is $\hat{7}$ 3. E is $\hat{5}$ 4. E is $\hat{6}$

D. The relative major scale of:

1. G minor 2. C♯ minor 3. B♭ minor 4. G♯ minor

E. The relative minor scale (melodic form) of:

1. F major 2. A major 3. E♭ major

F. The parallel major scale of:

1. E minor 2. A minor 3. A♭ minor

1.11 Scale Degrees and Transposition

Determine the major or minor key implied by the short melodic fragments, and label each pitch using scale degree numbers. Then, using accidentals (not a key signature), transpose each example to the key implied by the given starting pitch.

1.12 Scalar Membership

Determine the major and minor scales that contain the following three- and four-pitch fragments. For example, given the pitches F–G–A, there are at least six keys that contain these pitches (three major and three relative minor, shown by connecting slurs). *Note:* consider all forms of the minor scale.

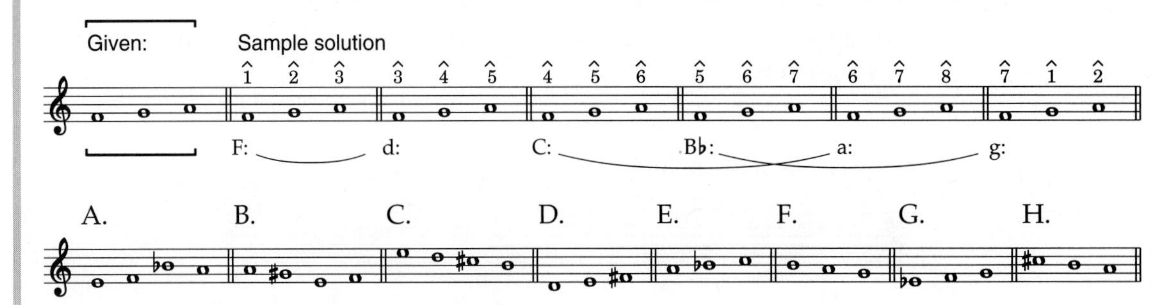

ANALYSIS

DVD 2
CH 1
TRACK 6

1.13 Minor Scale Forms

Label the type of minor scale(s) that appear in each of the examples. Circle and identify the following scale degrees using these labels: $\flat\hat{3}$, $\flat\hat{6}$, $\sharp\hat{6}$, $\flat\hat{7}$, $\sharp\hat{7}$. When you encounter the harmonic minor scale, do $\flat\hat{6}$ and $\sharp\hat{7}$ occur in the same voice? If so, does one lead to the other, or does $\flat\hat{6}$ arise from and return to $\hat{5}$ (i.e., $\hat{5}$-$\flat\hat{6}$-$\hat{5}$) as $\sharp\hat{7}$ is connected with $\hat{8}$?

A. Beethoven, String Quartet in F minor, op. 95, *Allegro con brio*

B. Bach, "Herr Jesu Christ, du höchstes Gut"

C. Haydn, Piano Sonata in D major, Hob. XVI/33, *Adagio*

D. Brahms, Clarinet Quintet, op. 115, *con moto*. The clarinet in A sounds three half steps lower than written. For example, a notated C would sound as A.

DVD 2
CH 1
TRACK 7

1.14 Comparing Tonal Relationships: Relative, Parallel, and Dominant

Each pair of examples shown here is taken from the same piece. Identify their relationship as relative, parallel, or dominant.

- You may encounter parallel relationships in which the enharmonically equivalent key is used for reading ease. For example, a modal shift from A♭ major to its parallel minor would require playing in the seven-flat key of A♭ minor; composers would often renotate such a passage in the five-sharp key of G♯ minor.
- Do not assume that the keys implied by the given key signature necessarily apply to the passages.

A. Beethoven op. 31/1, mm. 66ff

B. Haydn, Piano Sonata in F major, Hob. XVI/47

1.

2.

C. Schubert, Moments Musicale in C♯ minor, D. 780

1.15 Scrambled Major and Minor Scales

Determine which major and/or minor scale is used in the exercises shown, and notate the ascending and descending form of the scale on a separate sheet of manuscript paper. Recall that every major scale contains the same pitch classes as its relative natural-minor form. Adhere to the following guidelines:

- Look for accidentals, since their type (sharps or flats) and number will reduce the 12 possible keys to only one or at the most two. For example, given two sharps (F♯ and C♯), the major key would be D and the minor key would be B (natural minor).
- For harmonic and melodic forms of minor: To create ♯$\hat{6}$ and ♯$\hat{7}$, minor keys will add sharps as accidentals or will add naturals as accidentals (which omit flats from the key signature).
- Notate the pitches in ascending order, beginning with $\hat{1}$. Make sure that the key-defining half- and whole-step pattern conforms to one of the patterns that has been discussed. Label the key and the mode, and, when appropriate, specify the type of minor scale used.

The sample solution contains B♭ and E♭, which means that either B♭ major or G minor (natural) could be the scale.

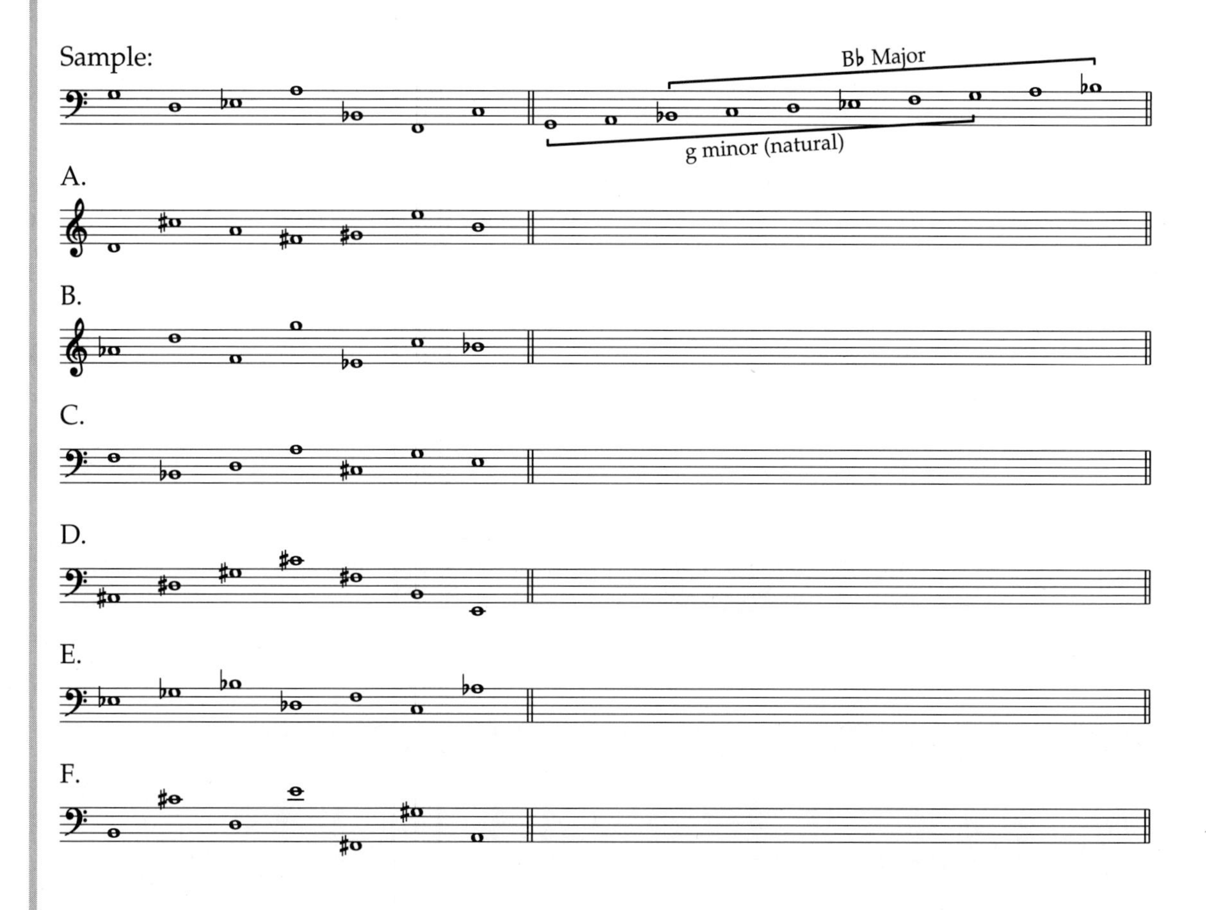

KEYBOARD

1.16 Reading in Bass and Treble Clefs, Ledger Lines

1. Say the names of the following pitches, including their octave designations (e.g., the D above middle C is D^4).
2. Play the pitch in the notated octave.
3. Sing each of the pitches in a comfortable octave after you play it.

4. Play half steps (diatonic and chromatic) and whole steps above and below each pitch, saying aloud the pitch name.
5. Viewing each given pitch as scale degree 1, play one-octave ascending and descending major and three forms of minor scales (in a comfortable octave).

1.17 Sing and Play (I)

Continue the given scale degree patterns until you return to the tonic. Alternate playing and singing such that you begin a pattern by playing it, then sing the first repetition, then play again, and so on until the end. Use scale degrees or solfège when you sing. Be able to transpose the patterns to major and minor keys up to two flats or two sharps.

A. $\hat{1}$–$\hat{2}$–$\hat{3}$, $\hat{2}$–$\hat{3}$–$\hat{4}$, $\hat{3}$–$\hat{4}$–$\hat{5}$, . . .
B. $\hat{1}$–$\hat{7}$–$\hat{1}$–$\hat{2}$–$\hat{3}$, $\hat{2}$–$\hat{1}$–$\hat{2}$–$\hat{3}$–$\hat{4}$, $\hat{3}$–$\hat{2}$–$\hat{3}$–$\hat{4}$–$\hat{5}$, . . .
C. $\hat{1}$–$\hat{3}$–$\hat{2}$–$\hat{1}$, $\hat{2}$–$\hat{4}$–$\hat{3}$–$\hat{2}$, $\hat{3}$–$\hat{5}$–$\hat{4}$–$\hat{3}$, . . .
D. $\hat{3}$–$\hat{4}$–$\hat{3}$–$\hat{2}$–$\hat{1}$, $\hat{4}$–$\hat{5}$–$\hat{4}$–$\hat{3}$–$\hat{2}$, $\hat{5}$–$\hat{6}$–$\hat{5}$–$\hat{4}$–$\hat{3}$, . . .
E. $\hat{1}$–$\hat{3}$–$\hat{5}$–$\hat{2}$–$\hat{1}$, $\hat{2}$–$\hat{4}$–$\hat{6}$–$\hat{3}$–$\hat{2}$, $\hat{3}$–$\hat{5}$–$\hat{7}$–$\hat{4}$–$\hat{3}$, . . .

WORKBOOK
1.1–1.4

1.18 Sing and Play (II)

Perform the exercises as required. Use the right hand to play in the treble clef and the left hand to play in the bass clef. Since the piano part guides what you will then sing, listen carefully as you play.

Analytical Application: Tonality and Hierarchy in Bach's Violin Partita no. 3, Prelude

We will use the opening passage of the Prelude from Bach's Violin Partita in E Major (Example 1.22) as a springboard to launch our studies. The purpose of this brief discussion is to connect some of the basic musical knowledge you have already acquired in your instrumental and vocal lessons with specific instances of those terms and concepts. Listen to the excerpt and consider the following questions: What is the most aurally important or prominent pitch in the phrase? How did you come to this decision?

The basic criteria for determining the importance of a pitch include how often the pitch appears, the degree to which other pitches are drawn to it, and its prominence as part of musical gestures. Perhaps you determined that B was the most important pitch, because it occurred most frequently. Or perhaps you chose E, since it might have stood out aurally. In fact, E often occurred conspicuously just after the **bar lines**, which indicate the beginning and end of **measures** (mm.); see Example 1.22. Pitches occurring after the bar lines have a special function in tonal music because they are **accented**. Accented musical events stand out because our attention is drawn to them. We will encounter a variety of ways that composers create accents in their music.

EXAMPLE 1.22 **Bach, Violin Partita 3 in E Major, BWV 1006, Prelude**

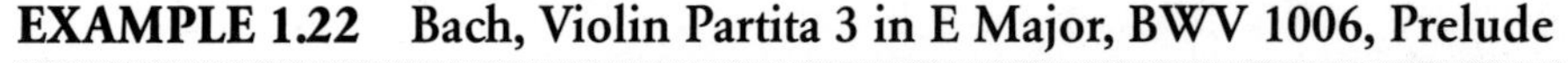

DVD 1
CH 1
TRACK 6

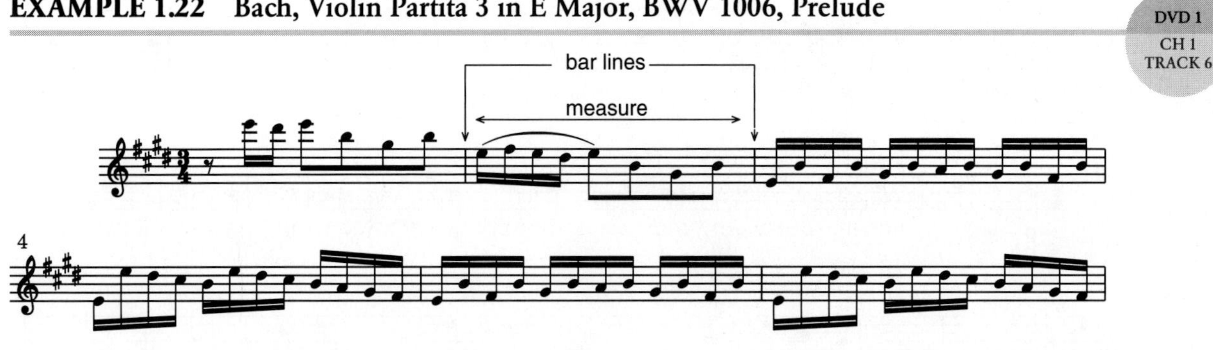

Continued

One reason our attention is drawn to an event is that it heralds something new or different, such as a change in pattern. However, many changes in a short time span are confusing, so composers balance the new (contrast and motion) with the familiar (similarity and stability). Bach uses a variety of melodic gestures and contours: Some fall while others rise; some comprise a series of skips, while others have no skips at all, and some gestures seem to go nowhere. When one of these melodic gestures ends and another begins, the change draws our attention. For example, the Prelude begins with a falling gesture. The next gesture, in mm. 3-6, is rhythmically and melodically repetitive. In m. 7, a two-measure rising gesture begins. The pitches that initiate these changes are audibly distinguished from the surrounding pitches and thus are accented.

Pitch prominence and melodic patterning may be only part of what you heard as you listened to Bach's composition. You may have also noticed that some of the pitches occupied more time than others. Longer pitches generally create a musical accent called **agogic**. Also, pitches that occur on beats are generally more accented than those that occur between beats, just as pitches that occur on a strong beat (beat 1 in a measure of $\frac{3}{4}$) are more accented than those that occur on weaker beats (beats 2 and 3). If we compare the pitches that occur between the beats to the pitches that occur on the beat, we notice that E is again emphasized. When an accented duration (i.e., a longer pitch) and metric placement (i.e., a pitch that occurs on a beat) align, one senses a particularly strong accent. Such powerful accents help the listener group musical events into intelligible units.

If you relate the rising, falling, or static contours to their temporal placement, you will notice that most measures begin after a large leap in the musical line. Leaps, like longer durations and dynamic accents, attract our attention more when they occur on a downbeat. When two or more different types of accented musical events are coordinated, we have a powerful standard by which to measure pitch prominence. A glance at the score reveals that E is in fact the most important pitch, since it is a focal point of several types of musical accent. Further, E, unlike any of the other pitches in the passage, is able to invoke a feeling of arrival and stability, a sense of "home" or "rest."

Finally, you might have sensed a deeper, slower-moving type of accent characterized by the completion of longer melodic gestures. Such accents occur over two or more measures (as on the beginning of mm. 3, 5, 7, 9, 10, and 12), and they can project one of the strongest types of musical emphasis. We can musically represent the preceding remarks concerning pitch prominence, accent, and melodic contour in the notated summary in Example 1.23A and B. Example 1.23A shows the pitches that occur on each beat of each of the 12 measures. Phrasing slurs group the two-measure patterns. Example 1.23B reveals the two types of melodic activity: sweeping gestures that fall (mm. 1–2) and rise (mm. 7–8), and more stationary gestures, which themselves are repeated to create longer, four-measure groupings (mm. 3–6 and mm. 9–12).

EXAMPLE 1.23 **Bach Prelude, Accented Pitches**

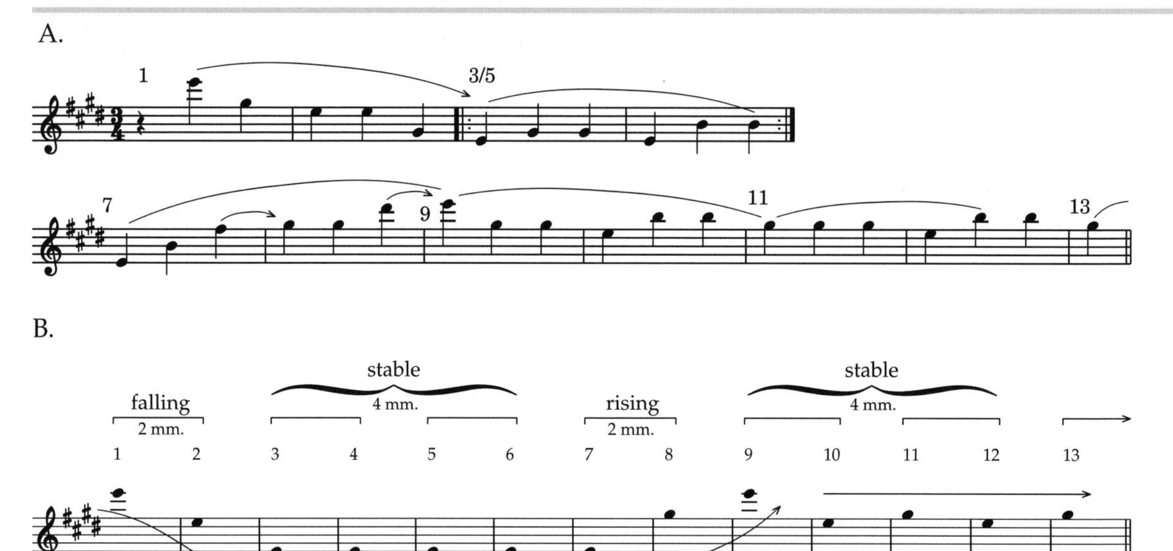

Clearly, there is a **hierarchy** of pitch and meter in Bach's piece, and we shall learn that hierarchy is a defining feature of tonal music. Since E is the most important pitch in the passage, we call it the **tonic** pitch. The only other prominent—albeit less important—pitches to emerge in the foregoing analysis are G♯ and B. Because the remaining pitches occur only within the melodic gestures and because they function merely as the glue that connects E with its satellites G♯ and B, they are less important in the hierarchy.

EXERCISE INTERLUDE

ANALYSIS

1.19 Scale and Key Analysis: Major Mode

The following examples are taken from the literature. Each fragment is in a major key other than C, lacks a key signature, and may begin and end on a note other than the tonic. Based on the given pitches, determine the key for each example. This exercise is slightly different than the previous exercises, given that not every member of the scale may be used in an example. Place the name of the key at the beginning of each example, and label each pitch by scale degree number.

A. Sample:

What are the possible keys? E♭, A♭. Why? Because there are three flats present (which means a key that contains at least three flats is used), indicating E♭ major. Why is A♭ possible? Because there is no D or D♭ in the melody, which would reduce the options to just one. Why couldn't the key be D♭? Because a G♭ would be required, given that D♭ contains five flats, and a G♮ is encountered in the example. What are the clues to narrow it down? E♭ sounds like a resting point more than A♭ does.

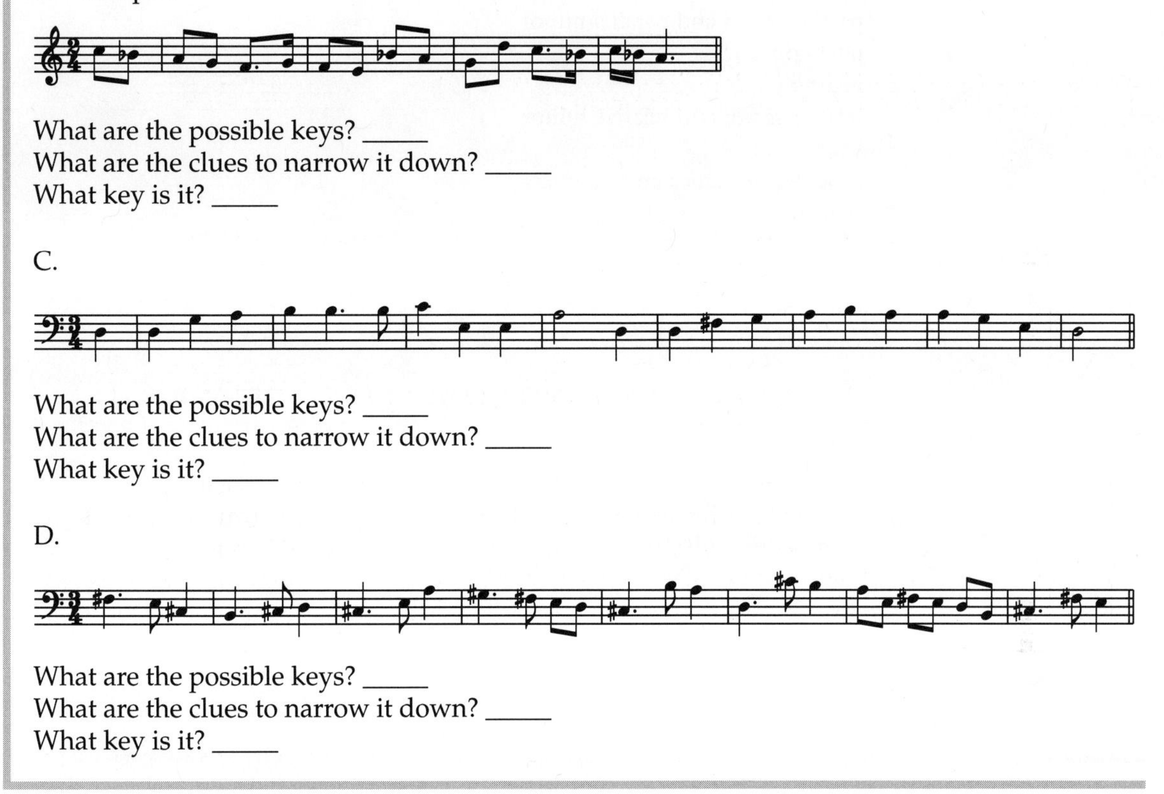

B. Sample:

What are the possible keys? _____
What are the clues to narrow it down? _____
What key is it? _____

C.

What are the possible keys? _____
What are the clues to narrow it down? _____
What key is it? _____

D.

What are the possible keys? _____
What are the clues to narrow it down? _____
What key is it? _____

TERMS AND CONCEPTS

Each chapter of this book concludes with a section that lists the important terms and concepts. Be able to define each of these in one or two sentences.

- accidentals:
- sharp (♯), flat (♭), natural (♮), double sharp(𝄪), double flat (𝄫)
- agogic
- bar line
- chromatic, chromatic system, chromatic scale
- chromatic alteration
- clef (treble, bass, C)
- diatonic
- enharmonic equivalence
- frequency
- grand staff

- interval: half step and whole step; diatonic and chromatic half steps
- key
- key signature
- ledger line
- major scale
- minor scales:
  - natural, harmonic, and melodic
- mode, major and minor
- octave sign
- parallel major and parallel minor
- pitch, pitch class
- register
- relative major and relative minor
- scale
- scale degree names and numbers
- staff
- step
- tonic
- transposition

ADDITIONAL TERMS AND CONCEPTS TO DEFINE

- chromatic scale
- circle of fifths
- common-practice period
- tonal, tonal center, tonality
- relative and parallel major and minor

CHAPTER 2

Pulse, Rhythm, and Meter

The time, or temporal (horizontal), aspects of music and the pitch (vertical) aspects of music are intimately intertwined and complement each other. This chapter concentrates on the essential concepts and terminology related to temporality. First, some basic terminology. Undifferentiated (e.g., same quality, loudness, and length) and equally spaced clicks or taps are called **pulses**. When you nod your head or tap your foot at a steady rate when listening to music, these pulses are called **beats**, because they now occur within a context that differentiates them; for example, some beats feel stronger than others. The **tempo** is the speed of the beat; that is, how fast or how slowly you nod or tap. **Meter** refers to the grouping of both strong and weak beats into recurring patterns. **Rhythm** refers to the ever-changing combinations of longer and shorter durations and silence that populate the surface of a piece of music. Rhythm is often patterned, and rhythmic groupings may divide the beat, align with the beat, or extend over several beats. The following discussion proceeds from temporal events that take place on the rhythmic surface of a piece to the metric grid that regulates the rhythmic surface.

Rhythm and Durational Symbols

We use two basic notational devices to provide rhythmic information to performers (see Example 2.1): the **notehead**, which may be unfilled or filled (blackened), and the stem, which is added to the notehead. One or more **flags** may be added to stems of filled noteheads. Each added element—stem, filled-in notehead, and flag—shortens a pitch's duration. The unfilled notehead may occur by itself, but in the common-practice period, the filled notehead is always accompanied by a stem. In order to balance notehead and stem on the staff, there is the following notational convention: If the notehead appears on or above the third line of any staff, the stem points down. Conversely, if the notehead appears on or below the third line of any staff the stem points up.

By itself, rhythmic notation does not indicate how long a note lasts, but it always precisely identifies the proportional relationships among notes. For example, each successive note in Example 2.1 has a duration precisely half that of the preceding note. Each additional flag decreases a pitch's duration by half. But it is only when rhythms occur in a context regulated by meter and tempo (described later)—that performers know the actual rhythmic durations.

EXAMPLE 2.1 Rhythmic Notation

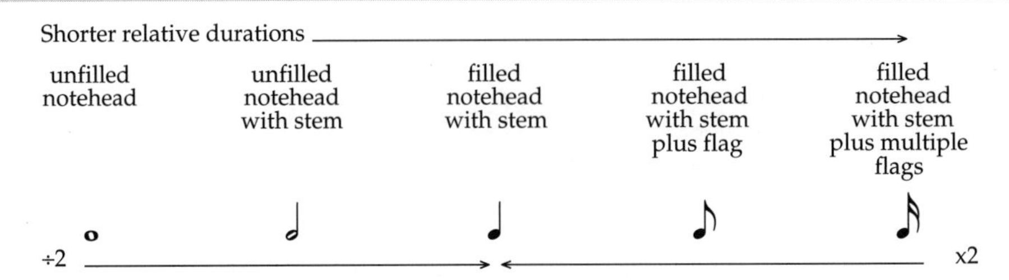

In contrast to notes, **rests** indicate a silence in music, and, as you see in Example 2.2, they correspond exactly to the durational symbols for notes. For example, the quarter rest (𝄽) indicates a silence that occupies the duration of a quarter note. The "hook" characterizes the eighth rest. Like the flag that characterizes the eighth note, each successive hook shortens the rest's duration by half. Example 2.2 summarizes the relationships between notes and rests. Note that each durational symbol is twice as long as the symbol directly below it.

EXAMPLE 2.2 Notes and Rests

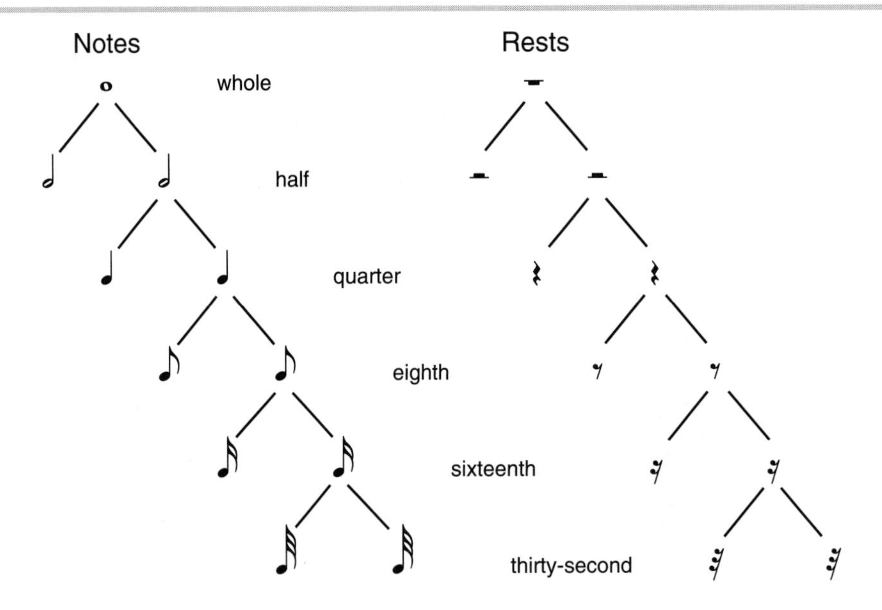

Dots and Ties

We can fine-tune the rhythmic system with additional features that permit more subtle rhythms by using dots and ties. The **dot** occurs after a pitch or rest, and it lengthens the value of the pitch or rest by half. For instance, if a half note is equivalent to two quarter notes, a dotted half is equivalent to three; a dotted quarter rest is equivalent to a quarter rest plus an eighth rest.

In general, undotted notes and rests are divided evenly into twos—a quarter note is divided into two eighth notes, for example. Dotted notes and rests are usually divided evenly into threes; for example, a dotted half note is divided into three quarter notes (Example 2.3A). Like each added flag and hook, which reduces a duration by one-half, each successive dot adds one-half the duration of the preceding dot, as shown in Example 2.3B.

EXAMPLE 2.3 Dotted Notes and Their Divisions

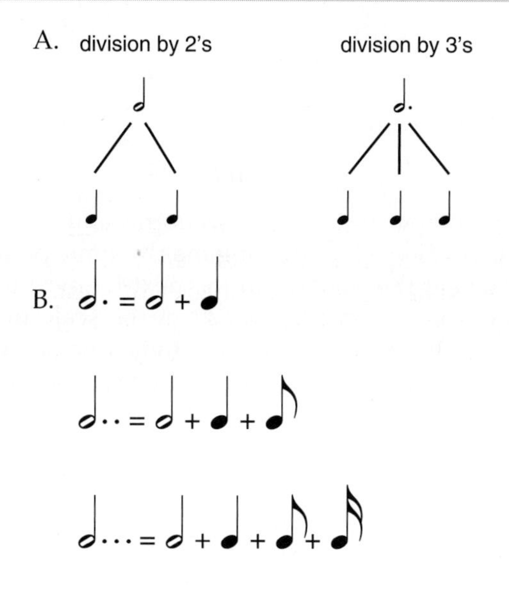

Like dots, **ties** lengthen the duration of a pitch. The tie's curved line combines the duration of two or more adjacent identical pitches. Ties are commonly used in two musical contexts: to sustain a pitch whose duration would exceed the normal length of the measure and to clarify rhythmic groupings in a measure. Listen to Example 2.4, which illustrates the use of dots and ties.

EXAMPLE 2.4 Beethoven, String Quartet no. 9, op. 59, no. 3, *Andante con moto*

DVD 1
CH 2
TRACK 1

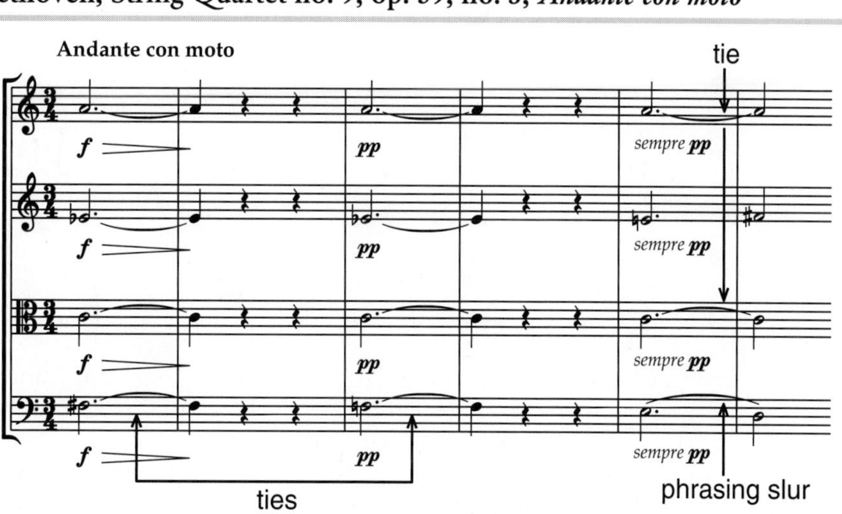

As you heard in Example 2.4, the tie sustains the first note by extending its duration without rearticulating it. Ties are distinguished from **phrasing slurs**, which connect two or more different pitches but which are also shown by curved lines. Phrasing slurs indicate that the grouped pitches should be played as a single musical idea. This is usually accomplished by playing the notes connected and uninterrupted, or *legato*. A phrasing slur is labeled near the end of Example 2.4.

EXERCISE INTERLUDE

PERFORMING

2.1 Singing Rhythmic Fragments in the Major and Minor Modes

Begin by singing major and minor ascending and descending scales in a comfortable octave. Then clap and sing the rhythmic pattern that appears in each exercise. Repeat the pattern on the next-higher scale degree, making sure to sing only the diatonic pitches from the scale in which you began. Continue the pattern until you reach the tonic one octave above the initial tonic. Then return to the tonic by descending the scale, continuing to sing and clap each pattern.

A. $\hat{1}$ $\hat{2}$ $\hat{3}$ $\hat{2}$ $\hat{1}$ ($\hat{2}$ $\hat{3}$ $\hat{4}$ $\hat{3}$ $\hat{2}$, etc.)

B. $\hat{1}$ $\hat{7}$ $\hat{1}$ $\hat{3}$ $\hat{2}$ $\hat{3}$ $\hat{4}$ ($\hat{2}$ $\hat{1}$ $\hat{2}$ $\hat{4}$, etc.)

C. $\hat{1}$ $\hat{3}$ $\hat{2}$ $\hat{4}$ $\hat{3}$ ($\hat{2}$ $\hat{4}$ $\hat{3}$, etc.)

D. $\hat{1}$ $\hat{5}$ $\hat{3}$ $\hat{2}$ $\hat{1}$ ($\hat{2}$ $\hat{6}$ $\hat{4}$, etc.)

E. $\hat{1}$ $\hat{2}$ $\hat{3}$ $\hat{2}$ $\hat{4}$ $\hat{3}$ $\hat{2}$ $\hat{7}$ $\hat{1}$ ($\hat{2}$ $\hat{3}$ $\hat{4}$, etc.)

ANALYSIS AND WRITING

2.2 Matching

Match a rhythm from column X with one in column Y that has the same total duration. Use all options in column Y (i.e., avoid duplicating any answers). The first example in Column X is completed for you.

X		Y
1.	C	A.
2.	____	B.
3.	____	C.
4.	____	D.
5.	____	E.
6.	____	F.
7.	____	G.
8.	____	H.
9.	____	I.
10.	____	J.

2.3 Pattern Durations

Write a *single duration* that is equivalent to the notes and/or rests in each of the given patterns. *Be aware*: One answer requires the use of double dots.

Sample: =

A. =

B. =

C. =

D. =

E. =

F. =

G. =

H. =

I. =

J. =

2.4 Brahms, Intermezzo in F minor, op. 118, no. 4 Ties Versus Phrasing Slurs

Label ties and phrasing slurs in the given example.

2.5

Perform the following rhythmic passages. Then determine how many of each of the given rhythmic durations would be required to represent the total length of each passage.

WORKBOOK
2.1–2.2

sample solution: ♬♩ ♩ ♪♬𝅗𝅥 ♩ = 6 ♩ 3 𝅗𝅥 4 ♩.

A. ♫ 𝄽 ♪ ♩ ♪ = ___ ♩ ___ 𝅝 ___ 𝅗𝅥

B. ♬♬ ♪.♬ ♪ 𝄾 = ___ ♪ ___ ♩. ___ 𝅗𝅥.

C. 𝄽 ♪‿♩ 𝅗𝅥. ♬ = ___ ♩ ___ 𝅗𝅥 ___ 𝅗𝅥.

D. ♩ ♩ ♪♩. ♪ 𝄿 ♪ 𝄿 = ___ 𝅘𝅥𝅯 ___ ♩ ___ ♪

E. ♩ 𝄽. 𝄾 ♪ ♬ = ___ 𝅝 ___ 𝅘𝅥𝅯 ___ 𝅗𝅥

Meter

Meter provides the framework that organizes groups of beats and rhythms into larger patterns of **accented beats** and **unaccented beats**. The patterns, commonly found in groups of two, three, or four beats, are collected into **measures**, which are demarcated by **bar lines**. But what creates meter? A series of identical pulses does not group into larger units but remains an undistinguished stream that simply punctuates the passage of time. For example, the following dots represent a series of pulses; tap them out with your right hand:

. . . .

You can hear and feel that each pulse is the same as every other; there is no differentiation between them. It is impossible to establish a meter because the pulses do not form groups. But if we add another level of pulse, one that moves proportionally faster or slower, then meter arises based on the interaction of the two hierarchical levels. *Meter* means "to measure," and the regularly recurring strong beat separated by a consistent number of weaker beats creates a **metrical accent**.

Perform the following series of pulses, the right hand tapping the faster pulses and the left hand tapping the slower pulses:

. . . .
● ● ● ● ●
s w w s w w s w w s w w s

Now we can hear and feel that the faster pulses are grouped into regularly recurring units of three beats. Notice that there is a distinction between accented, or strong (*s*), beats and unaccented, or weak (*w*), beats, as illustrated. Accented beats occur when both hands tap at the same time; unaccented beats occur when only the right hand taps. This hierarchy is crucial in creating meter. A clear meter emerges only through the addition of a second level of pulse (just as when you tapped both hands). Listen to Example 2.5. It includes a pattern of repeating quarter notes around which rhythms of quarter notes, eighth notes, and sixteenth notes occur. Can you identify a prevailing meter?

EXAMPLE 2.5

1/4 note pulse:

Most likely, you did not hear a strong sense of meter, even though there are two levels of activity. This is because only one level of a pulse regularly recurs, instead of the minimum of two. Once we add another level of pulse in the form of a half note, then the hierarchical relationship is clarified. With the third line added in Example 2.6, the rhythmic irregularity does not undermine the prevailing meter. Notice that bar lines—which identify the beginning of a metric group as well as the span—have been added, since there is now a clear metric patterning.

EXAMPLE 2.6

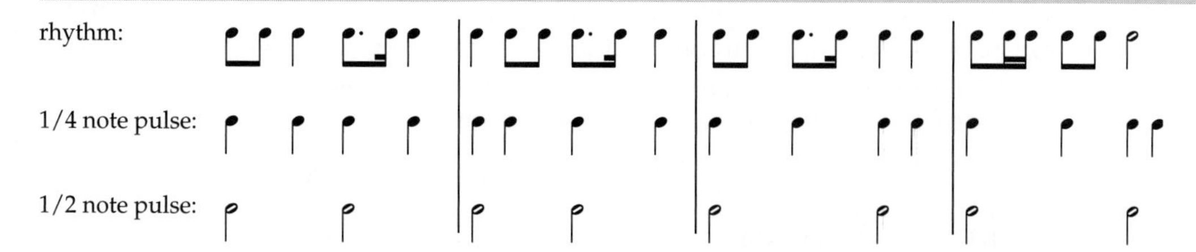

Now it is possible to sense either a **duple** (strong–weak) or **quadruple** (strong–weak–semistrong–weak) meter. You can usually distinguish between a two-beat or four-beat measure by rhythmic patterning. In Example 2.6, the dotted eighth–sixteenth pattern recurs every four beats in the first part of the example, creating four-beat, rather than two-beat, patterns. Further, in duple meter, a simple alteration of strong and weak occurs; but in quadruple meter, an intermediate type of metrical accent occurs on the third beat—one that is weaker than the downbeat but stronger than the second or fourth beat, as shown in Example 2.7.

EXAMPLE 2.7 **Mozart, Piano Sonata in C minor, K. 457, *Allegro***

Example 2.8 shows how using a dotted half note can create a different level of pulse. Here the quarter notes are grouped into threes to create a triple meter (strong–weak–weak).

EXAMPLE 2.8

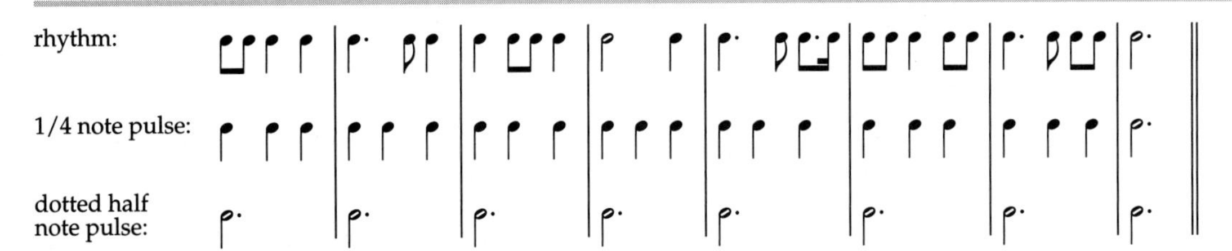

Accent in Music

From our brief exploration of Bach's Prelude in Chapter 1, we learned that there are many ways to create musical accent, including metric placement and changes of patterning. We now explore this important topic in more detail. We broadly define **musical accent** as a musical event that is **marked for consciousness** such that the listener's attention is drawn to it. The ways a composer marks events are diverse, but in general they all arise from a single source: thwarting the listener's expectations. We will learn that this is accomplished simply by changing an established pattern. Indeed, pattern changes create an accent, surprising us and drawing our attention. Accents can be produced not only in the domains of time (rhythm and meter) and pitch (melody and harmony), but also in the areas of dynamics, register, and texture.

Temporal Accents

We learned that meter arises when pulses are grouped into recurring patterns of accented and unaccented beats. Such accented beats are called **metrical accents**, since they occur at important points in a metrical unit (e.g., a beat or a measure). An **anacrusis** is an unaccented musical event that leads into an accented musical event. The anacrusis is often called an **upbeat** because a conductor's baton will be on its way up, in anticipation of the upcoming metrical accent. The following **downbeat**—the first and strongest metrically accented beat of a measure—is represented by the conductor's baton in the lowest position of the conducting pattern. Metrical accents provide the foundation for and standard by which we will consider other types of accent, both temporal and nontemporal.

Rhythmic accents occur throughout the surface of a piece of music and take many forms. The most important form of rhythmic accent arises from rhythmic duration—a long note tends to sound accented. Such **durational** (or **agogic**) **accents** usually coincide with metrical accents in order to support the prevailing meter. Given that longer notes are accented, they are often followed, rather than preceded, by notes with shorter durations. That is, when a beat (or other metric unit) is divided, a long–short division is more likely to occur than a short–long division. Example 2.9 illustrates: the first example (A) follows the typical "long–short" durational pattern, while the second (B) reverses the pattern, placing shorter durations before longer durations. Clap each example to see how the first is easier to perform and more natural sounding. Like metrical accents, durational accents occur at different levels. They occur not only on downbeats, but also on other accented beats (e.g., the third beat of m. 2 of Example 2.9A) and even within beats (the rhythm dotted eighth–sixteenth is more common than its reverse).

EXAMPLE 2.9

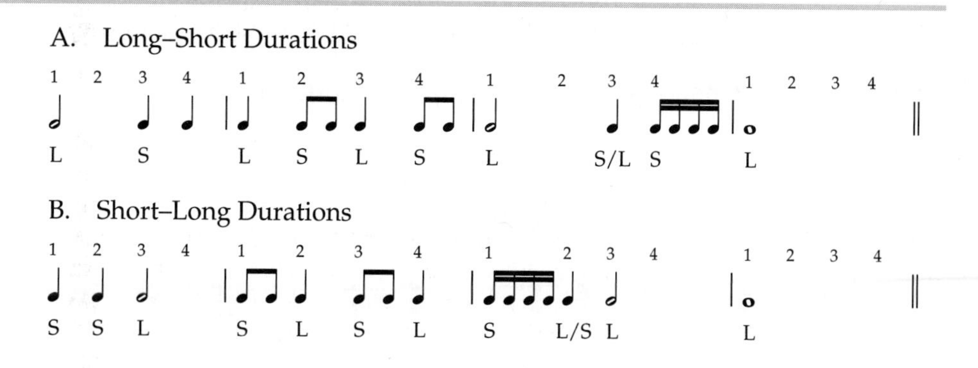

Nontemporal Accents

Every nontemporal element of music has the potential to create accents. We will examine six common types of nontemporal accent, all of which arise from a single source, pattern change: harmonic change and registral, articulative, textural, melodic contour, and pitch accents.

Harmonic change creates a powerful accent. Although we do not begin to explore harmony until Chapter 5, the following cursory discussion should not be problematic. Listen to the opening of Chopin's Waltz in A minor, in which a different chord appears in each measure (Example 2.10). Notice that the metric accent on beat 1 is accompanied by a different bass note in each measure (A–D–G–C); the chords on beats 2 and 3 fill out harmonies that are implied by the bass pitches. Metric accents are shown by the ">" sign above the treble staff.

EXAMPLE 2.10 Chopin, Waltz in A minor, BI 150

Composers usually balance the accent created by harmonic change with a consistent pattern in the rate of harmonic changes. (The rate at which harmonies change is called **harmonic rhythm**, a large topic that we explore throughout this text.) That is, once the speed of harmonic change is established, a composer will usually continue this pattern. Further, the changes usually align with the metric accents, as we saw in Chopin's waltz.

Since a pattern change creates an accent, let's see what happens when we modify Chopin's waltz slightly (Example 2.11 contains two recompositions). Example 2.11A begins like the original, with harmonic changes once per measure. However, in this modified version, the bass G and its harmony in m. 3 continue through m. 4, disrupting the established pattern of one harmonic change per measure and thereby marking the effect for consciousness and creating an accent. Example 2.11B does the opposite: Rather than extending the G harmony over two measures, it is shortened by the premature appearance of the C harmony. The question marks that accompany the beat patterns indicate the metric confusion that arises with breaking of the harmonic rhythm pattern.

EXAMPLE 2.11 Chopin, Waltz in A minor (modified)

A.

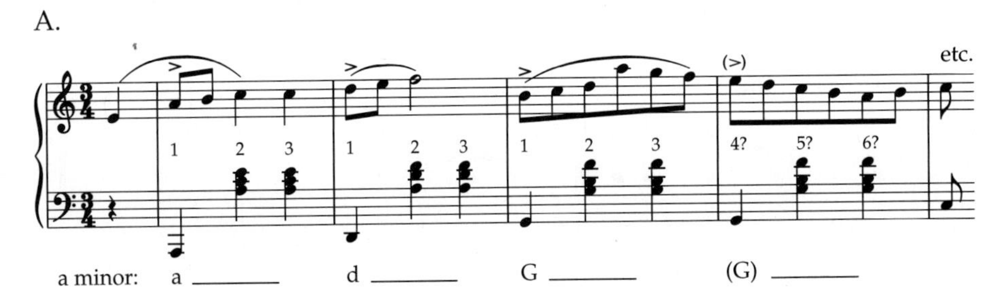

B.

You might have noticed that a strong left-hand accent occurs on beat 1 of each measure, nicely aligning with the metric accent, yet you might have also wondered how such an accent is created when beats 2 and 3 consistently contain three times as many pitches while remaining quite unaccented. Such **registral accents** occur because the first-beat low notes occur in a lower register than the rest of the left-hand notes, thus setting it in bold relief. Registral accents are very powerful, and when they do not align with the meter or when there is a pattern change, they become marked ever more strongly for consciousness. Example 2.12 establishes the registral accents in mm. 1–2 and then deviates, with accents occurring instead on weak beats. The low pitch followed by a single chord creates two-beat groupings that cut across the triple meter.

EXAMPLE 2.12 Chopin, Waltz in A minor (modified)

DVD 1
CH 2
TRACK 5

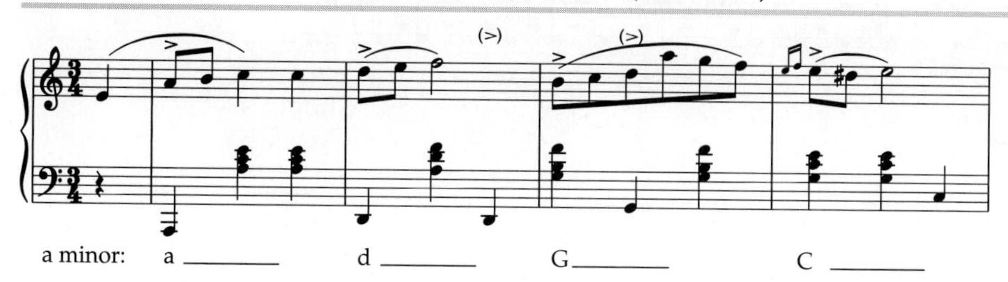

Registral accents may occur in any register. In fact, registral accents in the high register often appear to be more accented than accents in the low register, given that their frequency (vibration rate) is faster, and they stand out as brighter than pitches with slower frequencies. Registral accents are often intensified by **articulative** (or **phenomenal**) **accents**, which include changes in *dynamics* (both gradual and immediate, such as *sforzandi*)), and various types of articulations, such as *staccato/legato, pizzicato,* slurring, *tenuto,* and ornamentation (such as trills, turns, and mordents).

Beethoven was fond of such accents, as can be seen in the excerpt from his "Tempest" sonata (Example 2.13), where the *sforzandi* (marked *sf* and which signify a strong accent) occur mid-measure and are attacked by the left hand, which dramatically crosses over the right hand. Notice that registral accents actually begin in m. 21, where the left hand's low, sustained D^3 begins the excerpt. An actual line is created by the left hand's registral accents: D rises to E (m. 25) and then to F (m. 29). Notice that the articulative accents (that is, the *sforzandi* in the highest register starting at m. 30) are the same pitch classes but are moving at a rate twice as fast as the left hand (encompassing two measures instead of four).

EXAMPLE 2.13 Beethoven, Piano Sonata in D minor, op. 31, no. 2, "Tempest"

DVD 1
CH 2
TRACK 6

Continued

Most often the mood, general tessitura, accompanimental figures, and number and general character of voices (often referred to as *density*) remain consistent throughout long passages of a piece or even throughout an entire piece. We refer to the combination of these elements as **musical texture**. A **textural accent**, then, involves a change in the overall patterning of a piece and, as you might imagine, can be quite striking. In fact, entire style periods, such as the Baroque, are predicated on creating music that maintains a single mood, or *affect*, which in large measure is created by a consistent and unchanging texture. For example, Bach's C minor Prelude (Example 2.14) is a study in fast sixteenth notes that are relegated to the same register and melodic patterning (Example 2.14A). Thus, when the texture changes drastically to a more improvisatory, single-line, registrally roving *cadenza* near the end of the piece, the accent created certainly draws the listener's attention (Example 2.14B).

EXAMPLE 2.14 Bach, C minor Prelude, from *Well-Tempered Clavier*, Book 1

DVD 1
CH 2
TRACK 7

A.

B.

From the Classical period on, composers filled their works with textural accents, sometimes between sections, as in Schubert's song "Der Lindenbaum," where the plaintive major mode, soft dynamic level, and soothing accompaniment give way to the stormy section in the parallel minor (see Example 2.15).

EXAMPLE 2.15 Schubert, "Der Lindenbaum," from *Winterreise*

DVD 1
CH 2
TRACK 8

Continued

Finally, textural changes and the accents they create can be very subtle, as in the opening of Mozart's piano sonata in F (Example 2.16). The gentle rocking accompaniment supports a rising melody, but in m. 5 the melody falls, without any aid from the accompaniment. This textural change is intensified by the left hand's abandoning its accompanimental role and imitating the right hand in the falling gesture in m. 7. In m. 9 both hands are reunited. Finally, in m. 12 yet another new texture appears, as all of the voices participate in the same rhythmic gestures. These textural changes are not capricious but, rather, are carefully planned, occurring every four measures.

EXAMPLE 2.16 Mozart, Piano Sonata in F major, K. 332, *Allegro*

DVD 1
CH 2
TRACK 9

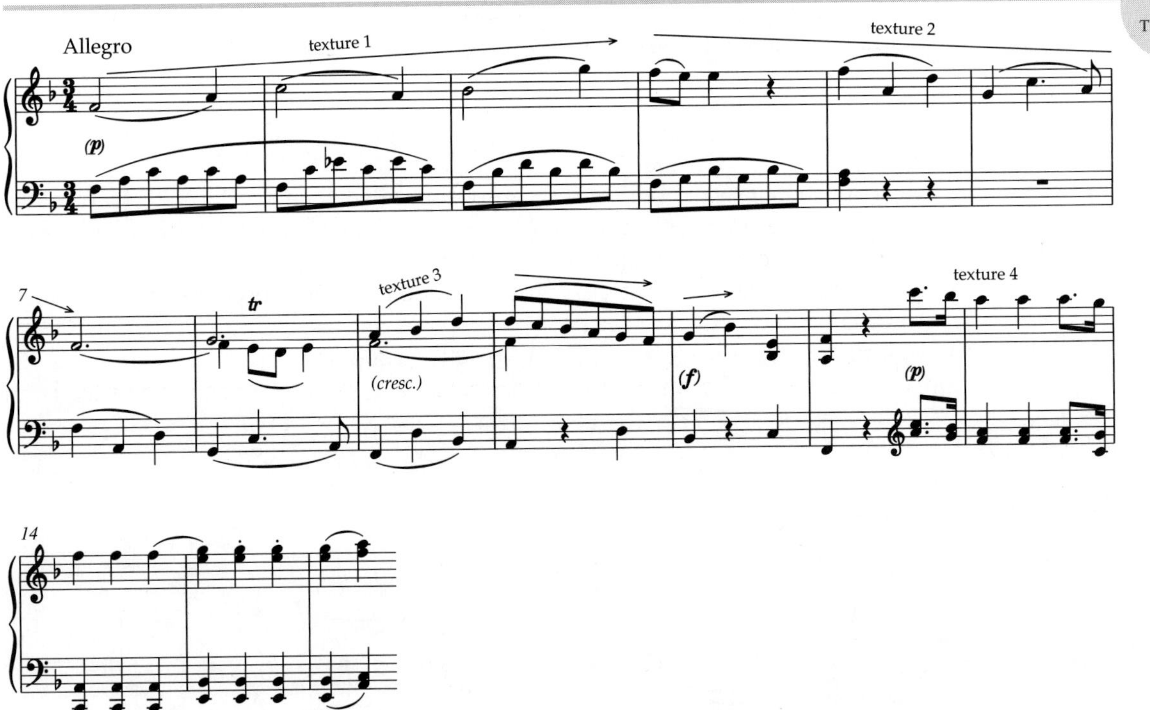

Staying for a moment with the Mozart excerpt, we discover other types of nontemporal accents. The first type involves melody, specifically its shape, which is created by changes in melodic direction. These shapes are part of a melody's **contour**, and changes in melodic contour create **contour accents**. They can be quite obvious (as in the overall rising line of mm. 1–4 that is followed by the descending contour in mm. 5–8, represented by arrows) or very subtle (as in the falling scalar line in m. 10, which changes direction on the downbeat of m. 11). Like most accents, contour accents usually align with metric accents.

Finally, when you listened to Example 2.16 for the first time, was your attention drawn to the E♭4 in m. 2, even though it occurred as part of the prevailing eighth-note pattern, on a weak beat, and hidden inside the texture? If this single pitch did catch your attention—that is, if it was accented—then you were aware of the last category of accent: **pitch accent**. Such accents arise when one or more pitches are perceived as unstable. Unstable pitches are accented because they are foreign to the immediately surrounding pitch environment; the term **dissonant** refers to musical events that are in one or more ways unstable. Pitch accents can occur in unaccented or accented metrical contexts. Compare the effect of the unaccented E♭4 in Mozart's F-major sonata with the unprepared, strongly accented D♯5 that opens his A-minor sonata (Example 2.17).

EXAMPLE 2.17 Mozart, Piano Sonata in A minor, K. 310, *Allegro maestoso*

DVD 1 CH 2 TRACK 10

EXERCISE INTERLUDE

ANALYSIS

2.6 Rhythmic Correction

Except for the first measures of each example, every subsequent measure contains the incorrect number of beats: Some measures have too many beats, while others have too few. You must determine how many beats should be in each measure by studying the correct first measure of each example. Then modify each measure so that it contains the correct number of beats by adding or changing a single rest (R) or note value (N), as requested.

2.7 Analysis of Musical Accent

The examples shown, all taken from Chopin's Waltzes, contain various types of accents. Find and label at least one example of each type of accent. Your choices are: durational, harmonic, registral, articulative, textural, contour, and pitch. Are these accents coordinated with the metrical accents?

A. Waltz in B minor, op. posth. 69, no. 2

B. Waltz in D♭ major, op. 64, no. 1

C. Waltz in E minor, BI 56

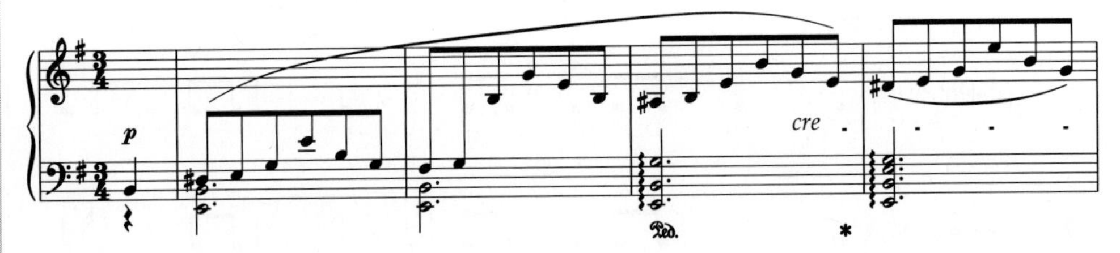

D. Waltz in A♭ major, op. 64, no. 3

Beat Division and Simple and Compound Meters

Most music contains note values that are shorter than the basic beat. **Beat division** refers to the equal division of the beat into either twos or threes. Recall that undotted note values divide naturally into twos (Example 2.18A) and that dotted note values divide equally into threes (see Example 2.18B). We refer to further division of the beat as **subdivision of the beat**. At the level of the subdivision, beats divide naturally only into twos (Example 2.18C).

EXAMPLE 2.18

A. 𝅝 = 𝅗𝅥 𝅗𝅥

𝅗𝅥 = ♩ ♩

♩ = ♪ ♪

♪ = 𝅘𝅥𝅯 𝅘𝅥𝅯

B. 𝅗𝅥. = ♩ ♩ ♩

♩. = ♪ ♪ ♪

♪. = 𝅘𝅥𝅯 𝅘𝅥𝅯 𝅘𝅥𝅯

C. ♩ = ♪ ♪ = 𝅘𝅥𝅯 𝅘𝅥𝅯 𝅘𝅥𝅯 𝅘𝅥𝅯

♩. = ♪♪♪ = 𝅘𝅥𝅯𝅘𝅥𝅯𝅘𝅥𝅯𝅘𝅥𝅯𝅘𝅥𝅯𝅘𝅥𝅯

We refer to meters in which the beat is divided into twos as **simple meters**. **Compound meters** refer to meters in which the beat is divided into threes. Recall that there are three basic metrical accent patterns: duple (strong–weak), triple (strong–weak–weak), and quadruple (strong–weak–semistrong–weak). Example 2.19 shows the six possible types of meters (most common beat values shown).

EXAMPLE 2.19

	Simple	Compound
Duple	♩ ♩, 𝅗𝅥 𝅗𝅥	♩. ♩., 𝅗𝅥. 𝅗𝅥.
Triple	♩ ♩ ♩, ♪ ♪ ♪	♩. ♩. ♩.
Quadruple	♩ ♩ ♩ ♩	♩. ♩. ♩. ♩.

Using duple as a model, we see in Example 2.20 the two ways that the beat can be divided. Examples of both simple and compound triple and quadruple meters are shown in Example 2.21.

EXAMPLE 2.20

EXAMPLE 2.21

DVD 1
CH 2
TRACK 12
A. Simple Triple ("Flow Gently")
beat:
division:
Flow gen - tly sweet Af - ton, a - mong thy green braes;
B. Compound Triple ("Down in the Valley")
beat:
division:
Down in the val - - ley, the val - ley so low,
Hang your head
C. Simple Quadruple ("Adeste")
beat:
division:
mf
Ad - es - - te fi - de - - les, lae - ti tri - um - phan - - tes;
O come, all ye faith - - ful, joy - ful and tri - umph - ant;
D. Compound Quadruple (Brahms "An den Mond")
beat:
division:
Geuß, lie - - ber Mond, geuß dei - ne Sil - ber-flim - mer
pp

Note that simple meters can have beats of any duration that are *not dotted;* compound meters have beats that are *dotted*. For example, both excerpts in Example 2.22A are in simple duple. However, the beat in "A Mighty Fortress" is the half note, while that in the slow movement from Beethoven's seventh symphony is the quarter note. Similarly, Example 2.22B shows two examples in simple triple: The quarter note is the beat unit in B1 and the eighth note is the beat unit in B2.

EXAMPLE 2.22

DVD 1
CH 2
TRACK 13

A1. "A Mighty Fortress Is Our God"

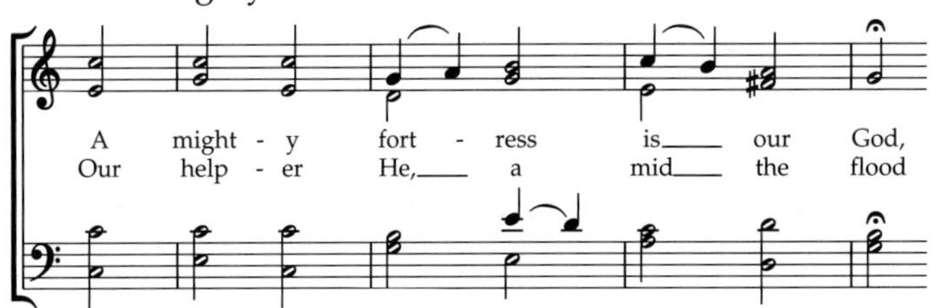

A2. Beethoven, Symphony no. 7 in A major, *Allegretto*

B1. Bach, French Suite in B minor, *Menuet*

B2. Bach, French Suite in B minor, *Gigue*

The Meter Signature

Composers indicate the *number of beats* in a measure (accented and unaccented), the *beat unit* (the rhythmic value that is assigned the beat), and the *beat division* (i.e., whether the beat value is divided into twos or threes) in the **meter signature**. The meter signature, or *time signature*, appears once, at the beginning of the piece, immediately after the key signature. A composer may change the meter within a piece or section, in which case the new meter signature will appear at the point of change.

The meter signature takes the form of two numbers, one on top of the other (see Example 2.23).

EXAMPLE 2.23 Meter Signatures for Simple Meters

Top number	2 = *two* beats per measure 3 = *three* beats per measure 4 = *four* beats per measure
Bottom number	2 = one *half note* makes up the beat unit 4 = one *quarter note* makes up the beat unit 8 = one *eighth note* makes up the beat unit 16 = one *sixteenth note* makes up the beat unit *and so on*

A meter signature of $\frac{3}{4}$ indicates three beats in each measure and that the quarter note is assigned the beat. Since Example 2.22B1 is felt strongly in three, a "3" would appear as the upper number. The basic beat is the quarter note (the piece begins with three quarter notes in the left hand (and attendant division by eighth notes); thus a "4" would appear as the lower number. Similarly, since Example 2.22B2 is also felt in three, albeit a fast three, and the eighth note is the basic pulse, the meter signature would be $\frac{3}{8}$.

Common simple meter signatures include $\frac{3}{8}$, $\frac{4}{8}$, $\frac{2}{4}$, $\frac{3}{4}$, and $\frac{4}{4}$, $\frac{2}{2}$, $\frac{3}{2}$, and $\frac{4}{2}$, where, respectively, the eighth note, the quarter note, and the half note are the beat unit and measures contain two, three, and four beats. There are two simple meter signatures that do not use numbers: C and ₵. C stands for $\frac{4}{4}$ and is sometimes known as **common time**. The ₵ stands for $\frac{2}{2}$ and is known as **cut time** or ***alla breve***. Both these symbols were used before meter signatures with numbers were established.

One determines the meter signature for compound meters in a slightly different way than one would determine simple meter signatures. This is because we do not have numbers that can represent dotted notes; we choose to represent *beat divisions* (rather than beats) in the meter signature.

Consider Example 2.24, where Beethoven employs the dotted quarter as the beat unit (two per measure to create the duple meter), its three eighth-note divisions creating a lilting effect that contributes to the *pastorale*, outdoors feeling.

EXAMPLE 2.24 Beethoven, Piano Sonata in D major, op. 28 "Pastorale," *Rondo, Allegro ma non troppo*

DVD 1
CH 2
TRACK 14

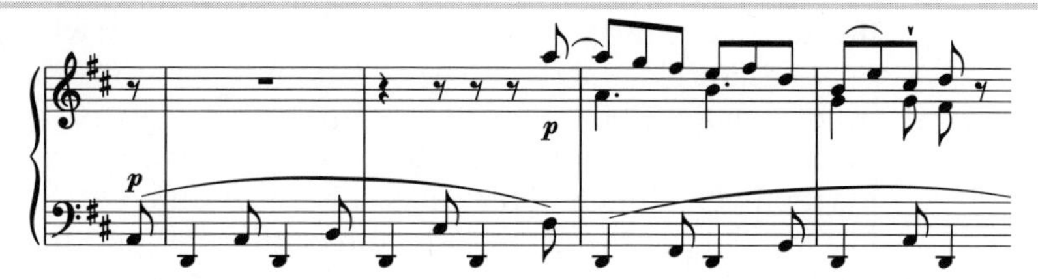

One must wonder, then, why Beethoven would write $\frac{6}{8}$, which seems quite unable to represent the actual two-beat measures (and compound division). The disparity arises because it is not possible to represent the dotted-value beat units that characterize compound meters (e.g., dotted quarter and dotted half). The solution, then, is to show the total number of beat divisions per measure, leaving the performer the job of determining the actual number of beats within a measure. This is accomplished by dividing the upper number by three (since compound meters divide the beat into threes). To determine the beat unit, divide the lower number by 2: the 8 (of $\frac{6}{8}$) would be 4. However, one must remember that this quarter note is dotted (see Example 2.25).

EXAMPLE 2.25 Meter Signatures for Compound Meter

Top number	6 = *two* dotted beats per measure 9 = *three* dotted beats per measure 12 = *four* dotted beats per measure
Bottom number	2 = three *half notes* make up the beat unit (𝅝.) 4 = three *quarter notes* make up the beat unit (𝅗𝅥.) 8 = three *eighth notes* make up the beat unit (♩.) 16 = three *sixteenth notes* make up the beat unit (♪.) *and so on*

The chart in Example 2.26 shows the most common simple and compound meters for duple, triple, and quadruple accent patterns. Notice that all meters with an upper number of 4 or smaller are simple (e.g., 2, 3, 4) and that all compound meters contain an upper number of 6 or larger (e.g., 6, 9, 12).

EXAMPLE 2.26

Common duple meters:
simple: $\frac{2}{4}$ and $\frac{2}{2}$ compound: $\frac{6}{8}$ and $\frac{6}{4}$
Common triple meters:
simple: $\frac{3}{4}$ and $\frac{3}{2}$ compound: $\frac{9}{8}$ and $\frac{9}{16}$
Common quadruple meters:
simple: $\frac{4}{4}$ and $\frac{4}{2}$ compound: $\frac{12}{8}$ and $\frac{12}{4}$

Asymmetrical Meters

In the vast majority of common-practice tonal music, the number of beats per measure is dependent on multiples of *either* 2 or 3 (e.g., $\frac{2}{4}$, $\frac{12}{8}$, $\frac{3}{8}$, $\frac{4}{2}$, $\frac{6}{4}$, and $\frac{9}{8}$). On occasion, however, composers write in **asymmetrical meters**, which are defined in one of the following two ways: as measures whose number of beats is not divisible by either 2 or 3 (such as $\frac{5}{8}$ and $\frac{7}{4}$) or as measures whose number of beats combines both 2's and 3's (such as $\frac{10}{4}$, created from 2 + 3 + 3 + 2). In moderate-to-fast tempi, such meters are usually performed so that the combination of 2's and 3's create larger beats of different durations. For example, in a fast tempo, $\frac{5}{8}$ would be felt (and conducted) in 2; that is, a combination of one 2 and one 3, either 2 + 3 or 3 + 2. Composers who use such signatures often indicate in their meter signatures the way they wish the large beats to be grouped; for example, the common meter signature of $\frac{9}{8}$ combines the divisions of the dotted quarter note into three equal groups of 3. However, a composer might wish to divide the beats asymmetrically, such as 2 + 3 + 2 + 2.

Folk music of Eastern Europe and the Balkans makes constant use of such asymmetrical meters. The opening of the Greek folk song in Example 2.27 is cast in the asymmetrical meter of $\frac{7}{8}$. Often the meter signature of asymmetrical meters clarifies the recurring patterns within each measure. The repetition pattern in the tune shown in Example 2.27 feels like a combination of $\frac{3}{8}$ and $\frac{4}{8}$ (although one could also hear the pattern as 3 + 2 + 2).

EXAMPLE 2.27 Greek Folk Song

DVD 1 CH 2 TRACK 15

EXERCISE INTERLUDE

LISTENING AND ANALYSIS

DVD 2 CH 2 TRACK 3

2.8 Meter and Mode Identification: Simple Meters

Identify the meter and mode (major or minor) of each of the following excerpts. First, identify the basic pulse; then locate the regularly recurring accented beat that is followed by one or more weak beats. Next, determine the generic meter, which will be duple or triple. Finally, refine your decision by assigning $\frac{2}{4}$ or $\frac{3}{4}$.

Example:
Schumann, "Einsame Blumen," *Waldscenen*, op. 82 — Meter: $\frac{2}{4}$ Mode: Major

A. Traditional, "Amazing Grace" — Meter: _____ Mode: ______
B. Beethoven, Piano Sonata, op. 28, *Andante* — Meter: _____ Mode: ______
C. Haydn, String Quartet, op. 64, no. 5 — Meter: _____ Mode: ______
D. Beethoven, Piano Sonata, op. 14, no. 1, *Andante* — Meter: _____ Mode: ______

DVD 2 CH 2 TRACK 4

2.9 Meter and Mode Identification: Simple and Compound Meters

This exercise requires you to identify both simple and compound meters. Your choices are $\frac{2}{4}$, $\frac{3}{4}$, $\frac{4}{4}$, $\frac{6}{8}$, and $\frac{9}{8}$. Each exercise contains a recurring rhythmic pattern. Based on the meter you choose, notate the rhythmic pattern.

A. Haydn, String Quartet in G minor, op. 74, no. 3 (Hob. III/74), *Allegro*
B. Wagner, *Liebestod*, from *Tristan und Isolde*
C. Brahms, Intermezzo in E minor, op. 119, no. 2
D. Bach, Minuet II from Suite no. 1 in G major for Cello, BWV 1007
E. Schubert, Moment Musical no. 6, D. 780
F. Beethoven, Symphony no. 7 in A major, op. 92, *Allegretto*

2.10 Beat Groupings in Simple and Compound Meters

A. Provide the note value for divisions of the following beats, and specify whether the meter is simple or compound.

Solution: beat = ♩. division = [♪♪♪] compound — simple or compound

1. beat = ♪, division = [ ] ________ simple or compound?

2. beat = ♪, division = [ ] ________ simple or compound?

3. beat = 𝅗𝅥, division = [ ] ________ simple or compound?

4. beat = ♪, division = [ ] ________ simple or compound?

B. The meter type and beat are given. Provide a meter signature, and notate one full measure of the given rhythm and the division of the given beat.

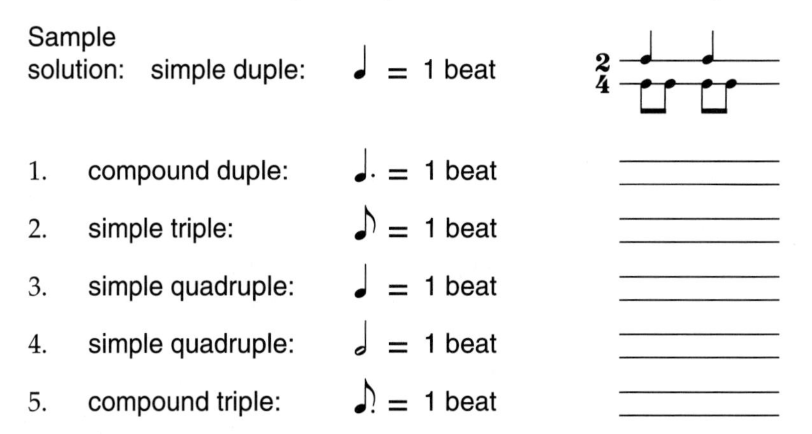

2.11 Determining Meter

Supply an appropriate meter signature for each of the following examples. Consider both the number of beats in each measure and their division and subdivision. *Hint:* Consider the beaming patterns.

2.12 Meter Identification and Rhythmic Correction

Perform each exercise in order to determine the meter. Then supply an appropriate meter signature and bar lines. All examples begin on downbeats, but some of the characteristic metrical groupings (e.g., beams) are missing. Discuss this in a sentence or two. Once you have determined the meter for each example, rewrite it using proper notation. There may be more than one possible meter for some examples. There are no examples of asymmetrical meters.

Clarifying Meter

It would be frustrating to identify meter if rhythmic durations were not organized into logical groups that would help you immediately see both the number of beats in each measure and their divisions. Rhythmic symbols must visually organize the beat unit for the performer. For example, the three-beat units of the $\frac{3}{4}$ meter in Example 2.28A are not visually clear because there is no grouping of rhythms. In Example 2.28B, however, the grouping becomes clear with the addition of **beams**, which are horizontal lines that connect two or more flagged notes (i.e., eighth notes or any combination of shorter rhythmic values). The number of beams corresponds to the number of flags such that one beam will connect two eighth notes, two beams will connect two sixteenth notes, etc.

EXAMPLE 2.28 Beams to Clarify Simple Meter

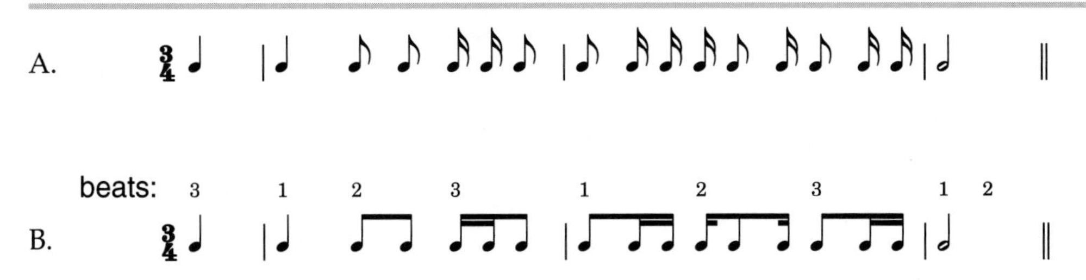

Example 2.29A presents an example of compound $\frac{9}{8}$ without grouping beams. Again, the underlying three beats are difficult to discern, but the addition of beams and longer note values in Example 2.29B instantly reveals the three beats within each measure. Beams generally do not connect across beats; a new beam starts with each beat in order to clarify the meter.

EXAMPLE 2.29 Beams to Clarify Compound Meter

In vocal music, however, beams are often used differently. Rather than highlighting the meter, beams connect two or more pitches that are to be sung on a single syllable. Therefore, pitches and their rhythms are, for the most part, separated from one another. This older convention—which has recently been replaced by the regular beaming tradition found in instrumental music—makes it difficult to perceive rhythmic patterns and their placement within and between beats. Notice in Example 2.30, from Berlioz's *L'Enfance du Christ*, how difficult it is to group beats in a single $^4_4$ measure of recitative (Example 2.30A). The renotated version in Example 2.30B makes it much easier to negotiate the rhythms.

EXAMPLE 2.30 Berlioz, *L'Enfance du Christ*, recitative of the Father, scene 2

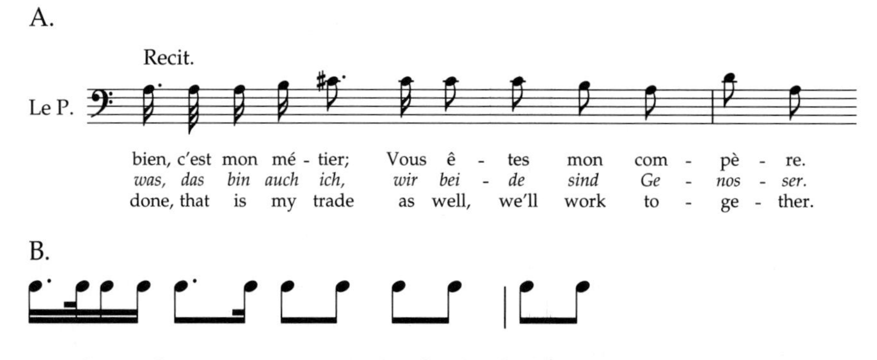

Thus, always attempt to clarify the location and grouping of each beat within a measure, avoiding long durations or dots that can obscure natural groupings by connecting rhythms across beats. Example 2.31A shows a sampling of incorrectly notated rhythms; Example 2.31B clarifies the notation.

EXAMPLE 2.31

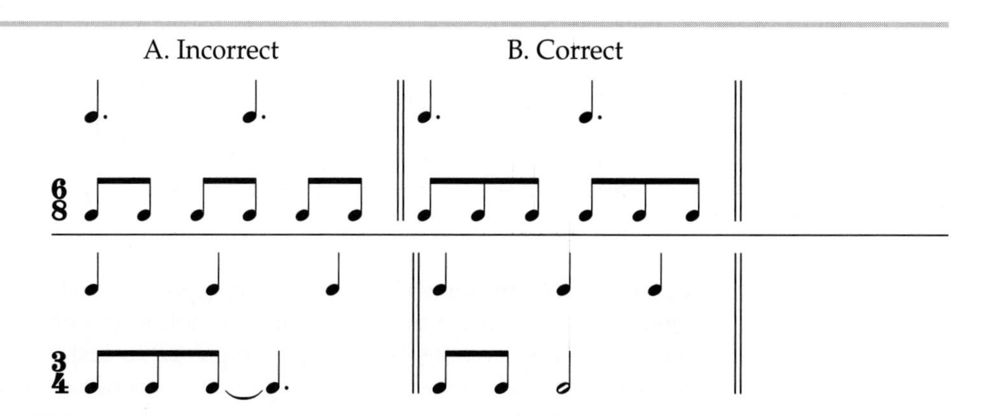

More Rhythmic Procedures

Although we know that the division of the beat unit in simple meters is by 2 and the division of the beat unit in compound meters is by 3, composers often import the 3's from compound into simple and the 2's from simple into compound. Such **borrowed divisions** permit considerably more rhythmic flexibility. Borrowed from compound meter, three-note divisions are called **triplets**. Triplets may occur not only at the primary division of the beat (see Example 2.32A), but also at the subdivision (for example, as triplet sixteenth notes in $\frac{4}{4}$). Triplets also occur over two or more beats. Example 2.32B illustrates several types of triplets in $\frac{4}{4}$. Measure 1 contains an eighth-note triplet, which occurs within one beat unit and therefore is at the level of the beat division. Measure 2, with its sixteenth-note triplet, illustrates triplets at the subdivision (i.e., within an eight-note division). Triplets are illustrated in mm. 3-4: The triplet occurs first at the half-measure level and then at the measure level.

EXAMPLE 2.32

A. Brahms, "Von ewiger Liebe," op. 43, no. 1

B. Several Types of Triplets

Similarly, though not as common, the two-note divisions found in simple meter are imported into compound meters. Such **duplets**, like triplets, can occur within divisions and subdivisions of the beat as well as encompassing more than one beat unit (Example 2.33).

EXAMPLE 2.33 Schumann, "Schlummerlied," from *Albumblätter*, op. 124

DVD 1
CH 2
TRACK 17

Less common divisions, called **irregular divisions**, include fives (called **quintuplets**) and sevens (**septuplets**). Most borrowed and irregular divisions are shown with a bracket that groups the note values and the appropriate number into which the beat is divided. Example 2.34 illustrates several types of divisions against its unwavering and very clear dotted eighth-note pattern in the accompaniment of this $\frac{6}{8}$ piece. In m. 138, an eight-pitch right-hand figure (**octuplet**) is juxtaposed with the three-pitch bass figure, followed two measures later with a quintuplet against the bass. In measure 141, septuplets occur, followed by more-standard sixteenth-note triplets. Finally, in m. 145, quadruplets appear against the three pitches in the bass.

EXAMPLE 2.34 Chopin, Nocturne in B major, op. 9, no. 3, mm. 136–147

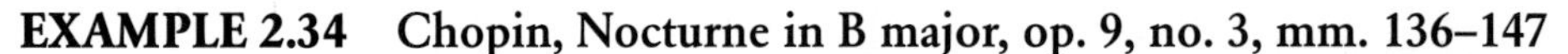

DVD 1
CH 2
TRACK 18

Composers, especially in the nineteenth century, delighted in presenting duple and triple divisions of the beat simultaneously, their juxtaposition lending a remarkable fluidity—if not metrical confusion—to a piece. Chopin, Schumann, and Brahms are three of the many composers who utilized this procedure. In Example 2.35A, Chopin has cast his etude in the simple duple meter of $\frac{2}{4}$, with the natural division of the beat into two parts (see the eighth notes in the left hand). However, superimposed on this bipartite structure are triplets (marked, in the right hand). Such a play of rhythms is called **two against three**. Finally, composers often go so far as intentionally to write patterns that cut across a meter, such that each hand is written in a distinct meter. Chopin's Waltz in A♭ clearly presents a left hand in a simple triple meter, with two eighth notes for every quarter note, as one would expect in a well-behaved waltz (Example 2.35B). However, the right hand is cast in the compound duple meter of $\frac{6}{8}$, whose two beats and division into 3's make very strange bedfellows with the left hand.

EXAMPLE 2.35

DVD 1
CH 2
TRACK 19

A. Chopin, Etude in A♭ major, op. posth.

B. Chopin, Waltz in A♭ major, op. 42

Metrical Disturbance

Syncopation

We have seen that longer durations—which are inherently accented—usually are coordinated with accented beats or accented parts of beats, and shorter durations usually follow, occurring on weak beats or weak parts of beats. This pattern is often reversed, and while the established meter continues, it is challenged by a new, conflicting accent. This phenomenon—in which a musical accent occurs on a metrically unaccented beat or part of a beat—is called **syncopation**. Example 2.36 presents two examples in which a regularly recurring pulse stream or series of accents occurs off the beat.

EXAMPLE 2.36

DVD 1
CH 2
TRACK 20

A. Mozart, Symphony in G minor, K. 183, *Allegro con brio*

B. Mozart, Piano Concerto in D minor, K. 466, *Allegro*

Syncopation is a mainstay in popular and commercial music, one example of which appears in Example 2.37, which contains accents not only at the beat unit, but also within the beat unit. Note that the left hand is regular and that it aligns with the natural accentual pattern of $\frac{4}{4}$: the lower of the two notes, marked by a registral accent, occurs on the metrically strong first and third beats. This stable left hand provides the metrical grid above which the right hand and vocal line playfully deviate, highlighting the fanciful lyrics. Syncopation appears already in the first vocal utterance: "Say" occurs on a weak part of the division of the first beat, and its quarter-note value cuts through the accented part of the second beat. The same situation is heard in the second half of the measure, up one octave. Articulative accents intensify the right hand of the piano part. The horizontal slashes, called *tenuto marks*, indicate that the note beneath should be sustained for its full value and also imply an accent; notice that these accents all occur on weak parts of beats. Similarly, the staccato marks, which shorten notes and thus weaken accents, occur on the accented parts of beats. Finally, notice how the semistrong accented third beat is weakened in mm. 2 and 3, since they occur as tied notes.

EXAMPLE 2.37 Arlen, "It's Only a Paper Moon"

DVD 1
CH 2
TRACK 21

Hemiola

Another important type of metrical disturbance, closely related to syncopation, is the **hemiola**. In a hemiola, the established meter temporarily is displaced by a competing meter. It occurs most often when a duple meter is imposed on a triple meter. To create this effect, accents are placed on every other beat rather than on every third beat, either by literal accent markings, by duple durations, or by one or more of the nontemporal accentual techniques, such as harmonic accent, dynamic accent, or registral accent. In Example 2.38A, hemiola is created by articulative accents: The regular placement on every other quarter note creates a duple accent pattern, effectively weakening if not overtaking the triple pattern. Only in the penultimate measure is the triple pattern reinstated. In Example 2.38B, hemiola arises through the durational accents.

EXAMPLE 2.38

A. Hemiola by Surface Elements

B. Hemiola by Duple Durations

Let's look briefly at the opening of the Menuetto from Mozart's *Eine kleine Nachtmusik*, which contains a clear example of a hemiola (Example 2.39). The first five measures of Mozart's eight-measure unit unfold as expected. The downbeat of each measure is well accented, and the following two beats are quite weak. The three-beat groups behave just as the meter signature indicates they will. But in the last three measures, something happens: The surface gesture changes with the trill figure that occurs first on beat 2 and then on beat 1, giving an odd feel to the triple meter. Now we sense groupings in 2's. Instead of **1** 2 3 | **1** 2 3 | **1** . . ., we feel **1** 2 **1** | 2 **1** 2 | **1**. Hemiola tends to occur in the approach to a final cadence, especially in the Baroque period. As an event marked for consciousness, it heralds the approach to closure, which brings welcome relief from the consistent texture and avoidance of musical articulations.

EXAMPLE 2.39 **Mozart, *Eine kleine Nachtmusik*, K. 525, "Menuetto"**

EXERCISE INTERLUDE

WRITING

2.13 Borrowed divisions

Write a *single duration* that is equivalent to the combined durations of the given patterns.

Sample solutions: = ____ 3 = ____

A. = ____

B. = ____

C. = ____

D. 3 = ____

E. 3 = ____

F. 3 = ____

G. 2 = ____

H. 5 = ____

I. 3 = ____

J. 7 = ____

2.14 Fill in the Blank

For each equation, fill in the missing information.

Sample solutions:

♩ = 2 ♪'s; ♩. = 6 𝅘𝅥𝅯's;

A. ____ = 6 ♪'s

B. 𝅝 = 16 ____

C. ♩ = 3 ____

D. 𝅗𝅥 = ____ ♪ (triplet, 3)'s

E. ♪. = ____ 𝅘𝅥𝅯's

F. ♩. = 6 ____

G. ____ = 12 ♪'s

H. ♩ (triplet, 3) = ____ ♪ (triplet, 3)'s

2.15 Correcting Rhythmic Notation to Clarify Meter

The examples shown employ the improper use of ties and beams. There are no examples of hemiola.

For Parts A–E: Determine the key, and on a separate sheet of paper, correct the rhythmic notation to align with the meter.

For Parts F–G: Determine and add the meter signature; then correct beams, ties, and dots in each example and add bar lines. Exercises begin on downbeats, and there are no examples of hemiola.

2.16 Meter Identification and Beaming

For each example:

1. Determine the most logical meter.
2. Provide a meter signature and bar lines.
3. Add beams to clarify the meter. Remember that notes within one beat should be beamed together. There are no examples of hemiola.

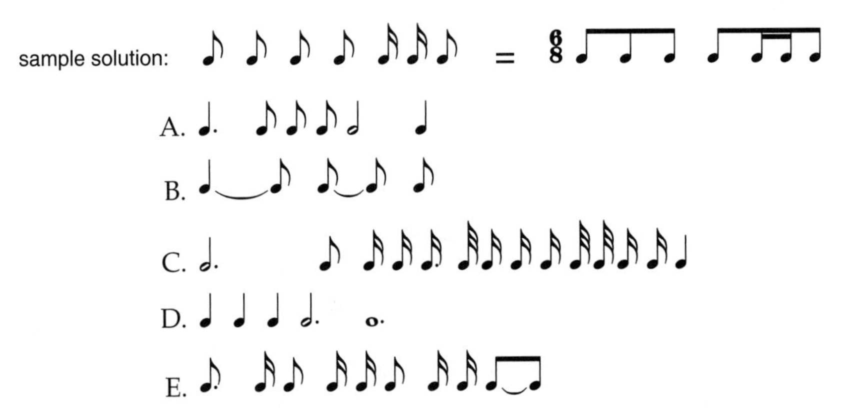

ANALYSIS

2.17 Syncopation and Hemiola

Identify instances of syncopation and hemiola in the following excerpts.

A. Brahms, "Wenn du nur zuweilen lächelst," op. 57, no. 2

B. Beethoven, Piano Sonata in E♭ major, op. 31, no. 3, Trio

C. Beethoven, Piano Sonata in A♭ major, op. 110, *Allegro molto*

D. Tchaikovsky, from *Sleeping Beauty*

PERFORMING

2.18 Integrating Rhythm, Meter, Singing, and Keyboard

Complete the following tasks while sitting at the keyboard.

A. Tap quarter notes on any pitch. Sing ascending and descending scales in quarter notes, then in eighth notes, and again in dotted-quarter-plus-eighth rhythms.
B. Tap quarter notes with one foot and eighth notes with one hand on any pitch on the keyboard. Sing ascending and descending scales in quarter notes, and then in eighth notes, and then in dotted quarter-plus-eighth rhythms.
C. Tap the following rhythms on any pitch on the keyboard while singing scales in even quarter notes and then eighth notes:

D. Tap a series of pulses at a tempo of one pulse per second (for example, the same as a metronome set to 60). The quarter note receives the pulse.
   1. Sing ascending and descending scales in eighth notes and then in triplet eighth notes.
   2. Sing ascending and descending scales in eighth notes. Start with an accent, and then accent every fourth note to create a $\frac{2}{4}$ meter; then accent every sixth note to create a $\frac{3}{4}$ meter.

WORKBOOK 2.5–2.7

E. Tap a series of quarter-note pulses on any note of the keyboard at a tempo of two pulses per second (for example, the same as a metronome set to 120). Sing ascending and descending scales in quarter notes. Create meters of $\frac{3}{4}$, $\frac{4}{4}$, and $\frac{6}{8}$ by accenting the appropriate members of the scale.

TERMS AND CONCEPTS

- accent
  - durational, metrical, rhythmic
  - nontemporal:
    - articulative, contour, dynamic, harmonic, pitch, registral, textural
- accented v. unaccented
- anacrusis
- bar line
- beam
- beat
- borrowed divisions (duplets, triplets, irregular)
- common time, cut time (*alla breve*)
- downbeat, upbeat
- dot
- durational values:
  - whole, half, quarter, eighth, sixteenth, and thirty-second notes
- flag
- harmonic rhythm
- hemiola
- measure
- meter:
  - simple v. compound
    - simple duple, simple triple; simple quadruple, compound duple, compound triple, compound quadruple
  - asymmetrical
- meter signature
- musical patterning
- notehead
- phrasing slur
- pulse
- rests:
  - whole, half, quarter, eighth, sixteenth, thirty-second
- rhythm
- stem
- strong and weak
- syncopation
- tempo
- tie

CHAPTER 3

Intervals and Melody

In our discussion of scales in Chapter 1, we explored various relationships between pairs of pitches. We now call a pair of pitches a **dyad**, and we refer to the distance between the pitches in a dyad as the **interval**. In this chapter you will learn that intervals are the basic building blocks of tonal music. Indeed, the one-measure excerpt in Example 3.1 contains dozens of intervals, some formed between pitches in the same voice, others formed between pitches sounding simultaneously between different voices; Example 3.1B shows the six intervals in the first beat.

EXAMPLE 3.1 Handel, *Allegro,* Concerto Grosso in C minor, op. 6, no. 8, HWV 326

Naming Generic Intervals

The distance between one pitch and any other pitch is represented by a number derived from the number of pitch letter names that separate the two notes and is measured by the number of lines or spaces on the staff that are spanned. (When we *speak* of intervals, we use the ordinal number, such as third, fifth, and seventh. When we label intervals, we use cardinal numbers, such as 3, 5, and 7). The numerical label that identifies the distance between letter names is called a **generic** name. So far we have focused on those intervals that are formed by successive scale degrees in major and minor scales. The distance between adjacent scale degrees, or steps, is called a second because it involves two successive letter names (for example, A up to B or E down to D). Example 3.2A presents the interval from G^4 up to E^5. Given that there are six different letter names, G–A–B–C–D–E, we refer to the interval as a sixth. Notice that we reckon the generic size by including both the first and last notes. Further, contour and accidentals do not change an interval's generic size. For example, whether you ascend from G^4 to E^5 or descend from E^5 to G^4, the interval remains a sixth; and no matter what combination of G, G♭, or G♯ up to E, E♭ or E♯, all are sixths (see Example 3.2B)

EXAMPLE 3.2 Generic Sixths

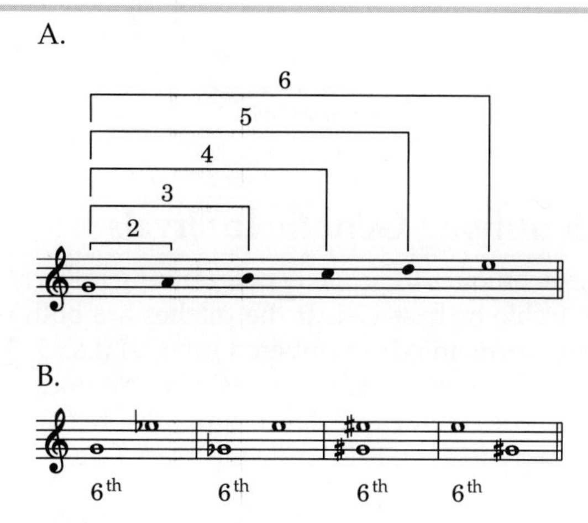

Melodic and Harmonic Intervals: Simple and Compound

When one pitch follows another in time, the interval is called a **melodic interval**, or linear interval. And we often specify the direction, or contour, of the interval by reading from left to right. For example, we would call the first interval in Example 3.2B an "ascending sixth" and the last interval a "descending sixth." If the two pitches are sounded simultaneously, as in the sixth formed by G♯ and E♯, the interval is called a **harmonic interval**. We cannot specify contour for harmonic intervals because they sound together.

The smallest interval is the **unison**, or **prime**, and it is the interval from a pitch to the same pitch—for example, the distance from middle C to middle C. The **octave** is the interval from a pitch to the pitch with the same letter name that lies seven steps away.

Intervals no larger than the octave are called **simple intervals** (Example 3.3). Intervals larger than the octave are called **compound intervals**. Since the labeling of compound intervals can become cumbersome (for example, the distance from C^2 to C^4 would be an unwieldy "fifteenth"), we use the names of these larger intervals only up to the distance of a twelfth, and we reduce to their simple forms intervals larger than the twelfth, but we append the adjective "compound" before the generic size. Thus, the interval from C^4 to E^5 is a tenth, while the interval from C^2 to C^4 is a compound octave. You are also free to use "octave plus" instead of "compound;" thus, the distance from D^4 to B^5 would be called either a "compound sixth" or an "octave plus a sixth." See Example 3.4.

EXAMPLE 3.3 Simple Intervals

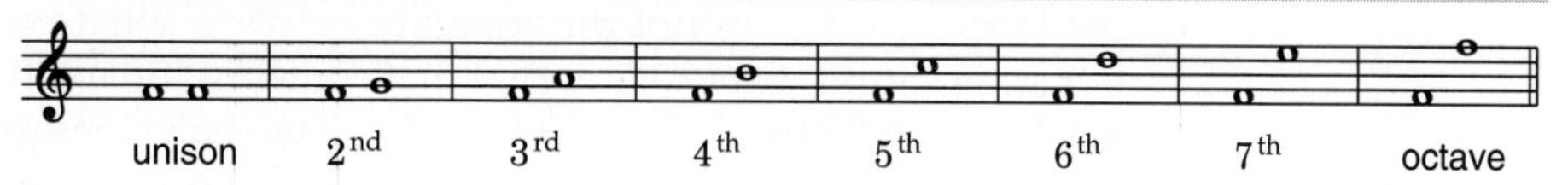

EXAMPLE 3.4 Compound Intervals

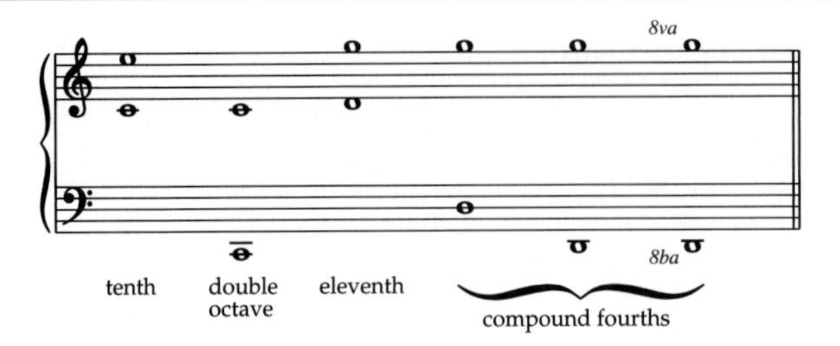

Tips for Identifying Generic Intervals

Here are some techniques for quickly determining intervals up to a twelfth for pitches in the treble or bass clef. If the pitches are both on lines or both on spaces, they will form an odd-numbered interval (i.e., 1, 3, 5, 7, 9). For example, a third is formed when pitches are on adjacent lines or spaces, and a fifth is formed when one line or one space separates the two pitches. This technique works when accidentals precede the notes (see Example 3.5).

EXAMPLE 3.5 Odd-Numbered Intervals in Various Clefs and with Accidentals

(*Note:* Both pitches on lines or both pitches on spaces form odd intervals: 3, 5, 7, 9.)

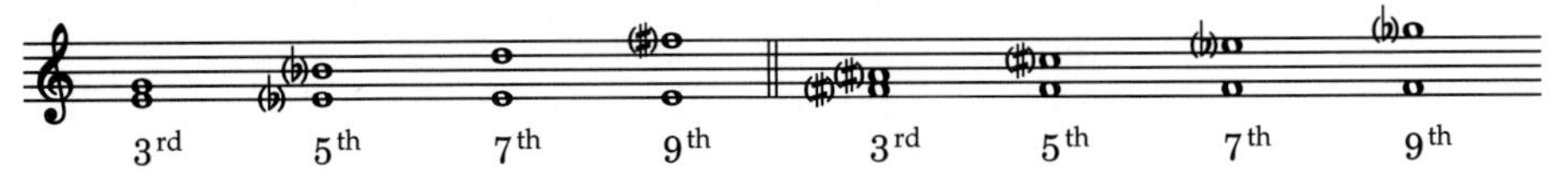

By contrast, if one of the pitches falls on a line and the other falls on a space, the result will be an even-numbered interval (i.e., 2, 4, 6, 8, 10). For example, pitches on an adjacent line and space form a second, and an interval occurring on a line and a space that is separated by one line is a fourth. Two lines separating an interval will result in a sixth, and three lines separating an interval produce an octave (see Example 3.6).

EXAMPLE 3.6 Even-Numbered Intervals in Various Clefs and with Accidentals

(*Note:* One pitch on a line and one pitch on a space form even intervals: 2, 4, 6, 8, 10.)

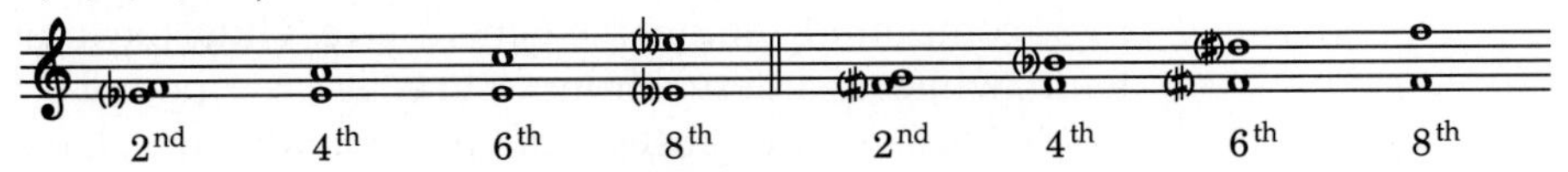

Naming Specific Intervals

A generic label is usually not specific enough to be of much use. For example, the label *second* does not differentiate between what we already know from our scale studies to be an interval that comes in three different sizes, spanning one half step (between $\hat{3}$ and $\hat{4}$ in major), two half steps (between $\hat{1}$ and $\hat{2}$), and even three half steps (between $\hat{6}$ and $\hat{7}$ in harmonic minor). Further, and more importantly, a generic label in no way reflects the audible differences in sound between these various forms of a second.

Indeed, aural comparison of a harmonic second comprising only one semitone with seconds comprising two or three semitones is striking, since the smaller second sounds more unstable and harsher than the larger seconds. Thus, we must identify intervals not only by their generic name, but also by their **quality**, which, together, will produce their **specific size**.

We will use the major and minor scales to identify intervals precisely. We group intervals into two basic categories: **perfect** (P) and **major** (M)/**minor** (m). See Example 3.7. In the example, each interval of the C major and C natural minor scale above $\hat{1}$ is identified by a generic name in conjunction with a modifier (here uppercase P or uppercase M or lowercase m):

EXAMPLE 3.7

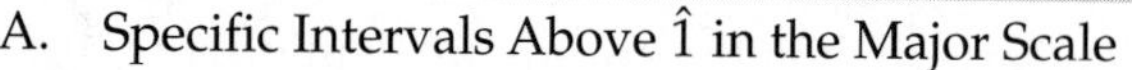

A. Specific Intervals Above $\hat{1}$ in the Major Scale

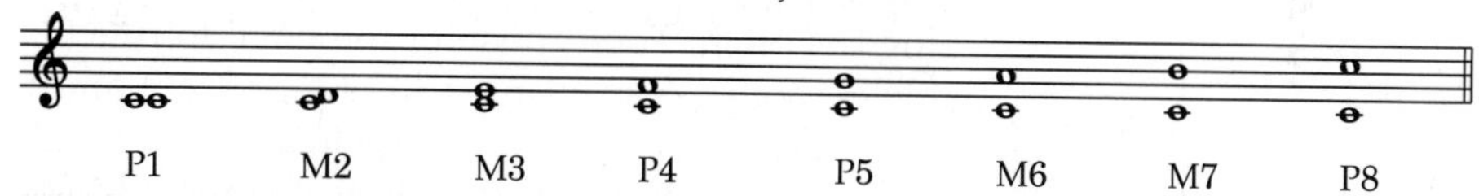

B. Specific Intervals Above $\hat{1}$ in the Minor Scale

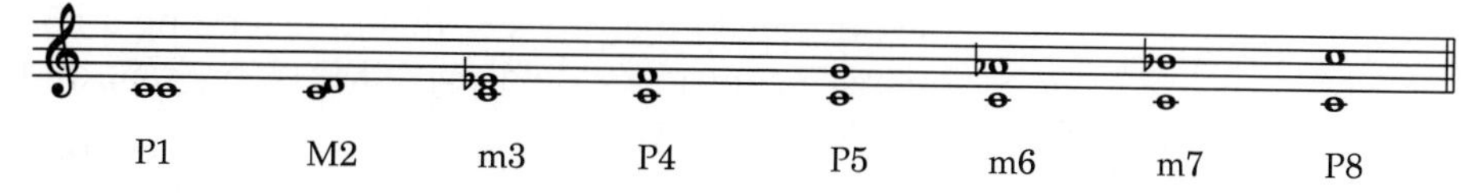

- P designates a perfect interval (which includes the unison (P1), the fourth (P4), the fifth (P5), and the octave (P8). Perfect intervals retain their specific size in both major and minor modes.
- Uppercase M designates major intervals, and lowercase m designates minor intervals; major and minor are applied to seconds, thirds, sixths, and sevenths. Major intervals occur above the tonic in the major scale, and minor intervals occur above the tonic in the minor scale (except for the second from $\hat{1}$ to $\hat{2}$, which is major).

Note that not all intervals are generated from $\hat{1}$ in major and natural minor scales. We will investigate other **diatonic intervals** (intervals found in either major or minor mode) later in this chapter.

To find the specific size of a diatonic interval, follow this two-stage process:

1. Determine the generic size of the interval.
2. Determine whether the interval's upper pitch is a member of the major or the minor scale of the lower pitch.

Example 3.8 presents several examples. In Example 3.8A, the generic interval size is a fourth (D–E–F–G). The upper pitch, G, lies in the scale of D (major and minor), so the interval is a perfect fourth. In Example 3.8B, C is a third above A♭ (A♭–B–C) and C is a member of the A♭ major scale, so the interval is a major third. In Example 3.8C, G lies a third above E, and G is a member of the

E minor scale, so the interval is a minor third. In Example 3.8D, G♯ lies a sixth above B, and since G♯ is a member of the B major scale, the interval is a major sixth.

EXAMPLE 3.8

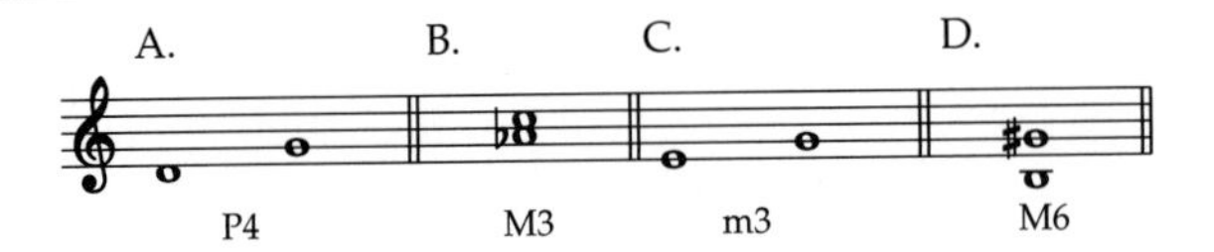

EXERCISE INTERLUDE

SINGING AND PLAYING

3.1

- Play any pitch in the approximate middle of the piano.
- Sing the pitch. Then consider the pitch to function as $\hat{1}$ ("do" in moveable do solfège) and sing a M2 ($\hat{2}$, or "re") and then a P5 ($\hat{5}$, or "sol") *above* the given pitch. Transpose to at least five different major keys.
- Then repeat the process, this time singing a M3 ($\hat{3}$, or "mi"), a M2 ($\hat{2}$, or "re"), and then a M6 ($\hat{6}$, or "la"), and transpose to five different major keys.
- Finally, repeat the process, this time singing a P5 ($\hat{5}$, or "sol"), a m3 ($\hat{3}$, or "me") a m6 ($\hat{6}$, or "le"), and a M2 ($\hat{2}$, or "re"), and transpose to five different minor keys.

ANALYSIS, PLAYING, AND SINGING

3.2

- Label each given interval using its specific name. [The specific name includes the generic (numerical) size and the specific quality (perfect, major, or minor)].
- Then play the lower pitch and sing the upper pitch.
- Finally, play the upper pitch and sing the lower pitch.

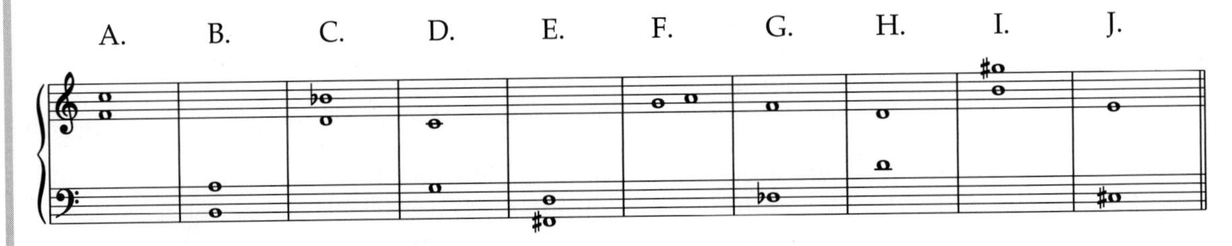

DVD 2
CH 3
TRACK 1

LISTENING

3.3 Aural Identification and Notation of Seconds, Perfect Fifths, and Octaves

In each example you will hear intervals in either melodic (successive) or harmonic (simultaneous) settings. You will hear the given pitch alone, followed by the interval. For harmonic intervals, the given pitch will always be the lower pitch of the interval. Notate the missing pitch, and identify the resulting interval. Your choices are m2, M2, P5, and P8. You might wish to employ the following listening procedure:

- Determine the approximate size of the interval; major and minor seconds are small intervals, the fifth is a medium-size interval, and the octave is a large interval.
- Differentiate between major and minor seconds in both harmonic and melodic contexts. Think about:
  - For intervals played harmonically, determine the level of dissonance. Minor seconds are very dissonant and major seconds are less dissonant.
  - For intervals played melodically, imagine that they are two pitches in a major scale; a *major* second will sound like $\hat{1}$ moving to $\hat{2}$ (or vice versa) and a minor second will sound like $\hat{7}$ to $\hat{1}$ (or vice versa).

WRITING

3.4 Generating Diatonic Intervals

- Notate the required interval above each given pitch.
- Transpose each interval a major third lower and a minor third higher than written.

3.5

Given the following series of intervals, notate the pitches, beginning on the given pitch. You will create a melody that you probably know. Arrows indicate the direction of the interval. Once you recognize the tune, add appropriate key and meter signatures and rhythmic values. Finally, transpose each tune up a major third using two methods. The first method is by scale degree (e.g., if you are in D major and find yourself on the pitch A, you know that it is $\hat{5}$ in D. If you wish to transpose a line that contains this pitch up a major third, then you would be in the key of F♯, and $\hat{5}$ in F♯ is C♯). The second method is by interval (e.g., given the pitch A in the key of D, the pitch a major third higher than A is C♯).

WORKBOOK
3.1–3.2

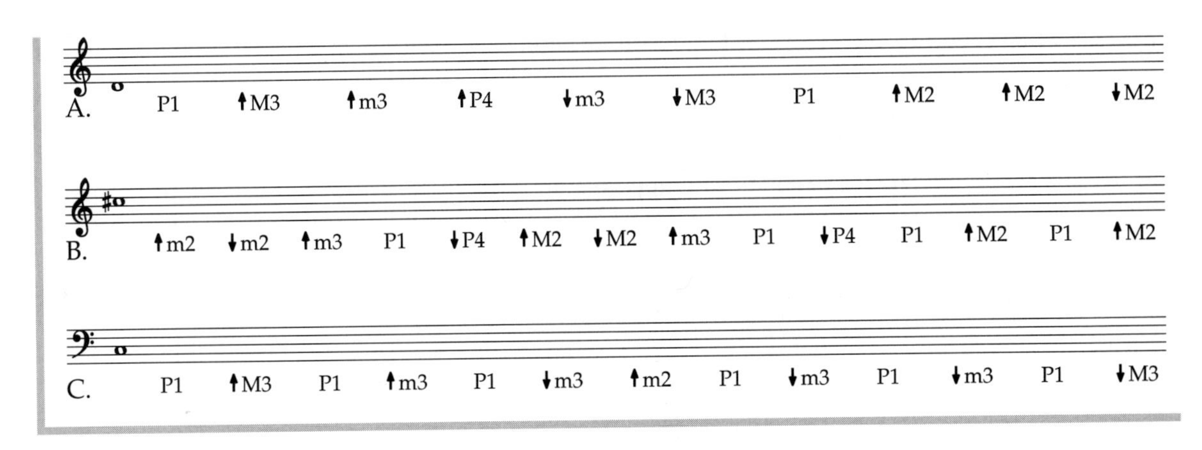

Transforming Intervals: Augmented and Diminished Intervals

Since minor intervals are a half step smaller than major intervals, one can transform any minor interval into a major interval by *increasing* its size by a half step, by either raising the upper note or lowering the lower note. Example 3.9A increases the size of a m3 to a M3 by raising the upper note a half step (A1) or lowering the lower note a half step (A2). Likewise, a major interval can be transformed into a minor interval by *decreasing* the size of the major interval by a half step. In this case, the upper note can be lowered by a half step or the lower note can be raised by a half step. Example 3.9B1 decreases the size of a M6 to a m6 by lowering the upper note, and B2 decreases the M6 to a m6 by raising the lower note a half step.

EXAMPLE 3.9

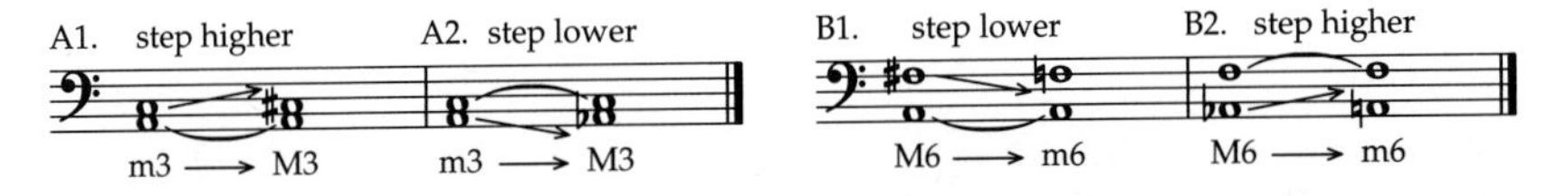

Further, it is possible to *increase* the size of major and perfect intervals by a half step (Example 3.10A and B), resulting in **augmented intervals**. We can also *decrease* the size of minor and perfect intervals (Example 3.10C and D), resulting in **diminished intervals** (see Example 3.10A–D). We find several augmented and diminished intervals in major and minor scales (the given intervals are ascending):

INTERVAL	MAJOR SCALE DEGREES	MINOR SCALE DEGREES
A2	none	$\flat\hat{6}$–$\sharp\hat{7}$
A4	$\hat{4}$–$\hat{7}$	$\hat{4}$–$\sharp\hat{7}$; $\flat\hat{6}$–$\hat{2}$
d5	$\hat{7}$–$\hat{4}$	$\hat{2}$–$\flat\hat{6}$; $\sharp\hat{7}$–$\hat{4}$
d7	none	$\sharp\hat{7}$–$\flat\hat{6}$

EXAMPLE 3.10

A. Augmenting a M3

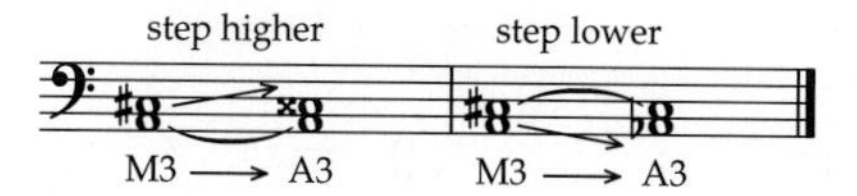

B. Augmenting a P5

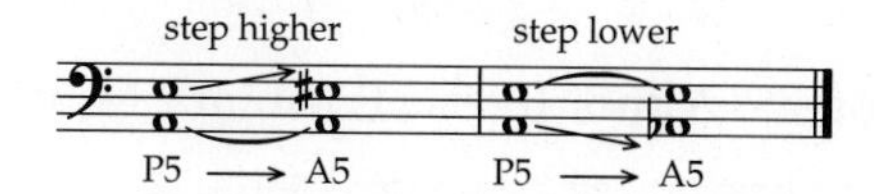

C. Diminishing a m3

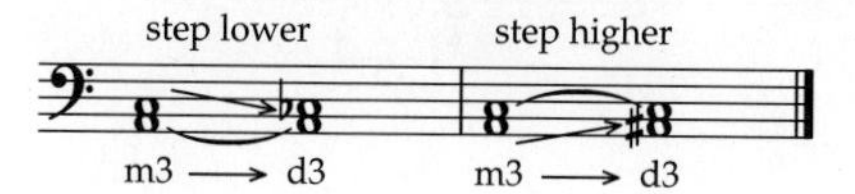

D. Diminishing a P5

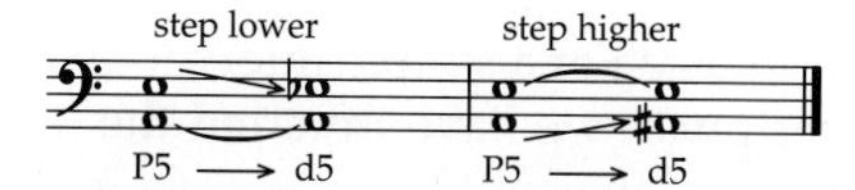

Thus, major, minor, and perfect intervals can all become augmented or diminished (except for the unison, which can only be augmented). However, major and minor intervals can never become perfect, and perfect intervals can never become major or minor.

The complete list of labels and abbreviations that reflect an interval's quality are as follows: *P* for perfect, *M* for major, *m* for minor, *A* (or +) for augmented, and d (or °) for diminished. Let's work through four intervals for practice (Example 3.11).

EXAMPLE 3.11

In Example 3.11A, the fourth from E♭ up to A is not perfect, since A♭, not A natural, lies in the E♭ scale. Since the interval is a half step smaller than a perfect fourth, it is a diminished fourth (d4, or °4). In Example 3.11B, the fifth from C up to G♯ is also not perfect, since G, not G♯, lies in the C scale. The interval is a half step larger than a perfect fifth; therefore, the interval is an augmented fifth (A5, or +5). In Example 3.11C, A♭ is not a member of either the F♯-major or F♯-minor scales; it is a half step smaller than a minor third, so the interval is a diminished third (d3, or °3). In Example 3.11D, B♯ is a half step higher than B natural, which lies in the D-major scale. Since D to B natural is a major sixth, D to B♯ would be an augmented sixth (A6, or +6).

Example 3.12A shows how perfect intervals may be increased or decreased in size; Example 3.12B summarizes how major and minor may be increased or decreased in size.

EXAMPLE 3.12

A. Transforming **Perfect** Intervals (P1, P4, P5, P8)

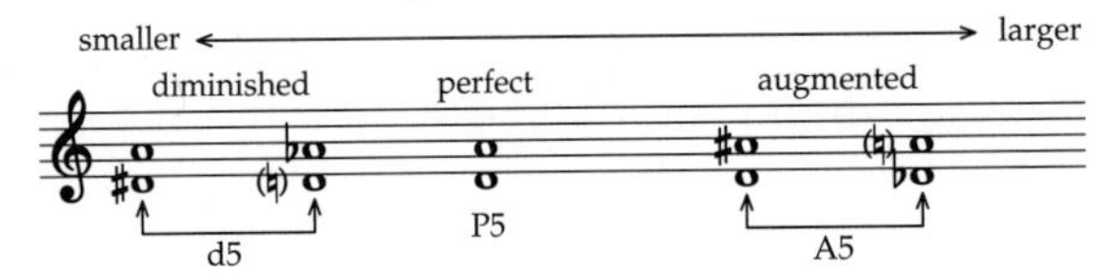

B. Transforming **Major** and **Minor** Intervals (M/m2, M/m3, M/m6, M/m7)

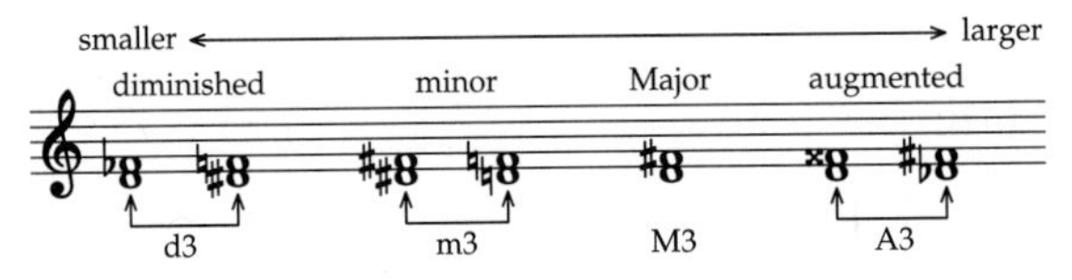

Interval Inversion

When we move the lower pitch of a simple interval up one octave so that it is placed above the higher pitch, we have **inverted** the interval. Inversion also occurs when we place the higher pitch of a simple interval below the lower pitch. Example 3.13A shows what happens when we invert generic intervals; Example 3.13B does the same for an interval's quality. Arrows represent the inversion process. Note that the inversion process can move in either direction (e.g., a second becomes a seventh, or vice versa). Notice that the inversion of *generic* intervals always sums to 9 (e.g., a third becomes a sixth: 3 + 6 = 9). Also note in Example 3.13B that perfect intervals retain their quality when inverted. However, quality is swapped for augmented/diminished and major/minor intervals.

EXAMPLE 3.13

A. Generic Interval Inversion

Unison ⟷ octave (1 + 8 = 9)

Second ⟷ seventh (2 + 7 = 9)

Third ⟷ sixth (3 + 6 = 9)

Fourth ⟷ fifth (4 + 5 = 9)

B. Quality

Perfect ⟷ Perfect

Augmented ⟷ diminished

Major ⟷ minor

Finally, the number of *half steps* between inversionally related intervals always sums to 12 [for example, the single half step of the minor second becomes 11 half steps when inverted as a major seventh (1 + 11 = 12)]. Example

3.14 shows the resulting pattern. There is only one inversional pair of intervals whose number of half steps remains the same following inversion: both the diminished fifth and the augmented fourth contain six half steps. The augmented fourth is a **tritone**, since it contains three whole steps; we also refer to the diminished fifth as a tritone, even though it actually spans five letter names (e.g., B–C–D–E–F). Notice also how inversionally related pairs of intervals in effect "repeat" themselves in reverse order from the center point A4/d5; for example, the P4/P5 pair becomes a P5/P4 pair.

EXAMPLE 3.14

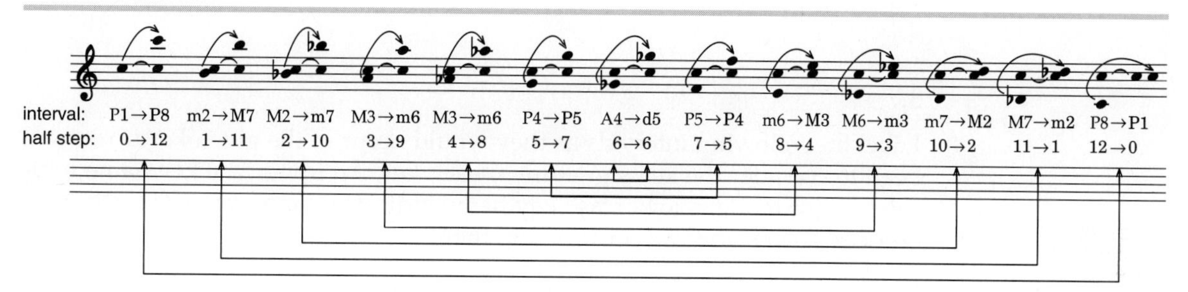

Now play each inversionally related pair of intervals, noticing how their sound quality and level of stability remain relatively the same. For example, the inversional pair of a minor second and a major seventh are both very unstable sounding, while a major third and a minor sixth are much more stable, and the octave and unison are absolutely stable.

EXERCISE INTERLUDE

WRITING

3.6 Intervallic Transformations

A. Identify the following intervals when you increase their size by one semitone without changing their generic name (e.g., a major second would become an augmented second, not a minor third).
   1. M3
   2. M2
   3. P4
   4. M6
   5. d3
   6. m7

B. Identify the following intervals when you decrease their size by one semitone without changing their generic name.
   1. m2
   2. P5
   3. A2
   4. M6
   5. A4
   6. A3

C. Identify the following intervals when you increase their size by two semitones without changing their generic name.
   1. m2
   2. d3
   3. d5

D. Identify the following intervals when you decrease their size by two semitones without changing their generic name.
   1. M6
   2. A5
   3. A2
   4. M3

3.7

Label the following intervals as they would occur in the given keys. You will need to consider the key signature of each key. An uppercase key name indicates major mode; a lowercase key name indicates minor mode. The first exercise is solved for you: in f♯ minor, there is a G♯, and G♯ up to B is a minor third.

Consider key signature for each example

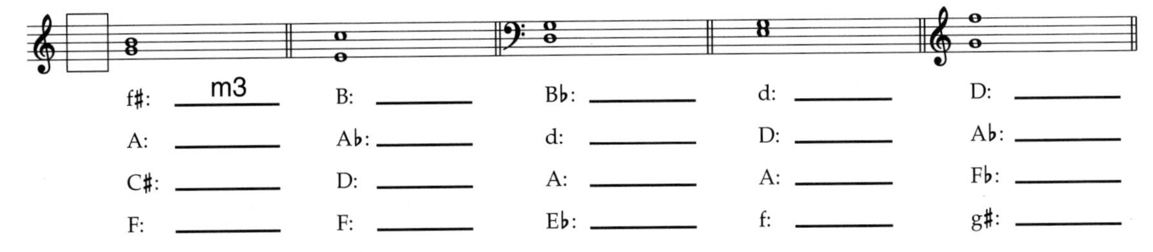

LISTENING

DVD 2 CH 3 TRACK 2

3.8 Error Detection

The following examples include intervals of M2 (M9), m2 (m9), M3 (M10), m3 (m10), P4, A4, P5, d5, and P8. Listen to each interval as it is played. If what you hear is correctly notated, write "Y" (yes). If what you hear is not notated, write "N" (no) and correctly notate what you hear by changing the upper pitch and maintaining the lower pitch.

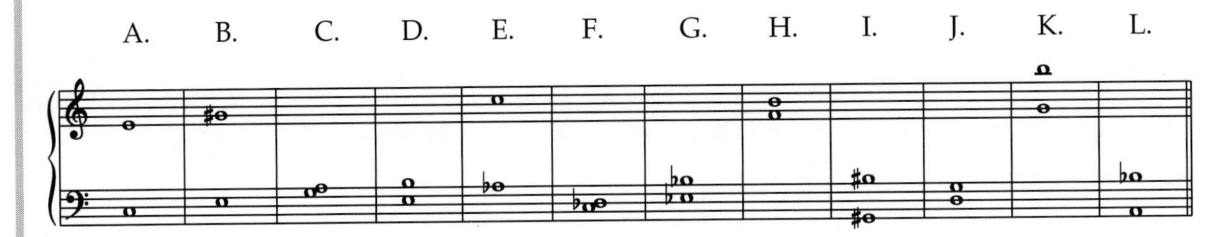

PLAYING

3.9

- Using the given pitches, play the intervals requested *above* each given note.
- Identify the inversion.
- Then increase and decrease the size of each interval by a half step and identify the resulting interval. (Remember, you can increase the size of an interval by raising the upper note or lowering the lower note, and you can decrease the size of an interval by lowering the upper note or raising the lower note.)

WORKBOOK
3.3–3.4

Construct above the pitch D: P5, m3, M6
Construct above the pitch B♭: M2, M7, P4
Construct above the pitch G: M6, P4
Construct above the pitch F♯: M3, M7, P5

Generating All Intervals

So far we have generated intervals only *above* a given pitch, a process based on (1) the generic size of the interval and (2) the quality (the specific size of the interval, based on whether the upper pitch lies in the major or minor scale of the lower pitch). When we create an interval *below* a given pitch, we still begin by calculating the generic size. However, to determine the quality (i.e., whether any accidentals are needed), we must use one of the two following methods.

Method 1

This method draws on our knowledge of inversion and is especially helpful in constructing large intervals.

1. Take the requested interval and invert it so that you are looking for a note above the given pitch.
2. Find the appropriate note above the given pitch, using scale membership. (Is the upper note a member of the major or minor scale of the lower pitch?)
3. Transpose this inverted pitch down one octave.

For example, to find the pitch that lies a major seventh below C, first determine the inversion of a M7, which is a m2. Then, generate a m2 above C, which is D♭. Finally, notate D♭ one octave lower to create a major seventh below C. You may wish to check your work using our method of scale membership: C is indeed a seventh above D♭, and C is a member of the D♭ major scale. See Example 3.15.

EXAMPLE 3.15

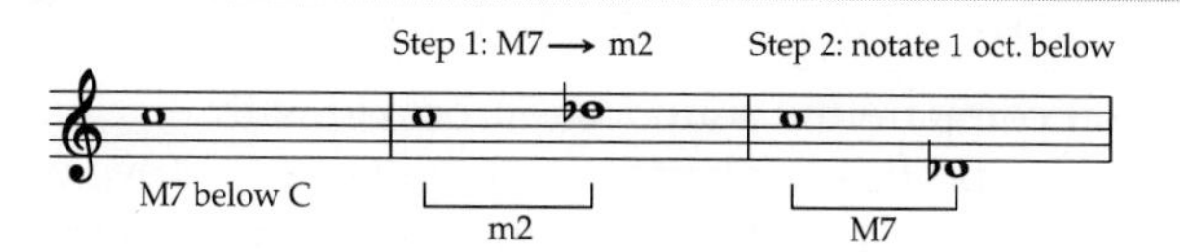

Method 2

This method requires adjusting the lower pitch.

1. Count down by generic interval from the given pitch—do not worry about accidentals yet.
2. Determine the resulting specific interval using the scale membership.
3. If the interval you have constructed is the requested interval, you are finished! If not, add an accidental to the lower pitch to change the specific interval. If the interval is too small, add a flat to the lower pitch (which increases the size of the interval). If the interval is too large, add a sharp to the lower pitch (which decreases the size of the interval).

For example, given the pitch F, construct the interval of a perfect fifth below it. First, determine the generic fifth, which is B. Second, ask yourself whether or not F is a perfect fifth above B. If it is, you're done. However, F is a diminished fifth above B. Thus, we must lower B to B♭ to increase the diminished fifth to a perfect fifth. Again, check your work: F is indeed a perfect fifth above B♭. See Example 3.16.

EXAMPLE 3.16

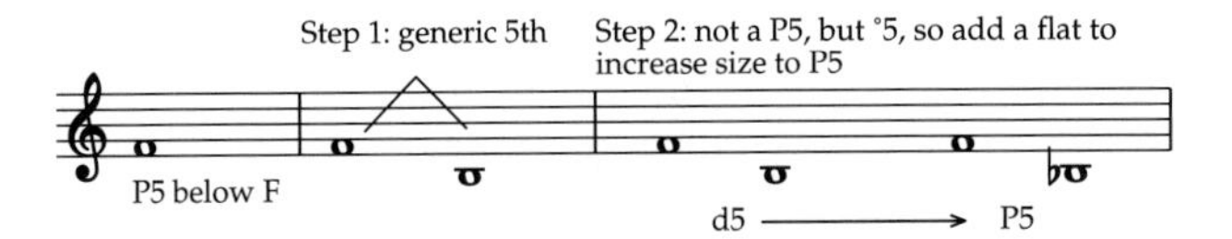

Enharmonic Intervals

Just as there are enharmonic pitches (discussed in Chapter 1), so too are there enharmonic intervals. For example, the minor third from C up to E♭ sounds identical to the augmented second from C up to D♯ (see Example 3.17A; dotted slurs indicate enharmonic pitches). The notation of intervals depends entirely on the musical context. For example, one would expect to find many instances of the minor third C–E♭ in any number of major and minor keys that contain flats because the interval is diatonic in these keys. However, the more unusual augmented second C–D♯ would occur only in the scale of E minor and only if its harmonic form were used. See Example 3.17B.

EXAMPLE 3.17

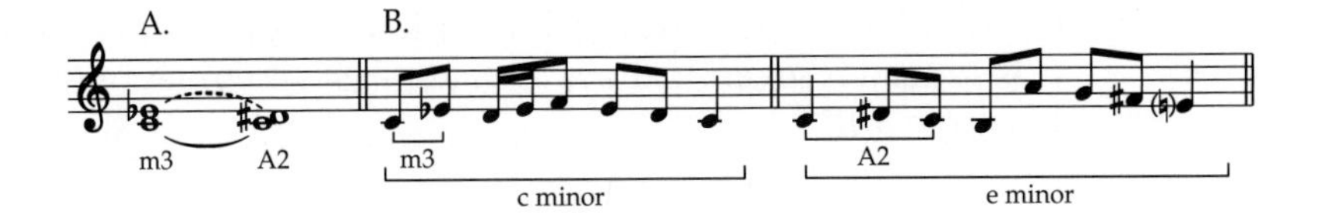

Consonant and Dissonant Intervals

When you compare the sound of an octave with that of a seventh, the octave seems stable and firmly planted, with no need to move on to some other, more stable interval. On the other hand, the seventh seems active, unstable, and even tense, as if it were searching for something to resolve its inherent discontent. At least as early as the ancient Greeks, Western musicians have felt that different-size intervals provoked certain feelings, ranging from a pleasing stability to a restless yearning. These musicians also discovered that the same interval in two different musical contexts could be perceived as either stable or unstable.

For example, Example 3.18 presents the perfect fourth C–F in four different contexts. Listen to each, and order the examples from most stable to least stable. If you heard D and the first chord in E as most stable and C as least stable (with B and the second chord in E somewhere in between), you were sensitive to the fact that intervallic stability and instability is highly determined by musical context.

EXAMPLE 3.18

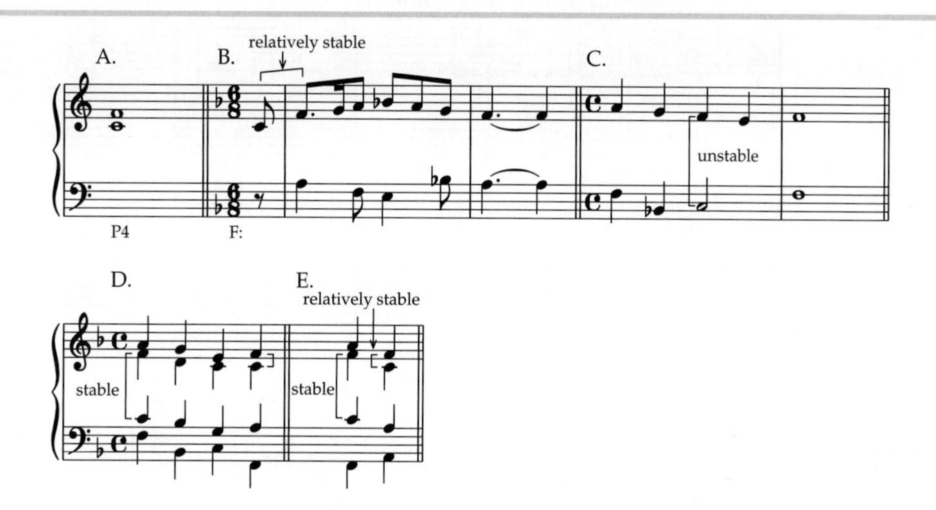

Although we usually consider intervallic stability and instability to be on a continuum, we will place all intervals into one of two categories. The stable intervals [including the diatonic forms of the unison, the third, the fifth (perfect only), the sixth, and the octave] are called **consonant intervals**; unstable intervals are called **dissonant intervals**. Dissonant intervals include the second, the seventh, and all diminished and augmented intervals. The perfect fourth is usually viewed as a dissonant interval.

The five consonant intervals are further divided into two types. The first type, known as **perfect consonances**, is the most stable and includes the perfect unison, the perfect octave, and the perfect fifth. **Imperfect consonances** include major and minor thirds and sixths, which are moderately stable yet more fluid than the perfect consonances. Imperfect consonances are central to moving the music forward. Example 3.19 summarizes the types of intervals. Composers create motion in their music by circulating through the various types of intervals; for example, from perfect consonances and imperfect consonances to dissonances, and back.

EXAMPLE 3.19

consonant intervals	**dissonant intervals**
perfect: P1, P5, P8	all forms of 2nds, 4ths, and 7ths
imperfect: M3, m3, M6, m6	all augmented and diminished intervals

EXERCISE INTERLUDE

ANALYSIS

3.10 Beethoven, String Quartet no. 14 in C♯ minor, op. 131, *Adagio ma non troppo e molto espressivo*

Identify the interval of each boxed pair of pitches, label its inversion, and specify whether the interval is a perfect consonance (PC), an imperfect consonance (IC), or a dissonance (DISS).

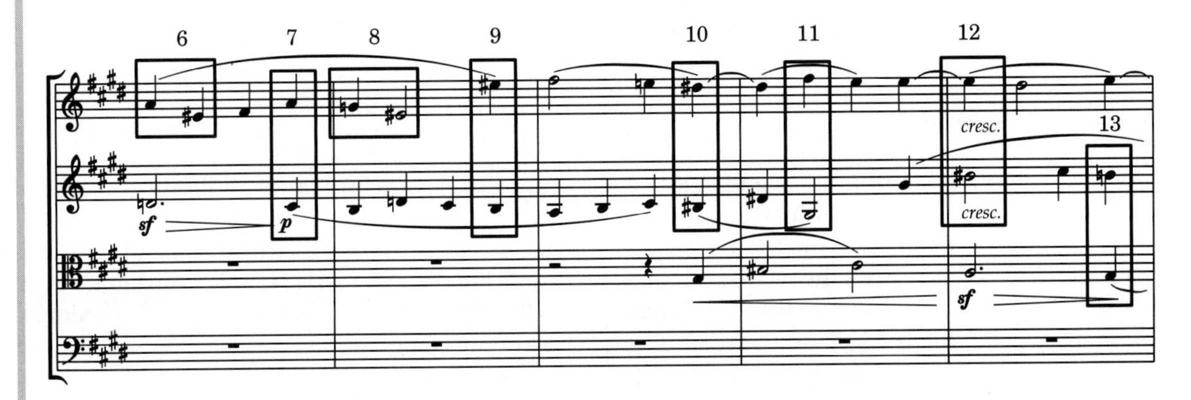

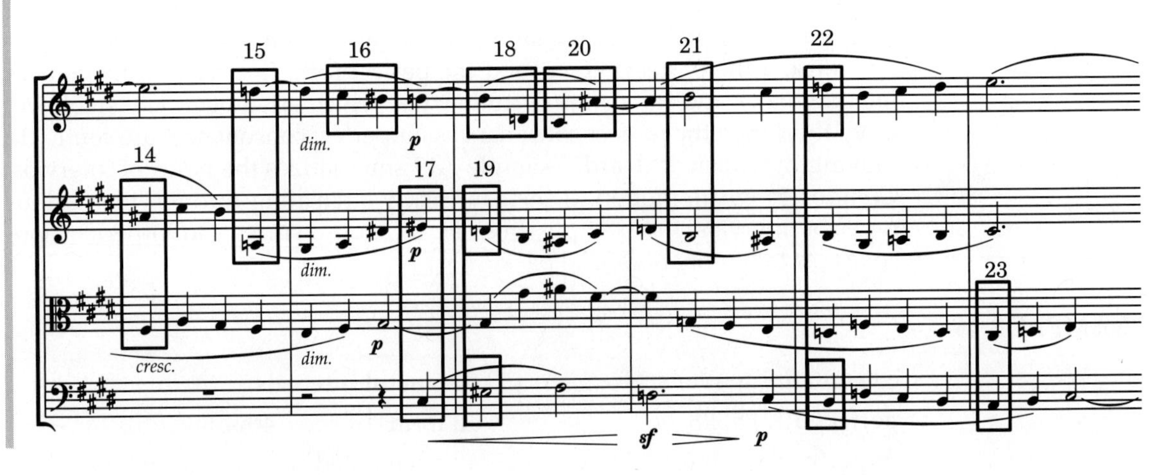

WRITING

3.11

Name all possible intervals requested in the given key. For example, "In A major, name all possible perfect fifths." *Answer:* A–E, B–F♯, C♯–G♯, D–A, E–B, and F♯–C♯.

A. In F major, name all possible major seconds.
B. In B♭ major, name all possible minor seconds.
C. In the C harmonic minor scale, name all possible major thirds.
D. In F♯ major, name all possible minor sixths.

3.12

Notate the requested intervals *below* the given pitch, and label each interval's inversion and whether it is a perfect consonance, an imperfect consonance, or a dissonance.

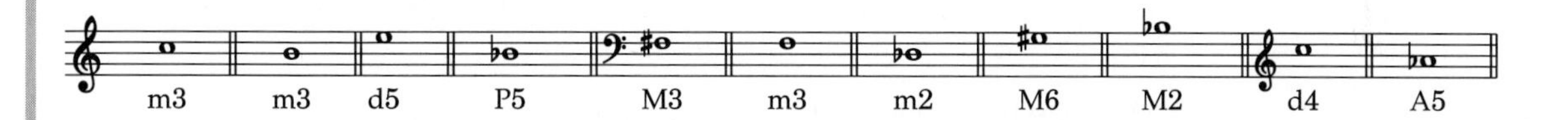

3.13

Identify each of the given intervals. Then, maintaining the tied note, renotate the interval using an enharmonic pitch. Label the new interval. *Note:* The enharmonically renotated interval must retain the same number of half steps as the original interval, and do not use pitches that require double sharps or double flats.

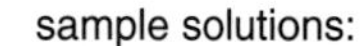

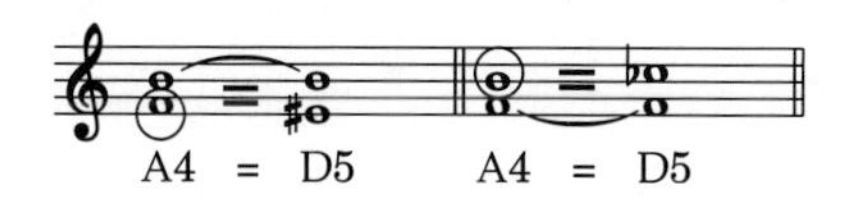

PERFORMING

WORKBOOK 3.5

3.14 Intervals from Scales

Sing and/or play all possible perfect, major, and minor intervals within major and minor keys. That is, perform all intervals between all possible scale degree combinations. For example, build intervals above and below each scale degree, such as from $\hat{1}$, as follows: ascending: 1–2, 1–3, 1–4, . . .; and 7–1, 6–1, 5–1; as well as descending: 1–7, 1–6, 1–5, . . .; and 2–1, 3–1, 4–1, . . . Continue this exercise by beginning on each of the seven scale degrees in both major and minor modes.

Melody: Characteristics, Writing, and Listening

As we've learned, intervals do not occur in isolation; rather, they are simply the stuff of all music. Beethoven employs streams of melodic intervals to create the haunting melody of the opening of his String Quartet in Exercise 3.10. Further, he uses this same series of intervals again and again, first as the source of the melody in the second violin, then in the entrances of viola, and, finally, cello. At the same time, Beethoven has also vertically combined each line's melodic intervals to create first two, then three, and finally four voices moving simultaneously against one another. Such a process, whereby one or more melodies are combined, is called *counterpoint*, and the vertical pillars that result are called *harmonies*. This process will be the focus of the rest of this book.

Before we delve into the world of counterpoint and harmony, we will first apply our knowledge of key, scale, and interval to writing and hearing single-line melodies. Example 3.20 contains numerous short melodic excerpts from a wide variety of music that spans the last 1,000 years. The examples are drawn from both vocal music (including both solo song and opera) and instrumental music (ranging from solo piano to full orchestra). Listen to the short melodic excerpts with the following questions in mind.

1. Are they in a key? If so how do you know?
2. Do the melodies have a shape or contour? You might want to trace the general flow of each melody, "connecting the dots" with a pencil.
3. What sorts of melodic intervals occur between pitches? Do the composers prefer some intervals more than others?
4. Are there accented events in the melodies, that is, events that draw your attention, such as leaps, chromaticism, and longer durations? If so, are these events isolated, or does the composer prepare them in some way?

EXAMPLE 3.20

DVD 1
CH 3
TRACK 1

A. Wipo, Victimae pachali laudes (c. 1020)

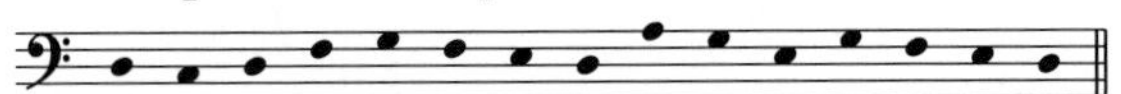

B. Byzantine chant (c. 1200)

C. Guillaume Costeley "Allon, gay, gay" (c. 1575)

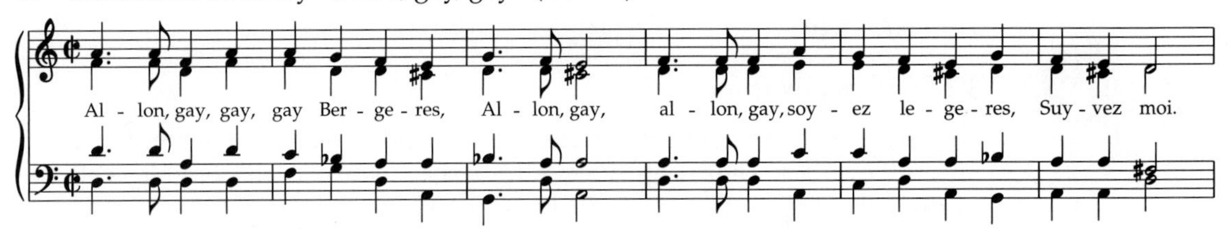

D. Denis Gaultier, piece for lute (c. 1650)

E. Bach, "Bereite dich, Zion," from *Christmas Oratorio* (1735)

F. Haydn, String Quartet in C major, op. 76, no. 3 ("Emperor"; 1796)

G. Beethoven, Piano Sonata in C major, op. 53, "Waldstein" (1803)

H. Schubert, Symphony no. 9 in C major (c. 1827)

I. Scriabin, Etude in C♯ minor, op. 2/1 (1887)

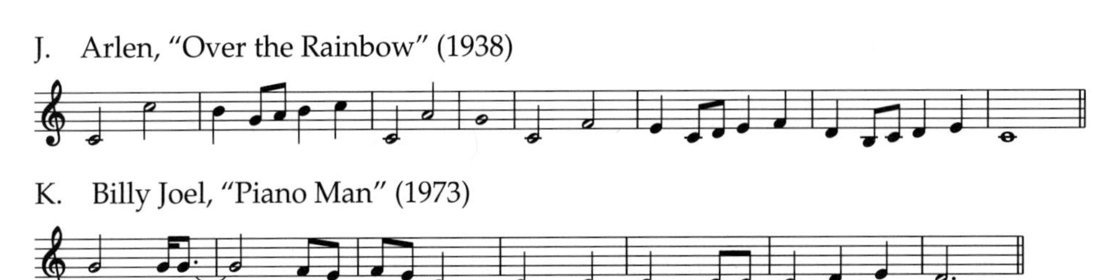

J. Arlen, "Over the Rainbow" (1938)

K. Billy Joel, "Piano Man" (1973)

Each example—whether written for voice or for instrument—is singable. The pitches follow one another in what seems to be a logical and goal-oriented flow. The intervals are mostly steps, and leaps are usually small. Large leaps are followed by change of direction. Notice also that large leaps often tend to be filled in, in effect retracing and completing a musical space that was left open. Such balance and the creation and dissipation of energy are important components of melody. These melodies are almost entirely diatonic, and they begin with a strong sense of key, always a member of the tonic triad and usually on $\hat{1}$. Most of the melodies end on $\hat{1}$; those that end on $\hat{2}$ or $\hat{5}$ will continue and eventually lead to $\hat{1}$. Their contours usually produce arches, often taking the form of an ascent followed by a descent; but sometimes, as in Beethoven's Waldstein Sonata, an ascent follows a descent. Finally, even though all of the melodies share these basic characteristics, each one possesses a distinct character. Melodic uniqueness is accomplished via relationships between segments of the melody, most of which are formed from short rhythmic and melodic patterns called *motives*, a topic that we take up in later chapters.

For our first studies in melody writing, we will explore a few specific attributes shared by many melodies written in the tonal style. Further, we will focus exclusively on the pitch domain, without the stylistic elements of repeated rhythmic and melodic patterns that characterize individual melodies. Following are the general guidelines for melody writing that we will apply, at least for now. Our melodies will be very short, about 12–18 pitches. They will also be entirely diatonic (except for raising $\hat{7}$ to create a leading tone in minor) and will be unmetered, with no rhythmic profile. Refer to Example 3.21 for examples of each of the following points.

1. Begin your melody on a member of the tonic triad ($\hat{1}$– $\hat{3}$– $\hat{5}$) and end with either $\hat{2}$– $\hat{1}$ or $\hat{7}$– $\hat{1}$. The approach to the final pitch by step is called a **melodic cadence**.
2. Limit the range of your melody (the total span of pitches) to a tenth, and try to maintain a general tessitura (the comfortable, most used span) of about a sixth.
3. Move primarily by steps (called **conjunct motion**). You can also move with occasional skips (jumps of a third) or leaps (jumps of a fourth or more) to add interest. It is fine to use skips and leaps (called **disjunct motion**) if they fit any of the following constraints.
    a. They are generally confined to small intervals, such as thirds, although one or two larger leaps may be used if they are no larger than a minor sixth.
    b. They traverse consonant melodic intervals (for example, do not use dissonant leaps, such as a diminished fourth). Be aware that the augmented second between $\hat{6}$ and $\hat{7}$ in harmonic minor is a dissonance and therefore should be avoided.

c. Some scale members have strong melodic pulls toward another member lying usually a half step away. Such **tendency tones** create an important tension, but they also should have their tendency resolved. The most important tendency tone is the leading tone, which should ascend by step to $\hat{1}$, except when $\hat{7}$ is part of the descending melodic line $\hat{1}$–$\hat{7}$–$\hat{6}$–$\hat{5}$.

d. They lead to a change of direction in order to fill in at least some of the musical space that was created by the leap (not essential in the case of skips of a third, but mandatory with larger leaps, such as a fifth). An aesthetic bonus is to prepare a leap by a change of direction (in addition to following a leap with a change of direction). Change of direction by step before and after a leap, called the **law of recovery**, is considered an important characteristic of good melody.

e. You may use two skips in a row if they are both thirds and you change direction after the second skip.

4. Avoid repeated notes and repetitive patterns, or *sequences* (for example, $\hat{1}$– $\hat{2}$– $\hat{3}$, $\hat{2}$– $\hat{3}$– $\hat{4}$, $\hat{3}$– $\hat{4}$– $\hat{5}$). Because such patterns result in a highly predictable melody (and perhaps even loss of listener interest), it is best to restrict the use of such patterns to one repetition.
5. Aim for a logical shape. An arch is commonly created by a melody that slowly rises to a single high point, or **melodic climax**, and then returns to the starting point. There should only be one such climax in your melody. Since climaxes take time to build and diminish, they usually occur about midway through the melody. It is an aesthetic bonus to lead to and from the climax pitch by step rather than by leap.

Example 3.21 illustrates that even the main tune from an instrumental *presto* movement embodies the basic tenets of good melody. The movement opens with a stepwise descent in the melody past $\hat{1}$, to $\sharp\hat{7}$, followed by change of direction, which satisfies the need for the leading tone to resolve to the tonic and to balance the falling motion with rising motion. Note that this ascent leads back to $\hat{3}$, but not as an arrival; instead the line falls to $\hat{2}$, a half step below $\hat{3}$, in exactly the same way that the line turned on $\hat{7}$ and rose to $\hat{1}$ in mm. 2–3. Mozart then dramatically pushes the line higher, first to D and then to F, the climax of the melody. Note that after the leap to D, the line changes direction and falls to C, thus balancing the leap with a contour change. Further, the climax on F is followed by a stepwise descent to the melodic cadence on B ($\hat{2}$), which leaves the listener hanging, waiting for a resolution to $\hat{1}$. Mozart repeats the melody from mm. 1–4 in mm. 9–12, but then immediately dramatically leaps to F without the intermediary skip through B, from which he descends again by step, this time closing strongly on the expected A ($\hat{1}$).

EXAMPLE 3.21 Mozart, Sonata in A minor, K. 310, *Presto*

DVD 1
CH 3
TRACK 2

Continued

Melodic Dictation

In addition to composing, analyzing, and performing melodies, counterpoint, and harmony, we will learn to memorize and notate these structures without the aid of a score. This crucial process, called **dictation**, will be of tremendous value to you as a musician, informing your sight-reading and memorization, your intonation and ensemble playing, your ability to learn a score quickly, your knowledge of musical style and notation, and every other facet of your music making.

Here are some things to keep in mind when you take dictation. Do not write down each note the instant you hear it. It is an ineffective way to develop your ear because, by focusing on a single pitch, you lose all sense of the musical context. A note-by-note approach to dictation also diminishes the development of musical memory. In addition, there are practical reasons why you wouldn't want to notate as the music is being played: If you make a mistake notating one of the pitches, each following pitch might also be incorrect. Or if the example is played at a faster tempo, you will find you are remembering and writing only a few notes at a time—requiring many more than the three or four playings recommended. Thus, an important goal is to develop a long-range memory. Indeed, it will be particularly satisfying to hear a musical passage, store its formal, melodic, and harmonic contents in your memory, and then leisurely reconstruct it on paper or on your instrument.

Let's go through the process of listening.

- Begin by quietly singing $\hat{1}$ and then $\hat{1}$–$\hat{3}$–$\hat{5}$ to situate yourself in the key.
- Listen to the first playing of the example. During the first hearing of a passage, you should listen for the musical features that seem to jump out at you—for example, beginnings and endings. Consider whether the example is a single unit or whether it is subdivided into smaller units.
- Notate each of the short melodies that you hear only after you are able to sing it from memory.

EXERCISE INTERLUDE

ANALYSIS

3.15 Melody Comparison

Listen to the following two melodies. Although A and B both contain the same number of pitches and each unfolds a melodic contour that rises toward the middle and then falls at the end, they could hardly be more different from one another. Which one do you like more? Try to sing each one. Which is more singable and memorable. Why? In a page or two, compare and contrast the two melodies by working through the list of melodic attributes given on pages 88–89.

3.16 Melodic Criticism

The following melodic contours (tunes without rhythm or meter) contain weaknesses or problems. Melodies A–D are in G major; melodies E–G are in D minor. Be able to explain the problems with each example.

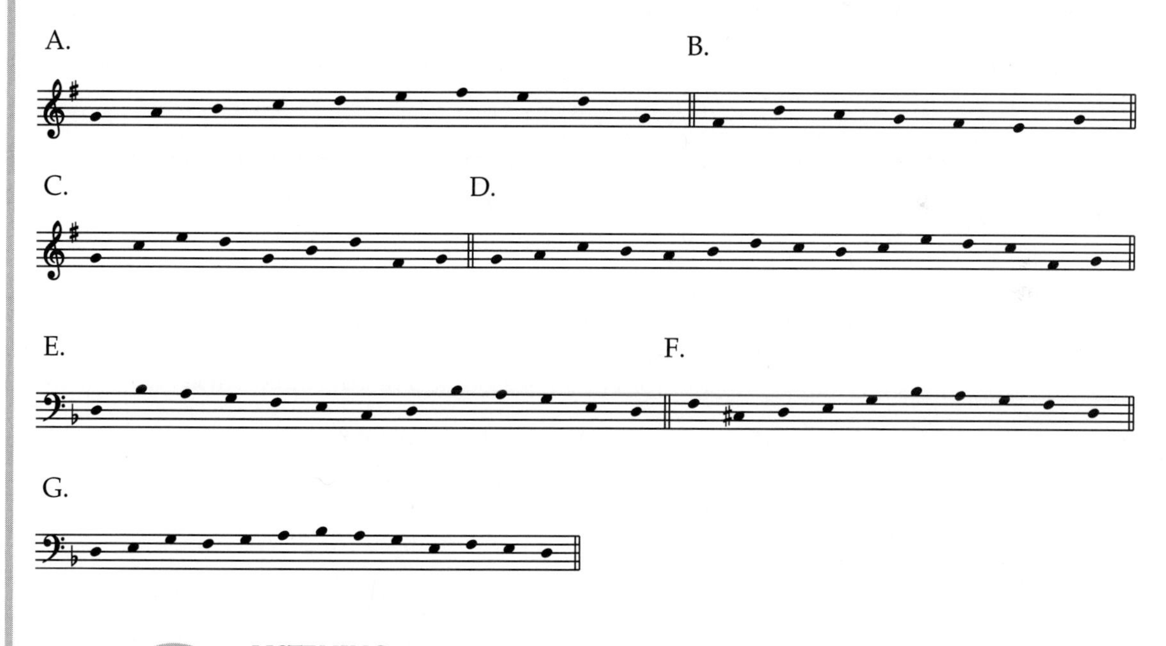

DVD 2
CH 3
TRACK 4

LISTENING

3.17 Profiles of Diatonic Melodies

You will hear six short melodic fragments. These are not necessarily complete melodies, so the final pitch may not be $\hat{1}$. For each example, determine the following: (1) mode (major or minor), (2) predominant motion (conjunct or disjunct), (3) scale degrees of first pitch, last pitch, and highest pitch.

	mode	conjunct or disjunct?	scale degrees of: 1st pitch	last pitch	highest pitch
A.	1 ________	2 ________	3 ________	________	________
B.	1 ________	2 ________	3 ________	________	________
C.	1 ________	2 ________	3 ________	________	________
D.	1 ________	2 ________	3 ________	________	________
E.	1 ________	2 ________	3 ________	________	________
F.	1 ________	2 ________	3 ________	________	________

3.18 Additional Elements Within Melodies

Listen to and memorize the following five melodies. For each example, determine the following: (1) meter, (2) first and last note, (3) lowest and highest notes (use scale degree numbers).

	meter	1st note	last note	lowest	highest
A.	1 ________	2 ________	________	3 ________	________
B.	1 ________	2 ________	________	3 ________	________
C.	1 ________	2 ________	________	3 ________	________
D.	1 ________	2 ________	________	3 ________	________
E.	1 ________	2 ________	________	3 ________	________

3.19 Notation of Melodic Fragments

Parts A–E are not in a meter; simply notate the pitches in the keys given using whole notes. Parts F–J are in simple meters; notate them using appropriate durational symbols in the keys given. You will hear the tonic triad before each exercise is played, and for Parts F–J assume a quarter-note pulse.

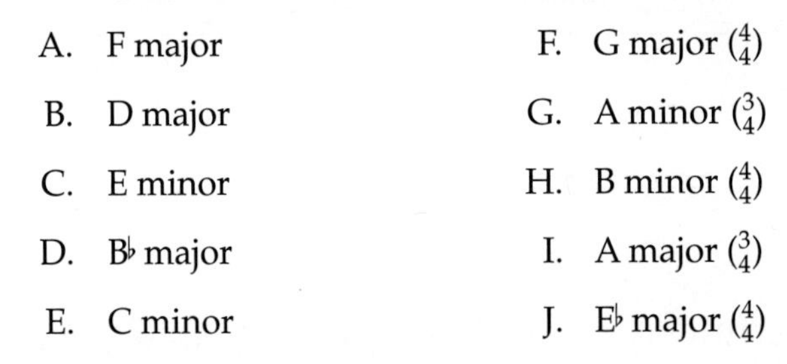

A. F major
B. D major
C. E minor
D. B♭ major
E. C minor

F. G major ($\left({4 \atop 4}\right)$)
G. A minor ($\left({3 \atop 4}\right)$)
H. B minor ($\left({4 \atop 4}\right)$)
I. A major ($\left({3 \atop 4}\right)$)
J. E♭ major ($\left({4 \atop 4}\right)$)

WORKBOOK
3.6–3.7

TERMS AND CONCEPTS

- chromatic and diatonic half steps
- climax, melodic
- compound and simple intervals
- conjunct and disjunct motion
- consonances: perfect vs. imperfect
- diatonic intervals

- dissonance, dissonant intervals
- enharmonic intervals
- generic interval vs. specific interval; intervallic quality
- harmonic interval vs. melodic interval
- interval types: augmented, diminished, major, minor, and perfect intervals
- intervallic consonance vs dissonance
- inversion of intervals
- law of recovery
- tendency tones
- tritone

CHAPTER 4

Controlling Consonance and Dissonance: Introduction to Two-Voice Counterpoint

The study of harmony concerns how chords connect to one another and move through time. But chords and their connections are dependent on how individual members, or **voices** (or **parts**), move from one chord tone to the next and how they combine with one another. Listen to the excerpts in Example 4.1, all of which sound very different from one another, but each of which shares many common features, including:

1. At least four simultaneously sounding voices. These voices are labeled "Soprano," "Alto," "Tenor," and "Bass" in Example 4.1A and in their abbreviated forms in Example 4.1B–D ("SATB").
2. Individual voices that are melodic, moving from one pitch to another, usually by steps or small leaps.
3. Voices that combine vertically with one another, forming, for the most part, consonances with the other voices (octaves, fifths, thirds, and sixths).
4. The highest- and lowest-sounding pitches as aurally the most prominent. That our ears are drawn to these **outer voices** is very important. Outer voices provide the structural skeleton in tonal music, and we will learn that harmony is most easily viewed as the filling in of the musical space between these two melodic voices—the soprano and the bass—with usually two additional voices (alto and tenor).
5. Voices that often move in opposite directions to one another, especially the outer voices; when one voice ascends, the other descends, and vice versa. When voices move in the same direction, it is usually by imperfect consonances (i.e., thirds and sixths).

EXAMPLE 4.1

DVD 1
CH 4
TRACK 1

A. Bach, *St. Matthew Passion*, "O World, I Now Must Leave Thee"

B. Schumann, "Armes Waisenkind," from *Album for the Young*, op. 68, no. 6

C. Chopin, Prelude in C minor, op. 28

D. Beethoven, Symphony #1 op. 21 in C major

E. Mendelssohn, *Midsummer Night's Dream*, Overture

As you can see, the specific pitches, their combination into sonorities, their individual movement, and their interaction with other voices are not haphazard. Rather, they are part of a well-regulated and thoughtful procedure. The relationship between and movement of two or more voices is called **counterpoint** ("melody against melody") or **polyphony** ("multiple sounds"). Counterpoint has been the focus of Western music study since the tenth century and it continues to serve musicians to this day. Contrapuntal relationships depend on two elements: (1) the behavior of consonant and dissonant intervals, and (2) the harmonies implied by their interaction. In this brief introduction to two-part counterpoint, we focus exclusively on the first element: how consonance and dissonance create musical motion. Our study of harmony, the second element, begins in Chapter 5.

By the early eighteenth century, musicians had developed user-friendly ways to teach counterpoint. Johann Fux is credited today with a particularly succinct pedagogy. In fact, his book *Gradus ad Parnassum* was closely studied by composers of the late eighteenth century, including Haydn, Mozart, and Beethoven, as well as composers throughout the nineteenth century, including Brahms. The book and its concepts continue to this day to be a fundamental part of music theory instruction. Many composers, including Mozart, taught composition using a healthy dose of the ideas presented in *Gradus*. The compositional exercises of some of Mozart's students have been preserved, including several hundred pages from the pen of a wealthy Englishman named Thomas Attwood. Mozart considered Attwood as possessing some talent, remarking that he "is a young man for whom I have a sincere affection and esteem. . . . He partakes more of my style than any scholar I ever had." However, Mozart wasn't always complimentary, as we can see in Example 4.2, in which he has crossed out Attwood's entire exercise and, in English, expressed his frustration in no uncertain terms.

EXAMPLE 4.2

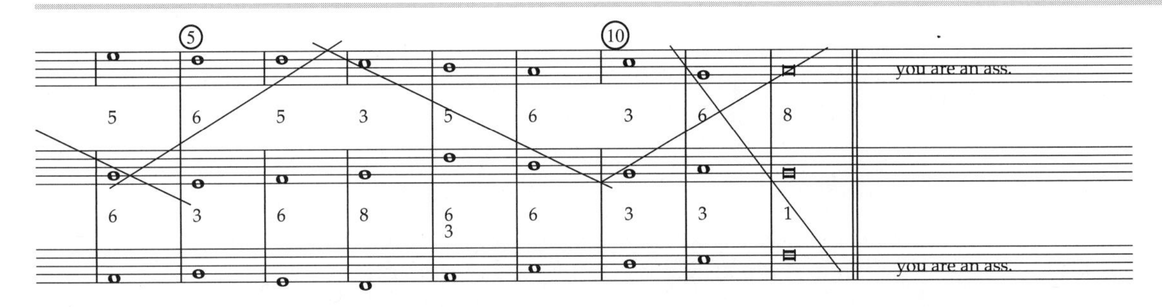

Fux begins with a study of melody (we have already dealt with this topic to some degree in Chapter 3). In subsequent chapters he uses these melodies, called **cantus firmi** ["fixed songs"; singular: **cantus firmus (CF)**], as the structural pillars against which he teaches how to add first one voice, later two, and, still later three, creating a total of four parts.

In order to make these studies as pedagogical as possible, Fux presents a series of five steps—or **species**—each of which isolates the way that an added voice would move against the CF. These five species begin, logically enough, with the addition of a single pitch above or below each pitch of the CF, resulting in **note-against-note-counterpoint**, or **first-species counterpoint** (also called 1:1 counterpoint). The newly composed voice is called the **contrapuntal voice** (or **counterpoint**). This voice can be written above or below the CF (see Example 4.3A). In **second-species counterpoint** (also called 2:1 counterpoint), two pitches are written against a single pitch of the CF (see Example 4.3B). Subsequent species add more pitches to the contrapuntal voice as well as new rhythmic procedures. Fifth-species counterpoint combines all of the techniques of the previous four species.

EXAMPLE 4.3

DVD 1
CH 4
TRACK 2

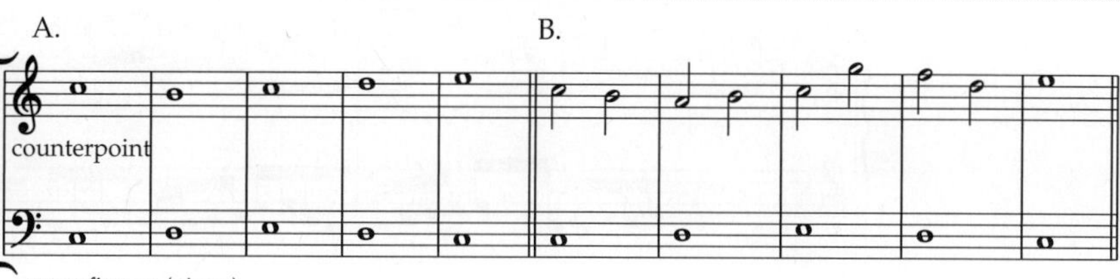

This highly controlled environment allows the musician to focus on the primary goal of writing counterpoint: to create a melody that simultaneously combines with the CF. Such harnessing of the horizontal plane in music (i.e., the linear, temporal domain) and the vertical plane in music (i.e., the spatial, harmonic domain) is actually the goal of your entire theory studies. Our counterpoint studies will focus only on first and second species in two voices and will provide the springboard for our upcoming harmony studies, which draw heavily on principles of melody and intervals. The study of species counterpoint (slightly modified in order to link up with our later harmonic studies) will help you to develop your ear and understand the difference between rules, which must be obeyed, and guidelines, which are more aesthetic options, and provide the best hands-on introduction to the subtle and crucial processes that underlie all of tonal music.

To demonstrate briefly that thinking in terms of two-voice counterpoint is central to Western music, the excerpts in Example 4.4 were taken from nearly 600 years of music; they range from the early Renaissance to the Baroque and Classical periods and span the entire nineteenth century. Each excerpt depends on the relationship between two voices moving in either 1:1 counterpoint, 2:1 counterpoint, or a mixture of the two. If there are more than two voices, the outer voices will, like those in Example 4.1, be most prominent. As you listen to these excerpts, notice that each voice is a melody unto itself and that when combined, the voices maintain their independence.

EXAMPLE 4.4

DVD 1
CH 4
TRACK 3

A. Dufay, *Missa Sancti Jacobi*, Communion (ca. 1428)

B. Josquin des Pres, *Missa Pange Lingua*, Kyrie (ca. 1517)

C. Bach, Invention in C minor (c. 1723)

D. Mozart, Sonata in C minor, K.475 (ca. 1775)

E. Beethoven, Violin Sonata in A Major, op. 23, *Allegro molto* (1800)

F. Brahms, "Unüberwindlich," op. 94, no. 5 (1884)

First-Species Counterpoint

We already know that one melodic tone most often moves to another in the smoothest manner: by step or by third. By extension, when we combine two voices, we must consider not only the intervallic movement *within* an individual voice, but also the intervals formed *between* the two voices. Example 4.5 presents an example of first-species counterpoint. The horizontal (melodic) intervals formed within each line are marked above the upper voice and below the lower voice. The vertical (harmonic) intervals formed between the two lines are labeled between the lines. All compound intervals are reduced to their simple forms (e.g., a tenth is labeled as a third). The direction and resulting shape, or contour, of each voice is traced by straight lines that appear between the pitches.

EXAMPLE 4.5

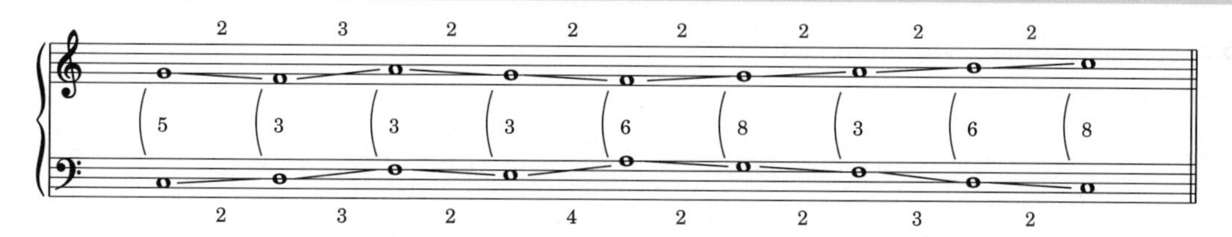

We'll begin our analysis of Example 4.5 by examining individual lines, and then we'll address the ways the lines combine.

1. Each line moves primarily by step (major and minor seconds); leaps are restricted to small consonant intervals (mostly thirds and a single fourth).
2. Each line's contour is varied such that the direction changes after every pitch or two.
3. The combination of lines produces only consonant harmonic intervals, most of which are imperfect (thirds and sixths). The example begins and ends with perfect consonances, and there is only one perfect consonance within the example (an octave). Notice that there are no perfect fourths; they are very unstable in two-voice counterpoint and considered to be a dissonance.
4. The two melodies rarely move in the same direction; rather, each melody maintains its own independence.

Consonant harmonic intervals (P8, P5, and M and m thirds and 6ths, and P1) are the only intervals permitted in first-species counterpoint. The perfect fourth may not be used. Melodic lines must be melodic and independent of one another, yet they must work together, using only consonant intervals. The source of successful counterpoint is the contrapuntal motion that results from the combined play of voices, to which we now turn.

Contrapuntal Motions

Contrapuntal motion refers to the contours produced between two or more voices. Note-against-note counterpoint involves three types of contrapuntal motion.

> Type 1. Voices that move in opposite directions from one another create **contrary motion**. For example, contrary motion is used in all but two cases in Example 4.5. Another example of contrary motion appears in Example 4.6A.

EXAMPLE 4.6

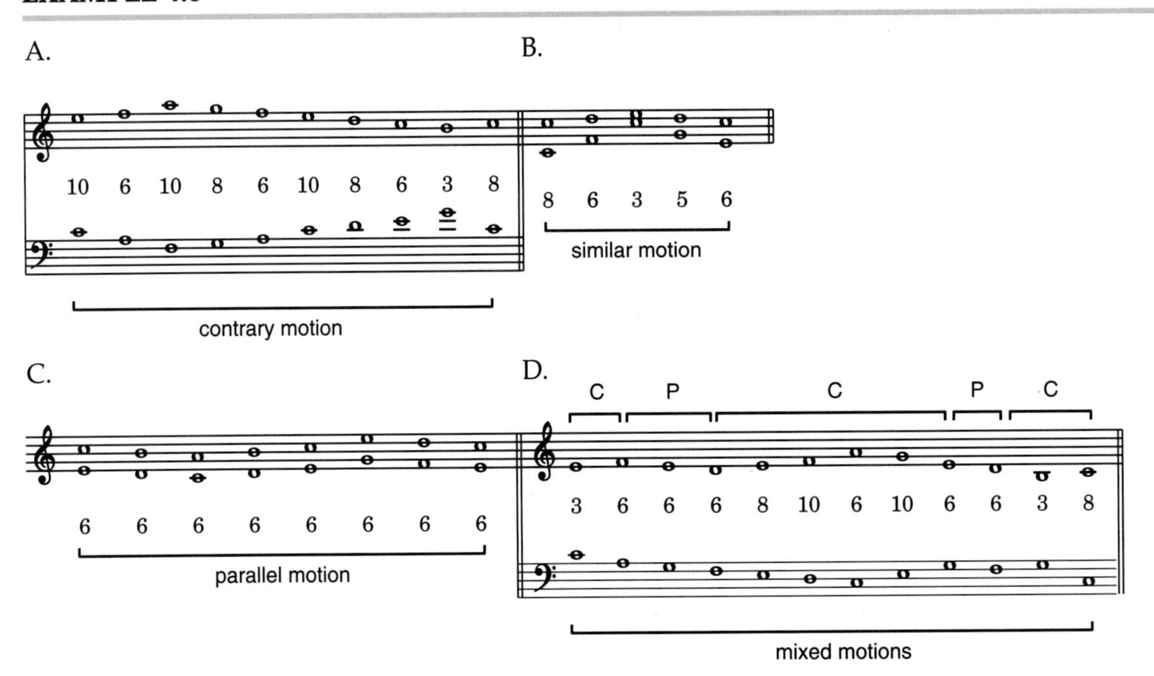

> Type 2. Voices that move in the same general direction produce **similar motion**. Example 4.6B shows similar motion.
>
> Type 3. Voices that move in the same direction and maintain the same generic interval create **parallel motion**. For example, parallel thirds and tenths characterize the motion between the second, third, and fourth intervals in Example 4.5. That these intervals are both major and minor does not affect the designation *parallel*; only the generic intervallic size needs to be repeated. Example 4.6C shows a string of parallel sixths.

Contrary motion creates the most independence between voices. You should therefore incorporate it as much as possible. Parallel motion can be very beautiful. But given that the voices are heard as shadowing one another, parallel motion substantially reduces voice independence and general motion. In order to maintain as much independence and momentum as possible in parallel motion, you may use only imperfect intervals (thirds and sixths). Further, parallel motion in thirds or sixths should be limited to a maximum of three consecutive uses (6–6–6, or 3–3–3) in order to avoid monotony. Music is made up of a mixture of these various motions to create a balanced and pleasing structure (Example 4.6D).

While parallel sixths and thirds are allowed, moving directly from one perfect interval between the CF and the counterpoint voice to another perfect interval of the same size is forbidden. Listen to Example 4.7, which contains several examples of such **parallel perfect intervals**, each of which is marked with parallel lines.

Notice how such parallels ruin line independence and, in the case of parallel octaves, create the unfortunate effect of one voice dropping out of the texture.

EXAMPLE 4.7

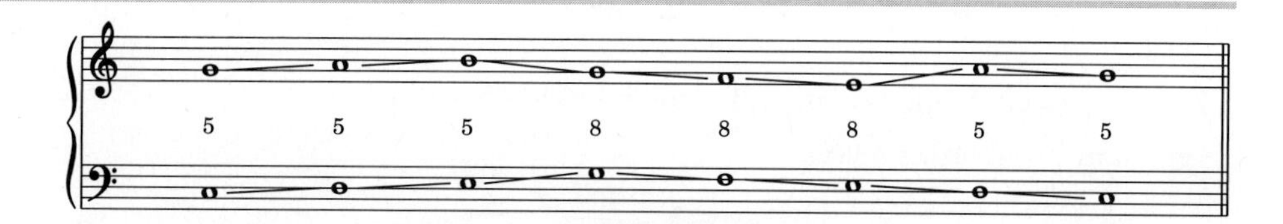

Finally, **similar motion** provides more drama to your counterpoint because both voices ascend or descend but by different-size intervals. Similar motion (like parallel motion) is most effective when you use imperfect consonances.

We must be careful when we approach perfect consonances. Of course, we may not move in parallel motion from a perfect consonance to another of the same size, but also we may not approach a perfect consonance by similar motion. Such **direct intervals** (also called **hidden intervals** or **similar intervals**) draw attention to perfect fifths and octaves, emphasizing their hollow sound (see Example 4.8A). Further, direct intervals often give the impression of parallels (hence the synonymous term *hidden*) because the ear tends to fill in the intervening intervals. Example 4.8B shows how the hidden fifths of Example 4.8A can be heard as hidden parallel fifths. To avoid direct intervals, approach perfect intervals by using contrary motion.

There is one situation in which you may move to an octave or a fifth in similar motion: when the upper voice moves by step to the perfect interval. In Examples 4.8C and 4.8D the direct motion to the octave and the fifth are permissible, given the step motion in the upper voice. Example 4.8E contains an example of a special setting of legal direct fifths, where the upper voice moves by step and the lower voice leaps. Given their rustic, hollow sound such *horn fifths* are popular referential devices throughout the common practice. Notice how Scarlatti, Schumann, and Paganini cast their horn fifths in a playful manner, while Beethoven's somber setting evokes the title that he gave the sonata ("The Farewell").

EXAMPLE 4.8 Hidden Intervals

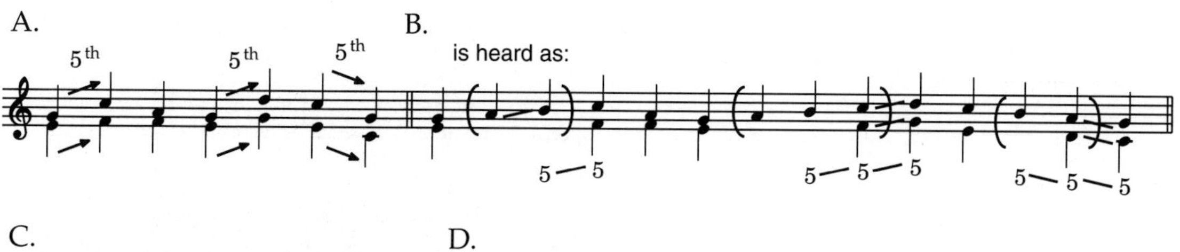

C.

5 — 8 10 — 8

D.

3 — 5 6 — 5

E1. Scarlatti, Sonata in D major, K. 96

E2. Beethoven, Piano Sonata in E♭ major, op. 81A

E3. Schumann, "Waldesgespräch," from *Liederkreis*, op. 39

E4. Paganini, Caprice for Violin, op. 1

Finally, aim for smooth lines, and avoid simultaneous leaps (fourths or larger) in both voices (Example 4.9A). When you do leap, change direction, just as you did in your melody writing (Example 4.9B).

EXAMPLE 4.9 Treatment of Leaps

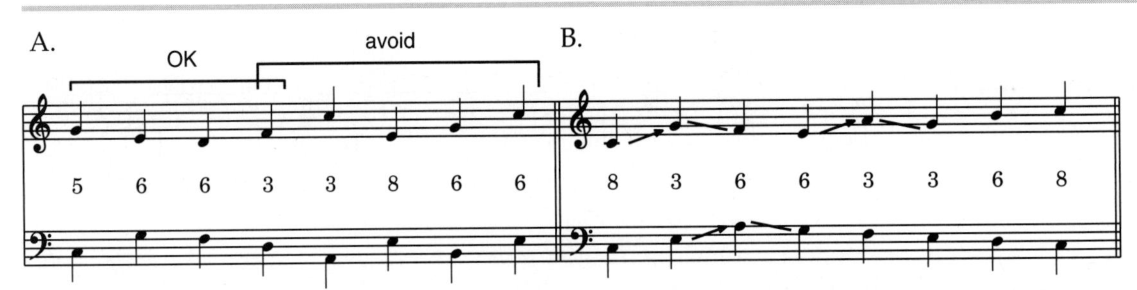

Beginning and Ending First-Species Counterpoint

We are almost ready to begin writing first-species counterpoint. But before we do, it is necessary to know how to begin and end each exercise. The contrapuntal voice must begin on $\hat{1}$. However, if the contrapuntal voice occurs above the CF, you may begin on $\hat{5}$ (see Example 4.10A). Your counterpoint must end, or **cadence**, on an octave or unison ($\hat{1}$ in both voices; see Example 4.10B). The penultimate (next-to-last) measure must contain $\hat{2}$ and $\hat{7}$, which move in contrary motion to the octave on $\hat{1}$. In minor, raise $\hat{7}$ to create a leading tone; if $\hat{6}$ precedes $\hat{7}$, raise it, too (see Example 4.10C). However, use only the lowered form of $\hat{7}$ (and $\hat{6}$) within the exercise. See Example 4.10 for examples of cadences. The CF is marked in each case.

EXAMPLE 4.10

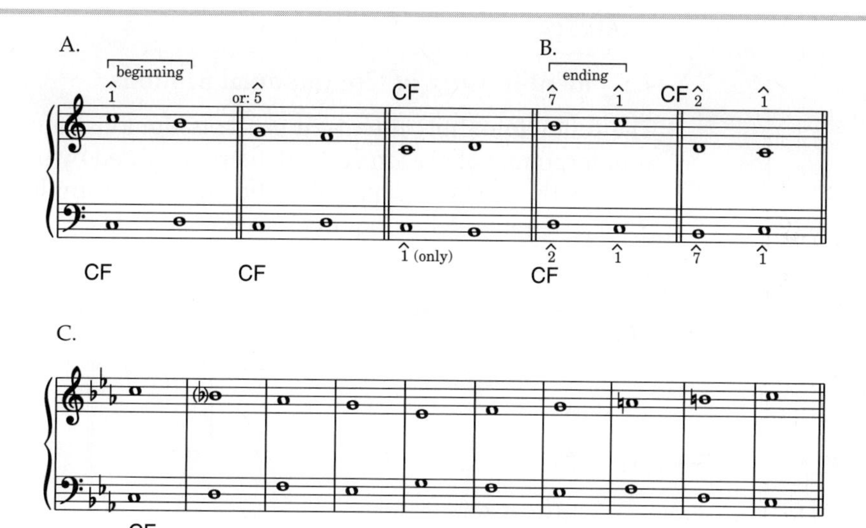

Rules and Guidelines for First-Species (1:1) Counterpoint

What follows is a summary of the rules and guidelines for first-species counterpoint. Rules are absolute and guidelines are suggestions. Rules create a structural foundation for your piece; guidelines, when followed, create a more aesthetically pleasing music surface.

Rule 1 Harmonic (vertical) intervals must be consonant (the perfect fourth is a dissonance in two-voice counterpoint).

Rule 2 Parallel perfect intervals (unisons, fifths, and octaves) are forbidden.

Rule 3 Approach perfect consonances using contrary motion; the single context in which similar motion is permitted occurs when the upper voice moves by step to the octave or fifth.

Rule 4 Begin and end your counterpoint on $\hat{1}$ (unless the counterpoint appears above the CF, when it may begin on $\hat{5}$).

Rule 5 In minor, use the lowered form of $\hat{6}$ and $\hat{7}$; raise $\hat{7}$ to create a leading tone only in the penultimate measure, and raise $\hat{6}$ when it precedes the leading tone.

Guideline 1 Use step motion as much as possible in the contrapuntal voice, with occasional skips (jumps of a third) or leaps (jumps of a fourth or more) to add interest. Change direction and move by step after a leap.

Guideline 2 Since the goal of counterpoint is voice independence, use contrary motion as much as possible. Parallel motion is restricted to imperfect consonances; limit to three consecutive uses.

Guideline 3 Use imperfect consonances as verticalities when possible. Restrict the use of octaves and fifths to only one or two within the exercise.

Guideline 4 Avoid two perfect consonances in a row since they create a hollow sound (e.g., a fifth to an octave, or vice versa).

EXERCISE INTERLUDE

ANALYSIS

DVD 2
CH 4
TRACK 1

4.1 Identification of Contrapuntal Motions

The following short literature excerpts demonstrate primarily first-species counterpoint. Label each vertical interval created by the outer voices, and then identify the prevailing type of motion in each example as contrary, parallel, or similar. Ignore pitches in parentheses.

A. Victoria, Kyrie, 1592

B. Quantz, Duet no. 4, from *Six Duets for Two Flutes*

C. Schumann, "Wichtige Begebenheit," from *Kinderscenen*, op. 15

D. Beethoven, Violin Sonata in G major, op. 96, *Scherzo*. Consider the lowest voice of the accompaniment and the violin part (i.e., ignore the right hand of the piano).

4.2 Error Detection

The given first-species counterpoint contains three types of errors:

1. Melodic (e.g., dissonant or multiple leaps)
2. Vertical intervals (e.g., dissonant intervals)
3. Motion from one interval to another (e.g., parallel perfect intervals or direct intervals)

WORKBOOK
4.1–4.2

First, label each vertical interval. Then mark each error using the following method: *D* for dissonant vertical interval and *P8* and *P5* for parallel perfect octave and fifth, respectively. Use *Dir* for direct intervals. For melodic errors in the counterpoint voice, use your own system, such as "too many leaps," "too big a leap," or "must change direction after leap."

counterpoint

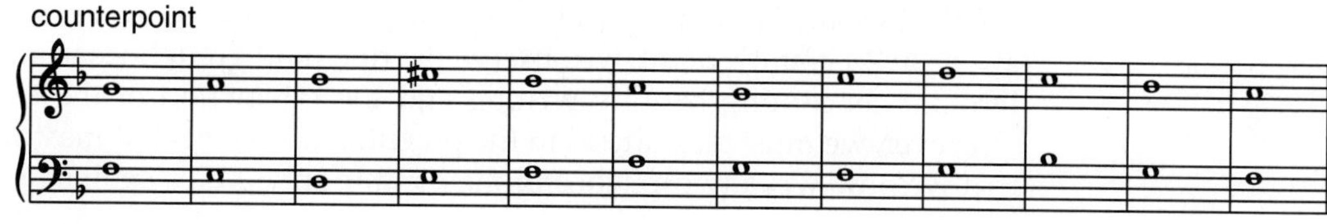

cantus

Key:

WRITING

4.3 Adding a Counterpoint to CF Fragments

Four three-note cantus firmus fragments are given. They are not taken from the beginning or the end of a longer CF but, rather, from the middle. Write four (4) different first-species solutions above and below each of the given CFs. Label each interval. A sample solution is given.

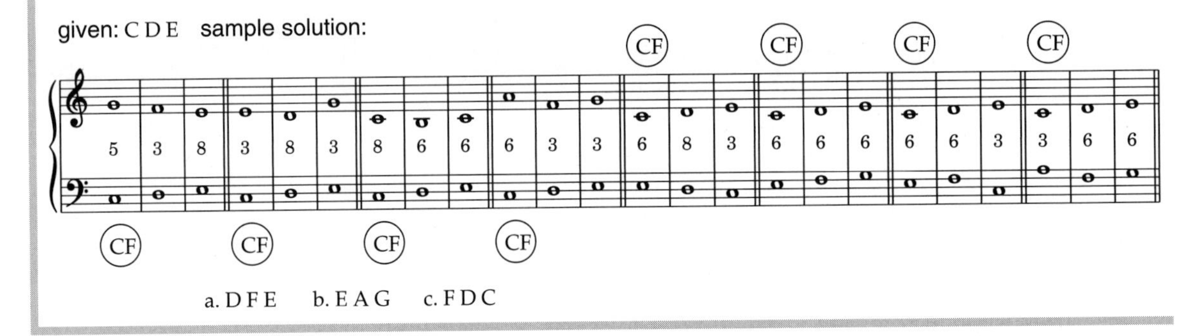

Second-Species Counterpoint

In second-species counterpoint, the contrapuntal voice uses rhythmic values that are twice as fast as those of the CF, so for every note of the CF, there are two in the contrapuntal voice. The contrapuntal motion of one voice moving while the other voice remains stationary is called **oblique motion**. See Example 4.11, which, in addition to similar and contrary motion, contains oblique motion. Oblique motion, along with parallel, similar, and contrary motion, completes the list of ways that voices may move against one another.

EXAMPLE 4.11 Oblique Motion

Given that there are now strong beats (where both the CF and the added counterpoint move to new pitches) and weak beats (where only the counterpoint moves to a new pitch against the sustained CF), a metric hierarchy arises. In 2:1 counterpoint, we observe the rules and guidelines from 1:1 counterpoint concerning melody writing and the interaction of the two voices. However, we must also attend to the potential problems that may arise given that we now write two pitches in the contrapuntal voice against a single CF pitch.

As with first-species counterpoint, the downbeat must be consonant, and successive downbeats must not contain parallel fifths or octaves. The weak beat, however, may be consonant *or* dissonant.

Weak-Beat Consonance

You may move to a weak-beat consonance by step or by skip. There is only one way to create a consonant step motion: by moving from a fifth to a sixth or a sixth to a fifth, since only this intervallic combination contains two adjacent consonances. The generic term for such step motion is **5–6 technique** (see Example 4.12, mm. 1–2 and m. 5). The consonant second pitch may continue its motion in the same direction, in which case we call it a **consonant passing tone**, or it may return to the pitch heard on the downbeat, in which case we call it a **consonant neighbor tone**. Example 4.12 presents examples of each.

Consonant skips are motions by a third. **Consonant leaps** are motions by intervals larger than a third. To skip or leap, the weak-beat note must be consonant with both the preceding melody note and the CF. Examples of consonant skips and leaps are found in mm. 3–4 and 6–9. Consonant skips and leaps are also possible from the weak beat to the strong beat, but, again, they must be consonant with the preceding melody note and the CF; see Example 4.12, from mm. 1–2 and mm. 4–5. Notice that the majority of leaps take place *within*, rather than *between*, measures. This is because leaps draw attention to themselves; when they occur on an accented beat, they are particularly noticeable, thus detracting from the flow of the line.

EXAMPLE 4.12 Second-Species Counterpoint Using Intervallic Consonance on All Strong and Weak Beats

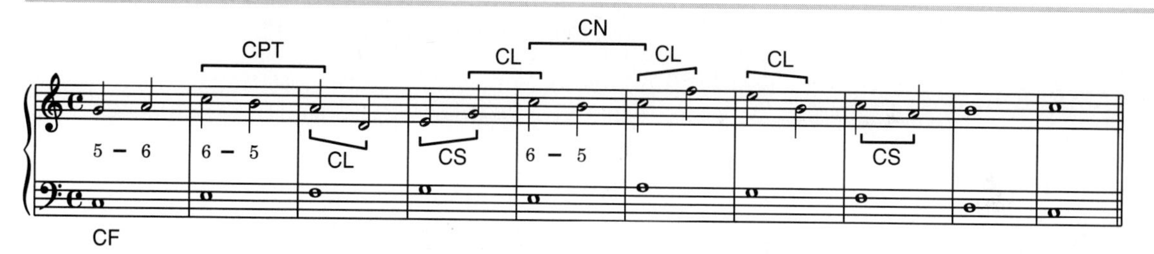

Weak-Beat Dissonance

Dissonance is the most important new feature of second-species counterpoint. Indeed, dissonance is the source of much expression in tonal music and a powerful way to create a dynamic flow. But dissonance, like any great force, must be carefully controlled.

Second-species counterpoint uses a single type of dissonance: the **unaccented passing tone.** Passing tones (PTs) occur on a weak beat in 2:1 counterpoint, and they fill the space within the interval of a third, creating a smooth, stepwise motion. (We saw an example of the consonant passing tone using the 5–6 technique in Example 4.12.) The motion into and out of the dissonant passing tone must occur in a single direction, either ascending or descending. Since the PT may only occur on the weak beat, it will lie between two strong-beat consonances that are a third apart. Note in Example 4.13 that there are also consonant passing tones.

EXAMPLE 4.13 Consonant and Dissonant Passing Tones

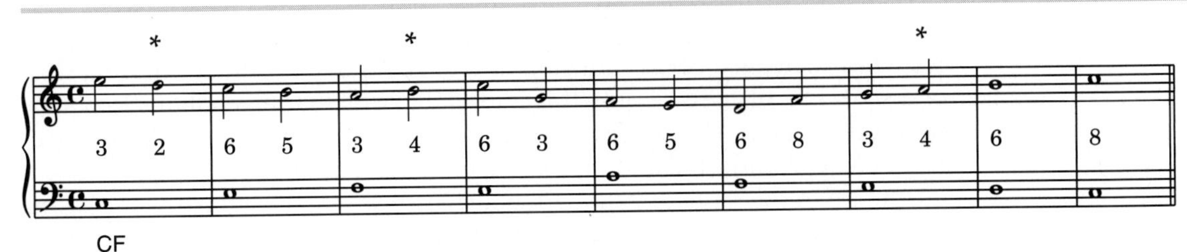

The 2:1 counterpoint in Example 4.13 contains both dissonant and consonant passing tones. Dissonant passing tones are marked with asterisks. Consonant passing tones are not marked, but you can spot them by their telltale intervallic labels "6 5" or "5 6." The first dissonant PT occurs in m. 1. The pitch D fills the third between E and C and creates a strong major-second dissonance that is discharged by the following sixth (m. 2). The next measure contains a consonant passing tone; B fills the third between C and A. Study the rest of the example, noting how both consonant and dissonant passing tones are used. The goal in second-species counterpoint is to include as many passing tones as possible.

More on Perfect Consonances

In second-species counterpoint, you must be especially vigilant to avoid writing parallel and direct perfect consonances. For example, you might be tempted to think that the intervening weak-beat interval reduces the effects of the strong-beat parallels, but this is not the case, as demonstrated in Example 4.14.

EXAMPLE 4.14

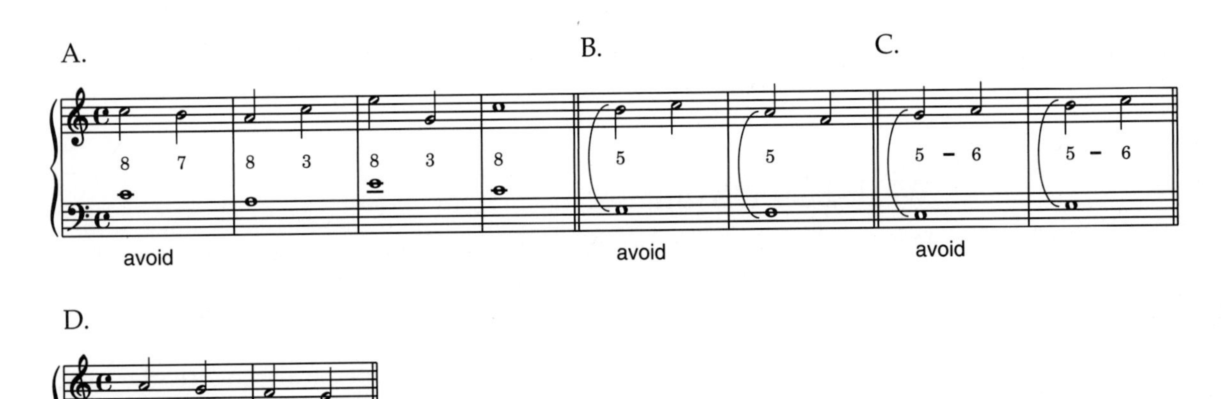

Example 4.14A contains four strong-beat octaves, none of which is obscured by the weak-beat pitch. In the first measure, the dissonant PT B is unable to conceal the octave motion between C and A on the downbeats of mm. 1 and 2. Note that a dissonance can never mediate poor voice leading. Nor is the consonant skip in m. 2 able to obviate the octaves A to E between mm. 2

and 3. Even the dramatic chordal leap of a falling sixth from E to G and change of direction cannot diminish the audible octaves on the downbeats; the metric accent from one measure to the next is simply too strong to hide the perfect intervals. Example 4.14B shows a similar situation with the perfect fifth. Example 4.14C illustrates that the important 5–6 technique is not powerful enough to hide downbeat fifths. However, a 6–5 motion is permissible, since the ear hears parallel sixths on the downbeats rather than fifths (see Example 4.14D).

Finally, be aware of creating parallel perfect and direct intervals when adding a weak-beat note. In Example 4.15A, parallel fifths and octaves arise because of the added weak-beat note. Similarly, in mm. 2–3 of Example 4.15B, what was a successful strong-beat counterpoint (a third moving to a perfect fifth in contrary motion) is now flawed by the addition of the weak-beat G, which creates a direct fifth with the following downbeat.

EXAMPLE 4.15 Avoid Parallel and Direct Intervals on Weak Beats

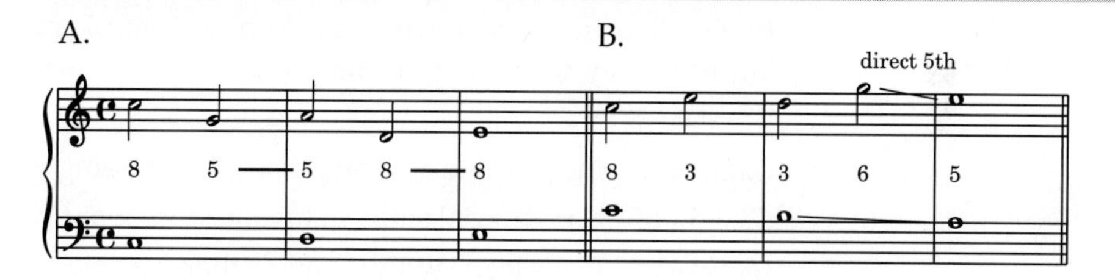

Beginning and Ending Second-Species Counterpoint

Like first species, you must begin on $\hat{1}$ if the contrapuntal voice is below the CF. When the contrapuntal voice is above the CF, you may begin on $\hat{1}$, $\hat{3}$, or $\hat{5}$. In addition, you may begin with either a half note or a half rest. The half rest is particularly effective since it immediately highlights the independence of voices and it creates a strong sense of forward motion. See Example 4.16A. The last measure must be a whole note on $\hat{1}$. However, the penultimate measure may be two half notes or a whole note. As with first-species counterpoint, the move to the final octave must be stepwise and in contrary motion. In the minor mode, use the lowered form of $\hat{7}$ within the exercise, reserving the leading tone for the penultimate measure. See Example 4.16C.

EXAMPLE 4.16

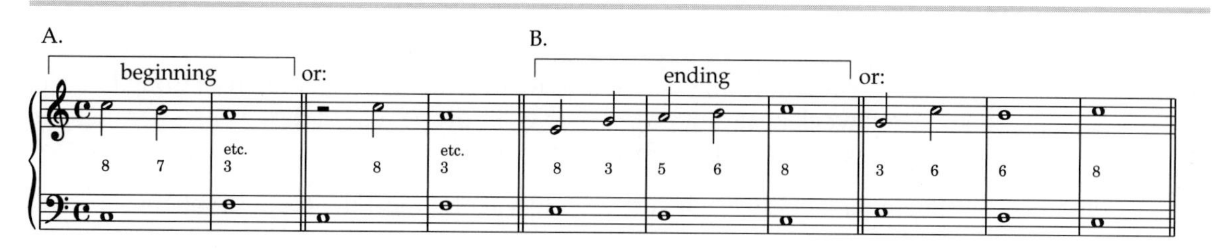

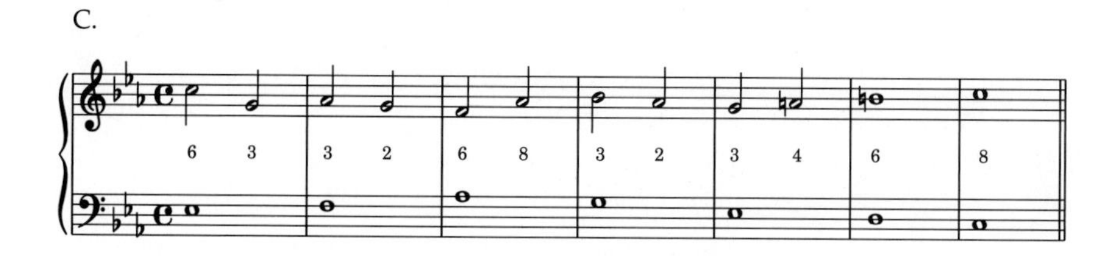

Rules and Guidelines for Second-Species Counterpoint

Rule 1 Strong beats must be consonant.

Rule 2 Avoid parallel perfect intervals between:

a. successive strong beats (downbeats).
b. weak beat and strong beat (upbeat and downbeat).

Rule 3 Avoid direct motion to perfect intervals from weak to strong beats.

Rule 4 The only permitted dissonance is the weak-beat passing tone (i.e., the dissonance must fill the space of a melodic third by step between two downbeats).

Rule 5 The added voice must begin on $\hat{1}$ when it appears below the CF, but it may begin on $\hat{1}$, $\hat{3}$, or $\hat{5}$ when it appears above the CF. You may begin with a half rest, and the penultimate measure may contain either one or two pitches. The final measure must contain a whole note.

Rule 6 In minor, use the lowered form of $\hat{6}$ and $\hat{7}$; raise $\hat{7}$ to create a leading tone only in the penultimate measure, and raise $\hat{6}$ if it precedes the leading tone.

Guideline 1 Incorporate as many dissonant passing tones as possible.

Guideline 2 Use chordal skips to balance dissonant passing tones.

Guideline 3 Place leaps within, rather than between, measures.

Guideline 4 Label every interval, and mark each dissonant passing tone with an asterisk.

EXERCISE INTERLUDE

ANALYSIS

4.4 Analysis of Second-Species Counterpoint

Based on the model analyses of A 1 and A2, you can see that the first example is error free, while the second is error ridden. Study these two models carefully; then analyze the following example using the labeling system shown in the models. Make sure you label all musical events, correct or incorrect. You will encounter three basic types of errors:

1. Melodic (e.g., dissonant or multiple leaps).
2. Vertical (e.g., improper use of dissonance).
3. Motion from one interval to another, either successive strong beats or weak beat to strong beat (e.g., improper use of dissonance, parallel perfect intervals, or direct intervals).

Begin by labeling each vertical interval and marking each dissonance.

A. Model Analysis

1.

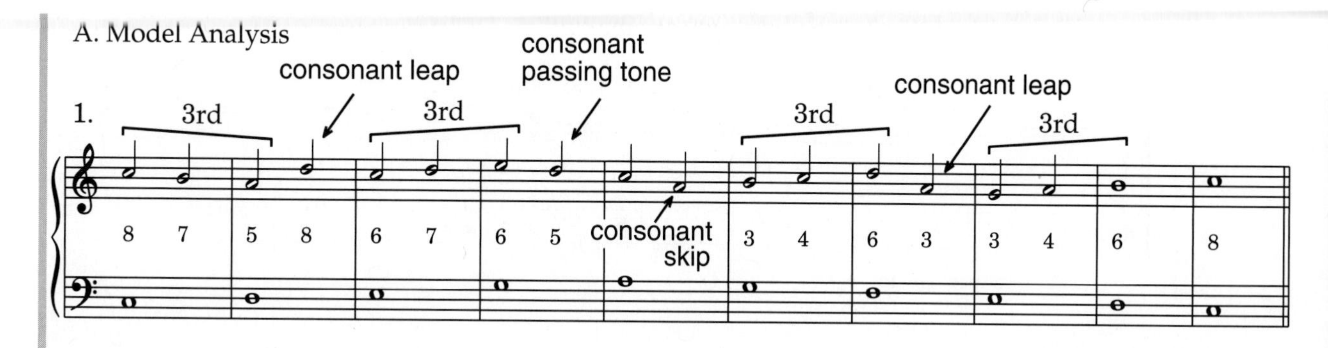

2.

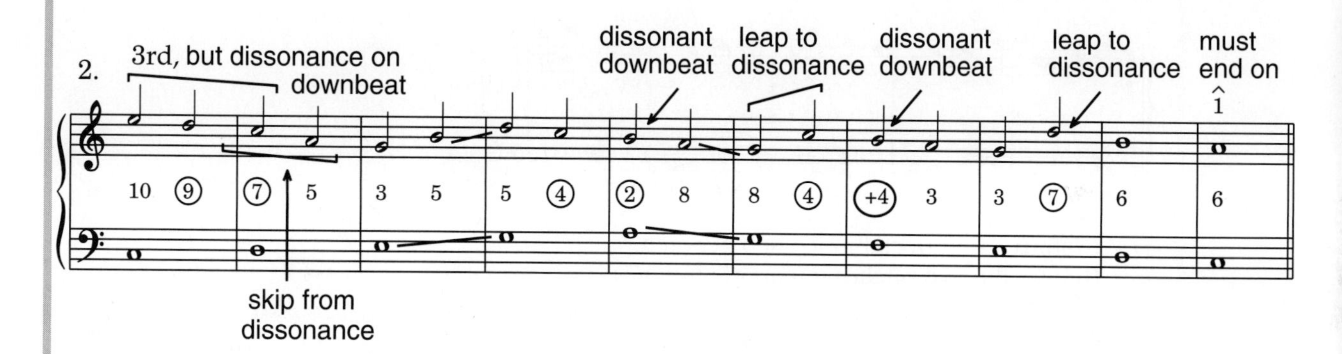

B.

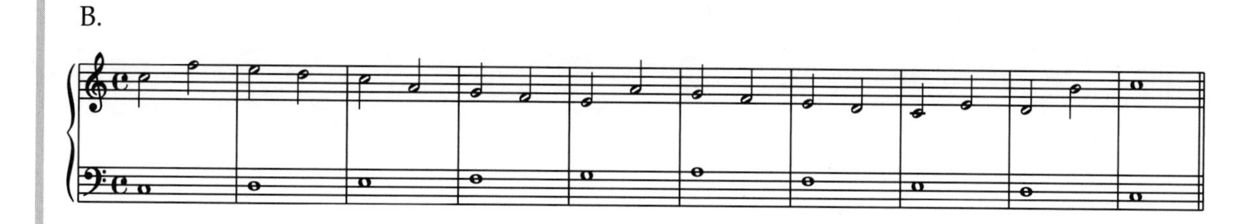

4.5 Analysis of Outer-Voice Counterpoint

Determine whether the given examples demonstrate primarily first- or second-species counterpoint. Then label each interval. Some examples involve two voices, others three to four voices; examine only the outer voices of examples with three or more voices. Finally, some examples shift the 2:1 relationship between voices.

A. Handel, *Water Music*, Minuet

B. Willaert, "And if out of jealousy you are making me such company"

C. Mozart, Minuet in D major, K. 94

D. Brahms, "und doch bin ich neu geboren."
(Ignore the two pitches in parentheses.)

WRITING

4.6 Adding a Counterpoint to CF Fragments

Given are four three-note cantus firmus fragments. They are not taken from the beginning or the end of a longer CF but, rather, from the middle. Write four (4) different second-species solutions above and two (2) below each of the given CFs. Label each interval, and mark passing dissonance with an asterisk. Use a whole note in the final measure of each pattern. A sample solution is given.

sample solution: F D E

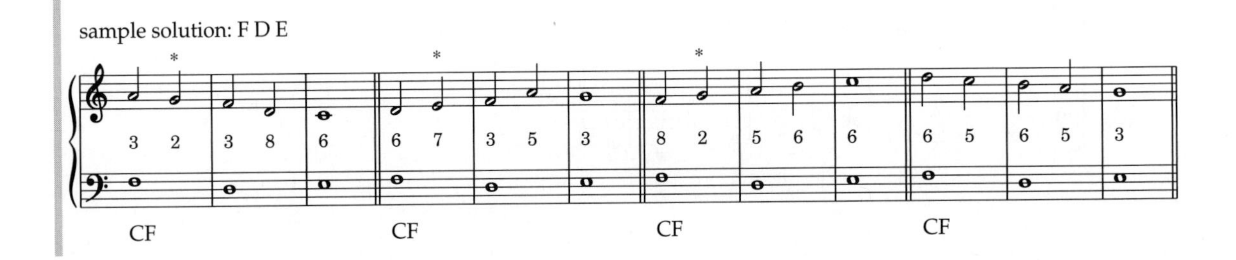

Continued

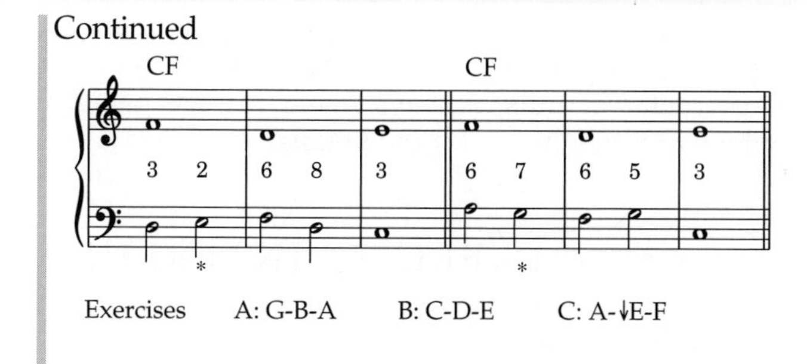

Hearing Two-Voice Counterpoint

You are now ready to listen to and notate two-voice counterpoint examples. As you learned when taking single-line dictation, it is important to postpone writing any pitches until you understand the musical context in which they occur. For example, if you listen to an eight-measure melody that you feel divides into two units, and you have memorized the first unit (by being able to sing it), then you are ready to write it down. Thus, always begin your listening with more general and global considerations, leaving the details until later hearings.

As always, begin by quietly singing $\hat{1}$, followed by the remaining scale members to situate yourself in the key; then listen to the first playing of the example. When listening to examples with multiple voices, focus on the following elements:

1. The opening and closing scale degrees in each of the two lines.
2. The motion of the individual lines and whether they are predominately by step or by leap.
3. The harmonic intervals formed by the two parts. Listen for consonance and dissonance and how dissonance is approached and left.

Another strategy you might wish to use (at least in the initial stages of notating two-voice counterpoint) is to concentrate on individual lines. Of course, this method somewhat defeats the goal of hearing multiple voices simultaneously. However, if you can sing an entire line and notate it and then turn to hearing how lines combine (begin with short units of one or two measures), you will soon be able to hear these two voices simultaneously.

Before you listen to two-voice lines, keep in mind the following tips and remember that notation is the last step, not the first.

1. *Be prepared.* Make sure you understand and anticipate clues, such as the key, the mode, and the number of measures in the example.
2. *Trust yourself.* It is a common mistake to write down an answer and then to assume it is wrong. More often than not, your initial impressions are correct.
3. *Play the odds.* A great deal of successful hearing is accomplished by means of informed guessing. For example, if you are trying to determine the final pitch of a melody but you know only that "it sounded convincing," you can rely on the odds that it is probably $\hat{1}$, since passages close there more often than on any other scale degree.
4. *Listen actively and with a goal.* Many times you might want music's dramatic power and beauty simply to wash over you. But taking dictation requires thoughtful, concentrated listening and parsing of the music

into intelligible units. Tonal music is built on a specific grammar and syntax that create powerful aural expectations. Thus, it moves forward in goal-oriented, predictable units. Always listen for the general, larger musical context, and then listen for the details.

EXERCISE INTERLUDE

LISTENING

4.7 Dictation of 1:1 Counterpoint Fragments

Notate the 1:1 counterpoint voice against the given cantus. Exercises A–E are in G major (the CF is in the bass). Exercises F–J are in E minor (the CF is in the treble). Use both your ear as well as your knowledge of permissible intervals.

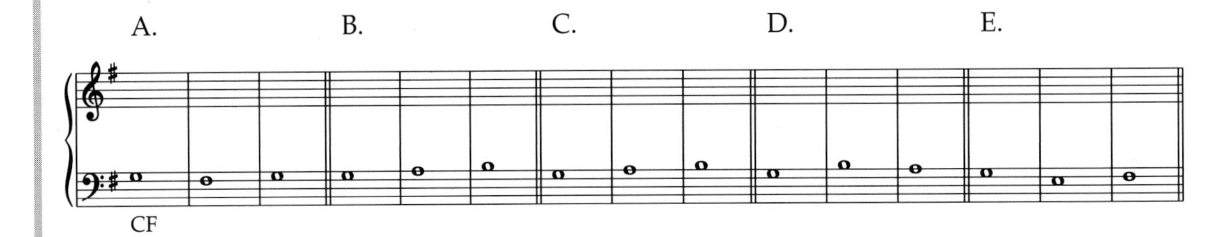

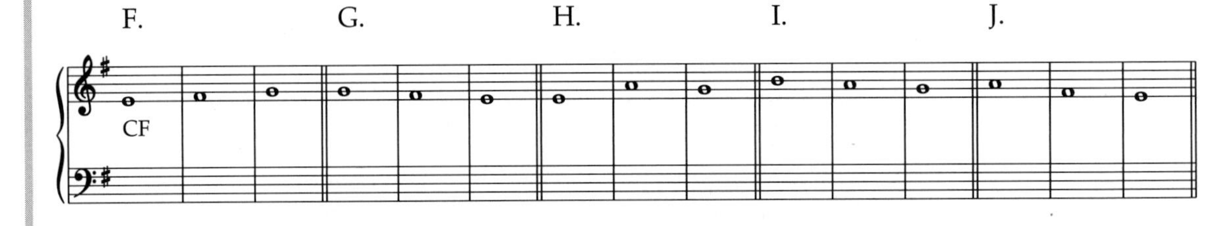

DVD 2
CH 4
TRACK 4

4.8 Dictation of 2:1 Counterpoint Fragments

Notate the 2:1 counterpoint voice against the given cantus. Exercises A–E, in F major, place the CF in the bass, and Exercises F–J, in D minor, place it above.

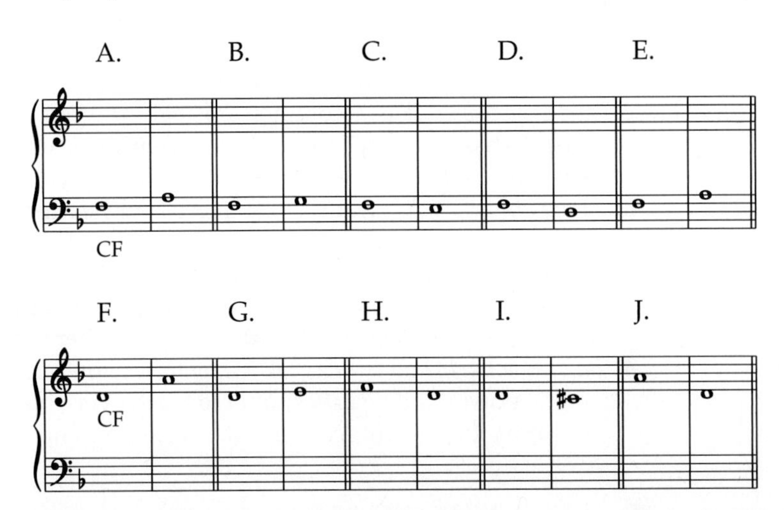

Review and Synthesis of Terms and Concepts

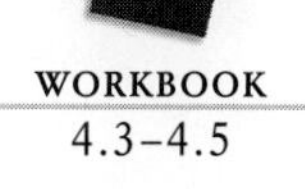

WORKBOOK
4.3–4.5

1. Compare and contrast the following pairs of terms:
   a. direct interval and parallel perfect interval
   b. cantus firmus and contrapuntal voice
   c. first-species and second-species counterpoint
   d. consonant passing tone and dissonant passing tone
   e. part and polyphony
   f. species and contour
2. Arrange the following list of contrapuntal motions in order of independence, from most independent to least: oblique motion, contrary motion, parallel motion, similar motion.
3. Find an example of each of the following procedures in the example given (there may be more than one correct answer).

summary/synthesis

a. cadence
b. consonant skip
c. direct/hidden interval
d. dissonant leap
e. dissonant (forbidden) neighbor
f. first species, second species
g. forbidden harmonic interval
h. forbidden melodic interval
i forbidden parallel intervals
j. neighbor tone
k. passing dissonance
l. 5–6 technique

CHAPTER 5

Triads, Inversions, Figured Bass, and Harmonic Analysis

So far our studies have led us through melody and counterpoint. We now move into the third and final building block of tonal music: harmony.

Triads

The combination of three or more different pitches creates a **chord**, the basic unit of harmonic organization in music. Although the combination of any three different pitches can create a chord, certain combinations—specifically those based on the interval of a third—are of special importance in tonal music. Chords that comprise three distinct pitches stacked in thirds are called **triads**, while chords that have four distinct pitches stacked in thirds are called **seventh chords**. We discuss triads in this chapter, seventh chords in Chapter 6.

Triads are identified by the lowest pitch name in a stack (see Example 5.1). When a triad is stacked in thirds as in Example 5.1, we say that the chord is in **root position**, and the lowest pitch is called the **root** of the chord. The note a third above the root is called the **third**; the note a fifth above the root is called the **fifth**.

EXAMPLE 5.1 A Triad on C

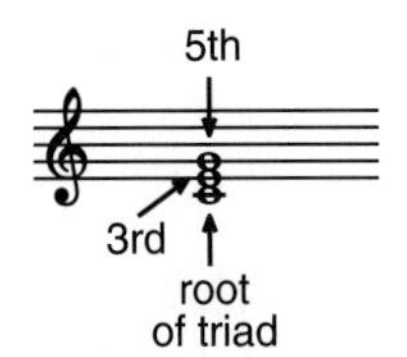

Using the diatonic thirds—major and minor—we can build four types (or **qualities**) of triads above a given root (see Example 5.2A). **Major (M)** and **minor (m)** triads are so called because of the quality of the interval between the root and third. Both major and minor triads are **consonant triads**, because they span a consonant interval: a perfect fifth. By contrast, augmented and diminished triads are **dissonant triads**, because of their dissonant fifth: an **augmented (A)** triad spans an augmented fifth; a **diminished (d)** triad spans a diminished fifth (see Example 5.2A). Example 5.2B orders the four triad types from smallest intervals spanned (diminished) to largest (augmented).

EXAMPLE 5.2 Four Types of Triad

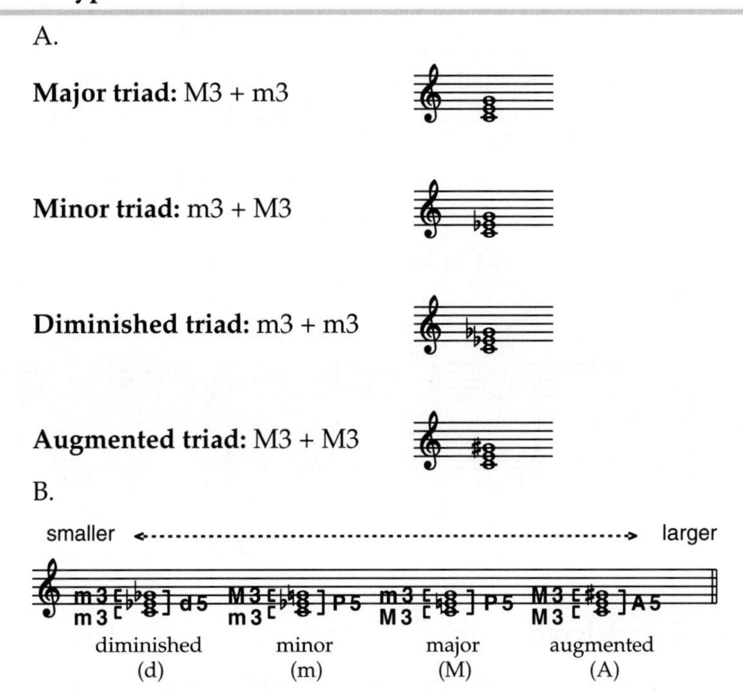

Only major, minor, and diminished triads are used as units of harmony in common-practice music. The augmented triad is not an independent sonority, but one that results from the convergence of contrapuntal lines; we explore this triad more fully in Chapter 35.

Voicing Triads: Spacing and Doubling

In Example 5.2 the third and the fifth of each triad are arranged directly above the root. This tight **spacing** (or *voicing*) of chordal members is called **close position**. However, the pitches of a triad do not always appear in close position. Instead, they might be variously distributed in register in order to create a different effect. When this occurs, the triad is in **open position**. Such spacing is generally wider between the lowest-sounding pitch and the pitches that appear above it because tightly spaced triads in the bass are hard to hear clearly. Listen to the sound of the root-position major, minor, and diminished triads in Example 5.3. Carefully study each example, and label each triad's members using 1, 3, or 5 for root, third, or fifth. As you will notice in Example 5.3A, by placing the third above the fifth, a new interval (a sixth) arises between the notes of the upper voices.

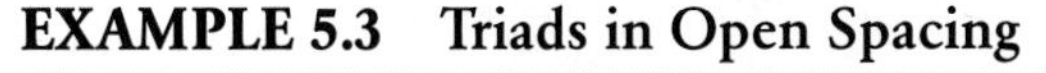

DVD 1
CH 5
TRACK 1

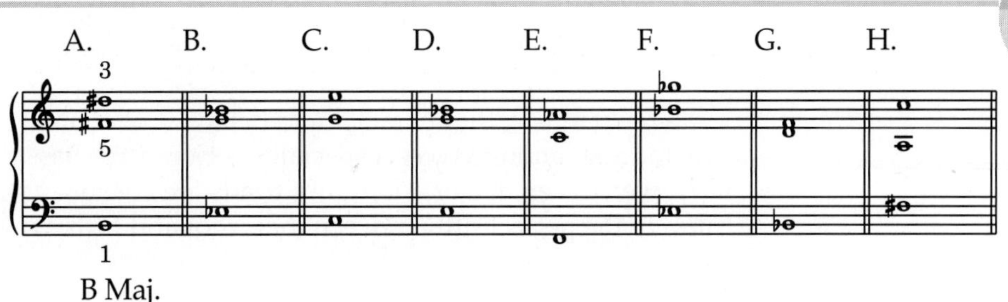

Composers can thicken the sound of triads by increasing the number of voices and **doubling** one or more members of the triad. Doubling one member increases the number of sounded notes from three to four. The most stable member of the triad, the root, is the note most often doubled, though we will often encounter doubled fifths and thirds. Example 5.4 illustrates root-position triads in a four-voice texture with one member doubled. Identify the triad type, circle doubled pitches, and label their chordal membership.

EXAMPLE 5.4 Root-Position Triads in Four-Voice Texture

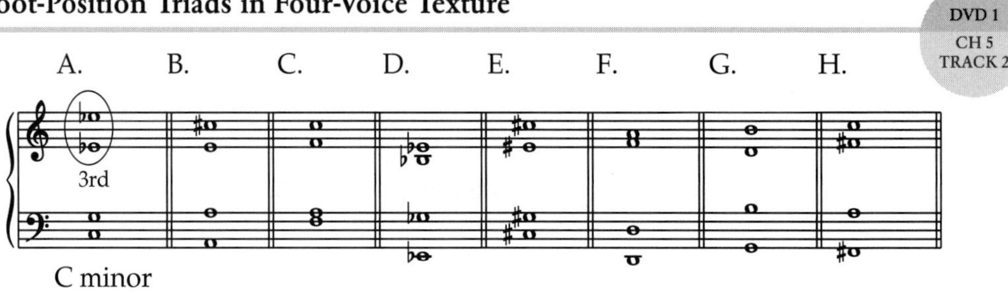

Triad Inversion

A triad is said to be **in root position** if the root is the lowest-sounding pitch, that is, if the root is in the bass. However, the root of a triad need not be the lowest-sounding note. Either the third or the fifth may instead appear in the bass. When the third or the fifth of a triad appears in the bass, the triad is said to be in **inversion**. When the third of the triad appears in the bass, the chord is in **first inversion**. When the fifth is in the bass, the triad is in **second inversion**. Thus, when triads are in first or second inversion, the root of the chord appears somewhere above the bass. Example 5.5 contains examples of major, minor, and diminished triads in root position, first inversion, and second inversion. It doesn't matter how the pitches above the bass are distributed; it is only the pitch in the bass that determines root position or inversion.

Root-position major and minor triads are stable by virtue of the perfect fifths (perfect consonances), while inverted triads are less stable because they are bound by sixths (imperfect consonances). This results in a desire to hear them move forward toward a cadence, where a root-position triad is usually found.

EXAMPLE 5.5 Triads and Their Inversions

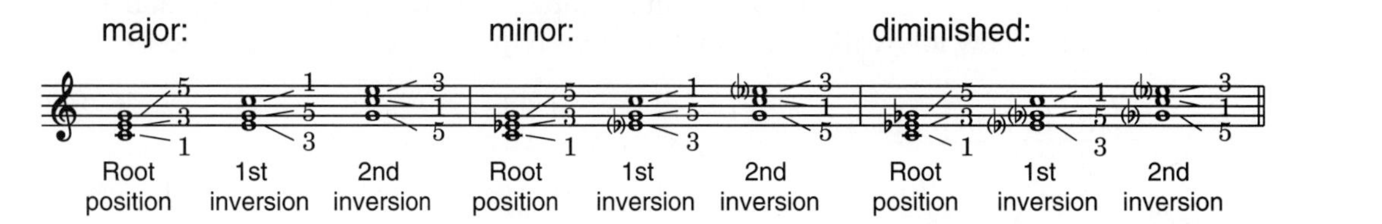

In tonal music, the character and behavior of chords depends on the intervals formed among voices, especially between the bass and the voices above it. As we've seen, major and minor triads are consonant (relatively stable) because of the perfect fifth between their root and fifth, whereas diminished triads are dissonant (relatively unstable) because of the diminished fifth between their root and fifth.

When inverted, each type of triad becomes progressively less stable. For example, in first inversion, major and minor triads are less stable than in root position because they include the intervals of a perfect fourth and a minor or major sixth. This is not true, however, for diminished triads. In root position they are highly dissonant because of the diminished fifth; but in first inversion, only consonant thirds and sixths sound above the bass (the tritone is less audible, given that it does not involve the bass). In second inversion, major and minor triads are regarded as dissonant because the perfect fourth is now formed with the bass, which drives the harmony. You may recall from the counterpoint discussion in Chapter 4 that in two voices, the perfect fourth is considered dissonant. Even in textures of three or more voices (as in the present case), when a perfect fourth is formed with the bass, we hear it as dissonant. Both root-position and first-inversion triads are common in tonal music; however, second-inversion triads, due to their greater instability, occur only in restricted contexts. As we shall see, whereas triads in root position and first inversion are more or less interchangeable, second-inversion triads are in a class of their own.

> **Note**
> The *root* is the generating pitch on which a triad is built and the *bass* is the lowest-sounding pitch in a sonority. For example, in the sonority E♭–G–C, E♭ is the bass and C is the root. In order to identify a triad, stack its members in thirds.
>
> 
>
> 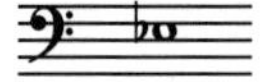

EXERCISE INTERLUDE

PERFORMING

5.1 Singing Root-Position Triads

Sing (arpeggiate on "la") root-position major, minor, and diminished triads from any pitch.

LISTENING

5.2 Identifying Chord Quality

Identify the type of root-position triad that you hear (major, minor, diminished). Sing, by arpeggiating, each triad after you have labeled it.

A. _______ B. _______ C. _______ D. _______ E. _______ F. _______

5.3 Aural Discrimination of Triad Members and Constructing Triads

Each of the given pitches is either the root, the third, or the fifth of a major, minor, or diminished triad. Listen to the pitch and then to the triad. Identify the type of triad and whether the given pitch is the triad's root, third, or fifth.

Notate the triad, labeling the type of triad and the function of the given pitch (root, third, or fifth).

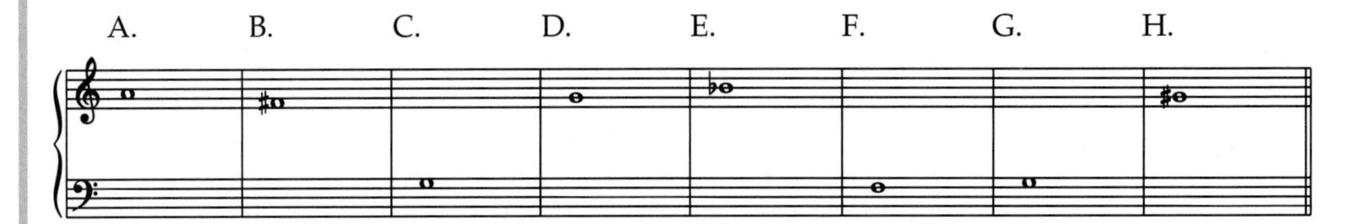

5.4 Aural and Visual Analysis of Root-Position Triads (I)

Listen to and identify each of the following close-position triads. Your choices are major (M), minor (m), diminished (d), and augmented (A). Then renotate each given triad as follows:

- Major becomes diminished, and vice versa.
- Minor becomes augmented, and vice versa.

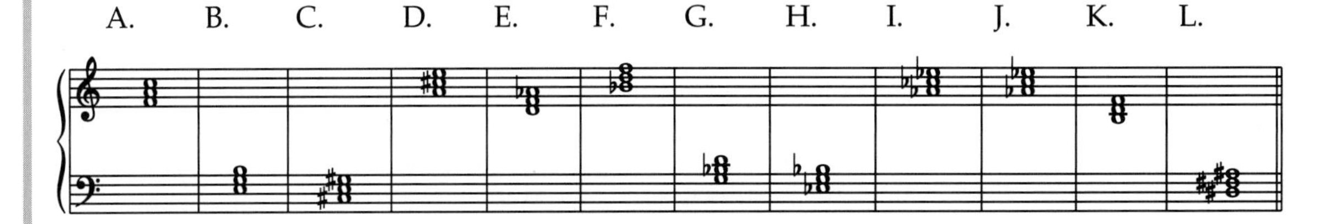

DVD 2
CH 5
TRACK 4

5.5 Aural and Visual Analysis of Root-Position Triads (II)

Listen to and identify each of the following open-position triads. Again, your choices are major (M), minor (m), diminished (d), and augmented (A). Then renotate each given triad as follows:

- Major becomes diminished, and vice versa.
- Minor becomes augmented, and vice versa.

WRITING

5.6 Writing Triads

Complete the following tasks on manuscript paper. Write odd-numbered exercises in treble clef, even-numbered exercises in bass clef.

A. Notate root-position major triads based on the following pitches:
   1. A
   2. B
   3. D

4. F
5. B♭
6. F♯

B. Notate root-position minor triads based on the following pitches:
1. C
2. B
3. G
4. E♭
5. B♭

C. Notate root-position diminished triads based on the following pitches:
1. D
2. E
3. B♭
4. F♯
5. B

D. Given the triad quality of one member of the triad (root, third, or fifth), notate the complete triad in root position.
1. C is the third of what major triad? the fifth of what minor triad?
2. A♭ is the third of what major triad? the fifth of what diminished triad?
3. E is the third of what minor triad? the fifth of what major triad?
4. G is the third of what diminished triad? the fifth of what diminished triad?
5. F♯ is the third of what minor triad? the fifth of what minor triad?

ANALYSIS

5.7

Each of the following triads is in root position or is an inversion. Identify the root of the chord quality (major, minor, or diminished) and the member of the chord that appears as the lowest and the highest pitch (root [1], third [3], or fifth [5]).

	A.	B.	C.	D.	E.	F.	G.	H.	I.	J.	K.	L.
root:	D^3											
quality:	m											
highest:	5											
lowest:	1											

ANALYSIS AND LISTENING

5.8 Error Detection and Notation

The labels that appear beneath the following root-position and inverted triads do not agree with the pitches above each label. On a separate sheet of manuscript paper, renotate the pitches in order to agree with each label.

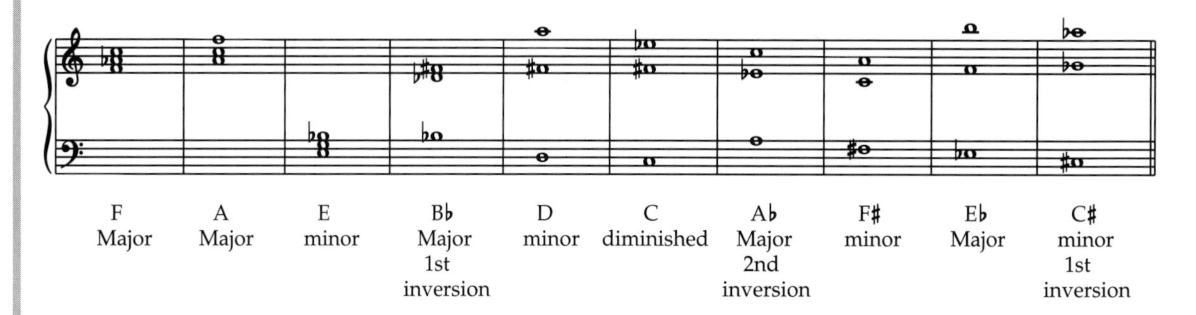

PERFORMING

5.9 Arpeggiation of Inverted Triads

Given any pitch, sing or play root-position major, minor, or diminished triads. Next, arpeggiating from the root-position triad, sing or play first-inversion then second-inversion triads, ending with root position. For example, to arpeggiate a minor triad from the pitch D, you would sing or play **D**–F–A, **F**–A–D, **A**–D–F, and end by ascending to root position (**D**–F–A).

5.10 Reinterpreting Pitches to Create Triads

WORKBOOK 5.1–5.3

Given a pitch, treat it as the root, the third, or the fifth of a major, minor, or diminished triad. For example, given the pitch G, consider it to be the root of major, minor, and diminished triads. Then treat it as the third of an E♭-major triad and the third of E-minor and E diminished triads. Finally, treat G as the fifth of C-major and C-minor triads and as the fifth of a C♯-diminished triad.

Figured Bass

Many composers who were writing between 1600 and 1800 used a shorthand notation to describe the intervals above bass notes. This type of shorthand, known as **figured bass** (or sometimes *thoroughbass*), is a handy way of understanding chordal construction as well as the melodic movement between chords. Today, the lead-sheet symbols of jazz and popular music serve a similar purpose.

Analyzing and Composing Using Figured Bass

Figured bass is predicated on the fact that the bass, the lowest-sounding voice, is harmonically the most important voice of any texture. To create a figured bass, count the generic (numerical) intervals that appear between the bass and the upper voices, from the top to the bottom, and list them from the largest to the smallest. For example, in a root-position triad, a third and a fifth sound above the bass; ordering these two intervals from the larger to the smaller gives a figured bass of $^{5}_{3}$. Chords in first inversion are labeled $^{6}_{3}$; chords in second inversion are $^{6}_{4}$.

By convention, we place the larger number above the smaller one, so the numbers do not necessarily reflect the specific placement of the notes above the bass; rather, they represent how the chord members would appear in close position. Using this system, a composer writes a bass note with figures, and the performer knows what notes are needed above the bass. The performer builds a chord with the specified intervals while always observing the prevailing key signature. For example, in the key of E major, an E in the bass with the figure $^{6}_{3}$ would tell the performer to add C♯ and G♯, since these notes appear in the key signature.

Example 5.6A shows how to analyze a given chordal structure in the key of D major using figured bass; Example 5.6B shows how to fill out, or **realize**, a given bass with figures to create a succession of four-voice chords. (Notice the greater incidence of root-position triads as compared with inverted triads.) You will learn to work in both directions, *analytically* (from full harmony to figured bass) and *compositionally* (from figured bass to full harmony).

EXAMPLE 5.6 Figured Bass: Analysis and Realization

Additional Figured Bass Conventions: Abbreviations and Chromaticism

Because root-position and first-inversion triads are so common, their figured bass notation is often assumed or abbreviated. Normally the symbol $^{5}_{3}$ is omitted entirely; thus the absence of a figure under a bass note signifies root position. Similarly, 6 by itself is often used instead of $^{6}_{3}$ for first inversion. However, second inversion is always written $^{6}_{4}$.

Figured bass also shows the melodic motion of individual voices, especially voices that move by step. For example, some of the triads that appear in Example 5.7 seem to do so through melodic motion, which is shown in the figured bass: The D-major triad that begins the excerpt moves to a G-major triad on beat 3. However, the melodic motion A–B in the soprano can be shown in the figured bass: The A (a fifth above the bass) moves to B (a sixth above the bass). The figures "5—6" capture that motion, and the dash makes this melodic motion explicit. There are two more of these 5—6 motions in the example. In fact, we can even show dissonant melodic motion in a figured bass, as illustrated by the alto's G that is sustained past the change to the D chord. The G is a dissonant fourth above the bass, so we label its melodic behavior 4—3.

EXAMPLE 5.7

If there is an accidental on a pitch above the bass, the same accidental is attached to the corresponding interval in the figured bass; if the accidental occurs on the interval "3" in the figured bass, the number 3 is omitted and only the accidental is written. These accidentals are called **chromatic alterations**. For example, a composer writing in the key of C major would indicate the E♭-major and B-major triads as shown in Example 5.8. In Example 5.8A, the "♭6" in the figured bass indicates that the E (a sixth above the bass) should have a flat; the "♭" by itself refers to the third above the bass (B, which becomes B♭). You do not have to put anything in the figure when there is an accidental in the bass (such as the D♯ in Example 5.8B); the figures apply only to the notes *above* the bass. Chromatic alterations in the figured bass are applied only to the pitches that appear directly above; that is, they do not carry through the measure, as do accidentals that appear in the score.

EXAMPLE 5.8 Chromatic Alterations

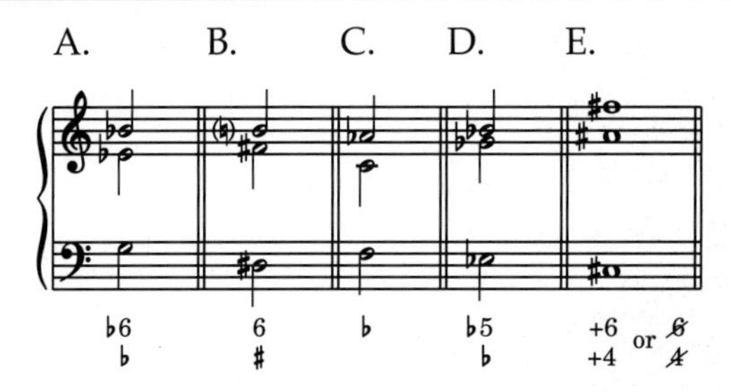

In the key of C major we would write the figured bass for a root-position F-minor triad and an E♭-minor triad as in Example 5.8 C and D. Since these are root-position triads, the figured bass $\frac{5}{3}$ normally would be assumed. However, because of the chromatically altered third, we must show the accidental in the figured bass. Since the third is one of the assumed intervals, we simply abbreviate this figure with the accidental alone (although it is not uncommon to see the redundant "♯3" or "3♯"). Additional symbols include the plus sign (+) and the slash through a number (/), which raise the pitch to which the number refers one half step (Example 5.8E).

Following is a summary of the most common figured bass symbols for triads, followed by their shorthand abbreviations. Note that there is some redundancy, given that many of these notations are alternate ways to indicate the same thing.

- Accidentals that appear next to the figure:
  - ♭ the specified pitch as a flat accidental (this can also have the generic meaning of "lower by a half step")
  - ♯ the specified pitch has a sharp accidental (this can also have the generic meaning of "raise by a half step")
  - /, + raise by a half step
  - ♮ the specified pitch has a natural sign on it
- Accidentals appearing alone refer to the third above the bass.
- Chromaticism in the bass voice cannot be shown in figured bass notation.
- The figures do not determine the placement of notes in the upper voices.
- Chromatic alterations in the figured bass apply only to the pitches that lie directly above the chromaticism—they do not carry through the measure.
- The dash (—) indicates that a single voice moves by the intervals indicated on each end of the dash.

Example 5.9 shows a sample of figured bass symbols and their realization using F^3 and E^3 in the bass, including various transformations of those bass notes.

EXAMPLE 5.9 Figured Bass

(*FB* = figured bass; *CP* = close position; *OP* = open position)

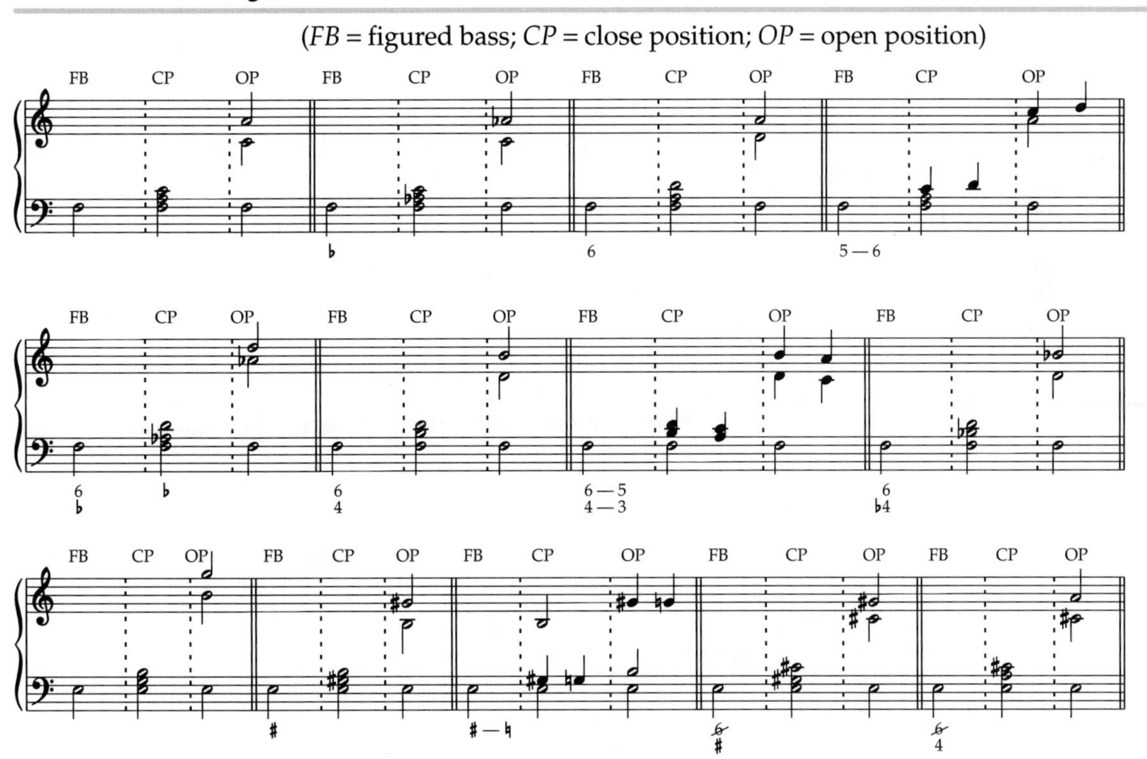

In keeping with the notion of abbreviations, compound intervals larger than a ninth are represented in figured bass notation by their smaller representative (for example, a tenth would be shown as a third). Usually it is not necessary to indicate doublings, and it is never necessary to indicate a chromatically altered octave, since it would be apparent from the given bass pitch (see Example 5.10). There are two Ds and one A written above the lowest note of the first chord (F♯), forming a sixth and a third above the bass. It is not necessary to account for the duplicate D. This is a $^6_3$ chord with D as its root. In the next chord, the lowest note (E♭) supports the intervals of a fourth, a sixth, and an octave above. Again, we ignore the octave, which duplicates the bass. It is a $^6_4$ chord with A♭ as its root.

EXAMPLE 5.10 Chromatically Altered Bass Notes

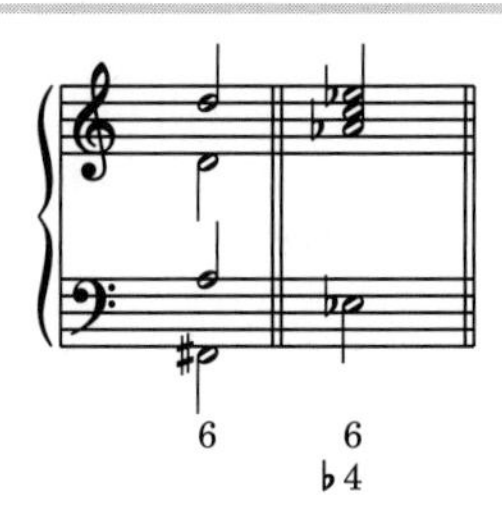

EXERCISE INTERLUDE

ANALYSIS

5.11 Figured Bass Practice

The following triads are in root position or inversion. For each one, identify the following:

- the root
- the triad quality (major, minor, or diminished)
- the member of the chord that is in the bass—root (1), third (3), or fifth (5)
- the complete figured bass symbols. Remember that the figures reflect generic sizes of intervals, not exact sizes, and that they are written with the largest interval above the bass on top and smaller intervals below.

Show chromatic alterations (consider there to be no key signature).

	A.	B.	C.	D.	E.	F.	G.	H.	I.	J.
root:	C									
quality:	M									
member of chord in bass:	3rd									
figured bass:	6 3									

5.12 Triads in Various Spacings

The three voices of the following root-position and inverted triads appear in various registers. For each one, identify:

- the root
- the quality of each
- the member of the chord that is in the bass—root (1), third (3), or fifth (5)

And provide a full figured bass analysis that shows any chromatic alterations (consider there to be no key signature).

	A.	B.	C.	D.	E.	F.	G.	H.	I.	J.	K.	L.
root:	E♭											
quality:	M											
member of chord in bass:	3rd											
figured bass:	♭6 ♭3											

5.13

In this exercise, you will provide two pieces of information:

1. a figured bass (chromaticism above the bass must be shown)
2. the root of each chord. If the chord is inverted, include the appropriate inversion. Ignore pitches in parentheses.

Sample solution:

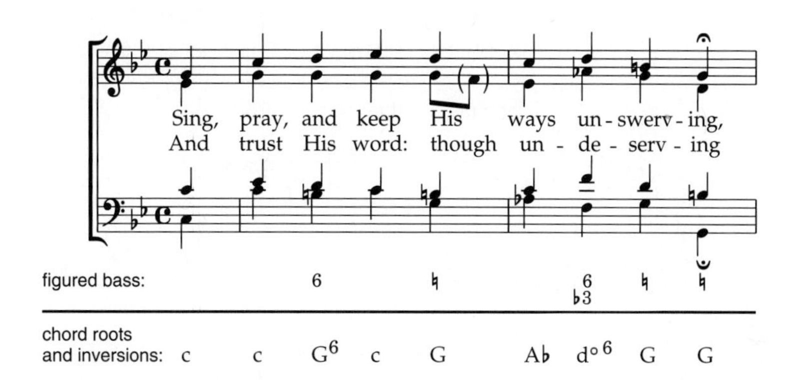

A. Bach, "Kommt her zu mir, spricht Gottes Sohn"

B. Bach, "Schwing' dich auf zu deinem Gott"

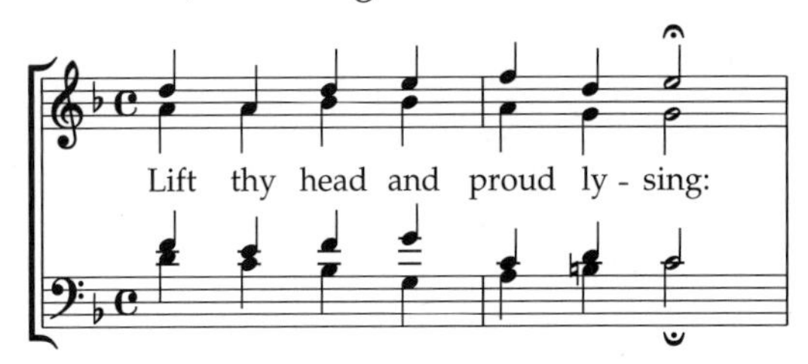

C. Bach, "Nun lasst uns Gott dem Herren"

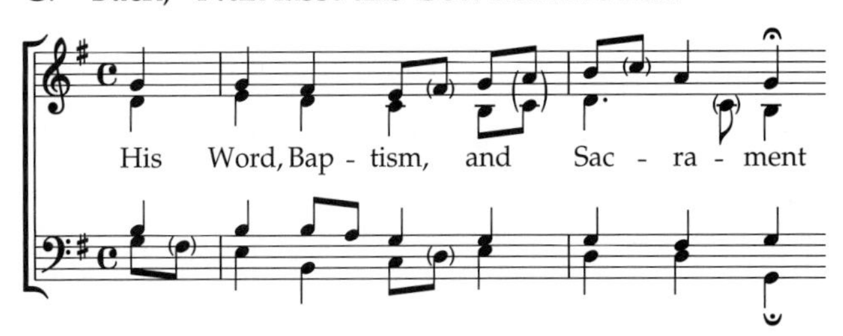

PERFORMING

5.14

On piano, play the given bass pitches with the left hand and create two-voice counterpoint by playing a note taken from the triad that is indicated by the figured bass with the right hand. Move from one upper-voice pitch to the next by the shortest possible distance; however, make sure the counterpoint is correct (e.g., avoid parallel perfect intervals). Then sing one of the voices while playing the other. Play each exercise in the parallel minor, and transpose each to one other key of your choice. Exercises A–E are entirely diatonic and permit few choices.

sample solution: A. or B.

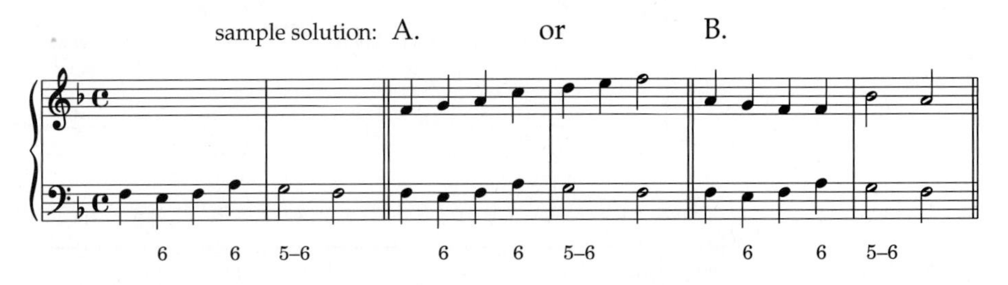

WORKBOOK 5.4

Exercises F–J contain some chromaticism and allow for more melodic choices for the upper voice.

Triads and the Scale: Harmonic Analysis

Each scale degree of a major or minor scale can support a triad constructed of pitches from that scale. In all major keys, for example, $\hat{4}$ supports a major triad and $\hat{2}$ supports a minor triad. In C, these end up being F major and D minor. In the key of A♭, they would be D♭ major and B♭ minor. Example 5.11 illustrates which type of triad—major, minor, or diminished—occurs on each scale degree in the major mode. As you learn to recognize the sound of each individual triad, it is also important that you memorize the types of triads generated from each scale degree in major and minor scales. Note that the triads built on the tonic ($\hat{1}$), the dominant ($\hat{5}$), and the subdominant ($\hat{4}$) are all major triads; the supertonic ($\hat{2}$), the mediant ($\hat{3}$), and the submediant ($\hat{6}$) triads are minor. The leading tone triad ($\hat{7}$) is the only dissonant chord; it is diminished.

EXAMPLE 5.11 Scale Degrees and Triad Types in Major

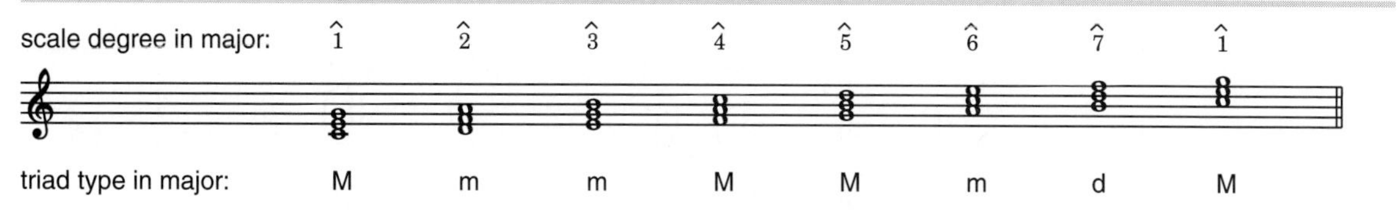

Because there are various forms of the minor scale, many more possibilities result from the raised and lowered forms of $\hat{6}$ and $\hat{7}$. Example 5.12 summarizes the most common types of triads that occur in the minor mode. The submediant, $\hat{6}$, usually occurs in its lowered form in the minor scale, thereby affecting the triads in which it is used (that is, triads built on $\hat{2}$, $\hat{4}$, and $\hat{6}$). Although triads built off of $\hat{5}$ and $\hat{7}$ are found in both their lowered and raised forms, the most common forms (V and vii°) incorporate the leading tone. In minor scales, triads built on the tonic ($\hat{1}$) and the subdominant ($\hat{4}$) are minor;

triads built on the mediant ($\hat{3}$), the dominant ($\hat{5}$), the submediant ($\hat{6}$), and, occasionally, the subtonic, or lowered form of $\hat{7}$, are major. Diminished triads result from chords built on the supertonic ($\hat{2}$) and the leading tone (raised $\hat{7}$).

EXAMPLE 5.12 Scale Degrees and Triad Types in Minor

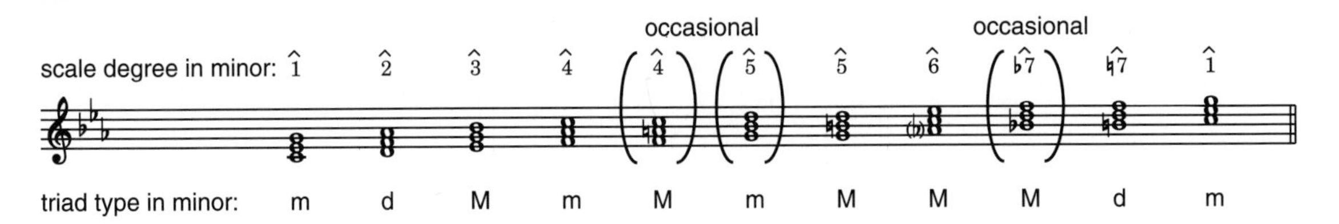

Roman Numerals

Individual pitches can be represented using scale degree numbers that identify their function within a given scale. Similarly, triads are represented by roman numerals that indicate the scale degree on which they are built. For example, a B♭ major triad in the key of F major is written as IV to show that it is built on the fourth scale degree in that key. Uppercase roman numerals are used for major triads; lowercase roman numerals are used for minor triads. Diminished triads are represented by lowercase roman numerals, with the addition of a small degree sign, "°." Example 5.13 shows the triads that occur on each scale degree for the keys of D major and D minor, with the appropriate roman numerals. Note that, given the various forms of the minor scale, it is possible to build two different triads on both $\hat{4}$ and $\hat{5}$ and two different triads (with two different roots) on $\hat{7}$.

EXAMPLE 5.13 Roman Numerals in Major and Minor

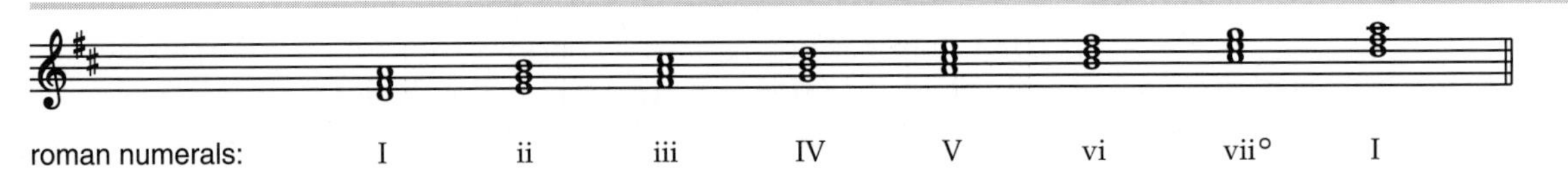

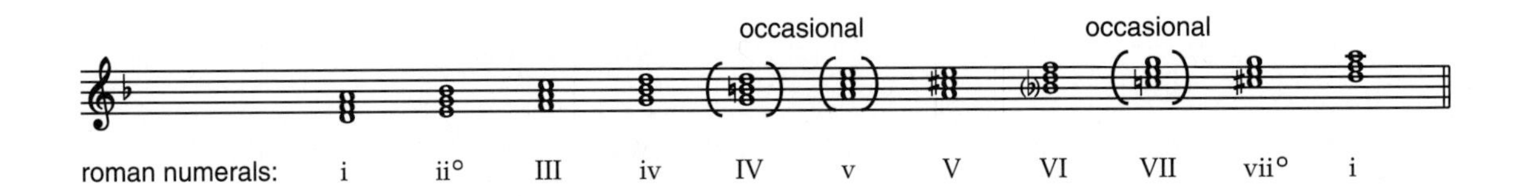

Introduction to Harmonic Analysis

A complete harmonic analysis combines roman numerals and figured bass; we use a roman numeral to identify the root (by scale degree) and quality of a chord, and we use the figure from figured bass (usually without accidentals) to identify the inversion of the chord and melodic motion (such as 5—6 or 4—3). Here is a step-by-step procedure to follow.

1. Determine the key of the exercise, because the key signature alone implies two possible keys: either the major or the relative minor. A helpful hint is provided by chromatic alterations of pitches that often indicate leading tones in minor. *Note:* Some key signatures do not agree with the key of the music.
2. Write out the letter name of the key, immediately followed by a colon, at the beginning of the exercise, under the bass staff. Use uppercase letters to represent a major key and lowercase to represent a minor key (except for C major and minor, for which you will write "C maj." and "c min."
3. Identify triad roots, and place the appropriate roman numeral under each harmony. Note that in most cases, you do not have to calculate the quality of a chord; most of the diatonic chords have one distinct quality (e. g., IV in major usually appears as a major triad; review Example 5.13). In minor keys, chords with $\hat{6}$ and $\hat{7}$ have different forms, and you will have to determine which quality of chord is being used.
4. You do not have to renotate the roman numeral if a chord is immediately repeated; you can simply draw a horizontal line that indicates the harmony is repeated.
5. If the triad is in root position, you need do nothing more. However, if the triad is inverted, supply a figured bass. Use the abbreviation "6" for the figure "$^6_3$." Example 5.14 shows sample harmonic analyses.

EXAMPLE 5.14

DVD 1
CH 5
TRACK 3

A.

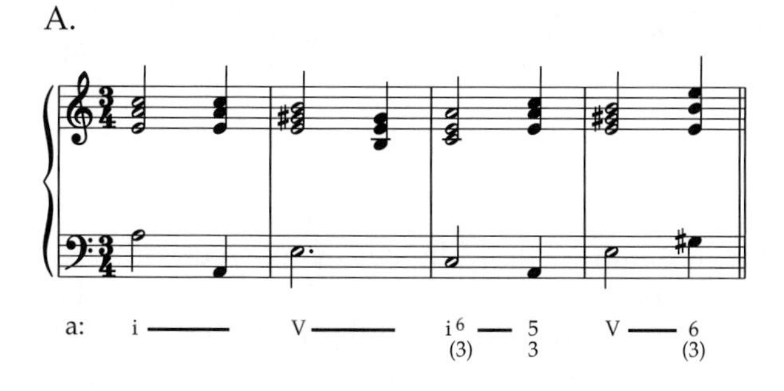

B. "Gunhilde," from Brahms, *German Folk Songs*, vol. 1

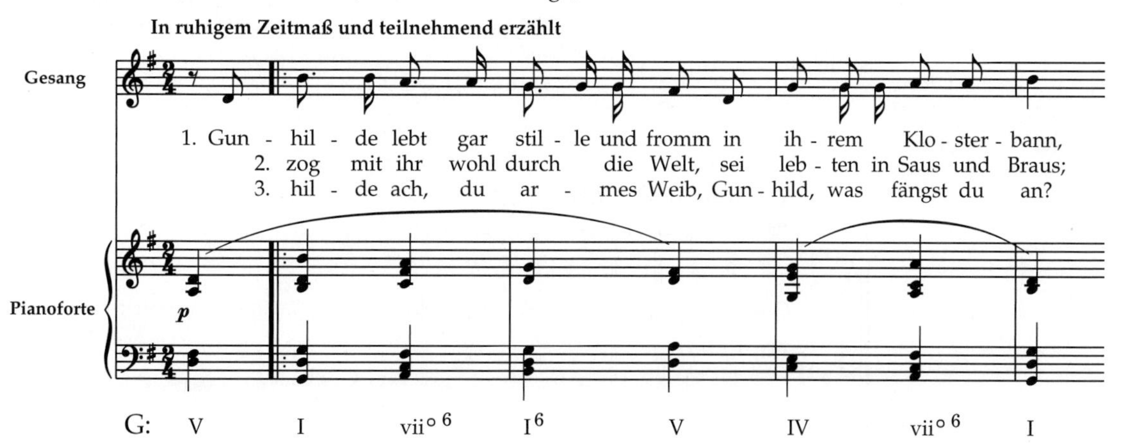

C. Brahms, "Es wohnet ein Fiedler," from *German Folk Songs*, vol. 6

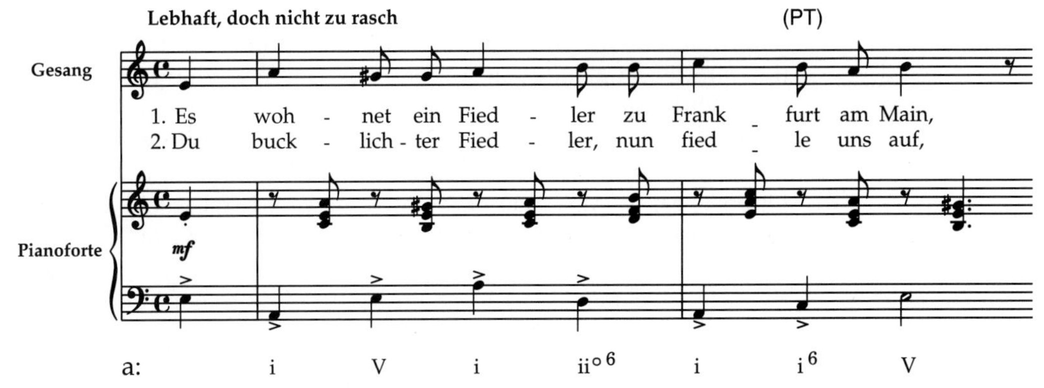

We will learn throughout this text that while roman numerals relate harmonies to a tonic (and thus can be considered a hierarchical analytical system), figured bass reveals how intervals connect one harmony to another (and is considered to be a highly context-sensitive analytical system).

Harmony and the Keyboard

We will apply each harmonic concept to both the keyboard and to your own instrument, since such work greatly helps our hearing and allows us to apply concepts in a musical medium. Adding the keyboard and your instrument completes the third side of what we can consider the learning triangle: hearing, thinking, and feeling. By activating the tactile sense a powerful synthesis of concepts will result.

Keyboard style is a four-voice texture in which three notes (voices) are played in the right hand, and within the space of one octave, and one note (voice) is played in the left hand. The notes in the right hand are labeled (from highest to lowest) soprano, alto, and tenor. The bass is played with the left hand. This helps to emphasize the outer voices, and keyboard style will be the most common hand position we will use throughout our studies. Further, on occasion you will be writing in keyboard style, although most of our writing will place the two upper voices (soprano and alto) in the treble clef and the two lower voices (tenor and bass) in the bass clef, a distribution called **chorale style**. Example 5.15 shows the harmonic progression I–V–I in both keyboard style and chorale style.

EXAMPLE 5.15

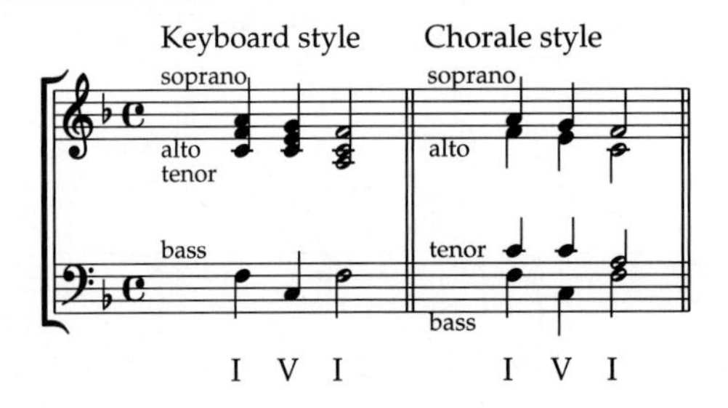

EXERCISE INTERLUDE

ANALYSIS

5.15

Analyze using roman numerals, and provide a figured bass for each boxed chord.
Mozart, from *The Magic Flute*:

A. "Drei Knäbchen"

B. "In Diesen Heiligen Hallen"

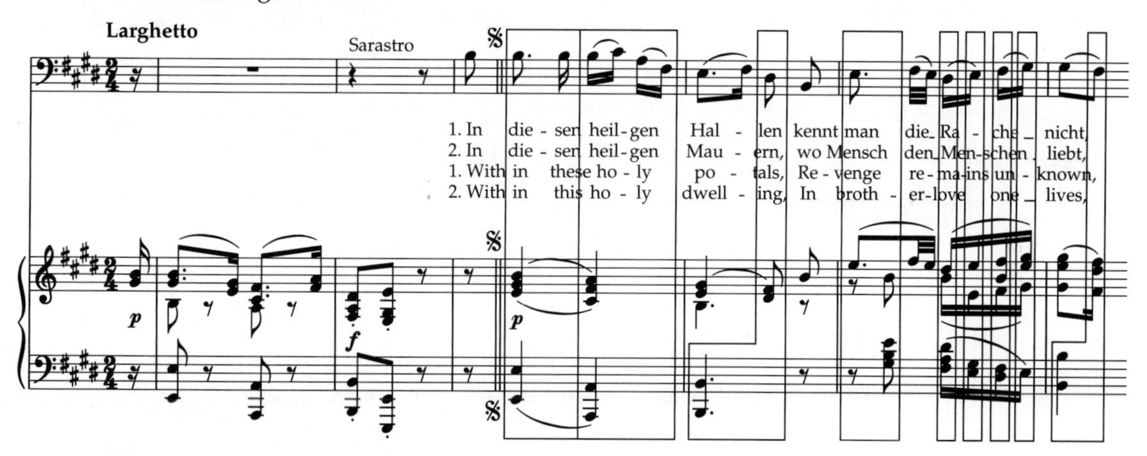

C. "Wie? Wie? Wie?"

Continued

D. Mozart, String Quartet in B♭ major, K. 458, *Allegro vivace assai*

PERFORMING

5.16 Singing Triads from Given Scale Degrees

Complete the following tasks in the order given:

1. Arpeggiate a tonic triad (I) upward from the root to the fifth.
2. Sing a dominant triad (V), also beginning with the root. (This should be easy, for the root of the dominant triad is the fifth of the tonic triad.)
3. Return to the tonic triad, arpeggiating it downward from the fifth.
4. Sing the subdominant triad (IV), arpeggiating downard from scale degree 1 (its fifth, and the root of the preceding tonic) to scale degree 4 (its root) and then up again.
5. Reestablish the tonic triad by arpeggiating it up and down, beginning with its root.

Thus, you'll sing:

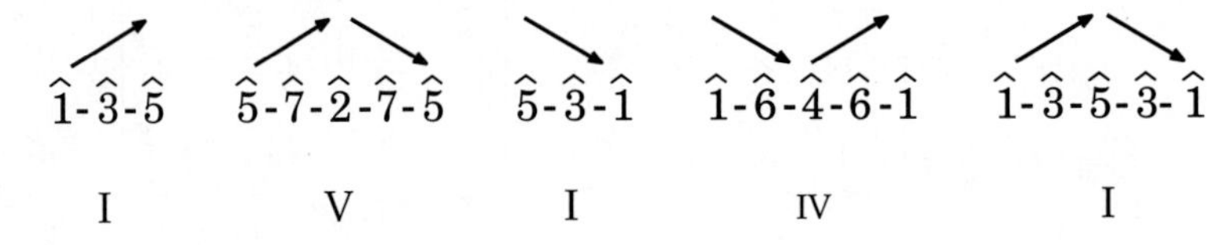

KEYBOARD

5.17 Building Triads at the Keyboard

First with the right hand and then with the left hand, play the following arpeggiation exercises as written (in broken chords) and as vertical chords. Be able to retrace your steps by descending as well. Transpose the patterns to major and minor keys up to five flats and sharps. Use the fingerings provided.

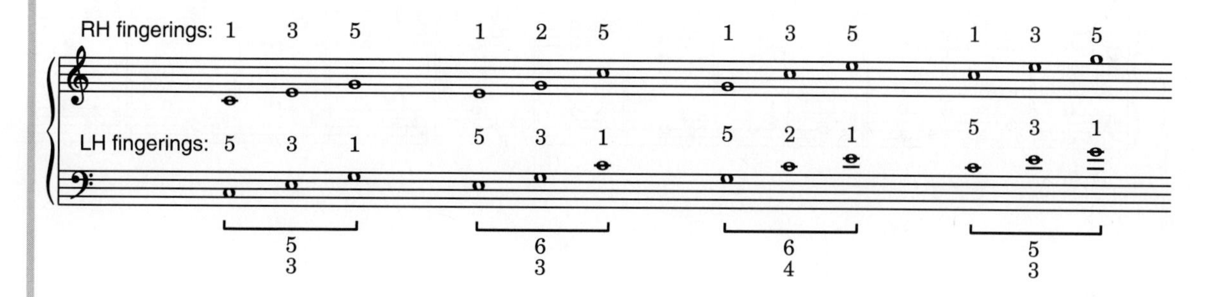

5.18 Building Triads at the Keyboard Using Figured Bass

In three voices, construct triads from the figured bass. Play the bass voice with the left hand and the upper two voices with the right hand. Remember that figured bass indicates intervals above the bass but does not indicate spacing. Be aware of accidentals. Identify root and triad type for each example.

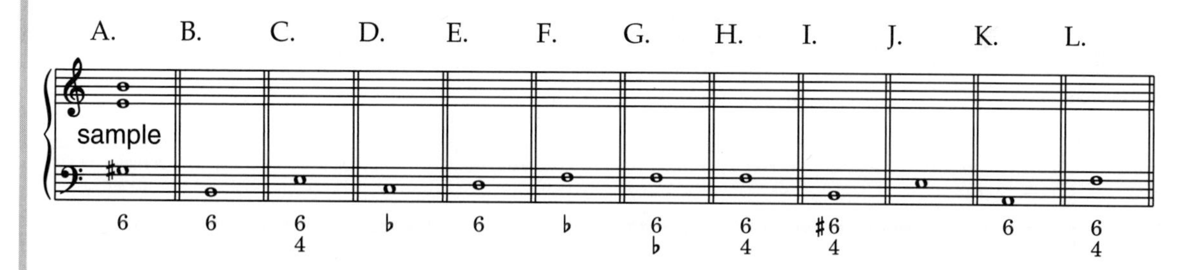

5.19 Playing in Keyboard Style

Given are both incomplete and complete three-voice root-position triads. Create complete four-voice sonorities with doubled roots. After playing the chords in keyboard style, revoice the right-hand notes to create three different voicings.

A. B. C. D. E. F. G. H.

ANALYSIS

5.20

For each of the following, label the *major* key, the roman numeral, and the full figured bass of the given chord within that key.

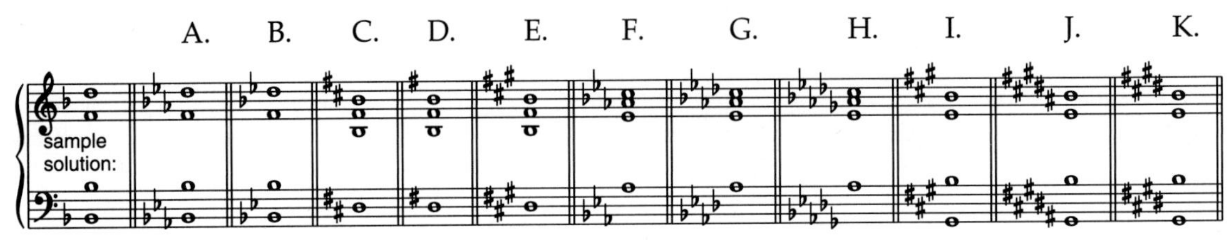

WRITING

5.21

Notate triads based on the given key and the roman numeral. Use accidentals, not key signatures. Voice chords in close or open spacing as required. Create a four-voice setting by doubling the root for open-spacing chords. Exercise A is solved for you.

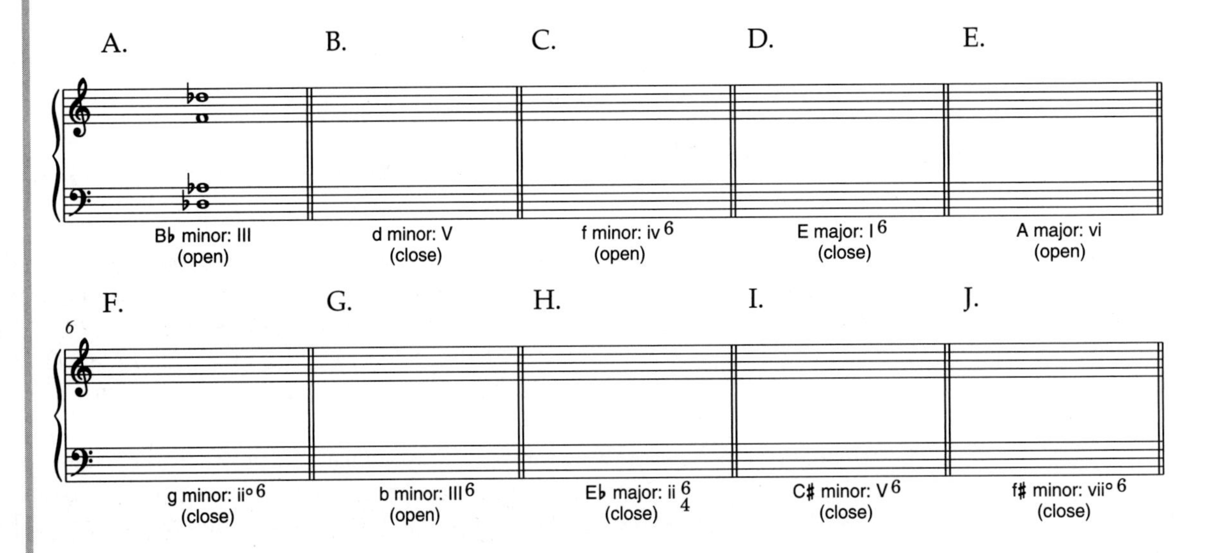

5.22 Illustrations

Complete the given writing tasks, and analyze your work.

WORKBOOK
5.5–5.7

A. In D minor, write the following root-position triads in four voices, close position (tightly compressed), doubling the bass: i, III, V, VI
B. In B♭ major, write the following root-position triads in four voices, using a wide spacing and doubling the bass note: ii, IV, vi, vii°

C. In C minor, write the following root-position and inverted triads in a spacing of your choice, doubling the root: i_6, ii°, III, iv_6, V, V_6, VI, $vii°_6$. For vii° and ii°, double the chordal third.

TERMS AND CONCEPTS

- chord vs. triad
- chromatic alterations
- close position and open position
- consonant triad
- dissonant triad
- doubling
- figured bass, figured bass realization
- harmonic analysis
- inversion, triadic [root position, first inversion ($^6_3$); second inversion ($^6_4$)]
- keyboard style vs. chorale style
- quality
- roman numerals
- root position ($^5_3$)
- root, third, fifth
- spacing, voicing (open position, close position)
- triad

CHAPTER 6

Seventh Chords, Musical Texture, and Harmonic Analysis

In this chapter we conclude our studies of theory fundamentals by exploring common four-note sonorities, called *seventh chords*. The second half of the chapter places all of what we've learned, including scales, melody, intervals, counterpoint, and harmony, in various musical contexts, called *musical texture*.

Listen to the chords in Example 6.1A and then play them on the piano. How many different pitch classes does each chord contain? Is it possible to stack the notes in thirds, as we did with the triads? What is the sound quality of these chords? Describe their effect in terms of stability and instability. Only the first and last chords are triads. The majority of the remaining chords contain four different pitches, which can be stacked in thirds. The few three-pitch class sonorities are not triads, but they can still be stacked in thirds, although there is a "gap" between the second and third pitches (see Example 6.1B, which stacks each of the chords in thirds, with the root as the lowest pitch). Finally, all but the first and last chords contain the dissonant interval of a seventh (again, see Example 6.1B). Because the chord spans the interval of a seventh, this sonority is known as a **seventh chord**. And because a seventh is a dissonant interval, all seventh chords are dissonant—though to varying degrees, as we shall see.

EXAMPLE 6.1 A Progression with Seventh Chords

A.

B.

We label seventh chords by their two most audible features: the type of triad (major, minor, diminished) and the type of seventh above the root (major, minor, diminished). There are five important types of seventh chords, though, like the triad types, they are not used with equal frequency. They are listed here and named according to the quality of the triad and the size of the seventh.

1. major-major seventh chord (MM 7th), called a major seventh chord
2. major-minor seventh chord (Mm 7th), called a major-minor seventh chord
3. minor-minor seventh chord (mm 7th), called a minor seventh chord
4. diminished-minor seventh chord (dm 7th), called a half-diminished seventh chord
5. diminished-diminished seventh chord (dd 7th), sometimes called a fully diminished seventh chord but most often simply called a diminished seventh chord

Example 6.2 shows an example of each type of seventh chord built on the root C.

EXAMPLE 6.2 Five Types of Seventh Chord

Musical Characteristics of Seventh Chords

The major-minor seventh chord (Mm 7th) is the most common seventh chord used in tonal music. It can be found regularly in music written from the early seventeenth century, and it is commonplace in popular music to this day, particularly the blues. The Mm 7 is often called the **dominant seventh chord** because it so regularly appears on the dominant scale degree ($\hat{5}$), for example, in the key of C major, V^7 is G–B–D–F.

The major seventh chord (MM 7th), with its major seventh, is more strident than the major-minor seventh chord. It appears occasionally in common-practice music but more regularly in twentieth-century popular music and jazz. The minor seventh chord (mm 7th), on the other hand, is a very soft-sounding chord, because its minor seventh creates a less dissonant sound than that of the major seventh.

The half-diminished seventh chord (dm 7th, or ø7) is a mix of effect. The dissonant triad is balanced with a less dissonant minor seventh. The chord occurs in both common-practice music—especially in Romantic vocal music, where it is often associated with anguish—and twentieth-century popular music.

The diminished seventh (fully diminished) chord (dd 7th, or °7) is the most dissonant of the seventh chords that we will study. It is found in late-Baroque works and throughout the Classical and Romantic eras. In addition, the diminished seventh chord is an asset to silent movie scores, where it often signals trouble, such as the train quickly approaching the maiden tied to the tracks. It is the only seventh chord that contains all the same types of thirds and fifths: three minor thirds and two diminished fifths.

EXERCISE INTERLUDE

ANALYSIS

6.1 Aural and Visual Analysis of Root-Position Seventh Chords

DVD 2
CH 6
TRACK 1

A. Identify the root and the type of root position seventh chord, choosing among Mm (major-minor), MM (major), mm (minor), dm (ø7), and dd (°7). Identify the chord member in the soprano (1, 3, 5, or 7).

B. Listen to and study the following series of root-position seventh chords that are written in open position. Identify the type of seventh chord from among the choices listed in part A.

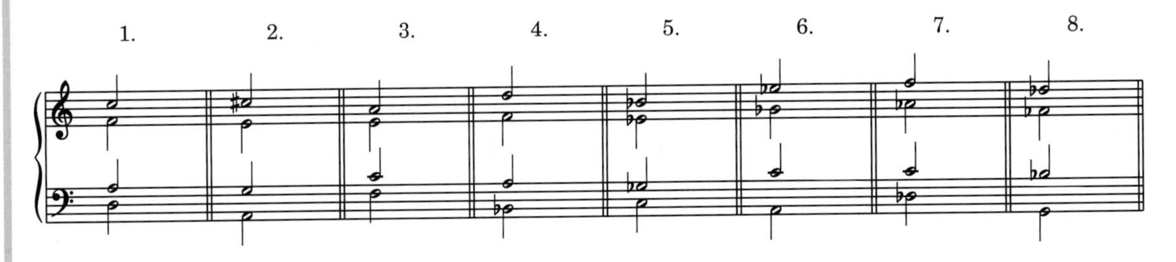

WRITING

6.2 Writing Seventh Chords

Complete the following tasks on a separate sheet of manuscript paper. Write even-numbered exercises in treble clef, odd-numbered exercises in bass clef.

A. 1. Notate root-position Mm seventh chords with the following roots: A, D, E♭
2. Notate root-position mm seventh chords with the following roots: G, B♭, D♭
3. Notate root-position dd (°7) seventh chords with the following roots: C, F, A
4. Notate root-position MM seventh chords with the following roots: B, E, B♭
5. Notate root position dm (ø7) seventh chords with the following roots: G, F, A♯, G♯

B. 1. F is the third of which Mm seventh chord? the fifth of which Mm seventh chord? the seventh of which Mm seventh chord?

2. D is the third of which dd seventh chord? the fifth of which mm seventh chord? the seventh of which MM seventh chord?
3. B♭ is the third of which mm seventh chord? the fifth of which Mm seventh chord? the seventh of which MM seventh chord?

6.3

Fill in the following chart by spelling the type of seventh chord requested using letter names.

	Root	*Third*	*Fifth*	*Seventh*
a. Mm:	______	F♯	______	______
b. mm	B♭	______	______	______
c. dd:	______	______	A♭	______
d. dm:	______	D	______	______
e. MM:	______	______	C♯	______
f: dd:	______	______	______	G♭
g. MM:	______	______	______	G
h. Mm:	______	______	E♭	______
i. dm:	E	______	______	______
j. mm:	______	______	______	A

PERFORMING

6.4

A. Play the seventh chords from Exercise 6.1.
B. Sing and play root-position Mm, MM, mm, dm, and dd seventh chords from any pitch.

WORKBOOK 6.1

6.5 Keyboard

In the following exercise, the bass is the root of a specified type of seventh chord. At the keyboard, add the two missing voices below the soprano to create the required chords in close spacing.

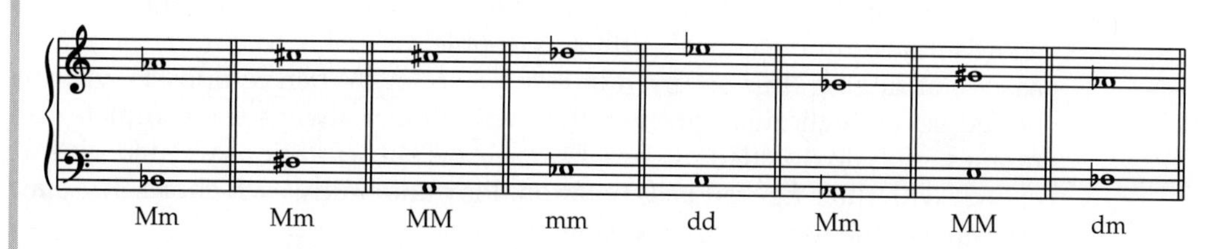

LISTENING

6.6 Identifying Chord Quality

Identify the type of root-position seventh chord (Mm, MM, mm, dm/ø7, dd/°7). Then, when you listen to each exercise, consider the musical characteristics of each chord presented earlier. Sing the chord's root once you hear it played, then arpeggiate the chord in order to determine its type.

A. _______ B. _______ C. _______ D. _______ E. _______ F. _______ G. _______ H. _______

Inverted Seventh Chords

Seventh chords often appear in inversion. Example 6.3 shows the three inversions of a major-minor (Mm) seventh chord with the root F. For each inversion, both the full and the abbreviated figures are given.

EXAMPLE 6.3 Seventh Chord in Root Position and Inversion

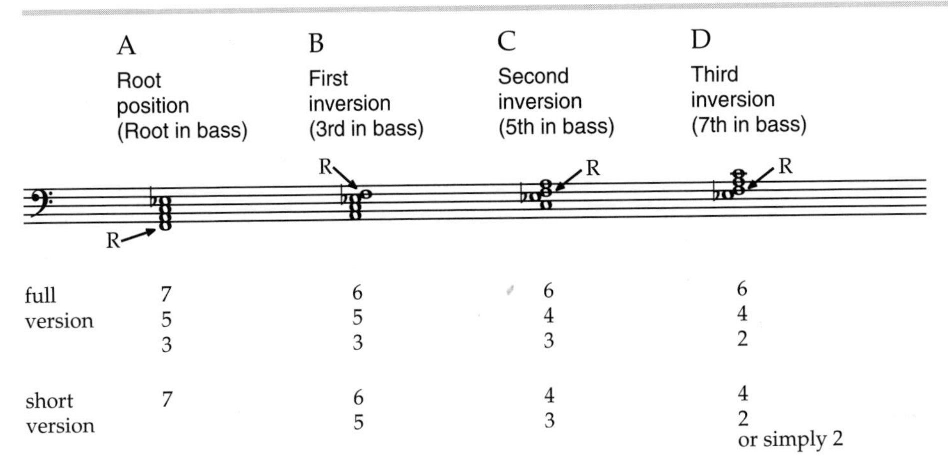

Analytical Tips

Determining the root of an inverted seventh chord is not difficult if you look first for the seventh—the defining interval of the chord—or its inversion, the second. The root of the chord will be the lower note of the seventh or the upper note of the second. For example, in Example 6.3A, the lower note of the seventh F–E♭ is the root. In Example 6.3C, the upper note of the major second (E♭–F) is the root.

To memorize the inversion labels of seventh chords, remember that as the chords move from root position up through the inversions, their numbers steadily decrease: 7–6–5–4–3–2 (7 = root position; $^{6}_{5}$ = first inversion; $^{4}_{3}$ = second inversion; 2 = third inversion). Composers writing root-position seventh chords may omit the chord's fifth and double the stable root for reasons such as ease of singing (this occurred in Example 6.1A). When composers write inverted seventh chords, however, they will almost always use complete harmonies, with no doubled pitches. Example 6.4 shows various notated seventh chords with their figured bass notation. Play and study each chord. Try playing three of the four voices and singing the fourth voice.

EXAMPLE 6.4 Seventh Chords in Root Position and Inversions

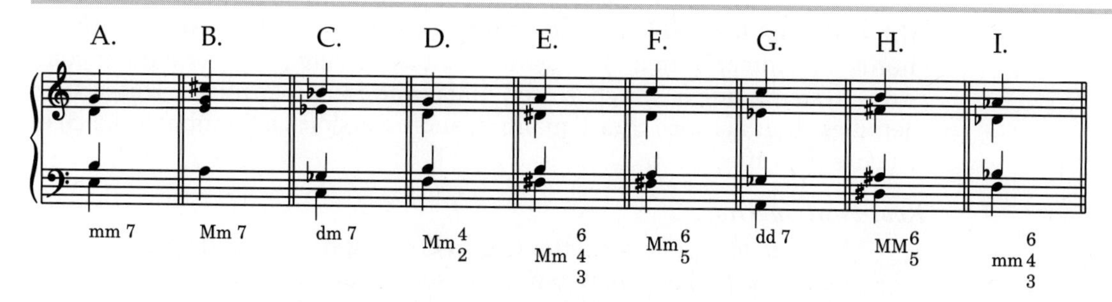

Seventh Chords and Harmonic Analysis

All five principal types of seventh chord arise in the major and minor scales, and, just as with triads, particular seventh chord types are associated with particular scale degrees. As you begin to listen to progressions within the context of a key, it is important to be able to identify instantly the quality of each chord and to know the scale degree from which each is built. When we analyze seventh chords using roman numerals, we follow a procedure similar to that used for analyzing triads:

- Mm and MM seventh chords require uppercase roman numerals.
- mm, dm, and dd seventh chords require lowercase roman numerals.
- dd seventh chords also require a degree sign (°) to indicate a diminished triad and seventh.
- dm seventh chords require a slash through the degree sign (ø) to indicate that the sonority is half diminished.

Example 6.5 shows the most common types of seventh chords that occur in major and minor keys.

EXAMPLE 6.5 Seventh Chords in Major and Minor Keys

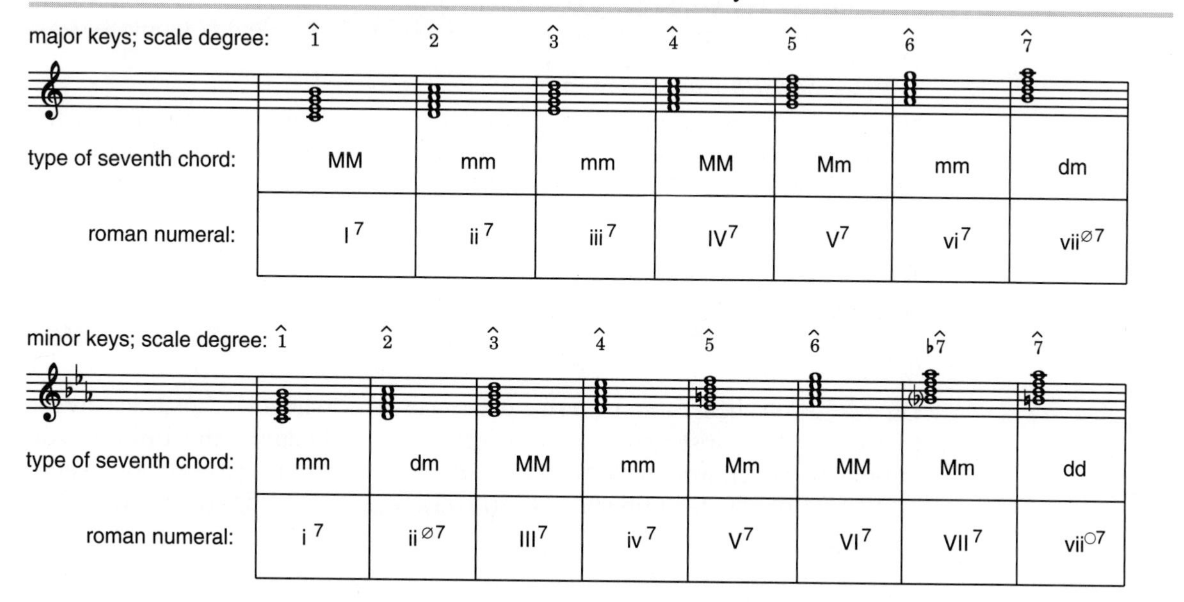

major keys; scale degree:	$\hat{1}$	$\hat{2}$	$\hat{3}$	$\hat{4}$	$\hat{5}$	$\hat{6}$	$\hat{7}$
type of seventh chord:	MM	mm	mm	MM	Mm	mm	dm
roman numeral:	I^{7}	ii^{7}	iii^{7}	IV^{7}	V^{7}	vi^{7}	vii^{ø7}

minor keys; scale degree:	$\hat{1}$	$\hat{2}$	$\hat{3}$	$\hat{4}$	$\hat{5}$	$\hat{6}$	♭$\hat{7}$	$\hat{7}$
type of seventh chord:	mm	dm	MM	mm	Mm	MM	Mm	dd
roman numeral:	i^{7}	ii^{ø7}	III^{7}	iv^{7}	V^{7}	VI^{7}	VII^{7}	vii^{o7}

Lead-Sheet Notation

Although this text will use the common-practice symbols for identifying chords (i.e., roman numerals plus figured bass), there are several other competing systems, one of which is used for jazz and popular music. This system identifies chordal roots, chord qualities, and inversions, a thumbnail sketch of which is presented next.

Root-Position Triads

- *Major triad:* uppercase letter (e.g., a C-major triad would be C)
- *Minor triad:* There are two ways to show a minor triad:
  - i. uppercase letter followed by a horizontal slash (e.g., a C-minor triad would be C—)
  - ii. lowercase letter (e.g., a C-minor triad would be c)
- *Diminished triad:* uppercase letter followed by the degree sign (e.g., a C-diminished triad would be C°)
- *Augmented triad:* uppercase letter followed by the plus sign (e.g., a C-augmented triad would be C+)

Inverted Triads

Inverted sonorities are not nearly as common in popular music as they are in classical music. Thus, the root is still indicated in inverted chords, but it is followed by the pitch required in the bass, showing the inversion [e.g., a first-inversion C-diminished chord would be written C°/E♭, indicating that C is the root and that E♭ (the third of the chord) is in the bass].

Root-Position Seventh Chords

- *Mm seventh:* uppercase root plus 7 (e.g., a C Mm7 would be C7)
- *MM seventh:* uppercase root plus triangle plus 7 (e.g., a C MM7 would be C Δ 7"). One also encounters the symbol M (e.g. CM7).
- *Mm seventh:* lowercase root plus 7 (e.g., a C mm7 would be cm7) or c7 or c − 7 or even Cm7
- *dm seventh:* uppercase root plus degree sign with strikethrough (e.g., a C dm7 would be (Cø7") or c7 dim 5
- *dd seventh:* uppercase plus degree sign plus 7 (e.g., a cdd7 would be C°7)

Inverted Seventh Chords

Like triads, inverted seventh chords are labeled as follows: root and quality followed by slash and bass note, indicating the pitch that is to be played in the bass (e.g., a Cmm seventh chord in second inversion would be labeled Cm7/G).

EXERCISE INTERLUDE

WRITING

6.7 More Seventh Chord Writing

On a separate sheet of manuscript paper, construct seventh chords according to the following instructions. For example, given D as the third of a major-minor seventh chord, you would write B♭–D–F–A♭. Another example: Given D as the fifth of a half-diminished seventh chord, you would write G♯–B–D–F♯.

A. Spell seventh chords in which E functions as the:
   1. root of a dd seventh
   2. fifth of a mm seventh
   3. seventh of a Mm seventh
   4. third of a MM seventh
B. Spell seventh chords in which A functions as the:
   1. seventh of a mm seventh
   2. third of a dd seventh
   3. fifth of a Mm seventh
   4. seventh of a MM seventh
   5. fifth of a dm seventh
C. Spell seventh chords in which F♯ functions as the:
   1. fifth of a Mm seventh
   2. third of a MM seventh
   3. seventh of a MM seventh
   4. third of a dm seventh

6.8 Inversions of Seventh Chords

On a separate sheet of manuscript paper, construct the required seventh chords. For example, given the bass note D and the instruction to spell a Mm $^6_5$, you will write D–F–A♭–B♭. You know this because the third of the chord is in the bass in first-inversion chords; and since a major third occurs between the bass and the root of a Mm $^6_5$ chord, then B♭ is the root.

A. With a given bass note of C, spell the following chords:
   1. a MM 7th chord
   2. a mm $^6_5$ chord
   3. a dd 7th chord
   4. a Mm $^4_2$ chord
B. With a given bass note of F, spell the following chords:
   1. a Mm $^6_5$ chord
   2. a MM 7th chord
   3. a mm $^4_3$ chord
   4. a dm $^4_2$ chord
C. With a given bass note of E♭, spell the following chords:
   1. a dd 7th (°7) chord
   2. a Mm $^4_3$ chord
   3. a mm $^4_2$ chord
   4. a MM $^6_5$ chord

ANALYSIS

6.9

Identify root, type, and inversion of each of the following seventh chords.

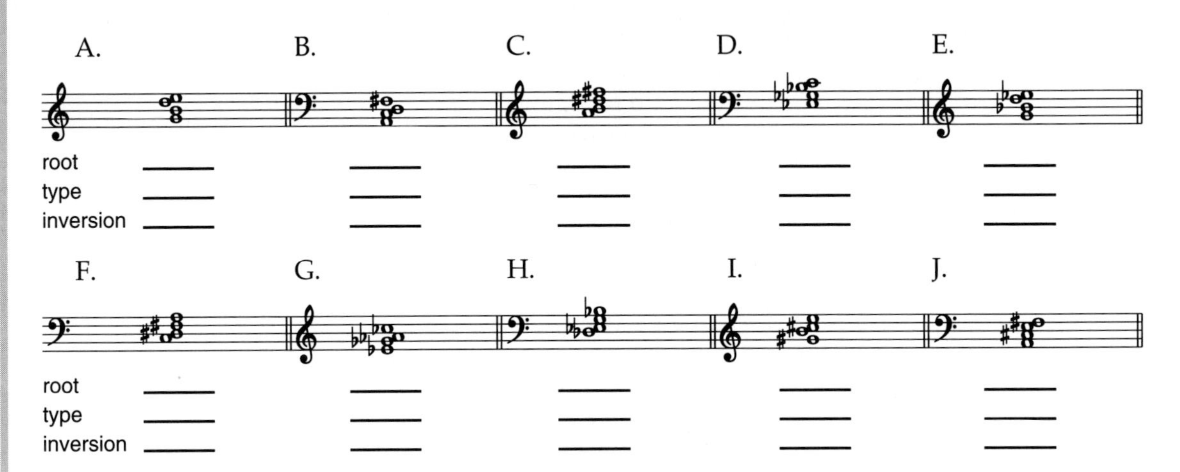

6.10 Distinction Between Scale Degrees, Figured Bass, and Chordal Members

In each of the examples, determine the following:

1. full figured bass
2. type of seventh chord
3. member of chord that is circled
4. member of chord in the bass
5. scale degree in the bass

A.

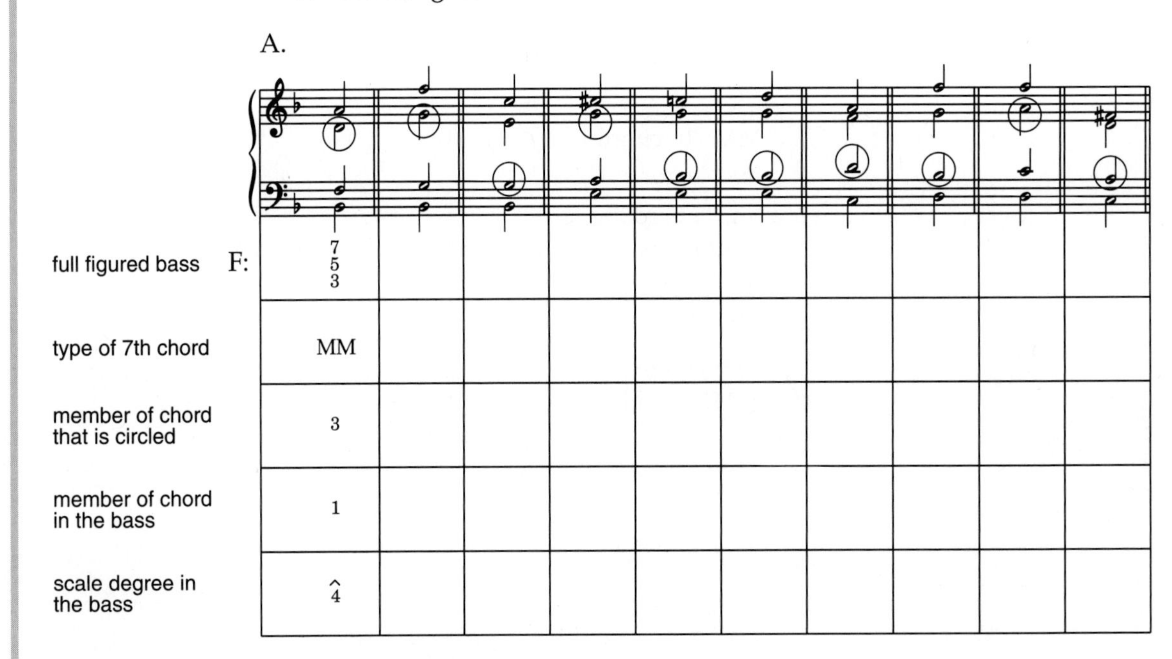

full figured bass F:	7 5 3									
type of 7th chord	MM									
member of chord that is circled	3									
member of chord in the bass	1									
scale degree in the bass	$\hat{4}$									

Continued

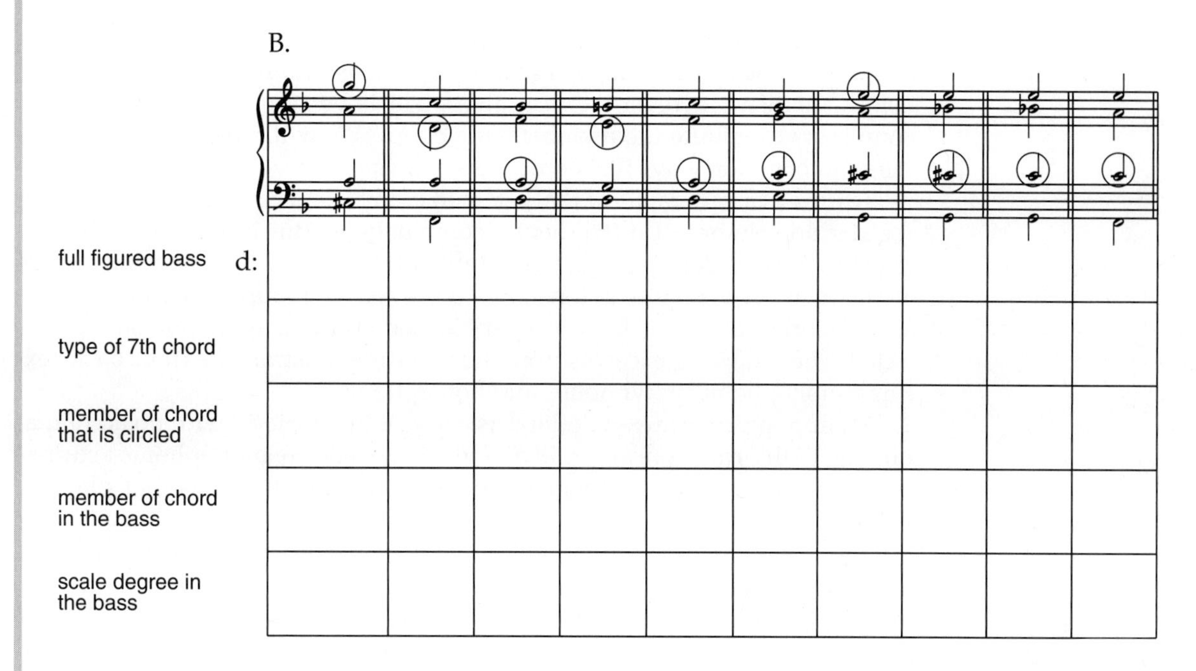

DVD 2
CH 6
TRACK 3

6.11 Functional Analysis of Seventh Chords

First, circle and label the root (1) and the seventh (7) in each chord. Then, after identifying the key of each exercise, provide a harmonic analysis (using roman numerals and figured bass). (Recall that root-position seventh chords need not contain a fifth).

WORKBOOK
6.2–6.4

Musical Texture

So far we have explored triads and seventh chords in their most simple form: as simultaneously sounding vertical sonorities, one chordal member above or below another. However, vertical alignment is but one of many ways that composers distribute the members of a chord. We will now explore some of the most common ways that composers activate chords in space and time.

Texture is a general term that refers to many elements of music, including register and timbre of instrumental combinations. But in particular, texture refers to music's density (e.g., the number of voices and their spacing). There are many types of texture in tonal music, but we can group them into three basic categories, each of which is distinguished by the way the melody is projected. The following excerpts from the literature illustrate the three basic textures: monophonic, polyphonic, and homophonic.

Monophonic texture is defined as a single-line melody with no accompaniment. Both a cantus firmus and a tune you whistle are monophonic textures. Schubert's last symphony begins monophonically with horns that play the primary melody of the first movement (see Example 6.6). Note that a texture can be monophonic even though it might be played (e.g., in octaves) by more than one instrument.

EXAMPLE 6.6 **Schubert, Symphony no. 9 in C major, *Andante***

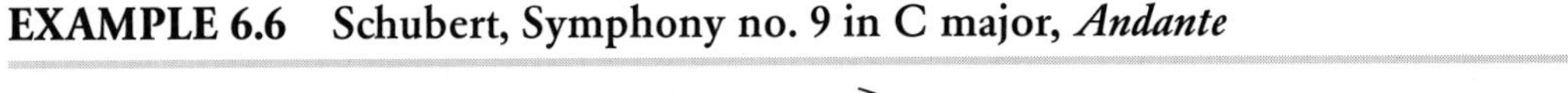

The second type of musical texture is shown in Example 6.7. Taken from one of Bach's fugues, it illustrates **polyphonic**, or **contrapuntal, texture**, which we define as the combination of two or more melodies such that there is no clear distinction between melody and accompaniment. Although polyphonic texture features greater independence of voices, such transparent textures as the two-voice counterpoint that we studied in Chapter 4 are considered polyphonic because two independent melodies were combined.

EXAMPLE 6.7 **Bach, Fugue in G minor, *Well-Tempered Clavier*, Book 1, BWV 861**

We can view the third type of musical texture, called **homophonic texture**, as a cross between monophonic and polyphonic textures, given that there is usually a clear melody accompanied by additional voices. The accompaniments can be highly varied, and it is because of the richness of possibilities that homophonic texture is the most widespread of the three texture types in common-practice music. The various types include the vertical, block-chord format that we have been studying. This chorale texture is one of the simplest types of homophonic textures, given that the accompanying voices are rhythmically aligned with the primary voice, which usually appears in the highest register (see Example 6.8A). In most homophonic textures, however, single harmonies are spread out over time, with their chordal members distributed over one or more beats, measures, or even multiple measures, as shown in Example 6.8B, where the pulsing F-major triad holds forth for three measures.

EXAMPLE 6.8

DVD 1
CH 6
TRACK 4

A. Hassler, "O Haupt voll Blut und Wunden"

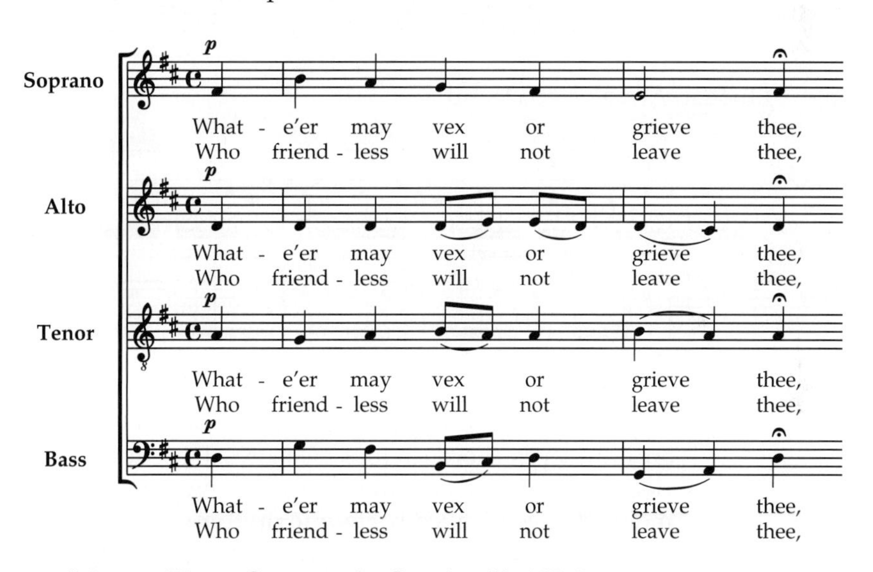

B. Mozart, Piano Concerto in C major, K. 467, ii

C. Mozart, Piano Sonata in C major, K. 545, *Allegro*

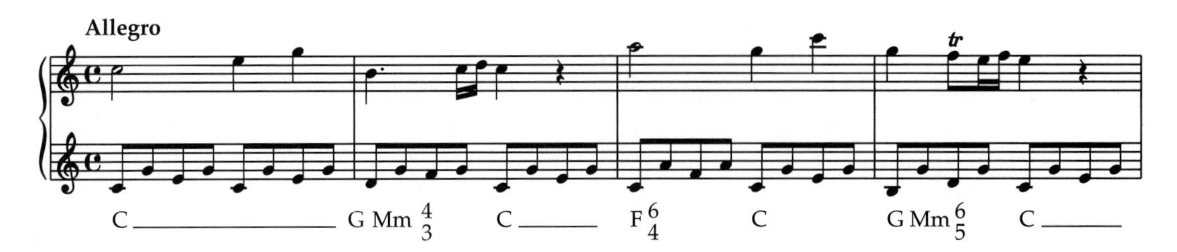

D. Schubert, *Impromptu* in G♭ major, op. 90, no. 3, D. 899

E. Chopin, Etude in A♭ major, op. 25, no. 1

The harmonies in Example 6.8C unfold at a leisurely pace, given that there are only seven chords in four measures. Depending on the composer, style period, and type of piece, chords may change slowly or quickly. The rate of harmonic change is called **harmonic rhythm**.

The preceding clunky analysis is improved by a more concise and informative roman numeral analysis, beneath which are note values that correspond to the duration of each harmony and thus reveal the harmonic rhythm:

mm:	1	2	3	4
	I	V^4_3 I	IV^6_4 I	V^6_5 I
	𝅝	𝅗𝅥 𝅗𝅥	𝅗𝅥 𝅗𝅥	𝅗𝅥 𝅗𝅥

Mozart is able to write such a slow harmonic rhythm because of the rhythmic interest created by the accompanimental figures, which—along with the tune—contain each of the chord members. The broken-chord accompanimental pattern in Example C, called an **Alberti bass**, is common in the Classical style. The Alberti bass and other accompanimental patterns are effective because our ears collect the individual pitches of the broken-chord figure into a single harmony.

Examples 6.8D and E illustrate some of the variety possible in homophonic textures that involve accompanying a single melody. The Schubert *Impromptu* opens with a harmonic rhythm of one chord per measure, while Chopin's is even slower: a single A♭ major triad extends for both of the excerpt's measures.

Very often the members of a chord in a homophonic texture are distributed between various registers (and therefore clefs) and different instruments. In such cases, we need to examine each part in order to get a complete harmonic picture. Often, however, you will be able to determine the harmony even if you see only one or two chordal members, because the harmonic implications are clear from the musical context. Beethoven's Piano Trio provides a simple illustration (Example 6.9). The piano [which moves in a basic 2:1 (second-species) motion] contains most, but not all, of the chord tones for each harmony. The first sonority is the perfect fifth E♭/B♭. However, we have strong suspicions that it implies a root-position E♭-major triad (rather than, say, a C mm seventh chord in $^6_5$ position) given that the key is E♭ major and the piece is just starting, therefore requiring the establishment of the underlying tonality. Our suspicions are corroborated by a glance at the violin part, which presents the missing third (G). Similarly, the incomplete V_7 harmony in the piano in m. 9 (B♭–D–A♭) is completed by the violin's F, which provides the fifth of the chord. Further, since the violin carries the melody, and given that melodies move primarily by step, Beethoven must consider voicing, doubling, register, and instrumentation in order to distribute most effectively this opening tonic triad in this homophonic texture.

EXAMPLE 6.9 Beethoven, Piano Trio in C minor, op. 1, no. 3, ii

DVD 1
CH 6
TRACK 5

Harmonic analysis of homophonic textures requires that you group members of a harmony quickly. In order to do so, you must be able to read pitches fluently in both bass and treble clefs. It is also helpful to have a solid working knowledge of both alto and tenor clefs. The ability to scan music quickly and identify patterns and repetitions is a crucial skill we will develop.

For example, the thirty-second notes and rests in Example 6.10 certainly look intimidating. However, a quick scan of the excerpt should console us. First, we discover a straightforward broken-chord texture (rather than a complicated multivoiced contrapuntal texture), one in which we can easily identify underlying harmonies. Second, we see that some chords are repeated within a measure or even for an entire measure (e.g., in m. 25 a root-position F-minor triad controls the harmony). Further, if the literal position of the chord (i.e., inversion) is not maintained, there are relations by inversion, such as the D♭ harmony in m. 27, which begins in first inversion, moves to second inversion, and in beat 3 lands on root position. Finally, revoicings of the same chord (such as in m. 24) show us that harmonic motion is not as fast as we might have initially thought. An analysis of the chord types and inversions of the first four measures would look like this:

m. 24	25	26	27
g ø7 C	f	A♭Mm $^4_2$	D♭ 6, $^6_4$, $^5_3$

EXAMPLE 6.10 **Beethoven, Violin Sonata no. 3 in E♭ major, op. 12, no. 3, *Adagio con molto espressione***

DVD 1
CH 6
TRACK 6

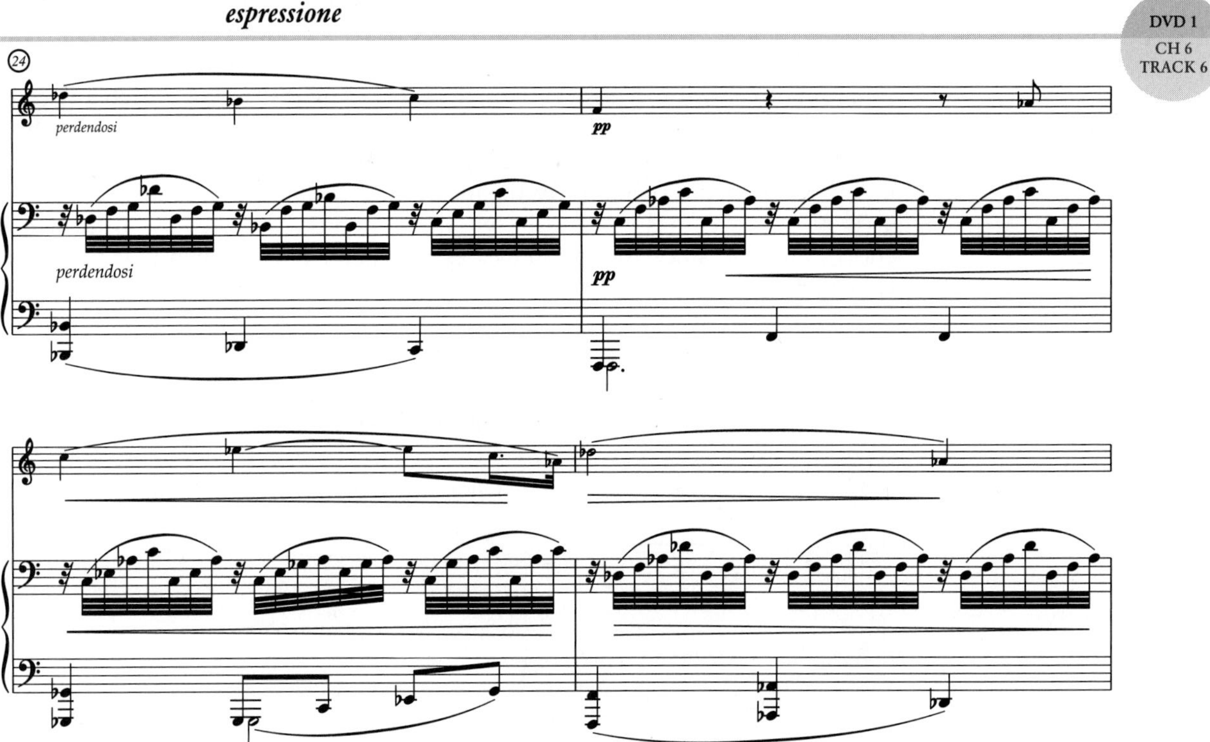

Often it is helpful to simplify dense homophonic and polyphonic textures by notating the underlying harmony in close position on a piece of manuscript paper. Such "reductions" capture harmonic motions and repeating patterns, and in time you will be able to negotiate these reductions in your head. This ability will be very useful not only in your theory and analysis, but also in your sight-reading and learning of pieces. For example, the first section of Mozart's "Catalogue Aria" from *Don Giovanni* contains a sixteenth-note passage, which can be rendered easily if reduced to its harmonic outline (Example 6.11). First, we scan the passage for patterns and repetitions and we discover that the left hand contains repeating chords (e.g., m. 77 contains two E-major triads) and that the right hand contains an ascending broken-chord figure that outlines the same chords as in the left hand. Further, the right-hand descent is identical to its ascent.

EXAMPLE 6.11 Mozart, "Madamina," *Don Giovanni*, act 1, no. 4

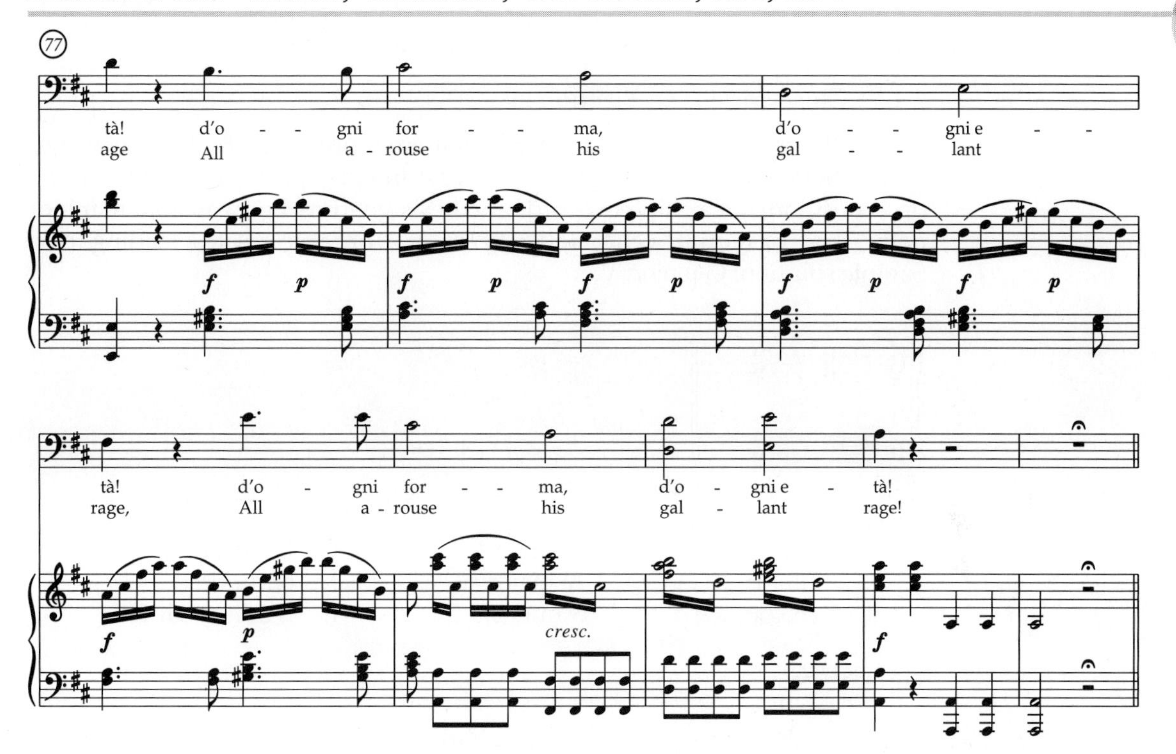

Next, we notate the bass notes (there is no need to notate the entire left-hand chord since it is easy to see its structure) and the right-hand chord, omitting pitch repetitions and, if possible, maintaining the highest pitch (the soprano), which we already know to be structural. The reduction in Example 6.12 shows this procedure and includes two kinds of analysis: the chord names (with uppercase letters indicating major triads and seventh chords that contain major triads, and lowercase letters indicating minor triads and seventh chords that contain minor triads) and inversions, and roman numerals. The bracket indicates that the progression is grouped into two parts; the first ends on vi, and the repeated second progression closes on the tonic. (The reduction, written in the key of A major, represents Mozart's key within the score.)

EXAMPLE 6.12 Reduction of Mozart

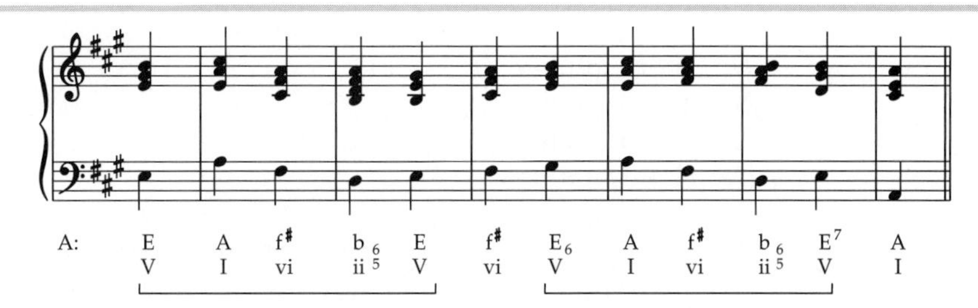

EXERCISE INTERLUDE

WRITING

6.12 Close and Open Position

Notate the triads and seventh chords that are represented by the roman numerals below. Write each chord twice, first in close position and then in an open position. Use complete chords and key signature. Be aware that in minor both V and V7 require a chromatic alteration in order to create a leading tone. Sample solution: G major: V7

A. D major: vi	B. c minor: V7	C. B♭ major: ii7
D. f minor: iv7	E. A♭ major: V7	F. b minor: iv7
G. E major: iii7	H. e♭ minor: V7	I. f♯ minor: vii°7

LISTENING

6.13 Triads and Seventh Chords in Various Textures: Aural Identification

We will now continue developing aural and analytical skills using various textures. Let's begin by varying the texture, that is, by altering spacing, instrumentation, density, register, and rhythmic pattern. All chord members will be present, but one or more members will be doubled or even tripled.

1. For A–D, identify the type of sonority (triads and seventh chords). All chords are in root position.
2. For E–H, identify the type of sonority and the member of the chord in the bass. (*Hint:* the only inverted sonorities you will hear are triads and the Mm seventh chord.)
3. For I–L, complete the tasks in (2), but now two sonorities will be played. Identify which member of the triad or the Mm seventh is in the bass, and sing the bass.

Use figured bass notation to denote inversions ($^6_3$, $^6_4$ for triads; $^6_5$, $^4_3$, $^4_2$ for seventh chords).

A. chord quality _______
B. chord quality _______
C. chord quality _______
D. chord quality _______
E. chord quality _______ chord member in bass _______
F. chord quality _______ chord member in bass _______
G. chord quality _______ chord member in bass _______
H. chord quality _______ chord member in bass _______

I. chord qualities _______ _______ chord members in bass _______ _______
J. chord qualities _______ _______ chord members in bass _______ _______
K. chord qualities _______ _______ chord members in bass _______ _______
L. chord qualities _______ _______ chord members in bass _______ _______

ANALYSIS

6.14 Harmonic Analysis in Various Textures (I)

Given next are short excerpts of various homophonic textures. Complete the following tasks:

1. Box each harmony, and label the root, the type of harmony (for triads: Maj, min, dim; for seventh chords: Mm, MM, mm, dm, dd) and the inversion, if any (for triads: $^6_3$, $^6_4$; for seventh chords $^6_5$, $^4_3$, $^4_2$).
2. Describe the harmonic rhythm in terms of its rate of change (fast or slow) and whether or not it is regular.
3. Using the manuscript paper provided beneath each example, make a reduction that includes the following:

   a. bass note (which may or may not be the root, depending on whether or not the chord is inverted)
   b. two added upper voices to complete triads and three added upper voices to complete seventh chords. Use close position, with the highest note of the texture functioning as the soprano.

An example from Corelli's Concerto Grosso no. 8, is provided.

A. Corelli, Concerto Grosso in G minor, op. 6, no. 8, *Allegro*

B. Haydn, String Quartet in F minor, op. 50, no. 4, *Andante*

6.15 Harmonic Analysis in Various Textures (II)

This exercise is identical to Exercise 6.14, but you will also include a roman numeral analysis of each excerpt.

DVD 2
CH 6
TRACK 6

A. Corelli, Concerto Grosso in D major, op. 6, no. 4, *Allegro*

B. Haydn, String Quartet in G minor, op. 20, no. 3, *Poco Adagio* (III)

C. Corelli, Concerto Grosso in B minor, op. 6, no. 1 *Largo* (#2)

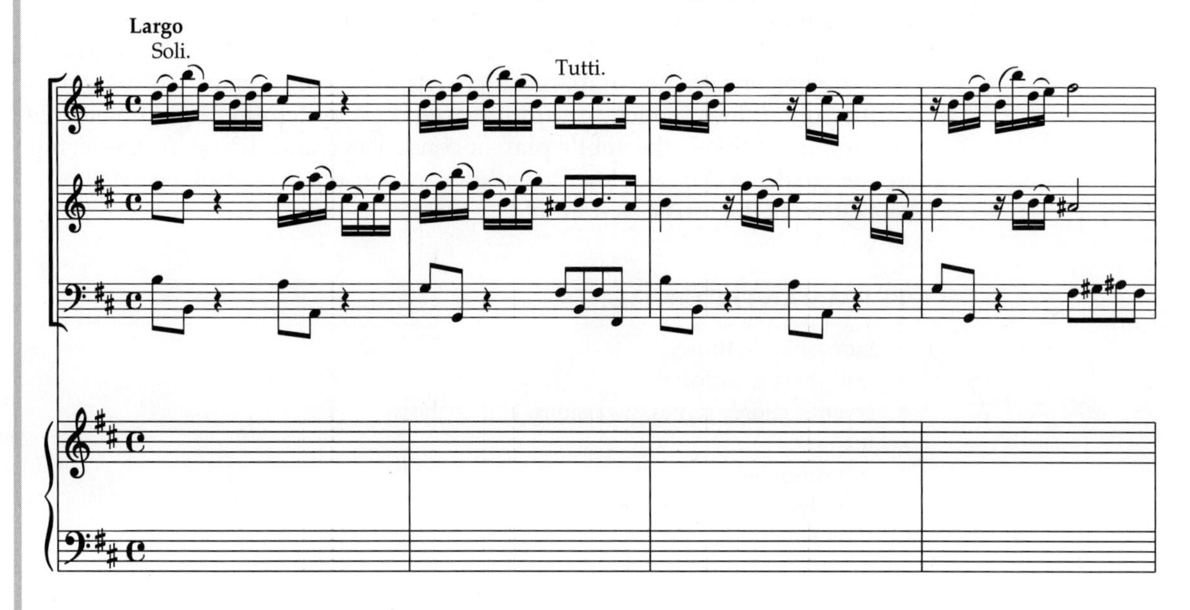

6.16 Composition

Using one of the pieces in either Exercise 6.14 or Exercise 6.15 as a textural model (or create your own texture), write a piece that:

1. contains eight measures
2. is in D minor
3. is in $\frac{4}{4}$ meter
4. contains only chord tones
5. has a harmonic rhythm of one chord per measure
6. contains the following chords and soprano pitch:
   m. 1: d minor (F in soprano)
   m. 2: g mm 7 (F in soprano)
   m. 3: A Mm 7 (E in soprano)
   m. 4: B♭ major (D in soprano)
   m. 5: g minor (D in soprano)
   m. 6: E dm $^6_5$ (E in soprano)
   m. 7: A Mm 7 (C♯ in soprano)
   m. 8: d minor (D in soprano)

WORKBOOK
6.5–6.6

Summary of Part 1

You now possess the basic knowledge that is the foundation of tonal music. The terminology and concepts you have learned will be the basis for exploring the rich and varied compositional techniques of the music written over nearly four centuries. Tonal music is a complex art form in which single pitches are combined in a carefully regulated fashion that is dictated by the way humans tend to perceive stimuli.

Pitches and their temporal placement are intertwined to such a degree that we find it helpful to acknowledge that tonal music exists in two dimensions: the temporal, or horizontal, and the spatial, or vertical dimension. Music's two-dimensionality occurs because chords and their connection depend on contrapuntal lines, which in turn are governed by temporal placement. The conduit in all this is the subtle play of consonance and dissonance, which together create an ebb and flow that allows composers to control the tension and relaxation of the music as it unfolds.

TERMS AND CONCEPTS

- harmonic rhythm
- lead-sheet notation
- seventh chords (types, inversions, and analysis)
- texture
  - homophonic
  - polyphonic (contrapuntal)
  - monophonic

PART 2

MERGING MELODY AND HARMONY

Now that we have completed our study of fundamentals, we can begin to apply this knowledge to the common-practice repertoire. Not only will you refine your keyboard skills, but you will also have regular opportunities to transfer these concepts directly to your own instrument. This part begins to develop new analytical techniques that illuminate the hierarchical nature of music and that will help you develop a basis for making critically informed interpretations about musical structure. We will work with ever-larger musical units and will eventually compose in the common-practice style by combining small harmonic progressions, which are the building blocks of larger musical forms.

We'll discover firsthand how melody, counterpoint, and harmony are interdependent, to the point of being inseparable. And we'll see that not all chords are created equal. Despite the large number of possible triad and seventh chords, composers of common-practice music tend to use some more than others. Indeed, the tonic and dominant triad or seventh chord are the most important harmonies. These two chords form the harmonic axis of practically every phrase of tonal music. However, very little music includes only root-position tonic and dominant chords, and in Part 2 we explore ways in which composers use these and other chords, in both root position and inversion, to create harmonic variety and thus to increase musical interest. Variety, however, does not come at the expense of musical coherence, and so we also learn how these new chords and inversions relate to the underlying tonal axis. What we'll discover is that each of these larger functions can be embellished over time with other chords, which thereby "expand" or "prolong" the axial harmonies. Thus we shall proceed systematically, introducing how melody and harmony are dependent on one another, the role of rhythm and meter, and the resulting hierarchy.

CHAPTER 7

Hierarchy in Music: Consonance, Unaccented Dissonance, and Melodic Fluency

This chapter provides a bridge that leads from our study of fundamentals to our exploration of harmony and form. Fundamentals included the terminology and concepts for the basic building blocks of tonal music (including notation, scales, rhythm, intervals, and melody). In our studies of two-voice counterpoint, triads, and seventh chords, we learned the importance of intervallic consonance and dissonance. In this chapter we begin to extend these concepts so that we will be able to hear and comprehend not only the note-to-note behavior of pitches, but also how certain pitches connect to other pitches, despite the fact that there are intervening pitches. These steps are crucial because they not only pave the way for subsequent chapters, but also inform our approach to the music we play and sing.

Consonance and Dissonance

Consonance and dissonance are traditionally defined by the intervals formed between voices. The perfect consonances (unison, octave, and fifth) are the most stable. The imperfect consonances (major and minor thirds and sixths) are less stable but more fluid, so we may use them in any voice-leading context, including parallel motion. Dissonant intervals include seconds, sevenths, the perfect fourth, and all augmented and diminished intervals. However, the distinction between consonant and dissonant intervals is not ironclad, since their status depends entirely on how they function within the musical context. For example, the minor sixth C–A♭ in Example 7.1A can be rendered consonant *or* dissonant, depending on its context. The sixth is consonant if either F or A♭ appears below it (creating an F minor triad or an A♭ major triad; Example 7.1B), but it is unstable if C appears in the bass (the sixth yearns for resolution to the perfect fifth; Example 7.1C). With E♭ in the bass, both pitches comprising the sixth require resolution down by step (Example 7.1D).

EXAMPLE 7.1

DVD 1 CH 7 TRACK 1

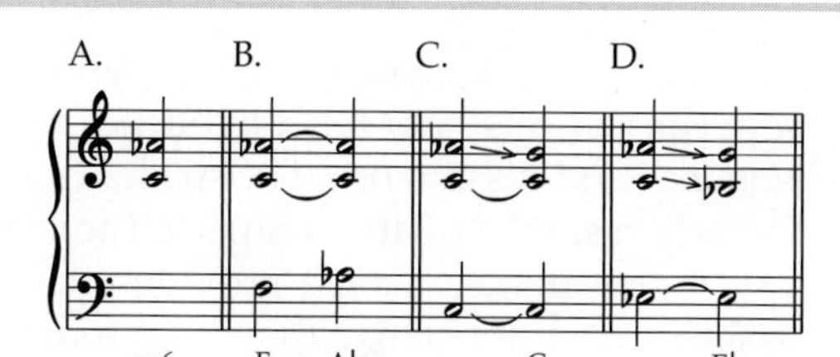

Another example could be drawn from the perfect fourth—which we viewed as a dissonance in our counterpoint studies. Indeed, the F above C in Example 7.2A is dissonant; as an active pitch, the F strives toward resolution to a consonance by falling a step. However, when the bass voice does not participate in the formation of the perfect fourth, the interval becomes consonant, as seen in Example 7.2B, where the addition of either A or A♭ below the fourth creates a first-inversion triad. And by adding another F below the C, the upper F becomes stable, since it is now consonant with the bass, as part of an implied F-major or -minor triad (Example 7.2C).

EXAMPLE 7.2

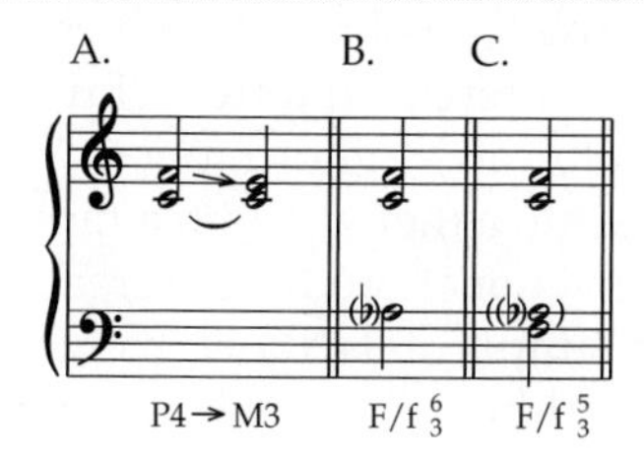

In addition to adding color, dissonant intervals—with their harmonic and melodic instability—provide musical tension and energy. Only through resolution can this energy be discharged. Example 7.3 illustrates where perfect consonances (labeled *PC*), imperfect consonances (labeled *IC*), and dissonances (labeled *D*) occur within a descending major scale over a sustained bass note. The label *P* indicates which pitches are passing between, and therefore subordinate to, more important notes.

EXAMPLE 7.3 Consonances and Dissonances

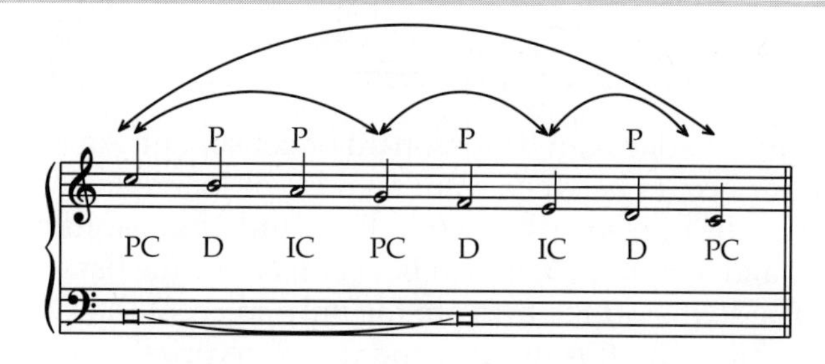

Of course, the interval of the octave is completely stable. The dissonant major seventh (B over C) meanwhile requires resolution. Depending on the direction of the line, $\hat{7}$ will either ascend to $\hat{8}$ or descend to $\hat{6}$, where, in the latter case, it forms a consonant sixth with the bass. Yet is the sixth really an arrival? Yes, but not a particularly strong one; as an imperfect consonance, it is less stable than the perfect fifth that results when $\hat{6}$ in turn passes to $\hat{5}$. We can see that the dependence between various intervals establishes a hierarchical relationship between consonance and dissonance. The strident sound of the dissonant seventh is only relatively resolved by the sixth, itself an imperfect consonance. It is the fifth, a perfect consonance, which provides stability. As we have already seen, the passing tone $\hat{4}$, forming a dissonant fourth with the bass, also has a strong need to resolve, and it does so to $\hat{3}$, which forms a major third with the bass. However, because this imperfect consonance is not completely stable, $\hat{3}$ descends via the dissonant passing tone $\hat{2}$ to $\hat{1}$, which forms an octave with the bass.

Thus the notes that are consonant with the bass note C in Example 7.3 are C, E, G, and A. If we ranked these consonances, C and G would be the most stable, followed by E. A is the least stable consonance because it has a tendency to fall to G. Thus the major tonic triad is a stable entity that is surrounded by unstable forces, as we heard in Bach's E Major Violin Partita in Chapter 1.

If we view this scale as a crude melody, we now see that the passing tones B, A, F, and D ($\hat{7}$, $\hat{6}$, $\hat{4}$, and $\hat{2}$) appear between and therefore connect the stable pitches C, E, G, whose combination results in a triad. Since these passing tones are not members of the underlying C-major triad, which is implied by the sustained C in the bass, we call them **nonchord tones**. Thus passing tones tend to create tension that requires resolution by chord tones.

If we turn the C-major scale into a melody with a more interesting contour, as in Example 7.4, another type of nonchord tone is created: the **neighbor tone** (also called **auxiliary tone**, or simply **neighbor**). Neighbors that lie above a stable pitch are called **upper neighbors** (UN), whereas those that lie below are called **lower neighbors** (LN). Since it modifies a single pitch, a neighbor-tone figure is more static (i.e., less dynamic) than the more fluid passing tone, which moves to a new pitch that lies a third above or below the original pitch.

EXAMPLE 7.4 Neighbor Tones and Arpeggiations

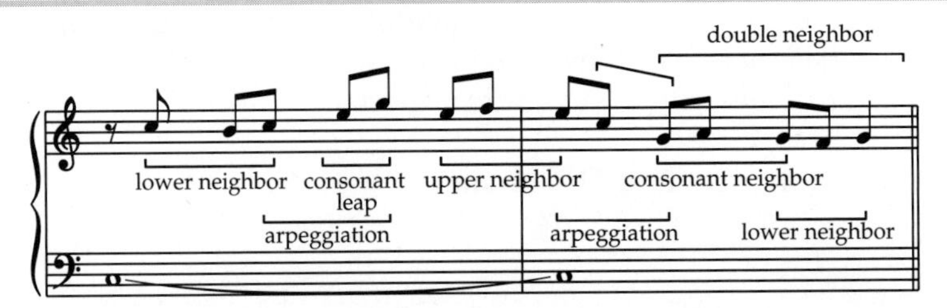

Neighbor tones can be dissonant or consonant. An example of a **dissonant neighbor** occurs between mm. 1 and 2 of Example 7.4; F, which is a fourth above the bass, resolves down to E, a third. A **consonant neighbor** occurs on beats 2 and 3 of m. 2; A, which is a sixth above the bass, resolves down to G, a fifth. The sixth and the fifth are the only adjacent intervals that are consonant above a bass, and this unique, and therefore privileged, relationship has huge compositional ramifications that we first discovered in our studies of second-species counterpoint (Example 4.11), but which we will encounter regularly in our later studies. For now we will simply refer to it as the *5–6 technique*. Dissonant neighbors form intervals of a second, fourth, or seventh above the bass.

Finally, a double neighbor results from the combination of the upper neighbor and lower neighbor in m. 2.

The melody in Example 7.4 also contains leaps that are consonant with the bass note, C. We refer to leaps that are members of the underlying harmony as **consonant leaps** or **chordal leaps**. [In our study of counterpoint in Chapter 4 we distinguished between leaps of thirds (called *skips*) and larger leaps; we will now refer to all nonstepwise motions simply as leaps.] If three or more tones from the same harmony appear in succession, they form an **arpeggiation** (ARP). We already learned in our counterpoint studies that leaps are permitted only if they are consonant with the cantus. Similarly, triadic skips and leaps are possible as long as they are members of the underlying harmony.

Because we have encountered both consonant embellishments (including the chordal leap and arpeggiation) and dissonant embellishments (the dissonant passing tone and neighbor tone), we will *not* use the term *nonharmonic tone*, given that the consonant embellishments are members of the underlying harmony and therefore are chord tones. Rather, we refer to all melodic embellishments generically as **tones of figuration** and you may add the prefix *consonant* or *dissonant*, depending on their function within the specific musical context.

There is very little tonal music written whose texture is characterized by a single sustained bass note and rambling melody above it, as shown in Example 7.4. In fact, as we learned in Chapter 6, much tonal music is homophonic, and, given the strong harmonic underpinning that is usually characteristic, it is not difficult to separate dissonant tones of figuration from consonant tones of figuration. Indeed, composers are careful to clarify the dissonant and consonant status of melodic pitches. For example, in Vivaldi's Sonata in C minor for oboe (Example 7.5), the Allegro's harmonic structure is made explicit by the underlying chordal accompaniment. Given that C-minor triads control mm. 1–2, we then know that the oboe's second pitch, F^4 (m. 1), is not a member of the chord. Since F descends from G and immediately returns to G, we understand it to be a dissonant neighbor note, just as we understand the D on beat 3 of m. 1 that fills the space of a third between two chordal members—$E\flat^5$ and C^5—to be a dissonant passing tone. However, these same pitches ($E\flat^5$ and C^5) in the oboe of m. 3 have become dissonant passing tones, given that the underlying harmony has changed to the dominant (G–B♮ –D–F) chord. Note that the remaining tones of figuration are all consonant skips within the C-minor harmony. Thus, if we identify underlying harmony (consonance), then we can distinguish between melodic tones that are members of chords and those that are embellishments (just as we did in our 2:1 contrapuntal studies, where, for example, passing tones connected two consonances).

EXAMPLE 7.5 Vivaldi, Sonata in C minor for Oboe and Basso Continuo, *Allegro*

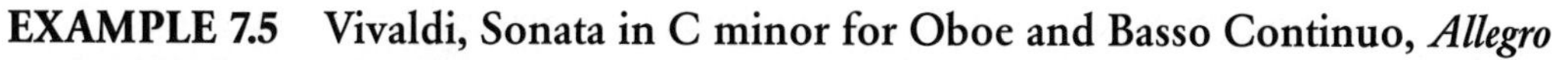

DVD 1
CH 7
TRACK 2

Harmonic underpinning is not limited to multivoiced textures. In fact, even solo instrumental music consisting of but a single line often unfolds within a strong, albeit implied, underlying harmonic context that still allows us to distinguish consonant and dissonant tones of figuration. For example, Bach's Presto in G minor (Example 7.6) opens with a cascading G-minor broken-chord figure that unfolds over five measures. In m. 6 a V_7 (D–F♯–A–C) chord succeeds the tonic, but only for two measures before G minor returns in m. 8. The acceleration of harmonic rhythm continues, with chord changes at least once per measure: m. 9 contains a C mm7 chord, m. 10 a B♭ major-minor, and m. 11 an A dm7 chord, all of which lead to the V_7 in m. 12 and back to tonic in m. 13. Notice that mm. 5, 7, and 12 contain pitches that are not members of the underlying harmony within that measure. For example, in m. 5, the C^5 and A^4 are not members of the G-minor triad but, rather, are passing tones; and in m. 7, $B♭^4$ is a passing tone within the D7 chord (the parenthetical $E♭^5$ and, in m. 12, the G^5, are tones of figuration that we'll discuss at a later point). In each case, these nonchord tones function identically to the dissonances encountered in our counterpoint studies.

EXAMPLE 7.6 Bach, Sonata for solo violin in G minor, *Presto*

The Importance of Contextual Analysis

We have learned that the tonic pitch and its accompanying triad are central to tonal music. But do composers always give priority to $\hat{1}$, $\hat{3}$, and $\hat{5}$? That is, can we always assume that the tonic triad primarily controls melody? And might we be able to study melody without having to consider the implied harmony or the supporting voices? Listen to an excerpt from one of Schubert's songs (Example 7.7).

EXAMPLE 7.7 Schubert, "Der Lindenbaum," from *Winterreise*, op. 89, no. 5, D. 911 (melody only)

DVD 1
CH 7
TRACK 4

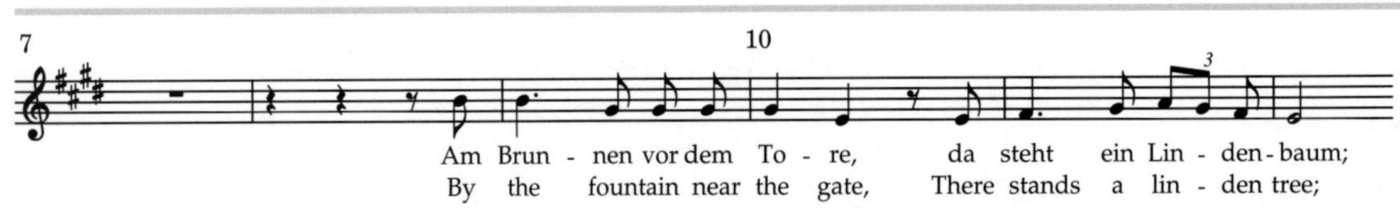

Because "Der Lindenbaum" ("The Linden Tree") is in E major, we might assume that E, G♯, and B are the primary structural tones and that the remaining pitches will be embellishments of the tonic triad. To be sure, the vocal line opens with an arpeggiation of the tonic. The following F♯^{4} (m. 11) appears to be a dissonant passing tone that leads to G♯^{4}, and A^4 would then be viewed as an upper neighbor to the stable G♯^{4}, as shown in Example 7.8.

EXAMPLE 7.8 Schubert, "Der Lindenbaum," from *Winterreise*, op. 89, no. 5, D. 911 (melody only)

Now listen to the excerpt again, this time with the accompaniment (Example 7.9). The underlying chords in mm. 9 and 10 are, indeed, all tonic. Because the harmony changes in m. 11 to a dominant harmony (B–D♯–F♯), however, the E^4 in the right-hand accompaniment is not a chord tone but merely delays D♯^{4}. Similarly, the F♯^{4} that begins m. 11 in the vocal line is not a dissonant passing tone at all. Rather, it is a member of the B-major triad and thus is consonant. The following G♯^{4}, which we originally said was related to the E-major triad, instead turns out to be a dissonant passing tone, since it is not a member of the underlying B-major harmony. Finally, the A^4 that we labeled as an upper neighbor to G♯^{4} turns out also to be a chord tone; it is the seventh of the dominant harmony, B–D♯–F♯–A.

EXAMPLE 7.9 Schubert, "Der Lindenbaum" (with accompaniment)

DVD 1
CH 7
TRACK 5

Our initial analysis of "Der Lindenbaum" was incorrect. Because we did not consider the underlying harmonic support or the rhythm, we had no standard to measure a pitch's function within a musical context. As a result, we confused a pitch's consonant or dissonant status.

EXERCISE INTERLUDE

DVD 2
CH 7
TRACK 1

ANALYSIS

7.1 Harmonic and Melodic Analysis (I)

Given are short excerpts of various homophonic textures. Complete the following tasks:

1. Circle each harmony, and label the root, the type of harmony (for triads: Maj, min, dim; for seventh chords: Mm, MM, mm, dm, dd), and the inversion, if any (for triads: $^{6}_{3}$, $^{6}_{4}$; for seventh chords $^{6}_{5}$, $^{4}_{3}$, $^{4}_{2}$).
2. Label each tone of figuration in the melody; use the following abbreviations: passing tone: P; neighbor tone: N; chordal leap: CL; arpeggiation: ARP.

A. Vivaldi, Sonata in C minor for oboe

B. Corelli, Sonata no. 11 in F for two flutes, after op. 5 Violin Sonata in E major, *Allegro*

DVD 2
CH 7
TRACK 2

7.2

This exercise is identical to Exercise 7.1, but this time you will add roman numerals.

Haydn, String Quartet in B♭ major, op. 50, no. 1 *Adagio non lento*

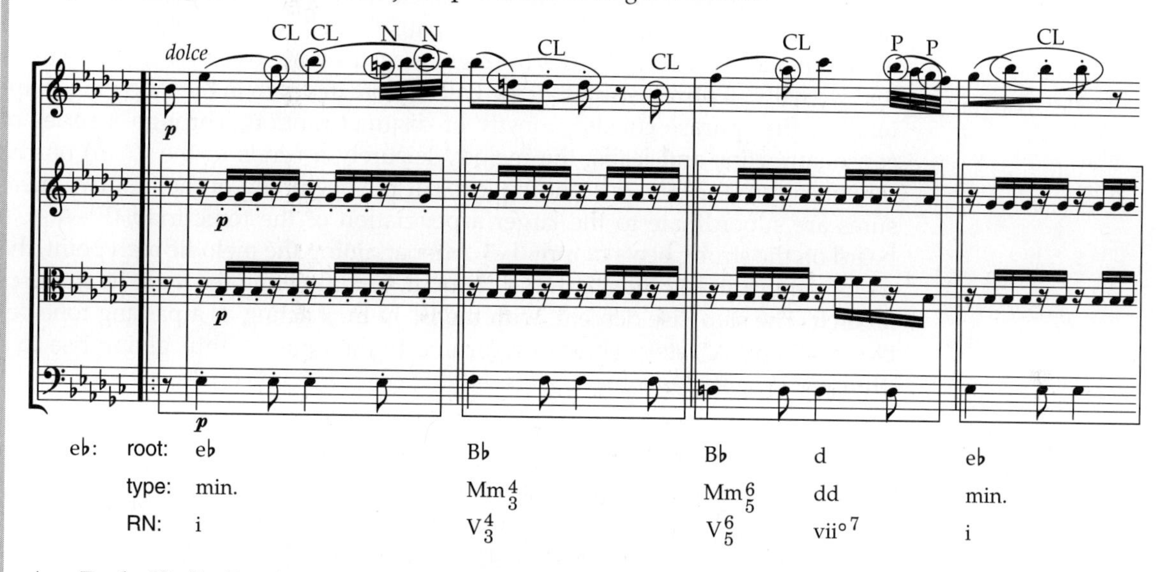

A. Bach, Violin Partita in D minor, BWV 1004, Giga, mm. 1–13 (you must first determine the harmonic rhythm and then label the harmonies)

B. Bach, Violin Partita in D minor, BWV 1004, Giga

C. Bach, Partita in D minor, BWV 1004, Giga

Sample Analyses

Let's develop our understanding of the hierarchy of melodic tones by exploring how they are used in two familiar melodies. Sing the opening of the well-known ballad "Clementine" (Example 7.10). The piece is in F major, and the first phrase begins on $\hat{1}$. The controlling harmonies for each measure are represented by bass pitch and roman numeral. The lengthy pause on G^4 in m. 4, which provides a natural place to breathe, divides the eight measures into two four-measure units that we will call **phrases** and that we will explore in depth in the following chapter. The first phrase consists mostly of disjunct motion. Through a series of consonant skips and leaps, the melody leisurely ascends to the C^5 ($\hat{5}$) on the downbeat of m. 3. The descending leaps at the beginning of the first two measures are subordinate to the larger arpeggiation of the tonic triad (F^4–A^4–C^5) heard on the strong beats of mm. 1–3. After attaining the melodic high point, the melody quickly descends to the G^4 ($\hat{2}$) in m. 4, completing the melodic shape of an arch. The stepwise descent, with the $B\flat^4$ in m. 3 acting as a passing tone between C^5 and A^4, stops short of returning to the tonic F^4, thus giving rise to a phrase ending that is somewhat unsettled because it ends on $\hat{2}$.

EXAMPLE 7.10 **"Clementine"**

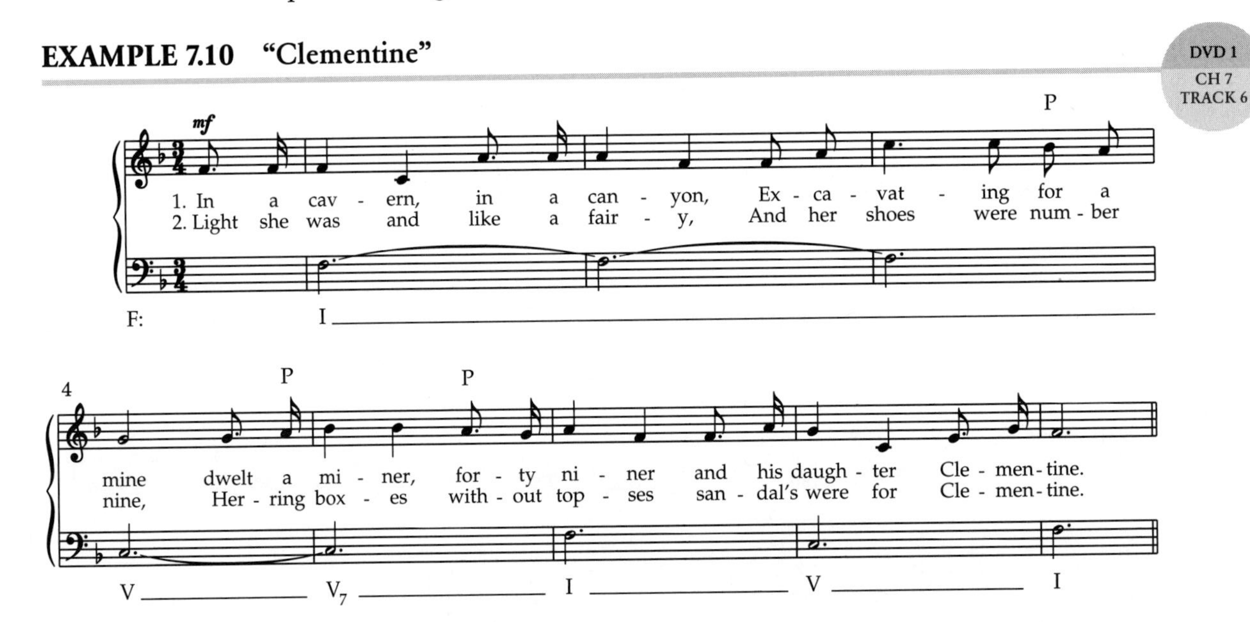

The second phrase begins as the G^4 on the third beat of m. 4 ascends by step to $B\flat^4$ via the passing tone A^4. Another passing A^4 traces the descent from $B\flat^4$ to G^4 in m. 5. The consonant skips of the first phrase return in mm. 6–7: first A^4 falls to F^4, then G^4 falls to C^4, C^4 skips up to E^4, and finally E^4 skips up to G^4. As in the opening phrase, the emphasized downbeats in mm. 5–8 reveal a melodic pattern—this time a stepwise descent from $B\flat^4$ (m. 5) to F^4 (m. 8). The F^4 at the end of the second phrase "resolves" the G^4 "left hanging" at the end of the first phrase. These larger motions are revealed in the structural analysis in Example 7.11.

The notation in Example 7.11 reflects the relative importance of pitches. The most important notes have stems and beams, and the less important notes consist only of noteheads. The slurs either connect less important notes to more important notes (as in a neighbor) or connect one member of a chord to another member.

EXAMPLE 7.11 Structural Analysis of "Clementine"

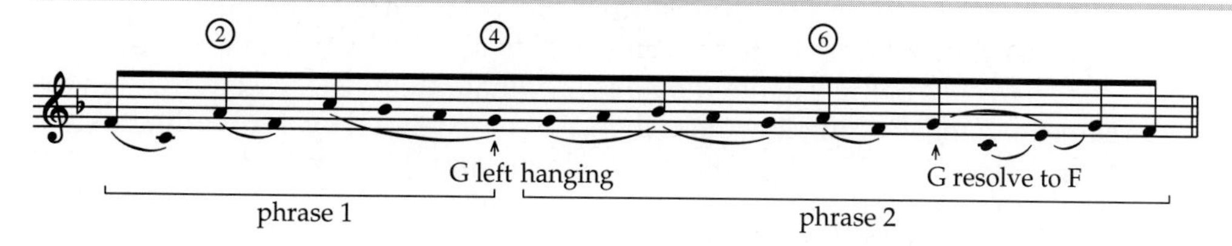

Having analyzed the long-range pitch structure of "Clementine," it may be illustrative to compare it to "God Save the King" (Example 7.12). This piece is also in the key of F major and has two phrases (once again, harmonic changes are represented in the bass); the first phrase contains six measures, the second phrase contains eight.

EXAMPLE 7.12 "God Save the King"

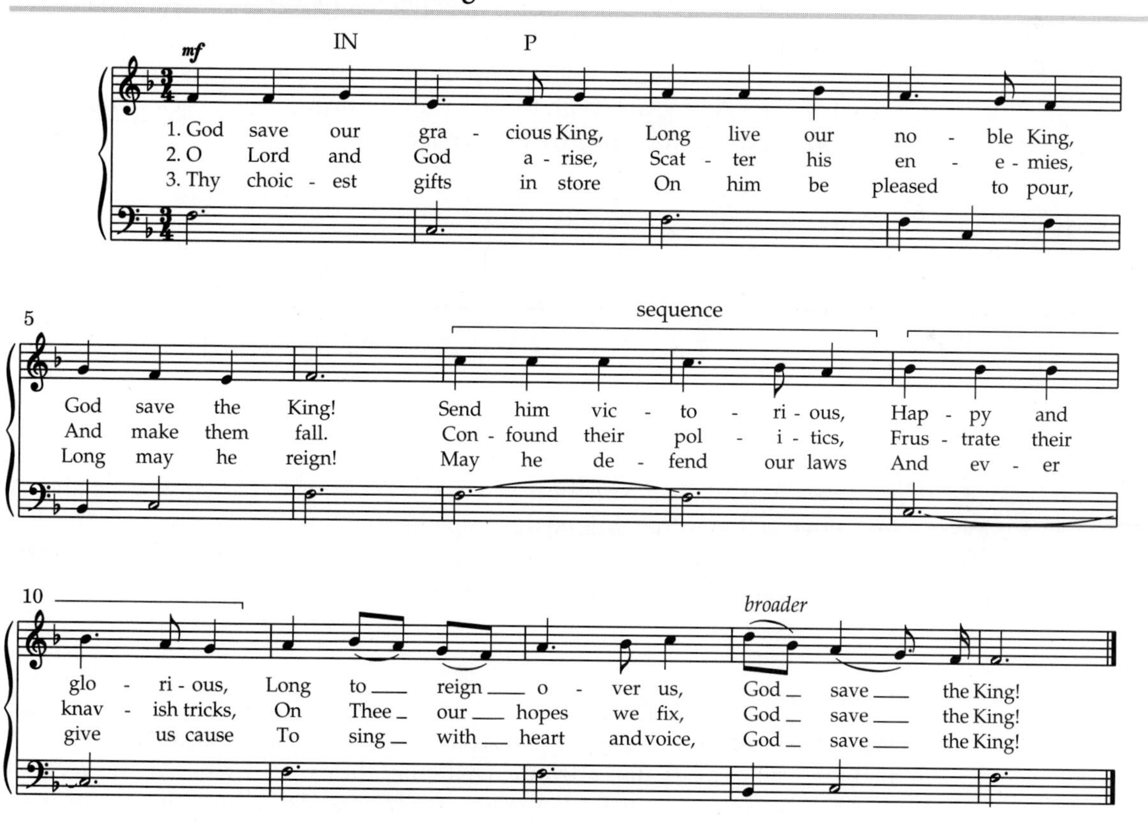

For the most part, the melody moves in stepwise motion, using passing and neighbor tones. However, the G^4 in m. 1 is neither a passing tone nor a typical neighbor. Since G^4 neighbors F^4 but does not return to F, it is called an **incomplete neighbor**. The E^4 in m. 2 leads through the passing tone F^4 to G^4. Since the G^4 sets the end of the first line of text ("King") (note the comma in the text) and leads to the A^4 that is the focal pitch in mm. 3 and 4, we may consider G to be a slower-moving passing tone, which connects the F of m. 1 with the A of m. 3. $B\flat^4$ is an upper neighbor to the A^4 in m. 3. There is a quick descent through G^4, which again functions as a passing tone and leads back to F^4. The phrase continues, and closure occurs in m. 6. Given that the more important stepwise descent from A^4 to F^4 occurs only in mm. 4–6, we can view the A^4 that begins m. 4 as being extended by a subordinate stepwise descent to F^4. In the same manner, we can view the G in m. 5 to be extended by a subordinate stepwise descent to E^4. Thus, the same slowly unfolding passing motion that opens the song on F^4–G^4–A^4 (mm. 1–3) is mirrored at the close of the first phrase with A^4–G^4–F^4 (mm. 4–6).

The second phrase begins on C^5 ($\hat{5}$) in m. 7. The passing tone $B\flat^4$ connects C^5 to A^4 in m. 8, and mm. 9 and 10 imitate mm. 7 and 8 by repeating the material down the interval of a second. This immediate restatement of a musical idea on different scale degrees is called **sequence**. The A^4 returns to C^5 in mm. 11 and 12, and the melody ends with a consonant skip from D^5 to $B\flat^4$, followed by a stepwise line that descends from A^4 through G^4 to F^4.

Once again, let's step back and collect our observations (refer to Example 7.13). The first phrase of the melody (mm. 1–6) begins on F ($\hat{1}$), ascends to A ($\hat{3}$, m. 3), and returns to $\hat{1}$. The second part of the song descends from C ($\hat{5}$) to F ($\hat{1}$).

If we compare "Clementine" and "God Save the King," we see that both tunes contain two phrases. More important, both first phrases arpeggiate the tonic triad, F^4–A^4–C^5, and both second phrases bring the C^5 back to its resting place on $\hat{1}$ through long stepwise descents.

EXAMPLE 7.13 Structural Analysis of "God Save the King"

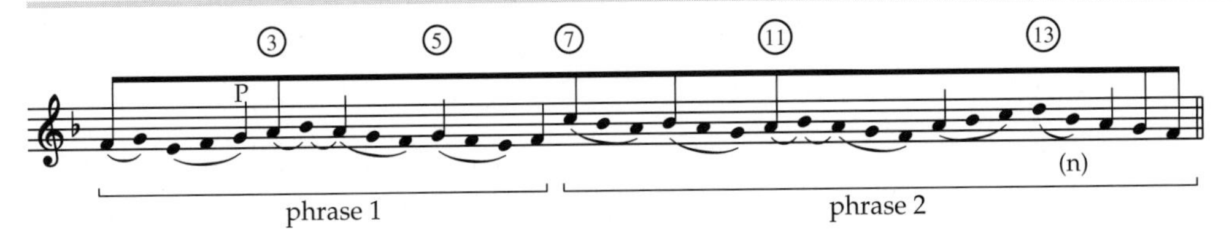

WORKBOOK
7.1–7.2

These two analyses function as a preview of the sort of contextual and interpretive analysis that will be developed in the text. Our analyses in this text will always go deeper than simply labeling surface events, for it is these deeper relationships that actually control the surface events.

Melodic Fluency

We have seen throughout our study of melody and counterpoint that melodies share particular attributes, whether they were written in the year 800 or 1990. For example, melodies often rise from a stable initiating point (usually $\hat{1}$) that is supported by the tonic triad. The melody eventually ascends to a climax that is followed by a descent that leads to a point of repose. Melodies move primarily by step, and any large leaps are balanced by stepwise changes of direction. One such melody is heard in Example 7.14, where a rapid ascent to $\hat{5}$ is followed by a long neighbor note on $\hat{6}$ that returns to $\hat{5}$. The following leisurely stepwise descent convincingly closes on $\hat{1}$.

EXAMPLE 7.14 Smetana, "Moldau," from *My Country*, mm. 40–46

DVD 1
CH 7
TRACK 7

We discovered that a given melody (e.g., a cantus firmus) or harmony provides a standard against which we can measure dissonance and consonance. Such a foundation allows us to **embellish** the given melody with consonant and dissonant pitches that include chordal skips and leaps, passing tones (dissonant and consonant), neighbor tones (complete, incomplete, and double), and arpeggiations. Conversely, by pruning away, or **reducing**, these embellishing pitches we discover structural lines and that the resulting nonadjacent stepwise pitches provide the underlying skeleton of the piece. We also learned that analysis reveals similar underlying melodic trajectories in works with very different musical surfaces, such as "Clementine" and "God Save the King." We invoked a single criterion to support our findings: that a pitch's function depends entirely on the context in which it appears. That is, all pitches are not created equal, and subordinate pitches embellish more important pitches.

Step motions occurring below the embellished surface of a melody are central to tonal music. Indeed, they are reflections of a larger human preoccupation to elaborate and dramatize forms of discourse and communication. For example, nothing particularly interesting is learned when someone is described as balding and middle aged. However, when these generic attributes are augmented by the mention of prominent scars and tattoos, a curious gait, and that third thumb, the listener's interest is certainly piqued. The same desire to embellish music is age old, as we can see from the highly decorated portions of thousand-year-old chant to classical theme and variations, to jazz and contemporary commercial music.

Further, all humans possess the basic desire to make sense of the myriad stimuli presented to them in their day-to-day activities and therefore subconsciously to group these stimuli into meaningful shapes. In order to accomplish this, we must ignore superfluous and confusing stimuli, give priority to the most logical, clear, and useful bits of information, and fill in incomplete yet necessary pieces, all in order to create an entity that makes the most sense. The rise of Gestalt psychology in the 1920s and its flowering in the second half of the twentieth century is predicated on the specific ways humans make sense of a world of nonstop stimuli. Composers and performers instinctively invoke these rules, which include various types of balance, expectation, and realization (e.g., the buildup toward a climax and the subsequent release) the thwarting of expectations, surprise, ambiguity, etc. We have already invoked several of these Gestalt principles in our discussion of musical accent in Chapter 2, and we now encounter a few additional types in the following discussion of below-the-surface step motions.

Melodic fluency refers to underlying scalar patterns that support the infinite variety of melodic embellishments that lie on the music's surface. Most likely you intuitively sense these lines, and you may use them to guide your interpretations of phrases; you might even choose to project them in performance. Indeed, composers guide our ears by aurally "marking" these underlying melodic lines in a variety of ways. Recall from Chapter 2 that we equated marking with "accent" and that there are many ways to accent a musical event, including duration, metric placement, dynamics, articulation, harmonic and contour changes, etc. Powerful goal-oriented motions arise when accented musical events are coordinated with hierarchical pitch structures (such as the tonic triad).

As you listen to Example 7.15, ask yourself whether or not the melody's register and general contour are static, or whether there is an ascent or descent over the course of the excerpt. The melody begins on B, and you probably noticed that it slowly descends during the phrase to close a fifth lower on E. That you heard this descent is noteworthy, given that many of the pitch-to-pitch melodic gestures actually *ascend* (e.g., the piece opens with a leap up to E (m. 3), and ascending gestures occur in mm. 3, 5, and 7). By tracing the accented pitches in this phrase, we understand why you heard the underlying descent (see Example 7.15B): B, which holds forth in mm. 1–2 falls first to A and then to G♯ (m. 4). G♯, like the preceding B, is a member of the tonic triad that is sustained in m. 5. G♯ then falls to F♯ (which is extended in mm. 6–7) and on to E. Each of these pitches is accented in specific ways: B by duration and metric placement, and A by metric placement and the fact that as $\hat{4}$ it is inherently predisposed to function as a passing tone between the more stable $\hat{5}$ and $\hat{3}$. Further, A is counterpointed by the unstable leading tone, D♯, which creates a dissonant diminished fifth: D♯ fulfills its responsibility to ascend to E as A in turn falls to G♯. The following G♯, F♯, and E are either metrically accented, durationally accented, or both.

EXAMPLE 7.15

DVD 1 CH 7 TRACK 8

A. Donizetti, Lucrezia Borgia, act 1, no. 3

B. Donizetti, *Lucrezia Borgia*, act 1, no. 3 (reduction)

Let's briefly look at the embellishments Donizetti uses to elaborate the fifth descent. A chordal leap of a fourth in m. 1 (from B to E) is filled in as the fourth retraces itself by stepwise motion. We have learned that changing direction after a leap is an important means of creating melodic balance. The specific procedure of filling in a leap is called **gap-fill**, another Gestalt law that is predicated on the listener's expectation that a melodic leap will eventually be filled in by stepwise motion in the opposite direction. Notice that the change of harmony to V_7 (B–D♯–F♯–A) in m. 2 renders the melodic D♯ and B chord tones, with C♯ a weak-beat passing dissonance. In fact, this falling passing motion characterizes mm. 4 and 6.

We have, of course, encountered gap-fill in our previous counterpoint studies. But it is a crucial component of successful composition, as we can see in the Chopin excerpts in Example 7.16A–D, the openings of several of Chopin's nocturnes, each of which begins with a leap that opens a musical space that is immediately filled in—and in contrary motion to the leap.

EXAMPLE 7.16 Chopin Nocturnes

DVD 1
CH 7
TRACK 9

A. in F major, op. 15, no. 1

B. in F minor, op. 55 no. 1

C. in E minor, op. posth. 72, no. 1

D. in G minor, op. 15, no. 3

Composers, of course, also create rising structural lines. Placed in the first half of phrases, such lines produce a subtle tension that is balanced and discharged by the later cadential falling. See Example 7.17. The phrase divides into two two-measure units. The second unit is a transposition (up a step) of the first. Further, the rising and falling passing figures that pervade each measure reflect the gradual rise in the line from E to G♯: E is embellished by the ascending third, while F♯ in m. 2 is embellished by the falling third (A–G♯–F♯). In the modified transposition in mm. 3–4, where the F♯ from m. 2 is picked up in m. 3, the line closes on G♯. Notice that these measure-to-measure thirds reflect the larger ascending third, E–F♯–G♯, that spans the entire excerpt. Thus, a slow structural ascent from E to G♯ in the first phrase (mm. 1–4) is embellished by various thirds (E–G♯, F♯–A, B–G♯), with a single neighbor motion (B–C♯–B) in m. 4 embellishing the high point of the phrase.

EXAMPLE 7.17 **Beethoven, Piano Trio, in E♭ major op. 1, no. 2, *Largo, con espressione***

DVD 1 CH 7 TRACK 10

The descending stepwise contour of the second phrase (mm. 4–9) nicely balances the ascending stepwise contour of the first phrase: The downbeat of m. 5 restates the first phrase's highest pitch, C♯, from which the descent unfolds from C♯ back to the passage's opening pitch, E.

Many phrases exhibit archlike contours, in which both ascending and descending subsurface lines occur. In Example 7.18A, each member of the stepwise ascending fourth line from C to F appears on the accented downbeat. The arrival on F is followed by an equally clear descent in the second half of the excerpt. Notice also that within the web of pitches in each measure (composed mainly of upper and lower neighbors) one hears miniature ascending thirds that mimic the larger passing motion in the line (for example, in m.1: **C** B **D** C F **E**). Arches that ascend and then descend are not the only possible types; composers often employ a descent followed by ascent, as shown in Example 7.18B. Notice that Chopin parallels the melodic contour in the bass.

EXAMPLE 7.18

DVD 1 CH 7 TRACK 11

A. Mozart, Symphony no. 41, in C major, "Jupiter" K. 551, *Andante cantabile*

B. Chopin, Etude in A♭, op. posth.

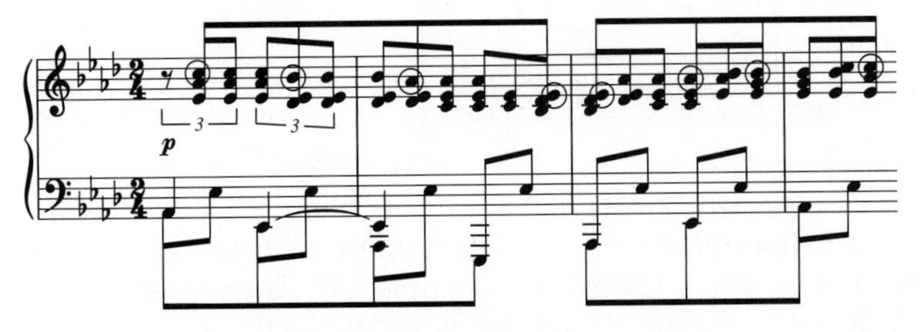

Finally, single-line melodies alone often present explicit or strongly implied harmonic underpinnings, as we discovered at the end of Chapter 6. As might be expected, such works also depend on the concept of melodic fluency. See Example 7.19. The first step in grappling with this excerpt is to determine the underlying harmonies. It is also helpful to find patterns in the speed of harmonic change (the *harmonic rhythm*), since composers will usually continue an established pattern, whether it be the texture, the mood, or the rate of harmonic change, yet another Gestalt principle, referred to as **good continuation**. This knowledge—combined with the fact that changes in harmony usually coincide with metric accents—provides a powerful standard of measurement that guides analysis.

EXAMPLE 7.19 Bach, Sonata no. 3 for Solo Violin in C major, BWV 1005 *Allemande*

Most likely you heard two harmonic changes in each measure. The incomplete first measure establishes the two-beat harmonic rhythm. Example 7.20 presents a harmonic verticalization of the chords, from which we can see the steadily rising chromatic line that begins on C (C–C♯–D–D♯–E) and eventually arrives on F (m. 47). Notice that given the pattern of rising half steps, we expect it to continue from the E^5 in m. 47, even though E is sustained for one and a half measures. This expectation arises because E is a member of the E-major, A-minor, and A-major harmonies that control the second half of m. 46 and all of m. 47. That the pattern is not continued creates a dramatic moment, and listeners are rewarded for their patience: F arrives over the D-minor harmony. Note that we are able to hear the retention of the previous E and its ascent to F in spite of 25 intervening pitches, given that we expect the previously established pattern to continue. The attentive performer will most likely exploit such a moment in performance.

EXAMPLE 7.20

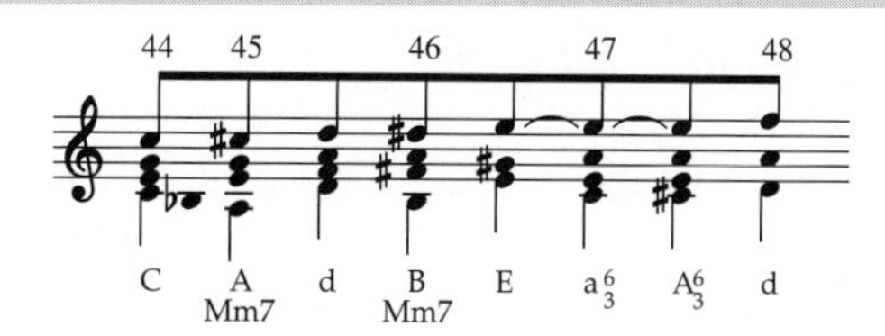

Another method that composers use to delay ascending and descending lines is momentarily to change a line's direction, which postpones and even thwarts what listeners assume will happen. The longer the postponement, the more dramatic its effect. This process, called **expectation/fulfillment** in Gestalt psychology, is central to the unfolding of a musical work. Listen to Example 7.21. The clear stepwise fifth descent from A to D accelerates, so four of the five pitches of the descent occur in mm. 3–4. The descent is postponed, however, by the upper-neighbor A–B♭–A that follows the initial descending arpeggiation in m. 1. Notice that the upper-neighbor B♭ is consonant, given that it is supported by the tenth, G.

EXAMPLE 7.21 Corelli, Sarabande in D minor from Sonata no. 7, op. 5

DVD 1
CH 7
TRACK 13

Our final example traces a third descent and provides a notational means to illustrate such descents. Haydn presents a two-measure tune that is sequentially repeated down a second in mm. 3–4. The D^5 from m. 1 moves via passing tone E$\flat^5$ to F^5 and via arpeggiation to B$\flat^4$ in m. 2, generating a B♭ triad. Haydn balances the ascending motion in m. 1 with the descent in m. 2.

This can be seen at X in Example 7.23. When the idea is repeated in m. 3, D^5 is the passing tone that links C^5 and E$\flat^5$. The stepwise-third descent that occurs over the four measures from D^5 through C^5 to B$\flat^4$ can be seen at Y in Example 7.23.

EXAMPLE 7.22 Haydn, String Quartet in B♭, op. 33, no. 4, *Allegretto*

DVD 1
CH 7
TRACK 14

EXAMPLE 7.23 Structural Analysis of Haydn, *Allegretto*

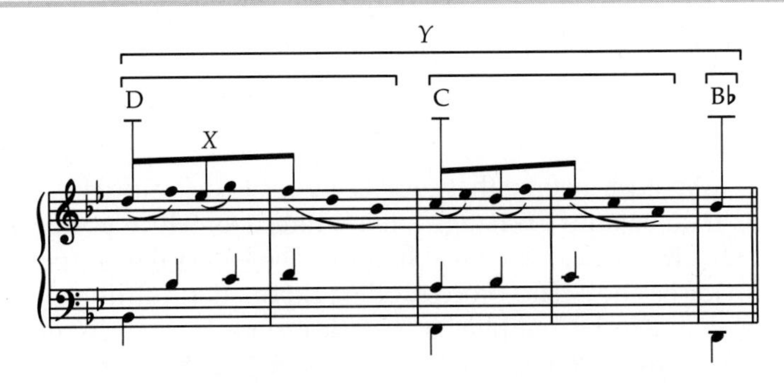

Analysis is not a casual, prescriptive endeavor. It must reflect what actually takes place in the music and what you, the analyst, bring to that music in terms of your own instincts. We must consider an entire musical texture, because harmony provides a foundation that allows us to understand what is stable and what is unstable in the melody.

EXERCISE INTERLUDE

ANALYSIS

DVD 2
CH 7
TRACK 3

7.3 Melodic Fluency, Harmony, and Tones of Figuration

The florid soprano melody of each of the following examples depends on slower-moving stepwise lines that emerge when we listen to and study the examples. Complete the following tasks.

1. Listen to each example, and circle and stem each note of the structural stepwise line; then beam them together.
2. Identify harmonies using roman numerals for those bass notes with horizontal lines beneath them.
3. Label the type of tone of figuration for each soprano pitch beneath an arrow.

A. Haydn, String Quartet in E♭ major, op. 50, no. 3, *Allegro con brio*

B. Jean Philippe Rameau, Rondino

C. Beethoven, Piano Concerto no. 1 in C major, op. 15, *Allegro con brio*

COMPOSITION AND PERFORMANCE

7.4 Embellishment

The first-species counterpoints given here are composed of slow-moving, primarily stepwise melodies, along with their implied harmonies (in parentheses). You are to add figurations to the upper voice to create a florid melody that embellishes the given underlying, melodically fluent line. You may add the following tones of figuration: passing tones, neighbors (both upper and lower), and chordal skips and leaps. You may also combine two or more of these tones of figuration. An example and solution are also presented.

Given is a 1:1 counterpoint in D minor, with implied chords in parentheses. You are to do the following:

1. a. If the implied missing chordal members are given (in parentheses, as in the sample solution), then analyze each chord with roman numerals (so that you will have a clear idea of the types of tones of figuration you can add and how they will function in the given harmonic environment.)
   b. If the roman numerals are given (below the bass staff), then notate the missing pitch (or pitches) of the chord above the given bass pitch in the bass clef so that you can see all of the chordal members, and enclose within parentheses (as in the sample solution).
2. Add tones of figuration. The sample shows how one can add specific types of figuration to each measure (e.g., m. 1 = passing tones, m. 2 = a combination of neighbor tones and chordal leaps, etc.). Here are guidelines for adding tones of figuration.
   a. Use a primary rhythmic value in your solution along with those values that are at the next-faster and -slower levels. For example, the eighth note is the basic rhythmic value in the given solution, along with quarter and sixteenth values (the quarter note is the next-longer value and the sixteenth note is the next-shorter value).

WORKBOOK 7.3–7.5

b. Create a logical and unified embellished melody by using only two or three rhythmic and melodic ideas. For example, the sample solution uses primarily eighth notes and the melodic ideas are mostly passing tones and chordal skips that fill in the interval of the third.

c. Don't forget the contrapuntal rules and guidelines you learned in Chapter 4. These include melodic principles (e.g., no dissonant leaps) and the way the voices combine (e.g., parallels).

TERMS AND CONCEPTS

- arpeggiations
- chordal leaps (consonant leaps)
- embellishment vs. reduction
- Gestalt concepts: expectation/fulfillment, gap-fill, good continuation
- hierarchy
  - melodic fluency
- neighbor tone (auxiliary tone or neighbor)
  - upper neighbor, lower neighbor
  - incomplete neighbor, complete neighbor
  - consonant neighbor, dissonant neighbor
- nonchord tones
- passing tones
- phrase
- resolution
- tones of figuration
- transposition

CHAPTER 8

Tonic and Dominant as Tonal Pillars and Introduction to Voice Leading

Tonic and dominant chords provide the harmonic foundation of tonal music. By themselves they can define a key. When used in conjunction with other chords, these two pillars create a sense of arrival and departure. Compositions and the phrases they comprise generally begin with the tonic chord and progress through nontonic chords. Eventually the harmonies lead to the dominant and then on to the concluding tonic. The tonic that is stated at the opening of a phrase or piece need not progress to any particular chord. The dominant, however, inevitably leads back to the tonic.

In the V chord, melodic and harmonic functions work together to create a powerful expectation of the tonic's return (see Example 8.1). The dominant's tendency to resolve to tonic stems from the relationship between its chordal members and those of the tonic. Recall from Chapter 7 that the V harmony comprises active scale degrees, called *tendency tones*, that are less stable than those of the tonic triad. $\hat{7}$ and $\hat{2}$ are melodic tendency tones: $\hat{7}$ wants to ascend to $\hat{1}$, and $\hat{2}$ can move to either $\hat{1}$ or $\hat{3}$. Although $\hat{5}$ is stable as a member of the tonic harmony, it is unstable as the root of the dominant harmony and has a tendency to return to $\hat{1}$. The V_7 chord, which we will encounter in Chapter 9, contains a fourth tone, $\hat{4}$, which forms the dissonant seventh of the chord. Although the progression I–V–I is simple, it is the basis for much great and imaginative music. We will listen to some excerpts from the literature that rely exclusively on the tonic and dominant. Note the different psychological effects that are created when tonic and dominant chords are used in isolation.

EXAMPLE 8.1 The V Chord: Harmonic and Melodic Functions

An E♭-major triad slowly emerges out of the sustained E♭ at the beginning of Wagner's *Das Rheingold* (Example 8.2). The chordal fifth is added in m. 5, and the chordal third does not enter until m. 18. This introduction (less than one-tenth of which is reproduced in Example 8.2) contains a single sonority: the tonic triad of E♭ major. Note that the single stable sonority does not create the expectation that it needs to move on to another harmony, in spite of the growth of the triad through register and textural changes; forward motion is achieved instead by rhythmic means.

EXAMPLE 8.2 Wagner, *Das Rheingold*, Prelude

Now listen to Example 8.3, the climactic passage from the last movement of Beethoven's *Eroica* Symphony. Beginning with the arrival of the B♭-major triad in m. 328, dominant harmony unfolds over the remainder of the excerpt. Compared with Example 8.2, this passage sounds much less stable, because the dominant gives rise to a powerful expectation to resolve to tonic harmony, which occurs after the fermata. Further destabilizing the passage is the addition of the dissonant minor seventh (A♭), heard first in m. 330 but then incessantly from m. 336 to m. 348, which turns the dominant triad into a dominant seventh chord and which creates an even more powerful impulse to resolve.

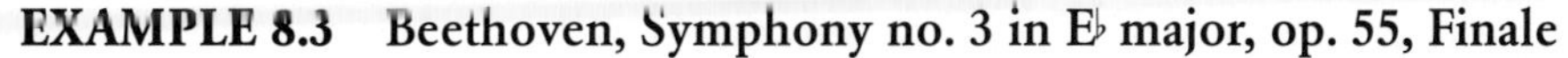

EXAMPLE 8.3 Beethoven, Symphony no. 3 in E♭ major, op. 55, Finale

Of course, lengthy passages of a single harmony are not the norm in tonal music. The following examples juxtapose the two harmonic forces of tonic and dominant. The forceful opening of the last movement of Beethoven's Fifth Symphony (Example 8.4) is created by the simple alternation of tonic and dominant harmonies. As indicated in the example, tonic harmony supports the opening arpeggiation ($\hat{1}$–$\hat{3}$–$\hat{5}$ in mm. 1–2) in the melody, after which I and V_7 alternate as the melody descends through the scale back to $\hat{1}$ and tonic harmony (mm. 2–4) and I–V–I supports a scalar ascent to $\hat{3}$ (mm. 4–6). Notice further how the changing harmonic rhythm is correlated with the rhythm of the melody and the use of V_7 chords (as opposed to V triads) to create a sense of both breadth and vigor. That is, after the broad statement of the opening tonic, Beethoven changes chords every quarter note from the end of m. 2 to the beginning of m. 4 and uses the less stable V_7 chord to propel the music forward. Beginning in m. 4, both melody and harmonic rhythm broaden again, and Beethoven's choice of the dominant *triad* in m. 5 underscores the grand ascent to $\hat{3}$ over the tonic.

EXAMPLE 8.4 Beethoven, Symphony no. 5 in C minor, op. 67

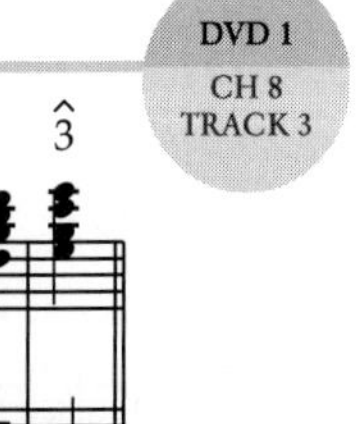

Although the tonic is the ultimate goal of all tonal motions, small yet important arrivals often occur on the dominant, heightening musical drama and propelling the music forward. Listen to the opening of Beethoven's Sixth Symphony (Example 8.5). The four-measure phrase leads from the tonic to the dominant, creating the effect of a musical question that needs an answer.

EXAMPLE 8.5 Beethoven, Symphony no. 6, "Pastorale," in F major, op. 68, *Allegro ma non troppo*

DVD 1
CH 8
TRACK 4

We have seen such stops before, both melodically and contrapuntally, and have identified them as *cadences*. Let's add a final component to the mix, harmony, so that we can expand our knowledge of this most important musical event.

The Cadence

A cadence is a point of arrival that usually occurs at the end of a phrase. We first encountered cadences in our exploration of two-voice counterpoint. In the previous examples in the present chapter we discovered that a sense of closure occurs, regardless of whether or not an example ends on I or V. This is because the forward motion of the music often stops on these chords, given the changes in the rhythm and the completion of larger metrical patterns. Further, specific soprano scale degrees are coordinated with these harmonic arrivals such that the entire musical fabric of melody, harmony, counterpoint, rhythm, and meter participates in this phrase-defining moment.

Mozart's Rondo contains examples of the two structural cadences used in tonal music (see Example 8.6). It can be divided into two parallel four-measure phrases. The reason we divide this excerpt's phrases into four-measure spans rather than two-measure spans is that the two-measure spans do not give the impression of a tonal motion in which two or more harmonies succeed one another and lead to a tonal goal. Harmonic as well as melodic motion is necessary to create a phrase. The first phrase closes on the dominant of C major (m. 4), and the second phrase closes on the tonic (m. 8). The melody begins on the downbeat $\hat{5}$, arpeggiates a tonic triad (G^5–E^5–C^5), and arrives in m. 4 on the correspondingly accented $\hat{2}$. At this point, another shorter arpeggiation unfolds, this time on the dominant (D^5–B^4–G^4). The opening idea on I returns in m. 5. When the tonic occurs in m. 8, the soprano strengthens the arrival by firmly stating $\hat{1}$. Notice how changes in the harmonic rhythm help articulate each phrase. In the first phrase, after three measures of tonic harmony, the dominant arrives in m. 4, supporting the arpeggiated D^4–B^3–G^3 in the melody. Leading to the final cadence, the harmonic rhythm speeds up even more noticeably as the chords change every half note beginning in m. 7.

EXAMPLE 8.6 Mozart, Rondo in C major, K. 144

DVD 1
CH 8
TRACK 5

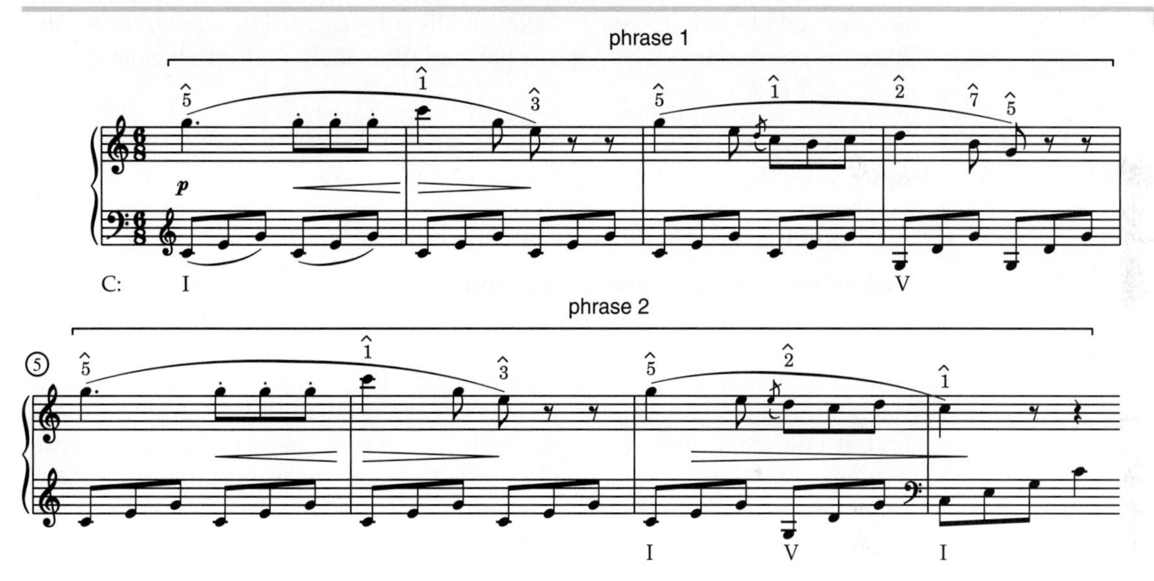

Mozart's example illustrates the two main types of cadences in tonal music. Those that close V–I (dominant to tonic in root position) are called **authentic cadences**, or full cadences, and are labeled AC. Those that close on a root-position dominant are called **half cadences** and are labeled HC.

EXAMPLE 8.7 Perfect and Imperfect Authentic Cadences; Half Cadences

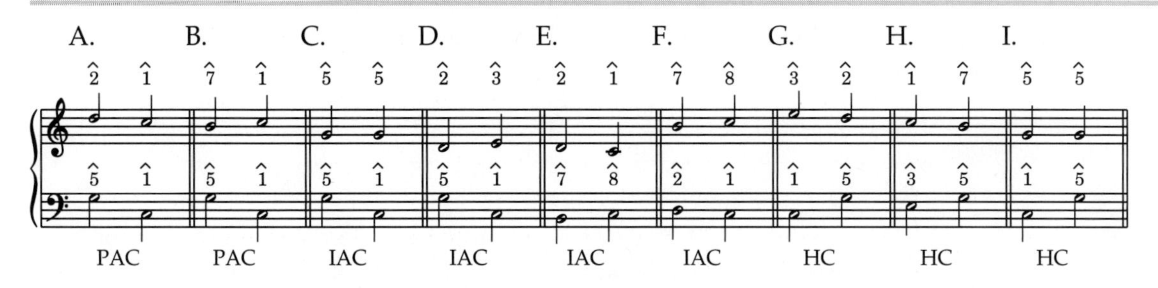

Authentic cadences are graded in strength based on the outer voices. If the soprano moves $\hat{2}$–$\hat{1}$ or $\hat{7}$–$\hat{8}$ while the bass moves $\hat{5}$–$\hat{1}$, the cadence is called a **perfect authentic cadence** and is labeled PAC (see Example 8.7A–B). If the soprano closes on $\hat{5}$ or $\hat{3}$, it is part of an **imperfect authentic cadence** and is labeled IAC (see Example 8.7C–D). Any bass motion other than $\hat{5}$–$\hat{1}$ (such as $\hat{7}$–$\hat{8}$ or $\hat{2}$–$\hat{1}$) also creates a special type of IAC called a **contrapuntal cadence**. Contrapuntal cadences, so named because of their relation to the cadences we used in our contrapuntal studies, are harmonically weaker than the more common leaping bass motions of $\hat{5}$ to $\hat{1}$ (see Example 8.7E–F). In contrast, no formal terms are in use to distinguish different types of half cadence, although the root-position dominant usually supports $\hat{2}$ in the soprano. Example 8.7G–I shows common HCs.

In minor, two common chromatic alterations occur. First, the dominant will be a major triad, so $\hat{7}$ must be raised to create a leading tone. Second, the tonic harmony that closes a piece will sometimes contain a raised third to form a major triad. This idiom is called a **Picardy third;** late-Renaissance and Baroque composers viewed it as a particularly satisfying form of closure.

EXERCISE INTERLUDE

PERFORMING

8.1 Singing and Playing on Your Instrument

Beginning with this chapter and continuing throughout the rest of the text, each Exercise Interlude will include one or more groups of exercises that summarize newly presented topics within the chapter. These arpeggiations of common harmonic patterns should both be sung, using either solfège or scale degree numbers (depending on which system is employed at your school) and, if you are a single-line instrumentalist (e.g., brass, woodwind, or string player), played and transposed to keys that contain up to three sharps and three flats in their signatures. Unless otherwise indicated, each should be performed as written in the major mode and in the parallel minor mode. In minor, raise $\hat{7}$ to create a leading tone.

DVD 2
CH 8
TRACK 1

ANALYSIS

8.2

The following excerpts employ only tonic and dominant triads in root position. Listen to each example; then locate and label the cadence that closes each excerpt. Some examples are longer than others and may contain multiple cadences that you must label. Provide roman numerals for the remaining chords, and label passing and neighbor tones in the soprano. Finally, choose two contrasting excerpts and write a paragraph that describes their differences, focusing on harmonic rhythm, textural and accompanimental patterns, melodic tones of figuration, or underlying two-voice counterpoint.

A.

B.

C. Vivaldi, Violin Sonata in F major, Ryom 176

D. Clara Schumann, "Les Ballet des Revenants," from *Quatre pieces caracteristique*, op. 5

Although the melody occurs in the left hand, the harmony should be clear from the metrically accented notes and the chords in the right hand.

E. Beethoven, Violin Sonata in G major, op. 30, no. 3, *Allegro assai*

The sixteenth-note figuration is governed by the implied harmony that is represented by the metrically accented notes (i.e., those notes that occur every half measure).

DVD 2
CH 8
TRACK 2

LISTENING

8.3 Cadence and Meter Identification

Examples A–D are in homophonic texture. Examples E–G are from Haydn's "Sun" Quartets. Determine a possible meter, and label the final cadence of each excerpt. Remember that you must listen to the outer-voice counterpoint to determine the type of cadence. Your choices are perfect authentic cadence (PAC), imperfect authentic cadence, (IAC), contrapuntal cadence (CC), and half cadence (HC).

A. _______ _______

B. _______ _______

C. _______ _______

D. _______ _______

E. _______ _______

F. _______ _______

G. _______ _______

DVD 2
CH 8
TRACK 3

8.4 Progressions from the Literature

The following excerpts employ tonic and dominant harmonies. The harmonic rhythm is one chord per measure (except as noted in exercise E). Write the correct roman numeral for each measure. Label cadences.

A. Quantz, Trio Sonata in G major for Oboe and Bassoon, *Adagio*

Note: Consider only the downbeat harmonies of each measure, which are in root position; ignore the bass line's chordal leaps on beat 2, which seem to create inversions.

m. 1 2 3 4
3/4 ____ ____ ____ ____

B. Corelli, Concerto Grosso in D major, op. 6, no. 1, *Allegro*

m. 1 2 3 4
3/4 ____ ____ ____ ____

C. Handel, Concerto Grosso in G minor, op. 6, no. 6, *Largo*

m. 1 2 3
3/4 ____ ____ ____

D. Corelli, Sonata, op. 1, no. 9, *Allegro*

m. 1 2 3 4 5 6 7 8
3/4 ____ ____ ____ ____ ____ ____ ____ ____

WORKBOOK
8.1–8.2

E. Schubert, "Waltz," from *38 Waltzes, Ländler, and Ecossaises*, D. 145

m. 1 2 3 4
3/4 - - - ____ - - - ____

Introduction to Voice Leading

Now that you are aware of how the tonic and the dominant are used in tonal music, wouldn't you like to create your own music? Granted, you have at your disposal only these two harmonies. But they are crucial ones, and you will have plenty of opportunities to incorporate the remaining harmonies once they too are introduced. You needn't worry that you may not be a composer, because our goal will be to write smooth and logical homophonic progressions and not to replicate a particular style of music, such as that of Bach or Haydn. Such style composition is not the focus of this book; it requires many years to learn. And we will discover that when we strip away the surface of compositions written in various styles throughout the common-practice period, a small core of tonal principles occurs over and over. These principles are not limited to so-called "serious" or "art" music but extend to popular and commercial music heard today.

The idea of an underlying harmonic foundation includes both the permissible chords (harmonic vocabulary) and the order in which chords appear (harmonic progression). The connection between chords must be smooth; therefore, we will focus on how members of one chord connect to members of the following chord. **Voice leading** refers to the way individual voices move. Voice-leading rules are derived from the principles that we learned in Chapter 4 concerning two-voice counterpoint.

Texture and Register

Tonal music of the common-practice era was generally conceived in four voices. This is not to say that every piece of tonal music literally uses four voices at every possible moment, although some do. Rather, it means that a four-voice framework underlies compositions that may have many more than four voices, such as works for large forces, including the symphony and the concerto, or those that may have fewer than four voices, such as solos, duets, and trios in which the framework is implicit (though no less audible). The four-voice texture represents a happy medium because it nicely accommodates the triads and seventh chords of which tonal harmony is made.

Because we do not all have the same vocal range, singing is divided into four voices, which are ordered from highest to lowest: soprano, alto, tenor, and bass (SATB). Composers notate these four voices in one of three ways: In **open score** (or **full score**), each voice appears on its own staff, and clefs specific to each voice are used (Example 8.8A). A **short score** is notated on two staves, the women's voices (SA) in the treble and the men's voices (TB) in the bass. The soprano and tenor pitches always have upward stems; the alto and bass always have downward stems (Example 8.8B). We refer to open score and short score as **chorale style**. The third method of notation is **keyboard style**, which uses bass and treble staves but places soprano, alto, and tenor in the treble voice and the bass alone in the bass clef (Example 8.8C). The three upper voices will fit within an octave in order to fit comfortably in the right hand. In keyboard style, the soprano stems point up, alto and tenor stems point down; the bass voice follows general stem-direction rules of melody writing. In our writing we will rely almost exclusively on the two-stave short-score format.

EXAMPLE 8.8

A. Bach, "Nun ruhen alle Wälder" from *St. Matthew Passion*

B1. Bach, "Nun ruhen alle Wälder"

B2. Beethoven, Symphony no. 9 in D minor, *Adagio molto*

C.

Voices, like most instruments, are limited to particular registers. The total span of pitches that a voice can sing is called the **range,** which covers roughly the interval of a twelfth. Composers utilize this "unrestricted range" when writing for solo voice (see Example 8.9). Of course, the entire range of one's voice is not called on at all times; rather, the voice will spend most of its time in a more comfortable register, referred to as its **tessitura.** This "optimal range" is much better suited to accommodate four voice parts simultaneously sounding. **Ambitus** refers to the specific range of a melody (as opposed to the range of the instrument playing the melody).

Example 8.9 shows both the range and the tessitura for each of the four vocal parts. We will observe the narrower tessitura spans, since we will be writing for four voices. A helpful rule of thumb is to write for a voice's midrange and to restrict its tessitura to about a sixth or a seventh for the upper voices. Note that the bass's register is usually approximately one octave below the alto and the tenor's register is usually one octave below the soprano. The leaps in a soprano melody are fewer and smaller than those in a bass line. Tenor and alto lines contain even fewer skips than does a soprano line. The larger range of the bass voice reflects its dual function as both melodic line and guiding force of the harmonic progression.

EXAMPLE 8.9 Vocal Ranges and Tessituras

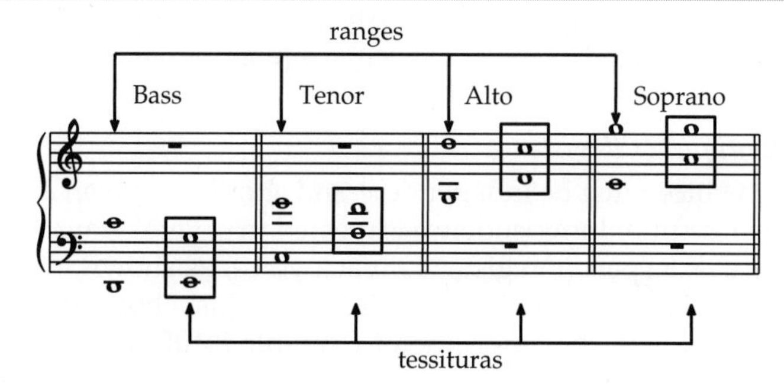

Three Techniques to Create Voice Independence Within a Four-Voice Texture

Just as we learned when writing for two voices, we face a continual paradox between maintaining the melodic and independent nature of individual voices and making sure voices work well with each other. In this section, we take up three techniques for reaching this goal. Example 8.10 presents two four-voice examples. Both examples use only tonic and dominant harmonies, yet they sound different. Listen carefully to each one. Which do you prefer? Why? What criteria are you using to support your opinions?

EXAMPLE 8.10 Voice Leading in Four-Part Texture

DVD 1 CH 8 TRACK 6

A.

B.

Technique 1: Smoothness

You may have preferred the first example because of its overall smoothness; the upper three voices of Example 8.10A move primarily by step and never leap more than a third. (The bass moves by leap because it is limited, for now, to the roots of the tonic and the dominant harmonies.) The tenor is remarkably static, because the tonic and dominant share $\hat{5}$ (the fifth of the tonic and the root of the dominant). However, given that our chief concern is for minimal movement of voices, this stasis is an asset. Always try to maintain common tones between chords by either tying or repeating them in a single voice. Inspection of Example 8.10B reveals melodic lines that are angular and disjunct. Smooth melodic motion is a primary requirement when connecting chords.

Technique 2: Register

Each voice must be independent and should be given a consistently comfortable tessitura. Independence is created in several ways, including the maintenance of a specific register for each voice, as shown in Example 8.10A. Note how the tenor elegantly controls the area just above and below C^4. Now compare this with the tenor line of Example 8.10B, which not only contains unnecessary leaps of fifths and sixths but forces the voice into an exceptionally low register.

Excessive leaping and registral shifting within a voice usually has very serious consequences, as we see when we examine the soprano and alto lines in Example 8.10B. Problems start as early as the third beat of m. 1, where the alto intrudes into the soprano's tessitura by hopping up a sixth to C^5, and actually extends beyond the soprano's previously established A^4. Such intrusions are called **voice overlaps**, additional examples of which occur between the tenor and alto in m. 2 as well as between the bass and tenor in mm. 3 and 4. Another kind of registral intrusion, known as **voice crossing**, occurs on the first beat of m. 3. The alto appears below the tenor C^4. Crossed voices occur again in the last chord of m. 4, where the tenor C^4 is higher than the alto A^3. Avoid overlapping and crossing voices.

Technique 3: Counterpoint

Another means of creating voice independence is derived from our study of counterpoint, in which we aimed for contrary and oblique motion when possible. However, recall that parallel motion in thirds and sixths is perfectly acceptable, as seen in Example 8.10A, where soprano and alto move primarily in parallel thirds. Notice that all the other intervals in Example 8.10A are approached by contrary or oblique motion. Further, in each case of similar motion, at least one voice moves smoothly by step. In Example 8.10B we encounter the most serious of voice-leading errors: Pairs of voices move in parallel octaves in every measure, creating the effect of one or more voices dropping out of the texture. Further, the soprano and bass move in parallel fifths in m. 2. We learned about the inherent weakness of parallel motion by perfect fifths and octaves; we now avoid parallel motion by perfect consonances (unisons, fifths, and octaves) between any pair of voices.

It is possible to avoid clumsy vocal lines that contain excessive leaping, intrusion of one voice into another's musical space, and parallels by following a single rule: Move the voices the shortest possible distance when changing chords. A symptom that there may be something wrong in your voice leading is the appearance of leaps of fifths or even fourths, particularly when you see leaps in two voices simultaneously. It is often possible simply to switch the pitches in the two voices in order to smooth out the individual lines and correct voice leading between lines.

EXAMPLE 8.11 Correcting Errors in Voice Leading

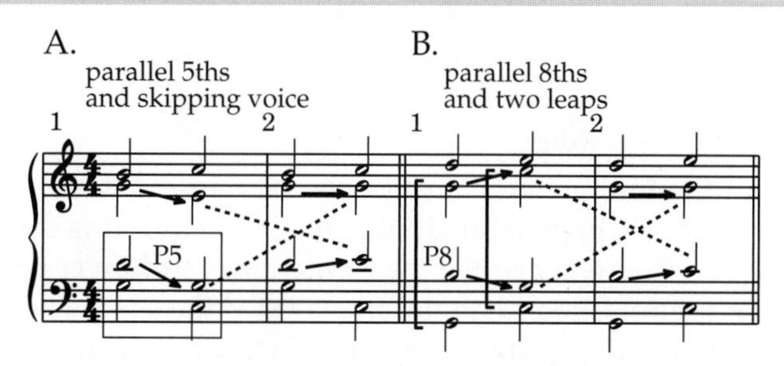

Example 8.11 shows corrections for two instances of faulty voice leading. In A1, the awkward tenor forms parallel fifths with the bass; in A2, correct voice leading results by switching tenor and alto. In B1, we encounter parallel octaves between alto and bass, and the awkward alto and tenor diverge to create a very wide spacing; in B2, the problem is easily solved simply by maintaining the common tone G in the alto and resolving the tenor's leading tone ($\hat{7}$) up by step.

Creating the Best Sound: Incomplete and Complete Chords, Doubling, and Spacing

Omitted Chord Tones

In general, write complete chords. This is easy, since you have four voices in which to include the three members of a triad. If you must write an incomplete chord for the sake of smooth voice leading or the requirements of dissonance treatment, you may only omit the fifth; all chords must contain a root and a third. Example 8.10A contains an example of an incomplete chord on beat 4 of m. 3: Here, the fifth (E) is missing and the root (A) has been tripled in order to avoid a leaping alto (A–E–G♯). Because the alto remains on A⁴, stepwise voice leading is maintained in the upper voices. Example 8.12 shows the two versions.

EXAMPLE 8.12 Incomplete vs. Complete Chords

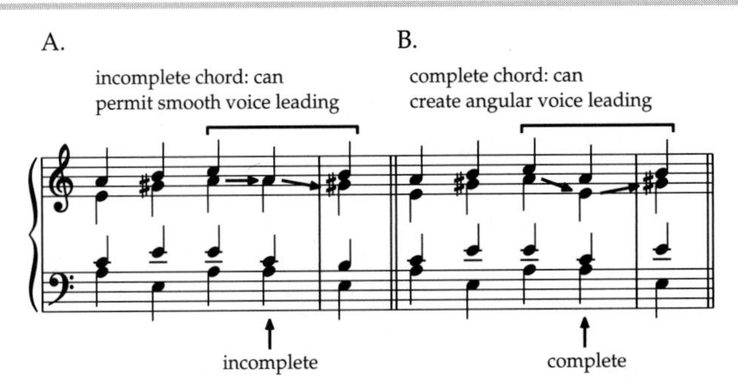

Instances of "illegal" incomplete chords abound in Example 8.10B. For example, there is no third in the first chord of m. 1, and the following chord has three thirds. How many more examples of chords with missing thirds can you identify?

Doubled Chord Tones

Most of the time when we write for four voices, we must double one of the triad members. In general, double the root, since it is the most stable member of a chord. (Later, when we use new chords and inversions of chords, we will learn other doublings.) Again, however, if the voice leading is smoother, you may double the fifth and, as a last resort, the third. In Example 8.10A, the first chord in m. 4 contains a doubled fifth (B), which allows the tenor in the following chord to move a half step from C to B and then maintain the B in the next chord. If the root was doubled in the chord, the tenor would then skip from the preceding C up to E and then down a fourth to the B. Example 8.13 shows the two versions.

EXAMPLE 8.13 Doubling the Fifth

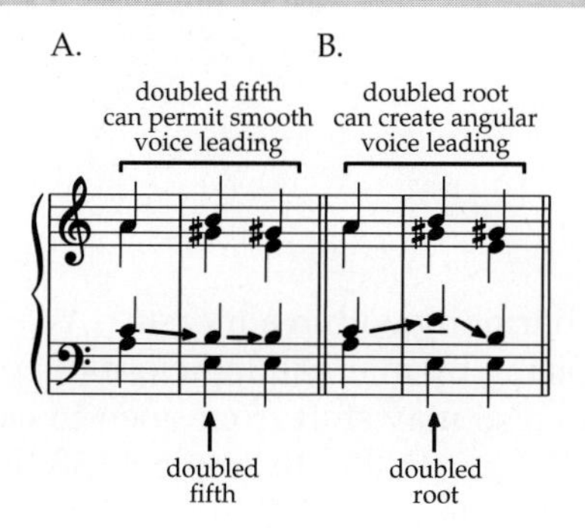

Tendency tones are aurally marked and therefore usually require special treatment. Do not double them because (1) they are already aurally prominent and inherently unstable and (2) correctly resolving both instances of them will necessarily result in parallel octaves. For example, $\hat{7}$ is the most important tendency tone for now. Harmonized by V, it has a strong tendency to resolve to $\hat{1}$ (harmonized by I). As a rule, never double the leading tone.

Spacing and Voicing

There is one more problem in Example 8.10B. The sound seems muddled in m. 3 as the tenor falls to C. This places the chordal third next to the root in a low register. To avoid this sound, keep adjacent upper voices (i.e., soprano, alto, and tenor) within one octave of one another. As we already know, we can pack the three upper voices within a single octave such that it is not possible to insert additional chord tones between any voice, a spacing referred to as **close position**. For a chord to be in close position, we consider only the upper three voices and not the bass, which must necessarily leap more than the upper voices, given that it is entrusted with defining the harmony. When the total spacing of the upper voices is an octave or more, we call this **open position**. It is a good idea to begin an exercise in close position; to accomplish this, keep the inner voices relatively high. Then, as you continue, it is perfectly acceptable to move the upper voices to open position, which results in a fuller, nicely contrasting sound. Try to return to close position, however, because in open position one can more easily write problematic parallels, which are more difficult to detect than when writing in close position. For example, parallel fifths are more easily avoided if you use close position, because potential parallel fifths will be rendered as harmless perfect fourths. See Example 8.14.

EXAMPLE 8.14 Benefits of Close Position

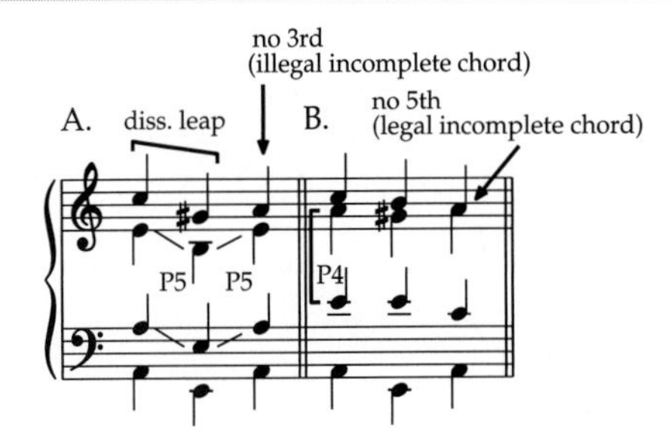

It is common to repeat a harmony within a measure. When this happens, you may change a chord's voicing by maintaining close (C) or open (O) position, as in Example 8.15A. You also may shift from open to close position, or vice versa, as in Example 8.15B. Note that in Example 8.15B the tenor and soprano voices have exchanged the notes C and E in the revoicing that moves from open to close position; this exchange is marked by the diagonal lines that form an X. This swapping is called a **voice exchange**. In such cases, two or even all three of the upper voices may leap. Note that the sustained perfect fifth (C–G) in the bass and the alto voices is perfectly acceptable and isn't considered a parallel. Parallels occur only when a pair of voices moves from one perfect interval to the same perfect interval on different pitches, as in Example 8.15C.

EXAMPLE 8.15 Revoicing Repeated Harmony; Parallel Motion

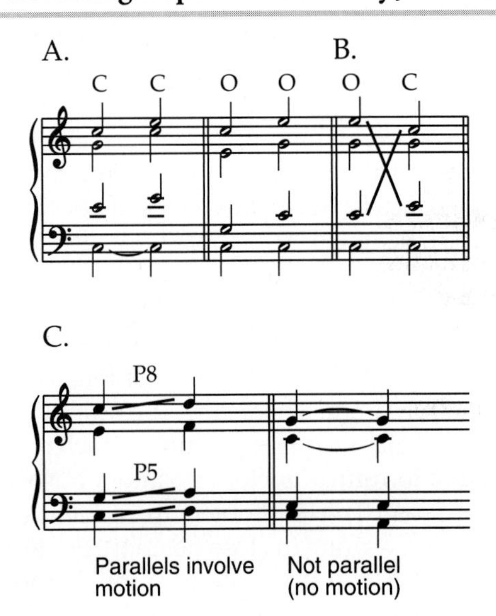

Summary of Voice-Leading Rules and Guidelines

The most important part-writing and voice-leading guidelines, summarized next, will remain in effect for our entire study of harmony. Asterisks denote rules that cannot be broken for any reason (there are only two). You will recognize many of these rules, which were first introduced in the counterpoint studies in Chapter 4.

Move the Voices as Little as Possible When Changing Chords

RULE 1 Resolve tendency tones (the leading tone and chordal dissonance) by step. Note that the leading tone, $\hat{7}$, does not need to resolve upward when it appears in an inner voice; it may fall to $\hat{5}$ to create a complete triad. However, the chordal seventh ($\hat{4}$) in a V_7 chord must always resolve down by step, no matter which voice it is in.

GUIDELINE 1 Generally retain the common tone between two chords.

GUIDELINE 2 Move the upper three voices mostly by seconds and thirds; follow leaps larger than a fourth with a step in the opposite direction.

GUIDELINE 3 Avoid melodic leaps involving augmented intervals. Leaps involving diminished intervals (such as the diminished fifth) are fine, as long as a stepwise change of direction follows.

GUIDELINE 4 If any pair of upper voices leaps simultaneously by more than a third, something may be wrong. Try reversing the pitches.

Maintain the Independence and Musical Territory for Each Voice

**RULE 2* Do not move from one unison, octave, or perfect fifth to another in parallel or contrary motion.

**RULE 3* Do not double tendency notes ($\hat{7}$, chordal dissonances, or chromatically altered tones).

RULE 4 Keep adjacent upper voices (S–A and A–T) within an octave of each other. There may be more than an octave between the tenor and bass.

GUIDELINE 5 Avoid voice crossings (for example, moving the alto line below the tenor line). Avoid voice overlappings between adjacent chords (for example, moving the alto below the tenor's previous note).

GUIDELINE 6 Avoid similar motion to octaves and fifths between the soprano and bass, unless the soprano moves stepwise (called direct octaves and fifths).

Construct Chords Logically

GUIDELINE 7 In general, use complete chords (although you may omit the chordal fifth if it smoothes the voice leading).

GUIDELINE 8 Double the root of root-position chords. You may double other members of root-position chords only if it makes for smoother voice leading. Prefer doubling the fifth to doubling the third. However, you may never double the third in V because it results in a doubled leading tone. Doubling the third emphasizes the least stable member of the triad, which by its nature does not require reinforcement because it is the most active member of the chord.

Tips for Avoiding Problems

1. Write the outer voices first. Their counterpoint controls everything.
2. Move the upper voices in contrary motion to the bass, and use a generally stepwise soprano line.
3. Begin part-writing exercises with a complete chord in close position, and try to maintain close position as much as possible.

EXERCISE INTERLUDE

WRITING

8.5 Chord Completion

The following chords are incomplete root-position tonic and dominant triads, each of which appears in a different major or minor key. Complete the following tasks (the first exercise is completed for you):

1. Label each key, and use a roman numeral to identify whether the chord is tonic or dominant.
2. Determine which voice (SATB) of the chord is missing, and add it, in open or close position, as specified. (*Hint*: To help identify the missing voice, examine stem directions.)
3. Rewrite each example next to the original presentation using the opposite spacing and a different soprano voice; that is, close position becomes open position, and vice versa.

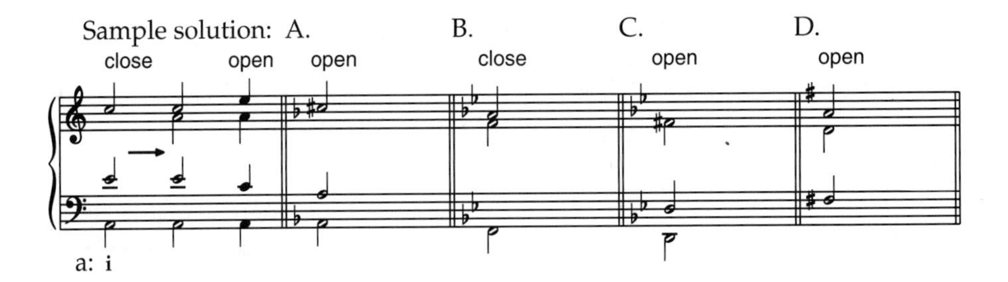

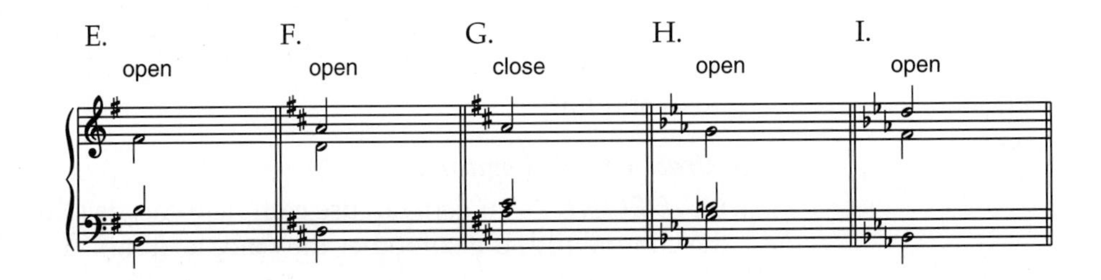

8.6 Review of Analysis and Voice Leading

1. Label the key and harmonies with roman numerals.
2. Label the soprano pitches using scale degree numbers.
3. Label similar (S) and/or parallel (P) motion between any of the six possible voice pairs (bass/tenor, bass/alto, bass/soprano, tenor/alto, tenor/soprano, and alto/soprano).

4. For any parallel motions, label the generic interval. The first exercise is completed for you.

8.7 Writing Cadences

On a separate sheet of manuscript paper, write cadences using only I and V in root position. Begin with the outer voices; then fill in alto and tenor lines. Analyze each chord with roman numerals.

A. Imperfect authentic cadences (IAC) in B♭ major and F♯ minor
B. Half cadences (HC) in G minor and E♭ major
C. Perfect authentic cadences (PAC) in C minor and A major

KEYBOARD

8.8 Keyboard: Authentic Cadences

WORKBOOK
8.3–8.6

Study the following chord progressions, in which the soprano voice either remains stationary or features a passing tone or neighbor note. The arrows in exercises A, B, and C show how the three upper voices simply circulate through the three positions of soprano, alto, and tenor. Note that $\hat{5}$ is held as a common tone between the tonic and the dominant (and shown by dotted lines), except in exercise D (stepwise motions between chords are shown with solid lines).

At the keyboard:

1. Play the progressions as written, in C major and C minor.
2. Transpose the progressions to major keys up to one sharp and one flat and in the relative minors of these keys.

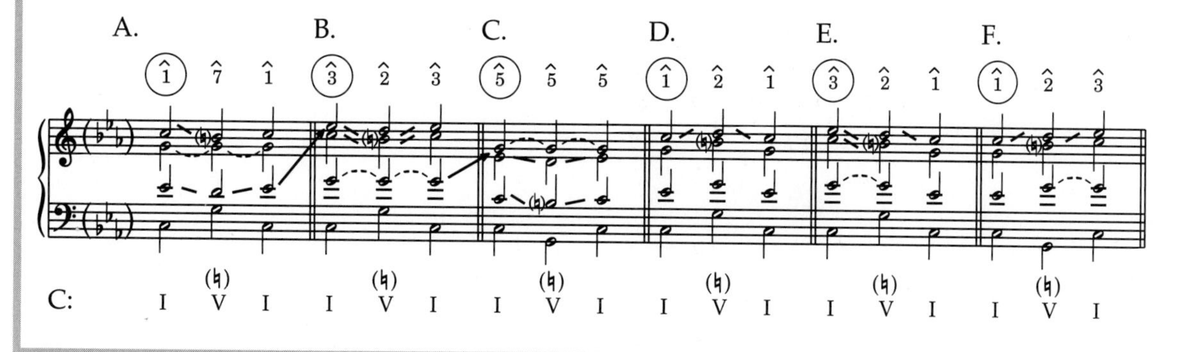

TERMS AND CONCEPTS

1. Define and then compare and contrast the following terms:
   a. range v. ambitus v. tessitura
   b. parallel v. hidden intervals
   c. perfect authentic cadence, imperfect authentic cadence, half cadence, contrapuntal cadence
2. Using the corresponding number, label one instance of each of the following terms or concepts in the given summary exercise.

1. close position
2. open position
3. common tone
4. contrapuntal framework
5. doubling
6. harmonic rhythm
7. hidden (or direct) fifths or octaves
8. parallel fifths
9. parallel octaves
10. Picardy third
11. tendency tone
12. voice
13. voice crossing
14. voice exchange
15. voice overlap
16. illegal doubling
17. excessive space between voices

CHAPTER 9

The Impact of Melody, Rhythm, and Meter on Harmony, and Introduction to V_7

In this chapter we explore two topics. The first revisits tonal hierarchy, this time through the lens of harmony. We see how the melodic, contrapuntal, rhythmic, and metric domains determine how we perceive harmonic flow and its impact on harmonic rhythm. The second topic is an introduction to chordal dissonance, and we explore the ramifications of adding a seventh to the dominant triad.

The Interaction of Harmony, Melody, Meter, and Rhythm: Embellishment and Reduction

Tonal music—a composite of harmony, melody, rhythm, meter, dynamics, and register—is crafted through a series of checks and balances. For example, the bass (or harmonic foundation) often contains large leaps that are a result of the alternation of root-position tonic and dominant harmonies. These leaps are, in a sense, compensated for and balanced by a soprano line that moves primarily by step. Meter and rhythm help to coordinate all this activity. For example, not only is harmony governed by the ebb and flow of weak (unaccented) and strong (accented) beats, but the counterpoint between bass and soprano is also dependent on meter and rhythm. Let us explore these two coordinated elements in turn.

Harmonic rhythm is intimately tied to and helps reinforce the meter. There will be times in your writing when you will need to make a choice between using one chord and another. For example, when deciding whether to harmonize $\hat{5}$ with tonic or dominant harmony, you must consider its metric placement, since a change to a new harmony creates an accent, and such harmonic accents usually align with metric accents. In general, it is advisable to change chords when moving from a weak to a strong beat (see Example 9.1A). Avoid a syncopated harmonic rhythm (Example 9.1B)

EXAMPLE 9.1

DVD 1
CH 9
TRACK 1

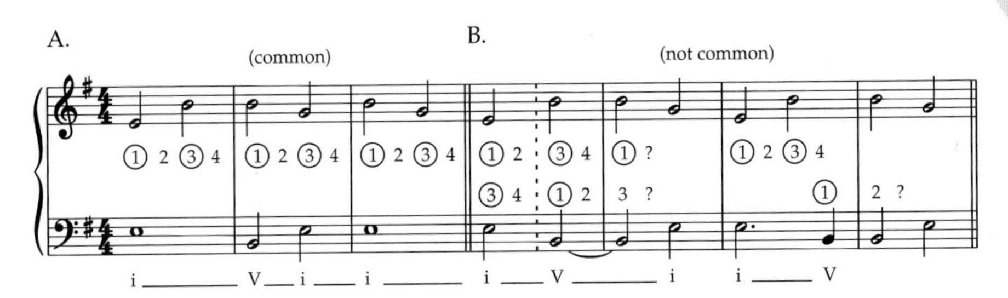

In $\frac{3}{4}$ you will often encounter a harmonic change on beat 3, creating the familiar accentual pattern of long–short, which helps to underscore the triple meter (Example 9.1C1). One exception to avoiding a syncopated harmonic rhythm occurs in $\frac{3}{4}$ at a cadence, when the dominant enters on beat 2 and is sustained through beat 3 (Example 9.1C2).

Another aspect of pitch organization that is dependent on meter and rhythm is the outer-voice framework arising from the combination of bass and soprano voices. We have already encountered the importance of this contrapuntal relationship: For every change of harmony (bass note), there is a single, primary soprano note. We now place the outer-voice framework in a rhythmical-metrical context, one that is fleshed out with complete chords and textural embellishments. Such embellishments are much like the leaves on a tree, which can decorate but not obscure the structural branches on which their existence depends.

Embellishment and Reduction

In order to see how we might embellish a basic outer-voice structure, we begin with a single implied harmony, the tonic, which supports $\hat{1}$ (Example 9.2A). We can elaborate this soprano pitch with tones of figuration to create a melody of sorts; one dissonant neighbor and two passing tones appear in Example 9.2B. The hierarchy is clear, since not only are the tones of figuration dissonant, but they fall on unaccented beats or parts of beats. We can also stabilize these tones of figuration by harmonizing them with chords that render them consonant. Since the neighbor (B) and passing tone (D) are members of the dominant harmony, we simply place the root of the dominant, G, in the bass (Example 9.2C).

EXAMPLE 9.2

DVD 1
CH 9
TRACK 2

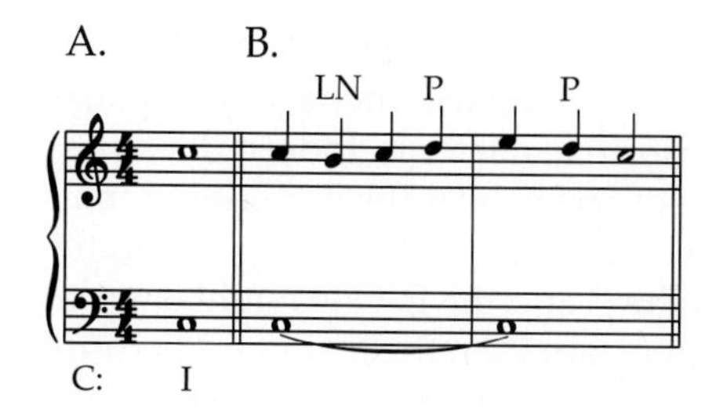

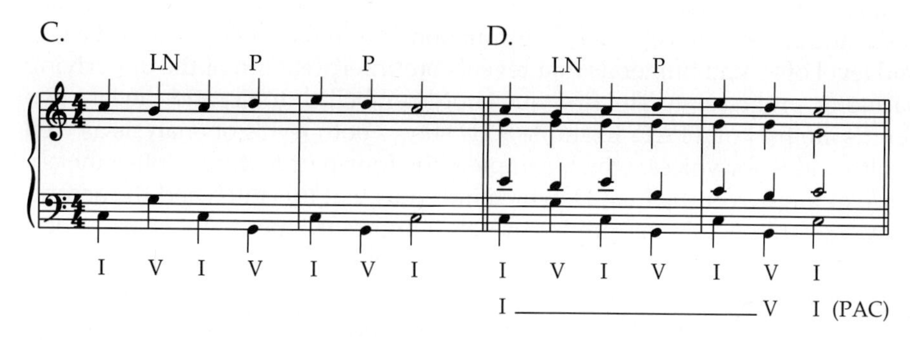

While it's true that each soprano pitch is now consonantly harmonized, we can still distinguish aurally between the more important melody notes that are members of the tonic triad (the soprano C and E) and the subordinate tones of figuration (the neighbor (B) and passing tones (D). This is because both the contour of the soprano line and the weak metric and rhythmic placement of the dominant harmony strongly prioritize the tonic. Indeed, these less important melodic and harmonic events allow us to hear the underlying tonic harmony. Specifically, the neighbor B is there to extend the flanking C, and the passing Ds provide a bridge that connects the C and the E. One might even go so far as to say that the D^5 in m. 1 is less important than the D^5 in m. 2 because the second D^5 is a member of the perfect authentic cadence. It is possible to illustrate this hierarchy in our harmonic analysis. After labeling every chord and standing back to consider their function within the context, we add a second level of roman numerals that reveals our interpretation of the underlying harmonic progression. The first five chords embellish tonic, and the last two chords are part of a PAC. Example 9.2D shows both levels of analysis as well as alto and tenor voices, which complete the four-part texture. Notice the absence of the *P* over the final D, which indicates that this pitch and the accompanying harmony are interpreted as very important, since the V chord is part of the structural authentic cadence and the soprano D is not just another harmonized tone of figuration.

It is possible to repeat the procedure of adding tones of figuration and then harmonizing them; done enough times, we could generate an actual piece of music. However, we shall merely embellish Example 9.2D twice more with tones of figuration to show that neighbors, passing tones, chordal leaps, and one or two tones of figuration we will soon learn can be used to create examples in contrasting styles. In Example 9.2E, notice how the E^5 on beat 2 in m. 2 delays the arrival of the D^5 by a sixteenth note just as the D^5 on beat 3 displaces the C^5 by a whole beat. Our understanding of the harmony once again helps us to interpret melodic features.

Although both the harmony and the outer-voice counterpoint of the original model are preserved in Example 9.2F, the surface of the music in this example is even more altered than in Example 9.2E. Cast in the parallel mode of C minor, with each chord change occupying an entire measure rather than a single beat, Example 9.2F is in a freer texture; the arpeggiated figuration creates a seamless flurry of sixteenth notes that is punctuated by the sparse upper-neighbor figure on the fourth beat of each of mm. 1–3.

Example 9.2 has demonstrated how a soprano voice can help distinguish structural from ornamental harmonies and how a basic two-voice structure might be ornamented, a process called **embellishment**. Embellishment takes many forms, including the simple process of sustaining and revoicing a tonic harmony that leads to a dominant chord (Example 9.3A). By adding a recurring eighth-note rhythmic figure we energize the texture (Example 9.3B). Finally, with a few passing tones, we have the opening of "Spring" from Vivaldi's *Seasons*.

EXAMPLE 9.3

DVD 1
CH 9
TRACK 3

A. Tonic Harmony Revoiced

B. Eighth-Note Figures Added

C. Passing Tones Added

Let us now reverse the process by using the harmony as a means of distinguishing structural tones from embellishing tones. This process, called **reduction**, reveals the underlying two-voice contrapuntal framework of a musical passage. Listen to Example 9.4 On the downbeat of m. 8, the musical unit sounds relatively complete, as if closure had been achieved. There are two reasons why we hear a strong arrival in m. 8, in spite of the fact that there are no obvious visual clues. First, the eight measures can be subdivided into two symmetrical harmonic and metrical units of four measures each. Given the change to dominant harmony in m. 4 (following three measures of tonic), we expect a similar change to occur in the corresponding spot four measures later, which indeed does occur. At the end of m. 4, the addition of the high G in the melody creates a V_7 chord that destabilizes the dominant and sends it forward into the next musical unit, which reverses the harmonic process of mm. 1–4: Three measures of dominant-seventh harmony lead to one measure of tonic. The return to tonic in m. 8 is what creates the sense of resolution.

EXAMPLE 9.4 Beethoven, Piano Sonata in D minor, "Tempest," op. 31, no. 2, *Allegretto*

DVD 1
CH 9
TRACK 4

Second, the relationship between the melody and the harmony enhances the effect of closure. The opening D^5 ($\hat{1}$) over tonic harmony repeats on the downbeats of mm. 2 and 3, after which E^5 ($\hat{2}$) arrives over the dominant on the downbeat of m. 5. Thereafter, E^5 is similarly emphasized over a repeated V_7 chord until it ascends to F^5 ($\hat{3}$), coinciding with the return of tonic harmony in m. 8. Thus, a sense of harmonic arrival is balanced by the forward motion of the melody: Tonic harmony returns at the moment the melody dramatically attains $\hat{3}$.

At the deepest melodic level, we can view the E^5 as a large-scale passing tone that connects $\hat{1}$ and $\hat{3}$. The recurring sixteenth-note soprano figure contains both arpeggiation (A^4–F^5–D^5) and passing motion (F^5–E^5–D^5). The notes of the large-scale ascent in the melody are in counterpoint with bass notes, and the large-scale melodic ascent ($\hat{1}$– $\hat{2}$– $\hat{3}$) is reflected in reverse order within the sixteenth-note figuration (see Example 9.5). The extended upper-voice passing motion (D–E–F) is represented by the beamed pitches, which are supported by the bass voice, a technique used in previous chapters. Literal repetitions of patterns are not shown. Ties illustrate restatements of important pitches (such as the two D^{5}s and the three E^{5}s), whereas slurs convey the dependency of less important melodic pitches on the important pitches. Notice too that the pitches aligned with a slur's beginning and ending points are members of the same harmony. Finally, the least important pitches in the contrapuntal fabric occur within the less important slurs. In this example, these pitches are dissonant passing tones. We refer to embellishing figures (like the large-scale melodic passing figure D–E–F) whose durations extend beyond the value of the beat as **supermetrical figurations**. These figurations are always made consonant by the supporting bass notes, as seen in the harmonization of the passing figure with the bass D–A–D, creating the overarching i–V–i progression.

EXAMPLE 9.5 Structural Analysis of Beethoven, *Allegretto*

With an understanding of the important roles played by meter, rhythm, melody, harmony, and their contrapuntal combinations, we have a standard by which to measure the relative strength and weakness of certain chords. Even when they appear in root position, as we saw in previous examples, we can distinguish between structural and ornamental harmonies. Example 9.6A reminds us to postpone interpretive decisions until we carefully consider the musical context.

EXAMPLE 9.6A Two Levels of I–V Harmonies

DVD 1
CH 9
TRACK 5

Up to this point, we have seen that tonic harmony usually falls on strong beats within a measure. But is this true for Example 9.6A? Tonic and dominant harmonies alternate on two levels: on the downbeat of each measure (level 2A) and within each measure (level 1). Tonic does indeed control m. 1 since the dominant appears on a weak beat and is outnumbered by the tonic harmonies that flank it on beats 1 and 3. Symptomatic of the weaker V, the D^5 is a harmonized passing tone that connects E^5 and C^5. Since D occupies one metrical unit (in this context one beat), we call it a **metrical passing tone**. We call any figurations whose duration occupies one metrical unit **metrical figurations**. Note that for a tone of figuration to occupy an entire metrical unit, it must be rendered consonant. Thus, metrical figurations are usually harmonized.

The relationship between the tonic and the dominant is reversed in m. 2. Now it is the tonic harmony that helps to extend the dominant: The soprano C^5 is a harmonized passing tone between B^4 and D^5. And given its identical function as the passing tone D^5 in m. 1, it too can be labeled as a metrical figuration (again, harmonized). We refer to the eighth-note passing tone A^4 as a **submetrical passing tone**. We call any figuration whose duration occupies less than one metrical unit **submetrical figurations**. That A^4 is not harmonized is common for submetrical figurations, although, as we will see, submetrical figurations may be harmonized.

Although m. 3 begins and ends with tonic harmony, it differs in two important ways from the previous measures. First, rather than a single harmony between the flanking chords, as in mm. 1 and 2, there are three root-position harmonies between the two flanking tonics. Second, accented beat 3 is occupied by a different harmony from that on the downbeat of the measure. For the first time, deciding which harmony is most important within the measure is more difficult. For example, if metrically accented harmonies are more important than unaccented harmonies, then we can assume that the dominant on beat 3 is more important than the tonic on beat 4. This would mean that the tonic on beat 4 (and the C^5 in the soprano) becomes a passing tone between the dominant chord on beat 3 and the dominant arrival in the next measure. This interpretation is reflected in Level 2B. If, however, we view the two tonic harmonies that begin and end the measure as important, then the dominant on beat 3 extends the tonic by harmonizing the lower neighbor B^4, in spite of the neighbor note's metric prominence. This interpretation is shown in Level 2A.

Clearly, these are two very different, yet plausible, readings, and each carries important performance implications. For example, we may favor the Level 2A interpretation, which takes into account patterns established in the preceding measures. Since a single harmony controlled each of the preceding two measures and a pattern of alternation of harmonies was established (i.e., m. 1 begins on I, m. 2 begins on V, and m. 3 begins on I), the listener may expect a *continuation* of the pattern. Thus, we would interpret it the same way we did mm. 1 and 2, with the tonic controlling m. 3. Since this interpretation postpones the dominant arrival until m. 4, the performer will shape m. 3 accordingly and play down the importance of the dominant chords. However, we might instead prefer the interpretation in Level 2B, given that the greater rhythmic complexity of m. 3 *breaks* the pattern of the repeated rhythm in mm. 1–2. Given that surface changes create an accent, the listener is drawn to this moment, and the performer would exercise the opportunity to highlight the dominant's control that would begin midway through m. 3.

We now briefly consider the harmonic changes on the eighth notes in m. 3. We will adopt interpretation 2A (in which tonic governs all of m. 3) because of the strength of pattern continuation over expected change. The soprano's B would be labeled a neighbor; given its strong metric placement, we call it an **accented neighbor note**. Further, since the neighbor is made consonant by the V, it is a **harmonized accented neighbor note**, analogous to the harmonized passing tones discussed earlier. Finally, given its short duration, this accented neighbor note is a submetrical tone of figuration.

EXAMPLE 9.6B Second-Level Analysis of Example 9.6A

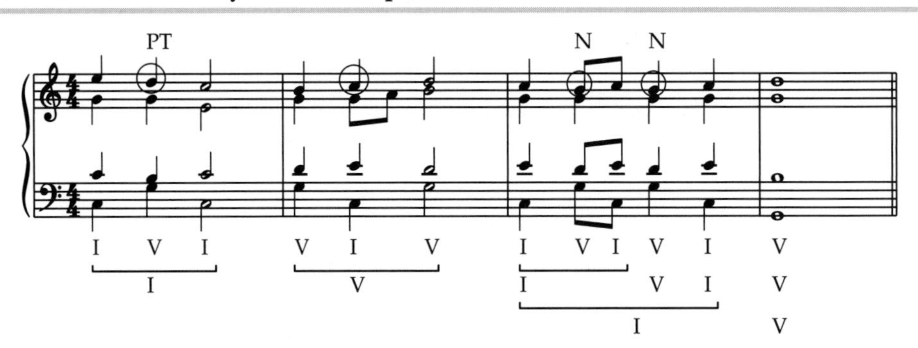

Example 9.6B summarizes our analysis so far. Notice two things. First, the soprano pitches in each measure that we interpreted as being subordinate to more structural pitches are now circled and labeled according to their melodic roles in extending the structural pitches, that is, as harmonized passing tones (PT) and harmonized neighbor tones (N). Second, each chord is labeled with a roman numeral, and the bracketed groups of chord symbols indicate the larger harmonic units (which in the present example occupy one measure). The controlling harmonies are labeled beneath the bracket. Multileveled analysis, which distinguishes more important harmonies from less important musical harmonies, is called **second-level analysis**. Second-level analysis is also referred to as **interpretive analysis**, given that the deeper you understand the function of counterpoint and harmony within a passage, the more it becomes a matter of interpretation. Finally, depending on the number of musical events within a measure or a passage, there may be more than one level of reduction required. For ex-

ample, in m. 3 the submetrical I–V–I harmonies that occur on beats 1 and 2 require their own interpretation before it is possible to interpret the next level.

If we consider the possibility of a melodically fluent large- scale soprano controlling the entire passage, we can view the E^5 in m. 1 moving to the C^5 in m. 3 through a large-scale supermetrical passing tone in m. 2 (see Example 9.6C). Finally, since our attention will be naturally drawn to the opening E, and, given the extension of the tonic over mm. 1–3 and the accent created by the change to the dominant harmony on the half cadence in m. 4, our ears might connect the opening E to the final D in the melody. Such deep-level melodic fluency is a feature of musical unity, one that composers were well aware of.

EXAMPLE 9.6C Structural Analysis of Example 9.6A

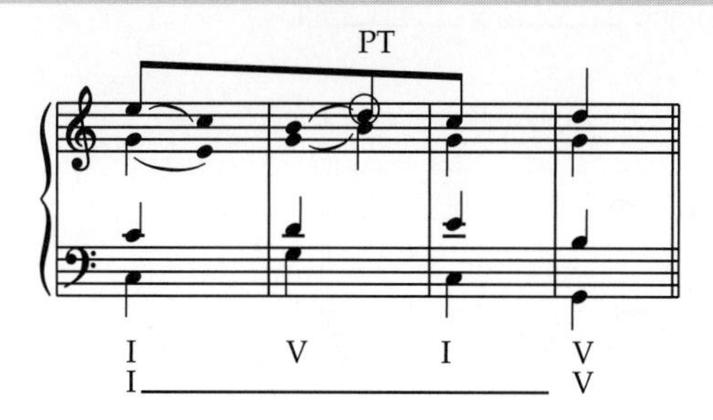

As we have just seen, the harmonies in a progression are not always of equal structural value. Indeed, there are many musical contexts in which I and V, chords that are usually viewed as structural, may become subordinate to each other and to other harmonies. The key to hearing and analyzing music is being sensitive to the musical context, especially the meter, the rhythm, and the counterpoint between bass and soprano. Think of analysis as a musical triangle; each side is intimately connected with and dependent on the other two sides.

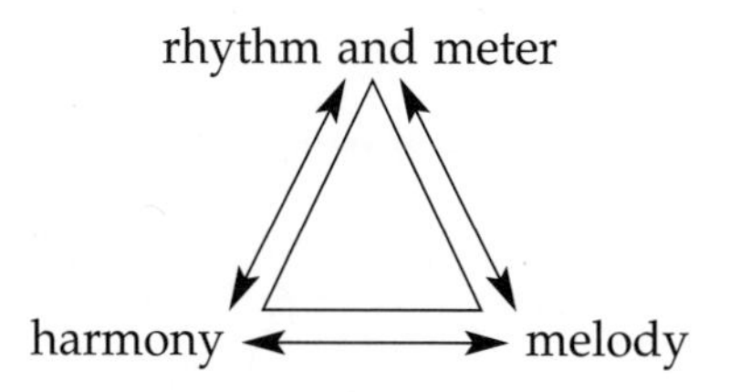

Taking these elements into account makes analysis a creative enterprise and, as we shall see in future chapters, informs musical interpretations and therefore performance.

EXERCISE INTERLUDE

ANALYSIS

DVD 2
CH 9
TRACK 1

9.1

Provide a two-level roman numeral analysis of each of the following examples. Only root-position I and V are used. In order to derive your second-level analysis, in which either tonic or dominant controls one or more measures, you will need to consider metric placement (i.e., whether or not the harmony occurs on a metrically stressed beat) and the soprano (whether the chord provides consonant support of a soprano passing tone or neighbor tone).

Sample solution:

A.

B.

C.

COMPOSITION

9.2

WORKBOOK 9.1

The relative importance of individual harmonies depends on their function within the musical context. For example, metrically stressed, durationally extended, and contrapuntally strong chords are more important than the surrounding chords, whose subordinate role is to extend the more important chords' control. Given here are short unmetered two-voice counterpoints without rhythm. You are to:

1. Select a meter for each counterpoint.
2. Write two different rhythmic settings using the selected meter such that one setting places tonic in control (with dominant as subordinate har-

mony) and the second setting places dominant in control (and tonic as subordinate harmony). See the following sample solution.

Sample solution:

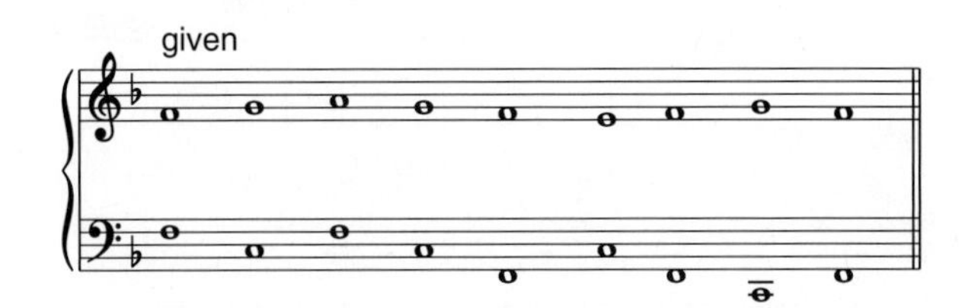

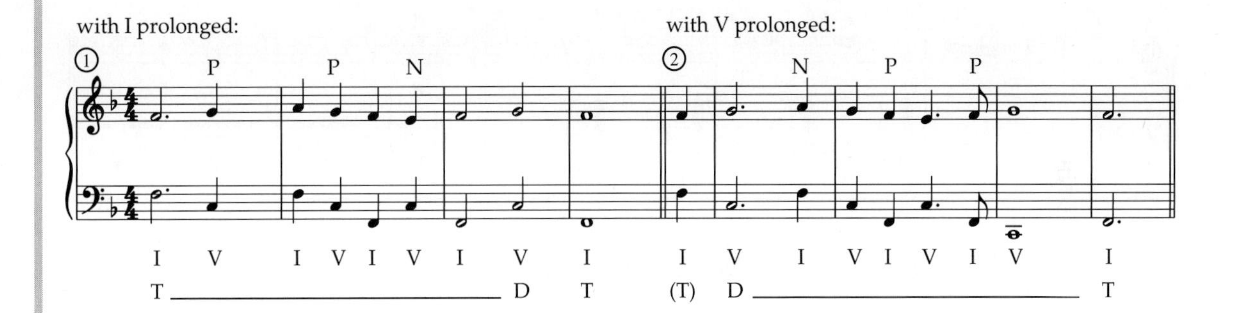

A.

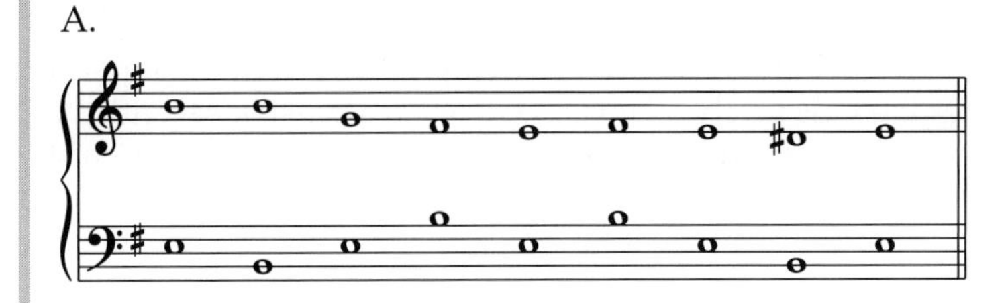

B.

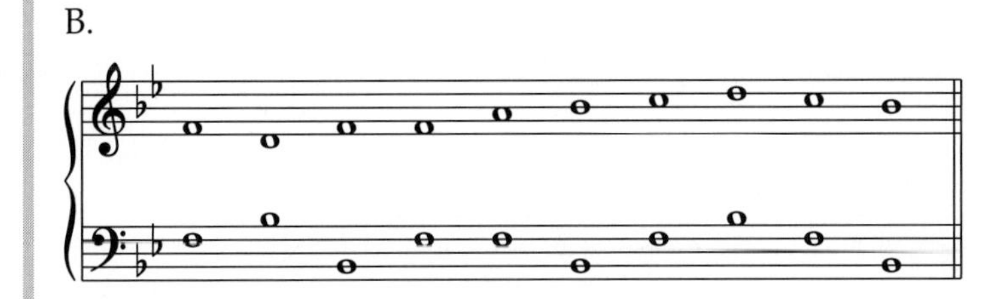

The Dominant Seventh and Chordal Dissonance

We know from earlier chapters that the seventh is a dissonant interval. We also know that chords that contain dissonant intervals, such as seventh chords, are dissonant. Just as dissonant intervals resolve to consonant ones, so dissonant chords are active sonorities that seek resolution and, in so doing, create tension and heighten expectation in tonal music. Indeed, in the opening measures of Beethoven's Fourth Symphony, the repeated V_7 chord that links the end of the slow introduction with the following *Allegro vivace* provides a powerful springboard to the eventual tonic that arrives seven measures later (see Example 9.7)

EXAMPLE 9.7 Beethoven, Symphony no. 4 in B♭ major, op. 60, *Adagio/Allegro vivace*

DVD 1
CH 9
TRACK 6

Derivation and New Melodic Possibilities

Example 9.8A is the basic model, showing a I–V–I progression with G^4–G^4–E^4 ($\hat{5}$– $\hat{5}$–$\hat{3}$) in the soprano voice. Example 9.8B is nearly identical, except that the skip from G^4 to E^4 in the soprano voice has been filled in by a passing F^4. Notice how the "8–7" in the figured bass acknowledges the voice leading of the soprano voice over the bass G: The octave G moves to a passing seventh. Notice further that the F^4 is introduced inconspicuously on a weak beat, in the same way we wrote passing dissonance in second-species counterpoint. In Example 9.8C the seventh now enters the harmonic domain and appears on a strong beat. Melodic motion remains intact; F^4 still passes between G^4 and E^4, but now it is accented.

EXAMPLE 9.8

DVD 1
CH 9
TRACK 7

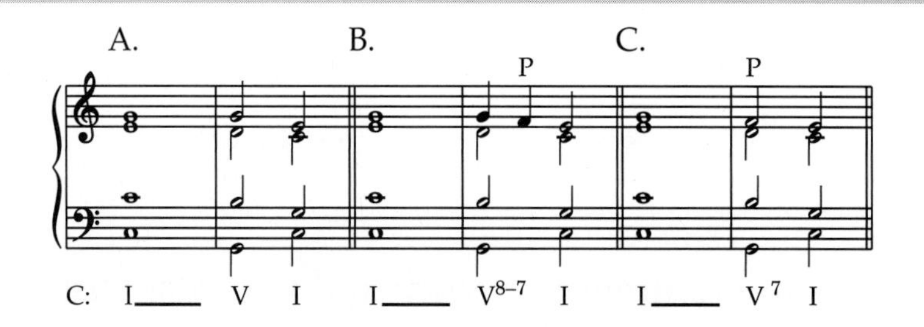

Chordal sevenths also participate in neighboring motions. In Example 9.9A, F functions as a neighbor to the surrounding Es. The treatment of the chordal seventh in Example 9.9B significantly differs from the preceding examples: F is not preceded by step; rather, it enters by leap (from C) and then falls by step, creating an incomplete-neighbor motion in the soprano. For V_7, how the dissonance is approached (its **preparation**) can occur in different ways. But there is one way to leave the dissonance (its **resolution**): by descending step. Preparation by step is the preferred method to use. The unprepared entrance of the seventh in Example 9.9B is not very common; avoid it.

EXAMPLE 9.9

DVD 1 CH 9 TRACK 8

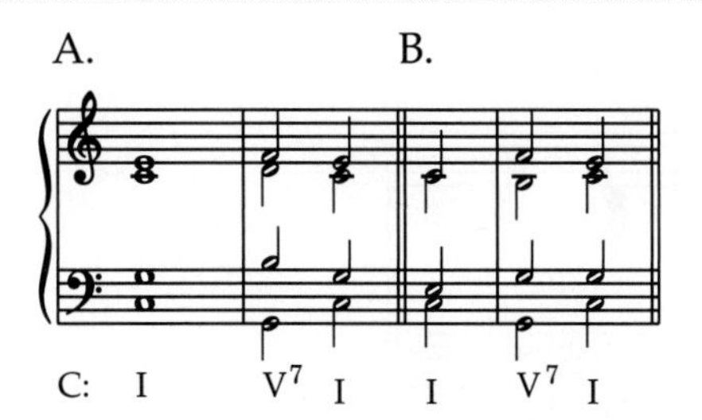

Schubert's song "Wasserfluth," from the song cycle *Winterreise* (Example 9.10), demonstrates how V_7 works within a musical context. Note how the tonic controls mm. 4–5 and the vocal line mostly arpeggiates the F♯-minor triad. Dominant harmony enters in m. 6 and returns to the tonic in m. 7. In m. 6, C♯^{5} in the vocal line descends by step to B^4, which is the dissonant seventh, which resolves appropriately to A^4. Thus, B^4 functions as a passing tone that connects C♯^{5} and A^4. Once again, we label the figured bass "8–7" to show the voice leading, with respect to the bass C♯, of the passing seventh from the octave. The dash connecting the two numbers means that this voice leading takes place *in a single voice*, any one of the upper voices, or, as here, in the vocal part (for a review of figured bass symbols, refer to Chapter 5). Note also how the V_7 chord can participate in an authentic cadence (here, the IAC in mm. 6–7); the addition of a seventh only enhances the dominant triad's tendency to resolve to tonic. Therefore, in your part writing, always use the dominant triad at a half cadence.

EXAMPLE 9.10 Schubert, "Wasserfluth" ("Torrent"), *Winterreise*, op. 89, no. 6, D. 911

DVD 1 CH 9 TRACK 9

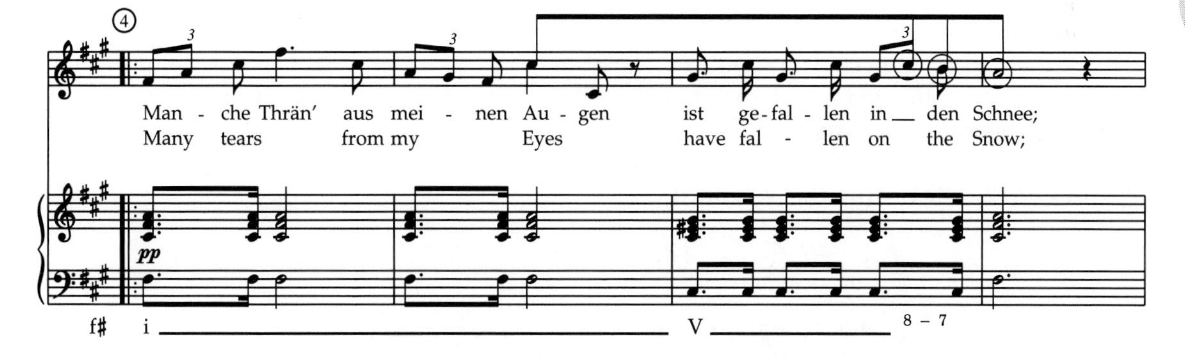

With the addition of the V_7 chord to our harmonic palette, we can add $\hat{4}$ to the soprano scale degrees that can be harmonized by the chords discussed thus far: $\hat{1}$, $\hat{2}$, $\hat{3}$, $\hat{4}$, $\hat{5}$, $\hat{7}$. Using $\hat{4}$ opens up the possibility of harmonizing a descending line from $\hat{5}$ to $\hat{3}$. Since we are already familiar with linking $\hat{3}$ down to $\hat{1}$, we can now harmonize a complete descending-fifth soprano melody from $\hat{5}$ to $\hat{1}$ (Example 9.11). The passing motion from $\hat{5}$ to $\hat{3}$ in the soprano is imitated in the tenor over the last three beats.

EXAMPLE 9.11 Harmonizing the Falling Fifth: $\hat{5}$–$\hat{1}$

DVD 1
CH 9
TRACK 10

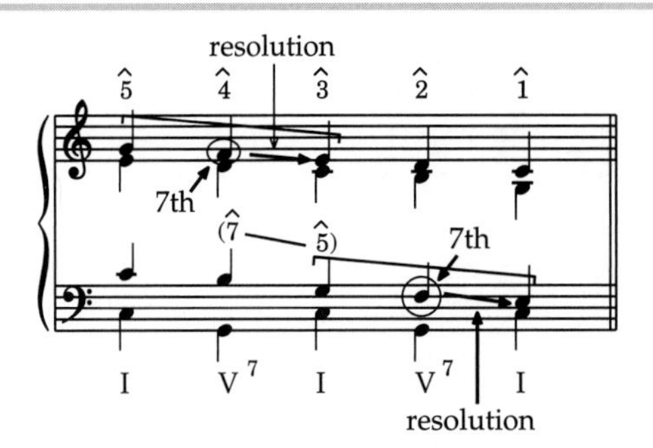

Finally, remember that the dominant triad contains two tendency tones: $\hat{7}$ (which returns to $\hat{1}$) and $\hat{2}$ (which moves to either $\hat{1}$ or $\hat{3}$). $\hat{5}$ in the bass provides a harmonic tendency that is resolved by leap to $\hat{1}$. With the addition of a seventh ($\hat{4}$) that returns to $\hat{3}$ by step, the dominant-seventh chord contains four tendency tones ($\hat{5}$, $\hat{7}$, $\hat{2}$, and $\hat{4}$). Thus, the progression V to V_7 is not reversible, because adding the seventh intensifies the triad built on V. Moving from V_7 to V would contradict the natural drive to the tonic that is created when the seventh is added.

Part Writing with the Dominant Seventh Chord

Generally connect the upper voices of V_7 to the preceding chord (for now, I) by step. Then resolve the chord's dissonances and tendency tones. Thus, in V_7, the chordal seventh ($\hat{4}$) *always descends* in any voice (as a *dissonant* tendency tone there are no other options), and the chordal third ($\hat{7}$) *always ascends* when it occurs in the soprano. These two members of the V_7 chord create a tritone, either a diminished fifth or an augmented fourth, which resolves to I by moving in contrary motion: The diminished fifth contracts to a third, and the augmented fourth expands to a sixth. Tritones and their resolutions occur in the upper voices of Example 9.12.

EXAMPLE 9.12 Resolving the V_7 chord

DVD 1
CH 9
TRACK 11

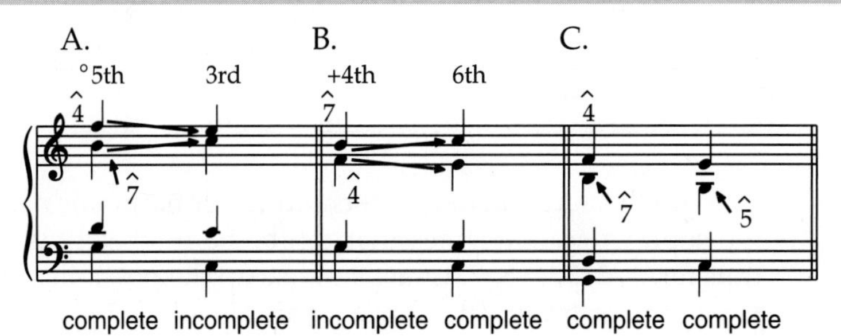

We will observe the following rule throughout this text: The only member of a triad or a seventh chord that you may omit is its fifth. Incomplete chords are important at this point, because they occur often in V_7–I progressions. Let's take a closer look at the construction of the dominant-seventh chords in Example 9.12. The V_7 chord in Example 9.12A is complete, in that each member of the chord appears once and none is omitted. In Example 9.12B the V_7 lacks a fifth and is thus incomplete; the root is correctly doubled. Now look at the tonic triads to which they resolve. The tonic in Example 9.12A is incomplete (in that it lacks the fifth and adds instead a third root), while that in Example 9.12B is complete (with the root correctly doubled). Both examples are perfectly correct. Generally, a complete V_7 resolves to an incomplete tonic, and an incomplete V_7 resolves to a complete tonic.

There is, however, one way to have both the V_7 and I chords complete (see Example 9.12C). While the seventh (in the soprano) resolves correctly, the leading tone (in the alto) doesn't ascend to $\hat{1}$; rather, it skips down a third to $\hat{5}$ in order to create a complete triad on I. This exception to the rule that the leading tone must ascend by step to $\hat{1}$ is permissible because the leading tone occurs in an inner voice, where its skip to $\hat{5}$ is less audible than it would be had it occurred in an outer voice.

The final part-writing issue concerns I moving to V_7, where the perfect fifth in I moves to the diminished fifth in V_7 (see Example 9.13). These fifths are not parallel perfect fifths, but **unequal fifths**, and they are permissible as long as the diminished fifth resolves to a third. Note that the reverse—a diminished fifth moving to a perfect fifth—is generally not permitted, since it contradicts the natural tendency of the diminished fifth to resolve to a third.

EXAMPLE 9.13 Approaching the V_7 Chord

DVD 1 CH 9 TRACK 12

An Analytical Interlude

We return to Beethoven's "Tempest" Sonata to provide an analytical model for upcoming exercises (Example 9.14). As we listen, our focus will be the context in which the dominant-seventh chord appears and how it intensifies the musical drama and enriches the voice leading.

EXAMPLE 9.14 Beethoven, Piano Sonata in D minor, op. 31, no. 2, "Tempest," *Allegretto*

DVD 1 CH 9 TRACK 13

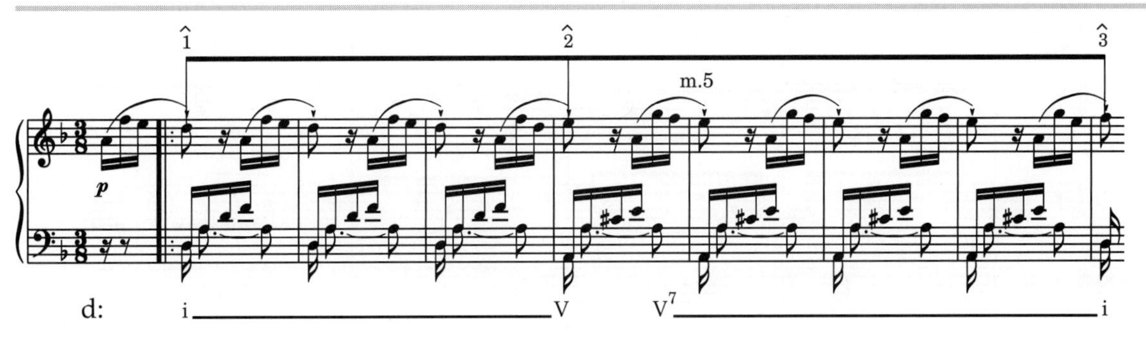

As we saw in Examples 9.4 and 9.5, this excerpt is built out of two four-measure units; the second unit mirrors the first in its 3 + 1 harmonic rhythm:

mm. 1–4: mm 5–8
(i–i–i–V) | V_7–V_7–V_7–i)

The dominant seventh chord that appears in the upbeat to m. 5 (G^5 in the soprano) intensifies the sound of the dominant triad in the beginning of m. 4. The harmonic motion is i–V–| V_7 –i. The V provides the musical glue that binds the two units to create a single phrase.

Above the staff of Example 9.14, the long beam connects the three pitches of the large-scale melodic ascent in the right hand from D^5 via E^5 to F^5. The reverse of this melodic line (F^5–E^5–D^5) occurs in sixteenth notes in mm. 1–3 and is answered by another filled-in third, G^5–E^5, in each of mm. 4–7. The imperfect authentic cadence in m. 8 spotlights the all-important arrival on the soprano's F^5, because this pitch is a point of arrival that is simultaneously secured from both above and below. E^5 rises to F^5, and G^5—the crucial seventh of the dominant harmony—falls to F^5. See the summary in Example 9.15.

EXAMPLE 9.15

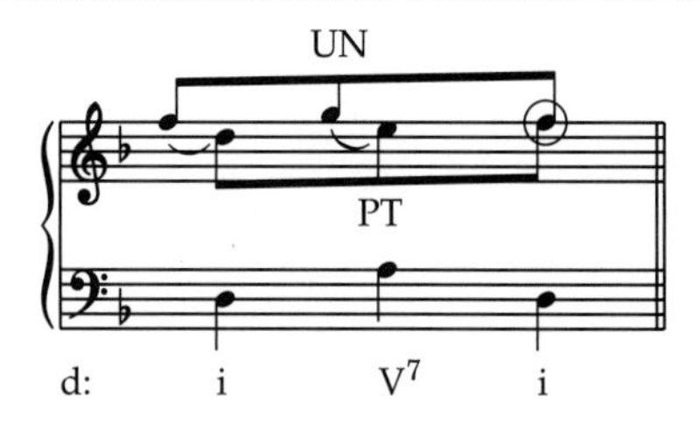

Notice that the seventh, G, does not resolve to the sixteenth-note F that immediately follows it in each of mm. 4–6. This is because the harmony at this point is still dominant and the F is a passing tone between G and E. Resolution of G occurs only in m. 8, where the F has the support of the underlying tonic harmony. Given that the basic soprano motion of the example is an ascent from D^5 to F^5, we view both E and G as supermetrical tones of figuration. A second example of supermetrical passing motion can be seen in Example 9.16.

EXAMPLE 9.16 Mozart, *Eine Kleine Nachtmusik*, K. 525, Trio

DVD 1
CH 9
TRACK 14

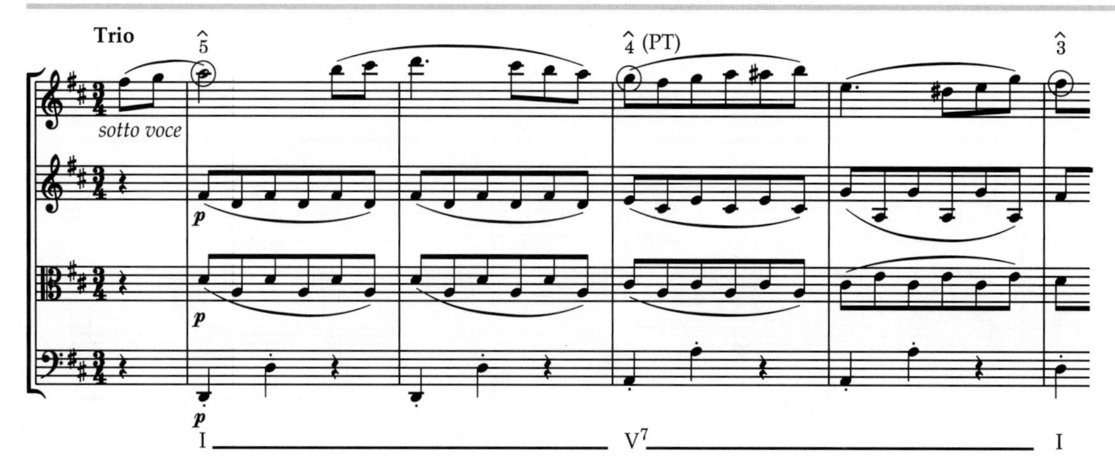

It is generally unproblematic to identify submetrical and metrical figurations. Supermetrical figurations can be more difficult to perceive. If, however, you locate the entrance and resolution of the seventh (recall that the resolution always requires a chord change), then you should be able to trace the deeper-level passing or neighbor motion.

Harmonizing Florid Melodies

Up to this point we have harmonized melodies in chorale style, a procedure in which every soprano pitch is harmonized. Such settings resulted in very fast harmonic rhythm, with up to four or even more chord changes within each measure. However, composers regularly slow the harmonic rhythm so that there is only one chord change in each measure or even in a group of measures. This is possible because the listener hears the single underlying harmony that controls the span (whether it be part of a measure, an entire measure, or a group of measures) and the underlying pattern of harmonic changes expressed in the harmonic rhythm. The vast body of folk songs is an important repertory that relies on a few basic harmonies—such as I, V and V_7—to accompany the countless examples. Let us work through a method that will allow you to harmonize folks tunes easily.

Example 9.17 presents the popular tune "Simple Gifts." We begin by singing the tune, noting the key and where cadences (and thus phrase endings) occur. The key is F major, and melodic repetitions, sustained pitches, and particularly the underlying four-measure "feel" of musical units reveal four-measures phrases, with cadences in mm. 4, 8, 12, and 16. We can determine the type of cadences as follows. Measure 4 ends on C ($\hat{5}$), and while this could be harmonized with a I chord, such a weak authentic cadence would not be as common as a half cadence, implying V. In addition, m. 4 arpeggiates a V chord and there is no sign of F anywhere. The choice of dominant harmony is supported by the beginning of the next phrase (m. 5), which—given that it starts on F—strongly implies a I chord. An authentic cadence is implied in m. 8, given the strong repeated Fs. Measure 12 again suggests a HC and m. 16 an authentic. Notice the pattern of cadences:

EXAMPLE 9.17 Simple Gifts

mm. 1–4	mm. 5–8	mm. 9–12	mm. 13–16
HC	PAC	HC	PAC

We finish identifying the harmonies that begin each phrase and then look for an underlying harmonic rhythm. In order to determine the controlling harmony for a span, we look at accented pitches, which will be stressed in a variety of ways, including metrically, durationally, and by repetition. We need to be aware which scale degrees can be harmonized with which harmony: $\hat{1}$–$\hat{3}$–$\hat{5}$ implies a I chord, and $\hat{5}$–$\hat{7}$–$\hat{2}$ and often $\hat{4}$ imply a V$^{(7)}$ harmony. The greater the number of stressed scale degrees that belong to a single harmony, the greater the chance that that harmony will work best for that span. Let's try out this method.

The accented pitches in m. 1 are F (on beat 1) and A (on beat 3), which imply a tonic harmony; since this is the first full measure of the piece, we can almost assume it will be tonic. Further, the upbeat eighth notes (on C) imply a dominant harmony, and, as we know, chords generally change from a weak beat to a strong beat. Using this method, we arrive at the following summary of harmonies that begin and end phrases:

Phrase 1:	Phrase 2:	Phrase 3:	Phrase 4:
mm. 1–2–3–4	mm. 5–6–7–8	mm. 9–10–11–12	mm. 13–14–15–16
I HC	I PAC	I HC	I PAC

Finally, looking at melodic patterns and starting to feel the implied harmonic changes, we find that the harmonies change no more often than once per measure. Phrase 1 contains harmonic changes every two measures. Phrases 2 and 4 share the same harmonic rhythm: two measures of tonic, one measure of dominant, and cadence on tonic. Phrase 3 has three measures of tonic and one measure of dominant.

Phrase 1:	Phrase 2:	Phrase 3:	Phrase 4:
mm. 1–2—3–4	5–6–7–8	9–10–11–12	13–14–15–16
I V	I V I	I V	I V I

Of course, folk song is but one type of music that depends on a relatively slow rate of harmonic change and the use of only a few basic chords (see Example 9.18). Using our analytical method, we see that there are two phrases, the first of which implies a HC and the second a PAC. The remaining harmonies are clearly implied, given that most of the melody is composed of chordal leaps. Thus, mm. 37–38 are tonic harmony, mm. 39–40 are dominant, and m. 40 is the HC. Measures 41–42 are dominant, with m. 41 adding A♭, the seventh of the chord. Measure 42 begins with A♭, implying a V_7 chord, and the rest of the measure could certainly be harmonized all by V_7 (the tones of figuration are strongly accented and therefore obscure the implied harmony).

EXAMPLE 9.18 Haydn, String Quartet in E♭ major, op. 76, no. 6, Trio (melody only)

Let's see how Haydn actually harmonizes these eight measures, with special attention to m. 43 (Example 9.19). Haydn has indeed followed the hints in the melody and harmonized at least most of it the way we had imagined.

However, he fooled us a bit in m. 43: He begins the measure with a I chord, treating the downbeat A♭ as a dissonant tone of figuration. Only at the very end of the measure does he move to the expected V chord.

EXAMPLE 9.19 Haydn, String Quartet in E♭ major, op. 76, no. 6, Trio

Summary

The central point of this chapter has been to show that tonal music is hierarchical. That is, certain events are more important than others. And what is remarkable is that these events need not be literally sounding in order for them to control a musical passage. For example, an underlying tonic may guide a tonal progression even if the actual tonic triad is not present. This notion of hierarchy can trickle down so that chords helping to extend a harmony may themselves be more important than surrounding harmonies, a process that can continue to the surface of the music. How composers extend more important contrapuntal and harmonic events by those that are less important is one thread we will follow in Chapters 10 and 11.

EXERCISE INTERLUDE

PERFORMING

9.3

The following arpeggiations create progressions that incorporate V_7. Sing them and/or play them on an instrument. Next, transpose the arpeggiations to other major and minor keys—remember that in minor keys, you raise $\hat{7}$ for the leading tone.

LISTENING

9.4

Distinguishing between V, V_7, and V8–7. For each short harmonic progression that you hear, identify the following:

1. mode (major or minor)
2. scale degree of first soprano pitch
3. type of cadence (IAC, PAC, HC)
4. whether V, V_7, or $V_{8\text{-}7}$ is used at the cadence

	mode	scale degree of 1st pitch	cadence type	type of V
A.	______	______	______	______
B.	______	______	______	______
C.	______	______	______	______
D.	______	______	______	______

ANALYSIS

9.5

Listen to the following melodies, observing how often the harmonies change. Analyze the progressions with roman numerals. Be able to sing each example.

DVD 2
CH 9
TRACK 3

9.6

The following excerpts demonstrate I, V, and V_7.

1. Listen to each example and complete a two-level harmonic analysis. Be sure you are able to distinguish between V and V_7.
2. As you analyze each example, note if the sevenths are prepared (not a requirement) as a common tone or by step. Draw a line from each seventh to its resolution.

A.

B. Schubert, Waltz in B major, from *36 Originaltänze*, op. 9, no. 24, D. 365

C. Schubert, Minuet in A minor, from *20 Minuets*, D. 41, no. 8, Trio.

The dissonant notes in the sixteenth-note figure found in mm. 2, 3, 6 and 7 are upper and lower neighbors around the chord tones. Together they constitute a double neighbor figure.

KEYBOARD

9.7

Play the following broken-chord exercise, which features a dominant-seventh chord in root position and each inversion. Transpose to major keys up to three sharps and three flats.

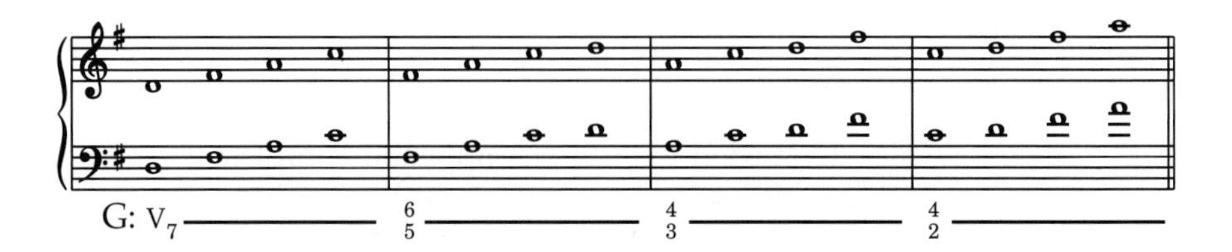

9.8

Identify the major key of each example, and play authentic cadences in *three* voices from the given V_7. Focus on resolution of tendency tones. Be able to sing any of the three voices while playing the other two.

e.g.:

G:

9.9

The two-voice models demonstrate common settings of I–V_7–I. Add inner voices, and play in four-voice keyboard style in C and in major and minor keys up to and including three sharps and flats. Be able to sing either the bass voice or the soprano voice while playing the other three voices.

$\hat{3}$ $\hat{2}$ $\hat{1}$ | $\hat{5}$ $\hat{4}$ $\hat{3}$ | $\hat{5}$ $\hat{4}$ $\hat{3}$ $\hat{2}$ $\hat{1}$ | $\hat{1}$ $\hat{7}$ $\hat{1}$ | $\hat{3}$ $\hat{4}$ $\hat{3}$ | $\hat{1}$ $\hat{4}$ $\hat{3}$

10 5 8 | 5 7 10 | 5 7 10 5 8 | 8 10 8 | 10 7 10 | 8 7 10

9.10

Play the progression I–V_7–I in four voices, keyboard style, in any major or minor key up to three sharps and three flats. Be able to demonstrate the various complete and incomplete voicings. Also, be able to sing either the bass voice or the soprano voice while playing the other three voices.

WRITING

9.11

Harmonize any three of the following tunes using usually one chord per measure. However, some tunes may permit the same harmony to continue for two or more measures, while others may require two chords within a single measure. Use only root-position I, V, and V_7. Apply the following method:

WORKBOOK
9.2–9.7

1. Determine the key.
2. Sing or play the tune.
3. Find cadences.

4. Determine the harmonic rhythm.
5. Determine individual harmonies by looking at accented pitches. Remember, $\hat{1}$– $\hat{3}$– $\hat{5}$ implies a I chord and $\hat{5}$– $\hat{7}$– $\hat{2}$ and often $\hat{4}$ imply a $V(_7)$ harmony. Arpeggiations and chordal skips imply a single harmony.

Note: Most tones of figuration occur on weak beats or weak parts of beats.

A. Mozart, "Longing for Spring," K. 596, *Giocoso*

B. Mozart, Symphony no. 39, K. 543, *Allegretto*

C. Haydn, "Surprise" Symphony in G major, no. 94, *Allegro*

D. Russian folk tune, *Andante grazioso.*

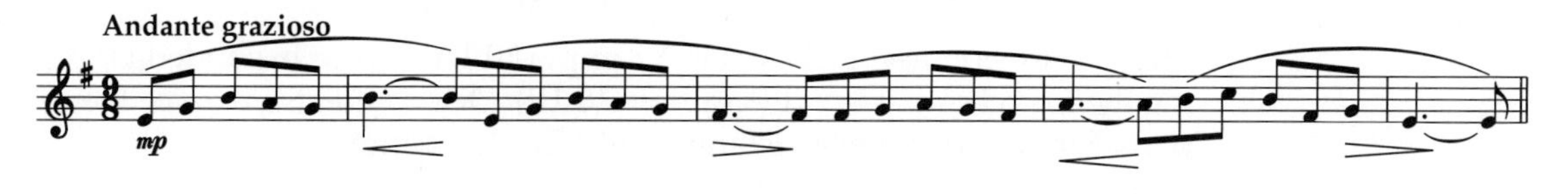

TERMS AND CONCEPTS

- embellishment/figuration: metrical, submetrical, supermetrical
- analysis: descriptive v. interpretive
- chordal dissonance
- dominant seventh chord
- 8–7
- preparation and resolution
- unequal fifths

CHAPTER 10

Contrapuntal Expansions of Tonic and Dominant: Six–Three Chords

In this chapter we explore how inversions of tonic and dominant triads enrich musical structure by elaborating the tonic–dominant axis within a phrase. Because inverted triads are less stable than their root-position counterparts, they allow for greater harmonic nuance. And by using inversions, composers turn the bass line into a melody.

Chordal Leaps in the Bass: I_6 and V_6

The progression I–V–I (shown in Example 10.1A) can be expanded by repeating the first chord: I–I–V–I (Example 10.1B). One could also revoice the upper parts for added interest (Example 10.1C). But a more dramatic and contrapuntally interesting way to expand the tonic is to use the first inversion I_6 chord: I–I_6–V–I (Example 10.1D). Instead of the leap of a fifth, the bass first skips to another note in the tonic chord, called, as we know, a chordal leap (CL). The I_6 chord is less stable than the root-position I chord; this instability helps to push the music forward. Play the inversions in Example 10.2, listening closely for tension.

EXAMPLE 10.1

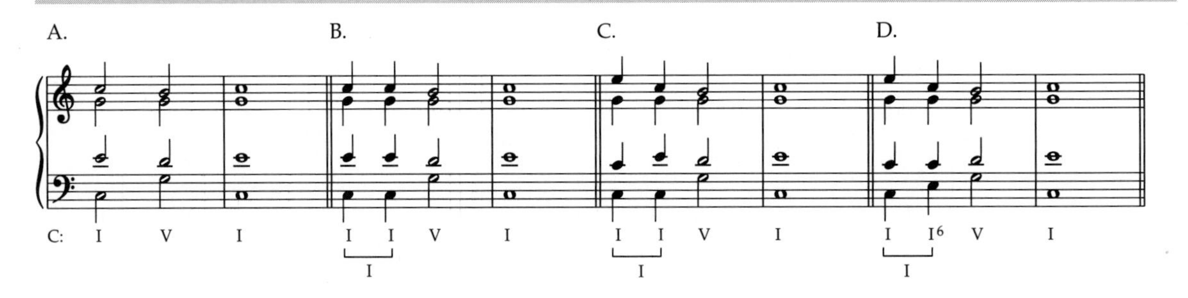

EXAMPLE 10.2

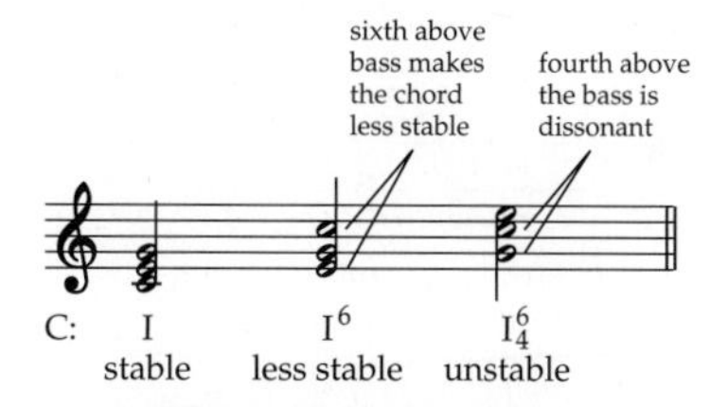

Whereas root-position and first-inversion triads can often be interchanged, second-inversion triads are not an effective substitute for either root position or first inversion, given their dissonant fourth above the bass. As we shall see later, triads in second inversion function quite differently from those in root position and first inversion. For the time being, we will use only root-position and first-inversion chords.

The folk song excerpt in Example 10.3A may be harmonized exclusively by means of tonic and dominant chords. Indeed, the chordal leaps and single weak-beat passing tone in m. 3 imply a harmonic rhythm of one chord per measure, with an alternation of tonic and dominant chords (see Example 10.3B). The excerpt closes with a half cadence. Although this is a passable harmonization, it is not very inspired, given the predictable bass. More problematic is the rather heavy and static sound created by the consistent root-position harmonies. Indeed, the half cadence sounds less like an arrival and more like just another dominant harmony.

EXAMPLE 10.3 A–C

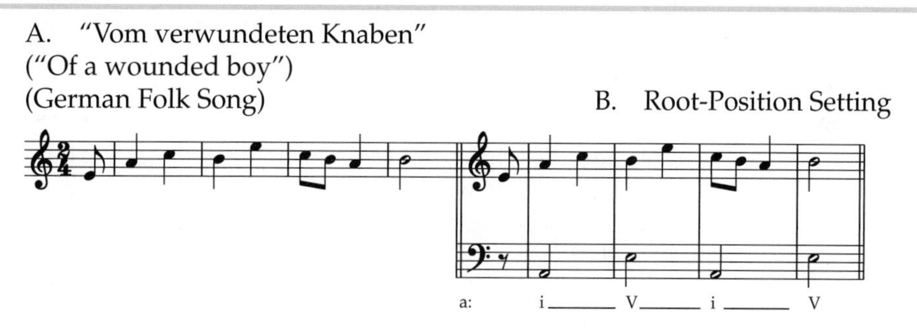

C. Brahms' Setting of "Vom verwundeten Knaben," op. 14, no. 2

D. Brahms, with Voice Exchanges

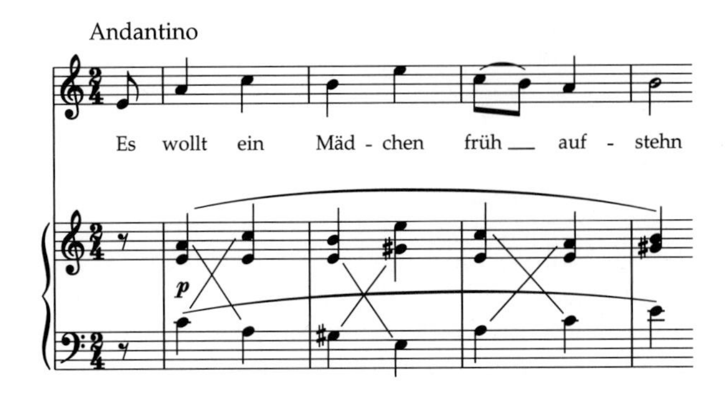

In Example 10.3C, Brahms restricts the harmonies in his setting to the very tonic and dominant chords heard in the previous example. But rather than relying exclusively on root-position triads, he includes their first-inversion counterparts. This visually unobtrusive change actually aurally alters the piece to the degree that it is now buoyant and strongly directed toward the half cadence.

First-inversion chords energize phrases because they render the bass more melodic. A brief look at the lowest voice in Brahms's setting reveals a melodic arch created by the descent of a sixth from C to E and the ascent of an octave to the half cadence. Thus, the bass plays multiple roles, fusing harmonic function with melodic interest, as it becomes a counterpart to the soprano, with which its underlying counterpoint controls the flow of events.

Indeed, a glance at the downbeat intervals of the root-position harmonization in Example 10.3B reveals an octave, a fifth, a tenth, and a fifth; only the tenth is active. Now compare this with Brahms's setting in Example 10.3C. Not only are the downbeat intervals all active (sixths and tenths, except for the half cadence's fifth), but so are nearly all of the weak-beat intervals. Note that the piece begins with tonic in first inversion, as does the second measure, where the leading tone, G♯, is prominently displayed in the bass's V_6 chord. The relationship between bass and soprano is intensified by the fact that the intervals in mm. 1 and 3 are inverted, and the pitches are swapped, creating voice exchanges (the voice exchange in m. 2 occurs between the piano's bass and tenor parts). Example 10.3D shows these voice exchanges.

Moving between a chord's root position and first inversion is analogous to revoicing the upper voices of a harmony. That is, there is no harmonic change, but rather, the extension or prolongation of a single harmony. That this can occur in the bass simply makes the change more dramatic. As a rule, it is much more common to extend the tonic harmony using its first inversion than it is to extend the dominant with its first inversion.

Example 10.4 presents common bass and soprano settings for motions between I and I_6, all of which are applicable to expanding V with V_6 (as shown in Example 10.4A2). Notice that the motion both to root position from first inversion and from first inversion to root position involves at least one and often two imperfect consonances (thirds and sixths). The fluid nature of the inverted chords helps propel a phrase and therefore these chords are best used within a phrase rather than at the beginning or end of a phrase, where the stability of root-position chords is desired [although Brahms began his song in this very way (see Example 10.3), with a i_6 chord!].

EXAMPLE 10.4

DVD 1
CH 10
TRACK 1

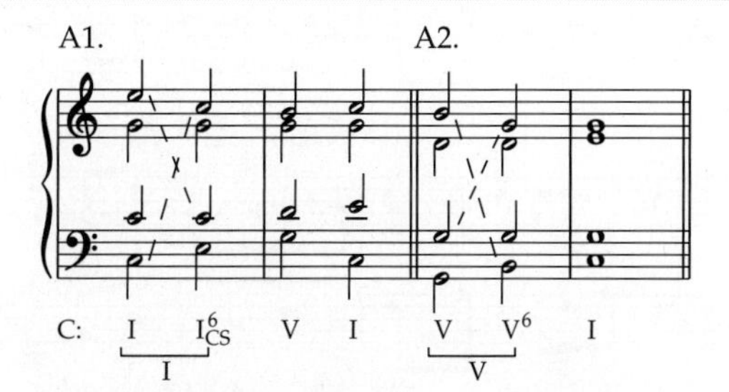

B. Schubert, Impromptu in B♭ major, Thema, *Andante*

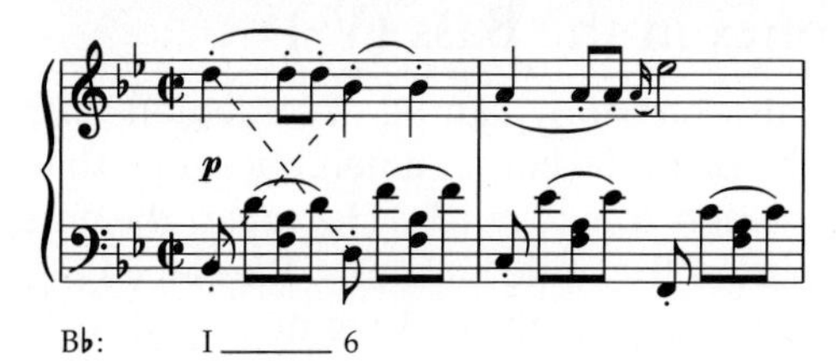

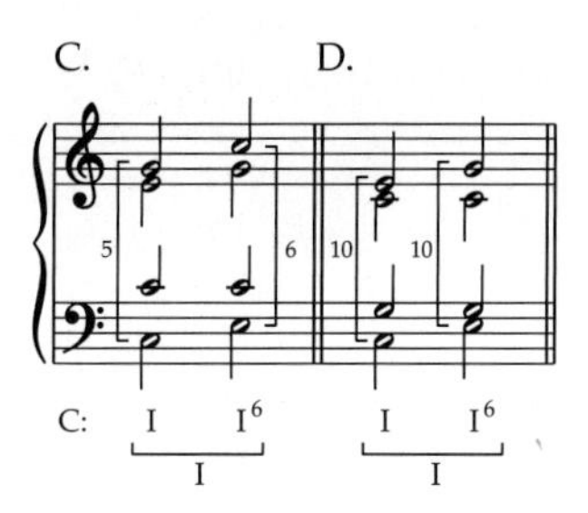

In addition to the voice exchange in Example 10.4A1 (in which the bass motion of $\hat{1}$ up to $\hat{3}$ is mirrored in the soprano, which descends from $\hat{3}$ to $\hat{1}$), using I_6 between I and V breaks up the large leap of a fifth into two smaller leaps of a third. To be sure, just as $\hat{1}$ in the soprano is most often harmonized by the tonic, $\hat{3}$ in the bass overwhelmingly appears as part of the tonic triad. By virtue of its greater instability, the inverted triad contrasts nicely with the more stable pillars of the harmonic progression, the root-position I and V. The pitches retained through the voice exchange make it clear that a single harmony, the tonic, has been extended by chordal leaps, as in Example 10.4B.

The contrary-motion voice exchange is one of many possible outer-voice configurations. Example 10.4C shows a similar-motion outer-voice counterpoint, and Example 10.4D shows parallel-tenth motion. Not only are these chordal leaps reversible ($^5_3 \rightarrow ^6_3$ or $^6_3 \rightarrow ^5_3$), but they may work in tandem, their combination creating entire phrases, as shown in Example 10.5. Telemann draws exclusively on I, I_6, V, and V_6, reserving V_7 for the cadence.

EXAMPLE 10.5 Telemann, Domenica, from *Scherzi Melodichi, Vivace*

Neighbor Tones in the Bass (V_6)

We have seen that a harmony can be ornamented with a neighbor tone; in Example 10.6A, the B2 in the bass is a neighbor tone that ties together the surrounding root position tonic chords. However, the pitch B is dissonant because it is not a part of the tonic harmony. We can change the upper voices to pitches that are consonant with the bass note B, thus **harmonizing** the bass note. The result is a V_6 chord (see Example 10.6B). Although we have created a new chord, it is still ornamental and subordinate to the surrounding chords. We refer to the V_6 harmony as a **neighboring chord**.

EXAMPLE 10.6

A.

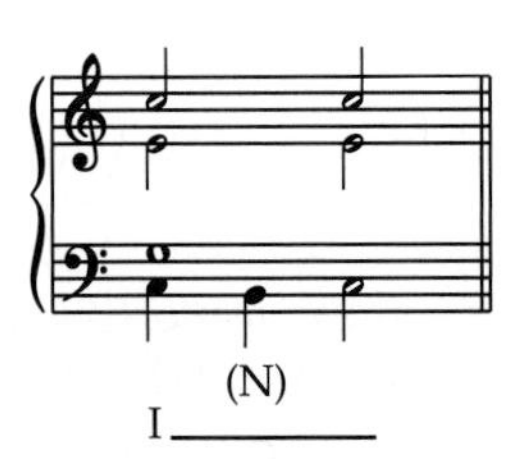

B.

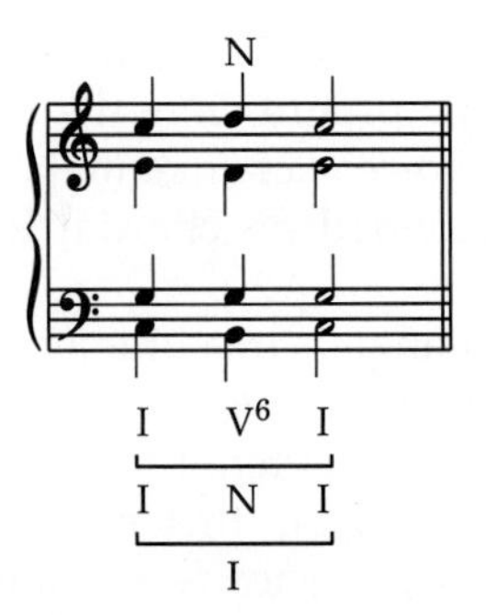

Often $\hat{5}$ is prominently displayed in the soprano when V_6 extends I, since this common tone secures their kinship. In addition, the musical drama is intensified because the outer-voice perfect fifth of the tonic harmony ($\hat{1}$ in the bass and $\hat{5}$ in the soprano) is destabilized by the sixth of the first-inversion dominant harmony, an effect taken advantage of by Beethoven in the first sonorities of the slow movement from his seventh symphony (Example 10.7A). A different effect is created when the soprano begins on $\hat{3}$, joining the bass in its own neighboring motion; the result is the gently rocking pair of lines moving in parallel tenths. Schubert opens one of his slow movements in just this way (Example 10.7B).

EXAMPLE 10.7

DVD 1
CH 10
TRACK 2

A. Beethoven, Symphony no. 7, *Allegretto*

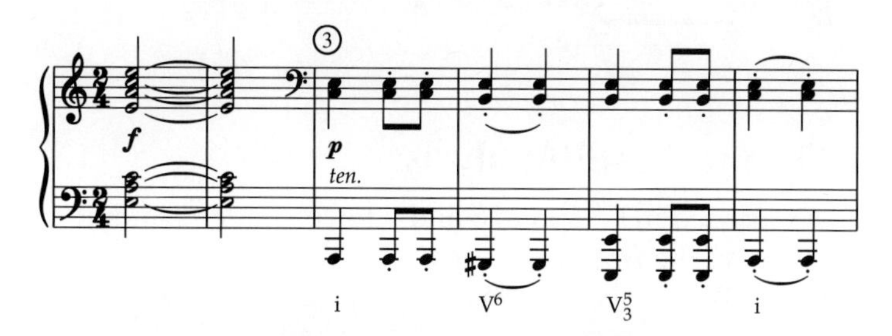

B. Schubert, Piano Sonata in A major, D. 959, *Andantino*

The V_6 can also be used as an **incomplete neighboring chord**. The most common type of incomplete neighbor occurs when I_6 is followed by V_6, which then returns to I (see Example 10.8A). In minor, the bass leap from $\hat{3}$ to $\hat{7}$ forms a diminished fourth, which, given its extreme pathos and that the leading tone is immediately resolved, is permitted. See Example 10.8B, in which Corelli presents a dramatic diminished-fourth leap from E♭ (the bass of i_6) to B natural (bass of V_6).

EXAMPLE 10.8

A. "V as Neighboring Chord"

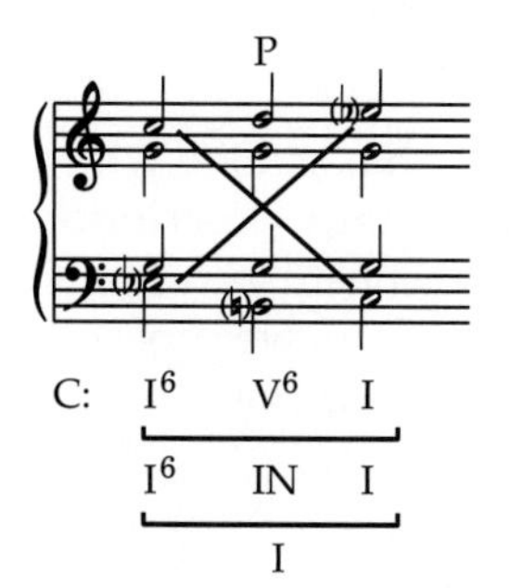

B. Corelli, Concerto Grosso no. 8 in F major, *Allegro* no. 2

Second-Level Analysis

We learned in Chapters 8 and 9 to consider harmonic analysis as a two-stage process. The first stage (or **first-level analysis**) identifies each sonority with roman numerals; such labeling represents the **descriptive** analysis of the progression. The second stage—or **second-level analysis**—reflects the functions of the sonorities. Some harmonies are structural, and other harmonies are ornamental. Structural harmonies are **progressional** because they indicate movement from one harmonic function (such as tonic) to another (such as dominant); structural harmonies keep their roman numerals in second-level analysis. Subordinate harmonies—such as the neighboring chord in Example 10.8—help to extend or prolong a single structural harmony. We call such harmonies **prolongational**. In second-level analysis, prolongational chords are labeled by melodic function, as this chart shows.

Structural harmonies . . .	*Subordinate harmonies . . .*
• are progressional	• are prolongational
• have harmonic function (tonic, dominant)	• have melodic function (chordal skip, neighbor tone)
• are usually on strong beats	• are usually on weak beats
• are usually in root position	• are usually in inversion
• are part of a harmonic progression	• are part of a contrapuntal progression
• keep their roman numerals in second-level analysis	• are labeled as ornaments ("N," "CS") in second-level analysis

As you can see, merely labeling each harmony with a roman numeral does not constitute an analysis; rather, it is more a description. An analysis with the sole aim of placing roman numerals beneath every chord is a mechanical and dull exercise, one that is doomed to fail. As we proceed, you will see the merits of multilevel analysis; fascinating compositional processes will emerge as you explore contrapuntal relationships between the bass and the soprano. Analysis is a creative, thought-provoking activity whose goal is to penetrate deep into the musical structure to reveal important correspondences between the surface and the underlying structure of a composition.

Writing and Playing First-Inversion Triads

Rules for Voice Leading and Doubling of First-Inversion Triads

- Keep common tones (unless you use a voice exchange which often requires movement in all voices)
- When possible, double the root (you can double the third or fifth if it smoothes the voice leading)
- You may find it useful to follow this general guideline: In first-inversion triads, double scale degrees $\hat{1}$, $\hat{5}$, $\hat{2}$.
- Never double the leading tone, $\hat{7}$ (the third of a dominant chord).
- Embellishing chords, especially those that neighbor, usually appear on metrically weak beats or parts of beats.

Up to this point, your keyboard chord progressions have been restricted to root-position triads and seventh chords. When the chord's root was in the bass, your right hand played a close-position chord that automatically doubled the root. However, the strategy of doubling the bass won't work for a first-inversion dominant triad (V_6), because doubling its third means doubling the leading tone.

Two Techniques for Playing and Writing First-Inversion Triads

- Double unisons (Example 10.9A and B).
- Use "neutral position" (Example 10.9C).

EXAMPLE 10.9

A. doubled unison

B. doubled unison

C.

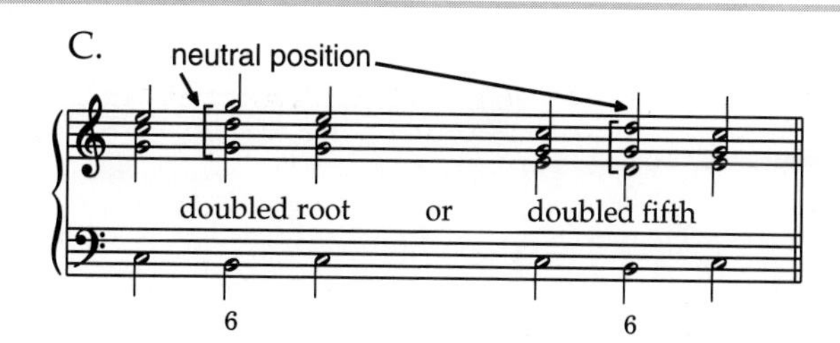

EXERCISE INTERLUDE

PERFORMING

10.1

The following arpeggiations create progressions that incorporate common uses of I_6 and V_6. Sing them and/or play them on an instrument. Listen to how often harmonies change; then analyze the progressions with roman numerals. Next, transpose the arpeggiations to other major and minor keys—remember that in minor keys, you raise $\hat{7}$ for the leading tone.

A.

B.

KEYBOARD

10.2

The following figured basses incorporate I_6 and V_6 chords. Play each in four-voice keyboard style (bass note in the left hand; upper voices in the right hand). Apply "doubled unisons" and "neutral position" when possible. Next, transpose the progressions to major and minor keys with key signatures up to two sharps or flats—remember that in minor keys, you raise $\hat{7}$ for the leading tone.

A.

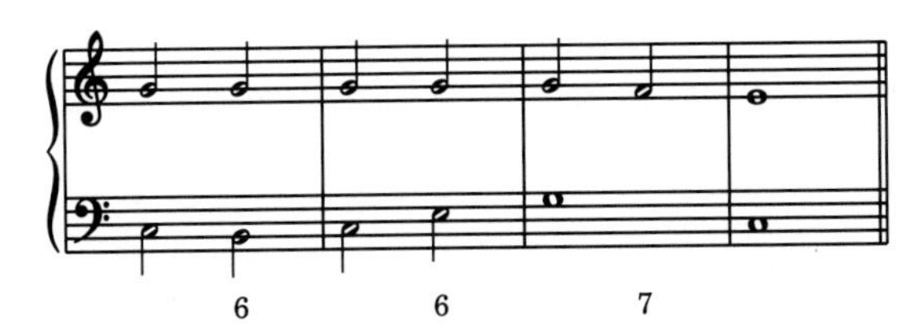

B.

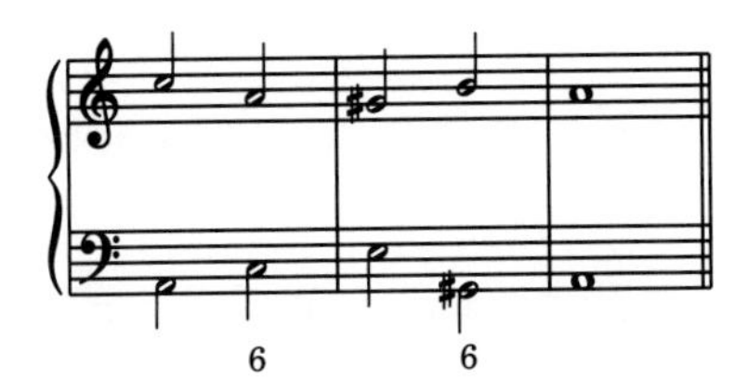

C.

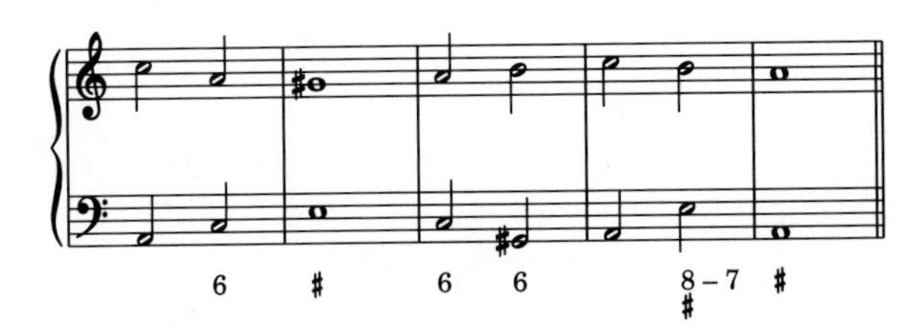

WRITING

10.3

In four-voice chorale style, set the following soprano scale degree fragments and bass scale degree fragments in the keys listed. Each progression must contain a tonic expansion. Some progressions, however, may contain both a tonic expansion and a cadence. Use only I (i), I_6 (i_6), V, V_6, V_7.

Soprano scale degrees

- In A minor: $\hat{1}$–$\hat{2}$–$\hat{3}$
- In F major: $\hat{3}$–$\hat{1}$–$\hat{5}$–$\hat{4}$–$\hat{3}$
- In B minor: $\hat{3}$–$\hat{2}$–$\hat{1}$–$\hat{7}$–$\hat{1}$

Bass scale degrees

- In C minor: $\hat{1}$–$\hat{7}$–$\hat{1}$–$\hat{2}$–$\hat{3}$
- In E♭ major: $\hat{1}$–$\hat{3}$–$\hat{7}$–$\hat{1}$
- In A major: $\hat{3}$–$\hat{2}$–$\hat{1}$–$\hat{5}$–$\hat{1}$

DVD 2
CH 10
TRACK 1

WORKBOOK
10.1–10.2

LISTENING

10.4

Listen to, memorize, and then notate the bass lines in the following examples, which use I, (i) I_6 (i_6), V, V_7, and V_6. Provide a two-level harmonic analysis. All exercises have two sharps in their key signatures. Exercises A and B are in $\frac{4}{4}$; C and D are in $\frac{6}{8}$; and E is in $\frac{4}{4}$.

Passing Tones in the Bass: vii°$_6$

So far we have seen contrapuntal expansions using neighbor tones (I–V_6–I) and chordal leaps (I–I_6 and V–V_6). A third contrapuntal motion, **passing**, expands the tonic by inserting a bass passing tone between I and I_6 chords.

Example 10.10 presents the opening of one of Handel's flute sonata movements. Each of the tonic's bass tones ($\hat{1}$ and $\hat{3}$ in m. 1 and the reverse in m. 2) is harmonized by root-position and first-inversion triads; in m. 1 a voice exchange is created between the bass and flute Bs and Ds. Notice, in addition, that Handel has harmonized the bass and soprano passing tones C♯ ($\hat{2}$) with first-inversion chords built on vii°. Given that vii°$_6$ harmonizes the passing tone C♯, it is called a **passing chord**, as shown below the example in the second-level analysis. Just as we learned for neighboring embellishing chords, passing chords usually fall on metrically weak beats or parts of beats. Before we leave the Handel example, notice in m. 3 that the tonic harmony first appears on a weak part of the beat; sandwiched between two dominant harmonies and harmonizing D, a weak-beat passing tone in the flute (we interpret the tonic chord as an incomplete neighbor that helps to extend the dominant that began its control on the second beat of m. 2 and that remains in force until the strong-beat arrival of tonic at the end of the excerpt). Standing back even further, we might assign the extended V_6 chord a neighboring function, given that it is flanked by the opening and closing tonic chords in root position.

EXAMPLE 10.10 Handel, Flute Sonata in B minor, HWV 367b

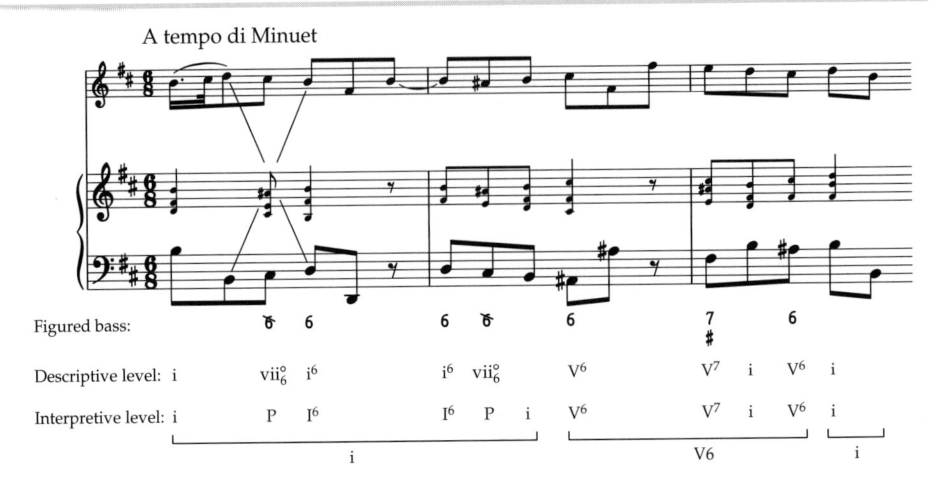

Example 10.11 shows common settings of vii°$_6$ with both first- and second-level analysis. Again, each of the contrapuntal chords occurs on a metrically unaccented beat, while the underlying harmony that is expanded usually occurs in a metrically accented position.

EXAMPLE 10.11

DVD 1
CH 10
TRACK 3

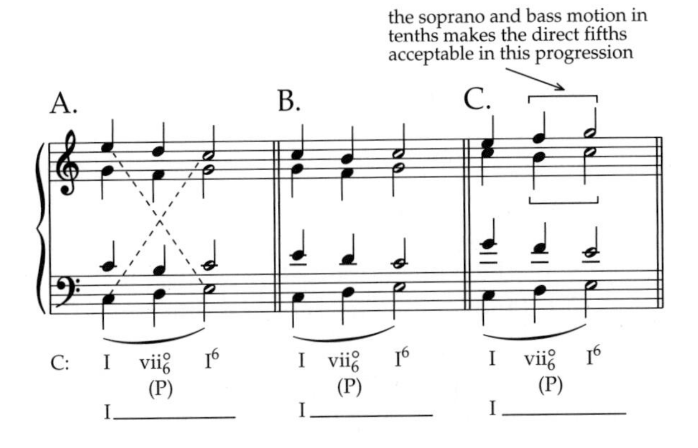

You might wonder why vii° in first inversion—rather than ii in root position—was preferred when harmonizing the bass passing tone $\hat{2}$. The ii is a strong harmony that draws attention away from the tonic and therefore is not a suitable contrapuntal chord. By contrast, vii°$_6$ is a perfect passing chord because:

- It is unstable—it has a diminished sonority.
- It shares notes with V and V$_7$, which work well as passing chords (we call vii°$_6$ a **dominant substitute**).
- It is in first inversion and therefore is more likely to be a contrapuntal chord.

Voice Leading for vii°$_6$

- **Never** double the leading tone, $\hat{7}$.
- Try to double the third of the chord ($\hat{2}$), which may move to either $\hat{1}$ or $\hat{3}$ (you may double $\hat{4}$, but only to make the voice leading smoother).
- If possible, resolve the tritone (as you did with V^7)—but it is common not to resolve the tritone if:
  - It leads to a complete tonic triad (Example 10.11A, B, and C).
  - It does not involve the bass (Example 10.11A and B). This is especially true if the tritone is expressed as an augmented fourth (rather than a diminished fifth).
  - The bass and soprano move by parallel tenths (Example 10.11C).

When we write vii°$_6$ in the minor mode, there is one addition to our figured bass vocabulary. We must raise the sixth above the bass of a vii°$_6$ chord—this is $\hat{7}$—in order to create a leading tone. Example 10.12 presents the figured bass you will encounter for vii°$_6$ in major and minor modes and, below that, the harmonic analysis that you should use.

EXAMPLE 10.12

DVD 1
CH 10
TRACK 4

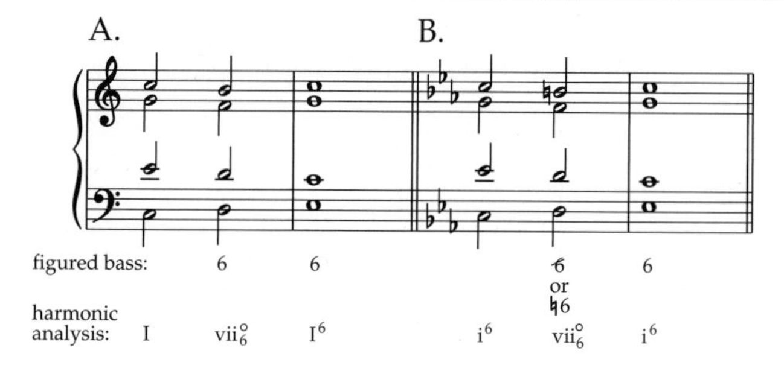

Tonic Expansion with an Arpeggiating Bass: IV$_6$

We know that I$_6$ expands I, with the bass *ascending* by a *third* (from $\hat{1}$ up to $\hat{3}$). Sometimes, for reasons of drama or range, the bass moves from I to I$_6$ by *falling* a *sixth*, from $\hat{1}$ down to $\hat{3}$, as in Example 10.13. Notice the large-scale voice exchange that results in the process: The soprano uses a passing tone ($\hat{3}$–$\hat{2}$–$\hat{1}$), and the bass uses a chordal leap or arpeggiation ($\hat{1}$–$\hat{5}$–$\hat{3}$). See Example 10.13B. The resulting V chord is subordinate to the surrounding tonic chords.

EXAMPLE 10.13 Handel, "Comfort Ye," from *Messiah*, HWV 56

DVD 1
CH 10
TRACK 5

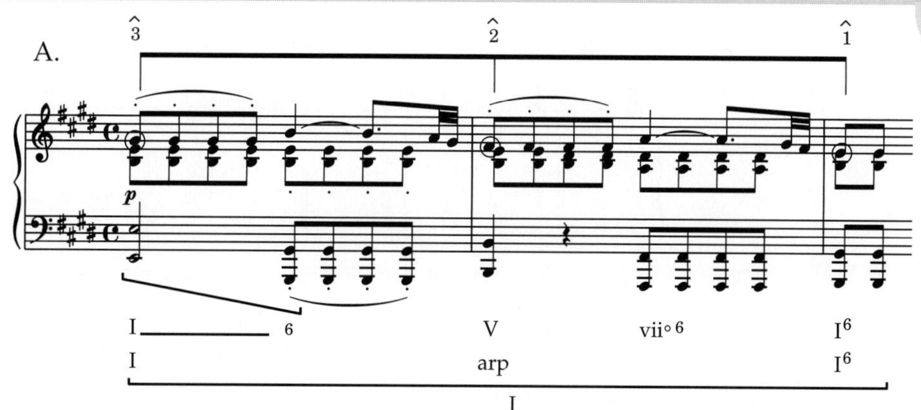

Continued

B.

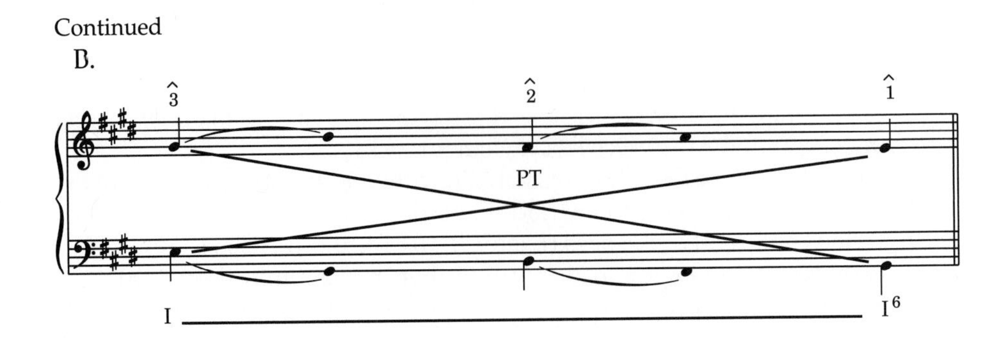

The large leap of a sixth is often split into the arpeggiation $\hat{1}$–$\hat{6}$–$\hat{3}$ by the addition of a new chord: IV_6 (see Example 10.14). Notice the stepwise ascent, $\hat{3}$–$\hat{4}$–$\hat{5}$, in the soprano; this ascent of $\hat{4}$ to $\hat{5}$ provides an important contrast to its more usual descent, as the dissonant seventh in dominant harmony. When you write IV_6, it is common to double $\hat{1}$ (the third above the bass), but you are free to double any member of the chord since smooth voice leading must always take priority over doublings in our writing.

EXAMPLE 10.14

DVD 1 CH 10 TRACK 6

Dominant Expansion with Passing Tones: IV_6

Just as tonic may be expanded with a passing $vii°_6$ chord, so too may the dominant be expanded by a first-inversion IV_6 chord. Observe in Example 10.15 how V–IV_6–V_6 is used in major and minor keys.

EXAMPLE 10.15

DVD 1 CH 10 TRACK 7

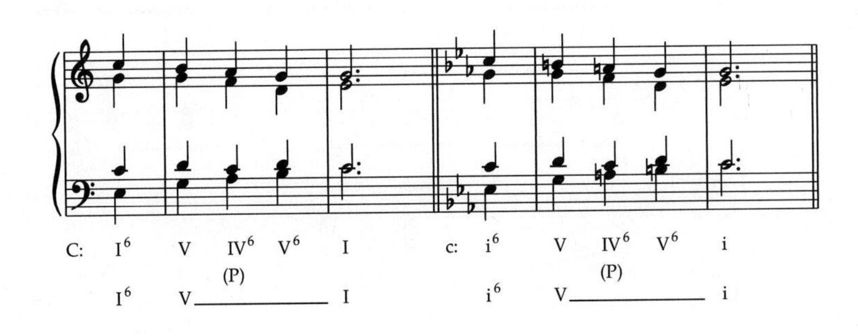

Voice Leading for V–IV$_6$–V$_6$

- In minor keys, $\hat{6}$ must be raised to avoid an augmented second between $\hat{6}$ and $\hat{7}$—this results in a major IV$_6$ chord.
- Avoid parallel fifths and octaves in IV$_6$–V$_6$ by moving the upper voices in contrary motion to the bass.

Combining First-Inversion Chords

Extended prolongations of tonic are common, and they often involve combinations of the first-inversion chords we have discussed (I$_6$, V$_6$, vii°$_6$, and IV$_6$). Example 10.16 shows how a neighboring V$_6$ and vii°$_6$ create a double-neighbor figure in the bass.

EXAMPLE 10.16

DVD 1
CH 10
TRACK 8

Example 10.17, from one of Telemann's flute sonatas, opens with an expansion of the G-minor tonic using the same chords as Example 10.16: V$_6$ and vii°$_6$. However, V$_6$ is now an incomplete neighbor and vii°$_6$ passes between I and i$_6$.

EXAMPLE 10.17 Telemann, Sonata for Flute in B♭ major, *Dolce*

DVD 1
CH 10
TRACK 9

Summary

In this chapter we continued our exploration of two basic types of harmonies: structural (which we hear as controlling the underlying harmonic flow of the music) and embellishing (which ornaments and extends the structural harmonies through their derivation as byproducts of melodic and contrapuntal events). Indeed, by considering melody, harmony, and the resulting two-voice counterpoint, we have a powerful standard by which to interpret each harmony. The importance of determining the function of each harmony is underscored in our second-level analysis, which carries with it performance implications. To be sure, composers did not create their artworks because of some burning desire to insert a I_6 or vii°_6 chord. Rather, their choice of harmony came from artistic efforts to make their pieces goal directed and integrated. They accomplished this in a variety of ways, including sharing the same melodic figures (such as passing and neighbor tones), passing them from one instrument to another to create recurring gestures or motives. When they fleshed out the harmonies implied by the melodic lines, the result was a tightly knit and organic structure. The two Corelli excerpts in Example 10.18 reveal this process. Indeed, if one considers the act of labeling each chord with a roman numeral (m. 1: (i)—V—i—vii°_6; and m. 2: i_6—V_6—i—etc.) to be the limits of analysis, one would have missed the "point," or premise, of these pieces, because the harmonies are actually the byproducts of a compositional process. In Example 10.18A, Corelli has simply transferred the melodic figure of F♯–B–C♯–D–A♯–B from violin 1 to the keyboard. The same process is seen in Example 10.18B, where the I–IV_6–I_6 progression is the result of the transfer of the violin's tune to the harpsichord.

EXAMPLE 10.18

DVD 1
CH 10
TRACK 10

A. Corelli, Violin Sonata in F major, op. 2, no. 7, *Allegro*

B. Corelli, Violin Sonata in F major, op. 5, no. 4, *Grave*

Example 10.19 graphically summarizes the way tonic and dominant functions are elaborated by means of first-inversion chords.

EXAMPLE 10.19 Chart of Chords

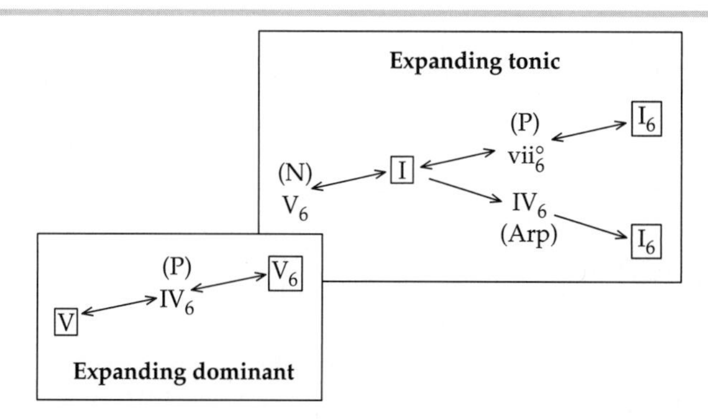

EXERCISE INTERLUDE

PERFORMING

10.5

A.

B.

C.

The following arpeggiations create progressions that incorporate common uses of I_6, V_6, vii°$_6$, and IV_6. Sing them and/or play them on an instrument. Listen to how often harmonies change. Then analyze the progressions with roman numerals. Next, transpose the arpeggiations to other major and minor keys—remember that in minor keys, you raise $\hat{7}$ for the leading tone, unless $\hat{7}$ passes down to $\hat{6}$, in which case $\hat{7}$ is not a leading tone, so we use its lowered form.

DVD 2 CH 10 TRACK 2

ANALYSIS

10.6

Each given analytical snapshot contains tonic expansions using the first-inversion triads I_6, V_6, vii°$_6$, and IV_6. Analyze each example using two levels where appropriate.

A. Mozart, String Quartet in F major, K. 590, *Andante*

B. Mozart, String Quartet in D minor, K. 173, *Menuetto*

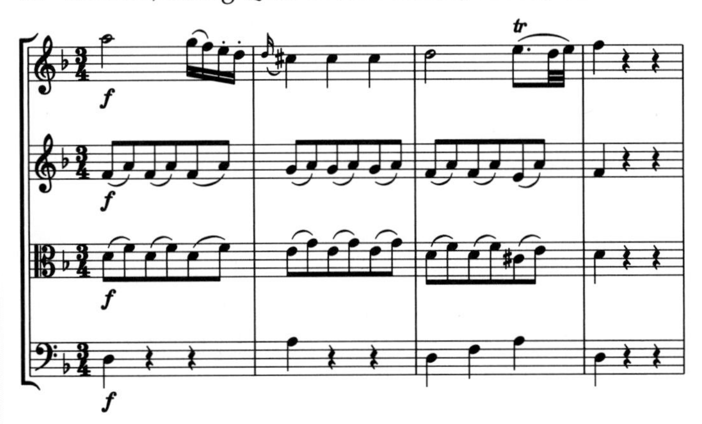

C. Mozart, String Quartet in C major, K. 157, *Andante*

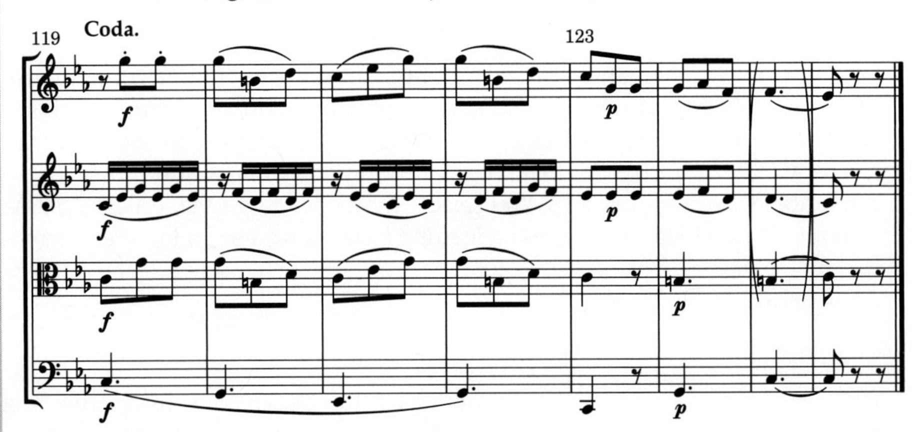

D. Johann Jacob Bach, Allegro from Flute Sonata in C minor

E. Haydn, String Quartet in D major, op. 76, no. 2, *Andante o piú tosto allegretto*

F. Beethoven, Violin Sonata no. 8 in G major, op. 30, no. 3, Minuet

KEYBOARD

10.7

Harmonize each soprano melodic fragment in two different ways. Your chord choices are I (i), I_6 (i_6) V, V_6, V_7, vii°$_6$, and IV_6 (iv_6). Harmonize all in D minor.

A. B. C. D. E. F.

10.8

Create a single melody by arranging the fragments from Exercise 10.7 in a logical order. Harmonize this melody in D minor using only i, i_6, V, V_6, V_7, and vii°$_6$, and IV_6. Be able to sing either outer voice while playing the other three voices. *Optional:* Add figuration to the upper voices of your homophonic setting.

WRITING

10.9

On a separate sheet of manuscript paper, complete the following tasks in four-voice chorale style. Analyze everything using first- and second-level analysis.

A. In D major, set I–vii°$_6$–I_6 three times. Each time use a different soprano melody.
B. In D minor, set the following progression in $\frac{3}{4}$ time, remembering that structural chords tend to be on stronger beats and subordinate chords tend to be on weaker beats: i–vii°$_6$–i_6–V_6–i–V_7–i
C. Set the progression from letter B in $\frac{4}{4}$ time.
D. Harmonize the following soprano fragments, and include vii°$_6$ chords where appropriate.
   1. In b minor, $\frac{2}{4}$ time: $\hat{3}$–$\hat{2}$–$\hat{1}$–$\hat{7}$–$\hat{1}$ (remember to raise $\hat{7}$ to create the leading tone in minor).
   2. In F major, $\frac{6}{8}$ time: $\hat{7}$–$\hat{1}$–$\hat{2}$–$\hat{3}$–$\hat{5}$–$\hat{4}$–$\hat{3}$.

E. In G major, set the following progression in $\frac{6}{8}$ time: I–V_6–I–IV_6–I_6–V^{8-7}–I.
F. In the key of G major and a meter of $\frac{4}{4}$, write a four-measure progression using a mixture of half notes and quarter notes in the soprano, each of which is harmonized. Remember, contrapuntal chords usually occur in unaccented metric positions. Include the following: (1) an expansion of the tonic with a passing chord, (2) a voice exchange, (3) an expansion of the tonic by a neighboring harmony in the bass, and (4) a PAC at the end.

LISTENING

10.10

On a separate sheet of manuscript paper, notate the bass part for each example. Then place a roman numeral that best fits each bass note, and also provide a second-level analysis. Each example has a key signature of one flat. All examples are cast in either $\frac{3}{4}$ or $\frac{4}{4}$; you will need to determine which of the two meters best fits each example. Listen first to an entire example without notating anything. Focus on:

1. Whether the meter is $\frac{3}{4}$ or $\frac{4}{4}$.
2. The location of the tonic harmonies—there should be a sense of return to the pitches of the tonic chord.

WORKBOOK
10.3–10.5

3. The location of first-inversion embellishing chords (V_6, vii°_6, IV_6) and how they expand tonic. Listen for metrical (harmonized) passing tones, neighbor tones, and chordal leaps in the outer voices.
4. Whether or not there is a root position, structural V chord near the end of the excerpt—does it sound like the excerpt ends with a strong V–I, or does it sound like the excerpt ends on V, which sounds open and unresolved?

TERMS AND CONCEPTS

- descriptive vs. interpretive analysis
- dominant substitute
- harmonic vs. contrapuntal progression
- incomplete neighboring chord
- neighboring chord
- passing chord
- passing motion
- structural harmonies vs. embellishing harmonies
- voice exchange

CHAPTER 11

More Contrapuntal Expansions: Inversions of V_7, Introduction to Leading Tone Seventh Chords, and Elaboration and Reduction

In this chapter, we explore the compositional possibilities of inverting V_7 and vii°$_7$ chords, which results in unstable chords that are used primarily to expand tonic. We will then look at the more limited functions of vii$^ø{}_7$.

V_7 and Its Inversions

Root-position V_7 generally does not expand the tonic. It is a progressional harmony that often signals a cadence; thus, it should be used sparingly. Inverted chords are inherently unstable and give rise to the kind of motion that is needed within a phrase. The inversions of V_7 are ideal embellishing chords. The voice leading for inverted V_7 chords is similar to that for root-position chords: The chordal third ($\hat{7}$) rises (to $\hat{1}$), and the chordal seventh ($\hat{4}$) resolves by step down (to $\hat{3}$) (Example 11.1).

EXAMPLE 11.1

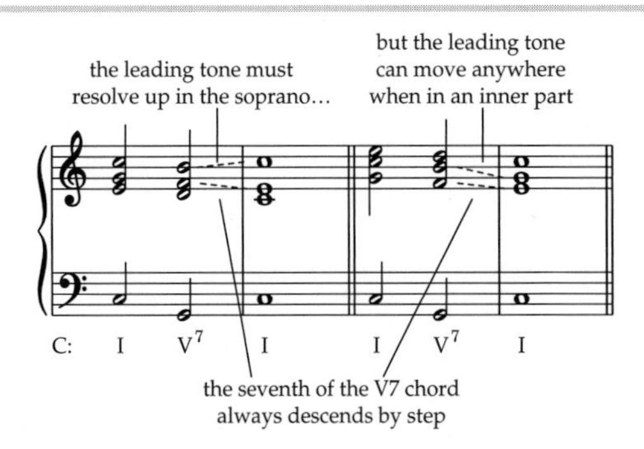

V^6_5

V^6_5 (first inversion) places the chordal third ($\hat{7}$) in the bass; thus it is usually a neighboring chord (like its first-inversion triadic cousin, V_6). The single difference between V_6 and V^6_5 is the presence of the chordal seventh ($\hat{4}$) in the latter, which often appears in the soprano. Example 11.2 presents the derivation of the V^6_5 chord from the V_6. The soprano in Example 11.2A skips down a third (from $\hat{5}$ to $\hat{3}$). The third is filled with the unaccented *passing seventh* in Example 11.2B. In Example 11.2C, the passing seventh is metrically accented.

EXAMPLE 11.2

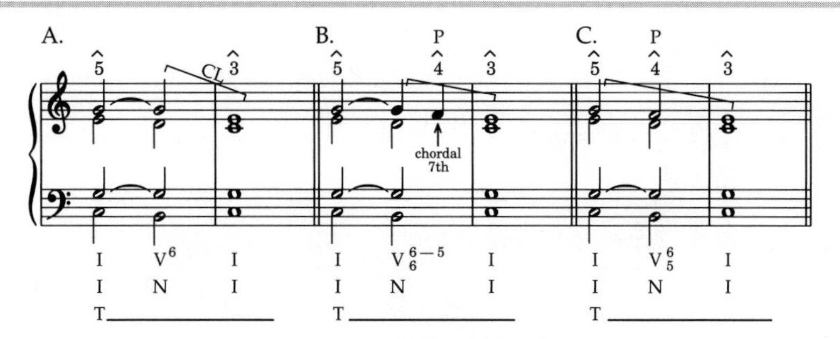

D. Mozart, Piano Sonata in E♭ major, K 282, *Allegro*

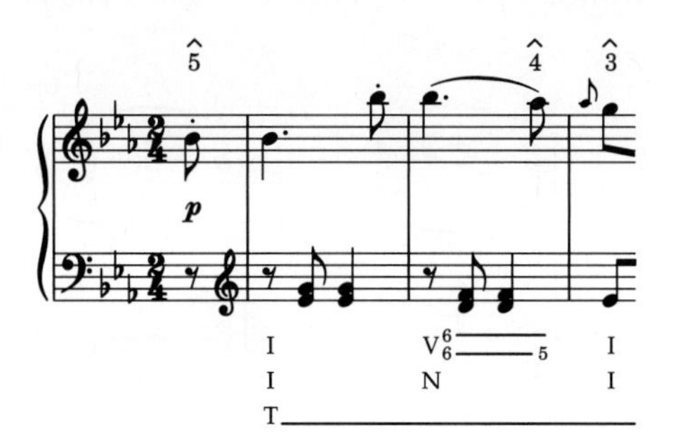

E.

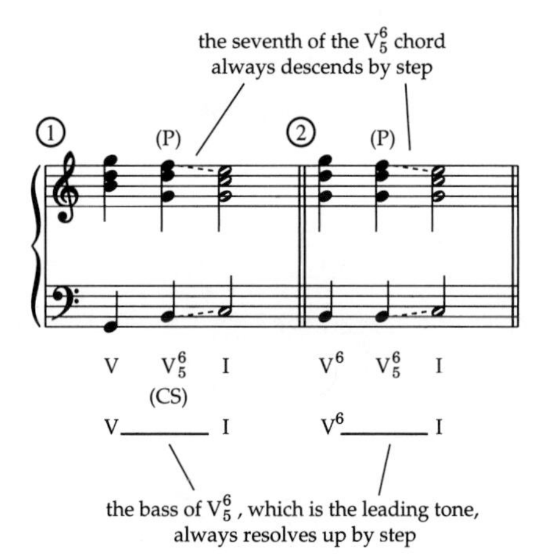

Example 11.2D illustrates the smooth entrance of the seventh: Mozart's movement begins on tonic, with B♭ ($\hat{5}$) prominently stated and then repeated as a dramatic octave leap. The sustained B♭ accompanies a harmonic change to a neighboring V_6 chord, which prepares the weak-beat passing seventh (A♭) that leads to the return of tonic in m. 3. Finally, V^6_5 can also follow V or V_6 (as shown in Example 11.2E) because the addition of the seventh intensifies a triad.

The seventh often appears within a *neighboring* configuration, where it mirrors the neighboring bass in contrary motion, as shown in Example 11.3A and B. With the anchoring neighbor motion of the fifth in an inner voice, a number of creative soprano lines are possible, one of which is shown in Example 11.3C, in which Mozart counterpoints the first violin and cello in parallel tenths.

EXAMPLE 11.3

DVD 1
CH 11
TRACK 2

A.

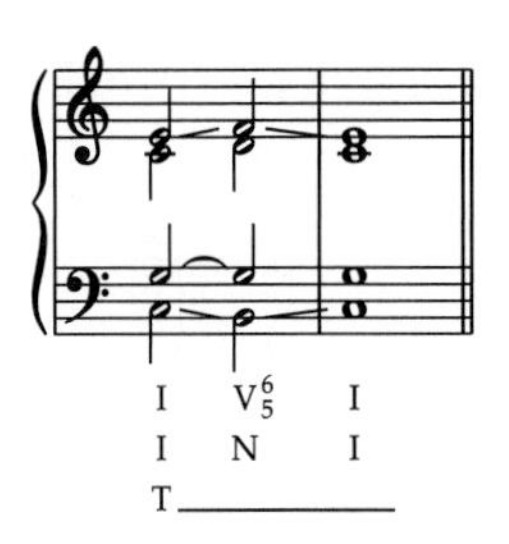

B. Beethoven, Symphony no. 7 in A major, *Assai meno presto*

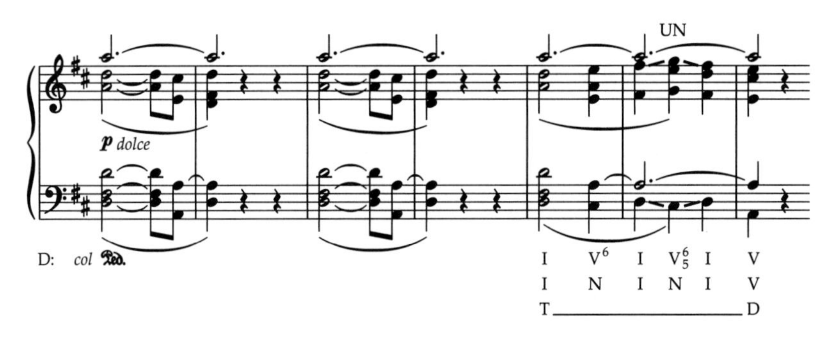

C. Mozart, String Quartet in B♭ major, K. 159, Rondo

V$^4_3$

V$^4_3$ (second inversion) places the chordal fifth ($\hat{2}$) in the bass. Since $\hat{2}$ also appears in the bass of vii°$_6$, V$^4_3$ functions in much the same way—as a neighboring chord to I or, more often, as a passing chord between I and I$_6$. Example 11.4A shows this passing motion as V$^4_3$ connects I$_6$ and I. The soprano moves in parallel tenths with the bass.

EXAMPLE 11.4

DVD 1 CH 11 TRACK 3

A.

B1.

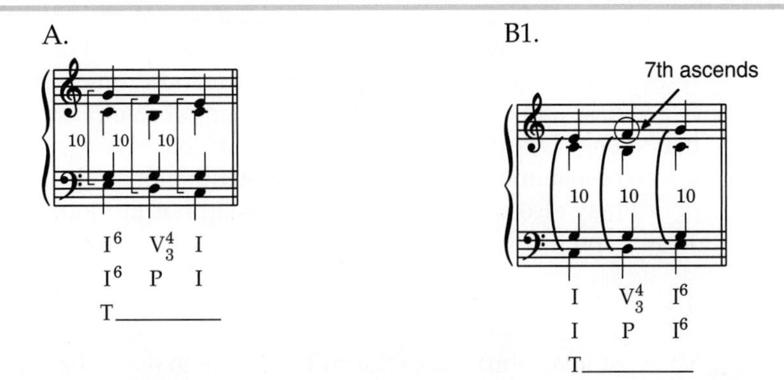

B2. Schubert, "Des Müllers Blumen," from *Die Schöne Müllerin*

C1.

C2. Schubert, "Wasserfluth," from *Winterreise*

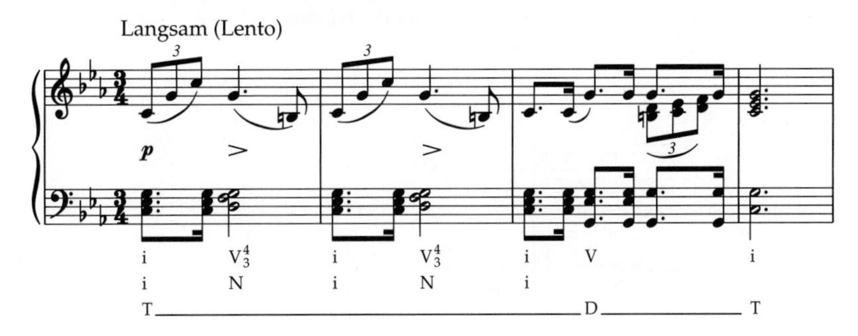

In Example 11.4B, the contour is reversed: V_3^4 is part of an ascending line, connecting I and I_6. Notice that the chordal seventh (F) *ascends* to G instead of resolving normally to E. This exception to the rule that chordal dissonance must resolve by step *descent* is permitted because the strong parallel-tenth motion between bass and soprano overrides the normal resolution of the seventh. Schubert's song "Des Müllers Blumen" opens in just this way, with the outer voices of the accompaniment tracing the parallel-tenth motion (Example 11.4B2).

V_3^4 may also prolong the tonic by neighbor motion, as shown in Example 11.4C1 and C2.

V_2^4

V_2^4 (third inversion) places the chordal seventh ($\hat{4}$) in the bass. Given the prominent placement of the seventh, V_2^4 is the least stable of the inverted dominants. Example 11.5A presents a setting of V_2^4 in which it participates in a tonic expansion from I to I_6 that includes a voice exchange. Composers often soften the effect of V_2^4 by preparing the seventh as a passing tone, as shown in Example 11.5B. It is also possible to use V_2^4 as an upper neighbor to I_6, which creates a less stable, more fleeting prolongation of the tonic (see Example 11.5C).

EXAMPLE 11.5

DVD 1
CH 11
TRACK 4

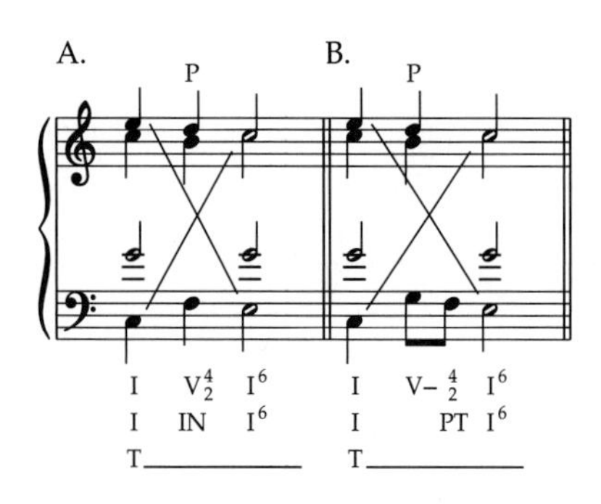

C. Mozart, Piano Sonata in C major, K. 545, *Allegro*

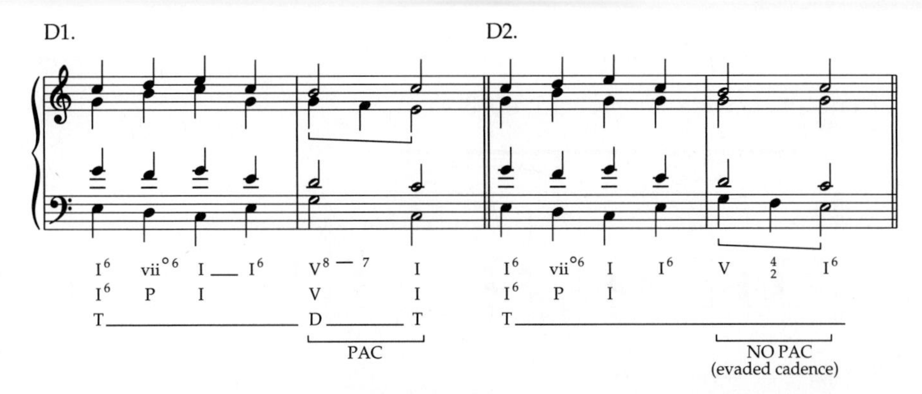

Finally, placing the passing seventh in the bass at a cadence destabilizes the dominant and transforms it into part of a tonic prolongation. Example 11.5D1 shows a tonic expansion and typical PAC (with passing seventh in the alto). Example 11.5D2 presents the passing seventh in the bass, creating an **evaded cadence**.

Voice-Leading Inversions of V_7

There are no new voice-leading rules for the inversions of V_7, but do not lose sight of the tenets of good part writing that have already been discussed.

1. Move most, if not all, of the voices by step or common tone when leading to and from inversions of V_7.
2. Inversions of V_7 should appear as complete chords.
3. Inversions of V_7 tend to fall on metrically unaccented beats, connecting the more stable tonic triads, which tend to fall on strong beats.
4. Resolve tendency tones: $\hat{7}$ (the leading tone) *must* ascend when it occurs in an outer voice (but may fall to $\hat{5}$ when it occurs in an inner voice). $\hat{4}$ (the seventh of V) *must* descend to $\hat{3}$ (except in the progression I–V^4_3–I_6, harmonizing a $\hat{3}$–$\hat{4}$–$\hat{5}$ soprano).

Combining Inversions of V_7

Extended prolongations of tonic are common, and they usually involve two or more inverted V_7 chords. A Donizetti aria (reproduced in Example 11.6A) opens with a tonic expansion using both V^4_3 and V^6_5. These expanding inverted dominant sevenths link the two-measure subphrases by creating the overall effect of double neighbors, as shown in the second-level analysis. Notice how Donizetti moves from an inversion with a less active tone in the bass ($\hat{2}$) to one with an active tone ($\hat{7}$), and not the reverse (i.e., V^6_5–V^4_3). The melodically fluent soprano line, B–A–G♯, enhances the connection between the two subphrases.

EXAMPLE 11.6

DVD 1
CH 11
TRACK 5

A. Donizetti, *Lucrezia Borgia*, act 1, no. 3

B. Mozart, Piano Sonata in F, K. 280, *Presto*

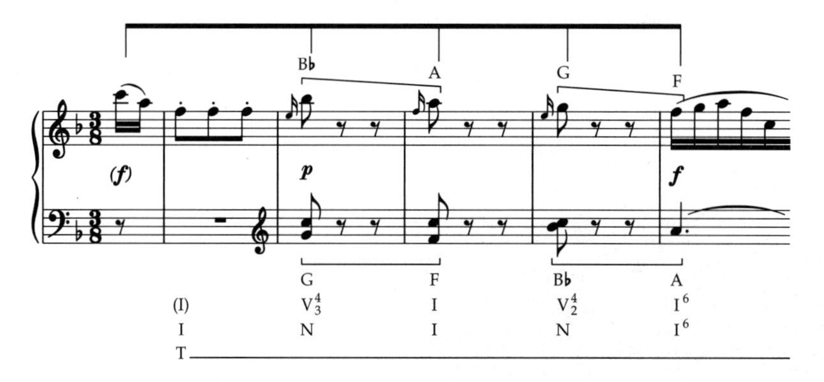

C. Beethoven, Symphony no. 5 in C minor, *Allegro*

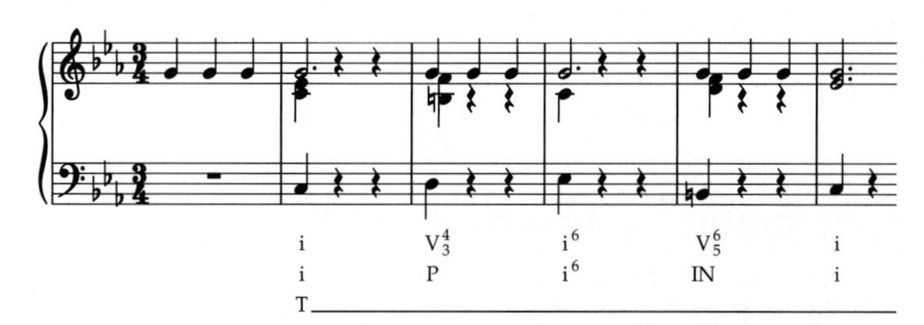

Example 11.6B shows how V^4_3 and V^4_2 expand the tonic in the opening of a Mozart *Presto*. Notice that their contrapuntal functions are made clear in the melodic swapping of the two-note pairs B♭–A and G–F. We learned that single-pitch swappings are called *voice exchanges*. Multiple-pitch swappings are called **part exchanges**. Further, the part exchanges in the upper voice are members of a longer stepwise falling fifth from the opening C down to F. Example 11.6C shows how Beethoven expands the tonic by moving from i to i_6 through V^4_3 and then dramatically leaps by a diminished fourth from $\hat{3}$ to $\hat{7}$ and back to $\hat{1}$ through a neighboring V^6_5 chord.

Compositional Impact of Contrapuntal Chords

You most likely have noticed that new concepts have been introduced in musical contexts as short as three chords, providing models that you can remember. These models, or **harmonic paradigms**, are crucial to the unfolding of all music written in the common-practice periods (including the Baroque, Classical, and Romantic periods and the late nineteenth century) as well as the commercial and popular music of today. You must, then, be intimately acquainted with each of these paradigms so that you are able to recognize them immediately no matter what the key, the mode, the meter, the instrumentation, the texture, or the like. Let's look at an excerpt by Chopin, a romantic composer credited with expanding the Classical harmonic palette by experimenting with unusual sonorities and progressions. However, he still relied heavily on these paradigms at the surface as well as the deeper levels of his works. Listen to the excerpts in Example 11.7.

EXAMPLE 11.7

DVD 1
CH 11
TRACK 6

A1. Chopin, Etude in F major, op. 10, no. 8, BI 42

A2.

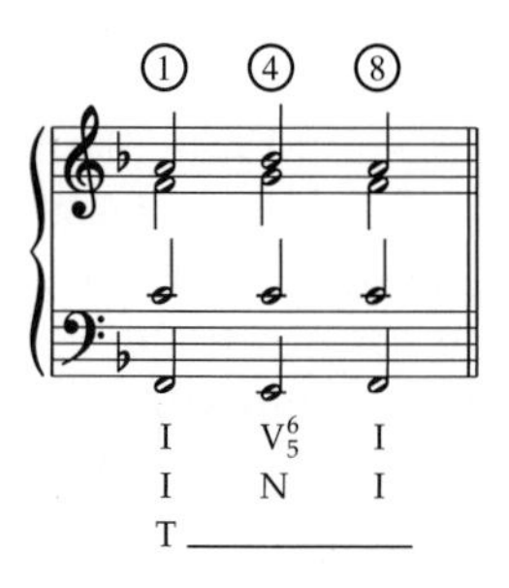

B1. Chopin, Impromptu no. 1 in A♭ major, op.29, BI 110

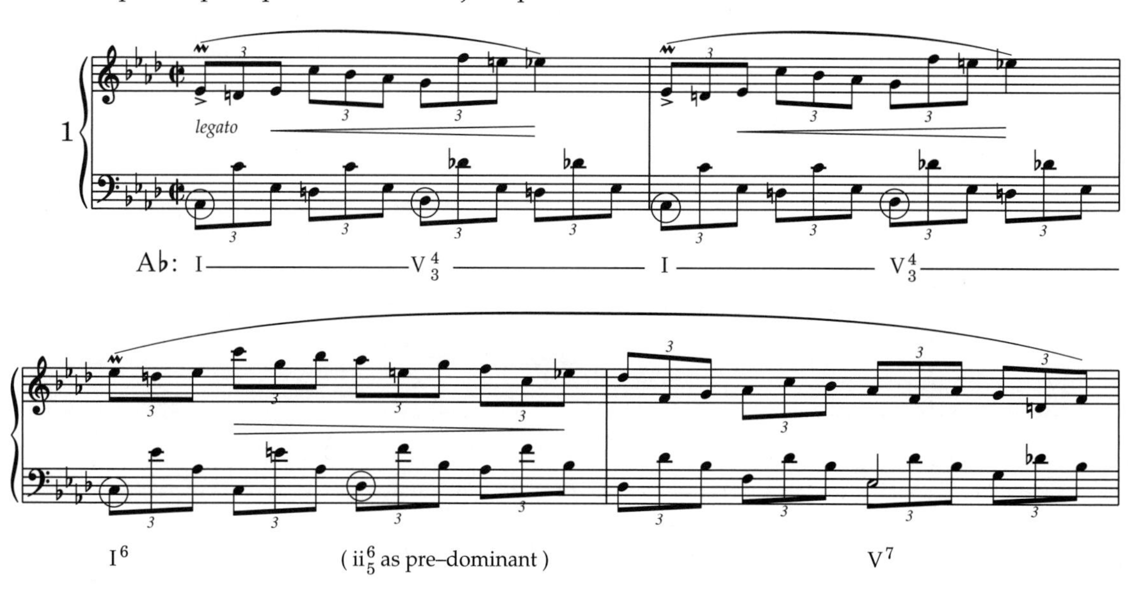

B2.

The progression in the etude is simple, an eight-measure phrase that consists entirely of tonic in root position, a neighboring V_5^6 that extends the tonic, and a return to tonic. In Example 11.7B, the tonic is also prolonged by linear chords. In mm. 1–3, two instances of V_3^4 help prolong the tonic—the first as a neighboring chord, the second as a passing chord. The cadential dominant arrives in the second half of m. 4. Indeed, these crucial harmonies are the skeleton that composers from various stylistic periods flesh out with their own distinctive figurations.

EXERCISE INTERLUDE

PERFORMING

11.1 Singing and Playing Inversions of V_7

The following arpeggiations create progressions that incorporate inversions of V_7. Sing them and/or play them on an instrument. Listen to how often harmonies change; then analyze the progressions with roman numerals. Next, transpose the arpeggiations to other major and minor keys—remember that in minor keys, you raise $\hat{7}$ for the leading tone.

A.

B.

DVD 2
CH 11
TRACK 1

ANALYSIS

11.2 Analytical Snapshots

Each of the following short excerpts contains expansions of the tonic and the dominant using inversions of V_7. Expect to encounter $vii°_6$ and V_6 as well. Analyze each, using two levels where appropriate.

A. Schubert, "Morgengruss," from *Die Schöne Müllerin*

B. Mozart, String Quartet in B♭ major, K. 172, *Allegro assai*

C. Beethoven, Violin Sonata no. 3 in E♭ major, op. 12, no. 3, *Adagio con molta espressione*

D. Brahms, Horn Trio, *Andante* (What harmony is prolonged in mm. 1–4?)

E. Thomas, Gavotte, from *Mignon*

WRITING

11.3 Spelling Inversions of V_7.

Given here are unordered inversions of V_7 chords. The first boldfaced pitch is the bass. Determine the *major* key in which each chord functions as V_7, and, using figured bass, provide the inversion based on the given bass note.

Example: given: **G♯**–*D–B–E* *Answer: A major:* V^6_5

A. **F**–D–B♭–A♭
B. **C**–A♭–E♭–G♭
C. **F**–B–D–G
D. **A♭**–F–D♭–C♭
E. **D**–G♯–E–B
F. **A**–F–C–E♭
G. **A**–D–C–F♯
H. **A**–D♯–F♯–B
I. **G♯**–C♯–E♯–B
J. **E♭**–C♭–G♭–B♭♭

11.4 Resolving Inversions of V_7.

Determine the key in which each inverted V_7 chord functions. Then resolve each to a form of the tonic chord. Since V^4_3 may resolve either to I_6 or I, include both possibilities. Examples A–F are in major keys, and G–O are in minor keys.

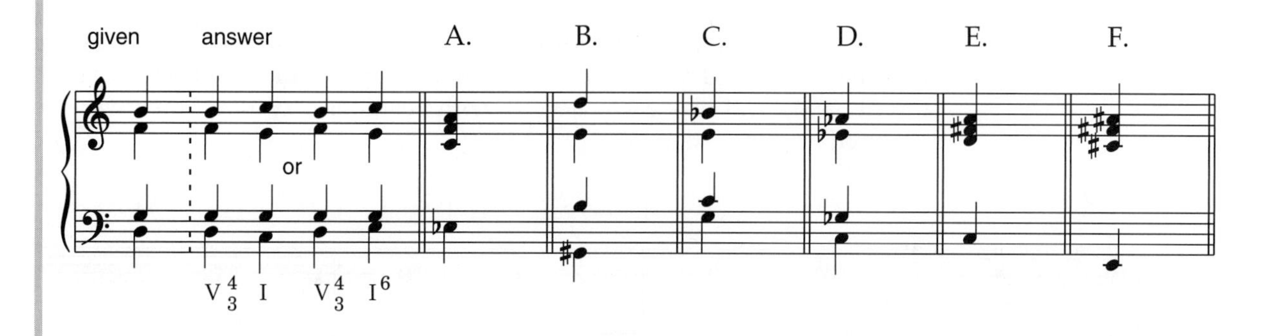

Continued

11.5 Harmonic Paradigms: Adding Inversions of V_7

Determine the key; then use inversions of V_7 to create P, N, or IN bass motions that expand the tonic.

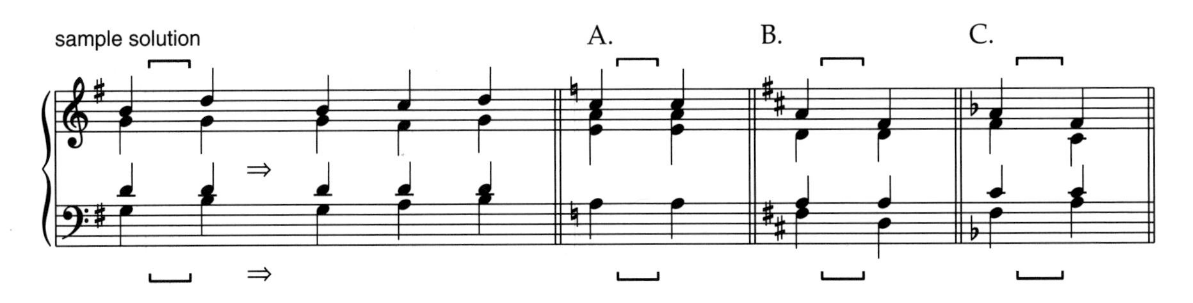

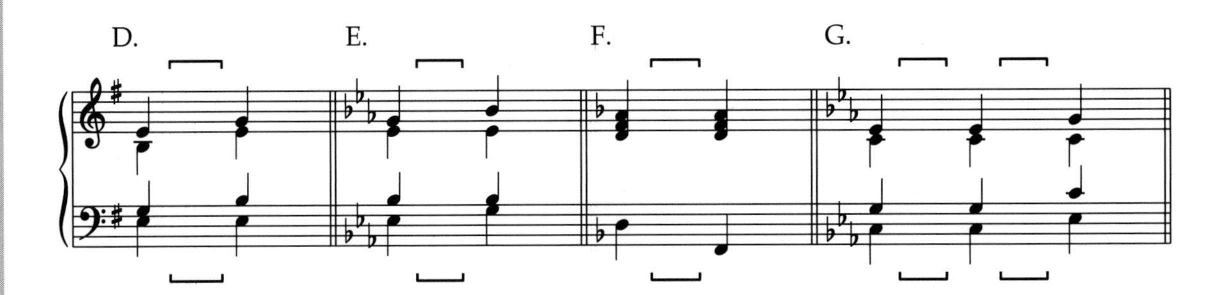

PLAYING

11.6 Completing Dominant Sevenths

Given are three notes of a dominant seventh chord. Determine the missing member, and then add it to the right hand to create four-voice chords. Be aware of inversions. Regard the missing note as either soprano or tenor (top or bottom of right hand), and play each chord in both positions. Say aloud the inversion or figured bass. An example is provided.

WORKBOOK
11.1–11.3

11.7 Figured Bass

Realize the figured basses in four voices. Transpose to the keys of C major and F major. Play each example in parallel and relative minor keys.

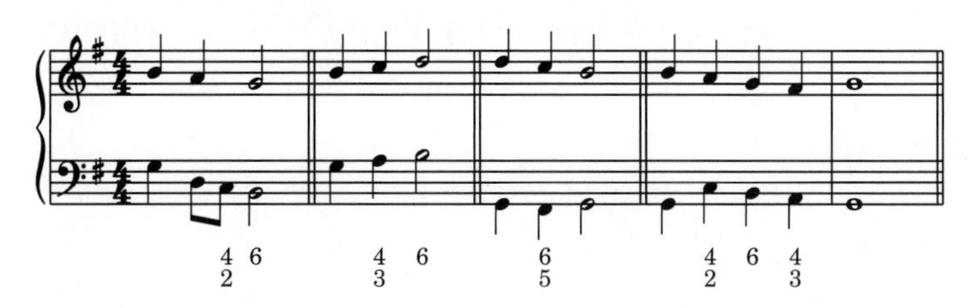

Leading Tone Seventh Chords: vii°$_7$ and viiø$_7$

A glance at the bass line of Gluck's *Orfeo* in Example 11.8 reveals contrapuntal expansions of the tonic similar to inversions of V_7. However, when you listen to the example, you will hear that each neighboring and passing sonority is a form of vii°$_7$. vii°$_7$ and its inversions are much more dissonant than V_7 and its inversions. This is because vii°$_7$ contains the interval of the diminished seventh as well as two tritones (in C minor, B–F and D–A♭). Further, V_7 shares one common tone with the tonic ($\hat{5}$), but vii°$_7$ does not share any common tones with the tonic ($\hat{7}$, $\hat{2}$, $\hat{4}$, $\hat{6}$).

EXAMPLE 11.8 Gluck, *Orfeo*, act 1, no. 1

DVD 1
CH 11
TRACK 7

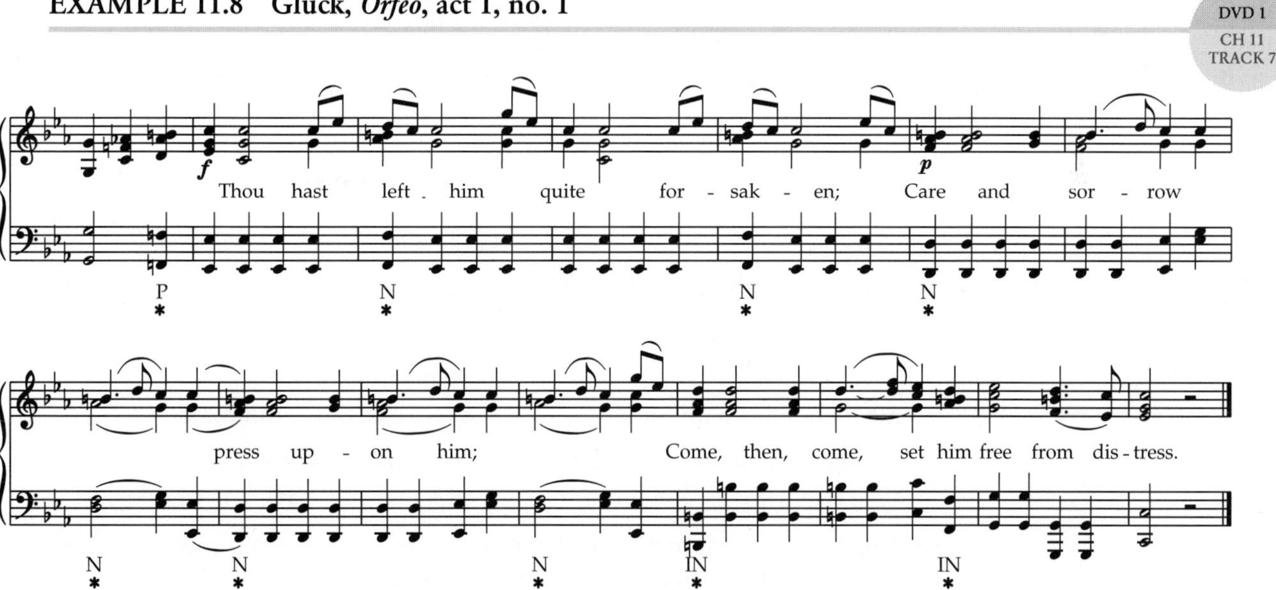

vii°$_7$ and its inversions function the same way as V_7 and its inversions because they share three pitches ($\hat{7}$, $\hat{2}$, and $\hat{4}$). vii°$_7$ and V_7 are interchangeable, as follows:

- vii°$_7$ behaves just like V^6_5—it is a neighboring chord to root-position tonic.
- vii°$^6_5$ behaves like V^4_3—it is a passing chord between i and i_6.
- vii° $^4_3$ behaves like V^4_2—it is a passing chord between V and I_6, or it is a neighboring chord to I_6.
- vii°$^4_2$ is rare and usually is a neighboring chord to root-position V.

Example 11.9A shows the contrapuntal functions of vii°$_7$ and its inversions. Example 11.9B compares V$_7$ with vii°$_7$; unfilled noteheads show common tones, and filled noteheads show the pitch difference between V$_7$ and vii°$_7$. Composers often take advantage of this subtle semitone shift between $\hat{5}$ and $\hat{6}$, as we will see. Finally, Example 11.9C compares and contrasts V$_7$ and vii°$_7$ in chart form.

EXAMPLE 11.9

DVD 1
CH 11
TRACK 8

A.

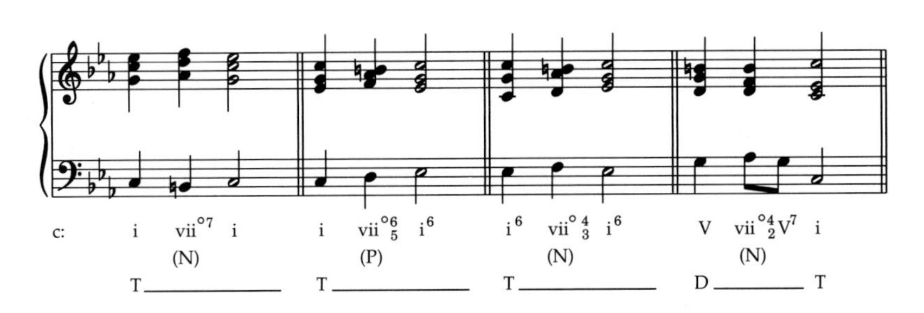

B.

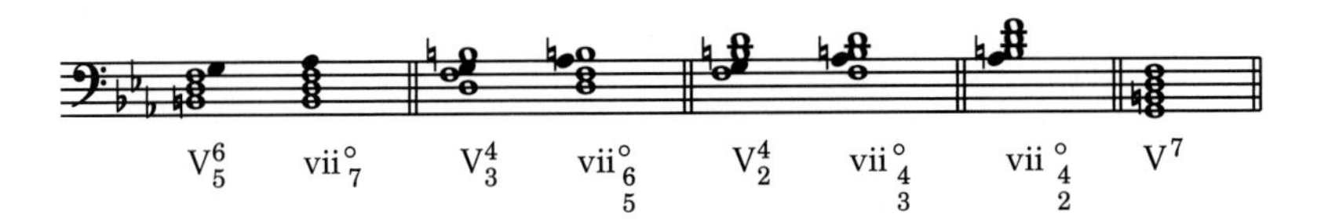

C.

vii°$_7$ chords . . .	V$_7$ chords . . .
• expand tonic	• expand tonic
• occur in minor keys	• occur in major and minor keys
• have $\hat{7}$–$\hat{2}$–$\hat{4}$ plus $\hat{6}$	• have $\hat{5}$ plus $\hat{7}$–$\hat{2}$–$\hat{4}$
• share no notes with tonic	• share one note with tonic
• are highly unstable because they have two tritones, $\hat{7}$–$\hat{4}$ and $\hat{2}$–$\hat{6}$	• are somewhat unstable because they have one tritone, $\hat{7}$–$\hat{4}$

The diminished seventh chord appears more often in minor-mode compositions because the chord appears within the minor scale. Finally, the diminished seventh provides support of $\hat{6}$, a scale degree that we have not harmonized before and that is particularly expressive when it occurs in the soprano voice.

Voice Leading for vii°$_7$

The best way to approach writing vii°$_7$ is first to think of the inversions of V$_7$ and then to substitute $\hat{6}$ for $\hat{5}$. Since all notes in vii°$_7$ are tendency tones, here is a guide to resolving the vii°$_7$ chord to tonic (see Example 11.10):

EXAMPLE 11.10

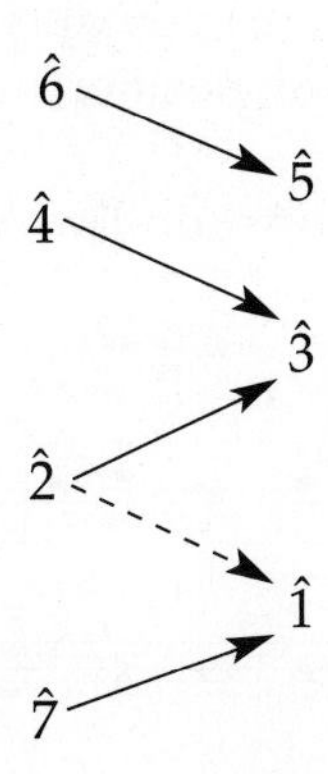

- Prepare $\hat{6}$—approach by step or with a common tone.
- $\hat{6}$ moves down to $\hat{5}$.
- $\hat{4}$ moves down to $\hat{3}$.
- $\hat{2}$ usually moves up to $\hat{3}$ (resulting in the common doubled third in the tonic chord), or it can move down to $\hat{1}$.
- $\hat{7}$ moves up to $\hat{1}$.

Example 11.11 demonstrates these voice-leading guidelines. Review Example 11.9 to confirm that these guidelines are consistent regardless of inversion [e.g., $\hat{6}$ (the chordal seventh) is always prepared by step (from $\hat{5}$) and always resolves by step (to $\hat{5}$)].

EXAMPLE 11.11

DVD 1
CH 11
TRACK 9

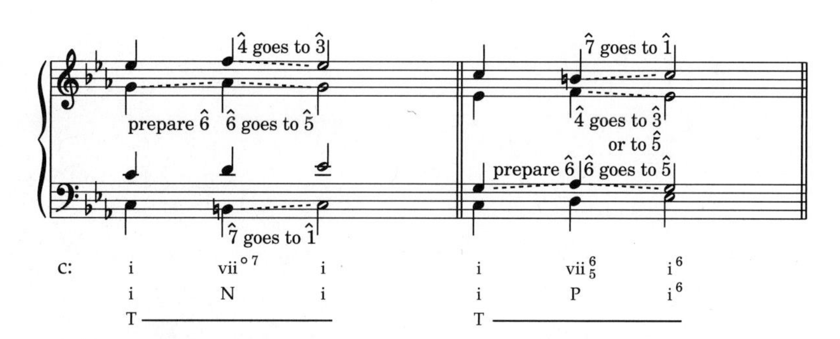

Alternatively, we can consider the resolution of $vii^{\circ}{}_7$ and its inversions from the perspective of chord tone pairs and their resolution. For example, the interval of the diminished seventh (or augmented second when the chord is inverted) between $\hat{7}$ and $\hat{6}$ must resolve by contrary motion to $\hat{1}$ and $\hat{5}$. Further, resolve the tritones normally: A diminished fifth contracts and an augmented fourth expands. Remember that resolution to tonic chords with doubled thirds is common.

Just like V_7 and its inversions, $vii^{\circ}{}_7$ and its inversions often appear in combination, not only with one another but also with V_7 and its inversions. Example 11.12 presents $vii^{\circ}{}_7$ as part of an expansion of tonic (in m. 4). In m. 5, $vii^{\circ 4}_{3}$

moves to vii°$_7$ and on to V$_7$ before resolving to tonic. Given that the dominant function controls mm. 5–8, vii°$_7$ is a substitute for V$_7$ rather than an elaboration of the tonic. Thus, because vii°$_7$ is a contrapuntal chord that usually expands the tonic, it occurs in a metrically weak position.

EXAMPLE 11.12 Jean-Marie Leclair l'Aine, Sonata in G minor for Two Violins and Basso Continuo, op. 4, no. 5, *Andante*

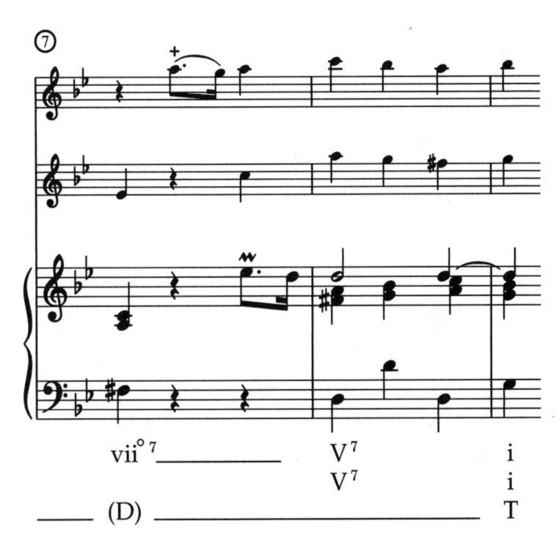

A compelling example of vii°$_7$ occurs in Mozart's E♭ major symphony (Example 11.13). Each of the four possible positions of vii°$_7$ occurs, with tonic playing a subordinate role in the passage. Beginning with the highly unstable vii°$^4_2$ and falling through $^4_3$, $^6_5$, and finally $_7$, inversions of the tonic (C) occur as passing chords that help to extend the dramatic vii°$_7$, which functions as an upbeat gesture that leads eventually to the arrival on C minor. Notice that the outer voices move in contrary motion, each spanning the interval of the diminished seventh (B♮–A♭). Since the initial interval is an augmented second (A♭–B♮) and the final interval a diminished seventh (B–A♭), a voice exchange results (see Example 11.13B).

EXAMPLE 11.13

A. Mozart, Symphony in E♭ major, K. 132, *Andante*

B. Reduction

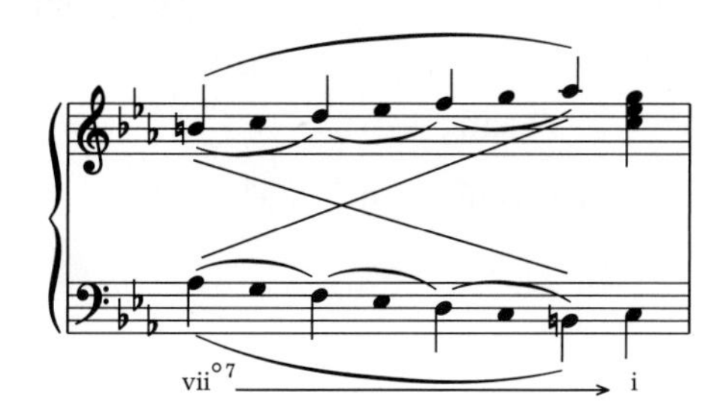

viiø7

The leading-tone seventh chord in major is a half-diminished seventh chord (e.g., B–D–F–A in C major). The minor seventh between $\hat{7}$ and $\hat{6}$ is much less dissonant than the diminished seventh found in the fully diminished seventh chord. However, because of its less goal-oriented tendencies, the vii$^{ø}_{7}$ chord in major occurs much less often than its minor-mode counterpart in minor does. In fact, composers often import the fully diminished seventh chord from minor into their major-mode works by borrowing ♭$\hat{6}$ from the parallel minor, a technique we will learn more about in chapter 27.

Example 11.14 illustrates vii$^{ø}_{7}$ used to expand the tonic. Here, vii$^{ø}_{7}$ appears as part of a larger neighboring process that unfolds in the melody: The line B–C–B (in which C is harmonized by V^{6}_{5}) is transposed up a third to D–E–D. Since no inversion of V_7 contains $\hat{6}$, Mozart must use the vii$^{ø}_{7}$. Notice also the unusual treatment of the seventh of the root-position V_7 chord in m. 28: It *rises*, rather than falls, in order to pass up to the D in m. 29.

EXAMPLE 11.14 Mozart, Symphony in G major, K. 97, Trio

$\text{vii}^{ø}_{7}$ appears much more often in root position than in any of its inversions. Follow the part-writing rules for vii°_{7}.

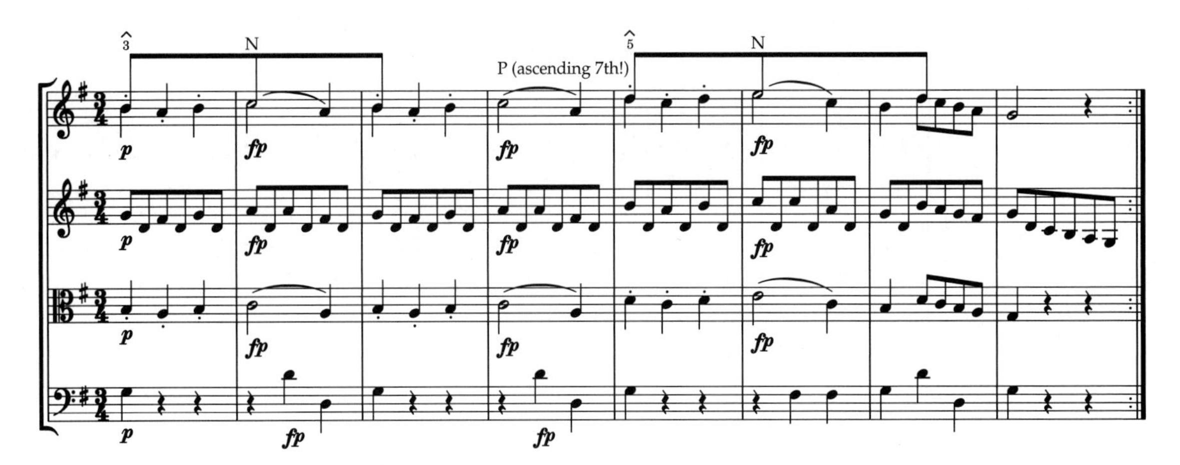

Example 11.15 presents a summary of the various contrapuntal expansions of tonic and dominant that involve chordal skips, passing, neighboring, and their combinations. These involve the following chords:

I and I_6	V_7, V^6_5, V^4_3, and V^4_2
V and V_6	$\text{vii}^{\circ 6}$, vii^{7} ($\text{vii}^{ø}_{7}$), $\text{vii}^{\circ 6}_{5}$, vii^{4}_{3}, and vii^{4}_{2}
IV_6	

EXAMPLE 11.15 Summary of Contrapuntal Expansions

A.

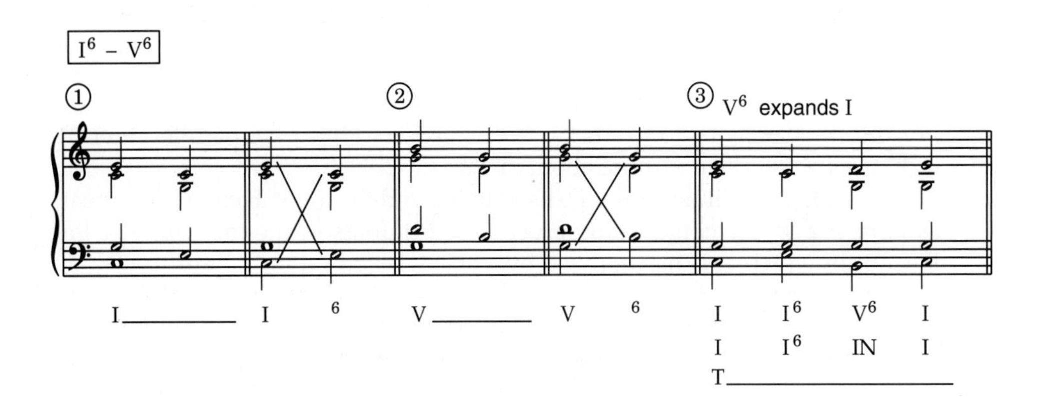

B.

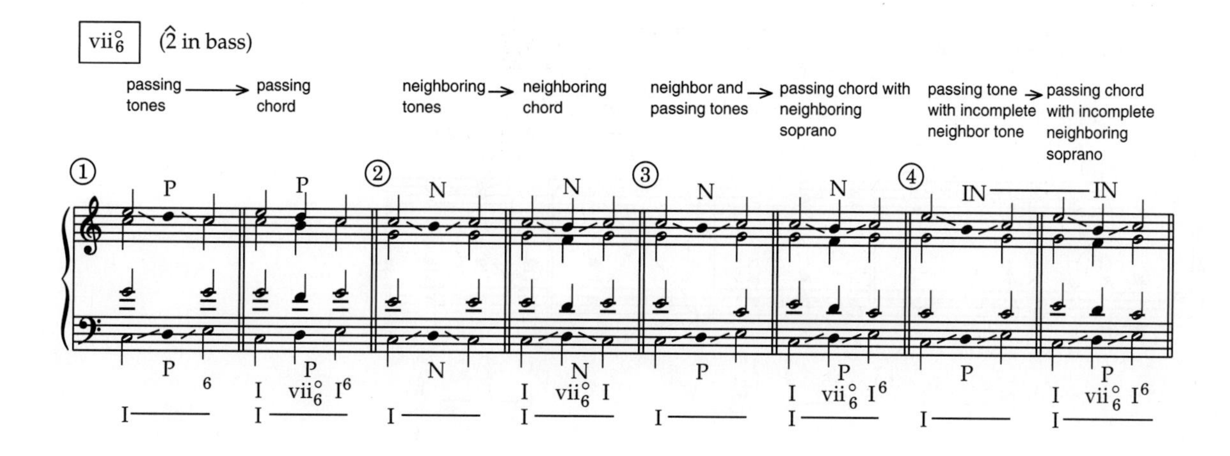

C.

$\boxed{V^6_5}$ + $\boxed{vii^{\circ 7}}$ ($\hat{7}$ in bass)

Note: examples show V^6_5. For vii°7, substitute $\hat{6}$ (A♭ in minor only) for $\hat{5}$ (G).
For viiø7, substitute $\hat{6}$ (A♮ in major only) for $\hat{5}$.

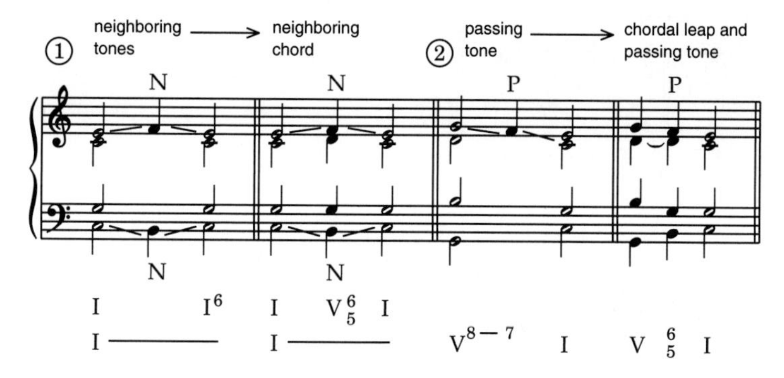

D.

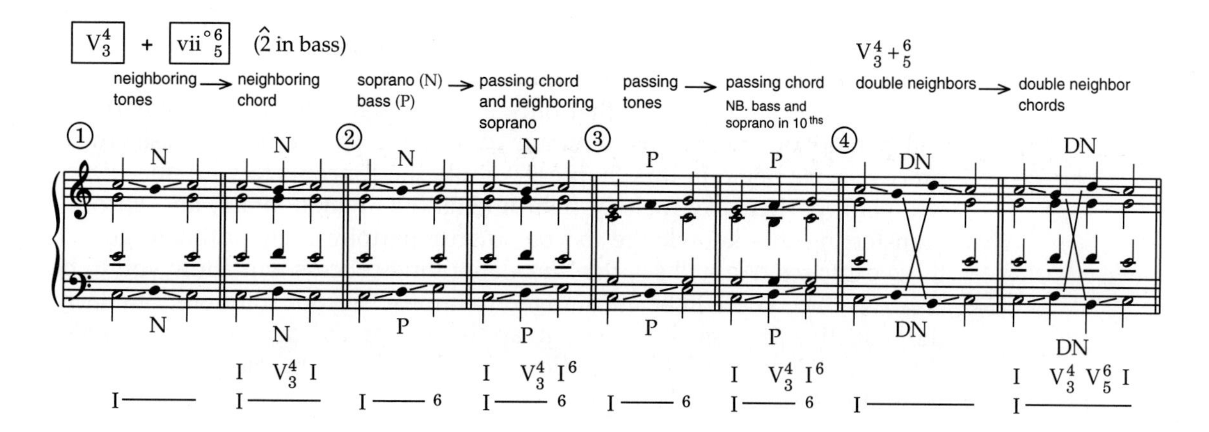

E.

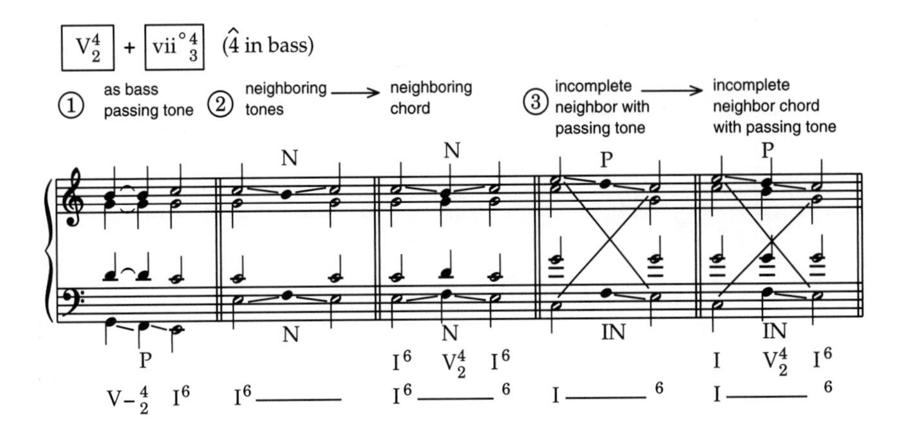

F.

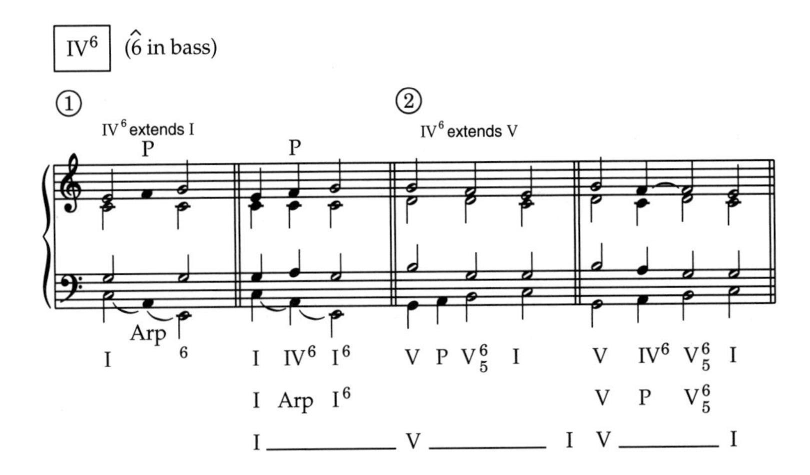

Elaboration and Reduction

In this chapter and Chapters 8–10, we have explored the complementary processes of **elaboration**—in which a skeletal two-voice counterpoint or four-voice homophonic texture was embellished with tones of figuration, florid accompaniments, etc.—and **reduction**—in which a florid example from the literature was simplified so that only the essential outer-voice counterpoint and homophonic inner voices remained. In order to internalize these crucial processes, we begin in this chapter to apply the concepts to your specific instrument, particularly melody instruments (i.e., winds, brass, and strings). Transferring this knowledge to your own repertoire is the ultimate goal of these exercises. We will see that the elaborating process will allow you to be creative, since you will be encouraged to improvise your solutions. Similarly, the reductive process allows you to apply your analytical and aural skills so that you will discover the melodic, contrapuntal, and harmonic commonalities in tonal pieces.

Let's briefly see how these two processes would be applied to a melody instrument like the violin. We'll begin with the process of reduction. The orchestral excerpt of Example 11.16, with its seven staves, three different clefs, dense texture, and highly varied rhythmic complexity, looks formidable. Let's go through a procedure that will allow you to tackle any score and find its basic harmonic structure and voice leading.

EXAMPLE 11.16 Mozart, Symphony in C major, K. 200, *Allegro*

First, we determine the key. This is necessary because an example may not be taken from the opening of a movement but, rather, excerpted from an interior portion of the movement where a key other than the main key of the movement holds forth. In the Mozart excerpt, we see that G major is the key, given the single sharp and the emphasis on dominant and tonic harmonies.

Second, we determine the function of each harmony, beginning with the harmonic rhythm, which seems to change once per measure. It is best to focus on the accented bass notes, which are usually the lowest-sounding pitches. As you know from looking at other large scores, there is often a great deal of pitch doubling, especially between the strings and the woodwinds. So it is usually easiest to focus on the four string parts (violins 1 and 2, viola, and cello/bass) and merely glance at the winds to confirm that they are doubling the strings. Of course, you will need to reduce out the tones of figuration, including dissonant as well as consonant types. We see that the chords unfold as follows: V^6_5 (two measures)—I—IV_6—I_6. This contrapuntal progression expands I (G major), first with a neighbor figure (F♯–G in the bass) and then with a descending arpeggiation (G–E–B in the bass).

Third, we find the spacing of the upper voices and determine how these voices lead from one chord to another. We begin with the soprano in order to establish the outer-voice counterpoint, and we discover a lot of activity around C natural, in both the first violin and the upper winds (Example 11.17). C is the seventh of the dominant; as such, it should resolve by descending to B, the third of the tonic chord, just as the bass F♯ (as the leading tone) must resolve to $\hat{1}$. Indeed, Mozart follows the standard voice leading. We continue this process to see that the main soprano pitches, doubled in high strings and winds, are C–D, as shown in Example 11.17. We have encountered this very counterpoint in our earlier studies (e.g., Example 11.4).

EXAMPLE 11.17

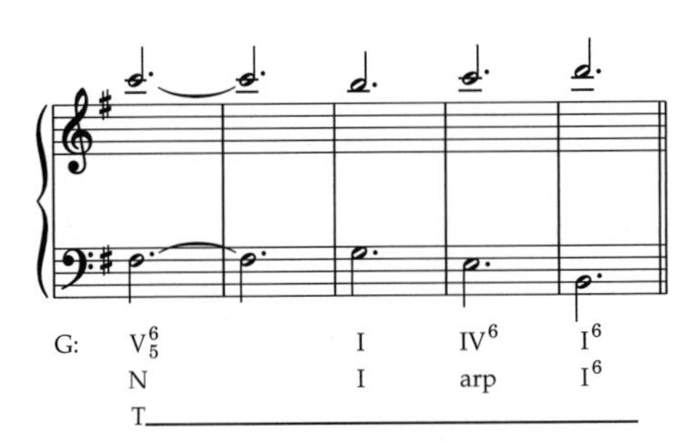

Fourth, we add the inner voices. But before we do, we must review the outer-voice counterpoint in order to have a general idea of what pitches are missing in the chord and therefore what to expect to find in the actual composition. Given that the root (D) and the fifth (A) are missing in the outer-voice counterpoint of the V^6_5 chord, we would expect those pitches to be prominent in the remaining instruments. Indeed, we see that the missing A appears immediately beneath the soprano's C in winds and strings and that the root, D, appears on the downbeat in four other instruments. We can then trace the voice leading from one chord to the other, as shown in Example 11.18 (note that the upper voices are notated one octave lower).

EXAMPLE 11.18

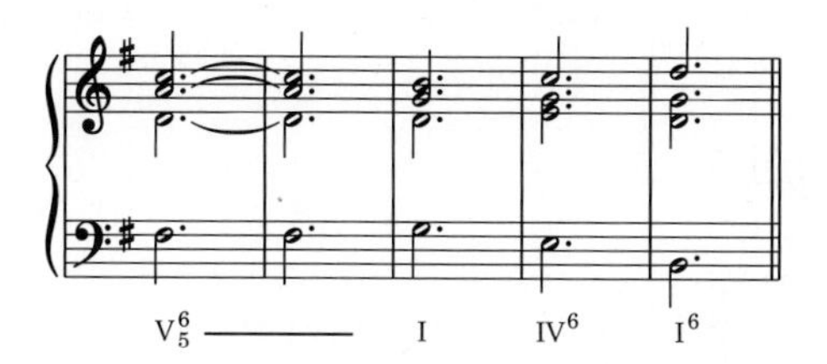

Thus, we have reduced Mozart's surface embellishments to the generating four-voice structure. You are strongly encouraged to play it on the piano. However, this chordal structure cannot be played on a melody instrument, so, as we have seen in earlier chapters, we must "horizontalize" the homophonic chords, as shown in Example 11.19, by playing them as arpeggiations. Note, however, that the strict four-part voice leading in Example 11.18 is maintained. You need not play your arpeggiations within the meter, and feel free to find a register that suits your instrument (e.g., in order to play Example 11.19 on the violin, you would have to transpose it up one octave, since the bass lies below the range of the instrument). When you reduce an embellished score from the literature, you will need to be flexible. You will need to omit tones of figuration, normalize the registers of pitches, infer the existence of missing pitches, etc. Remember, you have learned a great deal about how voices move, chordal behavior, etc., so be ready to draw on this information.

EXAMPLE 11.19

We now turn to elaboration of a given model. There will be three types of models: a four-voice chord progression, a soprano melody (with or without given roman numerals), and a figured bass (with or without a given soprano). We will work through this third type of model, a figured bass (without a given soprano); see Example 11.20.

EXAMPLE 11.20

DVD 1
CH 11
TRACK 10

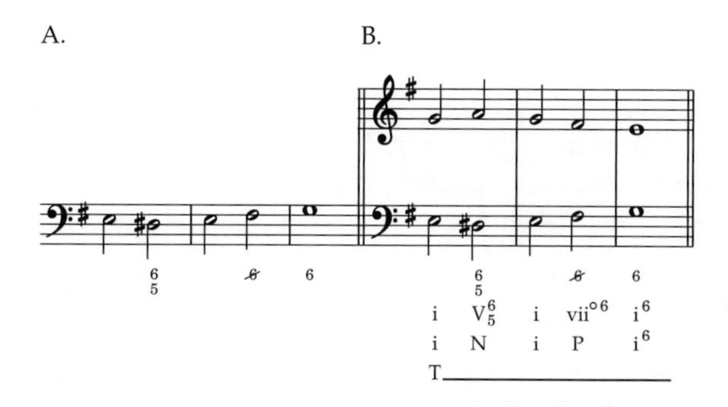

C.

Example 11.20A contains four bass notes and figures that could be the opening of a progression. Again, we can use a multistage procedure to bring this figured bass to life.

Step 1 (Example 11.20B). Determine the chord progression based on the figures, and add a soprano voice. Again, we encounter an expansion of the tonic, one that begins with a neighbor and then passes up to i_6 (i—V^6_5—i—vii°$_6$—i_6).

Step 2 (Example 11.20C). Add the inner voices to create a four-part structure.

Step 3 (Example 11.21). We are now at the performing stage, where, as in our reductions, we horizontalize the progression into broken chords. However, rather than being the end of the exercise, as it was when we reduced, the arpeggiation of the chords is the beginning of the elaborations.

EXAMPLE 11.21

DVD 1 CH 11 TRACK 11

There are many ways to play these arpeggiations. In example 11.21A, only an ascending arpeggiation occurs, but in Example B there are changes of direction incorporated that align with the strong beats. In Example 11.21C, a mix of directions is possible; in Example D, triplets replace the sixteenth notes. However, if you choose to use triplets, you must be conscious of the need to leave out one of the chord tones in seventh chords, even if they are inverted. For example, in the V^6_5 chord (measure 1), only the third, the root, and the seventh occur, a necessity if you use strictly triplets. In Example 11.21E, an alteration of *arco* and *pizzicato* differentiates the bass and the upper voices. In Example 11.21F, shorter note values increase the possibilities not only of contour, but also for the addition of tones of figuration (in this case neighbors and passing tones). Finally, feel free to increase the duration of each chord so that you slow the harmonic rhythm to two or even more times its given length. Particularly expansive examples of slowing the harmonic rhythm occur in many of Corelli's concerto grossi; an excerpt of one in the key of D major is given as Example 11.22. Note the single tonic harmony that unfolds over eight measures.

EXAMPLE 11.22 Corelli, Concerto Grosso in D major, op. 6, no. 7, *Allegro*

Continued

Summary of Part 2

In Part 2, you have learned that a great deal of music can be made from the tonic and the dominant harmonies. In addition to their use as vertical harmonic pillars, their contrapuntal expansion allows them to participate in melodic construction. Melodic passing tones and neighbor tones in the outer voices, when harmonized, become passing and neighboring chords. In a similar manner, the succession of these chords is often dependent on melodic processes.

We saw that dissonance and consonance still regulate musical flow and that inverted triads, derived from melodic passing and neighboring motions, are effective means for creating musical drive. The six-three chord is a versatile sonority often used to expand the tonic or the dominant function or to lead from the tonic to the dominant, or vice versa. We also used seventh chords, including those built on $\hat{5}$ and $\hat{7}$, both of which served to expand the tonic. We discovered that these underlying tonal principles and processes are not limited to any one style period but can be found in musical examples written by composers over two centuries, for our examples have been taken from the music of Bach, Mozart, Beethoven, Schubert, Chopin, and Brahms.

In Part 3, we will explore the third and final harmonic function in tonal music, the pre-dominant; learn how dissonance can occur in metrically accented contexts; witness how counterpoint can generate harmonic progressions; and, finally, see how the smallest melodic ideas can affect every facet of a composition.

EXERCISE INTERLUDE

ANALYSIS

11.8 Analytical Snapshots

Each of the following short excerpts contains expansions of the tonic using vii°$_7$ and vii$^{ø}_7$. Expect to encounter other chords that expand tonic, including vii°$_6$, V$_6$, and inversions of V$_7$ as well. Analyze each, using two levels where appropriate.

A. Mozart, Rondo, in F major K. 494

B. Strauss, "Ach lieb, ich muss nun scheiden"

C. Johann Helmich Roman, Flute Sonata in B minor, op. 1, no. 6, *Grave*

D. Haydn, String Quartet in G minor, op. 74, no. 3, ii, *Largo assai*

E. Wagner, *Das Rheingold*, scene 1

WRITING

11.9 Writing vii°$_7$ and vii$^{ø}_7$

On a separate sheet of manuscript paper, complete the following tasks in four-part chorale style, and provide a two-level harmonic analysis.

A. In D minor, use root position vii°$_7$ to expand the tonic.
B. In E minor, use the passing chord vii°$^4_3$ to expand the tonic.
C. In B♭ major, use root position vii$^{ø}_7$ and V$^4_3$ to expand the tonic.
D. Harmonize the following bass line in G minor: $\hat{1}$–$\hat{7}$–$\hat{1}$–$\hat{2}$–$\hat{3}$–$\hat{4}$–$\hat{3}$. Include at least two different inversions of vii°$_7$.
E. Harmonize the following soprano line in B minor: $\hat{5}$–$\hat{6}$–$\hat{5}$–$\hat{4}$–$\hat{3}$. Use two different versions of vii°$_7$.

F. In C♯ minor, expand the tonic with an upper and lower (double) neighbor that uses vii°$_7$. (*Hint:* A voice exchange with $\hat{7}$ and $\hat{2}$ would work well.)

11.10 Resolving Inversions of vii$_7$ (and Inversions of V$_7$)

For Parts A–E, determine the *minor* key in which each inverted vii°$_7$ chord functions. Then precede and follow each with a form of the tonic chord. For Part E, add inner voices based on the implications of the given outer voices.

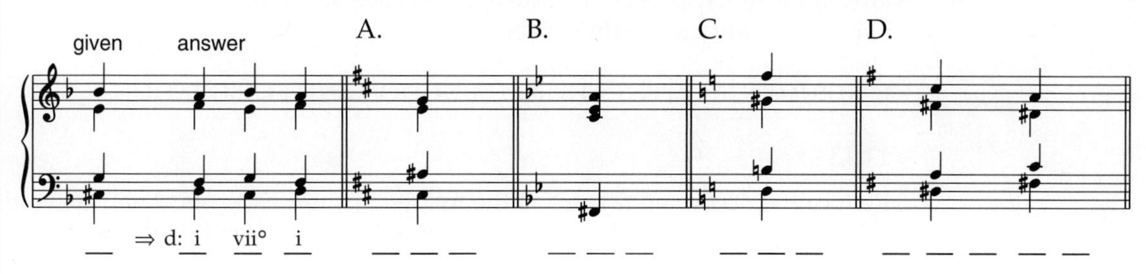

E.

PLAYING

11.11 Keyboard: Warmup with vii°$_7$ and vii$^{ø}_7$

Complete the following tasks in four voices. You may use either close or open position with keyboard or SATB spacing. Play:

A. i–vii°$_7$–i in minor keys up to five sharps and five flats (begin with $\hat{5}$ in the soprano)
B. i–vii°$^6_5$–i$_6$ in C, A, and F♯ minor (begin with $\hat{1}$ in the soprano)
C. i–vii°$^4_3$–i$_6$ in C♯, E, and G minor (begin with $\hat{3}$ in the soprano)
D. I–vii$^{ø}_7$–I in B♭, D, and C major (begin with $\hat{5}$ in the soprano)

11.12 Keyboard: Completion of vii°$_7$ and V$_7$ Chords

The following examples consist of incomplete (three-voice) vii°$_7$ and/or V$_7$ chords. Determine to which harmony—V or vii°$_7$—the missing note belongs; then resolve to tonic. Depending on the given pitches, it might be possible to construct both vii°$_7$ and V$_7$ chords; at other times only one might be possible. A good way to tell a chord's three-note potential is to stack intervals in thirds. In example A, the third stack, C♯–E–G, fits within a diminished fifth, so it might be part of vii°$_7$ (C♯–E–G–B♭) or V$_7$ (A–C♯–E–G). If the given notes stack into a minor seventh or a major second, the sonority can only be a V$_7$. Similarly, if the given notes stack into a diminished seventh or an augmented second, the sonority can only be a vii°$_7$.

INSTRUMENTAL APPLICATION: REDUCTION AND ELABORATION

11.13

Reduce the decorated texture of the following short excerpts. Analyze, verticalize (into a four-voice homophonic texture), and then arpeggiate each example. Refer to the discussion in this chapter for a detailed procedure. Play each reduction.

A. Corelli, Concerto Grosso in F major, op. 6, no. 12, Sarabanda

B. Handel, Concerto Grosso in D major, op. 3, no. 6, *Allegro*

C. Handel, Concerto Grosso in A minor, op. 6, no. 4, *Allegro*

D. Handel, Concerto Grosso in G major, op. 6, no. 1, *Allegro*

11.14

WORKBOOK
11.4–11.5

Elaborate the following figured basses and scale degree melodies (with roman numerals) by arpeggiating in strict ascending four-voice chords that maintain good voice leading between chords. Then embellish your solution by adding changes in contour and tones of figuration. Refer to the discussion in this chapter for a detailed procedure.

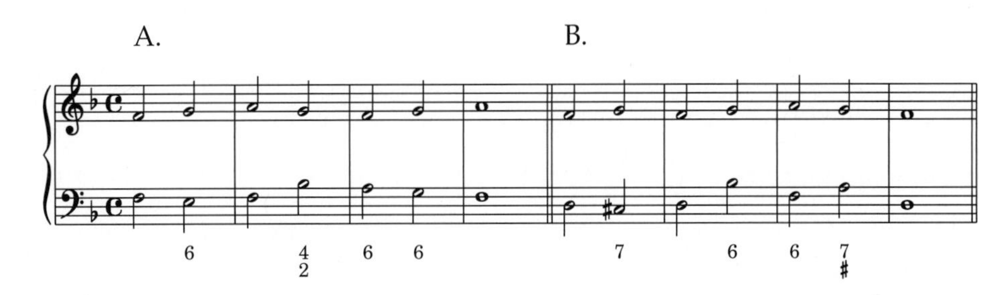

C. In G major, $\frac{3}{4}$:

$\hat{3}$	$\hat{2}$	$\hat{1}$	$\hat{2}$	$\hat{3}$	$\hat{4}$	$\hat{3}$
i	V	I_6	vii°$_6$	I	V^6_5	I

D. In E minor $\frac{4}{4}$:

$\hat{5}$	$\hat{6}$	$\hat{5}$	$\hat{4}$	$\hat{3}$	$\hat{2}$	$\hat{1}$
i	vii°$_7$	i	V^4_3	i	V_7	i

TERMS AND CONCEPTS

- Elaboration and reduction
- Evaded cadence
- Harmonic paradigms
- Part exchange

PART 3

A NEW HARMONIC FUNCTION AND ADDITIONAL MELODIC AND HARMONIC EMBELLISHMENTS

In Part 3 you have the opportunity to spread your harmonic wings as you learn how composers incorporate the third and final harmonic function, the pre-dominant. This harmonic function introduces a new way of enhancing the listener's expectations and also new ways of fulfilling or even thwarting those expectations. Your keyboard, singing, analysis, dictation, and composition exercises will be considerably enriched by incorporating the two harmonies that are used in this function. You also learn new techniques for elaborating both melodic lines and harmonic functions as well as techniques composers use to drive their pieces forward and unify them.

You also explore a new type of melodic figuration predicated on metric accent and chromaticism. And the ongoing assertion that melody and counterpoint generate harmony will be further illustrated in the study of six-four chords, invertible counterpoint, compound melody, and, finally, the smallest of musical gestures, the motive.

CHAPTER 12

The Pre-Dominant Function and the Phrase Model

Whereas tonic and dominant functions are sufficient to create coherent musical passages, a third harmonic function adds a new dimension to our sense of harmonic tension and resolution.

Listen to the excerpts in Example 12.1. Each excerpt contains a chord between the tonic and the dominant that we have not studied before. Unlike the contrapuntal chords we learned about in Part 2, these chords are independent sonorities that provide the connective tissue between the tonal skeleton of tonic and dominant. We call these chords **pre-dominants** since they usually precede the dominant. The most important pre-dominant chords are IV and ii, which we see in Example 12.1. Go back to the excerpts and listen to the intensified harmonic drive that results from these pre-dominant chords. When analyzing pre-dominants at the first level, use the appropriate roman numeral and figured bass. At the second level, use the symbol *PD.*

EXAMPLE 12.1

DVD 1
CH 12
TRACK 1

A. Meyerbeer, "Se non ti moro allato," *Sei canzonette italiane*, no. 5

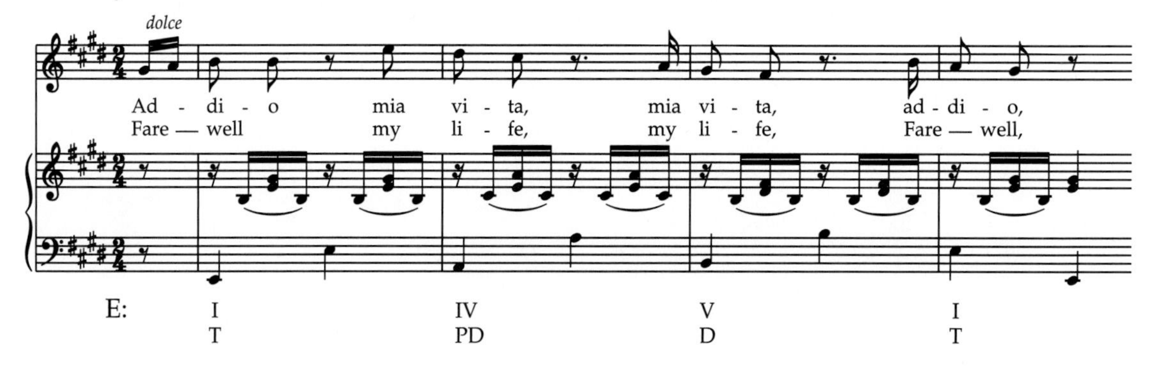

B. Foster, "Beautiful Dreamer"

C. Verdi, Overture to *La forza del destino*

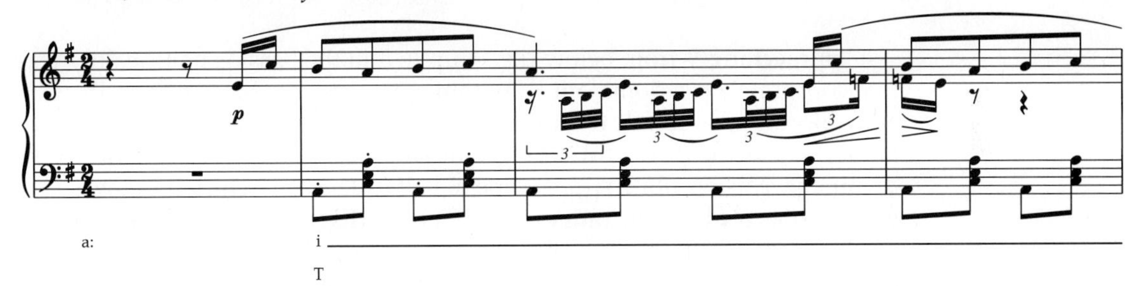

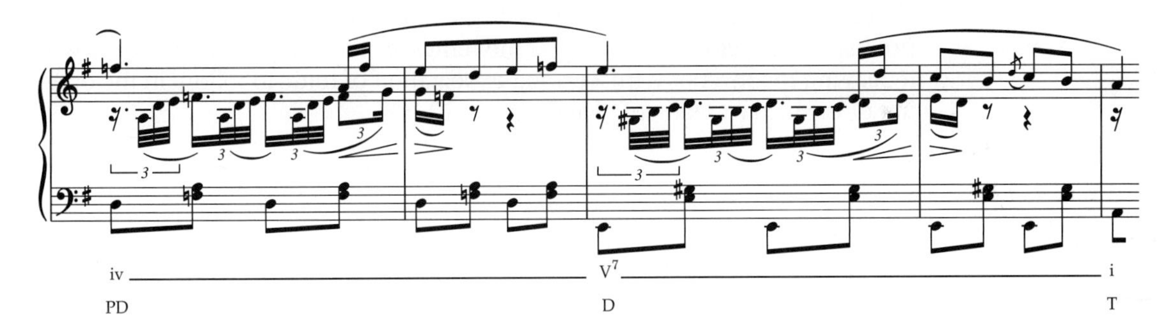

The Subdominant (IV in Major, iv in Minor)

EXAMPLE 12.2

DVD 1 CH 12 TRACK 2

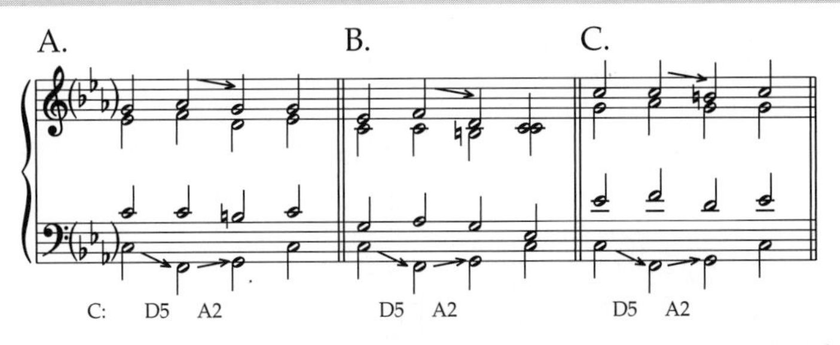

Composers frequently choose the subdominant as the pre-dominant chord because the I–IV motion proceeds by descending fifth (the most convincing root motion in tonal music) and the bass's ascent from $\hat{4}$ to $\hat{5}$ creates a smooth motion to the dominant (see Example 12.2). As the bass ascends by step, the upper voices usually descend, to avoid voice-leading problems. Example 12.3 shows how IV can move to V_7. Note in Example 12.3 that the soprano's $\hat{4}$ prepares the seventh of the upcoming dominant as part of an IAC.

EXAMPLE 12.3

DVD 1
CH 12
TRACK 3

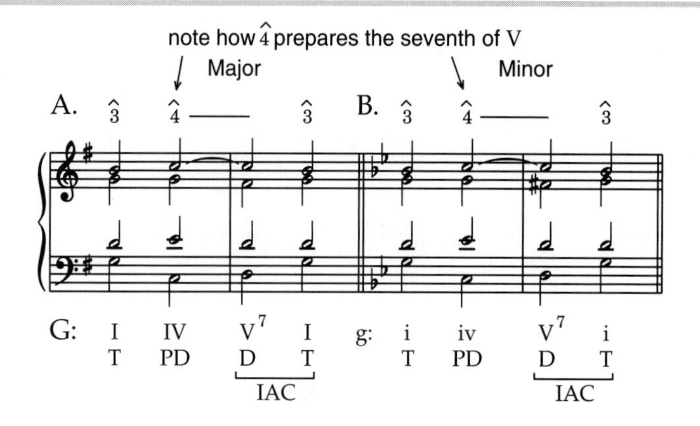

Approaching V from below (i.e., $\hat{4}$ up to $\hat{5}$ in the bass) is not the only way to incorporate a pre-dominant IV within a progression. Motion from IV_6 to V, allowing the bass to fall from $\hat{6}$ to $\hat{5}$, is very useful, especially in the minor mode, where the powerful falling half step intensifies tonal motion to the dominant. This resulting special type of half cadence, in which iv_6 moves to V, is known as a **phrygian cadence** (PHRY) (see Example 12.4A). Listen to the characteristic sound of the phrygian cadence in Example 12.4B, and note how the upper voice moves from $\hat{4}$ to $\hat{5}$ against the bass's descent from $\hat{6}$ to $\hat{5}$. Given the musical tension of the phrygian cadence, Baroque composers were predisposed to closing slow inner movements of multimovement works with it, leaving the listener with a strong expectation of tonic to follow in the opening of the next movement. See Example 12.4C.

EXAMPLE 12.4

DVD 1
CH 12
TRACK 4

A.

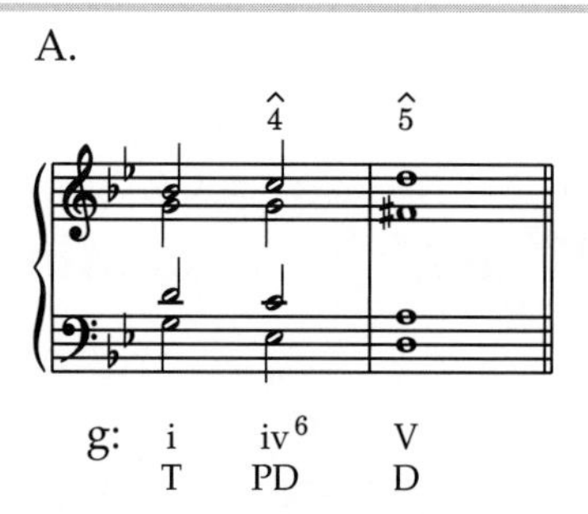

B. Bach, "Wo soll ich fliehen hin," Cantata no. 5, BWV 5

C. Corelli, Violin Sonata in A minor, op. 1, no. 4, *Presto/Adagio*

a:
♯ 6 6 6 ♯
i V i^6 V^6 i iv^6 V
T________________ PD D

The Supertonic (ii in Major, ii° in Minor)

The supertonic is the most common pre-dominant chord. There are at least three reasons why composers consider the supertonic to be an effective pre-dominant:

1. The progression ii–V proceeds by descending-fifth (or ascending-fourth) motion, the strongest root motion in tonal music.
2. The supertonic introduces a striking sonority and modal contrast in progressions:
   a. In major keys, ii is minor. I and V are major.
   b. In minor keys, ii° is diminished. i is minor and V is major.
3. The progression ii–V–I is often set to $\hat{2}$–$\hat{7}$–$\hat{1}$ in the soprano, versus the less dynamic $\hat{1}$–$\hat{7}$–$\hat{1}$ when IV functions as the pre-dominant. This double-neighbor melodic motion encircling the upcoming $\hat{1}$ makes the cadence especially powerful (see Example 12.5).

EXAMPLE 12.5

DVD 1
CH 12
TRACK 5

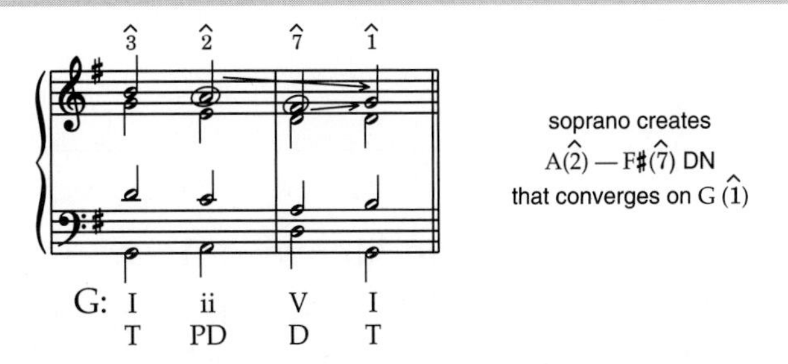

Composers write ii and ii_6 in the major mode, but they almost always use the first inversion $ii°_6$ chord in the minor mode. This is because ii° is a dissonant diminished triad, and (as we learned with vii°) any root-position diminished triad has an unsettling effect, given its exposed tritone between the bass and an upper voice. The tritone is softened when first-inversion ii°$_6$ is used, and $\hat{4}$ occurs in the bass (see Example 12.6).

EXAMPLE 12.6

DVD 1
CH 12
TRACK 6

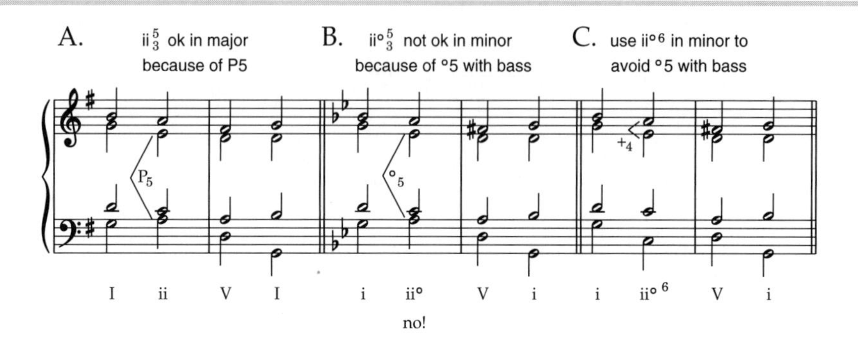

The use of ii in first inversion raises an important issue. Recall that root-position ii lacks the smooth melodic step progression to V in the bass that is enjoyed by IV (Example 12.3). The first-inversion supertonic (ii$_6$) embodies the best attributes of ii and IV: We get the modal contrast from ii, the descending-fifth root relation of ii–V, and the smooth bass voice leading of $\hat{4}$–$\hat{5}$ from IV. See Example 12.7.

EXAMPLE 12.7

DVD 1
CH 12
TRACK 7

Haydn, String Quartet in F minor, op. 20, no. 5, Hob. III.35,
Allegro moderato

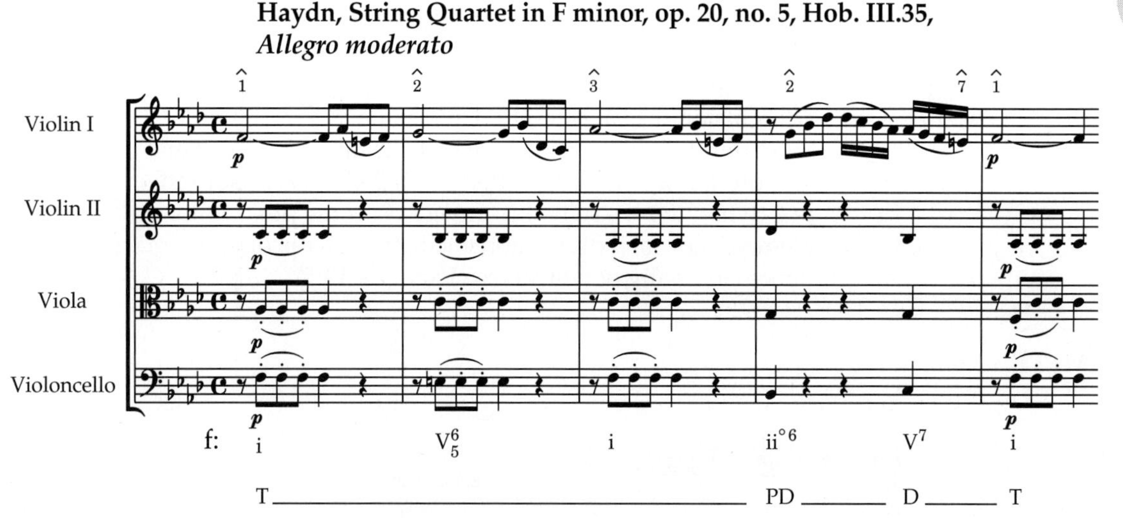

Pre-Dominants and the Stepwise Ascending Bass

Remember that when we first used V$_7$, we harmonized stepwise motions between $\hat{1}$ and $\hat{5}$ in the *soprano* (see Chapters 9 and 11). With the addition of pre-dominants, we can now write a stepwise line in the *bass* that ascends from $\hat{1}$ to $\hat{5}$. Thousands of musical phrases, from the early Baroque to today's popular music, feature this bass line, as shown in Example 12.8. The ascending bass line has an especially powerful effect in major-mode pieces, given that the bass of I$_6$ ($\hat{3}$) lies only a half step from the pre-dominant on $\hat{4}$.

EXAMPLE 12.8 Chopin, Nocturne in F♯ minor, op. 48, no. 2

DVD 1
CH 12
TRACK 8

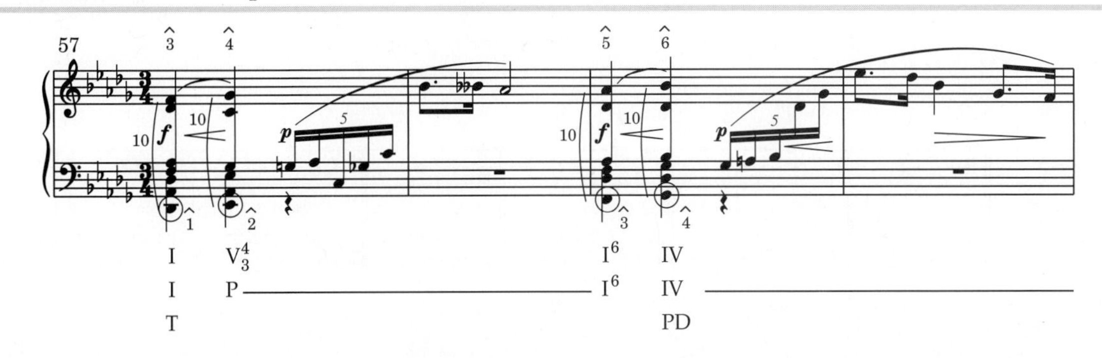

Part Writing for Pre-Dominants

Keep the following in mind when writing pre-dominants.

1. Pre-dominants move to V. Keep this model close to your heart: tonic→pre-dominant→dominant→tonic.
2. When the bass of a pre-dominant chord approaches the dominant by step ($\hat{4}$ to $\hat{5}$ or $\hat{6}$ to $\hat{5}$), the soprano moves in contrary motion with the bass (see the arrows in Example 12.9A–E).
3. Try to double the root of pre-dominant chords that are in root position (see Example 12.9E).
4. Try to double the bass ($\hat{4}$) when writing a ii_6 chord (see Example 12.9E).
5. In a phrygian cadence (iv_6–V), the bass moves from $\hat{6}$ to $\hat{5}$, the soprano usually moves from $\hat{4}$ to $\hat{5}$, and the other voices double $\hat{1}$ to avoid errors in voice leading (see Example 12.9C).
6. When writing in minor, approach the leading tone ($\hat{7}$) in the V chord from above. Example 12.9 F shows both problematic and good voice leading.

EXAMPLE 12.9

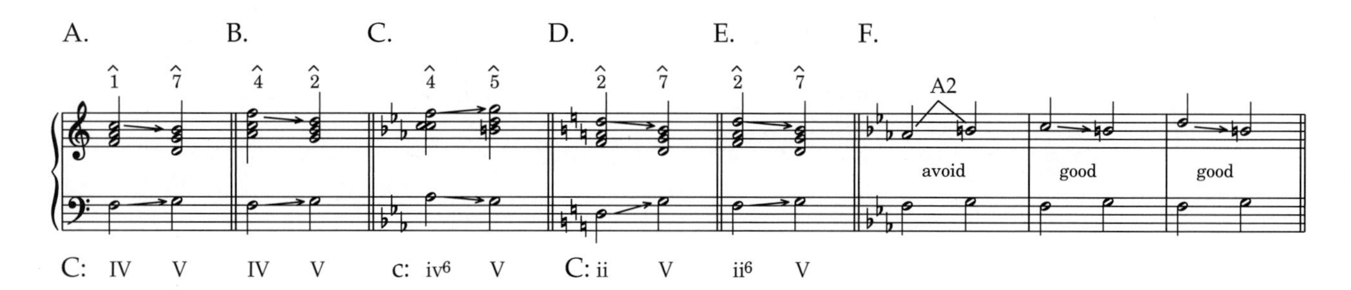

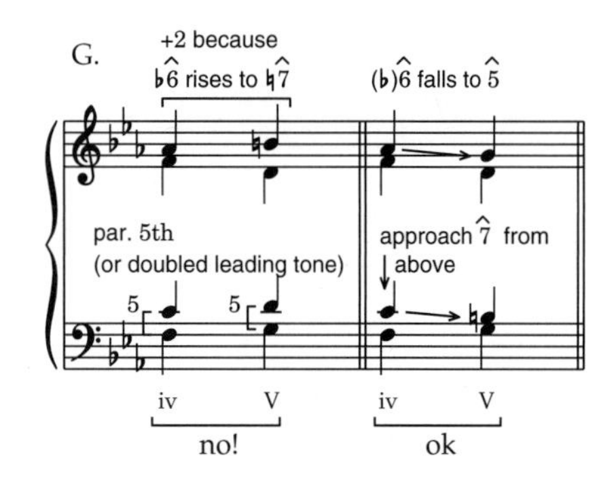

EXERCISE INTERLUDE

PERFORMING

12.1

The following arpeggiations create progressions that incorporate the predominant function. Sing them and/or play them on an instrument. Listen to how often harmonies change. Then analyze the progressions with roman numerals. Next, transpose the arpeggiations to other keys (Exercise C should be performed only in the minor mode).

LISTENING

DVD 2
CH 12
TRACK 1

12.2 Aural Identification of Pre-Dominants

Listen to the following phrases in the minor mode, and identify the pre-dominant with a roman numeral. Your choices are ii°$_6$, iv, and iv$_6$. In addition to the hints for the previous exercise, here are some more tips.

- If the bass steps into the V chord from above, the pre-dominant must be a iv$_6$ chord.
- Remember that there will be no root-position ii° chords in minor.

A. _____ E. _____

B. _____ F. _____

C. _____ G. _____

D. _____ H. _____

12.3

Listen to each of the following short phrases in the major mode, and identify the pre-dominant chord with a roman numeral. Your choices are ii, ii$_6$, and IV. The following hints will be helpful.

- If there is a bass leap into the V chord, the pre-dominant must be a root-position ii chord.
- If the pre-dominant harmonizes $\hat{2}$ in an upper voice, it must be a supertonic chord.
- If the pre-dominant harmonizes $\hat{1}$ in an upper voice, it must be a subdominant chord.

A. _____ E. _____

B. _____ F. _____

C. _____ G. _____

D. _____ H. _____

WRITING

12.4

On a separate sheet of paper, write the following progressions in four voices, using only half notes. Analyze your work using two levels.

A. i–iv–V–i (in D minor)
B. ii$_6$–V$_7$–I (in F major)
C. I–ii–V–I (in B♭ major)
D. i–iv$_6$–V (in A minor)
E. I–I$_6$–ii$_6$–V–I (in A major)

12.5 Harmonizing Soprano Fragments

On a separate sheet of paper, harmonize the following soprano fragments in four-voice chorale style: First use D major—then go back and harmonize the fragments in D minor. Include one pre-dominant chord in each progression.

A. $\hat{3}$–$\hat{2}$–$\hat{2}$–$\hat{1}$
B. $\hat{5}$–$\hat{4}$–$\hat{2}$–1
C. $\hat{5}$–$\hat{6}$–$\hat{5}$–$\hat{4}$–$\hat{3}$
D. $\hat{1}$–$\hat{2}$–$\hat{3}$–$\hat{4}$–$\hat{5}$ (minor only)
E. $\hat{3}$–$\hat{4}$–$\hat{3}$–$\hat{2}$–$\hat{7}$–$\hat{1}$

ANALYSIS

12.6 Snapshots

Listen to and study the following excerpts. Identify the harmonic rhythm. When do chords change? Identify the tonic part of each excerpt: Some excerpts contain just one tonic chord, and others expand the tonic with contrapuntal chords. Identify the pre-dominant chords, some of which may be ornamented with nonchord tones (strong-beat dissonances are indicated by parentheses). Provide a two-level harmonic analysis.

A. Beethoven, Piano Sonata in G major, op. 14, no. 2, *Andante*

B. Mozart, Piano Sonata in D major, K. 284, "Variation VII, Minore"

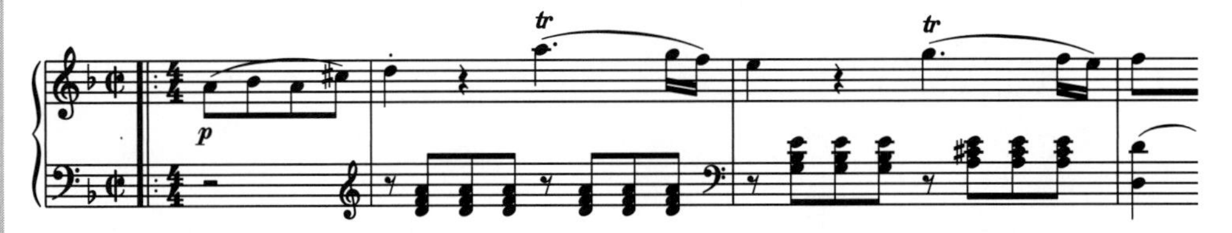

C. Haydn, String Quartet in B minor, op. 64, no. 2, Hob. III/68, *Adagio ma non troppo*

D. Haydn, Symphony no. 88 in G major, *Allegro*

E. Mozart, "Wer ein Liebchen hat gefunden," from *Die Entführung aus dem Serail* ("The Abduction from the Seraglio"), K. 384

12.7 Keyboard

Each of the following two-voice cadential models moves through tonic, pre-dominant, dominant, and back to tonic. Realize the figured bass, and play in four-voice keyboard style. Then transpose each to major and minor keys (up to two flats or sharps). You should not play parts B1 and C2 in minor keys. Why not?

12.8

Determine logical meters and progressions for the given melodic fragments. You may change the rhythms of the fragments. Parts A–D are soprano fragments; Parts E–H are bass fragments. Harmonize in four-voice keyboard style. Be aware that progressions may work in major and/or minor mode.

WORKBOOK
12.1–12.2

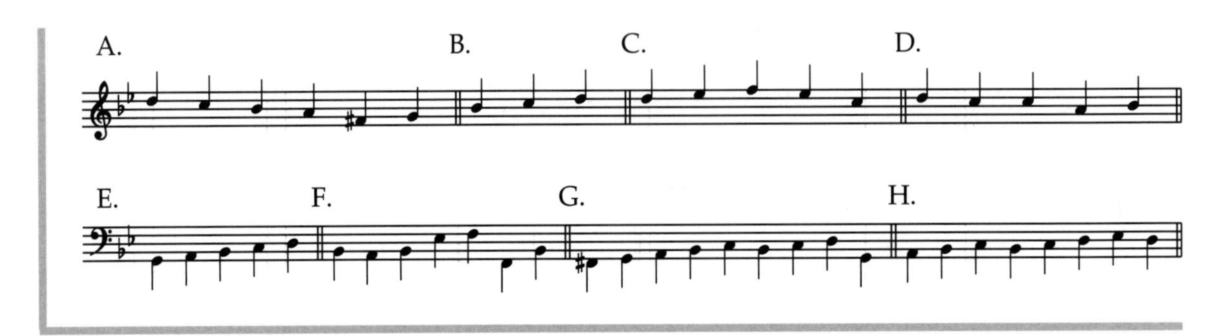

Extending the Pre-Dominant

Just as the tonic and the dominant functions may be extended by embellishing chords, so too may the pre-dominant. We will focus on two techniques that extend the pre-dominant function.

The first technique involves the use of a chordal skip in the bass, that is, moving from ii to ii^6 or vice versa. Example 12.10 illustrates this simple technique. Notice the resulting voice exchange between the outer voices.

EXAMPLE 12.10 Beethoven, Piano Concerto in G major, op. 58/I

DVD 2
CH 12
TRACK 9

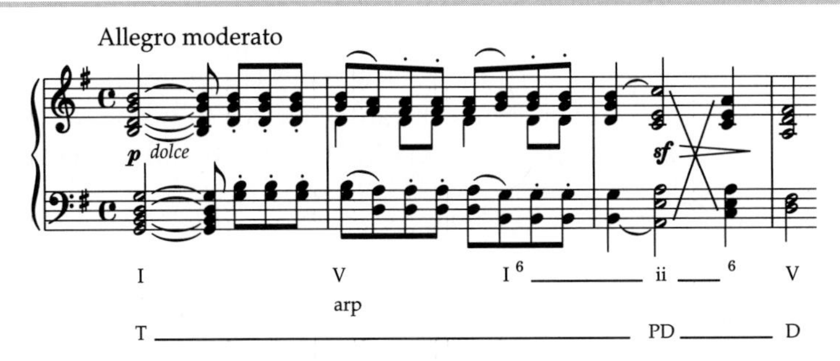

The second technique is subtler, yet arguably more important. We know that progressions whose roots move by step (e.g., IV–V) are especially vulnerable to parallel perfect intervals in voice leading, especially when the outer voices are moved in the same direction (see Example 12.11A). Yet, for motivic reasons, composers often wish to write bass-soprano gestures that move exactly in this way. In order to avoid poor voice leading, they often use what are called **helping chords** or, more commonly, **voice-leading chords**. In Example 12.11B, the soprano quarter-note motion creates a contrapuntal 5–6 motion above the bass that anticipates the dominant pitch G and avoids the parallel fifths seen in Example 12.11A. The 5–6 motion above the bass is a common device that gives the impression that two chords—IV and ii$_6$—are working seamlessly together to extend the pre-dominant function. Though it appears that the IV moves to ii$_6$, we interpret this motion as a subtle shift in voice leading (IV$^{5-6}$) rather than as a functional chord change, and we refer to the process as the **IV–ii complex**. This interpretation is reflected in the second-level analysis, which groups the IV–ii under a single functional heading: *PD*. In Example 12.11C the bass falls from $\hat{4}$ to $\hat{2}$, yet even this apparent chord change (IV to ii) is still motivated by the same voice-leading concerns as in Example 12.11B. Note that the goal-oriented melodic motion in the succession IV–ii$_{(6)}$ is very common but that the weaker motion of ii–IV is not. Example 12.11D, from Mozart's "Haffner" Symphony, shows how the pre-dominant, IV, moves to V using the iv–ii complex. Keenly aware of effective voice leading, Mozart would never move in parallel fifths from IV to V (as shown in Example 12.11D2). Rather, he shifts the upper note of the fifth, D, by step up to E, creating a consonant sixth and a resulting ii$_6$ chord. E is sustained as the bass raises to A (the root of the V), where it functions as the fifth of the chord (see Example 12.11D2).

DVD 2
CH 12
TRACK 10

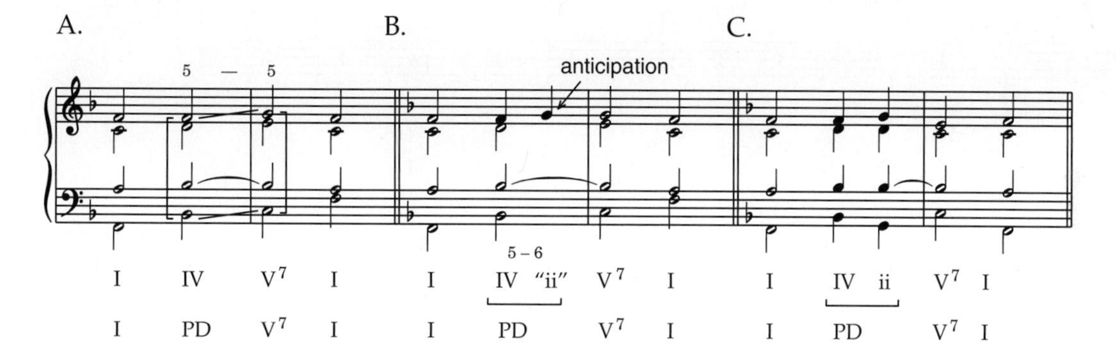

D1. Mozart, Symphony 35 in D major ("Haffner"), K. 385, *Menuetto*

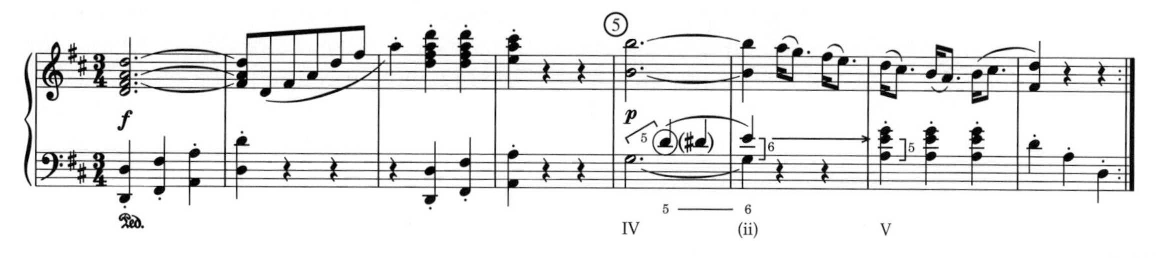

D2.

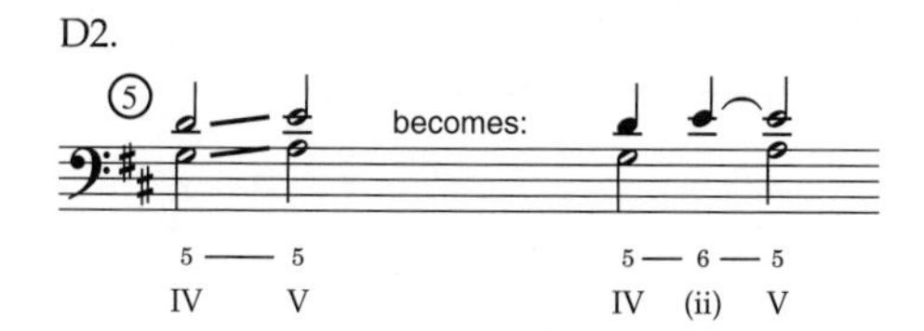

Introduction to the Phrase Model

Complete musical statements can rely exclusively on tonic and dominant chords. These units, called *phrases*, are always punctuated by strong closing gestures called *cadences*. Although there are many examples of phrases built exclusively on tonics and dominants, most phrases incorporate the pre-dominant function to create a richer harmonic progression. The harmonic motion of T–PD–D –T that guides a phrase from its beginning to its cadence is called the **phrase model**.

EXAMPLE 12.12 **Haydn, String Quartet in D major ("Der Frosch"), op. 50, no. 6, Hob. III.49, *Menuetto***

DVD 1
CH 12
TRACK 11

Although the phrase model can occupy any number of measures, four measures (or some multiple of four) is common, as seen in Example 12.12. Here, a balanced motion is clearly felt as the harmonic rhythm shifts once every measure. There is much room for variation in this model, however, and the harmonic rhythm of the tonic, pre-dominant, and dominant may vary considerably. For instance, the opening tonic often occupies at least as much time as the pre-dominant and dominant combined. Example 12.13, the opening four-measure phrase from one of Mozart's piano sonatas, extends the tonic for three and a third measures, with the PD and D occupying barely more than one beat. (Notice that the bass and soprano begin at the interval of a tenth; then, in parallel motion, they descend by step together and then return to the root-position tonic harmony, making the expansion of tonic explicit.)

EXAMPLE 12.13 **Mozart, Piano Sonata in A major, K. 331, *Andante grazioso***

In Example 12.12 the phrase model closed with an authentic cadence. Example 12.13 closed with a half cadence. These two basic models are represented schematically in Example 12.14. Models 3 and 4, which close with a half cadence, are as grammatically complete as the first two models, yet their harmony implies that the piece will go on eventually to resolve the tension of the dominant.

EXAMPLE 12.14

Four-measure phrase models

measures:	1	2	3	4	*cadence*
model 1:	T	PD	D	T	authentic
model 2:	T		PD — D	T	authentic
model 3:	T		PD	D	half
model 4:	T			PD — D	half

Note how in all four models it takes much more time for the tonic to move to the pre-dominant than for the pre-dominant to move to the dominant. It is common for the dominant to occupy two or even three times more time than the pre-dominant. Example 12.15 (closely resembling model 3) illustrates a four-measure phrase with five and three-quarter beats of tonic and two beats of dominant, but only half a beat of pre-dominant.

EXAMPLE 12.15 Schubert, Violin Sonata no. 2 in G minor, D. 408, *Andante*

DVD 1
CH 12
TRACK 13

Although the phrase models shown in Example 12.14 might seem to constrain a composer's creativity, they actually generate unlimited compositional possibilities. Composers from the Baroque era through the late nineteenth century, writing in very different styles, employed these models tirelessly. For example, listen to the two excerpts in Example 12.16. Both excerpts share the same harmonic structure; but because of their different figurations on the musical "surface," they could not sound more different. Each contains a single phrase (Example A is four measures and Example B is eight) that begins with a tonic expansion (i–V_6 (or V^6_5)–V_7–i). This is followed by a pre-dominant on ii, ornamented with strong-beat upper-voice dissonances and followed by a half cadence (also embellished by strong-beat dissonances). Even motivic details unfold identically in both examples. Note the $\hat{5}$–$\hat{6}$–$\hat{5}$–♯$\hat{4}$–$\hat{5}$ motion that extends the tonic in both examples and the embellishing harmonies.

EXAMPLE 12.16

DVD 1
CH 12
TRACK 14

A. Mendelssohn, *Lied ohne Worte* ("Song Without Words"), no. 5 in F♯ minor, op. 19

B. Mendelssohn, *Lied ohne Worte* ("Song Without Words"), no. 8 in B♭ minor, op. 30

T–PD–D–T Within the Tonic Prolongation

We have seen how musical events, including melodic figurations, tonal progressions, and especially motivic development, can coexist at various hierarchical levels. The tonal progression of the phrase model is no different. Composers often incorporate the T–PD–D–T model within the tonic prolongation.

In order to accomplish this without confusing the listener that it may be the actual structural cadence, composers weaken the progression through the use of inversions, a technique we have often seen already. For example, the strong cadential power of V_7–I can be undermined by placing the seventh of V_7 in the bass; the resultant V^4_2–I_6 motion delays the music's closure. One common technique is to follow IV or ii_6 with V^4_2, which maintains $\hat{4}$ in the bass that must fall to $\hat{3}$. This progression can be seen in Example 12.17A, where the tonic expansion includes a mini, noncadential PD–D–T. In Example 12.17B, we see a standard four-measure phrase model closing with a HC. Tonic and dominant alternate in mm. 1–2, until i_6 appears at the end of m. 2 and signals the upcoming predominant, which enters in m. 3. Through the iv–ii complex, the PD moves to the embellished HC. This example is nothing more than a pedantic recomposition of what the actual composer of this passage, Franz Josef Haydn, *could* have done. Rather, Haydn extends his phrase to six full measures by evading the HC in m. 4. He does so by sustaining the bass pitch, C, which becomes the dissonant seventh of V, which must resolve weakly to i_6, thus extending the tonic for two more measures before cadencing on V.

EXAMPLE 12.17

DVD 1
CH 12
TRACK 15

A.

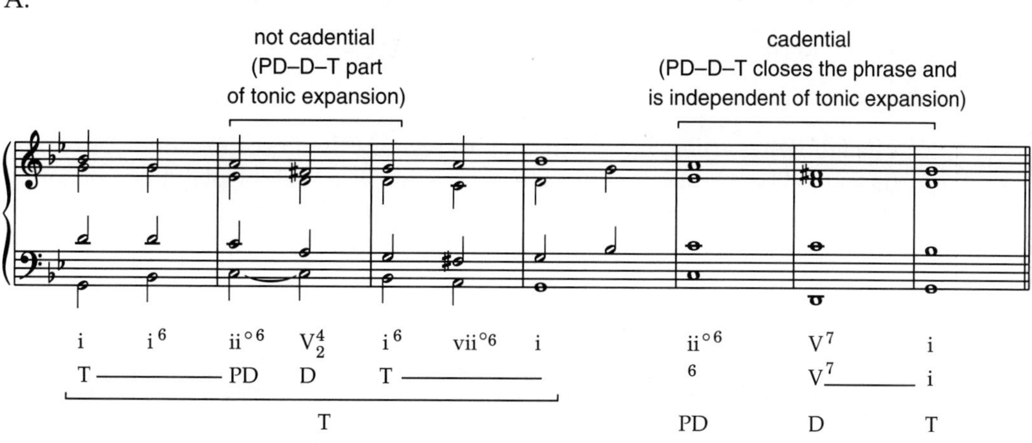

B1.

B2. Haydn, Piano Sonata in G minor, Hob. XVI/44, *Allegretto*

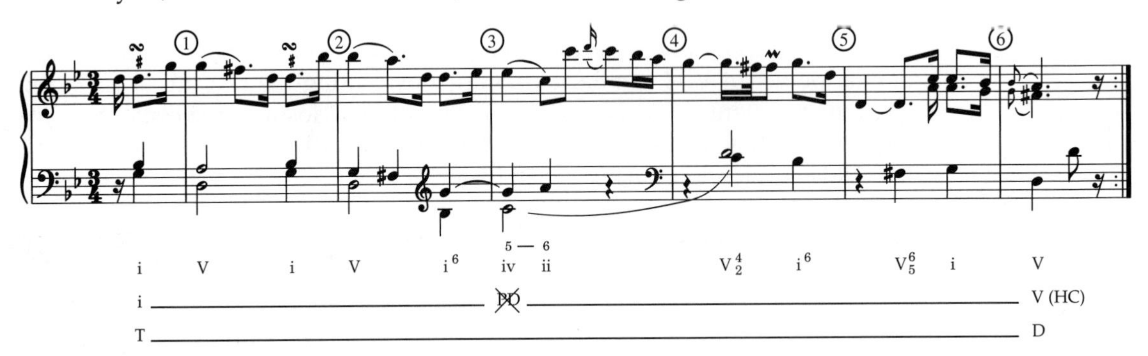

Final Checklist for Pre-Dominant Function

- The T–PD–D–T order is not reversible.
- Use contrary motion in the outer voices when writing I–ii, IV–V, or ii_6–V.
- In minor, $\hat{6}$ must descend to $\hat{5}$, and $\hat{7}$ must be approached from above.

EXERCISE INTERLUDE

PERFORMING

12.9

The following arpeggiations create progressions that incorporate the pre-dominant function within the phrase model. Sing them and/or play them on an instrument. Listen to how often harmonies change. Then analyze the progressions with roman numerals. Next, transpose the arpeggiations to other keys.

ANALYSIS

DVD 2
CH 12
TRACK 4

12.10

Determine the cadence, harmonic rhythm, and pre-dominant (ii, ii_6, or IV) for each of the following excerpts. Also, answer the following questions for each excerpt.

1. How is the tonic expanded?
2. Is there more than one pre-dominant harmony used (for example, IV–ii)? Circle and label each PD harmony.
3. What phrase model does each example most resemble?

A. Mozart, Piano Sonata in B♭ major, K. 333, *Allegro*

B. Handel, Concerto Grosso, op. 6, no. 9, *Largo*

C. Haydn, String Quartet in G major, op. 33, no. 5, Hob. III.42, *Largo cantabile*

WRITING

12.11 Recipes

The following lists of "ingredients" and steps are for "recipes" that incorporate pre-dominants. The lists do not appear in a logical order; if you carry out the instructions in the order in which they appear, the progressions will not work. First, arrange the instructions in logical order; then write the progressions in four-voice chorale style. Use a separate sheet of manuscript paper, and choose an appropriate meter for each progression.

A. Write a progression in D minor that:
- includes the pre-dominant $\text{ii}^{\circ}{}_{6}$
- expands tonic with a $\text{vii}^{\circ}{}_{7}$
- includes a perfect authentic cadence

B. Write a progression in F major that:
- includes a half cadence
- includes a form of $\text{vii}^{\circ}{}_{7}$ in a tonic expansion
- includes the pre-dominant IV
- includes the following bass in the tonic expansion: $\hat{1}$–$\hat{7}$–$\hat{1}$–$\hat{2}$–$\hat{3}$–$\hat{4}$–$\hat{3}$

C. Write a progression in B minor that:
- includes a phrygian cadence
- expands the tonic with a voice exchange
- includes a V^{6}_{5} chord

12.12 Composition

Play the following excerpts, each of which is a phrase that closes with a half cadence. Excerpt A is eight measures long, and excerpt B is four. For each excerpt, write a matching phrase on a separate sheet of manuscript paper that closes on tonic for each basic style, character, general harmonic rhythm, and figuration of the given phrase. (*Hint:* Most of the material in the first phrase can return in the second phrase. Consult the list of phrase models to see what part of the first phrase must be rewritten to end with an authentic cadence.)

A.

B. Vivaldi, Concerto in C major for Violin, Ryom 176, *Largo*

INSTRUMENTAL APPLICATION: REDUCTION AND ELABORATION

12.13

Reduce the textures in the following Mozart symphonic excerpts. Analyze, verticalize (into a four-voice homophonic texture), and then perform each example as follows. If you are a pianist, simply play your four-voice realization. If you are a melodic instrumentalist, arpeggiate each example. If necessary, refer to the discussion in Chapter 11 for a detailed procedure. Play each reduction in the key in which it is written; then transpose to one other key of your choice.

A. Mozart, Symphony in D major, K. 81, *Andante*

B. Mozart, Symphony in D major, K. 95, *Andante*

WORKBOOK 12.4–12.5

12.14

Elaborate the following four-voice progressions and figured basses by arpeggiating in strict ascending four-voice chords that maintain good voice leading between chords. Then embellish your solution by adding changes in contour and tones of figuration. Refer to the discussion in Chapter 11 for a detailed procedure.

TERMS AND CONCEPTS

- IV–ii complex
- four-measure phrase model: with perfect authentic cadence and with half cadence
- helping chords (or voice-leading chords)
- phrase model
- phrygian cadence
- pre-dominant
- use of IV
- use of ii

CHAPTER 13

Accented and Chromatic Dissonances

Tones of figuration enhance music's motion, grace, and drama. Their presence on the immediate surface of the music means that they are the first events to which the listener's attention is drawn. Tones of figuration flesh out the basic harmonic and contrapuntal structures in infinite ways, and, finally, composers use them in specific ways, to the degree that they provide stylistic fingerprints and helpful cues for performance practice.

So far we have encountered three types of melodic figuration: chordal skips, passing tones, and neighbor tones. The Corelli excerpt in Example 13.1 contains examples of each of these types of figuration. As you listen to the example (below which each harmony is indicated by its root name), label each tone of figuration and consider its rhythmic placement. Chordal leaps are heard in the first two beats of m. 9. Passing tones occur in beat 3 of m. 9. The upper-neighbor figure G–A♭–G on beat 2 in m. 10 is followed by an incomplete neighbor in violin 1 and a passing tone in violin 2. All dissonances are metrically unstressed; as such, they create a light and buoyant sound.

EXAMPLE 13.1 Corelli, Sonata for Two Violins in E♭ major, op. 2, no. 11, Giga

DVD 1
CH 13
TRACK 1

Now listen to Example 13.2, taken from the slow movement of another Corelli sonata. Again, the letter names of chord roots appear below the score. Compare Corelli's use of tones of figuration in this example with their use in the previous example. The tones of figuration in Example 13.2 are much more striking than those heard in Example 13.1. This is because the dissonances occur on accented beats or accented parts of beats. Most seem to arise through a rhythmic delay. For example, in m. 29 the chordal seventh, G, extends into the following measure, where it forms a dissonance against the D-major harmony. However, one beat later, G falls by step to F♯, where it functions as the third of the D-major chord. Another type of dissonance occurs in m. 31: The second violin plays an accented neighbor figure C♯–D–C♯ over the F♯ triad. The appearance of this dissonant neighbor *on* a beat rather than *between* beats makes it much more striking.

EXAMPLE 13.2 Corelli, Sonata for Two Violins in E minor, op. 2, no. 4, Preludio

We group tones of figuration into two categories, based on their rhythmic placement. The first category, called **unaccented tones of figuration** (Example 13.1), includes metrically unstressed tones of figuration. We have already studied the most important of these, including the chordal leap, the passing tone, and the neighbor tone (both complete and incomplete). We further categorized the unaccented tones of figuration into those that are consonant (chordal leaps) and those that are dissonant (most passing tones and neighbor tones). We learned that consonant tones of figuration may appear without preparation or resolution. However, dissonant tones of figuration must be carefully controlled, nearly always occurring between consonances and moving by step.

Tones of figuration that belong to the second category, called **accented tones of figuration** (Example 13.2), occur in metrically stressed contexts (e.g., on, rather than between, beats). Accented tones of figuration are some of the most emotive elements of music; recognizing them can influence your performance significantly. In fact, given that Baroque and Classical-period composers expected performers to add various types of tones of figuration to their published scores, it is possible for the performer to enhance the music's drama. Accented dissonances occur in many forms, but the most important are the accented passing tone, the accented neighbor tone, the suspension, the pedal, and the appoggiatura.

Since tones of figuration often fill the space between chordal members, then, by extension, **chromatic tones of figuration** fill the smaller intervallic space that occurs between stepwise motions. We also explore such unaccented and accented chromatic figures.

The Accented Passing Tone (APT)

Just like a passing tone, an **accented passing tone** (APT) fills in a melodic third; however, the APT occurs on, rather than between, beats. The usual metric positions of consonance and dissonance are reversed with the APT.

EXAMPLE 13.3

DVD 1
CH 13
TRACK 3

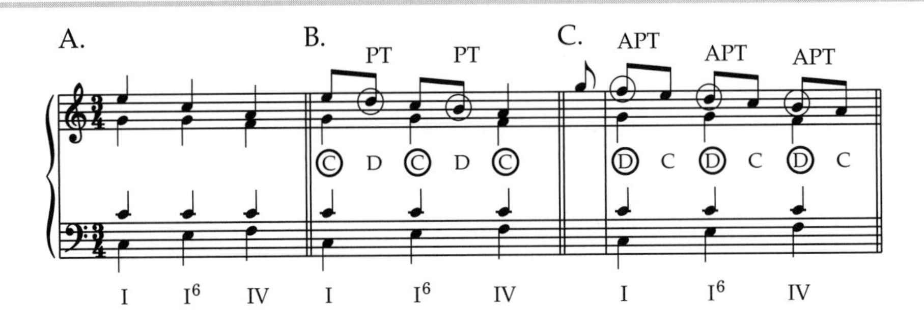

Example 13.3A shows an unelaborated SATB progression; Example 13.3B elaborates the progression with unaccented PTs. Note that consonance is aligned with metrical stress and that dissonance is reserved for the metrically weak offbeat. Example 13.3C demonstrates accented PTs; dissonance is highlighted because it occurs on the beat, whereas the consonance now occurs on the offbeat. Accented passing tones impart a new level of tension, since consonance and metrical accents do not align.

Example 13.4A presents the opening of Schumann's song "Am leuchtenden Sommermorgen," in which the accented passing tone A at the downbeat of m. 4 forms a dissonant fourth with the E♭ harmony before resolving to the chordal third. Imagine if Schumann had instead written the more mundane unaccented passing tone, as shown in Example 13.4B.

EXAMPLE 13.4

DVD 1
CH 13
TRACK 4

A. Schumann, "Am leuchtenden Sommermorgen," from *Dichterliebe*, op. 48

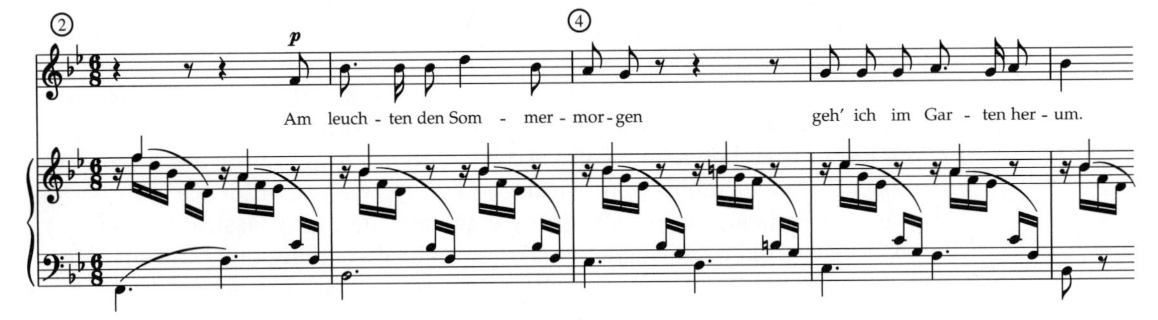

B. Schumann, "Am leuchtenden Sommermorgen," from *Dichterliebe* (modified)

Accented passing tones most often occur in descending lines, and they usually are part of either a 7–6 or 4–3 contrapuntal motion against the bass voice.

The Chromatic Passing Tone (CPT)

Chromatic passing tones fill the space between two diatonic pitches. Most often, the diatonic pitches are separated by a major second, creating a series of half-step motions. Example 13.5A1 illustrates how the diatonic passing tone E♭ fills the space between D and F. Example 13.5A2 illustrates the chromatic passing tone E natural, which fills the space between the major second E♭ to F. Less often CPTs can fill the space between diatonic pitches a third apart, as in Example 13.5A3.

EXAMPLE 13.5

DVD 1
CH 13
TRACK 5

A.

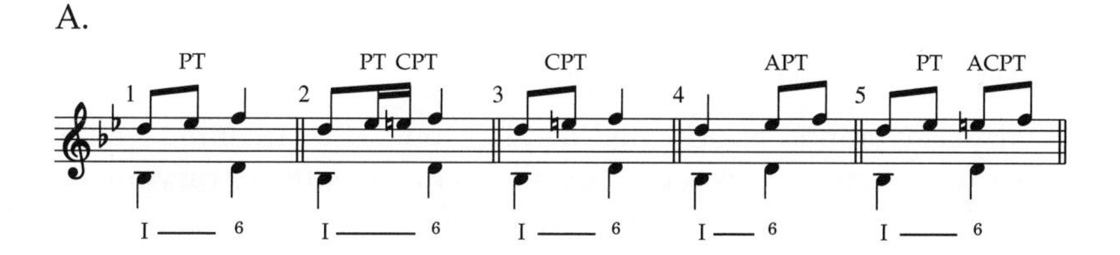

B. Mozart, Piano Sonata in B♭, K. 570, *Allegretto*

Like diatonic passing tones, chromatic passing tones occur in both unaccented and accented contexts. Ascending chromatic passing tones are more common than those that descend because ascending CPTs create miniature leading tones to the pitch they precede, thereby intensifying the melodic direction. Example 13.5A4 illustrates a diatonic APT, and Example 13.5A5 illustrates a chromatic APT. Notice how all of the five passing tones in Example 13.5A increase their aural prominence as they move along a continuum from unaccented and diatonic to accented and chromatic.

Example 13.5B presents the opening phrase of a Mozart piano sonata that contains both unaccented and accented CPTs. We'll begin with m. 3, where two unaccented CPTs (B♮^{4} and C♯^{5}) fill the space between B♭^{4} and D^5 ($\hat{1}$ and $\hat{3}$). Because these CPTs are unaccented, our ears are not nearly as drawn to them as they are to the accented CPT E♮^{5} that occurs on—rather than between—the strong part of beat 2 in m. 1 and that fills the space between E♭ and F. Notice that Mozart has written a two-note slur, indicating that E♮ is to receive an emphasis (both dynamic and articulative), whereas the unaccented CPTs in m. 3 are marked as the second pitches in two-note slurs, indicating that dynamic stress should be given to the first pitch in a two-note slur and that the second pitch is released and played without emphasis.

Mozart's phrase unfolds in the standard phrase model: T is prolonged for the vast majority of the excerpt, over three measures, until the PD enters for only an eighth-note duration and leads to D, on which the phrase closes in a half cadence. The strong, double APTs (B♭^{4} and D^5) at the end of m. 4 (Example 13.5B) postpone and therefore draw the listener's attention to the HC (both B♭ and D lead to the chord tones A and C of the dominant). Notice that the tonic prolongation is made clear by the soprano's line that falls a third from D to B♭ ($\hat{3}$–$\hat{2}$–$\hat{1}$) and ascends to recapture D. The counterpoint with the bass creates two voice exchanges (B♭–D). D finally falls to C ($\hat{2}$) in the HC.

The Accented Neighbor Tone (AN)

While not nearly as common as accented passing tones, the **accented neighbor tone** occurs with some frequency, especially in nineteenth-century music. Example 13.6A presents a neighboring expansion of the tonic without melodic embellishment. Example 13.6B contains an unaccented neighbor (G–A–G) and passing tone (G–F–E). In Example 13.6C, the neighbor A^4 is metrically accented, since it sounds on the beat. The second accented event occurs when F^4, as passing seventh of the dominant harmony, becomes an APT (4–3) over tonic harmony. Just as unaccented upper neighbors are more common than unaccented lower neighbors, so too are accented upper neighbors more common that accented lower neighbors. Finally, notice that the displacement (postponement) of the soprano's G in the V_6 chord results in what might be mistaken as a $vii^{ø}_7$ chord. This interpretation ignores the nonharmonic—and therefore aurally marked—function of the soprano's A and instead views it as the chordal seventh. This analytical error has performance repercussions, for the nonchord tone A begins a pattern of implied two-note slurs that carries over into the next beat of the soprano's line, where F clearly displaces E.

EXAMPLE 13.6

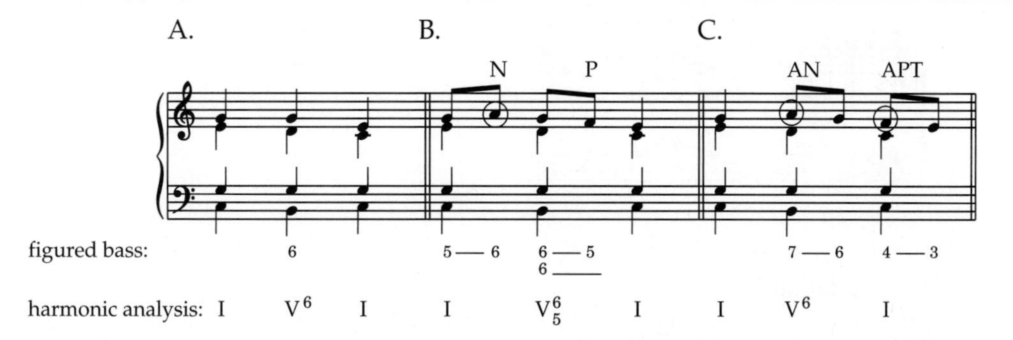

The Chromatic Neighbor Tone (CN)

The chromatic neighbor is highly dissonant yet very beautiful. Example 13.7 recasts the diatonic neighbors from Example 13.6 as chromatic neighbors.

EXAMPLE 13.7

DVD 1 CH 13 TRACK 7

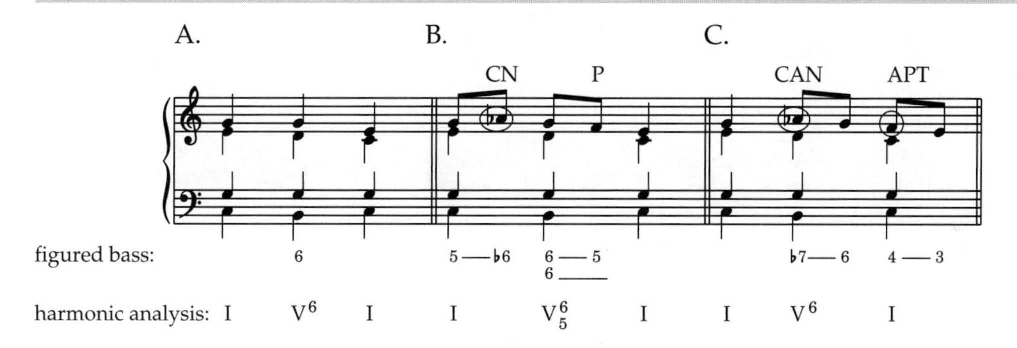

One frequently encounters accented and chromatic passing and neighboring tones in variation sets written in the late Classical and Romantic periods, where such variation and intensification of rhythmic and diatonic regularity provide contrast and drama. For example, Schubert's Impromptu in B♭ is cast as a theme followed by a series of variations. The theme (Example 13.8A) opens with a simple alteration of tonic and dominant, each of which is elaborated by inversion.

EXAMPLE 13.8 Schubert, Impromptu no. 3 in B♭, D. 935

DVD 1 CH 13 TRACK 8

A.

B. Variation 1

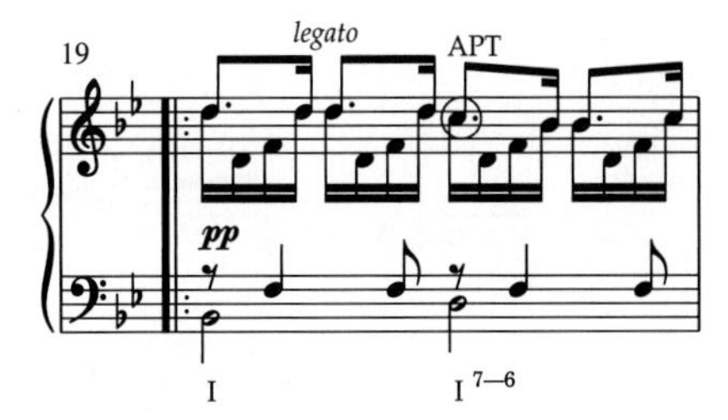

C. Variation 3

D. Variation 2

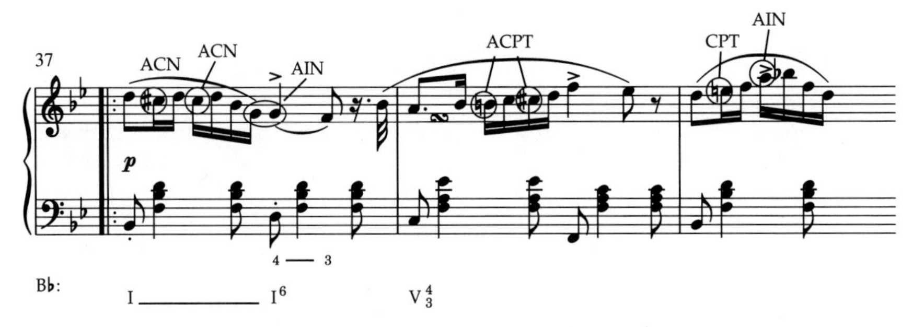

Variation 1 (Example 13.8B) is characterized by a broken-chord figure in which the melodic third D–B♭ from the theme is filled by the APT C^5, creating a 7–6 contrapuntal motion with the bass.

Variation 3 (Example 13.8C) contains the same APT figure in the right hand, but this variation is cast in the parallel minor, so the 7–6 figure is more dissonant, given that the seventh is major and more intense than the minor seventh found in variation 1. The upper part of the left hand contains faster-moving chromatic, unaccented neighbors that together form a larger, double-neighbor figure.

Variation 2 (Example 13.8D) contains nearly every possible tone of figuration, including chromatic neighbors (both unaccented and accented), two examples of which occur in m. 1. The variation opens with the complete neighbor D–C♯–D. This variation also presents something new, the **accented incomplete neighbor** (AIN). Incomplete neighbors move by step to a chord tone in only one direction; that is, rather than moving from a diatonic pitch and returning to the same pitch, incomplete neighbors usually leap from a diatonic pitch and move by step (up or down) to a different diatonic pitch. For example, in m. 2 beat 3, G is an incomplete upper neighbor: It leaps down a third from the chord tone B♭ and then falls by step to the chord tone F as its incomplete upper neighbor. An incomplete lower neighbor is heard near the end of the example, where A leaps from F and resolves in neighbor fashion to B♭.

The Appoggiatura (APP)

The appoggiatura is an important and striking type of figuration. Different than passing tones and complete neighbor tones (which are flanked by chord tones), appoggiaturas enter by leap and are dissonant and accented. They are related to other tones of figuration only in that they resolve by step to a chord tone (and usually in the direction opposite of their leap in order to balance the melodic contour; a number of important exceptions exist, such as the "Maria" motive from Leonard Bernstein's *West Side Story*). Thus, the appoggiatura behaves very much like the accented incomplete neighbors we encountered in Example 13.8. We will tend to refer to accented incomplete neighbors as appoggiaturas. Example 13.9 illustrates appoggiaturas and their labeling.

EXAMPLE 13.9

DVD 1
CH 13
TRACK 9

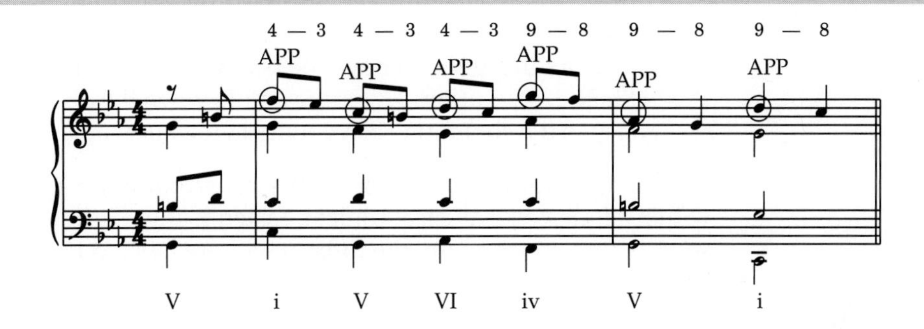

The Suspension (sus)

EXAMPLE 13.10

DVD 1
CH 13
TRACK 10

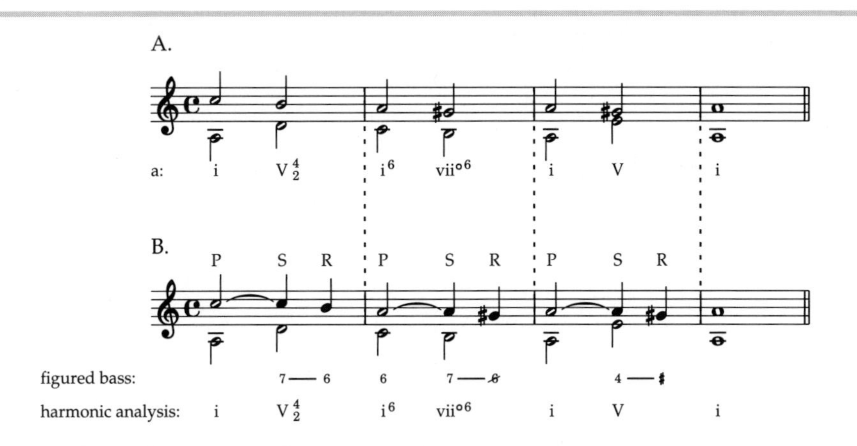

Listen to Example 13.10A, which presents a two-voice example that we'll consider to be the outer voices of the implied progression whose roman numeral analysis is given. Example 13.10B presents a modified version of Example 13.10A; in four instances the soprano voice is sustained, where it intrudes into the following implied chord change. The accented dissonant pitch creates a great deal of musical tension, which is then discharged, or resolved, as it falls by step to a chord tone. We refer to such expressive nonchord tones as **suspensions**; they are the most important type of accented tone of figuration, one found consistently in music from the fifteenth century to today's commercial and popular music.

The contrapuntal setting and metric placement of suspensions is prescribed and cannot be altered. Suspensions are composed of two pitches that are governed by a three-stage process. The first pitch progresses through two of the stages: a weak-beat *preparation* (P) followed by a strong-beat *suspension* (S). The second pitch consists of one stage: a weak-beat *resolution* (R). Each suspension in Example 13.10B illustrates the two-note figure and the three stages. In m. 1, for example, the two pitches of the suspension figure are C and B. The first pitch, C, participates in the two stages of preparation and suspension. The second pitch, B, participates in stage 3: resolution. Details of each stage follow.

- **Stage 1, preparation:** C is initially consonant (a tenth above the bass) on the weak beat (beat 2) so that it prepares for its transformation into a dissonance.
- **Stage 2, suspension:** The prepared pitch is held, by means of a tie or a dot, as the bass moves to the implied V^4_2. The C is now transformed from a third (tenth) above the bass into a seventh above the bass.
- **Stage 3, resolution:** This stage occurs when the dissonant seventh falls by step to the chord tone B, resulting in the interval of a sixth above the bass.

Example 13.11 demonstrates the most common types of suspensions within a four-voice musical context. Listen to the example, which contains five suspensions. Once again, the three stages are labeled *P*, *S*, and *R*.

EXAMPLE 13.11

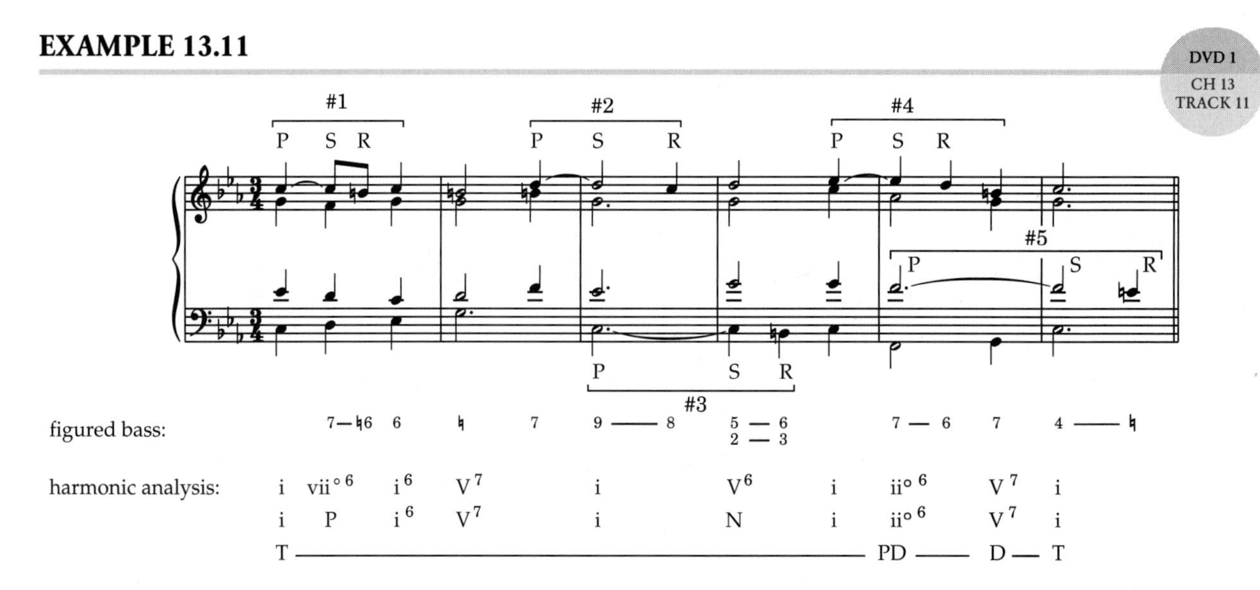

- Suspension 1 occurs in m. 1 as the harmony expands the tonic by moving from i to i_6 using a passing vii°$_6$. The motion in the soprano to its lower neighbor is delayed past the onset of beat 2 as C^5 in the soprano is suspended over the changing chord to create a seventh above the bass (D^3). The resolution to B occurs on the following weak-beat eighth note.

- Suspension 2 occurs in m. 3, as the soprano's D5 from m. 2 is suspended over the tonic chord in m. 3 to form a ninth above the bass; it resolves on the weak third beat.
- Suspension 3 appears in the bass in m. 4, as C3 is sustained from m. 3 to the downbeat of m. 4, thereby delaying for one beat the B♮2 (as chordal third of V_6).
- Suspension 4 appears in the soprano voice between mm. 4 and 5. Given its aural prominence, it coincides with, and thus highlights, the change from T to PD. Here, E♭5 is suspended and forms a dissonant seventh before resolving to the chord tone D, the root of $ii°_6$. Notice that the pre-dominant harmony appears to be an incomplete iv_7 chord, given the pitches F–A♭–E♭. As we discussed in relation to Example 13.6, however, context must determine function: Given the example's pattern of suspensions, the tie, and the fact that ii_6 is a far more common pre-dominant chord than iv_7, we interpret E♭5 as a nonchord tone that resolves to D.
- Suspension 5 occurs in m. 6: The tenor finally gets a chance to suspend, imitating the alto. A dissonant fourth (F4) against the bass (C3) is created as the tenor holds F4 and the bass moves to C2; the tenor resolves down to E♮4 on the final beat of the excerpt.

Labeling Suspensions

We use figured bass numbers to label the melodic motion of the suspension and resolution stages of the suspension figure. The names of the four upper-voice suspensions in Example 13.11 are based on the intervallic content of the suspended voice reckoned with the bass. Thus, the figured bass indications are 7–6, 9–8, 7–6, and 4–3, respectively. We label compound suspending intervals by their reduced, noncompound forms (an 11–10 suspension is called a 4–3, for example). By convention, however, the 9–8 suspension retains its compound label. The 2–1 suspension, while possible, is uncommon, given that the dissonance is sounding immediately adjacent to its resolution. The 2–3 suspension in Example 13.11 (mm. 3–4) is the figured bass label given to the most common bass suspension. Note that the suspension in the bass voice is represented by "2–3"; but in a four-voice texture, there is always another voice that creates the "5–6" motion above the suspending bass. In mm. 3–4 of Example 13.11, the alto and tenor G4 create the 5–6 motion against the bass's C–B. Note that in bass suspensions, the numbers increase in size, because the upper voices remain stationary, whereas the bass, in its descending resolution, naturally increases the size of the interval.

We place the figured bass numbers immediately below the moving pitches, and we show the melodic motion by using the dash so as not to confuse the suspensions with inversions of chords. For example, a "7" appearing by itself indicates a root-position seventh chord; thus the "7" is a chord member. However, a "7–6" indicates a 7–6 suspension (such as in m. 1 of Example 13.11) in which the seventh displaces the sixth of a first-inversion chord. That is, the second chord is not ii_7; rather, it is a $vii°_6$ chord with a suspended seventh. Conversely, the V_7 in m. 5 indicates that the dominant includes a chordal seventh above the bass. Depending on your teacher's preference, you can represent the suspension (and other accented tones of figuration) within a figured bass analysis (immediately below the bass staff), or you can incorporate them in your roman numeral analysis.

Writing Suspensions

The only upper-voice suspensions available to you are the 9–8, 7–6, and 4–3. The only bass suspension is the 2–3. The following guidelines will help you to write suspensions.

1. Suspension figures logically work best with chords whose intervals contain the interval of resolution. For example, 7–6 suspensions work well with $^6_3$ chords, given that all first-inversion chords contain the interval of a sixth and that chords with a sixth above the bass are most often first-inversion chords (e.g., vii°$_6$, V$_6$, and I$_6$). Similarly, 4–3 and 9–8 suspensions work best with root-position chords. The bass suspension (2–3) works best with a $^6_3$ chord (especially in the progression I–V$_6$).
2. Suspensions may occur in any voice at any time as long as the voice is moving down by step to the next chord tone. For example, in the chord progression in Example 13.12A, the three upper voices in the first chord all lie a second above the corresponding voice in the second chord, which means that the resolution is already set up. Now we consider the second chord in order to find an appropriate voice to suspend. Given that the second chord is a first-inversion sonority, the 7–6 suspension would work best (see Example 13.12B). Study Examples 13.12A and B to see how suspensions are generated.
3. If the voice in which you want to write a suspension is moving up by step, consider inserting an ascending chordal leap, which would allow for the preparation and resolution of the suspension downward. For example, say that you wanted to insert a soprano-voice suspension, as in Example 13.12C. However, F♯^{4} lies below G^4, which prevents the use of a suspension. A chordal leap from F♯^{4} to A^4 solves the problem, since the A^4 can now resolve to G^4 in a 7–6 suspension.

EXAMPLE 13.12

DVD 1 CH 13 TRACK 12

4. Make sure that the resolution pitch is not doubled in any other voice, for if it were, it would be sounding against the dissonant suspension and thus would anticipate the suspension's tone of resolution and ruin its intended effect. The one exception to this rule is the 9–8 suspension, which falls to the octave, because the dissonance is far enough away from the sounding note of resolution (see stage 2 from earlier). Finally, the duration of the dissonant suspended note should be at least as long or longer than the preparation and the resolution.

Additional Suspension Techniques

Having learned the basics of suspensions, it is easy to spot variations on suspension technique in musical works. There are six common modifications of the basic suspension pattern that we will encounter in our analyses. Example 13.13, which is an elaboration of Example 13.11, illustrates each of these suspension modifications.

EXAMPLE 13.13

DVD 1
CH 13
TRACK 13

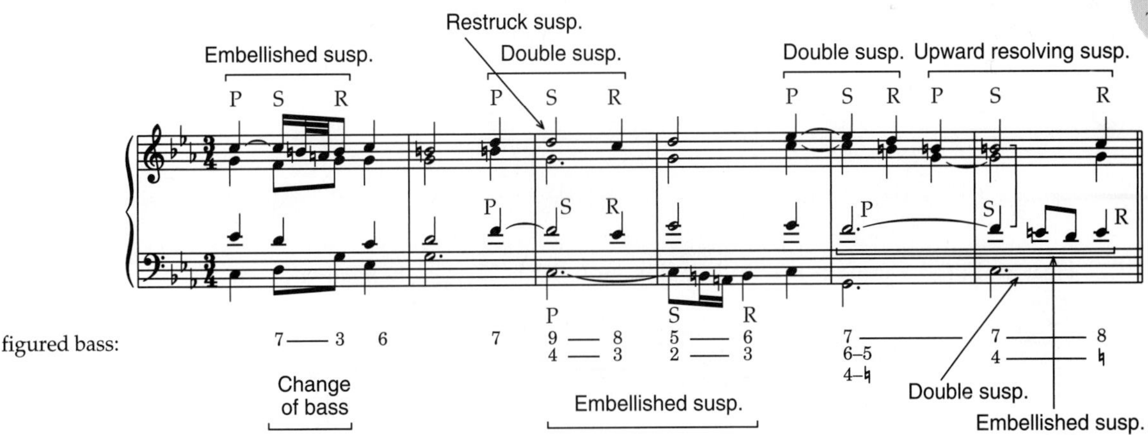

1. **Embellished suspensions**, as seen in mm. 1, 4, and, 6 use submetrical figurations to embellish the dissonant note.
2. **Suspensions with a change of bass**, as seen in m. 1, involve a bass leap to another consonance at the same time that an upper-voice suspension resolves. Since the bass is changing, this often results in a harmonic change. The figured bass notation for bass suspensions follows our established rules. Make sure you include the horizontal dash in order to make clear that the dissonance resolves (as seen in the 7–3 in the example).
3. **Restruck suspensions**, as seen in m. 2, omit the tie, permitting the suspended note to be resounded at the point of dissonance.

4. **Double and triple suspensions**, as seen in mm. 2–3, 4–5, and 6, involve two or three simultaneous dissonances, each of which resolves correctly.
5. **Retardations** (upward-resolving suspensions), as seen in m. 6, are relatively rare. We will use only one type: 7–8.
6. The **suspension chain** is a patterned series of suspensions that interlock. An example can be derived from a series of falling $^6_3$ chords (Example 13.14A), which in the hands of Haydn has been transformed into a suspension chain in Example 13.14B. In the reduction of Example 13.14C, we see how such motions are much more contrapuntal and melodic than harmonic. With all the submetrical figuration removed, Example 13.14C reveals outer-voice parallel tenths that descend by step, which provide an outer frame for the suspensions that occur in the alto voice. Haydn begins the series of 7–6 suspensions in m. 63 by moving the fifth of the E-minor chord, B^4, up to C^5. This is an effective preparation that creates a sixth that is tied over the bar to become the suspended seventh in the next measure. The 7–6s continue until m. 67, where Haydn uses a change of bass to create a V_7 harmony that intensifies the cadence on G major. Had he maintained the suspension pattern, the less conclusive vii°$_6$ chord would have occurred as the cadential chord. Notice how the parallel fifths in the alto and soprano of Example 13.14A are disguised by Haydn.

EXAMPLE 13.14

DVD 1
CH 13
TRACK 14

A. Parallel six-three chords

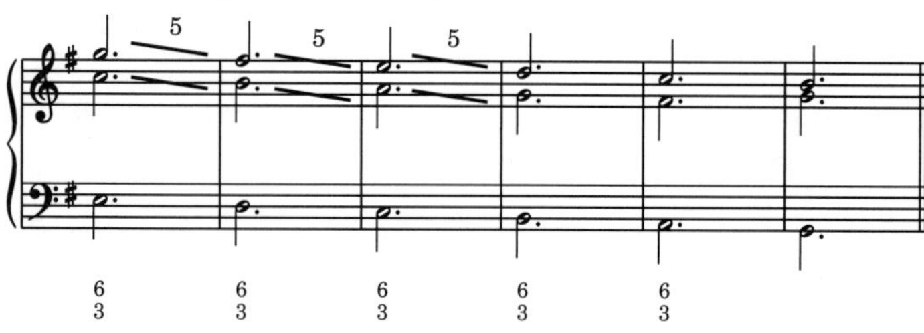

B. Haydn, Piano Sonata no. 37 in E major, Hob. XVI/22, *Allegro moderato*

C. Reduction

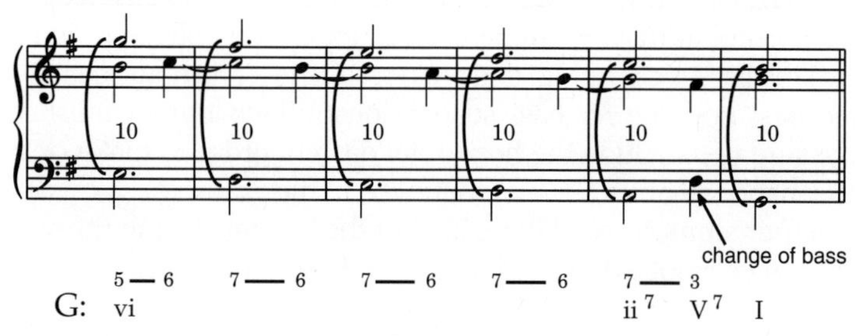

The Anticipation (ANT)

The **anticipation** is an unaccented nonchord tone, but, given that it can be considered the "mirror opposite" of the suspension, it is included at this point. The anticipation appears before the chord to which it belongs actually sounds, usually creating a dissonance with the already-sounding chord. Because it occurs on a weak beat and is premature, it can be viewed as a tone of figuration that functions in the exact opposite manner of the suspension, which is an accented tone that delays a chord tone's resolution. It is most effective at cadences, when the final chord is strongly expected. Example 13.15 presents an example of a double anticipation: The phrygian cadence (iv_6–V) is intensified by the entrance of C♯ and A (members of V) prematurely, while iv_6 is still sounding. This example also contains a hemiola and another double suspension.

EXAMPLE 13.15 **Corelli, Violin Sonata no. 11 in D minor, op. 1, *Adagio***

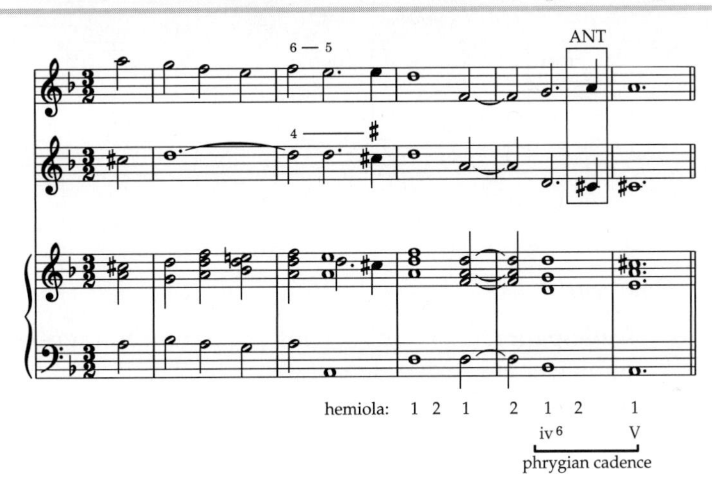

The Pedal (PED)

A sustained pitch or harmony that sits motionless during multiple harmonic changes is known as a **pedal** or **pedal point**. Derived from the organ's ability to sustain a pitch indefinitely, the pedal tone usually occurs in the bass and almost always is a tonic or dominant scale degree, which slows down the harmonic motion and firmly grounds the music on one static harmony. Pedals often occur in cadential situations (see Example 13.16), in which harmonic successions can unfold over a single held note. As the two levels of analysis in the Bach excerpt show, such harmonic successions are subordinate to the pedal.

EXAMPLE 13.16 **Bach, Fugue in C minor, from *The Well-Tempered Clavier*, Book 1, BWV 847**

DVD 1
CH 13
TRACK 16

Summary of the Most Common Tones of Figuration

EXAMPLE 13.17

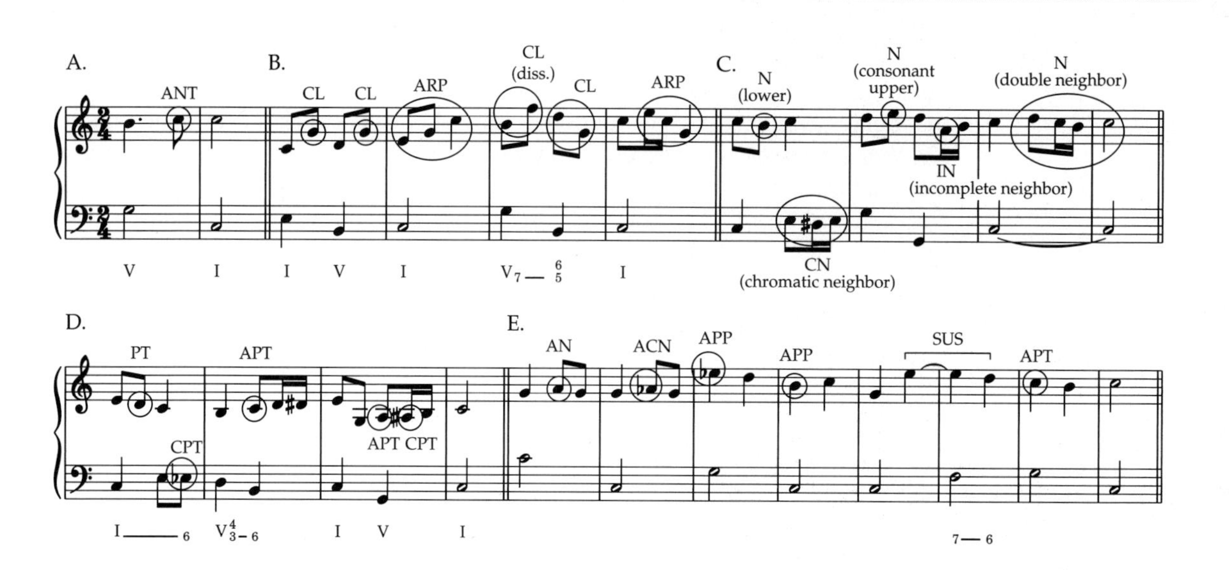

Unaccented

Anticipation (ANT): dissonant, premature entrance of a member of an upcoming chord (Example 13.17A).

Arpeggiation (ARP): successive chordal leaps that occur in a single direction and that include all members of the triad or seventh chord (Example 13.17B).

Chordal leap (CL; called consonant leap in contexts such as sixteenth-century counterpoint)

1. A leap from one chord tone to another within a single harmony (Example 13.17B).
2. Dissonant leaps are permitted if the pitches are members of V_7 (e.g., the tritone between scale degrees $\hat{7}$ and $\hat{4}$) (Example 13.17B).

Neighbor tone (N, IN, DN)

1. Stepwise ascent or descent from a chord tone, followed by a change in direction and return to the initial chord tone (N) (Example 13.17C).
2. *Incomplete neighbor* (IN): a leap to a note that neighbors a chord tone, followed by resolution to that chord tone by step (Example 13.17C).
3. *Double-neighbor figure* (DN): stepwise ascent or descent from a chord tone, followed by a balancing motion to the opposite neighbor and return to the initial chordal tone (Example 13.17C).
4. *Chromatic neighbor* (CN): includes one or more nondiatonic pitches.

Passing tone (PT)

1. Stepwise motion in a single direction that fills in an interval of a chord, most often a third (Example 13.17D).
2. *Chromatic passing tone* (CPT): fills the space between two diatonic tones a major second apart (or between two chord tones a third apart) (Example 13.17D).

Accented

Accented neighbor note (AN)

1. A three-note figure identical to the unaccented neighbor but occurring on accented beats (Example 13.17E).
2. *Accented chromatic neighbor* (ACN): A three-note figure identical to the chromatic neighbor but occurring on accented beats (Example 13.17E).

Accented passing tone (APT): a dissonant member of a passing figure that occurs on an accented beat. Usually occurs in descending lines. Most common intervallic structure is 7–6 and 4–3 (Example 13.17D).

Appoggiatura (APP): unprepared dissonance occurring on a strong beat; essentially an accented incomplete neighbor. Resolves by step, usually in the direction opposite that of its leap; 4–3 and 9–8 are most common (Example 13.17E).

Pedal (PED)

1. A sustained pitch, most often in the bass, with tonic or dominant function; surface harmonic succession usually unfolds above.

Suspension (SUS)

1. Most important accented tone of figuration, in which a stepwise melodic descent is temporarily postponed and that creates a dissonance before the line continues (Example 13.17E).
2. Unfolds in three stages:
   a. preparation (P): weak-beat consonance (chord tone)
   b. suspension (S): sustained preparation note continues into strong-beat chord change. In this environment it is a nonchord tone (usually dissonant).
   c. resolution (R): sounding dissonant suspension falls by step on a weak beat to a chord tone.
3. Three common upper-voice types: 9–8, 7–6, 4–3.
4. One common bass-voice type: 2–3 (9–10).

EXERCISE INTERLUDE

PERFORMING

13.1 Singing Accented and Chromatic Tones of Figuration

Be able to sing either voice while playing the other using scale degrees or solfège in major and minor modes up to and including two sharps and two flats. Label all tones of figuration.

13.2 Improvising Suspensions in Two Voices

A. Play the lower voice and sing the upper voice as written. Then add suspensions as shown in the figured bass. The result will be a continuous 2:1 counterpoint; the faster note values may occur in either voice.

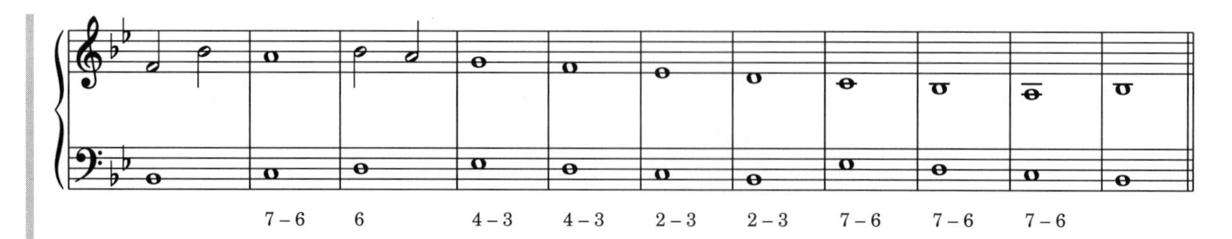

B. Same as in Part A, but no figured bass is given. Add a minimum of one each of the typical suspension figures (9–8, 7–6, 4–3, and 2–3). Analyze, using roman numerals. The result will be a continuous 2:1 counterpoint; the faster note values may occur in either voice.

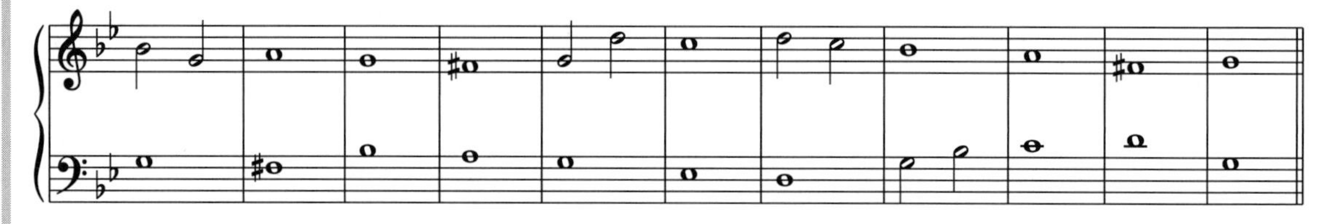

DVD 2
CH 13
TRACK 1

ANALYSIS

13.3 Suspensions

Analyze the given excerpts. Include the following.

1. Circle and label each component of the suspension (P, S, and R).
2. Figured bass (*no roman numerals unless specified*) that specifies the melodic motion of the suspension.

A. Beethoven, Symphony no. 1 in C major, Finale

B. Haydn, Piano Sonata in D major, Hob. XVI: 4, Menuetto

C. Felize Giardini, Six Duos for Violin and Cello, no. 2 (add roman numerals)

D. Mozart, Symphony in B♭ major, K. 172, *Adagio* (add roman numerals)

E. Beethoven, Piano Sonata, in E♭ major, op. 31, no. 3, Menuetto (add roman numerals)

F. Giovanni Battista, Twelve Sonatas for two Cellos, no. 9 in A major

13.4 All Tones of Figuration

Analyze the following examples. Circle and label all tones of figuration. Add roman numerals when specified.

A. Schubert, Waltz in C♯ minor, no. 27, from *36 Original Dances*, D. 365 (add roman numerals)

B. Corelli, Church Sonata, op. 3, no. 2

C. Mozart, Variations on "Ah vous dirais-je, Maman," K. 265

D. Haydn, String Quartet in G major, op. 33, no. 5, iii

E. Tchaikovsky, Symphony no. 4, op. 36, ii, *Andantino in modo di canzona*

DVD 2
CH 13
TRACK 3

WRITING

13.5 Corelli, Trio Sonata in G minor, op. 1, no. 10

Add as many of the following tones of figuration as possible to Corelli's trio sonata: PT, APT, SUSP. Label and analyze using figures (no roman numerals).

A.

B.

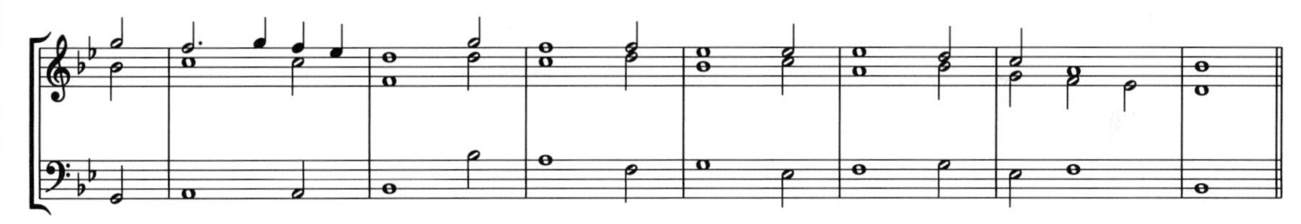

13.6

Write the following progressions and include the required suspension(s).

A. In D major, $\frac{4}{4}$: I–ii–V_7–I. Include *one* 9–8 and *one* 4–3 suspension.
B. In A minor, $\frac{4}{4}$: i–vii°$_6$–i_6. Include *two* 7–6 suspensions.
C. In F major, $\frac{4}{4}$: I–ii_6–V_7–I. Include *one* 7–6 and *one* 4–3 suspension.
D. In C minor, $\frac{4}{4}$: i–V_6–i–ii_6°–V. Include *one* 2–3 and *one* 7–6 suspension.
E. In G major, $\frac{4}{4}$: I–V^4_2–I_6. Include *two* 7–6 suspensions.

KEYBOARD

13.7 Adding Tones of Figuration

Study the given counterpoint and look for opportunities to add passing tones and suspensions. Particularly appropriate spots are marked with asterisks (*). Play the resulting embellished two-voice counterpoint. Next, add inner voices to create a four-part texture. Analyze your work by labeling harmonies and suspensions.

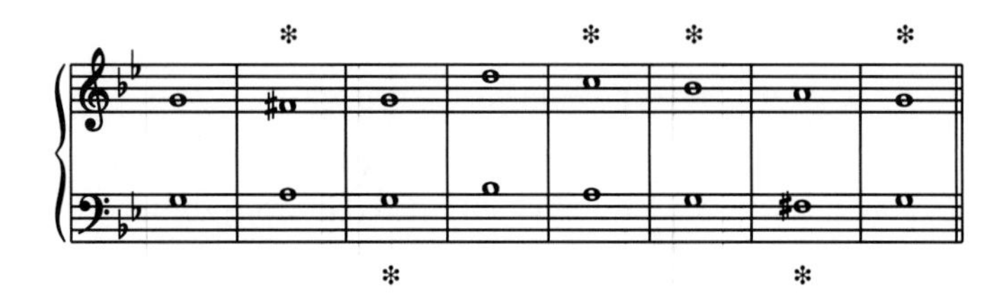

DVD 2
CH 13
TRACK 4

LISTENING

13.8

Determine the prevailing type of tone of figuration in each of the following examples. Your choices include PT, APT, NT, SUSP, APP, ANT, and CL.

A. _______
B. _______
C. _______
D. _______
E. Mozart, *The Magic Flute* _______
F. Verdi, *Nabucco*, Terzetino _______
G. Mozart, Symphony in F major, K. 75 _______
H. Bach, *Mach's mit mir. Gott, nach deiner Güt* _______
I. Handel, Sarabande from Keyboard Suite XI in D minor _______
J. Telemann, *Fantasie* _______
K. Haydn, Symphony no. 104 in D major, *Allegro* _______

13.9

Based on what you hear, add missing tones of figuration to or fix incorrectly notated pitches in the following two-voice examples.

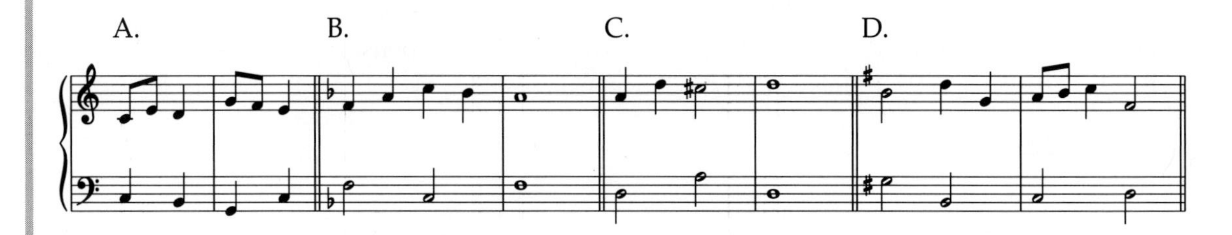

Continued

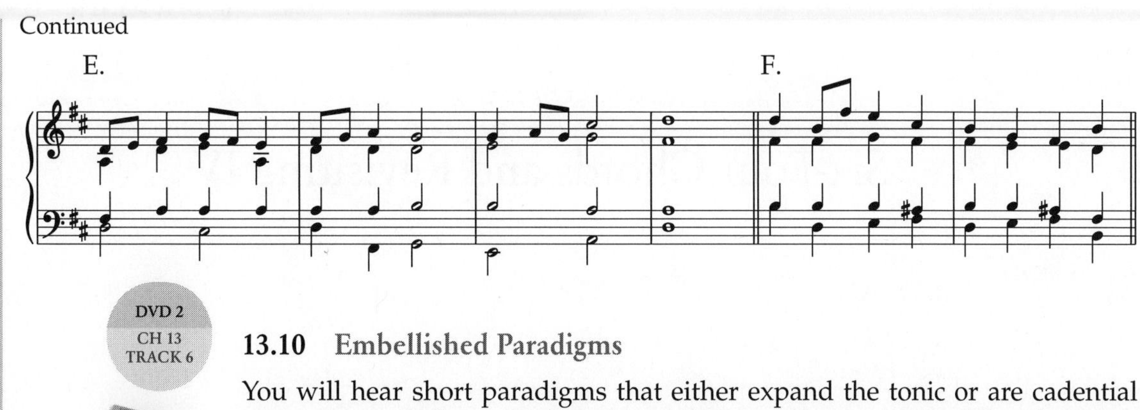

DVD 2
CH 13
TRACK 6

13.10 Embellished Paradigms

You will hear short paradigms that either expand the tonic or are cadential progressions. Refer to the list of paradigms in Chapter 12. Each has from one to three accented tones of figuration. Notate the outer voices, and provide roman numerals and figured bass. Exercises A through E are in A minor and contain no more than three chords. Exercises F through H are in G major and Exercise I is in D major.

WORKBOOK
13.1–13.5

TERMS AND CONCEPTS

- accented dissonances (accented tones of figuration)
  - accented neighbor
  - accented passing tone
  - appoggiatura
  - pedal
  - suspension
- unaccented dissonances (unaccented tones of figuration)
  - anticipation
  - passing tone
  - neighbor
- chromatic dissonances
  - chromatic neighbor
  - chromatic passing tone
- suspension
  - preparation, suspension, and resolution
- suspension chains
- suspension patterns
- double and triple suspension
- embellished suspension
- suspension with change of bass
- upward-resolving suspensions (retardation)
- restruck suspensions

CHAPTER 14

Six-Four Chords and Revisiting IV

You might have noticed that we have not discussed any six-four ($^6_4$) chords in our studies (save for their simple definition in Part 1). They occur much less often than root-position and first-inversion chords because of their dissonant interval of a fourth above their bass; root-position and first-inversion triads contain only consonant intervals (octaves, thirds, fifths, and sixths). While their intervals stack into second-inversion triads, they rarely function as do their root-position and first-inversion cousins. In fact, we will see that six-four chords are often only apparent harmonies resulting from the coincidence of passing and neighboring tones in two or more voices. Thus, six-four chords require careful contextual analysis and writing. Six-four chords occur in either unaccented or accented contexts; we discuss them next, in that order.

Unaccented Six-Four Chords I: Pedal

Unaccented six-four chords usually occur on weak beats within a measure or on weakly accented measures in four-measure groups. Listen to the short excerpt in Example 14.1, noting the six-four chord's function. You probably heard the opening of this famous Christmas carol as a single prolonged tonic harmony. If so, you would have interpreted the two IV$^6_4$ chords as sonorities that elaborate the much stronger-sounding tonic chords, rather than as some sort of structural chords. These six-four chords arise when the bass holds B♭ and the inner voices ascend from D^4 and F^4 to E♭^{4} and G^4, followed by a return to D^4 and F^4. Thus, the apparent IV$^6_4$ arises through a neighbor figure exhibited simultaneously in two voices. Given the sustained bass over which the neighbor figure appears, we assign the name **pedal six-four chord** (Ped$^6_4$). We label pedal six-four chords at the first level as IV$^6_4$ and at the second level either as I-Ped$^6_4$-I or, with figured bass, I$^{5-6-5}_{3-4-3}$.

EXAMPLE 14.1 Gruber, "Stille Nacht" ("Silent Night")

EXAMPLE 14.2 Schubert, Minuet in D major, D. 41

Pedal six-four chords can prolong not only tonic, but also the dominant, as shown in Example 14.2. It is crucial to recognize that this apparent tonic harmony (I$^6_4$) in m. 3 arises as the byproduct of two upper neighbors that move in parallel thirds.

So far, we have seen how pedal six-fours can arise out of upper-voice neighboring motion. Pedal six-four chords can also arise from passing motion. The expansion of V$^{(7)}$ is often accomplished through a Ped$^6_4$, with the upper voices ascending or descending a third (from $\hat{7}$–$\hat{2}$ and $\hat{2}$ to $\hat{4}$), as shown in Example 14.3.

EXAMPLE 14.3 Mozart, Symphony in A major, K. 385, *Menuetto/trio*

Unaccented Six-Four Chords II: Passing

We learned that pedal six-four chords derive their name from a sustained bass and upper-voice motion. The **passing six-four chord** (P^6_4) derives its name from the bass passing motion that fills the interval of a third. Listen to Example 14.4 and locate the passing six-four chord. Measures 1-5 act as a tonic prolongation from i to i_6 featuring an arch-shaped bass line (A–B–C–D–C). Within the arch, the passing six-four chord occurs in m. 2, where it connects root-position tonic with first-inversion tonic by the stepwise bass line A^2–B^2–C^3. Notice that this passing six-four chord functions identically to the passing vii°$_6$ chord, which also fills the space between the tonic and its first inversion. On the second level of analysis, we label the chord a P^6_4 to reflect its passing function. Here, it is important to consider how this P^6_4 is unaccented. Unlike that of Example 14.2, which occurs on a weak *beat*, this chord occurs on a weak *measure* within a quickly moving four-bar group. Similarly, in very slow tempos such chords may occur on weak *parts of beats*.

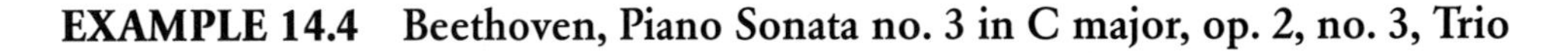

EXAMPLE 14.4 Beethoven, Piano Sonata no. 3 in C major, op. 2, no. 3, Trio

Passing six-four chords may be used to connect any five-three chord with its six-three inversion. Example 14.5 demonstrates a P^6_4 to extend both the tonic (d minor) and the subdominant (g minor). The Allegro opens with a series of restruck suspensions; once we remove them from the texture in Example 14.5B, we easily see the implied P^6_4s connecting i to i_6 and iv to iv_6.

EXAMPLE 14.5

DVD 1
CH 14
TRACK 4

A. Beethoven, Piano Sonata in D minor, op. 31, no. 2 Largo/Allegro

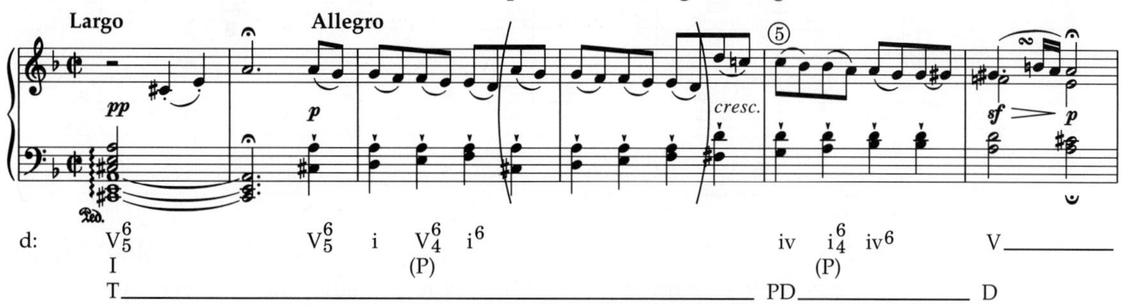

B. Reduction

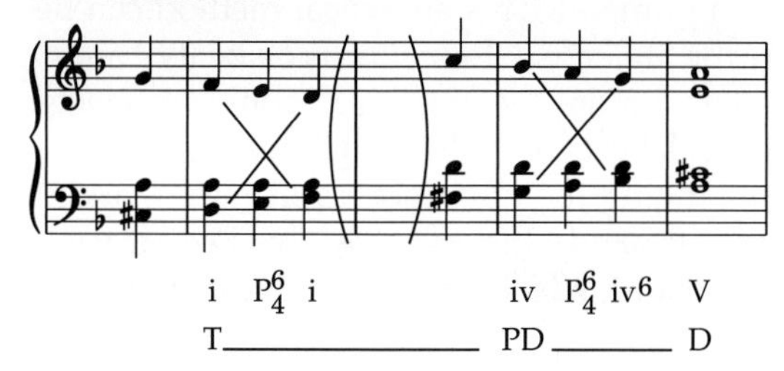

Unaccented Six-Four Chords III: Arpeggiating

Emerging from figurated textures and accompanimental patterns, the **arpeggiating six-four chord** is common in marches, waltzes, and folk tunes. See Example 14.6. In fact, the arp^6_4 chord is sometimes referred to as a **waltz-six-four chord**. In both the Schubert and Beethoven examples, the six-four chords that appear are consonant and are merely part of arpeggiations of the harmony that controls each measure. Arpeggiating (consonant) six-four chords fill chords whose root lies a fifth lower.

EXAMPLE 14.6

DVD 1
CH 14
TRACK 5

A. Schubert, Ländler, D 336, op. 67, no. 16

B. Beethoven, Symphony no. 3, in E♭ major, op. 55, III, Trio

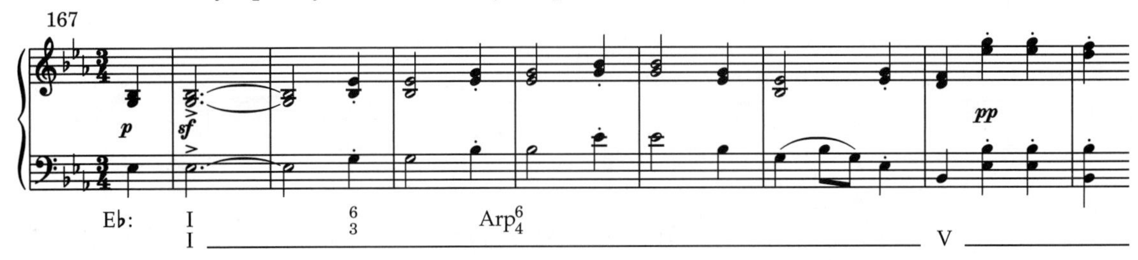

In fact, in pieces such as waltzes, where one could easily imagine the first (low) bass note sustained through the entire measure, the (higher) apparent six-four chords are heard as completing a root-position harmony. Thus, when analyzing arpeggiating six-fours, you need not label the actual chords; it is sufficient to draw a dash after the initial roman numeral. This analytical method can be seen at work in Example 14.7, where the "filler" six-four chords on beats 2 and 3 of mm. 1 and 3 are effectively ignored. Example 14.7 contains not only the arpeggiated six-four (which occurs on the weak beats of mm. 1 and 3) but also a pedal six-four (m. 2), which expands the flanking tonic harmonies in mm. 1 and 3 through neighboring motion (see the left hand). Interestingly, this Ped$^6_4$ is itself expanded by the arpeggiating six-four chord, which occupies the rest of m. 2.

EXAMPLE 14.7 Schubert, Waltz in A minor, from *12 Grazer Walzer*, D. 924, no. 9

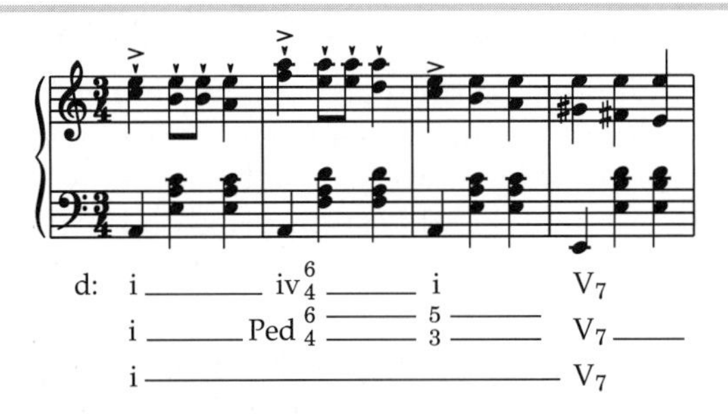

Accented Six-Four Chords

We will explore only one type of accented six-four chord, which is usually found at cadences. For that reason, we call it the **cadential six-four chord**. The cadential six-four chord is regularly heard in early Classical-period music, beginning in the early eighteenth century and continuing through the late nineteenth century.

The cadential six-four chord was an outgrowth of two metrically stressed dissonant events: the suspension and the accented passing tone. Example 14.8 provides a possible evolution of the cadential six-four chord from the suspension. In Example 14.8A, the progression is I–I$_6$–V–I; each harmonic function occupies one measure. The tied G^4 in the alto shows the common tone between the dominant and the tonic. In Example 14.8B, the progression is ornamented by a 4-3 suspension, as the soprano C^5 sustains into a measure of dominant harmony. In Example 14.8C, the tenor voice links up with the soprano voice by suspending into the next measure of dominant harmony and creating a $^{6-5}_{4-3}$ double suspension. The sixth then falls to a fifth and the fourth falls to a third. Example 14.8D revoices the upper voices so that the suspended $\hat{3}$ appears in the soprano voice. Example 14.8E adds the PD function by incorporating a IV chord, since $\hat{1}$, the chordal fifth, continues to serve as preparation for the suspension.

EXAMPLE 14.8

DVD 1
CH 14
TRACK 7

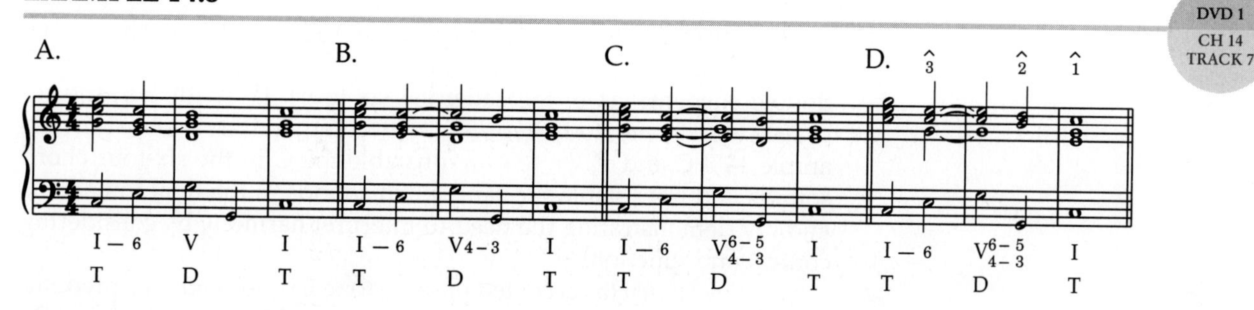

Example 14.9 presents an evolution of the cadential six-four chord through the second type of dissonant event: the accented passing tone. Recall that a melodic gap occurs in the soprano between $\hat{2}$ and $\hat{7}$ (see Example 14.9A) or between $\hat{4}$ and $\hat{2}$ (see Example 14.9B) when moving from $\text{ii}_{(6)}$ to V. The cadential six-four chord fills this gap of a third as a powerful accented passing tone that intensifies the motion to $\hat{7}$ or $\hat{2}$. IV, with $\hat{4}$ in the soprano, also works well in this situation.

EXAMPLE 14.9

DVD 1
CH 14
TRACK 8

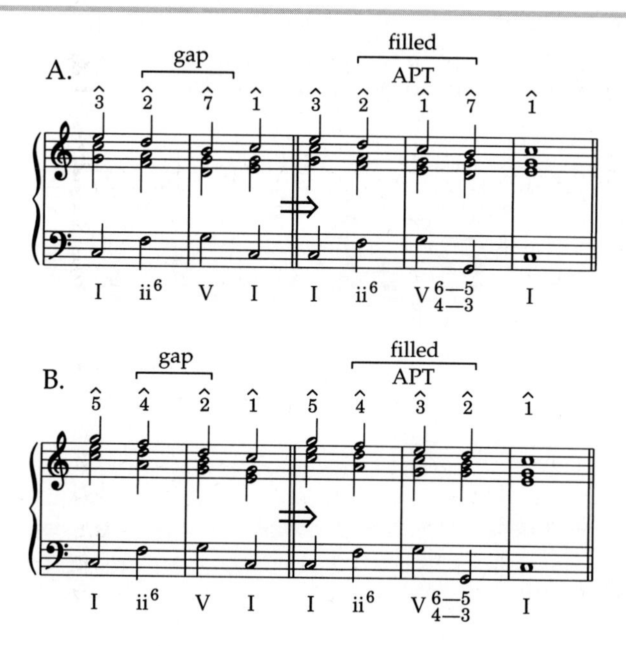

The cadential six-four chord, then, is a root-position dominant harmony whose chordal fifth and third are temporarily postponed by a dissonant fourth and sixth. These upper-voice, nonharmonic tones are both prepared and resolved. Resolution always occurs by step down. Preparation can occur in one of two ways:

1. *Preparation by common tone* (as suspensions) occurs when I precedes the cadential six-four (given that $\hat{1}$ and $\hat{3}$ appear in tonic and become the double suspensions in the cadential six-four). IV (with $\hat{1}$ in the soprano) works well, too. Preparation by common tone is shown in Example 14.8 C and D. Note how unstable the C in the six-four chord sounds and how stable the same pitch sounds in the final tonic, thus audibly demonstrating the need to interpret harmony by considering context and function.
2. *Preparation by step* (as accented passing tones) is used when a predominant harmony precedes the cadential six-four (Example 14.9A and B).

Notice that all cadential six-four chords occur on accented beats, in exactly the same ways as all accented tones of figuration (e.g., suspensions and accented passing tones), in order aurally to highlight their dissonance. Their resolution, again, like all accented tones of figuration, occurs on metrically weaker beats.

Additional Uses of Cadential Six-Four Chords

As Part of Half Cadences and Authentic Cadences

Not only do cadential six-four chords participate in authentic cadences, but they also intensify the dominant at half cadences, given the accented strong-beat dissonance that draws attention to the chord. Example 14.10 shows cadential six-four chords in half and authentic cadences. The first phrase closes in m. 4 with a HC that includes the cad$^6_4$, which permits a full measure for the horn to move from D♭ through the APT C and eventually on, to resolve to B♭. The second phrase closes with an acceleration of the harmonic rhythm: Both the cad$^6_4$ and the tonic occupy m. 8 as the horn balances the previous falling motion with a rise to $\hat{1}$.

EXAMPLE 14.10 Mozart, Concerto in E♭ for Horn and Orchestra, K. 447

Continued

Preceding V_7

Notice that the cad$^6_4$ in m. 8 of Example 14.10 leads not to a triad on V but, rather, to V_7: E♭ (the root of V_7) appears not only in the bass but also in the top voice of the accompaniment, where it participates in the common 8–7 motion.

Within a Phrase

Just as V_7 may occur within a phrase, so too do accented six-four chords. Example 14.11 presents an example. The six-measure phrase closes with a half cadence that is strengthened by a cad$^6_4$. However, Haydn peppers his phrase with sustained dominants, the first of which (m. 1) contains a 4–3 suspension, while the second example intensifies the single suspension with two suspensions, creating the characteristic cad$^6_4$.

EXAMPLE 14.11 Haydn, Piano Sonata in G minor, Hob. XVI/44, *Allegretto*

Evaded Cadences: Elision and Extension

We have seen that composers can thwart a listener's expectations of a strong cadence by changing the direction of the line at the last second. For example, a root-position V chord setting up an authentic cadence can be weakened by the addition of the chordal seventh *in the bass* (resulting in a V^4_2 chord), as we saw in Example 12.17. This common procedure of circumventing a cadence is called an **evaded cadence**. Evading the cadence occurs even more often when the most powerful dominant, the cadential $^6_4$ chord, is used as the dominant. Indeed, the addition of a simple passing seventh in the bass effectively dissolves a strong cadence, given that this seventh must resolve to the far-weaker I_6 chord rather than to a root-position tonic. There are two common reasons why composers would want to evade a cadence when using a cadential six-four chord: They wish to hide the seams between two independent phrases in order to create one large phrase, a technique called **elision**, or they wish to intensify a cadence by repeating certain elements of it, including the pre-dominant function and the dissonant, first part of the cadential six-four chord, before finally stating the authentic cadence, a technique called **cadential extension**. Listen to Example 14.12 for an example of the first type of V^4_2 chord. Mozart creates a single expansive eight-measure phrase rather than two four-measure phrases by converting the cadential $^6_4$ (m. 12) into a V^4_2. Indeed, the required resolution to I_6 averts the potential HC and thus covers any seam between mm. 12 and 13. Notice that the final cadence includes another cad$^6_4$, this one, however, participating in the PAC.

EXAMPLE 14.12

DVD 1
CH 14
TRACK 10

A. Mozart, Symphony in A major, K. 114, *Allegro moderato*

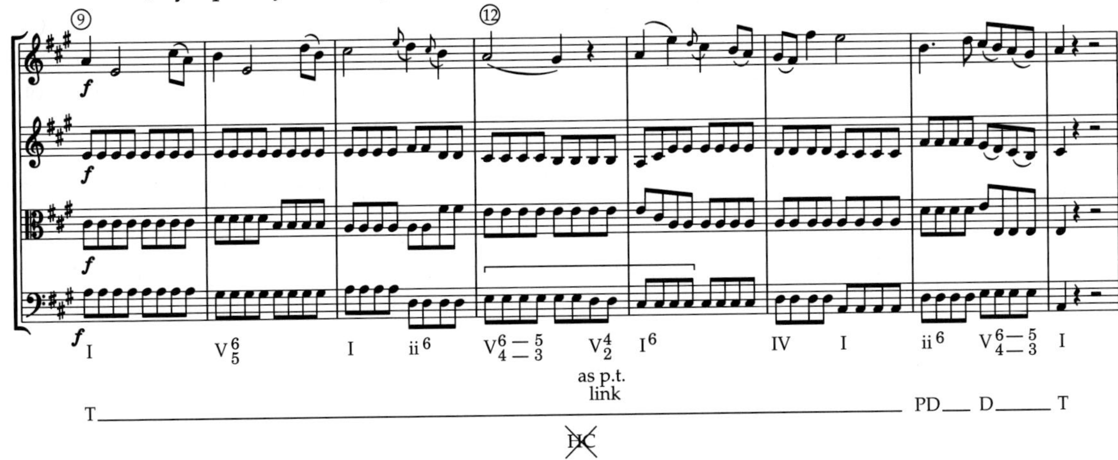

B. Mozart, Quintet "Hm! Hm! Hm!" from *The Magic Flute*, Act I

Continued

Postponing a cadence using V^4_2 dramatically intensifies the listener's desire for closure and sets up what amounts to a harmonic crescendo that heralds the impending structural cadence. Example 14.12B illustrates how Mozart is able both to suspend and to intensify an expected cadence. In the close of an aria from his *Magic Flute*, we hear the powerful cadential six-four chord lead not to a five-three chord, but rather to V^4_2, which necessarily leads to I_6 and another attempt to close the phrase. In the second try, the cadential six-four is extended, lasting almost two measures (rather than two beats, as in the first attempt). It is only in the third attempt that the V^6_4 finally resolves to the root-position V_7 chord and moves on to tonic.

Triple Meter

In triple meter, the cadential six-four chord may appear on either beat 1 or beat 2, since both are metrically stronger than beat 3. The last movement of Mozart's B♭ major Bassoon Concerto in $\frac{3}{4}$ often emphasizes beat 2, through durational accents (see Example 14.13). The first appearance of a cadential six-four moves to V^4_2. However, different than in Example 14.12, we still hear two phrases, given the parallel melodic construction. Nonetheless, Mozart smoothes the seam between the two phrases. Notice that the cadential six-four chord (m. 7) appears on beat 2 and falls to $^5_3$ on beat 3.

EXAMPLE 14.13 Mozart, Bassoon Concerto in B♭, K. 191, Rondo, *Tempo di Menuetto*

Writing Six-Four Chords

Based on the models of unaccented and accented six-four chords, we can now summarize their functions and formulate writing rules.

1. *Unaccented six-four chords* are embellishing chords that prolong another harmony, usually the tonic. These include the pedal (Example 14.14A), passing (Example 14.14B), and arpeggiating six-four chords (Example 14.14C).
2. The one type of *accented six-four chord* we have learned is the cadential six-four. The cadential six-four occurs over the root-position dominant and is formed by two nonchord tones above the root of V: the sixth and the fourth, postpone the chordal fifth and third.

The cadential six-four chord:

   a. may be used at either a HC or an AC (Example 14.14D).
   b. is usually immediately preceded by a pre-dominant, although sometimes by a form of the tonic, but *not* by another dominant-function chord (e.g., vii°$_6$ or vii°$_7$) since it weakens the impact of the cad$^6_4$ arrival.
   c. occurs on a metrically accented beat (either beat 1 or beat 3 in $\frac{4}{4}$ or beat 1 or beat 2 in $\frac{3}{4}$.)
   d. may lead to V (in a HC *or* an AC) or V$_7$ (in an AC).
   e. may be used within a phrase or between phrases (use V$^4_2$ to elide phrases by weakening cadential motion).

3. Approach and leave all six-four chords by step or common tone.
4. Double the bass in six-four chords.

EXAMPLE 14.14

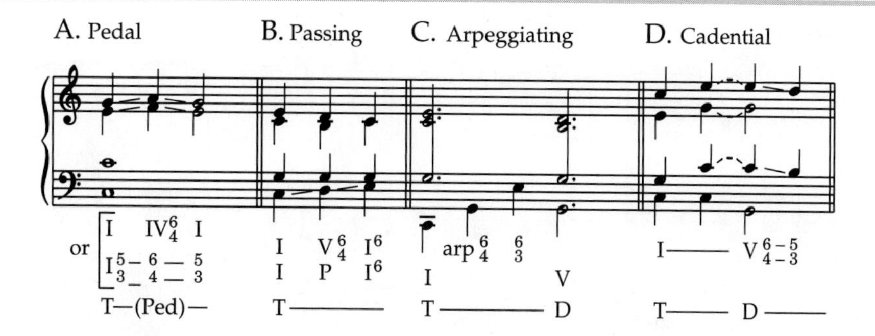

Revisiting the Subdominant

We have learned that the subdominant harmony can function in two very different ways. In its root position or first inversion (as part of the phrygian cadence), it occurs as a strong harmonic function: the pre-dominant. In its first inversion, it regularly occurs as a weak contrapuntal chord that expands either I or V. (Recall that IV_6 participates in tonic expansions as part of a bass arpeggiation ($\hat{1}$–$\hat{6}$–$\hat{3}$) and as dominant expansions as a passing chord between V and V_6.) We now see how IV in root position may be used to expand tonic.

Remember that the pedal six-four chord contains the same pitches as the subdominant, yet we refrained from labeling it a IV harmony because of its neighboring motion in the upper voices. Consider the situation in Example 14.15. The central sonority in Example 14.15A clearly acts as a pedal six-four chord. The central chord in Example 14.15B looks similar, yet the neighbor notes (G and E♭) are less dissonant. In fact, the chord is a stable root-position triad on IV since the bass leap to E♭ renders G and E♭ in the upper voices temporarily consonant. Thus, even though IV appears in root position, we still hear tonic controlling the example, and we label the IV an **embellishing chord (EC)**. Example 14.15C illustrates Haydn's use of IV to expand tonic.

EXAMPLE 14.15

As we do with every musical event, we must consider the context in which the subdominant appears and interpret it accordingly. For example, the Menuetto from Mozart's Symphony no. 39 opens with multiple statements of the IV chord (see Example 14.16). It appears as a pre-dominant in mm. 3–4, leading to the dominant function in m. 5ff. However, in m. 2, IV prolongs I through a neighboring motion.

EXAMPLE 14.16 Mozart, Symphony no. 39 in E♭ major, K. 543, Menuetto

DVD 1 CH 14 TRACK 11

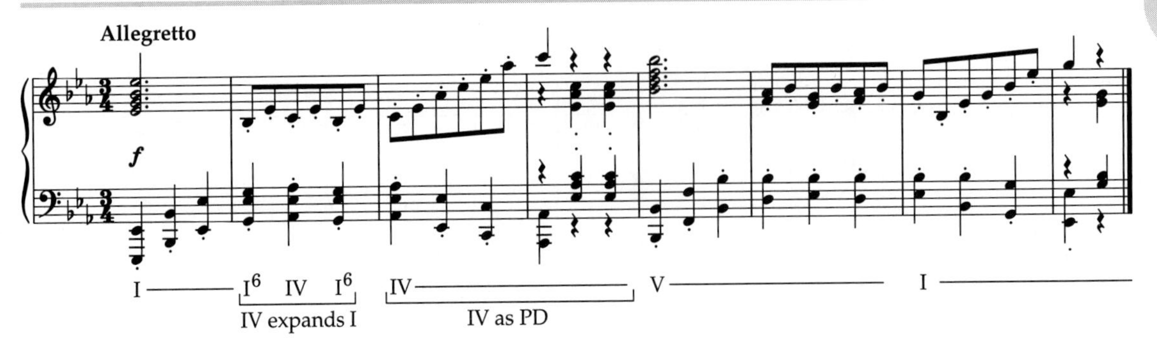

In addition to being an embellishing chord, IV sometimes can have an important cadential function. In Example 14.17, IV participates in closing the hymn. The two-chord motion IV-I is called a **plagal cadence**; because it often appears in church music, it is also known as the "amen cadence." Note how the plagal cadence immediately follows an authentic cadence, almost as if it were tacked on to the end of the piece. The plagal cadence is often a cadence in name only, since a strong authentic cadence usually precedes it.

EXAMPLE 14.17 Dykes, "Holy, Holy, Holy"

DVD 1 CH 14 TRACK 12

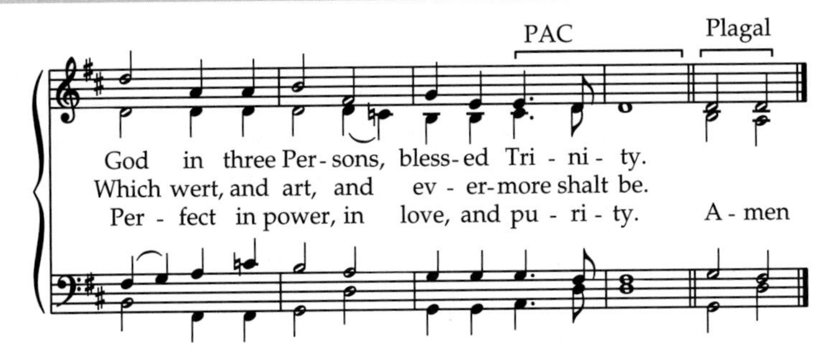

The plagal cadence is much weaker than the authentic cadence because the motion of IV to I is not nearly as goal directed as the motion from V to I heard in the authentic cadence. Whereas the authentic cadence contains the tonally defining *descending-fifth* root motion coupled with the equally strong melodic resolution of $\hat{7}$ to $\hat{1}$, the plagal cadence has only a *descending fourth* in the bass and a static common tone above, $\hat{1}$. Therefore, IV is peripheral to the harmonic motion and instead extends the tonic through double upper-neighbor motion.

Summary of Harmonic Paradigms

We have now completed our study of contrapuntal expansions. Although we have focused exclusively on ways that such embellishments expand the tonic and the dominant, we will see in later chapters that the principles can be applied to all of the other harmonies. Example 14.18 summarizes neighboring, passing and leaping bass motions, the possible contrapuntal chords used to harmonize them, and common soprano pitches used in setting these contrapuntal expansions. Progressions occur in major and minor, except those that involve vii°$_7$, which (for now) occur only in minor.

EXAMPLE 14.18 Summary of Bass and Soprano Harmonic Paradigms

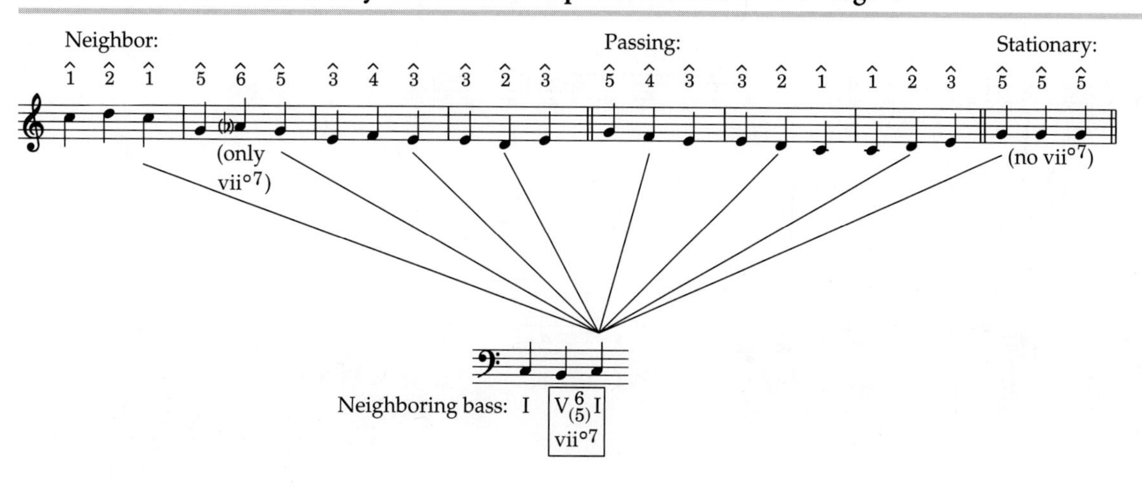

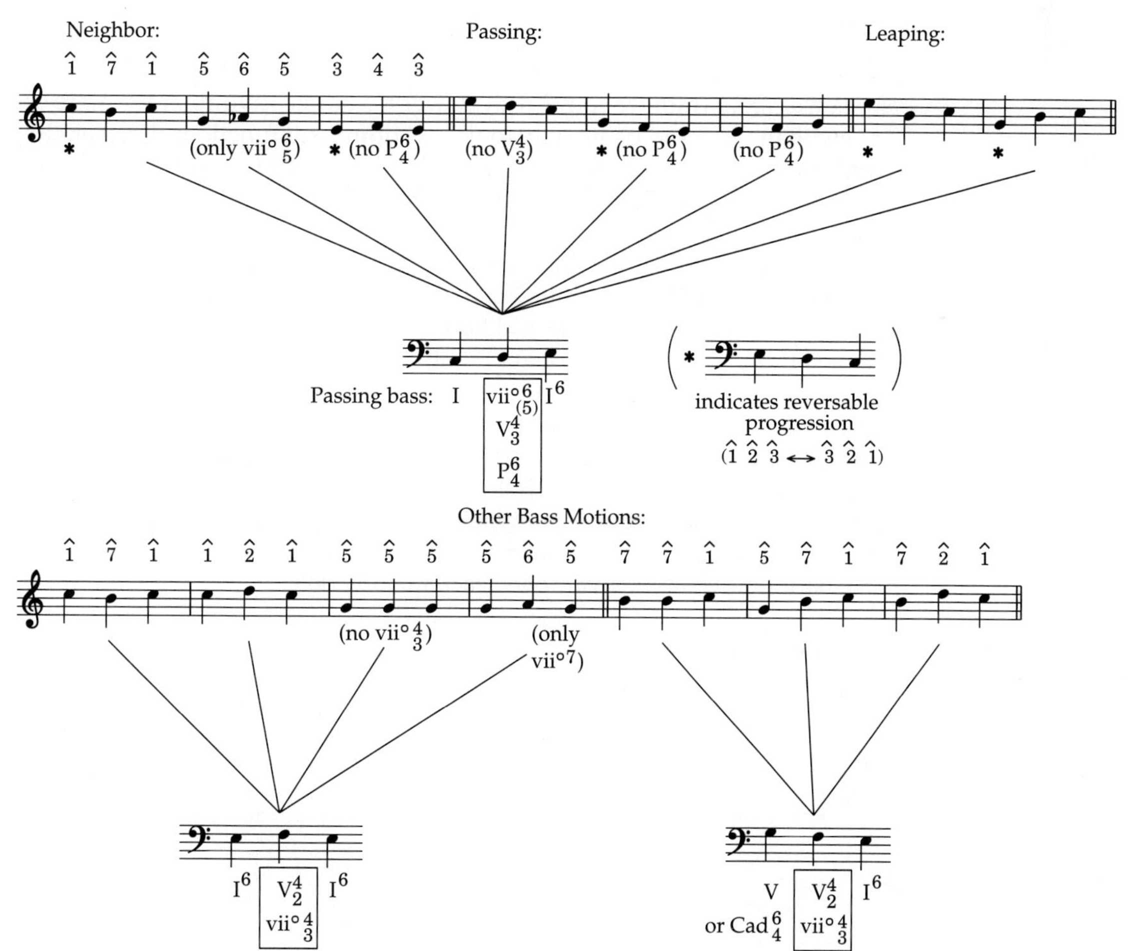

Continued

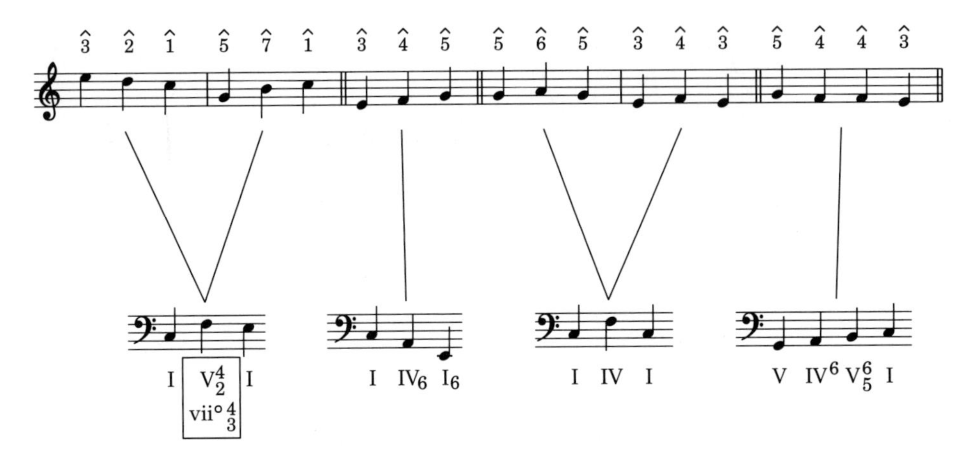

Harmonizing Florid Melodies

Now that the pre-dominant function has been added to your harmonic palette, we can harmonize tunes with slower harmonic rhythm much more effectively than we could using only tonic and dominant functions. Further, this chapter's discussion of six-four chords and the use of IV to expand I allows us to add these additional sonorities to our vocabulary and use them when harmonizing florid melodies.

For example, in "My Gentle Harp" (also called "Danny Boy") (Example 14.19), we see how a IV chord in m. 2 embellishes the tonic harmonies that extend from mm. 1–3. Note the possible addition of either a root-position IV or a pedal six-four chord in m. 3 to embellish the eighth-note A. A HC closes the first phrase in m. 4. A single V chord will work well here, although the falling line in the bass allows a stepwise motion back to tonic in m. 5, and it nicely harmonizes the upbeat figure in the tune. The second phrase opens the same as the first phrase but closes with a strong cadential six-four chord that is part of a PAC. Recall that in previous chapters we harmonized tunes with implied chord changes only once each measure or even less often. Such melodies contrast vividly with those whose harmonic changes accompany each melody note.

EXAMPLE 14.19 "My Gentle Harp"

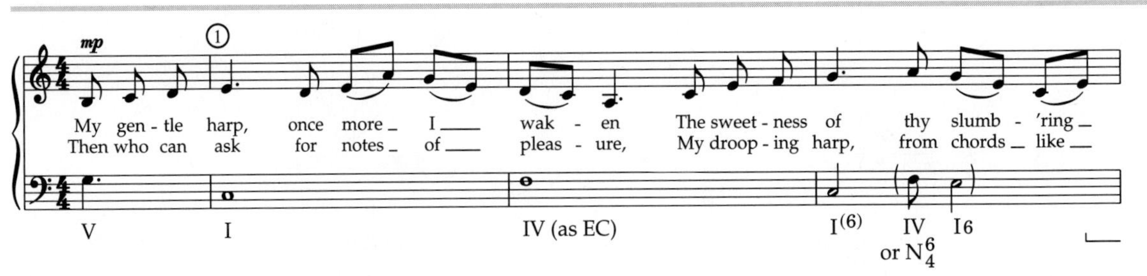

Continued

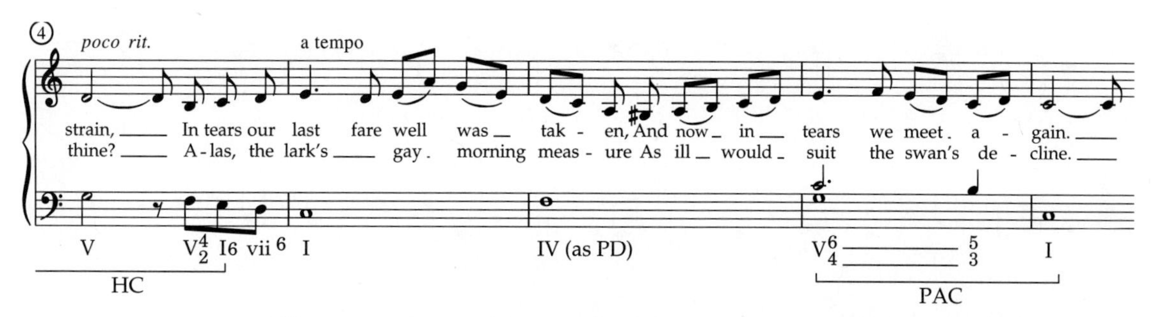

We review the working method that was presented in previous chapters.

1. Begin by singing the tune, noting the key and locations of cadences, since cadences imply the ends of phrases. Recall that phrases that end $\hat{2}$–$\hat{1}$, $\hat{7}$–$\hat{1}$, $\hat{4}$–$\hat{3}$, or $\hat{2}$–$\hat{3}$ imply authentic cadences. Phrases that end on $\hat{2}$ or $\hat{7}$ imply half cadences. Cadences on $\hat{5}$ usually imply a half cadence, but they can imply an authentic cadence; you will need to consider the preceding pitches and implied harmonies before making a decision.
2. Identify harmonies that begin each phrase, and determine the pattern of harmonic rhythm. In order to determine the controlling harmony for a group of pitches, focus on accented pitches. Recall that accented musical events take many forms, but the most important are metric (i.e., they fall on accented beats) and durational (i.e., they are longer notes) and are repeated. Keep in mind what scale degrees can be harmonized with what harmony, because the greater the number of stressed scale degrees that belong to a single harmony, the more chance that that harmony will work best for that span. In general, change harmonies on strong beats rather than on weak beats.
3. Keep the phrase model in mind, and remember that T–PD–D (T) is not reversible. T is usually prolonged for the majority of the phrase, and PD–D usually occur together as part of a cadential gesture (either a HC or an AC).

EXERCISE INTERLUDE

These exercises address not only material from the current chapter (including six-four chords and IV as prolonging chord), but also all concepts we have covered before, including contrapuntal expansions, the phrase model (T–PD–D–T), and tones of figuration.

PERFORMING

14.1

Sing the following harmonic progression using scale degrees or solfège in any major or minor key. Analyze.

A.

KEYBOARD

14.2

Realize each figured bass in four voices, and then transpose to keys up to and including two sharps and two flats. Analyze each example.

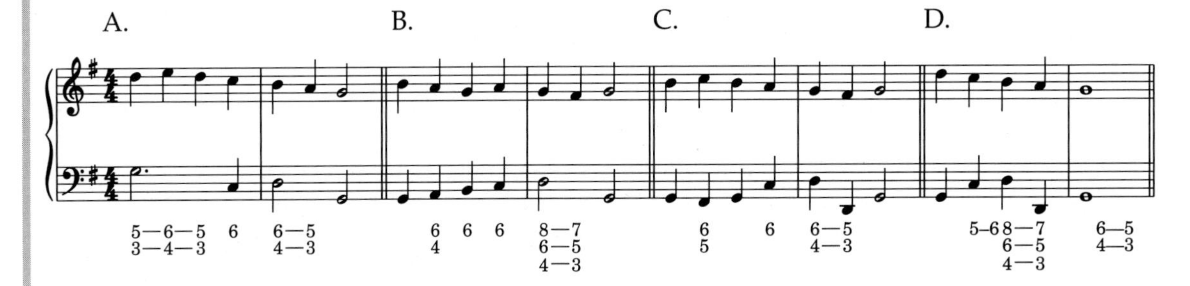

WRITING

14.3

Complete the following tasks in four voices (SATB).

A. In D major, write I–P$^6_4$–I$_6$–IV–V$^{6-5}_{4-3}$–I

B. In F minor, set the melody $\hat{5}$–$\hat{6}$–$\hat{5}$–$\hat{4}$–$\hat{3}$–$\hat{2}$–$\hat{1}$. Include two six-four chords

C. In A major, write a progression that expands tonic with a six-four chord. Close your progression with a PAC that includes a cadential six-four chord.

14.4 Unfigured Bass

Study the outer-voice counterpoint and, based on harmonic implications, analyze and add inner voices. Add as many six-four chords as possible.

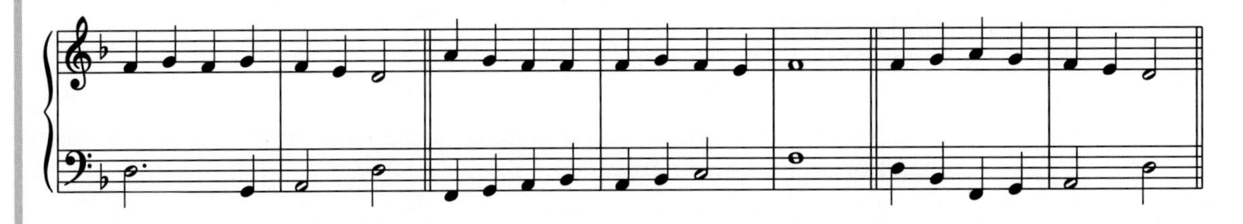

14.5 Harmonic Filling

The pitches given for each exercise represent beginning and ending points of contrapuntal expansions and harmonic progressions. You are to insert one chord or no more than two chords between the given pitches (marked with brackets). The resulting progression must be logical. The goal is to find as many solutions as possible. For example, in the sample solution, the pitches G and B are given, implying a tonic expansion of I–I$_6$. Seven different solutions are given. Analyze each of your solutions. Add a soprano melody for parts A–D and a bass line for parts E–H. Do *not* add inner voices.

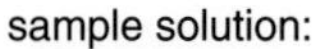

14.6 Harmonizing Florid Melodies

Study the given folk and classical tunes; then harmonize them with one to two chords per measure. Analyze your work.

A. "Home Sweet Home"

C. "Flow Gently, Sweet Afton"

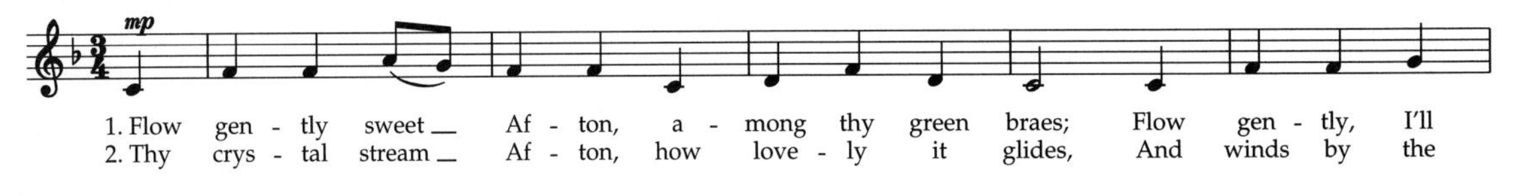

D. Beethoven, "Ich liebe dich," WoO 123

E. Mozart, Violin Concerto no. 3 in G major, K. 216, Rondeau

F. Mozart, Violin Concerto no. 2 in D major, K. 211, Rondeau

DVD 2
CH 14
TRACK 1

ANALYSIS

14.7 Analytical Snapshots of Six-Four Chords and IV

Using first and second levels, analyze the following excerpts, which illustrate various types of six-four chords.

A. Mozart, "In diesen heiligen Hallen," from *The Magic Flute*

B. Mozart, String Quartet in F major, K. 173, Trio

C. Daniel Gottlob Turk, *Serenade*

14.8 Analytical Potpourri

Given are numerous excerpts that include the following:

1. all harmonic expansions
2. the phrase model (T–PD–D–T)
3. all types of tones of figuration (including six-four chords)

Using two levels, analyze each excerpt.

A. Haydn, Piano Sonata in C major, Hob. XVI: 35 *Allegro con brio*

B. Beethoven, Piano Sonata in E♭ major, op. 31, no. 3, Trio

C. Schubert, Waltz in D major, from *Belles Viennoises*

D. Beethoven, Piano Sonata in F minor, op. 2, no. 1, *Adagio*

E. Mozart, Piano Sonata in C major, K. 330/i, *Allegro moderato*

F. Mozart, "Lacrimosa," *Requiem*, K. 626

G. Schubert, "Gesang des Harfners III," D. 480, no. 3

DVD 2 CH 14 TRACK 3

LISTENING

14.9

Identify the types of six-four chords in the progressions you will hear. Your choices are passing (P), pedal (PED), arpeggiating (ARP), and cadential (CAD). Parts A-F are homophonic and contain a single six-four chord; exercises F and G are taken from the literature.

14.10

This exercise requires quick recognition of basic contrapuntal expansions. Each example will be played twice: The first time you will hear bass and soprano only, the second time will include the inner voices to create a four-voice SATB texture. Examples A-F contain a single expansion of tonic. Examples G-L contain two or more expansions of tonic. All examples are either in G minor or B♭ major.

14.11

This exercise is similar to Exercise 14.10. However, each excerpt contains not only one tonic expansion but also a cadential progression (i.e., the PD–D or PD–D–T portion of the phrase). Notate outer voices, and provide a two-level analysis. Use the following procedure.

Step 1. Label events:
- a. cadence type _______ includes cadential $^6_4$ chord _______?
- b. PD type _______
- c. tonic expansion type:
  - *passing* (bass scale degrees either $\hat{1}$–$\hat{2}$–$\hat{3}$ or $\hat{3}$–$\hat{2}$–$\hat{1}$)
  - *neighboring* ($\hat{1}$–$\hat{7}$–$\hat{1}$, $\hat{1}$–$\hat{2}$–$\hat{1}$, $\hat{3}$–$\hat{4}$–$\hat{3}$)
  - *chordal skip* ($\hat{1}$–$\hat{3}$)

Step 2. Notate bass and add RNs.
Step 3. Notate soprano.

DVD 2 CH 14 TRACK 4

INSTRUMENTAL APPLICATION: REDUCTION AND ELABORATION

14.12

Reduce the textures in the given excerpts. Analyze, verticalize (into a four-voice homophonic texture), and then perform each example as follows. If you are a pianist, simply play your four-voice realization. If you are a melodic instrumentalist, arpeggiate each example. If necessary, refer to the discussion in Chapter 11 for a detailed procedure. Play each reduction in the key in which it is written; then transpose to one other key of your choice.

A. Mozart, Symphony in D major, K. 95, Trio

B. Mozart, Symphony in A major, K. 114, Trio

WORKBOOK
14.1–14.5

14.13

Elaborate the following four-voice homophonic examples and the figured bass by arpeggiating in strict ascending four-voice chords that maintain good voice leading between chords. Then embellish your solution by adding changes in contour and tones of figuration. Refer to the discussion in Chapter 11 for a detailed procedure.

A.

B.

TERMS AND CONCEPTS

- cadential extension
- elision
- embellishing chord
- plagal cadence
- six-four chord
  - pedal $^6_4$
  - passing $^6_4$
  - arpeggiating $^6_4$ (waltz $^6_4$)
  - cadential $^6_4$

CHAPTER 15

Invertible Counterpoint, Compound Melody, and Implied Harmonies

We have already learned that the intimate contrapuntal relationship between the bass and the soprano is the foundation of the standard four-voice harmonic texture. Composers take advantage of an important aspect of this contrapuntal relationship that allows them to spin out their musical material.

EXAMPLE 15.1 Mozart, Piano Sonata in G major, K. 283, *Allegro*

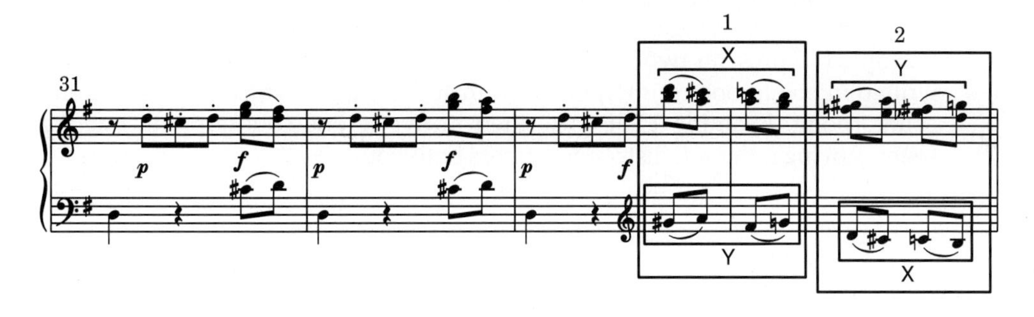

Listen to Example 15.1. The sections marked "1" and "2" have similar sounds, and, in fact, there is a very strong relationship between them. If you compare the outer-voice counterpoint in section 1 with that of section 2, you will discover that the soprano and bass melodies swap places: What was on top is now on the bottom, and vice versa. Thus, even though the lines trade places, they retain their original contour. This swapping of parts between voices is called **invertible counterpoint** or **double counterpoint**, and it is an important compositional procedure, for two reasons. First, economically, it allows composers to reap twice as much musical value from a single idea. Second, it allows the music to remain clearly unified because the listener is repeatedly exposed to material in different ways. The registral exchange of figures in invertible counterpoint creates sections of music that, although strongly related, have their own distinctive sound. The result is a perfect mix that satisfies the listener's desire for variety and contrast. Listen to the example several more times so that you are able to sing fragments X and Y and their transfer to the opposite register.

In the music of Example 15.1, Mozart has inverted his tunes at the octave (or its compound, the double or triple octave); that is, the rearrangement of upper and lower material is accomplished solely by octave leaps in one or both voices. This octave switching is called **invertible counterpoint at the octave**. It is also possible to invert two-voice counterpoint at other intervals, most commonly the twelfth, but we will restrict the following discussion to the octave.

EXAMPLE 15.2

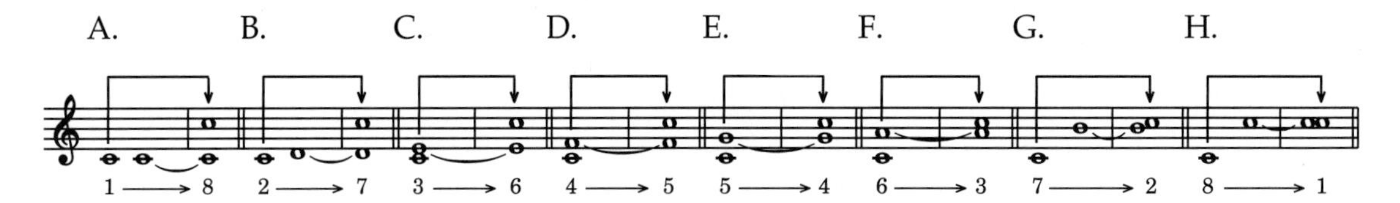

Remember from Chapter 3 that when intervals are inverted *at the octave*, they maintain their consonant or dissonant characters (see Example 15.2). This retention of consonance and dissonance is what allows for invertible counterpoint. For example, any dissonant seventh in an upper voice that properly resolves downward to a sixth will in inversion resolve in the same way; thus a second will resolve to a third because the moving voice is now in the bass. Dissonances can be treated correctly in inversion if they were treated correctly in the original version. The only potential danger is the interval of a fifth, which turns into a dissonant fourth when inverted. Thus, composers writing invertible counterpoint must be careful to treat all perfect fifths as potentially dissonant intervals (by preparing and resolving them and by generally placing them on the weak beats). Example 15.3 presents two instances of invertible counterpoint. Example 15.3A is written in one-to-one counterpoint that includes a few examples of two-to-one counterpoint. Example 15.3B is written in two-to-one counterpoint, but the faster-moving notes are distributed across both voices.

EXAMPLE 15.3

DVD 1
CH 15
TRACK 2

A.

B.

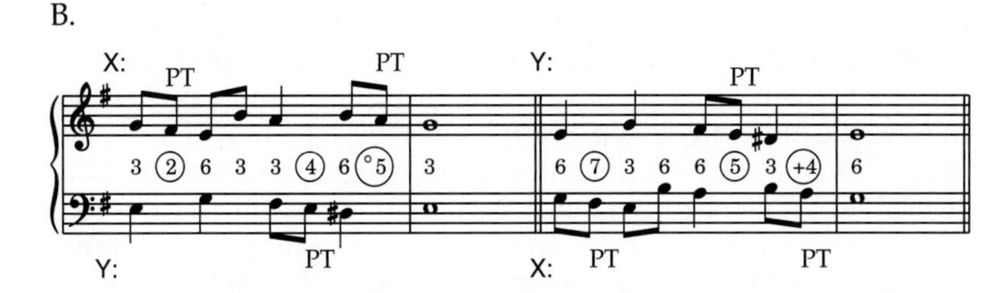

Of course, the use of invertible counterpoint is not restricted to piano music, but is found in all genres, including large symphonies, as illustrated in Example 15.4, which is taken from the developmental section of one of Haydn's late symphonies.

EXAMPLE 15.4 Haydn, Symphony no. 91 in F major, Hob. I/98, *Allegro assai*

The technique of invertible counterpoint is found throughout common-practice music. In fact, the late-nineteenth-century composer Johannes Brahms, regularly employed invertible counterpoint in his older-style imitative pieces (such as fugues and chorale preludes) and in his forward-looking piano works, such as the intermezzi. When Brahms was in his mid-twenties he invited his close friends Clara Schumann (arguably the most famous pianist in Europe at the time and the wife of Robert Schumann) and Joseph Joachim (the leading violinist in Europe) to form a "counterpoint club" in which each musician would write various contrapuntal exercises and pieces. Needless to say, invertible counterpoint was at the center of their activities. Example 15.5 presents a passage of one of Brahms's later pieces for piano, in which recognition of the inversion of melodies (at the octave) is far more revealing of his compositional procedure than trying to determine roman numerals. That Brahms both closes and begins the passage on C major indicates that the invertible counterpoint is there in order to extend that underlying harmony contrapuntally.

EXAMPLE 15.5 Brahms, Intermezzo in A minor, op. 76, no. 7

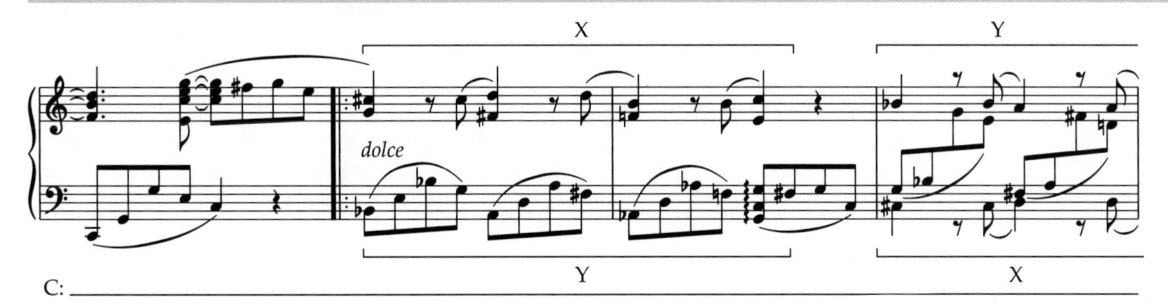

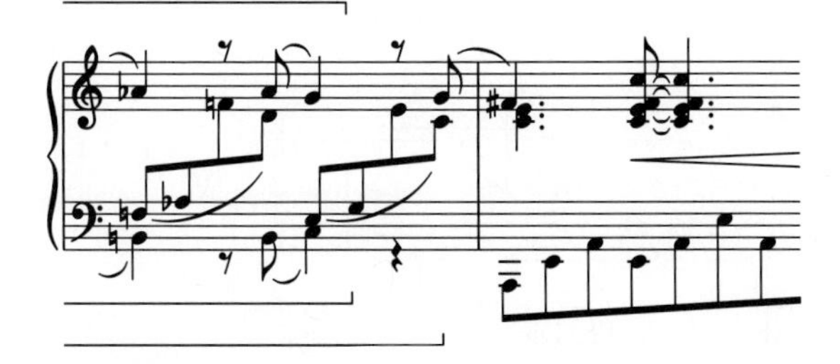

Invertible Counterpoint Below the Music's Surface

Occurrences of invertible counterpoint are often far subtler than the literal contrapuntal switch seen in the previous examples. Through various embellishing processes, composers camouflage their use of invertible counterpoint as a structural agent, in which it becomes the backbone of the harmonic progression itself. In Example 15.6, Schubert uses a full, homophonic texture that disguises the invertible relationship between the soprano and the bass.

EXAMPLE 15.6 Schubert, Impromptu in A♭ major, D. 935

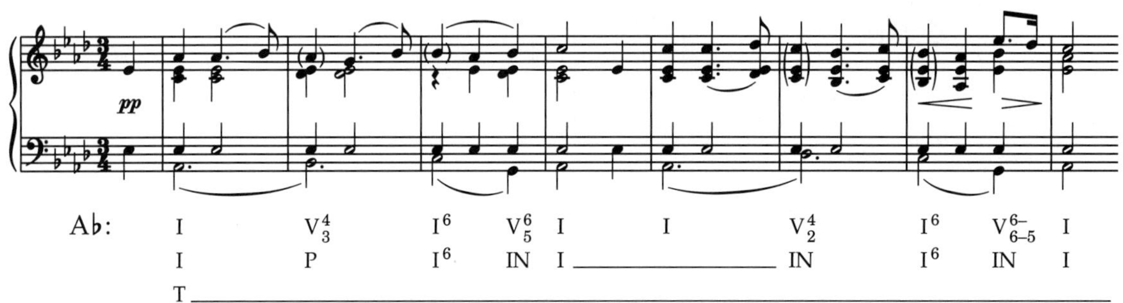

The first six measures serve to expand tonic, first by V^4_3, then V^6_5, and finally by V^4_2. But one might go so far as to say that identifying roman numerals in this context identifies symptoms more than causes as to what motivates this passage's unfolding. Indeed, we seem to be missing the forest for the trees here, since an important melodic relationship between the bass and the soprano governs these measures. Example 15.7A shows a two-voice contrapuntal reduction that reveals a large neighbor figure ($\hat{1}$– $\hat{7}$– $\hat{1}$) occurring over a large passing motion ($\hat{1}$– $\hat{2}$– $\hat{3}$). These figures can be seen in the stemmed pitches, which represent the structural counterpoint. Unstemmed pitches, such as the suspension $A\flat^4$ on the downbeat of m. 2, do not participate in the large-scale voice leading. The swap is literal, except that the neighbor (N) in mm. 1–3 of the soprano is followed in the bass by an incomplete neighbor (IN) in m. 3.

An understanding that invertible counterpoint holds together mm. 1-4 can bring new meaning to how we hear mm. 5-8. First, the large $A\flat^4$–C^5 passing motion in the soprano from mm. 1–4 reverses direction in mm. 5–7. The descending portion is loosely mirrored by the bass ($A\flat^2$–C^3), thus creating a large-scale voice exchange. Second, the use of V^4_2–I_6 in the bass (mm. 6–7) brings out the $D\flat^3$–C^3 motive, which is immediately imitated two octaves higher in the soprano.

EXAMPLE 15.7

A. Mm. 1–8

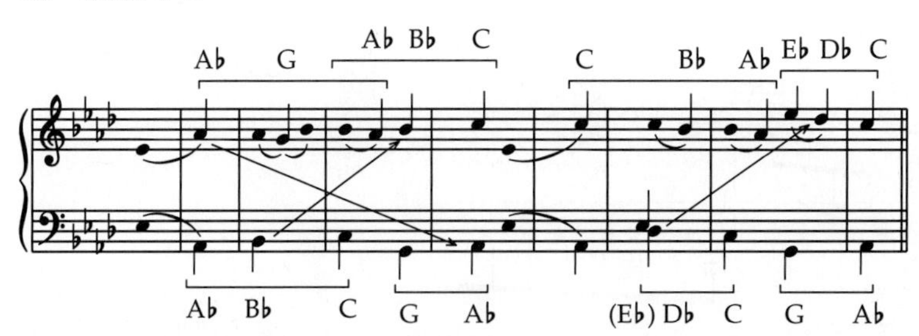

B. Mm. 5–8

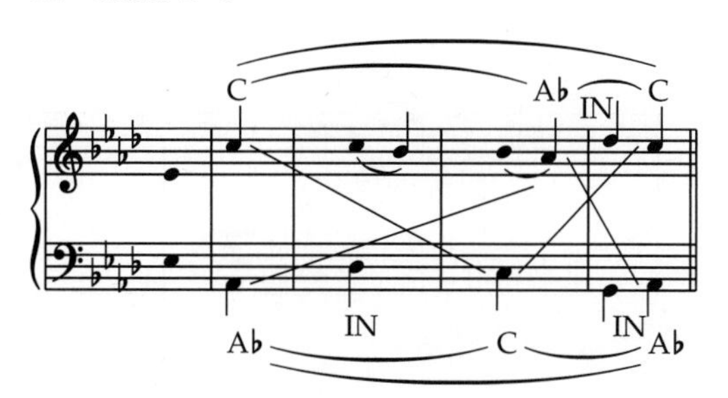

EXERCISE INTERLUDE

ANALYSIS

15.1 Analysis of Invertible Counterpoint

In the following excerpts, label any invertible counterpoint by using brackets and *X* and *Y* for the material in the upper and lower voices, showing how they are exchanged in the repetitions. Do *not* analyze with roman numerals.

A. Handel, Suite no. 7 in G minor, HWV 255, Passacaglia

B. Bach, Two-Part Invention no. 6 in E major, BWV 777

C. Giardini, from *Six Duos for Violin and Cello*, op. 14

D. Beethoven, Piano Sonata in E major, op. 109, "Gesangvoll, mit innigster Empfindung," Variation 3

E. Handel, Sonata no. 1 for Flute and Continuo in E minor, op. 1, HWV 359b, *Allegro*

F. Mozart, Piano Concerto in E♭, K. 482

WRITING

15.2 Writing Chord Progressions That Create Invertible Counterpoint

From the following models, on a separate sheet of manuscript paper:

1. Provide an outer voice to complement the given voice, such that the voices will produce invertible counterpoint at the octave.
2. Swap the voices to create invertible counterpoint.
3. Determine the contrapuntal/harmonic progression that is implied from the outer-voice counterpoint.
4. Add roman numerals and inner voices.

The first exercise presents one possible solution. Write at least one more for the first exercise and two solutions for B and C. Play solutions, first the outer voices only and then in four voices.

Optional: In a meter and a rhythmic setting of your choice, string together two or three of the progressions to create a four- to eight-measure piece.

A. Given: bass scale degrees $\hat{1}$–$\hat{2}$–$\hat{3}$–$\hat{4}$–$\hat{3}$

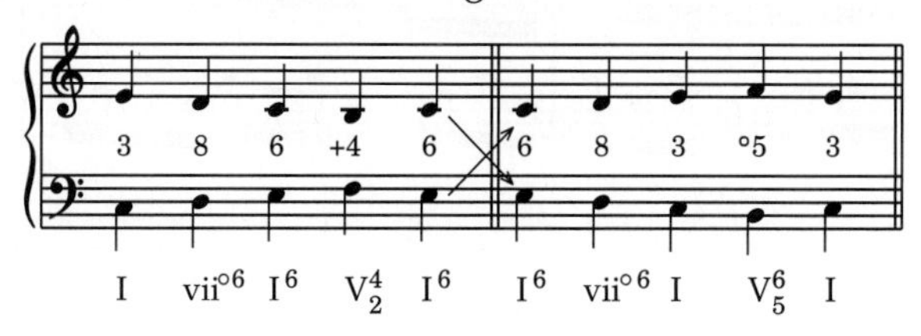

B. Given: bass scale degrees $\hat{1}$–$\hat{7}$–$\hat{1}$–$\hat{6}$–$\hat{3}$–$\hat{2}$–$\hat{1}$

C. Given: soprano scale degrees $\hat{3}$–$\hat{1}$–$\hat{2}$–$\hat{7}$–$\hat{4}$–$\hat{3}$–$\hat{2}$–$\hat{1}$–$\hat{7}$–$\hat{1}$

Harmonic Implications of Single Melodic Lines: Compound Melody

You often will encounter compositions written for one or two voices that do not present explicit harmonies (triads and seventh chords). Indeed, much Baroque music, particularly that of Johann Sebastian Bach, is presented linearly rather than harmonically. Even though such pieces are written for three or fewer voices, however, their construction strongly implies a clear harmonic structure, just as in the most traditional homophonic compositions.

Numerous compositional techniques allow composers to imply harmonies without using a fully voiced chord. The most important of these is called **compound melody**. A compound melody occurs when a single melodic line implies two, three, or even four voices. A composer achieves this illusion by means of registral leaps in the melody so that a single line splits into multiple voices delineated by register. When performing such music, it is important to consider the possibility that two or more voices are implied by a single melodic line. An understanding of compound line will help you hear the implied chord progression, thus allowing you to control and shape more effectively the energy of the music you play (see Example 15.8).

EXAMPLE 15.8 Mozart, Piano Sonata in D major, K. 284, *Andante* (Polonaise en Rondeau)

DVD 1 CH 15 TRACK 6

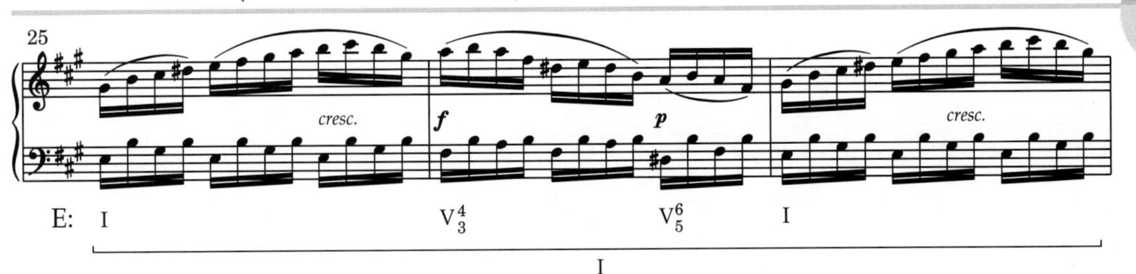

If you were to analyze the chord progression in Example 15.8 simply by moving from note to note, the result would be unmusical, in that you would be forced to label the second sixteenth note in m. 1 a dominant chord and the third sixteenth note as a six-four chord on C♯. Such an approach ignores the fact that three voices, which group together to form harmonies, unfold *temporally* rather than *spatially* in the left hand. Thus, a single tonic harmony unfolds in m. 1. The tonic is then contrapuntally expanded in m. 2 by upper and lower neighbor harmonies (V^4_3 and V^6_5), only to return in m. 3. The accompanimental figure seen in the left hand of Example 15.8, called an *Alberti bass* (we encountered this type of figure before, in Example 6.7), is an important type of compound melody seen in much music of the high Classical period. Beyond this, each of its voices follows standard voice-leading rules to progress to the next harmony. See Example 15.9 for a reduction of the excerpt's left hand, which shows the smooth connections between each chord and its voices.

EXAMPLE 15.9 Reduction of Mozart, Piano Sonata in D major, K. 284

A second example illustrates the role of compound melodies in the upper voices. Listen to Example 15.10. As you can hear, the right-hand voice is partitioned into two clear voices that move primarily in parallel sixths. The procedure provides the sensation of full three-note triads in a two-voice texture, and it rhythmically animates a one-to-one bass–soprano framework composed of the circled pitches in Example 15.10.

EXAMPLE 15.10 Handel, Suite no. 3 in D minor, HWV 428, "Air and Variations," Variation 5

DVD 1
CH 15
TRACK 7

So far we have considered only instances of compound lines that emerge from broken-chord formations where all voices play harmonic tones. Sometimes the effect of two-voice counterpoint can be disguised through arpeggiations and nonchord tones, as in Example 15.11. Although it may not appear so at first, Mozart constructs the compound melody in the opening of this remarkable movement similarly to the previous example. Again, this example illustrates a soprano melody that is composed of parallel sixths in descending motion (see Example 15.12).

EXAMPLE 15.11 Mozart, Piano Concerto in A major, K. 488, *Andante*

DVD 1
CH 15
TRACK 8

EXAMPLE 15.12 Mozart, Piano Concerto in A major, K. 488, *Andante*

In Example 15.13 the voices are stacked to show the three-part harmonic structure.

EXAMPLE 15.13

Some of the most interesting examples of compound melody occur in music written for solo melody instruments, in which knowledge of the harmonic structure is essential for effective performance and listening. And, arguably, the best examples of this type of writing appear in Bach's solo violin and solo cello works. Listen to Example 15.14. The solo violin plays an arpeggiated pattern with a few passing tones. As the analysis of the example shows, the harmonic rhythm moves at the speed of one chord per measure, unfolding a tonic in m. 1, a lower neighbor V$^6_5$ in m. 2, and a return to tonic in m. 3. In m. 4, an A dominant seventh chord in $^6_5$ position is followed by a D major harmony. What is remarkable about this passage is not so much the logical harmonic progression that unfolds but, rather, that the chord members move by strict voice leading from harmony to harmony. The highest and lowest of these independent melodic strands form "outer voices," which move in note-against-note counterpoint (see the reduction in Example 15.15).

EXAMPLE 15.14 Bach, Partita for Solo Violin in B minor, BWV 1002, Corrente

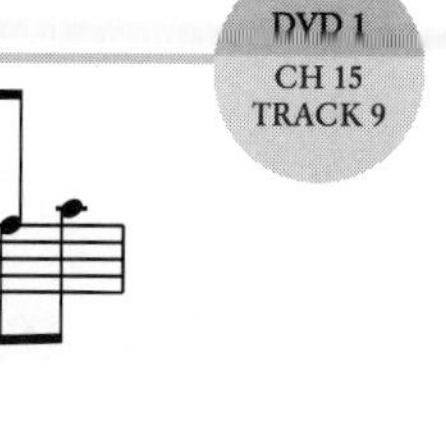

EXAMPLE 15.15

Analysis of compound melody is an essential tool that allows performers to understand the underlying harmonies and to communicate their meanings in performance through the informed and inspired projection of melodic line. Such knowledge of how a piece works will also necessarily affect their rendering of dynamic shape, influence their decisions to use contrast and color, and help them coordinate the ebb and flow of rubato. This type of analysis also illuminates important motives as well as parallel elements within and even between movements.

EXAMPLE 15.16 Bach, Partita for Solo Violin in B minor, BWV 1002, Corrente, Double

DVD 1
CH 15
TRACK 10

Now listen to Example 15.16. Notice that the Double's line consists mostly of stepwise motion, a dramatic contrast to the arpeggiations of the preceding Corrente (Example 15.14). Also different are the melodic contours of the two openings: The descent and ascent of mm. 1 and 2 in the Double are the opposite of the ascent and descent that characterize mm. 1 and 2 of the Corrente. A look at the compound line at the opening of the Double will help us discover important similarities between the movements that we missed by considering only the surface figurations. Once again, the harmony unfolds at the rate of one chord per measure, and, again, the tonic harmony is prolonged in mm. 1–3, with m. 2 functioning as a lower neighbor V^6_5, exactly as we saw in the Corrente. The similarity continues in the following measures with the A dominant seventh harmony moving to D major in m. 5. The similarities do not stop with the chord progression; the voice leading confirms the connection. After extracting the structural pitches in all the voices (Example 15.17A), Example

15.17B verticalizes this structure for comparison. Notice that the compound melody, pacing, and harmonic implications are identical. Yet the surface rhythm and contours are wildly different. Bach creates a perfect blend of variety at the surface and organic consistency below.

EXAMPLE 15.17

Implied Harmonies

In analyzing works using compound line, discerning the harmonic progression is often only a matter of locating all the voices. Once you do, you frequently find that full triads and seventh chords are literally present in the music. But sometimes you will encounter compound melodies in which the harmonies—even when all voice-leading strands are considered—are still incomplete. Then you will need to infer missing chord members.

EXAMPLE 15.18 Schubert, Piano Sonata no. 16 in A minor, op. 42, D. 845, Rondo

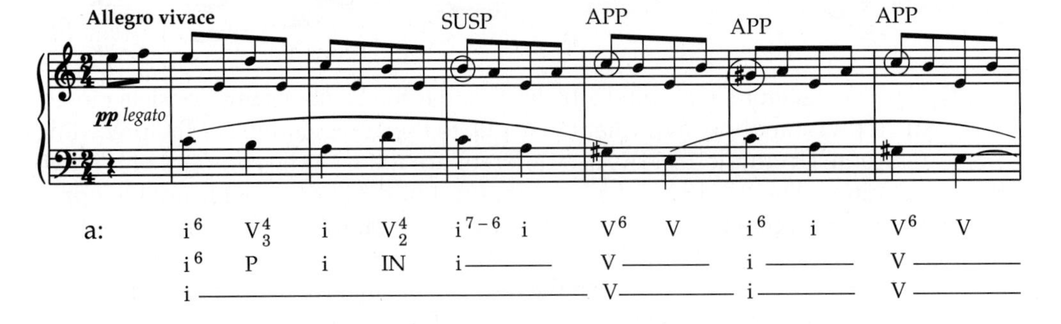

Listen to Example 15.18. The right-hand compound melody implies two voices, the lower of which is essentially a pedal. The combination of this compound melody with the single line in the left hand results in a three-voice texture. As you can see, many of the chords are incomplete, and harmonies must be determined by implication. A cursory glance at m. 1 reveals that the harmony is ambiguous. We may suspect initially that the implied harmony is C major, yet this intuition is contradicted in m. 2, when we discover that the key is A minor. Thus, the opening sonority is i^6_3, a not uncommon occurrence in the Romantic period. Now, because the entire example expands the tonic, we can apply our knowledge of what usually occurs in such a situation to decipher other partial harmonies. For example, a i_6 in m. 1 moves to i^5_3 in m. 2. The intervening chord with B^3 in the bass also contains E^4 and D^5 in the treble. Although the chord is incomplete, we can easily deduce that it is a seventh chord with a missing third (G♯). Thus, the contrapuntal chord on beat 2 of the first measure implies V^4_3. A similar situation occurs on beat 2 of m. 2, in which we suspect that the chord with D^4, E^4, and B^4 is a dominant sonority with a missing third (G♯): an implied V^4_2. In m. 3, the 7–6 suspension (B^4 to A^4) disguises the move back to tonic, but the bass resolution of the seventh (D^4) to the third of the tonic (C^4) confirms our suspicions that we've heard a V^4_2 properly resolve to i_6.

EXERCISE INTERLUDE

PERFORMING

15.3 Singing Compound Melodies

Sing the following compound melodies in C major and C minor and analyze by using roman numerals.

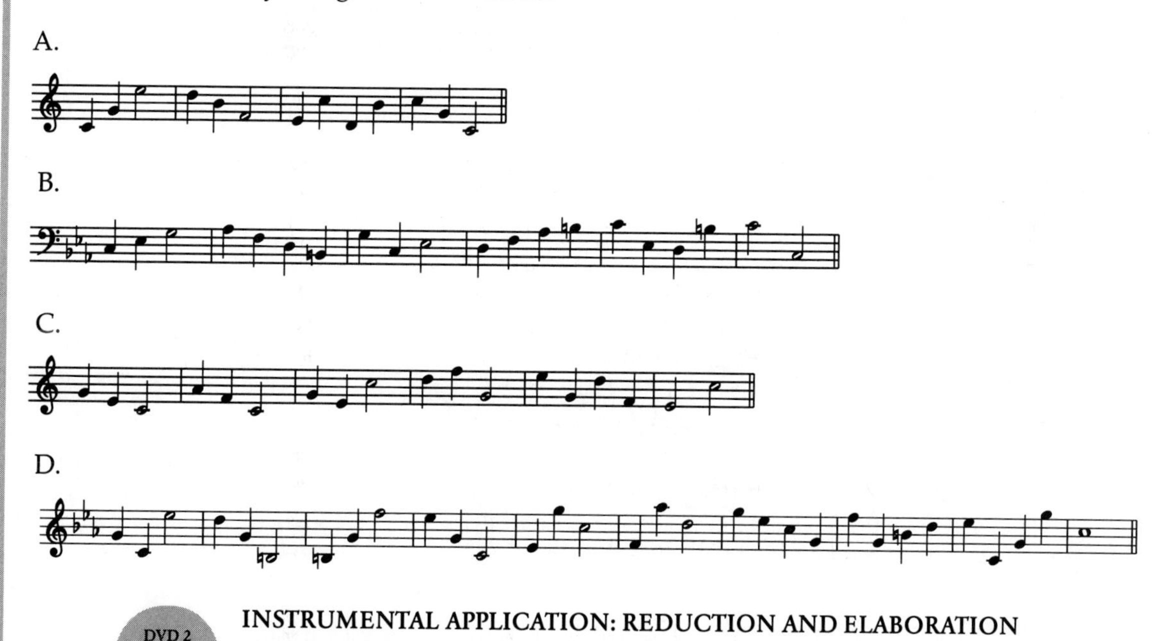

DVD 2
CH 15
TRACK 2

INSTRUMENTAL APPLICATION: REDUCTION AND ELABORATION

15.4

These embellished examples—all taken from Bach's solo violin and cello works—differ from previous reductive examples, in that compound melody is involved; that is, more voices are implied than there are instruments playing. Analyze, verticalize (into a three- or four-voice homophonic texture), and then perform each example as follows. If you are a pianist, simply play your four-voice realization. If you are a melodic instrumentalist, arpeggiate each example. If necessary, refer to the discussion in Chapter 11 for a detailed procedure.

Play each reduction in the key in which it is written; then transpose to one other key of your choice. The sample solution presented shows how Corelli's *Vivace* can be verticalized to create four voices.

Sample: Corelli Violin Sonata, op. 5, no. 2, *Vivace*

A. Bach, Violin Partita in D minor, BWV 1004, Gigue

1.

2.

B. Bach, Violin Sonata in C major, BWV 1005, *Allegro*

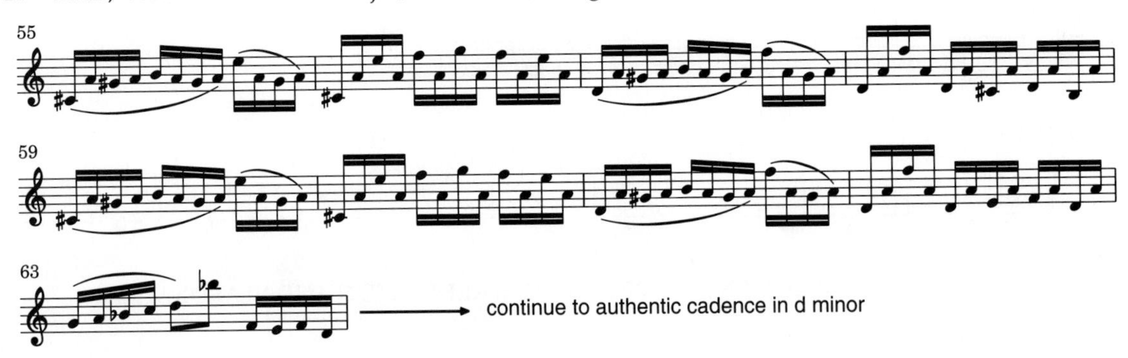

C. Bach, Violin Sonata in A minor, BWV 1003, Fuga

1.

2.

15.5

Elaborate the following figured basses and scale degree melodies (with roman numerals) by first arpeggiating in strict ascending four-voice chords that maintain good voice leading between chords. Then change the contours and add tones of figuration to create a compound melody.

Sample:

Given:

Elaboration:

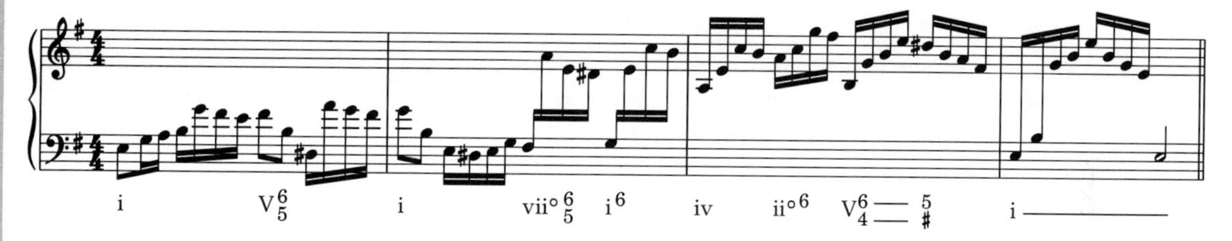

A.

B.

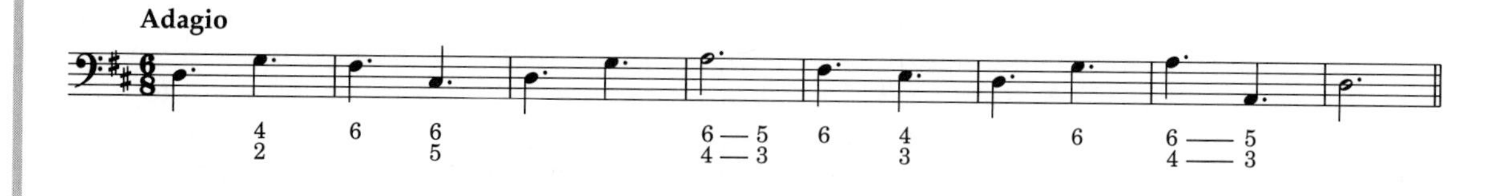

TERMS AND CONCEPTS

- compound melody
- invertible counterpoint (double counterpoint), invertible counterpoint at the octave

CHAPTER 16

The Motive

In this chapter we explore music's smallest units, called *motives*. These units provide substance, logic, coherence, and dramatic energy in music. As building blocks of larger structures, motives are the manifestation of our basic human need to organize and group, and we will see how the multilevel melodic, contrapuntal, and tonal events in music owe their very existence to these modest, often-overlooked musical elements.

Introduction

Music is an art form whose making depends on the temporal domain. That is, the element of time is required in order to play and perceive music, and, as such, music's content is utterly governed by time. Dance is another such art form. The plastic arts, such as painting and sculpture, are in stark contrast to the temporal arts, given that they rely on the spatial domain and that our perception of these art forms depends on their occupying a physical space.

Given that individual musical sounds are fleeting, quickly being replaced by ever-new sounds, composers are saddled with the task of ensuring that each new event is heard as a logical consequence and development of previous events. They must consider not only their own interests in creating a dramatic narrative, but also the listeners' abilities to perceive such a drama. Composers must maintain the delicate balance between repetition and its many degrees of variation, on the one hand, and the introduction of new material on the other.

It is within the melodic domain that we tend to find the most helpful clues that guide us through a developing musical drama. We know that a melody is constructed of a number of phrases, each of which is generally a self-contained unit that expresses a musical idea, is supported by a tonal progression, and closes with a cadence. However, we have yet to focus on the actual building blocks of melodies, those recurring pitch, intervallic, and rhythmic patterns that lie both on and below the music's surface. In this chapter we explore **motives**, which we define as the smallest formal units of musical organization. A motive, like its cousin *motif*, indicates a distinctive idea that unifies an object, whether the paisley wallpaper pattern that pulls together a room or the famous opening of Beethoven's Fifth Symphony. The term *motive*, however, actually comes from the Latin *motus*, meaning "motion," so even though music borrows the term from everyday language, it seems to have its origin in the musical notion of time and in a pattern's developing itself over time. One might liken motives to the amino acids that are the basic building blocks of our bodies. Indeed, motives combine to form phrase members, which in turn combine to form complete phrases. Phrases, by extension, combine to form periods. This hierarchical process can continue all the way to the piece level.

Motives must be audible, so composers imbue them with a clear identity and profile unique to the piece. Thus, motives are short, ranging in length from one beat (in a slow tempo) to one or more measures (in a faster tempo). They are composed of characteristic pitch contours (shapes) and/or rhythms. Since they are restated in different contexts, they must be flexible enough to permit various transformations. However, in order for these transformations to remain linked to the motive, its original statement must be defined well enough to withstand elaborations and transformations. Since motives are important to the development of a piece, they are given a prominent position: at the work's beginning. Pieces may, and usually do, contain more than a single motive. In such cases, they might all be presented near the beginning, or they may enter later at strategic places, often as components of new thematic material, and they may or may not be related. Motives are powerful enough to be able to represent specific characters, events, or situations, as we hear in the music of Wagner, where the appearance of *Leitmotiven*, or "leading motives," immediately conjures up images, whether the specific image is onstage or not. Indeed, weary music students on spring break in south Florida might think twice about going into the water should they hear wafting from someone's boombox a motive comprising only the following two-note figure in the low register: D–E♭ . . . D–E♭ . . . D–E♭–D–E♭–D–E♭ . . .

Motive Types

We begin by distinguishing two types of motive: those that are independent figures and those that are components of themes.

Listen to Example 16.1. Beethoven opens his first string quartet with a unison statement of the work's central motive, a four-beat gesture comprising both pitch and rhythmic elements. The pitch motive involves a turn figure around F followed by a falling skip. The rhythmic element includes two longer note values, which, given that they appear at the beginning and end of the motive, provide a frame that is filled with shorter note values. The motive itself is set off by rests. The recurrences of the motive are rarely identical to its initial presentation. Rather, they are transformed in a variety of ways, which we will soon explore and generalize. Beethoven's motive is self-standing, an independent pitch-and-rhythm construction that generates much of the piece.

EXAMPLE 16.1 Beethoven, String Quartet in F major, op. 18 no. 1, *Allegro con brio*

Beethoven also combines motives to create themes. The main tune of his "Pastorale Symphony" provides an example (Example 16.2). The three motives that comprise the thematic components of the tune are marked *X, Y,* and *Z* (see Example 16.2A). Each is articulated by metric placement (they all are the first events in successive measures) and duration (they all occupy one measure). Thus, while they are distinct (and later in the movement each motive appears separately and is developed) and therefore identifiable, they share musical features. To be sure, the motives relate to one another not only in length, but also in general contour (X rises a fourth, Y falls by a fourth (not counting the large leap at the end), and Z rises a fourth and then falls). Such close relationships make sense, since unrelated motives would jeopardize the logical unfolding of the tune. A quick look at the harmony reveals a single F-major tonic harmony. If we separate the chord tones from the nonchord tones, we see that each motive outlines the interval of a third, with motive Z outlining two thirds, the second of which leads directly to the final pitch, G (see Example 16.2B). And if we consider the melodic fluency of this opening tune in conjunction with the underlying tonic harmony, we can see the underlying descending stepwise line from C^5 to G^4. Thus, multiple motives that are components of longer thematic motions are no haphazard stringing together of ideas; rather, they are carefully ordered members in the linear unfolding of the tune.

EXAMPLE 16.2 Beethoven, Symphony no. 6 in F major, op. 68, *Allegro ma non troppo*

DVD 1
CH 16
TRACK 1

A. X Y Z HC

I V

B.

IN CL

C.

underlying motion

Since motives are characterized by a striking profile in either or both of the pitch and rhythmic domains, would you consider the recurring patterns in Example 16.3 to be a motive? Again, we see a pitch pattern, this time a broken-chord figure, and a rhythmic pattern of nonstop sixteenth notes. However, this recurring gesture is not regarded as a motive. Rather, we refer to it as a **figure**, since it recurs unchanged throughout the piece as part of the texture and general patterning. We are not able to distinguish it from other pitch and rhythmic events since it is the basis of them all. In effect, this undifferentiated figure becomes a background on which other—more striking—events would be set into bold relief.

EXAMPLE 16.3 Bach, Prelude in C major, from *The Well-Tempered Clavier*, Book I

Motivic Repetition

There are three main types of motivic repetitions, based on the degree of change between the initial statement of the motive and successive statements. Exact, or **strict motivic repetition** means that the same pitch-and-rhythm structure is maintained between statements of a motive. However, strict repetition is much less common than **modified motivic repetition**, in which repetitions of the motive's pitches and/or rhythms are varied. Modified repetitions can usually be traced back to the initial motive without difficulty. **Developmental repetitions** involve significant transformation. They often require the most effort to uncover, yet at the same time they are often the most important, having far-reaching consequences in the unfolding of the piece. We now take up each of these types of motivic repetition.

Strict Repetition

Strict motivic repetitions preserve both the pitch and the rhythm of the original motive. Obviously, such repetitions impose significant limitations on the way a composer can shape a piece, and for this reason strict repetitions are relatively rare. One place where strict repetition works well, however, is in the initial moments of a piece, when a listener must grapple with the diverse stimuli of meter, texture, instrumentation, etc. Literal repetition of various elements lessens the potential for information overload. Example 16.4 contains the initial statement of a two-measure motive that is strictly repeated immediately thereafter.

EXAMPLE 16.4 Loeillet, Sonata for Oboe in A minor, op. 5, no. 2

DVD 1
CH 16
TRACK 3

Composers use several different techniques when repeating a motive strictly. They may state the motive first in one voice and then in one or more different voices, a procedure called **imitation**. Clearly, the pacing, density, and overall musical drama are intensified when the imitation occurs in distinct registers and especially in different instruments. See Example 16.5A.

EXAMPLE 16.5

DVD 1
CH 16
TRACK 4

A. Bach, Invention in D minor, BWV 775

B. Schubert, "Die Nebensonnen," from *Winterreise*

Continued

Another way composers avoid the potential monotony of strict repetition is to repeat at pitch the melodic motive, but to cast it in a new harmonic environment, a technique called **reharmonization**. Example 16.5B illustrates. The first appearance of the C♯–B–(C♯)–D–C♯ double-neighbor motive occurs in the home key of A major, where C♯ = $\hat{3}$. Soon thereafter, Schubert reharmonizes the motive in the dark and tragic-sounding key of F♯ minor, in which C♯ = $\hat{5}$.

Modified Repetition

Modified motivic repetitions, a large and varied category, transform a motive in both degree and kind. One of the most important transformations is **embellishment**, defined as the process of adding one or more pitches to a motive. Depending on the context in which the added pitches appear, the transformations can range from being barely noticeable to actually distorting the motive beyond recognition. In Example 16.6A, Grieg opens his piano piece "Erotikon" with a two-beat motive whose immediate repetition contains a repeated F and a neighbor-note figure. However, given compensating factors such as the motive's length and that the addition of pitches leaves the overall contour unaffected, the listener easily hears a relationship between the original form of the motive and its modified repetition.

EXAMPLE 16.6

DVD 1 CH 16 TRACK 5

A. Grieg, "Erotikon," from *Lyric Pieces*, op. 43, no. 5

Lento molto X X′

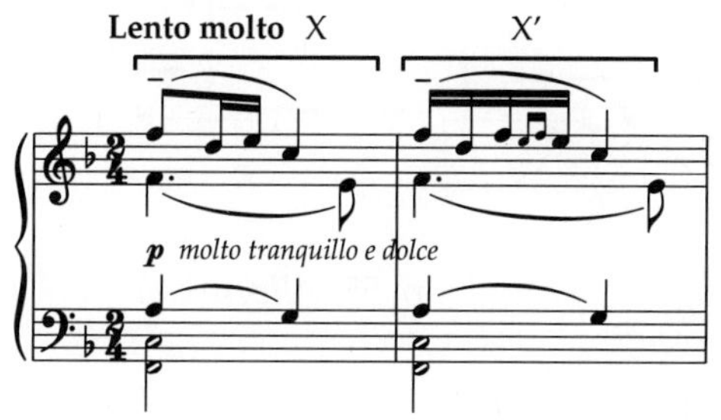

B. Haydn, String Quartet in B minor, op. 64, no. 2, *Adagio ma no troppo*

1.

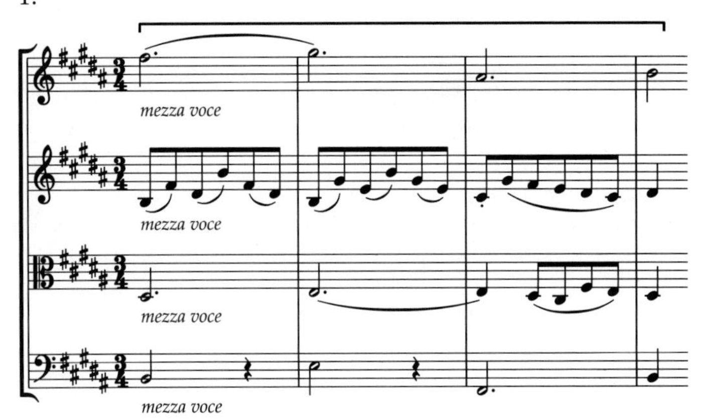

2.

3.

C. Beethoven, Symphony no. 3 in E♭ major, "Eroica," op. 55, *Allegro con brio*

1.

2.

Composers often embellish motives by adding diminutions, such as chordal skips and passing tones, which risk compromising the motive's integrity and audibility. For example, Haydn uses a simple four-note scalar figure (F♯–G♯–A♯–B) as the primary motive in one of his string quartet movements, and, in order to create a more distinctive contour, he displaces the final two pitches one octave lower, resulting in the angular minor-seventh leap from G♯ to A♯ (see Example 16.6B1). Haydn then embellishes the motive in its next statement by filling in not only the falling seventh with stepwise motion, but also the whole step between F♯ and G♯ (with the chromatic passing tone F𝄪 Example 16.6B2). Note that this rather substantial modification does not jeopardize the audible connection between this version of the motive and its initial presentation. Later, Haydn humorously recasts the increasingly embellished motive in an almost precompositional form: as a simple stepwise ascending fourth (Example 16.6B3).

On the other hand, what one might think would be the subtlest alteration of a motive—the simple transposition of one pitch up an octave—can actually undermine the character and connection between a motive and its repetition, as in the opening of Beethoven's "Eroica" Symphony and the following contrived repetition (Example 16.6C).

Although shifting a portion of a motive (e.g., a single pitch) by an octave weakened the Eroica theme, the most common form of modified repetition is **transposition**, in which the *entire* motive is restated on different pitches. Example 16.7 again presents the opening gesture of Beethoven's "Eroica," but this time the entire motive is transposed up a major second. Notice that the relationship between motive and repetition is not compromised when the entire structure is transposed by a consistent interval to a different pitch level. Examples 16.7B and C present two motives by Mozart, each of which he transposes up by a second.

EXAMPLE 16.7

A. Beethoven, Symphony no. 3 in E♭ major, "Eroica," op. 55, *Allegro*

B. Mozart, Symphony no. 40 in G minor, Trio

C. Mozart, Piano Sonata in D major, K. 576, *Allegro*

Continued

There are two types of transposition, tonal and real. **Tonal transposition** maintains the generic (numerical) size of the intervals but alters the quality of the intervals in order to remain within the key. **Real transposition** maintains the specific (both generic and quality) interval size between each member of the motive and the transposed repetition of the motive. For example, given the motive E–F–G in the key of C major, a *tonal transposition* up a third would yield the pitches G–A–B; we sacrifice the exact intervals of the original (m2 followed by M2) in order to stay firmly in the key of C major. A *real transposition* would yield the pitches G–A♭–B♭. Here, the exact intervals are maintained (m2 followed by M2), but we sacrifice the underlying key of C major. See Example 16.7A for an example of real transposition and Examples 16.7 B and C for tonal transposition.

When a motive is transposed two or more times successively *and* at a consistent interval (e.g., each repetition occurs at the tonal transposition of a second), we refer to the process as **sequence.** Example 16.8 reproduces the opening theme of Mozart's A-major symphony, comprising the sequential repetition of a two-measure motive. The motive is restated in rising steps from A to D ($\hat{1}$–$\hat{4}$), followed by the rapid return to $\hat{1}$ to close the eight-measure theme. Since most transposition of motives is by step, the resulting melodic fluency—coupled with the restatement of the unifying motive—creates a powerful musical unity and forward motion.

EXAMPLE 16.8 Mozart, Symphony no. 29 in A major, K. 201, *Allegro moderato*

Imitation—the restatement of material in different voices—is not limited to the octave (or its compound), but it can occur at any interval, the fifth being the most common (see Example 16.9A). The movement begins with a simple neighbor motion (C–D♭–C), which is imitated at the fifth above, on G (although stated a fourth lower). The next statement of the motive is at the original pitch level. Notice that a trill opens the movement. Since most trills occur in cadential gestures rather than as the first-sounding melodic event, we might wish to explore its possible significance. Since trills alternate the given note and the diatonic pitch that lies a second above the main note, we understand Mozart's reason for beginning the movement with this ornamental neighboring gesture: It prepares for the series of upper-neighbor motivic figures that appears in each of the voices. In fact, the falling-neighbor gesture, heard first in the soprano and subsequently in alto and tenor, is actually continued in the bass, albeit much more slowly. And because it alternates D♭ and C twice, we see that it is actually a written-out version of the trill that begins the movement.

EXAMPLE 16.9

DVD 1
CH 16
TRACK 7

A. Mozart, Sonata in F major, K. 280, *Adagio*

B. Bach, G minor Fugue, *The Well-Tempered Clavier*, Book 1

1.

2.

Composers often combine techniques, such as imitation and sequence. One favorite device of composers is to overlap imitative statements of the motive so that another voice enters with its statement before the previous voice has completed its own statement, a process called **stretto** (see Example 16.9B). In Example 16.9B1, Bach presents his motive, which in this piece is called a "subject." He immediately transposes the motive up a fifth (except for the first pitch, which enters on G rather than A). In Example 16.9B2, near the end of the piece, Bach states the motive three times in three voices and in as many octaves, each statement entering before the previous statement is completed.

Additional Pitch Transformations

Some of the most important motivic repetitions transform contour. However, motives are able to withstand many types of transformation without ill effect.

An example of one such transformation is the **change of interval**, which was heard in Example 16.1A; the first statement of the motive closed with a falling fourth, the second statement with a falling third. Yet the listener is still able to hear the kinship between the statements, given their contour and especially their rhythmic identity. And in the violin's solo statement of the motive (m. 5), which closes with an *ascent* rather than the expected descent, we still hear a strong connection. In fact, later sequential statements of the motive incorporate the modified, rather than the original, version of the motive.

Like transposition—which raises or lowers to the same degree every pitch of a motive—the alteration of contour and order that affects every element of a motive is common. **Inversion** is a transformation that projects the interval between pitches in the opposite direction. For example, if an interval between two pitches is an ascending major third, the inversion would be a descending major third. Since this procedure creates an intervallic reflection, it is often called **mirror inversion**. Inversion is a common compositional device because of its audibility: The contour is maintained, albeit in mirror form. Example 16.10A begins with three statements of the four-note motive, each of which is transposed by a third to traverse the tonic (B♭ major) triad. The viola follows suit; however, its inverted statements balance the cello's ascent with a descent.

EXAMPLE 16.10

A. Beethoven, String Quartet in E♭ major, op. 127, *Scherzando vivace*

B. Haydn, String Quartet in B minor, op. 64, no. 2, *Adagio ma no troppo*

Usually the rhythm and contour of a motive are strong enough to withstand even drastic intervallic change. Indeed, the predominantly rising whole-step motion that we encountered earlier in the opening of Haydn's op. 64 String Quartet (Example 16.6B) is recast in an inverted form that is composed exclusively of half steps; but the relationship between the two versions is maintained (see Example 16.10B).

Retrograde reverses the order of the motive's pitches: what was the first pitch becomes the last, and vice versa. As you can imagine, recognizing that a melodic line has been played backwards is not easy, since both contour and pitches are significantly altered between the original presentation and that of the retrograde. Thus, retrograde is not nearly as common a transformation as inversion. In order to project a retrograde relationship, composers provide visual clues for the performer and aural cues for the listener in the form of accents, rests, and leaps, as Haydn does in his "Minuet in Reverse" (see Example 16.11). Such palindromic structures occur occasionally in music, but not nearly as often as they do in language, which include such gems as "step on no pets" and "doc note, I dissent, a fast never prevents a fatness; I diet on cod."

EXAMPLE 16.11 Haydn, Piano Sonata no. 41 in A major, Hob. XVI. 27, "Menuet al rovescio"

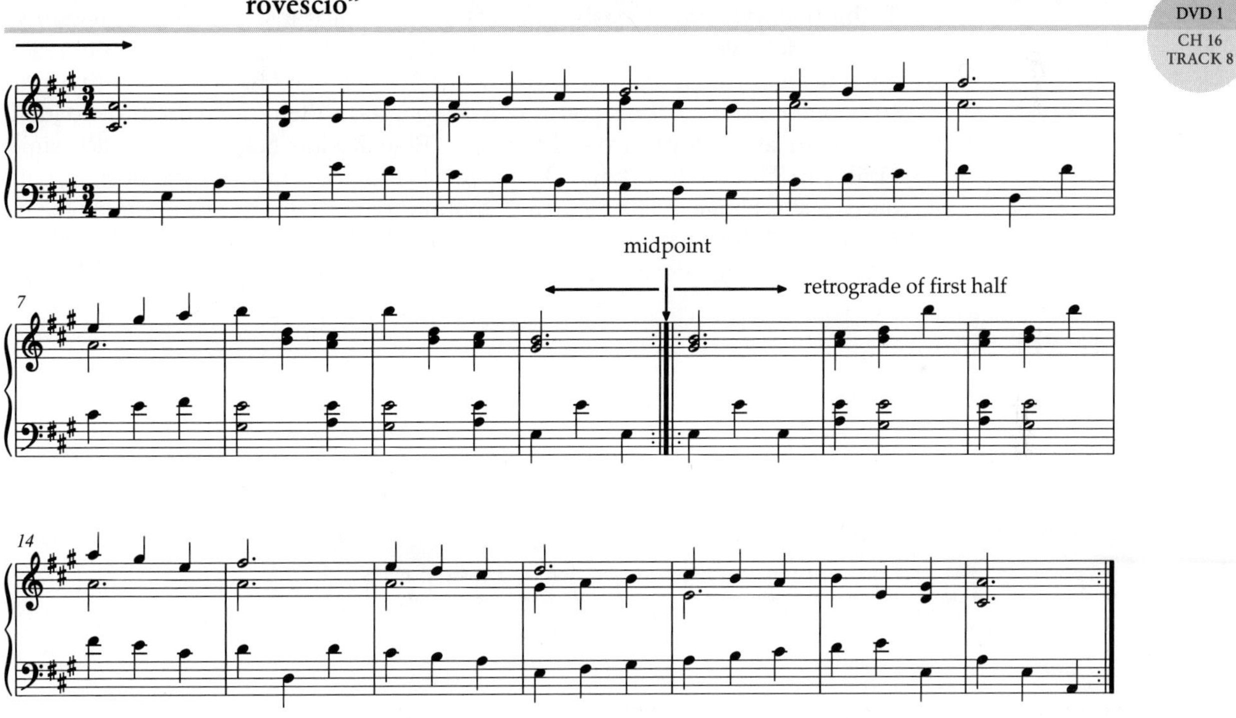

Retrograde inversion is a transformation that combines inversion and retrograde. Thus, one performs an inverted form of the motive backwards. Composers rarely employ retrograde and retrograde inversion, given how difficult they are to aurally recognize. We can summarize these transformations using a contour diagram such as the one shown in Example 16.12. Notice that since the model (taken from one of the *cantus firmi* in Chapter 4) creates an arch (ascent followed by descent) and that the first three pitches (G–A–C) are reversed at the end (C–A–G), the retrograde version and the model are quite audibly related. Study each of the transformations, all of which are tonal (as opposed to real, and thus remain within G major), and note how pitches and intervals are related in each of the transformations.

EXAMPLE 16.12

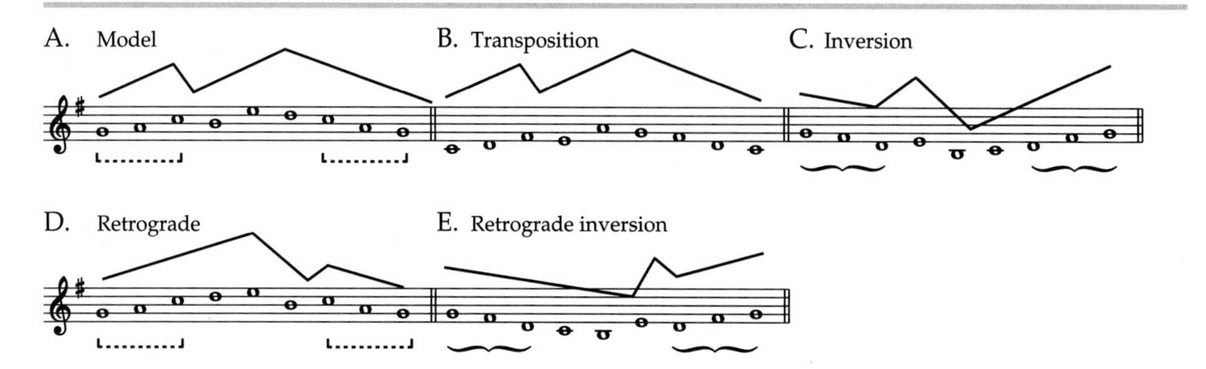

Rhythmic Transformations

To this point, we have focused primarily on motivic transformations that involve pitches. However, rhythm is certainly as important as pitch, at least in terms of aural recognition of repetitions. For example, one need hear only the rhythmic component from the three pieces of Example 16.13A to be able instantly to identify them as excerpts from Mozart's "Eine Kleine Nachtmusik," Rossini's "William Tell Overture," and Bernstein's "America" (from *West Side Story*). Indeed, pitch change over a recurring rhythmic pattern does not undermine the integrity of the motive (see Examples 16.13B1 and B2). The reverse, however—rhythmic change over a recurring pitch pattern—often will (Example 16.13B3).

EXAMPLE 16.13

A1. Mozart, "Eine Kleine Nachtmusik," K. 525, *Allegro*

A2. Rossini, "William Tell Overture"

A3. Bernstein, "America," from *West Side Story*

B. Schubert, "Aufenthalt," from *Schwanengesang*

1.

Composers often increase or decrease proportionately the overall duration of motivic repetitions. A proportional increase is called **augmentation**, and a decrease is called **diminution**. Instances of each are shown in Example 16.14A. Example 16.14B presents the opening of the *Adagietto* movement from Mahler's Symphony no. 5. The first statement of the well-known main motive occurs in the first violin. The subsequent restatement of the tune in the cello is augmented by a factor of 2.

EXAMPLE 16.14

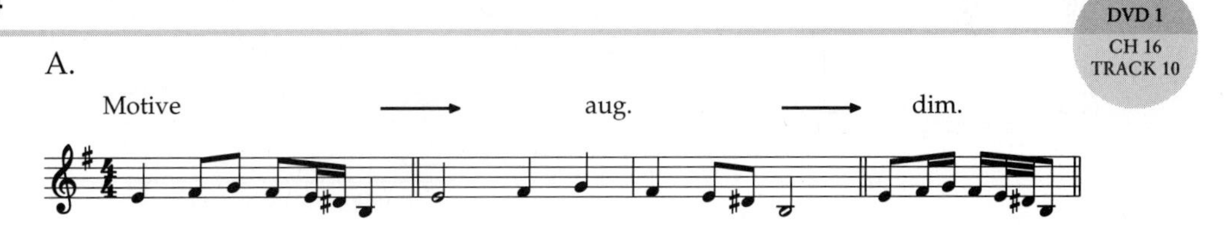

B. Mahler, Symphony no. 5, *Adagietto*, mm. 1–4 and 10–14

Both augmentation and diminution (and other transformations, such as inversion and transposition) may occur simultaneously. When they do, the listener is treated to what amounts to a "motivic saturation." Brahms is particularly fond of juxtaposing, often simultaneously, multiple, transformed versions of a motive that include augmentation, diminution, stretto, and transposition, examples of which all occur in his song "Mein wundes Herz" (see Example 16.15). Since the piano introduction's texture is already quite dense (four voices), we first focus on the initial single-line vocal melody and then return to the more complicated introduction. The vocal line opens with a falling figure that outlines the tonic triad (B–G–E), embellished by the passing tone F♯. Brahms balances this descent with a dramatic arpeggiation that spans an ascending tenth (E–B–G). The phrase closes by step descent to B.

EXAMPLE 16.15 Brahms, "Mein wundes Herz", op. 59, no. 7

Returning to the introduction, we see this motivic contour in the right hand, which begins on C: C–A–G–F♯. Brahms shadows this line a sixth above in imitation (A–F♯–E–D♯) at the eighth note, which begins a process that culminates in motivic saturation. The piano accompaniment echoes the soprano's initial pitches one octave lower, but in diminution, as eighth notes. This imitation extends through the balancing leaping gesture E–B–G–E. Immediately following, in m. 7, the piano restates the motive, this time beginning on D.

The following piano interlude (mm. 11–12) presents three versions of the motive, the first of which includes several preliminary falling thirds. The second and third statements present exact repetitions of m. 1; however, the voices that formed the sixths that open the piece have now swapped places, resulting in falling parallel thirds. This *intervallic* inversion sets up *contour* inversion that is explicitly stated in m. 13 and prepares the vocal line's entrance with its statement of the inversion of the motive, against which the accompaniment returns to its original falling contour.

Developmental Repetitions

The third category of motivic repetition—which we refer to as **developmental repetitions**—includes motivic repetitions whose pitch and/or rhythmic content are significantly altered. We will see that although developmental repetitions may not be as readily audible as modified repetitions, they often ultimately prove to be more important, given their ability to operate at different levels of the musical structure. Further, such motives can be transformed to the degree that they spawn new motives. We will limit our discussion to three procedures, the first two of which are interpolation and fragmentation. The third type, called *hidden motivic repetitions*, is particularly important, given the ability to operate within a musical texture to the degree that the repetitions determine not only the motivic, but also the harmonic trajectory of the music. We will also explore how a motive can migrate not only from one section of a piece to a contrasting section, but also from one movement to another.

Interpolation involves the substantial addition of pitches to a motive, creating the effect of an insertion rather than a mere embellishment. The effect is equivalent to parentheses or an independent clause in language. Musical interpolations can actually appear at a variety of musical levels within a piece, from the phrase level all the way to structures such as the cadenza in a concerto. **Fragmentation** develops only a portion of a motive, such as a neighbor gesture or even a single interval. Often it is the opening, or the "head," of the motive that is fragmented, given its prominent placement and relative memorableness. Further, composers often repeat the fragments sequentially.

Example 16.16A presents a one-measure motive followed by various transformations. First, the motive is inverted (and transposed up a step). The following two measures fragment the motive, stating only its first two beats in rising seconds, with the last note (D) acting as a pedal. The motive is restated in its original form in m. 5; m. 6 maintains the rhythm but alters the contour. A two-measure interpolation begins in m. 7 as a new rhythmic figure (triplets) and pitch motive (broken-chord figure and passing motion) unexpectedly enters. Measures 9–10 return to the original motive's rhythm, which supports a new contour that leads to the final cadence.

EXAMPLE 16.16

DVD 1
CH 16
TRACK 12

A.

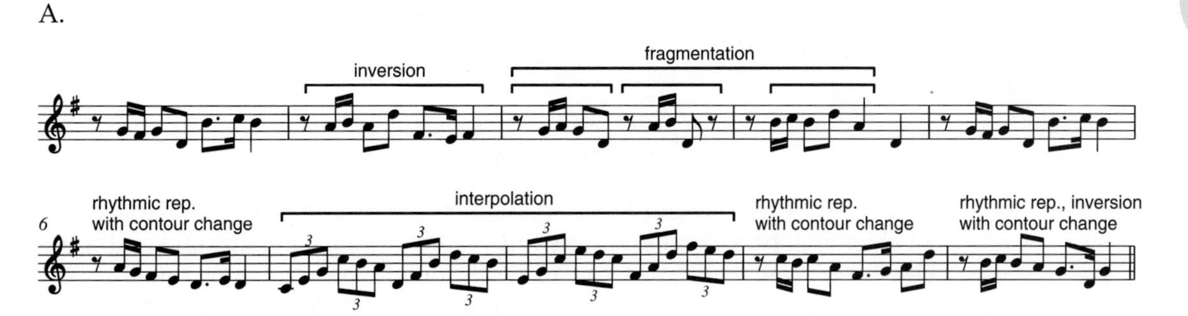

B. Haydn, String Quartet in B♭ major, op. 33, no. 2, Scherzo

The Haydn example (Example 16.16B) contains one phrase (the addition of the chordal seventh of V, A♭, "undoes" the cadential effect of the preceding V triad); the first phrase closes with a HC in m. 4 and the second a PAC in m. 10. The first phrase presents the one-measure motive: an incomplete-neighbor figure followed by a descending leap of an octave, with two chords that punctuate the end of the motive. The motive is repeated over the ii^6 chord and the V chord (although the descending leaps are smaller). What follows is an interpolation that prolongs the dominant, in echo fashion, of mm. 3–4. Haydn clarifies the function of this material as an insertion by changing the prevailing dynamic level from *forte* to *piano* (returning to *forte* in m. 6) and by stating only the neighboring portion of the motive several times, with the addition of a chromatic pitch. The second phrase, then, does not begin until m. 6.

EXAMPLE 16.17 Bach, Invention in B♭ major

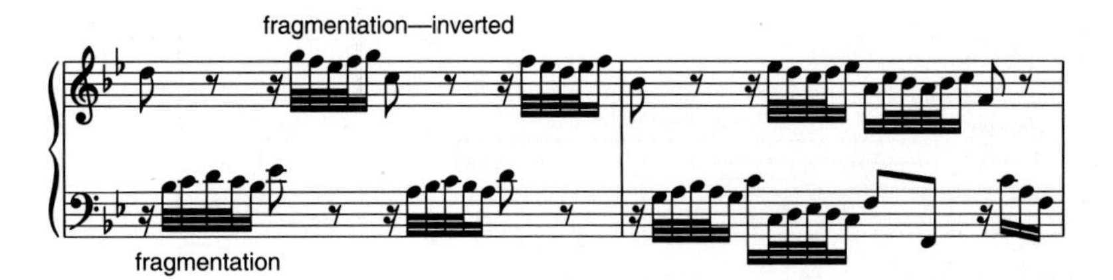

Listen to Example 16.17. The opening motivic gesture consists of two parts: an ascending broken-chord figure followed by a balancing descending figure. However, given that these two parts each contain the exact same rhythmic figure (thirty-second notes followed by sixteenth notes), we can refine our analysis and claim that the second part of the motive, the descending form, is a literal inversion of the first, thus altering our interpretation of what constitutes the actual motive: Rather than a single four-beat ascending and descending entity, the motive is better interpreted as a two-beat rising figure whose first repetition occurs in inversion. The first fragmentation of the motive occurs in m. 4, where only the opening thirty-second-note figure appears. Bach also states the inverted form of the thirty-second-note figure to create both imitation and, given that he repeats the figure down a step each time, sequence.

Intersection and Intermovement Motivic Repetitions

Composers unify their multisection and multimovement works in many ways, but one of the most important is through motivic connections. However, for a motive to migrate from one section of a piece (or from one movement to a contrasting movement), it must be highly malleable. For example, Mozart's Sonata in B♭ begins with the unharmonized upbeat incomplete upper-neighbor on $\hat{6}$, which falls to $\hat{5}$, which is followed by the stepwise descent to $\hat{1}$ (Example 16.18A). We hear a contrasting theme in the new key of F major in m. 23. However, a brief glance reveals that the opening gesture has migrated to this new section. This time the upper neighbor to $\hat{5}$ is complete, and the faster sixteenth-note D–C ($\hat{6}$–$\hat{5}$) mimics the grace-note figure G–F (again $\hat{6}$–$\hat{5}$) that began the piece (Example 16.18B). The first phrase of this new theme closes with a HC. The modified repetition that follows (mm. 31–38; not shown) carries the melodic line all the way down to F ($\hat{1}$ in F major).

EXAMPLE 16.18 Mozart, Piano Sonata in B♭ major, K. 333

DVD 1
CH 16
TRACK 14

Continued

Another, more dramatic example of motivic migration and development is found in Chopin's *Fantasie Impromptu,* a work that is cast in a large three-part form: The first and third related parts are virtuosic and tumultuous, while the second part is lyrical and restrained. However, a transformed motivic repetition connects the two sections and unifies the piece (see Example 16.19). The right-hand figure that opens the piece (m. 5) is composed of a rising one-octave arpeggiation of the tonic triad: G♯–C♯–E–G♯. This ascent is embellished by two turn figures, the first around G♯ (G♯–A–G♯–F^x–G♯) and the second around C♯ (D♯–C♯–B♯–C♯).

EXAMPLE 16.19 Chopin, *Fantasie Impromptu,* op. 66

DVD 1
CH 16
TRACK 15

A.

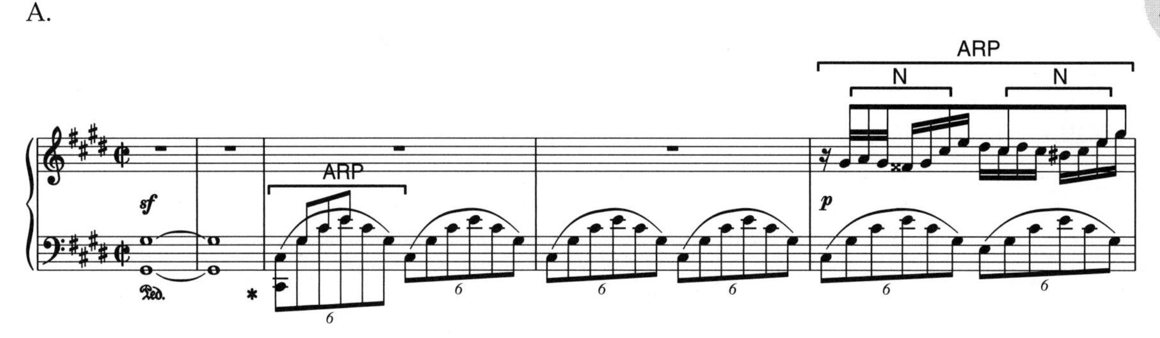

B.

Largo

ARP

N

ARP

tr

sotto voce

The contrasting section in the parallel major (notated enharmonically in the easier-to-read key of D♭ major) opens with a slow-moving tune that also begins on $\hat{5}$ (A♭) (Example 16.19B). Again, the melody sweeps upward, unfolding a tonic triad: A♭–D♭–F–A♭. Notice that this tune uses the nearly identical pitch classes and the order of the opening tune (save for the F^5, which, substitutes for the E in this major-mode section). To cement the motivic relationship, the D♭-major tune contains both the upper neighbor (B♭) and even the E♭, which was the repeated accented dissonance in the first theme. We may in turn work backwards from the work's opening right-hand material to the left-hand accompanimental figure, which contains the very pitches and contour that spawn the later themes. Note that Chopin reminds us of the left hand's importance by recycling it as the accompanimental figure in the D♭-major section.

Intermovement connections were common in the nineteenth century, yet such connections occur earlier in many Classical and even Baroque pieces, including the work of Italian Baroque composer Arcangelo Corelli. The movements within his trio sonatas are often linked by both melodic and rhythmic shapes; see Example 16.20. The Allemande opens with a dotted-note figure that arpeggiates the F-major triad, which is immediately imitated by the bass instruments (Example 16.20A). The second part of the movement recasts the tune in a modified inversion and places the bass instrument in the role of leader, with the first violin following close behind (Example 16.20B).

EXAMPLE 16.20 Corelli, Trio Sonata in F major, op. 2, no. 7

DVD 1
CH 16
TRACK 16

A. Allemande

B. Allemande

C. Corrente

D. Gigue

E. Prelude

F. Gigue

The Corrente uses this inverted form of the motive, filling in the leap that would have been from D down to A with steps (Example 16.20C). The Gigue returns to the imitative procedure first heard in the Allemande, in which Corelli restates the original ascending arpeggiated form of the motive (Example 16.20D). The added F in m. 2 and the skip to B♭ rather than C do not compromise hearing a connection between the original motive and the Gigue's restatement.

What remains intact in each movement is the dotted rhythmic figure that accompanies the fifth and fourth leaps. A brief glance at the sonata's opening Prelude reveals an emphasis on these very motives (Example 16.20E). They appear following each dramatic fermata: F–B♭, C–F, G–C. Note that the transposition of these leaps of a fourth and a fifth is by perfect fifths. That there may be a connection between these fourths and their expansion into the initial motive of each of the following movements, we can look at how Corelli develops the melody in the final movement. Beginning in m. 18, and just before the end of the Gigue, the rising perfect intervals occur in sequence: C–F, D–G, E–A, F–B♭, G–C, in effect explicitly announcing that the everyday interval of a perfect fourth/perfect fifth is a generating force in both the melodic and harmonic realms of the sonata.

In order to smooth the connection between contrasting sections of a piece, composers employ a technique referred to as **linkage**, whereby a motivic element is retained in both sections but is necessarily transformed in order to fit into the new musical environment (see Example 16.21). Three formal areas are shown in the example: the end of the tumultuous development section, characterized by sixteenth notes and off-beat *sforzandi* (through m. 132), a retransition whose function is to dissipate the energy of the development and prepare for the return of the opening material (mm. 132–143), and the restatement of the opening material in E minor (mm. 144ff). Notice how Beethoven converts the development's broken-chord figure into a scalar motive (G–F♯–E–D♯) that he repeats in rhythmic augmentation, first with sixteenth notes, then with eighths, then with quarters, and finally with half notes (mm. 132–137), all of which occurs in imitation at the octave, in stretto, and falling in register. Notice that the lowest note of the motive, D♯, is removed during this process and that the remaining pitches, G–F♯–E, begin to accelerate and regain the higher register and then rush headlong into the restatement of the original motive, which relies on this very third, G–F♯–E.

EXAMPLE 16.21

DVD 1
CH 16
TRACK 17

A. Beethoven, Piano Sonata in E minor, op. 90, *Allegro*

B. Mozart, Piano Sonata in F major, K. 332, *Allegro*

Mozart's use of linkage in his F-major sonata is a bit more concealed. The rising broken-chord figure that begins the development (G–C–E) has been subtly prepared in the preceding virtuosic cadential section (Example 16.21B).

Single-Interval Motives

The motives we have discussed so far possess distinct melodic and rhythmic profiles. Clear pitch contours supported by characteristic rhythmic settings help us to recognize the many transformations to which they are subjected. However, by the late eighteenth century, composers began to explore the power of a single interval. This type of motive can generate both melodic and harmonic material throughout a piece. When one stops to think about it, a single interval is highly versatile and can be employed in multiple musical environments. Consider the perfect fourth A♭–D♭, which can fit into any number of tonal contexts. At the same time, this perfect fourth is also ubiquitous in tonal music and therefore may not be motivic at all, but just a byproduct of melodic and harmonic motions. Composers such as Beethoven were drawn to single-interval motives because they could be used as the impetus to create longer and more involved motives. Indeed, this very perfect fourth is the seed Beethoven uses to generate the theme in the last movement of his Piano Sonata in A♭ (Example 16.22A). He also subjects the motive to various transformations, including inversion (Example 16.20B) and augmentation and diminution, *simultaneously* (Example 16.22C).

EXAMPLE 16.22 Beethoven, Piano Sonata in A♭ major, op. 110, fugue theme

DVD 1 CH 16 TRACK 18

A.

C.

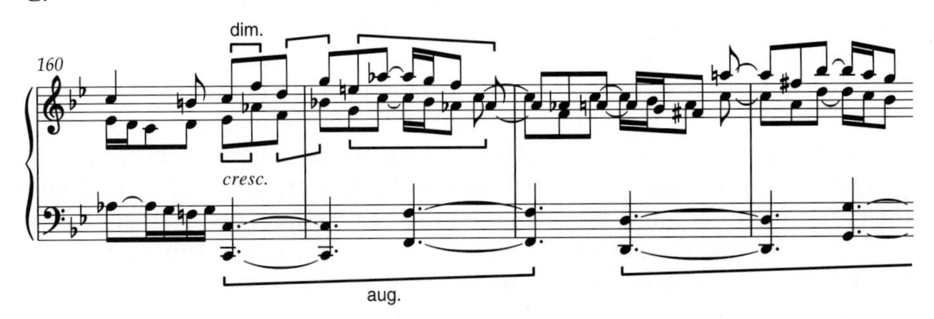

In order to create a motive composed of only a single interval or a pair of like intervals, composers often combine a more generic interval, such as the third or the fifth, with a more striking and immediately audible interval, such as the half-step neighbor. Example 16.23 presents the opening gestures of several well-known Chopin pieces, all of which depend on the upper-neighbor motive $\hat{5}$–$\hat{6}$–$\hat{5}$.

EXAMPLE 16.23

DVD 1
CH 16
TRACK 19

A. Chopin, Prelude in C minor, op. 28

B. Chopin, Nocturne in C minor, op. 48, no. 1

C. Chopin, Prelude in E♭ minor, op. 28

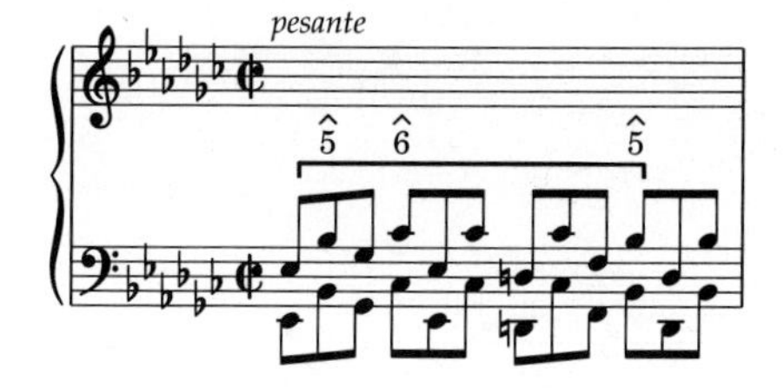

D. Chopin, Prelude in E minor, op. 28

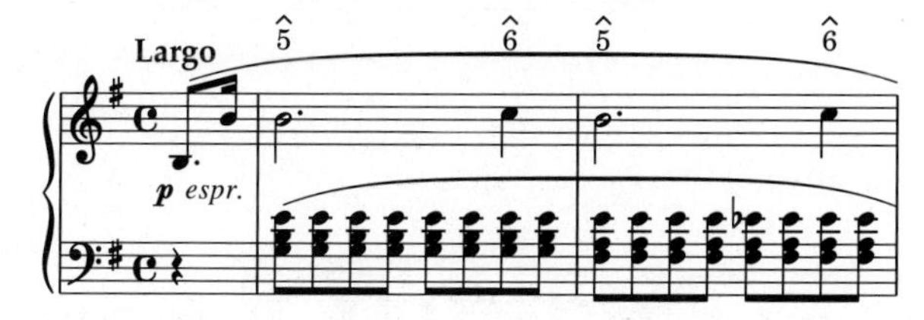

E. Chopin, Prelude in F♯ minor, op. 28

Finally, composers often combine a single-interval motive, such as the half-step neighbor, with a transformed version of itself, as seen in the Clementi excerpt in Example 16.24. The incomplete rising neighbor E–F ($\hat{7}$–$\hat{1}$) is combined with its inversion: D♭–C ($\hat{6}$–$\hat{5}$). Clementi subjects the motive not only to transposition and inversion, but also to **octave displacement**, in which a portion of the motive is shifted up or down by an octave. This procedure occurs early in the movement and coincides with the movement's first *crescendo*. Notice that the motive is dramatically augmented, occupying a full, rather than a half, measure. The following phrase opens with the motive in imitation, and from here Clementi develops it even further. The relentless motivic saturation, including many transposed versions, culminates in the final gesture of the movement, in which the motive appears at its original pitch level and with its characteristic half-step members tightly juxtaposed. However, its final statement in the piano's lowest register and at *pianissimo* dynamic seems to reflect the motive's utter exhaustion after its nonstop development throughout the movement (Example 16.25).

EXAMPLE 16.24 Clementi, Sonata in F minor, op. 13, no. 6

DVD 1
CH 16
TRACK 20

EXAMPLE 16.25 Clementi, Sonata in F minor, op. 13, no. 6

DVD 1
CH 16
TRACK 21

Octave displacement can transform a single-interval motive to the degree that it becomes unrecognizable. This technique, a favorite of Brahms, can be heard in his Fourth Symphony (Example 16.26). The interval of a falling third is prominent throughout the symphony. And in its closing moments, Brahms summarizes the motive's importance by dramatically stating these thirds in unison and in octaves, one after the other, in the following long series: E–C–A–F♯–D♯–B–G–E–C–A–F♯–D♯.

EXAMPLE 16.26 Brahms, Symphony no. 4, op. 98

DVD 1
CH 16
TRACK 22

Note that the pattern of falling thirds is broken only once, apparently because of range limitations. However, the nearly two-octave leap from the low B to the high G draws attention to this now-compound sixth. If we were to take advantage of the invertibility of sixths and thirds, we can keep this falling-third pattern within a more restricted tessitura. A glance at the melody that opens the symphony's first movement reveals this exact structure. In Example 16.27, after B^5 falls a third to G^5 and E^5, C^6 appears a sixth above, not a third below, E^5. Similarly, A^5, $F\sharp^5$, and $D\sharp^5$ fall by thirds from C^6, but B^5 rises a sixth from $D\sharp^5$. That Brahms subjects his tunes to such manipulation is clear from the following measures, where he changes direction and *ascends* through a series of hidden thirds.

EXAMPLE 16.27 Brahms, Symphony no. 4, *Allegro non troppo*

DVD 1
CH 16
TRACK 23

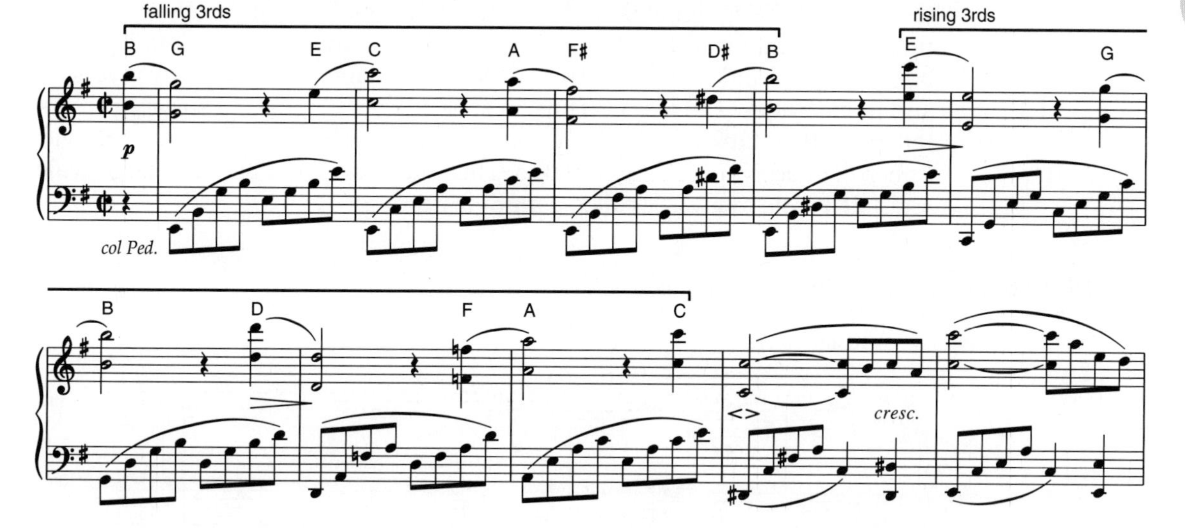

Hidden Motivic Repetitions

Developmental motives are the musical world's equivalent to the animal world's chameleons; motives are modified in order to fit within their musical environment. As such, they are remarkably powerful compositional tools. One reason that developmental motives are so important and interesting is that they are able to exist at various levels of musical structure (see example 16.28). Haydn begins his piece with the upper-neighbor figure D–E♭–D. The motive is innocuous, given its brevity (one beat) and that the E♭ (a dissonant fourth) is metrically unstressed. However, already in the next measure, the neighbor motive is expanded: E♭ is four times longer, occupying an entire beat, and now it is harmonically supported by the E♭ harmony (IV). Motives often gain structural importance as a piece unfolds. Recognition of such processes allows the performer to follow what amounts to a motivic path through a composition.

EXAMPLE 16.28 Haydn, Divertimento, "St. Anthony Chorale"

Sometimes composers state motives at various levels simultaneously. Beethoven begins one of his late bagatelles with what sounds like an accompanimental figure in the right hand: a gently rocking figure in parallel thirds supported by a pedal on G (see Example 16.29). The left-hand gesture that enters two beats later (above the right hand, in the high register) also sounds more accompanimental than thematic; as a triplet-sixteenth-note filigree, it is more commentary on the rocking figure than it is theme. Examination of the contours of both figures is revealing: The right-hand eighth-note figure outlines a double neighbor (E–F–D–E), and so does the triplet-sixteenth figure, transformed by inversion and transposition: G–F♯–A–G. Thus, in spite of their contrasting surface presentations, both figures are intimately related and, as such, should be given motivic, rather than accompanimental, status. This interconnection between large-scale and small-scale motives is called a **motivic nesting**.

EXAMPLE 16.29 Beethoven, Bagatelle, op. 126

DVD 1
CH 16
TRACK 24

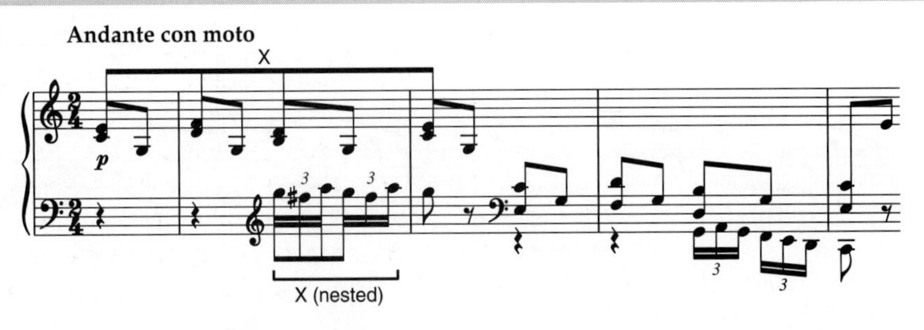

Depth and Surface: Motivic Parallelism

We have seen the importance of motives and how through transformation they can operate in any number of musical contexts. The most interesting transformations allow motives to migrate to different sections of a piece or to different movements and even to be hidden. We now explore the migration of motives to the harmonic domain, seeing how they control the composer's choice of chords. That is, we will see that the outer-voice counterpoint can project, at deep structural levels, the melodic figurations we hear at the musical surface. Listen to the excerpt by Mozart of Example 16.30 and consider the given roman numeral analysis. Note that there is no real harmonic progression in these four measures; rather, weak dominant harmonies expand the tonic.

EXAMPLE 16.30 Mozart, Piano Fantasy in D minor, K. 397, *Adagio*

DVD 1
CH 16
TRACK 25

Tonic harmony is expanded by an upper and a lower neighbor in the bass, harmonized by V^4_3 and V^6_5 (see Example 16.31). This static double-neighbor expansion of tonic is aligned with an equally static melodic framework that begins and ends on F ($\hat{3}$). The controlling upper-voice F is prolonged by the same double-neighbor melodic figure, mirroring the bass in inversion.

EXAMPLE 16.31

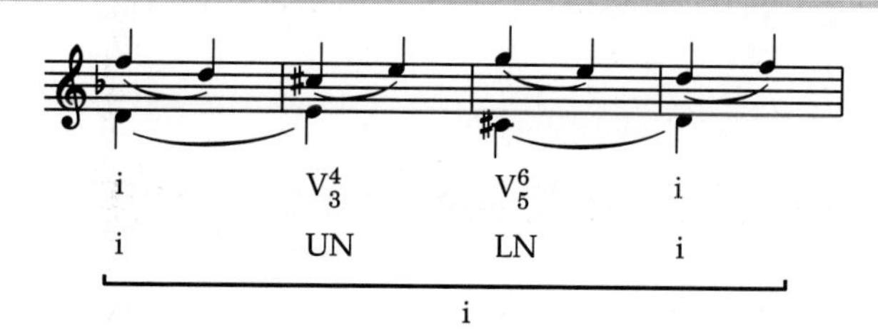

Example 16.32 summarizes the outer-voice counterpoint; stemmed notes represent structural notes.

EXAMPLE 16.32

An association links the surface tune to the underlying counterpoint. Example 16.33 shows how Mozart uses the same double-neighbor figure over two different time spans, both as a tiny figure in the melody (m. 1, beats 1–3) and as a large gesture controlling the melodic path of the first phrase (mm. 1–4). The result is an audible connection between the surface and the underlying counterpoint, made real through the ubiquitous presence of the motive. Thus, the initial melodic gesture becomes a shaping force not only over the entire melody but also in the bass, where it influences the harmony. The transformed repetitions of a motive and its harmonization at different structural levels is called **motivic parallelism**. Given that Mozart's initial motive occurs within the longer, more structural, version of the motive, this motivic parallelism is also nested.

EXAMPLE 16.33

Let's examine how motive works in conjunction with harmony, tonic expansions, counterpoint, and motivic parallelism in the opening of a late piano sonata by Beethoven (Example 16.34). Unlike Mozart's Fantasy, the first phrase of Beethoven's sonata contains a harmonic progression that unfolds in the standard phrase model (T–PD–D–T) as well as the expected tonic expansion. Beethoven uses inverted V_7 chords to expand the tonic, effectively surround the upcoming $\hat{3}$ in the bass of m. 3 from below and above. Examination of the pitch material and its interaction with the meter reveals yet another layer of structure. The underlying bass line is A♭2–B♭2–C3 ($\hat{1}$–$\hat{2}$–$\hat{3}$,) thus prolonging the tonic by movement from I to I_6.

EXAMPLE 16.34 Beethoven, Piano Sonata in A♭ major, op. 110, *Moderato cantabile molto espressivo*

The motive in this passage appears to be the third, given the large-scale third in mm. 1–3 and the smaller third in the opening interval in the bass (A♭2 to C3). Example 16.35 summarizes the bass motion for this passage.

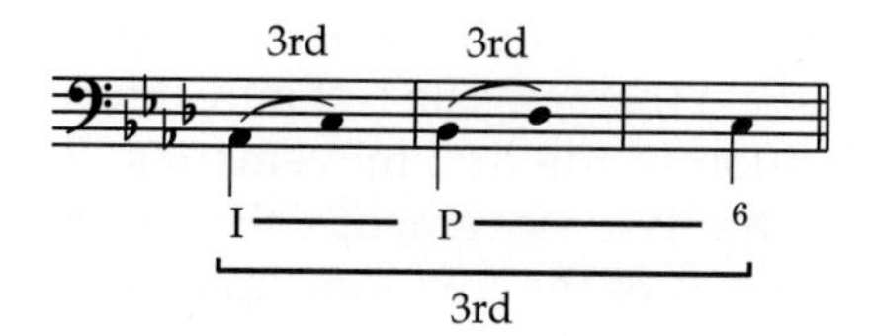

The two-voice contrapuntal scheme resulting from soprano and bass supports the assertion that the main motive is the third, for, at the surface, the melody in m. 1 mirrors the bass in contrary motion with the voice exchange of A♭ and C (Example 16.36). The pattern is continued in m. 2 with another voice exchange, this time involving D♭ and B♭. In m. 3 the voice-exchange pattern stops and E♭^{5} is extended with a double neighbor. The soprano plays C^5–D♭^{5}–E♭^{5} while the bass moves in parallel tenths over the first three measures. A final tenth (and another voice exchange) occurs at the pre-dominant, followed by a rapid descent that creates the balanced arch of the soprano line, C^5–D♭^{5}–E♭^{5}–F^5–E♭^{5}–D♭^{5}–C^5.

EXAMPLE 16.36

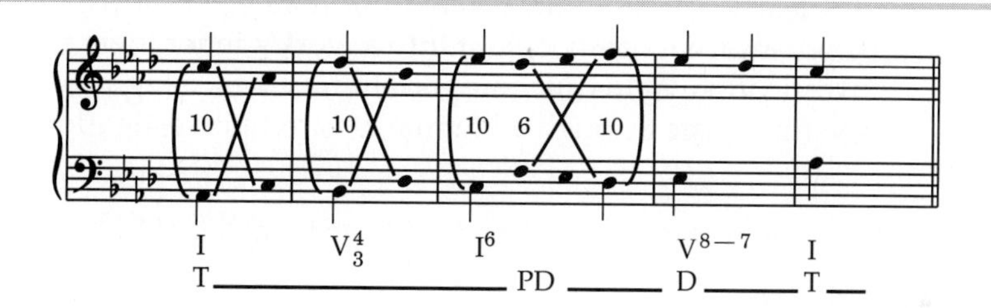

We have skirted over the short cadenza-like flourish in m. 4 that links the dominant back to the tonic. Indeed, pianists are often baffled by this curious figure. But if we review the structural contents of the soprano line in Example 16.36, we see a note-for-note correspondence between the structural soprano notes in the opening four measures and the thirty-second-note flourish (see Example 16.37).

EXAMPLE 16.37

Indeed, it seems as if Beethoven has provided the listener with a summary of exactly what took place in the first four measures, much in the same way that Mozart gave the listener an introduction to what was to follow in his Fantasy. Finally, lest the reader think that Beethoven limits the use of his motive to this one movement, let us return to Example 16.22 (reproduced here as Example 16.38), which presents the theme to the last movement. Comparing both themes based on their rhythms and metrical placement suggests that they are highly contrasting: The first movement is all "about" thirds and their transposition up seconds, while the last movement projects rising perfect fourths.

However, comparing only their pitch content, we see a note-for-note correspondence between the two themes. The last movement's theme, then, can be considered a recomposition of the first movement's. Beethoven has omitted the initial C, beginning the last movement's theme on A♭, which allows the unarticulated perfect fourths of the first movement's theme to emerge as the controlling interval. To cinch the connection between movements, both the high point of the first movement's theme, the F, and its stepwise return to C, recur in the last movement.

EXAMPLE 16.38

DVD 1
CH 16
TRACK 27

Clearly, analysis can reveal important musical correspondences that will help performers gain insight into a work's inner logic and structure. If a brief investigation yields such important findings, imagine what truths you'll discover in music through a lifetime of careful investigation.

EXERCISE INTERLUDE

WRITING

16.1

Transform the given motives as required.

A. D minor example

1. Transpose up a minor third (tonal transposition).
2. Invert (begin on D).
3. Retrograde.
4. Transpose down a minor second plus augmentation at 2:1 (real transposition).
5. Embellish using neighbor figures.
6. Embellish the motive to at least twice its length through fragmentation.

B. G major example

1. Invert (begin on G).
2. Sequence down by step at least twice; cadence on $\hat{1}$.
3. Add a one-measure interpolation.
4. Invert; then transpose down a major third (real transposition).
5. Retrograde plus diminution by 50%; then sequence the result up by step two times.

ANALYSIS

16.2

Label the transformation types that you encounter in the given excerpts, each of which is taken from J. S. Bach's *Art of the Fugue*. The main motive is boxed for you. Possible transformations include:

1. embellishment (adding pitches between main notes)
2. reharmonization
3. change of interval
4. transposition
5. sequence
6. inversion
7. retrograde
8. augmentation
9. diminution
10. imitation
11. interpolation
12. fragmentation
13. change of meter

A. Bach, Contrapunctus I

B. Bach, Contrapunctus IV

C. Bach, Contrapunctus V

D. Bach, Contrapunctus VI

E. Bach, Contrapunctus XII

F.

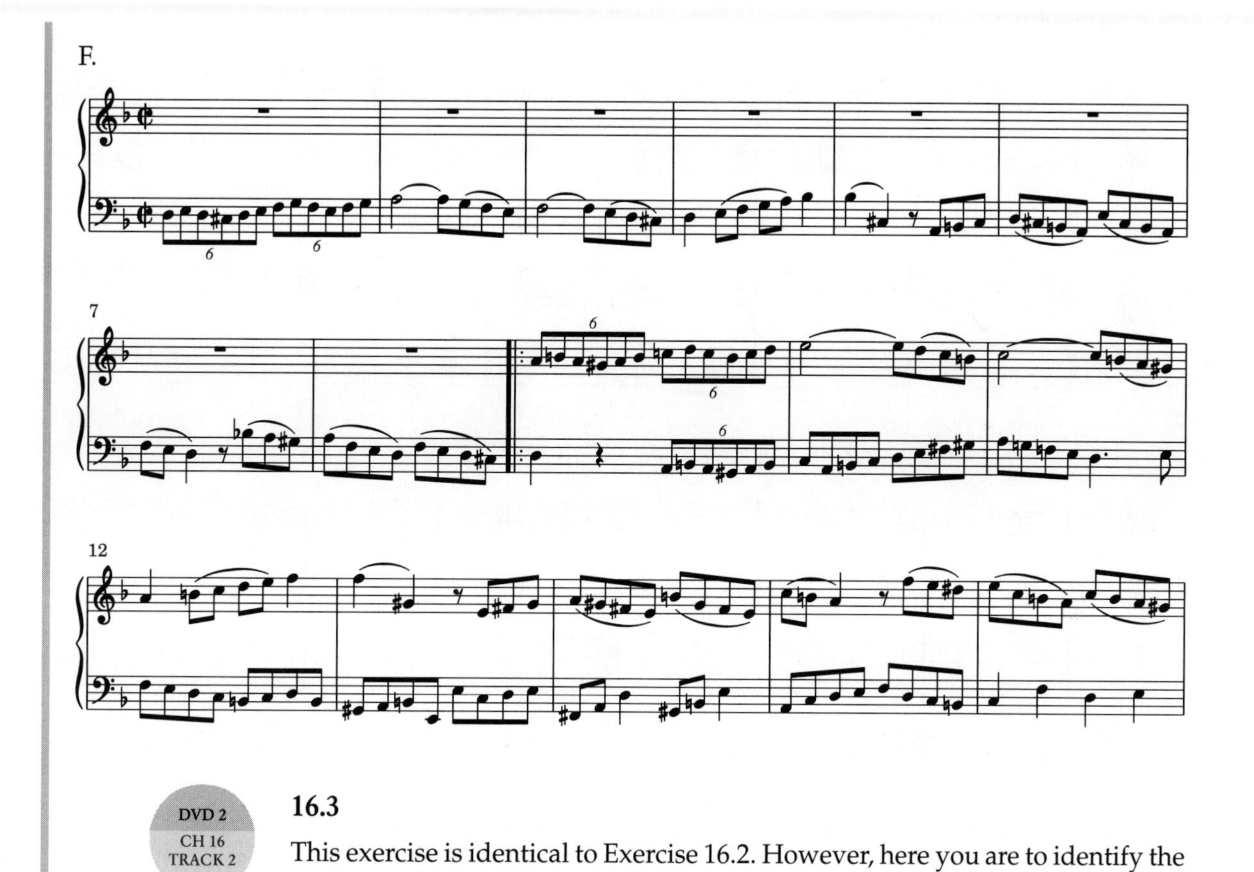

DVD 2
CH 16
TRACK 2

16.3

This exercise is identical to Exercise 16.2. However, here you are to identify the motive and subsequent transformations.

A. Beethoven, String Quartet in A minor, op. 132, *Assai sostenuto*

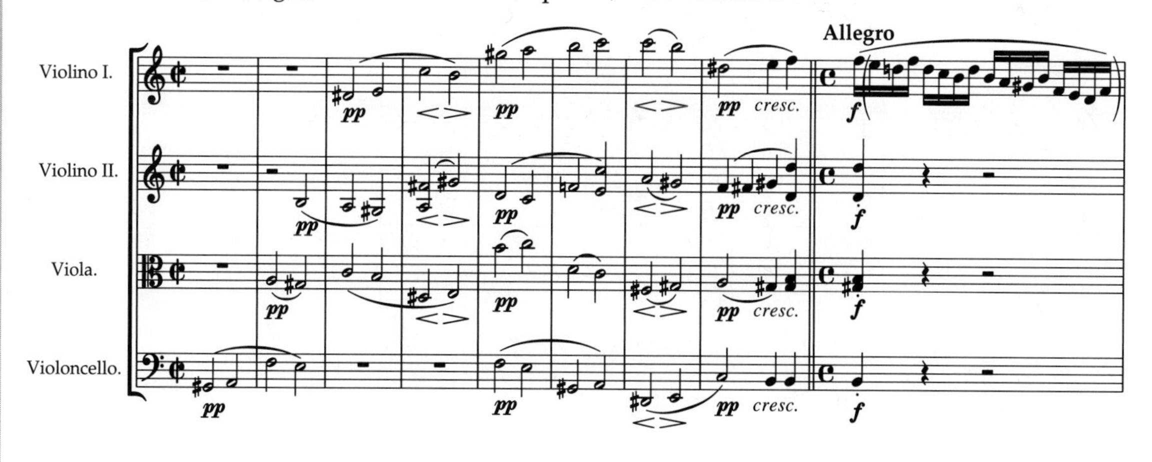

B. Corelli, Trio Sonata in C minor, op 1, no. 8, *Vivace*

C. Clementi, Sonata in G major, op. 40, no. 1

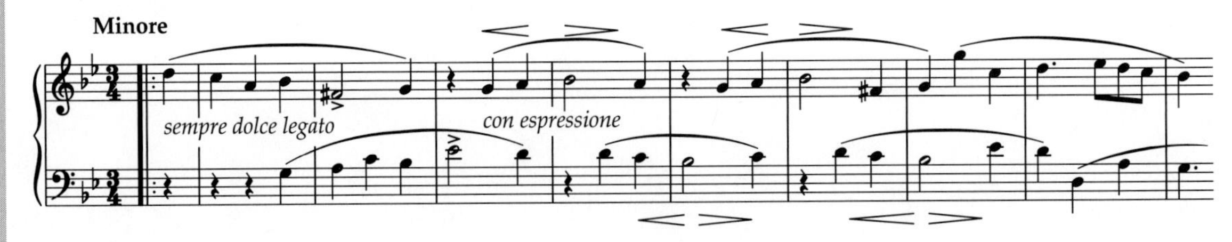

D. Beethoven, Piano Piece, WoO 61a

E. Beethoven, String Quartet in C major, op. 59, no. 3, Menuetto Grazioso

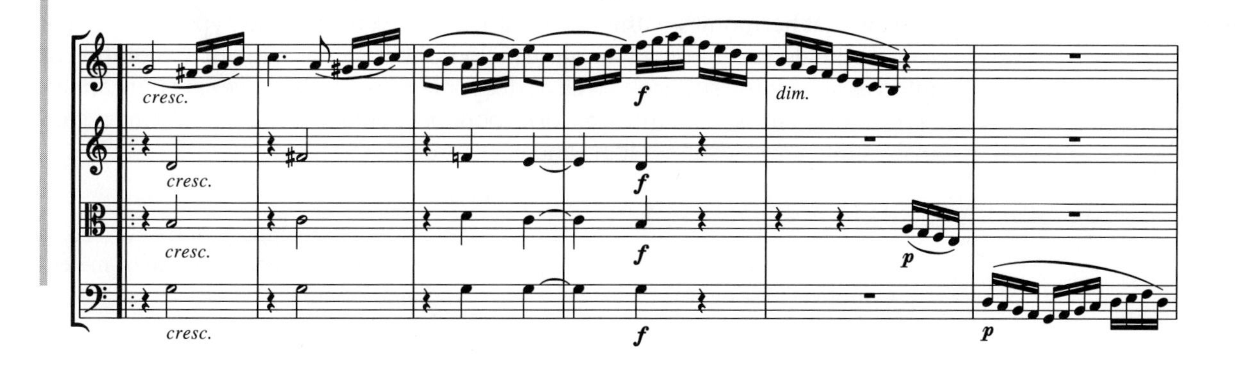

Continued

16.4 Prose Writing

Write a one- to two-page essay in which you define *motive* in your own words. Support your ideas with examples from the repertoire for your instrument.

Summary of Part 3

We explored several new topics in Part 3. First, the pre-dominant function is the third and final harmonic function in tonal music. This intermediate function, which occurs between the tonic and dominant functions, includes either or both the supertonic and subdominant harmonies. Pre-dominants provide contrast between the tonic and the dominant while at the same time become springboards to and aural signals for the upcoming dominant function. The three functions provide a goal-directed motion through the phrase, which we call the phrase model.

We also learned that metrically accented and chromatic dissonances provide the phrase with intensity and dramatic forward motion. Further, our discussion of the various six four chords confirmed importance of considering harmonies within a musical context, rather than just stacking thirds and adding roman numerals. In our study of invertible counterpoint, compound melody, and motive, we saw that harmonies within the phrase are often merely the byproducts of the contrapuntal motions of two or more melodic lines. Finally, in our exploration of motives at both the surface as well as deeper levels of a piece, we saw how analysis can reveal important musical correspondences that will help performers gain insight into a work's inner logic and structure.

TERMS AND CONCEPTS

- motivic processes
  - motivic nesting
  - motivic saturation
- motivic types
  - hidden motivic repetitions
  - intersection and intermovement types
  - motive vs. figure
  - motivic parallelism
  - strict, modified, developmental
  - tonal vs. real transposition
- motivic transformations
  - augmentation vs. diminution
- change of interval, change of meter
- embellishment
- fragmentation
- imitation
- interpolation
- inversion
- octave displacement
- reharmonization
- retrograde
- sequence
- stretto
- transposition (real and tonal)

PART 4

NEW CHORDS THAT COMPLETE THE DIATONIC SPECTRUM

We continue to explore the phrase model in the three chapters of Part 4. First, we add sevenths to the pre-dominant function. We then expand the pre-dominant function, just as we have expanded the tonic and dominant functions. We also complete our study of diatonic harmonies, including the submediant and mediant, and we learn how the internal components of phrases can be elaborated and how phrases can be extended.

CHAPTER 17

The Phrase Model Refined: Perception, Animation, and Expansion

We now know that the phrase model is central to tonal music. Composed of goal-oriented harmonic progressions and melodic structures, phrases are complete, organic entities. The ordered harmonic functions of tonic, pre-dominant, dominant, and return to tonic—and their accompanying contrapuntal expansions—underlie the musical phrase and provide it with a simple yet remarkably rich fabric on which composers over four centuries have relied.

We accomplish three tasks in this chapter:

1. We learn to hear entire phrases as single entities rather than a series of vertical sonorities.
2. We revisit the pre-dominant function to discover how it too can be enriched with seventh chords, how it can partner with the dominant to expand the tonic, and how it can be expanded by using contrapuntal (passing, neighboring) chords.
3. We see how phrases divide into smaller musical units called *subphrases*.

Hearing Phrases as Single Entities

When notating music from dictation, it is a good idea never to write the notes as they are being played. This is because the point of dictation is not to reproduce some correct answer, but to sharpen your skills as a listener. If you frantically try to capture every musical event as it happens (which is an impossibility anyway), your musical memory will not develop properly. Thus, the act of dictation can be compared to learning a role in a play: You do not memorize your lines letter by letter or word by word. Instead, you memorize in logical units driven by a context. Just as an actor must focus on the combining of words into phrases, sentences, and paragraphs, a musician must memorize units of music for successful dictation. So far most of these units have been small (one or two measures), but now you will learn to hear complete phrases and, eventually, combinations of phrases.

Because we are now going to work with phrases four measures in length, it is time to learn to stretch your memory to accommodate larger units. The techniques for memorizing units that we already covered are still in effect—however, now you will work at hearing hierarchically, with small units combining to create larger units. For example, at the end of Chapter 12 we learned that the tonic is usually considerably prolonged before moving to the pre-dominant in a phrase. The overall phrase structure can therefore be divided into two manageable units:

1. The first part of the phrase, composed of the initial tonic and its expansion through contrapuntal chords
2. The second part of the phrase, with faster harmonic rhythm comprising the pre-dominant (usually present), the dominant, and (if an authentic cadence) the final tonic.

Listening Guidelines

The first time you listen to a phrase, merely "take in" the phrase by asking yourself specific questions in order to obtain crucial information, such as:

- On what harmony and soprano scale degree does the phrase begin?
- What type of cadence is used?
- How is the cadence approached—where do I hear the final PD–D–T? This gives you an idea of the length of the two units of the phrase discussed earlier (tonic expansion and the remainder of the phrase).

After hearing the phrase for the first time, write the soprano pitches for the beginning chord and the cadence.

For the next two listenings:

- Memorize and notate the bass line for the tonic expansion. Remember that tonic chords will tend to be in metrically strong positions and that the subordinate chords will generally arise from neighboring or passing motion in the bass. Draw on the progressions we have already studied.
- Also focus on the soprano melody. Memorize it, sing it to yourself, and notate it.
- Make sure that the bass and soprano lines work together contrapuntally and create good voice leading.

For the final listening:

- Check your work. Listen for the placement of leaps and steps in the melodies. Listen for the return to tonic in the first part of the phrase and to the motion from T→PD→D→T.

EXERCISE INTERLUDE

LISTENING

DVD 2
CH 17
TRACK 1

17.1

On a separate sheet of manuscript paper, notate the bass and soprano for the given chorale-style exercises, following the listening guidelines just presented. All phrases have a key signature of three flats and are in $\frac{4}{4}$ meter (phrase D starts with a pickup note). Provide a two-level harmonic analysis.

17.2 Phrases from the literature

This exercise is similar to Exercise 17.1, except now you will hear phrases from the literature that include melodies with figurated accompaniments. On a separate sheet of manuscript paper, notate *only the bass* for each example, and provide a two-level harmonic analysis.

A. A♭ major, Chopin, *Grand valse brillante*, op. 34, no. 1
B. C minor, Schubert, Piano Sonata in C minor, op. posth., D. 958, *Allegro*
C. C major, Haydn, Piano Sonata no. 36 in C major, Hob. XVI.21, *Allegro*
D. D minor, Schumann, *Davidsbundlertänze*, op. 6, no. 10
E. E♭ major, Mozart, Symphony no. 24 in B♭ major, K. 182, *Andantino grazioso*
F. B♭ major, Mozart, Symphony no. 33 in B♭ major, K. 319, Minuetto
G. C minor, Mozart, Symphony no. 26 in E♭ major, K. 184, *Andante*
H. F major, Mozart, String Quintet in C major, K. 515, *Andante*

WORKBOOK
17.1–17.2

Pre-Dominant Seventh Chords: IV_7 (IV^6_5) and ii_7 (ii^6_5)

Just as a diatonic seventh can be added to the V triad to create V_7 in both major and minor keys, so too can a seventh be added to the pre-dominant ii and IV triads. Example 17.1A shows how ii becomes ii_7 and IV becomes IV_7 in major. Example 17.1B shows how ii° becomes $ii^{ø}_7$ and iv becomes iv_7 in minor. Example 17.1C shows the first measures of one of Chopin's nocturnes, in which he presents the cadential progression ii_7–V_7–I. Notice the tension created by the abrupt and unprepared entrance of the ii_7 chord. Further, the following V_7 chord sounds more like a *resolution* that discharges the tension of the ii_7 than a *dissonance*.

EXAMPLE 17.1 Chopin, Nocturne in B major, op. 62, no. 1

DVD 1
CH 17
TRACK 1

A. B.

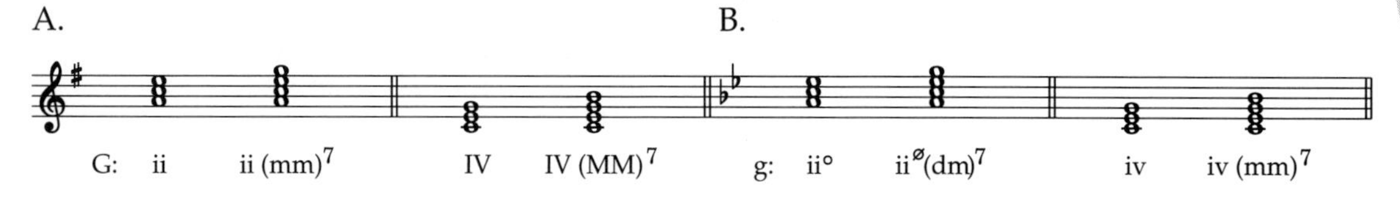

C1.

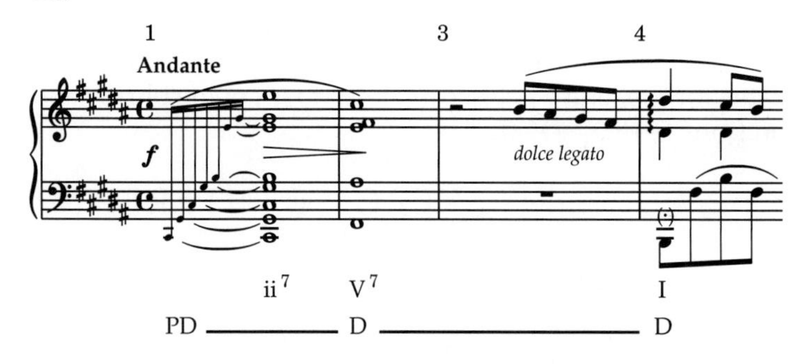

C2.

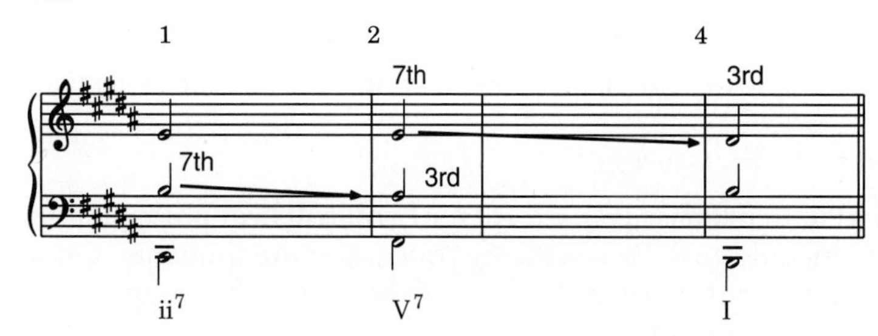

These pre-dominant seventh chords fall into a broad category of **nondominant seventh chords**—the chords in this category do not have a dominant (major–minor) or leading-tone (diminished–diminished) seventh chord quality. Nondominant seventh chords are widely used throughout the common-practice period; they provide color and contrast and are generally easy to implement.

Part Writing Nondominant Seventh Chords

1. You must *prepare* the seventh of the chord. This means that the note that becomes the seventh of the chord must be approached (in the same voice) by the same note (called *common-tone preparation* and the preferred means of preparation) or by the note one step higher.
2. You must *resolve* the seventh of the chord. As with the V_7 chord, the seventh of the nondominant seventh chord must step down in the next harmony.
3. Chords in inversion should be complete. Root-position seventh chords can omit the fifth (and double the root) in order to avoid parallels.

In general, pre-dominant seventh chords occur in all forms and inversions; however, we will see that ii^6_5 is the most common type and inversion of nondominant seventh chords. Example 17.2 illustrates ii^6_5 and the root-position ii_7 chord. Note how the seventh of the chord is prepared (marked with a *P*) and resolved (*R*). Also note that the ii^6_5 chord is complete but that the ii_7 chord omits the fifth and doubles the root to avoid parallels with the preceding tonic chord.

EXAMPLE 17.2

DVD 1 CH 17 TRACK 2

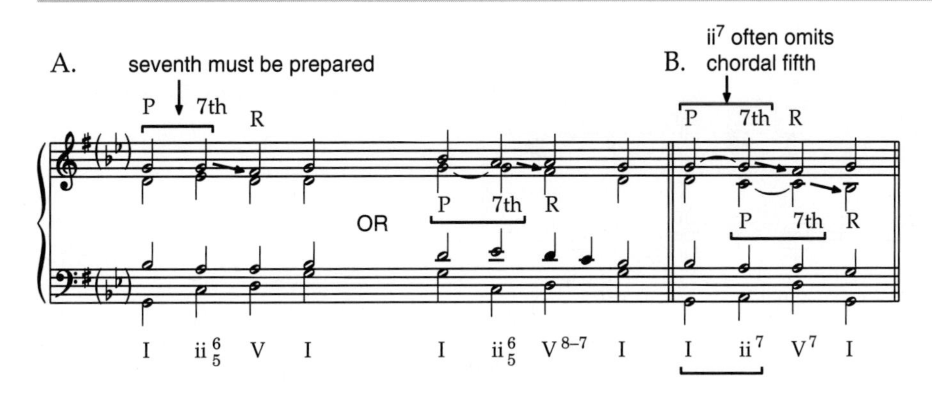

IV_7, not as common as ii_7, is a colorful sonority that may occur in root position. One must pay particular attention to the part writing from IV_7 to V; study Example 17.3A, where parallel fifths occur between IV and V. To avoid this part-writing error, IV_7 is often followed by V_7 (see Example 17.3B) or the cadential six-four chord (see Example 17.3C). Doubling the root of IV_7 ($\hat{4}$) and omitting the fifth not only helps to avoid parallels, but also prepares the seventh of V. Finally, the IV^6_5 chord, shown in Example 17.3D, typically resolves to a V^6_5 chord.

EXAMPLE 17.3

DVD 1
CH 17
TRACK 3

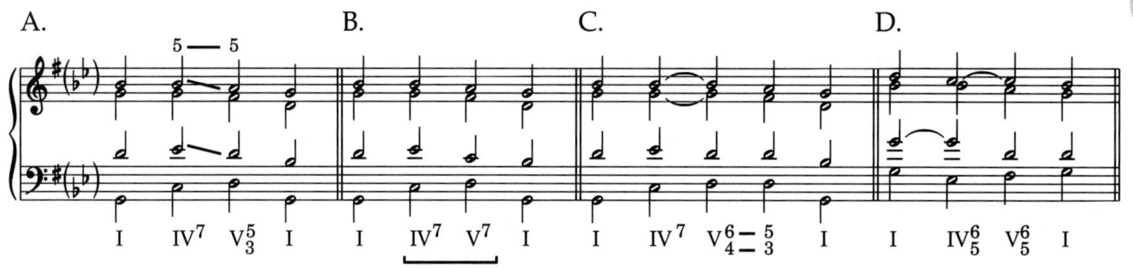

Analyzing Nondominant Seventh Chords

Composers often highlight nondominant seventh chords by suspending one of their chordal members. However, such suspensions can sometimes be misinterpreted as chord members, thus rendering a roman numeral label incorrect. Let's look at ii^6_5, a particular favorite of composers, to which suspensions can be applied. Since a form of the tonic usually precedes ii^6_5, $\hat{3}$ is the perfect candidate to suspend, since it will fall naturally to $\hat{2}$. See Example 17.4A. In Example 17.4A1, tonic moves to $\text{ii}^{\o 6}_5$, but in Example 17.4A2, $\hat{3}$ is suspended, displacing the chordal root of ii^6_5, $\hat{2}$. Notice that this suspended pitch ($\hat{3}$) *looks* like it could be a chordal member not of a ii_7 chord, but of a root-position iv_7 harmony. However, it *sounds* like a suspension that resolves correctly to the chord tone D ($\hat{2}$). As always, we must interpret music as it sounds and as those sounds fit into the context. Example 17.4B and C illustrate similar situations in two works by Schumann. Note that the suspensions are part of the motivic fabric of each example; therefore interpreting them in one context as chord tones but in another as nonchord tones is problematic.

EXAMPLE 17.4

DVD 1
CH 17
TRACK 4

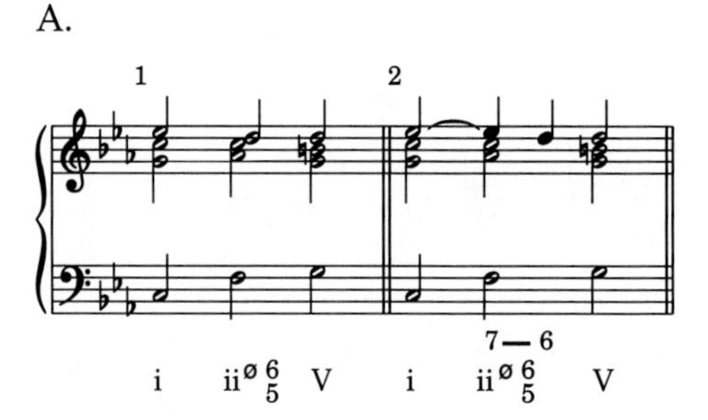

B. Schumann, "Winterzeit," from *Album for the Young*, op. 68

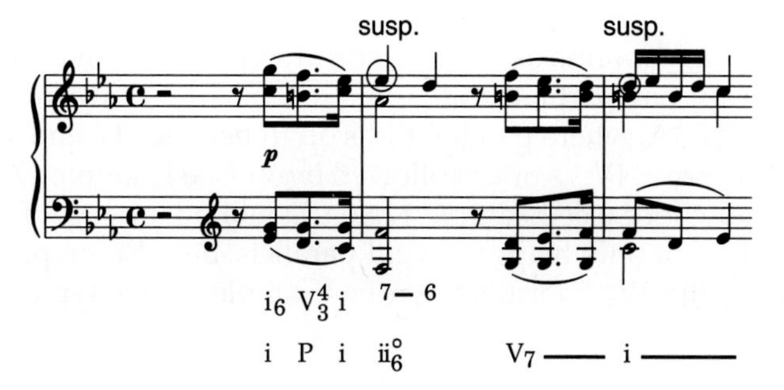

C. ***, From *Album for the Young,* op. 68

EXERCISE INTERLUDE

PERFORMING

17.3

The following arpeggiations create progressions that incorporate pre-dominant seventh chords. Sing them and/or play them on an instrument. Listen to how often harmonies change; then analyze the progressions with roman numerals.

WRITING

17.4 Error Detection and Correction

The short examples shown contain multiple part-writing and spelling errors. Label each error and then rewrite the example on a separate sheet of manuscript paper. Then play the correct version on the piano and transpose it to one other key of your choice.

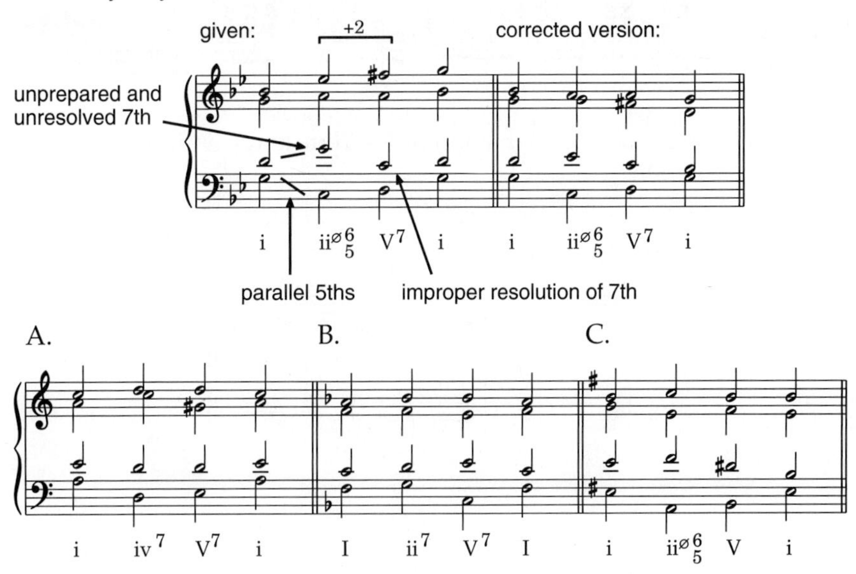

ANALYSIS

17.5

Provide a two-level harmonic analysis for the following excerpts. Next, circle and label the preparation and resolution of pre-dominant seventh chords.

A. Bach, "O Welt, ich muss dich lassen"

B. Corelli Violin Sonata no. 3, op. 2, no. 3, Preludio, *Largo*

C. Mendelssohn, *Lieder ohne Worte* ("Songs without Words"), no. 20 in E♭ major, op. 53

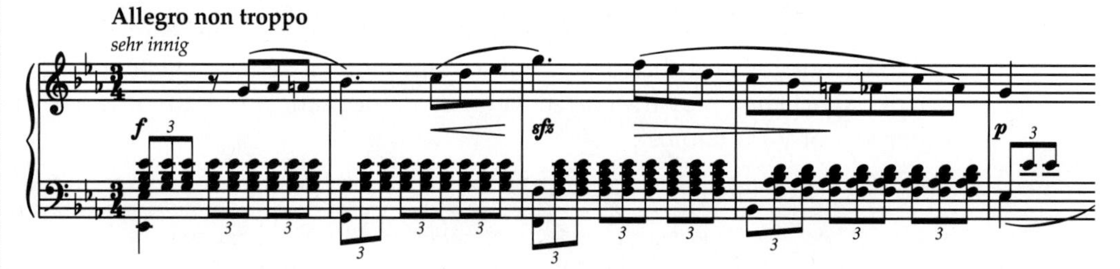

D. Michel Corrett, Sarabanda in E minor for Flute and Continuo

In m. 1, at the asterisk (*), which chord label is more appropriate for a tonic expansion: ii_7 or vii°_6?

E. Beethoven, Minuet for Piano in E♭ major, WoO 82

Is the chord in m. 3 IV_7 or ii^6_5? Your decision rests on the function of the G4 in the soprano.

WORKBOOK
17.3–17.4

F. Mahler, Symphony no. 4 in G major, bedächtig, nichteilen

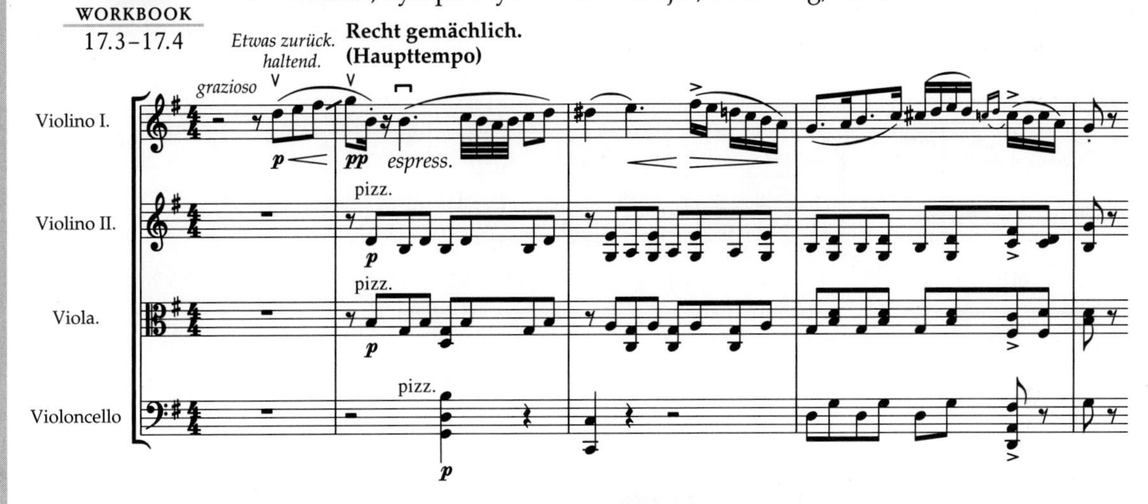

The Pre-Dominant in Embedded Phrase Models

The progression T–PD–D–T occurs not only over the course of the phrase but also—as we saw in Example 12.17—in microcosm within a phrase. In fact, one or more "mini–T–PD–D–T" progressions may occur anywhere within the initial tonic part of the phrase. Although these mini-progressions end with tonic (and are, therefore, tonally closed), they do not act as points of arrival in the same way cadences do. We will call such mini-progressions **embedded phrase models (EPMs)**.

Keep the following in mind when analyzing a phrase with multiple T–PD–D–T progressions: A second-level analysis has just one overall T–PD–D–T progression. Other occurrences of T–PD–D–T earlier in the phrase are not cadential—they are EPMs and expand the tonic.

Consider Example 17.5. Note that there are two sets of PD–D–T progressions within the phrase but that their functions are very different from one another. The first PD–D–T is within the first part of the phrase and expands the tonic. The second PD–D–T occurs at the end of the phrase and includes the cadence.

EXAMPLE 17.5

DVD 1
CH 17
TRACK 5

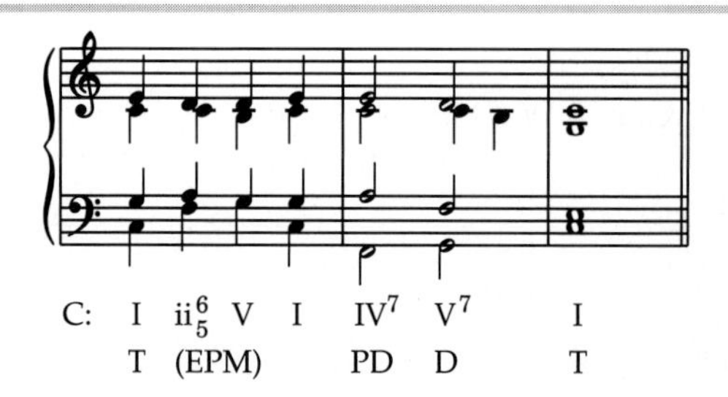

Composers often distinguish EPMs from actual cadences by making them sound more contrapuntal. This is achieved by weakening the PD and D harmonies through the use of inversions. Example 17.6 shows four important settings of EPMs.

EXAMPLE 17.6

DVD 1
CH 17
TRACK 6

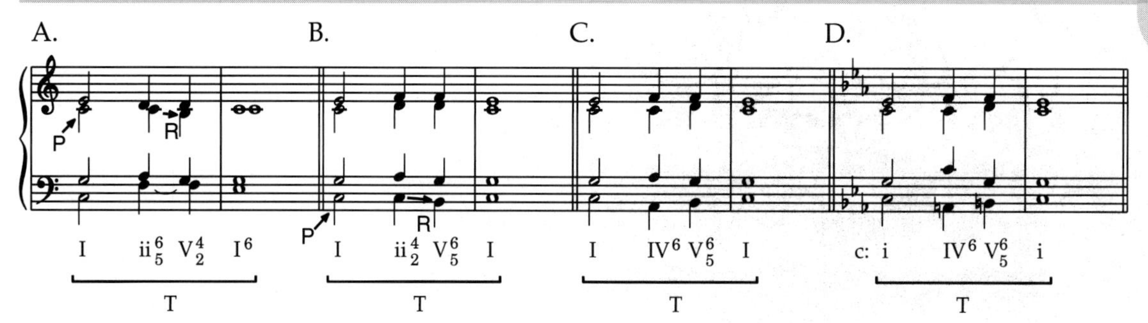

- Example 17.6A places the dominant in a weak inversion and thus evades a cadence.
- Example 17.6B shows an EPM that affords great stability and balance between outer voices, given the neighboring motion in the bass and soprano; it also includes a common and important use of the pre-dominant (ii^4_2, with the seventh prepared and resolved in the bass).
- In Example 17.6C, the bass leap of a third and stepwise return to $\hat{1}$ contrasts with the upper-voice neighboring motion.
- Example 17.6D shows the same progression as Example 14.6C, in minor. Note that $\hat{6}$ and $\hat{7}$ are raised to avoid awkward intervals in the bass melody.

Contrapuntal Cadences

As we know, structural cadences involve root-position dominant and tonic harmonies. However, composers occasionally close phrases using inverted dominant and tonic harmonies, often in order to save the powerful root-position V until a more dramatic and final-sounding cadence is required. Cadences in which either the dominant or the tonic or both are inverted are called **contrapuntal cadences**. Contrapuntal cadences often involve the very harmonies used in EPMs (e.g., I–IV_6–V^6_5–I) as well as others, including those shown in Example 17.7. Note that not only V, but also $vii°_6$ participate in the authentic motions.

Example 17.7C presents the first vocal phrase from Schubert's song "Die Krähe." The first three measures that expand tonic are followed by the very weak vii°$_6$–i to close the phrase. Clearly this four-measure excerpt has many of the hallmarks of a phrase: Both melody and accompaniment descend over the course of the excerpt and close on $\hat{1}$ (the voice and piano unisons dramatize the text; what better way to show the crow's attachment to the tired protagonist than to double—indeed, shadow—the voice and piano at the unison). We might hear the weak vii°$_6$—encountered much more often in tonic expansions—to substitute for, yet certainly function as, the dominant that helps to close the phrase. Of course it is also possible to view the four-measure excerpt as merely a tonic expansion and therefore not a phrase, since there is no strong root-position harmonic motion from T through D. We can see that even such apparently simple decisions as whether a musical unit is a phrase or not often become a matter of interpretation.

EXAMPLE 17.7

DVD 1
CH 17
TRACK 7

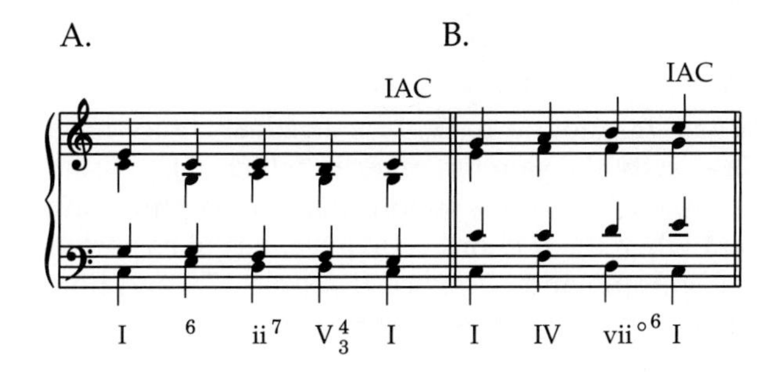

C. Schubert, "Die Krähe," from *Winterreise*

Expansion of the Pre-Dominant

Just as the tonic and the dominant can be expanded, so can the pre-dominant. An obvious way would be to move from ii$_6$ to ii, or vice versa, creating a voice exchange, as seen in the opening of Beethoven's fourth piano concerto (Example 17.8).

EXAMPLE 17.8 Beethoven, Piano Concerto no. 4 in G major, op. 58

DVD 1
CH 17
TRACK 8

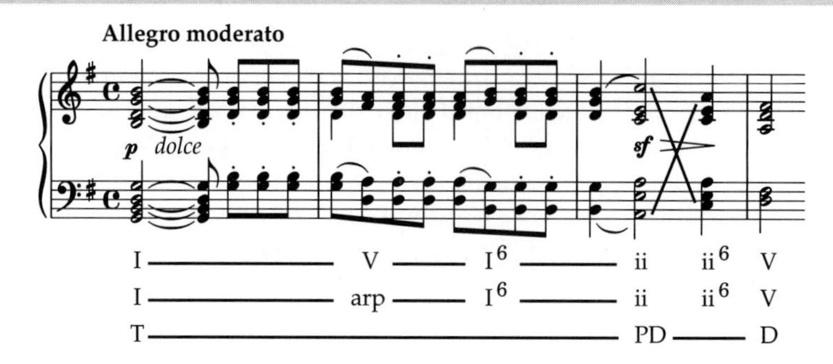

Another, more subtle and important technique used to expand the pre-dominant is the "IV–ii complex" described in Chapter 12. Pre-dominants may also be expanded through passing and neighboring chords, in the same ways as we have used them to expand the tonic and the dominant. We now look at four additional ways the pre-dominant can be expanded.

A Passing Chord Between ii and ii_6 (or Between ii_6 and ii)

If we wish to expand ii in a passing motion to ii_6, I_6 is an ideal choice for a passing chord. This works in exactly the same manner in which $vii°_6$ passes between I and I_6. Here, however, the I_6 chord is subordinate to the prevailing pre-dominant. This is apparent when the I_6 chord is on a weak beat as part of a voice exchange between the soprano and bass. See Example 17.9 and note the voice exchange, a common occurrence in this progression.

EXAMPLE 17.9 Expanding ii Using I as Passing Harmony

DVD 1
CH 17
TRACK 9

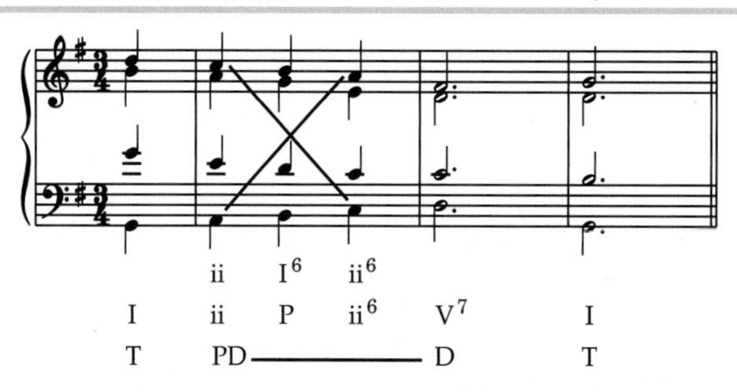

A Passing Chord Between IV and IV_6 (or Between IV_6 and IV)

A tonic chord helps to expand the subdominant as well. Listen to Example 17.10, an excerpt from Bach's *St. Matthew Passion* that contains an expanded iv. The vertical sonority—a passing i^6_4 chord—seen in beat 2 of m. 2 is on a weak beat and is in the middle of a voice exchange between the soprano and the bass. *Note*: A weak I_6 can be used to expand the supertonic (ii), but the reverse—$ii_{(6)}$ used to expand the tonic—is not possible.

EXAMPLE 17.10 **Bach, "Gerne will ich mich bequemen" ("Gladly Will I Take My Portion"), *St. Matthew Passion*, BWV 244**

DVD 1
CH 17
TRACK 10

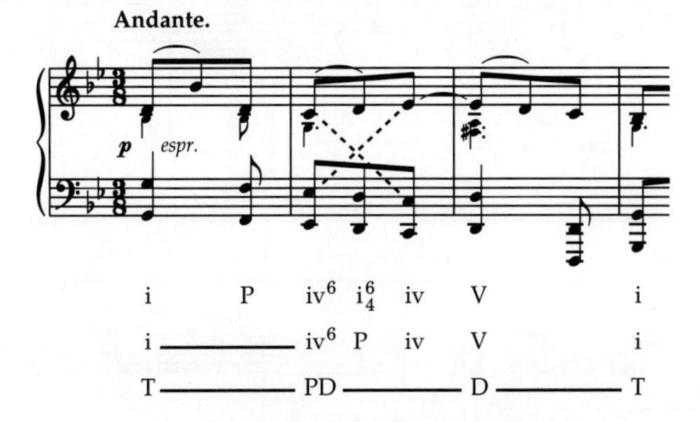

A Passing Chord Moving from IV$_6$ (IV$^6_5$) to ii$^6_5$

Expanding the pre-dominant by moving from IV$_6$ (IV$^6_5$) to ii$^6_5$ invokes both pre-dominant harmonies through voice leading. As you may remember, this technique embodies the expansion of the IV–ii complex in Chapter 12. The motion from IV$^6_5$ to ii$^6_5$ typically involves a passing $^6_4$ chord and a voice exchange. Note the smooth voice leading in Example 17.11: Three voices move by step, and the fourth holds a common tone.

EXAMPLE 17.11

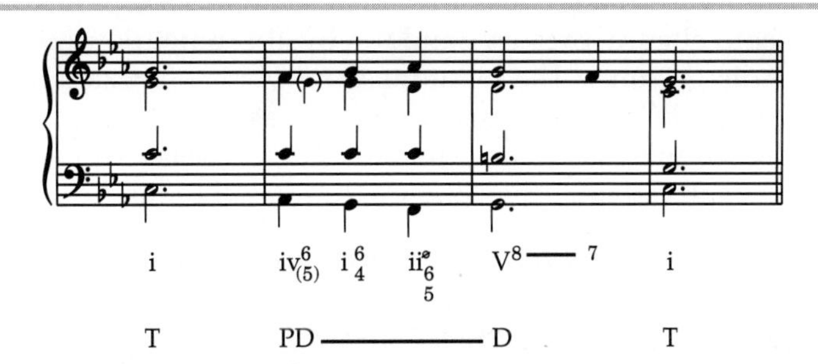

Restate Tonic Material Up a Step

One other way to expand the pre-dominant—specifically, the supertonic—is to restate, up a step, musical material that was initially stated in the tonic, before moving on to the dominant. Consider Example 17.12, where the initial material in mm. 1–2 repeats up a step in mm. 5–6. Note the expansion of the supertonic (E-minor harmony) in mm. 5–7. The chromatically altered pitch D♯^{5} (in m. 6) creates a temporary leading tone that belongs to the E-minor scale; thus, the power of the E-minor chord is expanded by invoking its leading tone. The expanded ii leads to the cadential dominant in m. 7. Note that the progression opens with an incomplete EPM: The opening tonic leads to a non-cadential PD–D. The dominant in m. 4 merely separates the motion from T (m. 1) to PD (m. 5) and does *not* lead directly to the ii in m. 5.

EXAMPLE 17.12 Mozart, Piano Sonata in D major, K. 576, *Allegro*

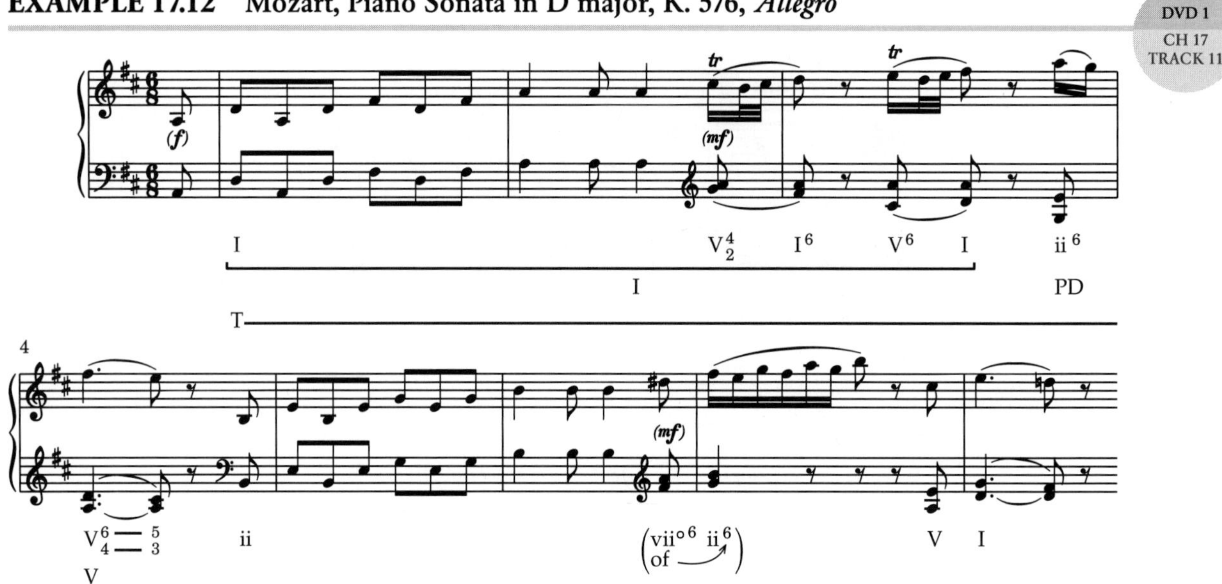

Subphrases

WORKBOOK
17.5–17.7

A complete phrase may comprise two or more smaller units called *subphrases*. A **subphrase** is a relatively independent part of a phrase that is marked by a pause (called a **caesura**) and/or by the repetition and variation of short melodic gestures. The eight-measure phrase in Example 17.13 divides into three subphrases. The first two subphrases are both two measures long, and each ends with a caesura. The final subphrase is four measures long and ends with a half cadence (thus ending the overall phrase).

EXAMPLE 17.13 Haydn, Symphony no. 100 in G major, "Military," *Allegretto*

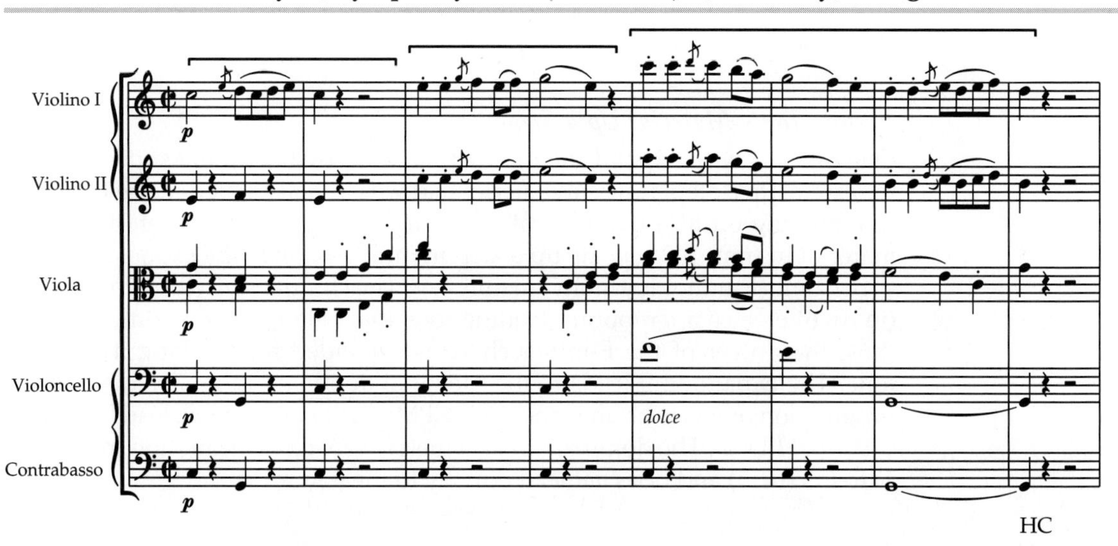

The presence of a caesura does not guarantee the presence of subphrases. For example, in the opening of Example 17.14, the vocal line is clearly divided into two gestures, where the initial gesture restarts in m. 3. However, a glance at the harmony reveals a single continuous harmonic motion over the four-measure phrase. The V^4_3 harmony in the second measure functions as a bass passing tone between $\hat{1}$ in m. 1 and $\hat{3}$ in m. 3. This I_6 then leads to the predominant-dominant in mm. 3 and 4. The contiguous stepwise-fifth ascent combined with a goal-oriented harmonic progression and cadence in m. 4 results in a phrase that does not contain subphrases.

EXAMPLE 17.14 Schubert, "Des Müllers Blumen" ("The Miller's Flowers"), from *Die schöne Müllerin*, D. 795

DVD 1
CH 17
TRACK 13

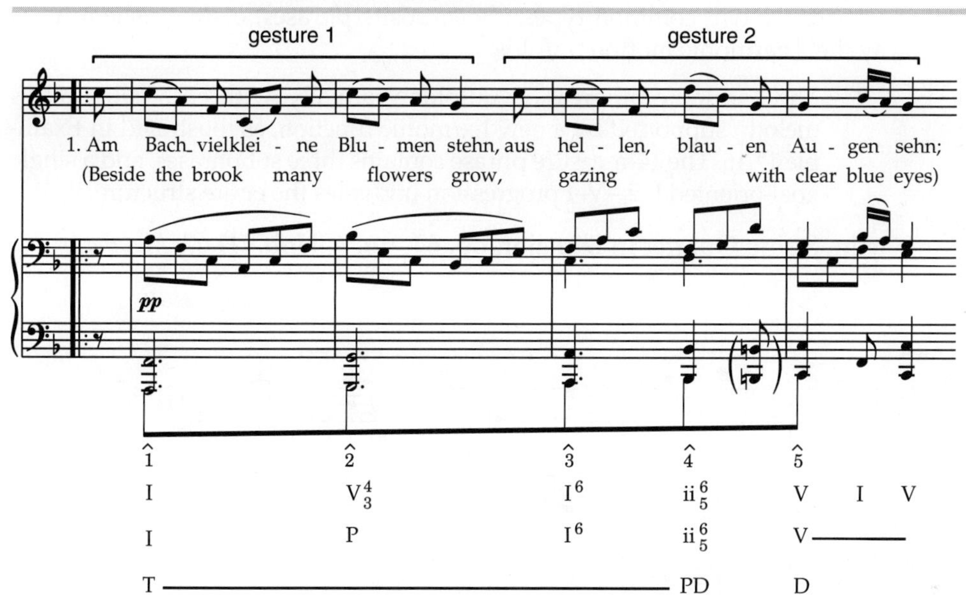

Conversely, there may be subphrases within a phrase, even if there are no caesuras present. The eight-measure phrase in Example 17.15 moves from the tonic to a half cadence. Despite the nearly continuous movement, the phrase contains three subphrases, the first two of which are two measures long (delineated by their motivic structure), and the third of which is four measures long. (Roman numerals are given only for harmonies that begin and end the subphrases since we have not yet covered some of the chords within the subphrases.)

EXAMPLE 17.15 Schubert, Symphony no. 4 in C minor, "Tragic," *Andante*

DVD 1
CH 17
TRACK 14

Composite Phrases

Phrases that comprise three or more subphrases are called *composite phrases*. The phrases in Examples 17.13 and 17.15 are both composite phrases. Composite phrases—like all phrases—contain only one structural harmonic progression and one cadence, but they are often longer than the more common four-measure phrases that we have encountered. Composite phrases are usually eight or more measures in length, and they give the aural impression of being composed in an additive, stage-by-stage process rather than as a single sweeping motion.

There are two common types of composite phrases, distinguished in the way their harmonic motion unfolds.

1. The harmonic progression unfolds gradually, with each subphrase's melody supported by a new harmonic function, as illustrated in Example 17.16. The 14-measure phrase contains three subphrases, and a single goal-oriented I–ii_6–V–I progression underlies the entire structure.

EXAMPLE 17.16 Haydn, String Quartet in B♭ major, op. 64, no. 3, Hob. III.67, *Menuetto*

DVD 1 CH 17 TRACK 15

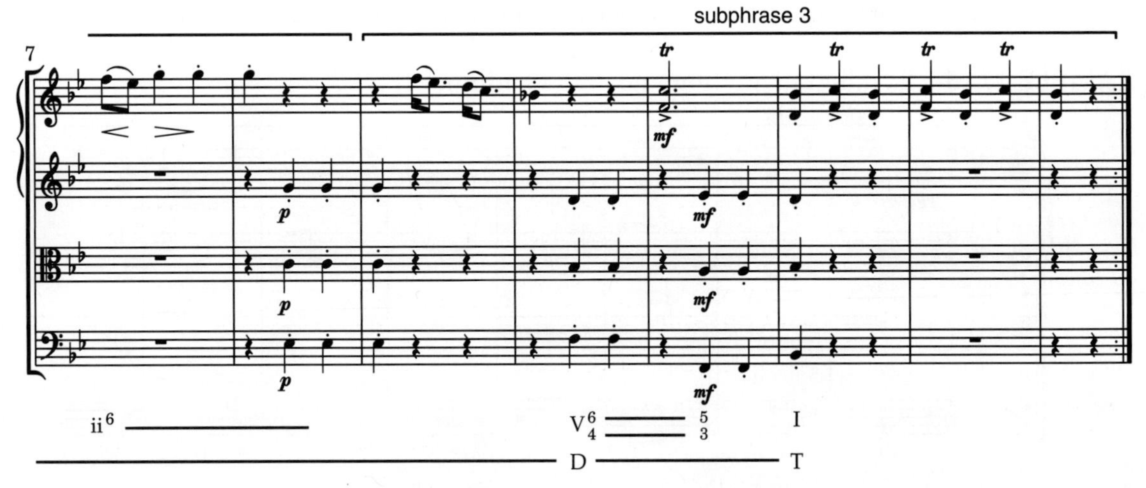

2. The harmonic progression stays on the initial tonic through most of the subphrases, changing to PD, D, and T only at the very end of the phrase. Pro-

jecting this structure in performance enhances the musical drama considerably. The first two subphrases in Example 17.17 close on the tonic. Subphrase 1 ends in parallel tenths, surely a weak conclusion, and subphrase 2, while featuring a ii–V_7–I ending, still feels more like the beginning of a new phrase that is cut short with a T–PD–D gesture that is more a harmonization of the soprano melody $\hat{3}$–$\hat{4}$–$\hat{3}$ than an actual cadence. It is only with the deceleration of the melody to quarter notes and the trill that the final subphrase brings the entire structure to a close in m. 8 (see Example 17.17).

EXAMPLE 17.17 Haydn, Piano Sonata no. 30 in D major, Hob. XVI.19, *Moderato*

DVD 1
CH 17
TRACK 16

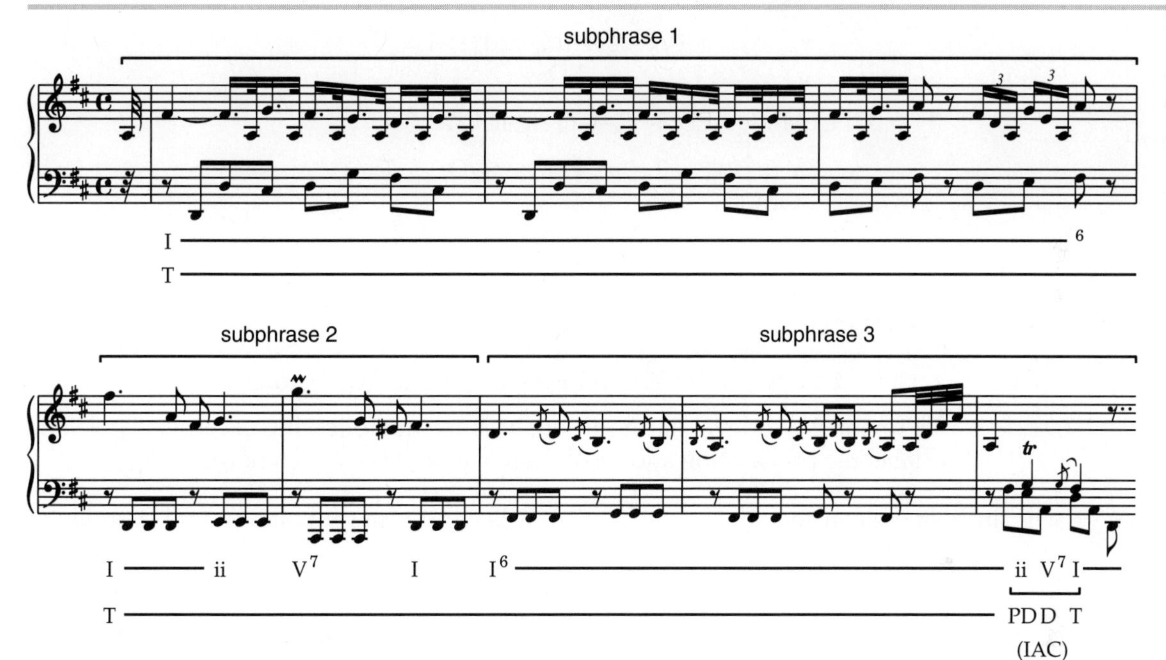

Notice in Example 17.17 how Haydn balances the varying subphrase lengths with an overall graceful symmetry. The last subphrase brings the melody back down from $\hat{5}$ to its resting place, $\hat{3}$. The symmetrical shape and harmonic and melodic structure of the passage are summarized in Example 17.18.

EXAMPLE 17.18

Identification and interpretation of subphrases and composite phrases is often, if not usually, a subjective enterprise. In fact, the interpretations of Examples 17.13–17.17 are all debatable to some extent, and alternate viewpoints are certainly possible.

EXERCISE INTERLUDE

WRITING

17.6

A. Write the given progressions that contain EPMs or expanded pre-dominants in the key of A major and a meter of your choice.

EPMS: $\text{I–ii}^4_2\text{–V}^6_5\text{–I–IV–V}_7\text{–I}$

T________PD D T

Or

$\text{i–IV}_6\text{–V}^6_5\text{–i–ii}^{\varnothing 6}_5\text{–cad}^{6}_{4}{}^{–5}_{–3}\text{–i}$

T________PD D T

B. expanded PD: $\text{I–V}^6_5\text{–I–ii}_6\text{–I}_6\text{–ii–cad}^{6}_{4}{}^{–5}_{–3}\text{–I}$

T_____PD______D____T

Or

$\text{i–i}_6\text{–V}^4_3\text{–i–iv}_6\text{–i}^6_4\text{–ii}^{\varnothing 6}_5\text{–cad}^{6}_{4}{}^{–5}_{–3}\text{–i}$

T_______PD________D____T

ANALYSIS

17.7 Analysis of EPMs and Pre-Dominant Expansions

Provide a two-level harmonic analysis for the following excerpts. Circle and label the preparation and resolution of any PD seventh chords.

A. Bach, "In allen meinen Taten"

B. Bach, "O Haupt voll Blut und Wunden"

C. Bach, "Des heil'gen Geistes reiche Gnad"

D. Mozart, Symphony no. 36 in C major, "Linz," K. 425, *Poco adagio*

E. Bach, Siciliana from Flute Sonata in E♭ major, BWV 1031

F. Mendelssohn, *Lieder ohne Worte* ("Songs Without Words"), no. 45, in C major, op. 102

G. Mozart, Symphony in C major, "Linz", K. 425, *Presto*

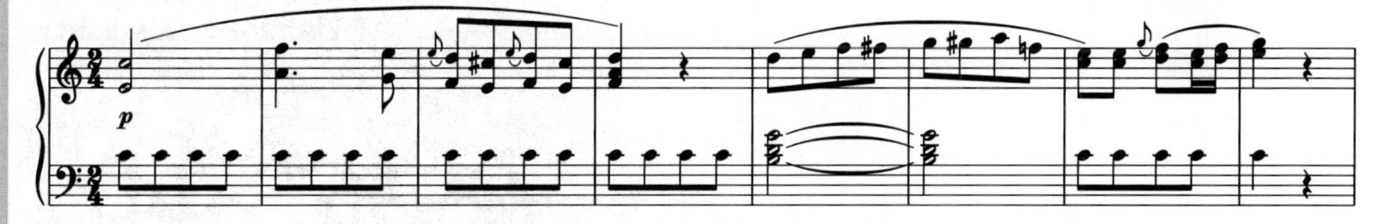

KEYBOARD

17.8 Embedded Phrase Model and Contrapuntal Cadences

The following progressions feature weak T–PD–D–T functions. Play each in major and minor keys up to and including two sharps and two flats. Be able to sing either outer voice while playing the other three voices.

A.

B.

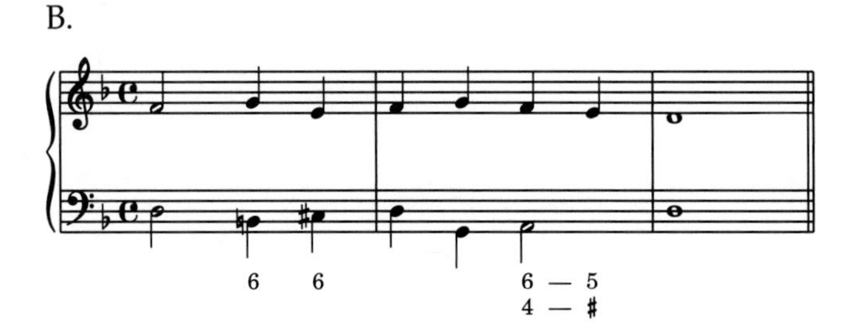

C.

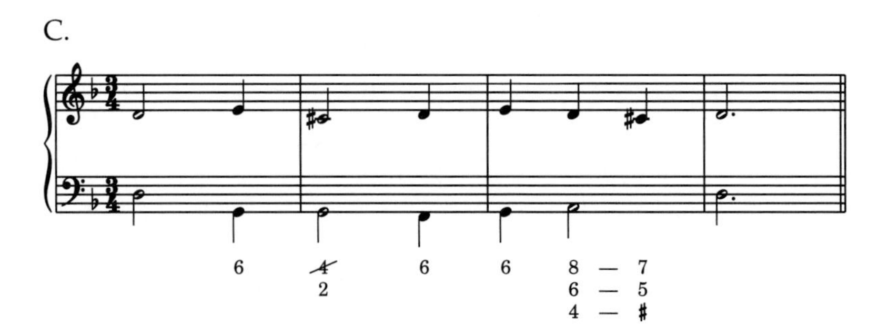

17.9 Soprano and Bass Harmonization

WORKBOOK
17.8–17.9

Harmonize each of the following soprano and bass scale degree fragments in four-voice keyboard style. Each fragment includes an EPM—use inversions of PD and/or D chord to weaken the cadential motion. Play at the keyboard in two keys of your choice.

Soprano fragments:

A. $\hat{3}$–$\hat{2}$–$\hat{1}$
B. $\hat{3}$–$\hat{4}$–$\hat{4}$–$\hat{3}$
C. $\hat{1}$–$\hat{2}$–$\hat{3}$–$\hat{4}$–$\hat{3}$–$\hat{2}$–$\hat{1}$

Bass fragments:

D. $\hat{8}$–$\hat{6}$–$\hat{7}$–$\hat{8}$
E. $\hat{1}$–$\hat{4}$–$\hat{4}$–$\hat{3}$
F. $\hat{1}$–$\hat{4}$–$\hat{2}$–$\hat{1}$

LISTENING

17.10

The following examples contain nondominant seventh chords, expanded predominants, contrapuntal cadences, and EPMs. Notate the bass lines and provide a first- and second-level analysis.

A. Mendelssohn, Concerto for Violin, op. 64, *Allegro, molto appassionato*

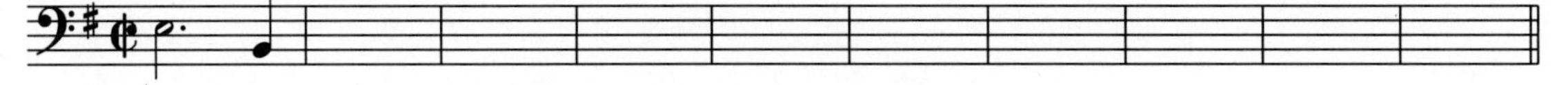

B. Marcello, Sonata no. 9 in A major for Harpsichord

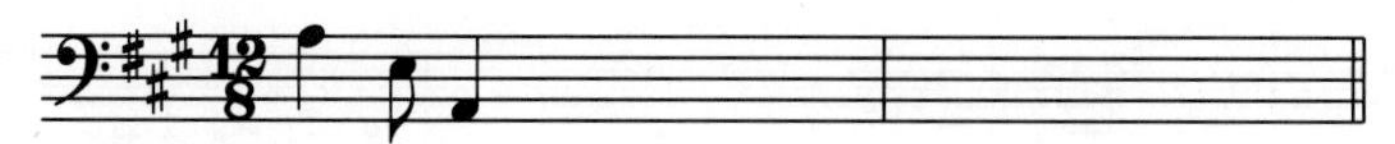

C. Bach, Chorale: "Nun Lob', Mein Seele', den Herren"

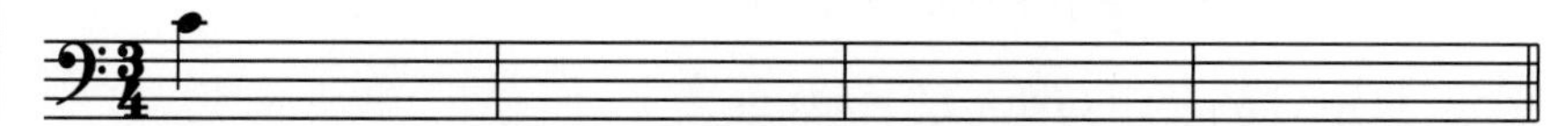

D. Haydn, Symphony in F♯ minor ("Farewell"), Hob. I:45 *Allegro*

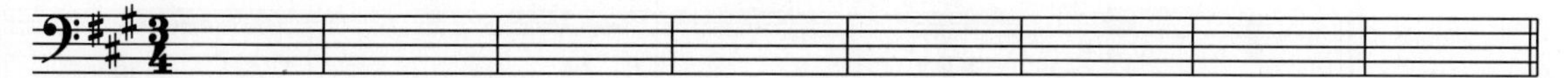

E. Corelli, Trio Sonata in C major, op. 2, no. 3, *Adagio*

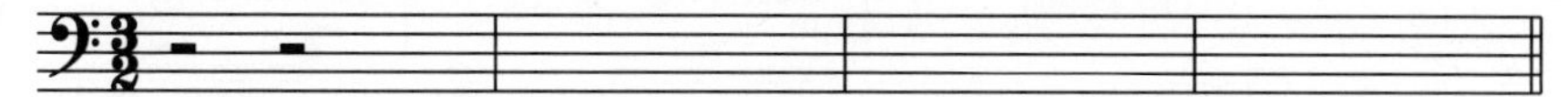

F. Bach, "Aus Liebe will mein Heiland Sterben," from *St. Matthew Passion*, BWV 244 (Note treble clef)

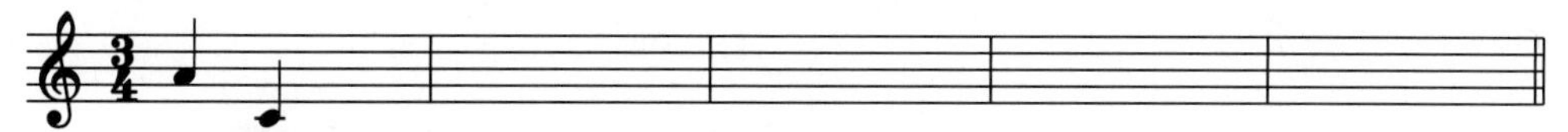

DVD 2
CH 17
TRACK 6

ANALYSIS

17.11 Subphrases

Bracket subphrases and provide a first- and second-level analysis that reveals T, PD, D, and T.

A. Schubert, Symphony no. 9 in C major, Scherzo

B. Haydn, Piano Sonata no. 29 in E♭ major, Hob. XVI:45, *Moderato*

C. Haydn, Symphony no. 92 in G major, "Oxford," *Andante*

TERMS AND CONCEPTS

- caesura
- composite phrase
- contrapuntal cadence
- embedded phrase model
- expansion of the pre-dominant
- nondominant seventh chord
- passing tonic
- subphrase

CHAPTER 18

The Submediant: A New Diatonic Harmony, and Further Extensions of the Phrase Model

The next two chapters introduce the last of the diatonic harmonies: the submediant and the mediant. These chords always provide dramatic color contrast to the prevailing key and play important roles supporting the tonic, pre-dominant, and dominant pillars of the phrase model.

The Submediant

In a major key, the submediant harmony (vi) is a minor triad. Because IV, V, and I are all major triads in a major key, the introduction of a minor sonority can provide a welcome relief from the prevailing harmonic color. In a minor key, the submediant harmony (VI) is a major triad, so again it offers contrast to the minor and diminished harmonies i, iv, and ii°. The harmonic contexts in which the submediant typically occurs are inextricably tied to the three basic **root motions** of tonal music:

- the **descending fifth**, previously seen in the authentic cadence, V–I
- the **ascending second**, which we have seen in the progession IV–V
- the **descending third**

The Submediant as Bridge in the Descending-Thirds Progression

Our discussion of the submediant's first function arises out of the root motion by descending thirds (Example 18.1).

EXAMPLE 18.1

Harmonies:	I	-	vi	-	IV	-
Bass:	$\hat{1}$					
			$\hat{6}$			
					$\hat{4}$	

Listen to Example 18.2. It demonstrates a progression that characterizes much of the rock and roll music of the 1950s and early 1960s. Take a moment to enjoy the voice leading of that style, which provides for a heavy dose of parallel perfect intervals. Example 18.2B illustrates the same progression but places it in the minor mode and uses common-practice voice leading to connect the chords. In these examples, the submediant is both attained and departed from by means of a descending third: I–vi and vi–IV. Taken together, the three roots $\hat{1}$–$\hat{6}$–$\hat{4}$ arpeggiate a triad of sorts. This progression is therefore often called a descending **harmonic arpeggiation**. The submediant in descending harmonic arpeggiations provides a way station, or bridge, connecting the tonic to the pre-dominant.

EXAMPLE 18.2

DVD 1 CH 18 TRACK 1

A.

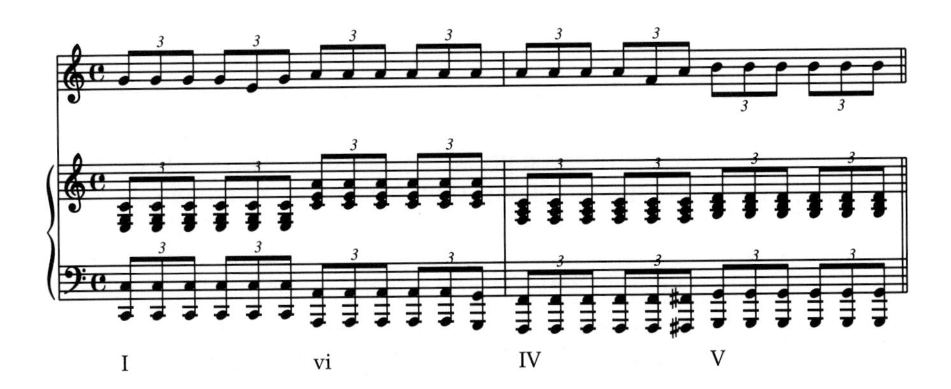

B.

Note: The submediant often acts in two seemingly contradictory ways within a phrase:

1. It acts as extension of the tonic. It has two common tones with the I chord and can be seen as arising from a contrapuntal 5–6 motion.
2. It acts as a pre-pre-dominant chord, because it prepares and precedes the PD chord.

Although vi exhibits both qualities, we will tend to analyze vi under "T" at the second level. However, the arrowhead is added to show the bridging function of vi.

The Submediant in the Descending-Circle-of-Fifths Progression

Another function of the submediant arises from its participation in descending-fifths progressions. It fits nicely into such a progression, extending the circle-of-fifths progression as seen in Example 18.3.

EXAMPLE 18.3

DVD 1 CH 18 TRACK 2

Listen to Example 18.4. The vi chord appears twice, first as part of an EPM that prolongs the tonic and then as part of the phrase's structural cadence. Both times it is part of a descending-fifths progression.

EXAMPLE 18.4 Beethoven, Violin Sonata no. 5 in F major ("Spring"), op. 24, *Allegro*

DVD 1 CH 18 TRACK 3

In Example 18.5 (Schubert), the vi–ii$_6$ progression blends the strong descending-fifths motion with a new means of obtaining a **melodic bass arpeggiation** : $\hat{1}$–$\hat{6}$–$\hat{4}$.

EXAMPLE 18.5 Schubert, "Frühlingstraum" ("A Dream of Springtime"), *Winterreise*, D. 911, no. 11

DVD 1 CH 18 TRACK 4

In Chapter 12 we praised the qualities of ii_6–V motion, in which a convincing descending-fifths root motion combines with smooth $\hat{4}$–$\hat{5}$ bass motion. We see the same ii_6–V motion in the major-mode progression I–vi–ii_6–V–I, as shown in Example 18.5.

The Submediant as Tonic Substitute in Ascending-Seconds Progressions

So far we have seen vi appear as a bridging harmony within a descending-thirds progression and as a harmony that initiates a descending-fifths progression. A third functional possibility is for vi to substitute for the tonic chord in the cadential progression V–I; the resulting progression is a root motion by ascending second (V–vi). This is shown in Example 18.6, where V moves to vi and the bass moves from $\hat{5}$ to $\hat{6}$. Haydn thwarts the arrival of the tonic by moving to vi. This suspenseful drama is intensified by the fermata as well as by the florid ascent in the first violin to a very high register. In general, the progression V–vi is called a **deceptive motion** (also called *evaded cadence*), since the listener expects one outcome (V–I) but hears another (V–vi).

EXAMPLE 18.6 Haydn, String Quartet in D minor ("Quinten"), op. 76, no. 2, Hob. III.76, *Andante o più tosto allegretto*

DVD 1 CH 18 TRACK 5

At this point, as we leave you suspended on vi and craving the tonic at the end of Example 18.6, you are likely wondering what happens next. In general, a deceptive motion seems to rewind the phrase model back to the pre-dominant and sometimes even to the tonic, which is followed by an authentic cadence. Listen to Example 18.7. The dramatic deceptive motion in m. 12 is followed by a return to tonic, at which point a varied repetition of the previous phrase leads to the PAC.

EXAMPLE 18.7 Mozart, Trio in E♭ major, K. 498, *Andante*

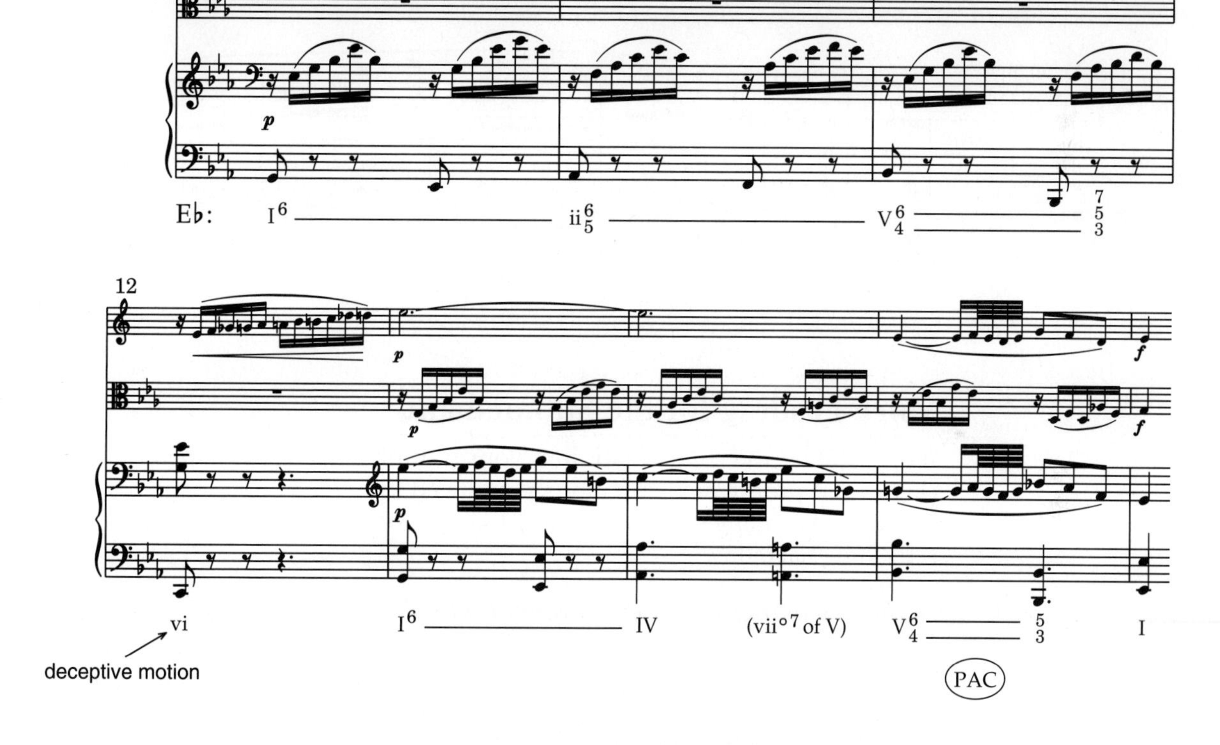

The Submediant as the Pre-Dominant

Occasionally, vi immediately precedes the dominant and, therefore, functions as the pre-dominant chord. Listen to Example 18.8; this famous opening features vi as a pre-dominant. As such, it allows for the motive of a descending second ($\hat{6}$–$\hat{5}$) to occur in the bass. We have already encountered the importance of this scale degree melodic motive in Chapter 16, but now we see how it can participate in the harmonic domain of the music. Given the strong outer-voice counterpoint—10–5–10—that undergirds the progression, composers often use this very progression in their works; see Example 18.8B for Chopin's 70-year-earlier setting of it, and in the same key as Mahler's movement.

EXAMPLE 18.8

A. Mahler, Symphony no. 2 in C minor ("Resurrection"), "Urlicht"

B. Chopin, Scherzo no. 2 in B♭ minor, op. 31

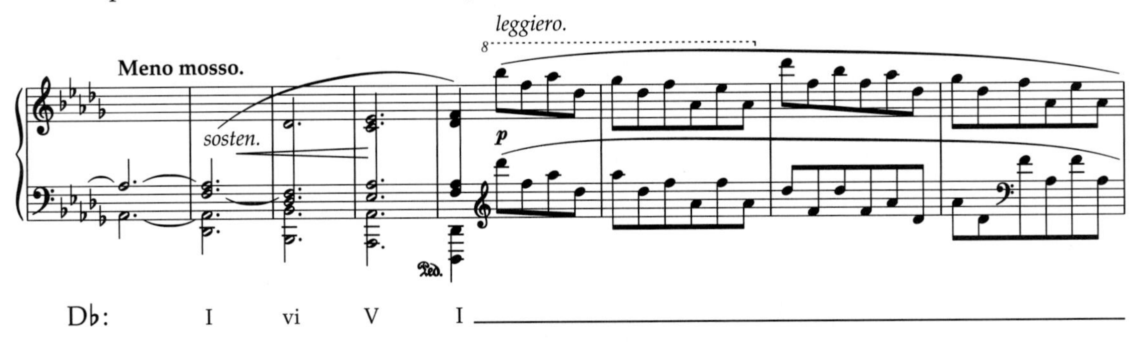

Voice Leading for the Submediant

Incorporating the submediant into your writing projects is simple. Also, because your progressions previously involved only tonic, dominant, and predominant harmonies, you will enjoy looking for interesting places to use this refreshing harmony.

In the Descending-Thirds Progression, I–vi–IV

The chords I and vi share two common tones ($\hat{1}$ and $\hat{3}$), and the chords vi and IV share two common tones ($\hat{6}$ and $\hat{1}$). So, when writing the descending-thirds progression, I–vi–IV, keep all of the common tones; any voice that moves should move up by step (Example 18.9).

EXAMPLE 18.9

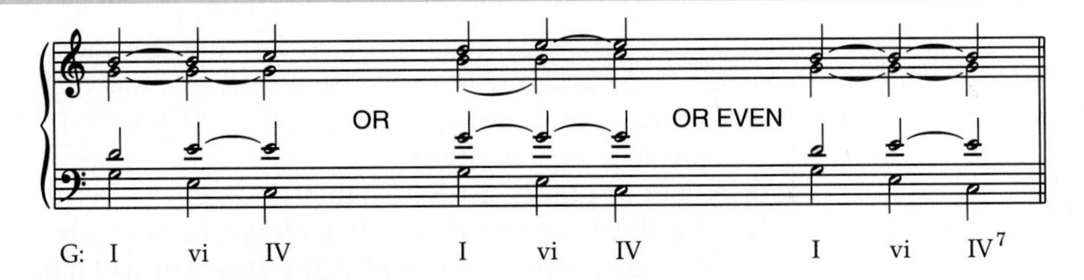

In the Descending-Fifths Progression, I–vi–ii (or I–vi–ii$_6$)

The chords I and vi share two common tones ($\hat{1}$ and $\hat{3}$), so keep all of the common tones in the progression I–vi. Since vi and ii share only one common tone

($\hat{6}$), there is more freedom in the voice leading; follow the voice-leading guidelines we have studied to avoid errors.

In the Ascending-Seconds Progression, V–vi

To enhance the deceptive effect of the progression V–vi, use $\hat{2}$–$\hat{1}$ or $\hat{7}$–$\hat{1}$ in the soprano. The voice leading varies slightly for major and minor keys because major $\hat{7}$ (as part of V) may *either* descend to $\hat{6}$ or ascend to $\hat{1}$. In minor, however, $\hat{7}$ may *only* ascend, since falling to $\hat{6}$ would create an augmented second.

- In major keys, if the soprano falls $\hat{2}$–$\hat{1}$, the remaining upper voices may all descend (as $\hat{7}$ falls to $\hat{6}$; see Example 18.10A) or $\hat{7}$ may rise to $\hat{1}$, in which case there will be a doubled third. If the soprano moves $\hat{7}$–$\hat{1}$, double the third ($\hat{1}$) in the vi chord. See Example 18.10B.
- In minor keys, all upper voices move downward, except for the leading tone, which must resolve upward to $\hat{1}$, regardless of its voicing. This will always result in a doubled third ($\hat{1}$) in the VI chord. See Example 18.10C.

EXAMPLE 18.10

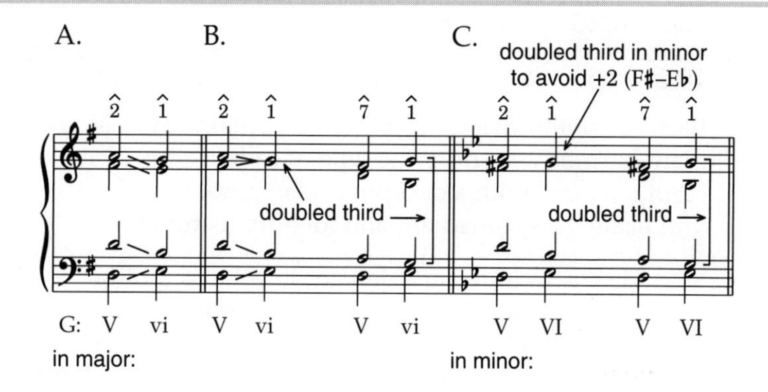

As with the progression V–vi, the voice leading for the progression vi–V varies slightly for major and minor keys.

- In major keys, all upper voices move upward against the descending bass. If the third is doubled, then the inner voice will follow the bass in tenths. See Example 18.11A.
- In minor keys, the VI chord must have a doubled third ($\hat{1}$) to avoid the augmented second. See Example 18.11B.

EXAMPLE 18.11

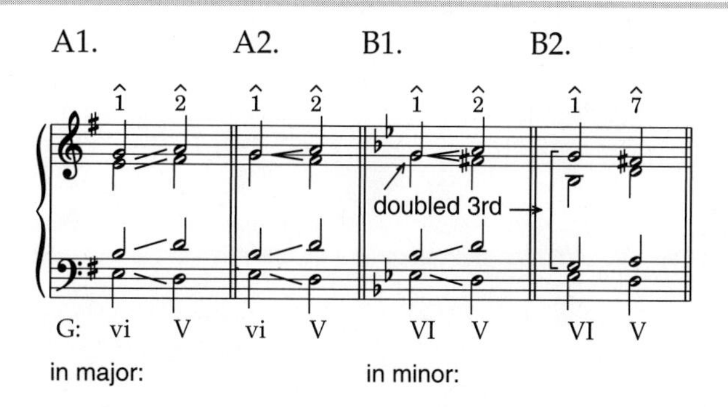

EXERCISE INTERLUDE

PERFORMING

18.1

The following arpeggiations create progressions that incorporate the submediant. Sing them and/or play them on an instrument. Listen to how often harmonies change; then analyze the progressions with roman numerals.

LISTENING

DVD 2
CH 18
TRACK 1

18.2

Each of the following progressions contains at least one instance of a submediant harmony. Identify the type of cadence for each excerpt (note that an excerpt may end with a deceptive V–vi motion).

Locate the submediant and identify its function:

- Is it a "bridge" in a descending-thirds motion?
- Does it start a descending-fifths motion?
- Does it substitute for tonic in a deceptive motion?
- Is it the PD chord?

Provide roman numerals for each chord (one roman numeral for each line given).

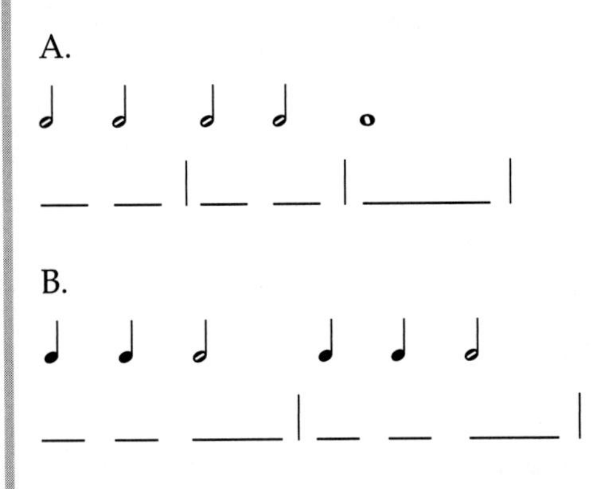

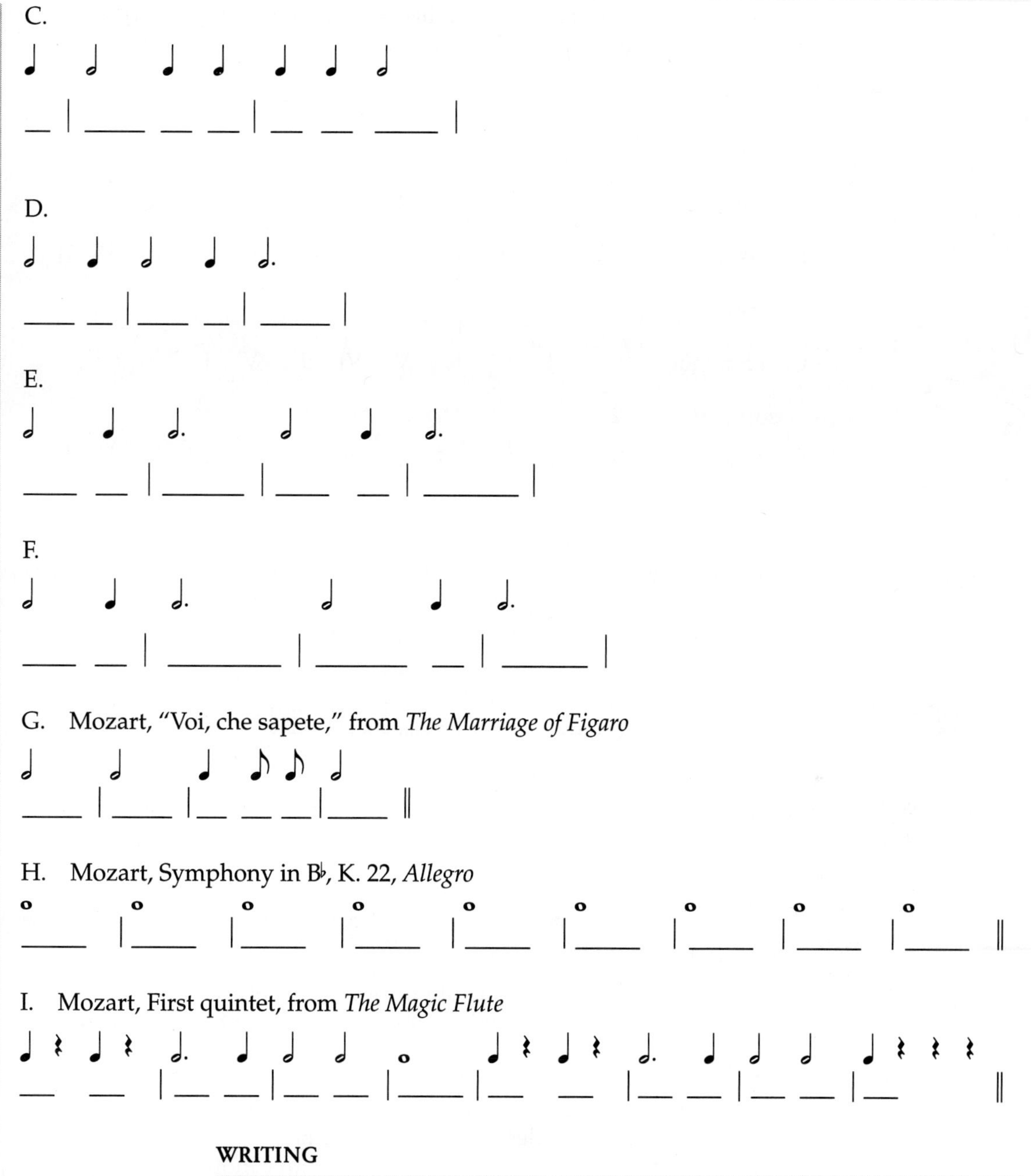

WRITING

18.3

The following progressions incorporate vi and include a few guiding soprano scale degrees. Select an appropriate meter and rhythm based on the progression (for example, cadential six-four chords must be placed on strong beats). Write the bass and then the soprano, and fill in the inner voices. Provide a two-level analysis, marking the function of vi (e.g., tonic substitute, harmonic bass arpeggiation, etc.). In many cases, this step will involve an interpretive decision with two or more possible answers.

soprano: $\hat{3}$

A. in A minor: i vii°$_7$ i VI iv V$^{6-5}_{4-3}$ i

soprano: $\hat{4}$ $\hat{5}$ $\hat{2}$

B. in B♭ major: V$^6_5$ I V$^4_3$ I$_6$ ii$_6$ V$^4_2$ I$_6$ I vi ii V$_7$ I$_{4-3}$

soprano: $\hat{3}$

C. in E minor: i ii$^4_2$ V$^6_5$ i$_{9-8}$ V VI ii°$_6$ V i

soprano: $\hat{2}$

D. in F major: V vi IV V$^4_2$ I$_6$ vii°$_6$ I vi ii ii$^6_5$ V$_7$ I

18.4

Study the following melody, noting the possibilities for inserting vi. On a separate sheet of manuscript paper, harmonize in major by adding lower voices; then reharmonize in the relative minor key. Analyze.

D/b

ANALYSIS

DVD 2
CH 18
TRACK 2

Exercise 18.5

Each of the given excerpts contains at least one example of the submediant. Complete the following tasks for each excerpt.

1. Bracket phrases and/or subphrases and label accordingly.
2. Analyze each chord with a roman numeral (first-level analysis).
3. Label cadences.
4. Specify the function of vi each time it appears:
   - Is it a "bridge" in a descending-third motion?
   - Does it start a descending-fifth motion?
   - Does it substitute for tonic in a deceptive motion?
   - Is it the PD chord?

A. Mozart, Violin Sonata in G major, K. 379, *Adagio*

B. Mozart, Piano Sonata in D major, K. 284, *Andante*

Label tones of figuration in this excerpt.

C. Wagner, "Der Augen leuchtendes Paar" ("Those eyes so lustrous and clear") (Wotan's Farewell), *Die Walküre*, act 3, scene 3

D. Schubert, Impromptu, op. posth. 142, no. 2, D. 935

This excerpt features many accented tones of figuration.

E. Beethoven, *Alla danza tedesca*, String Quartet no. 13 in B♭ major, op. 130

Describe the curious rhythmic effect in this excerpt.

WORKBOOK
18.1–18.3

KEYBOARD

Exercise 18.6

Realize the following figured bass in four-voice keyboard style. Include a two-level harmonic analysis.

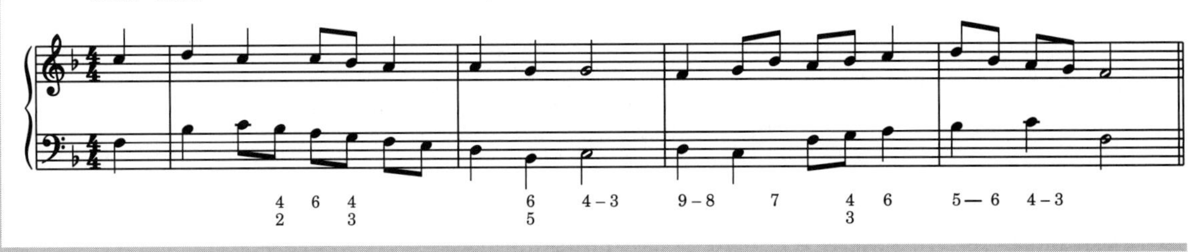

Contextual Analysis

Tonic and Dominant Embellish the Submediant

Although I and V are structural tonal pillars—usually more important than any other harmonies in a key—this is not always the case, because the importance of a harmony depends wholly on the musical context in which it appears. For example, in the progression I–V–vi, the vi chord often overshadows the dominant, which is demoted to being connective tissue between I and vi (see Example 18.12).

EXAMPLE 18.12 Mozart, Violin Sonata in F major, K. 377, Minuet

DVD 1
CH 18
TRACK 7

Note the deceptive motion in mm. 1–2 of Example 18.12. Because V is metrically weak (compared to the strong-beat tonic and submediant), it functions as a weak voice-leading chord (in this context it harmonizes the violin's G). Thus, the overall progression is I–vi–ii$^6_5$–V, with vi initiating a descending-fifth harmonic progression. This example also shows why we refer to such progressions as *deceptive motions* rather than as *deceptive cadences:* Clearly there cannot be a cadence after only three chords of a piece, and, most importantly, vi is not an independent entity but, rather, a member of the underlying progression that leads to the pre-dominant and dominant functions. The caesura on vi merely highlights the chord, but it does not take away its important role in the overall progression.

Not only can vi be more important than V, but it can even outrank the tonic. Listen to Example 18.13. Even though I_6 appears prominently at the end of m. 2, one can hear it as not being structural. To see why this is, consider the V_6 that occurs on beat 3 of m. 1: It acts as a passing chord between I and vi. Similarly, the I_6 on beat 3 of m. 2 is a voice-leading chord linking vi to the pre-dominant, ii_6, in m. 3. Recognition of the harmonic motion I–vi–ii_6 can influence the performance of this passage. Rather than dividing mm. 1–4 into two-measure units, we use the vi to fuse mm. 1–4 into a continuous idea.

It is also possible, however, to hear the I_6 outranking the submediant in m. 2. In this interpretation, the first two measures expand the tonic; a performance that considers the weakbeat I_6 as more important than vi might result in a more flexible and lilting rendering of the phrase, given that something other than downbeats is projected.

EXAMPLE 18.13 Mozart, String Quartet no. 6 in B♭ major, K. 159, *Andante*

DVD 1
CH 18
TRACK 8

Apparent Submediants

The submediant may occur as a byproduct of voice leading and therefore would not function as an actual harmony. We have seen voice-leading harmonies in several contexts, the most important of which is in progressions whose roots lie a second away from one another, such as the progression IV–V. The important 5–6 motion—in which the interval of a fifth above the bass moves to a sixth—allows IV to move to V, since the potential parallel fifths are broken up by the intervening sixth. The result of this 5–6 motion creates the ii_6 chord (see example 18.14A). We referred to this process as the "IV–ii complex," but it can occur in any progression where roots progress by an ascending second. In Example 18.14B, an analogous situation occurs when I moves to ii. Again, the 5–6 motion will help us avoid parallel fifths: F moves to G, which is already sounding as the bass rises to create the ii chord (Example 18.14B). Note that this 5–6 motion creates an apparent vi_6 chord; however, there is no "chord change." Rather, the vi_6 is a byproduct of the voice leading. Example 18.14C presents an example of the apparent vi_6 in an aria from Wagner's *The Flying Dutchman*.

EXAMPLE 18.14

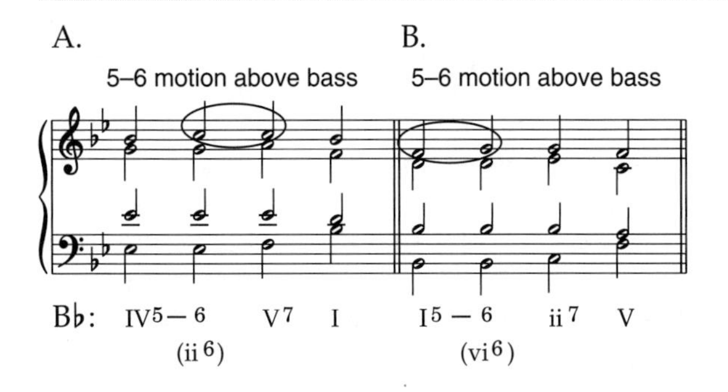

C. Wagner, "Mögst du mein Kind," from *The Flying Dutchman*

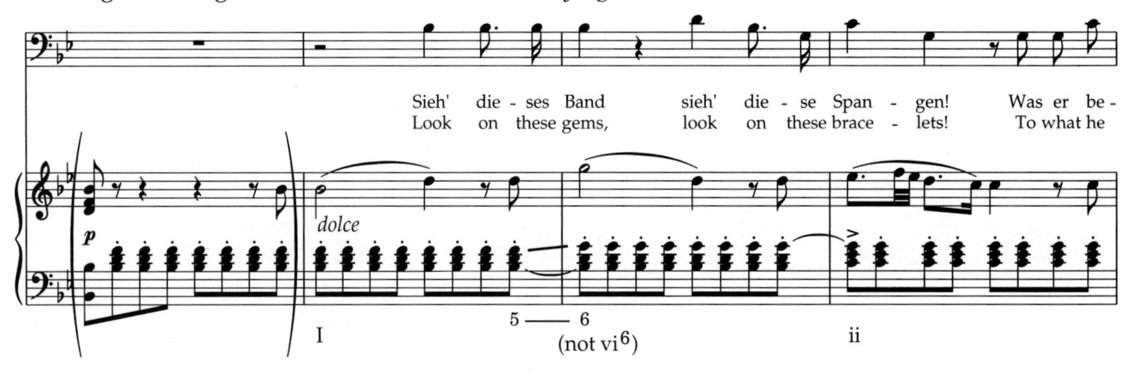

The Step Descent in the Bass

Although exceptions do occur, the most prevalent harmonic motion in phrases is from the tonic to the dominant. In Chapter 12, we saw a way to embellish I–V motion by means of stepwise ascent in the bass (see Example 12.8). It is now also possible to move from the tonic to the dominant by descending steps in the bass.

Composers have been creating phrases built on bass descents from $\hat{1}$ to $\hat{5}$ since the early seventeenth century. For example, the descending four-note scale segment $\hat{1}$–$\hat{7}$–$\hat{6}$–$\hat{5}$ appears regularly in Monteverdi's operas and madrigals, a late sixteenth- early seventeenth-century Italian composer. There are numerous paths of descent, ranging from diatonic ($\hat{1}$–$\hat{7}$–$\hat{6}$–$\hat{5}$) to descents that are chromatic (with multiple expressive chromatic passing tones), to descents that even overshoot $\hat{5}$ and then return to the dominant. Some well-known examples include "Dido's Lament" from Purcell's *Dido and Aeneas* and the "Crucifixus" from Bach's *Mass in B minor*.

Listen first to the diatonic descent in Example 18.15. Schütz's composition illustrates a characteristic stepwise descent: i→passing v_6→iv_6→V. Note that an especially strong gravitational pull downward to V is created by the descending melodic minor scale: This feel and the expressive half step ♭6–5 (D–C♯ in Example 18.15) show why such descents occur more often in the minor mode than in the major. Note that in minor, v_6 is used to precede minor iv_6 to give the bass line $\hat{8}$–♭$\hat{7}$–♭$\hat{6}$–5; the use of ↓$\hat{7}$ avoids the augmented second between ↑$\hat{7}$ and ↓$\hat{6}$. First-inversion minor v and root-position v do not function as dominants; rather, they are used as passing chords or voice-leading chords.

EXAMPLE 18.15 Schütz, "Nacket bin ich von Mutterleibe kommen" ("Naked I have come from my mother's womb"), *Musicalischen Exequien*, op. 7, SWV 279

DVD 1
CH 18
TRACK 9

We call step-descent basses that fall directly from tonic to dominant ($\hat{1}$–$\hat{7}$–$\hat{6}$–$\hat{5}$) **direct step-descent basses**. When direct step-descent basses are cast in the minor mode they are known as **lament basses**. Lament basses often accompany melancholy texts, which are not historically confined to the seventeenth century. Songs such as "Hit the Road, Jack," and "Erie Canal" are built on the same formula (Example 18.16).

EXAMPLE 18.16

DVD 1
CH 18
TRACK 10

A. Traditional, "Erie Canal"

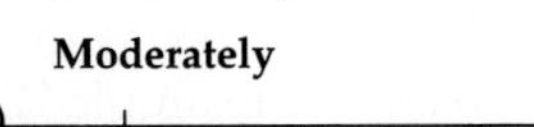

B. Rachmaninoff, Prelude in G minor, op. 23, no. 5

Step-descent basses are often repeated throughout a piece, providing the composition with a firm harmonic foundation. Such repetitions are called *ostinatos*, and the pieces based on them are often called **ground basses** or **chaconnes**.

As you have probably noticed from listening to the previous examples, the most common harmonic settings of these step-descent basses use the PD iv_6, which moves to V (see Example 18.17A). Because of the lurking parallels, a root-position VI usually does not lead directly to V (see Example 18.17E). It is first converted into a iv_6 chord via a contrapuntal 5–6 motion in order to avoid parallels (see Example 18.17B). Also, composers may opt to move $\hat{1}$–$\hat{7}$ in the bass while sustaining the tonic harmony; this creates a passing tone in the bass and the passing sonority i^4_2. (see Example 18.17C).

EXAMPLE 18.17

DVD 1
CH 18
TRACK 11

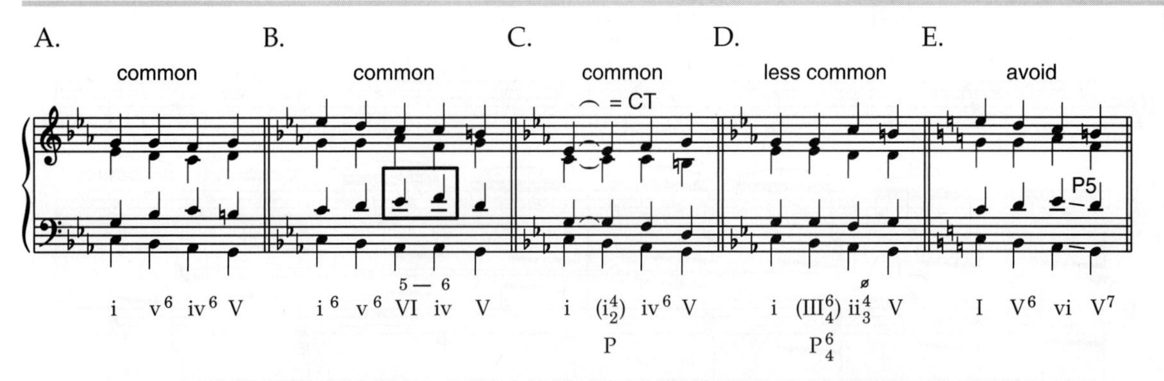

Finally, there are two less common variants of the step-descent bass. In Example 18.17D, note how $ii^{ø4}_{3}$ substitutes for iv_6; in Example 18.17E, note how the major mode may be used for the step-descent bass. There is less danger of awkward voice-leading intervals for the bass in the major mode than in the minor mode. Thus, the major V_6 can move directly to vi or IV_6 (but be aware of potential parallels).

Step-descent basses may be extended by passing through the dominant to reach a pre-dominant on $\hat{4}$, which is harmonized by iv or ii_6. Such **indirect step-descent basses** ($\hat{1}$–$\hat{7}$–$\hat{6}$–$\hat{5}$–$\hat{4}$→back to $\hat{5}$) therefore create a descent by fifth. Composers often harmonize the first $\hat{5}$ with a passing six-three or six-four chord to avoid any feeling of arrival on dominant (Example 18.18).

EXAMPLE 18.18

DVD 1
CH 18
TRACK 12

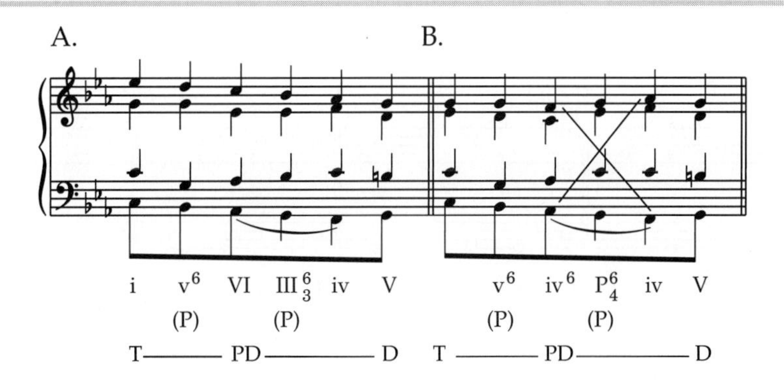

Descents can assume a number of different guises. Likewise, they can prolong any of the three harmonic functions. Listen to Example 18.19. Note that the bass descent, which prolongs the tonic, encompasses an entire octave. Notice that the dominant is converted to a V^4_2 that passes on to I_6, which expands the tonic in m. 3. The next passing V^4_3 connects I_6 with I, closing the octave descent and creating a large-scale tonic expansion. Note also the problematic parallels between vi and V.

EXAMPLE 18.19 **Tchaikovsky, "Za oknom v teni mel'kajet" ("At the window, in the shadow"), op. 60, no. 10**

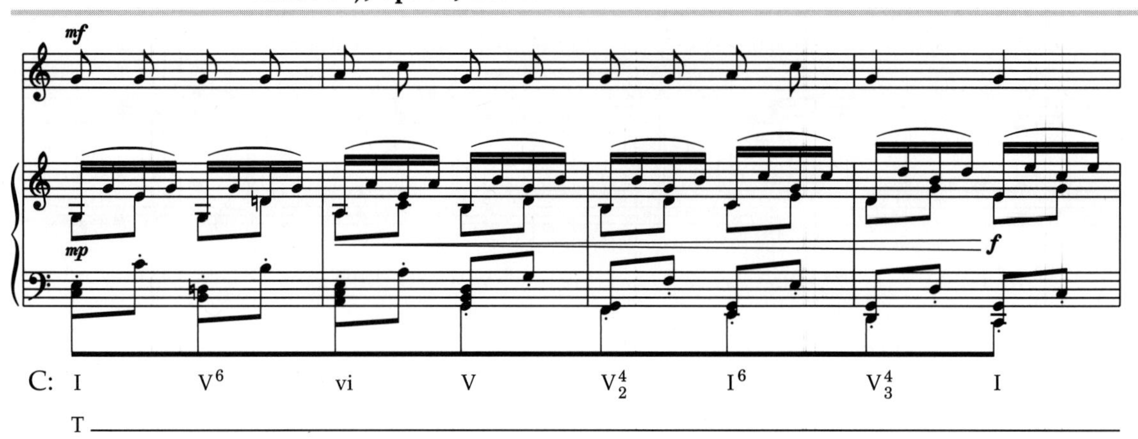

EXERCISE INTERLUDE

KEYBOARD

18.7 Contrapuntal Models

The following outer-voice models incorporate the submediant harmony. Realize each model in four-voice keyboard style. Note that when you play Exercise D in minor, the nonfunctional passing v_6 chord contains $\flat\hat{7}$ in the bass. This avoids the augmented second between $\sharp\hat{7}$ and $\flat\hat{6}$. Be able to sing either of the outer voices while playing the other three voices. Transpose each exercise to A major and F major and their parallel minors. Be aware of parallels in Exercise E.

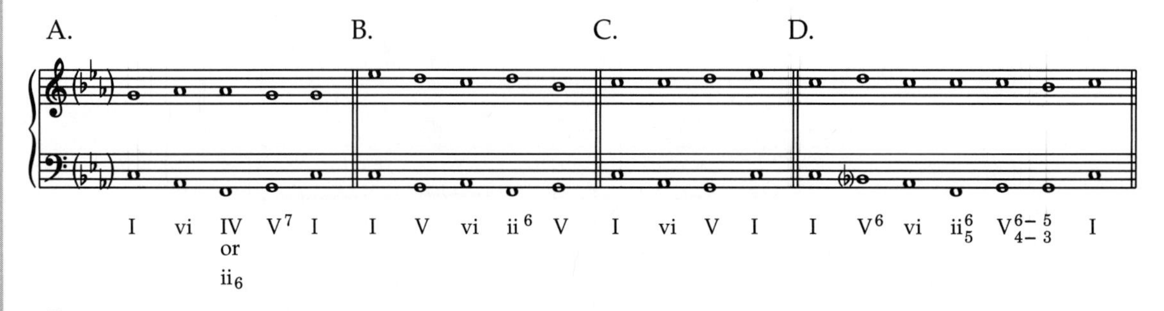

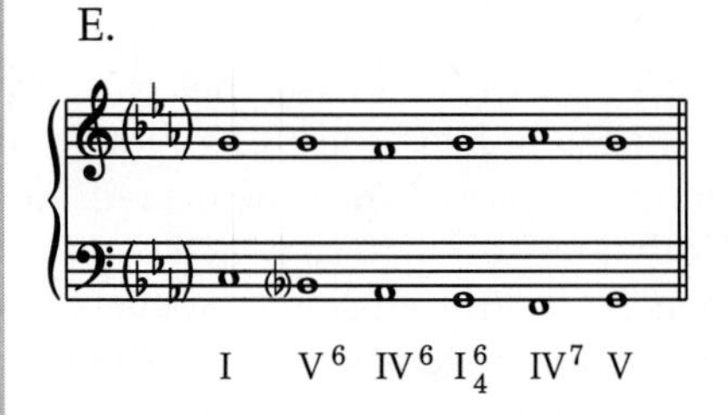

18.8 Figured Bass Using the Submediant

Realize and analyze the exercise in four-voice keyboard style. Be able to discuss the effects of the repetition of any harmonic patterns in the exercise, and label the numerous passing figures.

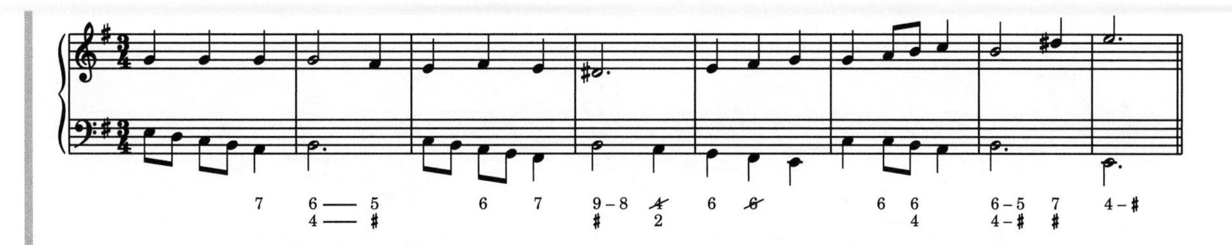

18.9 Keyboard: Figured Bass and Singing

Sing the following tunes. Next, realize the figured basses in four voices as you sing.

A. Bach, " Jesu, der du meine Seele," Cantata no. 78, BWV 78

B. Handel, "Let All the Angels of God Worship Him," *Messiah*, HWV 56

DVD 2
CH 18
TRACK 3

ANALYSIS

18.10

The following excerpts present vi in various contexts: as an independent harmony that leads to or is the pre-dominant (either as part of an EPM or as structural cadence) or as a voice-leading chord. Interpret each example based on how vi functions.

A. Bach, *Geistliches Lied*, "Beschränkt ihr Weisen"

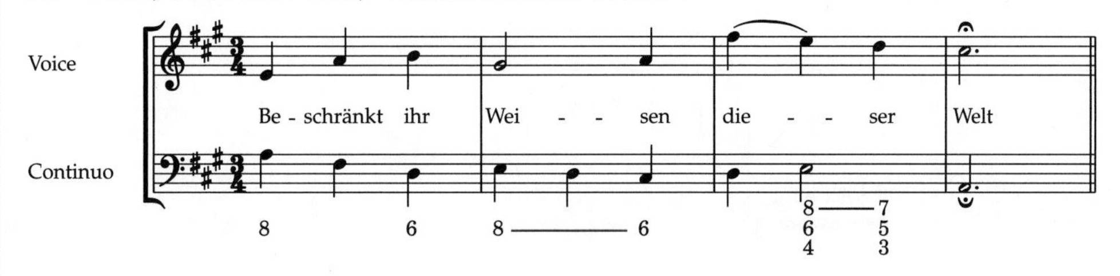

B. Mozart, Piano Sonata in B♭, K. 333, I

C. Mozart, Serenade in D major, K. 204

D. Mendelssohn, opening of Part I: *Elijah*

E. Bach, Flute Sonata in B minor, *Largo*

COMPOSITION

WORKBOOK
18.4–18.5

18.11

Study this broken-chord harmonic progression and the figuration. Then, on a separate sheet of paper, write three additional four-measure phrases in similar texture. Each phrase should use a different harmonic progression and should incorporate at least one example of the submediant harmony (e.g., an indirect step-descent bass or the submediant as a pre-dominant).

A. Schumann, "Hor' ich das Liedchen Klingen," from *Dichterliebe*

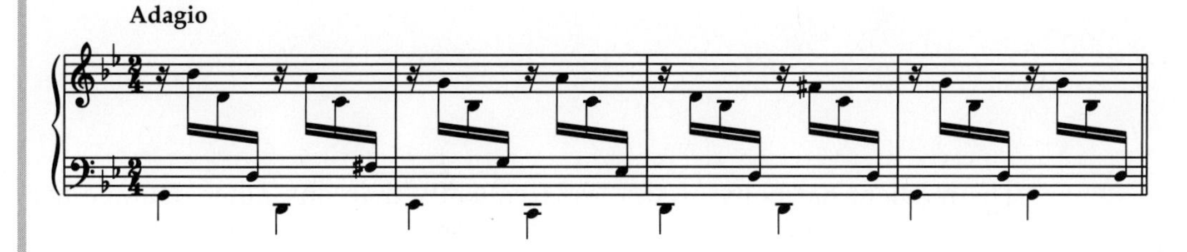

B. Corelli, Sonata, in D minor, op. 5

Using this lament bass as a model, write three variations that contain a more florid upper voice. Include chordal leaps, passing tones, neighbors, etc. Begin by analyzing the excerpt's structure; be aware of the bass suspension in m. 2.

TERMS AND CONCEPTS

- bass motion vs. root motion
- deceptive motion, deceptive cadence
- harmonic vs. melodic bass arpeggiation
- lament bass, step-descent bass (direct and indirect)
- tonic substitute

CHAPTER 19

The Mediant, the Back-Relating Dominant, and a Synthesis of Diatonic Harmonic Relationships

The mediant harmony occurs less frequently than any other diatonic harmony; this is not to say that the chord is unimportant, however. When we begin exploring the tonal plans of entire works, we will see that in minor-key pieces the structural significance of III is great—second only to that of tonic and dominant. The mediant harmony provides the same color contrast as the submediant: It is a minor triad in a major key and a major triad in a minor key. Within the phrase, the mediant usually appears in one of the following contexts: (1) ascending-bass arpeggiations and (2) descending-fifth progressions.

The Mediant in Arpeggiations

We have encountered the ascending-bass arpeggiation $\hat{1}$–$\hat{3}$–$\hat{5}$ under a I–I_6–V progression. We have seen how the contrapuntal motion of the bass can be filled with passing harmonies to create a stepwise ascent:

Bass: $\hat{1}$	$\hat{2}$	$\hat{3}$	$\hat{4}$	$\hat{5}$
I	vii°$_6$	I_6	IV	V
	or		*or*	
	V^4_3		ii_6	

Although $\hat{3}$ in the bass is most often harmonized by I_6, it can also be harmonized by a root-position mediant chord. In this way, iii may substitute for I_6 to create a tonic extension, just as vi may substitute for tonic. Example 19.1A illustrates the common tones in I–iii and I–vi progressions. The rest of the example shows some common uses of the mediant within phrases. The slurs show how the mediant divides the fifth from $\hat{1}$ to $\hat{5}$ in the bass. Just as we label vi's bridging function from T to PD with an arrow, so too will we use the arrow to show iii's bridging function leading from T to PD.

EXAMPLE 19.1

DVD 1
CH 19
TRACK 1

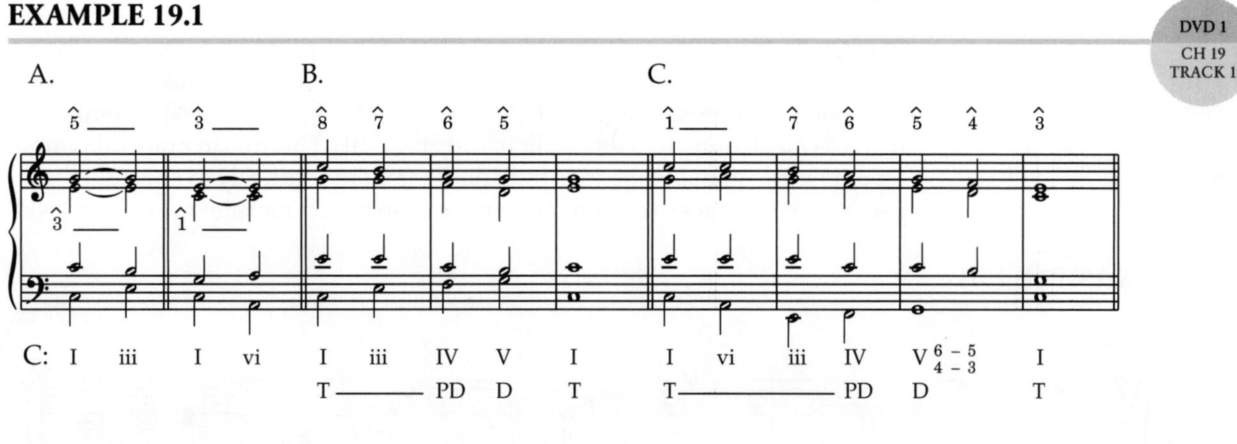

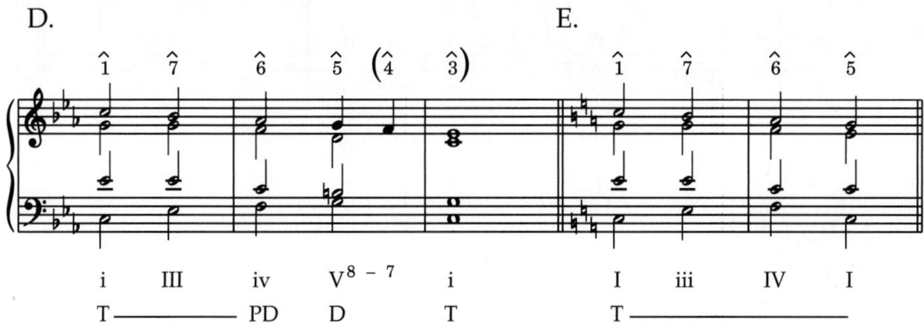

In Example 19.1B, the bass of the pre-dominant IV fills the space between $\hat{3}$ and $\hat{5}$. Note also how the soprano descends stepwise from $\hat{1}$ to $\hat{5}$, with $\hat{7}$ functioning as a downward passing tone rather than a leading tone. Example 19.1C shows how vi can be inserted between I and iii, resulting in an effective descending arpeggiation.

Example 19.1D recasts 19.1A in a minor mode. Example 19.1E illustrates a prolongation of tonic: iii and IV harmonize passing tones in the soprano ($\hat{7}$–$\hat{6}$) and lead back to I. The 1960s hit song "Puff the Magic Dragon" harmonizes its descending melody with this very progression (Example 19.2).

EXAMPLE 19.2 Yarrow, "Puff the Magic Dragon"

DVD 1
CH 19
TRACK 2

A Special Case: Preparing the III Chord in Minor

The mediant appears in the minor mode more often than in the major mode. Listen to Example 19.3. We are unfamiliar with the second harmony that appears in all three examples: a major triad built on $\flat\hat{7}$. Up to this point, we have seen chords built from a leading tone ($vii°_6$ and $vii°_7$) and a passing v^6 chord (in the step-descent bass). In Example 19.3, the root-position "VII" chord has a different function: It precedes the mediant harmony. The B♭ and E♭ chords form a close bond; they sound like a miniature V–I in the key of E♭ major. To reflect this motion of the V–I sound of B♭–E♭, we label the B♭ harmony as "V of III" (or "V/III"), indicating that B♭ is the dominant (V) chord that leads to E♭ (III). This roman numeral symbol represents the sound of the triad built on $\flat\hat{7}$ far more accurately than would the label "VII," which fails to capture its dominant function at the immediate, local level.

EXAMPLE 19.3

DVD 1
CH 19
TRACK 3

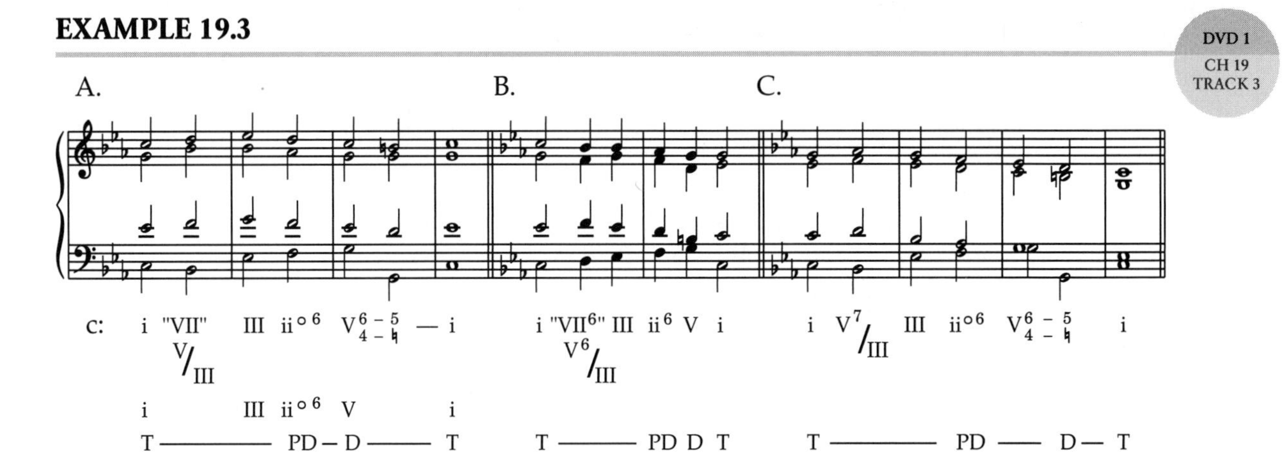

V/III often occurs in first inversion as V_6/III (Example 19.3B). The use of this inversion prominently places D—the temporary leading tone that leads to E♭ (III)—in the bass, thus intensifying the motion to III. In Example 19.3C, a seventh is added to create V^7/III, which further intensifies motion to III (since V_7–I is more powerful than V–I).

The use of chords such as V/III, which are called **applied chords**, will be further explored in Chapter 24. The reasons we have introduced them here arise largely out of convenience: III in a minor key is often preceded by its dominant (which is diatonic in the minor key).

The Mediant in Descending-Fifths Progressions

Because iii lies a perfect fifth above vi, in many progressions it descends by that perfect fifth, thus extending the descending-fifths progression back yet another notch: iii→vi→ii→V→I. Example 19.4 provides two settings of a descending-fifths progression from iii.

EXAMPLE 19.4

DVD 1
CH 19
TRACK 4

Voice Leading for the Mediant

Using the mediant with good voice leading is easy as long as you remember a few simple guidelines.

1. Try to move the upper voices in contrary motion to the bass when approaching and leaving iii (Example 19.5).
2. Use the soprano line $\hat{1}$–$\hat{7}$–$\hat{6}$ when iii supports the passing tone $\hat{7}$.

EXAMPLE 19.5

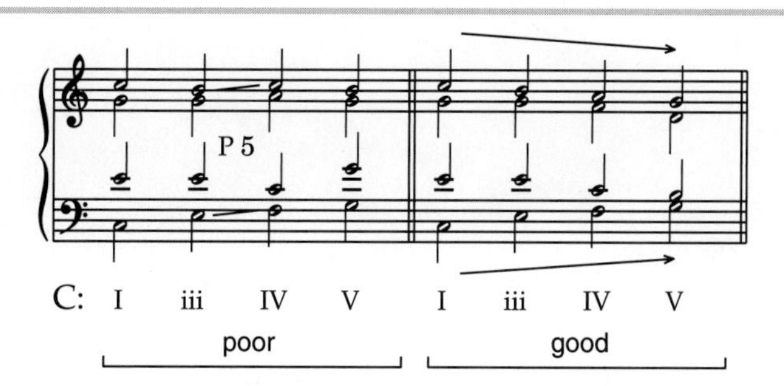

EXERCISE INTERLUDE

PERFORMING

19.1

The following arpeggiations create progressions that incorporate the mediant. Sing them and/or play them on an instrument. Listen to how often harmonies change; then analyze the progressions with roman numerals.

A.

B.

C.

LISTENING

19.2 The Mediant in Context: Two Voice Becomes Four Voice

You will hear the outer-voice counterpoint for one beat, immediately followed by the added inner voices, their combination resulting in four-voice harmony. You are to notate the outer voices only, using both their counterpoint and the addition of the inner voices to label the harmonies. Exercises are in $\frac{4}{4}$ meter and either D minor or F major.

A.

B.

C.

D.

E.

WRITING

19.3

The following exercises contain ascending-bass arpeggiations and descending-fifths motions using the mediant. Choose a meter and write the progressions in four-voice chorale style. Include a second-level analysis, and label the mediant's function (use a bracket and label with "arp. prog." or "fifths prog.").

A. In C minor: i–V/III–III–ii°$_6$–V–I (begin soprano on $\hat{1}$)

B. In A minor: i–V$^6_5$/III–III–iv–V–VI (begin soprano on $\hat{5}$)

C. in D major: I–iii–IV–ii$^6_5$–V$^4_2$–I$_6$–V$^6_5$–I–vi–ii$_6$–V$_7$–I (begin soprano on $\hat{5}$)

D. In D minor: i–V/III–III–VI–ii°$_6$–V–i (begin soprano on $\hat{3}$)

ANALYSIS

DVD 2
CH 19
TRACK 1

19.4

The following excerpts contain the mediant either in the context of an ascending-bass arpeggiation or as part of a descending-fifths progression. Analyze with roman numerals (first-level analysis).

A. Schubert, "Am Frühling"

Note the clef in the right hand.

B. Brahms, "Beim Ritt auf dem Knie," Volks- und Kinderlieder, WoO 31, no. 8.

Only the first portion of the phrase is given.

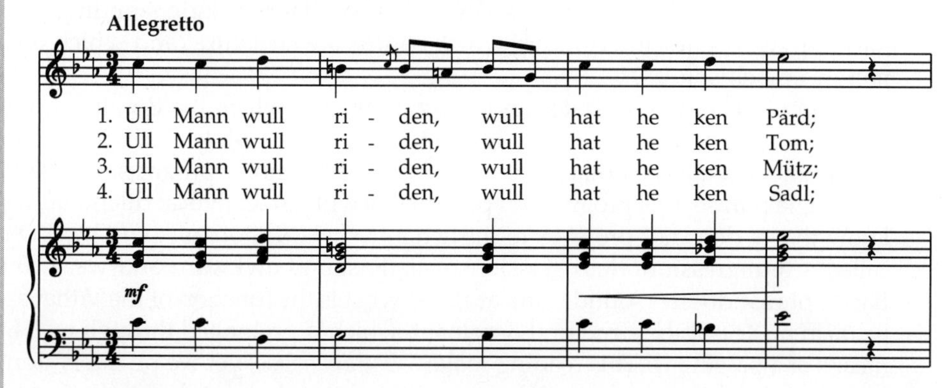

C. Marcello, Sonata in A minor, no. 8, Presto.

Consider the standard harmonic phrase model as you analyze this example.

D. Schumann, "Armes Waisenkind," from *Children's Pieces,* op. 68, no. 6

E. Brahms, Symphony no. 4, op. 98, *Allegro giocoso*

More Contextual Analysis

We know that a V chord may or may not function as a structural, cadential dominant. For example, for a phrase built on the progression I–V–vi–ii–V–I, the structural dominant is most likely the second one, while the first dominant is only a voice-leading chord that connects tonic and submediant harmonies and helps to avert potential parallels. Another example of a nonstructural dominant occurs in the step-descent bass progression i–v_6–iv_6–V. We observed that the minor v_6 was far removed from its dominant function; it harmonized the passing tone $\downarrow\hat{7}$, connecting $\hat{1}$ and $\hat{6}$ in the bass.

As always, such contextual analysis is essential for understanding how harmony works, for interpreting which chords are structural and which ones merely embellishing.

Example 19.6 demonstrates an important way in which the dominant may appear in a nonstructural context. Listen to the example while observing the roman numeral analysis. What is unusual about the harmonic progression? Heard as a single phrase, this progression presents us with an analytical dilemma. You know that V does not progress to ii; such a backward motion from D to PD is called a **retrogression**. Retrogressions usually sound awkward and weak. But Bach's phrase doesn't sound weak at all. So what is the function of the V that appears in m. 2? Is it the structural dominant, which is prolonged through m. 3 by means of a passing ii? This reading makes abstract sense, yet we probably don't hear the V in m. 2 as a structural V. Doesn't the ii chord sound as if it plays a harmonic role as a pre-dominant? Listen to the excerpt once again.

EXAMPLE 19.6

DVD 1
CH 19
TRACK 5

A. Bach, Prelude in E♭ Major, *The Well-Tempered Clavier*, Book 2, BWV 876

B.

To ignore the supertonic harmony is not a reasonable interpretation, since it clearly plays an important role in the excerpt. Given the prominence of ii, the harmonic importance of the first V now seems to wane. The excerpt begins on a soprano B♭4, but in m. 2—where the problematic V appears—the soprano leaps to E♭5 and then descends to D5. If we ignore the first dominant, the overall progression is I–ii_7–V_7–I, and each harmony supports the melodic descent in the soprano (B♭4–A♭4–G4). Example 19.6B shows this interpretation.

This analysis, which takes account of the phrasing and melodic continuity of the excerpt, reflects the perception of the music much better than the analysis that viewed the V in m. 2 as structural. The dominant chord in m. 2 prolongs the preceding tonic, but there is no connection between the dominant and the following ii chord. Dominants that prolong a previously sounding tonic without resolving to a following tonic are called **back-relating dominants (BRDs)**. BRDs can be shown only in second-level analysis:

1st-level analysis:	I	V	ii
2nd-level analysis:	T———	(BRD)———	PD

Given that the music following a half cadence is a restart and not a continuation, we will view the half cadence as a common and important type of back-relating dominant.

General Guidelines for Harmonic Progressions

We have learned that the phrase model, composed of three ordered harmonic functions (T–PD–D–T) lies at the heart of tonal progressions. And we have come to recognize that the tonic function usually occupies significantly more time and chords than the other two functions. Further, we have seen how standing back and considering how harmonies function within a musical context—rather than haphazardly scattering roman numeral labels over a score—allows us to see deeper connections.

You will apply these global analytical ideas to your compositions as well. However, you may find yourself in a situation where you simply can't figure out which chord could come next. For example, after you've completed a basic tonic expansion using contrapuntal chords, you might wish to use other diatonic harmonies within the tonic expansion. In general, diatonic harmonies (such as dominants, submediants, supertonics, and mediants) tend to follow one another in one of the three root motions that we have already learned:

1. by descending fifth (or rising fourth), which we abbreviate *D5*
2. by ascending second, which we abbreviate *A2*
3. by descending third, which we abbreviate *D3*

These root motions may be combined in an infinite number of ways. For example, a series of falling thirds from the tonic, I–vi–IV, may be followed by two successive A2s (IV to V and then, the deceptive motion V, to vi.) From the submediant, a set of D5 motions might follow, which will return the progression to tonic (ii–V–I). The sum total of all this motion is a large goal-directed progression: I–vi–IV–V–vi–ii–V–I, which may be set in many ways, depending on the progression's meter and harmonic rhythm. Most musical settings of this progression would likely reflect the following second-level analysis:

I–vi–IV–V–vi–ii_7–V_7–I
T————————PD-D—T

Let's try out some of these ideas by setting ourselves a task and then working through the compositional process.

Task: Write a piece for string quartet or vocal ensemble (SATB) that encompasses 12–20 measures and contains three or more phrases. The key (major or minor) and meter are your choice.

1. Begin with a compositional plan, one in which you envision the large-scale harmonic progressions. For example, if you write a four-phrase piece, consider how each phrase will close and how it will relate to succeeding phrases. Example 19.7 presents an example plan for a minor key.

EXAMPLE 19.7

	phrase 1:	phrase 2:	phrase 3:	phrase 4:
soprano:	$\hat{5}$	$\hat{3}$	$\hat{5}$	$\hat{2}$–$\hat{1}$
harmony:	i→HC	i→IAC	i→HC	i→PAC

2. Then decide on the length of each phrase; four measures is the most common. Think about the general harmonies that lead to each cadence. You are free to use all of the diatonic harmonies we have discussed, including EPMs, BRDs, and step-descent basses.

You may wish to lay out controlling harmonies for each measure by writing roman numerals, as in Example 19.8.

EXAMPLE 19.8

	phrase 1:	phrase 2:	phrase 3:	phrase 4:
measures:	1 2 3 4	5 6 7 8	9 10 11 12	13 14 15 16
harmonies:	i V^4_3 i_6–iv_6 V	i VI iv V_7–i	i III VI $ii°_6$–V	i iv–P^6_4–iv_6 V^{6-5}_{4-3}–i
second level:	T———PD D	T———PD D T	T————PD D	T—PD———D T

3. You may wish to go so far as to specify every harmony within each measure; their exact rhythmic placement will have much to do with your choice of meter and melodic motives. Example 19.9 presents a detailed plan for the first phrase only.

EXAMPLE 19.9

	phrase 1:			
measures:	1	2	3	4
harmonies:	i–$ii^{ø4}_{2}$–V^6_5–i	V^4_3–i_6–V^4_2	i_6–III–iv–iv_6	V
Structure:	i	V^4_3	i_6 iv_6	V
Second-level:	T————	————	PD————	D

Summary of Part 4

In Part 4 you have developed the skills to write, sing, play, and hear phrases containing diatonic harmonies. Even though we have begun to incorporate harmonies built on all seven scale degrees, we have consistently seen that hierarchy is still very much at the core of tonal music. Tonic, dominant, and predominant are still the most structural chords; the other chords in a progression play supporting, ornamental roles.

This hierarchy may always be represented through a multitiered analytical process. In first-level analysis, we *describe* all vertical sonorities using roman numerals. In second-level analysis, we *interpret* harmonic functions within the musical context to see larger connections. We have learned to interpret tricky harmonic successions by considering their overall tonal motion and effect (such as the back-relating dominant). We have seen how a second-level analysis mirrors our perception of the music. Thus, this type of analysis will surely influence the way we shape phrases in a performance.

EXERCISE INTERLUDE

PERFORMING

19.5

The following arpeggiations create progressions that incorporate the back-relating dominant. Sing them and/or play them on an instrument. Listen to how often harmonies change; then analyze the progressions with roman numerals.

A.

B.

C.

KEYBOARD

19.6

The following exercises contain mediant harmony and/or back-relating dominants. Realize the figured bass in four-part keyboard style, and provide a two-level analysis. Play each at the keyboard; try to sing either outer voice while playing the other three voices. Transpose each to any two other keys (Exercises A and D should be in major only, and Exercise C should be in minor only).

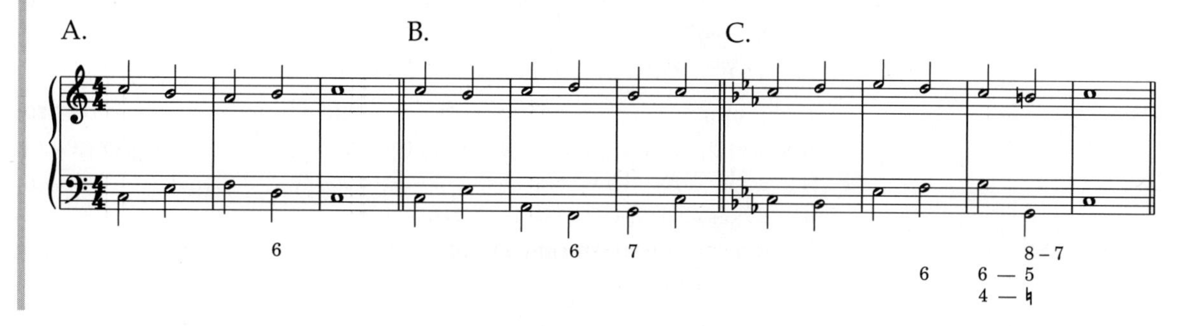

Continued

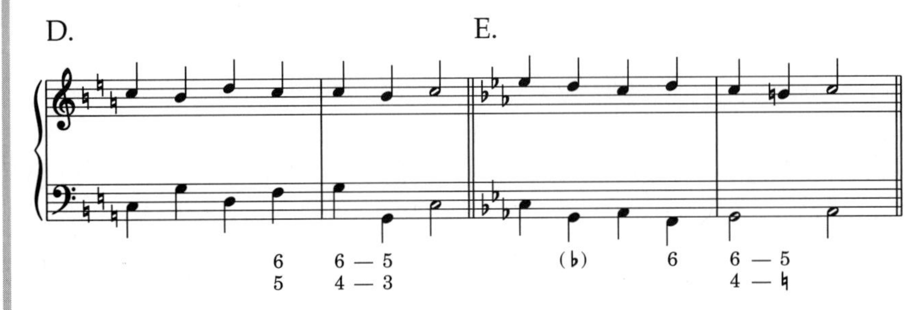

19.7

Realize and analyze the following figured bass.

COMPOSITION

19.8 Fluency Drills

Given here are tasks that involve the terms, harmonic paradigms, and concepts that we have learned so far. Complete each task quickly but carefully.

A. In A major, expand tonic in three to four chords, move to your choice of PD, and close your phrase with a HC.
B. In E minor, write a short chord progression (five to six chords) that includes a typical use of III.
C. In C minor, write a progression that includes an EPM and that closes with a PAC.
D. In A♭ major, expand tonic and include at least two suspensions.
E. In B minor and a meter of your choice, write a four- to six-measure progression that includes the following (not necessarily in the order given):
   i. a PAC
   ii. a typical use of both VI and III
   iii. a lament bass
   iv. four different types of tones of figuration in any of the voices (label each)
   v. a vii°$_7$ chord in any position
F. In B♭ major and a meter of your choice, write a four- to six-measure progression that includes the following (not necessarily in the order given):
   i. a HC and a PAC
   ii. ii$^4_2$ as part of the tonic expansion
   iii. descending harmonic arpeggiation
   iv. two examples of $^6_4$ chords
   v. an example of ii$^6_5$ and IV$_7$
   vi. a soprano neighboring motion within the tonic expansion

LISTENING

DVD 2
CH 19
TRACK 2

19.9 Aural Snapshots

You will hear numerous unmetered harmonizations of three-note soprano paradigms in G major and E minor. The goal is fluency: to be able to identify each three-chord paradigm in one but not more than two playings and to notate the outer voices and provide a first- and second-level analysis. There are only two types of soprano fragments: passing and neighboring.

Passing forms include: $\hat{3}$–$\hat{2}$–$\hat{1}$; $\hat{1}$–$\hat{2}$–$\hat{3}$; $\hat{5}$–$\hat{4}$–$\hat{3}$; $\hat{3}$–$\hat{4}$–$\hat{5}$

Neighboring forms include: $\hat{1}$–$\hat{7}$–$\hat{1}$; $\hat{1}$–$\hat{2}$–$\hat{1}$; $\hat{3}$–$\hat{4}$–$\hat{3}$

19.10 Combining Snapshots

The following exercises combine two or three short paradigms (for a total of six to nine chords). Notate the outer voices and provide a two-level harmonic analysis. As with Exercise 19.9, the goal here is fluency, but this time you may hear each example up to three times. Expect to hear both tonic expansions and complete progressions (T–PD–D–(T). All exercises are in $\frac{3}{4}$ and either in G major or E minor.

INSTRUMENTAL APPLICATION

19.11 Reduction

The following excerpts illustrate the melodic, contrapuntal, motivic, and harmonic techniques we have developed beginning in Chapter 8. These techniques include the phrase model and the three structural harmonic functions of T–PD–D as well as the various harmonies that work within the phrase model (e.g., iii and vi). Further, these excerpts illustrate the techniques composers used to prolong any of these structural harmonies (e.g., contrapuntal elaborations, including passing and neighboring chords).

Study the embellished literature excerpts in order to determine their harmonic and contrapuntal unfolding; then reduce them to their essential four-voice SATB chorale texture using good voice leading to connect each harmony. Perform each excerpt as follows: If you are a pianist, simply play your realization. If you are a melodic instrumentalist, arpeggiate each. If necessary, refer to the discussion in Chapter 11 for a detailed procedure. Play each reduction in the key in which it is written; then transpose to one other key of your choice.

Sample solution: Corelli, Church Sonata, op. 3, no. 5, *Allegro*

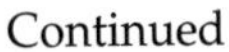

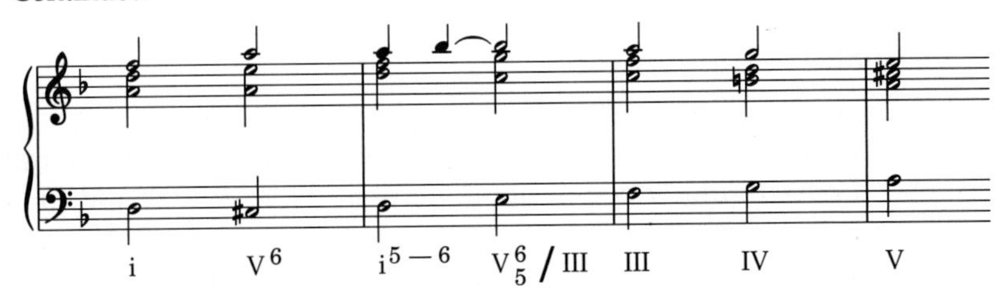

A. Corelli, Chamber Sonata in C major, op. 2, no. 3, Preludio, *Largo*

B. Corelli, Chamber Sonata in B minor, op. 4, no. 12, Giga

C. Handel, Concerto Grosso, "Alexander's Feast", *Andante, non presto*

WORKBOOK
19.1–19.6

19.12

Elaborate the given figured basses (with soprano) by first arpeggiating in strict ascending four-voice chords that maintain good voice leading between chords. Then change the contours and add tones of figuration to create a compound melody.

A.

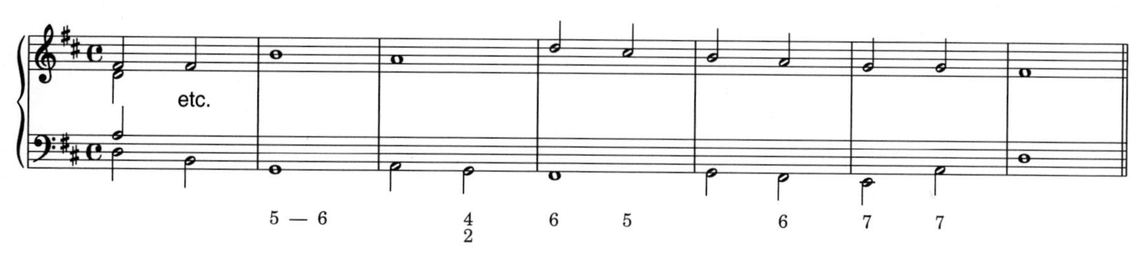

B.

TERMS AND CONCEPTS

- back-relating dominant
- iii in:
  - bass arpeggiations
  - motions of descending fifths
- retrogression
- V/III

PART 5

CREATING LARGER FORMS

In Part 5 we continue to explore how diatonic harmonies function within phrases, but our focus will be on learning how composers create larger formal structures by extending and combining phrases. We refine our understanding of how music is hierarchical and present new techniques that reveal how harmony and counterpoint are interdependent. We also incorporate more fully in our analyses the psychological phenomena of expectation and fulfillment. Analysis continues to be an essential activity in learning how subphrases and phrases can be strung together, but other skills also will be necessary. As you are given more creative responsibility, composition and instrumental application exercises will play a more pronounced role than ever before. You will learn how to write structures that balance repetition with contrast and stability with motion. The writing exercises depend on a rich and varied background of listening to and making music, since such activities provide a repository of common stylistic traits that can help guide your compositional choices.

CHAPTER 20

The Period

We have seen how contrapuntal and harmonic motions combine to create music: A phrase is not just a random succession of notes and chords, but a carefully balanced, goal-directed motion controlled by the outer-voice counterpoint and the pacing of the phrase model. According to the model, phrases often comprise one or more tonic expansions, a pre-dominant, and either a half cadence or an authentic cadence. Larger musical structures—those composed of multiple phrases—unfold logically as well. If this were not the case, music would move in unconnected, unmotivated chunks rather than in the smooth manner that connects the opening of the first phrase to the close of the piece.

One of the best ways to create continuity across a phrase boundary is to call on a listener's expectations for continuation. If somebody telling you a story abruptly stops mid-sentence, your immediate reaction is to want to know what comes next. We have already observed how a similar situation can arise in the harmonic realm. For example, the V and vi chords in a deceptive motion serve to heighten and thwart our expectations of tonic resolution. Few pieces—or even phrases—conclude with deceptive motions, because such motions create in listeners a desire to know what follows; the music is extended so that its eventual completion satisfies expectations. The half cadence also leaves phrases and the listener hanging in suspense.

Throughout the tonal era (and beyond), composers have relied on the pattern of incompleteness followed by completeness. Because a sense of incompleteness is crucial to the large-scale organization of tonal music, composers often avoid harmonically closed four-bar units. Instead, they rely on multiple four- or eight-bar phrases that hinge on one another.

EXAMPLE 20.1 Beethoven, Symphony no. 3 in E♭ major, "Eroica," op. 55, *Allegro vivace*: Trio

DVD 1
CH 20
TRACK 1

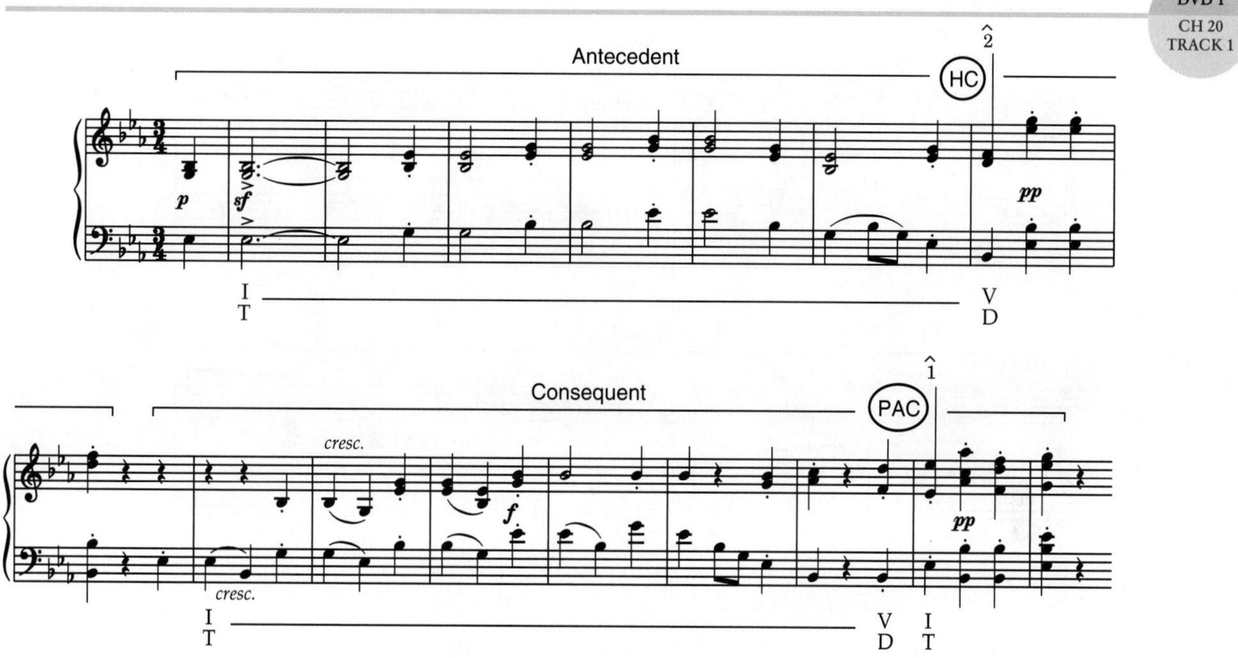

Listen to Example 20.1, noting how the phrases work together. The first phrase ends on a half cadence with $\hat{2}$ in the soprano; this leaves the listener craving tonic and the resolution of the melody to $\hat{1}$, which is achieved at the PAC of the second phrase. When a weakly conclusive phrase pairs with a stronger, more conclusive phrase, we call the resulting unit a **period**. The pairing is possible because the harmonic and melodic tensions left hanging at the end of the opening (**antecedent**) phrase resolve at the end of the final (**consequent**) phrase. Two phrases make a period only when they relate to each other musically and the second phrase ends with a strong authentic cadence.

An understanding of the period allows us to view musical spans of eight or sixteen measures (as in Example 20.1)—or even more measures—as a single musical idea. As we continue our studies, we will see how composers manipulate these units, increasing their size and linking them together to form complete musical works.

Aspects of Melody and Harmony in Periods

The cementing of two separate phrases is highly dependent on the interaction of melody and harmony. Listen to the two periods in Example 20.2, focusing on the following melodic and harmonic issues.

1. Do the two phrases in each period have melodies that resemble one another? If so, in what ways?
2. Locate and compare cadences.
3. What does the second-level harmonic analysis reveal about each phrase?

EXAMPLE 20.2

DVD 1
CH 20
TRACK 2

A. Mozart, Piano Concerto in D minor, K. 466, *Andante*

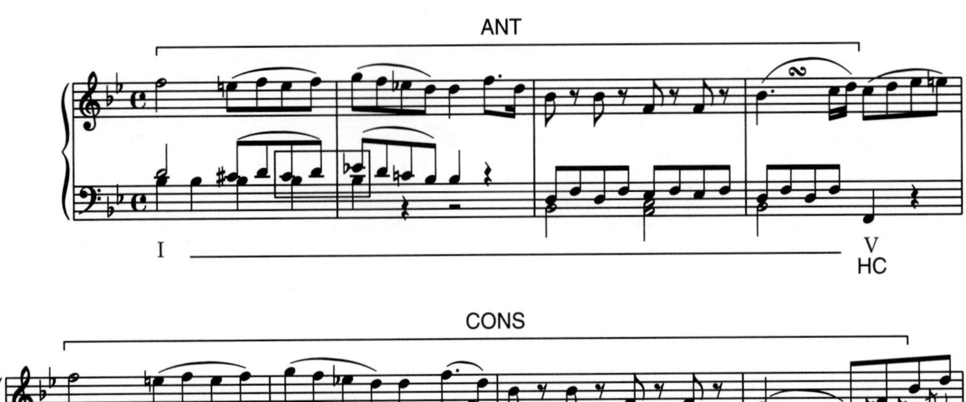

B. Beethoven, Piano Sonata no. 11 in B♭ major, op. 22, Menuetto

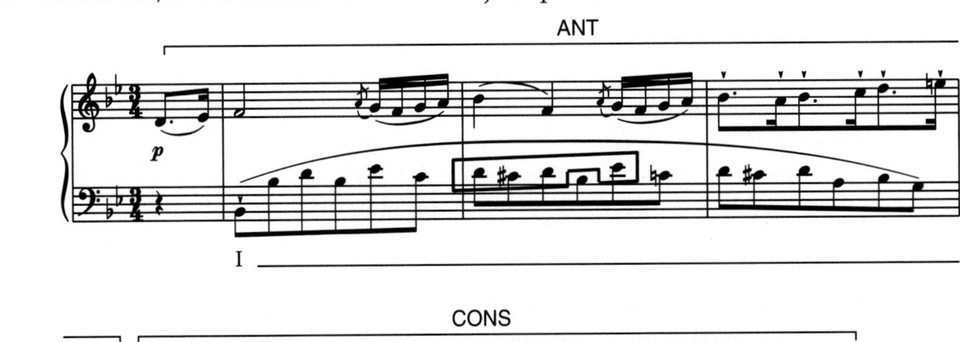

Both periods in Example 20.2 are in the key of B♭ major and divide into two four-measure phrases. Although the examples sound very different, they share several basic melodic features.

1. Both tunes begin with arpeggiations of the tonic triad.
2. The melody of the Mozart excerpt descends from $\hat{5}$ to $\hat{3}$ to $\hat{1}$ in mm. 1–3; the Beethoven melody ascends from $\hat{5}$ to $\hat{1}$ to $\hat{3}$ in mm. 1–3 and finally to the upper-octave $\hat{5}$ in m. 4.

3. The same accompanimental neighboring figure (boxed in both excerpts) gives a chromatic twist to each example.

However, there are important melodic differences: The second phrase of the Mozart excerpt begins exactly the same as the first, with only a slight change at the end. The Beethoven excerpt has no melodic repetition of material from mm. 1–3; instead, it begins its second phrase at m. 5 with relatively new-sounding material. When the two phrases of a period are melodically similar to each other, as in the Mozart example, we call them **parallel phrases.** Those that are melodically dissimilar, as in the Beethoven example, are called **contrasting phrases.**

Although the two periods in Example 20.2 have similar cadences (HC in m. 4; authentic cadence in m. 8), there are important harmonic differences. Mozart's first phrase has the harmonic structure T–PD–D. The second phrase begins again on the tonic, restating the same melodic idea of the first phrase. It is as if the music restarts after being interrupted at the half cadence:

phrase 1———————— phrase 2————
T PD D // T PD D T
←(BRD) phrase model interrupted starts over → resolves!

Only in the second phrase, after a restart of the phrase model, does the music push through the cadential dominant to attain the long-awaited tonic in m. 8. A pair of phrases with this harmonic structure creates an **interrupted period.** (Note that Mozart's half cadence does not resolve to the tonic; the dominant at the end of the first phrase is a back-relating dominant that extends the first tonic.)

Beethoven's first phrase also has the structure T–PD–D. The second phrase, by contrast, does not begin on the tonic with a statement of melodic material; it begins with a V_7 chord, which extends the dominant over the phrase boundary:

phrase 1———— phrase 2————
T PD D————(D)————T
phrase model continues →

Thus, there is only a single harmonic motion for the whole period. A pair of phrases that has a single, sweeping harmonic motion forms a **continuous period.** A favorite device of composers to create a continuous period is to lead to a HC in the first phrase but then follow it with the structural pre-dominant to begin the second phrase. In this case, the HC is strongly heard as a back-relating dominant:

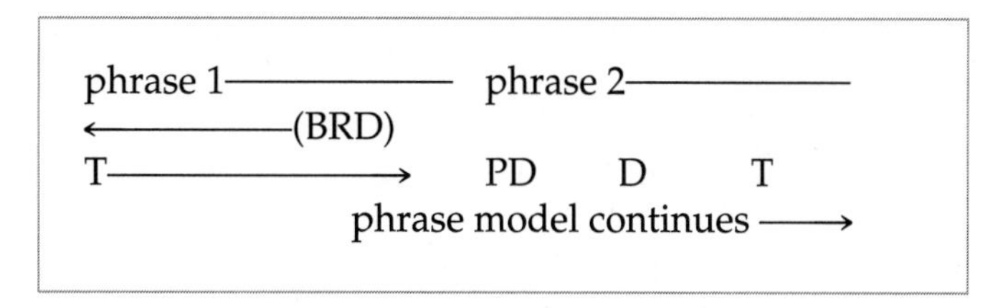

An alternate manner of creating a continuous period is to end the first phrase with an authentic cadence on a harmony other than tonic and then to continue the second phrase on the dominant, as shown here:

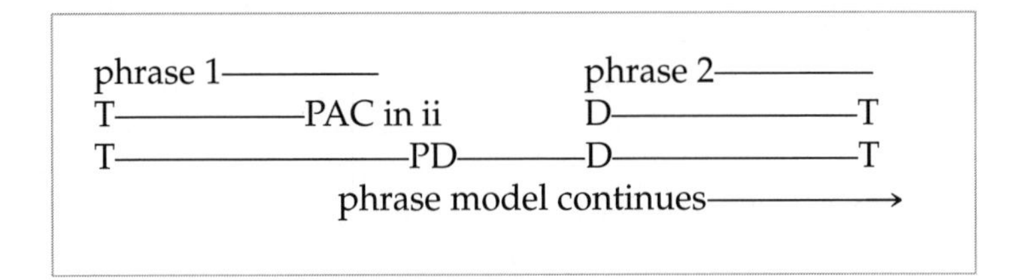

Again, a single harmonic sweep occurs, as shown by the second-level analysis, which is the same for both models: T–PD–D–T.

In addition to the harmonic paradigms we have seen so far for both interrupted and continuous periods, there exist two other possibilities. Listen to Example 20.3 and focus on the cadences that close each phrase.

EXAMPLE 20.3 Mozart, Piano Sonata in B♭ major, K. 281, *Allegro*

DVD 1 CH 20 TRACK 3

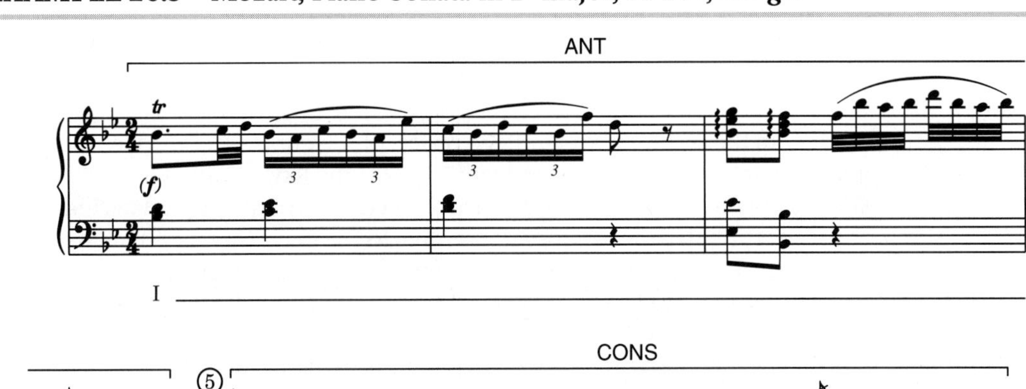

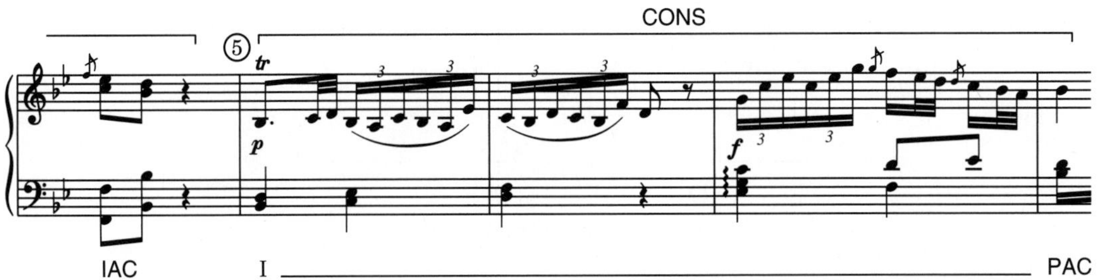

We have defined a period as a formal structure in which the final phrase closes something left open in the first phrase. In Example 20.3, both phrases close on the tonic, so you might wonder whether or not they form a period. It is indeed a period, because the second phrase subtly completes something left open in the first phrase: The melody—not the harmony—is left incomplete at the halfway point. This harmonic arrangement is called **sectional**.

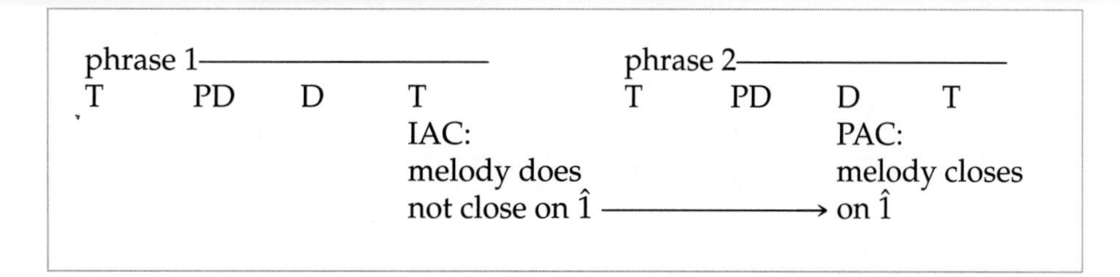

As an introduction to the final type of period, listen to Example 20.4 and observe each cadence. You probably heard two authentic cadences but may have been particularly struck by the sound of the second cadence, which is in a different tonal area—the key of III, the relative major. This idea may seem strange at first, but eventually we will see that it is quite common to close phrases, periods, and even whole sections of pieces in new harmonic areas. The technique of moving a composition through different tonal areas is called *modulation;* we explore this topic in Chapters 24 and 25. Periods that feature a second phrase closing with an authentic cadence in a different area or key are known as **progressive periods.**

EXAMPLE 20.4 Schubert, "Ständchen," from *Schwanengesang*, D. 957, no. 4

DVD 1
CH 20
TRACK 4

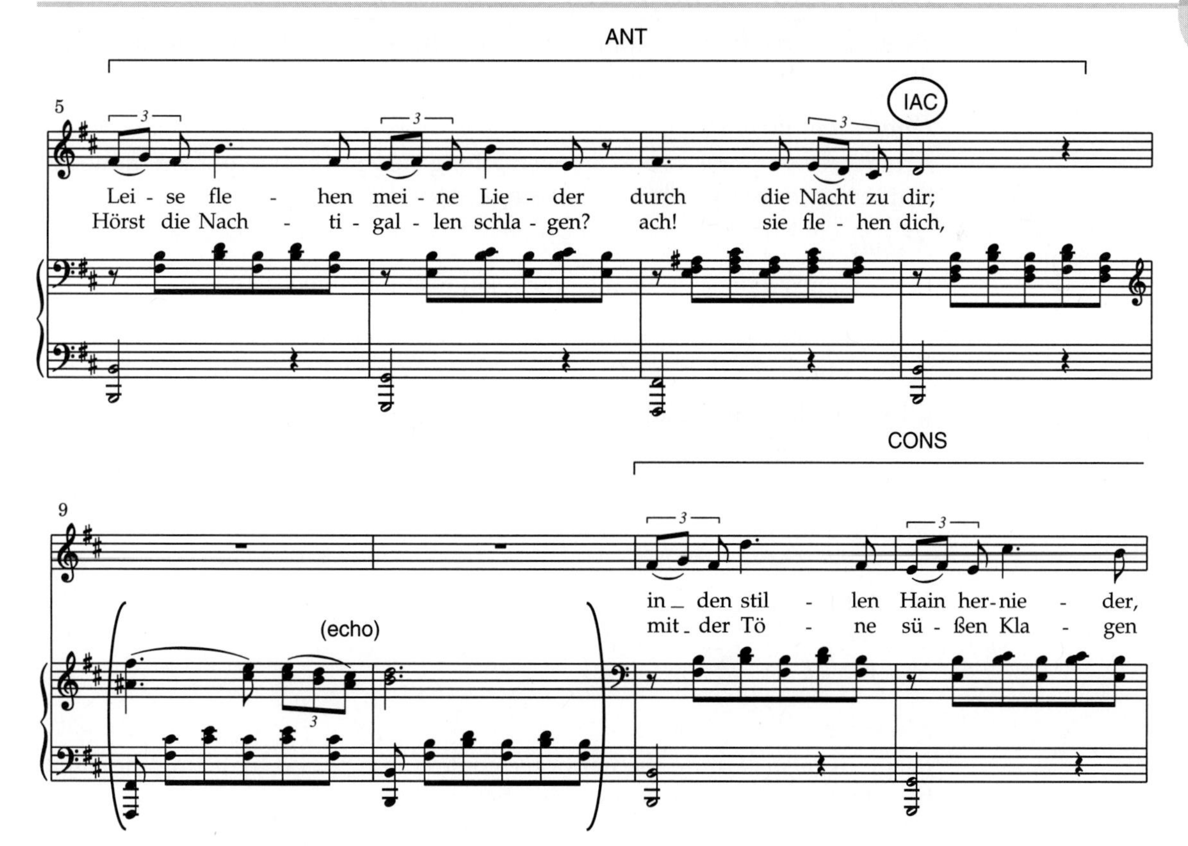

Continued

Representing Form: The Formal Diagram

We are now ready to diagram the relationships of phrases to capture visually the sense of how they combine to form periods.

Phrases and Periods

Arcs represent phrases, and an overarching curve over two phrases indicates that those phrases combine into a single period.

Melody

Letter names represent the melodic relationship between phrases:

For phrase 1: a = melodic material of the first phrase

For phrase 2:

a′ = melodic material similar to the first phrase

b = melodic material different from the first phrase

Compare the following diagrams with the melodic material in Examples 20.2A and 20.2B:

Harmony

Diagrams also capture the harmonic content of a period by listing the initial harmony and the cadence for each phrase.

Initial harmony: Typically, the first harmony is listed by roman numeral.

Cadence: Use HC, IAC, or PAC to identify the cadence.

A double slash (//) after a HC indicates a harmonic **interruption**—the second phrase restarts with tonic. Consider the diagrams for Examples 20.2A and 20.2B:

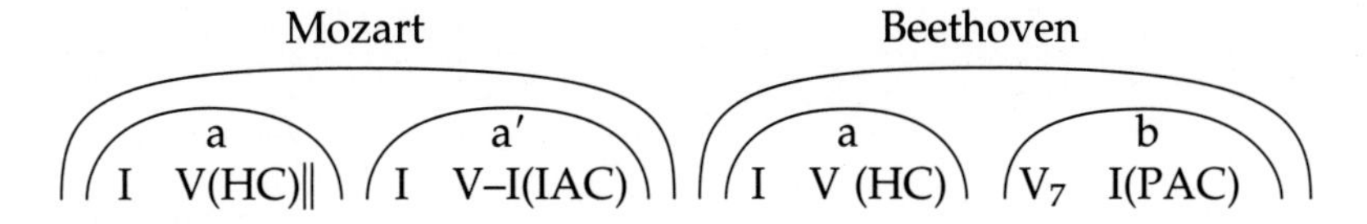

Period Label

We label a period with three words.

1. The first word describes the melodic relationship between phrases. The choices are:
   a. parallel
   b. contrasting
2. The second word describes the harmonic motion of the period. The choices are:
   a. interrupted
   b. continuous
   c. sectional
   d. progressive
3. The last word identifies the form: period.

As the completed form diagram from earlier illustrates, Example 20.2A is a **parallel interrupted period** and Example 20.2B is a **contrasting continuous period**. The following diagram represents the **parallel sectional period** and **parallel progressive period** of Examples 20.3 and 20.4, respectively.

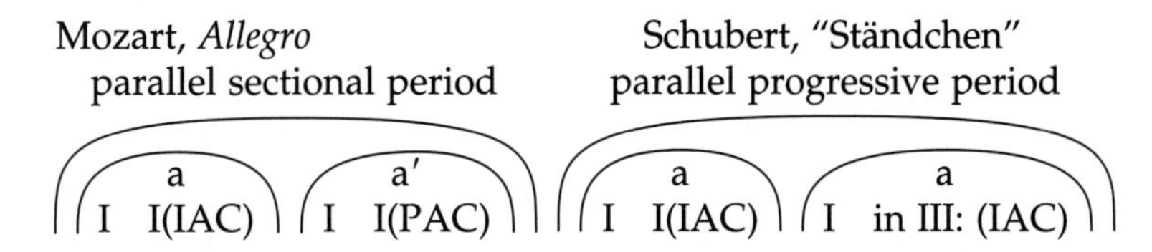

Period Diagrams and Their Labels

Period label	Abbeviation	Frequency of use	Formal diagram
parallel interrupted period	PIP	common	a: HC‖ / a′: I PAC
contrasting interrupted period	CIP	rare	a: HC‖ / b: I PAC
parallel sectional period	PSP	somewhat common	a: IAC / a′: I PAC
contrasting sectional periods	CSP	somewhat common	a: IAC / b: I PAC

Continued

Period label	Abbeviation	Frequency of use	Formal diagram
parallel continuous period	PCP	rare	a: HC, or AC on vi, ii, or IV — a′: phrase 2 begins somewhere other than tonic; PAC
contrasting continuous period	CCP	somewhat common	a: HC, or AC on vi, ii,or IV — b: phrase 2 begins somewhere other than tonic; PAC
parallel progressive period	PPP	common	a: HC or IAC — a′: phrase 2 ends with AC somewhere other than tonic
contrasting progressive period	CPP	common	a: HC or IAC — b: phrase 2 ends with AC somewhere other than tonic

Sample Analyses of Periods and Some Analytical Guidelines

Listen to Example 20.5 and consider the five questions and answers that follow. Strive to remember the questions, so you will be able to ask yourself the same questions when you begin your own analyses.

EXAMPLE 20.5 Mozart, *Die Zauberflöte (The Magic Flute)*, K. 617, act I, finale

DVD 1 CH 20 TRACK 5

Continued

1. Can the excerpt be divided into two or more phrases?
   Answer: Yes, it can be divided into two four-measure phrases, each of which ends with a cadence.
2. Do these phrases create an antecedent–consequent relationship?
   Answer: Yes, the first phrase sounds harmonically open (ending on a dominant chord) and melodically open (ending on the leading tone); the second phrase provides satisfying closure, with $\hat{2}$–$\hat{1}$ in the melody over a PAC.
3. Is the second cadence stronger than the first?
   Answer: Yes, the first phrase ends with a HC and the second ends with a PAC. *This forms a period.*
4. Are the melodies in each phrase related?
   Answer: Yes, they are clearly related. The second phrase is nearly identical to the first phrase except for embellishments at the cadence. *Thus, the melodic structure is parallel.*
5. What harmonies begin and end each phrase?
   Answer: Phrase I begins with tonic and ends with a HC. Phrase 2 restarts with tonic and ends with a PAC. *Thus, the harmonic structure is interrupted.*

From the answers to these five questions, we are ready to label the period as a PIP and diagram it in the following manner:

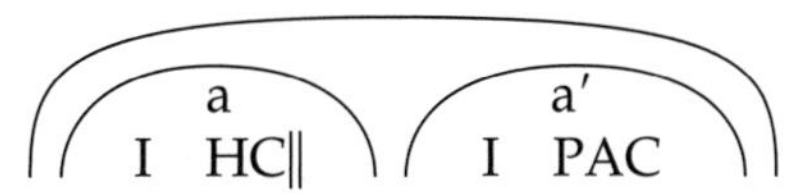

parallel interrupted period

Now let's try applying the same question-and-answer process to Example 20.6.

Example 20.6 Beethoven, *Moderato*, from *Klavierstück*, WoO 82

DVD 1
CH 20
TRACK 6

1. Can the excerpt be divided into two or more phrases?
   Answer: No. Although the excerpt divides into two musical units, they cannot be considered phrases because there is no cadence in m. 4, just a caesura on a dissonant ii$^6_5$ chord. There is only one cadence (m. 8), so there can be only one phrase.

We can end the question-and-answer series at this point, because this excerpt is simply an eight-measure phrase; it is not a period.

A Summary for Analyzing Periods

The following four steps will assist you in locating and identifying periods.

Step 1. Locate phrases and mark their cadences.

Step 2. Examine the cadence of phrase 1. If it is a PAC in the tonic, it cannot be part of a period. If the first phrase closes with a cadence that is weaker than the cadence found at the end of the second phrase, however, draw arcs and identify phrase lengths.

Step 3. Analyze the melodies of the phrases. There are two possible melodic structures: parallel and contrasting.

Step 4. Analyze the cadences of the phrases and write your answers to the right of each arc. Next, label the harmony that begins each phrase. There are four possible harmonic structures: sectional, interrupted, continuous, and progressive.

Composing Periods

Writing periods involves creativity and using your ear. It is a good exercise because it calls directly on your knowledge of diatonic harmonies, cadences, and construction of four-measure phrases. It also allows you to express your own musicality in deciding what melodies and harmonies sound best in your compositions. You should try to sing and play your compositions.

For the time being, we confine ourselves to three period types that end on the tonic. In beginning a composition, we start with the large harmonic picture using the following tonal models:

- I_____ HC I_____I (PAC or IAC)
- I_____ (IAC) I_____I (PAC)
- I_____ HC V(7) _____I (PAC)

Next we map out the harmonies within each phrase. Remember that, as a general rule, harmonic changes tend to occur on strong, accented beats (such as downbeats). For example, the harmonies in $\frac{4}{4}$ meter will change most often on beats 1 and 3. The following eight-measure structure reveals two potential harmonic solutions for an interrupted period (the first tonal model shown earlier):

Measure:	1	2	3	4	5	6	7	8
Solution 1:	I	vi	IV	V //	I–IV–I	iii–vi	ii–V^7	I
Solution 2:	I–I^6	V^4_2–I^6	ii^6	V //	I–iii	vi–IV	ii^6_5–V^7	I

Notice that the consequent phrases in both solutions open with harmonic settings different from their antecedents. Such harmonic contrast permits—in fact, almost demands—these periods to be contrasting melodically rather than parallel.

After our harmonic plan is in place, we can then add a melody that provides a good outer-voice counterpoint and exhibits a high degree of motivic consistency and melodic interest.

EXERCISE INTERLUDE

ANALYSIS

DVD 2
CH 20
TRACK 1

20.1

Following the question-and-answer procedure demonstrated earlier, label each of the following examples. The examples may be a single phrase or a period; if an example is a period, provide a formal diagram and period label. *Note:* You may find it useful to mark up the music to help you with your analysis.

A. Mozart, Piano Sonata in B♭ major, K. 333, *Allegretto grazioso*

B. Mozart, Symphony no. 39 in E♭ major, K. 543, *Allegretto*

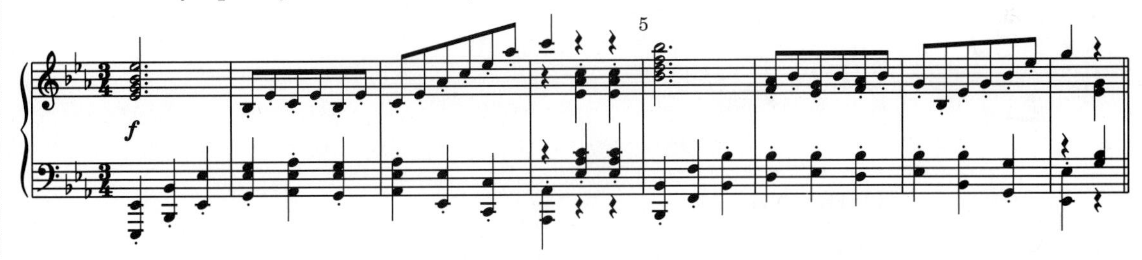

C. Beethoven, Piano Sonata in D major, op. 28 ("Pastorale"), *Andante*

D. Brahms, Waltz in A♭ major, op. 39, no. 15

E. Beethoven, Violin Sonata in G major, op. 30, no. 3, *Allegro assai*

DVD 2
CH 20
TRACK 2

LISTENING

20.2 Aural Identification of Periods

Listen to each of the following examples. For each:

1. Identify cadences (PAC, IAC, HC), and mark "x" to indicate that an example closes in a key other than the one in which it began.
2. Identify the relationship between the melodies of each phrase.
3. Provide a formal diagram and period label.

A. Rossini, *Il barbiere di Siviglia* (*The Barber of Seville*), Overture phrase 1 cadence ____; phrase 2 cadence _____; melodies ____ ; period _____

B. Schubert, "Der Lindenbaum," *Winterreise*, op. 89, no. 5, D. 911, in $\frac{3}{4}$ phrase 1 cadence; ____ phrase 2 cadence _____; melodies ____; period _____

C. Haydn, Piano Sonata no. 48 in C major, Hob. XVI: 35, Finale: *Allegro*, in $\frac{3}{4}$ phrase 1 cadence____; phrase 2 cadence ____; melodies ___; period _____

D. Mendelssohn, Symphony in A, op. 56, *Andante con moto*, in $\frac{3}{4}$ phrase 1 cadence ____; phrase 2 cadence ____; melodies ____; period _____

E. Haydn, Symphony no. 94 in G major ("Surprise"), *Andante*, in $\frac{2}{4}$ phrase 1 cadence __; phrase 2 cadence ___; melodies ___ period _____

F. Beethoven, Piano Sonata in C minor, op. 13 ("Pathetique"), Rondo (alla breve) phrase 1 cadence __; phrase 2 cadence ___; melodies ___; period _____

G. Mozart: Symphony no. 40 in G minor, K. 550, Menuetto: *Allegro*, in $\frac{3}{4}$ phrase 1 cadence __; phrase 2 cadence ___; melodies ___; period _____

PERFORMING

20.3 Instrumental Application and Improvisation

We will use the following phrases from the literature to create periods. Depending on their shape and harmonic implications, they will function as *either* antecedent phrases or consequent phrases in a two-phrase period. Your compositional choices include PIPs, CIPs, and CCPs. If you are not a pianist, find an accompanist to provide a harmonic setting for each tune. You will need to play the given phrase and your newly created antecedent or consequent phrase for your accompanist for him/her to be able to hear the implied harmonies and be able to accompany you. If you are a pianist, add either full chords or just a bass voice to accompany yourself.

A.

B. Beethoven, "An den Fernen Geliebten" op. 75, no. 5

C. Mendelssohn, "Wenn sich zwei Herzen scheiden"

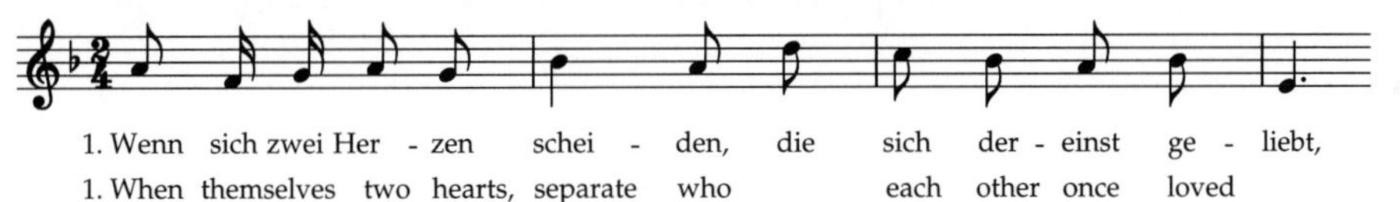

D. Schumann, "Volksliedchen", from *Children's Pieces*, op. 68

E. Mozart, Symphony in G major, K. 110

F. Haydn, String Quartet in E♭ major, op. 64, no. 6, Trio

G. Jean Baptiste Loeillet, Sonata in G minor, op. 2, no. 2

H. Beethoven, "Urians Reise um die Welt" op. 52, no. 1

I. Haydn, String Quartet in D major, op. 64, no. 5, Finale

J. Mozart, Symphony in D major, K. 97, Trio

COMPOSITION

20.4

WORKBOOK
20.1–20.5

Based on the given antecedent phrase, write two different period types. Make sure that your consequent phrases continue the basic texture of the antecedent phrase.

Type 1: a PIP
Type 2: a CCP

TERMS AND CONCEPTS

- period
- melodic types
  - parallel
  - contrasting
- harmonic types
  - interrupted
  - continuous
  - sectional
  - progressive
- phrase
  - antecedent vs. consequent

CHAPTER 21

Other Small Musical Structures: Sentences, Double Periods, and Asymmetrical Periods

Have you ever listened to the way that parents call their children inside on a hot summer evening? There is usually a consistency in their speech pattern, given that parents need to make their announcement more than once:

"Johnny, it's time to come in now."

"Johnny, you need to come in *now*."

"Johnny, I mean it. Get in right now or you'll be grounded for life."

While reading these three statements aloud, notice the pattern and the proportional length of each utterance. The first two declamations are related both in length and content: In eight syllables, each statement communicates that Johnny must come in, although slight emphasis is made in the second statement by leaning on the word *now*. The third statement, however, is very different. Not only is it exactly twice as long (16 syllables), but now the parent's level of insistence is communicated by a threat to the child. One would assume that other factors, such as the pitch and the dynamic level of the parent's voice, are correspondingly accentuated as well. As we all know, it is usually only the third statement—which intensifies the sentiments of the previous two—that is ever successful: Within 15 seconds, the child makes it breathlessly through the door.

This threefold process of communication is common in human interaction. For example, very young children (between the ages of 2 and 4) often improvise in exactly such a way: a short statement followed by a similar repetition and then an elaboration of the statement that occupies exactly twice as much time. Given that music is in many ways a communicative art filled with the same sorts of rhetorical characteristics, one frequently encounters this process as well. Whenever this rhetorical formal device of short–short–long (usually in the proportion 1:1:2) occurs within music, it is described as an instance of **sentence structure**.

Many folk and even popular tunes unfold using this pattern. Consider the pacing of "Clementine" (Oh My Darlin' | Oh My Darlin' | Oh My Dar——lin' Clementine). Entire genres of music are based on the sentence structure, including the blues, and—not to be left out—composers of art music from the seventeenth century to the present have consistently relied on the successful rhetorical device in contexts that we now explore.

The Sentence: An Alternative Musical Structure

Listen to Example 21.1. The phrase contains subphrases articulated by rests that create a breathy and halting effect. The analytical annotations represent the harmonic, melodic, and rhythmic content of each gesture in the Beethoven excerpt. We see that mm. 1 and 2, which move from I to V, are labeled A; mm. 3 and 4, which transpose the melody up a second, moving from V^6_5 to I, are labeled A′. The second contrasting gesture behaves as one continuous unit of four measures and is labeled B.

EXAMPLE 21.1 **Beethoven, "Lustig-Traurig" in C major, WoO 54**

DVD 1
CH 21
TRACK 1

We see in Example 21.1 how Beethoven has created a proportional, additive structure, in which a two-measure musical idea is stated, restated, and then embellished and extended, ending in a cadence. The excerpt is particularly satisfying because it develops so organically: The two two-measure subphrases become, in a sense, an integral part of the consequent unit.

Now listen to Example 21.2. This eight-measure excerpt comprises a single phrase that closes with a half cadence. The first half of the phrase contains two distinct yet closely related ideas (labeled A and A′); the second four measures seem to combine into a single unit, creating an overall 2 + 2 + 4 sentence structure. Yet there is more to this sentence. If we look at the harmonic rhythm, we see that the rate of change is relatively slow in the first four measures (two measures of tonic are followed by two measures of a neighboring dominant).

EXAMPLE 21.2 **Beethoven, Piano Sonata no. 1 in F minor, op. 2, *Allegro***

DVD 1
CH 21
TRACK 2

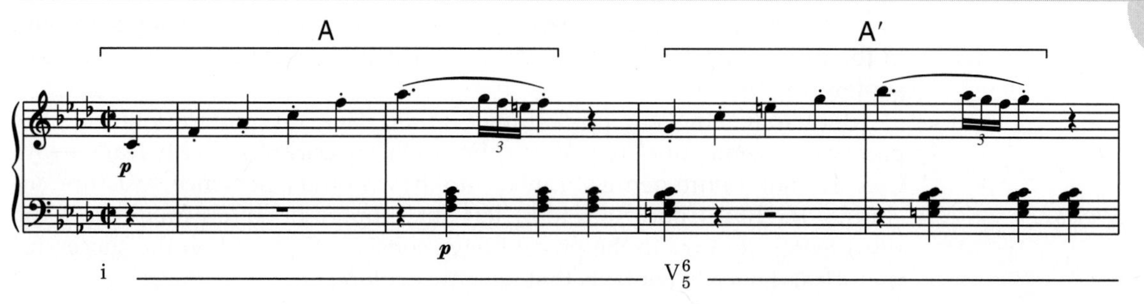

Continued

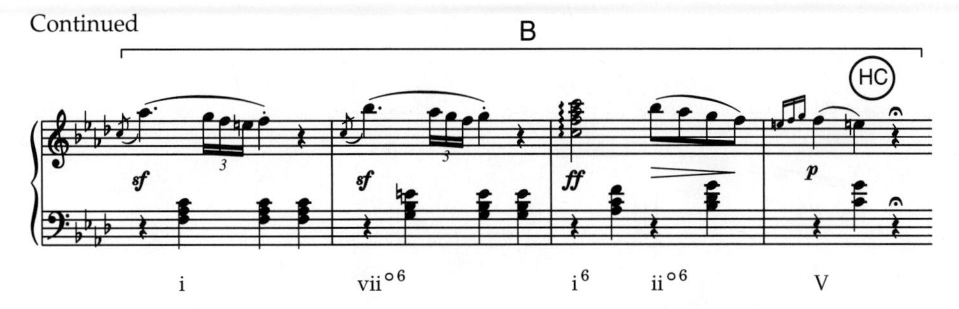

The harmonic rhythm speeds up in mm. 4–8, as illustrated here:

measure:	1	2	3	4	5	6	7	8
harmony	i______________		V^6_5______________		i	vii°$_6$	i6 ii°$_6$	V
	rate of harmonic change accelerates⟶							

Note how Beethoven creates a musical paradox in his sentence: As the initial two-measure units combine and lengthen into a single four-measure unit, the final four measures are fragmented by the acceleration of the harmonic rhythm. Further analysis reveals another layer of complexity: On the first pass, we labeled the melodic ideas in the first four measures A and A′, implying a close relationship (both consist of an arpeggiated, staccato ascent followed by a turn figure). Now, how would you describe the melodic content of mm. 5–6? Again, there is a close relationship, because m. 5 repeats a step higher in m. 6—but this melody goes by twice as fast as A and A′.

When the melody of mm. 5–6 (labeled a-a′) is followed by the climactic two-measure gesture of mm. 7–8 (labeled b), we see a miniature sentence develop (1 + 1 + 2) *within* the four-measure B of the larger sentence. This **nesting of sentences** is reflected in the following diagram. When nested structures occur within *both* the A and the B portions of the sentence, new letters (c and d) are assigned to the nested structures in the B portion of the sentence (e.g., A's nested structures would be labeled a, a′, b and B's nested structures would be labeled c, c′, d).

measure:	1 2	3 4	5	6	7	8
larger sentence:	A (2 mm) +	A′ (2 mm.)	B (4 mm.)			
smaller sentence:			a (1)	a′ (1)	b (2)	

Beethoven is not the only composer to use these elegant techniques. Examples 21.3A and B present sentences composed by Haydn and Mozart, respectively. Haydn's sentence illustrates a single four-measure phrase; Mozart's sentence (written in 1764 when he was only 8 years old) contains eight measures.

EXAMPLE 21.3

DVD 1 CH 21 TRACK 3

A. Haydn, Piano Sonata no. 38 in F major, Hob. XVI. 23, *Adagio*

Continued

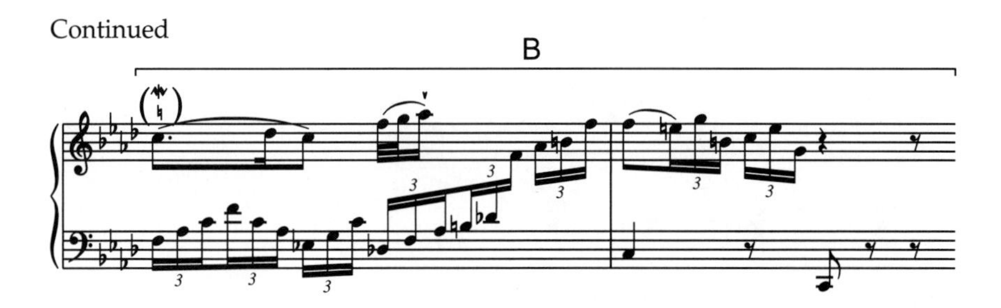

B. Mozart, Violin Sonata in C major, K. 14, Menuetto secondo en Carillon

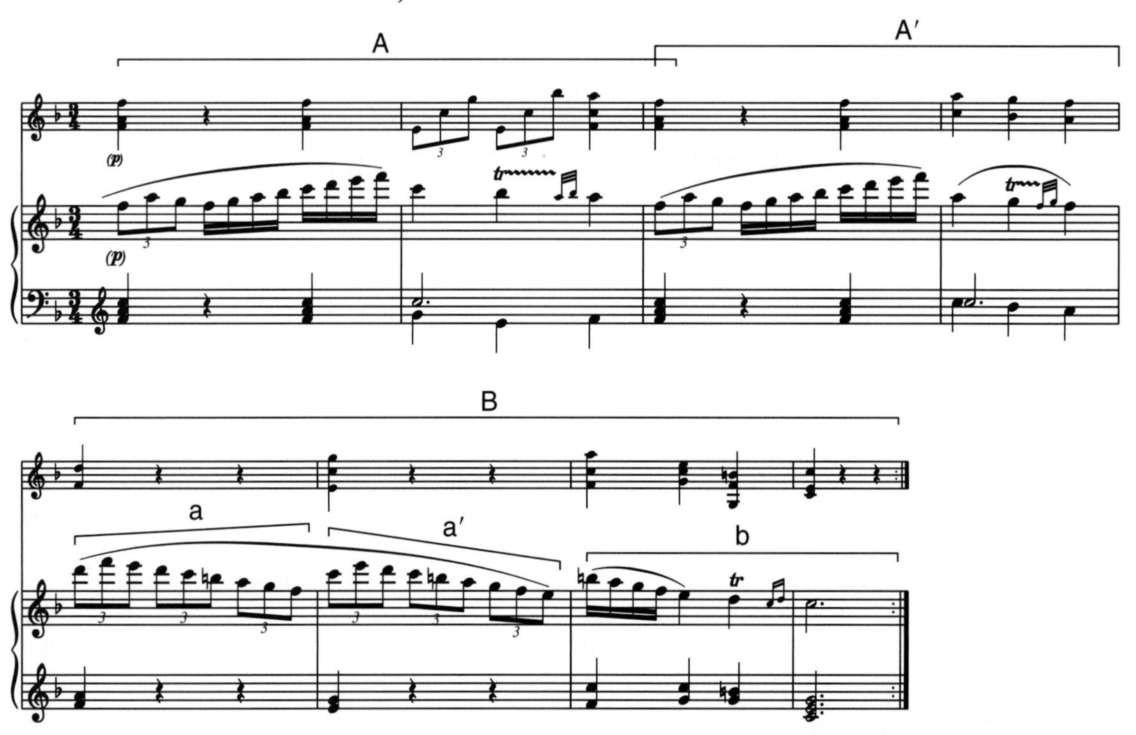

Given that phrases are often fashioned into sentence structures, it follows that periods draw on sentence construction. Listen to Example 21.4. The first phrase (mm. 1–4) is also a sentence, containing two one-measure ideas that are answered by a two-measure idea that moves to a half cadence. The material repeats in an ornamented form in mm. 5–8 and closes with a PAC. The idea of repeating a phrase with sentence structure is one of two common techniques for casting a period in sentence structure (see Example 21.5A). The second technique, which does not merely repeat the sentence structure, is more dramatic. The first phrase forms the A and A′ of the sentence; the second phrase comprises the B. Thus, a single sentence structure unfolds over the entire period (see Example 21.5B).

EXAMPLE 21.4 Mozart, Piano Sonata no. 3 in B♭ major, K. 281, Rondeau: *Allegro*

DVD 1
CH 21
TRACK 4

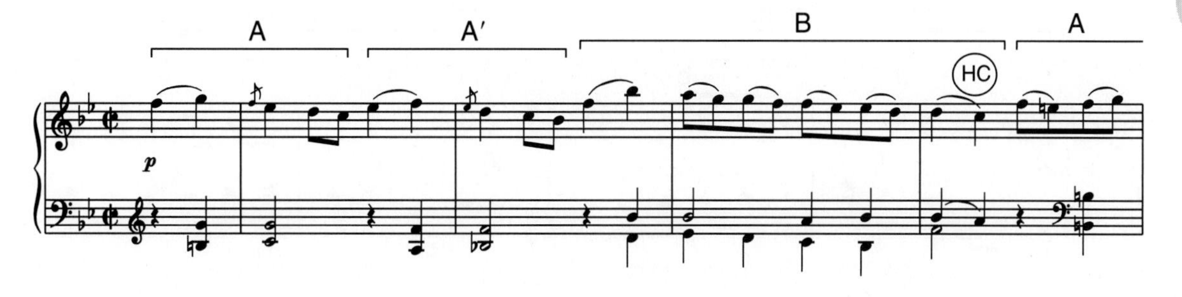

EXAMPLE 21.5

A. Period Composed of a Repeated Sentence

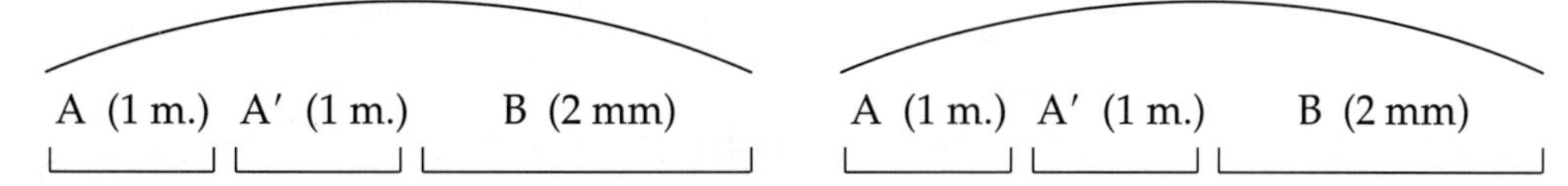

B. Period Composed of a Single Sentence

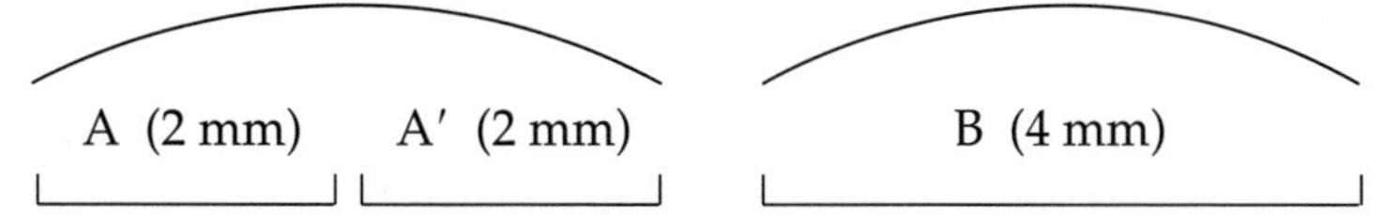

EXERCISE INTERLUDE

ANALYSIS

DVD 2
CH 21
TRACK 1

21.1

The following phrases and periods contain sentence structures. Do *not* analyze with roman numerals. Provide only a formal diagram for each. Include period labels, and clearly identify sentence structures with brackets. (When you encounter a nested sentence, as in Example 21.2, use uppercase letters for the larger sentence and lowercase letters for the smaller sentence. Further, if both the A and the B of the sentence contain nested structures, new letters (c and d) are assigned to the nested structures in the B portion of the sentence.) In a paragraph or two, compare or contrast any two examples.

Sample Solution: Beethoven, Piano Concerto no. 2 in B♭, Rondo

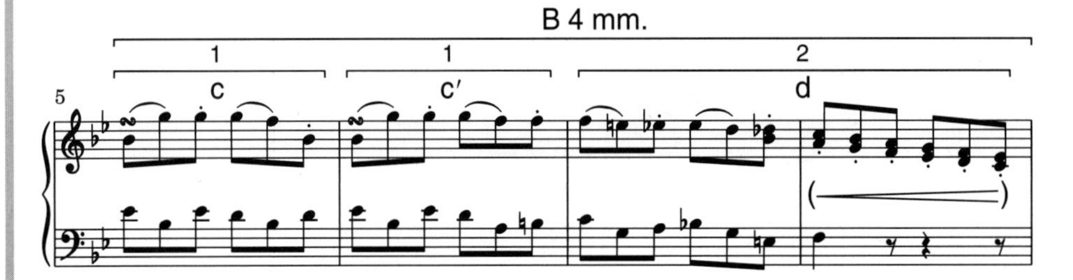

A. Beethoven, Violin Concerto in D major, op. 61, *Rondo: Allegro*

B. Haydn, String Quartet in D minor, op. 76, no. 2 ("Quinten"), Hob III: 76, I, *Adagio*

C. Schubert, Piano Sonata in A major, op. posth, *Trio*

D. Schumann, "Kind im einschlummern," *Kinderszenen*, op. 15, no. 12

E. Schumann, *Kreisleriana*, op. 16, no. 2

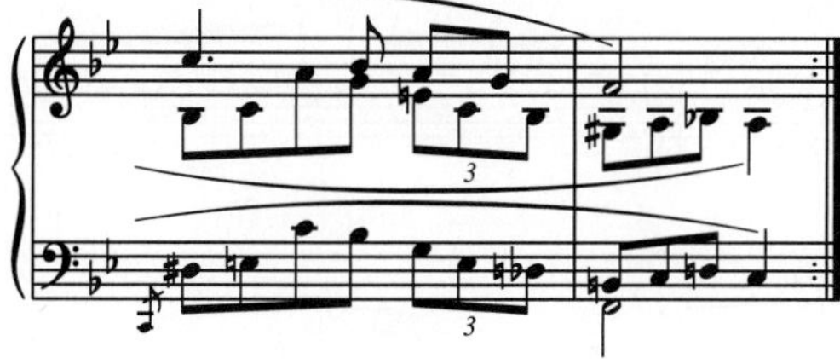

F. Chopin, Nocturne in F minor, op. 55, no. 1

The Double Period

By this point, you should feel comfortable in hearing the ways in which pairs of phrases combine to make periods. Your listening strategy will have included finding pairs of cadences in which the second arrival is more convincing than the first. This approach, however, is not a foolproof way to find periods.

In Example 21.6, Beethoven's 16 measures contain four distinct cadences. *Why wouldn't we say that there are two periods?* The cadence in m. 8 is not conclusive enough to close a period; it is only a half cadence, which requires a consequent authentic cadence. The necessary PAC does not appear until m. 16, so *why wouldn't we say that there is one giant period?*

EXAMPLE 21.6 Beethoven, Piano Sonata in A♭ major, op. 26

DVD 1 CH 21 TRACK 5

There is something to the intuition that mm. 1–8 and 9–16 each subdivide into four-measure antecedent–consequent segments; the cadences in mm. 8 and 16 are stronger than the cadences in mm. 4 and 12. For example, the half cadence in m. 4 comes about almost as an afterthought. The downbeat sonority of m. 4 is tonic, and the dominant enters only on the weak beat of the measure. The half cadence in m. 8, however, appears to be more confident; here, the bass rings on dominant $\hat{5}$ right from the downbeat.

As soon as we hear that m. 9 parallels the melody of m. 1, we gain a whole set of expectations for mm. 8–16. We anticipate that this second unit will take eight measures to close on the tonic. And indeed, the melody in mm. 9–16 is similar to the melody in mm. 1–8. The result is a parallel melodic structure, in which the PAC in m. 16 answers the HC in m. 8. The diagram in Example 21.7 summarizes the form of the four phrases. Measures 1-16 appear to be one giant parallel interrupted period, each half of which contains two contrasting phrases. This type of structure—the antecedent and consequent segments divide into antecedent–consequent phrases at a smaller level—is called a **double period**.

EXAMPLE 21.7

measures:	1–4	5–8	9–12	13–16
harmony:	I ------- HC	IV6 ------ HC ‖	I ------- HC	IV6 ------ PAC
smaller-level melody: large level melody:	a A ------------------	b ------------------	a′ A′ ------------------	b′ ------------------
smaller-level period structure: large level period structure:	"antecedent" Antecedent	"consequent" ------------------	"antecedent" Consequent	"consequent" ------------------

Just as we saw multiple strategies for integrating sentence structures into periods, there are a number of cadence formulas that composers use to create double periods. A common double-period structure is one with phrases that close as in Example 21.8. The structure of Examples 21.7 and 21.8 would be labeled a *parallel interrupted double period*. Notice that the IAC/HC relationship in mm. 1–8 does not set up a true antecedent–consequent relationship, because of the need for the cadence in m. 8 to create a sense of inconclusiveness that will require closure in m. 16.

EXAMPLE 21.8

measures:	1–4	5–8	9–12	13–16
harmony:	I ------- IAC	---------- HC ‖	I ------- IAC	---------- PAC
smaller-level melody: large level melody:	a A ------------------	b ------------------	a′ A′ ------------------	b′ ------------------
smaller-level period structure: large level period structure:	"antecedent" Antecedent	"consequent" ------------------	"antecedent" Consequent	"consequent" ------------------

Asymmetrical Periods

Occasionally, you will encounter periods that comprise an uneven number of phrases—three-phrase, five-phrase, or even seven-phrase periods; we call these **asymmetrical periods**. Each phrase of an asymmetrical period must close with a cadence that is weaker than the cadence of the final phrase. (Note that a series of phrases punctuated by weak cadences—none of which is strong enough to close a passage—does not constitute a period. Rather, it is just a phrase chain, or **phrase group**.)

In asymmetrical periods, composers distribute the unequal number of antecedent phrases in one of three ways.

1. They may immediately repeat either the antecedent or the consequent (for example, *aab* or *abb*). Example 21.9 presents the opening of a rondo

by Beethoven that has the structure antecedent–consequent–consequent. This type of asymmetrical period maintains a deeper-level two-phrase symmetry; the repetition of the consequent is more of an echo than an independent entity.

EXAMPLE 21.9 Beethoven, Piano Sonata in C minor ("Pathetique"), op. 13, Rondo

DVD 1 CH 21 TRACK 6

2. Composers may employ new material for each of the phrases (for example, *abc*). In such cases, the underlying asymmetry is easily perceived. Multiphrase periods that contain new material in each phrase often sound more like phrase groups or even subphrases; we must consider the strength of the final cadence to discriminate a period from a phrase group. Consider Example 21.10. There are three distinct sections, but only the first and third contain cadences. The second phrase—or, more accurately, subphrase—elaborates tonic. Yet, given that the final cadence is so strong and brings closure to the previous phrases and that each of the three components contains four measures, one could interpret the piece as an asymmetrical, three-phrase period.

EXAMPLE 21.10 Gruber, "Silent Night"

Continued

3. The third technique combines the repetition of material with statements of new material (for example, *aabbc*). Example 21.11 is an example of such a period. There are five four-measure phrases, but there is an underlying three-phrase structure:

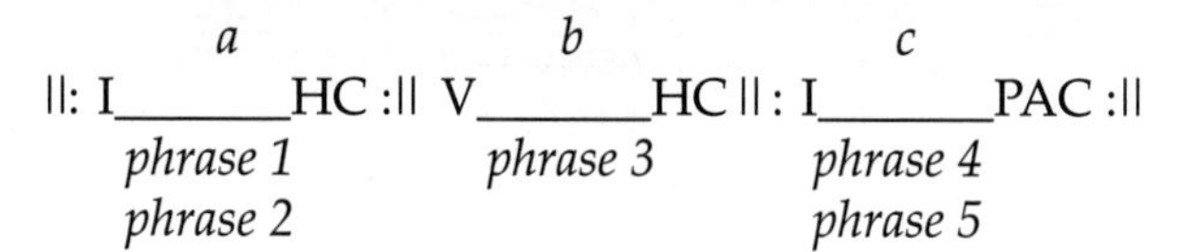

EXAMPLE 21.11 **Haydn, String Quartet in C major, "Emperor", op. 76, no. 3 Hob. III: 77, *Poco adagio; cantabile***

Continued

EXERCISE INTERLUDE

DVD 2
CH 21
TRACK 2

ANALYSIS

21.2 Aural and Visual Analysis of Periods

Analyze each of the following periods by providing a formal diagram. In some cases, the bass and soprano lines are incomplete, and you will need to add the missing pitches as indicated by arrows. Note that you may encounter sentences, double periods, and asymmetrical periods.

A. Mozart, Piano Sonata in D major, K. 284, Theme (*Andante*)

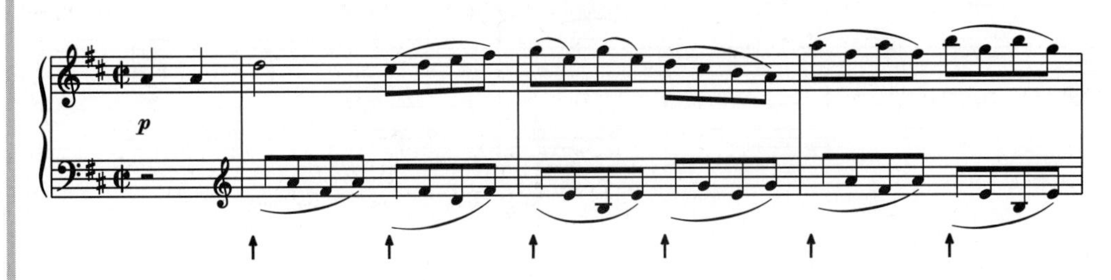

Continued

B. Brahms, Intermezzo in A minor, op. 116, no. 2

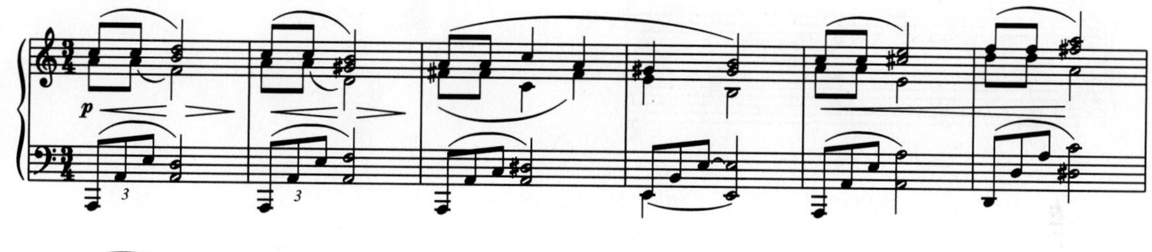

C. Chopin, *Grande Valse Brillante* in A minor, op. 34, no. 2, BI 64

Is this excerpt a double period or a single long period? Why?

D. Mozart, Piano Sonata in D major, K. 576, *Allegretto*

E. Tchaikovsky, "Sweet Reverie," *Children's Pieces*, op. 39, no. 21

Explain why this excerpt could be interpreted as containing sentence structure.

21.3 Aural Analysis of Periods

This exercise is identical to the previous exercise, except this time no scores are provided. Provide a formal diagram for each period.

A. Mozart, Piano Sonata in A major, K. 331, *Andante grazioso*
B. Rameau, "La Villageouise," Suite in E minor, *Pièces de clavecin, 1724,*
C. Beethoven, Symphony no. 7 in A major, op. 92, *Allegretto*
D. Mozart, "In diesen heil'gen Hallen," *Die Zauberflöte*, K. 620, act II, scene 3
E. Schumann, "Erster Verlust," from *43 Pieces for Children*
F. Mozart, Piano Sonata in D major, K. 576, *Allegro*
G. Mozart, Concerto in E♭ major for Horn and Orchestra, K. 447, *Larghetto*
H. John Stanley, Solo in D, op. 1, no. 1, Minuet

KEYBOARD, ANALYSIS, SINGING, AND COMPOSITION

21.4 Period Criticism

The given melody is in period form; there are three different figured bass harmonizations below the melody. Sing the melody and provide roman numerals for each of the harmonizations. Then accompany your singing by realizing each of the figured basses in turn. Which do you like best, and why? Are there portions of the figured basses that you particularly like? Create your own distinct figured bass setting by combining material from the three figured basses into a new setting.

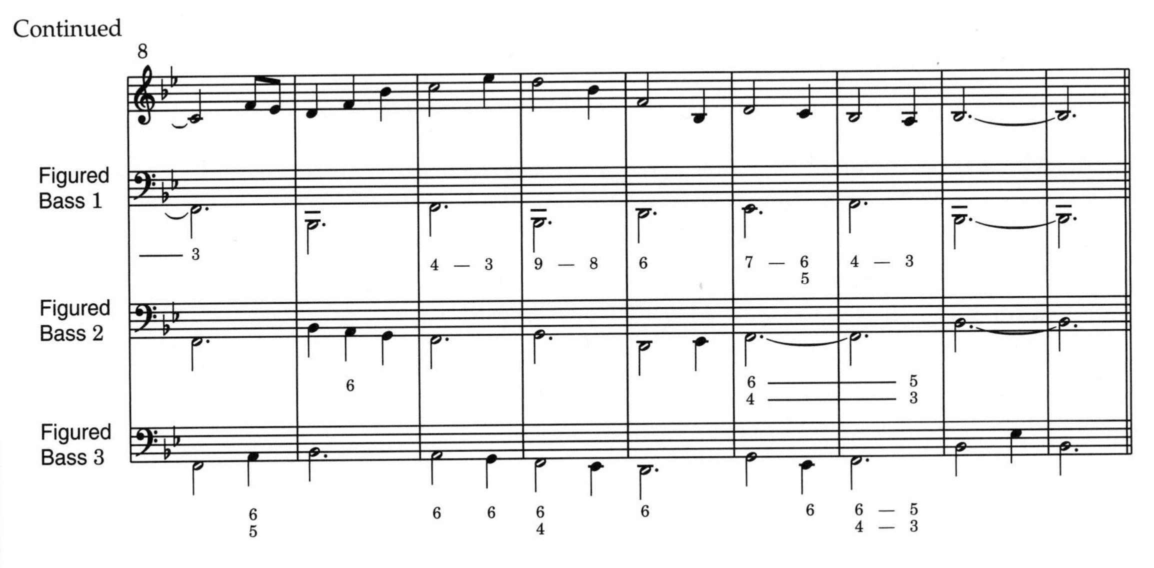

LISTENING

DVD 2 CH 21 TRACK 4

21.5

Notate the bass and provide roman numerals for the following phrases cast in sentence structure. Use a separate sheet of manuscript paper.

A. Felice Giardini, *Six Duos for Violin and Cello*, no. 2, *Allegro* ($\frac{6}{8}$; harmonic rhythm at the dotted quarter)

B. Marcello, Sonata in A minor, no. 8, Minuetto ($\frac{3}{4}$, usually two harmonic changes per measure)

C. Bach, Sonata in B minor, BWV 1030, *Andante* (slow $\frac{4}{4}$, eighth-note bass motion)

COMPOSITION

21.6

Given are the openings (*incipits*) of sentence structures. Some will work well as single phrases cast in the 1:1:2 proportion, while others will provide good models for a period cast in sentence structure. Sing each incipit to determine its implied harmonic rhythm and setting; then write a continuation that leads to a cadence. Write in the bass note and roman numerals; then accompany your singing of the solution.

INSTRUMENTAL APPLICATION

21.7 Improvising Sentence Structures

Given are the openings of potential sentences (i.e., the *a* portion of the overall *a-a′-b* entirety). Study the given examples, which demonstrate ways to develop the given material.

Example 1

Example 1 presents a falling triad (a), which is literally repeated (a′) and developed in the b by leading to a HC. Example 1B shows how the a′ can be transposed to IV. Example 1C adds a decorative PT to the a′, and the b closes with an AC

Example 2

WORKBOOK
21.1–21.4

Example 2 presents a melodically fluent structure in which a begins on $\hat{1}$ and leads to $\hat{2}$, a′ moves from $\hat{2}$ to $\hat{3}$; b reverses the contour and returns by step to $\hat{1}$.

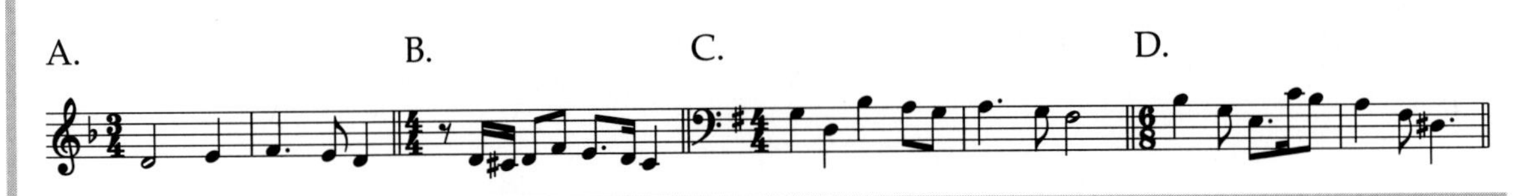

TERMS AND CONCEPTS

- asymmetrical period
- double period
- sentence
- sentence structure

CHAPTER 22

Harmonic Sequences: Concepts and Patterns

We have seen how diatonic harmonies in major and minor keys participate in the phrase model. Though each harmony may appear in a variety of musical contexts, its behavior is strictly regulated by counterpoint and the hierarchy of the phrase model. The three ordered harmonic functions and their expansion through contrapuntal chords rarely incorporated more than just a few diatonic harmonies within any phrase. In this chapter, we see how composers can employ all of the diatonic harmonies to fill a single phrase.

Listen to Example 22.1A, which presents the end of one phrase followed by a complete four-measure phrase. Example 22.1B presents the same structure as Example 22.1A, except the final phrase of Example 22.1B contains twice as many measures. The added measures, bracketed and labeled in the example, are interpolated between the i_6 that begins the final phrase and the $ii^{\circ}{}_{(6)}$–V^6_5–i that closes the phrase. However, the added chords fit nicely within the phrase and serve both to prolong the tonic function and to connect the tonic to the pre-dominant. Such patterns, called **harmonic sequences**, form seamless, goal-directed musical units that draw no attention away from the underlying harmonic progression.

EXAMPLE 22.1

DVD 1 CH 22 TRACK 1

A. Vivaldi, Concerto Grosso in C minor, F. 1, no. 2 ("Il Sospetto"), *Allegro*

B. Vivaldi, recomposed

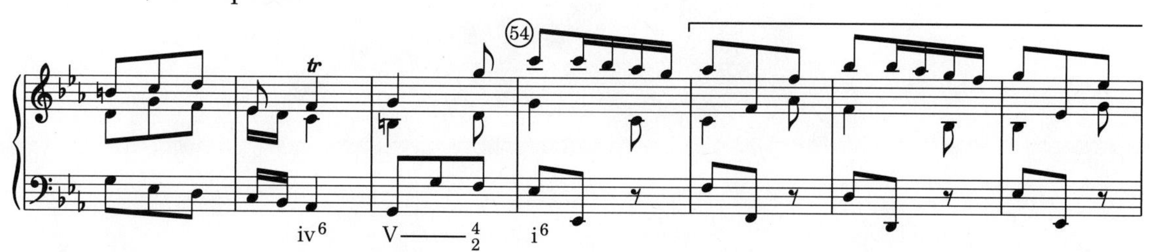

Sequences embody a paradox. Given their rapid harmonic rhythm, they provide the impression of intense musical motion. Yet, given their repetition, predictability, and subordination to harmonically functional chords, they slow harmonic motion. One might compare sequences to some of the art of M. C. Escher, whose paintings, such as *Ascending and Descending* (1960) (Example 22.2A), represent constant goal-directed motion. The observer who follows the course of these busy monks, however, discovers that at the end of the journey, he is back at the beginning point.

EXAMPLE 22.2 M. C. Escher (1898–1972), *Ascending and Descending*

A.

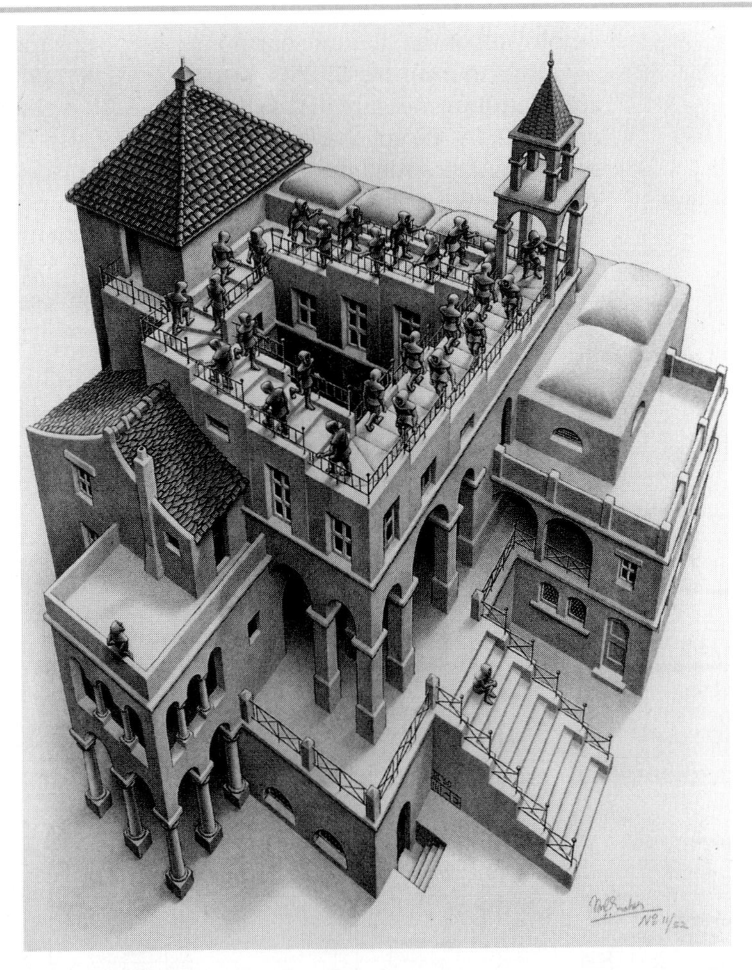

B.

model copy copy copy

a b c

-5 +4

Sequences first appeared during the Renaissance period (c. 1450-1600), but they played a much more important role in the Baroque (c. 1600-1750) and in successive musical periods, including in the popular and commercial music of today.

Components and Types of Sequences

One can divide a sequence into two parts: the **model** and its **copies** (which "copy and paste" the model at different pitch levels). The model presents the basic contrapuntal/harmonic pattern—this is usually two chords in length. Any melodic or motivic figuration used in the sequence will first appear in the model and will be repeated in each successive copy. Sequences typically have two or three copies of the model.

Sequence types are determined from harmonic and contrapuntal voice-leading patterns. Although there are many types of sequences, they fall into two categories: **descending** and **ascending** sequences. Each sequence is named and labeled according to three criteria, arranged from the general to the specific. Consider Example 22.2B.

There are three distances we have to know in order to produce this sequence:

1. The root distance from chord *a* to chord *c*. This is the amount that the model moves each time it makes a new copy—in this example, the distance is a descending second (**D2**).
2. Now we need to know the two steps that take us from *a* to *c* in our example. The first is the root distance from chord *a* to chord *b*—here, it is a descending fifth (−5). We label the chord-to-chord motions using negative numbers to indicate descent and positive numbers to indicate ascent.
3. Then we measure from chord *b* to chord *c*—here, an ascending fourth (+4).

The label for this sequence is **D2 (**−5/+4). The D2 indicates that each repetition of the model descends by step. The "−5" and "+4" show the root motion that takes us chord by chord from the model to the copy. We will now examine two sequences that descend and two sequences that ascend.

The Descending-Second (D2) Sequence

The D2 (−5/+4) sequence, as in our example, is called the **descending-second sequence.** It is also called the *descending-fifth sequence,* because the root motion from chord to chord follows the circle of fifths. We have seen this series of chords before: We began with V–I. Each time we added a new harmony, we backed up on the circle of fifths. The complete diatonic pattern of fifths is I–IV–vii°–iii–vi–ii–V–I. Range limitations preclude using descending fifths exclusively; therefore, we answer a descending fifth with an ascending fourth (see our earlier example again). Of course, composers might begin their D2 sequences by rising a fourth and then falling a fifth. For simplicity, we will call any sequence whose roots fall a fifth and rise a fourth *or* rise a fourth and fall a fifth, a D2 (−5/+4) sequence. Notice that this sequential two-chord pattern creates the deeper-level descent by second, as shown by the connecting beams in Example 22.3.

EXAMPLE 22.3

DVD 1 CH 22 TRACK 2

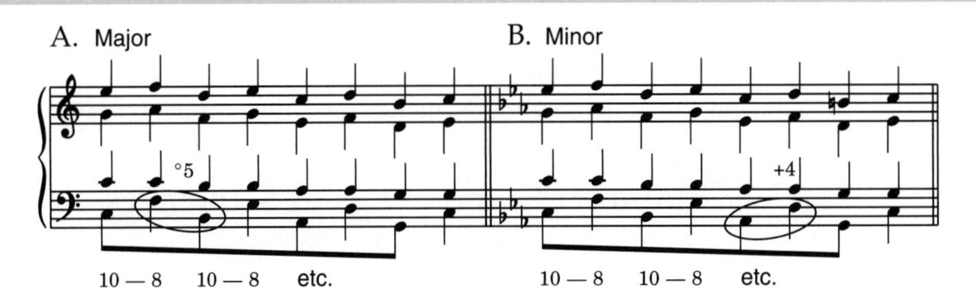

If we had only the beamed chords in Example 22.3, it would result in parallel motion in all voices. Thus, we discover another important function of sequences: The second chord of the model (and of each of its copies) breaks up the potential parallels that result from moving downward by step. We refer to these helping chords that appear in each sequence we study as **voice-leading chords**.

Note that the major-mode D2 (−5/+4) contains a melodic tritone in the bass near its beginning; in the minor mode, the tritone occurs near the end of the sequence (tritones are circled in Example 22.3). Given the need to keep the pitches from spiraling outside of the key, this bass tritone leap, though uncommon in traditional harmonic progressions, is both acceptable and necessary in this sequence. For example, in the key of C major, if the sequence were to move in strict perfect fifths, it would spin off into chromatic areas and require six copies of the model to return to the tonic (C–F–[B♭–E♭–A♭–D♭–G♭]–C♭/B–E–A–D–G–C).

In your analysis, you may have noticed that the harmonization of $\hat{7}$ in major and $\hat{2}$ in minor creates root-position diminished triads (vii° and ii°), which so far have not been permitted. Within sequences, these sonorities are members of a larger contrapuntal/harmonic pattern and not independent entities; they are allowed in order to participate in the overall repeating pattern. In Example 22.4, the stately D2 (−5/+4) sequence in G minor maintains its contrapuntal/harmonic pattern through the entire circle of fifths in that key, arriving back at the tonic. Thus, we hear not only the strong tritone E♭-A but also the ii° in root position.

EXAMPLE 22.4 Handel, Concerto in B♭ major for Harp, op. 6, no. 6, *Larghetto*

DVD 1 CH 22 TRACK 3

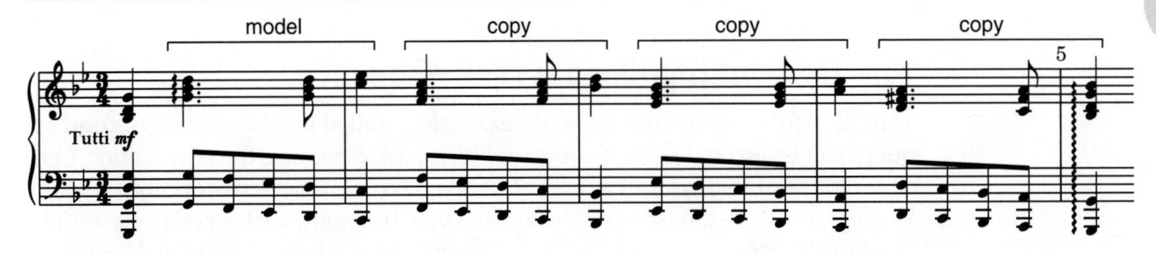

The Descending-Second Sequence in Inversion

Given the angular, disjunct bass that occurs in root-position D2 (−5/+4) sequences, composers often place one of the chords of the model—usually the second chord—in first inversion. This technique, as we know, creates a more melodic bass. We represent inversions by adding $^6_3$ to the label: D2 (−5/+4) + $^6_3$. See Example 22.5.

EXAMPLE 22.5

DVD 1
CH 22
TRACK 4

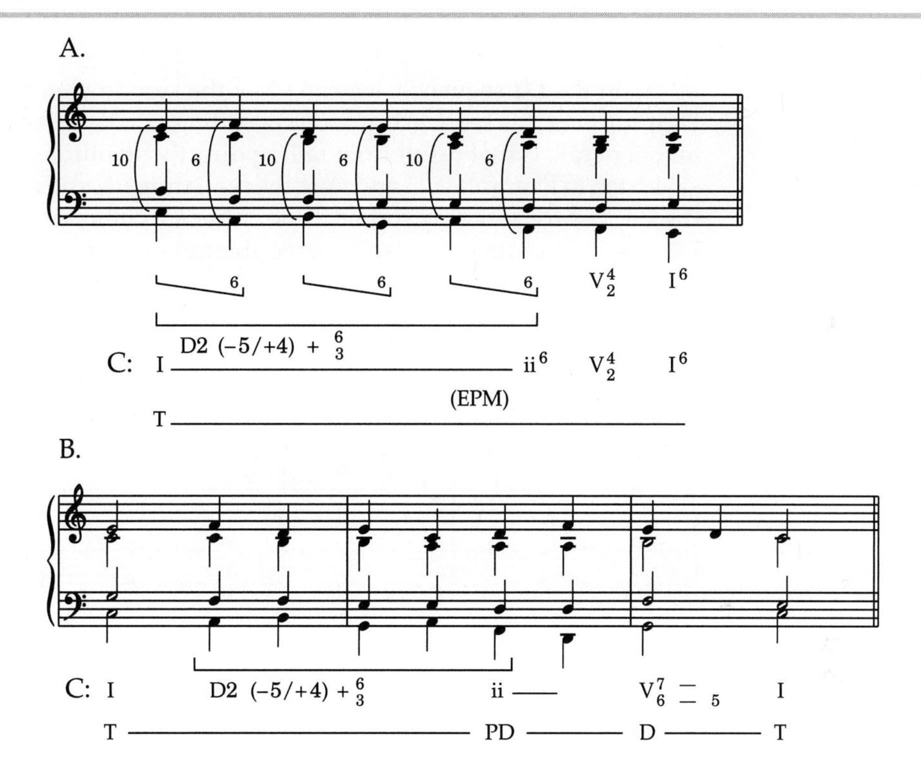

Compare the outer-voice counterpoint of Example 22.3 with Example 22.5. Notice that in the earlier example, an octave occurs on the second chord of the model and each copy. This is acceptable, but the bass is not smooth. The outer-voice counterpoint of Example 22.5 consists exclusively of imperfect consonances (10–6), which enhances the smooth, melodic sound.

Given the contrapuntal derivation of sequences, there is no need to analyze individual chords. You need only provide the following when analyzing a sequence:

- The roman numeral for the first chord in the sequence.
- The roman numeral for the final chord in the sequence.
- A sequence label, including overall motion [e.g., (D2)], specific root motions between chords [e.g., (−4/+2)], and inversions (e.g., +$^6_3$s).

The Descending-Third (D3) Sequence

The D3 (−4/+2) sequence contrasts nicely with the D2 (−5/+4) sequence, because it incorporates different root motions in each stage; none of the following root relations occur in the D2 (−5/+4) sequence.

EXAMPLE 22.6A

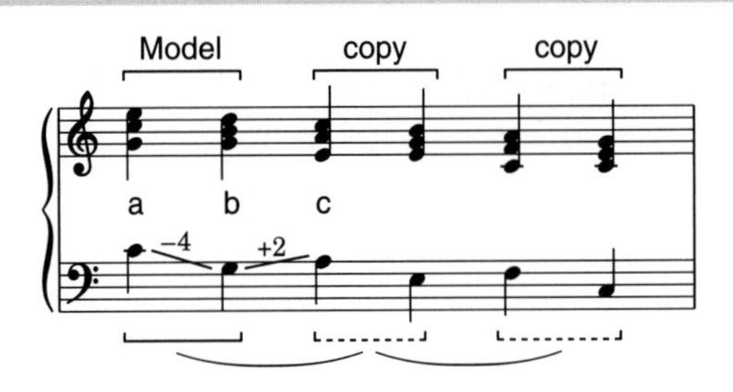

As in the D2 sequence, we can view the second chord of the model (and each copy) in this sequence as a voice-leading chord, because it avoids the potential parallels that result from falling directly by thirds.

Listen to Example 22.6 and note the miniature deceptive motion (V–vi) and the stepwise descending soprano line; these are common characteristics of the D3 (−4/+2) sequence. Also observe the minor v chord in m. 1 of Example 22.6B, which is necessary to avoid the augmented second between A♭ and B♮.

EXAMPLE 22.6B

DVD 1
CH 22
TRACK 5

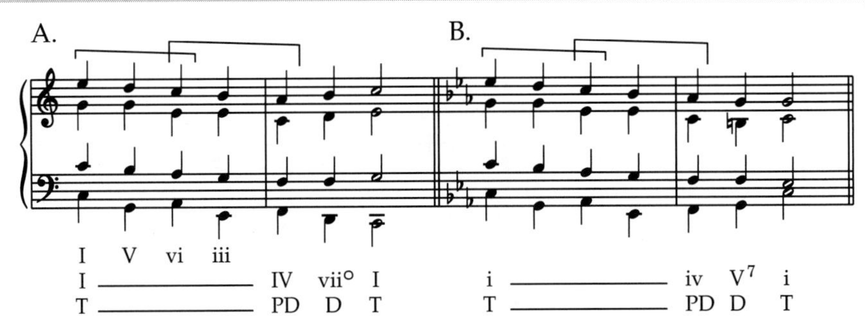

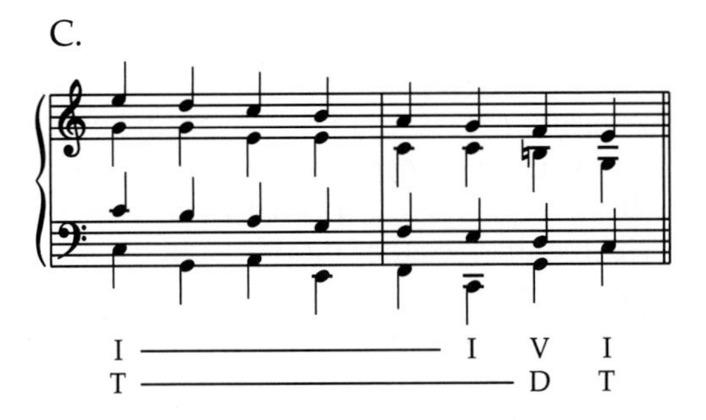

The Pachelbel Canon (Example 22.7) is a well-known example of this sequence. The sequence is two measures long, and three of the piece's many repetitions are included in the example. Both the model and its copies are bracketed in the first two measures, and important bass notes are circled. Notice that the sequence seems to serve a double function in the piece: It prolongs tonic (I is the first and last chord of the sequence), but it also leads to the PD (the tonic at the end of the sequence sounds less like an arrival than like a voice-leading chord to ii^6_5). D3 (−4/+2) sequences often function in this dual capacity.

EXAMPLE 22.7 Pachelbel, Canon in D major

DVD 1
CH 22
TRACK 6

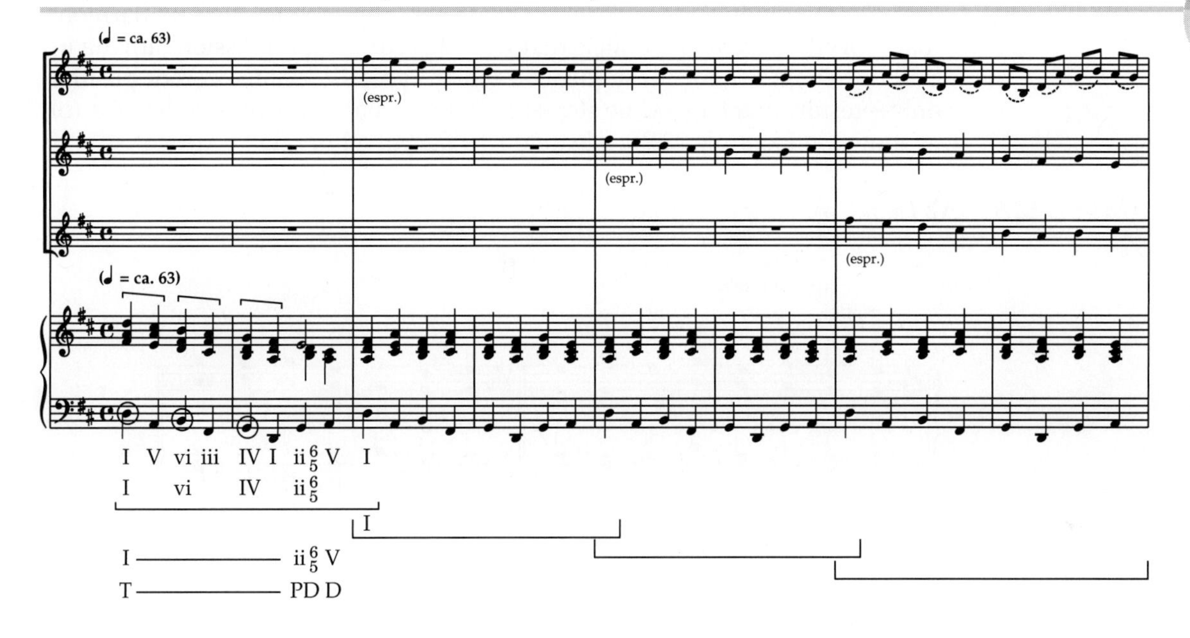

The Descending-Third Sequence in Inversion

Composers often use six-three chords to smooth the basses of D3 sequences (just as they do with D2 sequences). We will label D3 sequences that incorporate six-three chords as D3 $(-4/+2) + {}^{6}_{3}$.

EXAMPLE 22.8 D3 $(-4/+2) + {}^{6}_{3}$

DVD 1
CH 22
TRACK 7

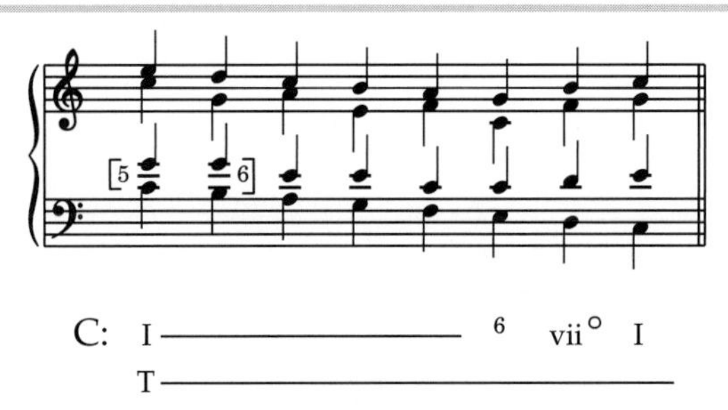

Consider Example 22.8. Notice the stepwise bass descent that moves in parallel tenths with the soprano. This sequence is also often called the *descending 5-6 sequence* because one voice (often the tenor, as in the example) remains stationary against the falling bass, forming first a fifth and then a sixth. The D3 $(-4/+2) + {}^{6}_{3}$ sequence is much more common than its root-position counterpart.

The Ascending-Second (A2) Sequence

This sequence, with ascending fifths and descending fourths, is much less common than the D2 $(-5/+4)$ sequence, because it is not nearly as goal directed.

Look at Example 22.9. In the progression I to V, the dominant's natural tendency is to return to the tonic to create a strong progression; but V ascending a fifth to ii creates a weak retrogression. For two reasons, however, common-practice composers occasionally use the A2 $(+5/-4)$ sequence. First, given its overall ascent, it provides some sense of drive. Second, the second chord of the model (and each copy) again serves as a voice-leading harmony that prevents potential parallels that would occur in a progression moving up by step. The A2 (+5/−4) sequence—which typically occurs in root position only—results in a large-scale step ascent that usually moves to a PD on $\hat{4}$ (or, as shown in Example 22.9B, a leap to $\hat{6}$ as part of a Phrygian cadence).

EXAMPLE 22.9 A2 (+5/−4)

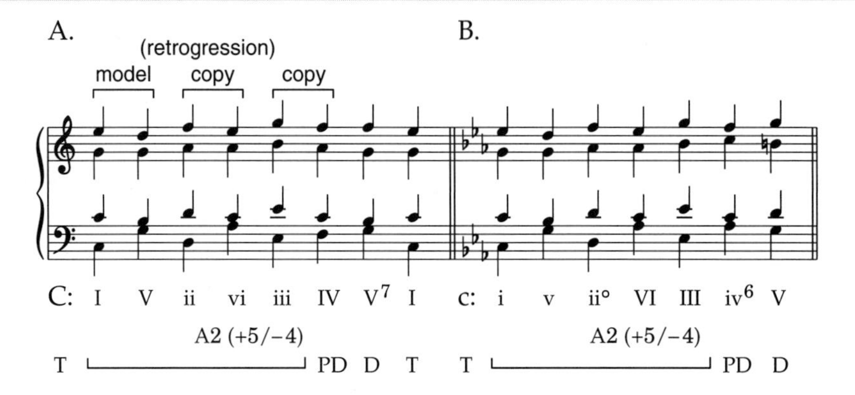

Another Ascending-Second Sequence: A2 (−3/+4)

Similar to the A2 (+5/−4) sequence, the A2 (−3/+4) sequence is characterized by rising seconds, as illustrated in Example 22.10. (Compare Examples 22.9 and 22.10.) Note that the A2 (−3/+4) sequence also leads to the PD function. It achieves this through the fall of the third, however, which prepares for the springboard motion up a fourth to begin the next copy of the model. Indeed, the propulsion for this sequence comes from this motion, as indicated by the arrows that appear in the roman numerals of Example 22.10.

EXAMPLE 22.10 A2 (−3/+4)

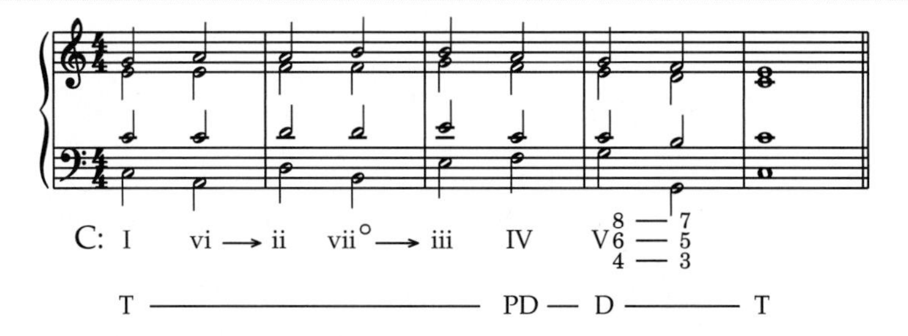

Listen to and study Example 22.11. As with the other sequences that employ first-inversion triads, the addition of the six-three chords allows the A2 (−3/+4) to be much smoother. In fact, the bass is sustained as a common tone throughout the model (and in each copy). This is, perhaps, the oldest of all sequences and can be found in the music of early-sixteenth-century composers such as Josquin Despres (d. 1521). As you can see in Example 22.11, parallels that would occur in a stepwise progression are averted by the intervening $^6_3$ chord, creating a 5–6 contrapuntal motion (which usually occurs in the outer voices). Thus, this sequence is also known as the *ascending 5–6 sequence.*

Diatomic sequences are summarized in example 22.12.

EXAMPLE 22.11

A. Major

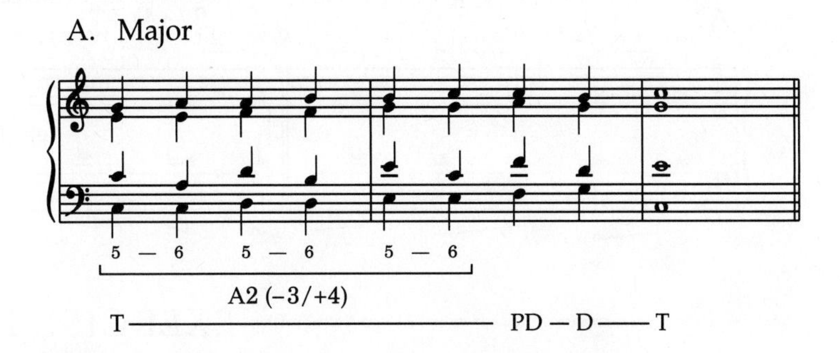

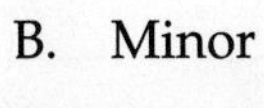

B. Minor

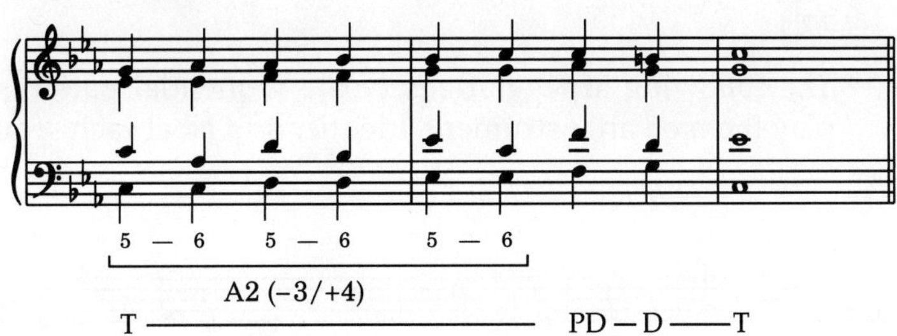

EXAMPLE 22.12 Summary of Diatonic Sequences

A.

D2 (−5/+4) D2 (−5/+4) + $^6_3$

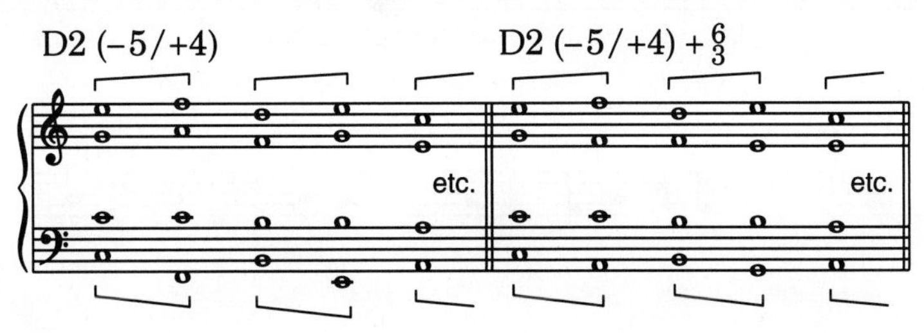

B.

D3 (−4/+2) D3 (−4/+2) + $^6_3$

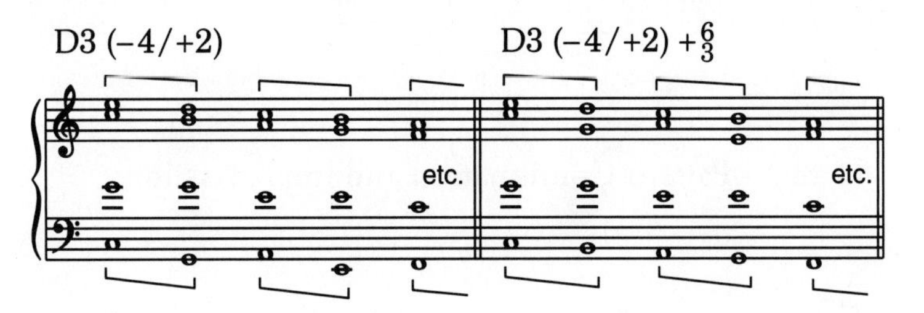

C.

A2 (+5/−4)

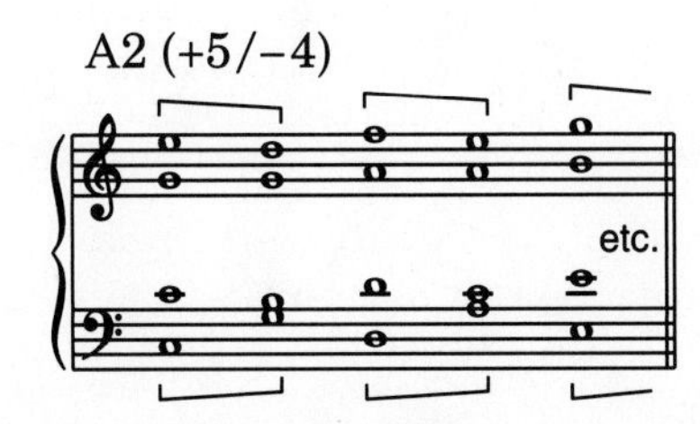

D.

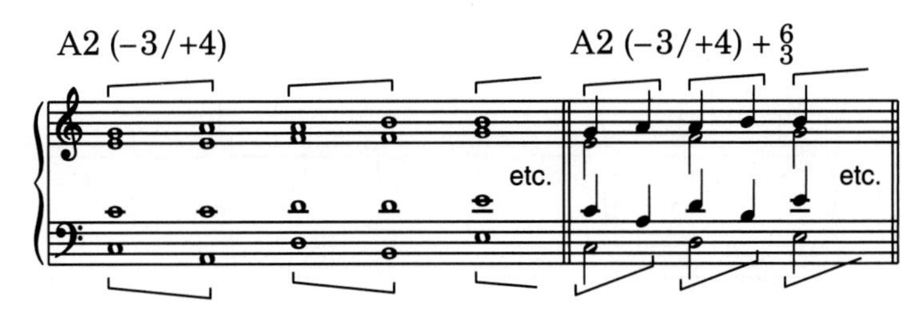

EXERCISE INTERLUDE

PERFORMING

22.1

The following arpeggiations create sequential patterns. Sing them and/or play them on an instrument. Identify and label each sequence.

A.

B.

C.

D.

22.2 Pattern Continuation and Improvisation

A.

B.

C.

D.

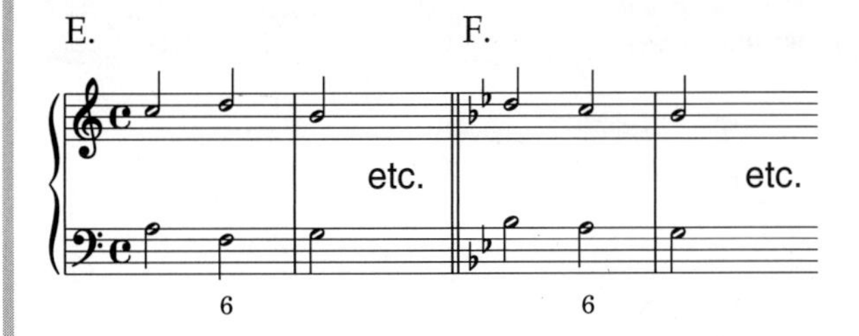

Study the sequential patterns in order to determine the type of sequence. Then, either on a keyboard or with a friend using two melody instruments, play (or sing) the given patterns (outer voices only if using melody instruments) and continue the pattern, leading to an authentic cadence.

For Exercises E and F, add various tones of figuration in order to create a more florid realization of the sequential pattern; refer to Exercises A and D for samples of such figurations. In Exercise A, a lower-neighbor, chordal leap and passing tone combine into a useful melodic pattern, and in Exercise D, passing figures lead to the sequence, which is ornamented with chordal skips and passing tones. Be able to transpose your solutions to two additional keys.

ANALYSIS

22.3

The following examples contain sequences using mostly root-position harmonies. Do not analyze the entire example—just bracket the model and copies for each sequence and provide a sequence label.

A. Mozart, String Quintet in C minor, K. 406, iii

B. Scarlatti, Sonata in D minor, K. 1, transcribed for guitar

C. Bach, Chaconne, from Partita no. 2 in D minor for violin solo, BWV, 1004

DVD 2
CH 22
TRACK 2

22.4

The following examples contain a mixture of the four sequence types. Also, all but the A2 (+5/−4) sequence may incorporate first-inversion variants. Bracket the model and copies for each sequence and provide a sequence label.

A. Handel, Keyboard Suite no. 7 in G minor, Passacaille

A single sequence type is repeated twice. Notice how Handel elaborates the underlying structure. Be able to discuss the relationship between the two hands in mm. 9–12 and mm. 13–16.

Continued

B. Mozart, Violin Sonata in G major, K. 379, *Andantino cantabile*

C. Pergolesi, "Il nocchier nella Tempesta," from *Salustia*, act 2, scene 9

D. Quantz, Flute duet in A minor, op. 5, no. 5

Compare the relationship between the instruments in mm. 9–16 and mm. 17–24.

E. Mozart, Flute Sonata no. 5 in C major, K. 14, *Allegro*

F. Mascagni, *Cavalleria rusticana*, Interlude

G. Brahms, Symphony no. 4 in E minor, op. 98, *Allegro non troppo*

DVD 2
CH 22
TRACK 3

LISTENING

22.5

Listen to and label the root-position sequences; identify with a sequence label. Follow these guidelines when listening.

1. Determine whether or not the sequence ascends or descends overall.
2. If the sequence descends:

a. Listen to the bass to determine whether the copies descend by second or third overall.
b. Note that the D3 sequence usually has a stepwise descending soprano, while the D2 sequence usually has a "sawtooth" motion in the soprano that moves in contrary motion with the bass.

3. If the sequence ascends:

a. Listen to the bass to determine whether the model has (+5/−4) or (−3/+4) motion.
b. Note that the A2 (+5/−4) sequence has bigger leaps in the bass and usually has a "sawtooth" motion in the soprano that moves in contrary motion with the bass
c. The A2 (−3/+4) sequence typically has a soprano that sounds like 5–6 motion in the model, and the soprano note will repeat as it starts the next copy. Listen for a repeating soprano note.

A.______ B.______ C.______ D.______

E.______ F.______

G. Mozart, Symphony in A major, K. 134 ______

H. Mozart, String Quartet in G major, K. 80, Trio ______

WORKBOOK
22.1–22.2

I. Heinichen, Sonata for Oboe and Bassoon, *Allegro* ______

J. Corelli, Concerto Grosso in C major, op. 6, no. 10, *Corrente* ______

Writing Sequences

In writing sequences, there are no new chords to conquer, nor are there any new voice-leading rules. In fact, given that each chord within a sequence must follow the voice leading and doublings in the model, you will encounter double leading tones, dissonant leaps, and diminished triads in root position. All of these are frowned on in the usual voice-leading situations, but they are perfectly acceptable within sequences (because of the overall repetition of the model). You must rely on your musical instincts, for if you write only nonstop sequences, the listener will soon tire. By contrast, the sequence is a compositional procedure that can be used without becoming stale. Witness the continued popularity of works such as Pachelbel's Canon. Here are three guidelines, which, if followed, will allow you to write successful sequences.

GUIDELINE 1 Make sure the voice leading in the first three chords is correct. Because the copies merely restate the model (at a different pitch level), any faulty voice leading in the opening will blemish every copy.

GUIDELINE 2 Always start with the bass and soprano voices; try to incorporate contrary step motion between the outer voices.

GUIDELINE 3 Include at least one imperfect consonance (3, 6, 10) between the outer voices in the model. Example 22.13 shows various intervallic patterns between the outer voices of the D2 (−5/+4) sequence. Letters A-C each employ one imperfect consonance, and Letter D employs two. Although the soprano becomes more disjunct with the nonstop tenths in letter D, such a contrapuntal framework has occurred often in music, particularly in popular music of the twentieth century (including Bart Howard's "Fly Me to the Moon" and Jerome Kern's "All the Things You Are").

EXAMPLE 22.13

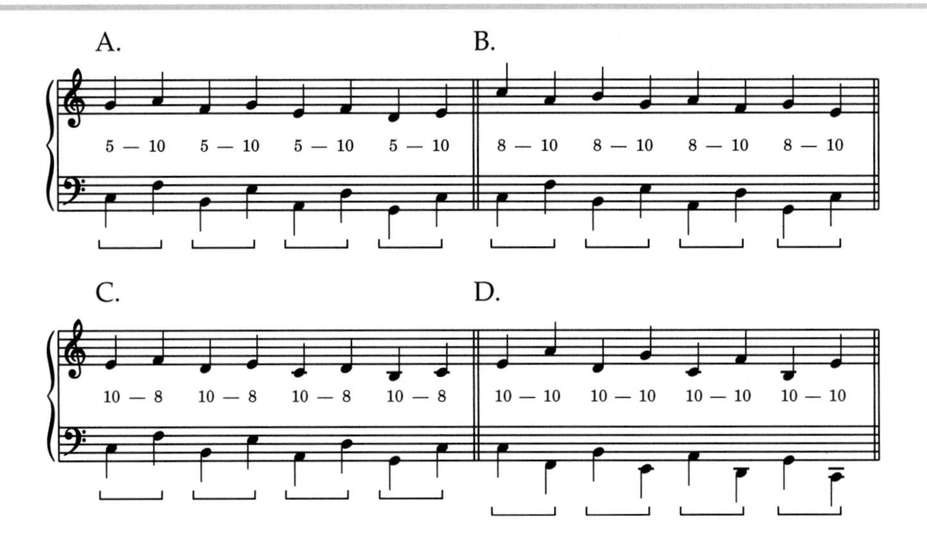

EXERCISE INTERLUDE

WRITING

22.6

On a separate sheet of manuscript paper, continue writing the following sequences, each of which starts on the tonic. The model is given, as well as (in some cases) its connection to the first chord of the copy. Label the intervals of the outer-voice counterpoint, as in Example 22.13. Begin by writing the bass and the soprano, filling in the tenor and alto parts only after you are sure that the repetitions replicate the model exactly. Do not use accidentals within the sequence. Label each sequence type; note that there may be first-inversion triads. Follow these guidelines when completing the sequences:

- For D2 (−5/+4): Write a complete diatonic cycle, leading back to the tonic.
- For the other sequence types: Stop the sequence on a pre-dominant chord.

A.

B.

C.

D.

KEYBOARD

22.7

Play each of the following sequence models in four voices and major and minor keys up to two sharps and two flats. All of the sequences are in root position, and voicings are given for the model. Be able to sing either outer voice while playing the remaining three voices.

A.

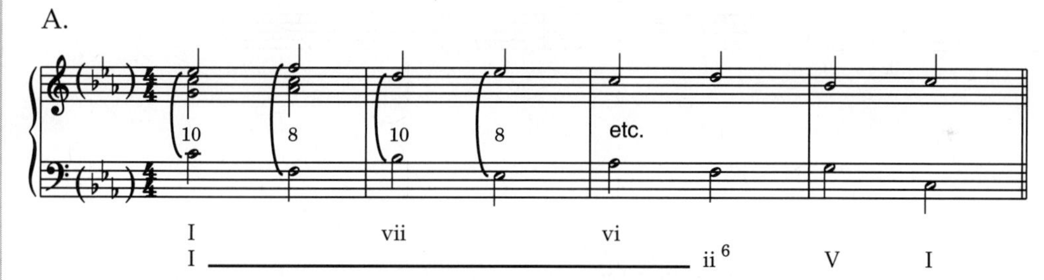

B.

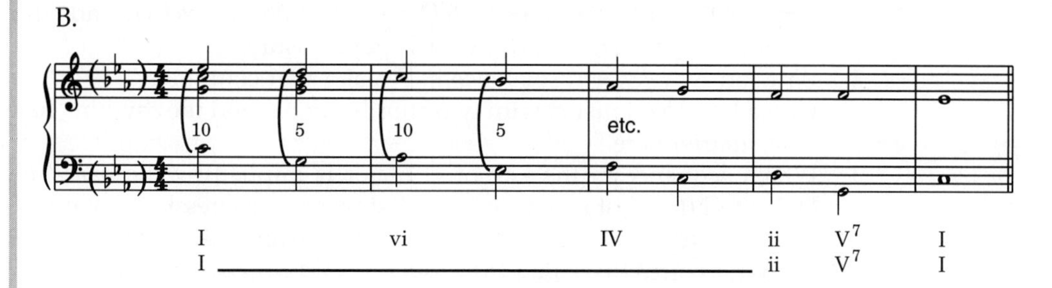

C.

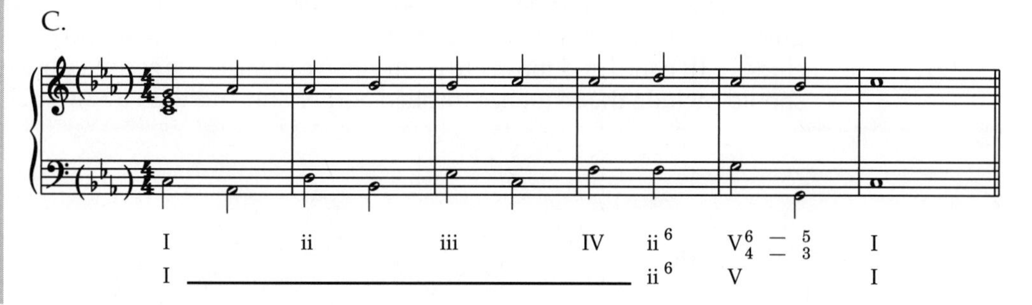

Continued

D. major only

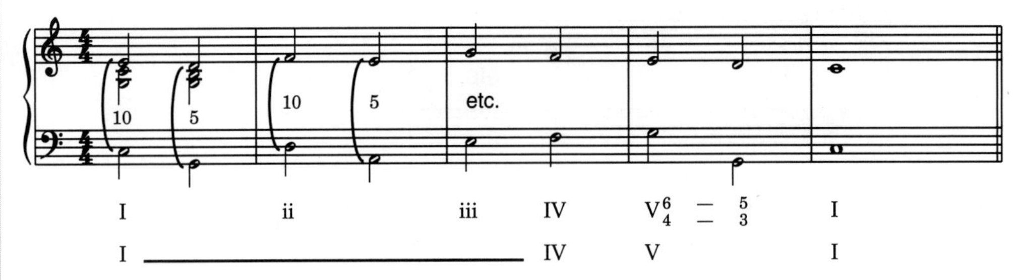

22.8

The following figured bass contains multiple sequences. Realize the figured bass in four-part keyboard style on a separate sheet of manuscript paper. Be able to sing either outer voice while playing the remaining three voices.

COMPOSITION

22.9

Complete the following tasks in four-part chorale style.

1. Write a D3 (−4/+2) sequence in D major that continues to ii; end with a PAC. Use $\frac{4}{4}$ meter, with two chords per measure.
2. Write an A2 (−3/+4) sequence in F major that continues to IV; close with a HC. Use $\frac{3}{4}$ meter, with two chords per bar and the rhythm "half note, quarter note."
3. Which sequence in the key of D major is implied by the bass line D–E–F♯–G (the first note is tonic)? First write a progression that establishes the key (with a tonic expansion); then begin the sequence (write the outer voices first). End the sequence, and close with an IAC.
4. Which sequence is implied by the soprano line $\hat{3}$–$\hat{2}$–$\hat{1}$–$\hat{7}$–$\hat{6}$? Write a progression in B minor and in a meter of your choice whose first phrase includes a III chord and moves to a Phrygian cadence. The second phrase should include the sequence implied earlier and end with a PAC.

TERMS AND CONCEPTS

- harmonic Sequence
- ascending sequences
  - A2 (+5/−4 or −4/+5); ascending second (by ascending fifth and descending fourth or descending fourth and ascending fifth)
  - A2 (−3/+4); ascending second (by descending third and ascending fourth) and A2 (−3/+4) with $^6_3$s
- descending sequences
  - D2 (−5/+4 or +4/−5); descending second (by descending fifth and ascending fourth or ascending fourth and descending fifth) and D2 with $^6_3$s
  - D3 (−4/+2); descending thirds (by descending fourth and ascending second) and D3 with $^6_3$s
- melodic sequence
- model and copy
- voice-leading chords (helping chords)

WORKBOOK
22.3–22.6

CHAPTER 23

Sequences Within Larger Musical Contexts and Sequences with Seventh Chords

In Chapter 22 we learned that sequences arise from the delicate balance that exists between counterpoint and harmony. Sequences are easily inserted into phrases. There are **prolongational** sequences (which expand one function, such as T–T) and **transitional** sequences (which move from one function to another, such as T–PD). Generally, sequences occur after a tonic expansion and before the PD and D functions, extending the phrase model. In this chapter we explore compositional techniques that composers and you can use to create elaborate phrases as well as ways to embellish sequences themselves.

Composing Sequences Within the Phrase Model

When we compose sequences within phrases, we must consider harmonic rhythm, balance, and proportion so that the sequence will fit logically within a musical context. First, we need to determine how long it will take for a sequence to unfold.

Example: Write a four-measure phrase that establishes tonic, contains a D2 (−5/+4) sequence, and ends with a PAC.

Given that the short tonic expansion before the sequence will occupy at least the first measure and that the PD–D–T will occupy mm. 3 and 4, the sequence must fit into the second measure—a tall order even for an accomplished composer. There are at least three solutions to the problem, albeit not necessarily equally effective.

1. You might use much faster rhythmic values for the chords of the sequence. However, this solution creates the very impression you are trying to avoid: an unmotivated insertion of chords, tightly wedged into a context in which they do not musically fit. Yet there are instances in which the acceleration of harmonic rhythm in sequential passages can be used effectively.
2. A better solution is to use only part of a sequence. For example, you might start the sequence on iii rather than on I, to reduce its length by almost half: (I–IV–vii°)–iii–vi–ii–V–I. You can also end the sequence early, perhaps on iii, which would immediately move to a PD. How you want your sequence to function will determine whether or not the

sequence begins on tonic and where the sequence ends. That is, will the sequence prolong one harmonic function (T–T, for example), or will it transition, leading to a new function?

3. A common solution is to increase the length of the phrase, perhaps to six measures. Many longer phrases, with extended interiors, result from inserted sequences.

We will merge the first two solutions as we write sequential phrases. Let's return to our original problem: writing a four-measure phrase that contains a D2 (−5/+4) sequence. We can partially solve the space problem by using a meter that accommodates more harmonic changes per measure, such as $\frac{4}{4}$ or $\frac{6}{8}$. We also can overlap the end of the tonic expansion with the beginning of the sequence, and we can end the sequence with the PD, leading to the PAC. This creates a transitional sequence, as seen in Example 23.1A.

EXAMPLE 23.1

DVD 1 CH 23 TRACK 1

A.

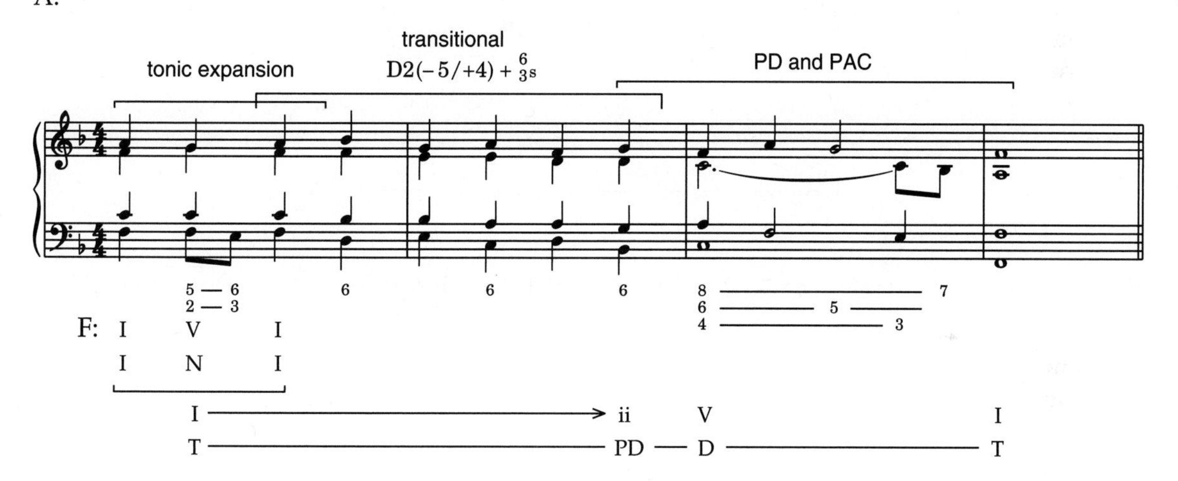

B.

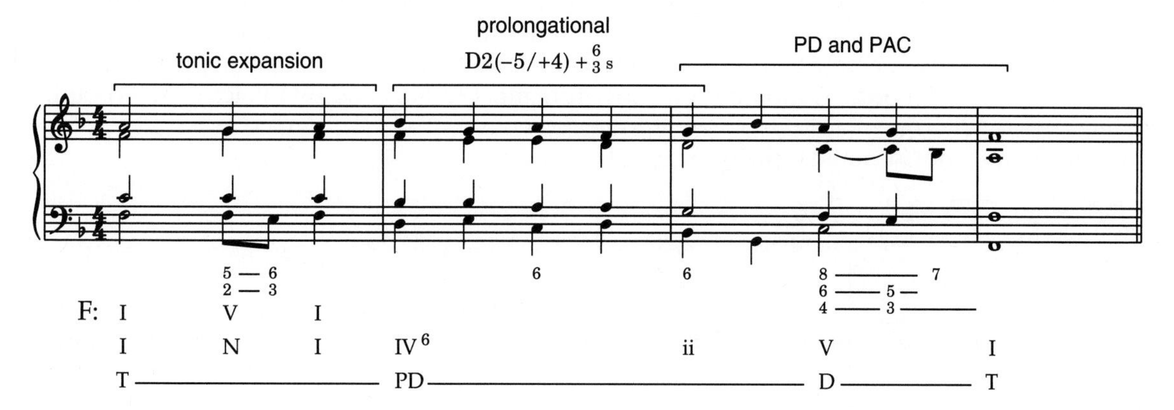

Composers often blur the distinction between prolongational and transitional sequences in order to create a seamless musical structure. Consider Example 23.1B. By simply changing the rhythm of Example 23.1A, the transitional sequence (T–PD) becomes a prolongational sequence (PD–PD). The repeating pattern still begins with the I chord, but because we hear a change to PD in m. 2 due to the strong metric placement of the IV_6 chord, the second-level analysis shows that the sequence expands the PD.

The four-measure phrase model can contain an enormous amount of material, as demonstrated in Example 23.2: A complete D2 (−5/+4) + $^6_3$ sequence prolongs the tonic, yet there is also an initial tonic expansion that precedes the sequence. Note that the first-inversion chords are used in the sequence. Also observe how the sequence leads back to the tonic in m. 3, followed by a strong cadential progression.

EXAMPLE 23.2

DVD 1 CH 23 TRACK 2

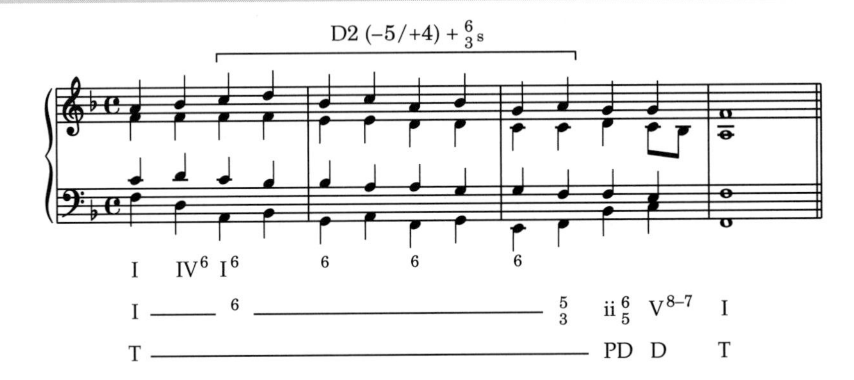

EXERCISE INTERLUDE

ANALYSIS

DVD 2 CH 23 TRACK 1

23.1

The following examples from the literature present sequences within larger musical contexts. Create a formal diagram for each example (which may include phrases, periods, and sentences). Bracket and label the following in the score: tonic expansion, sequence, and cadence. A sequence may occur at the beginning or at a later point within the tonic prolongation. Circle the bass and soprano pitches of the sequence (one bass note and one soprano note per chord). This outer-voice structure must create good two-voice counterpoint.

A. Mozart, Piano Sonata in C major, K. 545, I

B. Handel, Concerto Grosso in G minor, op. 6, no. 6, HWV 324, *Allegro*

C. Corelli, Concerto Grosso, no. 10 in C major, *Corrente*

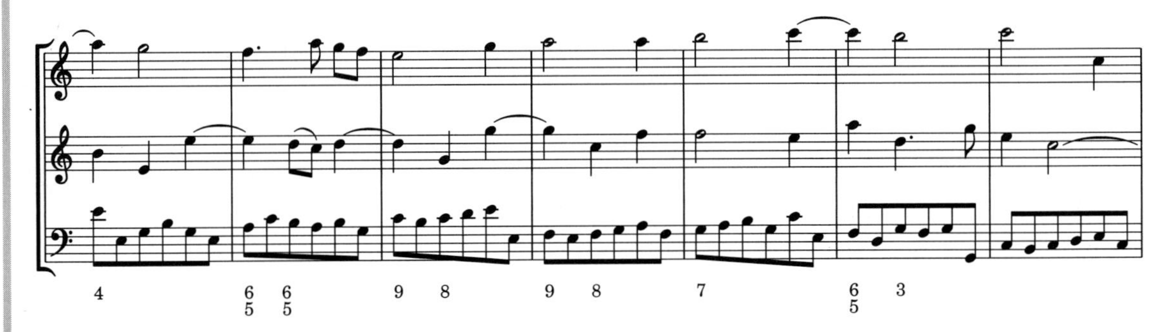

LISTENING

DVD 2
CH 23
TRACK 2

23.2

Each of the following six phrases includes a sequence. As you listen, focus on the three basic components of phrases that contain sequences: tonic expansion, sequence, and cadence. On a separate sheet of manuscript paper, notate the bass line and provide a second-level harmonic analysis. (Remember that only the first and last chords of a sequence receive roman numerals.) Identify and label each sequence type.

A. G minor, $\frac{4}{4}$; quarter note = 60
B. D major, $\frac{4}{4}$; quarter note = 90
C. A major, $\frac{3}{4}$; quarter note = 104
D. E♭ major, $\frac{4}{4}$; quarter note = 88
E. F major, $\frac{4}{4}$; quarter note = 76
F. Handel, Concerto Grosso in B minor, op. 6, no. 12, HWV 330, *Allegro*: F♯ minor, $\frac{4}{4}$; quarter note = 108. The sequence begins after two measures of music. Notate only the bass line of the sequence.

COMPOSITION

23.3

On a separate sheet of manuscript paper, complete the following tasks in four-voice chorale style. Each represents compositional guidelines only; you should not restrict your creativity. Use any major or minor key and either $\frac{4}{4}$ or $\frac{6}{8}$ meter. Begin with a compositional plan like the ones discussed earlier so that your sequences fit convincingly into the musical fabric rather than sounding as if they are merely wedged in. Then write the outer voices, making sure that the harmonic rhythm is logical. Finally, write the inner voices.

1. Write a four-measure phrase that contains a sequence: Establish tonic (m. 1)—sequence (mm. 2–3)—cadence.
2. Write an eight-measure interrupted period with a sequence:
   Phrase 1: Establish tonic (mm. 1–2), lead to PD and a HC.
   Phrase 2: Sequence, starting on tonic (mm. 5–6), lead to PD and a PAC.
3. Write an eight-measure period that has a sentence form:
   Phrase 1: Write two two-measure subphrases, the first of which moves from I to IV and the second of which moves from V to I and closes with an IAC.
   Phrase 2: Write a single four-measure gesture that develops the idea in the first subphrase; include a sequence in mm. 2–3 of the phrase.

WORKBOOK 23.1

23.4

Take any of the compositions from Exercise 23.3 and add a florid melody in the soprano voice. This melody will be played by a melody instrument, and the lower three voices will be played by either a small ensemble (strings or winds) or piano. Note that you may have to write parts for transposing instruments. *Optional:* Augment the rhythmic values of each chord by a consistent proportion (e.g., × 2 or × 4), and add more tones of figurations to the melody as well as the inner voices. The resulting 16- or even 32-measure pieces will sound terrific.

Sequences with Diatonic Seventh Chords

It is common to add sevenths to harmonies that are involved in sequences, resulting in a stream of seventh chords. We will limit our study of seventh-chord sequences to the D2 (−5/+4) sequence.

Listen to Example 23.3. Part A contains a D2 (−5/+4) sequence composed entirely of triads. Part B reproduces the opening of a movement by François Couperin, which also illustrates a D2 sequence, but this example contains diatonic seventh chords (the only triad to appear is the E-minor tonic harmony that begins and ends Example B). Notice the harmonic interest and richness in Example B compared with Example A, due in large part to the four different types of seventh chords used (mm, MM, dm, and Mm).

EXAMPLE 23.3

DVD 1
CH 23
TRACK 3

A.

B. François Couperin "Les Nations," *Premier Ordre: La Francoise*, XIV, Chaconne

Diatonic sevenths may be added to every chord, as we saw in Example 23.3B, or to every other chord in the D2 (−5/+4) sequence. There is one important voice-leading point to bear in mind: *You must prepare and resolve each seventh.* Refer back to Example 23.3B; notice that the circled sevenths of each chord have been prepared by common tone and resolved down by step (the soprano-voice seventh moves to its upper neighbor (actually the root of the chord) before resolving down).

Listen to and contrast the two D2 (−5/+4) sequences in Example 23.4. Example 23.4A has alternating triads and seventh chords; we refer to this sequence as a D2 (−5/+4) with **alternating** sevenths. Note that each seventh is prepared by a common tone (dotted slur in the example) and is resolved down by step (arrow in the example). Also note that once the series begins, the resolution pitch serves simultaneously as the next preparation pitch.

EXAMPLE 23.4

DVD 1 CH 23 TRACK 4

A. Preparation by step

B.

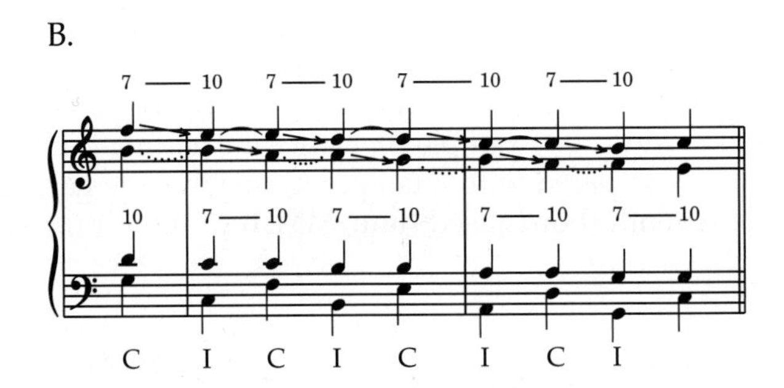

Every harmony in Example 23.4B contains a seventh; we call this type of sequence a D2 (−5/+4) with **interlocking** sevenths. The soprano and alto have interlocking sevenths above the bass: As the soprano resolves its seventh, the alto prepares its seventh; as the alto resolves its seventh, the soprano prepares its seventh; and so on.

Composing Sequences with Seventh Chords

You need to remember only one rule when writing D2 (−5/+4) sequences with seventh chords: *prepare and resolve each chordal seventh.* Follow this general procedure for writing sequences.

1. Work out careful voice leading in your model and into the beginning of the first copy.
2. Alternating seventh chords in D2 (−5/+4) may be complete.
3. When using interlocking seventh chords, every other chord will be incomplete. Refer to Example 23.4B, noting that the harmonies on beats 1 and 3 are incomplete (omitted fifth, doubled root).

Sequences with Inversions of Seventh Chords

Just as first-inversion triads are used in D2 (−5/+4) sequences, so too are first-inversion seventh chords. Listen to Example 23.5, in which Mozart writes two back-to-back D2 sequences with first-inversion chords. The first sequence contains only triads. But for the repetition of the entire sequence, Mozart intensifies the drama by adding a pair of oboes that soar above the strings to present the falling sixths, whose suspension figure includes the chordal seventh (circled and labeled in the score).

EXAMPLE 23.5 Mozart, Symphony in G major, K. 74, *Allegro*

Seventh chords in third inversion ($\frac{4}{2}$) are also common in sequences. They resolve to first-inversion triads or seventh chords. Listen to Example 23.6. As always, the seventh—this time in the bass—is prepared, giving the impression of a bass suspension. In general, when determining a sequence type, locate the root of each chord. In Example 23.6, the sequence unfolds with the roots E–A, D–G, C♯–F♯, B–E, revealing the underlying D2 (−5/+4) motion; figures reveal the interlocking inverted seventh chords ($\begin{smallmatrix}4\\2\end{smallmatrix}\ \begin{smallmatrix}6\\5\end{smallmatrix}$).

EXAMPLE 23.6 Leclair, Trio Sonata in D major, op. 2, no. 8, *Allegro*

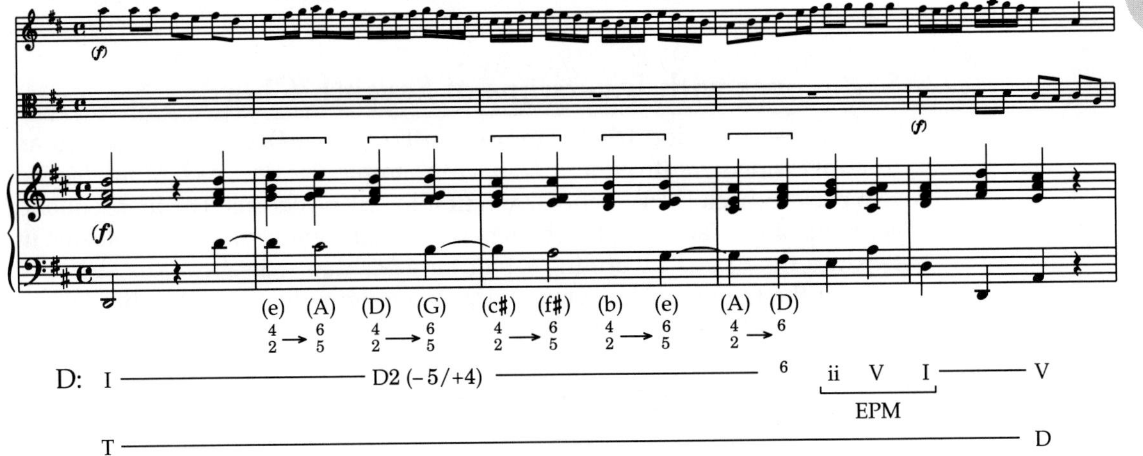

Finally, when you write sequences involving inverted seventh chords, make sure that each sonority is complete.

Compound Melody and Implied Seventh Chord Sequences

In earlier chapters we observed how composers wrote single melodic lines that gave the impression of two or more independent voices. This compositional technique, *compound melody*, is common in sequential passages. In many cases, there is a subtle play between consonance and dissonance. The reduction in Example 23.7 shows how one might hear the treble voice split into two voices, creating an implied three-voice texture. Taken together, a D2 (−5/+4) sequence with alternating triads and $\begin{smallmatrix}6\\5\end{smallmatrix}$ chords results. This is possible since (1) the two voices are in separate registers, (2) each voice maintains its independence by descending in stepwise motion, and (3) the voices combine to make good counterpoint.

EXAMPLE 23.7 Handel, Sonata for Flute and Continuo in A minor, op. 1, no. 4, HWV 362, *Adagio*

DVD 1
CH 22
TRACK 6

Continued

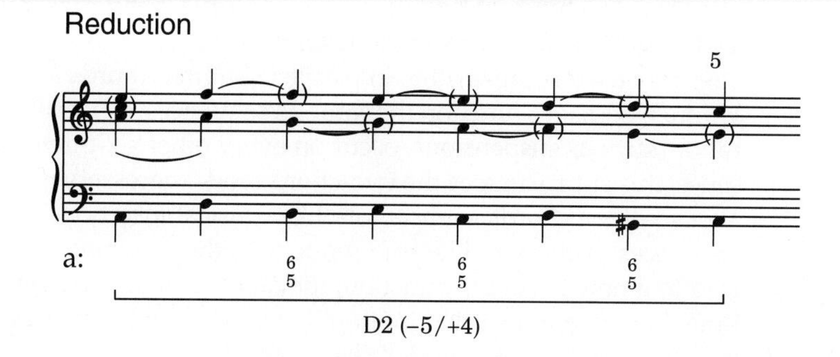

Parallel First-Inversion Triads

We know that the second chord in the model for a sequence often helps voice leading by avoiding potential parallels. Sometimes composers wish to use a parallel-motion chord stream. The only way to write a series of triads that move in strict parallel motion is to employ first-inversion chords (in three voices). This is the solution that composers have used since the sixteenth century. As with sequences, a series of parallel first-inversion triads serves either to prolong a harmony or as transition between harmonic functions.

EXAMPLE 23.8

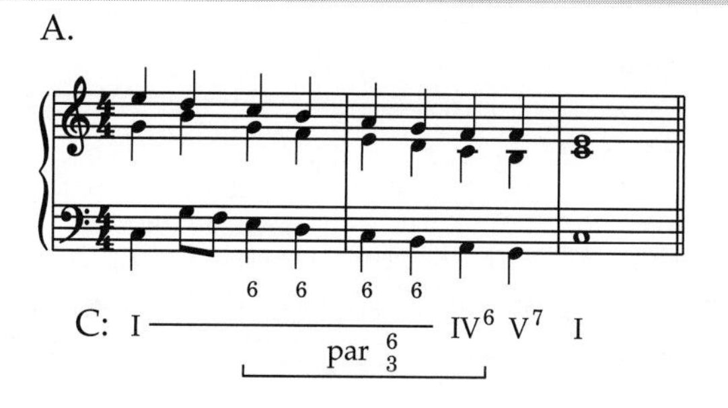

Composers who wished to write parallel first-inversion triads in four voices were faced with the problem of parallels. The solution is to have three voices in parallel motion and an inner voice use the following pattern: double the soprano, double the bass, double the soprano, double the bass, etc. (You can also start by doubling the bass.) Example 23.8B presents the voice leading and doublings (shown with brackets).

Passages that are written in parallel six-three chords are not strict sequences. Yet such passages function the same as sequences, especially when tones of figuration, such as suspensions, occur on every other six-three chord. Thus, in some sense, this approximates the two-chord model necessary for true sequences. Parallel six-three chords sound more like musical insertions or interpolations than sequences. Although, like true sequences, they prolong a harmonic function or lead to a new harmonic function, they create an impression more of stalling for time than of goal-directed motion. Let's examine two examples of parallel first-inversion triads from Handel's keyboard works (Example 23.9).

EXAMPLE 23.9

DVD 1
CH 23
TRACK 7

A. Handel, Suite IX in G minor, Gigue

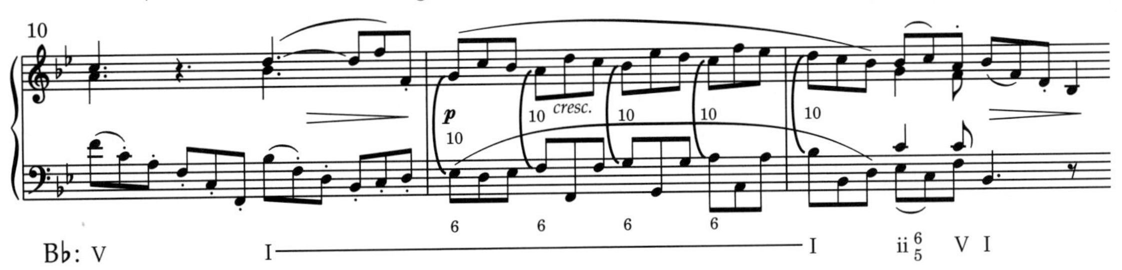

B. Handel, Suite XIII in B♭ major, Allemande

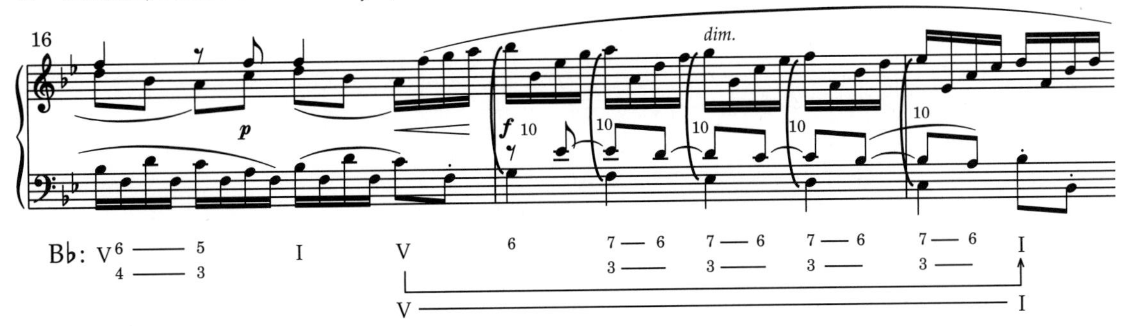

In Example 23.9A, the parallel first-inversion triads *ascend* and are part of a tonic expansion; ascending lines occur, but descending lines are more common. In Example 23.9B, the parallel first-inversion triads contain 7–6 suspensions, a common procedure in descending lines, and it provides a remarkable link to the D2 (−5/+4) sequence with sevenths.

Consider Example 23.10, which starts with descending parallel first-inversion triads that include 7–6 suspensions. By changing the bass notes as the suspensions resolve—as seen in Example 23.10B—the parallel first-inversion triads transform into the D2 (−5/+4) sequence with interlocking sevenths.

EXAMPLE 23.10

DVD 1
CH 23
TRACK 8

A. Descending six-three sequence with 7–6 suspensions

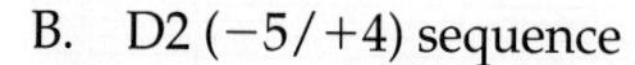
B. D2 (−5/+4) sequence

Sequences versus Sequential Progressions

Composers often write passages in which the harmonic structure follows a sequential pattern but the melodic structure does not. Such passages are referred to as **sequential progressions**. Sequential progressions are common because the root motions of three of the four basic sequence types are also common, and the D2 (−5/+4) sequential progression is particularly popular. Listen to Example 23.11, which presents two D2 (−5/+4) sequential progressions. We label sequential progressions by root, for example, "D2 progression."

EXAMPLE 23.11

DVD 1
CH 23
TRACK 9

A. Brahms, "Der Gang zum Liebchen" ("The Way to His Sweetheart"), op. 48, no. 1

B. Bach, French Suite in D minor, BWV 812, Menuet II

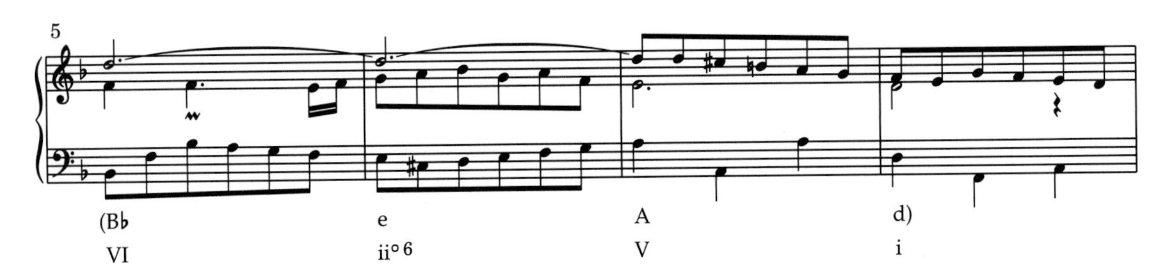

Summary of Part 5

Throughout Part 5 you were reminded that much of tonal analysis is based on interpretation and that right or wrong answers concerning how musical events function are often not possible. The simplest concepts that we may have learned as children and that we take for granted, such as what constitutes a phrase, became much more varied and complex in Part 5. Even though the components of music are relatively finite, their combinations, successions, and placement in time create endless compositional possibilities. Often, you must wrestle with opposing interpretations and contradictions.

You have learned fundamental concepts of grouping phrases and extending them, of the delicate balance in symmetrical phrases and periods, and of the dramatic proportional structure that is provided by the sentence form. Hierarchy was again evident in the way that basic root motions of fifths, seconds, and thirds were combined and extended through the sequence, creating patterns that provided elegant means for prolonging an underlying harmonic function or progressing to a new harmonic function.

EXERCISE INTERLUDE

PERFORMING

23.5

Using solfège syllables or scale degree numbers, sing each of the following sequences (as written and in the parallel minor) and label each sequence.

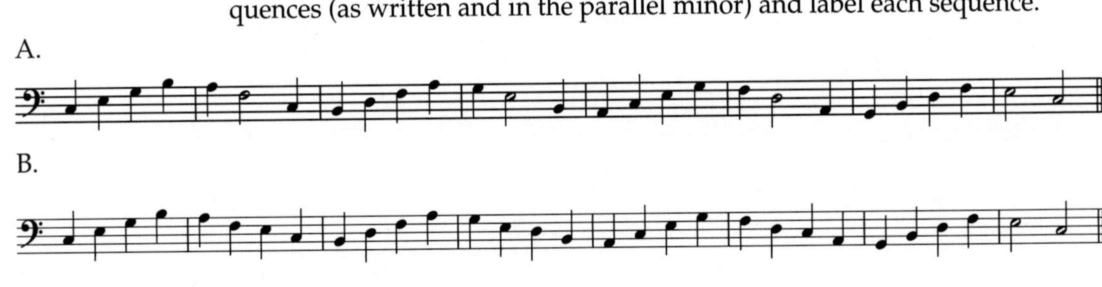

ANALYSIS

23.6

For each of the following examples from the literature, identify the sequence with brackets and label. Include figures that show the alternating or interlocking seventh chords. Be aware that you may encounter sequential progressions (label them "sequential prog." and use roman numerals as you usually would) in addition to sequences.

A. Brahms, "Wach auf, mein Hort," *Deutsche Volkslieder*, WoO 33, no. 13

What rhythmic device does Brahms use in this excerpt?

B. Haydn, String Quartet in C major, op. 20, no. 2, Hob. III. 32, Trio

C. Brahms, Intermezzo in B♭ minor, op. 117, no. 2

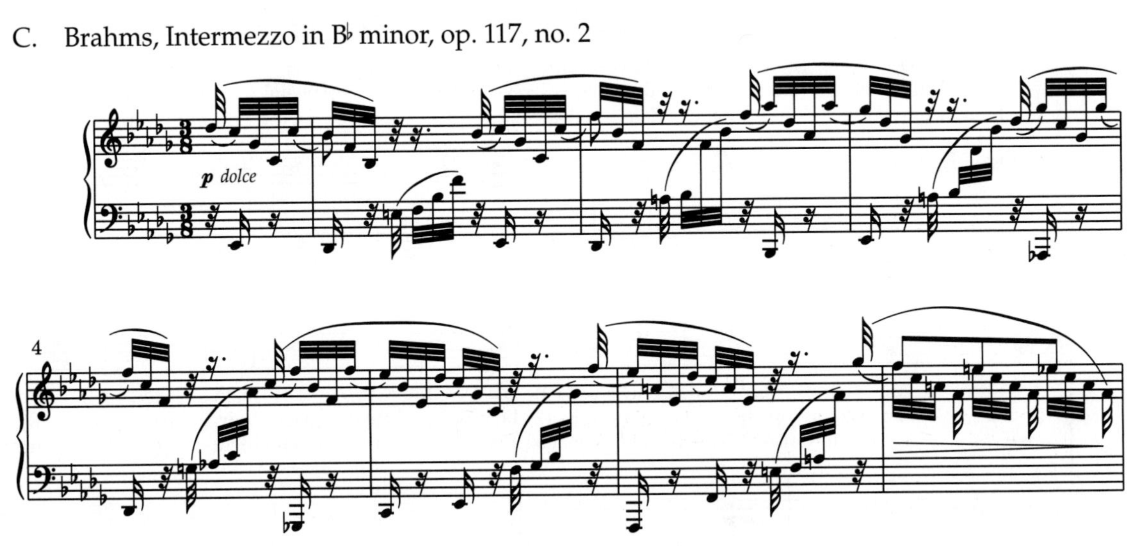

This example begins on a neighboring harmony that leads to the tonic in six-three position (m. 1). Be aware that incomplete chromatic neighbors appear in each measure, beginning with the E♮ in m. 1.

LISTENING

23.7

These examples contain the four types of triadic sequences and D2 sequences with seventh chords. Notate the bass lines of the sequential passages from the literature and label the sequence type.

A. Cimarosa, Concerto for Oboe (adapted by A. Benjamin): $\frac{3}{8}$; dotted quarter = 50
B. Corelli, Violin Sonata in F major, op. 5, no. 10; Sarabanda: $\frac{3}{4}$; quarter note = 72
C. Corelli, Violin Sonata in B minor, op. 3 no. 4, *Adagio*: $\frac{3}{8}$; eighth note = 96
D. Handel, Concerto Grosso, op. 3, no. 2: *quarter note* = 96
E. Mozart, Violin Concerto no. 3; alla breve: half note = 60
F. Handel, "He gave His back to the smiters," *Messiah*: $\frac{4}{4}$; quarter note = 69

G. Mozart, Serenade in C minor, K. 388, *Andante*: $\frac{3}{8}$; eighth note = 96
H. Corelli, Violin Sonata in D major, op. 4, no. 4: $\frac{4}{4}$; quarter note = 96

WRITING

23.8

Each of the following exercises contains one of the sequences we have studied. Exercises A–C present figured basses. Study the figures and bass pattern; then label the sequence type, add a soprano, and fill in the inner voices. Exercises D–F present unfigured basses with a soprano. Study the sequential implications of the outer-voice counterpoint; then label the sequence and add inner voices.

KEYBOARD

23.9

Play the following models for the D2 (−5/+4) sequences with seventh chords. Preparation and resolution of the chordal sevenths are indicated by dotted lines and arrows, respectively. The first model has alternating sevenths, the second has interlocking sevenths, and the third alternates triads with first-inversion seventh chords. Play each example in C major and C minor—remember how to use the leading tone in minor-mode sequences and note that the first chord of letter B should also use the leading tone.

A.

B.

C.

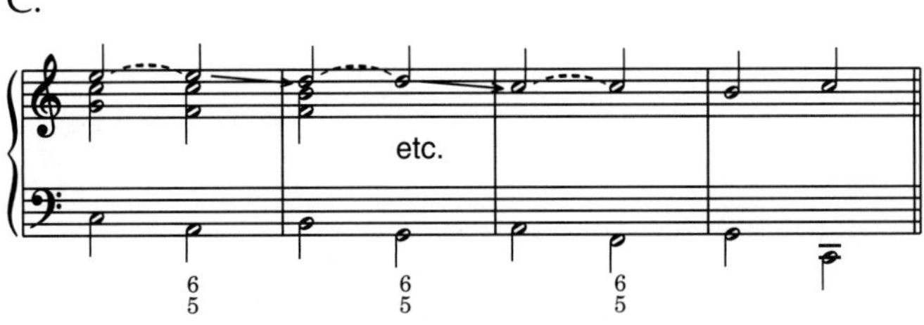

INSTRUMENTAL APPLICATION

23.10 Improvising and elaborating sequences

A. Duets (or one pianist)

One student plays the given bass while the second student arpeggiates the required chords based on the bass and the figures. Ascend on the first chord and descend on the second. Play in the parallel mode and transpose to two other keys. Finally, players should reverse voices.

given:

1.

Continued

given: (different solution from 1)

2.
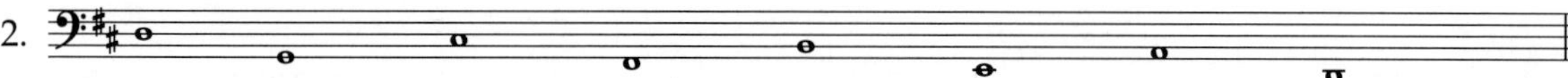

given:

3.
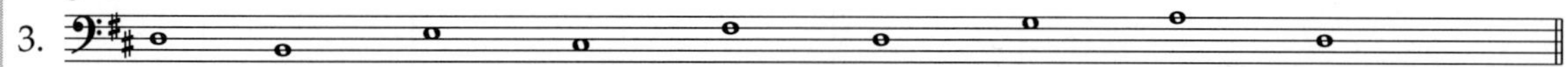

given:

4.

given:

5.
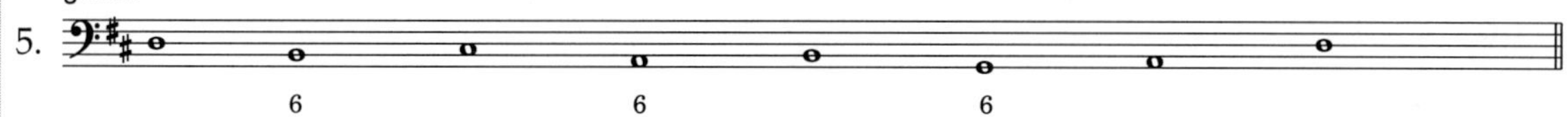

B. Figurated duets

Add tones of figuration to your melodic lines. Begin with chordal leaps and passing tones (see Example 1). Feel free to add combinations of these tones of figuration as well as neighbors and suspensions. Try to balance the faster motion between voices, a procedure called *complementation*.

given:

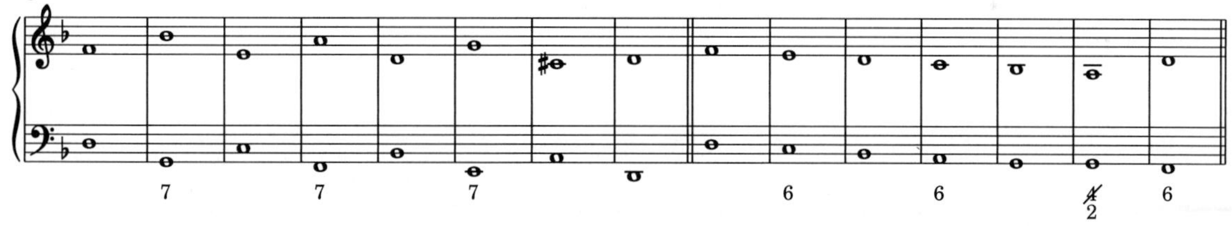

Example1:

DVD 2
CH 23
TRACK 5

23.11 Reduction of Sequences

Determine the sequence type in the given examples, and reduce the texture to three or four voices, which you will play as either vertical sonorities on the piano or arpeggiations on a melody instrument. A sample solution is provided, which contains three sequences.

Sample Solution

44
A2
51
D2
58
D2

A. Haydn, String Quartet in F♯ minor, op. 20, no. 6, *Allegro*

B. Corelli, Trio Sonata in A minor, op. 1, no. 4, *Allegro*

C. Corelli, Concerto Grosso no. 10 in C major, *Corrente*

D. Corelli, Trio Sonata in F major, op. 1, no. 1, *Allegro*

E. Corelli, Concerto Grosso no. 10 in C major, *Corrente*

F. Corelli, Chamber Sonata in C major, op. 4, no. 1, Preludio

WORKBOOK
23.2–23.5

TERMS AND CONCEPTS

- D2 (−5/+4) sequences with alternating sevenths
- D2 (−5/+4) sequences with interlocking sevenths
- parallel six-three sequential motions
- prolongational sequence versus transitional sequences
- sequential progressions

PART 6

CHROMATICISM

We have studied two types of chromaticism. The first type involves unharmonized chromatic tones of figuration (such as chromatic passing tones), which animate the texture, provide color, and intensify motion to the following diatonic chord tone. The second type—"harmonized chromaticism"—creates a leading tone in the minor mode by raising $\hat{7}$ a half step to give V a dominant function. Nearly all leading tones that we have seen resolve to tonic. Now, however, we will expand our understanding of leading-tone chromaticism by examining how it can be transferred to chords other than V in a key. In doing so, we will learn how this chromaticism is a useful voice-leading tool and how it can participate in musical events at deeper levels of the structure. We also will see that, although leading-tone chromaticism is powerful, it remains subordinate to the diatonic events in a piece.

CHAPTER 24

Applied Chords

Chromaticism colors diatonicism; therefore, chromatic pitches are generally not integral to the underlying diatonic structure. Instead, chromatic pitches take the place of diatonic pitches in a process called **chromatic alteration**. We have seen that diatonic passing tones can be harmonized by diatonic chords. In the same manner, chromatic passing tones can be harmonized by chromatic chords. Compare the two excerpts in Example 24.1. Example 24.1A presents a chromatic passing tone (C♯) between the tonic and ii chords, invigorating the melodic motion between $\hat{1}$ and $\hat{2}$. In Example 24.1B, the chromatic passing tone is harmonized by an intermediate harmony, an A-major chord. The chromatic passing tone is of little help in avoiding the parallel octaves and fifths in Example 24.1A, but when C♯ is supported with its own chord (A major in Example 24.1B), all of the parallels disappear and we have invigorated the harmonic motion to the ii chord.

EXAMPLE 24.1

DVD 1
CH 24
TRACK 1

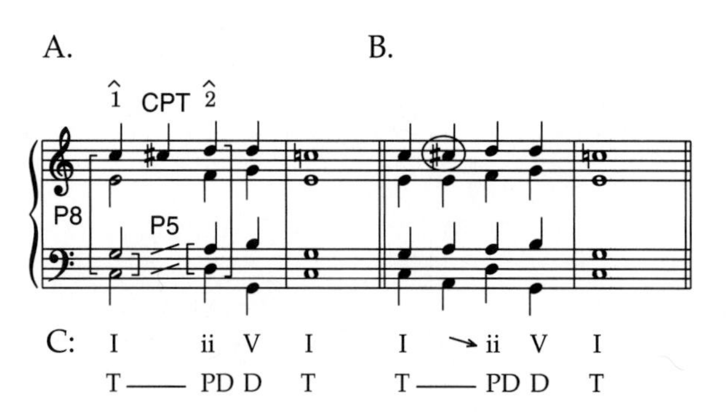

A tonic chord is fairly neutral with respect to direction: It might progress to ii or V, extend to vi, act as a neighbor to V, or go nowhere. The A-major sonority in Example 24.1B, however, is strongly directed to ii; in fact, it functions as the dominant of D minor. Because the A major chord functions as a dominant, it evokes the momentary impression that we are in the key of D minor. This sensation of briefly experiencing a key (e.g., for a few beats or even a measure or two) other than the tonic is **tonicization**, which is accomplished through the use of these **applied dominant chords** (also called **secondary dominant chords** or *applied* chords). The essential feature of tonicization is that it stretches out a diatonic harmony. For example, the tonicization above expands the PD: The realm of ii lists two chords (A major and D minor) rather than just one, but it still participates in the underlying structural harmonic progression of T-PD-D-T.

Applied Dominant Chords

For a chord to function as an applied dominant, it must behave like a dominant. In other words, it must be a major triad (V) or a dominant seventh chord (V_7) and it will usually move to its tonic. Any major or minor diatonic harmony can be preceded by its applied dominant chord.

Example: We are in C minor and would like to determine the applied dominant of V. V is a G major chord, so we need to determine the applied dominant of G major. The applied dominant of G major is D major. This is not in the original key, so we label the roman numeral as "applied dominant of V," or "V of V"—or simply "V/V." It is common for the dominant and pre-dominant to be preceded by their applied dominants. Just as common is the use of an applied dominant to III in minor—we have already seen this "V of III" chord in Chapter 19.

Another way to go about exploring the role of applied chords is to alter diatonic chords chromatically, changing them into applied dominants and seeing where they point to as dominant chords. Consider Example 24.2. Note that IV (in major) cannot be altered to create V/vii°, because vii° is dissonant (diminished harmony) and the root of IV lies an augmented fourth (rather than a perfect fourth) below the root of vii°. Similarly, VI (in minor) cannot be altered to create V/ii° because ii° is dissonant and the root of VI lies an augmented fourth below the root of ii°. Example 24.2 shows the diatonic triads in both C major and C minor and their transformation into applied dominants (in parentheses) and to what diatonic triad they would lead.

EXAMPLE 24.2

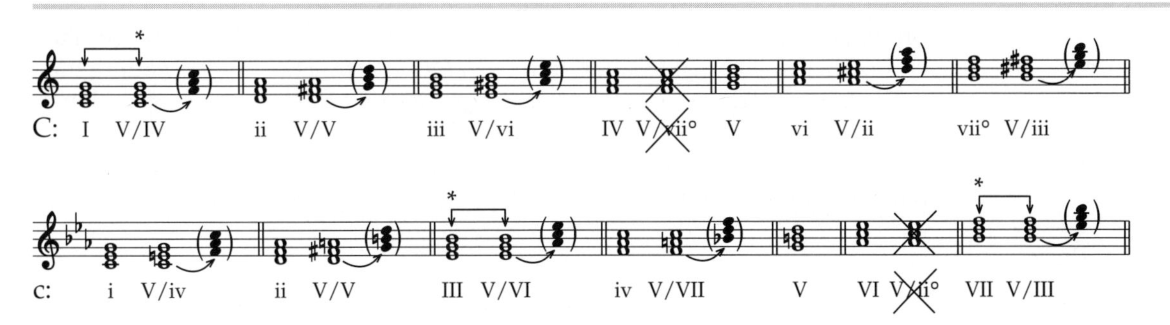

Notice in Example 24.2 that some diatonic chords are already major triads and therefore can be used as applied dominant chords (see the bracketed arrows): In major keys, V/IV (built on $\hat{1}$) is diatonic; in minor keys, V/VI (built on $\hat{3}$) and V/III (built on $\hat{7}$) are diatonic. In order to clarify their applied function, these chords typically appear as V_7 chords, adding the minor seventh above the root. For example, V/IV–IV in major will most likely be heard simply as tonic moving to IV rather than as IV's applied dominant. Adding the seventh transforms the diatonic harmony into an applied chord. Asterisks in

Example 24.2 indicate applied chords that require the added seventh. Because of their strong connection, applied dominant chords and their tonics occur under the same function in second-level analysis. For example:

I	V/ii	ii	V/V	V	I
T	PD——	——	D——	——	T

Applied Chords in Inversion

We have seen how root-position applied chords can enrich and enliven a progression. Example 24.3A presents a diatonic progression, which is elaborated with applied dominant chords in Example 24.3B. The bass line in Example 24.3B is rather angular; inversions can be used to smooth out bass lines of applied-chord progressions. Compare Example 24.3B to Example 24.3C, and notice that the latter sounds more polished.

EXAMPLE 24.3

DVD 1 CH 24 TRACK 2

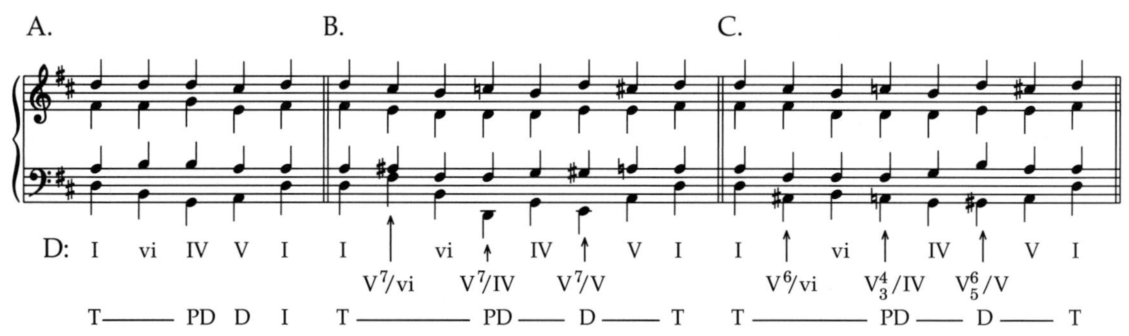

In the same way that inversions of V prolong I (e.g., V_6 usually expands I as a lower-neighbor chord), any other major or minor harmony in a key can be prolonged by its applied dominant chord. Example 24.4A reviews how tonic may be prolonged by any inversion of V_7. In Example 24.4B the supertonic is prolonged by its V_7 chord in precisely the same way. The only difference is the chromaticism: D must be altered to D♯ in order to function as the leading tone to the key of ii (E minor). However, no matter how extensive the expansion of a nontonic harmony, that harmony will ultimately figure into the tonal motion of the phrase model. For example, in Example 24.4C, ii is considerably expanded, but it still functions in the capacity of the phrase's pre-dominant.

EXAMPLE 24.4

DVD 1 CH 24 TRACK 3

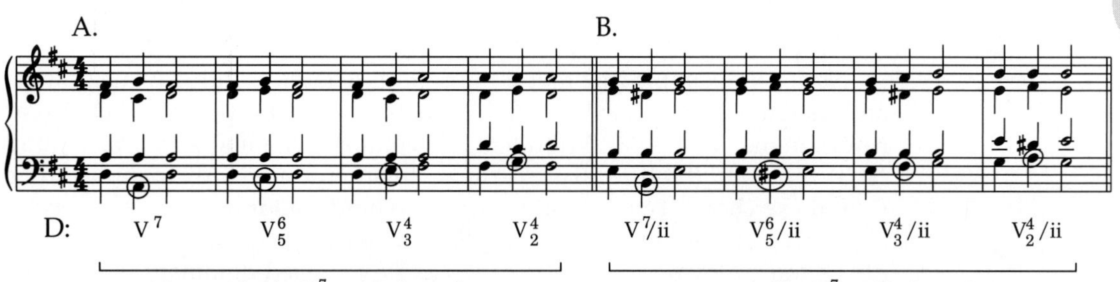

Continued

Hearing Applied Chords

It is not difficult to recognize applied chords: Aurally they have a distinctive dominant sound, and visually they have a distinctive notation. A chromatically raised note is often the third of an applied dominant chord (which is the leading tone for its key), and a chromatically lowered note is often the seventh of the applied dominant chord. In Example 24.5, the first chromatic pitch is F♯, and as a *raised* pitch it signals its function as a temporary leading tone to G, to which it leads (and, of course, G is iv in D minor, thus helping you analyze the chord as a V/iv). Similarly, the E♭ (diatonic E's *lowered* form; m. 1, beat 4) implies that it will function as the seventh of an F dominant seventh chord, as V_7/VI.

EXAMPLE 24.5

DVD 1
CH 24
TRACK 4

Voice Leading for Applied Chords

We have learned to identify and analyze applied chords in different musical contexts. The next step is to become comfortable with writing them in your own compositions. The following guidelines will help you achieve this goal with good voice leading.

We have encountered two chromatic alterations in applied chords, both of which are tendency tones. One is the third of the chord, which is often chromatically *raised* and acts as a *temporary leading tone*. The other is the *seventh of the chord*, which sometimes needs to be chromatically *lowered*. The voice-leading rules we know from our study of the V_7 chord apply to applied dominant chords as well.

- We do not double the leading tone or the seventh of the chord.
- The leading tone must resolve upward when in an outer voice.
- The seventh of the chord always resolves downward.

Example 24.6 shows the proper voice leading for applied dominant chords to vi and IV in C major. Note that root-position applied dominant chords can be complete (V_7/vi in Example 24.6A) or incomplete (V_7/IV in Example 24.6B).

EXAMPLE 24.6

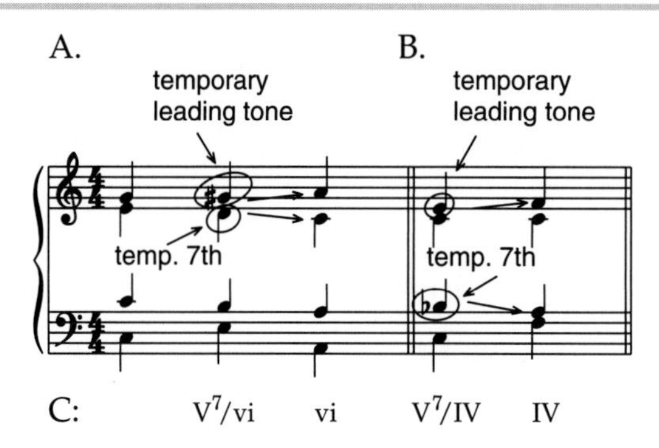

Look again at the soprano line of Example 24.6A. The leading tone (G♯) is a chromatic passing tone between G and A, which creates a smooth chromatic line: G–G♯–A. We **prepare chromaticism** by preceding a chromatic tone with its diatonic version in the same voice. Prepared chromaticism is always preferred in part writing, because it softens the harsh aural effect of the chromatic tone.

When a chromatic tone is prepared by another voice (instead of the same voice), it results in a **cross relation**. In Example 24.7, the chromatic G♯ is not prepared in the tenor; the diatonic G occurs in the soprano voice, and there is a cross relation. This produces a harsh aural effect due to the awkward leaps in the soprano and tenor.

EXAMPLE 24.7 Cross Relation

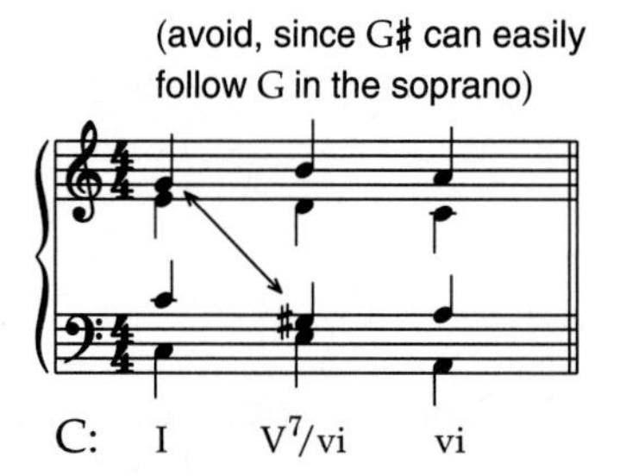

Despite the desirability of chromatic preparation, in many instances it is impossible for chromatic pitches to follow their diatonic forms in the same voice. Example 24.8 shows one such scenario. In a progression from I to V_6/vi in C major, the bass leaps down from C to G♯, which resolves as it should, to A. This leap of a diminished fourth in the bass is acceptable and quite expressive; in Baroque music with text, this leap often accompanies words of great sorrow or pain. Clearly, the alto G cannot move to G♯ when the bass sounds that pitch (since G♯ is a temporary leading tone). If you must write a cross relation, avoid writing the notes between the aurally prominent bass and soprano; instead, place the cross relation between inner voices or between one outer voice and an inner voice.

EXAMPLE 24.8 Common Cross Relation

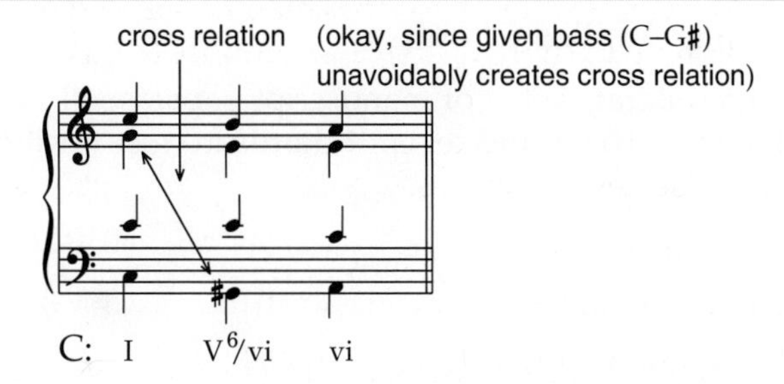

EXERCISE INTERLUDE

PERFORMING

24.1

Using solfège syllables or scale degrees, sing or play on your instrument the following progressions that incorporate applied chords. Label all applied chords, and circle their chordal thirds (temporary leading tones) and sevenths.

A. Major only

B.

C. Once without sharps in parentheses, once with

D.

E. Minor only

WRITING

24.2 Spelling Applied Chords

A. On a separate sheet of manuscript paper, spell the following applied dominant triads and seventh chords in close position on the treble clef staff. Use key signatures.

1. In G major: V_7/IV	V_7/vi	V_7/V
2. In D minor: V_7/iv	V^6_5/III	V_7/VI
3. In B minor: V_7/V	V_6/VI	V^4_3/iv
4. In E♭ major: V_6/iii	V_7/vi	V^6_5/ii
5. In C minor: V^4_2/III	V_7/iv	V/VII

B. On a separate sheet of manuscript paper, write the following applied dominant triads and seventh chords in four-part keyboard style. Use key signatures. Remember not to double temporary leading tones or chordal sevenths. Write the resolutions of the applied chords.

1. In F major: V_7/V	V^6_5/IV	V_6/ii	V_7/iii
2. In G minor: V_7/VI	V^6_5/III	V^4_2/V	V^6_5/iv
3. In E minor: V_6/III	V^4_3/V	V_7/VI	V^6_5/iv
4. In D major: V_7/vi	V^4_2/IV	V_6/ii	V^6_5/iii
5. In A major: V^4_3/IV	V^6_5/V	V_7/ii	V_6/iii

24.3

Write the following progressions in four-voice keyboard style. Choose any meter, but remember that applied chords are embellishing and often appear in weak metrical contexts.

A. F major: I–V_7/IV–IV–V_7/ii–ii–V

B. E minor: i–V^4_3/VI–VI–V^6_5/iv–iv

C. D major: V–V^6_5/vi–vi–ii_6–V^6_5/V–V

D. C minor: i–V^6_5/III–III–iv_6–V

LISTENING

24.4

Each of the following progressions contains one applied chord. Notate the bass and soprano lines and provide roman numerals on a separate sheet of paper. All examples are in $\frac{4}{4}$ time and two measures long. Exercise A contains one flat, B contains one sharp, C contains three flats, and D contains two flats.

Applied Leading-Tone Chords

We know from our studies that vii°$_6$, vii°$_7$, (and to a lesser degree vii$^{ø}_{7}$) are dominant substitutes that can participate in contrapuntal expansions of the tonic. Often, these harmonies are also used as applied dominant substitutes that tonicize other scale degrees.

Listen to Example 24.9, in which the applied chords in mm. 1–2 help tonicize ii of C major. Because of the varied types and inversions of the applied chords—vii°$_7$/ii, vii°$_6$/ii, and vii°$^4_3$/ii—the supertonic can be tonicized for some time (nearly half of the example's four measures). Note that the larger function of ii as a pre-dominant remains unchanged. The tonicized area functions as a way station that helps to connect tonic and dominant.

EXAMPLE 24.9

Up to this point, we have used only those diminished seventh chords that are built on $\hat{7}$ of the minor mode. With the introduction of applied dominant substitute chords, we now may use vii°$_7$ and its inversions to tonicize major and minor triads, two of which are asterisked in Example 24.9.

Incorporating Applied Chords Within Phrases

There are no new rules to learn when writing applied chords in phrases; however, you must consider metric and rhythmic issues in order to create a balanced and pleasing structure. Listen to Example 24.10, and determine its phrase structure and the metrical placement of the applied chords. Beethoven has created a parallel interrupted period, and every applied chord appears on a metrically weak beat. Weak metrical placement of applied chords is common because they contain leading tones that precipitate motion toward a metrically stressed goal. Beethoven uses three applied chords in the first phrase; only the first two applied chords appear in the second phrase, because the dominant is not the goal of motion and therefore is not tonicized as it was in m. 4 of the first phrase. Rather, the tonic occupies the entire last measure, using the dominant to intensify the PAC.

EXAMPLE 24.10 **Beethoven, String Quartet no. 9 in C major, op. 59, no. 3, Menuetto:** ***Grazioso***

DVD 1
CH 24
TRACK 6

Notice in Example 24.10 that there is a new notational symbol, the curved arrow (↷), which represents that the chord preceding the arrow is an applied dominant or dominant substitute that leads to the chord to which the arrow points. This shorthand label is often necessary when it may prove difficult to squeeze in complete labels for applied chords, as in this excerpt with such fast harmonic rhythm and so many chords in so few beats. However, sometimes applied dominants (like the actual $V_{(7)}$ chord) resolve deceptively to what would be vi in the temporary key. In such cases, you will need to supply the complete roman numeral for the applied chord since the arrow alone will not indicate a deceptive motion. Further, you may also use the following analytical shorthand for both applied dominants (and dominant sevenths) and applied diminished-seventh chords: For dominants, use only their figured bass symbols (e.g., $^6_3$, $_7$, $^4_3$); for diminished sevenths, add the accompanying diminished sign (e.g., $^\circ{}_7$, $^{\circ 6}_{5}$). It is also possible to use the complete roman numeral followed by the arrow (e.g., V_7↷).

An Example Composition

Let's write a contrasting continuous period, in $^4_4$ meter and G minor, incorporating several applied chords. We should first plan the big picture by mapping out the overall structure. We can construct a single large-scale harmonic progression by closing the first phrase with a deceptive motion, moving to a PD to begin the second phrase, and closing on tonic. A possible harmonic rhythm of this plan is illustrated in the following diagram:

	Phrase 1			(DC)		Phrase 2		PAC
mm:	1	2	3	4	5	6	7	8
G minor:	i—	—	V—	VI	iv—	—	ii°—V—	i

Measures 2 and 6 provide opportunities to insert embellishing harmonies. First, we should try to connect the i of m. 1 with the V of m. 3. We could use the bass arpeggiation i–VI–PD. But because the phrase closes on VI, an early appearance of VI might make m. 4 sound anticlimactic. Another option to link i and V is to use the following progression:

	Phrase 1			
mm:	1	2	3	4
	i———	III———	PD—V—	VI

Although this looks like a workable harmonic plan, it still might sound a bit bare and simplistic. At this point, adding some contrapuntal and applied chords will help to establish the tonic in m. 1 and to intensify the overall progression.

From this point on, we will envision our harmonic choices with the help of a bass line. First, let's try to arrange it so that every chord in the progression is preceded by an applied chord. (Remember that we can precede consonant (major and minor) harmonies with an applied chord, so only ii° may not be expanded by an applied chord.) In placing our applied chords, we should aim for weak beats so that the chord can resolve to structural chords on stronger beats, as in Example 24.11A. Most likely, however, we would not rely exclusively on root-position applied dominant chords, nor would we restrict ourselves solely to triads.

EXAMPLE 24.11

For variety, our taste demands a mix of applied chords as well as a smooth bass contour, as in Example 24.11B. A neighboring diminished seventh chord helps to establish the tonic in m. 1. In addition, the bass of the chord contrasts with the following F, the root of a V_7/III chord. III is prolonged with an applied dominant substitute that acts as a passing chord. Rather than moving directly to the PD at the end of m. 2, the bass skips dramatically up to F, creating a V^4_2/iv chord. The subdominant is then expanded with a simple chordal leap, and vii°$_7$/V nicely fills the space between iv and V with a chromatic passing tone in the bass. Now we will add a soprano melody and inner voices (Example 24.12).

EXAMPLE 24.12

DVD 1
CH 24
TRACK 7

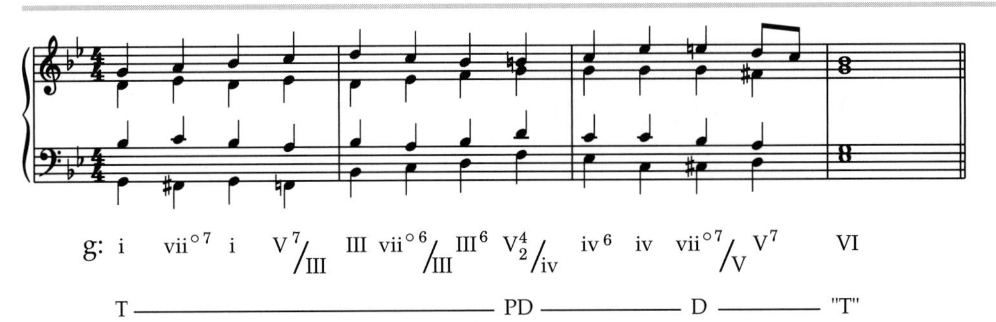

We can insert a sequence into the second phrase, because there is at least one measure—perhaps even two—to work with. A D2 (−5/+4) sequence starting on iv would lead to ii° in four chords (Example 24.13). The sequence unfolds in an unremarkable and rather clunky manner. It moves in heavy half notes, with ponderous leaps.

EXAMPLE 24.13

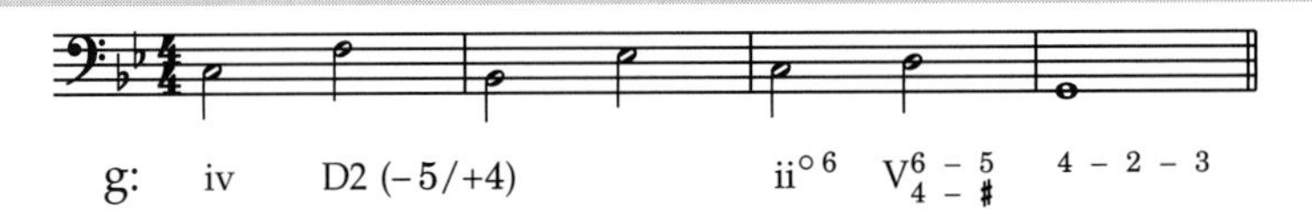

We can enrich the harmonic color and smooth the linear motion of the sequence by using first-inversion chords. We also can add an applied dominant chord leading to V in m. 3 (Example 24.14).

EXAMPLE 24.14

Finally, the seam between the two phrases—an entire motionless measure of VI—does not fit well in what is otherwise a robust harmonic progression. We can use an applied chord to integrate the two phrases: V^4_3/iv begins the second phrase and glues the disparate sections to form a continuous period, or, as interpreted, a single large phrase (Example 24.15). Since the chord-to-chord analysis has already been shown in previous versions of this example, only the underlying diatonic harmonic progression is shown in Example 24.15; brackets above the structural roman numerals show the extent of their control.

EXAMPLE 24.15

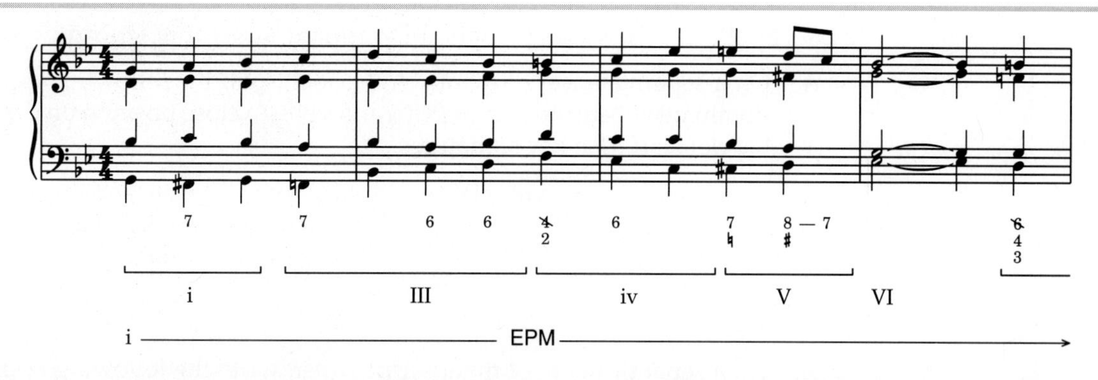

EXERCISE INTERLUDE

PERFORMING

24.5

Using solfège syllables or scale degrees, sing or play on your instrument the following progressions that incorporate applied dominant substitute chords. If you play these on your instrument, be able to transpose each to one other key.

A. Major only

B. Minor only

WRITING

24.6 Spelling and Writing Applied Dominant Substitute Chords

A. On a separate sheet of manuscript paper, spell the following applied dominant substitute chords (vii°$_6$ and vii°$_7$) in close position on the treble clef staff. Use key signatures.

1. In D major:	vii°$_7$/IV	vii°$_6$/vi	vii°$^4_3$/V
2. In E minor:	vii°$_7$/iv	vii°$^6_5$/III	vii$_6$/VI
3. In B minor:	vii°$^6_5$/V	vii°$_7$/VI	vii°$_6$/iv
4. In E♭ major:	V$_6$/iii	vii°$_7$/vi	vii°$^4_3$/ii

B. On a separate sheet of manuscript paper, write the following applied dominant substitute chords in four-part chorale style. Use key signatures. Remember not to double temporary leading tones or chordal sevenths. Write the resolutions of the applied chords.

1. In B♭ major:	(a) vii°$_7$/V	(b) vii°$^4_3$/IV	(c) vii°$_6$/ii	(d) vii°$_7$/iii
2. In G minor:	(e) vii°$_7$/VI	(f) vii°$^6_5$/III	(g) vii°$_7$/V	(h) vii°$^6_5$/iv

24.7

Write the following progressions in four-voice keyboard style. Choose any meter, but remember that all applied chords are embellishing and often appear in weak metrical contexts.

A. D major: I–I$_6$-vii°$_7$/IV–IV–vii°$_7$/ii–ii–V
B. A minor: i–vii°$^6_5$/III–III–iv$_6$–V—vii°$_7$/V–V

LISTENING

24.8 Comparison of Applied V$_7$ and vii°$_7$ in Short Phrases

Notate outer voices of the following progressions, and provide roman numerals.

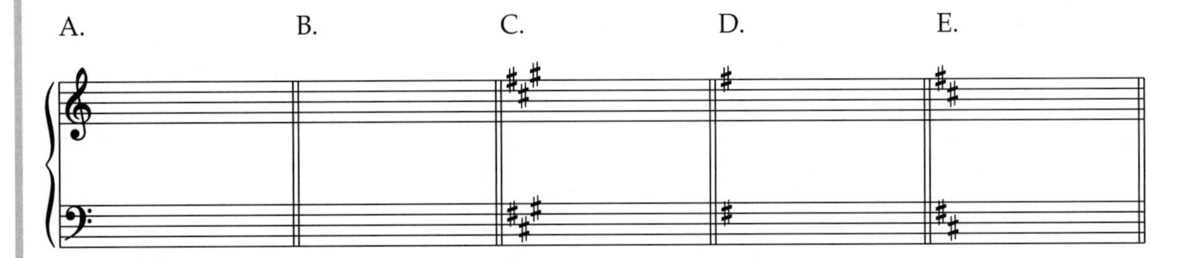

KEYBOARD

WORKBOOK
24.1–24.5

24.9 Brain Twister

Determine the major and (relative) minor keys for each example, and label the applied dominant or diminished seventh chord given. In four-voice keyboard style, play and resolve the applied chords; then lead each example to an authentic cadence, first in major and then in the relative minor key.

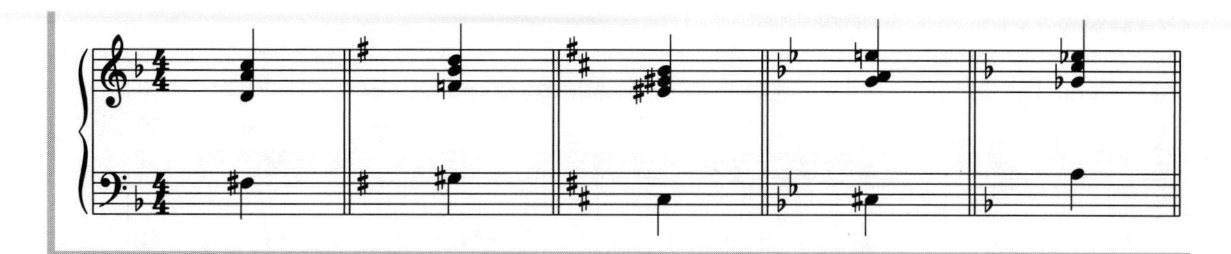

Sequences with Applied Chords

Listen to Example 24.16, an excerpt from a Baroque flute sonata. Did you hear the sequence that begins in m. 94 and ends at m. 100? Analysis of the chord roots (C–F, D–G, E–A) reveals that it is an ascending sequence. But it is different from the rising sequences we have studied: It contains applied-chord chromaticism. If we were to remove the chromaticism, what would remain is a form of A2 (−3/+4) sequence including first-inversion triads—the ascending 5–6 sequence. In the chromatic sequence, applied $^6_5$ chords alternate with diatonic triads. When applied chords are added to the sequence types we studied in Chapters 22–23, **applied-chord sequences**—which intensify sequential motion significantly—are created.

EXAMPLE 24.16 Leclair, Sonata in C major for Flute and Continuo, op. 1, no. 2, *Corrente*

DVD 1
CH 24
TRACK 11

The D2 (−5/+4) Sequence

Review the diatonic form of the D2 (−5/+4) sequence in Example 24.17A, then note that a chromatic version of it appears when applied chords substitute for diatonic chords. The result is the sequence seen in Example 24.17B.

EXAMPLE 24.17

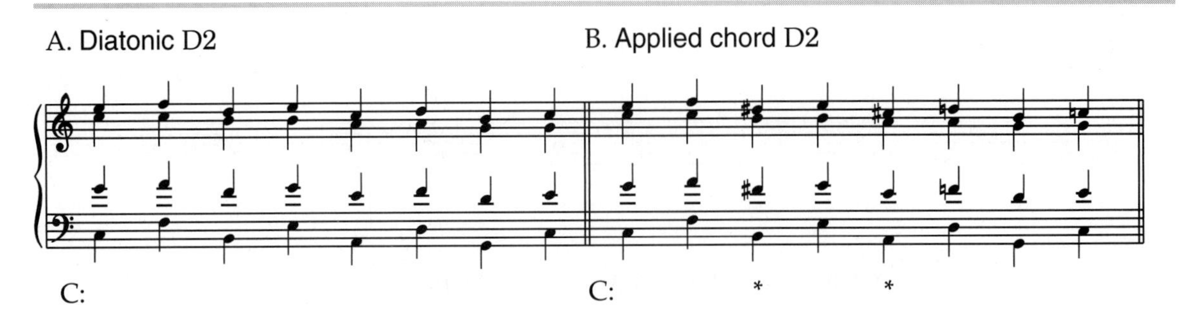

In a further twist, it is common to add sevenths to the triads of the D2 (−5/+4) applied-chord sequence, thus enhancing the sequence's goal-directed motion. These seventh chords may be alternating (Example 24.18A) or interlocking (Example 24.18B). Note the presence of parallel tritones in the upper voices of Beethoven's "Moonlight" Sonata (Example 24.19).

EXAMPLE 24.18

DVD 1
CH 24
TRACK 12

A. D2 (−5/+4) with alternating sevenths B. D2 (−5/+4) with interlocking sevenths

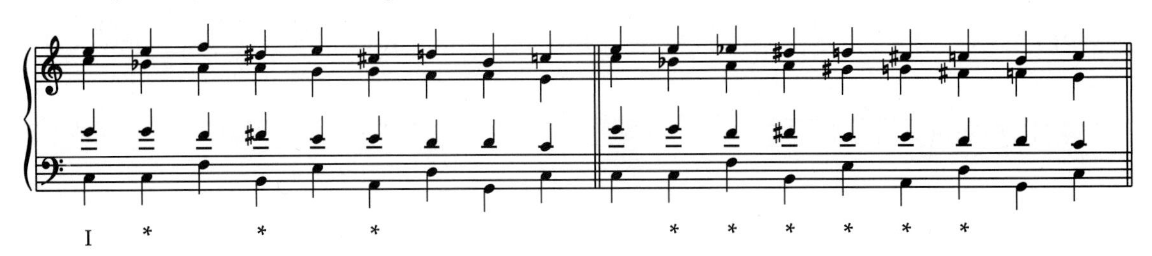

EXAMPLE 24.19 Beethoven, Piano Sonata in C♯ minor, op. 27, no. 1 ("Moonlight"), Trio

DVD 1
CH 24
TRACK 13

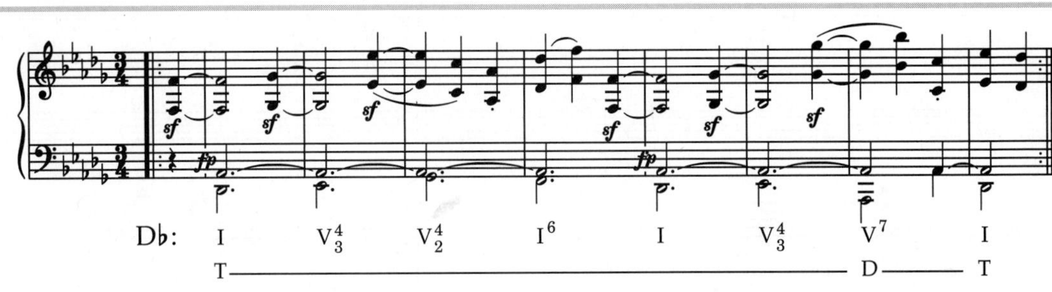

Continued

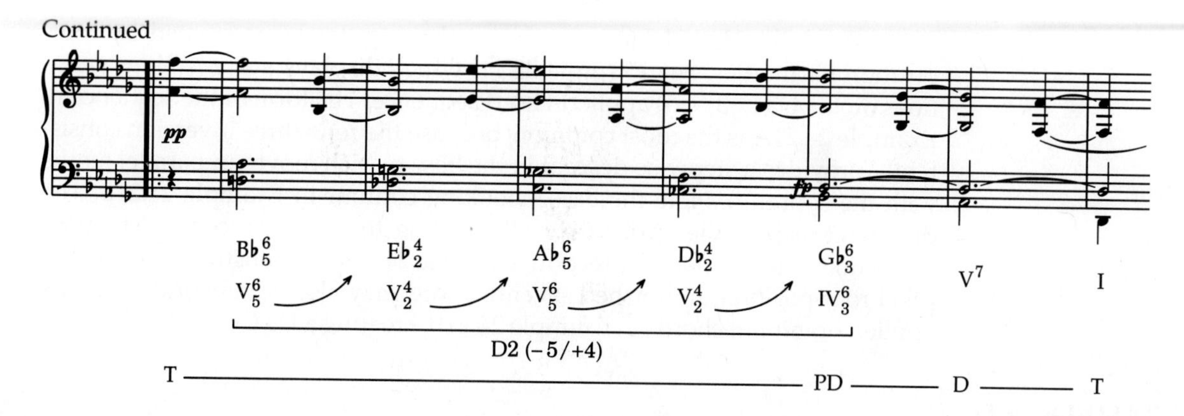

The D3 (−4/+2) Sequence

We have seen that in the diatonic D3 (−4/+2) sequence, the second chord of each pair lies a fourth below the first (Example 24.20A). (One could hear this either as a back-relating (or retrogressive) motion or as a slightly stronger forward deceptive motion). A dramatic forward motion occurs in the applied-chord form of this sequence, seen in Example 24.20. Because each applied chord creates a temporary leading tone that leads to its own following tonic, the second chord of each copy functions as a dominant of the following—and not the previous—chord. Consequently, the chords have different roots from their counterparts in the diatonic sequence. The diatonic D3 (−4/+2) is transformed into the D3 (+3/−5) applied-chord sequence. Applied chords in this sequence most often contain sevenths, as shown in Example 24.20B.

EXAMPLE 24.20

A. D3 (diatonic)

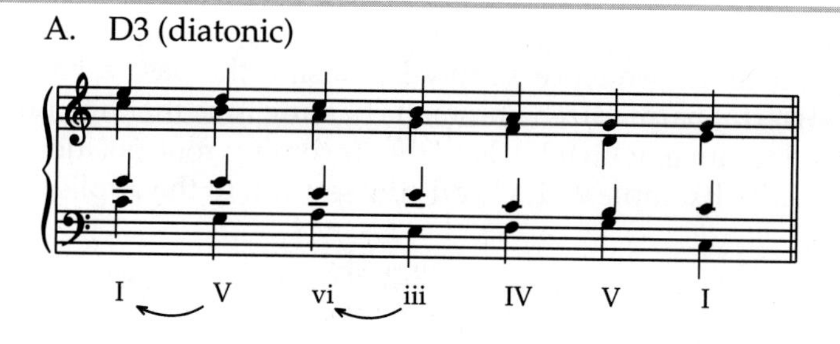

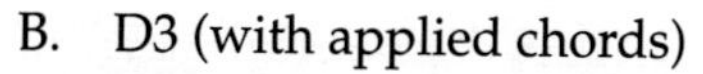
B. D3 (with applied chords)

Inverted chords help to smooth out the angular leaps created by root-position harmonies. See Example 24.21, which displays voice-leading variations on the D3 (+3/−5) applied-chord sequence. The form of the sequence in Example 24.21A is the most common, because the four-three inversion consistently provides a stepwise descent in the bass (which moves in parallel tenths with the soprano). Note the bass's hooking contour in Example 24.21B: The dissonant leap to the applied chord's leading tone is balanced by stepwise resolution in the opposite direction. Example 24.21C demonstrates that an applied root-position diminished seventh chord may also be substituted for the applied dominant chords in Example 24.21B, creating a D3 (−4/+1) sequence.

EXAMPLE 24.21

DVD 1
CH 24
TRACK 14

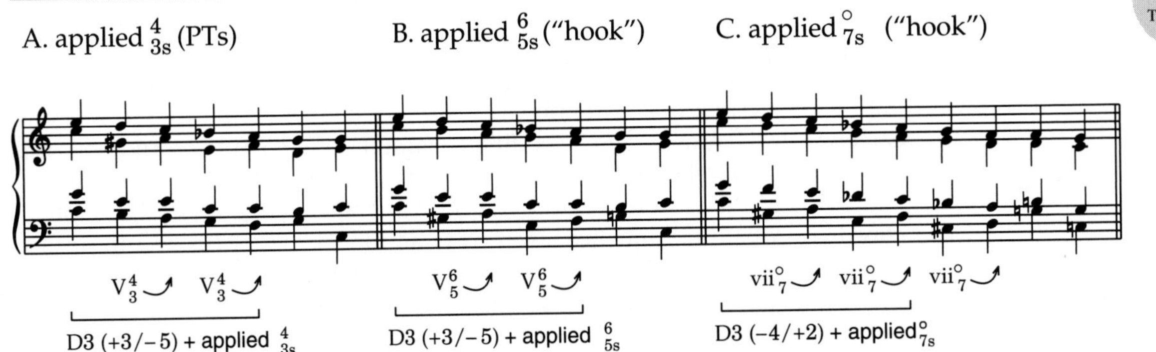

The A2 (−3/+4) Applied-Chord Sequence

Of the two A2 sequences, A2 (−3/+4) is much more likely to incorporate applied chords. The form of the sequence that includes first-inversion triads—the *ascending* 5–6 sequence (Example 24.22A)—may be converted into an applied-chord sequence simply by raising the bass a half step. This creates a powerful harmonized chromatic passing tone that functions as the temporary leading tone, which leads to the upcoming root-position triad step (Example 24.22B). Example 24.22C adds the seventh to the applied chords.

EXAMPLE 24.22

DVD 1
CH 24
TRACK 15

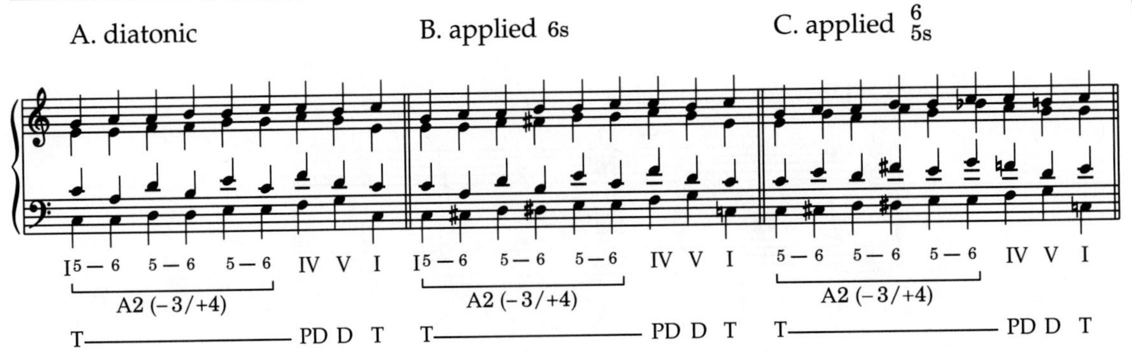

It is also common to find this sequence created through the use of root-position applied chords. In this case, the chromatic passing motion appears in the soprano rather than in the bass (Example 24.23).

EXAMPLE 24.23

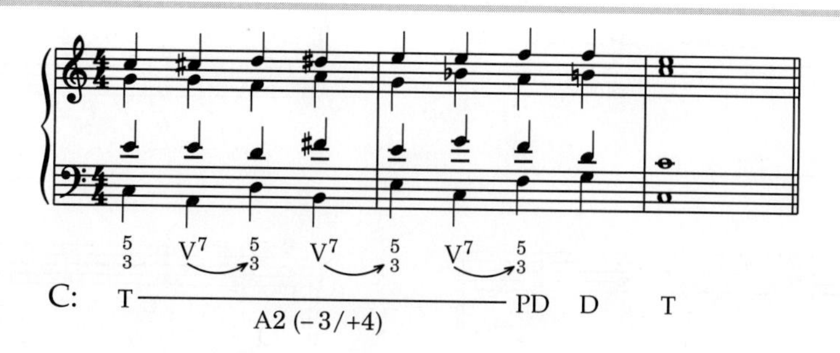

Writing Applied-Chord Sequences

There are no new voice-leading procedures involved in writing applied-chord sequences. Simply remember the following.

1. Construct the two-chord model carefully so that the voice leading between the two chords and the first chord of the copy is correct.
2. Copies must follow the voice leading of the model.
3. The root of each chord must be diatonic to the key.
4. Write complete seventh chords, especially when they appear in inversion. The only exception occurs in D2 (−5/+4) sequences with interlocking sevenths (see Example 24.18B).

Summary of Diatonic and Applied-chord Sequences

An example of each of the sequence types we have studied appears below. The examples are organized by the four generic types of sequences: descending by second and by third, and two forms of ascending by second. The modifications within each of the four types are organized as follows:

Diatonic: triads ($^5_3$, $^6_3$), seventh chords (root, inversion(s))

Applied: triads ($^5_3$, $^6_3$), seventh chords (root, inversion(s))

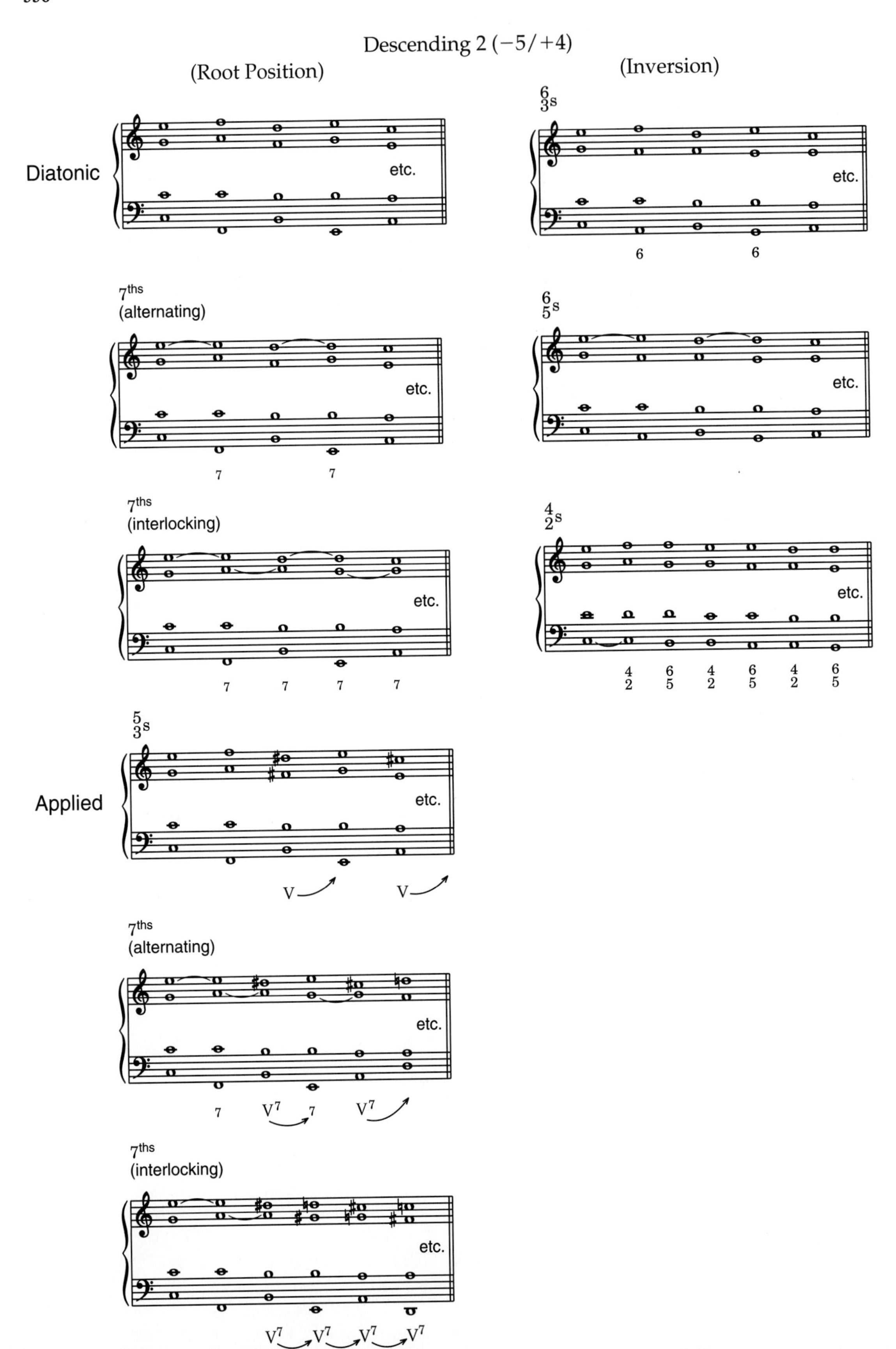
Descending 2 (−5/+4)
(Root Position)
(Inversion)
Diatonic
etc.
6
3s
6 6
7ths
(alternating)
7 7
6
5s
7ths
(interlocking)
7 7 7 7
4
2s
4 2 6 5 4 2 6 5 4 2 6 5
5
3s
Applied
V V
7ths
(alternating)
7 V7 7 V7
7ths
(interlocking)
V7 V7 V7 V7

Descending 3 (−4/+2)

(Root Position)

(Inversion)

$^5_3$s

Diatonic

etc.

$^6_3$s

etc.

$^5_3$ $^6_3$ $^5_3$ $^6_3$ $^5_3$

Descending 3 (+3/−5)

$^5_3$s

Applied

etc.

V → V →

$^6_5$s

etc.

V^6_5 → V^6_5 →

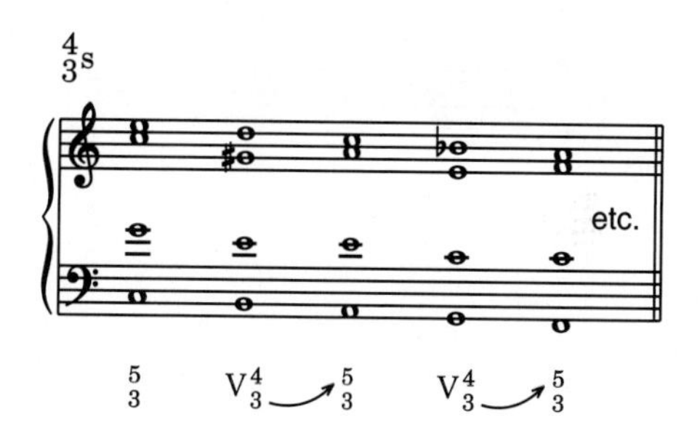

Ascending 2 (−3/+4)
(Root Position)
(Inversion)
5
3s
6
3s
6
5s
7ths
Diatonic
Applied
etc.
5 6 5 6 5
3 3 3 3 3
5 6 5 6 5
3 5 3 5 3
V V
V6 3 5 3 V6 3 5 3
V7 5 3 V7 5 3
V6 5 5 3 V6 5 5 3
Ascending 2 (+5/−4)
5
3
Diatonic
etc.

EXERCISE INTERLUDE

PERFORMING

24.10

Using solfège or scale degrees, sing the following harmonic patterns, which incorporate applied-chord sequences. Label all applied chords, and identify their chordal thirds and sevenths.

KEYBOARD

24.11

In keyboard style, play and resolve the following applied chords. Lead each example to an authentic cadence.

A. F major and D major: V_7/IV; vii$^{\circ}_7$/ii; V_7/vi
B. B♭ major and G major: V_7/V; V_7/vi; V^6_5/IV
C. E minor and D minor: vii$^{\circ 6}_5$/iv; vii$^{\circ}_7$/III; vii$^{\circ}_7$/VI
D. C major and E♭ major: vii$^{\circ}_6$/ii; V^6_5/iii; V^4_2/vi

24.12

Play the models for applied-chord sequences as written; then continue the given pattern. Analyze all progressions, and label sequence types. Be able to sing either outer voice while playing the remaining three voices. Transpose to major keys up to two flats and two sharps.

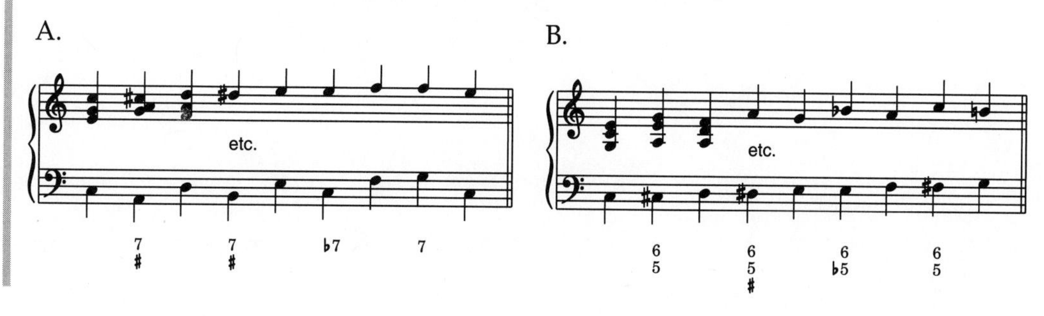

C. D.

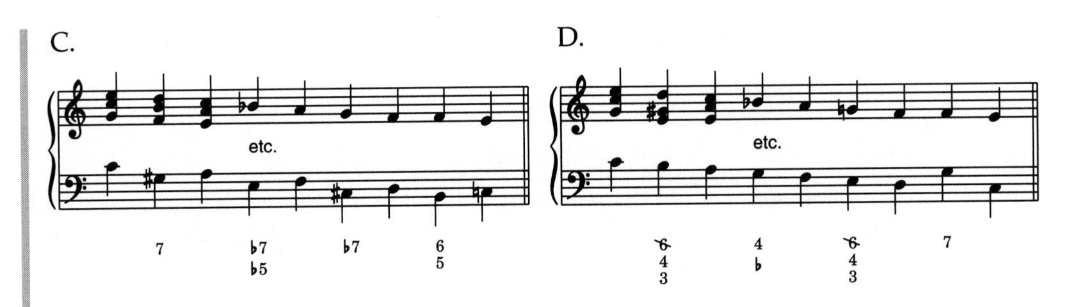

E.

LISTENING

DVD 2 CH 24 TRACK 3

24.13

Identify and label each applied-chord sequence that you hear.

A. _______ B. _______ C. _______ D. _______
E. _______ F. _______ G. _______ H. _______

Instrumental Application: Reduction and Elaboration

DVD 2 CH 24 TRACK 4

24.14

Reduce the textures in the following excerpts in order to determine the type of sequence used. Analyze, verticalize (into a four-voice homophonic texture), and then perform each example as follows: If you are a pianist, simply play your four-voice realization. If you are a melodic instrumentalist, arpeggiate each example. Maintain good voice leading.

A. Corelli, Sonata for Violin in B♭ major, op. 5, no. 2, *Vivace*

B. Corelli, Concerto Grosso in D major, op. 6, no. 1, Allegro

WORKBOOK
24.6–24.8

24.15

Improvise embellished versions of any of the sequences given in Exercise 24.12. In order to include various tones of figuration (PT, NT, CL, SUSP, or some combination of two or three of these), consider each chord as occupying one measure of $\frac{2}{4}$ or $\frac{3}{4}$. Maintain good voice leading. Play in the key given and in one other key of your choice.

TERMS AND CONCEPTS

- applied-chord sequences
    - D2 (−5/+4); A2 (+5/−4); D3 (+3/−5); A2 (−3/+4)
- applied dominant chord
- chromatic alteration
- cross relation
- temporary tonic
- tonicization
- voice leading of applied chords

CHAPTER 25

Tonicization and Modulation

In Chapter 24 we learned about applied dominant chords that led toward chords other than the tonic through tonicization. We will now explore **extended tonicizations** and **modulations.**

Extended Tonicizations

A tonicization is extended in the same way that a harmonic function is extended within a phrase. In Example 25.1B—an expansion of Example 25.1A—the ii chord in m. 2 is extended in precisely the same way as the tonic of m. 1: A passing vii°$_6$ chord connects I to I$_6$ in m. 1 and a passing vii°$_6$/ii chord connects ii to ii$_6$ in m. 2. The analysis should reflect the similarities in the two measures, but the roman numerals are more cluttered in m. 2 due to the extended tonicization of ii. Example 25.1C provides a clear way to analyze an extended tonicization:

1. Bracket where a tonicization occurs.
2. Label the temporary tonic chord under the bracket.
3. Label all chords within the bracket as if they were in the temporary new key.

EXAMPLE 25.1

DVD 1
CH 25
TRACK 1

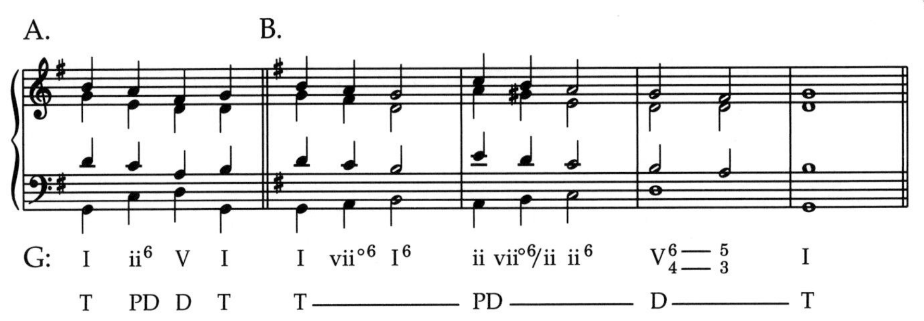

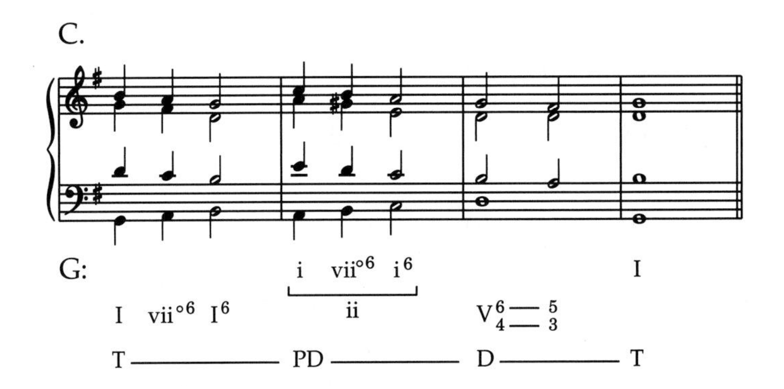

We try out this method of analysis in the next four examples from the literature, which demonstrate various types of extended tonicizations.

EXAMPLE 25.2 Beethoven, Piano Sonata in E♭ major, op. 27, no. 1, *Andante* (I)

DVD 1
CH 25
TRACK 2

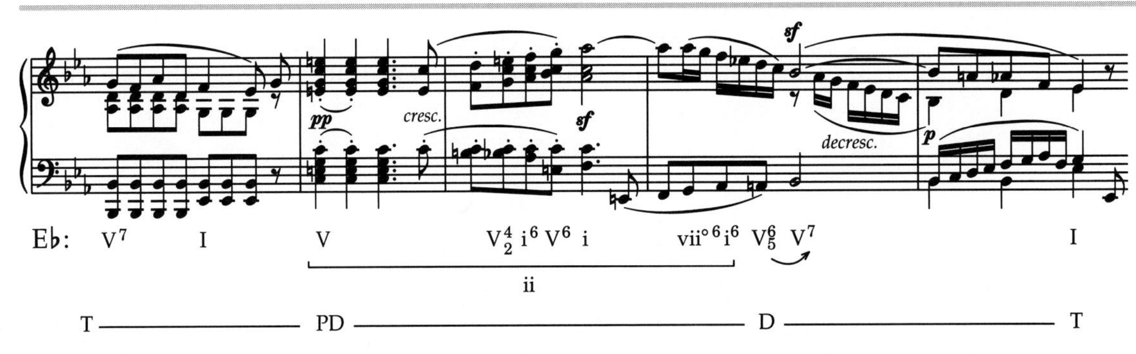

After a PAC closes a phrase in the first measure of Example 25.2, an unexpected and jarring C-major harmony appears in the second measure. When such an unusual event occurs, we must always look beyond individual harmonies to understand how it participates in the phrase. Given that the C-major chord becomes a dominant seventh in the third measure, it functions as an applied dominant chord leading to F minor. The tonicization of F minor (ii in the key of E♭ major) continues until the applied V/V chord. Thus, we see an expanded tonicization of PD.

EXAMPLE 25.3 **Robert Schumann, "Sängers Trost" ("Singer's Consolation"), *Fünf Lieder und Gesänge*, op. 127, no. 1**

DVD 1 CH 25 TRACK 3

The tonic in Example 25.3 is barely established before it moves to B♭ major (III) and D minor (v), in a repeating pattern (vi–V_7–I). This brief tonicization of G, B♭, and D results in a large-scale arpeggiation of the tonic G-minor chord. Notice that G minor is reinterpreted as vi/III and that III becomes VI/v.

EXAMPLE 25.4 **Clara Schumann, "Andante espressivo," *Quatre pièces fugitives*, op. 15, no. 3**

DVD 1 CH 25 TRACK 4

The excerpt by Clara Schumann in Example 25.4 is similar to—but slightly more complex than—the previous examples. An extended tonicization of ii follows a back-relating dominant in m. 4. Consequently, we can now understand the function of the A-minor chord in m. 4: It is a iv chord in the temporary key of E minor and not some sort of minor v chord in the home key of D. Finally, following the tonicization of ii, the structural dominant occurs in m. 7, which completes the excerpt's overall progression, I–ii–V.

The excerpt by Robert Schumann in Example 25.5 contains tonicizations of two harmonies, vi and ii, which are extended after the vocal entrance. As the second-level analysis reveals, over the course of the entire excerpt the tonicizations of vi and ii repeatedly expand the simple underlying harmonic progression, I–vi–ii–V–I.

EXAMPLE 25.5 Robert Schumann, "Mit Myrthen und Rosen" ("With Myrtle and Roses"), *Liederkreis*, op. 24, no. 9

DVD 1
CH 25
TRACK 5

EXERCISE INTERLUDE

PERFORMING

25.1

Sing (or play on your instrument) the following progressions using solfège or scale degrees. Given that the progressions contain expansions of nontonic areas, analyze each exercise before singing. Your instructor will give you analytical guidelines specific to the needs of your school's curriculum.

ANALYSIS

DVD 2 CH 25 TRACK 1

25.2

The following excerpts contain tonicizations. Listen to each example, and bracket the expanded harmony(ies); then provide a two-level roman numeral analysis.

A. Clementi, Prelude in A minor, op. 19

B. Chopin, Nocturne in G major, op. 37, no. 2

Continued

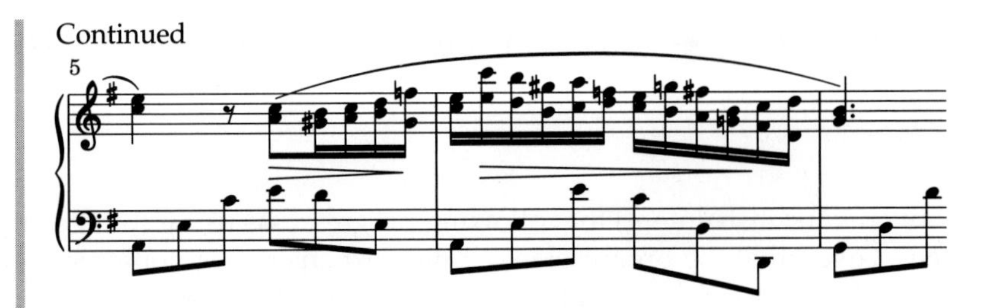

C. Brahms, *Hungarian Dance* no. 1, op. 102

D. Mozart, Symphony in D major, K. 504 ("Prague"), *Presto*

Continued

COMPOSITION

25.3

WORKBOOK 25.1

On a separate sheet of manuscript paper, complete the following tasks in a four-voice chorale style. Each task is a harmonic road map. Start by choosing the number of measures (four or eight). Then sketch out the phrase model for each phrase: Plan where the "structural" chords will fall. Finally, include the appropriate tonicizations, which can range from one applied dominant chord to extended tonicizations (these are typically tonic expansions or EPMs in the temporary keys).

A. In d minor: **Establish** tonic; **arpeggiate** through III to a phrygian cadence; **return** to **tonic;** tonicize iv using at least five chords; **lead** to a cadential six-four with an applied chord; **close** with a neighboring six-four chord to expand the final tonic.
B. In the following progression in B♭ major, tonicize chords with an asterisk (*) with at least four harmonies: I–iii*–vi*–ii*–V $^{6}_{4}{}^{-}_{-}{}^{5}_{3}$–I.
C. Write a progression in C minor that includes the following sequences (not necessarily in the following order): D3 (+3/−5) with applied chords, A2 (−3/+4) with applied chords, and diatonic D2 (−5/+4) with six-three variant.
D. Write a period of your choice in F major that briefly tonicizes ii, IV, and V.

Modulation

Longer tonicizations, which can occupy entire sections of a piece, are called **modulations**. Although it is difficult to draw a firm line between tonicizations and modulations, for our purposes:

Tonicizations usually occur within phrases. They do not disrupt the feeling of the home key; they do not have strong cadences in new keys, and they are fleeting.

Modulations include a strong cadence in the new key, and the new key continues after the cadence. They give the feeling that a new key has usurped the home key (at least for the moment).

Listen to the two excerpts in Example 25.6. Each excerpt tonicizes one or more keys, but the methods and degree of tonicization are fundamentally different. The Beethoven example contains extended tonicizations that are reminiscent of those we have already encountered: The first strong cadence occurs at the end of the excerpt, with the PAC in mm. 15–16. The first phrase is in the tonic key; phrase 2 is an extended tonicization of ii, IV is tonicized until the cadence at the end. There is one overall harmonic progression, I–ii–IV–V–I, and none of the fleeting tonicizations disrupts the sense that we are hearing an A-major piece.

EXAMPLE 25.6

DVD 1
CH 25
TRACK 6

A. Beethoven, Violin Sonata in A major, op. 12, no. 2, *Allegro piacevole*

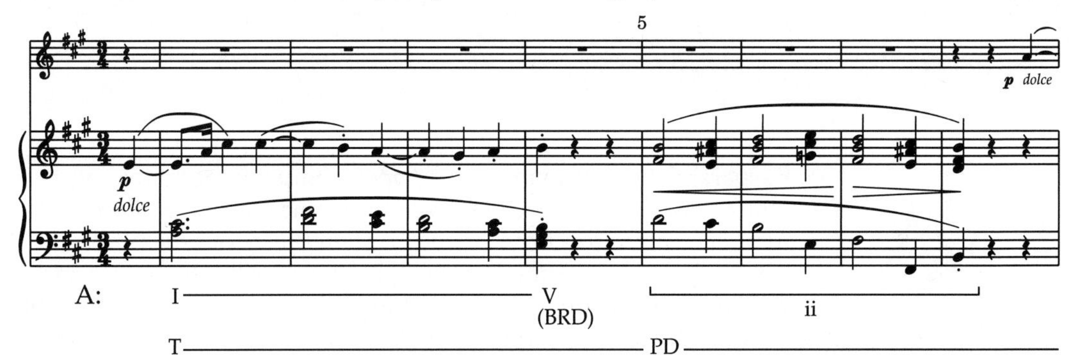

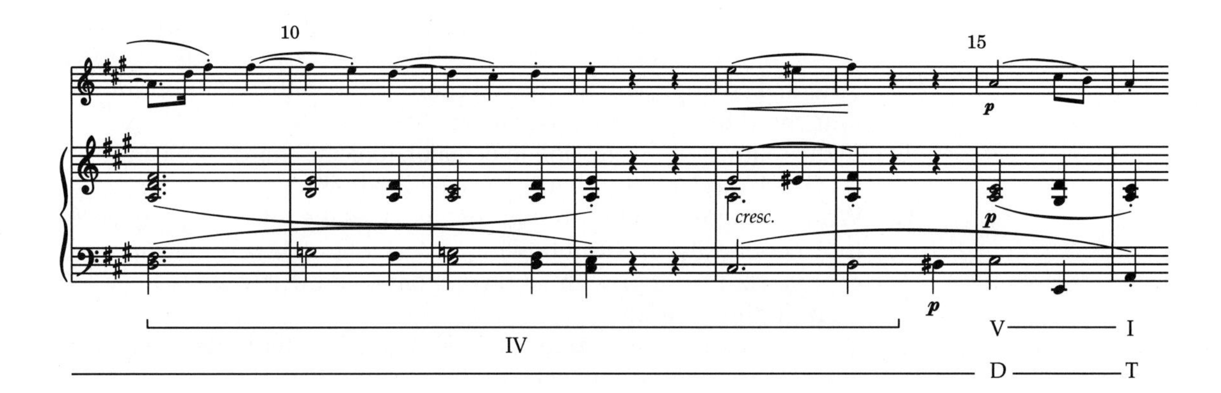

B. Haydn, Piano Sonata no. 53 in E minor, Hob. XVI.34, *Vivace molto*

The tonicizations of the Haydn excerpt, however, evoke a much different effect. The piece begins in E minor; but the second phrase closes in mm. 7–8 with a convincing PAC in G major (III). On reaching mm. 7–8, the listener feels for a moment that G has usurped the home key of E minor. The listener's sense of a G tonic is further confirmed when the music moves on to m. 9. This motion to a strong, new tonal area is an indication that the music has modulated.

A comment should be made concerning how the repeat sign alters the way that Example 25.6B is heard. One initially hears a short tonicization of III rather than a convincing modulation to III, because the music immediately returns to E minor at the repeat. After the second time through the first section, however, G major continues after the double bar, indicating a modulation.

Closely Related Keys

In general, modulations in tonal music move from a home key to any of its **closely related keys**. There are two ways to determine closely related keys.

1. Build a diatonic triad on each scale degree of the home key. All of the consonant triads (major and minor) form tonics for the closely related keys. For example, the keys closely related to C major are D minor (ii), E minor (iii), F major (IV), G major (V), and A minor (vi). The keys closely related to C minor—using the natural minor scale—are E♭ major (III), F minor (iv), G minor (v), A♭ major (VI), and B♭ major (VII).
2. Identify the major and minor keys whose key signatures differ by no more than one sharp or flat sign from the original key.

For example, the keys closely related to C major (0 sharps/flats) are: A minor (0 sharps/flats), G major (1 sharp), E minor (1 sharp), F major (1 flat), and D minor (1 flat). The keys closely related to C minor (three flats) are: E♭ major (three flats), F minor (four flats), A♭ major (four flats), G minor (two flats), and B♭ major (two flats).

Although it is possible to modulate to any major or minor diatonic key, our studies will focus on the most common modulations. They are listed in order of importance:

Major keys tend to modulate to V, vi, and iii.

Minor keys tend to modulate to III, v, and VI.

Hearing Modulations

When listening to a phrase, there are several ways to determine whether or not it has modulated.

1. Listen for the presence of new chromatic pitches that persist through the end of the phrase. This most likely signals a modulation.
2. If the first key is in major and the closing key is in minor (or vice versa), then a modulation has occurred. If you wish to know the specific harmonic motion of the modulation, you should be able to reduce your choices by a process of elimination. For example, if the music begins in a major key and ends in a minor key, the example probably has closed in either iii or vi. There will be exceptions, but this is the most common modulation strategy. Similarly, if the music begins in a minor key and ends in a major key, the example probably will have modulated to III (very common) or VI (less common).
3. To identify modulations in phrases that begin and end in the same mode, get a physical sense of how it feels to sing the tonic of the initial key. When the phrase ends, sing the closing tonic and compare it to the opening tonic. If the closing tonic is higher or lower than the opening tonic, a modulation has occurred. The possible tonal areas for modulation are very limited: If the opening and closing keys are major, you have likely modulated to V. If the opening and closing keys are minor, you have almost certainly moved to minor v.

Analyzing Modulations

In our study of modulation, we will identify three important musical events:

1. The location of the new key area in relation to the initial tonic (by roman numeral)
2. The function of the new key area within the overall harmonic progression of a piece or a section of a piece
3. The point where the original key and the new key are momentarily fused

Since roman numerals exist in only one key at a time, there must be a point in a modulation where the roman numerals "jump tracks" to the new key. We will use the following method for analyzing a modulation:

1. Start writing roman numerals at the beginning, in the original key.
2. Keep analyzing chords until the roman numerals become more complex or are nonsense, due to the change of key.
3. Write roman numerals for the new key, working backwards from the cadence. Keep analyzing chords until you come to the first chord that has a simple roman numeral in *both* keys. Draw a box around the roman numerals for this chord, which will act as a **pivot chord** between the keys.

Example 25.7A shows two phrases that—in spite of their unusually short length—have been interpreted as modulations in order to show the pivot chord. Example 25.7A1 moves from C to G (I–V), with the A-minor chord treated as a pivot chord: vi in the original key becomes ii in the new key. Example 25.7A2 presents a phrase that modulates from C minor to III (the relative major); once again, VI is the pivot, which this time becomes IV in the key of E♭ major. Erase the strange roman numerals in the original key. A chord should have only one roman numeral attached to it, except for the pivot chord (Example 25.7B). The *pivot chord is a diatonic chord in both keys*, so it has one roman numeral for each key it is in. *(Note that cadential $^6_4$s are not good candidates for pivot chords, because they are part of a strong cadential motion in the new key. Pivot chords are typically PD chords right before the cadence in the new key.)* The second-level analysis also "jumps tracks"—it will result in incomplete second-level analyses in both keys (Example 25.7C). We will see later in the chapter how modulations fit into larger musical contexts.

EXAMPLE 25.7

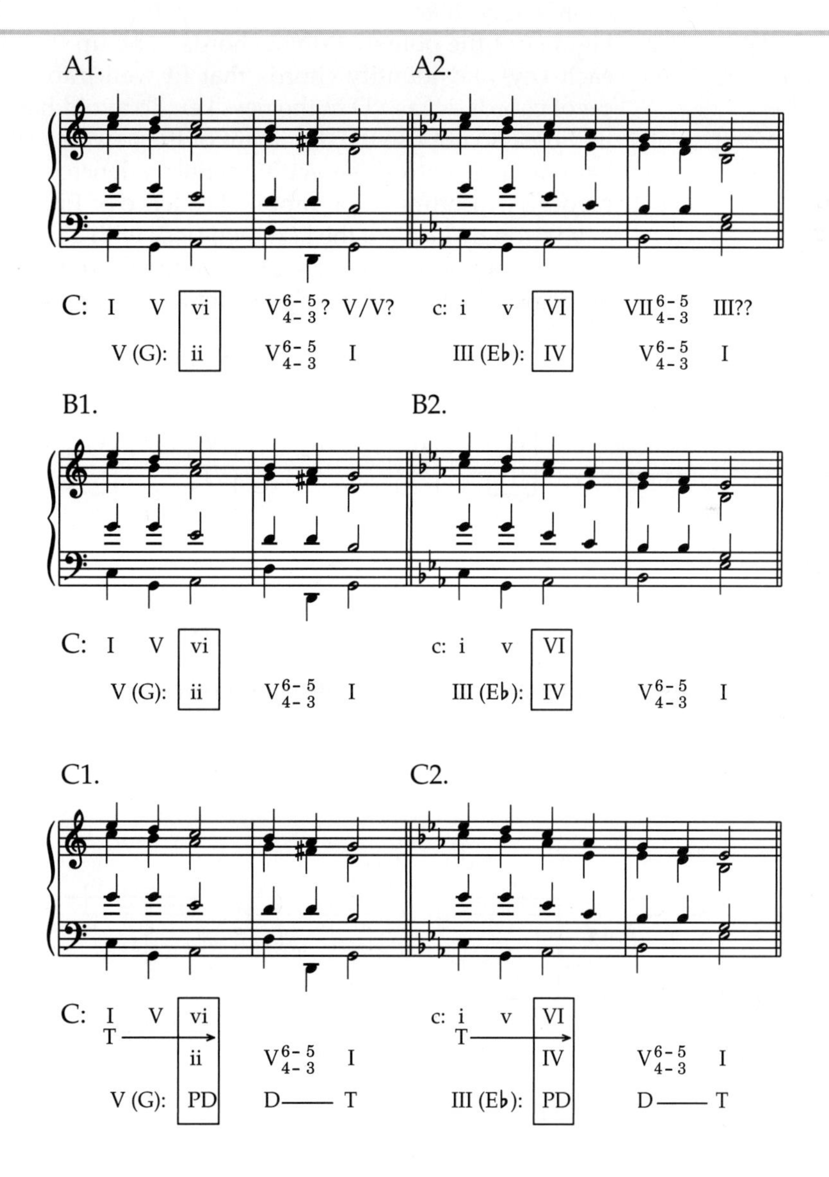

Writing Modulations

More than any of your other writing, modulations must be tested out on the piano. Often, what looks like a successful pivot chord may in actuality not work at all. This is because in addition to voice-leading rules—which you must continue to follow—you have before you the task of establishing two keys in a convincing manner. The following guidelines will help you to write modulations.

1. When establishing the original key and the new key, make sure that the duration of the two tonal areas is balanced. Place the pivot chord about halfway into a phrase that modulates, and use at least a few chords in each key.
2. Figure out the potential pivot chords. Line up the diatonic chords for each key, and identify chords that fit well into both keys. The best pivot chords act as PD in the new key. To avoid harsh-sounding modulations, do not use the dominant of the new key as a pivot chord.
3. Do not crash into a perfect authentic cadence immediately after the pivot. Try inserting a contrapuntal cadence or EPM, and only after you have strongly implied the key, then close with a structural cadence.
4. Use a stepwise soprano line to move to the strongest possible cadence in the new key: a PAC using a cadential six-four chord.

Let's set ourselves the task of creating a phrase that modulates from F major to D minor. We first identify the potential pivot chords:

F major:	I	ii	iii	IV	vi	vii°
D minor:	III	iv	v	VI	i	ii°
Best choices:		*		*		*
Good choices:	*				*	

We will start our progression with the descending bass arpeggiation, I–IV$_6$–I$_6$, and move to the pivot chord and a strong cadence in the new key. For comparison, we will try out five possibilities for a pivot chord (Example 25.8). Listen to and study each progression, and identify which pivot chords work well.

EXAMPLE 25.8

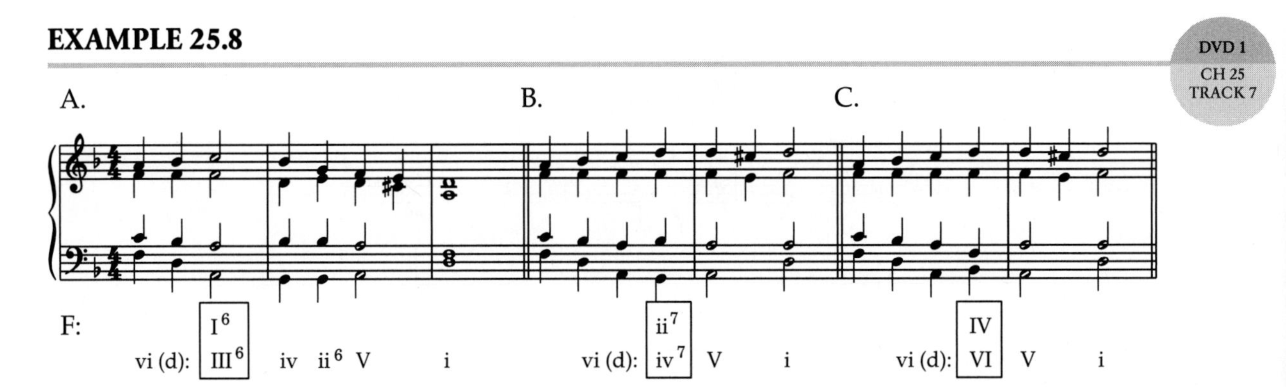

Continued

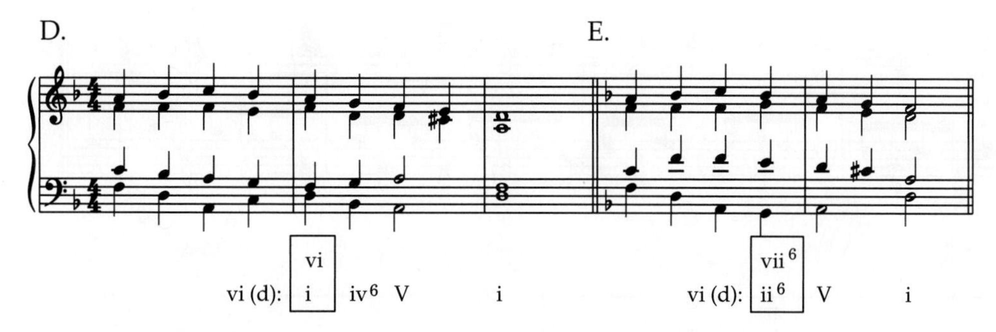

Modulation in the Larger Musical Context

Very few compositions end in a different key from the one in which they begin. In fact, considering a work as a whole, modulations will never displace the prevailing tonic. Thus, modulations in tonal music participate in a single overall harmonic motion. For example, a piece in C minor might modulate to E♭ major and F minor before leading to the dominant and returning to C minor to close the piece. This series of keys would constitute a large-scale progression in C minor: i–III–iv–V–i. As you analyze modulations, you should refer to the new key in its relationship to the original tonic. For example, a modulation from C major to G major should be viewed as a modulation from I to V; a modulation from F minor to D♭ major is a modulation from i to VI.

Example 25.9 contains several short tonal shifts that function in an underlying chord progression. It also illustrates the point that determining whether a tonal shift is a tonicization or a modulation is often a matter of personal interpretation. The initial key of C minor moves smoothly to E♭ major (III) in mm. 3–4. Although a potential pivot chord occurs in m. 3 that seamlessly binds the two tonal areas, the short duration of III and the lack of a good cadence favor calling this tonal shift a tonicization. By contrast, despite the missing pivot chord, the shift to G minor (v) can be considered a modulation because of its strong cadential arrival (and because G minor is the tonal goal of this excerpt), or it can be considered to be a tonicization (the interpretation given in the example).

EXAMPLE 25.9 Robert Schumann, *Davidsbundler Tänze*, op. 6, no. 7

DVD 1
CH 25
TRACK 8

Frisch ♩ = 100

sf

c: i VI ii⌀6/5 V i VI ii⌀6/5 V i VI iv7

i III ii7 V7

III

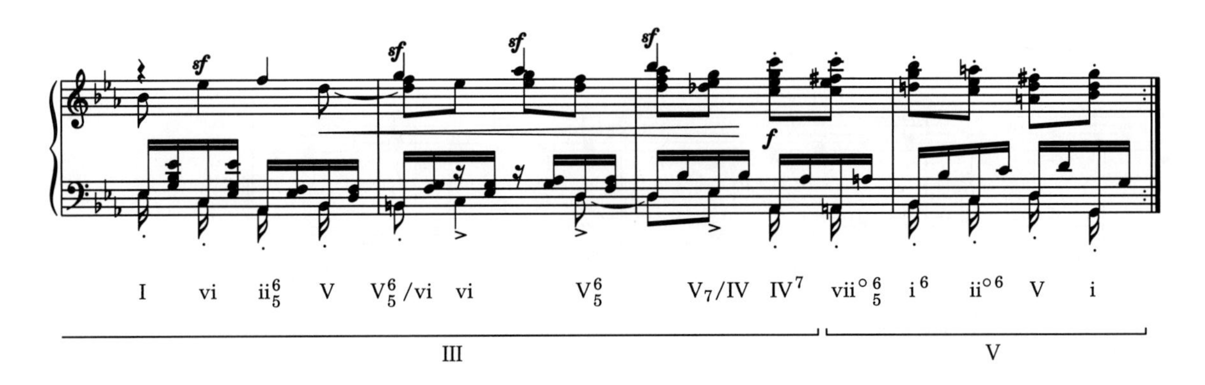

The Sequence as a Tool in Modulation

The function of a pivot is not limited to a single chord. Often, several chords that function in two keys will work together to create a **pivot area**. For example, a pivot chord might be expanded or tonicized. Or a group of chords that share the same harmonic function (such as pre-dominants IV and II) might be coupled through a voice exchange, creating a pre-dominant complex that works in both the starting and ending keys.

Sequences, too, make terrific pivots. In fact, we have already learned that one of the two functions of a sequence is transitional: It frequently takes the music from one harmonic area to another. There are many strategies of using sequences to modulate, given that a sequence touches on many chords, sometimes every chord within a key. Therefore, by prematurely quitting a sequence and reinterpreting one of its chords as a pre-dominant that moves to a dominant, one can effectively move to a new key. Listen to Example 25.10. Vivaldi invokes a D2 sequence that stops on VI (c–f–B♭–E♭–A♭). The A♭ chord functions as IV in the new key of E♭ (III of C minor).

EXAMPLE 25.10 Vivaldi, Trio Sonata in C minor, *Allegro*

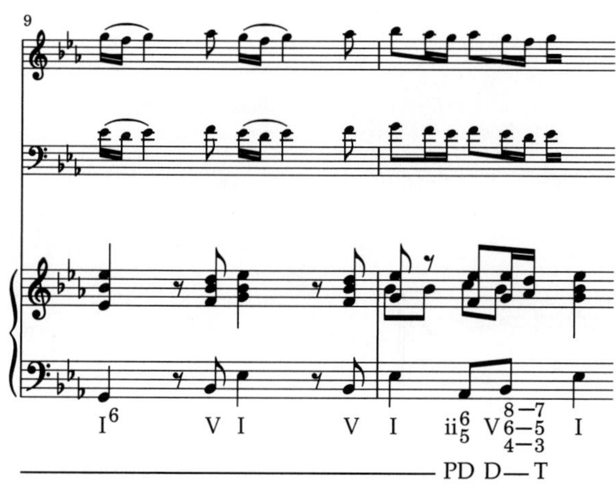

Example 25.11 demonstrates how easy it is to modulate to a variety of keys from within a sequence. Example 25.11A presents a D2 (−5/+4) sequence in G minor; Example 25.11B presents an A2 (−3/+4) sequence in B♭ major. Each sequence contains at least two repetitions of the model, marked by brackets. Beneath each sequence are progressions that modulate to several different keys, accomplished by incorporating some, but not all, of the given sequence. The G-minor example modulates to III (two examples), VI, and v (two examples). The B♭-major example modulates to iii, vi, and V. Play each solution on the piano.

EXAMPLE 25.11

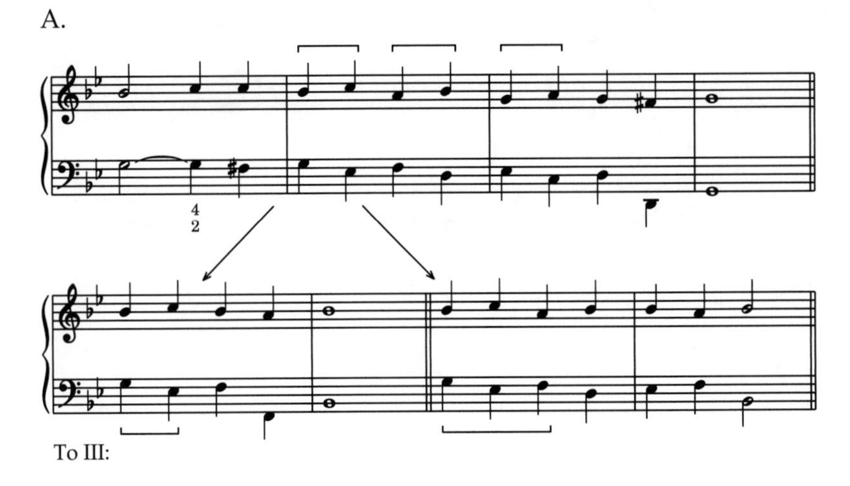

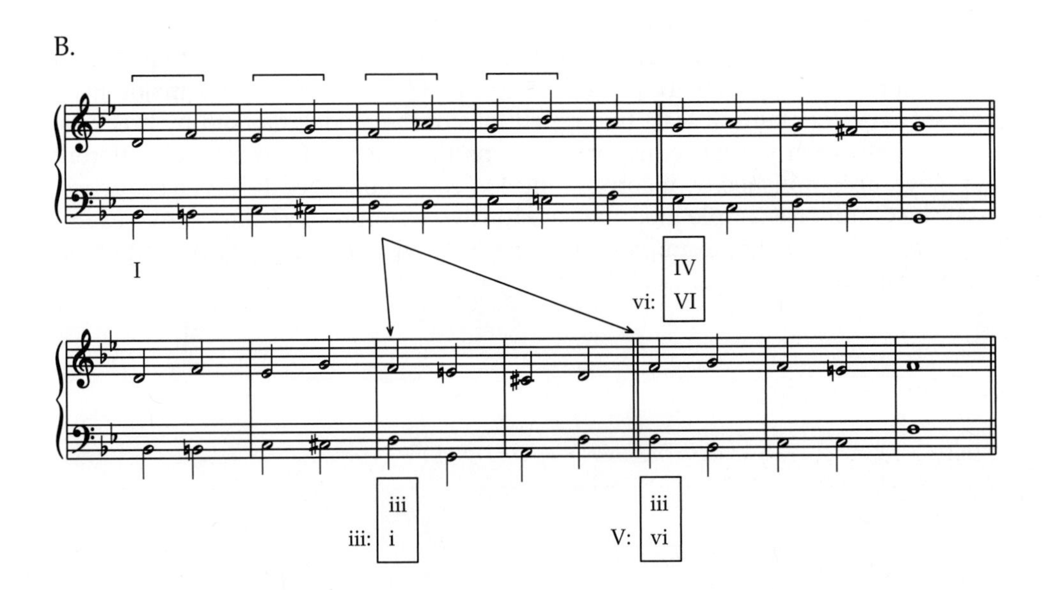

EXERCISE INTERLUDE

PERFORMING

25.4

Sing (or play on your instrument) the following progressions using solfège or scale degrees. Each progression modulates, closing in a different tonal area and containing a pivot chord. Analyze. If you play these exercises on your instrument, transpose each to one other key.

I. Bach, Flute Sonata in A minor, BWV. 1033, Menuett II

J. Marcello, Sonata no. 2 in E minor for Cello and Basso Continuo

K. Turk, Gavotte in A major

L. Andre, Sonatina in C major

M. Turk, Dance in G

N. De Fesch, Sarabanda for Flute in B minor

DVD 2
CH 25
TRACK 2

LISTENING

25.5 Hearing Modulations

1. Listen to the following progressions and determine whether or not they modulate (answer yes or no).
2. Label the mode (major or minor) that occurs at the beginning of the progression.
3. If there is a modulation, determine the mode at the end of the progression.

Does the example modulate?	*Mode (M or m) of opening*	*Mode (M or m) of closing (if example modulates)*
A. _______	_______	_______
B. _______	_______	_______
C. _______	_______	_______
D. _______	_______	_______
E. _______	_______	_______
F. _______	_______	_______

DVD 2 CH 25 TRACK 3

25.6 Determining Goals of Modulations

Listen to the following examples and determine to what key each excerpt modulates. Use roman numerals to represent the new key. In order to do this, we combine the two methods described earlier. Sing the opening tonic and determine the mode. Do the same for the closing tonic. Then ask whether the new tonic is above or below the original and if it is major or minor, which will tell you the goal of the modulation. For example, if you begin in C major and you end in a minor key that is below C major, you have modulated to vi; above C major you have modulated to iii. As you know from previous chapters, you must always listen to complete spans of music rather than focusing on individual pitches. Thus, listen to the entire harmonic progression before you determine to where it modulates.

DVD 2 CH 25 TRACK 4

25.7 Dictation of Two-Voice Modulations

On a separate sheet of manuscript paper, notate the modulating two-voice examples and provide a roman numeral analysis of the implied harmonic progressions. Each contains two phrases. The beginning key and meter are given.

A. in F major, $\frac{3}{4}$ B. in G minor, $\frac{4}{4}$ C. in C major, $\frac{4}{4}$

ANALYSIS

DVD 2 CH 25 TRACK 5

25.8

Given are examples that end in a different tonal area from the one in which they begin. Assume that they would continue in the new key. Provide a two-level harmonic analysis; remember to describe the pivot chord in both keys—draw a box around the roman numerals for the pivot chord.

A.

B.

C.

D.

E.

F. Scarlatti, Sonata in G minor, K. 64

G. Mozart, Piano Concerto in G major, K453, *Allegretto*

25.9 Analysis of Modulating Sequence

Bracket and label the following modulating sequence. Then determine, using pivot notation, how the last chord of the sequence functions in the new key.

Handel, Concerto Grosso in B♭ major, op. 3, no. 2, HWV 313, *Largo*

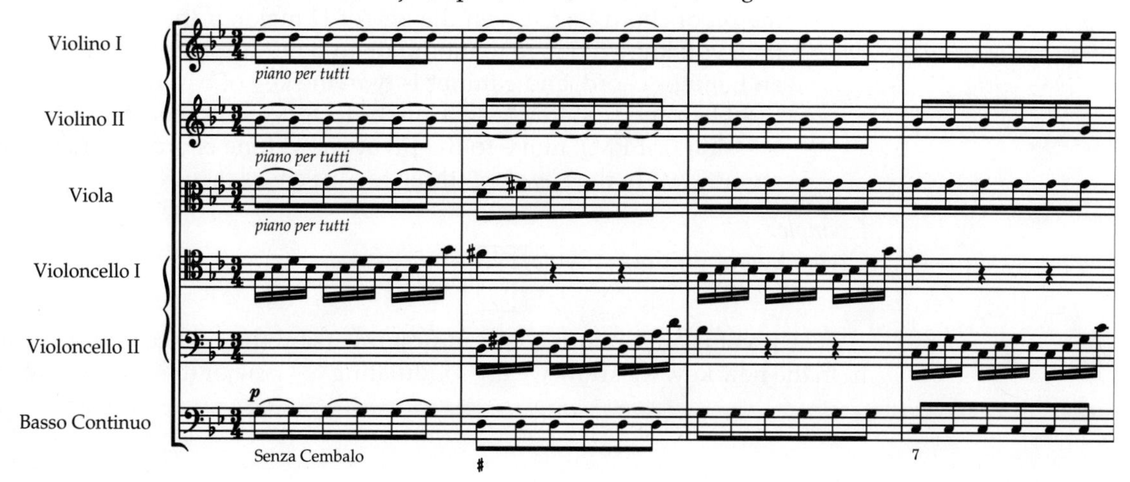

Continued

WRITING

25.10 Modulation Warmup: Pivot Choices

The pivot chord is important because it hides any abrupt motion that might result from a modulation and instead glues the musical seams together to create one fluid gesture. Given are several harmonic scenarios in which phrases modulate from the tonic to a closely related key. Determine (and list on a separate sheet of paper) all the possible pivot chords that will work between the two keys, and then mark with an "X" the pivot that you feel might work best.

A. D major: I to vi
B. C minor: i to v
C. G minor: i to III
D. A major: I to V
E. D minor: i to iv

25.11

Initial key and pivot chords are given. You will write short progressions (seven to nine chords) that modulate.

1. Determine what the new key is, based on the information provided by the pivot chord (e.g., given the key of D major, if the pivot is ii → iv, then you know you are to modulate to B minor, since, in D major, ii is an E minor chord, and e minor is iv in the key of b minor.
2. Establish the first key (use a three- to four-chord contrapuntal progression or EPM), move to the pivot chord (one chord), and lead to a strong PAC in the new key (three to four chords).

Example:
Given: key of E minor; pivot; $\frac{\text{iv}_6}{\text{ii}_6}$

The pivot is an A minor chord in first inversion (iv_6). Since it will become ii_6 in the new key, we know we are modulating to G major (because A minor is ii in G). We then establish E minor (three to four chords), lead to the pivot, and write a cadential progression in G major.

A. In B♭ major: pivot is | vi / ii |

B. In B minor: pivot is | VI / IV |

C. In C minor: pivot is | III / VI |

D. In F major: pivot is | ii / iv |

25.12

In approximately seven to nine chords, write the following modulations on a separate sheet of manuscript paper. Analyze—remember to identify the pivot chord. As you play your compositions, consider whether the new key is established convincingly.

A. In G major, modulate from I to V.
B. In D minor, modulate from i to III.
C. In A major, modulate from I to vi.
D. In F major, modulate from I to iii.
E. In B minor, modulate from i to v.
F. In E minor, modulate from i to VI.
G. In B♭ major, modulate from I to ii.

INSTRUMENTAL APPLICATION

25.13 Improvising Consequent Phrases in Two Voices

With another melody-line player or alone at a keyboard, improvise three consequent phrases to the given antecedent phrases to create the following period types: a PIP, a PPP, and a CPP. A sample solution of a PPP is given.

A. given antecedent:

added consequent forms PPP:

B.

C.

D.

E.

WORKBOOK
25.2–25.6

25.14 Improvising Modulations Using Modulating Sequences

Determine the type of sequence implied by the given pattern; then continue the sequence in order to modulate to a closely related key. Close each modulation with a strong cadence in order to secure the new key. Be able to use each sequence to modulate to at least two different closely related keys.

A.

B.

C.

D.

TERMS AND CONCEPTS

- closely related keys
- modulation
- modulating sequences
- pivot
- pivot area
- pivot chord
- tonicized area

CHAPTER 26

Binary Form and Variations

We can view the study of musical form in three stages. At the first stage, we gained familiarity with how the fundamental building blocks of music—the phrase and the subphrase—could combine to form units of modest length: the period and sentence. Here, at the second stage, we will explore how composers combine periods, phrases, and sentences to create binary form. (The third stage, encompassing rondo, ternary, and sonata forms, is discussed in Part 8.)

Binary form, a term describing a complete work that can be parsed into two sections, can be traced back to well before 1700. The Baroque suite, for example, comprises numerous dance movements, ranging from slow sarabandes to lively gigues, each of which is cast in binary form. One of these dance movements, the **minuet**, was maintained in compositions of the Classical period, where it may be found in instrumental sonatas, string quartets, and symphonies. In the nineteenth century, the **scherzo**, a more energetic cousin of the minuet, appeared more and more frequently in works by Beethoven and later nineteenth-century composers. It, too, is cast in binary form, as are the theme and subsequent subsections of many variation sets. Throughout the common-practice period, repeat signs almost always mark the two sections of pieces in binary form; for this reason, binary form is also known as **two-reprise form**.

Listen to Example 26.1 and ask yourself the following questions.

1. How many sections does the work contain, and what differentiates these sections musically?
2. What is the overall tonal structure?
3. Does material recur?

EXAMPLE 26.1 Hummel, Bagatelle in C major, op. 107

DVD 1
CH 26
TRACK 1

Most likely, your senses led you to consider this piece in two parts; the double bars indicate two sections. When we describe binary form, we apply a label in the same manner as a period label: We consider the melodic structure (or **thematic design**) and the harmonic structure. Notice that no thematic material recurs in Example 26.1. In cases like this, when the two sections of a binary form share no melodic material, the melodic design is called **simple**. As for the harmonic label, our first step is to consider the cadence that occurs at the end of the *first* section. When the cadence at the end of the first section ends on the *tonic*, the harmonic structure is called **sectional** (since both *sections* of the binary form are tonally closed). Thus, we can say that Hummel's Bagatelle is in **simple sectional binary form**.

Now listen to Example 26.2, which illustrates a different type of binary form. In what ways is the Weber piece similar to the Hummel, and in what ways is it different? Melodically, this binary form is simple. Harmonically, the tonicization of the dominant at the end of the first section clearly presents a significant difference from the previous example. The dominant continues after the double bar but is weakened by the addition of the seventh, which forces it back into the orbit of G major. In cases like this, when the first section closes *away from the tonic*, and the following section *continues* away from the tonic, the binary form's harmonic structure is called **continuous**. Thus, Weber's piece is in a **simple continuous binary form**.

EXAMPLE 26.2 Carl Maria von Weber, no. 1, *Six Ecossaise*, J. 29

DVD 1
CH 26
TRACK 2

Continued

Notice that so far we have used period terminology to describe the harmonic structure of binary forms. If both sections are tonally closed, binary forms (just like periods) are **sectional**. If the first section ends away from tonic, and the second section starts away from tonic, binary forms (just like periods) are **continuous**.

Listen to Example 26.3. In what ways does it differ from Examples 26.1 and 26.2? The first section closes on tonic; therefore, the piece's harmonic structure is sectional. However, a glance at the piece's relative proportions reveals a lopsided structure: The material after the first double bar occupies 16 measures, so it is exactly twice as long as the preceding material. If we look more carefully at the second section, we see a distinct HC in m. 16 that divides the second half. After the HC, there is a literal restatement of material that began the piece. Thus, the second section of Haydn's binary form is more complex than in Example 26.1 or Example 26.2. It features a new compositional tactic: Begin the second section with fragmented and unstable material that leads to a HC. We call this a **digression**, since it wanders from the preceding material but then quickly leads back to a restatement of the original material, called a **recapitulation**. When all or part of the *opening* material of a binary form returns in the second section after the digression, the binary form's thematic design is called **rounded**. This name derives from the cyclical effect created by the return of the opening material. The scherzo by Haydn is in a **rounded sectional binary form**.

EXAMPLE 26.3 Haydn, Sonatina no. 4 in F major, Hob. XVI.9, Scherzo

DVD 1
CH 26
TRACK 3

Continued

Look again at Example 26.3. The structure of a binary form resembles a parallel interrupted period. The music works to a structural HC (mm. 1–16), after which the music begins again in the tonic (mm. 17–24). We call the structural HC in m. 16 an **interruption** (marked with a double slash (||), since this is the point where the harmonic progression is interrupted and begins again in the tonic. (Note that the repeats complicate the form, so it is not the same as a PIP.)

Listen to Example 26.4, the theme that opens the variation movement of Mozart's Piano Sonata in D major, K. 284. Attempt to answer the following questions.

1. Is this thematically simple or rounded? If it is rounded, is there an interruption?
2. Is this harmonically sectional or continuous?
3. Are the sections similar in proportion (like the Hummel excerpt) or lopsided (like the Haydn excerpt)?

EXAMPLE 26.4 Mozart, Piano Sonata in D major, K. 284, Thema, *Andante*

DVD 1
CH 26
TRACK 4

Continued

Most likely you heard two nearly symmetrical sections (of eight and nine measures, respectively), each of which is articulated by repeats and by cadences. The harmonic structure is continuous, since the first section ends away from the tonic. Thematically, there is a digression in mm. 9–12 that leads to an interruption; this is followed by a repetition of part of the opening theme in the tonic. Thus, Mozart's piece is cast in **rounded continuous binary form**.

An interesting formal conflict arises when one compares the melodic design with the tonal structure. Mozart's piece has a three-part design that is based on the melodic structure and surface rhythm articulations:

Initial tune = A (mm. 1–8)

Sequential figuration = digression (mm. 9–12)

Restatement of tune = A′ (mm. 14–17)

However, it has a two-part tonal structure based on the large-scale interruption and restart on the tonic.

The following is a model of the most common two-reprise form, the rounded continuous binary form. The model shows the three-part thematic design and two-part harmonic structure in both major and minor keys.

Rounded Continuous Binary Form

thematic design in 3 sections:

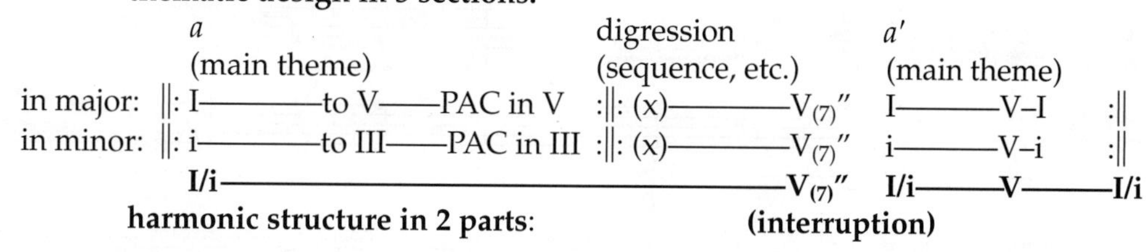

Simple and rounded binary forms can also be melodically balanced if the *closing* material in the first section is restated as the closing material in the second section. The term actually refers more to the harmonic underpinning than to the repeated melody. This is because, in most binary forms, the first section closes in a nontonic key. To provide convincing tonal closure at the end of the piece, the restatement of this material will naturally occur in the tonic.

Listen to Example 26.5. The first section closes in V (D major) in m. 8, making the harmonic structure continuous. In the digression (mm. 9–21), Handel develops the piece's opening gesture by reversing the order of scale and broken chord and placing them within two sequences. Handel is in a quandary: The extensive, 13-measure digression creates an imbalance with the first section, which occupies only eight measures, yet he must provide convincing melodic and harmonic closure. He does not return with the opening harmonic and melodic material as in rounded binary form; instead, his solution is to draw material that closes the piece from an analogous point in the close of the first section, to create a **balanced continuous binary form**.

EXAMPLE 26.5 Handel, Prelude in G major

DVD 1 CH 26 TRACK 5

Continued

Summary of Binary Form Types

The feature common to all two-reprise binary forms is the presence of two sections, often marked by double bars. We look at cadences to determine the harmonic structure:

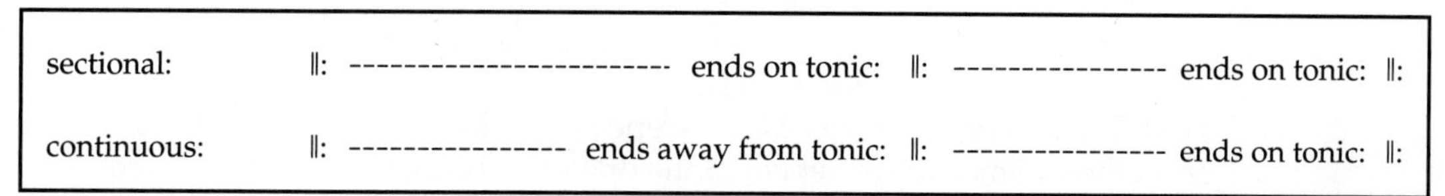

We discern whether material from the first section recurs in the second section to determine the melodic structure. Finally, we look at the closing material of each section to see if the binary form is balanced.

Like many specimens of tonal music, binary forms do not always fall neatly into one of our established theoretical categories. Categorization is merely an attempt to deal with the many and varied stimuli with which we are confronted at every moment of our lives. As such, categories are more general than specific. Given that music is an art form capable of multiple interpretations, we must be flexible and open-minded in our attempts to come to grips with it. In your analysis of form, always be sensitive to the music.

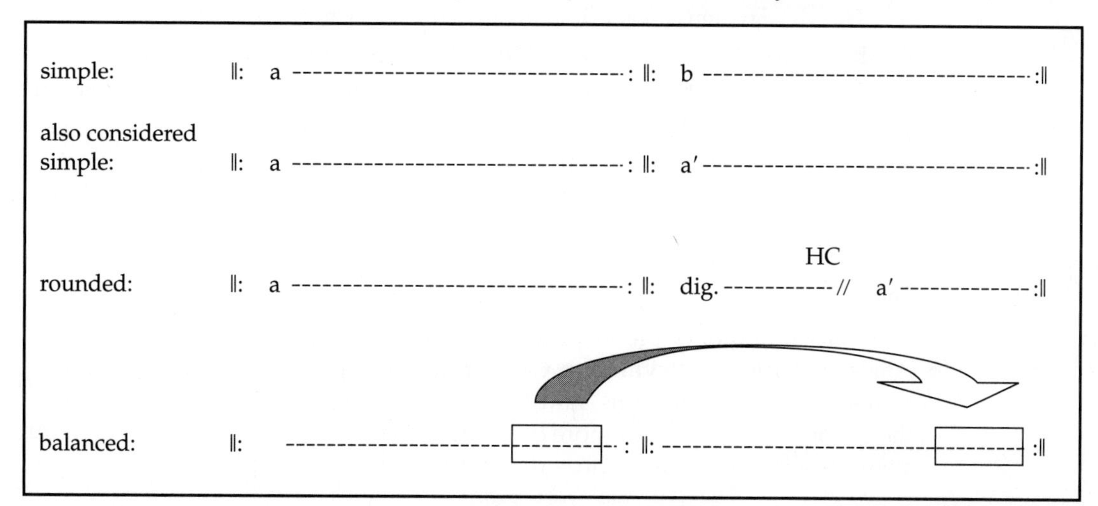

EXERCISE INTERLUDE

LISTENING

26.1

You will hear five short pieces, each of which is cast in binary form. You are to provide the full (two-part) label for each example. Ask yourself the following questions in order to determine their form:

1. Does the first large section cadence on the tonic (PAC or IAC)? If so, the form is **sectional**; if not, the form is **continuous**. Most binary forms are continuous, and they follow the modulatory schemes outlined in Chapter 25: In major, most pieces modulate to V; in minor, most pieces modulate to III, although modulation to minor v is fairly common too. Review the listening techniques presented in Chapter 25, and don't forget that listening is heavily dependent on educated guessing and the process of elimination. For example:
   a. If the first key is in *major* and the closing key is *major*, then most likely the modulation is to V.
   b. If the first key is in *major* and the closing key is *minor*, then most likely the modulation is to vi.
   c. If the first key is in *minor* and the closing key is *minor*, then most likely the modulation is to minor v.
   d. If the first key is *minor* and the closing key is *major*, then most likely the modulation is to III.

Hint: Usually each large section is repeated. Thus, if you hear a chord change from the cadence to the repeat of the opening chord, then the form is continuous. It there is no change of chord, then the form is sectional.

2. If the digression opens with the same motivic material as the first half *and* there is no literal return of the opening melody in the tonic later in the second half, then the form is **simple**. If the opening material returns in tonic after the digression, then the form is **rounded**. If the motivic material from the *cadence* of the first section recurs (transposed) at the end of the second section, then the form is **balanced**.

Note: If the entire first part returns at the end of the second part, the form is rounded.

A. Haydn, String Quartet in D major, op. 76, no. 5, Menuetto
B. Boismortier, *Vivace*, from Six Duets for Bass Instruments, op. 40
C. Loeillet, Menuet in C minor. Identify each of the sequences in the digression.
D. Mozart, "Eine kleine Nachtmusik," K. 525, Menuetto
E. Beethoven, Piano Sonata in D major, op. 28, ii

ANALYSIS

26.2

The following binary pieces present a variety of formal and harmonic issues. Analytical questions will take you through the process of analyzing binary forms. Study the questions, and then listen to the piece. Answer as many of the questions as possible before listening a second time. Finally, compare your answers with the answers provided at the end of the chapter.

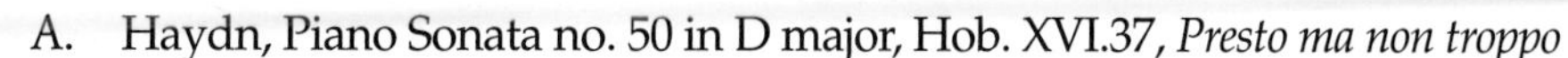

A. Haydn, Piano Sonata no. 50 in D major, Hob. XVI.37, *Presto ma non troppo*

1. What is the form? Be precise when labeling binary forms. Include harmonic and melodic labels.
2. What melodic figuration occurs in mm. 2 and 4?
3. How many phrases make up mm. 1–8? Do they form a period? If so, label the type of period.
4. What key is briefly tonicized in mm. 9–10?
5. What applied chord appears in m. 17?

B. Mozart, Piano Trio in G major, K. 496, *Allegretto*

Continued

1. What is the form?
2. How many phrases occur in mm. 1–8? Do they form a period? If so, label the type of period.
3. How long is the tonic expanded in the first phrase?
4. What sequential progression occurs in mm. 9–11? And to what harmony does it lead?
5. Since this is a trio, one would expect an equal division of melodic interest between the instruments. Is this the case? Why or why not?

C. Haydn, Piano Sonata in A major, Hob. XVI.12, Trio

Continued

1. What is the form?
2. What melodic figuration occurs throughout the piece?
3. How would you label the bass motion from i to V in mm. 1–6?
4. What type of sequence begins in m. 7? How long does it last? Is it transitional or prolongational?
5. What key is the goal of the first section? What key is tonicized in mm. 15–18?
6. What is the underlying tonal progression for the entire excerpt?

D. Handel, Concerto Grosso in F major, op. 3, no. 4, HWV 315, *Allegro*

Continued

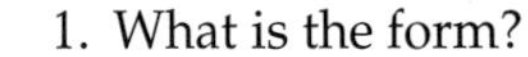

1. What is the form?
2. To what key does the first section modulate? What is the pivot chord?
3. Immediately after the double bar, there is a return to the tonic (F major), which seems premature, given the length of the second section. Is this a true return to the tonic, or is it part of a larger progression that leads to a new tonal destination?
4. The syncopated tune that appears in m. 9 looks new, yet one could argue that this syncopation is an explicit statement of rhythmic irregularity implied in the first tune. What are two other similarities between the opening four measures and mm. 9–13?
5. What sequence occurs in mm. 17–20? What is its function?

WORKBOOK
26.1–26.5

Variation Form

One of the most difficult and important tasks for a composer is to balance unity with variety. Fulfilling that task raises a central question in composition: How do you handle repeating melodic material? As master listeners, composers are keenly aware of the potential stasis that is created by literal restatement, on the one hand, and of the potential for aural chaos when a listener is constantly assailed with new material, on the other. One of the most important genres for exploring and developing this relationship between unity and variety is the variation set. **Variation sets** usually begin with an initial idea, or **theme**, from which a series of **variations** unfolds. These variation sets may be independent pieces, or they may be members of larger, multimovement works, such as suites and sonatas. Variation sets are found in just about all instrumental combinations, including works for solo instruments, chamber works, symphonies, and vocal pieces.

The two common types of variation sets are **continuous variations** and **sectional variations**. The difference between the two is based on how strong the division is between variations and how smooth the progression of events is from the opening to the close of the piece.

Continuous Variations

In a **continuous variation set**, the theme is relatively short (usually a phrase), and it gives the effect of being incomplete in order to permit each variation—there are usually many—to flow seamlessly into the next. This is often accomplished by an overlapping process whereby the ending tonic of one variation simultaneously acts as the beginning of the next.

EXAMPLE 26.6 Monteverdi, "Lamento della ninfa" ("Lament of the Nymph"), *Madrigali guerrieri et amorosi*

DVD 1 CH 26 TRACK 6

Listen to Example 26.6, which is the beginning of a continuous variation set. Note the repeating bass pattern (bracketed in the example) that forms the foundation for the variations (note also the brackets above the staves showing how some repetitions of the pattern are overlapped, for the initial arrival on V can be heard as part of an authentic cadence). Continuous variations are most often constructed through the use of a repeated idea, called an **ostinato**, rather than a lyrical tune. Ostinati provide the backbone of the variations, over which changes in register, texture, and motivic design occur. Ostinati generally appear in the lower voices and can be as simple as a repeating bass pattern, called a **ground bass**, a repeating harmonic pattern, called a **chaconne**, or both a repeating bass and a repeating harmonic pattern, called a **passacaglia**.

Often, all three terms are used interchangeably. The distinction between the repeating bass line of the ground bass and the repeating harmonic pattern of the passacaglia and chaconne is often artificial; composers use repeating harmonies to accompany a repeating bass, and vice versa. In Example 26.7, Purcell harmonizes his eight-measure ground bass (circled notes) with a harmonic pattern that is used in each repetition.

EXAMPLE 26.7 Purcell, Ground in G, theme and two variations

DVD 1
CH 26
TRACK 7

EXAMPLE 26.8 Bach, Partita no. 2 in D minor for violin solo, BWV 1004, Chaconne

DVD 1
CH 26
TRACK 8

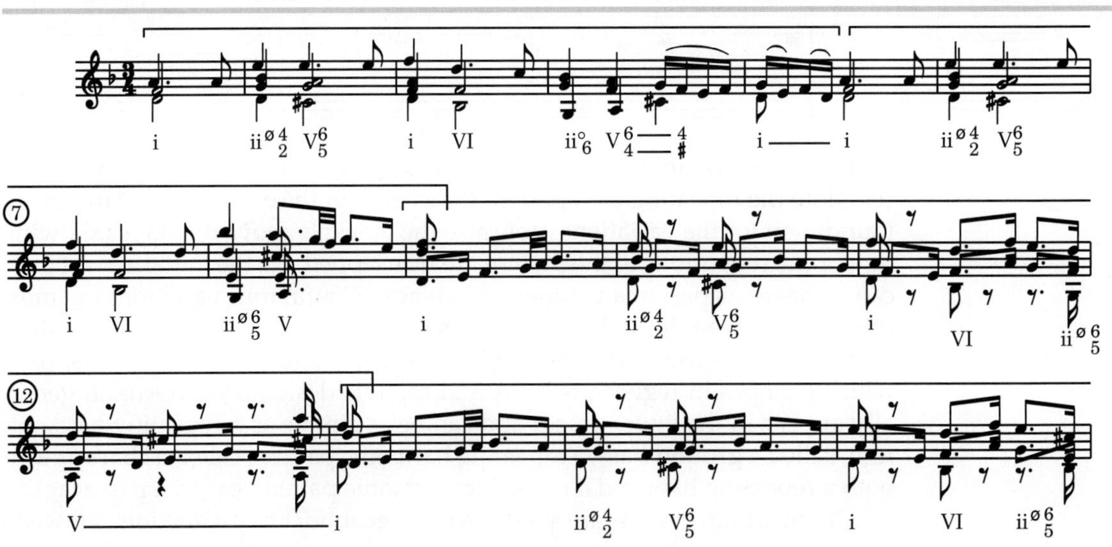

Examples 26.8, 26.9, and 26.10 illustrate how composers merge the two types of ostinati. Bach's famous Chaconne is based on a repeating series of harmonies (see Example 26.8). That the ostinato begins in midmeasure helps to maintain continuity between repetitions. Furthermore, the variations overlap, with each ending dovetailed with the beginning of the next statement; only the theme is not overlapped.

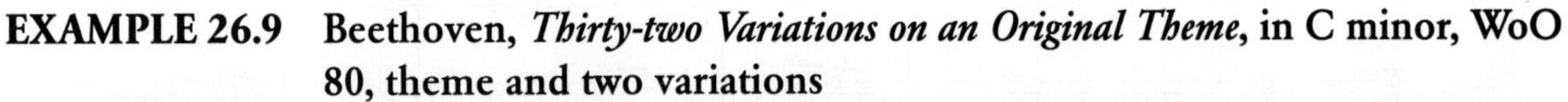

EXAMPLE 26.9 Beethoven, *Thirty-two Variations on an Original Theme*, in C minor, WoO 80, theme and two variations

DVD 1 CH 26 TRACK 9

In Example 26.9, Beethoven's eight-measure theme—a repeating harmonic ostinato—traverses an indirect step-descent bass to iv, followed by a two-measure cadential gesture. Although the theme is tonally closed and there is no dovetailing between repetitions, continuity is preserved by the continuous figurations.

EXAMPLE 26.10 Brahms, Symphony no. 4 in E minor, op. 98, *Allegro energico e passionate*

DVD 1
CH 26
TRACK 10

Brahms combines the idea of ground and chaconne in the last movement of his E-minor symphony (Example 26.10). The harmonic pattern (chaconne) of the opening continues in the first variations. But in the following several variations, it is the theme's upper-voice ascent (ground) that holds each variation together.

Sectional Variations

You may have noticed that in several of the continuous variation sets illustrated, the overlap between phrases was achieved largely through tonal means: Each ground bass tended toward V, whose resolution thus coincided with the next variation's start on tonic. In a **sectional variation set**, the theme and variations are usually in binary form (often a rounded continuous binary form) that is tonally closed, and therefore they are separated from one another. There are often more substantive changes among variations in a sectional variations set. In addition to changes in texture and figuration, there may be reharmonization, tonicization of diatonic and chromatic keys, and changes between major and minor modes.

In general, composers strive to balance musical unity with diversity in each variation by retaining one or more characteristic elements presented by the theme. For example, if a composer significantly alters the theme's melody by adding figuration or ornamentation, the harmonic underpinning will most likely not stray too far from its thematic presentation. If the harmony is dramatically altered, the melody will often remain unchanged. One musical element that tends not to be altered is the form of the theme, including its general proportions and length. When we analyze variations, it is precisely the degrees and types of changes in the variations that interest us. It is particularly rewarding to find the seeds for such alterations sown in the theme itself, seeds that lie dormant until a particular variation provides the environment for it to germinate and flourish.

By their very nature—that of repeating some musical idea—variation sets clearly run the risk of being merely a string of connected ideas devoid of any larger, goal-oriented musical process or development. To avoid such problems, composers use two common strategies. In the first strategy, they create a sense of drive that leads to a musical climax. The most common means of achieving such a drive is by using ever-smaller note values (sometimes referred to as a *rhythmic crescendo*) or increasingly elaborate textures and expanded registers and dynamics (in which there may be one or more arches of intensity). In the second strategy, composers group two or more variations to create another level of organization. Using this procedure, composers can create a large-scale ebb and flow in the unfolding of the entire set. For example, in a set of 12 variations, a composer might create three larger groups of five, two, and five variations respectively, with each group distinguished from the other by mode change (e.g., the central group may be cast in the parallel minor if the work is in major) and with each group unfolding in one of the processes described in strategy 1.

Example 26.11 presents excerpts from Beethoven's six variations on the duet "Nel cor più non mi sento," WoO 70 (1795), from Giovanni Paisiello's opera *La molinara*, which provides a clear and simple example of sectional variations. The theme lacks the typical double-bar signposts that are symptomatic of binary forms. Nonetheless, it meets all of the binary requirements. The theme opens with an eight-measure contrasting-interrupted period (4 + 4). The first phrase's initial descent is followed by a series of leaps that highlight $\hat{6}$ and $\hat{5}$ (E and D). The second phrase precisely balances these features by reversing the contour: It ascends by step to $\hat{6}$ and then descends to close on $\hat{1}$. This first period comprises the first half of the binary structure. Given its close on tonic, it is sectional.

EXAMPLE 26.11

Continued

82
VAR. IV.
86
fp
91
96
102
VAR. V.
105
109

VAR. VI.
122
125
129
133
137
141
L.H.

The following six measures are primarily sequential, though the bass is relatively static, given that the arrivals in mm. 10–12 occur on six-four chords. Perhaps this E–D neighbor motion in the bass is motivated by the same motion that occurred in the A section's upper voice. The sequential motion leads to the dominant, intensified by the applied chord and signaled by the fermata (mm. 13–14). Paisiello adds the seventh of the chord (C) to this stable dominant, which weakens and thus prepares the return to tonic. The following tonic in m. 17 is accompanied by the material from mm. 5–8, which creates a balanced sectional binary form.

Fast-note chromatic lower neighbors characterize the first part of Variation I, while broken-chord figures characterize the second part (mm. 9–11). Both melody and harmony remain faithful to the theme, save for minor deviations, which include a shift from root-position harmonies to more stepwise motion in the opening (resulting in parallel sixths), followed by a compensating alteration in the sequence, whose stepwise bass motion becomes more angular given the root-position harmonies. Contrapuntal features that were only implied in the theme are now made explicit, including the striking parallel-tenth motion in mm. 5–6, which creates a strong drive to the subdominant in m. 6. A mini-cadenza follows the fermata, in which the lower-neighbor motive from the opening of the variation becomes a trill; C♯ eventually leads to C♮ in order to destabilize the dominant.

Beginning in Variation II, Beethoven intensifies the musical drama. By swapping the material that occurred in the right and left hands of Variation I, both textural density and register are expanded. The sixteenth-note motion now occurs in the left hand, and the right hand's large leaps create compound melody, giving the impression that a third voice has been added to the texture. An added applied chord (V^6_5 of V in m. 3) not only intensifies motion to the dominant to close phrase 1, but also reminds us of the preceding variation's C♯–D neighbor motive and trill extension.

Variation III, the midpoint of the variation set, is climactic, in that Beethoven continues to expand the register (by a full octave in the bass and by dwelling in the high register of the right hand rather than merely touching those notes as he had done previously). Further, the hands are equal: They share all textural material and create the impression of a dialogue.

Variation IV provides a momentary respite from the mounting tension of the preceding figuration variations. However, the shift to the parallel minor mode combined with the highly dissonant appoggiaturas, suspensions, and accented passing tones creates a dark and introspective mood. Beethoven again thickens the texture by adding a fourth voice. This variation also contains the most significant harmonic departures from the theme in the entire set. Here, the subdominant rather than the dominant becomes the harmonic focus in each section. The harmonic tide turns already at the beginning of the second phrase (m. 5), where tonic becomes V_7/iv, which briefly tonicizes iv. The following sequential passage might have proven a minor obstacle for Beethoven, given that the D2 ($-5/+4$) applied chord sequence in the theme first tonicized ii and then returned to I. Now ii is a diminished triad and cannot be tonicized. Beethoven solved the problem by turning once again to the subdominant, which he tonicizes in m. 10 through a dialogue-like play between soprano and bass that is reminiscent of Variation III. This time, however, Beethoven inverts the relationships between the voices. He also develops the theme's 5–6 neighbor motive by reiterating E♭ and D at the variation's climax in m. 14. Sighlike echoes of the motive immediately follow in the inner voice (mm. 15–17). The variation closes with two more statements of the neighbor motive, which occur in invertible counterpoint, first in the tenor and then in the soprano.

Variation V's sudden shift to the high register, in which the tune is projected, accompanied by rapid scalar sixteenth-note triplets, and the out-of-doors, pastoral horn calls in the left hand dramatically contrast with Variation IV. Variation V also provides what feels like a giant upbeat to the final variation.

Variation VI not only summarizes the previous variations but also simultaneously provides a fitting climax for the entire set. To accomplish this, the prevailing texture is two voice; but, given the compound melody in each hand, four voices emerge. Thus, Beethoven has artfully summarized the two- to four-voice texture that occurred throughout the set. Further, the neighbor motive that was so important reappears. Variation VI rounds out the set by restating crucial features of the theme. For example, the applied V^4_3 of V reappears in m. 134, the harmony that had been replaced with others in preceding variations. Finally, Beethoven abandons the 20-measure theme and same-length variations by adding a 24-measure coda. This coda presents the opening gesture of the theme, scale degrees $\hat{5}$–$\hat{3}$–$\hat{2}$–$\hat{1}$ (D–B–A–G), which now becomes a closing gesture tossed between the hands in imitative fashion and in the extreme upper and lower registers of the piano. Such a drive to the end is fitting, given that it also summarizes events presented in earlier variations. The brief tonicization of IV beginning in m. 156 serves three purposes. First, it signals the close of the piece, since codas often touch on the subdominant to create a plagal effect. Second, it is reminiscent of the tonicization of minor iv that took place in Variation IV. And third, the IV–I motion permits one last statement of the E–D neighbor motive that played a central role in the variation set.

Summary of Part 6

In Chapter 24 we learned that *applied chords* function as dominants of nontonic harmonies, and as such they are powerful agents of *tonicizations*. A tonicization may contain just a single applied chord, or it may be an extended area consisting of numerous applied chords, all working under the influence of a single harmony. When a tonicized area is stabilized through one or more cadences, we call this larger expansion a *modulation*. Regardless of how extensive tonicizations and modulations are, however, the expanded harmonies always retain their function within the overall key and participate in the unfolding of the underlying harmonic progression.

We also have studied complete pieces for the first time in Part 6. In addition to simple, rounded, and balanced melodic plans, we built on large-scale motions from the tonic to one or more other tonal areas, followed by a return to (and closure in) the tonic. In labeling the harmonic content of binary forms, we saw how the large-scale cadences function analogously to the models of sectional and continuous periods.

Finally, we saw how extensive works may be constructed using building blocks composed of small binary-form movements. *Sectional variations* are one such type; we study several others in the chapters to come. We also encountered *continuous variations*, in which constant cadential overlappings permitted a nonstop musical effect.

EXERCISE INTERLUDE

INSTRUMENTAL APPLICATION

26.3 Improvisation on a Ground Bass

From the mid-seventeenth century to the mid-twentieth century, numerous composers were drawn to a particular melody and its specific harmonization. These are referred to as *folia* (a name originally meaning "crazy" or "empty headed," a reference to the fast tempo and the wild abandon that apparently issued from the dancers). Famous composers, including Lully, Handel, C. P. E. Bach, and even Carl Nielsen (*Maskarade*) and Rachmaninoff (*Variations on a theme by Corelli*), tried their hands at writing variations on this famous theme. Following is the opening of Corelli's Folia, from his op. 5 Violin Sonatas. It includes the theme and the opening of two variations. You will improvise three or four variations. Begin by studying the theme and its harmonic setting, form, and phrase structure.

Answers to Exercise 26.2

Exercise 26.2A

1. The material from the opening of the piece returns in m. 13, making the thematic design rounded. That the initial tune is slightly embellished by thirds and sixths does not interfere with the immediate perception that the tune recurs and is thus rounded. The dominant (A major) is tonicized at the double bar, leaving the section open on the dominant; therefore, the harmonic structure is continuous. This, then, is a rounded continuous binary form.
2. The contrapuntal technique employed is the suspension: in m. 2, a 7–6 suspension, and in m. 4, a 4–3 suspension, both of which are prepared.
3. There are two phrases, and they combine to create a contrasting progressive period.
4. The key of E minor is briefly tonicized (it is ii in the original key, leading to V^6_5 in m. 11).

Exercise 26.2B

1. The first section (mm. 1–8) closes on the tonic; therefore, the harmonic structure is sectional. The opening material returns in m. 13; therefore, the melodic design is rounded. Thus, the form is a rounded sectional binary.
2. The two phrases comprise a parallel interrupted period (PIP).
3. The progression is contrapuntal, since the tonic is extended through neighboring six-five chords (mm. 1–2) and passing vii°$_6$ (m. 3). The only harmonic motion in mm. 1–8 is the V_7 harmony that occurs in mm. 4 and 8.
4. This is a D2 (−5/+4) sequence with applied chords. Since the applied six-five chords resolve not to diatonic four-twos but to yet other applied chords, this is a D2 (−5/+4) int. applied $^{6}_{5}\,^{-}_{-}\,^{5}_{2}$ (i.e., V^6_5 of E resolves to V^4_2 of A, which moves to V^4_2 of D, etc.). Notice the telltale parallel tritones between the piano's left hand and the violin. This sequence leads to the pre-dominant, ii$_6$, in m. 11.
5. The piano and violin share the spotlight with their florid lines and melodies. The cello doubles the piano's bass line, providing harmonic support.

Exercise 26.2C

1. Since opening material returns in the last system, albeit altered in order to close in the tonic, the thematic design is rounded. Furthermore, the modulation to the mediant, C major, at the first double bar makes the harmonic structure continuous. The form is rounded continuous binary.
2. The contrapuntal technique is suspension, most often 7–6s. The suspensions are prepared in m. 1 in the tenor with the 5–6 motion (E^4–F^4) that ties over the bar line. The bass descends to G$\sharp^3$, creating the suspended interval of a seventh with the tenor, resolving on beat 3 to E^4.
3. The bass line is an example of the step-descent bass.

4. The sequence is an A2 (−3/+4) type. Beginning on E minor, the harmonic motion consists of ascending triads in root position: E^3–F^3–G^3–A^3–B^3–C^4. The 5–6 motion helps obviate the potential parallel fifths. This sequence is a transitional type, since it begins in the tonic key area and, through its ascent, helps to secure the mediant key.

5. and 6. The mediant (C major) is the added key area that gives way to iv (D minor) in mm. 18–19. Notice how D minor is strongly implied by its PD and dominant, beginning immediately after the double bar. In fact, in a clever allusion to the opening octave leaps, Haydn transfers the dissonant seventh, G, of the dominant of D (A–C♯–E–G) down an octave in m. 17, where it finally resolves to F (the third of D) in m. 18. D minor as large-scale pre-dominant moves to the dominant and the interruption. The tonal structure of the movement, then, is i–III–iv–V || i–V–i.

Exercise 26.2D

1. The first section does not close on tonic, so the harmonic structure is continuous. There is no obvious repetition of melodic material from the first eight measures, so the thematic design is simple. The form is simple continuous binary.
2. The new tonal destination is V, and the pivot may be traced to m. 4, the downbeat, at which point tonic becomes IV in the context of the dominant.
3. F major lasts only four measures but is followed by what sounds like a sequential restatement of the F-major material, the goal of which is to tonicize D minor (vi).
4. The new melody beginning in m. 9 is a loose inversion of the opening tune. Furthermore, the clear melodic ascent F^5–G^5–A^5, which occurs prominently at the downbeats of mm. 1–3, reappears in mm. 9–13 but now on the weak, second beats of each measure. This motivic restatement may help to explain why F major reappears after the double bar.

WORKBOOK
26.5–26.8

5. This is a D2 (−5/+4) sequence with applied dominants. D minor (m. 16) is converted to D major with an added seventh, creating a V^6_5 of G minor, to which it leads, followed by V^6_5 of F major, thus securing the return to tonic.

TERMS AND CONCEPTS

- binary form
- chaconne
- continuous variations
- digression
- ground bass
- harmonic structure
  - sectional
  - continuous
- interruption
- minuet
- ostinato
- passacaglia
- sectional variations
- thematic design
  - simple
  - rounded
  - balanced
- theme
- two-reprise form
- variation set

PART 7

EXPRESSIVE CHROMATICISM

Chromatic harmony in the form of the applied dominant chord has existed essentially from the beginning of tonality. Examples of V/V can be found in the output of early-sixteenth-century composers, such as Josquin. Yet as music moved into the late Classical and Romantic eras, composers began to focus on exploring the potential of pre-dominant, rather than dominant, harmony. For example, the off-tonic beginning—which typically involves starting a piece on a ii or IV chord and only eventually revealing the home sonority—is a hallmark of Schumann, Brahms, Wolf, and Mahler. A natural outcome of this new interest in pre-dominant harmony was that composers began investing pre-dominants with their own forms of chromaticism. In the following chapters, we explore the roles of these chromatic pre-dominants. We will see how they function both as expressive devices in local contexts and as stepping-stones to remote tonicizations at deeper levels. In fact, at the same time that these new chromatic harmonies were surfacing, so too were new motivic techniques and new genres (including the solo song with piano accompaniment). We also explore two special sonorities of remarkable pre-dominant power: the Neapolitan sixth chord and the augmented sixth chord.

CHAPTER 27

Modal Mixture

When we listen to music of the late eighteenth and early nineteenth centuries, we frequently encounter a type of chromaticism that cannot be said to derive from applied functions and tonicization. In fact, the chromaticism often appears to be nonfunctional—a mere coloring of the melodic and harmonic surface of the music.

Listen to the two phrases of Example 27.1. The first phrase (mm. 1–8) contains exclusively diatonic harmonies, but the second phrase (mm. 9–20) is full of chromaticism. This creates sonorities, such as the A♭-major chord in m. 15, which appear to be distant from the underlying F-major tonic. The chromatic harmonies in mm. 11–20 have been labeled with letter names that indicate the root and quality of the chord.

EXAMPLE 27.1 **Mascagni, "A casa amici" ("Homeward, friends"), *Cavalleria Rusticana*, scene 9**

DVD 1 CH 27 TRACK 1

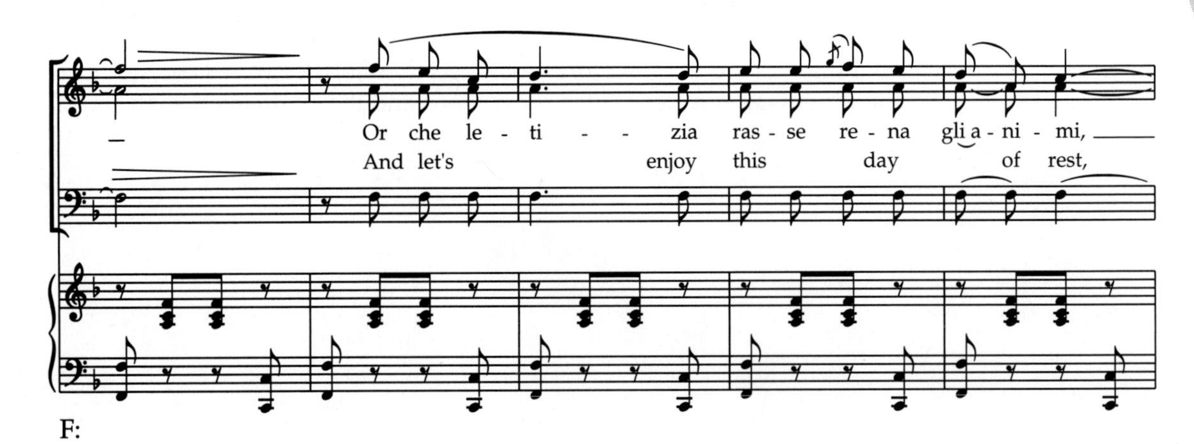

Continued

Perhaps you recognized the important feature these sonorities share: All but the cadential V–I are members of the parallel mode, F minor. Viewing this progression through the lens of F minor reveals a simple bass arpeggiation that briefly tonicizes III (A♭), then moves to PD and D, followed by a final resolution to major tonic in the major mode.

The Mascagni excerpt is quite remarkable in its tonal plan. Although it begins and ends in F major, a significant portion of the music behaves as though written in F minor. This technique of borrowing harmonies from the parallel mode is called **modal mixture** (sometimes known simply as **mixture**). Although the topic may seem entirely new, we have actually already encountered two instances of modal mixture. The first occurred as the "Picardy third," the cadence seen in minor works that raises $\hat{3}$ to end on a major chord. A second instance arose through the use of the fully diminished seventh chord in the major mode, which had ♭$\hat{6}$, as its seventh.

Although harmonies may be borrowed from either the parallel major or minor, *it is much more common for elements of the minor mode to be imported into the major mode*. A quick review of the possible pitch material in the major and minor modes reveals why: In the minor mode, $\hat{6}$ and $\hat{7}$ each have two forms, depending on whether the melodic line ascends or descends (See Example 1.16). Consequently, the importation of natural $\hat{6}$ into a minor piece results from good voice leading. By contrast, the major mode does not include the altered forms of $\hat{3}$, $\hat{6}$, and $\hat{7}$; thus, if a musical passage is forging ahead in a major key but then introduces ♭$\hat{6}$, the effect can be quite shocking.

Altered Pre-Dominant Harmonies: ii° and iv

The most common scale degree involved in modal mixture is $\hat{6}$. There are four reasons why this is so.

1. $\hat{6}$ is least likely to undermine the integrity of the home key and mode.
2. Lowering $\hat{6}$ permits a strong half-step motion to the dominant.
3. Modal mixture invoked on $\hat{6}$ colors all PD harmonies.
4. $\hat{6}$ is the only scale degree outside of the tonic triad that can be consonantly supported by a harmony with $\hat{1}$ in the bass. Thus, it is a component of the contrapuntal 5–6 motion that we know figures prominently in music.

Example 27.2 shows how ♭$\hat{6}$, which is drawn from the parallel minor, alters the most common pre-dominants, ii, ii_7, and IV; the supertonic harmony becomes a diminished triad (ii°), ii_7 becomes a half-diminished seventh, and the subdominant becomes a minor triad (iv). This type of chromatic alteration—which changes the quality of a chord but does not alter its root—is called **melodic mixture**. As you can see from the roman numerals in Example 27.2, the labeling of chords to reflect melodic mixture is easy: You label the chord as if it were in a minor key.

EXAMPLE 27.2

Application: Musical Effects of Melodic Mixture

We now explore the musical contexts for mixture chords. Listen to Example 27.3, and focus on the downbeat of m. 3, where mixture appears as the PD seventh chord incorporates ♭$\hat{6}$ to become ii^{ø}$_7$. One way to view this melodic mixture is to interpret the A♭ in the voice—a heartbreaking cry—as a surprising foreign tone to C major. This is a partially valid interpretation. When A♭ enters the melody in m. 3, it has a highly poetic function. Schumann is able to underscore the speaker's pain ("I bear no grudge, even if my heart breaks") by introducing dissonance through modal mixture. The jarring entrance of the A♭ shatters the major mode, just as the poet's heart ("Herz") is broken. Schumann leads the phrase to its high point on the word *heart*, extending the word for most of m. 3. The A♭ continues to intensify the pain by forming an even more dissonant minor ninth when the A♭ is sustained over the dominant (G).

EXAMPLE 27.3 Schumann, "Ich grolle nicht" ("I bear no grudge"), *Dichterliebe*, op. 48, no. 7

Finally, melodic mixture harmonies work very well in contrapuntal expansions of the tonic, especially as embedded phrase models (EPMs), shown in Example 27.4.

EXAMPLE 27.4

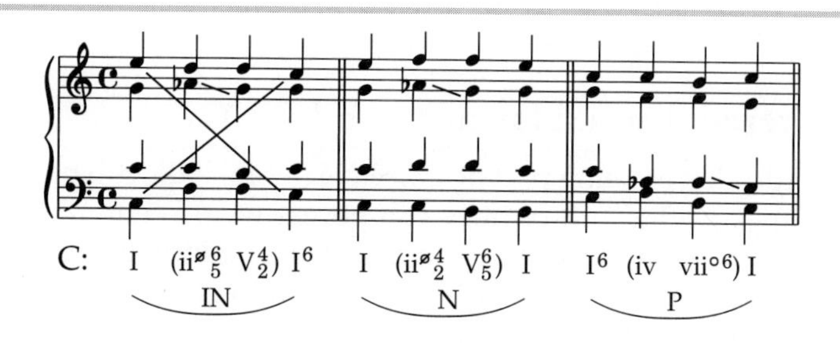

Altered Submediant Harmony: ♭VI

In melodic mixture, we have seen ♭$\hat{6}$ appear as the *third* or the *fifth* of a mixture chord. A different situation occurs when ♭$\hat{6}$ appears as the *root* of a mixture chord. In these cases, the root of the chord has been shifted down from where it usually occurs. We describe this as **harmonic mixture** and label the resulting chord ♭VI.

EXAMPLE 27.5

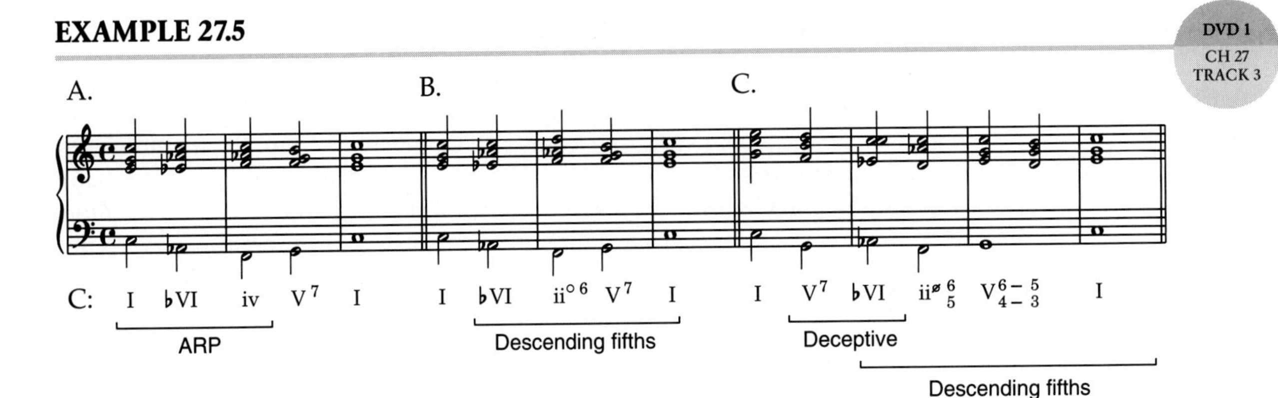

Take a moment to examine the nomenclature for harmonic mixture (Example 27.5). Note that the lowered root of the chord is indicated by a flat sign placed before the roman numeral. If the root ($\flat\hat{6}$) were the only altered pitch in the submediant chord, however, the resulting sonority would be a dissonant augmented triad (e.g., in C major, A♭–C–E♮), an unstable chord that common-practice composers never used as an independent harmony. Therefore, mixture is also applied to $\hat{3}$ in order to produce a consonant major triad on VI (just as it is in minor). We use the generic "♭VI" to refer to all major triads built on the lowered form of $\hat{6}$ and when generally describing the chord, even if a natural, rather than a flat, is used to notate the chord (e.g., in A major, the ♭VI chord is built on F natural, not F flat). Despite its new roman numeral and chromatic inflection, ♭VI continues to function as a submediant chord.

1. It participates in descending arpeggiations (Example 27.5A).
2. It participates in descending-fifth motions (Example 27.5B).
3. It precedes the dominant as a PD chord.
4. It follows the dominant (and substitutes for the tonic chord) in deceptive motions (Example 27.5C).
5. Because ♭VI lies a half step away from the dominant, composers often take advantage of this proximity by using ♭VI motivically as a dramatic upper neighbor that extends V.

Altered Tonic Harmony: i

In addition to being part of ♭VI, $\flat\hat{3}$ creates melodic mixture in altered tonic harmonies. Eighteenth-century composers were keenly aware of the ambiguity that can result from making a major tonic minor. Because this modal juxtaposition calls the mode of an entire piece into question, a minor tonic is more often only implied rather than literally stated. For example, in Example 27.6, the long chromatic line—which extends the dominant (before it returns to the tonic) and includes F♮—implies the parallel mode, D minor.

EXAMPLE 27.6 Mozart, Menuett in D major, K. 94

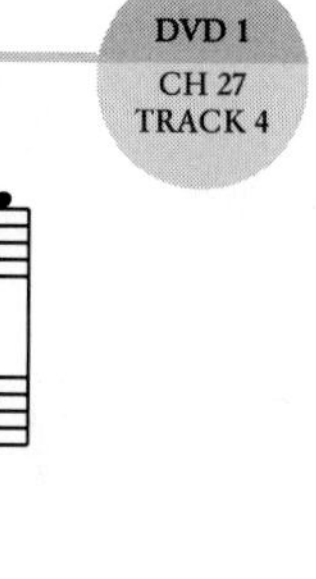

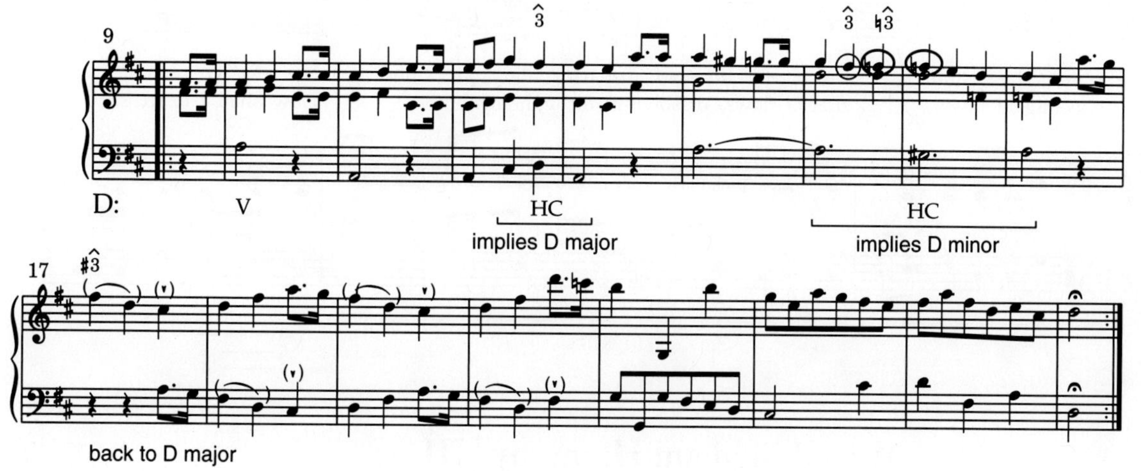

Despite this destabilizing effect, some eighteenth-century composers—including not only Bach but also later, Classical composers such as Haydn and Mozart—invoked modal mixture on the tonic. By the nineteenth century, some composers (such as Schubert) began to saturate their major-mode pieces with elements of the minor to such a degree that the 24 major and minor keys could be said to have fused into 12 major–minor keys. For example, it would be impossible to tell if a piece were in D major or D minor if it had equal numbers of F♯s/F♮s and B♭s/B♮s; you could only be sure it was in D. Listen to Example 27.7 and note how the key of F major is pervaded with elements of F minor, including a tonicization of ♭III (A♭), which is the final common mixture harmony we will study.

EXAMPLE 27.7 Schubert, "Schwanengesang" ("Swan Song"), op. 23, no. 3, D. 744

Continued

Altered Mediant Harmony: ♭III

Just as ♭VI arose from harmonic mixture, so too does the ♭III chord, which has $\flat\hat{3}$ as its root. The ♭III chord also borrows $\flat\hat{7}$ to create a consonant major triad. As Example 27.8 shows, ♭III continues to function as a mediant chord.

1. It divides the fifth between I and V into two smaller thirds (Example 27.8A).
2. It is a bridge between T and PD (Example 27.8B and D).
3. It participates in descending-fifths motion (Example 27.7C), although less often than the diatonic ii chord.
4. It is a PD chord, leading to V^4_3 (Example 27.8E).
5. It can be preceded by its dominant (in minor keys, V/III leads to III; in major keys, this progression becomes V/♭III to ♭III) (Example 27.8F).
6. It also is a substitute for I_6 (although not nearly as common as diatonic iii, given that $\hat{3}$ is lowered in ♭III; see Example 27.8D).

EXAMPLE 27.8

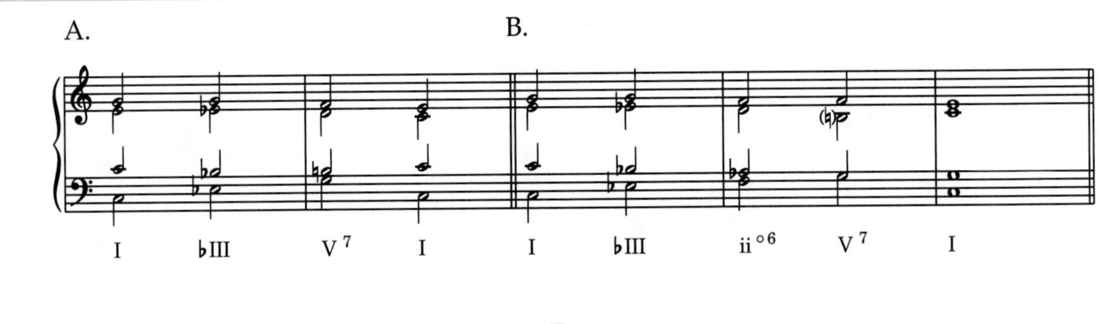

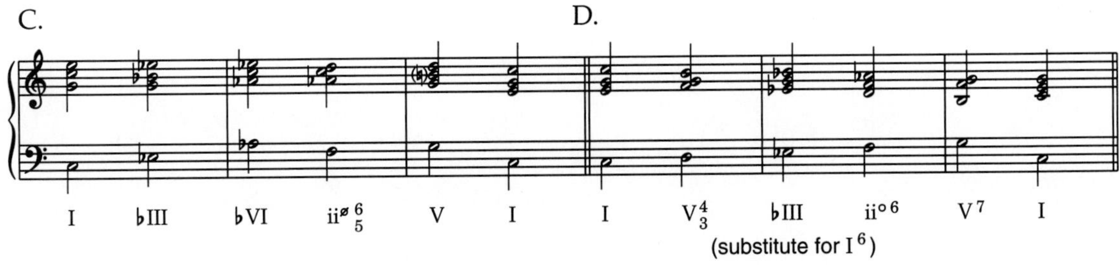

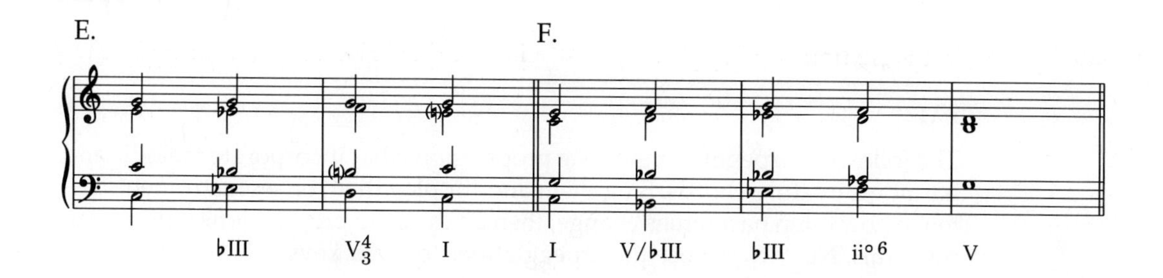

Voice Leading for Mixture Harmonies

Review the following guidelines, which restate and slightly develop the rules for writing applied chords.

- Avoid doubling a chromatically altered tone unless it is the root of the chord (as in ♭VI).
- Since ♭$\hat{6}$ will be either a neighbor tone ($\hat{5}$–♭$\hat{6}$–$\hat{5}$) or a descending passing tone ($\hat{6}$–♭$\hat{6}$–$\hat{5}$), prepare and resolve it by step motion. Keeping the chromatic line $\hat{6}$–♭$\hat{6}$–$\hat{5}$ in a single voice will help avoid outer-voice cross relations.
- Once you introduce modal mixture, continue its use until you reach the dominant function. This is because ♭$\hat{3}$ and especially ♭$\hat{6}$ possess such powerful drives to $\hat{2}$ and to $\hat{5}$, respectively, that any intrusion of their diatonic forms would not only create a jarring cross relation but also ruin the drive to the dominant (see Example 27.9).

EXAMPLE 27.9

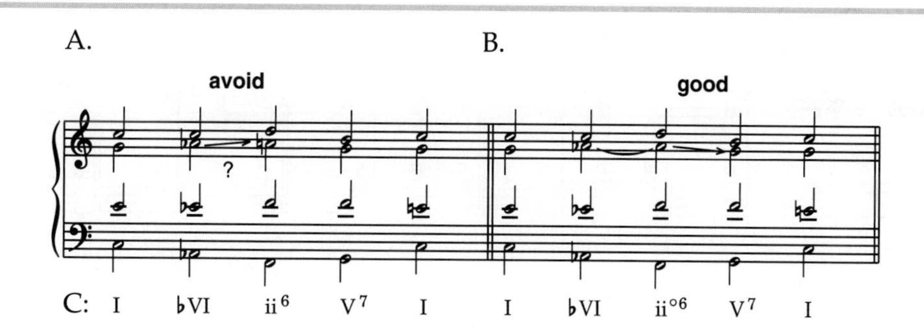

EXERCISE INTERLUDE

PERFORMING

27.1

The following arpeggiations create progressions that incorporate melodic and harmonic mixture chords. Sing them and/or play them on an instrument. Listen to how often harmonies change; then analyze the progressions with roman numerals. Next, transpose the arpeggiations to other keys.

LISTENING

DVD 2
CH 27
TRACK 1

27.2 Aural Comparison of Diatonic and Mixture Progressions

Short diatonic and mixture progressions are notated here. You will hear each of the progressions performed. However, the performance of each example may not be in the order notated. If what you see is what is played, then write "okay." If what you see is played in the wrong order, write "reversed." Analyze each example.

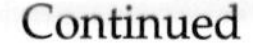
Continued

WRITING

27.3

Complete the following tasks on a separate sheet of manuscript paper. Use a key signature.

A. In the major keys of D, F, and A, write the following chords in four voices. You need not connect them to one another.

$\text{ii}^{ø6}_{5}$ iv ♭VI ♭III V_7/♭VI V^4_3/♭III

B. Write the following progressions in four voices and in your choice of meter.

1. In C major: I–♭VI–iv–V–I. Begin with $\hat{3}$ in the soprano.
2. In F major: I–ii°$_6$–$\text{V}^{6\,-\,5}_{4\,-\,3}$–I
3. In E♭ major: I–IV–iv–V_{8-7}–I
4. In G and E major: I–I_6–iv–I–♭III–iiø/$^6_5$–V–I
5. In C and A major: I–♭VI–iv–vii°$_7$/V–$\text{V}^{6-♭6-5}_{4\,—\,3}$♭VI–iv$_6$–$\text{V}_{8-7}$–I

ANALYSIS

DVD 2 CH 27 TRACK 2

27.4

Determine the locations and types of mixture harmonies in the following excerpts. In your analyses, remember that not all chromatically altered chords result from mixture; some are applied chords. Mixture harmonies are independent chords that participate in the harmonic progression and usually carry a pre-dominant function. Applied harmonies, by contrast, function as dominants and thus merely point to more important chords that are tonicized. Provide a two-level harmonic analysis.

A.

B.

C. J. S. Bach, "Christus, der ist mein Leben"

D.

E. Mizzou, Waltz in D major

WORKBOOK
27.1–27.3

KEYBOARD

27.5

Play the following progressions as written and in major keys up to and including three sharps.

Chromatic Stepwise Bass Descents

In Chapter 18 we encountered two types of stepwise bass descents leading to the dominant. Because there are two diatonic forms of $\hat{6}$ and $\hat{7}$ in minor, it is possible for this descent to be completely chromaticized (e.g., $\hat{1}$–$\hat{7}$–$\flat\hat{7}$–$\hat{6}$–$\flat\hat{6}$–$\hat{5}$) in a minor piece, as shown in Example 27.10A, where Geminiani is able to write a fully chromatic descending bass line by using an applied chord (V$^4_2$ of IV) that leads to major IV$_6$. With modal mixture, we can import this powerful progression into major-mode pieces. Examples 27.10B and C illustrate two common settings. Example 27.10B shows a direct descent to V, and Example 27.10C shows an indirect descent to PD on $\hat{4}$, followed by the dominant. Note that the use of a passing minor v$_6$ in Example 27.10C leads to the pre-dominant, which is expanded through a **chromatic voice exchange** (where the **A**/F in the IV$_6$ chord are exchanged by the F/**A♭** in the ii$^{ø6}_5$ chord.

EXAMPLE 27.10

DVD 1
CH 27
TRACK 6

A. Geminiani, *The Art of Playing on the Violin*, op. 9, no. 8

Notice that chromatic voice exchanges necessarily involve strong cross relations. In such cases, intervening passing chords diminish any harshness that would have occurred in a direct succession of chromatic tones. In general, as we learned with applied chords, it is best to avoid direct outer-voice cross relations; instead, keep the chromatic motion within a single voice (see Example 27.10D).

Plagal Motions

During the nineteenth century, the role of the dominant harmony gradually changed. For the most part, progressions still led to the tonic, but the dominant was often conspicuously absent from the cadence. This is due largely to nineteenth-century composers' obsession with creating novel harmonic combinations along with a general distaste for commonplace formulas such as V_7–I. The growing acceptance of mixture harmonies partially accounts for this change, since their dramatic effects made them popular substitutes for the dominant.

For example, iv leads convincingly to the dominant in both major and minor modes. In a way, though, because $\flat\hat{6}$ strongly desires resolution by half step to $\hat{5}$, iv also can move directly to the tonic at a cadence (Example 27.11A). Substitution for the dominant is not restricted to the subdominant. Both the supertonic and the submediant may move directly to tonic (Examples 27.11B and C). The cadence in Example 27.11B is commonly heard in popular music of the 1920s through the 1950s and in films today; we therefore label it a **Hollywood cadence**. Notice that the Hollywood cadence is a chromatically embellished plagal cadence (IV–I); a contrapuntal 5–6 motion and mixture transform IV into ii$^{ø6}_{5}$ before the resolution to the tonic chord. We use the term **plagal motion** and the abbreviation "**PL**" at the second level to describe progressions in which harmonies other than the dominant lead to the tonic.

EXAMPLE 27.11

DVD 1 CH 27 TRACK 7

Notice both the absence of dominant harmony (even at the final cadence) and the prominence of mixture in Example 27.12. The passage begins with an expansion of tonic harmony through an upper-neighbor figure G–A–G in the alto. Although a repetition of this figure is expected in m. 3, ♭VI instead participates in the upper-neighbor figure, now chromaticized (G–A♭–G). The mixture continues with ♭VI and minor iv resolving to the tonic in a plagal cadence.

EXAMPLE 27.12 Brahms, Symphony no. 3 in F major, op. 90, *Andante*

The prominence of the neighbor figure—in particular, the conflict between A♮ and A♭—indicates that this gesture is motivic. In fact, this motive is not restricted to the slow movement of Brahms' third symphony. The seeds are planted in the opening measures of the symphony's first movement (Example 27.13). The A♮/A♭ conflict is set into motion by the cross relation in mm. 1–2 and is intensified in mm. 3 by a voice exchange. This pitch-class conflict between A♮ and A♭ that takes place in the first and second movements seems especially important, given that the two movements are in different keys: A♮ and A♭ function as $\hat{3}$ and $\flat\hat{3}$ in F major; in C major they are $\hat{6}$ and $\flat\hat{6}$.

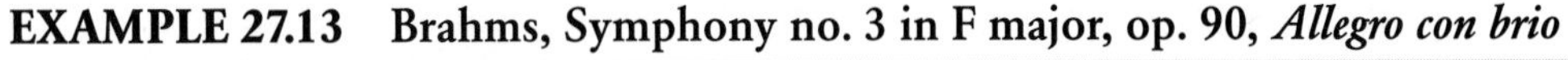

EXAMPLE 27.13 Brahms, Symphony no. 3 in F major, op. 90, *Allegro con brio*

Modal Mixture, Applied Chords, and Other Chromatic Harmonies

In this and the previous two chapters, we have learned two tonal processes that account for chromaticism in tonal music.

1. Tonicization is intimately associated with *dominant* function, as new chromatic tones act as *temporary leading tones*.
2. Modal mixture usually occurs within the *pre-dominant* function, as the new chromatic tones retain their scale degree function but in an altered form.

Occasionally, composers use two other chromatic harmonies on $\hat{3}$ and $\hat{6}$ of a major key, but they are not products of tonicization or modal mixture. The first is a major mediant chord (III) whose root is diatonic $\hat{3}$. Like diatonic iii and mixture ♭III, III most often is part of a rising bass arpeggiation (I–III–V), which may include a PD (I–III–IV–V).

Look at Example 27.14A. The piece is in E major. Note that G♯ is not an applied chord (V/vi). Rather, it is a self-standing harmony. The second chromatic harmony that one occasionally encounters is a major submediant chord (VI) whose root is the diatonic $\hat{6}$ (Example 27.14B). And, like vi and ♭VI, VI most often leads to IV. Note that had VI led to ii, it would be better interpreted as V/ii rather than VI [e.g., in C major, VI (A major) leading to ii (D minor) would sound more like an applied chord than an independent harmony]. That VI is an independent harmony is made clear by the behavior of C♯ (in the alto): Rather than ascending to D, as it would had it functioned as an applied chord, it instead descends to C natural.

EXAMPLE 27.14

DVD 1
CH 27
TRACK 10

A. Grieg, "Morning" from *Peer Gynt Suite*, op. 46, no. 1

B.

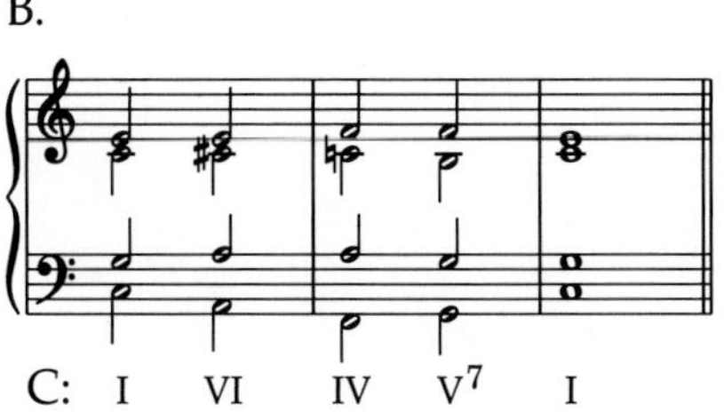

Indeed, it is important in your analysis that you discern between these chords and applied dominant chords. For a final example, if you encounter a D-major harmony in B♭ major, you must determine whether it is the applied V/vi or the chromatic III chord. In Example 27.15A, D major functions as a chromatic mediant chord (III), leading to the PD ii_6 chord. In Example 27.15B, D major is V/vi, an applied dominant chord leading to G minor (vi).

EXAMPLE 27.15

Summary

The major tonic now has access to three sets of third relations: to the *diatonic* upper and lower thirds (iii, vi), to the *raised chromatic* thirds (III, VI), and to the *lowered chromatic thirds* resulting from modal mixture (♭III, ♭VI). Notice that the minor tonic's options for third relations are very limited: A minor tonic will usually move only to its diatonic III and VI. Example 27.16 shows how the submediant and mediant harmonies fit into the common-practice tonal scheme. Upper thirds lead to $\hat{5}$ through arpeggiation, and lower thirds lead to $\hat{4}$ through arpeggiation.

EXAMPLE 27.16

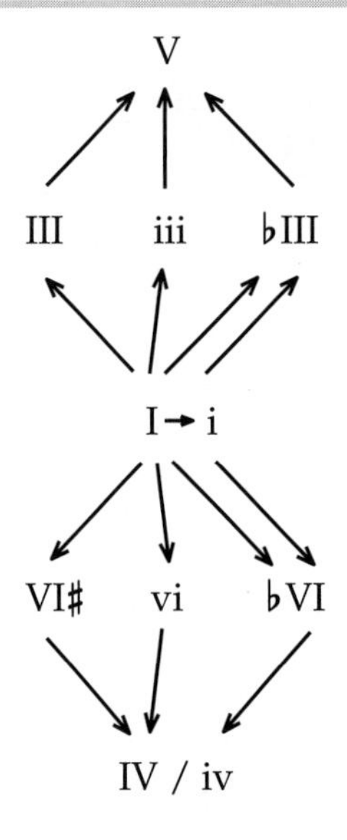

Modal mixture plays a central role in tonal music, one that is much more varied than merely coloring harmonies for musical contrast. When paired with their diatonic counterparts, mixture chords present the potential for powerful musical conflicts that are often dramatically worked out over the course of a work.

The complex workings of chromatic pitches became a critical feature of nineteenth-century compositions. Through modal mixture, a chromatic pitch may appear early and at the surface of a work. As the work progresses, the mixture accrues significance and evolves until it participates in the deepest levels of musical structure.

EXERCISE INTERLUDE

PERFORMING

27.6

Sing the following progression, which involves the chromatic step descent, using solfège syllables or scale degree numbers. Improvise a consequent phrase that closes on the tonic to create a period.

LISTENING

DVD 1
CH 27
TRACK 3

27.7

You will hear four longer examples; the last two are from the literature. Each contains two or more instances of modal mixture. On a separate sheet of manuscript paper, notate the bass line of the piano accompaniment and analyze with roman numerals. The examples may modulate.

A. Three sharps, $\frac{4}{4}$, 4 mm., Moderato
B. Five flats, $\frac{4}{4}$, 24 mm. (not counting two-measure introduction), Andante
C. Mozart, "Wahnsinn and Raserei" from *Cosí fan tutte;* three flats $\frac{4}{4}$, 13 mm., Allegro
D. Schubert Impromptu in E♭ major; three flats, $\frac{3}{4}$, 32 mm., Allegro molto (one beat p/measure)

ANALYSIS

27.8

Analyze the following examples, which illustrate plagal motions and other chromatic chords.

A.

B.

C. "Heartfelt Greeting Card"

What type of period is this?

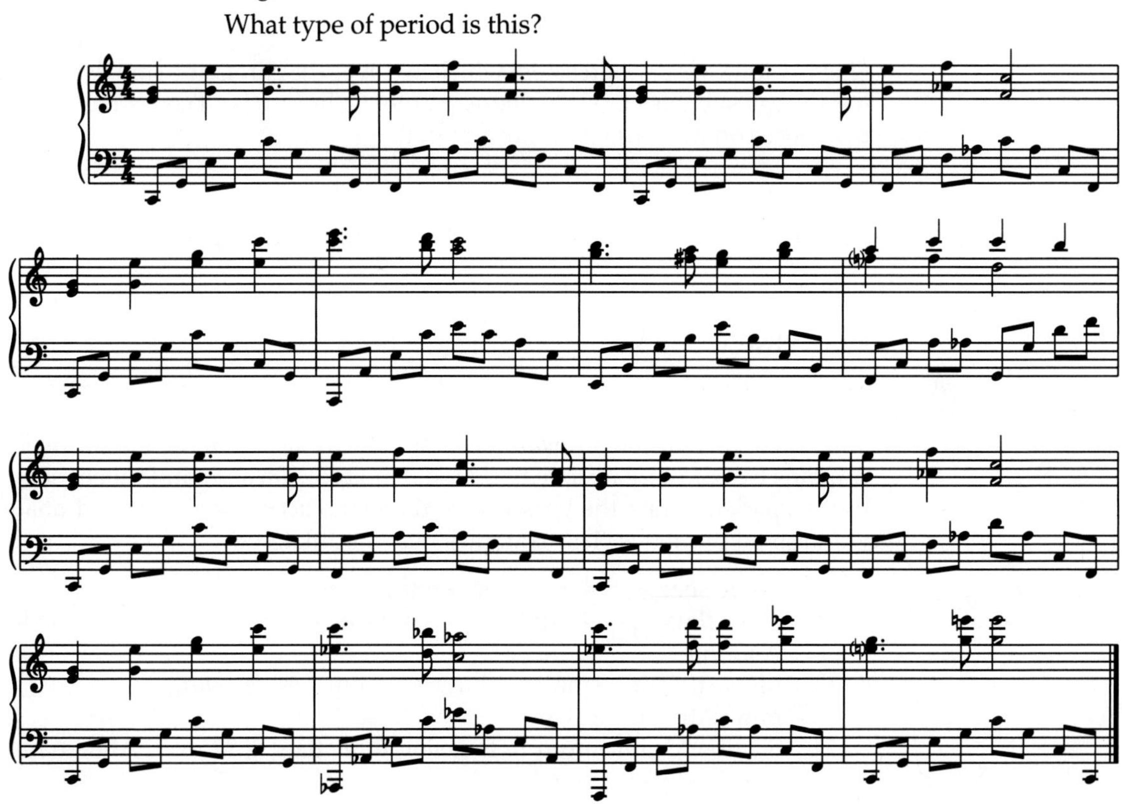

D. Chopin, Nocturne in C minor, op. 48, no. 1

KEYBOARD

27.9 Expansion of Harmonic Pillars

Given is a skeleton of harmonic structural chords, under which are instructions that will enable you to flesh out the structure with other harmonies, including mixture chords. Choose a meter, and play in four-voice keyboard style. Analyze.

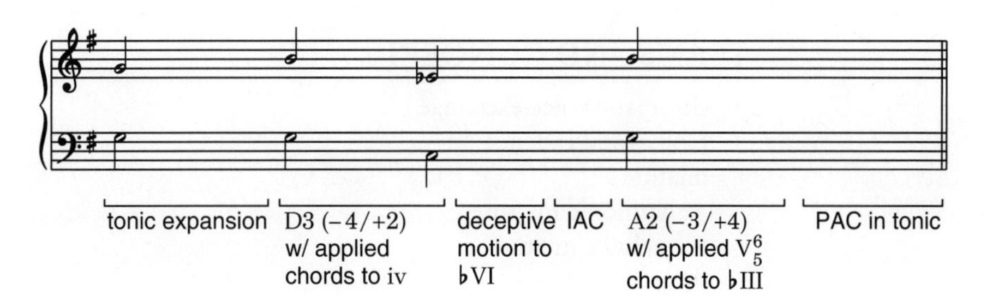

27.10

Sing the tune "Tiptoe thru the Tulips with Me" by Al Dubin. Then analyze the figured bass and realize in four-voice keyboard style to accompany your singing.

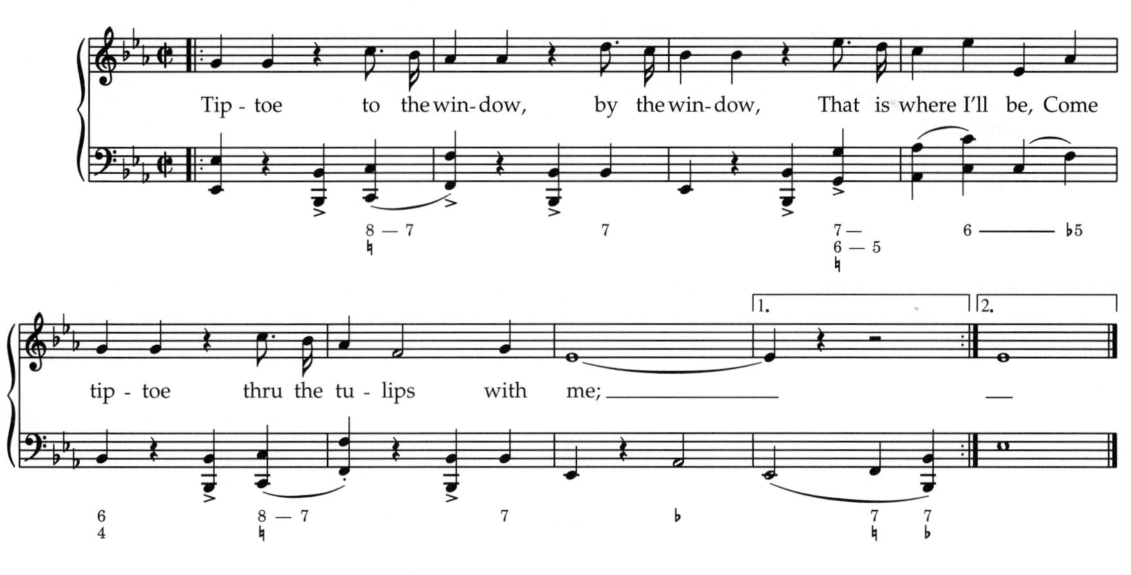

COMPOSITION

27.11

Complete the following tasks in four-voice chorale style (choose a meter) on a separate sheet of manuscript paper. Analyze; then play your solutions on the keyboard.

A. In D major, write a progression that expands tonic with a mixture chord, includes two suspensions, and incorporates ♭VI.

WORKBOOK
27.4–27.6

B. In A major, write a progression that contains two short phrases that create a PIP, includes $ii^{\text{ø}6}_{5}$ in the first phrase and iv in the second phrase, and includes an applied chord in each phrase.
C. Given an F-major triad, use it correctly within progressions in the keys of B♭ major, D minor, D major, and A major.
D. In E major, write a progression that includes a chromatic step-descent bass that leads to iv. Close with a PAC.

TERMS AND CONCEPTS

- chromatic voice exchange
- Hollywood cadence
- mixture
  - harmonic mixture
  - melodic mixture
  - modal mixture
- plagal relations

CHAPTER 28

Expansion of Modal Mixture Harmonies: Chromatic Modulation and the German *Lied*

Chapter 27 served as an introduction to the concept of mixture. It presented examples in which the mixture sonorities lasted only a moment or so and served to color a progression. Yet surely it is possible for modal mixture to be extended for more than a single chord. Remember the Mascagni example (Example 27.1), in which F minor intruded for several measures. Think back also to the discussion of applied chords versus mixture, which showed that when an applied dominant precedes a mixture chord, the two together serve as a mini-tonicization of a chromatic harmony.

In this chapter, we explore the possibilities of **chromatic modulations**. We will start from the assumption that ♭VI and ♭III are the most commonly tonicized chromatic harmonies in eighteenth- and nineteenth-century art music. Composers less often tonicize VI (e.g., C major to A major) and III (e.g., C major to E major), but we consider these relations as well.

We explore the means by which composers move smoothly from diatonic harmonies to expanded chromatic harmonies within progressions. Once this knowledge is gained, we then learn how extended chromatic tonicizations and modulations function logically within the harmonic progressions of entire works.

Chromatic Pivot-Chord Modulations

In order to move smoothly from one key area to another, composers usually employ a pivot harmony that is common to both keys. When we search for a suitable pivot for chromatic modulation, however, we encounter a problem: Often, there are no triads common to both keys. For example, there are no chords in common between C major and A♭ (♭VI; see Example 28.1). However, the knowledge that a major key often borrows from its parallel minor allows us to reenvision our move from C major as one from C major/minor to A♭ major (Example 28.2). Modal mixture introduces triads that appear in both keys.

EXAMPLE 28.1

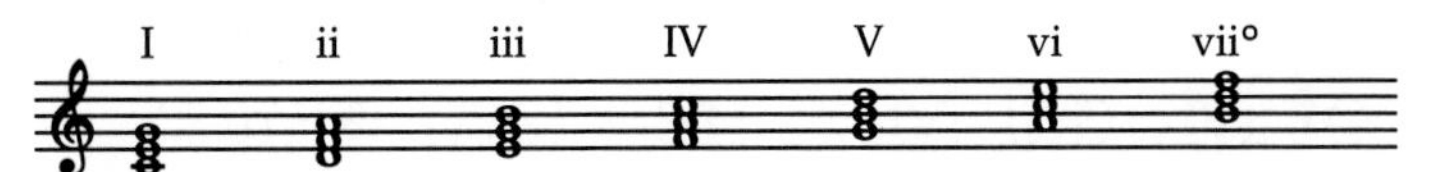

triads in A♭ major:

EXAMPLE 28.2

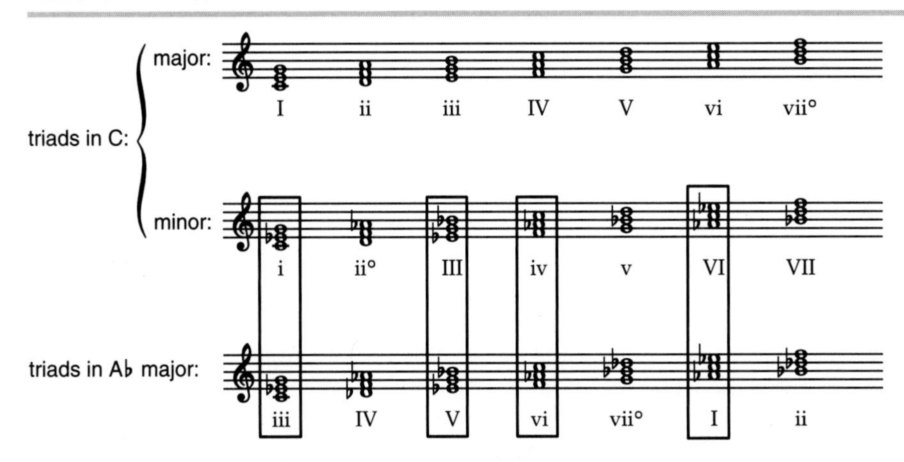

Permitting modal mixture to enter into the equation causes four potential pivot chords to emerge in Example 28.2. We can formulate the following rule for **chromatic pivot-chord modulations**: In a modulation to a chromatic key that results from modal mixture (such as ♭III or ♭VI), the pivot chord must be a mixture chord in the original key. This rule holds so consistently for music of the nineteenth century that the presence of modal mixture—particularly of the tonic—often signals an upcoming tonicization of a chromatic key. This is true because, owing to the modal shift, the tonic loses its anchoring power and instead begins to act as a pre-dominant to an upcoming ♭VI or ♭III. Listen to Example 28.3A and note how the modal shift from E major (I) to E minor (i) nicely prepares the motion from E-major to C major (♭VI). The E-minor chord functions as iii in C major and as a bridge that connects the two distantly related keys.

EXAMPLE 28.3

DVD 1
CH 28
TRACK 1

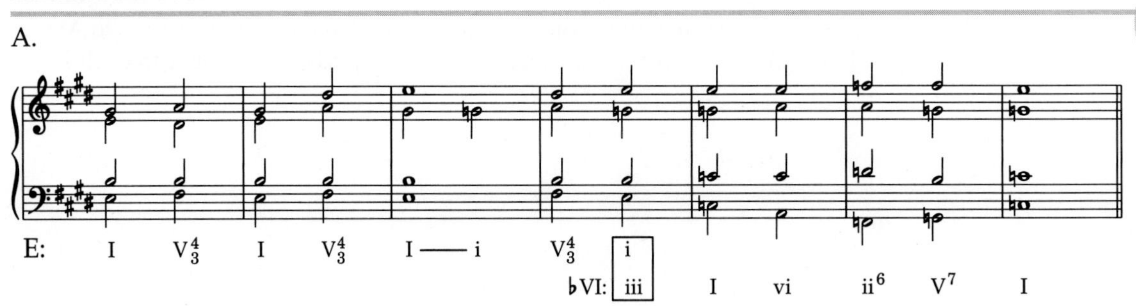

B. Beethoven, Piano Sonata no. 27 in E major, op. 90, *Nicht zu geschwind und sehr singbar vorzutragen* *(To be played not too fast and yet very songfully)*

Now listen to Example 28.3B to see how Beethoven artfully uses this very same strategy in his E-major piano sonata, considerably expanding it.

An Analytical Interlude: Franz Schubert's Waltz in F Major

Listen to Example 28.4 and determine the following.

1. Which chromatic harmony is the goal of the modulation: ♭III or ♭VI?
2. What is the pivot chord used to change to the chromatic key?
3. When does the original key return?
4. What is the function of the chromatic modulation in the overall harmonic plan of the work?

EXAMPLE 28.4 Schubert, Waltz in F major, *36 Original Dances*, D. 365, no. 33

After an alternation of I and V in F major, the major tonic is converted to minor in m. 13, where it functions as a pivot leading to A♭ major (♭III). The original key returns with a V_7 chord in m. 25. Given that chromatic modulation participates in the overall harmonic progression of a passage, we can step back and discover that the tonicized ♭III is part of a large tonal arpeggiation: I–♭III–V_7–I.

As we have seen in earlier analyses, a motive that appears early in a work and on the music's surface may reappear later at a deeper level. Thus, even the most common progressions or fleeting nonchord tones can provide the means for later development. This is just the case in Schubert's Waltz, which opens with a melody projecting the upper-neighbor motive C–D–C. The same upper-neighbor motive is restated in the parallel minor (C–D♭–C at m. 13) to prepare the entrance of ♭III. Notice also that the neighbor motion has been transferred to the harmonic domain at m. 13, where the bass F falls to E♭.

Writing Chromatic Modulations

There are no new part-writing rules, but keep the following in mind.

1. Add the necessary accidentals in the new key, or use the appropriate key signature. Given that you will often need many accidentals for several measures, it is recommended that you simply add a new key signature.
2. The pivot chord must always result from modal mixture. Often, it is effective to use minor i (as vi or iii in the new key).
3. Try to create a seamless musical process by expanding the PD in the new key, either through inversions or a brief tonicization. This postpones the cadence in the new key and therefore allows the ear to get acclimated to the new tonal environment.

EXAMPLE 28.5

C: I $ii^{\varnothing 4}_{2}$ V^{6}_{5} I V^{4}_{2}/iv [iv_6]
(EPM)
T -------------- PD --- [---]

A♭: [vi_6] V^{4}_{3}/vi vi ii_6 V^{6-5}_{4-3} I
(♭VI) [(T)] ----------- PD D ----- T

Example 28.5 shows one way to modulate from C major to A♭ major (♭VI), using the following steps.

1. Establish C major by means of an embedded phrase model; your EPM may even include mixture.
2. Introduce a mixture pivot chord (F-minor chord in Example 28.5 is iv in C major and vi in A♭ major).
3. Elaborate the PD in the new key with a passing contrapuntal harmony. Here, a passing V^{4}_{3} of vi chord connects vi_6 and vi.
4. Proceed to the dominant; then arrive on the tonic of ♭VI with a PAC.
5. (*Optional*) To return to the home key, use a chord in ♭VI that is a mixture chord in the original key. For example, a vi chord in A♭ major becomes iv in C major; iv is a PD chord that leads to a PAC in C major.

EXERCISE INTERLUDE

PERFORMING

28.1

Using solfège syllables or scale degrees, sing (or play on your instrument) the following progressions, which contain chromatic pivot-chord modulations. Analyze, focusing on the location of the pivot chord. If you play the examples, be able to transpose each to at least one other key.

A.

B.

C.

LISTENING

DVD 2
CH 28
TRACK 1

28.2 Aural Identification of Chromatic Third Modulations

You will hear progressions that begin in a major key. Determine whether or not each closes in another key. If it does not, write "No." If it does, provide the appropriate roman numeral for the chromatic key (♭III or ♭VI). You may wish to review the techniques for hearing modulations that were presented in Chapter 25.

A. _____ B. _____ C. _____ D. _____
E. _____ F. _____ G. _____ H. _____

DVD 2
CH 28
TRACK 2

28.3 Aural Identification of Diatonic and Chromatic Third Modulations

Now your choices include diatonic and chromatic third relations: iii, ♭III, vi, and ♭VI (in major), and III and VI (in minor).

A. _____ B. _____ C. _____ D. _____
E. _____ F. _____

WRITING

28.4

Answer the following questions.

1. Given the following major-key modulations, what pivot chords are possible?
   a. D to F (♭III)
   b. G to B♭ (♭III)
   c. E♭ to C♭ (♭VI)
   d. A to F (♭VI)
2. Complete the following chart.

In what key is the triad. . .

triads	*I*	*III*	*IV*	*V*	♭*VI*
D major	*D major*	*B♭ major*	*A major*	*G major*	F♯ major
C major					
E major					
B♭ major					
F major					
A major					

28.5

The following short progressions end with a chromatic pivot chord. To which chromatic keys could the chord lead? Choose one of your solutions for each example, and write a convincing bass voice that secures the new chromatic key.

Example: C major: I–I_6–iv

Answer: iv in C major can be vi in A♭ major (♭VI) or ii in E♭ major (♭III).

D major : I–V_6–I–V_7–♭VI

F major: I–♭VI–V^4_3/iv–iv

A major: I–V_6/♭III–♭III

KEYBOARD

28.6

Analyze and play the following progressions. Then transpose to E major and G major.

WORKBOOK 28.1–28.3

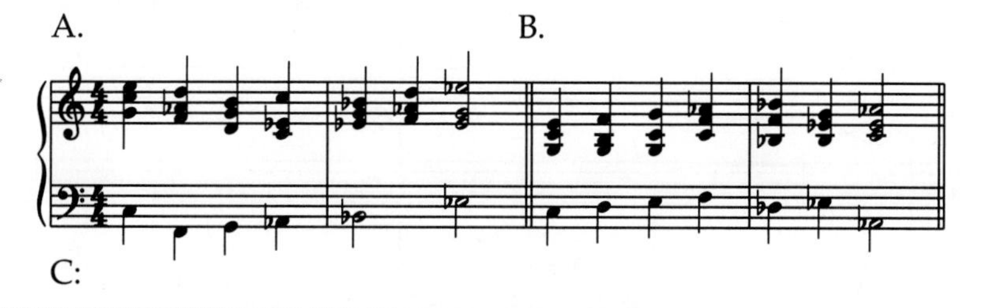

Unprepared Chromatic Modulations

Unlike tonicizations achieved smoothly by means of a harmony that simultaneously functions in multiple harmonic contexts, **unprepared chromatic modulations** occur without the aid of a pivot chord.

Listen for the unprepared chromatic modulation in Example 28.6. The opening 11 measures could be interpreted in two ways: as a single phrase that is divided into subphrases (I-V_7, V_7-I), or as a two-phrase parallel continuous period. After a grand pause in m. 12, the opening theme abruptly enters in A♭ (♭VI).

EXAMPLE 28.6 Haydn, String Quartet in C major, op. 54, no. 2, Hob. III. 58, *Allegro*

DVD 1 CH 28 TRACK 3

Continued

Chromatic Common-Tone Modulations

Most chromatic modulations are not as abrupt as that of Example 28.6. Often the composer will communicate by rhetorical means that a chromatic departure is on the horizon. This can be done by providing the listener with a thread that connects the two keys.

Listen to Example 28.7, in which Schubert juxtaposes D major (I) with B♭ major (♭VI). Even though there is no hint of the upcoming motion to ♭VI, the pitch D in the violins is common to both keys: It is heard in retrospect as $\hat{1}$ of D major and is reinterpreted as $\hat{3}$ in B♭ major. This type of modulation, which usually links two nondiatonic keys lying a third above or below one another, is called a **chromatic common-tone modulation**.

EXAMPLE 28.7 Schubert, String Quartet No. 3 in B♭ major, D. 36, Menuetto-Trio

DVD 1
CH 28
TRACK 4

Continued

Both chromatic common-tone modulations and motivic development are common in nineteenth-century music. Listen to Example 28.8, the opening of Schubert's last piano sonata, written just weeks before his untimely death in 1828 at the age of 31. Identify the location and type of chromatic modulation. The opening tune repeats in the key of G♭ major (♭VI) in m. 20, and it returns to the tonic in mm. 35–36. The chromatic common-tone modulation in mm. 18–20 is surprising; a written-out trill is all that separates I and ♭VI (except for C♭ and A♭, which help to prepare G♭ major). The written-out trill was in turn prepared by the preceding mysterious trill on ♭$\hat{6}$ in m. 8. Thus, the G♭ seed that Schubert planted in the trill germinates when the trill is written out in m. 19 and blossoms in the modulation in mm. 20–35. When Schubert boldly heads the tonicized G♭ major back to F in mm. 35–36, the listener is transported back to the initial measures of the piece and the moment when the neighbor motive, ♭$\hat{6}$–$\hat{5}$, was born.

EXAMPLE 28.8 Schubert, Sonata in B♭ major, op. posth., D. 960, *Molto moderato*

14
19
pp
21
24
27
pp
30
33
cresc.
f
augmented sixth chord
35

Analytical Challenges

You will sometimes encounter chromatic modulations that pose interpretive challenges. Listen to Example 28.9. The trio begins in D♭ major, with its first section closing strongly with a PAC in m. 58. A sudden shift to the parallel minor (m. 59) is followed by a section in A major. How should we interpret the modulation to A major (♯V)?

EXAMPLE 28.9 Schubert Impromptu in A♭, from *Four impromptus, D. 935, Trio*

DVD 1 CH 28 TRACK 5

Continued

For a moment, place yourself in Schubert's shoes. You feel this piece in D♭ major should modulate to ♭VI. Given that ♭VI is B𝄫 major—with a painful nine-flat key signature—you might back off and consider tonicizing some other scale degree. However, your artistic sensibilities and the piece's unity demand that the music move to ♭VI. What do you do? For over two centuries, composers have employed a simple and elegant solution to this problem: write in the enharmonically equivalent key. So, instead of composing a section of music in B𝄫 major, you write in A major, a much easier key to navigate.

Thus, we interpret the relationship between D♭ major and A major as I going to ♭VI (and not ♯V). This will be confirmed when the diatonic dominant (A♭ major) returns: A♭ remains a structural pillar and is never altered. We have a chromatic pivot-chord modulation: The shift to D♭ minor in m. 59 is a pivot that links D♭ to its ♭VI key.

EXAMPLE 28.10 Schubert, "Der Flug der Zeit" ("The Flight of Time"), op. 7, no. 2, D. 515

Continued

Now consider Example 28.10. There is an extended tonicization of C major in mm. 13–20. How does C fit into the overall progression? There are two potential interpretations:

1. There is a modulation from A major to E major in mm. 9–12, and E major goes to C major through a chromatic common-tone modulation.
2. The first 12 measures stay in A major. The E-major chord in m. 12 is a back-relating dominant and is followed by an extended tonicization of C major (♭III).

The best interpretation of C major rests on the fact that while V is a point of arrival in m. 12, it is one that involves being "on" rather than "in" V. Thus, V is understood as back-relating, and C major is connected to A major as its ♭III. This interpretation is supported by the fact that C major is prepared by the modal shift to A minor in m. 9. Study Example 28.11, which presents a tonal summary of "Der Flug der Zeit."

EXAMPLE 28.11

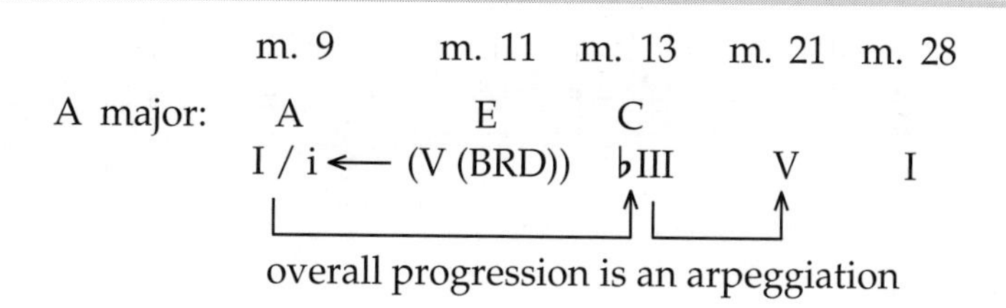

Modal Mixture and the German *Lied*

We have not yet explored text–music relations in any detail. Now we will look at songs written by two of the most important composers of the nineteenth century: Franz Schubert and Robert Schumann. We will see how modal mixture functions in larger contexts, and we will explore how composers control the interaction of music and poetry to project underlying poetic meaning in their vocal compositions.

In nineteenth-century Germany and Austria, the genre of song (*Lied*, pl. *Lieder*) became an important laboratory for experimentation. The idea was to develop musically expressive forces that would be capable of meeting the needs of communicating the emotionally rich poetry of the time. Modal mixture was often at the heart of these innovations. For example, the juxtaposition of mixture tones and harmonies against diatonic ones is almost always a sign of emotional conflicts, tensions, or contradictions. Consider the role of $\hat{6}$ (in both raised and lowered forms) in Schubert's song "Lachen und Weinen" ("Laughter and Tears") (Example 28.12). Note that each form of $\hat{6}$ is highlighted within its respective mode, but also listen to how $\flat\hat{6}$ occurs in the major tonic, where it is starkly juxtaposed with its diatonic counterpart.

The shift to the parallel minor prepares the listener for the substitution of $\flat\hat{6}$ for $\hat{6}$ at m. 25, where the new expressive tone underscores the melancholy text "and why I weep now." The specific placement of the F♭–E♭ sigh, where the upper note is a dissonant ninth over the bass, strongly highlights the word *weep*. The next development of the F♭ idea comes at m. 27, where $\flat\hat{6}$ then moves to the harmonic domain.

Example 28.12 shows where a ♭VI chord captures the protagonist's wonder at love's ability to arouse conflicting feelings of pain at twilight and joy at daybreak by means of a strange and wondrous-sounding chromatic harmony. In summary, the diatonic and mixed forms of $\hat{6}$ represent these two sides of his emotions. Both forms of $\hat{6}$ are neighbors to $\hat{5}$; that they share a common genesis in $\hat{5}$ may be analogous to the fact that love is the source of both his pain and his joy.

EXAMPLE 28.12 Schubert, "Lachen und Weinen" ("Laughter and Tears"), D. 777

DVD 1
CH 28
TRACK 7

Continued

9
La - chen und Wei - nen zu jeg - li-eher Stun - de ruht_ bei der lieb_ auf so
Laughter and tears at any hour rest on love
15
man - cher-lei Grun - de. Mor - gens lacht'_ich vor Lust;
in so many ways In the morning I laugh with joy
22
und wa-rum ich nun wei - ne bei des A - ben-des Schei_
and why I weep now In the evening glow,
decresc.
dim.
pp
♭VI
30
a tempo
ist mir selb'_nicht be-wusst, ist mir selb'_nicht be-wusst.
I myself do not know.
mf

EXAMPLE 28.13 Schubert, "Die liebe Farbe" ("The Beloved Color") and "Die böse Farbe" ("The Evil Color"), from *Die schöne Müllerin*

DVD 1 CH 28 TRACK 8

Continued

Schubert's song cycle *Die schöne Müllerin* furnishes another example of the role that mixture plays in projecting a poetic text. The drama begins with a roaming youth's discovery of a brook that leads him to a mill and ultimately to a young woman with whom he falls in love. As he begins to press his affections, he finds that she does not love him but rather someone else. What follows is the youth's downward spiral, characterized by anger, jealousy, bitterness, and finally, when nothing can quench his pain, suicide. In the second half of the cycle, the young miller points to the fact that his gifts of green objects, such as the sash from his guitar, delighted her, and her delight—and with it her love—was only intensified as nature, in all of its green beauty, resounded in him.

But with the entrance of the hunter, who symbolizes authority and physical power, the miller's idyllic world comes crashing down about him. The woman is immediately drawn to the hunter, who is dressed in traditional green. The color is now poisoned for the miller, and as he roams through the forest, nature's green only mocks him, providing a thorny reminder that his beloved's affections are directed toward someone else. In the songs "Die liebe Farbe" ("The Beloved Color"), and "Die böse Farbe" ("The Evil Color"), modal mixture plays crucial roles in projecting the powerful feelings aroused by the color green (Example 28.13). In fact, vacillations between the major and the minor modes through modal mixture become an important musical metaphor for Schubert in conveying the young miller's abrupt changes of mood.

Robert Schumann also used modal mixture to project poetic drama. In his song "Waldesgesprach" ("Forest Conversation"), from *Liederkreis*, op. 39 (Example 28.14), what appears at first as a simple chromatic tonicization is revealed through analysis to be an important dramatic moment. As the song gathers momentum, one sees how the motion to ♭VI reverberates throughout the song, foreshadowing and directing the surprising turn of events that follows. In familiarizing yourself with this work to begin analysis, start by reading the text carefully, and then listen to the song with the following questions in mind.

1. What musical techniques does Schumann employ in setting the scene of the forest?
2. How does Schumann differentiate the two characters musically?
3. What is the form of the song?
4. What is the relation of the chromatic tonicization to the overall key, and how does the composer secure the new key (i.e., is it prepared or unprepared)?

EXAMPLE 28.14 Schumann, "Waldesgesprach," from *Liederkreis*, op. 39, no. 3

21
Schmerz mein Herz ge - bro - chen ist, wohl irrt das Wald-horn
pain has broken my heart, the horn sounds
aug. 6th → V
27
her und hin, o flieh', o flieh'. du weisst nicht, wer ich bin.
here and there Oh flee! You do not know who I am
aug. 6th → V (as IV/E)
ii⌀ 6 5
V
33
So reich ge - schmückt ist Ross und Weib, so wun - der-schön, so wun-der-schön der
So richly covered are horse and woman, so beautiful her
39
ritard.
Im tempo
ritard.
Im tempo
jun - ge Leib; jetzt kenn' ich dich, Gott steh mir bei, du bist die He-xe Lo - re - lei!
young body Now I know who you are—God save me! You are the witch, Lorelei!

45
p
Du kennst mich wohl, du kennst mich wohl, von ho-hem
Indeed you know me—from rock's height
p
Ped.
51
Stein schaut still mein Schloss tief in den Rhein; es ist schon spät, es ist schon
my castle silently gazes deep into the Rhine. It is late, it is cold,
aug. 6th → "V" (P) aug. 6th →
58
f
ritard.
kalt, kennst nim-mer-mehr aus die-sem Wald, nim-mer-mehr, nim-mer-mehr aus die-sem
you will never leave this forest.
f
sf
"V"
64
ritard.
Wald.
fp

The story begins traditionally enough: A horseman comes across a beautiful woman deep in the forest, and, after informing her of the dangers of the woods and extolling her beauty, he offers to guide her home. The unsettling chromatic departure to C major to herald the woman's entrance is curious. This abrupt juxtaposition of E major and C major, coupled with the man's inability to complete the final word of his phrase, *heim* ("home"), in his key rather than in her foreign key, not only enhances the strangeness of this woman, cloaking her in tonal mystery, but also plants the seeds for his later demise.

The woman informs the man that she has been hurt in love before and by a hunter. Apparently, from her past unsuccessful encounters, she has now gained some sort of strength, intimating an otherworldly power, and warns the man that he does not know with whom (or what) he is dealing. She gives him one—and only one—chance to flee. Foolishly, the man stays and continues his flattery. But just as there was an abrupt shift in the first section, so too is there one here. As he realizes she is the infamous Lorelei, a demon in the form of a beautiful woman who lures men to their death, placid E major is thrown over by its parallel minor, the stark modal shift enhancing this terror-filled moment. In the final verse, the woman informs the man that he is ensnared and will never again leave the forest. He is hers.

The introduction to the song captures an out-of-doors feeling with its sprightly triple meter. The simple alternation of tonic and dominant in the bass lends a folklike quality to the song, while the syncopated upper voice of the left hand—with the emphasis on beat 2—creates a fifth drone and rhythmically suggests the feel of folk dances such as the mazurka and the polonaise. The lilting right hand also supports the rustic character of the introduction. In fact, the two-voice intervallic progression in the right hand with stepwise motion in the soprano (E–F♯–G♯) and leaps in the alto (G♯–B–E) is used by Schumann because of its connection with the sound of hunting horns. This trick of invoking the idea of the hunt has a double meaning in the song: Not only do we think immediately of the dense forest, its fauna, and the hunter's horn, but we are also reminded of another meaning of the hunt—that of seduction. By the end of the poem, however, we discover that our original expectations are shattered as the roles of hunter and prey are reversed.

The form of the song is dependent on the interaction of its two characters: A (he speaks) B (she speaks) A′ (he speaks) B′ (she speaks), coda. A number of musical features reinforce hearing the piece in this way: First, the piano interludes separate the sections; second, there is highly contrasting melodic, accompanimental, and tonal material in the B section. A motion from E major to ♭VI, C major, powerfully separates the A and A′ sections from the B section. This motion to ♭VI is quite surprising, yet, in retrospect, the listener realizes that it is prepared, in that the deceptive motion from V of E to ♭VI turns the flatted submediant into the tonic.

Analytical Payoff: The Dramatic Role of ♭VI

By virtue of its surprising arrival at m. 14 and its otherworldly sound, ♭VI obviously plays an important role in creating mystery and distance. Its appearance, like a rock thrown into a pond, creates musical ripples that extend to the outer reaches of the song. This strange new harmony seems to characterize the speech of the unknown woman in the piece's B section. But now let us turn to the moment in which he realizes who she is. The hunter begins his A′ section pretty much as his A began, seemingly oblivious to the woman's warnings. But at the moment of the modal shift to E minor, the man's tune moves in a new direction. His melody is strongly reminiscent of the Lorelei's tune, with her ascending line G-A-B-C recurring in his ascending motion. The effect is more than simple association. The witch's seductive powers have begun to permeate his being, and the decomposition of his melodic independence represents his loosening of will.

On the other side, the modal shift from E major to E minor, which places the Lorelei's key of C major within easy reach, further suggests that he is slipping into her tonal power. E minor is part of her tonal domain. It is diatonic to her C major, making his eventual abduction almost certain. The final step in his demise occurs in the Lorelei's closing strophe. Her musical texture returns unchanged, save for one crucial alteration: It is recast in his key, E major. His tonal foundation of E major, a metaphor for his physical being, has now been secured by Lorelei. Indeed, even his opening words, "Es ist schon spät, es ist schon kalt" ("it is late and cold"), are now possessed and sung ironically by the victor. It is clear that the man is ensnared in her forest arms, never to return home. That the postlude reprises the introduction—lilting, happy, and naive—shows that the forest returns to its placid and amiable state, but the Lorelei—like a Venus flytrap—awaits her next victim.

EXERCISE INTERLUDE

WRITING

28.7 Road Map

Following is a series of steps that should lead you away from the tonic and back to it. Complete the steps in the given order, and try to stay on the road.

Step 1. Tonicize D major.
Step 2. Tonicize ♭III using a mixture chord in D major as a pivot.
Step 3. Use a descending-fifth sequence in ♭III as a pivot to tonicize the dominant of ♭III.
Step 4. In the dominant of ♭III, use any sequence that will lead you to its diatonic mediant; tonicize it.
Step 5. In the mediant of ♭III's dominant, write a step-descent bass followed by a D2 (−5/+4) sequence that will lead you back to the original tonic, D major.

DVD 2
CH 28
TRACK 3

ANALYSIS

28.8

The given examples demonstrate various types of chromatic modulations. Analyze each.

A. Beethoven, Piano Sonata in C major, op. 2, no. 3, *Adagio*

B. Schumann, Symphony no. 2 in C major, op. 61. Scherzo; trio I

C. Beethoven, String Quartet, op. 18, no. 6, *Allegro con brio*

WORKBOOK
28.4–28.7

TERMS AND CONCEPTS

- chromatic third relations
- common-tone modulation
- *Lied, Lieder*
- prepared chromatic tonicization
- text–music relation
- unprepared chromatic tonicization

CHAPTER 29

The Neapolitan Chord (♭II)

Listen to the excerpt from one of Schubert's songs in Example 29.1. The music divides clearly into three phrases, which are marked by cadence type. As you follow along, try to keep a running tally of particularly striking chromatic harmonies. Where are they, and what contributes to their novel sound? A new chromatic harmony first appears in m. 8. This same chord then recurs in mm. 16 and 25. To understand the sound and function of a new chord, it often pays to dissect it into its individual voices (C–E♭–A♭). Let's begin with its bass, whose C ($\hat{4}$) functions like a standard pre-dominant that leads to V. The E♭ also functions as we'd expect it to, as a ♭$\hat{6}$ pulling down toward D ($\hat{5}$). A♭, however, is a chromatic pitch that substitutes for the diatonic A: Instead of creating a diatonic ii°_6 (C–E♭–**A**), Schubert has written a major triad that includes ♭$\hat{2}$ (**A**♭–C–E♭). A major triad built on ♭$\hat{2}$ is called the **Neapolitan** (♭II).

EXAMPLE 29.1 Schubert, "Der Müller und der Bach" ("The Miller and the Brook"), *Die schöne Müllerin*, D. 795, no. 19

DVD 1
CH 29
TRACK 1

Continued

Common Contexts for ♭II$_6$

The Neapolitan (named after a group of Baroque composers from the area of Naples who are said to have frequently used its sound) usually occurs in first inversion as the **Neapolitan sixth chord** (♭II$_6$). The Neapolitan is easy to write as long as you double stable chordal members, such as the bass ($\hat{4}$) (if necessary, you may double $\hat{6}$). Do not double ♭$\hat{2}$ in ♭II$_6$ (Example 29.2).

EXAMPLE 29.2

DVD 1 CH 29 TRACK 2

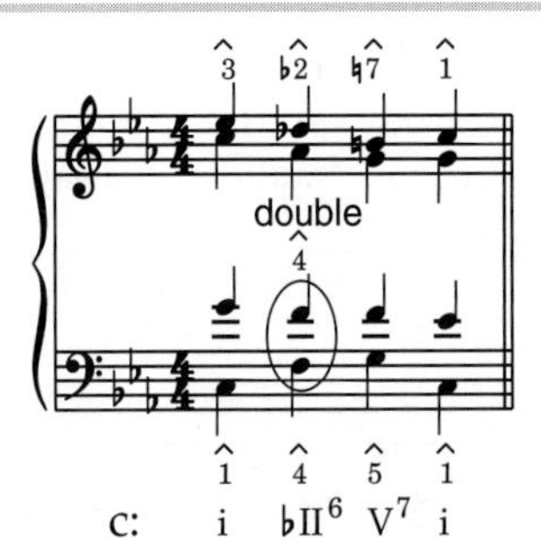

The Neapolitan sixth chord functions as a pre-dominant that pulls strongly toward V. It occurs more often in minor-mode pieces than in major-mode pieces. When it occurs in the major mode, it is as a product of modal mixture. In these cases, lower both $\hat{2}$ and $\hat{6}$ (see Example 29.3B). Avoid the augmented second that can occur between $\hat{3}$ and ♭$\hat{2}$ in a major mode by using the soprano $\hat{1}$–♭$\hat{2}$ (Example 29.3B). The ♭II$_6$ usually appears at cadences, but it can be used with EPMs (Example 29.3C).

EXAMPLE 29.3

DVD 1
CH 29
TRACK 3

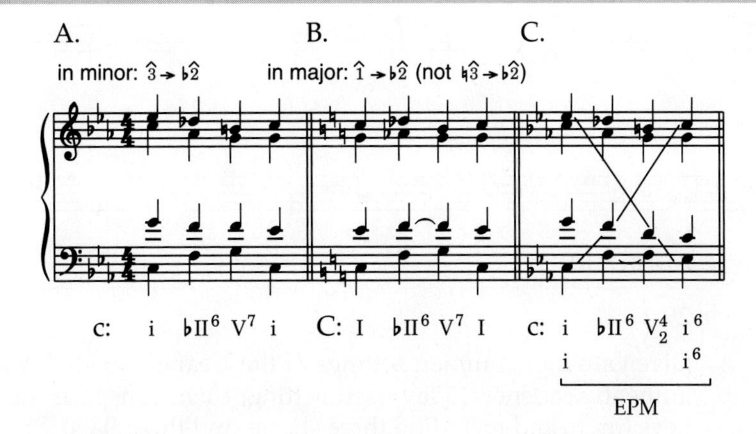

♭II⁶–V progressions typically have ♭2̂–7̂ in the soprano. The diminished third between ♭2̂ and 7̂ is perfectly acceptable, although it is possible to fill it with 1̂ that will function as a passing tone. There are two common ways to harmonize the passing 1̂, by using either a cadential six-four chord or an applied diminished-seventh chord, as shown in Example 29.4.

EXAMPLE 29.4

DVD 1
CH 29
TRACK 4

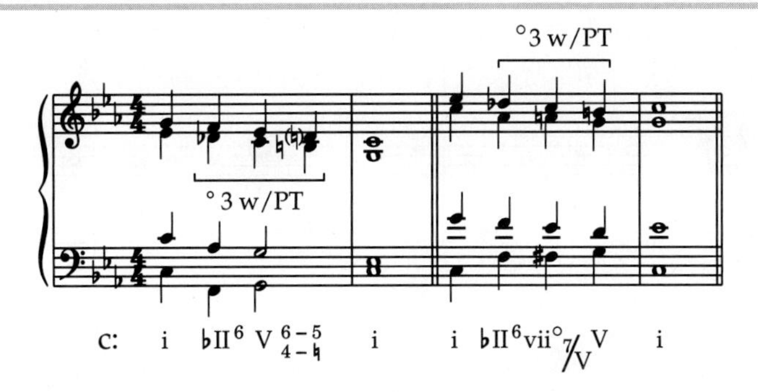

EXERCISE INTERLUDE

PERFORMING

29.1

The following arpeggiations create progressions that incorporate the Neapolitan sixth chord. Sing them and/or play them on an instrument. Listen to how often harmonies change; then analyze the progressions with roman numerals. Next, transpose the arpeggiations to other minor keys.

Continued

KEYBOARD

29.2

Given are four common settings of the Neapolitan sixth chord within perfect authentic cadences. Play each setting; then transpose the settings to minor keys (up to and including three sharps and three flats).

A. B.

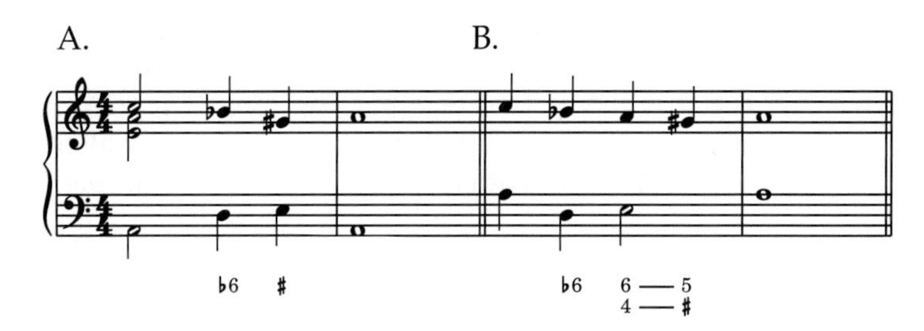

C. D.

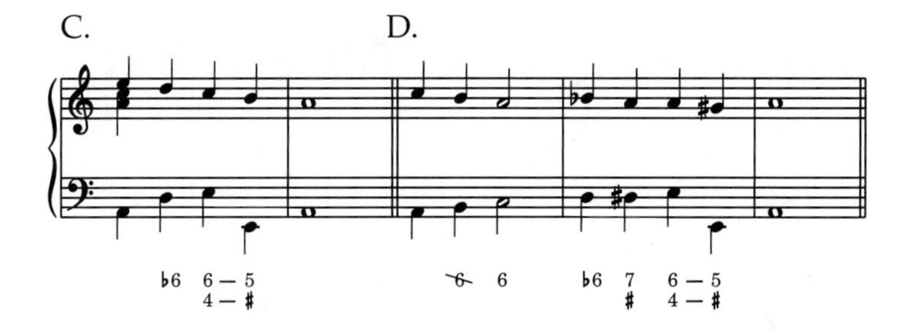

LISTENING

DVD 2
CH 29
TRACK 1

29.3 Aural Comparison of ii, ii$_6$, ii°$_6$, and ♭II$_6$

Listen to each of the following phrases, which have the following shape:

1. Either a single tonic chord or a short tonic expansion (no EPMs)
2. One of the following pre-dominant chords: ii, ii$_6$, ii°$_6$, ♭II$_6$
3. A perfect authentic cadence

Determine which pre-dominant chord occurs in each phrase; write the roman numeral of each pre-dominant chord on a sheet of paper. *Hint:* Each form of the supertonic is distinct:

♭II = major
ii (in major keys) = minor
ii°$_6$ (in minor keys) = diminished

DVD 2
CH 29
TRACK 2

29.4

This exercise is identical to the previous one, except that:

1. The possible pre-dominant chords also include iv (in minor keys).
2. The possible cadences are PACs and IACs.

DVD 2
CH 29
TRACK 3

29.5

The Neapolitan appears within larger musical contexts in the following examples. Listen to each example, and provide roman numerals in the blanks below the notes.

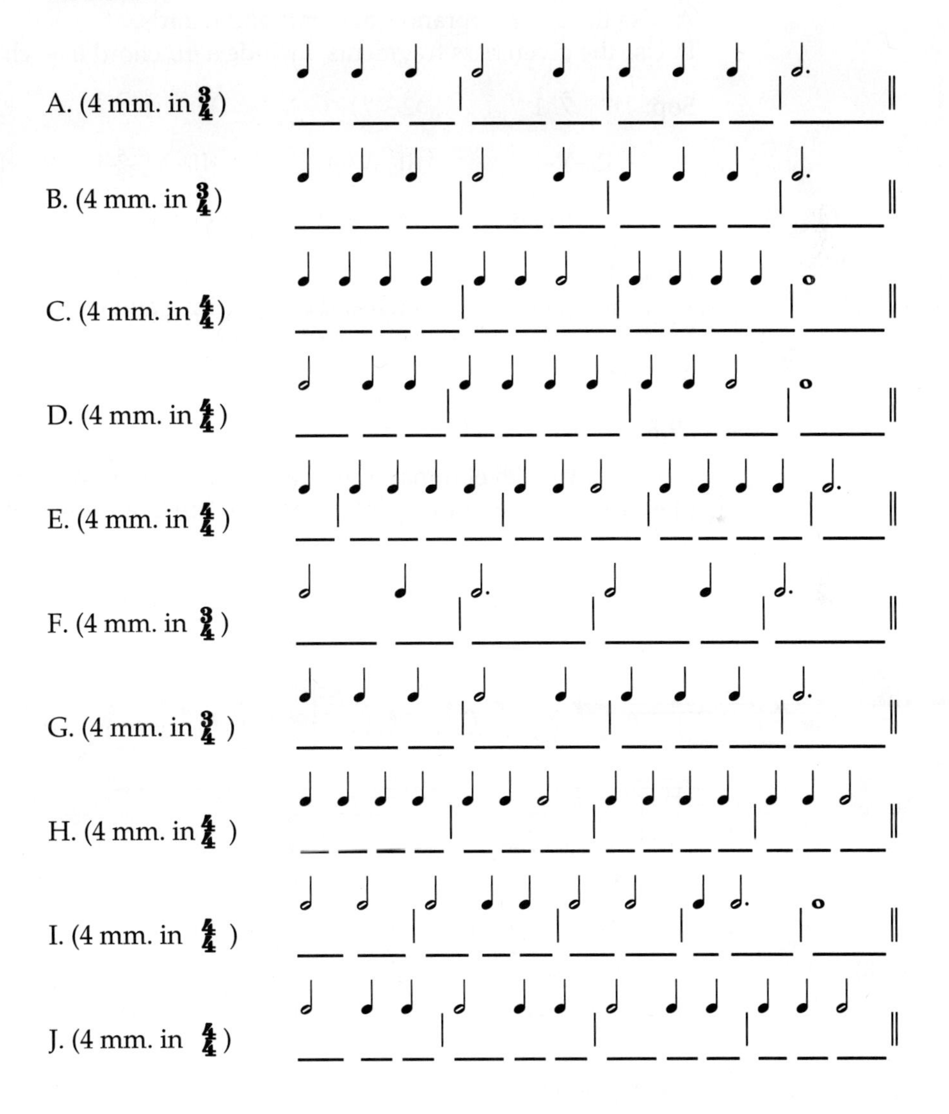

DVD 2
CH 29
TRACK 4

29.6

Listen to the following four examples, performed with a figurated texture. Provide roman numerals for each of the examples.

A. $\frac{4}{4}$ ______ ______ | ______ ______ | ______ ______ | ______ ______
B. $\frac{6}{8}$ ______ ______ | ______ ______ | ______ ______ | ______ ______
C. $\frac{3}{4}$ ______ ______ | ______ ______ | ______ ______ | ______ ______
D. $\frac{4}{4}$ ______ ______ | ______ ______ | ______ ______ | ______ ______

WRITING

29.7

On a separate sheet of manuscript paper, set the following progressions in the specified minor keys and in four voices.
A. Use the given soprano fragments and chords.
B. Use the given bass fragments; include a ♭II$_6$ chord in each progression.

Sop:	♭2̂ 7̂ 1̂	♭2̂ 7̂ 1̂	♭2̂ 1̂ 7̂ 1̂	♭2̂ 1̂ 7̂ 1̂
	♭II$_6$–V–i	♭II$_6$–V$_7$–i	♭II$_6$–V$^{6-5}_{4-3}$–i	♭II$_6$–vii°$_7$/V–V–i
	in: d, a, f♯	in: c, e, c♯	in: f, g, d	in: d, b, a
Bass:	1̂ 4̂ 5̂ 1̂ in: c and e	3̂ 4̂ 5̂ 1̂ in: b and d	3̂ 4̂ ♯4̂ 5̂ 1̂ in: g and b♭	

WORKBOOK
29.1–29.3

ANALYSIS

29.8

Provide a two-level roman numeral analysis for each of the following examples. To facilitate your chordal analysis, circle all tones of figuration in the melody.

Sample: Beethoven, Piano Sonata no. 14 in C♯ minor ("Moonlight"), op. 27, no. 2, *Adagio*

A. Beethoven, Bagatelle, op. 119, no. 9
Make a formal diagram.

Continued

B. Chopin, Mazurka in F minor, op. 63, no. 2, BI 162

C. Chopin, Mazurka in C♯ minor, op. 30, no. 4, BI 105

Include in your discussion the underlying harmonic progression in the excerpt.

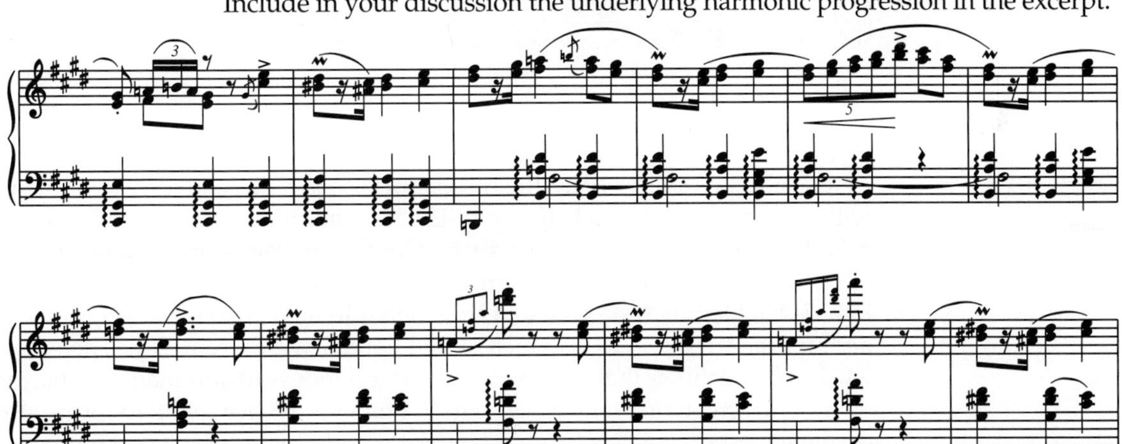

D. Rachmaninoff, Vocalise

What type of bass line does Rachmaninoff use? What keys are implied in m. 5?

Continued

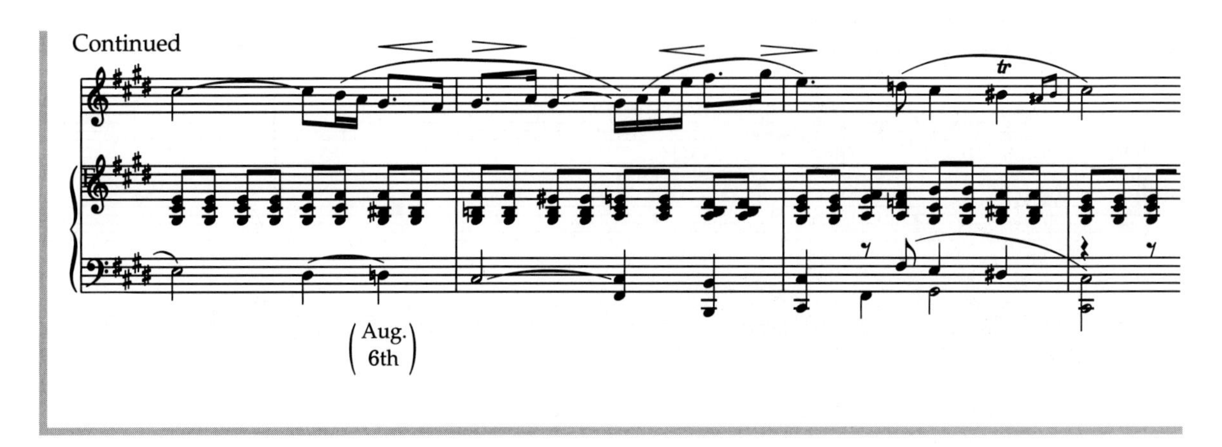

Expanding ♭II

Although the Neapolitan often occurs as a single ♭II6 chord, it is possible to prolong the Neapolitan within a phrase. For example, you can prolong the Neapolitan with a chordal leap in the bass (Example 29.5).

EXAMPLE 29.5

DVD 1
CH 29
TRACK 5

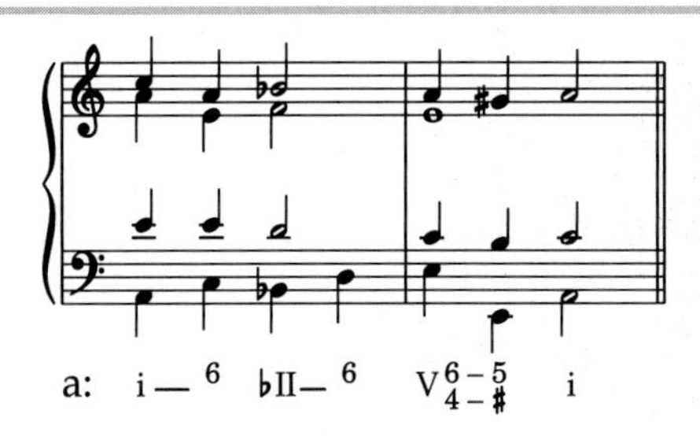

It is also possible to place the first subphrase of a piece in tonic and follow it with one transposed up a half step to ♭II. This particular procedure is common in middle-period Beethoven pieces, such as his String Quartet in E minor (Example 29.6). The root-position Neapolitan of mm. 6–7 occurs when the opening tune of mm. 3–4 is literally restated a half step higher in m. 6. Melodically, this presents an important motive, B–C, which is highlighted within mm. 3–6. The second-level analysis shows that the pre-dominant still moves to dominant function and on to tonic, creating a large-scale i–♭II–V–i motion. Notice that two forms of the dominant appear: vii°$_7$ is followed by V. The only two pitch classes involved in this subtle shift are C ($\hat{6}$) and B ($\hat{5}$), which can be heard as a melodic summary of the immediately preceding motion from tonic to the Neapolitan. Beethoven has thus returned the upper-neighbor C to B, its point of origin.

EXAMPLE 29.6 Beethoven, String Quartet no. 8 in E minor, op. 59, no. 2, *Allegro*

DVD 1
CH 29
TRACK 6

It is also possible to prolong ♭II by tonicization. One of the most common means of tonicizing the Neapolitan is to precede it with its dominant (VI in minor or ♭VI in major). (See Example 29.7.)

EXAMPLE 29.7

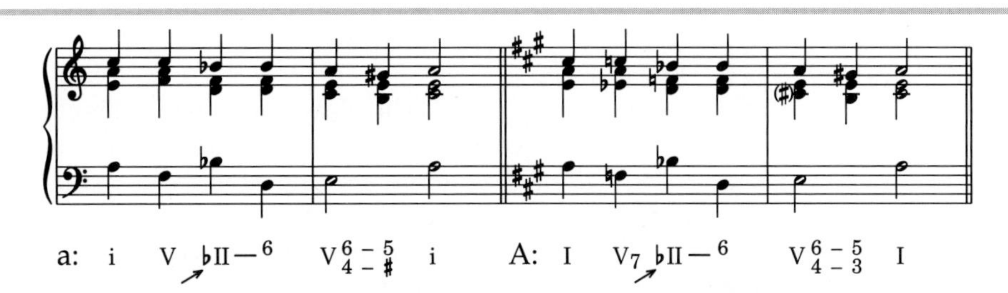

Extended tonicizations are common. No matter how extended the Neapolitan becomes, however, it almost always functions as a pre-dominant within the overall progression. Consider the first-level analysis of Example

29.8, which results in a confusing string of roman numerals. In order to make the roman numerals more meaningful in light of the second-level analysis, a bracket identifies the extended tonicization of the Neapolitan.

EXAMPLE 29.8

EXAMPLE 29.9 Chopin, Nocturne in B♭ minor, op. 9, no. 1

DVD 1 CH 29 TRACK 7

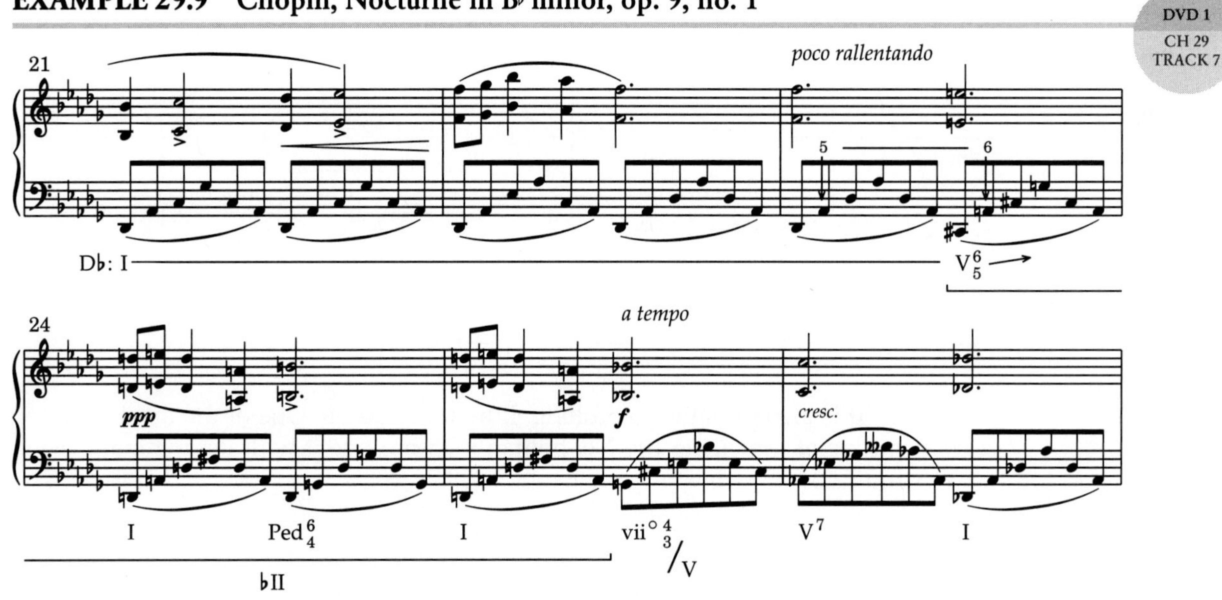

Listen to Example 29.9. The Neapolitan in m. 24 is contrapuntally prepared in the previous measure by the 5–6 motion from I; over the bass D♭/C♯ A♭ moves to A (the enharmonic spelling of $\flat\hat{6}$, B𝄫), creating a V^6_5/♭II. When the Neapolitan arrives at the downbeat of m. 24, Chopin spells it enharmonically as D major rather than as E𝄫 major. Chopin's *ppp* dynamic marking at this moment helps the performer interpret this special harmonic coloration. The Neapolitan's bass motion up to V is accomplished by the $vii^{\circ 4}_{3}$/V chord in m. 25; this chord is pivotal, for it sounds like a mixture coloring of the right-hand B natural in m. 24, yet the $vii^{\circ 4}_{3}$/V also leads to V_7 (A♭) as an applied chord.

The Neapolitan in Sequences

Look again at Example 29.9 and notice that chords in m. 23, leading to the Neapolitan chord in m. 24, are identical to the way A2 (−3/+4) applied-chord sequences begin. Example 29.10A continues Chopin's ascent, using an A2 (−3/+4) sequence with applied chords that continues all the way to V. The use of ♭II in the A2 (−3/+4) sequence is much more common in minor-mode works. A further bonus of incorporating the Neapolitan in sequences is that it allows for root-position ♭2 in minor pieces. Remember, when ii° is diatonic, it cannot participate in applied sequences, because dissonant triads cannot be preceded by an applied chord.

EXAMPLE 29.10

A.

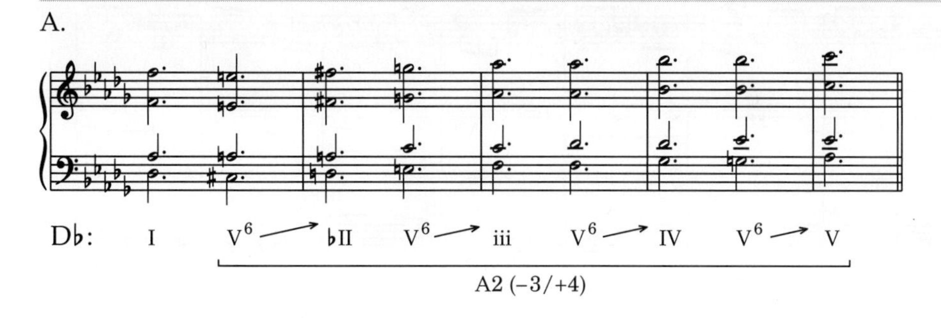

B.

The Neapolitan as a Pivot Chord

The Neapolitan is an effective pivot chord when modulating to diatonic as well as chromatic keys. Example 29.11 contains two statements of a D♭ sonority. The D♭ chord in m. 9 functions typically as a $♭II_6$, leading to V. But when it returns in m. 23, it functions as a pivot that precipitates the modulation to A♭.

EXAMPLE 29.11 Schubert, String Quartet in C minor ("Quartettsatz"), D. 703

DVD 1 CH 29 TRACK 8

Allegro assai

Violino I pp

Violino II pp

Viola

Violoncello

c:

Continued

EXERCISE INTERLUDE

KEYBOARD

29.9

Given are three common contexts in which the Neapolitan is expanded. Be able to describe each context. Play in four-voice keyboard style; then transpose each to one other key of your choice.

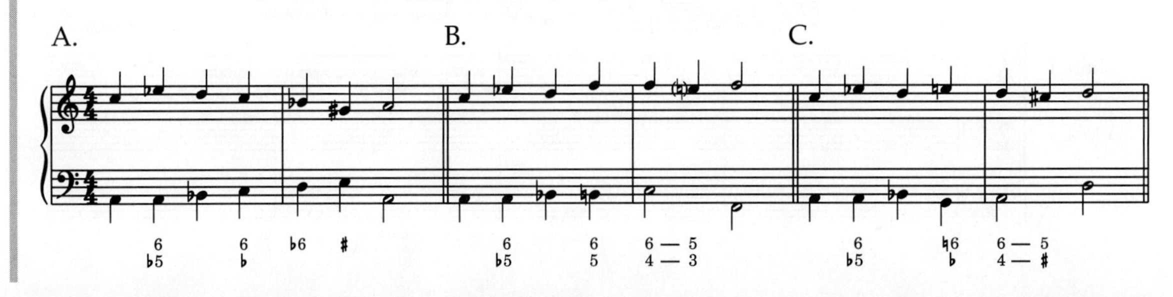

DVD 2
CH 29
TRACK 6

ANALYSIS

29.10

The following excerpts illustrate expanded ♭II. Provide a two-level analysis for each excerpt and a short paragraph that summarizes your analysis.
Sample analysis: Chopin, Nocturne in C minor, op. 48, No. 1, BI 142

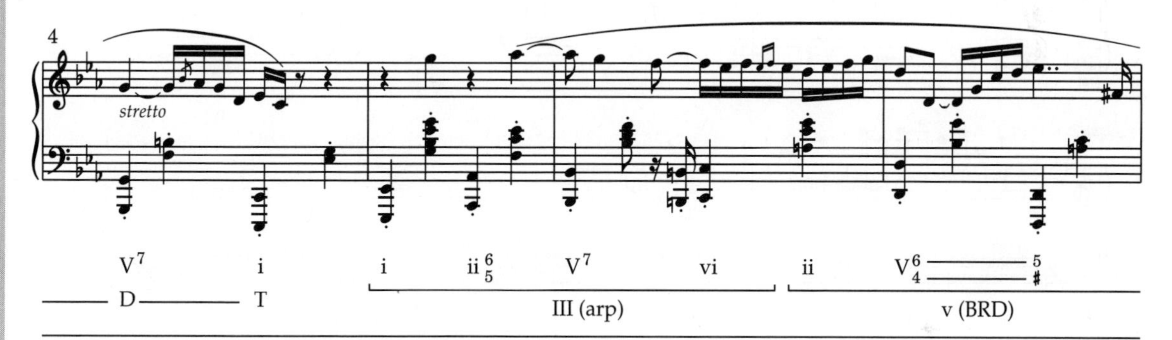

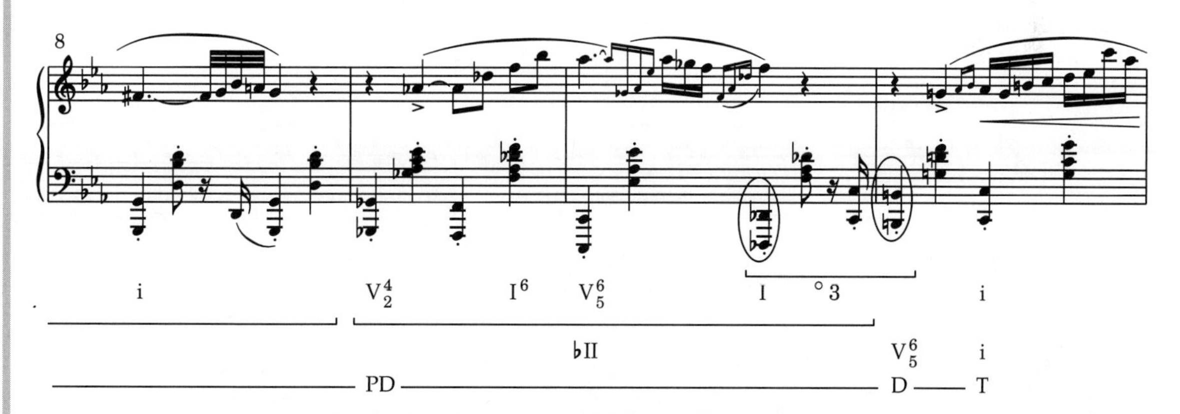

Sample paragraph: Chopin's C-minor Nocturne illustrates an extensive tonicization not only of ♭II, but also of several diatonic harmonies. The nocturne opens with a descending-bass arpeggiation (C–A♭–F) that returns to tonic, followed by a balancing ascending arpeggiation (C–E♭–G), each member of which is tonicized. The descent from G to G♭ begins the Neapolitan's expansion (m. 9). The G♭ in m. 9 is harmonized as V^4_2 of ♭II, and it becomes a chromatic passing tone that connects G and the following F (m. 9), which is harmonized as ♭II_6. Root-position ♭II follows its V^6_5 chord in m. 10, ending the tonicization of ♭II. The dominant (G) is secured in precisely the same way that ♭II was: through chromatic passing tones that lead to V_6 (D♭–C–B♮). Notice that this bass motion ♭ $\hat{2}$ to $\hat{7}$ is what usually takes place in the soprano when ♭II_6 moves to V.

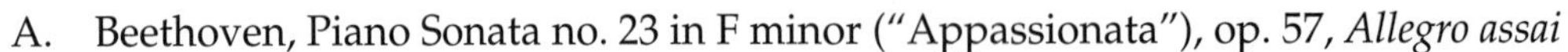

A. Beethoven, Piano Sonata no. 23 in F minor ("Appassionata"), op. 57, *Allegro assai*

B. Rachmaninoff, Prelude in G♯ minor, op. 32, no. 12
Be aware of the bass' D natural and the chord of which it is part in m. 8.

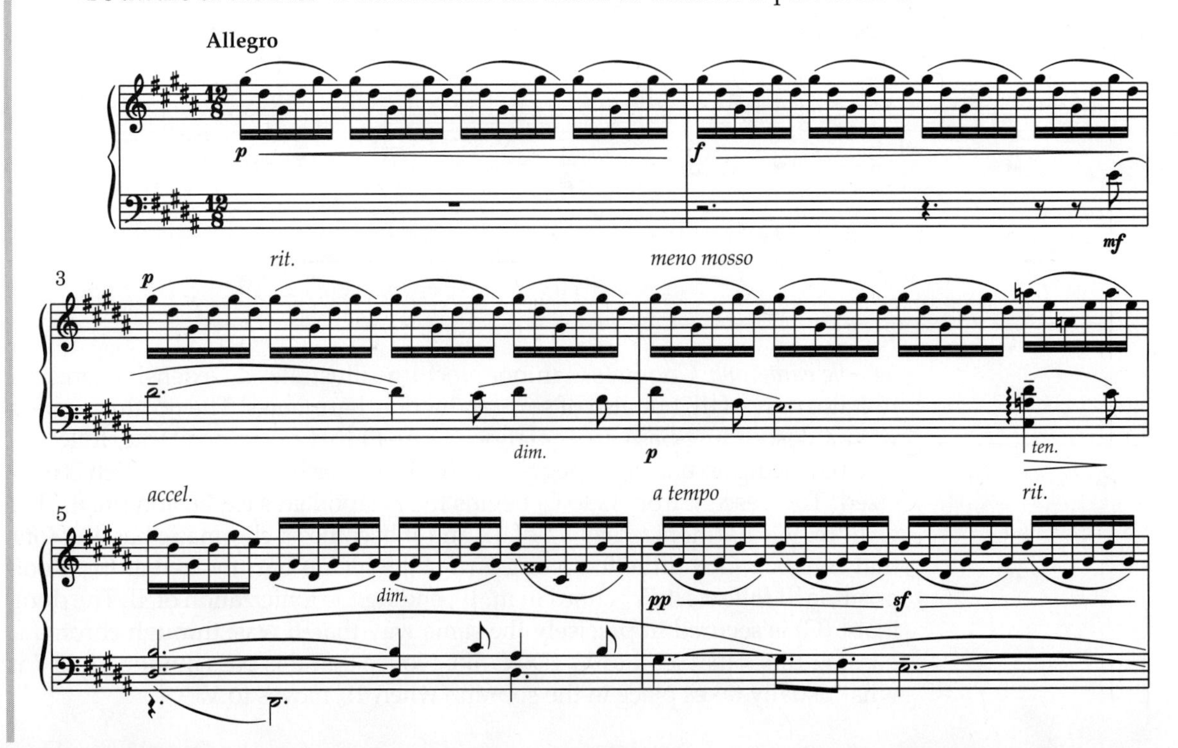

Continued

meno mosso
accel.
7
p
C. Beethoven, Rondo in C major, op. 51, no. 1
ri – tar – dan – do
104
pp
107
110
legato
112
cresc.
114
f
116
sfp

INSTRUMENTAL APPLICATION: EMBELLISHMENT AND REDUCTION

29.11 Embellishment

This exercise can be performed as follows: solo keyboard player, solo melodic instrumentalist, two instrumentalists (one plays the bass, the other adds the upper voices). Based on harmonic implications of the outer voices, add inner voices to the unfigured bass in the following manner:

a. Arpeggiate from the bottom to the top of the chord (i.e., bass, tenor, alto, and soprano).
b. Make sure the voice leading works from chord to chord (i.e., consider what you play to be linear versions of a homophonic progression).
c. Consider the arpeggiations to unfold in eighth notes, such that the given quarter notes now become half notes (i.e., four eighth notes to a half note).
d. In a freer texture, add passing tones and chordal leaps between alto and soprano voices, maintaining the half-note harmonic rhythm.

Follow this procedure:

1. This example moves through several keys, each of which is defined by a cadence that includes the Neapolitan harmony. Find cadences; then work from the beginning of phrases to understand the tonal motions within each phrase.
2. Intervals and accidentals are very helpful in determining harmonies. For example:

a. A perfect fifth usually indicates a root-position harmony, a sixth usually indicates a first-inversion harmony. A diminished fifth contracts and usually moves to a root-position triad. An augmented fourth expands and usually moves to a first-inversion triad.
b. Chromatically raised pitches indicate applied chords (they represent the temporary leading tone).

29.12 Reduction

The following examples contain the Neapolitan harmony. Reduce the texture by verticalizing it into four-voices. Play each reduction in the key in which it is written; then transpose to one other key of your choice. Instrumentalists who play single-line instruments will simply arpeggiate each of the harmonies (using good voice leading).

A. Schubert, Violin Sonata in A minor ("Arpeggione"), D. 821, *Allegro moderato*

B. Vivaldi, Concerto in E minor, F. XI, no. 43

TERMS AND CONCEPTS

- Neapolitan sixth chord (♭II_6)

CHAPTER 30

The Augmented Sixth Chord

The two excerpts in Example 30.1 are from different style periods, yet they share several features. In terms of form and harmony, both divide into two subphrases and close with strong half cadences. Further, the pre-dominant harmony in both examples is the same: an altered iv_6 chord. Indeed, we hear not a Phrygian cadence (iv_6–V), but rather some chromatic version, where the diatonic *major* sixth above the bass is raised a half step to create the strongly directed interval of the *augmented* sixth. The new half-step ascent ($\sharp\hat{4}$–$\hat{5}$) mirrors the bass's half-step descent ($\hat{6}$–$\hat{5}$). We refer to such chromatic pre-dominants as **augmented sixth chords** because of the characteristic interval between the bass $\hat{6}$ and the upper-voice $\sharp\hat{4}$. Listen to both excerpts in Example 30.1, noting the striking sound of the augmented sixth chords.

EXAMPLE 30.1

DVD 1
CH 30
TRACK 1

A. Schubert, Waltz in G minor, *Die letzte Waltze*, op. 127, no. 12, D. 146

B. Handel, "Since by Man Came Death," *Messiah*, HWV 56

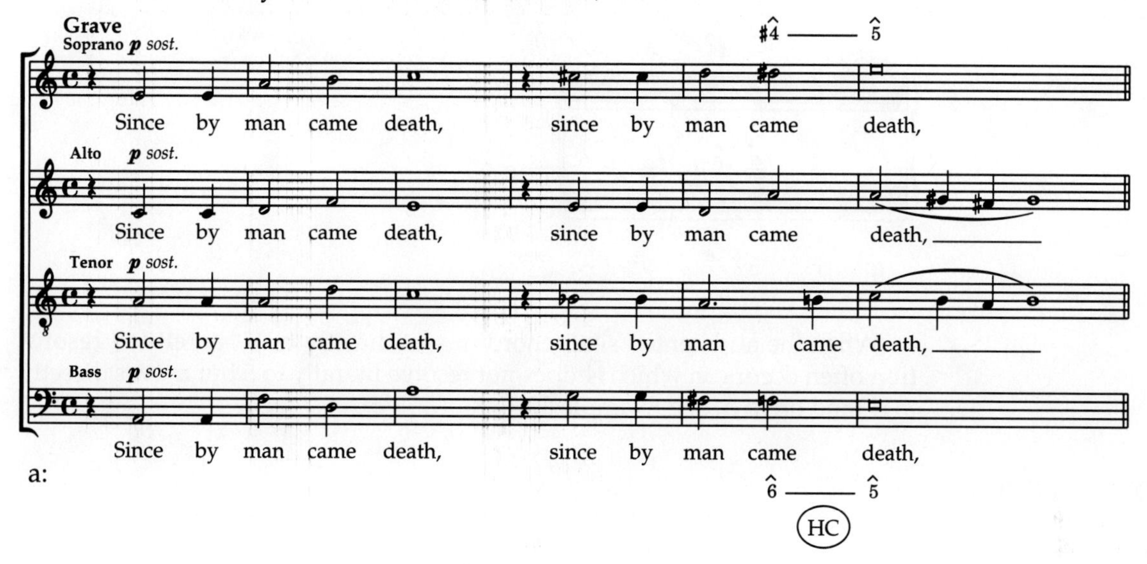

Example 30.2 demonstrates the derivation of the augmented sixth chord from the Phrygian cadence. Example 30.2A represents a traditional Phrygian cadence. In Example 30.2B, the chromatic F♯ fills the space between F and G, and the passing motion creates an interval of an augmented sixth. Finally, Example 30.2C shows the augmented sixth chord as a harmonic entity, with no consonant preparation.

EXAMPLE 30.2

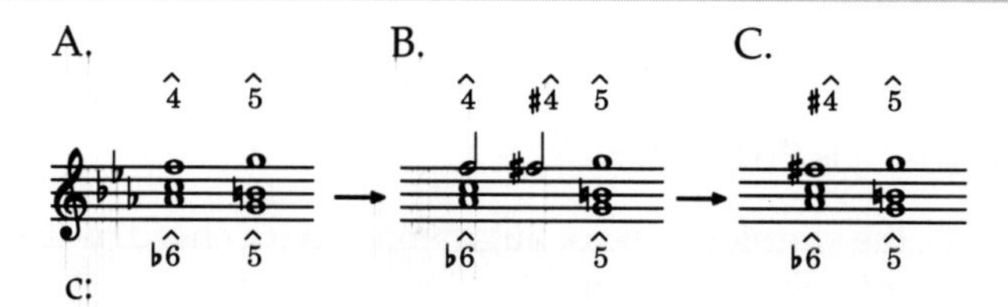

General Features

Like most of the other chromatic chords we have studied (such as the Neapolitan), the augmented sixth chord functions primarily as a pre-dominant harmony. In addition, it occurs more frequently in minor-mode pieces (again like the Neapolitan), where its characteristic ♭6̂–5̂ bass motion is diatonic. Because the augmented sixth chord derives from the iv_6 chord, it moves to V in like manner. Example 30.3 illustrates the characteristic voice leading: The bass ♭6̂ falls by half step to 5̂; ♯4̂—the augmented sixth above the bass, often found in the soprano—ascends by half step to 5̂. Notice that the remaining inner voices double 1̂ (the third above the bass) and move in contrary motion, the exact voice leading used in the Phrygian cadence.

EXAMPLE 30.3

When the augmented sixth chord moves directly to V_7, an **elided resolution** often occurs, in which $\sharp\hat{4}$ does not resolve literally to $\hat{5}$ but moves directly to $\natural\hat{4}$ (and on to $\hat{3}$) See Example 30.4.

EXAMPLE 30.4

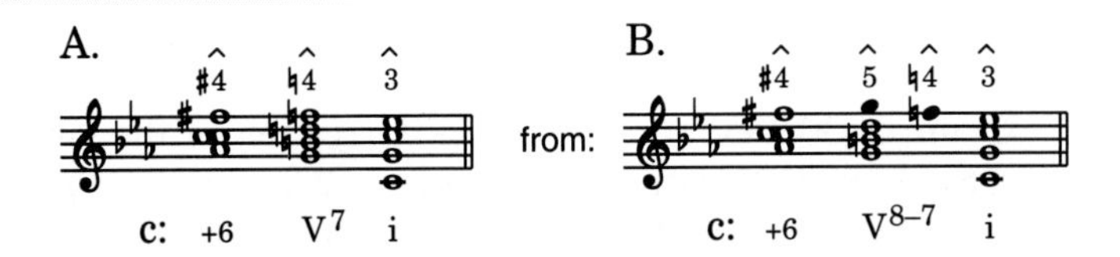

Types of Augmented Sixth Chords

The basic components of the augmented sixth chord are:

$\hat{6}$ in the bass

$\sharp\hat{4}$ in an upper voice (often the soprano)

$\hat{1}$, which is doubled

This, the simplest type of augmented sixth chord, is the **Italian augmented sixth chord** (labeled **It**$_6$), and it is shown in Example 30.5A. The two common variations of this sonority substitute a different pitch for one of the doubled pitches ($\hat{1}$). As Example 30.5 shows, the circled notes (in this case, located in the alto voice) indicate the subtle differences in construction among the three types of augmented sixth chords. Note the absence of roman numerals to describe these contrapuntal sonorities. It is common to represent them using figured bass, preceded by a long-standing tradition of names drawn from European regional geography.

The **German augmented sixth chord** (**Ger**$^6_5$), shown in Example 30.5B, is different from the Italian, in that it substitutes a perfect fifth above the bass ($\hat{3}$) for one of the doubled pitches on $\hat{1}$. The figured bass is $^6_5$.

The **French augmented sixth chord** (**Fr**$^4_3$), shown in Example 30.5C, contains an augmented fourth ($\hat{2}$) and is reflected in the figured bass: $^4_3$

EXAMPLE 30.5

Writing Augmented Sixth Chords: Approach and Resolution

Example 30.5 also illustrates how augmented sixth chords of all varieties can be approached from the tonic and resolved to the dominant. Augmented sixth chords can be approached easily from the tonic by step and common tone, and—given the number of tendency tones—their resolution is for the most part predetermined. For example, $\hat{6}$ in the bass resolves to $\hat{5}$, and $\sharp\hat{4}$ resolves up to $\hat{5}$ (unless, as we saw in Example 30.4, resolution to V_7 is elided). Notice that the Ger^6_5 (in Example 30.5B) should move first to a cadential $^6_4$ in order to offset the parallel fifths that would occur with a direct move to V. Note that in the French augmented sixth, illustrated in Example 30.5C, $\hat{2}$ is held as a common tone with V, where it becomes the chordal fifth of V.

Since both the Ger^6_5 and Fr^4_3 contain four different pitches, there is no concern for doublings in four voices. Given that the It_6 contains only three distinct pitch classes, always double the third above the bass ($\hat{1}$).

Although augmented sixth chords tend to occur more often in the minor mode, they occasionally occur in the major mode. Be aware that at least one additional chromatic alteration is necessary for augmented sixth chords to appear in major: The bass must be lowered to $\flat\hat{6}$. This holds for all three species of augmented sixth chords. In the special case of the Ger$^6_5$, $\hat{3}$ must also be lowered (see Example 30.5D). Finally, when a German $^6_5$ occurs in the major mode and it leads to a cadential $^6_4$ with a *major* sixth, composers will often notate this chromatic ascent (from $\flat\hat{3}$ to raised $\hat{3}$) using the enharmonic equivalent $\sharp\hat{2}$, which visually leads more effectively up to $\hat{3}$. See Example 30.5E. Given that the fourth above the bass is doubly augmented, this unfortunate-looking chord is referred to as the *doubly augmented sixth chord* or sometimes as the *Swiss* augmented sixth chord.

Hearing Augmented Sixth Chords

The French augmented sixth chord is the easiest to identify because of its distinctive sound. Not only do its two tritones create an exotic effect, but they also often create a major-second clash in the inner pitches. It is more difficult to distinguish the Italian from the German augmented sixth chord because they sound so similar. A starting point is to recognize that the It^6 is the simplest of the three chords and thus will sound less full than the others; the Ger$^6_5$ contains four distinct pitches and sounds like a complete dominant seventh chord (the significance of which we will take up soon). The resolution of the It^6 and Ger$^6_5$ chords will usually betray their nationality: The Italian sixth moves directly to V, but the Ger$^6_5$ usually resolves first to a cadential six-four chord (refer back to Example 30.5).

EXERCISE INTERLUDE

PERFORMING

30.1 Singing and Playing

Using solfège or scale degrees, sing or play on your instrument the following progressions, which incorporate the augmented sixth chord. Analyze the harmonic progressions in each example. The harmonic rhythm is generally one chord per measure. Part A has been analyzed for you. If you play the exercises on your instrument, transpose to one other key of your choice.

ANALYZING

30.2 Identification

Determine the key in which each of the augmented sixth chords would function; then identify the type of augmented sixth chord that is notated.

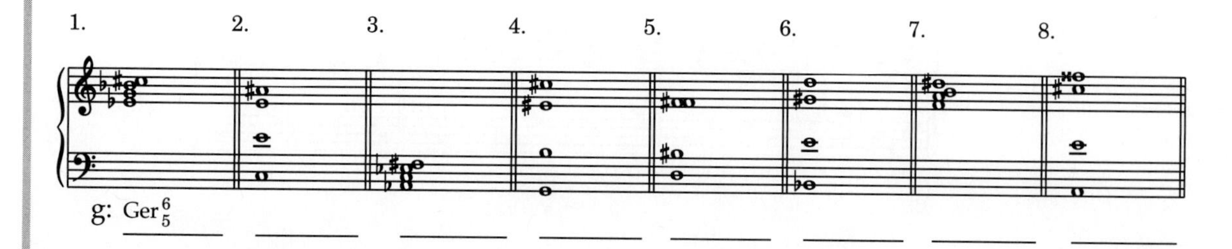

WRITING

30.3

A. For each given augmented sixth interval, label the minor key in which it would function as a pre-dominant and provide a key signature. Then add the missing chordal members to complete the sonorities as specified (the first one is completed for you).

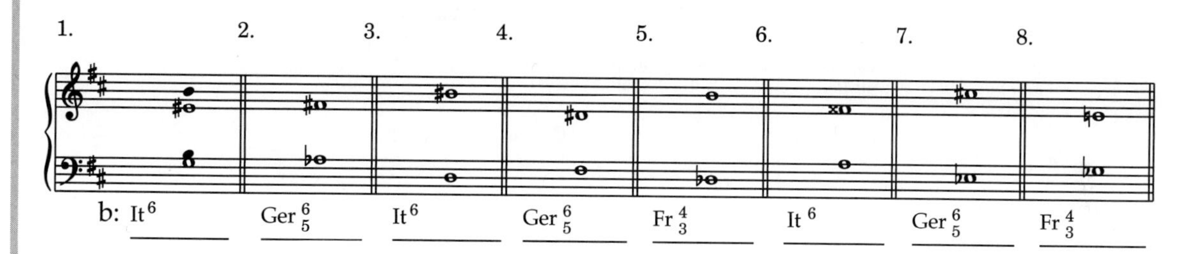

B. Assuming the bass is correct, determine the key and the type of augmented sixth chord that is notated, and correct any spelling errors.

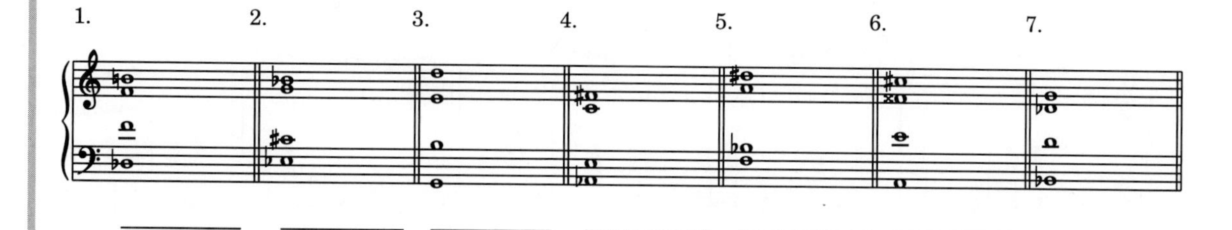

LISTENING

30.4 Aural Detection of Augmented Sixth Chords

These progressions may or may not use the augmented sixth chord as a predominant. Mark "Y" (yes) or "N" (no), depending on whether or not you hear an augmented sixth.

A. ___ B. ___ C. ___ D. ___ E. ___ F. ___ G. ___ H. ___

PLAYING

30.5 Augmented Sixth Chord Models

Play the four-voice augmented sixth chord models as written and in minor and major keys up to and including two sharps and two flats.

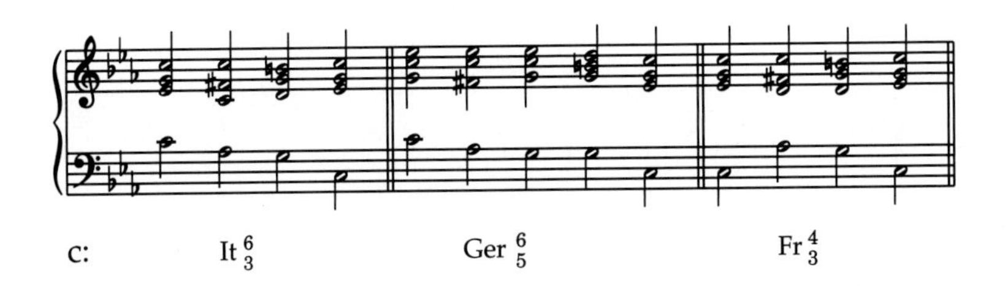

ANALYZING

DVD 2 CH 30 TRACK 2

30.6

Listen to and then provide a harmonic analysis for the following examples, which contain augmented sixth chords.

A. Mozart, "Wer ein Liebchen," from *Abduction from the Seraglio*

B. Verdi, "Stride la vampa," from *Il trovatore*, no. 8

(♭)VI and the Augmented Sixth Chord

Chords other than the tonic may approach an augmented sixth chord. One of the most important of these chords is the submediant. In either case, (♭)VI usually moves to a pre-dominant. Often, however, composers want to lead ♭VI directly to V in order to take advantage of the dramatic half-step motion (♭)$\hat{6}$–$\hat{5}$ in the bass. Since leading (♭)VI directly to V results in voice-leading problems of octaves and fifths, composers regularly convert (♭)VI into a German augmented sixth chord, because the two chords share three of four scale degrees. See this procedure in the second and third chords of Example 30.6.

EXAMPLE 30.6

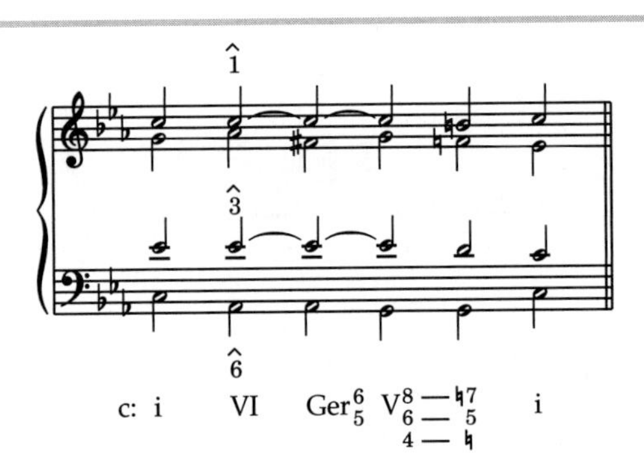

A second instance of this process is given in Example 30.7, in which a tonicized ♭VI (mm. 10–12) is converted to—and destabilized by—a Ger$^6_5$ (m. 13), which can then move smoothly to V (m. 14).

EXAMPLE 30.7 Schubert, Waltz in C major, *Valses sentimentales*, D. 779, no. 16

DVD 1 CH 30 TRACK 2

Augmented Sixth Chords as Part of PD Expansions

Augmented sixth chords frequently combine with other pre-dominant harmonies to expand the pre-dominant function; we have already seen this in Example 30.2. Given that two of its voices are so goal-directed toward $\hat{5}$, the augmented sixth chord is usually the last event before the dominant, following either iv$_{(6)}$ or VI. In Example 30.8 Beethoven drives home the arrival in B♭ minor by moving from iv$_6$ to a Ger$^6_5$ in mm. 129–30 (the vii$^{o6}_5$ appears as a neighb♭: i). The Ger$^6_5$–V motion is then reiterated seven times in the following nine measures and highlighted by the *sf* marking.

EXAMPLE 30.8 Beethoven, Piano Sonata no. 13 in E♭ major, op. 27, no. 1, *Allegro vivace*

Augmented sixth chords often appear in chromaticized bass descents as the final step before the dominant (Example 30.9).

EXAMPLE 30.9

We have already learned that one of the most important techniques for expanding the PD is to move from iv through a passing $^6_4$ chord to iv$_6$, as in Example 30.10A. It is also common for iv to move to a different PD harmony, such as the ii$^{ø6}_5$ in Example 30.10B. In both cases, the expansion of the PD involves a prominent voice exchange between the bass and one of the upper voices.

EXAMPLE 30.10

DVD 1
CH 30
TRACK 5

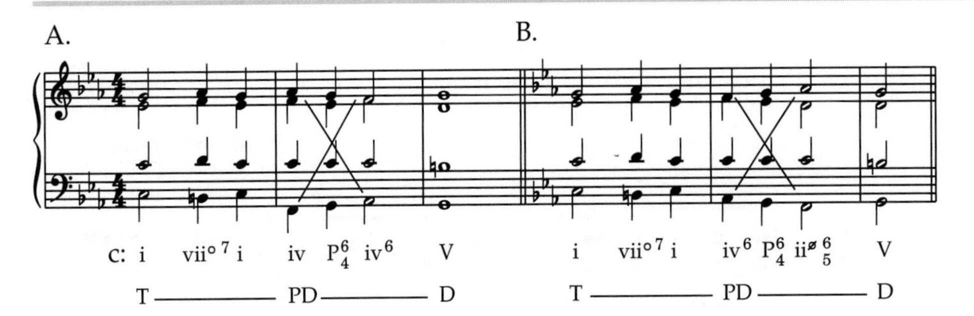

Since the augmented sixth chord is structured similarly to iv_6, it often participates as the final chord in PD expansions of the type shown in Example 30.10. However, when chromatic augmented sixth chords occur with other diatonic pre-dominants (such as iv and ii_6), the resulting voice exchange is not exact. This can be seen in m. 1 of Example 30.11A, in which the F and A♭ of the iv chord swap to become the A♭ and F♯ of the It_6 chord. This special type of swapping cross relations is called a **chromatic voice exchange**. Example 30.11B illustrates both a diatonic voice exchange (m. 108 to downbeat of m. 109) and a chromatic voice exchange (m. 109).

EXAMPLE 30.11

DVD 1
CH 30
TRACK 6

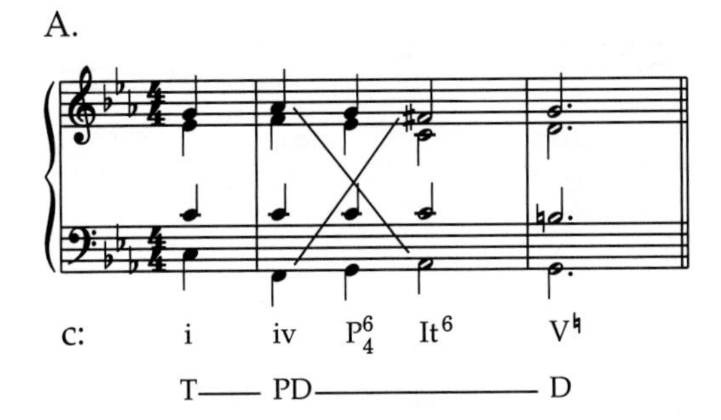

B. C.P.E. Bach, Flute Sonata no. 6 in G, Wq 134 H548, *Allegro*

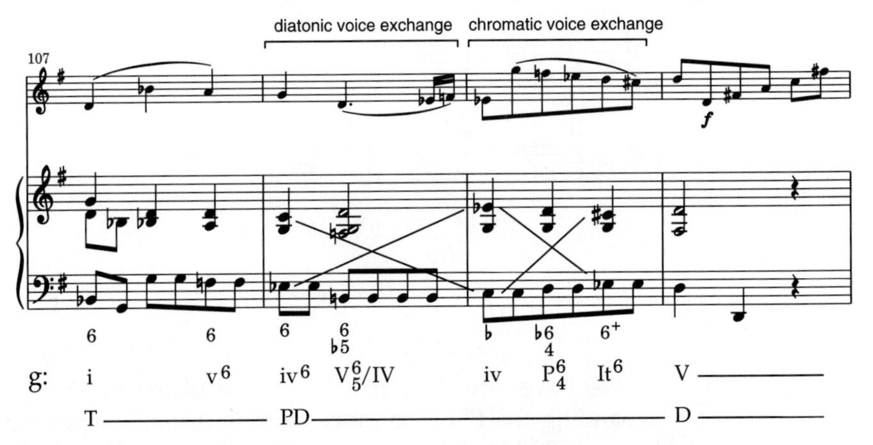

In rarer cases where the PD expansion involves only an augmented sixth chord, the resulting voice exchange is literal, as in Example 30.12. The chord on the downbeat of m. 1 in Example 30.12 is a Ger$^6_5$. The chord on beat 3 of that measure sounds like—and contains the same pitches as—a Ger$^6_5$, although the pitches have been reordered such that ♯$\hat{4}$ appears in the bass and ♭$\hat{6}$ in an upper voice. The resulting chord is therefore an inversion of the augmented sixth and is called a **German diminished third chord**.

Since the figure for this chord would be "7", we label the German diminished third chord as **Ger$_7$**.

EXAMPLE 30.12

DVD 1
CH 30
TRACK 7

EXAMPLE 30.13

DVD 1
CH 30
TRACK 8

The individual voices of this chord behave identically to those in any augmented sixth chord—$\hat{6}$ descends to $\hat{5}$ and ♯$\hat{4}$ ascends to $\hat{5}$. But given that the pitches are switched from the traditional Ger$^6_5$ arrangement, the voices contract on resolution instead of expanding (see Example 30.13).

In the first scene of Tchaikovsky's ballet *Sleeping Beauty* (Example 30.14), an extended PD involves IV, ii$_6$, and Ger$_7$, which Tchaikovsky marks *ff* in m. 72. The diminished third chord returns in m. 76, elaborating the V$^6_4$ as its neighbor.

EXAMPLE 30.14 Tchaikovsky, *Sleeping Beauty*, scene 1

Continued

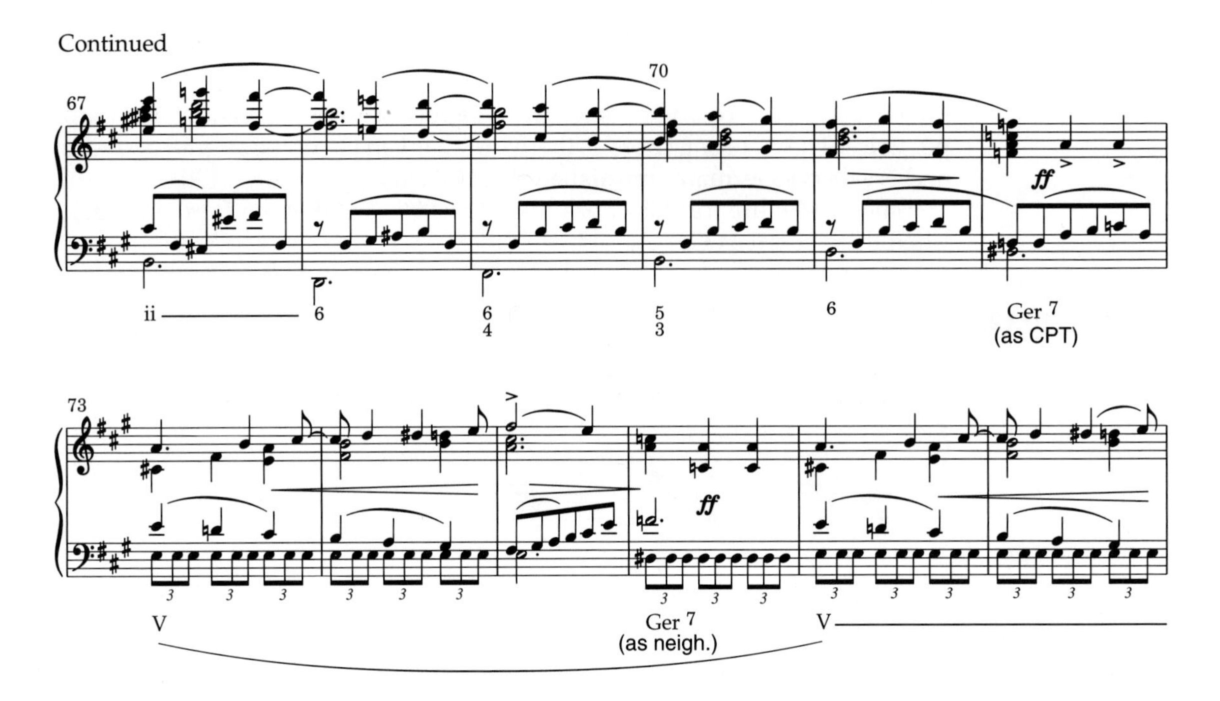

The Augmented Sixth Chord and Modulation: Reinforcement

Because of its half-step tendencies to $\hat{5}$, the augmented sixth chord contains more linear drive toward the dominant than any other PD harmony. Therefore, its appearance *after* a pivot chord is particularly helpful in securing a new key.

Listen to Example 30.15 and consider the following questions:

1. How many phrases does the excerpt contain?
2. What is their relationship (for example, do the phrases form a period)?
3. Is there a modulation? If so, where is (or are) the pivot chord(s)?

EXAMPLE 30.15 **Haydn, String Quartet in A major, op. 55, no. 1, Menuetto**

DVD 1
CH 30
TRACK 9

As the analysis of Example 30.15 shows, the excerpt's two phrases form a contrasting progressive period. The first phrase moves from the opening tonic to the dominant on the downbeat of m. 4. After a brief connective passage (over a passing V^4_2), the second phrase restarts on the tonic and modulates to V. At first glance, it might appear that there are two possible pivot chords in the excerpt: the tonic that begins the second phrase (m. 5) and the chord that follows in m. 6. Because the chord in m. 6 functions in only one way—as a Ger^6_5 in the key of E (V)—the tonic is best regarded as the pivot chord. Now we can understand why Haydn began the second phrase with the tonic in first inversion. As a pivot, it becomes IV_6 in the key of V, which smoothly moves by step to the Ger^6_5 in m. 6.

In most of the modulating passages we have examined, it seems that composers have taken special care to make the harmonic motion to the new key as smooth as possible. In situations where composers desire a more striking effect, they will often juxtapose radically different chromatic harmonies but then confirm the key of the second by means of the augmented sixth chord. In Example 30.16, Schubert boldly moves from the tonic D major to F (♭III) in m. 5. At this point, he reinterprets F major as ♭VI and converts it into an augmented sixth chord that resolves to V of A (V). (Note that all three types of the augmented sixth chord appear in m. 38 as the alto voice moves by step to G♯.)

EXAMPLE 30.16 **Schubert, Sonatina in D major for Piano and Violin, op. posth. 137, no. 1, D. 384, *Allegro molto***

DVD 1 CH 30 TRACK 10

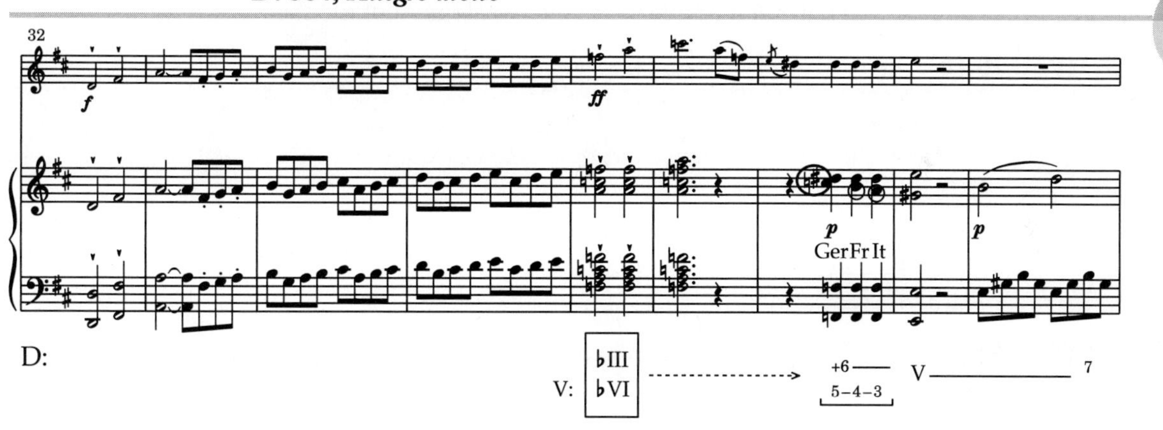

The Augmented Sixth Chord as Pivot in Modulations

At some point in your keyboard and listening exercises centered around augmented sixth chords, you may have already discovered that both the It^6_3 and Ger^6_5 chords are enharmonically equivalent to a V_7 chord; that is, the It^6_3 sounds like an incomplete V_7 (without fifth) and the German $^6_5$, shown in Example 30.17, sounds like a complete V_7 chord.

EXAMPLE 30.17

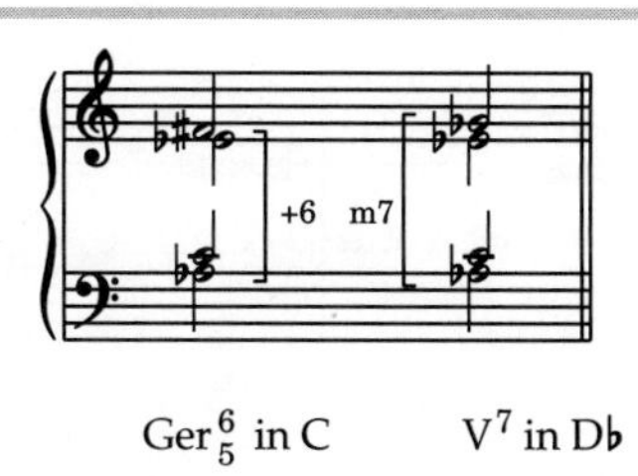

Ger^6_5 in C V^7 in D♭

Despite the aural similarity between the augmented sixth chords and their V_7 respellings, we understand their distinct functions based on their resolutions and voice leading.

- An augmented sixth chord is a PD chord and leads to dominant. The bass descends by half step to $\hat{5}$, and another voice ascends by half step to $\hat{5}$.
- A V_7 chord is a dominant chord that leads to tonic. The seventh of the chord descends by step as the bass leaps.

But the voice leading aside, we are left with two chords that are sonically interchangeable, the identities of which differ only by one enharmonic pitch. Look again at Example 30.17. See how the only difference between the augmented sixth in C and V_7 in D♭ is the shift of F♯ to G♭? To take advantage of this enharmonic relationship, composers sometimes modulate by treating this sonority as a pivot. Such **enharmonic reinterpretation** permits certain chromatic modulations, as shown in Example 30.18. For example, imagine that a Ger$^6_5$ chord is reached within a C-minor passage. Normally we would expect that chord to progress to the dominant. But instead it may be reinterpreted (via the enharmonic shift F♯4–G♭4) as a dominant of D♭ major—the Neapolitan to C. Example 30.18B illustrates how Beethoven's enharmonic reinterpretation allows him to tonicize ♭II effortlessly: A quick modal shift from G major to G minor prepares the Ger$^6_5$ (mm. 163–165). In m. 167, D♭ appears (rather than the previously notated C♯). As the chordal seventh of the E♭ chord, the D♭ resolves by step descent and leads to the restatement of the theme in A♭ (♭II).

EXAMPLE 30.18

DVD 1
CH 30
TRACK 11

A.

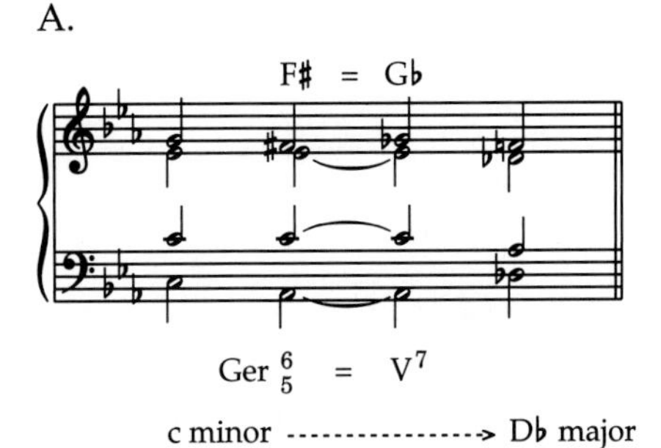

B. Beethoven, "Rage Over a Lost Penny," op. 129

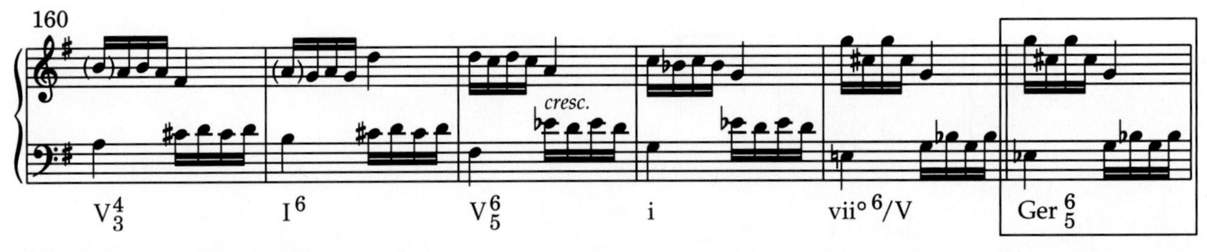

Continued

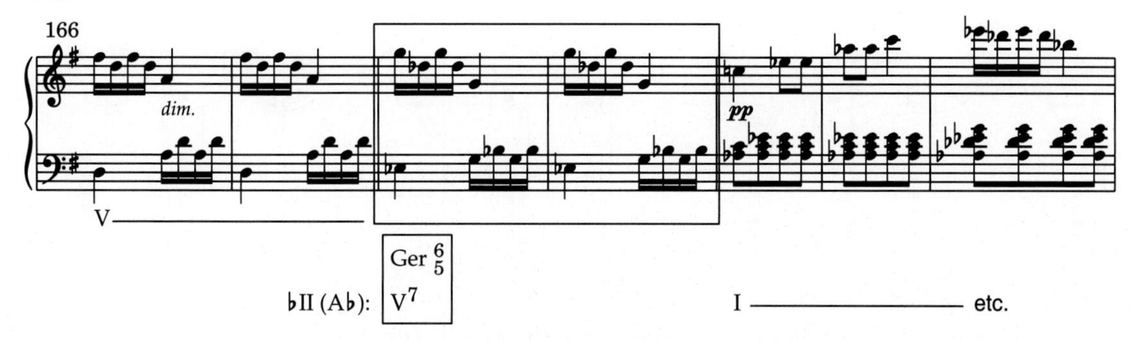

Composers do not always notate the Ger^6_5 and the V_7/♭II successively in their two forms, as in Example 30.18. Rather, they will notate one form, which functions as a pivot chord between the two harmonic areas. Example 30.19 shows how to label such a dual-functioning sonority.

EXAMPLE 30.19

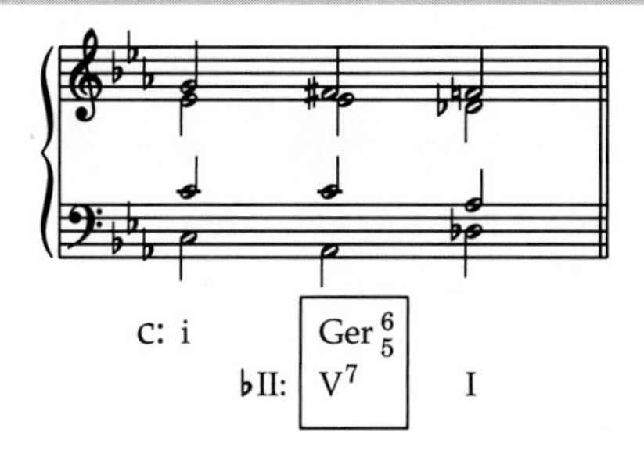

Just as the Ger^6_5 and V_7 are enharmonically equivalent, so too are the Ger_7 and V^4_2 chords. Example 30.20 illustrates how these chords can be used interchangeably. In m. 2 of Example 30.20A, the Ger_7 chord (labeled *x*) functions as part of a PD expansion that leads to V. In m. 2 the Ger_7 chord (labeled *y*) expands the dominant through chromatic neighbor motion. Its final appearance in m. 2 (labeled *z*) is sonically identical to its previous statement, but G♭ appears in the bass, transforming the chord into a V^4_2 of D♭ (♭II). This enharmonic pivot is boxed to show how it secures the tonicization of ♭II.

EXAMPLE 30.20

DVD 1 CH 30 TRACK 12

A.

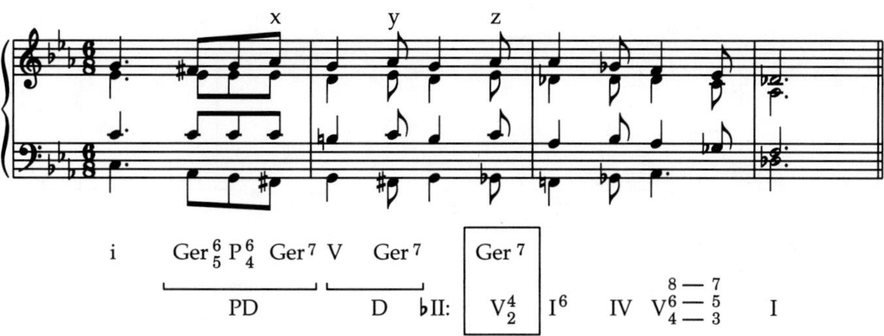

B. Tchaikovsky, *Sleeping Beauty*, Pas de Six, "Violente"

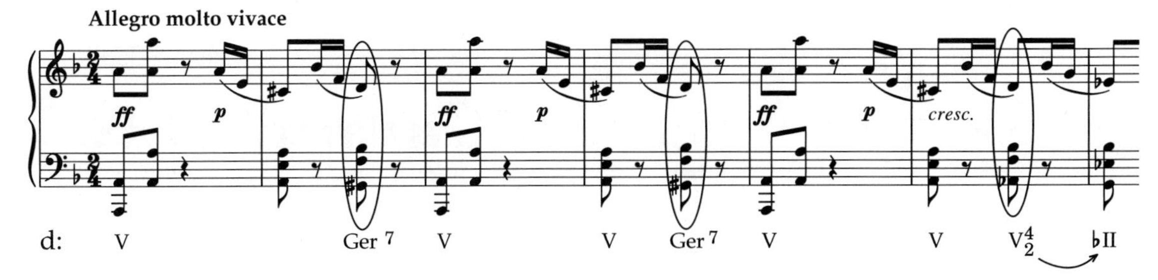

Example 30.20B, from Tchaikovsky's *Sleeping Beauty*, contains many examples of diminished third chords. The opening of the "Pas de Six" begins on V of D minor, which is expanded by the Ger_7 chord in mm. 2–4. In m. 6, the chord is respelled as a V^4_2 of E♭ (♭II), to which it resolves.

The reverse of this enharmonic reinterpretation is shown in Example 30.21. This procedure is not nearly as common as the move to ♭II, because the new tonic is $\hat{7}$, a scale degree that is rarely tonicized in tonal music.

EXAMPLE 30.21

DVD 1
CH 30
TRACK 13

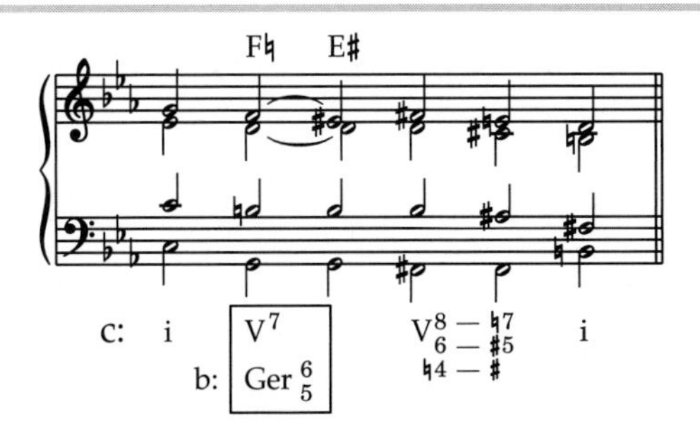

If you think back to Chapter 24, you will remember that it is possible to precede any consonant triad in a key with its own V_7. With enharmonic reinterpretation, it is now possible to change any of these V_7s into augmented sixth chords. The result of this transformation easily allows composers access to both closely and distantly related keys.

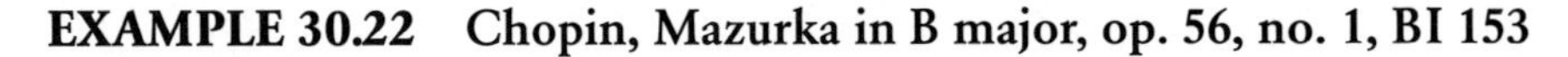

EXAMPLE 30.22 Chopin, Mazurka in B major, op. 56, no. 1, BI 153

DVD 1
CH 30
TRACK 14

Continued

Listen to Example 30.22. Note how B major (I) closes the phrase in m. 44. Immediately, a seventh is added to the tonic, creating the aural expectation that it will function as V_7 in the key of E (IV). Remarkably, this chord is resolved differently: It acts as a Ger$^6_5$ moving to the dominant of the new key D♯ major (III♯, enharmonically spelled as E♭). The roman numeral analysis below Example 30.22 shows how the pivot functions.

Enharmonic reinterpretation functions in the same way as does a pun. Based on traditional syntax, the listener has clear expectations. But a good pun leads the story in an entirely unexpected direction.

EXERCISE INTERLUDE

PERFORMING

30.7 Singing and Playing Augmented Sixth Chords versus V_7

Using scale degrees or solfège, sing (or play on your instrument) the following progressions, which incorporate enharmonic use of the augmented sixth chord. Be able to identify the starting and ending keys for each exercise.

A.

B.

ANALYZING

30.8 Analytical Snapshots from the Literature

Listen to and then provide roman numerals for the following excerpts, which contain examples of the following techniques: converting ♭VI into an augmented sixth chord, pre-dominant expansions using augmented sixth or diminished third chords, and enharmonic modulation using augmented sixth and dominant seventh chords.

A. Mozart, Adagio in C major K 356

B. Gluck, Chorus, "Bettet den Vater," from *Alceste*, act 1

C. Mendelssohn, "Weh mir!" Ariette, from *Elijah*, no. 18

D. Beethoven, Andante in F major, WoO 57

E. Schubert, Symphony no. 8 in B minor ("Unfinished"), D. 759, *Andante*

30.9 Reduction

The example given is a variation movement from Mozart's String Quartet in D minor, K. 421. It contains various chromatic harmonies, in particular Neapolitan and augmented sixth chords. Reduce the texture by verticalizing it into four voices. Play each reduction in the key in which it is written; then transpose to one other key of your choice. Instrumentalists who play single-line instruments will simply arpeggiate (using good voice leading) each of the harmonies.

Summary of Part 7

Having examined modal mixture, the Neapolitan chord, and augmented sixth chords, we have completed our study of common-practice harmony. In looking at its role in the composition of music, we have seen mixture to be a procedure through which pitches belonging to the parallel mode can be incorporated and—in the cases of ♭III and ♭VI—to be tonicized. Such stabilization is one of the hallmarks of nineteenth-century music. We also learned that these chromatic third tonicizations, so called because the tonicized keys lie a third away from the tonic, function identically to their diatonic counterparts. Furthermore, these new chromatic harmonies are often connected to an underlying musical narrative, or drama, whether or not a text is present. We learned that these chords can function in vocal music as musical analogues that highlight, clarify, or even expand on a text. Finally, we have seen yet again how counterpoint is a central force behind not only mixture sonorities but also both the Neapolitan and augmented sixth chords.

TERMS AND CONCEPTS

- augmented sixth chord
- chromatic voice exchange
- doubly augmented sixth chord
- enharmonic reinterpretation
- French augmented sixth chord (Fr^4_3)
- German augmented sixth chord (Ger^6_5)
- German diminished third chord (Ger_7)
- Italian augmented sixth chord (It_6)

PART 8

LARGE FORMS: TERNARY, RONDO, SONATA

Now that we have completed our study of common-practice harmony, we begin a journey through three important large forms: ternary, rondo, and sonata. Taken together, these forms fittingly describe the structure of vast numbers of instrumental and vocal works composed throughout the eighteenth and nineteenth centuries. Learning to recognize these forms and their local and large-scale harmonic procedures aurally will be a major step toward comprehending the design of classical works.

In addition to exploring formal strategies in large works, we also look at musical processes that unfold throughout a piece and that provide musical narratives for both listener and performer. Generally these processes are motivic, and they range from simple repetitions that are slightly obscured by the musical surface to significant transformations in which the motive is expanded at the very deepest level of structure.

CHAPTER 31

Ternary Form

Ternary and rondo forms are **composite forms**. That is, they are constructed of multiple sections that are self-contained. The independent sections feature strong melodic contrast and tonal closure; that is, the various sections usually begin and end conclusively in the same key. Binary form is not a composite form, since its sections are tonally dependent on one another and can be viewed as being more organic in its construction.

Ternary form has a three-part melodic design (ABA or ABA′) and a three-part tonal structure (original key–contrasting key–original key) (See Example 31.1A). Contrast the design of ternary form with the rounded binary form of Example 31.1B, which has a three-part melodic design (a–dig.–a′) but a two-part tonal structure.

EXAMPLE 31.1

A. Ternary form

A	B	A or (A′)
° original material	° contrasting material	° literal repetition of A (or altered restatement, labeled A′)
° original key	° contrasting key: (major mode: IV, vi, iv, ♭VI, i) (minor mode: III, iv, VI, I)	° original key

B. Rounded binary form

<table>
<tr><td>‖: a :‖</td><td colspan="2">‖: digression a′ :‖</td></tr>
<tr><td colspan="2">° in one key
I -- V //</td><td>I ------------------------------ V I</td></tr>
</table>

Listen to Example 31.2, which is in ternary form. The three distinct and autonomous parts in Example 31.2 may be labeled ABA′. The fast, folklike B part in the parallel major key highly contrasts with the brooding A and A′ parts. The piece is in ternary form because each of the three sections is harmonically and thematically closed and the B section is self-standing.

EXAMPLE 31.2 Grieg, "Hjemve" ("Homesickness"), *Lyric Pieces*, book VI, op. 57, no. 6

DVD 1 CH 31 TRACK 1

Molto più vivo
28
pp una corda
32
36
39
f
42
poco
fp
45
fp

48
fp
fp
51
55
f
58
poco
fp
61
fp
64
fp
fp
66
Tempo I
rit.
lunga
p

Continued

If each of the three sections of a ternary form closes in its respective tonic, as in the Grieg example, we call the form a **full sectional ternary form** (A || B || A ||). When either the A section (A || BA: not common) or the B section (AB || A: common) closes away from its tonic chord and this closure is integral to the tonal motion of the section, then we refer to the form as a **sectional ternary form**. When both A and B close away from their respective tonic chords, we call the form a **continuous ternary form** (ABA).

Sometimes it may not be easy to distinguish a continuous ternary form from a rounded binary form. To decide whether a form is rounded binary or continuous ternary, consider how much the B part is dependent on the A part. If there is little connection, a ternary form is indicated. By contrast, if there is a thematic or motivic connection and little or no change of key, it is better termed a binary form. Like much of your musical analysis, you must interpret such works according to how you hear them and then support your answer.

Transitions and Retransitions

Composers sometimes compose *bridging* sections in order to create a sense of continuity in a ternary form. Material that bridges between tonic and a new key (from A to B in ternary form) is called a **transition**. Bridging material that leads from a contrasting key back to tonic is a *returning transition*, or **retransition**. Note that a ternary form may have a transition and a retransition, a transition without a retransition, a retransition without a transition, or no bridging material at all. We will see that retransitions occur much more frequently than transitions.

Transitions and retransitions make for some of the most exciting music in a piece, because their material is completely unpredictable. They may be as simple as presenting the dominant of the upcoming key, or they may be considerably more involved, delicately foreshadowing motives and harmonies of the upcoming section. Note that it may be hard to determine whether a piece is in continuous ternary form or in sectional ternary form with a transition or retransition. If there is a conclusive end to a section followed by a modulation with the melodic fragmentation, this is most likely a transitional area. By contrast, if a section closes in another key but the closure is integral to the tonal motion of a section, then there is most likely no transitional area.

To familiarize yourself with the role of transitional material, consider the relationship between the A and B sections in Example 31.3, a work by Brahms. The outer parts of Brahms's Romanze are in F major, and the contrasting B section (beginning in m. 17) is in the remote key of D major (VI). The B part is further distinguished from A by a faster tempo and a meter change.

EXAMPLE 31.3 Brahms, Romanze in F, *Six Piano Pieces*, op. 118, no. 5, mm. 1–19

DVD 1
CH 31
TRACK 2

Continued

If we view the transition only as the final measure of the A section (m. 16), then it is present but quite short. Here, a bass arpeggiation of D minor prepares the upcoming D major section: All that is required is a modal shift to the parallel major. But Brahms has done much more than tack on a measure of D minor. We must scan the A section in order to see the musical process.

The A section contains four four-measure phrases with the relationship *a-a′-a-a′*. The first *a* (mm. 1–4) closes with a HC, and the first *a′* (mm. 5–8) moves to vi and closes with a HC in D minor. It is only the quick shift to A minor that prepares the return to F major in m. 9. The second *a* (mm. 9–12) is almost identical to mm. 1–4, but the second *a′* (mm. 13–17) closes on V of D, which leads nicely to the next section. Thus, the large A section closes in a different key from the one in which it began.

A retransition prepares for the return of A after the B section (Example 31.4). The retransition begins by shifting to the lullaby-like $\frac{6}{4}$ meter of the A section and by reprising the A section's two-note slurred chords in parallel sixths (m. 45). Yet elements of the B part are retained in the retransition, the most obvious of which are the key of D major and the trills that close the retransition. In m. 46, D major moves to D minor, which functions as diatonic vi in F major. This is followed by a cadential six-four chord in F major that resolves directly to the tonic (mm. 47–48). Thus, Brahms's work is a **sectional ternary form**.

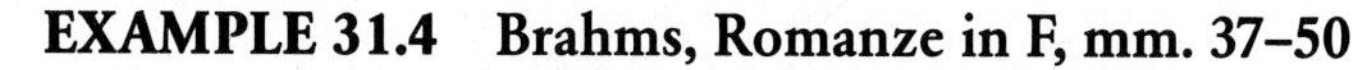

EXAMPLE 31.4 Brahms, Romanze in F, mm. 37–50

Da Capo Form: Compound Ternary Form

Ternary forms can be found in several genres and style periods. We will see examples in a Classical sonata, a da capo aria from the Baroque period, a minuet and trio from the Classical period, and a character piece from the nineteenth century. As we begin our exploration, be aware that ternary forms are found in many more genres and styles than we can explore here. For example, although **da capo form** is the primary form of the Baroque aria, it can be found in almost all genres, style periods, and instrumental combinations of the common-practice era.

The Presto by Haydn in Example 31.5 is in da capo form. The ABA structure of da capo works is realized by following the marking at the end of the score, *Da Capo (al* 𝄐), which in literal translation means "from the head to the fermata sign," telling the performer to return to the beginning of the piece and play to the fermata sign. It is the return that creates the final balancing A section; the da capo instruction merely saves space and ink.

EXAMPLE 31.5 Haydn, Divertimento in G major, Hob. XVI.11, *Presto*

DVD 1
CH 31
TRACK 4

Haydn's Divertimento is much like Grieg's work in Example 31.2: Both are full sectional ternary forms, and both include smaller binary forms within the larger ternary form. These are **compound ternary forms**, because larger parts divide into smaller forms (see Example 31.6).

EXAMPLE 31.6

A. Grieg

measures:	1–8	9–18	19–27	28–67	68–75	76–85	86–94
large parts:	A			B	A′		
small parts:	*a*	*dig.*	a′		*a*	*dig.*	a′
	(rounded binary)				*(rounded binary)*		

B. Haydn

measures:	1–8	9–16	17–24	25–32	33–40	41–48	1–8	9–16	17–24
large parts:	A			B			A′		
small parts:	*a*	*dig.*	a′	b	*dig.*	b′	*a*	*dig.*	a′
	(rounded binary)			*(rounded binary)*			*(rounded binary)*		

Da Capo Aria

Instrumental works are by no means the only type of da capo structures. In fact, the **da capo aria** is arguably the most important ternary structure in the Baroque period. One or more instrumental interludes, called **ritornellos**, usually punctuate formal parts and sections of text. Attempt the following tasks before you listen to Example 31.7.

1. Locate and mark the division between the A and B sections; remember that the third section is a repeat of the A, from the beginning up to the *fine*. What underlying keys control each section? Are the sections divided into subsections? If so, mark them and indicate the prevailing keys in each with roman numerals.
2. What sequential progression unfolds in the opening instrumental ritornello? Discuss relationships between the ritornello tune and the soprano's opening melody.
3. What musical events help to distinguish the B section of this aria from the flanking outer parts?

EXAMPLE 31.7 Bach, "Ich will Dir mein Herze schenken" ("Lord, to Thee my heart I proffer"), *St. Matthew Passion*, BWV 244

DVD 1 CH 31 TRACK 5

Continued

16
and dwell in me, O Lord, to Thee my heart I prof - - -
19
cresc.
- - - - - fer, en - ter Thou, and
f
22
dwell in me, en - - - ter Thou, and dwell in me.
f
25
f
tr
28
rfz
Fine.

Continued

31
mf
All I am or have I of - fer, My - self would I
p
34
lose in Thee. Know I not, They face to see, More than all the world.
cresc.
37
f
would be?
f
40
p
All I am, I am
rfz
p
p

The form in Bach's aria unfolds as is shown in Example 31.8. The A part, which remains in the tonic key, markedly contrasts with the B part, which begins after the instrumental ritornello. The B part is more transitory and sequential, similar to what we would see in the digression of a binary form. The B part closes in B minor, the minor dominant of E minor (or the mediant of the returning G major). Thus, this is a **sectional ternary form**.

EXAMPLE 31.8

section:	A			B			A (da capo)
measures:	1–6	7–24	25–30	31–37	38–41	42–48	1–30
subsection:	ritornello	voice	ritornello	voice	ritornello	voice	
keys:	I (G)	V–I	I	vi (e)	V–I	PAC in v of vi (b)	I

Minuet-Trio Form

The Baroque **minuet** was a type of dance that remained popular in the following Classical period, when it became a standard inner movement in symphonies and chamber pieces such as serenades, divertimentos, and sonatas. In the hands of first Haydn and Beethoven, the minuet was often transformed into a more spirited piece called the **scherzo**. The Classical minuet is followed without pause by a companion piece of lighter texture, called a **trio**, after which a *da capo* marking indicates that the minuet is to be repeated. The result is a large ternary form called **minuet-trio form**. As with many composite forms, the minuet-trio form is often a compound ternary, with nested binary forms.

Before listening to Example 31.9, a minuet-trio movement from one of Beethoven's early piano sonatas, review the following points and questions.

1. The minuet and trio are clearly delineated by Beethoven's use of titles. Yet even if no clues were provided, you would still be able to differentiate the A and B sections. Identify at least three features of the trio that distinguish it from the minuet.
2. Identify three features of the trio that are *shared* with the minuet.
3. What nested forms occur within the minuet and trio?
4. What is the underlying harmonic progression in the minuet?

EXAMPLE 31.9 Beethoven, Piano Sonata no. 1 in F minor, op. 2, no. 1, Menuetto-Trio: *Allegretto*

DVD 1
CH 31
TRACK 6

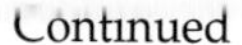

Continued

This movement is a **full sectional ternary form** and both the minuet and trio are rounded continuous binary forms (see Example 31.10). The minuet, in F minor, moves from i to III in the first *a* section. The digression is characteristically more transitory, tonicizing iv briefly in mm. 19–25 before the V and interruption in m. 28. The underlying tonal progression of the minuet is i–III–iv–V || i-V–i.

EXAMPLE 31.10

section:	**A (minuet)**			**B (trio)**			**A (minuet)**
measures:	1–14	15–28	29–40	41–50	51–65	66–73	1–40
	a	*digression*	*a′*	*b*	*digression*	*b′*	
keys:	i–III	iv–V //	i–V–i	I–V	–V7 //	I–V–I	i

To achieve variety in the rounded binary forms, material from the *a* section is often restated in invertible counterpoint in the *a′* section. Beethoven uses this contrapuntal technique in both the minuet and the trio; a common procedure thus ties the two together. In the minuet, the reprise of the *a′* section in m. 29 places the initial tune in the left hand rather than in the right. The right hand again takes over the melody in m. 31. Similar registral shifting takes place in the trio, where Beethoven intensifies the effect by introducing it immediately in back-to-back phrases (mm. 41–44 and 45–48). Invertible counterpoint and registral change become ever more explicit in the digression of the trio, which is shown in Example 31.11: The chromatic line C^4–B^3–$B\flat^3$–A^3 begins on C^2 in m. 51 and repeats one and two octaves higher than the tune (m. 55 and m. 65). One can find the seeds of registral shifting and invertible counterpoint planted in the opening of the minuet: The tenor-voice entrance at the end of m. 2 restates the soprano-voice entrance down an octave.

EXAMPLE 31.11 Beethoven, Piano Sonata no. 1, Trio, mm. 41–65

Ternary Form in the Nineteenth Century

Some of the species of ternary forms from the eighteenth century, such as the minuet-trio, continued to serve composers throughout the nineteenth century. Others, such as the da capo, fell out of favor and were replaced with new—or at least hybrid—forms whose very titles suggest the intense Romanticism that beget them. One new addition, the **character piece**, was a short, expressive work often written for solo piano. Examples of some important nineteenth-century character pieces include the bagatelles of Beethoven and the impromptus and *Moment musicales* of Schubert; and the ballades, nocturnes, polonaises, and mazurkas of Chopin. In addition, composers who were influenced by the literature of the time wrote entire cycles of piano pieces with highly descriptive titles, such as Robert Schumann's *Papillons* and *Carnival*. Character pieces continued to be composed throughout the nineteenth century by Liszt, Brahms, Scriabin, and Grieg, whose "Hjemve" ("Homesickness") we have already encountered in Example 31.2.

In the following examples from the cusp of the nineteenth century and onward, we will explore how composers used motives to link independent sections of ternary works—in particular, how apparently new musical material may be seen to be a concealed repetition or a transformation of earlier material. Although it reaches its apogee in the music of Liszt and Wagner, motivic transformation is not new to the nineteenth century. One often encounters instances of transformation in the music of late-Classical composers such as Mozart and Haydn, some of whose string quartets are unified through the recurrence of the same one or two motives in multiple movements.

Consider the minuet-trio pair from a Haydn string quartet shown in Example 31.12. On first glance, it is clear that the minuet and trio are highly contrasting. Not only are there dynamic and key changes (from C major to A minor), but the trio is more sparse in texture than the minuet, with the first violin given the lion's share of melodic material and the lower instruments merely punctuating the tune with the occasional chord. However, even a slightly more detailed look reveals important connections between the minuet and trio.

EXAMPLE 31.12 Haydn, String Quartet in C major, "Emperor", op. 76, no. 3, Hob. III. 76

DVD 1
CH 31
TRACK 7

A. Menuett: *Allegro*

B. Trio

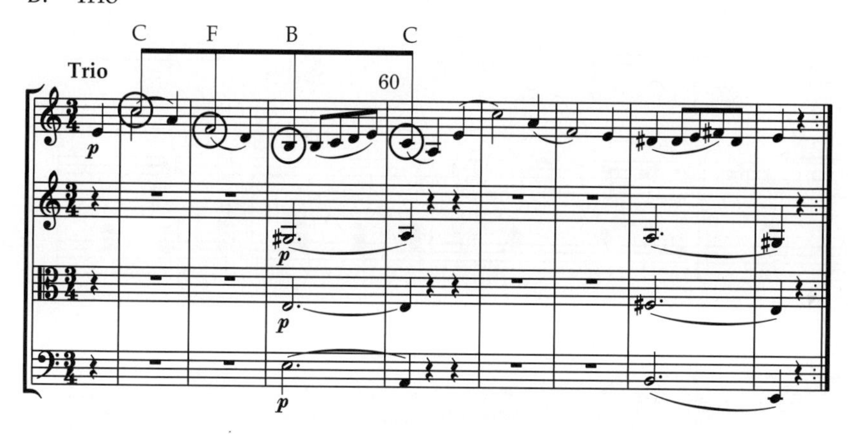

The minuet opens in C major with the angular violin falling by ever-increasing large intervals: a sixth, a seventh, and finally a ninth. The other instruments imitate the first violin's jaunty contour, but the cello line (C, F, B, C) is particularly exposed. The opening of the trio reveals a barely hidden repetition of the earlier cello figure in the first violin, even though the trio is cast in the relative minor. See Example 31.12. This important association between the minuet and trio is one that performers might wish to consider, since recognizing such motivic recurrences can render the performance of works more beautiful and insightful.

EXAMPLE 31.13 Chopin, Mazurka in A minor, op. 17, no. 4

DVD 1
CH 31
TRACK 8

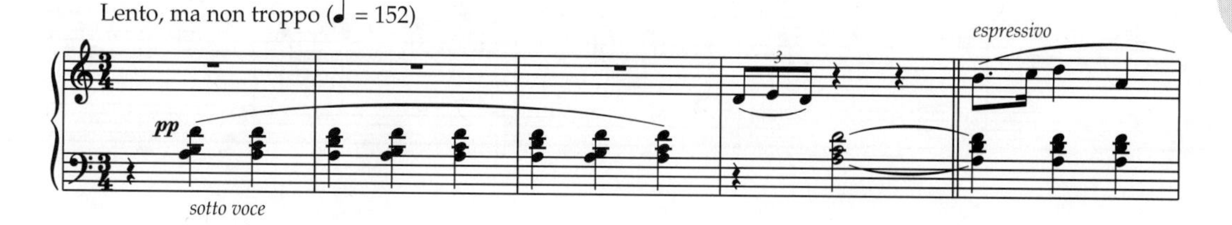

Continued

Let's now explore two of Chopin's mazurkas. Example 31.13 shows the opening A section of a mazurka in A minor, a section that contains a nested small ternary form (*aba*). After an ambiguous four-measure introduction, a wandering melody enters at m. 5. The opening notes of the right hand (B^4–C^5–D^5) help to explain the function of the introduction, where the middle voice moves with this same three-note figure, almost as if it were lying in gestation before flowering into an expressive melody at m. 5. The next seven measures are filled with chromaticism, including the descending line E^4–$D\sharp^4$–$D\natural^4$–C^4 in mm. 8–11 (Example 31.13). Again, the mood remains somber, such that we crave relief. It arrives in mm. 37–42, as a more sprightly tune unfolds over a dominant pedal—this is the *b* part of the nested *aba* form. Despite the contrast, one discovers a compressed repetition of the chromatic line from mm. 8–13 in mm. 37–42 (Example 31.14).

EXAMPLE 31.14 Chopin, Mazurka in A minor

In his late F-minor mazurka, also cast in ternary form, Chopin juxtaposes the very distant keys of F minor and A major in the two halves of the A section, yet he subtly links these disparate keys with a neighbor motive that he presents at various structural levels in the opening moments of the piece (Example 31.15). Following the initial statement of the neighbor C^5–$D\flat^5$–C^5 ($\hat{5}$–$\hat{6}$–$\hat{5}$) in m. 1, a chromatic descent from C^5 to G^4 (in m. 6) is compensated by an upward leap that recaptures the upper neighbor figure, $D\flat^5$–C^5, in mm. 6–7. The contrasting melody (m. 15ff) begins with a stepwise ascending line that balances the more angular, predominantly descending line that characterized the opening. It is not surprising that C♯ is the most prominent pitch in this section, since one might view it as a hugely expanded statement of its enharmonic twin, D♭. In fact, given that C♯ occupies the B section and returns to C in the restatement of the A material, one might say that Chopin's choice of A major for the contrasting melody is actually quite logical, given that it nicely harmonizes the expanded neighbor D♭ as C♯.

EXAMPLE 31.15 Chopin, Mazurka in F minor, op. 68, no. 4

DVD 1
CH 31
TRACK 9

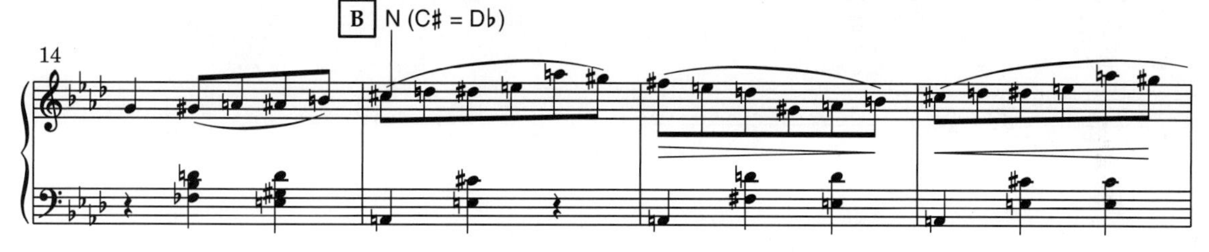

EXERCISE INTERLUDE

DVD 2
CH 31
TRACK 1

ANALYSIS

31.1

Draw a formal diagram for the following pieces. If a piece is a compound form, include the nested, smaller forms. Then answer the accompanying questions on a separate sheet of paper.

A. Haydn, Piano Sonata in C major, Hob. XVI.10, Menuet and Trio

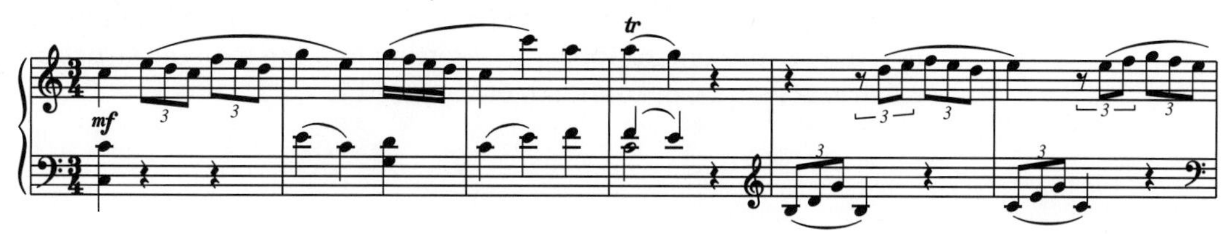

Continued

1. What type of period opens the minuet?
2. What is somewhat unusual about the harmony in the digression?
3. What harmonic and melodic technique occurs in the bass line that opens the trio?
4. Discuss the pre-dominant that occurs in the first phrase of the trio.
5. What key(s) is/are tonicized after the first double bar of the trio?
6. Why could one support the assertion that the melodic structure of the trio is simple, or rounded, or balanced?

B. Schumann, "Widmung" from *Myrthen*, op. 25

1. Discuss the phrase structure in the A section. How does it differ from Classical-style-period structure?
2. The contrasting section, while clearly different from the first section in key, texture, rhythm, etc., subtly draws on harmonic events from the first section in order to integrate the two sections. Discuss some of these connections.
3. Describe in detail how Schumann accomplishes the return to the tonic, A♭ major.

12
mei-nen Kum - mer gab!
Du bist die Ruh, du
ritard.
p
16
bist der Frie - den,
du bist vom Him - - mel
20
mir be schie - den.
Dass du mich liebst,
macht mich mir werth,
dein Blick hat
24
mich vor mir ver-klärt,
du hebst mich
lie - bend ü - ber mich,
mein
ritard.
Ped.
*

28
ritard.
f
gu - ter Geist, mein bess-res Ich!
Du mei-ne See - le, du mein Herz,
du mei-ne
ritard.
32
steigen und eilend
Wonní, o du mein Schmerz,
du mei-ne Welt,
in der ich le - be, mein Him - mel
steigen und eilend
36
ritard.
du, da-rein ich schwe - be, mein gu-ter Geist, mein bess res Ich!
ritard.
p
40
ritard.
ritard.

C. Paganini, Caprice no. 20, from *24 Caprices*, op. 1

WORKBOOK
31.1–31.4

TERMS AND CONCEPTS

- character piece
- composite form
- compound form
- da capo aria
- da capo form
- minuet
- minuet-trio form
- retransition
- ritornello
- scherzo
- ternary form
  - continuous
  - full sectional
  - sectional
- transition
- trio

CHAPTER 32

Rondo

"Variety is the spice of life" and "There's no place like home" are two popular sayings that convey very different meanings. Although most of us desire new experiences to keep life interesting, we also need frequent returns to the familiar so that our lives don't feel like they're becoming too chaotic. This balance of variety and return so fundamental to human nature is reflected not only in ternary form, but also in **rondo form**. Ternary form and rondo form are **composite forms**, constructed of multiple self-contained sections. The sections of a ternary form introduce variety (in the B section) and return (in the final A section). Rondo form continues the balance of variety and return as it incorporates more and more sections. We can think of rondo form as an extension of ternary form, or we can consider ternary as a small three-part rondo:

Ternary form (three-part):		A	B	A			
Rondo form (five-part):	A1	B	A2	C	A3		
Rondo form (seven-part):	A1	B1	A2	C	A3	B2	A4

Rondo form alternates sections of recurring material (A1, A2, A3, etc.), called **refrains**, with sections of contrasting material (B, C, etc.), called **episodes**.

The rondo is a common form in French Baroque instrumental music, where it is called **rondeau**. Works by Louis Couperin (*ca.* 1626–61), his nephew François Couperin (1668–1733), and Jean-Philippe Rameau (1663–1733) often consist of very short refrains and a variable number of episodes in the form ABACADA, and so on. These early works became the model for later eighteenth- and nineteenth-century compositions, and it is here where we will begin our study of rondo.

Listen to Example 32.1, which contains a rondeau by François Couperin. The refrain is the first thing heard and always occurs in the home key—this is common in most rondos. The refrain occurs three times:

EXAMPLE 32.1 François Couperin, *Les Goûts-réunis*, Concert no. 8, "Air tendre"

DVD 1
CH 32
TRACK 1

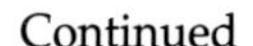
Continued

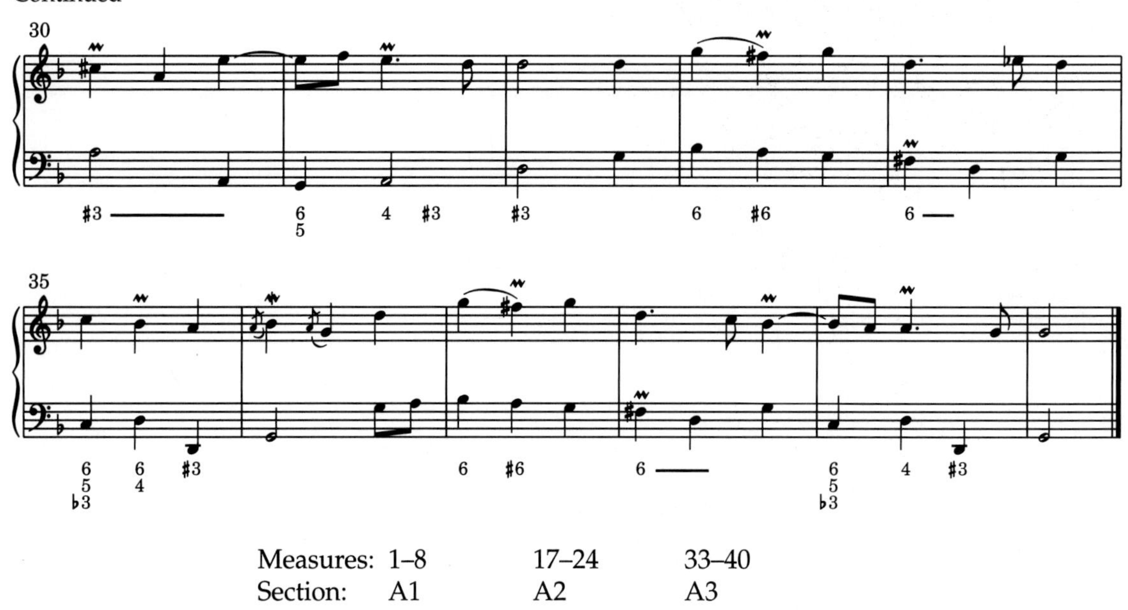

Measures:	1–8	17–24	33–40
Section:	A1	A2	A3
Key:	i	i	i

There are two episodes: The first, at mm. 9–16, is in B♭ major (III). Remarkably, this episode has an off-tonic beginning. The C minor chord of m. 9 is ii. The second episode begins at the upbeat to m. 25 and moves toward D minor (v) in m. 28. If we order our findings, we see that Couperin's piece follows a five-part structure that is very common in the later Classical period:

Measures:	1–8	9–16	17–24	25–32	33–40
Section:	A1	B	A2	C	A3
Key:	i	III	i	v	i

The Classical Rondo

Rondos in the late eighteenth century often occur at the end of larger multimovement works, such as sonatas, chamber pieces, and symphonies. With themes that are often taken from folk or popular sources or that at least imitate those sources, they provide a light finish and a welcome contrast to the usually more complex first movements and serious slow movements. Moreover, rondos provide an opportunity to demonstrate the player's ability to change style quickly between contrasting sections. We next explore the two most important types of Classical rondos: the five-part rondo and the seven-part rondo.

Five-Part Rondo

Before you listen to Example 32.2, the final movement of a Clementi piano sonatina, glance at the score to familiarize yourself with the key and the melodic shape of the refrain's opening. Now observe how Clementi articulates the beginnings of new sections with double bars. Do you see any significant changes in melodic contour, key, mood, and texture at these locations?

Next, listen to the work in its entirety at least twice. On a separate sheet of paper, start your own form diagram of the piece, indicating refrains with A1, A2, and A3; indicate episodes with the letters B and C. For each section, capture its location and duration in measure numbers and its key with the proper roman numeral.

EXAMPLE 32.2 Clementi, Sonatina in C major, op. 36, no. 3

DVD 1
CH 32
TRACK 2

Continued

Continued

Maggiore
97
102
p
108
f
p
112
f
117
121
125

Continued

Your form diagram should look something like this:

Measures:	1–24	25–46	47–70	71–104	105–119	120–end
Section:	A1	B	A2	C	A3	Coda
Key:	I	V	I	i	I	I

Coda, Transitions, and Retransitions

In listening to Example 32.2, you probably heard one final section that did not sound like a refrain but merely served to confirm the home key and provide a satisfactory ending. Technically, the final return of a refrain is the structural end of a rondo; however, when extra musical material occurs beyond the point at which a piece could have ended, it is called a **coda**.

The foregoing form diagram represents at the large scale how Clementi's five-part rondo is put together (ABACA–Coda), but it misses a lot of detail. First of all, rondo forms can have connecting sections that move from refrain to episode (**transition**) or return from an episode back to the refrain (**retransition**). Look at the end of section A1: There is no modulation, there is no new theme or thematic development, and the cadence in m. 24 serves as a strong close for the section; therefore, there is no transition section. Contrast this with the end of section B: There is a PAC at m. 40, and the remaining material is fragmented and leads back to the original key. Measures 40–46 form a retransition. A similar retransition occurs at the end of section C, beginning at m. 90, so the form now looks like this:

Measures:	1–24	25–40	40–46	47–70	71–90	90–104	105–119	120–end
Section:	A1	B	Retrans.	A2	C	Retrans.	A3	Coda
Key:	I	V	→	I	i	V→	I	I

Compound Rondo Form

The second important detail missing from the form diagram involves nested forms. As with ternary form, rondo form can be a **compound form** with nested forms. Note that A1, B, A2, and C are in rounded binary form.

Measures:	1–24	25–40	40–46	47–70	71–90	90–104	105–119	120–end
Section:	A1	B	Retrans.	A2	C	Retrans.	A3	Coda
Subsection:	*a-dig.-a'*	*b-dig.-b'*		*a-dig.-a'*	*c-dig.-c'*			
Key:	I	V	→	I	i	V→	I	I

The rondo in Example 32.3 is composed entirely of nested forms. Use the criteria of repetition and contrast of thematic and tonal materials to help group smaller sections into larger formal units that represent the refrain and contrasting episodes. Be especially wary of where 16-measure units may be interpreted as small binary forms, and be on the lookout for transitions and retransitions.

EXAMPLE 32.3 Mozart, Viennese Sonatina in C, *Five Divertimenti for Two Clarinets and Bassoon*, K. Anh. 229, *Allegro*

DVD 1
CH 32
TRACK 3

The following diagram summarizes both the form and the harmonic structure of the rondo. Note that each part contains two eight-measure units that together comprise a binary form. The refrain is a simple sectional binary form, and the episodes are balanced continuous binary forms.

Measures:	1–16	17–32	33–48	49–64	65–80	81–end
Section:	A1	B	A2	C	A3	Coda
Subsection:	*a a′*	*b b′*	*a a′*	*c c′*	*a a′*	
Key:	I	i→I	I	IV	I	I

Seven-Part Rondo

The seven-part rondo adds another episode and refrain to the five-part rondo. These two added parts create a symmetrical form, which some liken to a musical arch. The following diagram shows the symmetrical form and the typical keys for the seven-part rondo:

	A1	B1	A2	C	A3	B2	A4
in major keys:	I	V, i, or IV	I	i, IV, or vi	I	I or i	I
in minor keys:	i	III or v	i	iv, IV, III, VI, or I	i	I	i

As in the five-part rondo, the sections of the seven-part rondo are often cast in rounded binary forms.

Distinguishing Seven-Part Rondo Form from Ternary Form

Because of its symmetrical construction and because section C may be longer and distinct from the flanking ABA sections, the seven-part rondo can sound like a giant three-part ternary:

Seven-part rondo:	A1 B1 A2	C	A3 B2 A4
Ternary:	A	B	A′

It is possible to confuse a large ternary form with a seven-part rondo, especially if a ternary form contains its own nested binary form in the A section. Generally, the context will help you distinguish between the two.

- Consider when the work was written. Rondos were favored in the eighteenth century and ternary forms in the nineteenth century.
- Consider the tempo. One is less likely to encounter a slow rondo than a spirited one.
- Recall that seven-part rondos usually contain repeated, nested smaller forms, adding yet another level of structure that is sometimes absent from ternary forms.
- Be aware that seven-part rondos can be shorter than five-part rondos because the latter often have lengthy C sections, transitions, retransitions, and codas that appear less often in seven-part rondos.

Missing Double Bars and Repeats

Keep some additional points in mind as you continue to analyze rondos. First, because double bars demarcating large formal sections or subsections do not always appear in rondos, you may need to appeal to other musical signals (changes in key, motive, or texture) in defending your formal choices. Remember that transitions and retransitions may or may not be present in rondo form. Also, many rondos end with a coda that restates earlier material. Usually, codas are cadential and emphasize the tonic, but they may sometimes emphasize IV before returning to V and I.

Finally, after the statement of A1 and B1, composers often omit the repeats or write out ornamented repeats. An example of the latter may be seen in a comparison of A1 (mm. 1–16) and A2 (mm. 33–64) in the rondo from a Haydn string quartet, in Example 32.4. Notice that A2 occupies exactly twice as many measures as A1. This is because each of the two eight-measure repeated phrases of A1 have been written out and ornamented in A2.

EXAMPLE 32.4 **Haydn, String Quartet in D major, op. 33, no. 6, Hob. III.42, Finale**

DVD 1
CH 32
TRACK 4

A. mm. 1–16

45
p
f
mf
49
55
60

EXERCISE INTERLUDE

ANALYSIS

32.1

For each of the following pieces, listen to the recorded performance and study the score, then answer the questions on a separate sheet of paper.

A. Haydn, Piano Sonata in C major, Hob. XVI.35, Finale: *Allegro*

1. What is the form? Make a formal diagram that includes section labels and key structure. Make sure to show transitions and retransitions, and include measure numbers.
2. What is the period and formal structure of the opening refrain? Are there any changes in subsequent repetitions of this refrain?
3. Make a reduction of mm. 1–8 of the refrain that shows the contrapuntal relationship between the outer voices. In your analysis, distinguish between contrapuntal expansions and harmonic progressions.
4. Are there any motivic relationships between the refrain and episodes? Focus on contour.
5. If transitions or retransitions exist, describe their content (e.g., sequential) and function (e.g., modulatory, leading back to the refrain).

32
39
poco rit.
f
46
a tempo
p
f
54
p dolce
mf
60
1.
2.
f
p

66
f
p
73
f
p
80
f
86
p
92
f

B. Beethoven String Quartet in C minor, op. 18, no. 4, *Allegro*

48
p
sf
cresc.
f
56
sf
65
ff
72
fp
79

86
1.
2.
p
cresc.
sf
p
cresc.
p
f
p
f
p
cresc.
f
p
p
cresc.
f
p
f
93
1.
2.
f
p
p
cresc.
f
p
p
p
cresc.
f
p
p
cresc.
ff
p
ff
p
p
cresc.
101
f
p
cresc.
f
f
p
cresc.
f
p
cresc.
f
f
ff
p
cresc.
f
110
cresc.
6
6
6
6
ff
p
sf
sf
ff
p
sf
ff
p
sf
sf
sf
ff
p
119
pizz.

129
cresc.
cresc.
cresc.
cresc.
137
pp
pp
pp
arco
pp
145
cresc.
cresc.
cresc.
cresc.
f
f
sf
f
sf
f
154
f
f
sf
sf
f
f
sf
f
f
sf
f
decresc. p
f
f
f
163 Prestissimo.
ff
ff
sf
sf
sff
sf
sf
ff
sf
sf

171
sf
ff
p
180
cresc.
f
p cresc.
190
decresc.
200
pp
p
psf
sf
210
pp
ff

1. What is the form of the opening refrain? What is the period structure of the A section within the refrain?
2. What harmonic procedure occurs in the B section of the refrain?
3. In spite of the fact that two different chords are involved, the predominant in m. 15 encompasses two beats. Discuss how these chords are related.
4. What contrapuntal technique occurs in the first episode? *Hint*: What is the relationship between the instruments? You may wish to compare the opening second violin line with the first violin, cello, and viola lines. Why might this relationship be easier to hear in the B section of the first episode?
5. What is the major difference between A1 and A2?
6. How would you support the assertion that the C section (the second episode) is derived from both the refrain and the B section?
7. How would you explain the two dozen or so measures that occur before the final *Prestissimo*?
8. List at least three ways that the material in the *Prestissimo* section summarizes material presented earlier in the movement.

WORKBOOK
32.1–32.7

TERMS AND CONCEPTS

- coda
- episode
- five-part versus seven-part rondos
- refrain
- rondo (rondeau form)
- rondo aria

CHAPTER 33

Sonata Form

Sonata form is a process on which many of the greatest compositions from the late-eighteenth and nineteenth centuries are based. We explore its history, trace the evolution of its form, and analyze examples from the literature.

Originally, in the sixteenth century, the term *sonata* was used as a signal that a given musical work was to be performed instrumentally and not sung. To a large degree, this meaning has held constant for centuries. The term applies to multimovement works for solo instrument or a small ensemble of instruments (there are almost no sonatas for voice). But over the years, musicians also have extended the word *sonata* beyond its original meaning and have applied it to discussion of movements with a very particular form. This form is as important (and just as common) as the other forms we have learned: variation, binary, ternary, and rondo.

Since the 1780s all of the important genres of art music, including symphonies, concertos, operas, and instrumental sonatas, have featured movements cast in sonata form. The two terms often used as synonyms for sonata form—*sonata-allegro form* and *first-movement form*—are misnomers, because movements cast in sonata form may be in any tempo and occur in any movement of larger works. Furthermore, the first movements of these works may not even be cast in sonata form.

At a deeper level, even the term *sonata form* itself is problematic, given that it implies a rigid formal mold governed by a series of compositional rules that composers are required to follow. This most certainly is not the case. We consider sonata form as essentially a way of composing, one that is the outgrowth of a large-scale musical process that is dependent on a powerful yet simple tonal strategy:

1. State the opening material in the tonic.
2. State additional material in a contrasting key.
3. Restate all of the material in tonic.

This very general model harkens back to our study of binary form. We will see that it is from the merging of rounded and balanced elements of binary form that sonata form arises.

The Binary Model for Sonata Form

Just as our understanding of variation, rondo, and even the ternary form is dependent on our knowledge of binary form, so too will be our understanding of sonata form.

Sonata form may be seen as arising from a combination of balanced and rounded continuous binary forms (Example 33.1). Notice that both the exposition and recapitulation are divided into two sections that are defined by harmony. In the **first tonal area (FTA)**, material is presented in the tonic key; in the **second tonal area (STA)**, material is presented originally in the contrasting key (usually V in major mode and III in minor mode). The FTA is dependent on the rounded-binary characteristics, returning with the original material (**recapitulation**) after a digression (**development**) and a HC with an interruption. The STA is dependent on balanced-binary characteristics: Material (STA, usually with a new theme) presented at the end of the first section (exposition) returns at the end of the piece (recapitulation) in the tonic key. This is the **sonata principle**.

EXAMPLE 33.1

A. Balanced rounded continuous binary form (major mode)

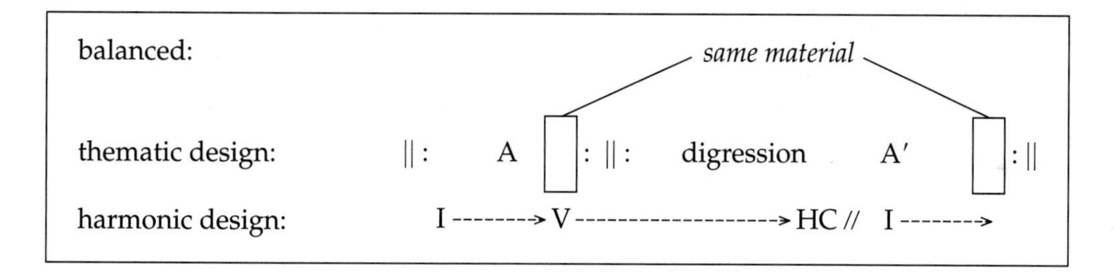

B. Sonata form (major mode)

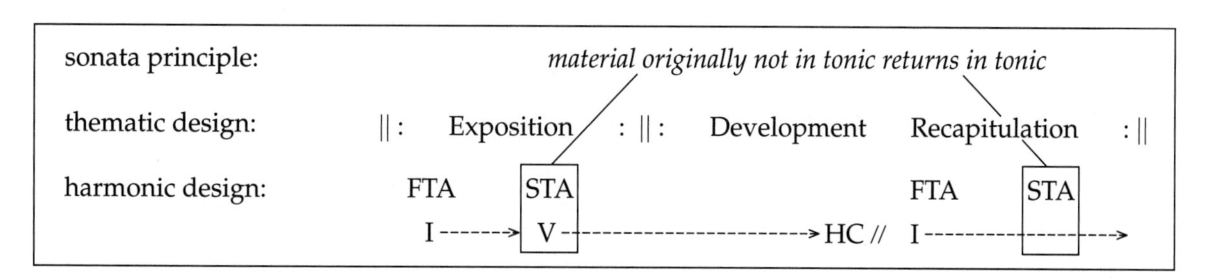

The FTA and STA sections may contain similar or contrasting thematic material; they may also contain multiple themes. To avoid confusion and ambiguity, each theme will be labeled such that the number 1 or 2 designate its tonal area and the letters a, b, c, etc. indicate its order. For example, given three themes in the FTA and two in the STA, the labels would be 1a, 1b, 1c, 2a, 2b, respectively.

Listen to the small sonata movement by Beethoven in Example 33.2 and see if you can label the thematic sections (exposition, development, recapitulation) and harmonic sections (FTA, STA). Be aware that you will encounter passages that seem not to belong to any of these five sections. For now, we'll ignore the additional passages. Keep the following questions in mind as you proceed. What is the large-scale tonal progression? Does it conform to our model of binary form? If not, what are the differences?

EXAMPLE 33.2 Beethoven, Piano Sonata no. 19 in G minor, op. 49, no. 1, *Andante*

DVD 1
CH 33
TRACK 1

39
44
49
f
p
54
59
sf
sf
p
65
sf
73
sf
sf

Continued

Beethoven's movement does indeed blend and expand aspects of rounded- and balanced-binary forms, but only the exposition repeats. The following diagram reveals why only the exposition is repeated: The development and recapitulation together are over twice as long as the exposition, and Beethoven achieves a proportional balance by repeating only the exposition.

measure:	1	16		34			64	80
thematic design:	||: Exposition		:||	Development			Recapitulation	||
	1a	2a		2a	x	2a	1a	2a
harmonic design	i ——→	III ——→		VI ——→			V// i ——→	

Transition

Now that we have determined the large-scale tonal and formal sections in Beethoven's movement, let's return to those passages that seem not to belong to the sections in the preceding diagram. Between the FTA and the STA (mm. 9–15) is a passage that begins identically to the opening of the piece. Given that this passage follows a half cadence, we might expect this to be a consequent phrase that makes a period in the FTA. Instead, there is an alteration in m. 13, and the passage modulates to B♭ major (III), ending on a half cadence and preparing for the entrance of the STA. This seven-measure passage that leads to the STA is called a **transition** (Tr). There are two types of transitions.

1. A **dependent transition (DTr)** begins with a restatement of the initial theme from the FTA.
2. An **independent transition (Itr)** uses new thematic material.

Both types of transition modulate to the STA and end either on the new tonic or the new dominant (in which case the actual statement of the tonic is reserved for the opening of the STA). The pause that very often occurs between the end of the transition and the beginning of the STA and that marks the approximate midpoint of the exposition, is called the **medial caesura**.

In the recapitulation, the FTA and STA remain in the tonic. There is no need for a transition, but transitions often reappear in the recapitulation. Since the ending key for the "transition" is now the original key, this passage is often altered (harmonically and/or melodically) to create a sense of motion. In Beethoven's example, the transition returns at m. 72. This time, there is more activity (in the right hand) and a quicker movement to III before a HC in the original key (at m. 79).

Closing Section

The contrasting tune of the STA ends with a PAC (in III) in m. 29 of Example 33.2. The following cadential section, which closes the exposition, is called the **closing section (Cl).** The closing section follows the appearance of contrasting thematic material in the STA and a conclusive cadence of that material. Because the closing section's purpose is to reinforce the new key, it usually contains multiple cadential figures that are cast in two or more subsections that may even contain new thematic material. As such, the closing section is often longer than the STA, which may occupy eight or even fewer measures. A double bar (or repeat sign) usually marks the end of the exposition, just as it marks the close of the A section in a binary form. Thus, the exposition for Beethoven's sonata has the following form:

measure:	1	9	16	29
thematic design:	FTA	DTr	STA	Cl
harmonic design:	i	i ——→	III	III

Development and Retransition

The development is usually the freest section in a sonata form and is analogous to the digression in a binary form. Material presented in the exposition is transformed, although composers are free to spread their wings and introduce one or more new themes, explore new and often remote harmonic areas, and develop thematic and motivic material through transformations that include thematic fragmentation and sequence. Given the improvisatory character of the development, there is often a complete absence of regular phrasing and periodicity. Thus, developments are often the most complex and dramatic sections of the movement. Underneath the chaotic surface, however, lies a logical unfolding of tonal and melodic events that imbue the form with a sense of coherence.

Beethoven begins his development with a variation of the theme from the STA, followed by a new melody in E♭ major (VI) that enters in m. 38 (labeled *x* in the diagram). The melody from the closing section enters in m. 46, ushering in a tonally unstable section that drives to the dominant and the interruption in m. 54. The **retransition** (**RTr**) is the final area of the development, where the dominant prepares the return of the tonic in the recapitulation. In major-mode sonata forms, the dominant would be secured much earlier (in the STA), and from that point is implicitly prolonged through the development. In this case, the retransition explicitly restates and expands the dominant at the end of the development and moves to the interruption that precedes the recapitulation.

Recapitulation and Coda

Almost always, the recapitulation repeats many events of the exposition, but it contains crucial changes, the most important of which is that not only the FTA's material but also that of the STA and Cl return in the tonic. We have also seen how transitions are altered so that they lead back to the tonic. In addition, composers often alter the recapitulation by compressing thematic material from the FTA, introducing brief tonicizations using modal mixture, or even reversing the order of themes from the exposition's FTA and STA.

Although Beethoven's movement could have ended in m. 97, Beethoven instead concludes the movement with cadential material from the STA in a **coda**. Codas occur after the recapitulation. They also can occur at the end of the exposition, where they are called **codettas**, since they are typically shorter and end away from the tonic key. Codas are optional, as their name implies (in English, "tail" or "appendage"). They serve to confirm the closing key and often incorporate material from the FTA or STA. Material is often stated over a pedal point, which creates a strong cadential feeling. Finally, codas often emphasize the subdominant, which provides a large plagal motion that extends the prevailing key.

The following diagram provides a complete summary of the prototypical events that occur in a sonata form written in either major and minor modes.

Sonata form

thematic design:	‖: Exposition					:‖: Development		Recapitulation			Coda:‖
harmonic design:	FTA	Tr	STA	CL	(Codetta)		RTr	FTA	"Tr"	STA	CL
keys (major mode):	I	→	V	V	V	———→	V //	I	→	I	I I
keys (minor mode):	i	→	III	III	III	———→	V //	i	→	i	i i

Additional Characteristics and Elements of Sonata Form

Monothematic Sonata Form

Example 33.3 illustrates one of Haydn's string quartets, in which the opening of the FTA theme reappears in the STA. Haydn frequently used the same theme (although often varied) in both the FTA and the STA, to create a form called a **monothematic sonata form**. The lack of differentiation between sections plays havoc with attempts to define a first theme and a second theme, but, as you will see, it poses no problem to our analytical labeling system.

EXAMPLE 33.3 Haydn, String Quartet in A major, op. 55, no. 1, *Allegro*

DVD 1
CH 33
TRACK 2

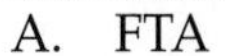

B. STA (using FTA theme)

The Slow Introduction

Some movements cast in sonata form contain slow introductions that touch on foreign harmonic territory and chromatic key areas and incorporate modal mixture. This is particularly common in large works, such as symphonies. Slow introductions usually begin on the tonic (although I is not well established) and eventually move to and close on a half cadence. Because the slow introduction wanders harmonically before moving to V, and because V is often extended, hovering with its added seventh, in anticipation of leading to the tonic, the introduction can be heard to function as a hugely extended upbeat that resolves to the tonic "downbeat" at the allegro FTA.

Example 33.4 shows the 12-measure introduction to Beethoven's Symphony no. 1 in C. A brief look at the opening four measures reveals Beethoven's game plan. Although the first sonority is a root-position C chord, it contains a seventh; as V_7/IV, it moves to F, conferring on this sonority apparent tonic status. Tonal clarification is not given in the following measure since the V_7 that appears (G^7) moves deceptively to vi. The following crescendo sets up the expectation of tonal stability, but yet again Beethoven thwarts our expectations by falling in fifths, as vi moves to V_7/V to V, where a seventh is added. Subsequent attempts to resolve V_7 are thwarted, and the closing cadential gestures in mm. 9–12 reinforce the dominant. At last, in m. 13, V_7 resolves to tonic, which signals the beginning of the exposition.

EXAMPLE 33.4 Beethoven, Symphony no. 1 in C major, op. 21, *Adagio molto*

Harmonic Anomalies

Two harmonic anomalies frequently appear near or at the point of recapitulation. The first is the **false recapitulation**, in which the theme from the FTA appears in the "wrong" key; the real recapitulation, in the tonic, usually follows soon thereafter. Thus, false recapitulations are actually part of the development. The first movement of Haydn's Op. 33/I String Quartet contains a false recapitulation (Example 33.5). The movement is in B minor (although tonal ambiguity is present from the movement's beginning, since D major is strongly implied). The apparent retransition strongly suggests a dominant. But rather than its being the V of B minor, it is instead V of F♯ minor. And the joke doesn't stop there. Haydn doubly fools the listener: Rather than the expected (albeit false) recapitulation beginning on F♯ minor, A major boldly enters, stating the original theme. Only the twists and turns leading through an augmented sixth chord and arrival on V of B minor in mm. 56–57 redirect the tonal trajectory to the true recapitulation in m. 59.

EXAMPLE 33.5 Haydn, String Quartet in B minor, op. 33, no. 1

DVD 1
CH 33
TRACK 4

The second harmonic anomaly is the **subdominant return**, in which the recapitulation begins not on I but on IV (Example 33.6). This procedure arose to create harmonic interest in the recapitulation since so much of it is traditionally cast only in the tonic. Given the exposition's tonal model of root motion up a fifth from I to V and given that the STA in the recapitulation must appear in the tonic to prepare for closure of the movement, composers begin the recapitulation down a fifth from the eventual tonic. Mozart's Piano Sonata in C major, K. 545, is an example of one such work with a subdominant return.

EXAMPLE 33.6

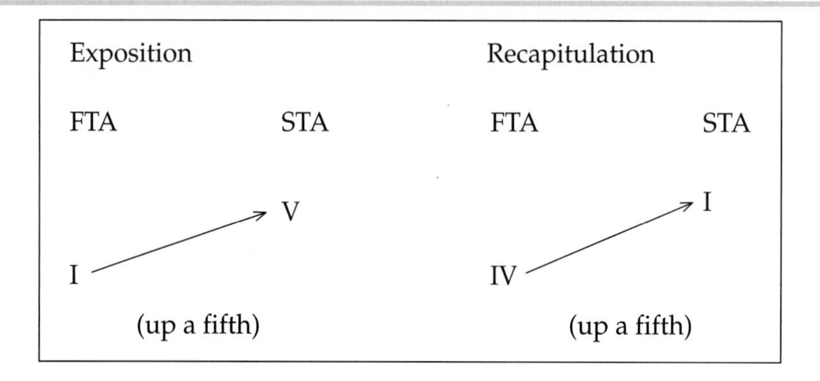

Other Tonal Strategies

Three-Key Exposition

Sonata form remained an important formal type in the nineteenth century. However, the opening years of the 1800s brought with them tonal innovations of many types, including supplanting the traditional tonic and dominant polarity with other tonal progressions. One of these, the **three-key exposition,** is found in major-mode works in which the STA moves to a diatonic third–related key, which bisects the traditional fifth motion from I to V. The motivation for such procedures may have been the century-old minor-mode binary and sonata forms whose overarching i–III–V || create an arguably more dramatic progression than the I–V——— || characteristic of major-mode works. For example, Bruckner's sixth symphony in A major moves from I-iii-V in the exposition and I-vi-IV in the recapitulation before returning to tonic. However, notice that the traditional dominant is secured by the end of the exposition.

Extended Third-Related STAs

An even more dramatic tonal strategy is to postpone the structural dominant until the retransition and to remain in the mediant for the entire exposition. For example, beginning in 1800, Beethoven explored such motion in his so-called "middle period" works, including his Piano Sonata in G-major, Op. 31, no. 1 (Example 33.7). The piece begins with a jaunty G-major gesture leading to the dependent transition, which we would assume would nicely place the STA in the traditional key of V (D major). Instead, the surprising arrival on F♯, with its dominant flavor, leads us to the chromatic third–related key of B major (III). However, Beethoven quickly downgrades the novelty of this tonal progression by converting the B major to B minor (iii), the diatonic key in which the rest of the exposition unfolds.

EXAMPLE 33.7 Beethoven, Piano Sonata in G major, op. 31, no. 1, *Allegro vivace*

DVD 1
CH 33
TRACK 5

Two years later, in his "Waldstein" sonata (Example 33.8), Beethoven again invokes the tonal tactic of moving from I to chromatic III. But this time, after the opening in C major, he remains in E major (III) throughout the exposition. The development focuses on various forms of IV, and V is really only secured at the retransition.

EXAMPLE 33.8 Beethoven, Piano Sonata in C major ("Waldstein"), op. 53, *Allegro con brio*

Continued

Analytical Interlude: Sonatas of Haydn and Mozart

To provide analytical models for your own analysis, we will continue with an analysis of two sonata movements, the first by Haydn and the second by Mozart. In addition to exploring the form of these movements, we will see how each composer fleshes out the structure. In the Haydn sonata, we will focus on tonal issues to see how surface events penetrate into deeper musical structures and influence the form. In Mozart's piece, we will discover how an analysis of motivic expansion helps to clarify the meaning behind what appears to be tonal chaos in the development.

Haydn: Piano Sonata no. 48 in C major, Hob. XVI.35, *Allegro con brio*

Haydn's well-known Piano Sonata in C major (Example 33.9) provides a good introduction to analysis of sonata form, although it does not always adhere strictly to traditional procedures. Remember that sonata form is really not a "form" at all, but a dynamic process in which certain conventions of form can often be counted on to appear. In beginning your study, listen to the piece, marking the following events (some may not be present) and providing roman numerals for keys:

Introduction
Exposition: FTA, DTr or ITr, STA, Cl, Codetta
Development: Retr
Recapitulation: FTA, "DTr" or "ITr," STA, Cl
Coda

EXAMPLE 33.9 Haydn, Piano Sonata no. 48 in C major, Hob. XVI.35, *Allegro con brio*

31
36
40
fz
p
pp
46
f
p
52
56
tr
60

64
68
p
f
fz
73
76
79
fz
83
87

91
95
99
Adagio Tempo I
p
103
fz
110
f
f
fz
114
fz

117
121
125
p
129
cresc.
134
p
pp
f
141
f
p
f
p
f
p
f

Exposition

The piece begins without an introduction. At m. 1, the exposition commences with the FTA in the tonic. The opening eight-measure theme begins with simple arpeggiations (mm. 1–4) followed by a mostly stepwise descent with incomplete neighbors (mm. 5–8). A bit of melodic reduction reveals a stepwise motion from the repeated G that descends a fifth to C in m. 8 (Example 33.10). Note that the final D^5 and C^5 do not really participate in the stepwise descent in m. 6 but wait until the final cadential motion in mm. 7–8; the contrapuntal motion and voice exchange in m. 6 simply prolongs the E^5 in m. 5.

EXAMPLE 33.10 Haydn, Sonata in C, mm. 1–8

Measures 9–16 are an almost literal repeat of mm. 1–8 except for the triplet accompanimental figure and the more varied harmonic setting in mm. 13–15. Thus, we are not finished with the FTA until at least m. 16 and the second PAC.

EXAMPLE 33.11 Haydn, Sonata in C, mm. 20–30

A new theme appears in m. 20 (Example 33.11). When F♯^{5} instigates a move to G major (V), we know that we have entered the modulatory transition. Thus, the proper label for this section is ITr. In general, the use of accidentals in a major-key sonata marks the beginning of the transition section, and the dominant of the key of the STA marks the end of the transition section (i.e., V/V in m. 35). In minor-mode pieces it is the opposite: The opening minor tonic requires an accidental (raising $\hat{7}$ to create a leading tone), but the move to the relative major reinstates the lowered form of $\hat{7}$ since it now functions as $\hat{5}$ in the new key.

Motivically, the beginning of the transition contains a stepwise ascent, C^5-D^5-E^5, E^5-F♯^{5}-G^5 (Example 33.11); this is reminiscent of the opening arpeggiation (now filled in with passing tones), as well as an inversion of the linear descent from G^5 to C^5. Another remarkable correspondence follows when, after G^5 rises a fifth to D^6 (mm. 24–26), D^6 descends a fifth to G^5 (mm. 26–28 and 28–30) in exact imitation of the opening stepwise-fifth descent from G^5 to C^5.

EXAMPLE 33.12 Haydn, Sonata in C, mm. 36–41

The STA begins in m. 36 with a new theme. However, even a cursory examination reveals that the ascending fifth recurs (Example 33.12). A strong cadence in mm. 44–45 closes the STA. The Cl, which occupies mm. 46–62, begins with yet another manifestation of the descending fifth (filled-in arpeggiation figure), which releases the tension of the exposition (Example 33.13).

EXAMPLE 33.13 Haydn, Sonata in C, mm. 44–48

A codetta (mm. 62–67) restates the opening theme in V. The following chart presents the exposition's formal and harmonic events.

measures:	1–19	20–35	36–45	46–62	62–67
thematic design:	FTA	ITr	STA	CL	Codetta
harmonic design:	I	⟶	V	V	V

Development

The development begins humorously, with an apparent return to the tonic, C major. However, the linear descent of a fifth in the soprano ends in an unexpected half cadence in A minor (vi) in m. 71. Haydn—a composer with a penchant for surprise—does not continue in A minor, but instead sets the opening theme in F major. Only after the theme is completely stated (mm. 71–79) and an A2 (−3/+4) sequence accrues dramatic tension (mm. 80–83) does A minor return, in m. 83.

Haydn next retraces his harmonic steps, using a D2 (−5/+4) sequence to return to F major (mm. 86–90). However, the F harmony continues to descend to E, the same chord that was abandoned in m. 71. A pedal point on $\hat{5}$ usually indicates the retransition, but the pedal here is on E (V/vi) rather than on G (V). A strong circle of fifths moves to the dominant (E-A-D-G in mm. 94–103), so the pedal on E in m. 94 may be regarded as the beginning of the retransition.

Recapitulation

The recapitulation begins in m. 104 with a restatement of theme 1a one octave lower than its original presentation. A dramatic change occurs in m. 111 when, just as the listener anticipates a literal restatement of the theme, it appears in the parallel minor. This use of modal mixture might suggest that Haydn is redeveloping material (i.e., that the movement has not really left the development and begun the recapitulation), but in m. 118 he returns to the established model by repeating the material of 1a first heard in m. 13.

Suddenly, Haydn skips ahead to the dramatic arpeggiations and half cadence that characterized the end of the transition section, thus compressing the second part of the FTA and the transition into a 15-measure phrase, nearly half the length it occupied in the exposition.

The STA is stated in the tonic (mm. 126–35), followed by the Cl (mm. 136–51), at which point a dramatic diminished seventh chord (m. 141) heralds an extended coda that closes the piece. The following diagram presents a complete formal and harmonic diagram of the movement.

measure:	1	20	36	46	62	68	94	104	111	126	136	152
thematic design:	Exposition					Development		Recapitulation				Coda
harmonic design	FTA	ITr	STA	CL	Codetta		RTr	FTA	"ITr"	STA	CL	
	I	⟶	V	V	V	I–vi–IV–vi–V//		I	⟶	I	I	I

This movement generally conforms to our model of sonata form. However, departures from the norm, such as the pedal point at the end of the FTA, the very short STA, the curtailed FTA in the recapitulation, and the dovetailing of the missing material in the transition of the recapitulation, demonstrate how composers might mold the sonata form to accommodate their creative impulses.

Mozart, Piano Sonata in B♭ major, K. 333, *Allegro*

In the first movement of Mozart's Piano Sonata in B♭ major, K. 333, we will grapple with interpreting what appears to be a random series of harmonies in the development.

Listen to and study Example 33.14, locating the important formal sections and their controlling key areas. The formal structure is extremely clear in this movement. The exposition, demarcated by the double bar and repeat signs, occupies mm. 1–63. The FTA closes at m. 10, the dependent transition begins at m. 11 and closes on the arpeggiating dominant of the new key, and the STA in F major (V) occupies mm. 23–38. The closing section divides into two smaller sections (mm. 38–50 and mm. 50–58), and a codetta closes the exposition (mm. 59–63). The recapitulation and coda (mm. 94–165) unfold in the same manner as the exposition. The chart following the score shows the main formal sections of the movement. Notice that the harmonic progression in the development (mm. 64–93) remains to be interpreted.

EXAMPLE 33.14 Mozart, Piano Sonata in B♭ major, K. 333, *Allegro*

17
20
23
28
32
36

39
fp
fp
f
fp
fp
42
f
p
46
50
53
56
tr
59
tr

64
68
71
74
tr
tr
77
tr
80
83

87
90
93
97
100
104

107
111
114
117
tr
120
tr
124

127
131
tr
134
fp
fp
f
137
fp
fp
f
139
p
143

measure:	1	11	23	39	59	64	87	94	104	119	135	161
thematic design:	Exposition					Development		Recapitulation				Coda
harmonic design:	FTA	DTr	STA	CI	Codetta		RTr	FTA	"DTr"	STA	CI	
	I	⟶	V	V	V	???⟶	V//	I	⟶	I	I	I

Exposition

We will now explore the thematic and motivic materials in Mozart's sonata. Let's make a contrapuntal reduction of the outer voices of the FTA theme in order to understand the underlying voice-leading framework from which motivic figures might emerge. A clear I-ii-V_7 progression opens the piece and is followed by a contrapuntal elaboration of the tonic (mm. 5–6). This movement does not initially appear to contain any clear-cut motives based on surface contours, except for the descending scalar sixth (comprising a fifth, preceded by an upper-neighbor grace note that should be played as a sixteenth note) that begins the piece.

Although the B♭^{4} in the upper voice of m. 1 is clearly an arrival point, the E♭^{5} (m. 2) that eventually moves to D^5 (m. 4) seems to be more important, given those pitches' durational, metrical, and registral prominence. Might the initial scalar descent be emerging and expanded over many measures? This is the interpretation given in Example 33.15. Note that the overall descent of a fifth (the same fifth that opened the movement) is bisected into thirds by range: F^5-E♭^{5}-D^5 and D^6-C^6-B♭^{5}. The F^5 in the upbeat of m. 1 is prolonged through the downbeat of m. 2 before it descends to Eb^5 (m. 2) and D^5 (m. 4). The continuing C^4–B♭^{4} in mm. 5–6 is not a strong arrival on tonic, because the tonic chord is in inversion and is not preceded by a PD–D; the chords in mm. 5–6 act as part of a voice exchange that prolongs tonic, which further indicates the subordinate nature of the B♭ in m. 6. The strong structural arrival of C^6–B♭^{5} in mm. 9–10 completes the fifth descent.

EXAMPLE 33.15

The theme in the STA literally repeats the same fifth-plus-neighbor descent from the FTA, in the key of F major (V). However, this time Mozart develops the upper neighbor to $\hat{5}$ by harmonizing $\hat{6}$ with B♭ major (IV) in m. 24, thus stabilizing the soprano D^5. Notice that just like the FTA's fifth-plus-neighbor descent, the STA's descent is interrupted by a pause on $\hat{3}$ (in F major, m. 26). The complete descent does not occur until m. 38.

Development

The development contains unusual modal shifts and curious tonicizations that make it difficult to determine any underlying harmonic progression. It begins with a simple right-hand restatement of the initial tune in F major (V), with the upper neighbor, D^5. A bass ascent begins with F^3 in m. 64 and moves through G^3, A^3, B♭^{3}, and C^4; the line continues with the D^4 (m. 69) and resolves to C^4 (m. 70). This results in another setting of the familiar motive of a stepwise fifth-plus-neighbor, this time in exact retrograde of the opening gesture of the STA and expanded over seven measures. Note that the chord in m. 69 sounds out of place, as if Mozart has marked it for our consciousness. Could he be preparing us for other hidden statements of the motive?

The unexpected cadence on F minor (rather than major) in m. 71 and motion to a G^7 harmony in m. 73 imply a tonicization of C minor. However, the "arrival" on C minor is greatly weakened when the bass is left unresolved on G, resulting in a six-four harmony (m. 75). $G\flat^3$ descends to an F^7 harmony (mm. 76–78), implying the beginning of the retransition. However, once again the listener's expectations are thwarted when F^3 rises to $F\sharp^3$ and then resolves to G minor in m. 80. There is no strong cadence in G minor; instead, V^4_3 of V suddenly appears in m. 87 and moves to V in mm. 88–89. The recapitulation begins in m. 93.

We now step back and interpret these events. We know that F major (V) controls the opening of the development and that C minor (ii) and G minor (vi) follow. Thus, a series of ascending fifths (F-C-G, and D, as V of G) underlies the development until the motion to F at m. 87. But many questions remain unanswered. For example, why are the tonal areas so weakly tonicized? And how can we explain the odd shift from the unusually long and unresolved D-major harmony that moves to the weak V^4_3/V chord in m. 87). Let's look to the eight-measure motivic expansion of the fifth-plus-neighbor motive for clues.

EXAMPLE 33.16

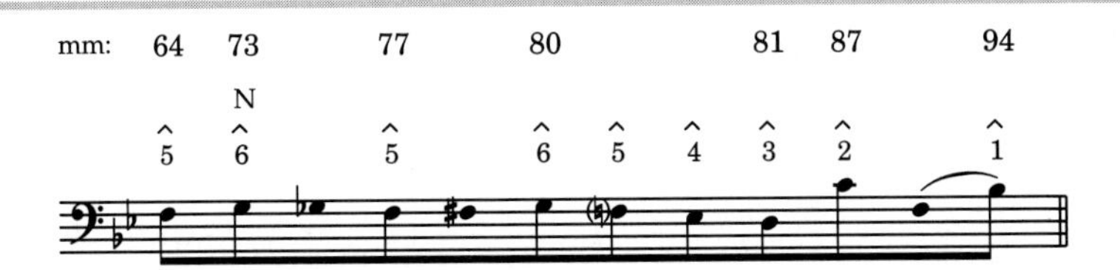

The bass F^3 ascends to G^3 in m. 73; the sustained G^3 was followed by the chromatic passing tone $G\flat^3$, which returned to F^3 (mm. 76–77). Again, the bass rose to G^3 through $F\sharp^3$, followed this time by a rapid descent to D^3, which was sustained from mm. 81–86. Through registral transfer, D^3 then fell to C^4 (V^4_3/V chord in m. 87), leapt to F^3 (m. 88), and finally returned to $B\flat^3$ at the opening of the recapitulation. Example 33.16 presents a notated summary of this progression.

From this bass-line summary, we see that Mozart is projecting the small opening gesture (G-F-E♭-D-C-B♭) over the entire development. Remember that the very first expanded statement of the descent (mm. 1–10) stopped on D for five measures. We now can understand why Mozart extended D major for so long (mm. 81–87) and didn't resolve it to its tonic. We also know why Mozart did not resolve the G^3 to C in m. 75, for to have done so would have obscured the remarkable linear parallelism. Finally, in light of the controlling nature of the motive, we understand why Mozart used the V^4_3 chord in m. 87 rather than the expected and much stronger root position: because the inversion (with C in the bass) preserves the motive's stepwise descent.

The goals of the preceding analyses were to understand the mechanics of sonata form, to show how sonata form is an outgrowth and expansion of binary form, and to demonstrate how sonata form is a flexible and fascinating process that composers employ to express uniquely personal musical statements. Discovering and interpreting hidden and transformed manifestations of motives are some of the rewards of analysis.

Summary of Part 8

We have seen that even though binary form lies at the heart of ternary, rondo, and sonata forms, there is a crucial distinction between sonata and the other two forms: Ternary and rondo are additive, composite forms, whereas sonata is an organic form. That is, ternary and rondo forms—while often demonstrating important motivic and harmonic connections between their various sections—contain tonally closed units, and thus the omission of one or more of these sections would not seriously jeopardize the structural integrity of the piece. Sonata form, by contrast, is a more continuous structure, each part of which depends on every other part, resulting in a single integrated whole.

We also learned that the basic root motions of tonal music, which we first encountered in the chord-to-chord progressions beginning in Chapter 8 and later learned may be expanded by tonicization, also were part of these large forms. Finally, motivic connections between the various strata of a piece create carefully woven webs that make each piece a unique artwork.

EXERCISE INTERLUDE

ANALYSIS

DVD 2
CH 33
TRACK 1

33.1 Platti, Sonata in C Major, *Six Sonatas for Harpsichord*, op. 4, no. 4

Listen to and study the following movement. On a separate sheet of paper, answer the series of questions that follows.

1. Make a formal diagram that includes names of sections and their respective measure numbers as well as the tonal plan (use roman numerals).
2. The phrase lengths in the exposition vary from four to eleven measures. Mark the phrases in the exposition. And when you encounter long ones, explain how they are extended. Consider the possibility that Platti has repeated small subphrases or inserted sequences. For example, the first phrase occupies six measures, but mm. 5–6 are a repetition of mm. 4–5, which help to reinforce the first cadence.
3. Bracket and label all sequences in the piece.
4. What contrapuntal technique is used in mm. 22–24?
5. The transition in the exposition prepares not only the new key but also the motivic and thematic material in the STA. Discuss at least two examples of how Platti achieves this preparation.
6. The development begins much the same way the exposition does. However, an important change occurs that sets into motion the fragmentation and tonal adventures that are characteristic of development sections. Discuss the relationship of the opening of the development to the opening of the exposition, and then focus on the changes that follow. Include in your discussion the motives used and the harmonic areas explored.
7. There appears to be no retransition that would prepare the recapitulation. However, a slight retard into the recapitulation just might allow

one to hear an implied dominant that leads to the recapitulation. Develop this idea in a few sentences.

8. Given that the tonic key is maintained throughout the recapitulation, you might assume that transitions are not necessary. In fact, they might be viewed as hindrances, for they must give the impression of motion, only to lead eventually back to the tonic, in which the tune from the STA is cast. However, Platti has written a transition that is much more interesting than the usual fare. List at least three differences between this transition and the transition in the exposition.

TERMS AND CONCEPTS

- closing section (Cl)
- false recapitulation
- first tonal area (FTA)
- monothematic sonata form
- second tonal area (STA)
- slow introduction
- sonata form
  - exposition
  - codetta
  - development
  - recapitulation
  - coda
- subdominant return
- three-key exposition
- transition (Tr)
  - dependent transition (DTr)
  - independent transition (ITr)

PART 9

INTRODUCTION TO NINETEENTH-CENTURY HARMONY: THE SHIFT FROM ASYMMETRY TO SYMMETRY

Far too often, people rely on general proclamations to characterize the new developments of nineteenth-century music. There is some truth both in effusive and subjective statements such as "It is a period evincing a lush hodgepodge of thick, wandering harmonies" and in technical and clinically objective statements such as "the chromatic tonal system replaces the diatonic system." The music of nineteenth-century composers is indeed lush, and it features thick, rapidly changing harmonies built from novel combinations of four and five voices. And later-nineteenth-century music is more chromatic than eighteenth- and early-nineteenth-century music. But neither proclamation provides us with examples of these new attributes or with tangible explanations of how early-nineteenth-century harmonic practice influences the music of the late nineteenth and early twentieth centuries.

These final four chapters explore some of the innovations of tonal composition that occurred from the early nineteenth century through the first decade of the twentieth century. These developments were naturally suited to the artistic sensibilities of the nineteenth century, an era in which sharp social, philosophical, political, and artistic changes took place. We start by tracing the seeds for these new harmonic tendencies in the music of composers such as Mozart, Beethoven, Schubert, and Chopin. From there, we witness the flowering of these harmonic techniques in the music of composers such as Wagner, Liszt, Brahms, Tchaikovsky, Wolf, Grieg, Scriabin, and Berg.

CHAPTER 34

New Harmonic Tendencies

Tonal Ambiguity: The Plagal Relation and Reciprocal Process

Modal mixture (Chapter 27) and tonicization (Chapter 25) allow chromaticism to permeate deeper levels of music. The free interchange of major and minor modes results in a compression from 24 major and minor keys to 12 "major-minor" keys. Such compression allows composers easy access to chromatically related keys such as ♭III and ♭VI. In the nineteenth century, this weakened the dominant function. As a result, the final structural cadence of pieces incorporated harmonies such as iv and $ii^{ø6}_{5}$—chords that substitute for the dominant—and moved directly to the tonic in a technique called the **plagal relation**. Paradoxically, this caused the dominant to become much more important as it retained its ability to signal where the tonic should be.

EXAMPLE 34.1 Chopin, Etude in C minor ("Revolutionary"), op. 10, no. 12

DVD 1
CH 34
TRACK 1

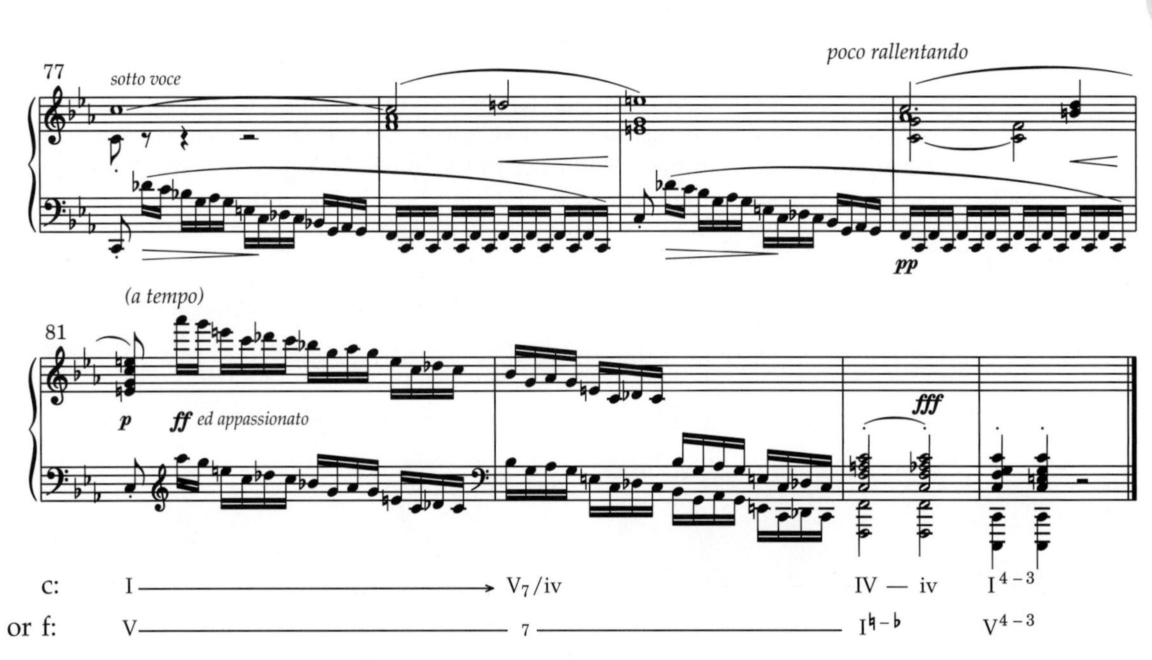

The rise of the plagal relation contributed to **tonal ambiguity**, an important aesthetic in the music of the nineteenth century. An example of this deliberate obscuring of the location of the tonic may be heard at the end of Chopin's Etude in C minor (Example 34.1). Note how the final section of the piece sounds like a coda, because the major tonic functions as an applied chord of F minor (iv). Because this coda-like section treats the tonic as an applied chord of iv, you might have heard the piece close not on a tonic harmony but rather on the dominant of iv. If, after careful listening, you can discern both functions of the progression, then you are being sensitive to an important type of nineteenth-century tonal ambiguity called the **reciprocal process**. The reciprocal process occurs when the listener loses tonal grounding because of conflicting tonal implications that confuse the three harmonic functions (T, PD, and D).

Composers such as Robert Schumann and Johannes Brahms were fond of incorporating the reciprocal process in their compositions. Study the close of Schumann's song "Auf einer Burg," which begins in E minor (Example 34.2); then listen carefully to the excerpt. Although the song *looks* like it ends in E major, does it *sound* like it ends in that key?

EXAMPLE 34.2 Schumann, "Auf einer Burg" ("In a Castle"), *Liederkreis*, op. 39, no. 7

DVD 1 CH 34 TRACK 2

Continued

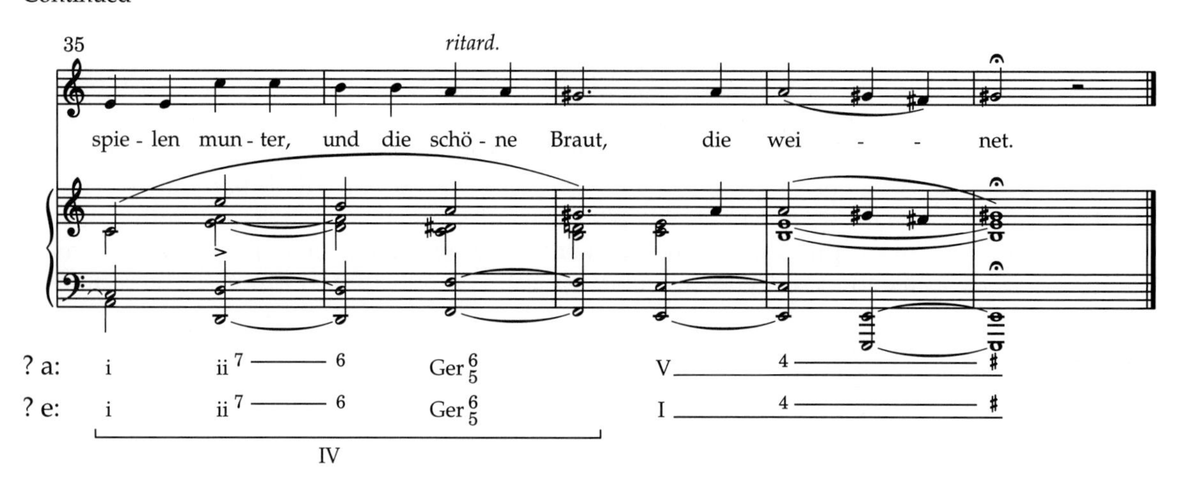

The closing five measures use augmented sixth and cadential six-four chords to tonicize a minor (iv), effectively transforming the E major into the V of A minor. Consistent with this transformation, the E-major triad that closes "Auf einer Burg" functions as a dominant preparation leading to the start of the next song of the cycle, "In der Fremde" (Example 34.3). Notice that the songs are linked not only by their large-scale dominant-tonic motions but also by the melodic motive that permeates both songs (marked by brackets in Examples 34.2 and 34.3).

EXAMPLE 34.3 "In der Fremde" ("In a Foreign Land"), *Liederkreis*, op. 39, no. 8

DVD 1
CH 34
TRACK 3

Tonal Ambiguity: Semitonal Voice Leading

Nineteenth-century composers often connected distantly related chords or tonal areas with a technique that transforms one chord chromatically into the next. **Semitonal voice leading** moves two or more voices by a half step while usually keeping one common tone in another voice.

EXAMPLE 34.4 Mozart, String Quartet in C major ("Dissonant"), K. 465, *Adagio*

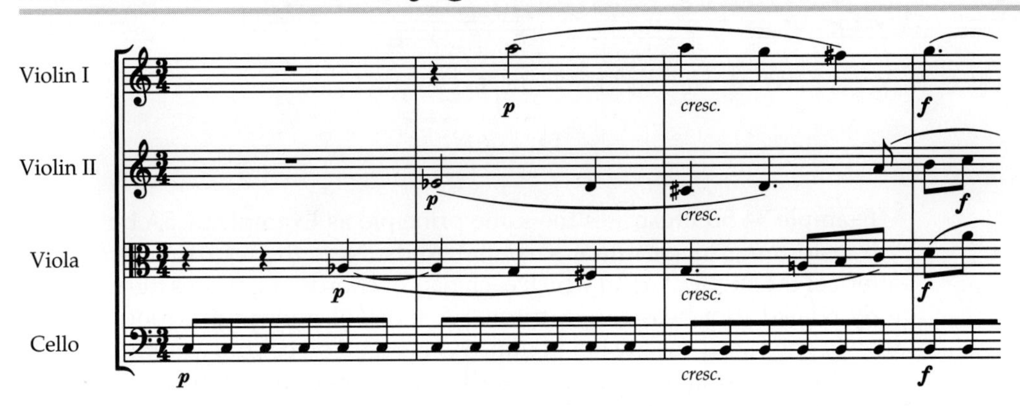

A good introduction to semitonal voice leading can be seen in the slow introduction of Mozart's "Dissonant" Quartet, shown in Example 34.4. Here, the sinuous motion of all the voices clouds the tonic of the piece, C major. The repeated C^3s in the cello that open the piece imply the key of C. But the entrance of the viola's A♭ calls into question the possibility of C major, especially given that the first complete sonority is an A♭-major triad in first inversion on the downbeat of m. 2. On the next beat, however, violin I boldly enters with A♮^{5}. The resulting pungent cross relation with A♭^{3} thwarts our expectations that A♭ major might be the key. Only at the downbeat of m. 4, when a G-major triad (in first inversion) occurs, is there any evidence to support our initial expectation that C major is the key. In retrospect, we can understand that both the A♭ and the A♮ displace G, postponing its arrival.

Example 34.5A illustrates a harmonic succession that involves chords whose roots lie a major third away from one another: C major-A♭ minor-E major-C major (note the presence of intense enharmonicism, shown by slurs that indicate retention of common tones). The chord-to-chord connections sound relatively smooth, given their consistent step motion, yet tonal stability evaporates; there is no sense of tonic, pre-dominant, or dominant. In fact, one might say that tonal function is suspended so that the harmonic motion is more a chordal succession than a functional progression. This sense is corroborated by the lack of cadence. See how the return to C major is not satisfying as an arrival, even though the opening voicing returns.

EXAMPLE 34.5

DVD 1
CH 34
TRACK 5

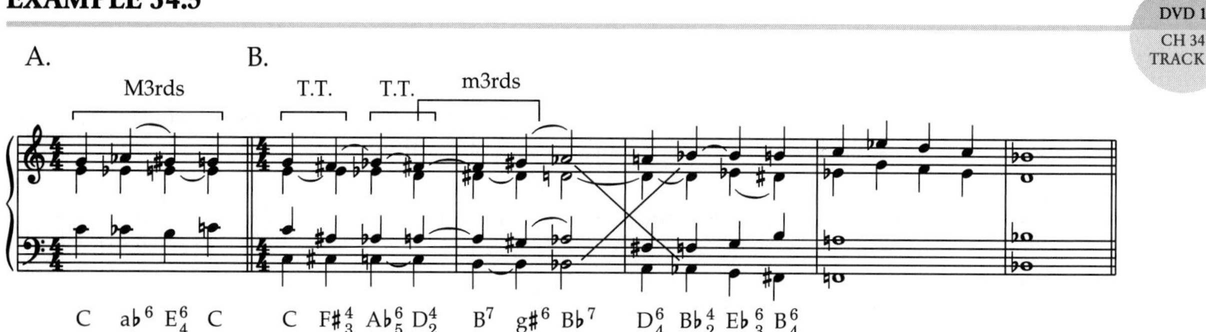

Example 34.5B illustrates the same principle as Example 34.5A but works by transforming major-minor seventh chords. Note the recurring two-chord pattern of the succession, in which each pair of chords juxtaposes the most distantly related root possible—a tritone. A series of minor-third root relations follows. The chord succession in mm. 3–5 is based on contrary motion that resolves to the new key, B♭ major. Overall, B♭ is secured by a stepwise chromatic descent from C (m. 1) to the new dominant (m. 4). Although the modulation could have been accomplished much more simply, its present form creates tonal ambiguity and demonstrates how its arrival on ♭VII of C is but one of any number of potential tonal destinations.

Let's look at a longer stretch of a slow introduction to see how modal mixture and semitonal voice leading create tonal ambiguity. In the opening of Beethoven's Fourth Symphony, the octaves strongly imply that B♭ is the tonic (Example 34.6). Just as in the introduction to Mozart's "Dissonant" Quartet, Beethoven uses $\flat\hat{6}$; to displace $\hat{5}$ and create tonal ambiguity. The interval of a sixth between B♭ and G♭ could imply the parallel minor or even a first-inversion G♭ harmony. The motion in the alto voice through E♭ and F to D♭ strongly implies the key of B♭ minor. By contrast, the melodic sequence of falling thirds in mm. 2-4 (G♭-E♭, F-D♭, E♭-C, D♭-B♭) takes us to the first stable, complete root-position harmony-on G♭ major (m. 5). The listener is therefore confronted with two possibilities. Is the melodic motion sufficient to establish the key of G♭ major? It is only when G♭ descends a semitone to F in a half cadence (m. 6) that the listener understands its role as a $\flat\hat{6}$, pre-dominant, and hears B♭ as the prevailing key, but B♭ minor, not major. This is reinforced in the subsequent measures when both G♭ and E♮ form double neighbors around the dominant F. From there, G♭ makes a last appearance, in m. 12, as the ninth of a dissonant chord, which finally moves to the tonic B♭ octaves in m. 13.

EXAMPLE 34.6 Beethoven, Symphony no. 4 in B♭ major, op. 60, *Adagio*

DVD 1
CH 34
TRACK 6

A.

p pp pp sempre

B♭: I ♭VI V (N)

Continued

8
pp
V
UN
LN
V
7
A′
13
fp
pp
pp
I
♭VI
UN
LN
20
pp
♭VI
UN
LN
♭VI ⇒ V7/♭ii
25
fp
VI/♭ii? V
C Major
V
d minor
A2 (−3/+4)
30
sfp
pp
V7/V
V/d
35
5̂ (in d) 7̂ (in B♭)
CT
cresc.
ff
ff
5
5
V
BRD
V
B♭ major

The tonal battle is far from over, however. At m. 13 the restatement of the material from the opening measures sets up the listener for a direct repeat, which will be denied. The difference this time is that G♭ is sustained in m. 17 and expanded by its upper neighbor, G♮, in m. 19. The G♭ is converted to F♯ in the following measures, and the addition of flanking double neighbors implies B minor, a sort of minor Neapolitan of B♭. The motion to G major (m. 25) then sounds like a deceptive progression (V to ♭VI in B major) that recalls the underlying V-♭VI motion of F-G♭ in the tonic, B♭ major. Next, an A2 ($-3/+4$) sequence climbs to d minor (mm. 25–29). At m. 36, A major, the back-relating dominant of D minor, yields to the dominant of B♭ major, the key of the symphony. It takes 39 long measures to establish the key, thus postponing the tonic for nearly two minutes.

A good place to look for moments that exhibit the power and potential ambiguity of semitonal voice leading are pieces that employ enharmonic transformations of the augmented sixth chord and dominant seventh chord. Example 34.7 illustrates this common procedure. Because Brahms's song begins on a C-major sonority, the first-time listener will most likely assume C major to be the tonic. However, the addition of A♯³ in m. 3 destabilizes the C-major triad. The attentive listener will probably hear the chromaticism as the lowered seventh (B♭), rather than the augmented sixth (A♯), and thus assume that C has become V_7/IV. The semitonal movement to the cadential six-four chord in m. 6 requires the listener immediately to revise this expectation. At m. 6 we head to E minor rather than C major; the following PAC in m. 9 confirms this key.

EXAMPLE 34.7 Brahms, "Parole" ("Password"), op. 7, no. 2

DVD 1 CH 34 TRACK 7

Continued

The listener, in an attempt not to be misled by the C Mm seventh chord when it returns at m. 9, is likely to interpret it this time as an augmented sixth chord. Brahms, however, fools the listener again by making the chord a V_7, which moves to an F-major sonority and a dominant pedal in ♭II rather than to the expected dominant of E minor. Only in m. 14 does the augmented sixth return. The ambiguity of the dominant seventh and augmented sixth chords, paired with semitonal voice leading, allows Brahms to fool the listener again and again.

EXERCISE INTERLUDE

ANALYSIS

34.1

Study the following excerpts, which contain ambiguities resulting from mixture, semitonal voice leading, the reciprocal process, and enharmonic puns. Bracket the area or areas in which ambiguity plays an important role. Then describe in prose the type of ambiguity involved.

A. Brahms, "Dämmrung senkte sich von oben" ("Twilight sank from high above"), op. 59, no. 1

While tonal ambiguity in this excerpt is minimal, a harmonized melodic motive appears in the introduction that somewhat obscures the surface harmony. What is this motive? Consider also the metric placement of the motive (i.e., where do the tones of figuration occur in relation to the chord tones? Is Brahms consistent in their metric placement?).

B. Dvořák, Symphony no. 9 ("New World"), *Largo*

C. Brahms, "Es hing der Reif" ("Hoarfrost was hanging"), op. 106, no. 3

Brahms implies two tonal areas simultaneously. What are they? Discuss how these keys are implied, juxtaposed, and discarded. For example, does the excerpt begin with a cadential six-four in A minor or with a simple 6-5 motion in C major? By the end of the excerpt, which key controls? Compare this excerpt with the final measures of the song. Why do these closing measures come as a surprise?

Continued

7
Lin - den - baum, wo - durch das Licht wie Sil - ber floß Ich
in the lime tree. Through which light streamed like silver I
13
sah dein Haus, wie hell im Traum ein bli - tzend Fe - en -
saw your house, as brightly as in a dream a sparkling
19
schloß ein bli - - tzend Fe - en - schloß
fairy castle
daß Frost und Win - - -
that it was actually
pp

Continued

D. Brahms, Symphony no. 1 in C minor, op. 68, *Allegro*

This excerpt, from the beginning of the development, starts in B major but ends in C minor. Make a bass-line reduction of the progression to determine how B major moves to C minor.

Continued

WRITING

34.2 Writing Progressions Involving Mixture, Reciprocal Process, Semitonal Voice Leading, and Enharmonic Reinterpretation

On a separate sheet of manuscript paper, complete the following tasks.

A. In B minor, write a chromatic voice exchange incorporating pre-dominant harmony and any augmented sixth chord.
B. Using a German sixth chord as your pivot, modulate in five chords or less from F minor to F♯ minor.
C. In D major, move to ♭VI, briefly stabilize (prolong) it, and then destabilize it by turning it into a Fr^4_3 that resolves to V.
D. Modulate from F major to its relative minor using an enharmonic pivot. (*Hint:* The chord is a pre-dominant in both keys.)
E. Given the key of G major, write short progressions in which the D dominant seventh chord functions as:
1. a German augmented sixth chord
2. part of an A2 (−3/+4) applied chord sequence
3. a German diminished third chord

WORKBOOK 34.1–34.2

F. Write a progression in D minor in which the closing D tonic sounds more like a dominant than a tonic. (*Hint:* A Picardy third alone does not imply a reciprocal process.)
G. Write a progression in C major that opens with a plagal progression, tonicizes E♭ major, and closes in E♭ major with a different plagal progression.

KEYBOARD

34.3 New Harmonic Procedures and Chromatic Chords

Complete the following tasks in four voices; analyze.

A. In D major and B♭ major play the progression I-iv-iv_6-V-♭VI-$ii^{ø6}_5$ I (begin with $\hat{5}$ in the soprano).
B. In G major, play a progression in which tonal ambiguity arises because of the confusion between the tonic and IV.
C. Modulate from E♭ major to D major using an enharmonic augmented sixth chord.

The Diminished Seventh Chord and Enharmonic Modulation

Beginning in the eighteenth century, composers used the diminished seventh chord both as a powerful goal-oriented applied chord and as a dramatic signpost. For example, a strategically placed diminished seventh chord could underscore a particularly emotional image from the text of a song. A vivid and painful example is heard in the last moment of Schubert's "Erlking." Immediately before we learn of the fate of the sick child ("and in [the father's] arms, the child. . ."), the previous 145 measures of frantic, wildly galloping music come to a halt. The fermata that marks this moment, and which seems to last forever, is accompanied by a single sustained diminished seventh, underscoring this crucial moment (Example 34.8). We learn immediately thereafter that in spite of his valiant attempts to rush his sick son home by horseback, the father was too late: The child was dead.

EXAMPLE 34.8 Schubert, "Erlkönig," D. 328

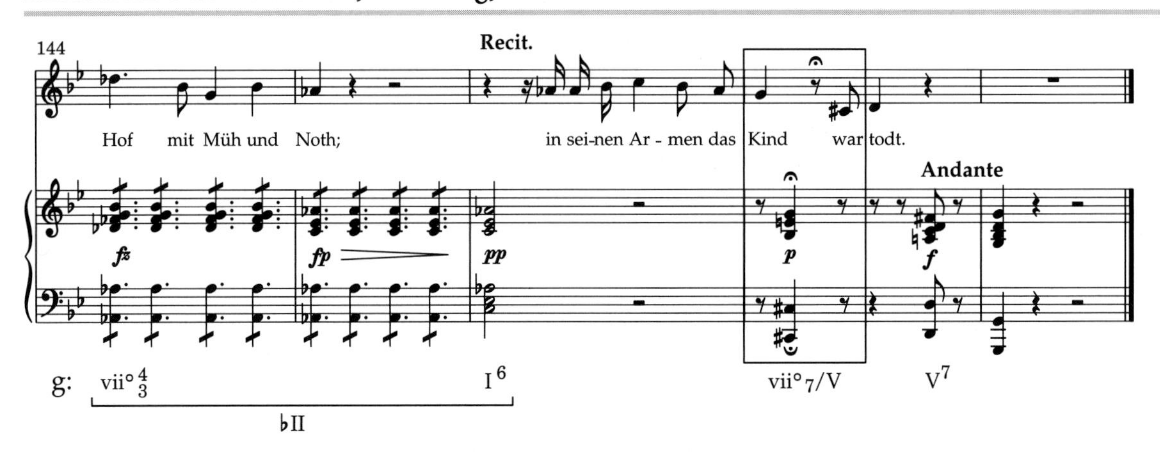

Since before Bach, composers also have used the diminished seventh chord to create tonal ambiguity. Ambiguity is possible because the chord in any of its inversions partitions the octave into four minor thirds (using enharmonicism). For example, given the diminished seventh chord in Example 34.9A, its three inversions produce no new intervals. This is not the case for other sonorities, such as the major triad, which contains six intervals through its inversions (m3, M3, P4, P5, m6, M6). See Example 34.9B. Chords that possess this special ability to partition the octave into identical intervals are known as **symmetrically constructed harmonies**.

EXAMPLE 34.9

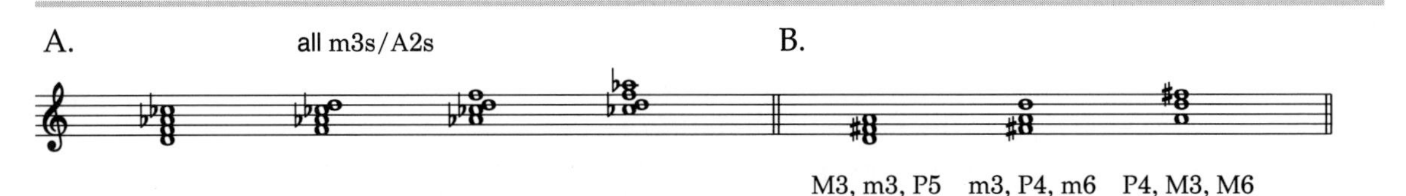

Composers exploit the potential of symmetrically constructed harmonies by using them to access both close and distant key areas. Example 34.10 contains a diminished seventh chord that implies C minor or C major. When we spell the same chord a bit differently (Example 34.10), it leans toward a different tonic: A minor.

EXAMPLE 34.10

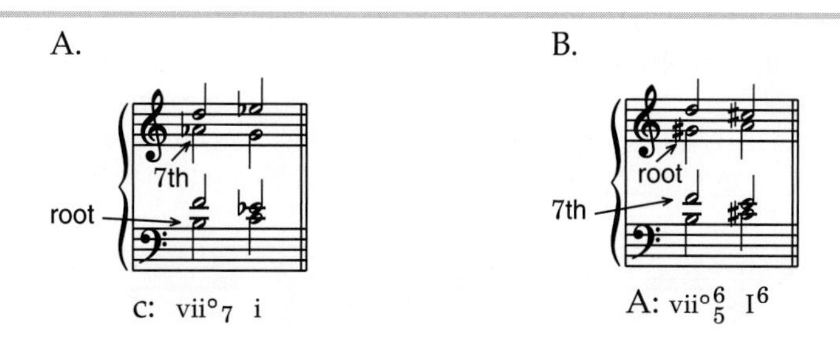

Consider the ramifications of what we've just seen: Within a given chord, the inaudible enharmonic alteration of a single note (here, A♭ becomes G♯) allows the chord to function in two remotely related keys. C minor and A major (six accidentals apart) both become instantly accessible by virtue of this single respelled pitch. In fact, through **enharmonic reinterpretation**, the vii°$_7$ becomes a vehicle that can modulate to many other key areas. This technique is similar to the reinterpretation of the German augmented sixth chord (respelled as a V$_7$ in Chapter 30); given that the German sixth is not symmetrical, its access to remote keys is limited.

Example 34.11 shows four different spellings of our diminished seventh chord, along with its resolutions. The diminished seventh is a remarkable pivot chord that can access distant tonal areas, even keys that lie a minor third or a tritone away from each other. A good way to determine the four accessible keys is to interpret each of the four pitches in the diminished seventh chord as a leading tone, as shown in Example 34.11.

EXAMPLE 34.11

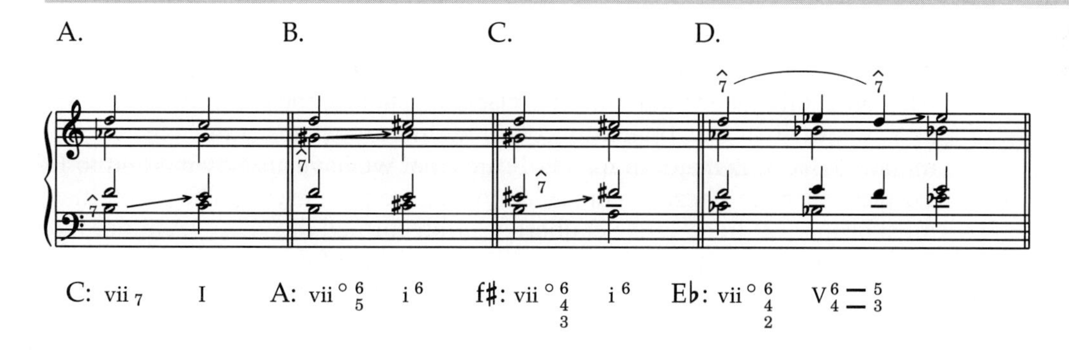

Analysis

When analyzing tonicizations that result from the enharmonic reinterpretation of a diminished seventh chord, use the same pivot chord technique that we employed in Chapters 25 and 28. It is important to show how the chord functions in both the original key and the new key. Example 34.12 begins in G major and ends with a tonicization of B♭ major (♭III). Note that the first appearance of the diminished seventh chord functions as a passing chord (m. 1). Arrows reveal the resolution of the root (F♯) and seventh (E♭). The enharmonically transformed diminished seventh chord in m. 3 is initially still heard as vii°$^6_5$; but because of where it progresses, it actually functions and is notated as a root-position vii°$_7$ in the new tonal area. Be aware that composers are not consistent in the way they notate enharmonic modulations using diminished seventh chords. They may notate the chord either as it functions in the new key or as it functions in the old key (in which case it would appear to have an unusual resolution).

EXAMPLE 34.12

DVD 1
CH 34
TRACK 8

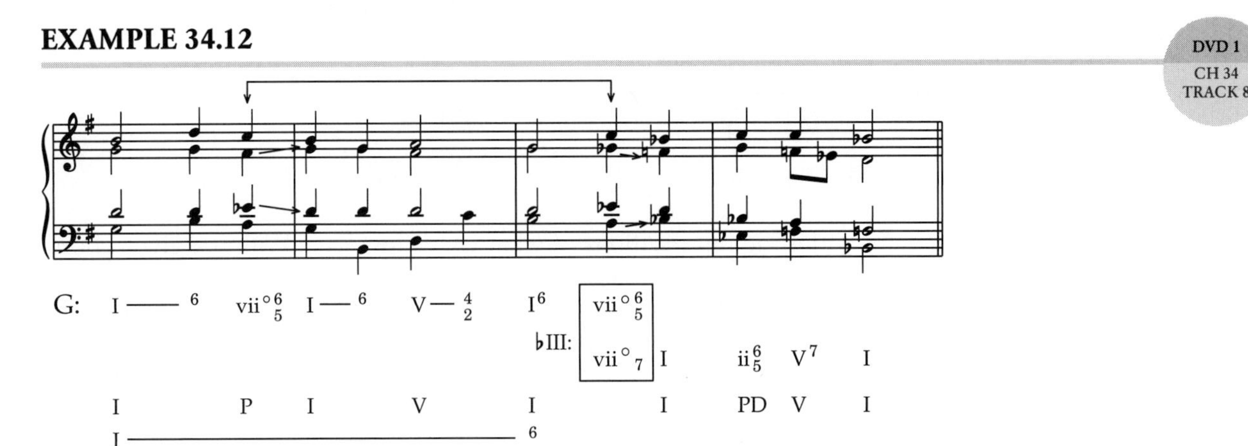

Example 34.13 illustrates two distant modulations from the literature that rely on the enharmonic potential of the diminished seventh chord. Example 34.13A, from the first movement of Beethoven's "Pathetique" sonata, is the passage that leads from the exposition to the development. The excerpt begins in G minor, yet it moves with little effort quickly into the remote key of E minor. Notice how m. 134 begins identically to the previous measure; but as the voice exchange unfolds, C^5 leads not to E♭5 but to D#5. This inaudible change has powerful ramifications, for the resulting enharmonic spelling sets the stage for E minor to enter. What was $vii^{\circ 4}_{3}$ in G minor has become $vii^{\circ 4}_{2}$ in E minor.

Example 34.13B contains a particularly bold modulation using vii°_{7} enharmonically in A minor that allows a tonicization of the tritone-related key, E♭ major. This example is particularly intriguing, given that not only is the enharmonic conversion inaudible, it is also not visible to the players! The excerpt begins with vii°_{7} that apparently continues in the next measure. However, the motion to V^4_2 of E♭ major in m. 3 indicates that we have already made it to E♭. We not only didn't hear the modulation, but we didn't see it. The pivot, then, must be in m. 2. To be sure, Schubert has transformed the vii°_{7} of A minor into $vii^{\circ 4}_{3}$ in E♭ major, only implying the correct spelling of the $vii^{\circ 4}_{3}$ chord.

EXAMPLE 34.13

DVD 1
CH 34
TRACK 9

A. Beethoven, Sonata in C minor, op. 13, i

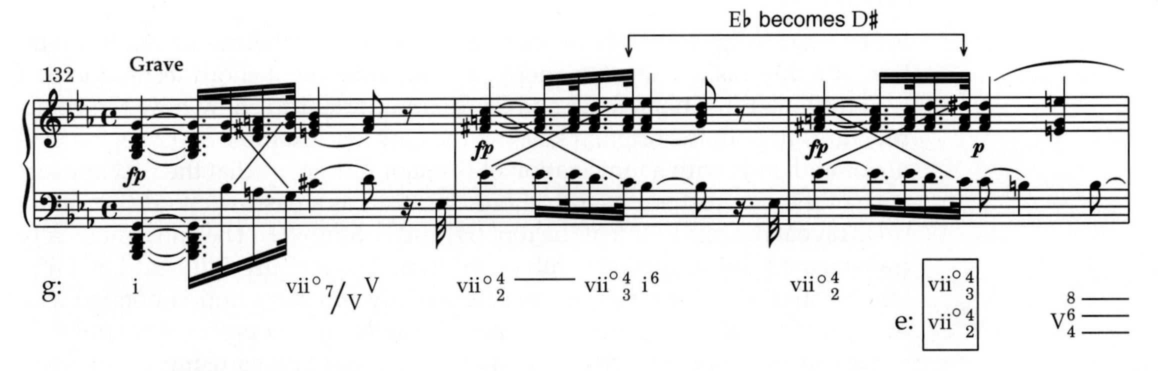

Continued

B. Schubert, String Quartet in A minor, D. 804, I

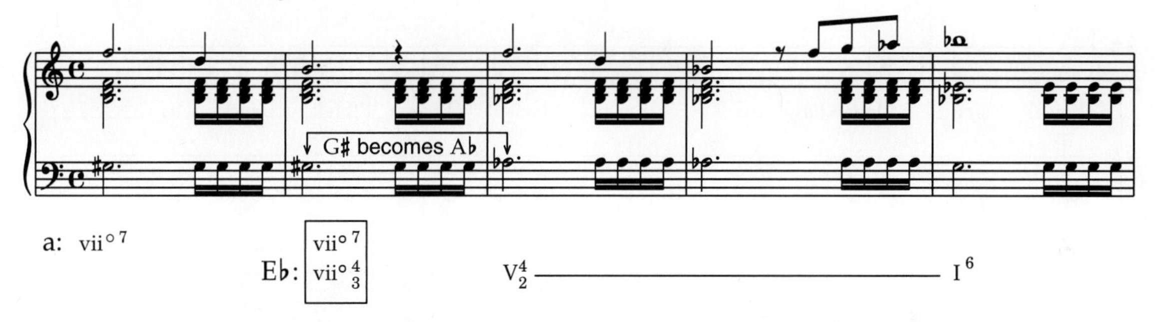

Tonal Clarity Postponed: Off-Tonic Beginning

Nineteenth-century composers often postpone tonal stability to create a sense of ambiguity and heightened expectation. Rather than beginning a piece (or an important subsection) with the tonic and its prolongation, composers may begin on a harmony other than the tonic. We have already seen examples of such an **off-tonic beginning**. For example, Brahms's song "Parole" in Example 34.7 began on an extended PD that occupied the entire introduction. In the Classical period, off-tonic beginnings were approximated in the slow introductions of works in which a weakly stated initial tonic was quickly displaced by chromatic harmonies that veered into distant regions, as in the Beethoven excerpt in Example 34.6. The tonal goal of the slow introduction was almost always the dominant, and the strong arrival on the tonic was thus postponed until the following *allegro* section. Off-tonic beginnings were often a mainstay of popular music in the twentieth century. The G-major refrain of "Sweet Georgia Brown" (Example 34.14) begins far away from the tonic; a series of applied dominants (E_7–A_7–D_7) finally leads to G in m. 33.

EXAMPLE 34.14 Pinkard, "Sweet Georgia Brown"

DVD 1 CH 34 TRACK 10

Continued

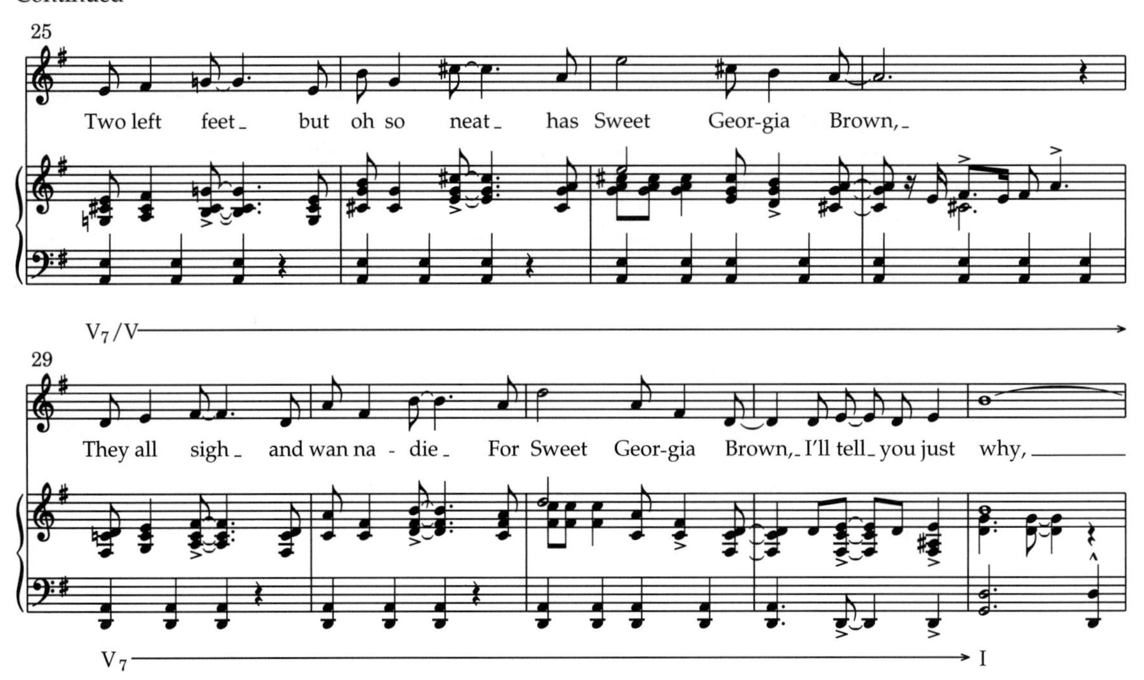

Double Tonality

Sometimes you may encounter pieces in which two keys vie for supremacy simultaneously. Often the ambiguity is acute, and the analyst has little choice but to interpret the piece in the key in which it ends. Some analysts conclude that highly ambiguous pieces are being controlled not by a single key but by the two keys juxtaposed throughout the piece. Such pieces display **double tonality**. For example, some of the songs by Schubert, scenes and acts of operas by Wagner, and orchestral works of late-nineteenth-century composers, including Liszt, Mahler, and Strauss, fall into the double-tonal category. Most of the time, double-tonal pieces are better interpreted as being in a single key: the key in which the piece closes. One might consider Brahms's song "Es hing der Reif" (See Exercise 34.1C) to be a double-tonal example, given that C major and A minor are set in conflict throughout. Although the interior cadences and tonicizations are all in C major, the closing key of the piece suggests that the song might best be interpreted in A minor.

EXERCISE INTERLUDE

WRITING

34.4 Enharmonic Modulations Using the Diminished Seventh Chord

Complete the following tasks on a separate sheet of manuscript paper.

A. Given the diminished seventh chord B-D-F-A♭, list the possible keys in which it and its enharmonic spellings can function. Then write and analyze, using pivot notation, two progressions, each of which employs the diminished seventh chord as an enharmonic pivot that helps move to a distantly related key. Begin the first progression in C major or C minor and the second in A major or A minor.

B. Begin three progressions in A minor and include a vii°$_7$ chord. Then enharmonically reinterpret the diminished seventh chord in order to move to the three distantly related keys that lie minor thirds and a tritone away from A minor.

C. Harmonize the following soprano fragments, each using an enharmonically reinterpreted diminished seventh chord on the pitch that occurs in boldface print in order to modulate to a distantly related key.
1. Begin in F major: A-B♭-A-**G**-G-F♯-E
2. Begin in D: D-C♯-D-**G**-F-E♭-D

D. Complete the following enharmonic modulations, based on the given key and the harmonic model (°$_7$;-I-V$_7$-I). See the Sample Solution.

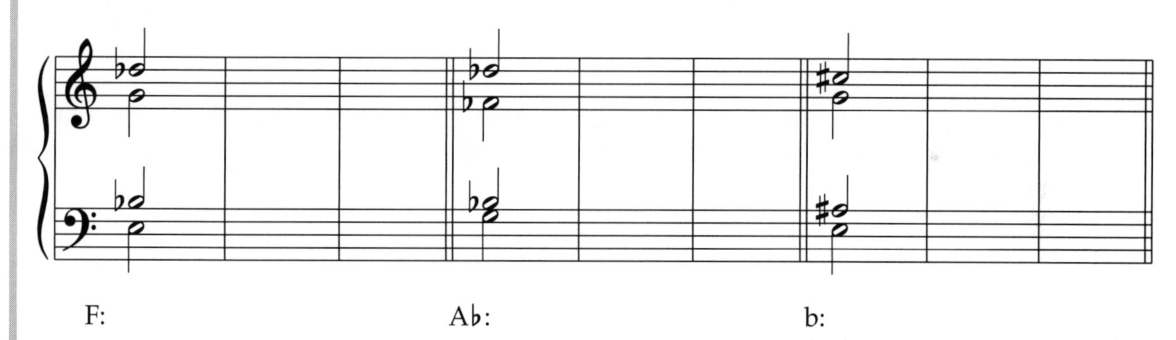

KEYBOARD

34.5

A. Figured Bass

Using four voices, realize the given figured bass, which begins off-tonic. Be aware of other types of ambiguity, including plagal relations, the reciprocal process, and semitonal voice leading as well as enharmonic modulation.

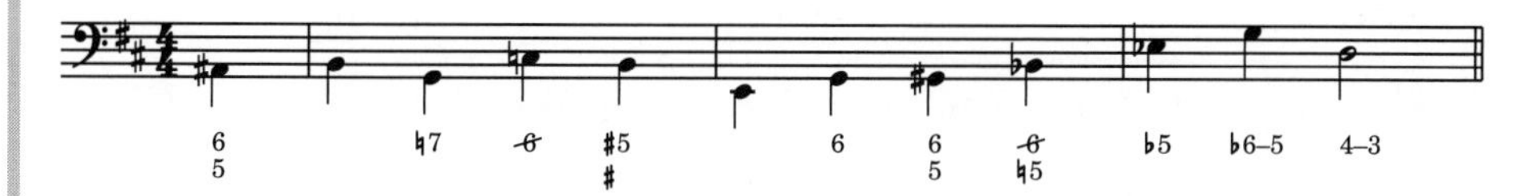

B. Play a progression in F major that begins off-tonic. You may wish to stabilize a chord such as vi for at least two measures before moving to the tonic.

ANALYSIS

34.6

Following are excerpts that either modulate using enharmonically reinterpreted diminished seventh chords or begin off-tonic. Analyze each. Mark the pivot in enharmonic modulations.

A. Schumann, Symphony no. 2, op. 61, iii

Be aware of the possibility of enharmonically reinterpreted Ger $\frac{6}{5}$ chords.

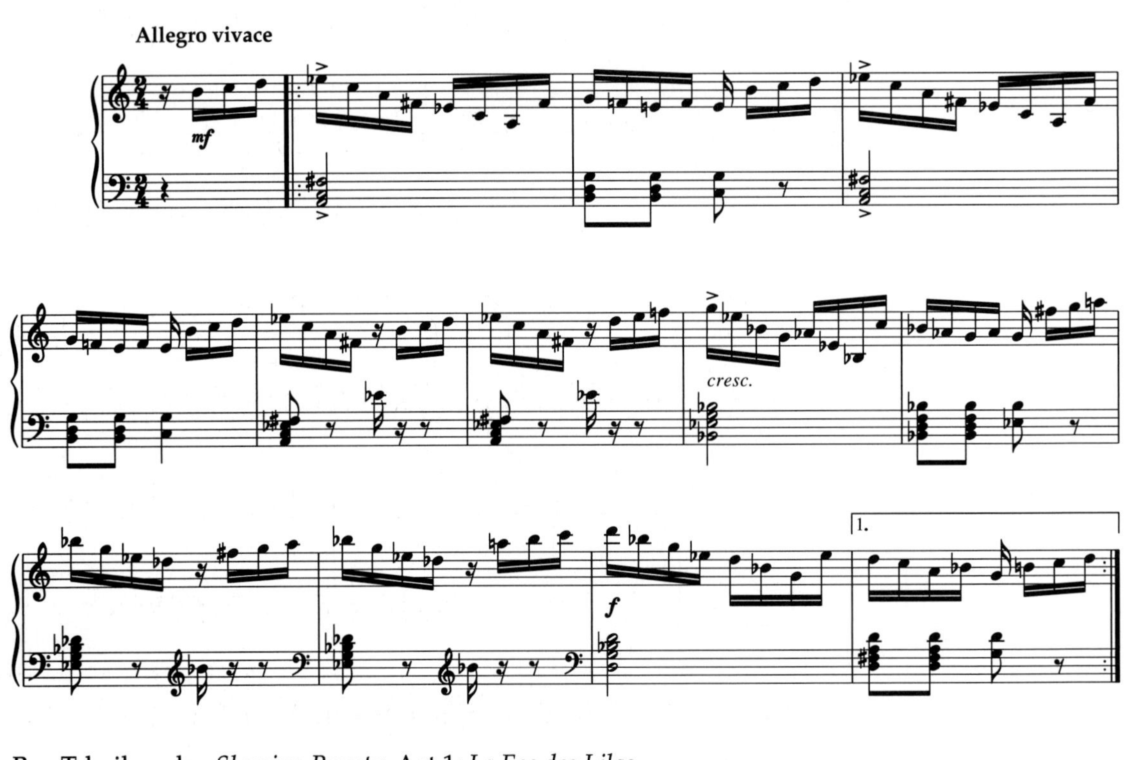

B. Tchaikovsky, *Sleeping Beauty*, Act 1: *La Fee des Lilas*

C. Lamm, "Saturday in the Park"

TERMS AND CONCEPTS

- enharmonic modulation
- enharmonic pun
- enharmonic reinterpretation
    - vii°$_7$
    - V_7/Ger$^6_5$
- off-tonic beginning
    - double tonality
- plagal relation
- reciprocal process
- semitonal voice leading
- symmetrically constructed harmonies
- tonal ambiguity

CHAPTER 35

The Rise of Symmetrical Harmony in Tonal Music

The use of compositional techniques such as modal mixture and semitonal voice leading to evoke a sense of ambiguity precipitated a rise in the use of **symmetrically constructed harmonies and tonal motions**. We have already explored one of these structures—the diminished seventh chord—and the way its potential for harmonic ambiguity could be realized through enharmonic reinterpretation. In this chapter, we learn how the interaction of symmetrical structures with traditional asymmetrical structures influenced other nineteenth-century compositional techniques.

A Paradox: "Balanced" Music Based on Asymmetry

Balance characterizes tonal music—especially Classical music, where the idea of symmetry pervades most aspects of composition. Melodically, the music moves in predictably proportioned patterns. Formally, we usually think of Classical musical units at all levels as structures featuring regularly recurring measure lengths, such as four-measure phrases and eight-measure periods. Metrical and formal symmetries allow a deeper level of periodicity to arise, in a phenomenon called *hypermeter*. At the level of whole works, the idea of perfect symmetry is replaced by tonal balance, as can be seen in both binary and sonata forms, which can be heard as harmonic arches progressing from tonic to dominant and back again.

It is consequently curious that the "well-balanced" tonal system itself is predicated on asymmetrical structures that contain unequal and asymmetrical intervallic divisions. Major and minor triads and dominant seventh chords are asymmetrical structures that consist of a mix of major and minor thirds. Even harmonic progressions in tonal music are asymmetrical. Root motions divide the octave unequally—V to I (ascending perfect fourth) answers I to V (ascending perfect fifth)—and common descending and ascending arpeggiations move in a mix of major and minor thirds. Most significantly, diatonic sequences are also highly asymmetrical. For example, the common D2 ($-5/+4$) sequence does not move exclusively by perfect fifths; a tritone occurs within the sequence in order to maintain the scale degrees of the key. Indeed, it is precisely the breaking of the perfect-fifth pattern by the diminished fifth that makes the progression so goal oriented, for without the tritone, the symmetrical sequence would wander over the entire 12 chromatic steps before returning to its beginning point.

Just as asymmetrical structures such as major and minor triads help to create tonality, the use of symmetrically constructed harmonies and harmonic progressions results in tonal ambiguity, an important feature of nineteenth-century music. But how does symmetry fit into our asymmetrical harmonic models? Actually, the tonal system contains the seeds for symmetry: Harmonic motions up to the dominant and down to the subdominant symmetrically flank the tonic. However, common-practice music will not usually permit the subdominant to lead directly back to the tonic, but rather to the dominant (Example 35.1).

EXAMPLE 35.1

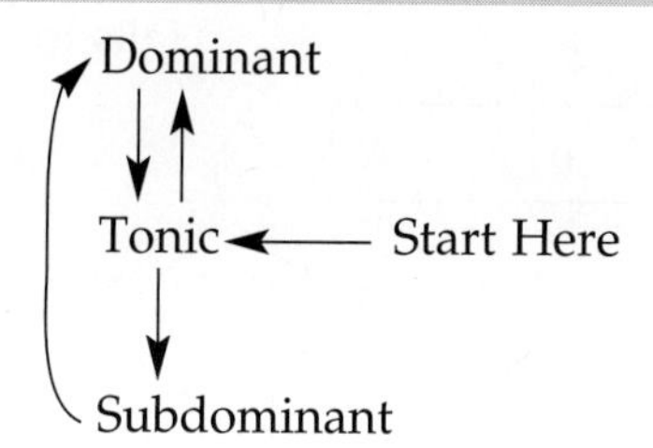

The model in Example 35.2 represents eighteenth-century diatonic motion, with the symmetrical perfect fifths asymmetrically divided by major and minor thirds.

EXAMPLE 35.2 Eighteenth-Century Tonal Paths

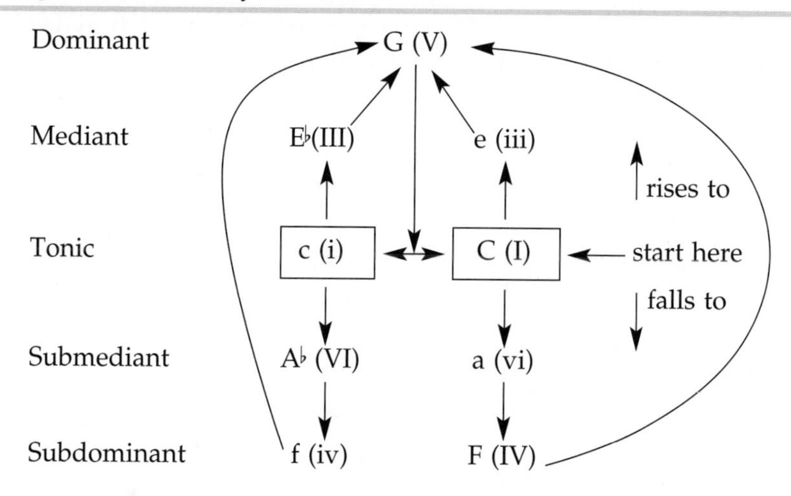

We have learned that chromatic third relations can emerge from the combination of parallel modes through mixture. The model in Example 35.3 represents the rise of chromatic third relations from the end of the eighteenth century to the first half of the nineteenth century. Notice that the combinations of major and minor thirds continue to form asymmetrical tonal progressions. Notice also that the subdominant need not progress to the dominant; rather, it may move directly to the tonic (through the plagal relation).

EXAMPLE 35.3 Late-Eighteenth- and Nineteenth-Century Tonal Paths: Mixture Incorporated

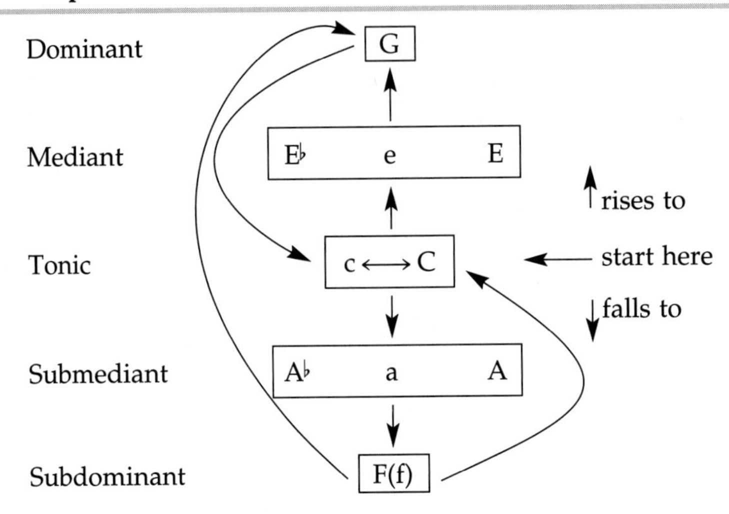

Symmetry and Tonal Ambiguity

The model in Example 35.4 is fundamentally different from the preceding models. The long diagonal lines represent symmetrical paths that circumvent both the dominant and the subdominant. Notice that root progressions move by a single repeating interval of either a major third or a minor third (or their enharmonic equivalents) until these intervallic cycles reach a perfect octave.

EXAMPLE 35.4 Late-Nineteenth-Century Tonal Paths: Symmetrical Third Relations Replace Asymmetrical Fifth Relations

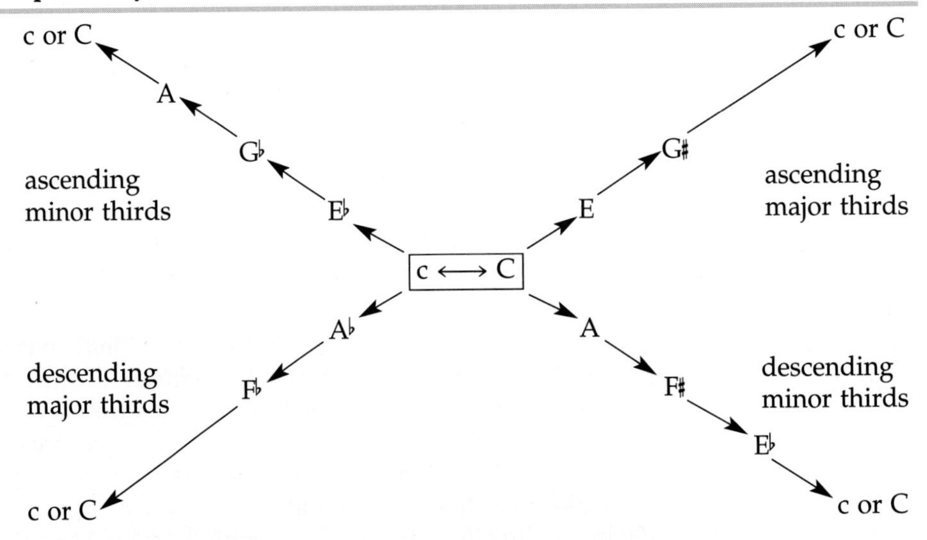

We can understand that the basis of tonality's gravitational field, which pulls scale degrees and harmonies toward tonic, is predicated on asymmetry—specifically the asymmetry associated with major and minor scales. Imagine what would happen to tonality if scales were composed solely of whole steps or half steps or of consistently alternating half and whole steps. If you try singing the scales in Example 35.5, you will soon discover that a sense of goal-directed motion and tonal grounding disappears because every scale step is as stable (or as unstable) as every other step.

EXAMPLE 35.5

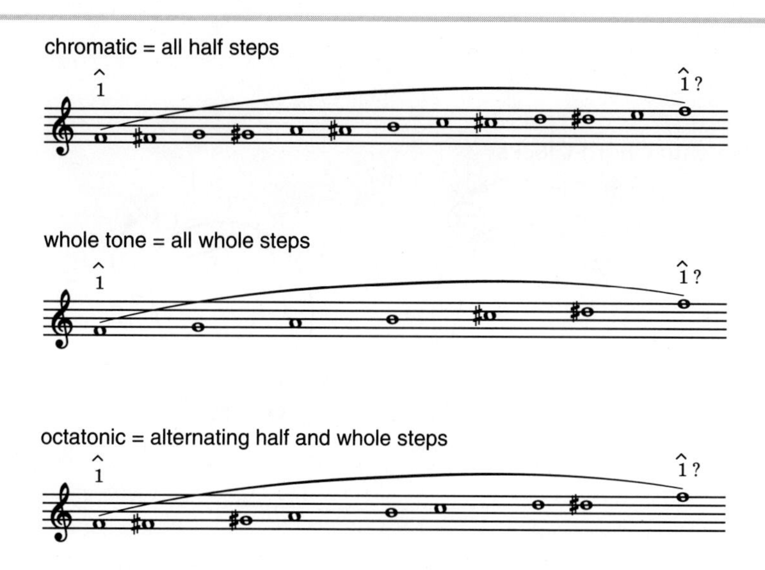

Just as symmetrical structures (major and minor triads) help to create tonality, the use of symmetrically constructed harmonies and harmonic progressions results in tonal ambiguity, an important feature of nineteenth-century music. Symmetrical harmonies and symmetrical tonal progressions develop from two late-eighteenth-century precedents: chromatically altered dominant harmonies and chromatic sequences. We devote the rest of this chapter to the exploration of chromatically altered harmonies.

The Augmented Triad

So far, we have considered only one symmetrical triad—the diminished triad. It has a symmetrical construction because its two component intervals are both minor thirds (Example 35.6A). It does not, however, equally partition the octave (since it spans a tritone, it only partitions half of the octave evenly). By contrast, the diminished seventh chord partitions the octave symmetrically (Example 35.6B). Notice how the lines connecting the pitch classes that make up a diminished seventh chord symmetrically partition the octave. Moving the diminished seventh chord up by one half step (i.e., starting the next "square" on C♯) does not, of course, alter its symmetrical structure. Transposition by three semitones (i.e., starting the chord on E♭) results in a restatement of the same pitch classes, thus revealing how there are only three distinct diminished seventh chords.

EXAMPLE 35.6

A. Diminished Triad Clock

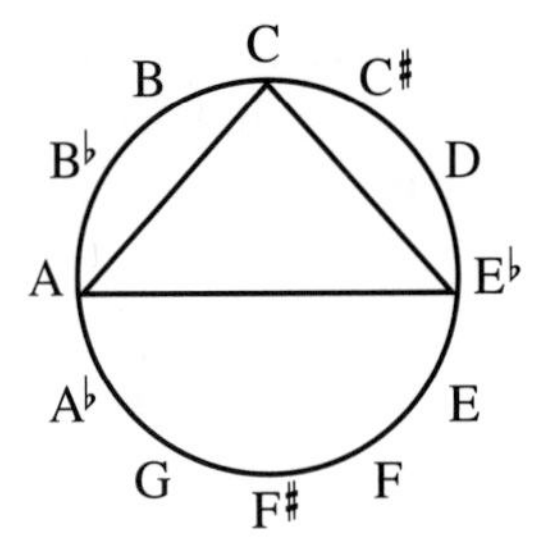

B. Diminished Seventh Chord Clocks

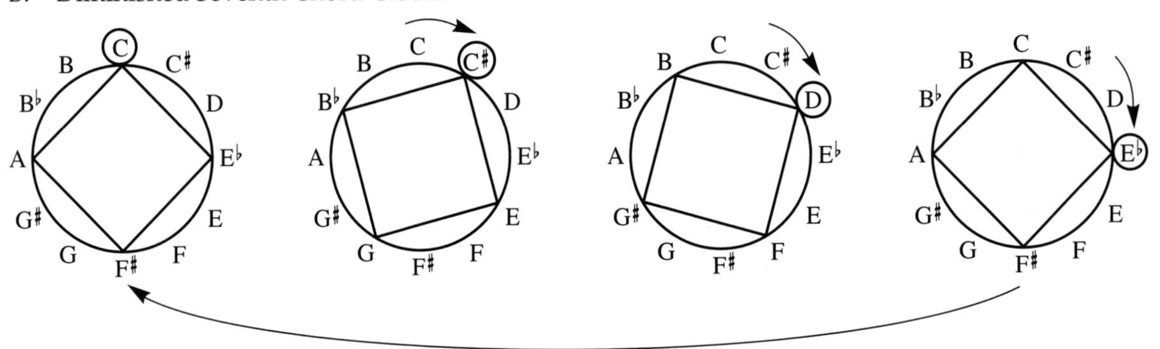

Like the diminished triad, the highly dissonant **augmented triad** (shown in Example 35.7) is symmetrical, consisting of two major thirds and spanning an augmented fifth. Moreover, like the diminished seventh chord, the augmented triad also partitions the octave equally. Unlike every other triadic structure, the augmented triad retains its major third and augmented fifth intervals (or their enharmonic equivalents) under inversion. Compare the inversions of the minor triad to the inversions of the augmented triad. A minor triad in root position contains a minor third (e.g., C–E♭) and a major third (E♭–G), which together span a perfect fifth (C–G). Its first inversion yields a major third (E♭–G) and a perfect fourth (G–C), which together span a major sixth. Its second inversion yields a perfect fourth (G–C) and a minor third (C–E♭), which together span a minor sixth. But when we invert an augmented triad (such as C–E–G♯), no matter how many times we cycle the three pitches around, only major thirds (or diminished fourths) and minor sixths (or augmented fifths) result. Thus, there is no way aurally to distinguish inversions of the augmented triad. Its symmetrical construction is harmonically ambiguous and thus well suited to the experimental works of the late nineteenth century.

EXAMPLE 35.7 Augmented Triad Clock

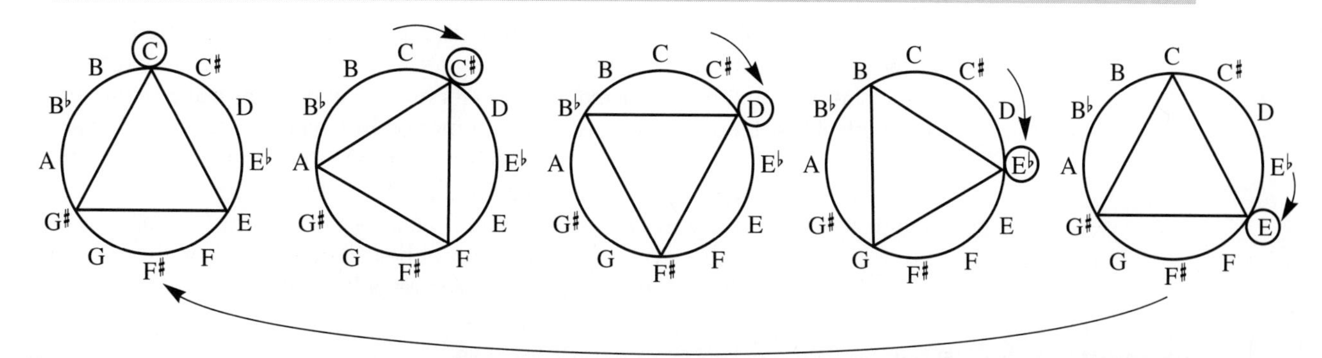

The augmented triad originally was a by product of melodic motion before becoming an independent sonority. Listen to Example 35.8. It is likely that you heard an augmented triad (G–B–D♯) on the upbeat to m. 1. It is metrically weak, with the D♯s arising from passing motion; thus, it is not an independent harmonic entity.

Now listen to Example 35.9, and note the function of the augmented triads. Again, the augmented triad in m. 2 is not an independent triad, because F♯ is functioning simply as an appoggiatura to the chord tone G.

EXAMPLE 35.8 Beethoven, Theme and Variations in G major, WoO 77, Thema: *Andante, quasi Allegretto*

DVD 1
CH 35
TRACK 1

EXAMPLE 35.9 Schubert, "Der Atlas," from *Schwanengesang*, D. 957, no. 8

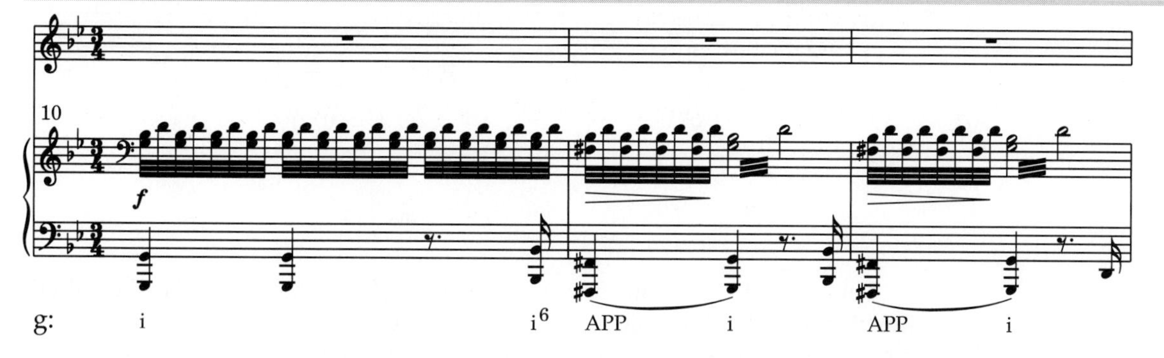

Often, augmented triads participate in sequential progressions, filling in the whole steps with chromatic semitones. Listen to Example 35.10 and identify all the augmented triads. Here is an example that plays on the augmented triad's harmonic ambiguity: The chromatic passing tone G♯ creates an augmented triad. At the same time, the tonic is extended to its first inversion on beat 3. An interesting effect results from the parallel-tenth motion between the bass and the soprano voices, where the G♯4 begins to sound a bit like a leading tone to A. This "applied dominant" to A minor is intensified by the fact that E is in the bass. Although it is customary to label this sonority as a C–E–G♯ chord (C-major triad with a raised fifth), there is no reason it cannot be called an E-major chord with raised fifth (E–G♯–B♯, with B♯ as an enharmonic respelling of C).

EXAMPLE 35.10 Beethoven, Bagatelle in C major, op. 119

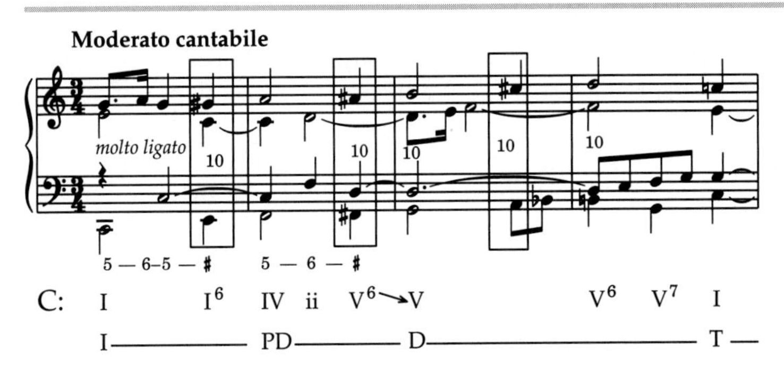

Some late-nineteenth-century composers exploited the harmonic ambiguity of the augmented triad. Listen to the opening of "Illusion" in Example 35.11 and determine the key, the location where the key is explicitly stated, and how Grieg earlier implies the key. What musical devices make the opening tonally ambiguous?

EXAMPLE 35.11 Grieg, "Illusion," *Lyric Pieces VI*, op. 57

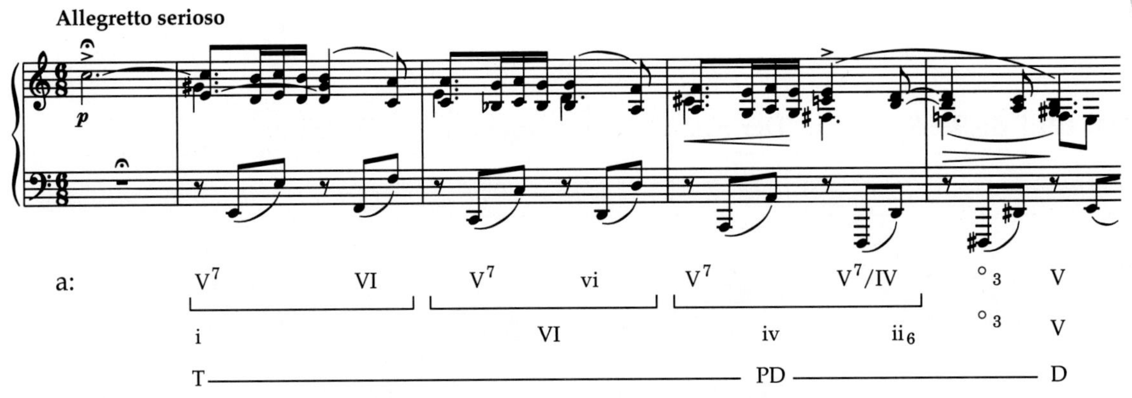

The excerpt closes on V of A minor, the tonic of the piece. The opening's unharmonized and ambiguous C5 could imply the key of C major or the dominant of F or any number of other keys. However, C5 turns out to be a dissonance that is first heard as the minor sixth above the dominant of A minor. (Note that the first sonority, E–G♯–C, is identical to the chord in the previous example, which we hypothesized could work just as well in A minor.) The V_7 resolves deceptively to VI; this pattern begins again in m. 2, transposed down a third. Only in m. 3 does a goal-directed progression begin, leading to a half cadence in A minor. It is difficult to miss the explicit connection between the meaning of the song's title and Grieg's musical setting.

Finally, the augmented triad can become an independent sonority. Listen to the opening of Liszt's "Nuages gris" (Example 35.12), in which all of the chords but the first take the form of augmented triads. As Liszt obscures all sense of tonality with chromatically descending augmented chords (m. 11), he brings to life the image of visible yet amorphous gray clouds.

EXAMPLE 35.12 Liszt, "Nuages gris" ("Gray Clouds"), S199, LW 305

DVD 1
CH 35
TRACK 5

Altered Dominant Seventh Chords

The fifth of the V_7 chord, $\hat{2}$, is a weak tendency tone when compared to the leading tone ($\hat{7}$) and the chordal seventh $\hat{4}$). But when $\hat{2}$ is raised—creating an **altered dominant seventh chord**—it forms an augmented sixth interval with $\hat{4}$, and, as a strong tendency tone, it must rise to $\hat{3}$ (Example 35.13). Because of the proper resolution of the chordal seventh, the following tonic chord has a doubled third.

EXAMPLE 35.13

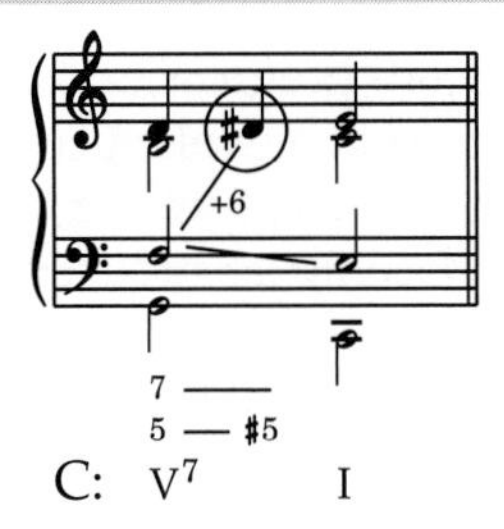

It is also possible to alter V_7 by lowering $\hat{2}$ a half step; this chord often plays a crucial role in late-nineteenth-century music (Example 35.14A). When $\hat{2}$ is lowered it forms an augmented sixth with the leading tone; composers place the chord in second inversion so that $\flat\hat{2}$ is in the bass. This inversion, shown in Example 35.14B, produces a chord that is identical to a French augmented sixth chord. Thus, the altered dominant seventh chord functions in a reciprocal process (Chapter 34): The chord sounds like it participates in a half cadence (Fr^4_3→V), but it actually functions as part of an authentic cadence (altered V^4_3 →I). For now, we will label this type of altered dominant as FrV^4_3, which shows its function as a dominant and its intervallic properties that are similar to the regular Fr^4_3.

EXAMPLE 35.14

A.

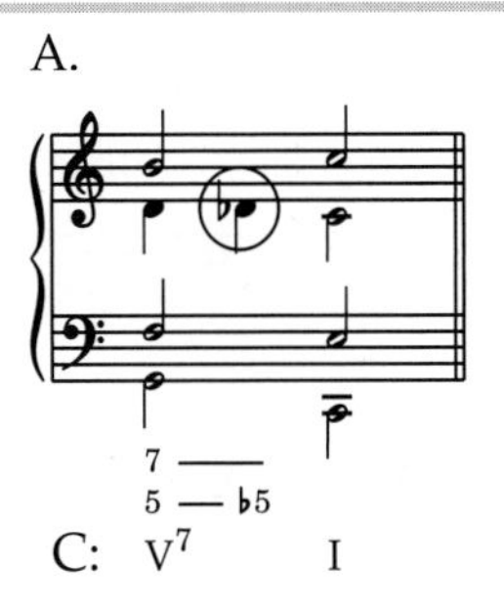

B.

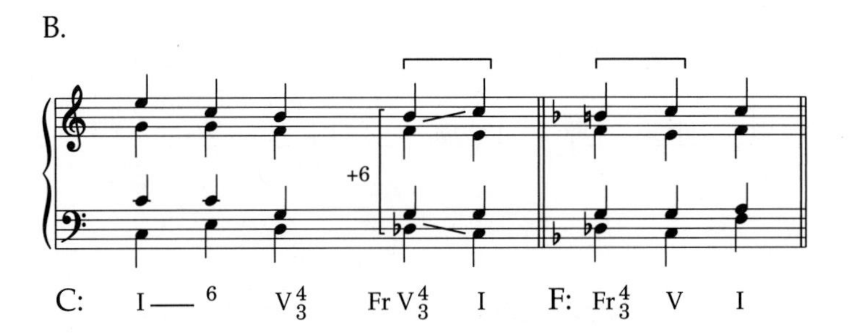

Listen to the opening of the last movement of Brahms's Fourth Symphony (Example 35.15). What is ambiguous about the cadence? Perhaps you were once again struck by a disparity between what you saw and what you heard at the cadence in m. 8. There are two reasons why what looks like a weak authentic cadence—in which V^4_3 (F replaces F♯) resolves to I—actually sounds like a half cadence. First, the altered V^4_3 chord (m. 7), with F♮ prominently placed in the bass (F♮–A–B–D♯) is identical to a Fr^4_3 chord in the key of A minor. Second, the Picardy third (G♯) in the final chord sounds like it participates in a half cadence (Fr^4_3–V) rather than an authentic cadence (V^4_3–I). This altered dominant seventh therefore functions in a reciprocal process. We will learn more about the wide-ranging enharmonic potential and other special properties inherent in this sonority when we look at the music of Alexander Scriabin and Alban Berg in Chapter 37.

EXAMPLE 35.15 Brahms, Symphony no. 4 in E minor, op. 98, *Allegro energico e passionato*

DVD 1
CH 35
TRACK 6

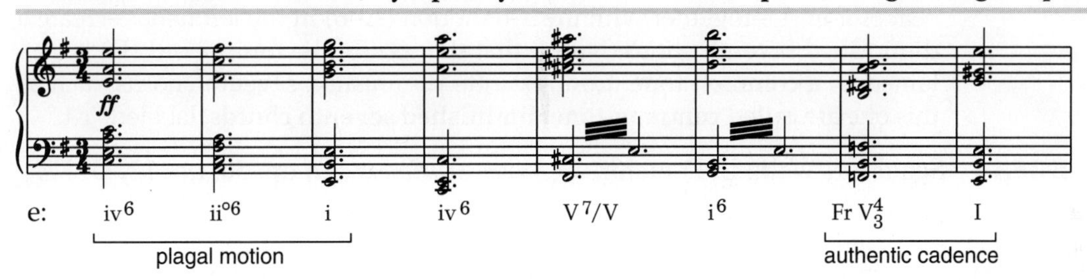

EXERCISE INTERLUDE

KEYBOARD

35.1 Augmented Triads

Indicate the function of the augmented triads in the following progression. Then play the progression as written and transpose to any two other keys.

35.2 Altered Dominant Seventh Chords

Play the following cadential patterns containing altered dominant sevenths. Transpose to major keys with signatures up to and including two sharps and two flats.

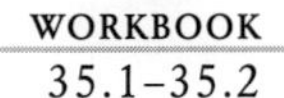
WORKBOOK
35.1–35.2

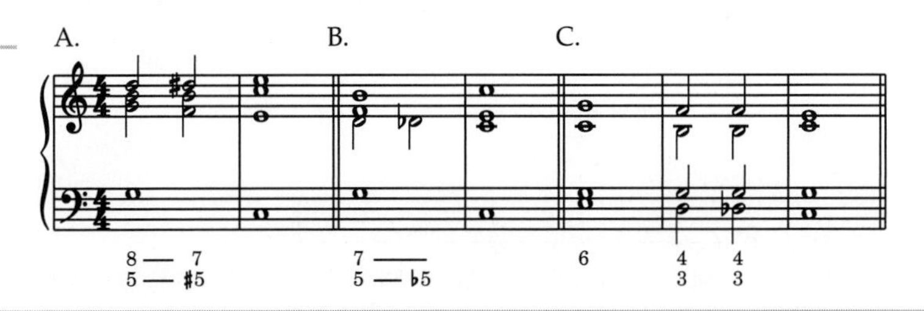

The Common-Tone Diminished Seventh Chord

We have encountered a number of ways to extend an underlying harmony contrapuntally. In addition to embedded phrase models (EPMs), we have learned about passing and neighboring chords, such as vii°$_6$, P$^6_4$, N$^6_4$, vii$^{\circ 6}_5$, and IV$_6$, which usually occur in first or second inversion so as to allow them smoothly to connect structural harmonies in root position.

We will now learn about two additional harmonies that can prolong I and V through neighboring and passing motions. These new chords contain chromaticism and *maintain the root of the harmony they extend.*

Example 35.16 shows the first type of harmony: The lower neighbors on beat 3 of m. 1—together with the 5–6 motion (A–B) in the left hand—create a diminished seventh chord. Notice that the root of the tonic chord (D) is sustained as a common tone. Contrapuntal diminished seventh chords such as this one are called **common-tone diminished seventh chords**, labeled "c.t.°$_7$."

EXAMPLE 35.16 Schubert, Waltz in D major, *34 Valses Sentimentales*, op. 50, no. 12, D. 779

We now have two functions for diminished seventh chords: They can be tonicizing (as a vii°$_7$ or an applied vii°$_7$) or contrapuntal (as a c.t.°$_7$ or an applied c.t.°$_7$) (Example 35.17). The following guiding principles may be useful when attempting to determine the function of a fully diminished sonority.

EXAMPLE 35.17

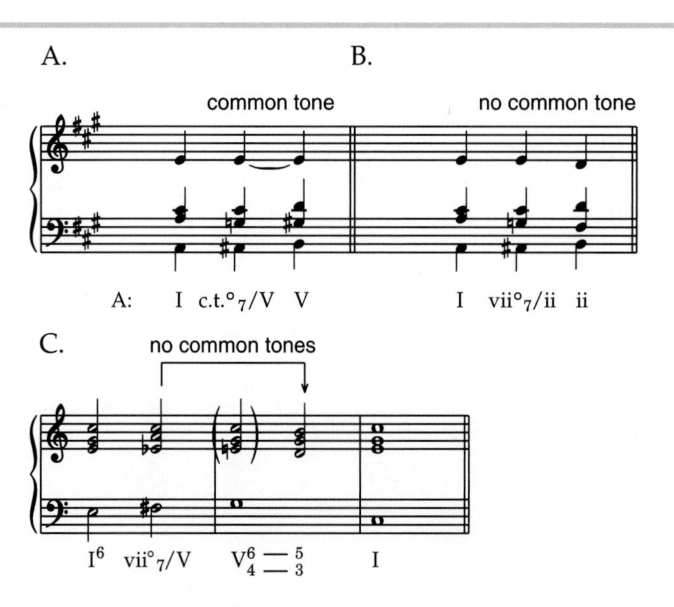

- Common-tone diminished seventh chords share a common tone with the following chord of resolution (Example 35.17A).
- vii$^{\circ}_{7}$ and applied vii$^{\circ}_{7}$ chords have no common tones with the following chord of resolution (Example 35.17B).
- Beware of the progression vii$^{\circ}_{7}$/V to cad. $^{6}_{4}$–$^{5}_{3}$. The vii$^{\circ}_{7}$/V chord shares common tones with the cadential $^{6}_{4}$ chord.
  The common tones, however, are misleading, for they are not chord tones but suspensions that fall to the $^{5}_{3}$ chord, which shares no pitches with the applied vii$^{\circ}_{7}$ chord (Example 35.17C).

It can be difficult to distinguish between the different types of diminished seventh chords. The chromatic bass line in Example 35.18 suggests that the diminished seventh chord will function as a vii$^{\circ}_{7}$/ii. However, B is not the root of the chord on the downbeat of m. 2; it is a V$^{4}_{3}$ chord. Further evidence against viewing the diminished seventh chord as vii$^{\circ}_{7}$/ii may be seen in the octave E, which is a common tone of both the diminished seventh chord and the following V$^{4}_{3}$ chord. As you know, there are no common tones between an applied vii$^{\circ}_{7}$ chord and its resolution, so this diminished seventh cannot be applied. Rather, it is a contrapuntal chord (c.t.$^{\circ}_{7}$ of V) that connects I and V$^{4}_{3}$ by means of a chromatic passing tone in the bass.

EXAMPLE 35.18 Brahms, "Heimweh III" ("Homesickness III"), op. 64, no. 9

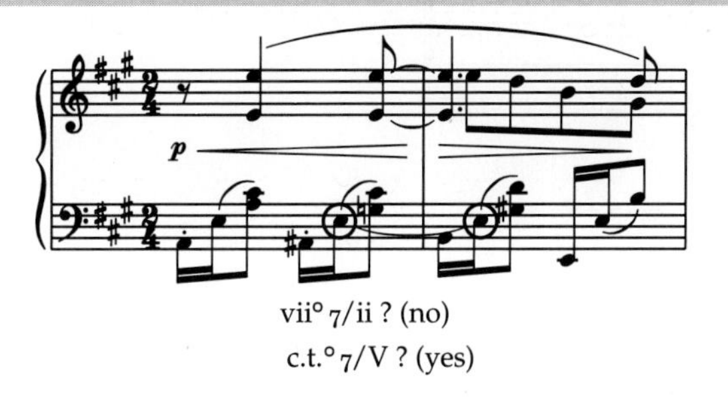

Common-Tone Augmented Sixth Chords

Example 35.19 contains another chromatic common-tone harmony over a tonic pedal that arises from contrapuntal motion, but it is not a diminished seventh chord. Look at the figure for the first chord. Does the presence of both flat and sharp accidentals remind you of any other chords we have learned? The sonority sounds and looks like a Ger$^{6}_{5}$ chord, since it contains an augmented sixth (A♭–F♯). It is a bit peculiar, however, not to have the $\flat\hat{6}$-$\hat{5}$ motion in the bass, for we expect an augmented sixth chord moving to its resolution. Instead, the bass voice sustains a common-tone C. The result of this voice leading is a chord that extends the tonic rather than leading strongly to the dominant. Such a chord is referred to as a **common-tone augmented sixth chord** (c.t.$_{+6}$).

EXAMPLE 35.19 Schubert, "Am Meer" ("By the Sea"), *Schwanengesang*, D. 957, no. 12

DVD 1
CH 35
TRACK 9

Continued

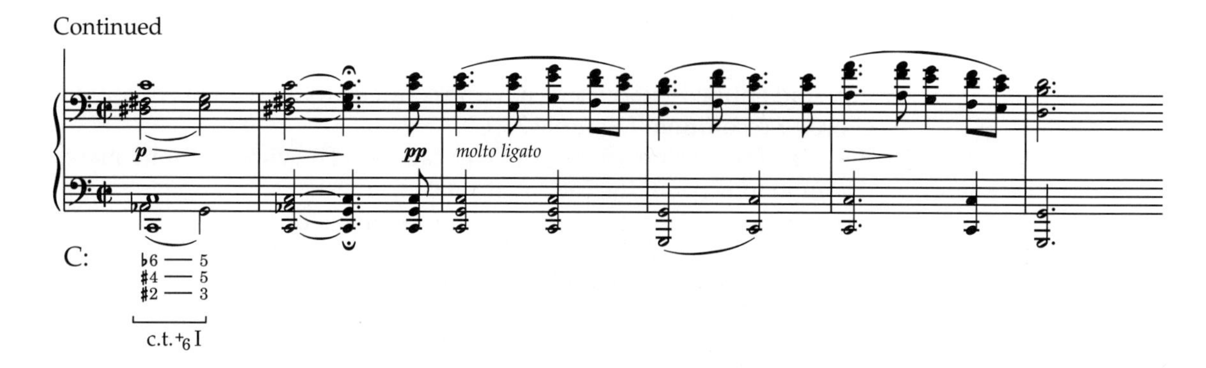

The bass in c.t.$_{+6}$ chords may skip down a major third to what would be the usual bass of an augmented sixth chord (Example 35.20). The fact that the augmented sixth chord returns to the tonic, however, demonstrates its common-tone function. Nineteenth-century music contains a variety of chromatic third–related vacillations.

EXAMPLE 35.20

Analytical Interlude

We have learned that composers do not choose harmonies in a capricious manner. Chords both progressive and prolongational play important roles in the harmonic and melodic domains, where they project motives at deep structural levels. We also have seen how harmonic and melodic choices in *Lieder* are often made to project images from the texts. Let's see what new effects are created in late-nineteenth-century songs by the incorporation of these common-tone chromatic harmonies (see Example 35.21).

EXAMPLE 35.21 Wolf, "Man sagt mir, deine Mutter woll' es nicht" ("They tell me your mother doesn't approve of it"), *Italienisches Liederbuch*, no. 21

DVD 1
CH 35
TRACK 10

Continued

The story is simple: A girl teases her lover, saying that because his mother disapproves of their relationship, he should simply stay away. But in the next phrase, the girl contradicts herself and says that her lover should ignore his mother's wishes so that he may secretly visit her even more often. The following analysis reveals how Wolf's musical setting reflects the text.

The key of the song is clearly A minor, in spite of the c.t.$_{+6}$ on beat 2 of the first measure, which creates a neighbor figure above and below the fifth of the tonic harmony. When the first harmonic change occurs in m. 4, an apparent altered V_7 of G major (Example 35.22A) actually functions as an altered augmented sixth chord when it leads to F♯ major (see Example 35.22B).

EXAMPLE 35.22 Augmented sixth chord resolution in m. 4, beat 4

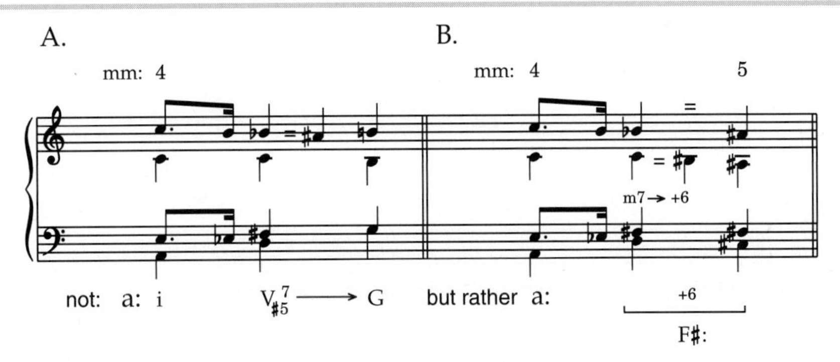

The key of F♯ major, with its six sharps, vividly contrasts with A minor's zero sharps. In fact, F♯ major and A minor are nearly as tonally distant as two keys can be. This unusual and very sudden shift occurs at the very point where the girl says, "den Willen" ("do what she wants"). In the very next phrase the girl reverses her proclamation, saying that the boy should ignore his mother's desires and visit her daily. The unexpected tonal shift from A minor to F♯ major could be Wolf's imaginative way of creating a musical analogue that reflects the girl's sudden change of mind.

EXERCISE INTERLUDE

DVD 2
CH 35
TRACK 1

ANALYSIS

35.3

Analyze the following excerpts, which contain augmented triads, altered dominant seventh chords, common-tone diminished seventh chords, and common-tone augmented sixth chords.

A.

The ending of this exercise is tonally ambiguous. Discuss.

B. Chopin, Nocturne in A♭ major, op. 32, no. 2

C. Brahms, "Unbewegte laue Luft" (Motionless, Tepid Air"), op. 57, no. 8

Continued

D. Brahms, Symphony no. 3 in F major, op. 90, *Allegro con brio*

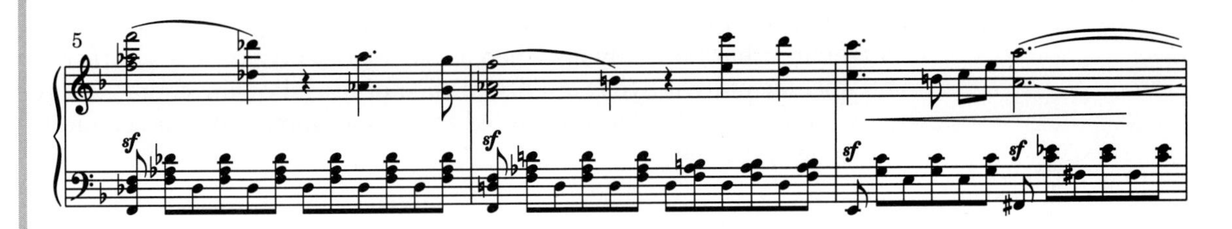

KEYBOARD

35.4 Common-Tone Chords

Play the given progression as written and in another major key of your choice. Determine whether common-tone (embellishing) diminished seventh chords are used in neighboring or passing functions and whether they expand the tonic or the dominant.

35.5 Figured Bass and Metrical Realization

Analyze the following two progressions. Then, based on the harmonic rhythm, contrapuntal expansions, and required metrical placement of certain harmonies, add a meter and rhythms. Expect to encounter enharmonic modulations, altered dominant sevenths, and various types and expansions of the augmented sixth chord.

WRITING

DVD 2
CH 35
TRACK 2

35.6 Composition Project

This assignment focuses first on generating a harmonic progression and then on transforming the progression into a piece for a melody instrument or voice with piano accompaniment. The passage must be at least one period in length and consist of at least two four-measure phrases. It must:

1. Modulate to a chromatic key of your choice and back to the original key. Each of the keys must incorporate a pivot chord that moves either to the new key or back to the original key. Use either a mixture chord or an enharmonically respelled augmented sixth as one of the pivots.
2. Include at least two examples of each of the following chords or procedures: plagal relations, altered triads and dominants, and common-tone harmonies.

Begin your work by determining a good progression; then animate it by working out an accompanimental pattern (for keyboard). Finally, add a melody above (refer to the following excerpts from Schubert songs and Beethoven violin sonatas).

A. Beethoven, Violin Sonata in A major, op. 30, no. 1, *Adagio molto espressivo*

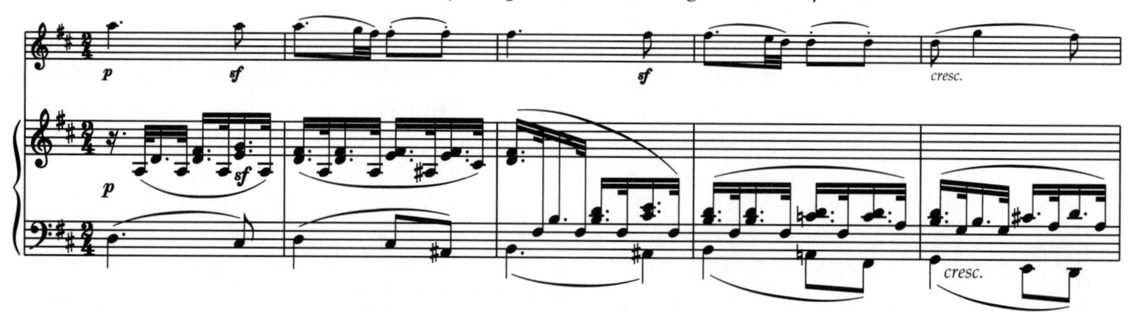

B. Beethoven, Violin Sonata in F major, "Spring," op. 24, *Allegro*

C. Schubert, "Des Müllers Blumen" ("The Miller's Flowers"), *Die schöne Müllerin*, op. 25, no. 9, D. 795

D. Schubert, "Auf dem Flusse" ("By the Stream"), *Winterreise*, D. 911

KEYBOARD

35.7 Figured Bass

A.

Realize the given figured bass in four voices. Be able to sing either bass or soprano parts while playing the remaining three parts.

B. Warren, "We're in the Money"

Sing only the tune while realizing the other voices at the keyboard. Analyze.

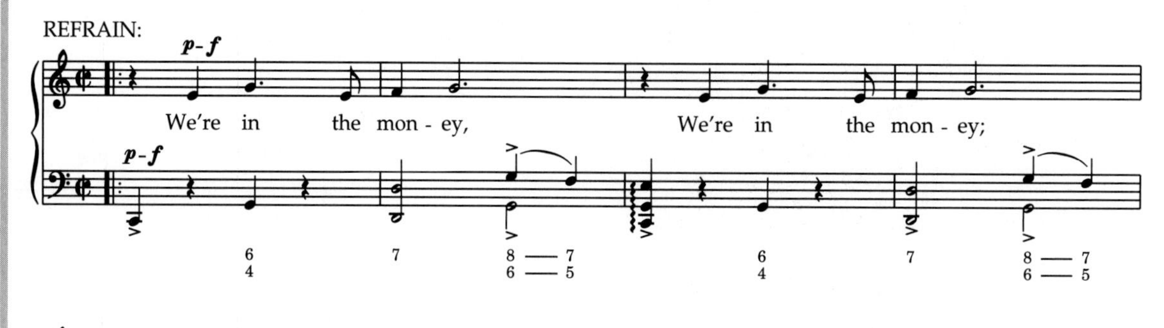

35.8 Composition

WORKBOOK 35.3–35.6

Write, then play, a parallel progressive period based on the given antecedent phrase, to which you will add a consequent phrase. Use the diminished seventh in m. 6 enharmonically to modulate to a minor-third-related key of your choice. This example is taken from Haydn's Divertimento in G major, Hob. XVI.11, mm. 33–40.

TERMS AND CONCEPTS

- altered dominant seventh chords
- augmented triad
- chromatic common-tone harmonies
    - common-tone augmented sixth chords
    - common-tone diminished seventh chords
- symmetrical versus asymmetrical relationships

CHAPTER 36

Melodic and Harmonic Symmetry Combine: Chromatic Sequences

Sequences are paradoxical musical processes. At the surface level they provide rapid harmonic rhythm, yet at a deeper level they function to suspend tonal motion and prolong an underlying harmony. Tonal sequences move up and down the diatonic scale using scale degrees as stepping-stones. In this chapter, we will explore the consequences of transferring the sequential motions you learned in Chapter 22 from the asymmetry of the diatonic scale to the symmetrical tonal patterns of the nineteenth century. You will likely notice many similarities of behavior between these new chromatic sequences and the old diatonic ones, but there are differences as well. For instance, the stepping-stones for chromatic sequences are no longer the major and minor scales. Furthermore, the chord qualities of each individual harmony inside a chromatic sequence tend to exhibit more homogeneity. Whereas in the past you may have expected major, minor, and diminished chords to alternate inside a diatonic sequence, in the chromatic realm it is not uncommon for all the chords in a sequence to manifest the same quality.

EXAMPLE 36.1

DVD 1
CH 36
TRACK 1

A.

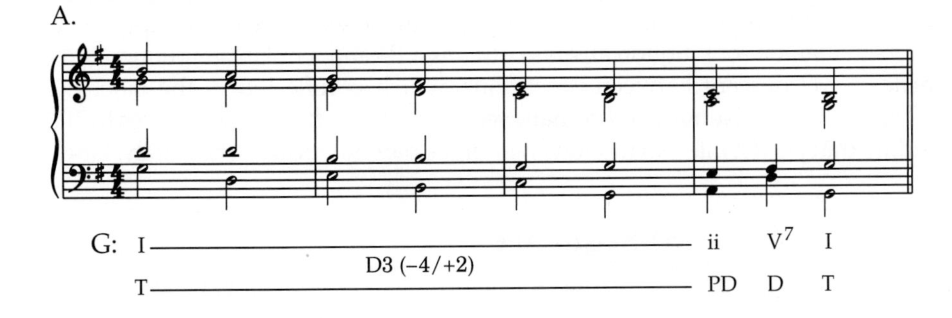

B.

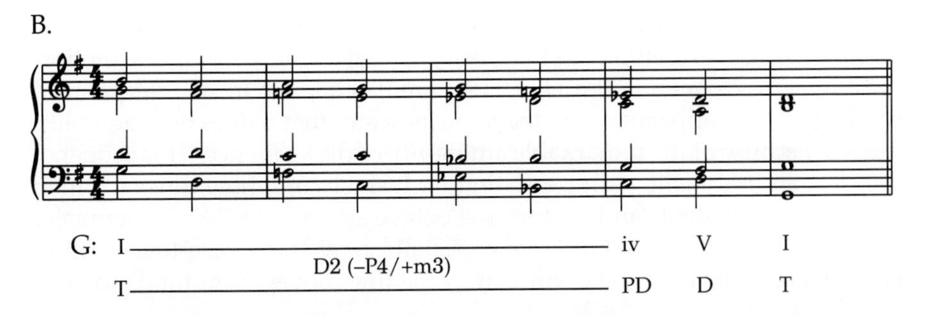

Consider Example 36.1A, which contains the D3 (−4/+2)—or "descending 5–6"—sequence. The sequence is strongly goal directed (progressing to ii) and diatonic (its harmonies are diatonic to G major). Chord qualities and distances are not consistent, since they conform to the asymmetry of G major. For example, see how the first chord of the model, G major, repeats down a minor third on E minor, while the next repetition begins down a major third on C major.

Example 36.1B illustrates a new chromatic sequence, and its sense of harmonic ambiguity and lack of direction might unsettle you as you hear it. The sequence is ambiguous (its harmonies do not fit into one key), and it is not goal directed (it ends on B♭ major, whose function as ♭III becomes clear only after the final strong cadence in G major). The two-chord model is identical to that of Example 36.1A, but the copies contain numerous chromatic alterations that result in harmonies foreign to G major. The model and its repetitions contain all *major* triads and each repetition occurs down a *major* second. It is as if the copying mechanism has been perfected so that every repetition reproduces exactly the harmonic pattern of the model.

The sequence in Example 36.1B is a type of **chromatic sequence.** Chromatic sequences are distinguished from diatonic sequences by the fact that their main chords—those chords we use to reckon the first portion of a sequence label such as D2 or D3—contain altered scale degrees. (*Note*: The designation *chromatic* has nothing to do with the mere presence of accidentals; many of the applied-chord sequences seen in Chapter 24 contain accidentals, yet they are still diatonic sequences because their main chords are diatonic.) Furthermore, chromatic sequences maintain strictly both chord quality and intervallic distance between repetitions, whereas diatonic sequences conform to the whole-step and half-step characteristics of the diatonic key. Because these chromatic sequences divide the octave into the same-sized intervals (such as the major seconds in Example 33.1B), they avoid the shifting whole steps and half steps that precipitate the goal-directed motion of traditional, diatonic sequences.

In studying the chromatic forms of the three common sequences we learned in Chapter 22, we shall see that the basic contrapuntal motion remains the same but that the overall root movements are often altered. For example, the diatonic sequence in Example 36.1A is labeled D3 (−4/+2) since the root movements change to conform to the diatonic key. The chromatic sequence in Example 36.1B differs in that the root motion always contains a P4 and a m3 in a repetition; this creates a M2 descent between repetitions, which is reflected in the label D2 (−P4/+m3). We distinguish chromatic sequences from diatonic sequences by including the specific interval motions within the parenthetical portion of the label.

The DM2 (−4/+3) Sequence

Both the diatonic D3 (−4/+2) sequences and the chromatic D2 (−P4/+m3) sequences are related by the underlying 5–6 motion that holds each sequence together. In Chapter 22 we learned that the diatonic form most often occurs with alternating six-three chords that clearly reveal the underlying 5–6 motion.

Example 36.2 contains the D2 (−P4/+m3) sequence in its alternating $^6_3$ form. The "?" that appears under the tonic indicates that it does not sound like an arrival because of the remarkable ambiguity of the sequence. This sequence carves out an intervallic path consisting exclusively of whole tones (or their enharmonic equivalent) and divides the octave symmetrically into six major seconds (G–F–E♭–D♭–C♭–A–G). Note especially how the whole-tone path of this sequence skips over the dominant as the line moves from the E♭ to D♭ in mm. 3–4. As it stands, the sequence is barely tonal. To reintroduce tonal focus, one must break off the sequence after the repetition of the pattern on ♭VI. From here it will lead to the pre-dominant function (Example 36.3).

EXAMPLE 36.2 Chromatic D2 (−P4/+m3) Sequence

DVD 1
CH 36
TRACK 2

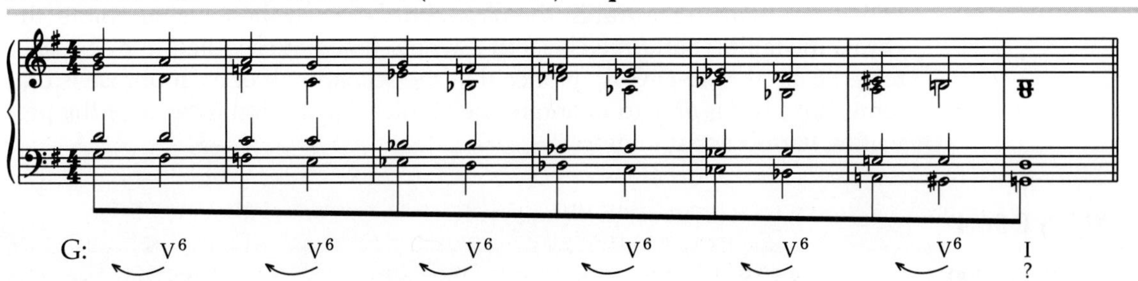

EXAMPLE 36.3

A.

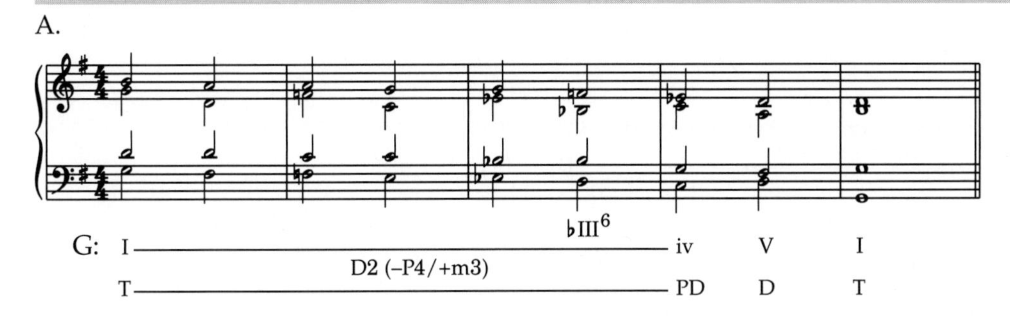

B.

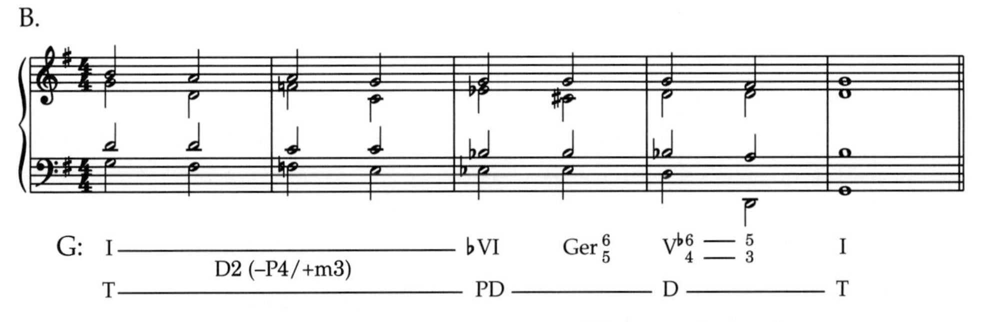

C. Schubert, String Quartet in G major, D. 887, *Allegro molto moderato*

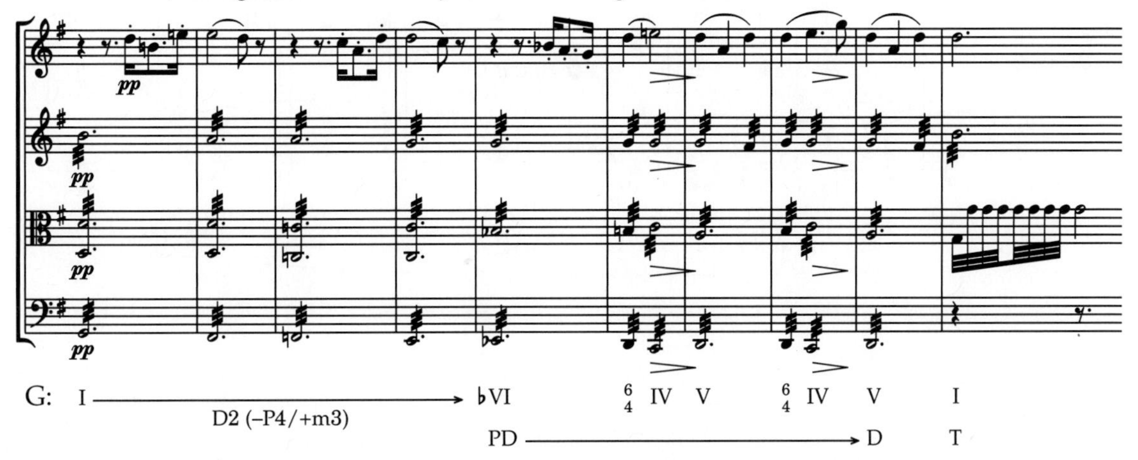

In general, chromatic sequences occur more often in the major mode than in the minor. Example 36.4 demonstrates the minor-mode form of the chromatic D2 (−P4/+m3) sequence. Example 36.4C, from a particularly evocative passage from a Franz Liszt piano piece, contains a phrase and its repetition down one octave using the chromatic D2 sequence. Each phrase begins and ends on I_6 (with B natural in the bass), but between these stable points, the chromatic falling pattern etches out a whole-tone pattern filled in by passing tones (**B**-B♭-A♭-F♯-E♭-D-C-**B**). Notice that the second half of each phrase is diatonic, but Liszt is able to maintain the whole-tone motion in spite of the prevailing harmonic asymmetry.

EXAMPLE 36.4

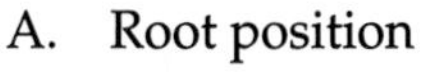
A. Root position

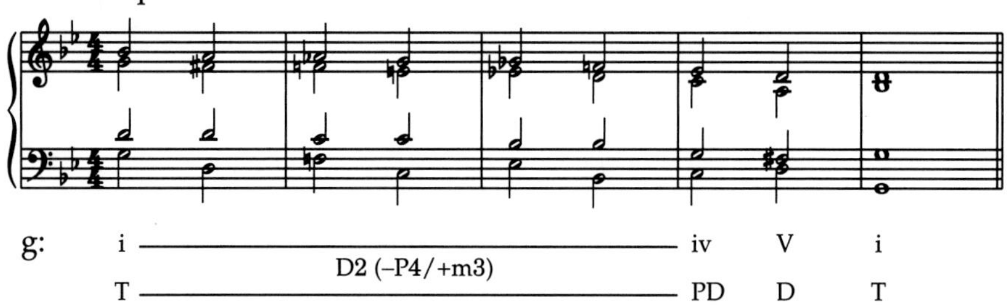

B. Alternating $^6_3$ chords

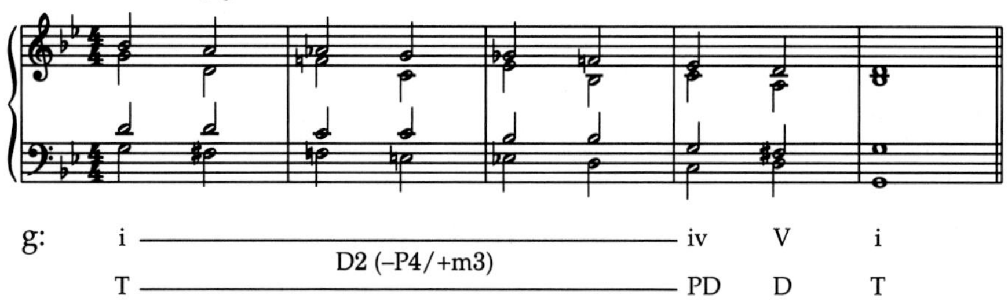

C. Liszt, "Aux cypres de la Villa d'Este I: Threnodie" (To the cypresses of the Villa d'Este), from *Annees de Pelerinage*, (*Years of Pilgrimage*); Third Year

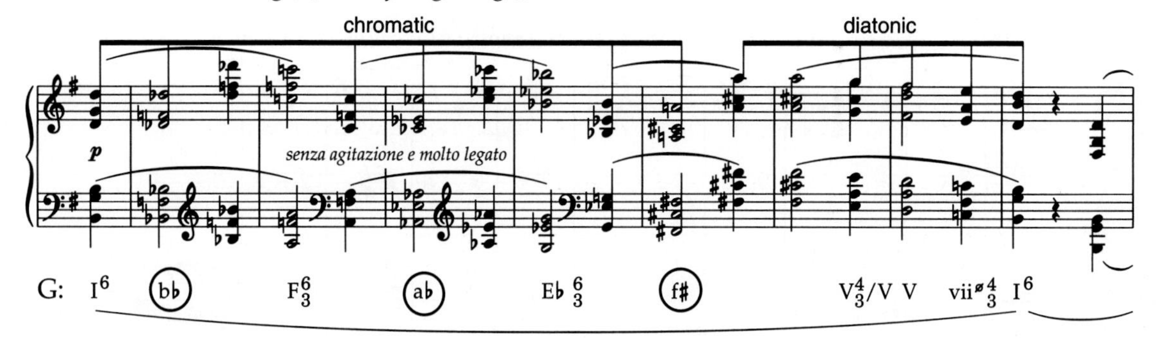

Continued

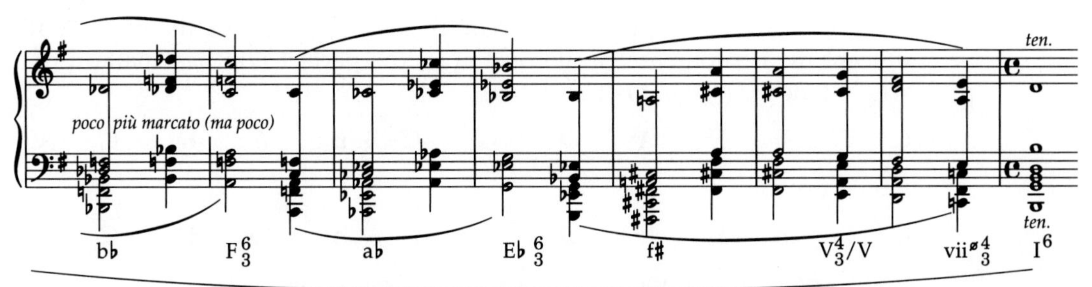

The Chromatic Forms of the D2 (−5/+4) Sequence

Recall that the D2 (−5/+4) sequence is asymmetrical because it contains perfect fifths and a tritone. To become symmetrical, the chromatic D2 (−P5/+P4) sequence contains exclusively perfect fifths. A secondary difference between the two forms of the sequence concerns length of time required to cycle back to tonic: A complete statement of the diatonic D2 (−5/+4) sequence requires seven diatonic steps, while a complete statement of the chromatic form requires 12 chromatic steps. This provides a compositional problem of sorts for the D2 (−P5/+P4) sequences, given that a complete statement of the sequence requires so many repetitions.

Composers use two techniques to avoid sequential stasis: (1) partial statements of the series (only one or two repetitions) and (2) three or more fifth-related chords within the model rather than two in order to reduce the number of repetitions. For example, a three-chord model would require only three repetitions to make it all the way through this chromatic sequence's 12 chordal members (Example 36.5).

EXAMPLE 36.5

DVD 1
CH 36
TRACK 4

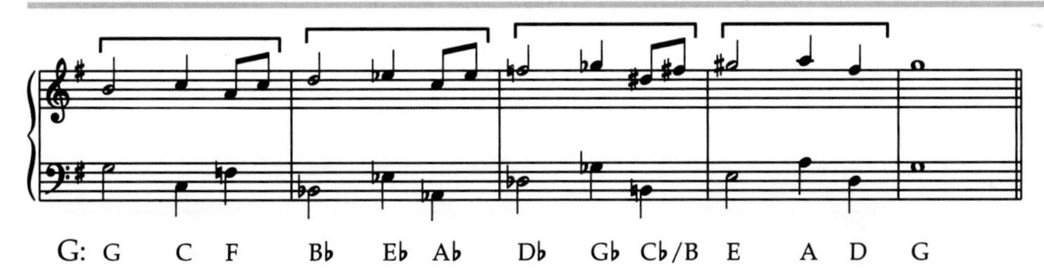

Now, let's compare this sequence to the other chromatic D2 sequence we have just studied. Both the D2 (−P4/+m3) and the D2 (−P5/+P4) fall by major second, but the latter is more goal directed, because it moves more naturally by descending perfect fifths. The D2 (−P4/+m3) sequence contains back-relating dominants, and the sequence itself never lands on the dominant V chord. To feel this distinction, try playing Examples 36.2 and 36.6 while noting the direction of the arrows.

EXAMPLE 36.6

DVD 1
CH 36
TRACK 5

It is also possible to have a chromatic sequence descending by minor seconds, D2 (−P5/+A4). This is accomplished by following the perfect-fifth descent by a tritone ascent. For example, the perfect-fifth bass pattern of a whole-tone D2 (−P5/+P4):

C F **B♭** E♭ **A♭** D♭ **G♭** C♭/B **E** A **D** G C

would become:

C F **B** E **B♭** E♭ **A** D **A♭** D♭ **G** C

Example 36.7 contains such a pattern, beginning on B. Members of the stepwise chromatic descent are circled and connected by slurs; the tritone leaps between them are bracketed.

EXAMPLE 36.7 Chopin, Mazurka in A minor, op. 59, no. 1, BI 157

DVD 1
CH 36
TRACK 6

The Chromatic Forms of the A2 (−3/+4) Sequence

Like the diatonic A2 (−3/+4) sequence, the chromatic forms derive from the contrapuntal 5–6 motion. Let's examine how the diatonic form evolved into the chromatic, symmetrical form. Example 36.8 reviews two forms of the diatonic A2 sequence: the simple diatonic form and a variation that uses alternating applied chords to tonicize briefly each diatonic scale degree. These sequences are diatonic because the structural chord of each two-chord repetition falls on a diatonic scale degree that is diatonically harmonized.

EXAMPLE 36.8

DVD 1 CH 36 TRACK 7

A.

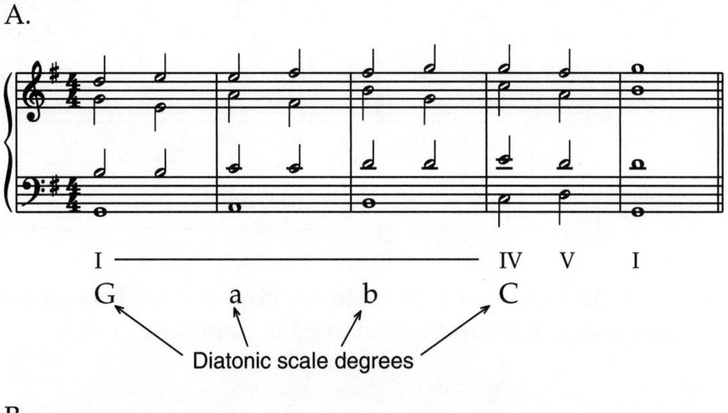

B.

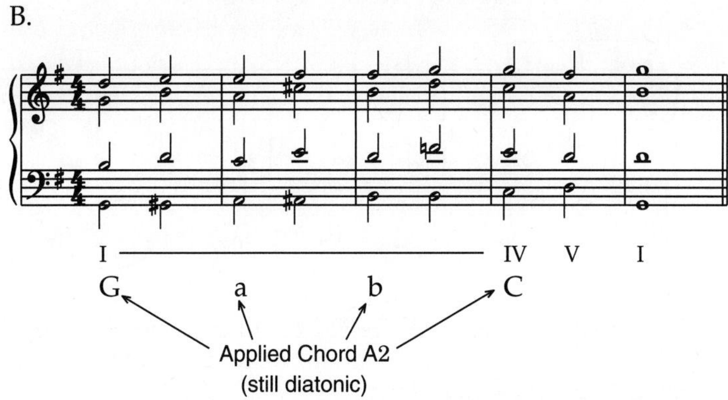

Two chromatic variants of this sequence are shown in Example 36.9. The first sequence lies somewhere between standard diatonic sequences and chromatic sequences: The root of every chord is diatonic (asymmetrical), but the structural chord of each repetition is chromatically altered (symmetrical). The second sequence is fully chromatic, A2 (−M3/+P4): The structural first chord of every repetition is major, and the sequence ascends by half step. Although the bass is sustained through the two-chord repetition, every second chord is transformed into an applied $^6_5$ chord. This is reflected in the enharmonic respelling of the bass in mm. 2 and 4, showing the leading-tone function of the bass.

EXAMPLE 36.9

DVD 1 CH 36 TRACK 8

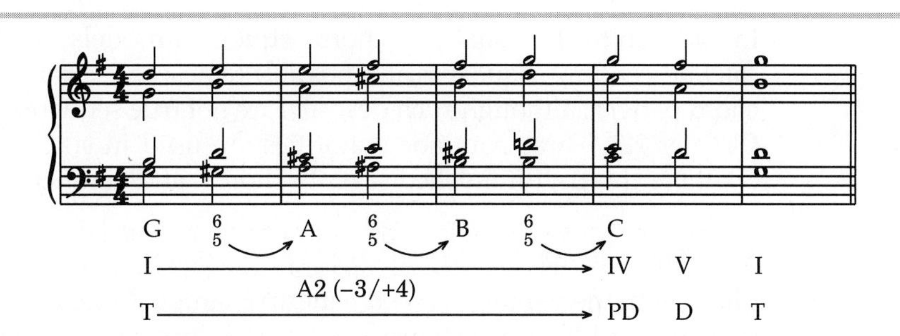

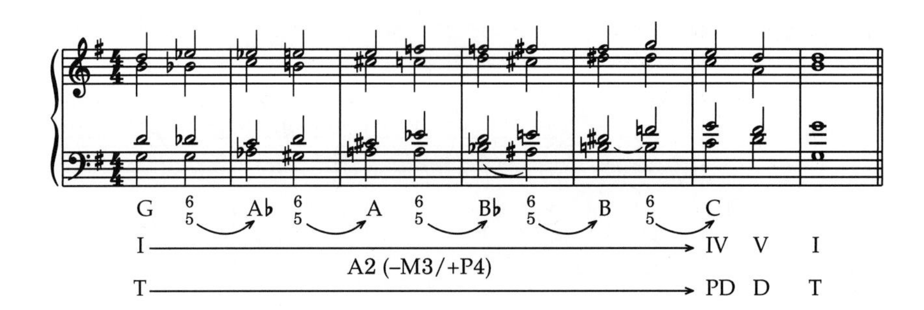

Example 36.10 demonstrates how the applied chords may appear in root position, a technique often used in popular music.

EXAMPLE 36.10

DVD 1
CH 36
TRACK 9

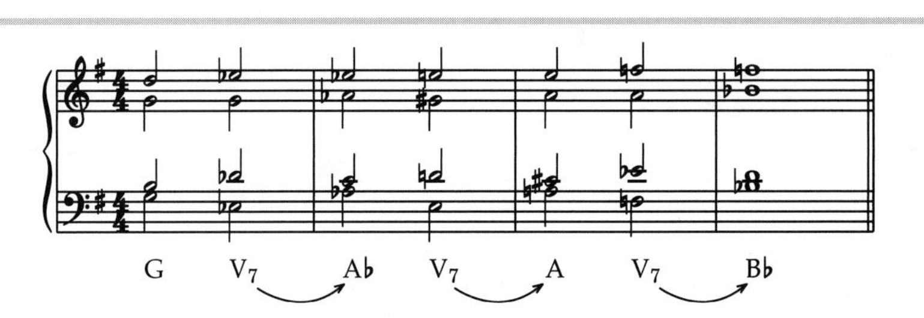

Finally, a second sustained common tone between the first chord and its transformation into a dominant results in an augmented triad on the second chord (see Example 36.11).

EXAMPLE 36.11

DVD 1
CH 36
TRACK 10

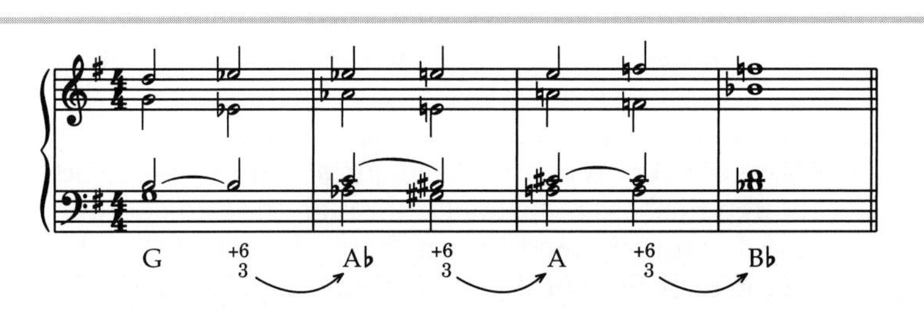

Other Chromatic Step-Descent Basses

In addition to the usual two-chord sequential models that become chromatically descending sequences, it is possible to descend chromatically using a one-chord pattern, although such descents are not true sequences (as we learned in Chapter 22). Three common sonorities are used in such chromatic descents. Six-three chords, diminished seventh chords, and augmented sixth chords.

Six-Three Chords

The diatonic descending $^6_3$ chord pattern (Example 36.12A), with 7–6 suspensions (Example 36.12B), can be transformed into a chromatic motion (Example 36.12C). The dissonant seventh usually occurs over a chromatic bass note and resolves over a diatonic bass note. This alignment of dissonance with chromaticism (and consonance with diatonicism) is common. Furthermore, the metrically emphasized beats on which the suspensions occur are harmonized by various types of seventh chords, making this pattern particularly expressive and useful in slow-tempo pieces with emotional texts. In Chopin's *Impromptu*, a chromatic $^6_3$ motion extends tonic before leading to the pre-dominant (Example 36.12D).

EXAMPLE 36.12

DVD 1
CH 36
TRACK 11

A.

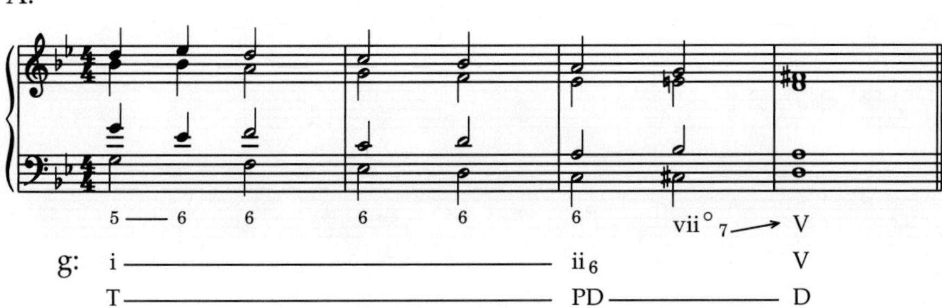

B.

C.

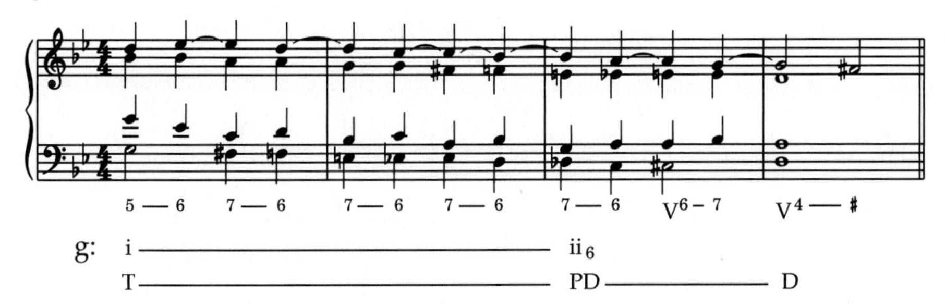

D1. Chopin, Impromptu in A♭

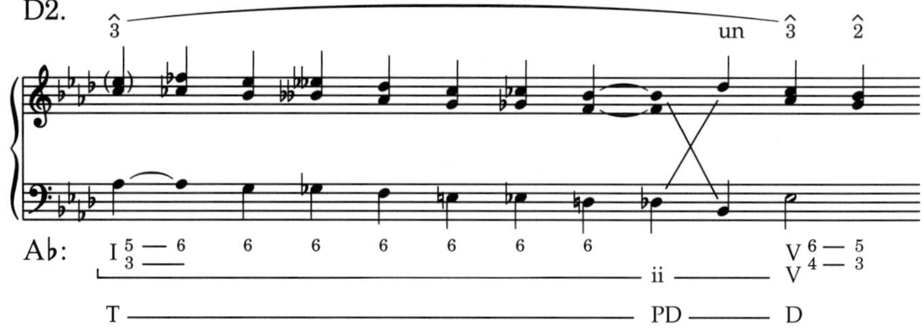

Diminished Seventh Chords

The diminished seventh chord may be used in descending chromatic sequences, such as the DM2 (+P4/−P5) sequence in Example 36.13. The notation in this example reflects careful voice-leading practice, but it is not possible aurally to differentiate root-position and inverted diminished seventh chords (due to the symmetry of the chord). Rather, the sequence sounds like a stream of root-position diminished seventh chords.

EXAMPLE 36.13

Augmented Sixth Chords

Example 36.14A illustrates the potential ambiguity between the German sixth and the dominant seventh chords. Without seeing the score, the listener will probably assume that these are streams of dominant seventh chords with an anticipation in the soprano voice. Yet one might also hear a descending PD–D progression, resulting in a descending series of keys related by half step. The analysis below Example 36.14A shows how V_7/IV (C) becomes a German sixth, a technique that we already know effectively lowers the temporary tonal center a half step. Notice that this PD–D progression is clarified at the end of each measure by the transformation of the ambiguous German sixth to the harmonically clearer French sixth. The French sixth's lowered fifth also avoids parallel fifths, in that it anticipates the perfect fifth of the following dominant seventh. Through all of this sequencing, the real underlying motion is from tonic to dominant in G major. Chopin uses this pattern in Example 36.14B.

EXAMPLE 36.14 Descending Augmented Sixth and Dominant Seventh Chords

DVD 1
CH 36
TRACK 13

A.

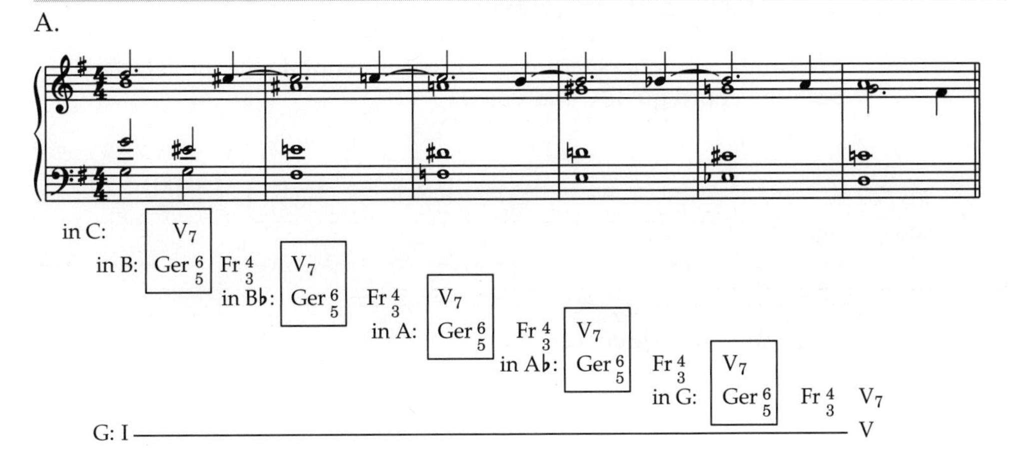

B. Chopin, Prelude in A♭ major, op. 28

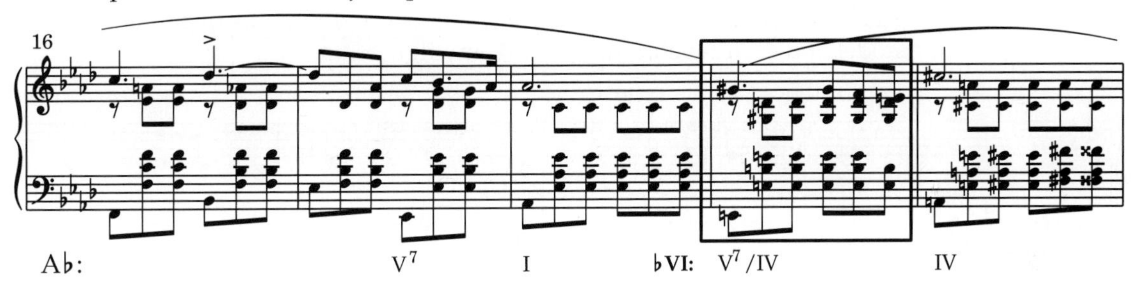

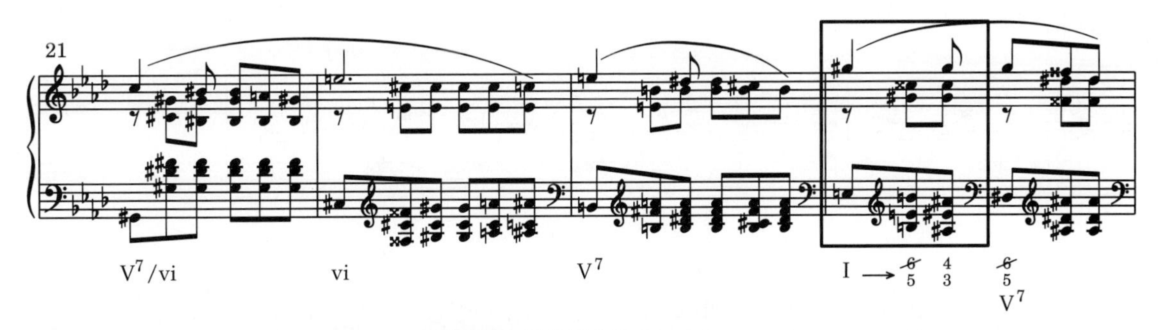

Writing Chromatic Sequences

Although there are no new guidelines for writing chromatic sequences, the following issues arise.

1. Use enharmonic notation instead of writing double flats or double sharps.
2. Like diatonic sequences, chromatic sequences usually break off at the pre-dominant, whether the sequences rise or fall.
3. Chromatic sequences require that copies maintain the model exactly—both the chord quality and voicing.

EXERCISE INTERLUDE

ANALYSIS

DVD 2
CH 36
TRACK 1

36.1

Analyze the following sequences. Your choices are:

1. descents by seconds, thirds, and streams of six-threes, diminished sevenths, and augmented sixths
2. ascents by seconds

You may also encounter examples of diatonic asymmetrical sequences. Bracket each sequence and label it. Then circle the notes of the outer-voice model and each repetition, ignoring any figuration.

D. Beethoven, Symphony no. 3 in E♭ major ("Eroica"), op. 55, *Allegro con brio*

E. Marcello, Lament in G minor for Cello and Continuo

Continued

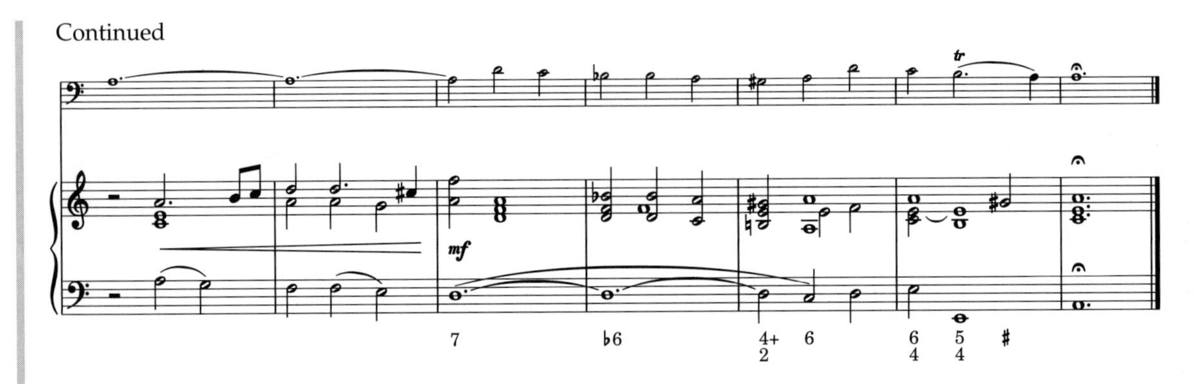

F. Mendelssohn, Etude in F minor, 1836

DVD 2
CH 36
TRACK 2

LISTENING

36.2 Sequence Identification

You will hear a variety of diatonic and chromatic sequences. All but the first two are taken from the literature. Label each sequence. (*Note*: There may be more than one sequence in an excerpt.)

A. ____________________

B. ____________________

C. Chopin, Piano Concerto in F minor, op. 21, BI 43, *Allegro*

____

D. Chopin, Piano Concerto in E minor, op. 11, BI 53, *Allegro*

____

E. Beethoven, String Quartet no. 7 in F major, op. 59, no. 1, *Allegro*

____

F. Schubert, Trio in B♭ major, D. 898, *Allegro moderato*

____

KEYBOARD

36.3 Sequences

Identify each sequence type. Realize A and C in three voices and B in four voices.

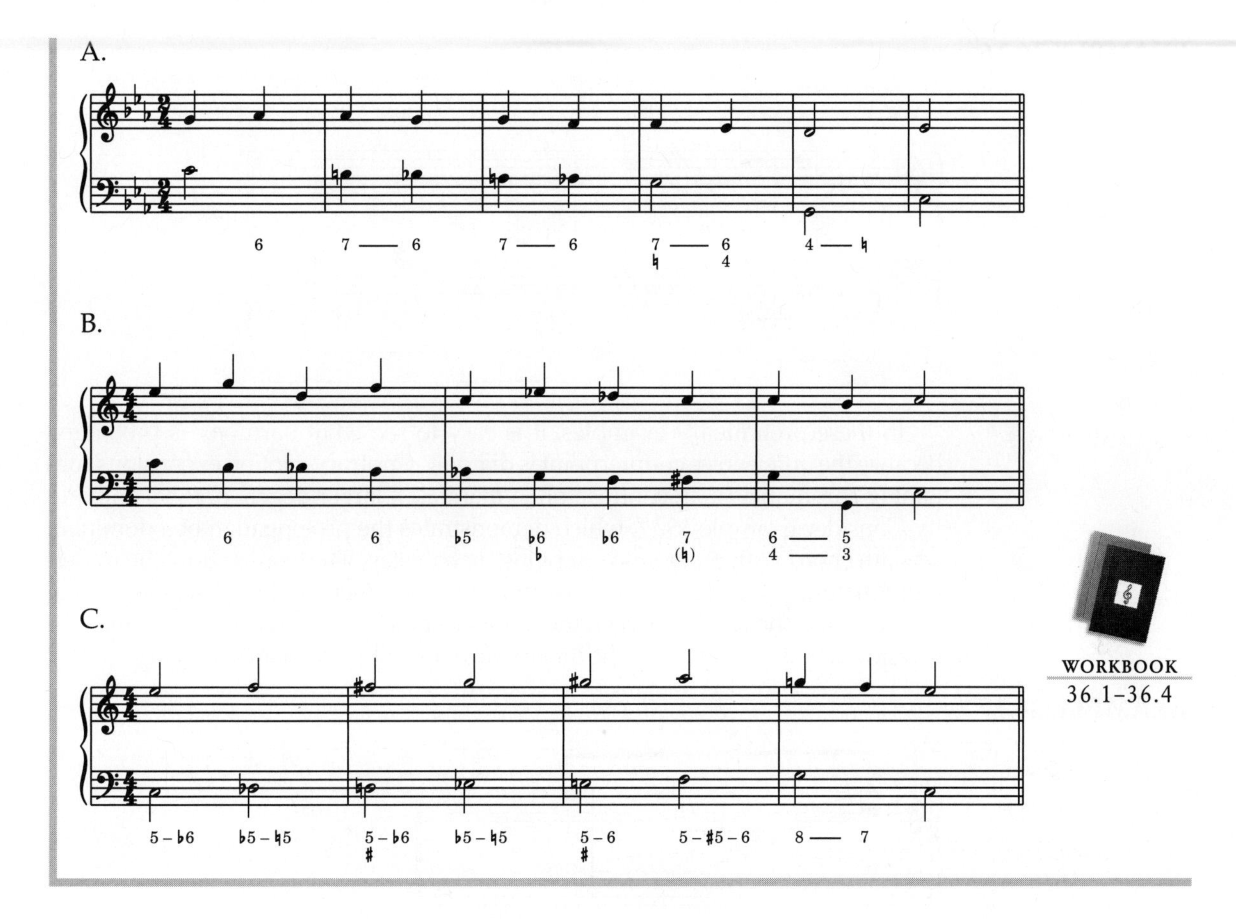

Chromatic Contrary Motion

We have learned many ways to extend an underlying harmony using contrary motion. We began with the chordal leap, which results in the most rapid voice exchange possible (Example 36.15A). Next we added passing chords, such as vii°$_6$, V$^4_3$, and vii$^{\circ 6}_{5}$ (Example 36.15B).

EXAMPLE 36.15

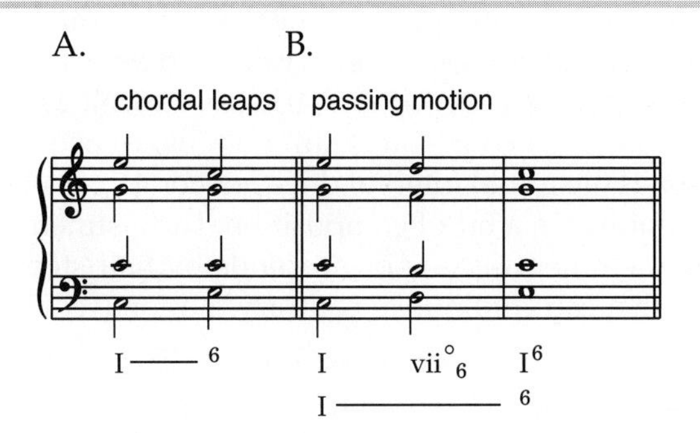

We can extend not only consonant triads but also dissonant harmonies—most often a dominant seventh chord—by contrary motion. The **dissonant prolongation** spans a third in Example 36.16A and a tritone in Example 36.16B. Note how little the inner voices move.

EXAMPLE 36.16

DVD 1
CH 36
TRACK 14

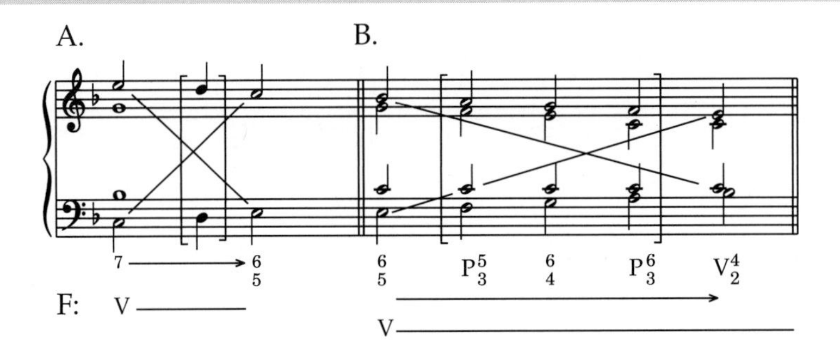

In these preliminary examples, it is easy to see what harmony is prolonged because the outer-voice counterpoint is diatonic. Contrary-motion expansions containing chromaticism, in contrast, often manifest a larger degree of tonal ambiguity. Consider Example 36.17, which demonstrates the prolongation of a dominant seventh chord with outer voices moving by half step. The beams show the underlying diatonic stepwise motion; the nonfunctional Ger_7 and Ger^6_5 act as passing chords filling the space between the diatonic chords. This densely chromatic progression works well because the inner voices are able to remain stationary.

EXAMPLE 36.17

DVD 1
CH 36
TRACK 15

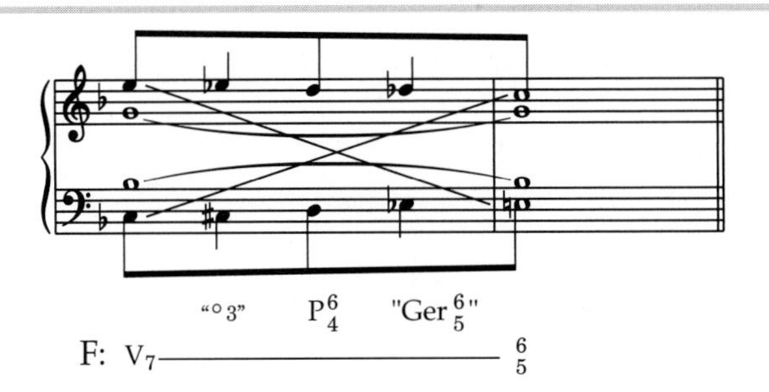

It is not a matter of luck that these particular soprano and bass lines work well together in contrary motion. For comparison, let's consider two lines that move in contrary motion starting from a minor tenth rather than a major tenth (Example 36.18). Almost from the beginning, the counterpoint is flawed. There is no suitable way to harmonize the minor ninth or the major seventh. In contrary-motion chromatic lines, the intervals with an even number of half steps are best harmonized: unison, M2, M3, tritone, m6, m7, and their compound-interval counterparts. Of course, it is still possible to use contrary-motion chromaticism even if the initial interval does not comprise an even number of half steps. All it requires is a bit of compositional adjustment: Suspend one of the voices while the other ascends or descends by half step, which will form an even interval that can continue in contrary motion (see Example 36.19).

EXAMPLE 36.18

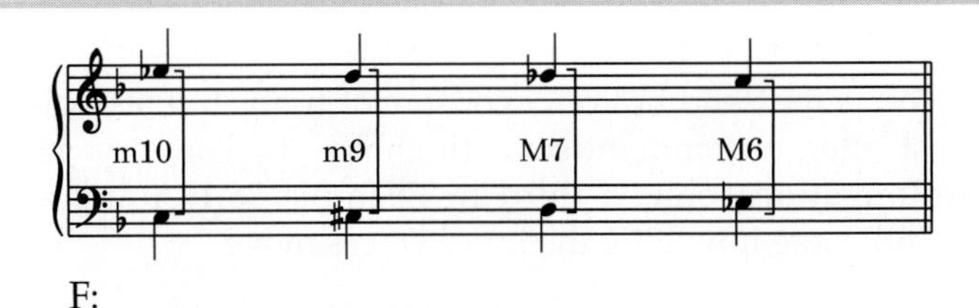

EXAMPLE 36.19

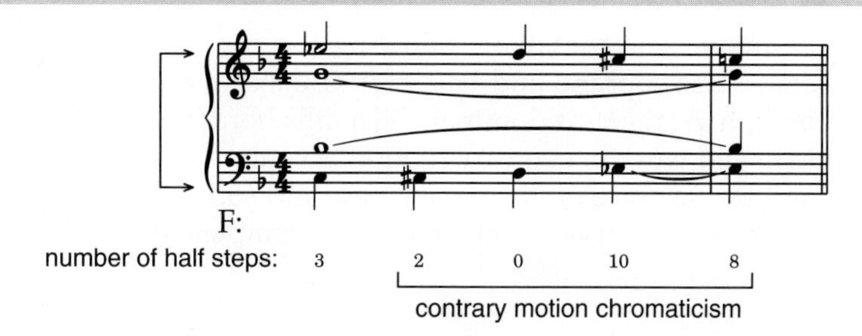

Examples 36.16 and 36.17 showed expansions of a dominant seventh chord from one position to an adjacent one—from $^{6}_{5}$ to $^{4}_{2}$ and from 7 to $^{6}_{5}$, respectively. Example 36.20 expands the previous models by demonstrating how a $^{6}_{5}$-to-$^{4}_{2}$ tritone can be expanded chromatically in a seven-chord progression.

EXAMPLE 36.20

DVD 1
CH 36
TRACK 16

Note that when we use these sequences, it is possible to begin and end the contrary motion at any point in order to prolong different diatonic entities. Example 36.21 shows how we can prolong tonic or a °3/+6 complex by using different spans of the sequence; depending on which portion is used, the chromatic contrary motion can prolong tonic, dominant, or pre-dominant.

EXAMPLE 36.21

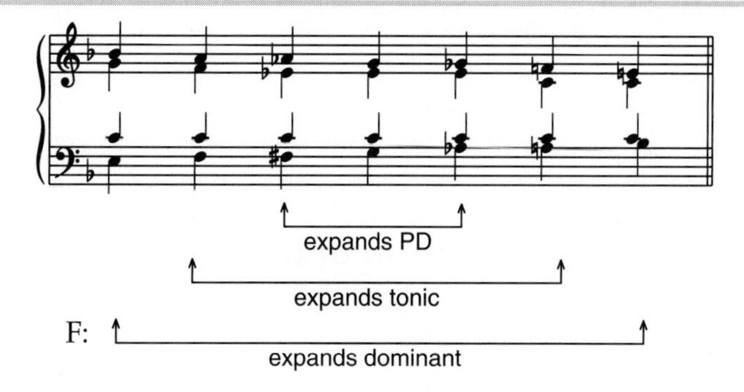

The Omnibus

In a final expansion, the same chromatic contrary motion that prolongs dominant (V_7 to V^{6}_{5}) can be stretched so that it traverses an entire octave (ascending or descending). In Example 36.22, the bass ascent partitions the octave into minor thirds: Different root-position dominant seventh chords appear on every third sonority (the dominant seventh chords are sometimes spelled enharmonically as Ger^{6}_{5} chords). At each dominant seventh chord, a remarkable enharmonicism is invoked, allowing the contrary chromatic motion to begin anew. The soprano and bass start a major tenth apart and work in contrary motion. At the next dominant seventh chord, the tenor and bass start with the M10 and work in contrary motion. At chord 7, the alto and bass are on a M10 and start a voice exchange; the bass and soprano return to a M10 at chord 10. The bass arrives on C3 at chord 13 to complete its one-octave ascent.

EXAMPLE 36.22

DVD 1
CH 36
TRACK 17

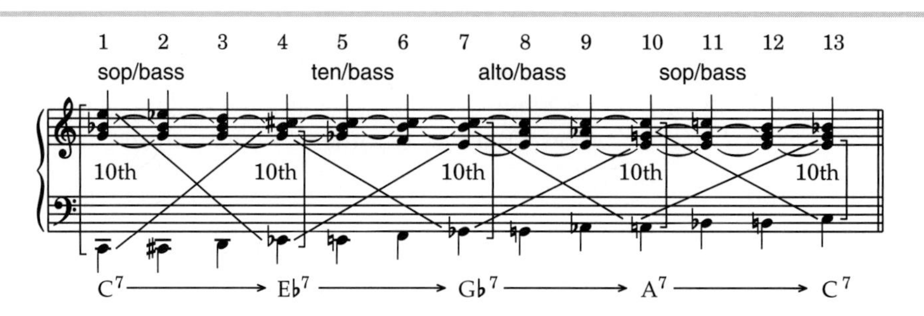

Example 36.23 reproduces the motions of Example 36.22 and demonstrates how the entire passage acts as a prolongation of a single harmony. In total, this prolongation is called the **omnibus**. The omnibus, first described by Viennese music theorists around 1800, was used by composers throughout the nineteenth century (such as Beethoven, Schubert, Chopin, and Liszt). In practice, composers generally used only part of the omnibus.

EXAMPLE 36.23

DVD 1
CH 36
TRACK 18

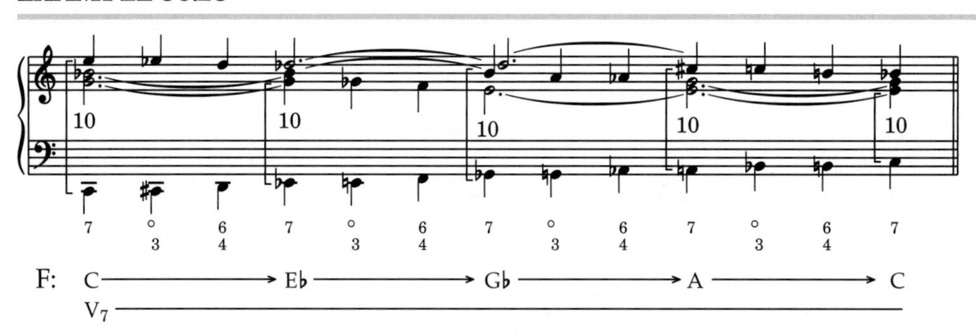

A Final Equal Division of the Octave

We have seen that chromatic parallel-motion sequences and contrary-motion progressions partition the octave into equal-sized intervals.

Descending minor seconds:	D2 (−P5/+A4)
Descending major seconds:	D2 (−P4/+M3) and DM2 (−P5/+P4)
Ascending minor seconds:	A2 (−M3/+P4)
Minor thirds:	Omnibus

We consider one more interval that can symmetrically divide the octave: the major third. Example 36.24 presents a slight variation of the diatonic D3 (−4/+2) sequence that partitions the octave into major thirds, D3

(−P4/+m2). The voice-leading irregularities result from maintaining the sequential progression exactly. The overall progression, which prolongs C major, contains descending major thirds (C–A♭–E–C) in the bass and a whole-step descent in the soprano.

EXAMPLE 36.24

DVD 1 CH 36 TRACK 19

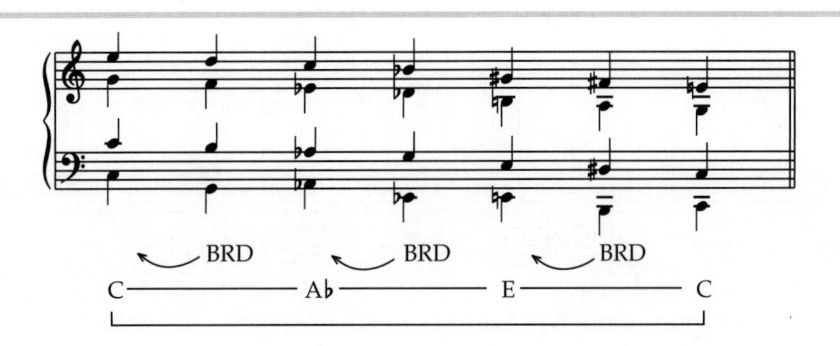

Chromatic sequences all create the temporary effect of tonal ambiguity. It was but a short and natural step for composers to begin to use autonomous symmetrical progressions independent of sequential motion. Such progressions, which we take up in the next chapter, extend ambiguity to deep structural levels of the music.

EXERCISE INTERLUDE

ANALYSIS

DVD 2 CH 36 TRACK 3

36.4 Contrary-Motion Progressions

Given are progressions that employ contrary-motion chromaticism. Determine the harmonic function that the chromaticism extends; then bracket and label that function (tonic, dominant, or pre-dominant). Circle the pairs of pitches involved in the contrary-motion chromaticism; for more extended examples, the pairs will change between voices. Is there a deeper harmonic pattern that emerges?

A.

B.

C.

D. Tchaikovsky, Symphony no. 5 in E minor, op. 64, *Allegro con anima*

DVD 2
CH 36
TRACK 4

36.5 Analysis Project

Schubert's song "Meeres stille" ("Still Sea," op. 3, no. 2, D. 216) contains part of an omnibus that expands (that is, moves outward in contrary motion) and a chromatic third relation that usurps a structural dominant. Both of these harmonic techniques project the poetry. Listen to the song and study the translation.

Continued

1. The subject of the poem is a sailor on a placid sea. The "deep calm" that "rules the water," however, carries with it the sailor's anxiety. Why? What is the sailor ultimately afraid of?
2. How does Schubert's accompaniment support the text? Do you think the sailor lands safely, or not?
3. Determine the key areas in the song. You will need to consider how E major functions. Is it an applied chord or a mixture chord? (Remember, an applied chord is subordinate to the following harmony, but a mixture chord participates in the underlying tonal motion.)

4. Is there an underlying harmonic progression in these key areas?
5. In spite of the clear cadences, how might the tonal structure reflect the uncertainty of the sailor becalmed at sea?
6. One might expect the dominant to appear somewhere after m. 16. Why? Instead, a chromatic passage follows. How does this chromaticism reflect the text? The text in this chromatic passage divides into two parts. What key is implied at the end of the first part (on the word *Seite*)? Based on what immediately follows (*Todesstille*, meaning "deadly calm"), what different key does Schubert imply? What is the relationship between this key and the song's primary key? Could the placement of this particular sonority influence your interpretation of the sailor's fate?

WORKBOOK
36.5–36.7

COMPOSITION

36.6

Write two consequents to the given antecedent to create a parallel interrupted period and a contrasting progressive period. Label your periods and analyze the harmonies.

36.7

Continue the given patterns until you return to the tonic. By what interval does each sequence partition the octave? Be able to perform your solutions with one or more of your colleagues.

36.8

Realize the following figured bass in four voices. Analyze.

TERMS AND CONCEPTS

- chromatic versus diatonic sequences
- chromatic A2 (−M3/+P4) sequence
- chromatic D2 (−P4/+m3) sequence
- chromatic D2 (−P5/+P4) sequence
- contrary-motion chromaticism
- dissonant prolongation
- omnibus

CHAPTER 37

At Tonality's Edge

In this final chapter, we conclude our study of the interaction of symmetry and ambiguity. The musical structures we examine here will lead us to the very frontier dividing tonal music from nontonal music. We will continue working from the premise that a work is tonal and organized by the subtle play of counterpoint and hierarchy. At this point, you may have doubts about using anachronistic terms such as *tonality*. Our definitions, however, will still equip us with tools that unlock the underlying structural principles behind music that remains within the tonal tradition but whose construction looks forward to nontonal practices. Our analyses permit us to see this music as part of a long historical tradition.

Sequential Progressions

Remember that the increased use of mixture resulted in the increased use of chromatic third relations in the late eighteenth century. Motion to the fifth above and below the tonic was often divided by chromatic thirds (I–♭III–V and I–♭VI–IV, for example). Although these progressions were goal directed, they were asymmetrical, because they contained root motions that were a mixture of major and minor thirds.

It is possible to incorporate two or more identical intervals into progressions that segment the octave into equal intervals, called **equal divisions of the octave**. See Example 37.1, which shows how intervals of one, two, three, four, or six half steps can equally divide the octave.

EXAMPLE 37.1 Equal Divisions of the Octave

By six half steps (tritone)	C						F♯						C
By four half steps (M3)	C				E				G♯				C
By three half steps (m3)	C			E♭			F♯			A			C
By two half steps (M3)	C		D		E		F♯		G♯		B♭		C
By one half step (m2)	C	C♯	D	E♭	E	F	F♯	G	G♯	A	B♭	B	C

Example 37.2 contains two important symmetrical progressions. Example 37.2A moves by descending major thirds from C major to A♭ major (♭VI), to E major (III or ♭IV), and back to C major. The two-chord model is exactly copied by

two-chord repetitions that preserve the motion of each voice. Notice how each major-third-related key is secured when the pivot (♭VI) becomes I in the new key.

EXAMPLE 37.2

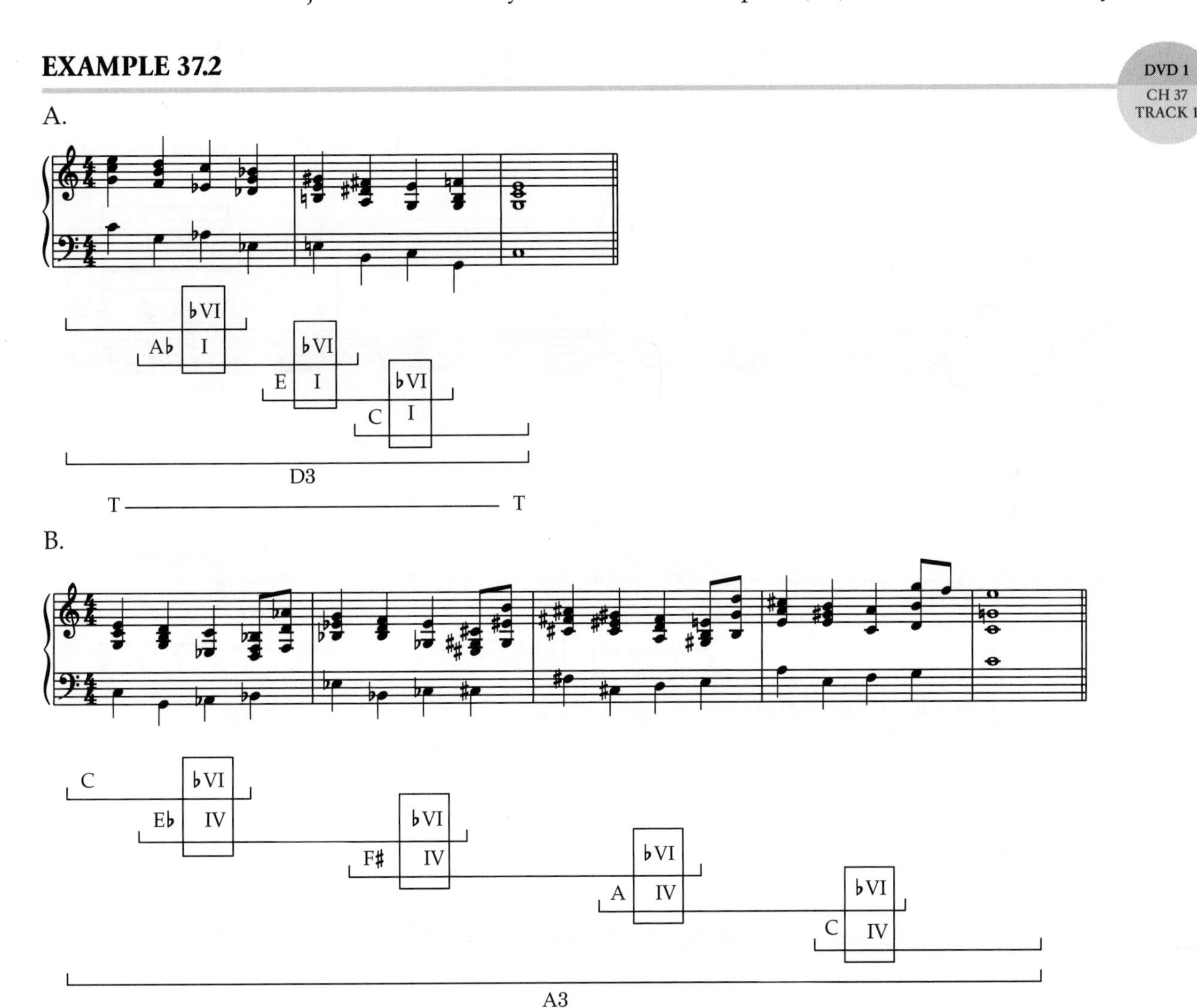

Example 37.2B ascends by minor thirds: C major (I)–E♭ major (♭III)–F♯ major (♯IV)–A major (VI)–C major (I). Given the progression's consistent transposition and sequential behavior, we call it a **sequential progression**. The sequential progression is symmetrical because it ascends by minor thirds. Roman numerals are not helpful in Example 37.2, because labels such as "♯IV" and "♭IV" reveal nothing about the interdependence within the progression. Each part of the progression is like a spoke on a wheel, supporting the final shape yet nearly meaningless when examined separately. When you encounter these kinds of progressions, do not focus solely on the roman numeral analysis but look instead for a larger pattern: Bracket sequential progressions, label the interval of transposition, and try to determine whether the chords prolong an underlying harmony or whether they progress to a new harmony.

Composers will not always use sequential progressions at deep structural levels. Example 37.3 contains a sequential progression that prolongs a surface harmony within a larger asymmetrical tonal progression. This passage is sequential and contains an ambiguous descending M3 sequential progression. One may interpret the descending major thirds either as prolonging the tonic (**I**–[♭VI–III♯]–**I**–♭VI–V–I) or pre-dominant (I–♭**VI**–[III♯–I]–♭**VI**–V–I). Given that the sequence ends on ♭VI, the latter interpretation is more convincing.

EXAMPLE 37.3 Schubert, String Quartet no. 14 in G major, D. 887, *Allegro molto moderato*

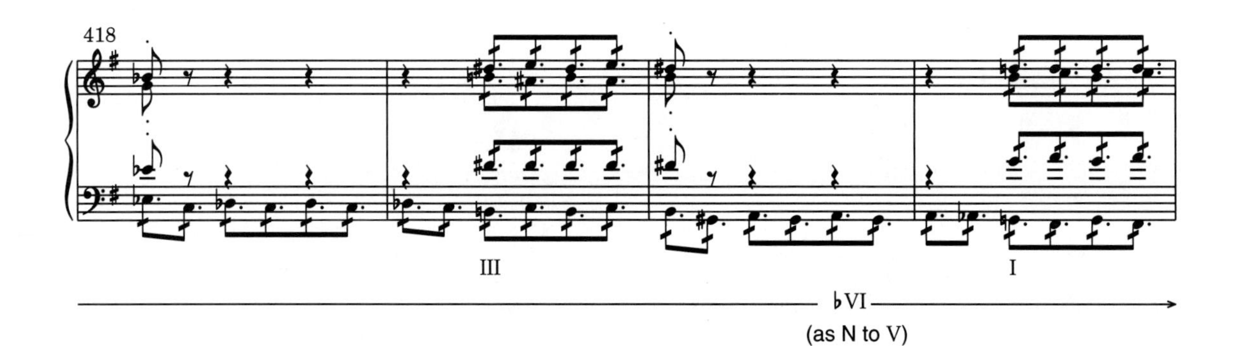

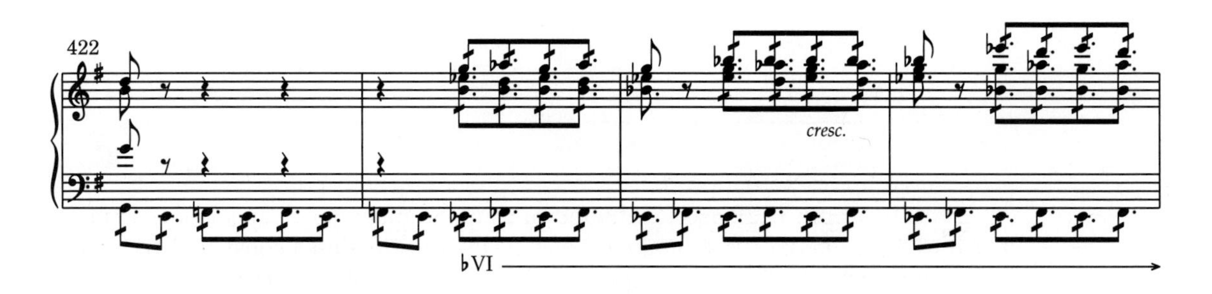

The Chopin nocturne in Example 37.4 contains a more complexly crafted sequential progression. You may have heard the sequential pattern unfolding in one of two ways.

- If you focused on the larger musical gesture, you probably discovered an ascending m3 sequential progression that occurred on metrically accented beats and partitioned the octave.
- If you focused on the smaller musical gesture, you probably found a chromatic D2 (−P5/+P4) sequence (see the circled pitches on the score).

You may recall that a complete statement of a 12-chord chromatic D2 sequence would require six repetitions of two-chord units. To avoid this sequential stasis, Chopin has cleverly grouped the sequence into three-chord units in mm. 130–131. In m. 132 the harmonic rhythm accelerates when Chopin includes a six-chord unit. As the acceleration intensifies the drama, the listener expects the inevitable arrival on the tonic, G major. Chopin, however, derails the progression by the completely unexpected return of motion to the dominant through the vii°$_7$/V. The effect is heightened by the following silence. Thus, this nocturne contains a particularly artistic juxtaposition of two sequences: A D2 sequence metrically unfolds in a manner that reveals a more global ascending m3 sequential progression.

EXAMPLE 37.4 Chopin, Nocturne in G major, op. 37, no. 2, BI 127

DVD 1
CH 37
TRACK 3

Nonsequential Progressions and Equal Divisions of the Octave

Example 37.5 demonstrates that equal divisions of the octave also occur in progressions that are not sequential. Notice that each tonicized area contains a different harmonic progression. Such progressions often occur over large spans of music, with intervening tonicizations of independent musical sections. Again, when analyzing such passages, you will need to interpret the tonal structure both within each section and between sections in order to see the deeper-level progression.

EXAMPLE 37.5

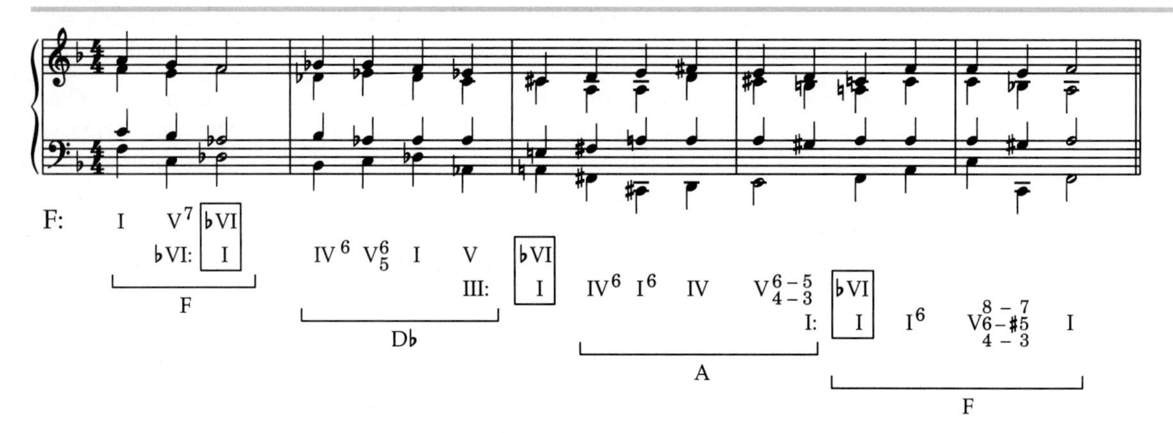

A series of falling major thirds divides the octave into three segments. The brief tonicization of each segment disrupts our sense of tonal orientation. D♭ major is easily accessed through mixture when ♭VI functions as the tonic in m. 1. Similarly, both the tonicization of A major and the return to F major are secured when ♭VI of the preceding key functions as the tonic.

EXERCISE INTERLUDE

PERFORMING

37.1 Singing Sequential Motions That Evenly Divide the Octave

Using scale degree numbers or solfège, sing (or play on your instrument) the sequential progressions, and continue until you return to the starting tonic. You will need to alter scale degree numbers and solfège syllables when you enter a new tonal area. If you play the progressions on your instrument, transpose each to two additional keys of your choice. You will need to consider octave shifts in order to maintain a single register as much as possible.

Continued

DVD 2
CH 37
TRACK 1

ANALYSIS

37.2 Sequential Progressions That Symmetrically Divide the Octave

Analyze the following sequential progressions, which divide the octave symmetrically into major and minor thirds, by bracketing the transpositions of material and labeling the tonicized area with key names (e.g., A major). Then label the interval of transposition between each statement of material.

D. Brahms, "Immer leiser wird mein Schlummer" ("Ever More Peaceful Grows My Slumber"), op. 105, no. 2

You will encounter several $^6_4$ chords. Some are cadential; others are consonant.

WRITING

37.3 Illustrations

Complete the following tasks on a separate sheet of manuscript paper.

A. **Modulation**. Compose a two-phrase period (either AA′ or AB) that modulates from D major to its relative minor.
   1. Phrase 1 must include a common-tone diminished seventh and any chromatic sequence.
   2. Phrase 2 must include an example of mixture in the original key, a clear pivot chord, and a Ger$^6_5$ chord in the new key.

B. In D major, accomplish the following in approximately 10–12 chords:
1. Establish D major.
2. Employing the enharmonic relation $\text{Ger}^6_5 = V_7$, tonicize ♭II (E♭) in D major.
3. Return to D using the Neapolitan as pre-dominant.
4. Once back in D, employ any fully chromatic sequence that moves to the dominant.

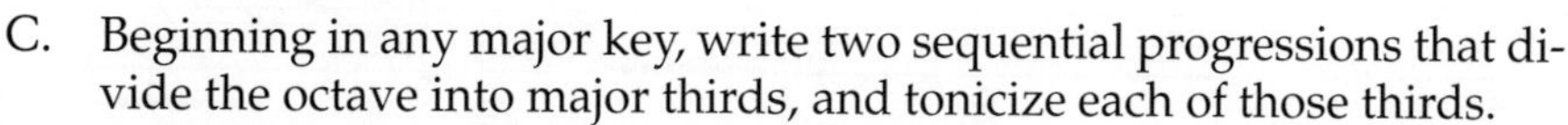

C. Beginning in any major key, write two sequential progressions that divide the octave into major thirds, and tonicize each of those thirds.
1. In the first progression, the pivot chords must be either an enharmonic diminished seventh chord or an enharmonic $\text{Ger}^6_5 = V_7$.
2. In the second progression, use any of the chromatic sequences in a transitional capacity to move from one major-third-related key to another.

WORKBOOK
37.1–37.5

The Intervallic Cell

Mixture and the structuring of passages based on symmetry are two of the three processes that create ambiguity and that underlie much late-nineteenth- and early-twentieth-century music. The third process involves a subtle yet unmistakable shift from easily singable, periodic constructions to more abstract collections of pitches that are defined by their intervallic structure and contour rather than by their melodic design. These malleable and motivic structures are called **intervallic cells**, or just **cells**. Cells can easily be developed in both the melodic and the harmonic domains, and there is a close relationship between musical events that unfold in time (melodies, which occupy the horizontal domain) and events that unfold in space (harmonies, which occupy the vertical domain). Such an emphasis on the intervallic aspect of music was a central focus of composers writing atonal music between 1900 and 1920. As the nineteenth century unfolded, melodic cells became more common because of their capacity for diverse harmonizations and because of their potential ambiguity. Like motives, cells appear early in a composition and are developed and transformed at various levels of the musical structure. Such transformations include *transposition, inversion* (reversing the contour of each interval of the cell), *interpolation* (adding pitch elements between some or all of the members of the cell), *rhythmic diminution* (shortening the rhythmic value of members of the cell), and *rhythmic augmentation* (lengthening the rhythmic value of members of the cell).

EXAMPLE 37.6 Brahms, Intermezzo in A minor, op. 118, no. 1

DVD 1
CH 37
TRACK 4

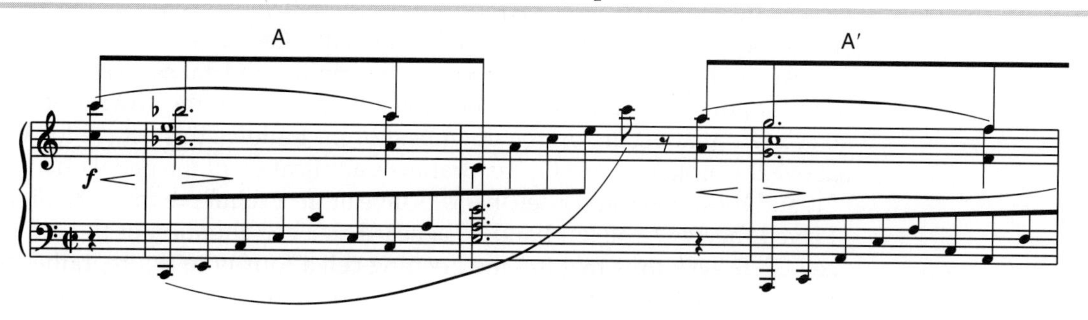

Listen to Example 37.6. It initially appears that much of Brahms's piece is composed of a descending three-note cell (C^6–$B\flat^5$–A^5). This cell is transposed down in thirds in mm. 2–3 (A^5–G^5–F^5) and mm. 4–5 (F^5–E^5–$D\sharp^5$). After the double bar (m. 10), the cell reverses direction and ascends chromatically (G^5–$G\#^5$–A^5). This contour inversion is enhanced by the descending broken-chord figure in the bass, which balances the opening ascending figure. Note that the cell appears longer after the double bar: The chromatic fragment is followed by a leap to C^6. The added length is confirmed in mm. 14–16, in which a chromatic fragment is followed by a leap (C^5–$C\#^5$–D^5–F^5).

At the beginning of the piece, as the right hand takes over the broken-chord figure in m. 2, the left hand attacks octave Es on the downbeat. The decrescendo that occurs on the downbeat of m. 1 allows this octave to be heard above the broken-chord figure. Brahms's application of the pedal on m. 1, beat $2\frac{1}{2}$, and the accent on the left-hand octave at m. 2 reinforce this interpretation. Played this way, the left hand E^4 is heard as a continuation of the right-hand cell C^6–$B\flat^5$–A^5, thus making the opening cell a four-note figure, rather than a three-note figure that is lengthened to four notes in the second half of the piece. Example 37.7 shows these figures.

EXAMPLE 37.7

Analytical Interlude: Chopin, Prelude, op. 28, no.2

EXAMPLE 37.8 Chopin, Prelude, op. 28, no. 2

DVD 1
CH 37
TRACK 5

Let's now analyze a short prelude by Chopin that incorporates intervallic cells. Listen to Example 37.8 with the following issues in mind.

1. Is this piece in a key? If so, which one or ones?
2. Is there an underlying harmonic progression? If so, what is it?
3. Is there a tune? If so, compare it to tunes we have encountered before.
4. Discuss the structure of the accompanimental figure that underlies the entire piece.

The prelude begins ominously in E minor but ends clearly in A minor. We may immediately wonder if this piece is double tonal (in both E minor and A minor) or progressive (moving from E minor to A minor). Or is it merely an off-tonic piece that begins on minor v and moves to the tonic, A minor? We must seek answers through analysis.

The first phrase (mm. 1–6) moves from E minor to G major (i to III in E minor). But could E minor simply function as vi in G major? Because E minor is not strongly established as a tonal area and because the progression works well in G major (vi–V–I), the prelude might begin off-tonic. The restatement of the opening tune abruptly begins in B minor. Given its relation to the opening, the listener accordingly anticipates that B minor will yield to D major, just as E minor led to G major. However, only the melody confirms our expectations. The left hand continues to repeat the bass note A^2 (mm. 9–12), which is sustained through a half-diminished seventh chord that is transformed into a fully diminished seventh chord (D♯–F♯–A–C) until it falls to an F♯^{2} in m. 13. In m. 14, when F♯^{2} yields to F♮^{2}, the Fr$^4_3$ chord (F–A–B–D♯) foreshadows the eventual resolution to A minor.

We must base our overall structural interpretation on how we view the first phrase and its modified repetition up a perfect fifth. In Example 37.9, path 1 illustrates the goal-oriented tonal progression G major–D major–a minor, in which the cadence of each phrase is considered to be more important than the opening harmony. This interpretation suggests that two large-scale fifth motions propel the music toward the tonal goal, A minor. Path 2 illustrates the progression E minor–B minor–A minor, in which the opening harmonies take precedence over the cadential harmonies. In this case, we might decide that the piece contains a large-scale modal shift from the minor to the major dominant. Neither interpretation is particularly revealing. All we know is that the large-scale progression is atypical, but we understand little about what motivates this progression.

EXAMPLE 37.9

Path 1:	vi V I	vi V (I)	
	G major	D major ↘	
		a minor:	vii°$^4_3$–$^6_5$ of V → Fr$^4_3$ → V → i
Path 2:	i V/III	III i V/III ↗	(III)
	E minor	B minor	

Let's look to the melodic domain for more answers. The opening right-hand melody is curiously disjunct, built of a three-note segment (E^4–B^3–D^4) in mm. 3–6, which is followed by a modified repetition (D^4–A^3–B^3). Because this melodic figure consists of only three notes, is repeated (with slight changes) down a major second, and appears consistently throughout the remainder of the piece, it can be said to function as a melodic cell.

While melodic contours are defined hierarchically with terms like *neighbor* and *passing* that render certain tones subordinate to others, ambiguous cells are often defined by their intervallic content. For example, the opening two-measure cell of Chopin's prelude comprises a falling fourth and rising third, with the result that the first and third pitches are a major second apart. (Thus, the perfect fourth contains a second within it.) Given that the intervals of the repetition recur, we can establish a close connection between the cell's model and its copies. Note, as in Example 37.10, that a copy need not be exact for it to be considered a melodic cell. If we compare E–B–D to D–A–B, we see that the position of the second has changed within. The overall intervallic content, however—a fourth, a third, and a second—remains constant. We can easily relate the two statements by simply saying that a small skip or step follows a larger leap.

If we look at the pitches that are strongly articulated at phrase beginnings and endings, we see that E^4 falls to D^4, which in turn falls to B^3. This expanded statement of the initial cell now occupies almost half of the prelude. Example 37.10 illustrates how the two statements of the cell in mm. 3–6 combine to make one super cell at a deeper level.

EXAMPLE 37.10

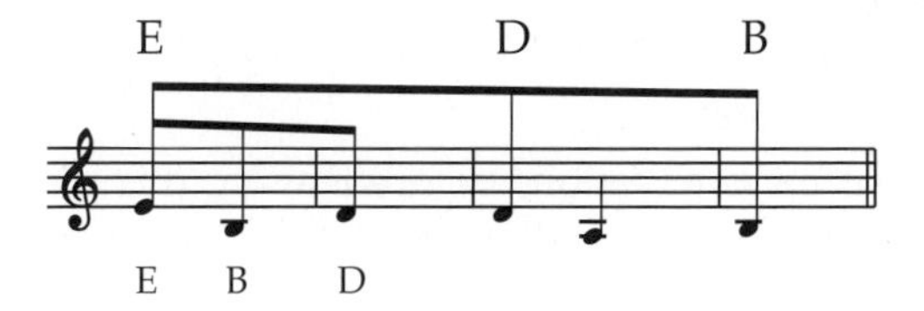

For further influence of the melodic cell, let's examine the left-hand ostinato that begins the piece. It comprises two voices. The lowest voice, which leaps a tenth (E^2–G^2), is counterpointed against a moving voice (B^2–$A\sharp^2$–B^2–G^2). It seems that Chopin is investing the moving voice with the generative potential of the intervallic cell, because it is composed of a small step (B^2–$A\#^2$) and a larger interval (B^2–G^2). Yet another manifestation of the cell, this time harmonic, appears in the bass in mm. 1–6: E^2–D^2–G^2 spans a perfect fourth (D^2–G^2) and contains a second (D^2–E^2) within the fourth. In fact, recognition of the existence of the cell helps to explain the deep-level parallel octaves (E–D) that occur between the outer voices, which are especially strange given that Chopin's counterpoint is impeccable and that such obvious voice-leading errors would never escape his perceptive ears and eyes.

Let's continue this tack of hearing the cell at ever-deeper levels of the musical structure. The melodic pattern is restated up an octave, on B (B^4–A^4–$F\sharp^4$) in mm. 8–9; the same expansion of those pitches also occurs over mm. 8–11. The anticipated arrival on D is derailed at the $F\#^4$, and the progression moves instead toward A minor. Thus far, the structural melodic units are the opening E^4 and the highly marked $F\#^4$: E^4–D^4–B^3, B^3–A^3–$F\#^4$. The next four statements of the melodic cell are accompanied by a traditional harmonic progression in which Fr^4_3 moves to V and then resolves to I. The beginning and ending points of these statements both occur on A: A^4 in m. 14

and A^3 in m. 23. The overall beginning and ending points (**E–F♯** and **A**), then, combine to create a final statement of the cell, one that lies at the deepest structural level of melody.

In addition to the connection we have drawn between different functions of the cell across Chopin's prelude, we also may consider extramusical factors in our analysis. For example, the inner line of the left-hand ostinato clearly invokes the opening portion of the well-known religious chant "Dies irae" (Example 37.11). The hymn, which appears in Berlioz's *Symphonie fantastique*, written around the same time as Chopin's prelude, is part of the Mass for the Dead, and its use here is particularly poignant, given that at the time of composing these preludes Chopin was sick with tuberculosis, a disease that eventually killed him.

EXAMPLE 37.11

Dies irae, dies illa — Day of wrath, day of doom

Let's ask two more questions before leaving this piece. Why is there harmonic ambiguity between relative minor and major modes, and why is the second phrase transposed up a perfect fifth? If we extend our analysis to consider that this is but one of a set of 24 preludes, the large-scale tonal plan reveals that each of the 12 major and minor pieces is connected by a pattern. The preludes are paired: A major-key piece is followed by one in the relative minor. The pattern continues by ascending a fifth through each of the keys (e.g., **C**/a, **G**/e, **D**/b). Notice that this pattern corresponds to both of our harmonic interpretations of the A-minor prelude, the second of the set. The opening is harmonically ambiguous because of the juxtaposition of the relative minor and major modes (e/G), which are repeated up a fifth (b/D). Might Chopin be giving the listener a glimpse of the harmonic model that will unfold over the next 22 pieces?

This analysis enables us to see that a short, three-note cell influences both surface and deeper-level melodic and harmonic events in this piece. Most important, exploring the generative role of the intervallic cell provides us with insight into a compositional process that transcends roman numeral analysis.

By 1880 an unprecedented explosion of radically different compositional aesthetics and styles flourished that boldly contrasted with all previous musical styles. During the preceding three centuries, for example, no matter what the stylistic changes, there were still basic points of intersection, not the least important of which was tonality. But during the closing years of the nineteenth century and the opening decade of the twentieth, a remarkable number of composers were writing highly contrasting music. In the year 1910, divergent composers such as Gustav Mahler, Maurice Ravel, Claude Debussy,

Richard Strauss, Carl Nielsen, Alban Berg, Anton Webern, Sergei Rachmaninoff, Paul Hindemith, Arnold Schoenberg, Belá Bartók, Igor Stravinsky, and Alexander Scriabin were creating some of their greatest works, but each took a unique path, with far-reaching consequences that greatly influenced the rest of the twentieth century.

Yet these same composers who carved their own niches in the twentieth century owed a tremendous debt to the past and, in particular, to the harmonic techniques that we have explored in this chapter. While any extended or even cursory treatment of these composers' contributions is beyond the scope of this text, we shall examine a single short piano piece by Alexander Scriabin, a transitional composer who bridges the tonal tradition and newly developing twentieth-century techniques. The musical materials and techniques found in Scriabin's Prelude, op. 39, no. 2, provide a summary of the trends we have explored in the previous three chapters—specifically, the notions of ambiguity, asymmetrical versus symmetrical structures, double tonality, and cells.

Analytical Interlude: Scriabin, Prelude, op. 39, no.2

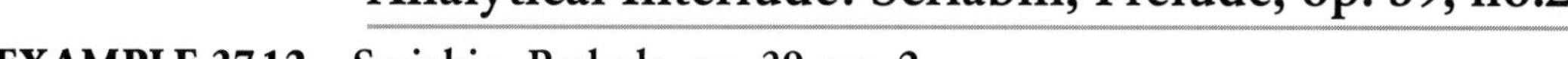

EXAMPLE 37.12 Scriabin, Prelude, op. 39, no. 2

DVD 1
CH 37
TRACK 6

Continued

This prelude (Example 37.12) is the most difficult work we encounter in this book. Written in 1903, it lies midway between Scriabin's earlier compositions (c. 1890–1900), which are in the style of Chopin, and his final works (c. 1908–12), which are often characterized as atonal. In its short 28 measures, the listener is flung into a sea of confusion, thrust this way and that with thwarted expectations brought about by nonstop chromatic shifts and misbehaving harmonic progressions. Listen to the piece with the following questions in mind.

1. Is this piece tonal? Why or why not? If it is in a key, what is it, and how and where is it established? Are there other important keys (either literally stated or only implied)? Do they support or undermine the main key? Do any of these keys compete with the overall tonic such that this work might be viewed as double tonal?
2. What is the form? Consider repetition of material as your main criterion.
3. Label phrases. Do they combine into periods?
4. Are there any motives or cells? If so, what are they? You should first focus on the opening musical idea and determine its length. (Composers usually invest great importance in the initial moments of a work.)
5. Are there focal points where events become either clarified or more ambiguous?

Pieces written in the nineteenth century often postpone harmonic clarity until the ends of musical units (phrases, periods, sections, or, as we saw in Chopin's A-minor Prelude, entire pieces). In Scriabin's prelude, an authentic cadence in the structural key, D major, is postponed until the final two measures of the piece. Why does Scriabin project the tonic only after going to great pains to obscure it? Could he have only frivolously tacked on the authentic cadence in a moment of wild abandon? It is likely that deliberate ambiguity is Scriabin's compositional premise and that this piece does not progress along a straight and clear path.

Both the prelude's form and harmonic motion are unusual. The material from mm. 1–12 is literally repeated and transposed down a major second in mm. 13–24. Measures 25–28 contain a cadential area in which E♭ major functions as the pre-dominant (♭II) that moves to the dominant. Why would Scriabin structure a piece in which the second half is a transposed restatement of the material from the first half?

Let's analyze the harmonic structure to make sense of the form. The opening progression (mm. 1–3) is ambiguous, but it eventually moves to a dominant seventh (in D major) with a 9–8 suspension in the uppermost voice (m. 3). In m. 2, a IV_7 moves to a modified Neapolitan on E♭, which functions as a predominant (♭II). (The ♭II in m. 25 also moves to the final dominant of the piece.) Scriabin is moving harmonically by fifth (V–I) and by tritone (♭II–V).

Now let's consider the opening sonority of the piece. Spelled in thirds, the chord is F♯–A♯–C–E. Such a chromatically altered chord is an unusual way to begin a piece. However, given its ambiguity and potential to imply any number of keys, Scriabin has chosen the perfect sonority to cloud his prelude in mystery. Let's look briefly at this chord's potential to function in several keys.

F♯–A♯–C–E can function as an altered V_7 chord in B (major or minor). See Example 37.13A.

F♯–A♯–C–E can be heard as a French augmented sixth chord in A♯ (major or minor) (notated, for convenience, in B♭: G♭–B♭–C–E). Its bass note, G♭, would fall by half step to F, which in turn is V of B♭. See Example 37.13B.

F♯–A♯–C–E can also function as a FrV $^4_3$ in F (that is, as the altered V_7: C–E–G♭–B♭. See Example 37.13C.

EXAMPLE 37.13

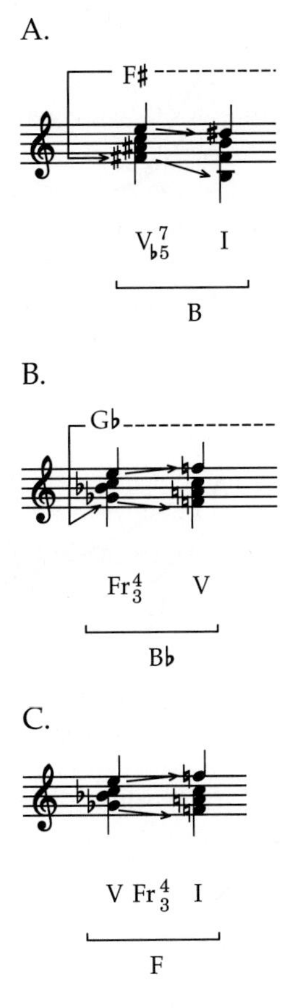

The reason that such diverse keys as B, B♭, and F are possible tonics is this chord's symmetrical intervallic structure. The chromatic clocks in Example 37.14 plots the chord's pitches, which are connected by lines that result in a rectangle shape.

EXAMPLE 37.14

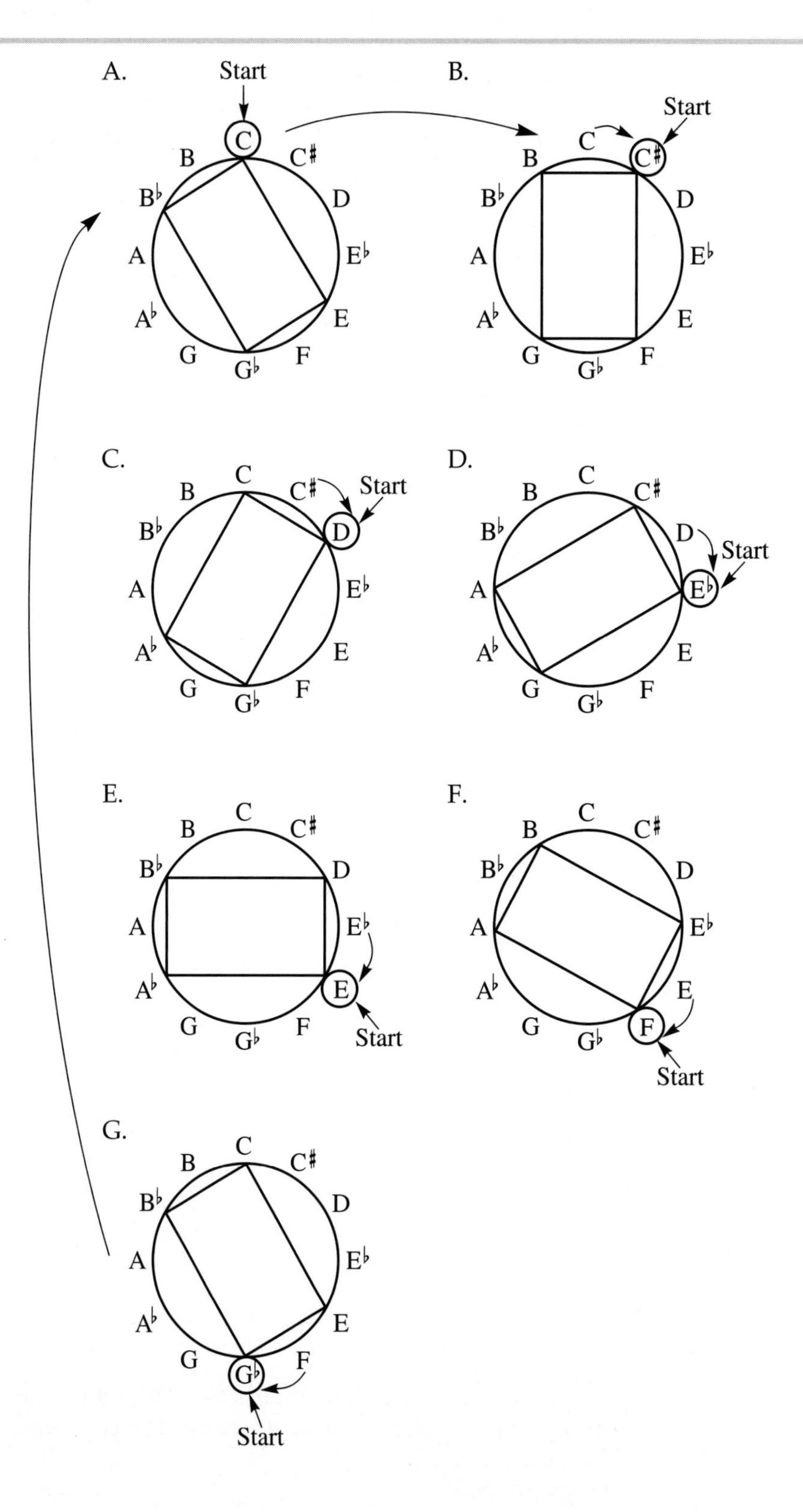

By transposing the sonority up by semitone (clockwise around the circle), we discover that all of the pitches return when we transpose the sonority at the tritone (i.e. F♯–A♯–C–E → C–E–F♯–A♯). Given that all of the pitches return, we can treat C as the bass note and derive another new set of tonal relationships, all a tritone away from the first set. For example:

C–E–F♯–A♯ can function as an altered V_7 chord in F (major or minor) (Example 37.15A).

C–E–F♯–A♯ can be heard as a French augmented sixth chord in E (major or minor) (see Example 37.15B).

C–E–F♯–A♯ can also function as a Fr V $^4_3$ in B major (that is, as the altered V_7: F♯–A♯–C–E) (Example 37.15C).

EXAMPLE 37.15

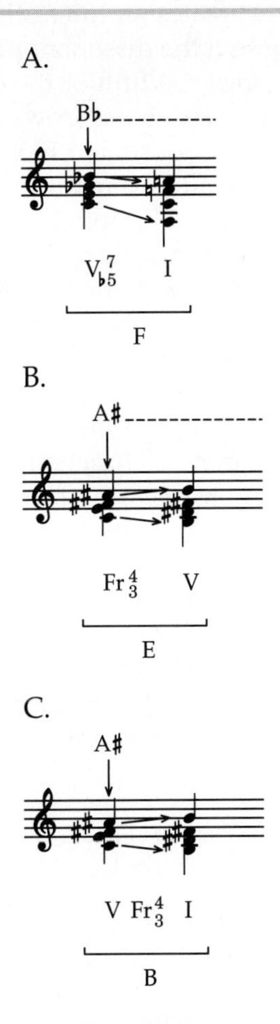

Notice that the first and third functions from each list are mirror images of one another, a tritone away. This is because when a tritone is transposed by a tritone (six semitones), the pitches are preserved. Thus, four of the 12 possible keys are implied by this single sonority: B♭, B, E, and F. They stem from hearing the sonority either as a PD (augmented sixth) or as a dominant (altered V_7) at two different pitch levels that lie a tritone apart.

Finally, we could imagine the chord functioning as a $^6_5$ chord with an implied root of D. This is possible, given that this would be an altered tonic triad, rather than a PD or D function, as described earlier. If the sonority were to function as an altered applied dominant of IV (with an implied root on D, a raised fifth, and a raised ninth, [D]–F♯–A♯–C–E, it would lead to a G-major chord, which, in fact, it does, in m. 2.

Notice that every interval in the sonority is a member of the whole-tone track that begins on C: major seconds/minor sevenths, major thirds/minor sixths, and tritones. (There are only two whole-tone tracks: one that begins on C [**C**–D–**E**–**F♯**–G♯–**A♯**] and one that begins on C♯ [C♯–D♯–F–G–A–B].)

So far, we cannot tell what the root of the initial chord is because of its inherent symmetry. We now explore the rest of the piece to determine whether Scriabin provides any hints for what the first chord is, and, if he does, whether this knowledge will help us to understand other curiosities in the piece. Let's study the harmonic progression in the first half of the piece (mm. 1–12). The dominant A^2 in m. 3 is prolonged by its upper neighbor $A\sharp^2/B\flat^2$ until m. 10. The chromatic line $D\sharp^4$–E^4–$E\sharp^4$ in m. 4 creates an interesting effect. Traditionally, the weak second beat would contain the dissonant passing tone. But our expectations are thwarted when the lowered fifth of the dominant harmony, E♭, spelled enharmonically as $D\sharp^4$, appears on the downbeat and the raised fifth, $E\sharp^4$, appears on the third triplet. The consonant E^4 sounds dissonant because of its location between the raised and lowered fifth.

In the bass of mm. 11–12, $B\flat^2$ moves to C^3 through the chromatic passing tone $B\natural^2$, in a gesture reminiscent of the chromatic ascent in m. 4. In m. 12, C^3 sounds like V of F major, and the harmony in m. 13 sounds like an altered V_6/F that resolves to F major in m. 14. Recall that m. 13 is the point at which the opening material appears transposed down a step. Because m. 13 contains a first-inversion extension of the C-major harmony that appeared in m. 12, we can retrospectively conclude that the opening sonority of the piece is also a first-inversion chord. As the harmony in m. 13 functions as a V^6_5, so the tonic harmony in m. 1 functions as a V^6_5 that moves to IV. Thus, we can answer our earlier question: The opening sonority is an altered D-major tonic that functions as V^6_5 of IV.

The second part of the piece is a literal transposition of the material in mm. 1–11, but a significant change occurs in m. 24, which one might have expected to correspond to m. 12. Rather than transposing the material down a step again, Scriabin moves by fifth to E♭ major (♭II). If we step back and view the harmonic motions in the piece, we discover a traditional pattern based on root motion by fifth:

form:	part 1	part 2	cadence
harmonies:	(D)–G–C–❘	F–B♭–❘	E♭–A–D

The underlying progression descends by step, from D major to C major (which ends the first section and begins the second section) and finally to B♭ major (the end point of the second section's repetition of the first section). Thus, the tonic moves to ♭VI, whereupon the final cadence reestablishes D major (♭II–V–I):

harmonies:	D — G — C — ❘ F — B♭ —— ❘ E♭ — A — D
functions:	I ——— PT ——— ♭VI —— ♭II —— V — I

This interpretation relegates much of the chromaticism to the periphery and illuminates the underlying traditional diatonic plan. However, the question of whether the chromaticism also plays a structural role remains unresolved. Before ending our explorations of this prelude, let's try a more radical approach that embraces the work's anomalies.

We can see that the opening sonority is a tonic chord (D) in first inversion with raised fifth (A♯) and an added ninth (E). Let's now consider the chord's spacing: F♯^{2} occurs in the lowest register and A♯^{4} in the highest, and the chord is sustained for one measure. The next sustained arrival point occurs on the F♯-major triad in first inversion in m. 5. Comparison of the opening sonority with the sonority in m. 5 reveals striking aural similarities. Scriabin emphasizes this association through the identical duration of the harmonies and by the voice exchange between F♯ and A♯. The next sustained harmony that occurs is in m. 9, where the same F♯-major chord again appears in first inversion. Now the A-major harmony appears to function as a lower neighbor to F♯$^6_{\sharp 3}$, an interpretation that contradicts our previous, more conservative interpretation in which the bass A♯^{1} was the upper neighbor to the A major harmony.

The bass A♯^{2}/B♭^{2} rises first to C^3 (m. 12) and then to E^2 (m. 13). We can now discover that the structural bass notes in mm. 1–13 comprise, note for note, the prelude's opening sonority, F♯–A♯–C–E. This projection of a dissonant, ambiguous, surface sonority over a considerable span is analogous to traditional motivic parallelisms. Remember that motivic parallelisms occur when a surface motive emerges in the harmonic domain and controls the unfolding musical events of a larger span of the work. (This technique has influenced many of the works we have explored in this book.) What distinguishes Scriabin's piece is the expansion of a dissonant harmonic structure rather than a diatonic, consonant harmonic structure.

EXERCISE INTERLUDE

KEYBOARD

37.4 Sequential Progressions

Continue the following short chromatic progressions for at least two repetitions. The result will be longer sequential progressions that divide the octave equally. Discuss the chords within each progression as well as the overall octave division.

Continued

C.

etc.

D.

etc.

E.

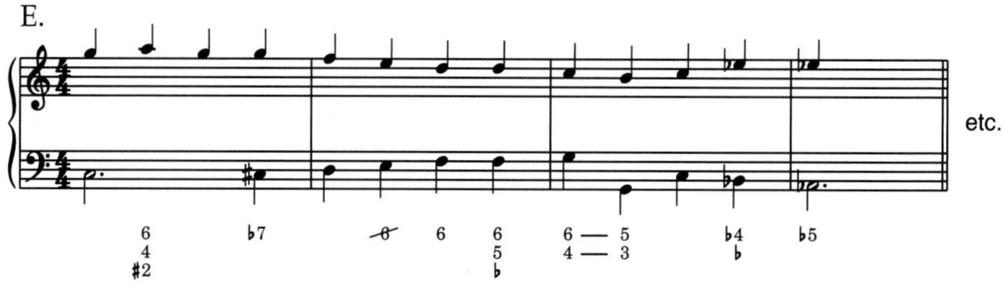

etc.

F.

etc.

37.5 Brain Twister

Employ an F-major triad in the various contexts and keys detailed here. Play each example in four voices. Each progression should establish the tonic and close with a cadence and contain approximately eight to ten chords. Use the F-major triad.

A. As a mixture chord in A major
B. As a pre-dominant in E minor
C. As part of a descending chromatic 5–6 sequence in G major
D. Tonicized in D minor
E. Expanded through voice exchange in B♭ major
F. As an applied chord in A minor

DVD 2
CH 37
TRACK 2

ANALYSIS

37.6 Nonsequential Symmetrical Progressions

Analyze the following passages. Mark the keys using letters of the alphabet; then summarize the interval used to subdivide the octave evenly.

A. Mozart, "Don Ottavio! Son morta!", from *Don Giovanni*, act 1, no. 10

Continued

B. Beethoven, Violin Sonata no. 5 in F major ("Spring,") op. 24, *Adagio molto espressivo*

WORKBOOK
37.6

Summary of Part 9

We have come to what appears to be the end of a long journey, along a road well traveled for centuries. Our journey began modestly, with no more than an introduction to the fundamental components of tonal music. We immersed ourselves in a sort of basic training that allowed us to develop the skills and to learn the concepts and terminology necessary for the journey. Soon we discovered why music is an art form: because, like any art, it must be not only perceived but also interpreted. We must examine music, as we do life itself, from various points of view. We had to make choices based on the context in which musical events took place and on our ever-growing knowledge of tonal norms. Our own interpretation might very well be quite different from someone else's.

We learned that music has depth and that this depth could be measured in levels, ranging from the surface all the way to the undergirding of an entire piece. And we discovered not only that the same principles were at work in each level but also that certain musical features, such as motives, actually provided the means to connect the various levels. For example, the surface-level chord-to-chord connections were precisely mirrored at successively deeper levels, and apparent departures from a key based on chromatic alterations or tonicizations merely turned out to be way stations, places that composers stopped at to view the harmonic terrain before returning to the main highway to continue their journey.

We learned that composers plant seeds early in a piece and that those seeds grow in various and wonderful ways. By creating a narrative or a dramatic story, composers then punctuate the piece with cadences, thwart expectations, clarify that which was ambiguous, and allow harmonic motion to be drawn out almost to a standstill or accelerated and intensified in order to create a natural ebb and flow common to all life.

We learned that theoretical concepts—whether voice-leading tendencies, compound melody, or sonata form—are drawn from musical practice, which in turn is motivated by human modes of perception. If we become aware of and develop these basic modes of perception by singing, playing, hearing, and seeing, then we have greatly deepened our understanding of what is taking place in a piece.

We learned that the tonal system and the principles it embodies are powerful enough that composers to this day continue to find it a source for developing musical ideas. Thus, whether the piece is written by Bach or Brahms, Mozart or Rachmaninoff, Beethoven or Ennio Morricone, a consistent set of core principles is at work. With our understanding of these principles, we are now able to negotiate these pieces with considerable success.

But it turns out that our journey hasn't concluded at all and that the road, which we thought finally ended, instead forks. Take one fork and we'll enter the world of twentieth-century music, a world of wonderful new sonorities, unique expressive gestures, innovative instruments and orchestration, and the migration of non-Western traditions. We will need to listen with different ears and to learn new sets of compositional and analytic principles in order to appreciate and grapple with this music. Take the other fork, and we will have many choices, one of which is to embrace earlier music, written between 1200 and 1600.

Music allows us to experience feelings that would otherwise have lain dormant. Thus, it plays a crucial role in one's development, as it reveals who and what we are. And, just as the study of music is an ongoing process, self-knowledge takes a lifetime to acquire. We must allow music to accompany us throughout this journey.

TERMS AND CONCEPTS

- sequential progression
- equal divisions of the octave
- intervallic cell
- whole-tone track

Index of Terms and Concepts

Index of Musical Examples and Exercises

(Exercises are identified with "*" to distinguish them from Examples)